CHILD WELFARE FOR THE

TWENTY-FIRST CENTURY

❖ ❖ ❖ ❖ ❖ ❖ ❖

CHILD WELFARE FOR THE TWENTY-FIRST CENTURY

A Handbook of
Practices, Policies, and Programs

Edited by

GERALD P. MALLON

AND PEG McCARTT HESS

COLUMBIA UNIVERSITY PRESS

New York

Columbia University Press
Publishers Since 1893
New York   Chichester, West Sussex
© 2005 Columbia University Press
All rights reserved.

Library of Congress Cataloging-in-Publication Data

Mallon, Gerald P.
Child welfare for the twenty-first century : a handbook
of practices, policies, and programs / edited by Gerald
P. Mallon and Peg McCartt Hess.
   p. cm.
  Includes bibliographical references and index.
  ISBN 978-0-231-13072-1 (cloth : alk. paper)
   1. Child welfare—United States.   I. Hess, Peg
McCartt. II. Title.
HV741.M336   2005
362.7′0973—dc22   2005049351

Columbia University Press books are printed on
permanent and durable acid-free paper.
Printed in the United States of America
10 9 8 7 6 5 4 3

To our parents and our children, who have
taught us so much about the meaning of family:

Gerald P. Mallon and Madge Gallagher Mallon
Travis Keller, Ian Keller, and Leslie Fuller
and
Rev. J. Spurgeon McCartt and Jan Taylor McCartt
Jeremy Hess and Kristen Hess

❖ CONTENTS

More than two decades ago, Joan Laird and Ann Hartman (1985:xvi–xvii) reminded us that "every society at every time must make some provision for its children in need." When Laird and Hartman, the editors of the classic text *A Handbook of Child Welfare: Context, Knowledge, and Practice,* wrote this statement, the field of child welfare was determinedly implementing a new federal mandate that outlined such provisions. The Adoption Assistance and Child Welfare Act of 1980 identified a range of management and practice requirements intended to prevent the unnecessary placement of children and reunify families when placement could not be prevented. The *Handbook of child welfare* outlined the philosophical underpinnings as well as the policy and practice emphases of that period. It provided detailed discussions that shaped the understanding and commitments of numerous cohorts of students who subsequently entered practice in the field. It is important for us as co-editors of this volume to acknowledge the influence Laird and Hartman's text has had in our teaching, in our professional child welfare practice, and in our development of this text. This volume is inspired by, and yet different from, that significant work.

Indeed, since 1985, when Laird and Hartman collected the essays in their volume, child welfare as an institution and a field of practice has continued to experience transformations in the provisions for children, youth, and families in need. Despite the hope associated with the passage of the Adoption Assistance and Child Welfare Act of 1980, the field has struggled during the intervening years with insufficient funding, increased public concerns about the safety of children, and generally disappointing outcomes with regard to achieving permanency for children and youth who enter care. Throughout the country, stresses within and on the child welfare system have kept many state agencies in the news and on the defensive.

Although in the past two decades many changes have occurred in practice and in ideological and planning orientations, change is perhaps most vividly seen in the primary legislation that currently forms the foundation of child welfare policy in the United States: the Adoption and Safe Families Act of 1997 (ASFA). This legislation replaced the Adoption Assistance and Child Welfare Act of 1980 (Title IV-E of the Social Security Act). The key principles that form the foundation for ASFA are conceptualized as the safety, permanency, and well-being of children and youth. ASFA puts into place legislative provisions that are intended to insure that child safety is the paramount concern in all child welfare decisionmaking, to shorten the time frames for making permanency planning decisions, and to promote the adoption of children and youth who cannot safely return to their own homes. This legislation also requires a focus on positive results for children, youth, and families, and promotes the strengthening of partnerships among child welfare agencies and other service delivery systems to support families at the community level.

Recognizing the significance of these multiple and complex changes, but especially attentive to ASFA's increasing influence on child welfare policy, programs, and practice, we decided to utilize these three concepts—safety, permanency, and well-being—as the primary framework for this text. It seemed timely to ask colleagues across the country—academics, policymakers, and practitioners, all of whom are deeply committed to child welfare—to commit to writing their views about the current status and changing complexity of services to children, youth, and families in twenty-first-century America. We believe that using this framework has permitted our contributors to thoroughly examine both the explicit and subtle challenges and opportunities to improving child welfare practice and offer practice and policy guidelines that fall

within the broad strokes of the ASFA decisionmaking framework.

We asked our contributors to outline the major assumptions and values of child welfare today and identify and elaborate the recent research and knowledge that currently support practice in a wide range of areas relevant to the field. Even as the contributors have been writing their chapters, the states and the U.S. Children's Bureau have been engaged in an extensive review process that has now been completed. The findings of the first 52 Child and Family Services Reviews, which have been integrated into the text where relevant, provide an additional source of information regarding the current strengths and concerns of child welfare, thereby further informing the agenda for future change efforts.

As child welfare practitioners, teachers, and researchers, both of us have, like Laird and Hartman (1985:xxiii), subscribed to an ecological perspective. This perspective provides an excellent framework for understanding and evaluating the nature of social and institutional responses to children, youth, and families in need. Furthermore, we both believe that it is important to emphasize family-centeredness in child welfare policy and practice. The philosophical concepts of family-centered practice and permanency planning are infused throughout this text. Both acknowledge the complex reality that, although a family is the best place for children and youth to grow up, for some, their families of origin may not be safe or nurturing. We believe that providing as much support as possible to birth families to assist them in being safe and nurturing permanent caregivers for their children, while at the same time planning for another permanency option if efforts are not successful, must be accomplished through a family-centered orientation. Furthermore, seeking the optimal connection a child can have to family, culture, and community in our efforts to achieve permanency reflects both an ecological and family-centered practice orientation.

Throughout this text, the contributors emphasize that strengthening and supporting all families—birth, kinship, guardian, adoptive, and foster—is the best way to insure children's safety, stability, continuity in family relationships, and timely permanence.

Through its provisions, ASFA legally reinforces the linkage between strenthening and supporting families and good outcomes for children and youth. Although it places the safety of children and youth first, it also provides for family preservation and family support services to prevent children from being removed from their families when it is safe to do so; maintains a commitment to agencies undertaking reasonable efforts to preserve families; encourages concurrent planning to insure permanency through either reunification or another permanent placement within shorter timeframes; and encourages the initiation of permanency planning efforts as children and their families have an initial contact with the child welfare system. Almost a decade after the passage of ASFA, practitioners continue working to change their policies and practices to better serve children, youth, and families while striving to comply with its complex legislative mandates and with other child welfare legislation. An urgent need remains for the adequate funding of child welfare agencies; sufficient resources are required to strengthen the capacity of child welfare practitioners to integrate policy and practices which are designed to reflect the field's developing knowledge base, increase accountability, and improve outcomes for children, youth, and families.

Another philosophical orientation that guided our work on this volume is that of evidence-based practices (Gambrill 2003; Gibbs 1989, 2003). Over the past 20 years, this orientation has increasingly permeated child welfare in ways that have moved the field of children, youth, and family services in new directions. We asked contributors to acknowledge and identify not only promising approaches to child welfare practice, but also those practices that are grounded

in empirical evidence. The profession of social work, as well as the society more broadly, has placed greater emphasis on evaluating to what degree identifiable outcomes have been achieved; that value on outcomes has also extended to the field of child welfare. Contributors were also asked to address the significant value and ethical issues relevant to their discussions, as well as the range of services and practice approaches required to address the needs and experiences of the diverse population of children and families served by the child welfare system. Where relevant, contributors were asked to include illustrative fictional or disguised case examples.

Utilizing safety, permanence, and well-being as its organizing and guiding principles, this text provides a framework for examining and exploring child welfare practices and policies in the twenty-first century. Within this framework, there are clearly differences of perspective among our authors. The field of children, youth, and family services and indeed social work embrace a wide array of diverse perspectives and practices. Although this edited volume has a unifying framework to provide structure for the authors and for the readers, it has been our intention that diverse perspectives and practices be incorporated.

A historical and legislative overview of child welfare grounds the text in time and place and provides elements of context critical to all subsequent parts of the volume. Following this overview, the main body of the text is divided into four sections, each of which is prefaced by an overview of the section. The overall introduction and four section overviews intentionally include few cited references to enhance the flow of these sections. The ideas contained in these introductory pages are cited extensively throughout the text.

Section I explores and examines the varied perspectives that frame what is currently known about child and adolescent well-being. Although safety is given prominence in AFSA legislation and language, we have intentionally situated the initial focus on child and adolescent well-being. Philosophically, we believe that without adequate attention to well-being, important developmental issues will be disregarded with a resultant weakening of the foundation for both safety and permanency. Assuring children's safety and achieving permanency for them requires that all those involved in their care and services understand their developmental and special needs; the care supports, and services required to support their ongoing development and well-being; and the ways in which resilience and both risk and protective factors are relevant to the assessment of and planning for each child and youth. Consistent with this philosophy, the chapters in Section I provide a needs-based approach to understanding experiences and services that support well-being. The first chapters address the broader issues of this area, beginning with an in-depth examination of resilience and risk, followed by assessment of children, youth, and their families and then by engagement of families and their communities in service planning. The section then enters into the various realms of children's and youth's health, mental health, and educational needs and concludes with issues pertaining to gay and lesbian youth, runaway and homeless youth, and spirituality.

Section II explores the critical issues pertaining to child and adolescent safety. Drawing from the theoretical literature, research, and best practices in the area of child maltreatment, this section begins with an overview of the salient issues pertaining to prevention of physical child abuse and neglect and moves into an extensive discussion of the areas of child protection. A thorough examination of risk assessment and of practice considerations for agency staff and others involved in answering the question, "will this parent abuse or reabuse his or her child in the near future?" follows. Section II also provides an extensive overview of the policies, practices, and research that provide a foundation for family preservation services and examines which children and parents are most and least

likely to benefit from such services. Over the past two decades, the field of child welfare has recognized the need to develop programs and practice approaches addressing particular problems that increasingly place large numbers of children and youth at risk of maltreatment and placement outside their homes. Therefore, Section II concludes with comprehensive reviews of the practices, policies, and research as these apply to two critical problems confronted daily in serving children, youth, and families: substance abuse and domestic violence.

Section III is devoted to a wide array of issues related to permanency for children and youth. This section provides an extensive overview on each of the major permanency goals—reunification, permanent placement with relatives, adoption, guardianship, and another planned permanent living arrangement—and on the primary out-of-home placement settings. These include foster family care, relative care, and residential programs. Other content areas relevant to the selection of permanency goals and achieving permanence are also explored, including kinship and sibling connections, adoption disruption, youth development, parent-child visiting, birth parent issues, and post-permanency services.

The volume concludes with a view of the systemic issues that affect children, youth, and family services. The initial chapters in Section IV focus on systemic issues that negatively affect all or specific groups of children and youth, including placement instability, the overrepresentation in the child welfare system of children and youth of color, immigration issues, and the role of fathers. Other practice-related systemic issues are also addressed, including the role of courts and the legal system in child welfare, the essential need for recruitment, development, support, and retention of foster families, a report on the process and outcomes of the federal Child and Family Services Reviews, and the roles of continuous quality improvement, strategic planning, and accreditation in child welfare.

References

Adoption and Safe Families Act. (1997). P.L. 105-89.

Adoption Assistance and Child Welfare Act. (1980). P.L. 96-272.

Gambrill, E. (2003). Evidence-based practice: Sea change or the emperor's new clothes. *Journal of Social Work Education, 39*(1), 3–23.

Gibbs, L. E. (1989). Quality of Study Rating Form: An instrument for synthesizing evaluation studies. *Journal of Social Work Education, 25*(1), 55–67.

Gibbs, L. E. (2003). *Evidence-based practice for the helping professions: A practical guide with integrated multimedia.* Pacific Grove, CA: Brooks/Cole–Thomson Learning.

Laird, J., & Hartman, A. (eds.) (1985). *A handbook of child welfare: Context, knowledge, and practice.* New York: Free Press.

❖ ACKNOWLEDGMENTS

Writing and putting together an edited volume can be a complicated business. From conceptualizing and developing the prospectus, to the call for abstracts and requests to potential contributors, to the review of the original and revised chapters, and finally, to the submission of the manuscript to the publishers is a lengthy journey. It is gratifying to complete these tasks and to know that others, especially students, will add to the development of their knowledge by using this text. One of the most pleasant aspects of the process is being able to acknowledge and thank those people who contributed to this effort and those who helped to sustain and encourage us along this journey.

Both of us began our careers in social work in child welfare: Gary as a child welfare worker in St. Dominic's Home, working on the front line with children, youth, and families in Blauvelt, New York, and Peg as a social work intern at the Juvenile Protective Association of Chicago, an agency providing intensive family-centered, home-based placement prevention services. Much of Peg's work subsequently continued to focus on placement prevention services, as well as on the critical importance of visiting in the lives of children in care and their families, particularly as it relates to family reunification. Gary's work has emphasized the importance of developing a lesbian and gay affirming perspective to working with children, youth, and families. We have both been blessed with good colleagues and friends along the way, as well as inspiring teachers; fine supervisors; and many, many children, youth, and families who have taught us much more than we ever could have imagined when we began our careers.

More recently, Gary's work at the Hunter College School of Social Work in New York, where he is the executive director of the National Resource Center for Family Centered Practice and

Permanency Planning, has brought him in touch with federal, state, and tribal leaders in child welfare throughout the country. These valuable associations and dialogues have provided a stimulating context for the planning, coordination, and completion of this text. The ideas, discussions, and principles presented in this text are those of the authors of each chapter and do not represent the official position of the Children's Bureau or the U.S. Department of Health and Human Services, nor were any funds from any grant used in developing this text.

While working on this text, Peg has been directing a multiphase review of case files of foster children in Fulton and DeKalb counties, Georgia, for Children's Rights, Inc. The findings of this review have served as reminders of the troubling gap between what is currently known about good child welfare practice and what many children and their families actually experience. Peg has also been consulting with several states concerning policies and practices related to family visiting of children in care. In contrast, these experiences have exemplified the creativity and dedication of many professionals laboring tirelessly on behalf of children and youth in the child welfare system.

Both of us recognize how much we have learned from our ongoing contacts with countless direct line staff, supervisors, out-of-home caregivers, and administrators in the child welfare agencies across the country and with child and family advocates as we have consulted, provided training, and studied a wide array of child welfare issues. We also acknowledge the profound lessons that we have learned from the countless children, youth, and families who have touched our lives with their courage and resilience in the least desirable of circumstances.

Our debt to our colleagues who contributed to this volume is inestimable. Both of us on many occasions have noted how fortunate we have been to have such knowledgeable and devoted child welfare professionals writing for this text. Each author has provided a rich and thoughtful contribution; as a group, the authors have had extraordinary patience as they waited to see their work in print. The depth of their knowledge and their willingness to share it with the students who will use this text is quite remarkable. Our contributors met their deadlines, were amiable about making edits quickly, and were delightful to work with. We are extremely grateful for their exceptional contributions to the field through their chapters in this volume.

About four years ago, Gary proposed working on this text with Peg; we met over coffee at a bagel store on Broadway near Columbia University in New York, where we both had worked as faculty and had come to know each other as colleagues and friends. Although there have been some coordinating challenges along the way, our collaboration as co-editors has been rich, rewarding, and satisfying from start to finish.

It is a particularly important to us to acknowledge the consistent strong support and encouragement provided by one of the finest people in academic publishing, our senior editor at Columbia University Press, the late John Michel. In the work on this volume as in our earlier publications with the press, John, in his own gentle and always humorous way, gave us wise counsel at every step in the process. We are deeply saddened by the recent loss of our colleague and friend and regret that John will not be able to see the published text he jokingly called "the mammoth volume."

We also gratefully acknowledge senior executive editor Shelley Reinhardt's attentive and very skillful guidance of the manuscript's movement through final reviews and editing to publication, as well as the remarkably efficient and competent editing provided by Cyd Westmoreland and her colleagues at Princeton Editorial Associates.

Our final thanks are extended to our partners Mike and Howard, to our children, and to our families (kin and fictive), who support, nurture, and sustain us in personal ways that in turn permit us to spend time away from them, immersed in professional endeavors that sustain us in different ways.

CHILD WELFARE FOR THE

TWENTY-FIRST CENTURY

❖   ❖   ❖   ❖   ❖   ❖   ❖

Introduction

The passage of the Adoption and Safe Families Act (ASFA) of 1997 (P.L. 105-89) marked the culmination of several decades of reform in the child welfare field. This legislation reinforces and clarifies the intent of the Child Welfare and Adoption Assistance Act (P.L. 96-272), which was enacted into law in 1980 due to growing concern that children and youth were being "lost" in foster care. The 1980 act reflected the belief that through the provision of family-centered services and permanency planning, the future for these children and youth would be more appropriate and positive. ASFA builds on earlier laws and codifies many innovative state policies and practices that have emerged to respond to the multiple, often complex, needs of children, youth, and families (see McGowan's chapter for the history and context of child welfare).

All children and youth need a stable, nurturing, and enduring relationship with at least one adult who assures that their physical, emotional, educational, and social needs are met and who protects them from harm. The major role of the child welfare system in the twenty-first century is to insure the safety, permanency, and well-being of children and youth whose families are not meeting these needs or protecting them. Increasingly, attention is being given to programs designed to prevent child abuse and neglect (see the chapter by Guterman and Taylor). Despite these efforts, however, every day, public child welfare systems across the country receive many reports about children who allegedly are not receiving adequate care and protection from their parents or other permanent caregivers. In 2001, child welfare agencies around the country received more than two and one-half million reports of alleged child abuse or neglect; more than 50% of these (1,789,000) were subject to investigation. Less than one-half of those investigations (578,051) were determined to be actual cases of abuse or neglect.

When such reports are received, the child welfare system's legally mandated first response is to immediately and thoroughly investigate the nature and degree of harm experienced by the child. This first response is crucial; in some instances, it has life-and-death consequences for the child involved. In almost all cases, the first response and the engagement of family members, as discussed in Altman's chapter, will shape the work with the identified family. At this initial juncture, agency staff must determine whether the child can safely remain at home if supportive services are provided to improve the parents' level of care (see the chapters by DiPanfilis and by Shlonsky and Gambrill).

Whether children and their families are served through in-home services or children are placed in out-of-home care, the public child welfare system is responsible for providing service to children, youth, and families who come to its attention, in partnership with the courts (see Hardin's chapter), private child welfare structures, and other service systems, such as mental health (see Dore's chapter), substance abuse (see the chapters by Cordero and Epstein, Fenster, and by Maluccio and Ainworth), healthcare (see McCarthy and Woolverton's chapter), education (see the chapters by Elze, Auslander,

1

McMillen, and Stiffman, and by Walsh), and family violence programs (see Postmus's chapter). Those practitioners serving children and families must insure that the array of services is individualized and culturally relevant (see the chapters by Cross and Fox, McRoy, Saltzburg, and Earner). The spiritual relevance of the services may also be of concern (see Hawkins's chapter).

In-Home Services

If, after the initial assessment, it is determined that the child can safely remain in his or her own home with services provided to improve the parents' level of care, the public child welfare system, which is state administered in some areas, county administered in others, is responsible for:

- Assisting families in solving the problems that caused abuse or neglect;
- Supporting families in their communities by helping children and youth to be maintained safely in their homes; and
- Preserving families by preventing separation of children and youth from their families.

To these ends, agency staff must develop an appropriate service plan with the goal of preventing out-of-home placement and monitor its implementation and the child's continuing safety in the home.

Services designed to help families stay together while insuring the well-being and safety of children and youth are sometimes called "in-home services." As the name implies, in-home services are provided in the homes and communities in which families reside. In-home services, discussed in the safety and well-being sections of this volume (see the chapters by Kemp, Allen-Eckard, Ackroyd, Becker, and Burke, and by Berry), assist families in learning the skills necessary for providing care and protection of children and youth and work to prevent out-of-home placements. In some cases,

participation in these services is voluntary; in others, in-home services are mandated. In states, tribes, and localities, these services are known by different names, but they are collectively most generally known as:

- Family support services;
- Family preservation services;
- Intensive home-based services;
- Family crisis services; or
- Family-centered services.

In-home services are based on the principles of client empowerment. Therefore, in-home services are designed to encourage families to take charge of their own lives and to be active partners in the process of supporting their own families. Such services first insure that the child and family's basic needs are addressed (e.g., food, shelter, clothing, health care, child care, employment training) and then attend to the problems that must be resolved to prevent the child's placement in out-of-home care.

Out-of-Home Services

When agency staff members determine that the young person cannot safely remain in his or her own home, the child welfare agency is required to provide for the child's welfare and protection by taking legal and physical custody of the child. These services are often called "out-of-home services." Out-of-home services provide 24-hour care by the child welfare system for children and youth who need to be temporarily separated from their families. Modeled after the 1977 Education of All Handicapped Children Act, these placements are mandated to be guided by the least restrictive setting principle; that is, placement settings are selected that most closely approximate a child's family setting. In addition, placement selections are to be based on sound ecological principles, taking into account the importance of placement in close geographic proximity to the child's own home, school, and other neighborhood supports. There are many different types of placements, which collectively are typically referred to as "foster care." The range of residential services (reviewed by Bullard and Johnson in their chapter) includes:

- Kinship care (sometimes known as "relative care placement");
- Family foster homes (with a licensed foster family not related to the child);
- Therapeutic and medical foster homes (licensed foster parents with additional training to meet the special needs of the child);
- Emergency shelters (very short-term temporary housing for children awaiting a more appropriate setting);
- Group homes (state licensed, community-based facilities with 24-hour staff, with eight to 12 children usually of the same age);
- Supervised independent living settings (state licensed, community-based settings, without 24-hour staff, for older adolescents preparing to transition to adulthood); and
- Residential treatment centers (RTC) (state licensed congregate care settings with an on-site educational facility and intensive health, mental health, and social services).

In making the determination that placement in out-of-home care is necessary, the public child welfare agency accepts the critical responsibility of functioning as the child's parent or caregiver. Consequently, the system staff is expected to insure that care and protection are provided at a level fully adequate to meet each child's basic and individual special needs (see the chapter by Weaver, Keller, and Loyek). The public child welfare agency is challenged further to always provide care at a higher level than that of the parent or caregiver from whom the child was separated.

Federal laws specifically mandate that states and local child welfare agencies take full responsibility for the children and youth in their legal custody. Agencies are responsible for:

- Insuring that children and youth are safe and protected from further harm while separated from their families;
- Insuring that while in care, children and youth receive adequate physical, emotional, and educational care and that their special needs are fully met;
- Working expeditiously to reunify children and youth with their families if they have been separated from their families; and
- Developing and implementing a plan (referred to as the child's "plan for permanency") to provide a safe, nurturing, and permanent home for children and youth who cannot return home to their families. This includes recruiting, retaining, and supporting suitable permanent homes.

In this volume, the section on permanency is extensive. The chapter authors in this section either examine a placement alternative or one of the various permanency pathways that may be utilized to develop plans to achieve the intended long-term, stable home for the child or youth.

Providing a Safe and Nurturing Placement

A child's family is at the center of his or her world. Therefore, for almost all children and youth, the experience of being removed from their family is extremely traumatic. No matter what harms children have experienced, they are attached to their parents/caregivers and thus experience profound loss and fear at being taken to live with strangers. Therefore, the public agency must be prepared to immediately provide the child a safe, nurturing placement and insure that in every way possible, the child is afforded support and stability. For example, every effort must be made to place children with caring relatives and with all siblings also in legal custody, which provides reassurance and comfort to them (see Hegar and Scannapieco's comprehensive overview of kinship care, and Hegar's chapter on siblings), and to place school-aged children near their own schools, thus preventing the loss of familiar teachers and friends. These important efforts reduce the negative impact of separation from family upon the child.

Within days of an out-of-home placement, the public agency must provide children contact with their parents/caregivers (see Hess's chapter on family visiting of children in care), including the child's paternal resources (see Pate's chapter on fathers and the child welfare system), preferably in person. This contact reassures children and youth that they have not been abandoned and that the adults responsible for their care understand their deep need to maintain a relationship with their parents and other family members.

If it is determined that children and youth cannot safely be placed with a relative or other familiar person, the public agency is responsible for identifying a placement with caregivers who are fully prepared to meet not only the child's basic needs but also his or her special needs (see Barbell and Freudlich's chapter on foster care). For example, a child who has been chronically neglected may have severe developmental delays or medical needs; a child who has been repeatedly abused and lived in a violent household may be withdrawn and uncommunicative or aggressive and unresponsive to typical household rules (see Postmus's chapter). A child or youth who has been sexually abused may relate to adults and other children in ways that place him or her at further risk for exploitation. Depending on their nature and extent, children's special needs may be met through placement in a relative or nonrelative foster family home or may require more specialized services, such as a therapeutic or medical foster home. Some children's special needs, including diagnosed mental illness, require the intensive services and structure provided in a group or residential treatment setting. Therefore, at the time of placement, an accurate and full assessment must be made regarding the level of caregiver training and competence, placement

structure, and medical, mental health, and educational services that are required to insure that the child's special needs are fully met while in custody (see Cohen, Hornsby, and Priester's chapter on assessment). Otherwise, children continue to be subjected to repeated traumatic events at a time of already heightened vulnerability.

To address all these issues, the child's public agency caseworker or case manager is charged with coordinating an assessment and service planning process, through which the child's service and placement needs are determined, an appropriate placement setting is selected, and a plan for delivery of needed service is developed. The child's plan for services (the "case plan") is developed in partnership with the child's family, monitored through court and other reviews every six months at a minimum, and revised as indicated by the parent's use of services and the child's needs. In addition, throughout the child's placement, the public agency caseworker/case manager is responsible for maintaining regular contact with the child, the child's parents, and the child's caregiver to insure that the child is safe, that caregivers have the information and support necessary to provide for the child's care, that the continuity of family relationships and connections is preserved for children, and that progress toward the permanent plan is taking place.

Family Reunification as a Permanency Goal

Because most children and youth want to live with their families and because both legally and morally, parents and other legal permanent caregivers have a right to raise their children when they can do so safely, the public agency is required to make reasonable efforts to provide services that enhance family's capacities and facilitate the child's safe return home. This placement outcome is called "family reunification" (see Pine, Spath, and Gosteli's chapter on reunification) and is to be achieved within 12 to 15 months of the child's entry into legal custody.

To achieve reunification, services must be individualized to address the family's particular needs, be accessible, and be provided in a timely manner by competent professionals. Thus it is the public agency's responsibility to insure that at or immediately following the child's placement, the family's service needs are identified, appropriate services are offered, and obstacles to service provision are addressed. Such services necessarily include frequent, regular parent-child (and when placed separately, sibling-sibling) visits and other contacts. Without frequent contact, already fragile family relationships cannot be maintained and children inevitably experience abandonment and deep loss. Without frequent contact, family reunification is much less likely to occur and to occur successfully. Again, the child's well-being and safety are at stake.

When it has been determined that a child may safely be returned to his or her home, an assessment must be made of the follow-up services required to support the family in this often difficult transition. Simply returning a child who has lived out of the home back into the family unit without services to support changes in parents' behaviors predictably results in further harm to the child due to neglect and abuse.

Adoption and Other Permanency Goals

In some instances, due to the severity of the neglect and/or abuse, a parent's diagnosed condition, or a family's history, it can be determined at the time of placement that family reunification cannot safely be achieved. In other instances, such a determination is made after reunification services have been provided and it becomes clear, based on the parents' inability or unwillingness to make the changes required for the child's safe return to their care, that reunification will not be achieved.

In either case, under timetables mandated by federal law, the public agency is responsible for identifying another viable plan for the child's future that provides the child with stability and

a sense of permanence (see D'Andrade's chapter). The agency must determine what plan is appropriate for the child—permanent placement with relatives; adoption; or in some cases, Another Planned Permanent Living Arrangement (APPLA). Steps to achieve this permanent plan must be identified, taken in a timely manner, and documented fully in the case record. For example, achieving the goal of adoption typically requires the legal termination of the parent's rights, recruitment of an appropriate adoptive family, and preparation of the adoptive family and the child for adoption (see Groza, Houlihan, and Wood's chapter on adoption).

Services designed to support birth parents when reunification cannot occur, although not mandated and generally underfunded, are also increasingly being made available by service providers (see the chapters by Hollingsworth and Cooper Heitzman).

In all instances, achieving permanency for the child through means other than family reunification will require services that support the child in working through the realization that he or she will not be returning to his or her parent's care (see Testa and Miller's chapter on guardianship). Permanency arrangements for youth have frequently been defaulted to what was known as "long-term foster care" or "independent living designations." More recently, services for youth have begun to be reconceptualized and to focus more on promoting lifetime connections for youth and less on a permanency goal of independent living services (see Nixon's discussion on youth development issues; Renne and Mallon's chapter on APPLA; and Staller's chapter on the unique needs of runaway and homeless youth).

In all instances, achieving permanency for the child or youth requires that the potential permanent caregiver is fully informed of the young person's basic and special needs and is willing and able to meet those needs. And once the child is placed with the potential permanent caregiver, services to support and to maintain the child's integration into the caregiver's family are essential (see Festinger's chapter on adoption disruption, as well as Wright and Freudlich's chapter on post-permanency services).

Placement of a child in foster care is intended to be a temporary measure. Children should be placed in out-of-home care only when a careful assessment determines that the child's safety and well-being cannot be insured even with the provision of intensive services to the family. In those instances, out-of-home family placement with relatives or others or in a group care setting, depending upon the child's special needs, is a time-limited measure, taken to protect the child until the child can be safely returned to his or her home. When the preferred placement outcome of family reunification cannot be achieved, placement then is necessarily extended. But placement remains a temporary measure, taken until the child can be permanently and legally placed with another family, either relatives or an adoptive family.

In only a few instances should children be required to stay for longer periods in legal custody, including those in which the child's special needs require treatment that cannot be provided in a family setting. The child welfare system is not intended to serve as a replacement for the families that children need and deserve. However, when the child welfare system fails to follow the legally mandated processes outlined above, it will inevitably fail to achieve the goals for permanency it is mandated to accomplish. As a consequence, children will predictably spend longer periods of their lifetimes in legal custody than is necessary or acceptable.

For more than 40 years, research has consistently found that the longer children are permitted to remain in care, the greater the likelihood that they will never return to their own families or move into another stable permanent home. And during lengthy stays in legal custody, if they are exposed to multiple placement changes and/or to other harms in care, including caregiver neglect and abuse, their emotional, physical, social, and educational status will

deteriorate, often markedly. Young children, particularly, who rely on a stable, continuous nurturing adult relationship to develop the capacity for healthy human attachments, are often irreparably harmed by multiple placement changes and neglect and abuse in care (see the chapter by D'Andrade on placement stability). Practice and accreditation standards and federal and state legislation have been devised to prevent such harms to already vulnerable children.

Children in custody necessarily rely on others to document their needs and experiences. Professionals in the child welfare system understand that if it is not written down, it is as if it never happened. Without a full and accurate record of the child's needs and experiences, the child's well-being and safety are in constant jeopardy. Given the life-altering nature of the decisions made in the child protection and permanency planning process, decisions based on incomplete or inaccurate documentation are not only likely to be unwise, but may also be seriously harmful and even life-threatening to a child.

In addition, without timely, accurate, and thorough documentation of the child's experiences while in care, critical aspects of the child's history will be lost. The agency will then be unable to fully and accurately inform others, such as placement caregivers or service providers, about children's needs while in care or to inform children's birth or adoptive families about their needs upon discharge from legal custody.

The circumstances that bring child welfare practitioners into the homes and lives of children, youth, and families are often ambiguous and challenging. The child welfare practitioner is asked to make decisions quickly, based on the best and most complete information available to him or her. This information will always have limitations, and yet decisions based on it will have profound, long-term consequences for children and families. The decisionmaking process is more effective when agency staff work together as a team within the agency and with the family and community partners (see the chapter by Chahine and Higgins) to develop service interventions that include the following elements of good child welfare practice:

- Child-focused: the safety, permanency, and well-being of children and youth are the leading criteria in all child welfare decisions;
- Family-centered: children, youth, parents, and extended family members are involved as partners in all phases of engagement, assessment, planning, and implementation of case plans;
- Strengths-based: practices emphasize the strengths and resources of children, youth, biological and extended families, and their communities;
- Attentive: practices take into account both risk and resilience factors for children, youth, and families (see the chapter by Fraser and Terzian);
- Individualized: case plans are individualized to address the unique needs of the child, youth, and family to appropriately address needs for safety and permanency;
- Culturally competent: problems and solutions are defined within the context of the family's culture and ethnicity;
- Comprehensive: services address a broad range of family conditions, needs, and contexts;
- Community partnership–oriented: planning and implementation of case plans are undertaken in partnership with staff and agencies from different systems that together make a formal commitment to provide the services and supports that the child and family need; and
- Outcome-based: there are measurable outcomes for services regarding the safety, permanency, and well-being of children and youth.

At every stage and for every child and family, the cornerstone of effective child welfare practice is formed by comprehensive and ongoing assessment, the competent and timely provision of appropriate services, and the complete and accurate documentation of service provision and outcomes.

Systemic Issues

On a systemic level, states and local child welfare agencies have had to make strategic decisions about how to use existing financial and staff resources (see the chapter by Sahonchik, Frizsell, and O'Brien), work in partnership with the courts, develop purposeful agreements to coordinate with community-based organizations and other child-serving agencies, and continuously redesign their service delivery so individualized case plans can be developed that will insure the safety of the children and youth.

The principles and provisions of ASFA, the most recent federal legislation concerning child welfare practice, are designed to insure child safety, decrease the time required to reach permanent placements, increase the incidence of adoption and other permanent options, and enhance states' capacity and accountability for reaching these goals. This law has had a significant impact on children and families, the child welfare and court systems, child welfare practice on the front lines, and community-based organizations that are enlisted to help meet the comprehensive needs of children and their families. The influence of this law has been made manifest in the key findings from the Child and Family Services Reviews (see Milner, Mitchell, and Hornsby's chapter), now completed in all 50 states as well as in the District of Columbia and Puerto Rico. The Child and Family Services Review process examines statewide data indicators and qualitative information to determine state achievement in two areas: (1) outcomes around safety, permanency, and well-being; and (2) systemic factors that directly impact the state's capacity to deliver services that support improved outcomes.

Seven systemic factors are also identified for examination by the federal review process:

1. Statewide information system: The state can readily identify the status, demographic characteristics, location, and goals for the placement of every child who is—or has been within the preceding 12 months—in foster care.

2. Case review system: The state provides a written case plan for each child to be developed jointly with the child's parent(s); provides a periodic review of the status of each child no less than once every 6 months; insures that each child in foster care has a permanency hearing no later than 12 months from the date the child entered foster care and not less than every 12 months thereafter; provides a process for termination of parental rights proceedings; and provides foster parents, preadoptive parents, and relative caregivers of children in foster care with notice of and an opportunity to be heard in any review or hearing.

3. Quality assurance system: The state insures that children in foster care placements receive quality services that protect their safety and health and evaluates and reports on these services (see the chapter by Sahonchik, Frizsell, and O'Brien).

4. Staff training: Development and training programs support the goals and objectives in the state's Child and Family Services Plan; address services provided under both subparts of Title IV-B and the training plan under Title IV-E of the Social Security Act; and provide training for staff that provide family preservation and support services, as well as child protective, foster care, adoption, and independent living services. Ongoing training is also provided for staff that addresses the skills and knowledge necessary to carry out their duties within the state's Child and Family Services Plan. Short-term training is also offered for current or prospective foster parents, adoptive parents, and the staff of state-licensed/approved child care institutions that care for foster and adopted children (see the chapter by Mori-son for a discussion of accreditation of child welfare organizations).

5. Service array: The state has an array of services that assesses the strengths and needs of children and families; addresses the needs of the family, as well as the individual child, to create a safe home environment; and enables children at risk of foster care placement to remain with their families when their safety and well-being can be reasonably assured. Services are designed to help children achieve permanency; be accessible to families and children in all political subdivisions covered in the state's Child and Family Services Plan; and be individualized to meet children's and families' unique needs.

6. Agency responsiveness to the community: The state engages in ongoing consultation, coordination, and annual progress reviews with a variety of individuals and organizations representing the state and county agencies responsible for implementing the Child and Family Services Plan and with other major stakeholders in the services delivery system, including, at minimum, tribal representatives, consumers, service providers, foster care providers, the juvenile court, and other public and private child and family servicing agencies.

7. Foster and adoptive parent licensing, recruitment, and retention: The state establishes and maintains standards for foster family homes and child care institutions, applies standards to every licensed/approved foster family home or child care institution that receives Title IV-E or IV-B funds, and complies with the safety requirements for foster care and adoption placements. In addition, each state has a process that recruits foster and adoptive families who reflect the racial diversity of children in the state, and develops and implements plans for the effective use of cross jurisdictional resources to facilitate timely adoption or permanent placement (see Pasztor, McNitt, and McFadden's chapter).

Each of these systemic factors is addressed at various points in this text. These factors greatly affect the experiences not only of those served by the system, but also of those who are responsible for serving them.

By and large, the keys to improving the experiences of children, youth, and families currently in or entering the child welfare system are to continue to identify evidence-based approaches to achieving child and youth safety, well-being, and permanency; to promote more effective methods of implementing those approaches regardless of the jurisdiction within which children and youth reside; and to adequately fund those services essential to achieving child safety, well-being, and permanency. Certainly evaluation of policies and practices resulting from the implementation of ASFA will help the field better understand how to promote the best interests of individual children and youth.

BRENDA G. McGOWAN

Historical Evolution of Child Welfare Services

The major forces shaping the provision of child welfare services in this country—the size and composition of the population at large and the child population at risk; social, economic, and technological demands on families; prevailing ideologies regarding the proper relationships among children, parents, church, and state; dominant views about the causes of poverty, illness, and crime; and the political influence of different interest groups—have all shifted significantly since early colonial days. Yet many of the issues that plague the child welfare field today reflect the unresolved tensions and debates of the past. These tensions include:

- Parents' rights vs. children's needs;
- Saving children vs. supporting families;
- Federal vs. state vs. local responsibility;
- Public vs. voluntary financing and service provision;
- Developmental vs. protective services;
- In-home vs. foster family vs. institutional care;
- Appropriate boundaries between the child welfare, family service, juvenile justice, mental health, and mental retardation systems vs. comprehensive, integrated services;
- Individualized, pluralistic modes of interventions vs. uniform standards and treatment;
- Specialized professional services vs. informal, natural helping networks; and
- Social costs vs. benefits of providing varying levels of care.

All of these issues appear repeatedly in the major historical documents on the American child welfare system.

The one theme that never disappears is the search for a panacea, a solution to the problems of children whose parents are unable to provide adequate care. The proposed solution of today is the concept of permanency planning, but a careful reading of history suggests that the implementation of this concept is no more likely to eliminate the need for extensive, ongoing public provision for children who are poor, neglected, unwanted, socially deficient, or disabled than the infanticide, warehousing, banishment, and foster home programs of the past. The earliest biblical accounts of Moses, Abraham, Isaac, and Jesus all refer in different ways to the problems of dependent and maltreated children. Therefore, although the concept of permanency planning seems to offer the most promising route for service provision in the next decade, it would be naïve to assume that movements in this direction will meet all the needs of the child welfare population without creating or drawing attention to still other problems.

In this chapter, I provide a broad overview of the historical evolution of the child welfare system via examination of the major trends and shifts in service provision for dependent, neglected, and troubled children. This historical overview will give readers a clearer understanding of the sources of some of the current dilemmas and strains in the child welfare field, thereby providing an analytical base for addressing problematic issues that are likely to arise in the future.

Social trends seldom fit into neat lines of demarcation. Unlike historical events, the beginnings of social movements can rarely be traced to a single action or a specific date. They are the result of numerous forces that come together over an extended period of time. Although century boundaries are used as the organizing framework for this chapter, such intervals should not be taken too literally. To do so poses the risk of historical distortion, for social movements and social changes often span more than one century.

Seventeenth and Eighteenth Centuries

The early American settlers were preoccupied with issues of freedom and survival for themselves and their new country. The demands of exploring, settling, and cultivating vast expanses of land were enormous, and because of the small size of the population, contributing members of society were at a premium. The family was the basic economic unit, and all members were expected to contribute to the work of the household.

The concept of childhood, as it is currently understood, was unknown except for very young children. Although there was a high birth rate, approximately two-thirds of all children died before the age of four. Those who lived past this age were expected to start contributing labor as soon as possible by helping with household and farming chores, caring for younger siblings, and so forth. Hence, children moved quickly from infant status to serving essential economic functions for their families. Children were perceived as a scarce and valued resource for the nation, but little attention was paid to individual differences or needs, and the concept of children's rights was nonexistent. As Hillary Rodham (1973:489) commented:

> In eighteenth century English common law, the term children's rights would have been a *non sequitur*. Children were regarded as chattels of the family and wards of the state, with no recognized political character or power and few legal rights.

Although there was no child welfare system as such in those early days, two groups of children were presumed to require attention from the public authorities: orphans and the children of paupers. Because of the high maternal mortality rates and high adult male death rates caused by the vicissitudes of life in the New World, large numbers of children were orphaned at a relatively young age and required special provisions for their care. Children of paupers were also assumed to require special care because of the high value placed on work and self-sufficiency and the concomitant fear that these children would acquire the "bad habits" of their parents if they were not taught a skill and good working habits at an early age. Parents who could not provide adequately for their children were deprived of the right to plan for their children and were socially condemned. To illustrate, a record of the selectmen's meeting in Watertown, Massachusetts, on March 3, 1671, describes the following incident (Watertown Records, as cited in Bremner 1970–1974:68):

> There coming a complaint to us the Selectmen concerning the poverty of Edward Sanderson's family: that they had not wherewith to maintain themselves and children either with supply of provision or employment to earn any, and considering that it would be the charge of the town to provide for the whole family which will be hard to do this year, and not knowing how to supply them with provisions, we [are] considering if we should supply them and could do it, yet it would not tend to the good of the children for their good education and bringing up so they may be useful in the commonwealth or themselves to live comfortably and usefully in time to come; we have, therefore, agreed to put out two of his children into some honest families where they may be educated and brought up in the knowledge of God and some honest calling or labor.

Social provisions for dependent children during this early period derived from the English Poor Law tradition. Children and dependent adults were treated alike and were generally handled in one of four ways:

1. Outdoor relief, a public assistance program for poor families and children consisting of a meager dole paid by the local community to maintain families in their own homes;
2. Farming-out, a system whereby individuals or groups of paupers were auctioned off to citizens who agreed to maintain the paupers in their homes for a contracted fee;
3. Almshouses or poorhouses, institutions established and administered by pubic authorities in large urban areas for the care of destitute children and adults; and
4. Indenture, a plan for apprenticing children to households where they would be cared for and taught a trade, in return for which they owed loyalty, obedience, and labor until the costs of their rearing had been worked off.

In addition to these provisions under the public authorities, dependent children were cared for by a range of informal provisions arranged through relatives, neighbors, or church officials. A few private institutions for orphans were also established during the early colonial period. The first such orphanage in the United States was the Ursuline Convent, founded in New Orleans in 1727 under the auspices of Louis XV of France (Folks 1978). However, prior to 1800, most dependent children were cared for in almshouses and/or by indenture, the most common pattern being that very young children were placed in public almshouses until the age of eight or nine, and then they were indentured until they reached majority.

Thus, the social provisions for dependent children during the first two centuries of American history can be characterized as meager arrangements made on a reluctant, begrudging basis to guarantee a minimal level of subsistence. The arrangements were designed to insure that children were taught the values of industriousness and hard work and received a strict religious upbringing. Provisions were made at the lowest cost possible for the local community, in part because of the widespread belief that indolence and depravity should not be rewarded. Parents who were unable to provide for their children were thought to have abrogated their parental rights, and children were perceived primarily as property that could be disposed of according to the will of their owners—parents, masters, and/or public authorities who assumed the costs of their care. The goal was to make provisions for dependent children that would best serve the interests of the community, not the individual child.

Nineteenth Century

Massive social changes occurred in the United States during the nineteenth century, all of which influenced the nature of provisions for dependent children. The importation of large numbers of slaves and the eventual abolition of slavery first reduced the number of requests for indentured white children and later created opposition to a form of care for white children that was no longer permitted for blacks. The emergence of a bourgeois class of families in which the labor of children and wives was not required at home permitted upper-income citizens to turn their attention to the educational and developmental needs of their own children, as well as those of the orphaned, poor, and delinquent. The large-scale economic growth of the country after the Civil War helped to expand the tax base and to free funds for the development of private philanthropies aimed at improving the lives of the poor. The massive wave of immigrants from countries other than England created a large pool of needy children, primarily Catholic and Jewish, from diverse cultural backgrounds. Finally, the Industrial Revolution changed the entire economic and social fabric of the nation. New industries required different, more dangerous types of labor from parents and youth and created a new set of environmental hazards and problems for low-income families.

The Rise of the Institution

Perhaps the most significant change in the pattern of care for dependent children during the early nineteenth century was the dramatic increase in the number of orphanages, especially during the 1830s. These facilities were established under public, voluntary, and sectarian auspices and were designed to care for children whose parents were unable to provide adequately for them, as well as for true orphans. Two reports issued in the 1820s contributed heavily to the decline of the earlier system of indenture and outdoor relief and to the expansion of congregate care facilities. The 1821 Report of the Massachusetts Committee on Pauper Laws concluded that "outdoor relief was the worst and almshouse care the most economical and best method of relief, especially when it provided opportunities for work" (Abbott 1938:121). The other report, known as the Yates Report of 1824, was issued by the secretary of state for New York following a year's study of poor laws. This report took an even stronger position against outdoor relief and indenture and advocated the care of dependent children and adults in county-administered almshouses. Mr. Yates concluded (Annual Report 1900, as cited in Thurston 1930:68):

1. Removal of human beings like felons for no other fault than poverty seems inconsistent with the spirit of a system professing to be founded on principles of pure benevolence and humanity.
2. The poor, when farmed out, or sold, are frequently treated with barbarity and neglect by their keepers.
3. The education and morals of the children of paupers (except in almshouses) are almost wholly neglected. They grow up in filth, illness, ignorance and disease, and many become early candidates for the prison or the grave.

A major expansion in almshouse care occurred in the years succeeding the publication of these reports. But what was not foreseen by the early advocates of the use of almshouses were the physical and social risks to children posed by housing them with all classes of dependent adults. Although facilities in some of the larger cities established separate quarters for children, most were mixed almshouses caring for young children, "derelicts," the insane, the sick, the blind, the deaf, the retarded, the delinquent, and the poor alike.

By mid-century, investigations of the living conditions of children in poorhouses had started, creating strong pressure for the development of alternative methods of care. For example, a Select Committee of the New York State Senate (New York State Senate 1857, as cited in Bremner 1970–1974:321) reported on a study conducted in 1856, just 32 years after the publication of the Yates Report:

> The evidence taken by the committee exhibits such a record of filth, nakedness, licentiousness, general bad morals, and disregard of religion and the most common religious observances, as well as of gross neglect of the most ordinary comforts and decencies of life, as if published in detail would disgrace the State and shock humanity.... They are for the young, notwithstanding the legal provision for their education, the worst possible nurseries; contributing an annual accession to our population of three hundred infants, whose present destiny is to pass their most impressible years in the midst of such vicious associations as will stamp them for a life of future infamy and crime.

State after state issued similar reports, characterizing almshouses as symbols of human wretchedness and political corruption and calling for special provisions for the care of young children in orphanages under public or private auspices. But reform came slowly, in part because public funds had been invested in the poorhouses and in part because there were no readily available alternatives for the large number of children housed in these facilities. Therefore, laws prohibiting the care of children in mixed almshouses were not passed until the latter part of the century (Abbott 1938).

Black dependent children who were not sold as slaves were cared for primarily in the local almshouses. They were explicitly excluded from most of the private orphanages established prior to the Civil War. Consequently, several separate facilities for black children were founded during this period, the first of which was the Philadelphia Association for the Care of Colored Children, established by the Society of Friends in 1822. To insure the survival of these facilities, their founders attempted to separate the orphanages from the abolitionist movement, with which they were identified. However, the shelter in Philadelphia was burned by a white mob in 1838 and the Colored Orphan Asylum in New York was set on fire during the Draft Riot of 1863 (Billingsley & Giovannoni 1972).

Beginnings of "Foster" Care

With the recognition of the condition of children cared for in mixed almshouses, the stage was set for a number of reform efforts. One such effort began in 1853, with the founding of the Children's Aid Society in New York by Charles Loring Brace. By the end of the century, Children's Aid Societies had been established in most of the other major eastern cities.

Loring Brace was strongly committed to the idea that the best way to save poor children from the evils of urban life was to place them in Christian homes in the country, where they would receive a solid moral training and learn good work habits. Consequently, Loring Brace recruited large numbers of free foster homes in the Midwest and upper New York State and sent trainloads of children to these localities (for an excellent review of the mission of Loring Brace, see O'Connor 2001). By 1879, the Children's Aid Society in New York City had sent 40,000 homeless or destitute children to homes in the country (Bremner 1970–1974).

A somewhat parallel development was the establishment of the Children's Home Society movement. These societies were statewide child-placing agencies under Protestant auspices, also designed to provide free foster homes for dependent children. The first such society was established by Martin Van Buren Van Arsdale in Illinois in 1883. His idea spread rapidly, and by 1916, there were 36 Children's Home Societies, located primarily in midwestern and southern states (Thurston 1930).

The free foster home movement was not without its critics for several reasons. First, although Brace and Van Arsdale viewed their programs as conceptually quite different from the indenture system of the past, in practice, it was difficult to make such a distinction. Their arrangements involved essentially the same three-part contract between the family, the child, and the agency officially responsible for the child. Children were expected to pay for their bread and board through their labor. Investigations of the receiving families were minimal, and many reports were received of children who received poor treatment and were exposed to bad influences during their placement.

A second concern voiced was that foster families, almost by definition, did not have the structure and specialized resources necessary to insure that children received a formal education and thorough training in the tenets of their own religion. Finally—and perhaps most significantly—a number of Roman Catholic leaders opposed this movement on the grounds that children were placed primarily in Protestant homes and were likely to lose their religious faith if they were not given the opportunity to be raised in Catholic settings.

Care of Delinquent Youth

Parallel to the recognition that children are different from adults and need different forms of care came the realization that not all children should be cared for in the same way. Although it had long been recognized that there were differences between dependent children who needed care because their parents could not provide for them and children who needed to be "punished" because they had committed criminal acts, early nineteenth-century America often cared for both groups in the same way—the almshouse. This had not been the case in colonial America; hence, reformers during this later period sought to reestablish differences in the care of these two groups of children.

Under English Common Law, children over the age of seven who committed criminal offenses were treated the same as adults and subjected to harsh, cruel punishments, such as whipping, mutilation, banishment, and even death. The early American colonies adopted very similar procedures and continued to use various forms of corporal punishment for children until the concept of confinement was introduced in the eighteenth century. The predominant mode of punishment shifted to various types of confinement, and by the beginning of the nineteenth century, many of the public almshouses and workhouses held a mixed population of juvenile and adult offenders, as well as the dependent children and paupers for whom the institutions were originally intended. This situation created pressure to establish special facilities for child offenders, and in 1824, the Society for the Reformation of Juvenile Delinquents established the New York City House of Refuge, an asylum for vagrant youth and juvenile offenders designed to provide work training and some formal education (Abbott 1938).

Other cities quickly followed the New York example, and Lyman School, the first state reform school in the United States, opened in Massachusetts in 1848. Numerous other states established separate institutions for delinquent children in the years preceding and following the Civil War, all of which emphasized rigid discipline and hard work. Although many of these facilities were designed as experimental efforts in the reformation of troubled youth, they were forced to derive much of their income from the contracted labor of the juvenile

inmates. This inevitably resulted in institutional corruption, exploitation, and brutal treatment of the youths. For example, one of the leading juvenile authorities of the day, William Letchworth, commented (Letchworth 1882, as cited in Bremner 1970–1974:321):

> While flogging has long been abolished in the Navy and the use of the "cat" in the state prisons, it is still thought necessary in order to realize a fair pecuniary return from the children's labor, for the contractor to inflict severe corporal punishment for deficiency in imposed tasks. One institution in the state, in order to meet the expectation of contractors, was forced in a single year to inflict on the boys employed . . . corporal punishment *two-thousand-two hundred-and-sixty-three times.*

During the latter part of the nineteenth century, there was a number of investigations and exposés of institutional abuse in reform schools, and many public officials and concerned citizens made valiant attempts to improve the quality of life for youngsters in these facilities. But these reform efforts had little impact. Attention gradually turned to developing voluntary institutions for juvenile offenders and finding alternative, community-based means of caring for these youth. Massachusetts and Michigan passed laws permitting the appointment of state probation officers for delinquents, and several other states authorized voluntary aid societies to represent youth in court and supervise their probation. The passage of the first juvenile court law in 1899 represented what Bremner termed "the culmination of various efforts to reform children without committing them to reform schools" (Bremner 1970–1974: 440).

The development of the juvenile court has long been viewed by authorities in the child welfare field as a landmark event in the history of services to dependent and delinquent children. As suggested above, it did not represent a major shift in orientation; the reform efforts of the nineteenth century had been moving in the direction of an approach that emphasized the concept of treatment rather than punishment for youth who had committed delinquent offenses and of separate, individualized services for different groups of children. However, the passage of this law did signal a significant change in the degree to which courts would sanction state intervention in the lives of children.

The first juvenile court law in Illinois resulted from the efforts of a coalition of middle-class reform groups representing a range of civic, feminist, and children's interests. Two of the best-known leaders of this coalition were Julia Lathrop and Jane Addams. Frustrated by their inability to effect any basic reforms in the institutions caring for delinquent youth, they decided that more fundamental changes were necessary to insure that youngsters could be removed from corrupting influences. But they needed to find a constitutionally acceptable basis for intervening in the lives of children considered at risk. After much effort, a bill was worked out with a committee from the Chicago Bar Association giving the Illinois courts of equity jurisdiction over juvenile offenders. These noncriminal courts of equity derive from the English chancery courts that exercise the privilege of the state as parens patriae and do not require the application of rigid rules of law to permit state intervention designed to protect the interest of children (Abbott 1938:330–332):

It was believed that if children were separated from adult offenders and the judge dealt with the problems of "erring children" as a "wise and kind father"—as the statute creating the juvenile courts sometimes directed—wayward tendencies would be checked and delinquency and crime prevented or reduced. Under these laws the child offender was regarded not as a criminal but as a delinquent, "as misdirected and misguided and needing aid, encouragement, help, and assistance." The challenging and seminal idea underlying the establishment which was the lack of the juvenile court, was that its function was to cure, rather than to punish, delinquency—a very much more difficult

task. (For a more detailed discussion, see Abbott 1938:331–332; Bremner 1970–1974:440–441.)

The concept of the juvenile court took hold quickly, spreading rapidly throughout the United States and to various European countries during the early twentieth century. It had a major impact on the development of children's services in the twentieth century. In fact, the debates engendered by the actions of the juvenile court regarding punishment vs. treatment of juvenile offenders and children's rights vs. children's needs, persist to this day.

Expansion of Services

Until the last quarter of the nineteenth century, state intervention in a child's life occurred, for the most part, only when the child threatened the social order. Dominant members of society feared that dependent children would grow up without the moral guidance and education necessary to enable them to become productive members of society. Children violating the law posed not only an immediate threat but also the fear that, without intervention, they would grow up to be adult criminals.

During the latter part of the nineteenth century, the focus of concern began to change. Voluntary organizations founded during this period recognized that families had an obligation to provide for their children's basic needs. If they did not, it was argued, society had the right and obligation to intervene. Thus, the concept of minimal social standards for child rearing was introduced.

The founding of the New York Society for the Prevention of Cruelty to Children in 1874 signaled the beginning of this broader concept of societal intervention on the child's behalf. Similar societies were quickly established in other areas of the country, and by 1900, there were more than 250 such agencies (Bremner 1970–1974). The New York society was established in the wake of the notorious case of "little Mary Ellen" (for a full discussion of this event, see Shelman & Lazoritz 1998). A friendly visitor named Etta Wheeler from the child's neighborhood was horrified by the abusive treatment the child had received from her caretaker and sought help from several child welfare institutions to no avail. Finally she turned to Henry Bergh, president of the Society for the Prevention of Cruelty to Animals, who promptly brought the case to court, requesting that the child be removed from her caretaker immediately. As reported in *The New York Times* (1874, as cited in Bremner 1970–1974:190), "the apprehension and subsequent conviction of the persecutors of little Mary Ellen . . . suggested to Mr. Elbridge T. Gerry, the counsel engaged in the prosecution of the case, the necessity for the existence of an organized society for the prevention of similar acts of atrocity."

Newspaper accounts of the early meetings of the society indicate that the founders saw their primary function as prosecuting parents, not providing direct services to parents or children; in fact, the society was denied tax-exempt status by the State of New York in 1900 because its primary purpose was defined as law enforcement, not the administration of charity (Bremner 1970–1974). However, this agency, as well as the other early child protection societies, quickly turned their interests to all forms of child neglect and exploitation, not confining their activities merely to the prevention of physical abuse of children in their own homes.

The establishment of the Charity Organization Society movement, starting in 1877, also contributed to the expansion of services to children. Founded as a response to unorganized outdoor relief and indiscriminant giving, these societies set out to rationalize charity. Initially their leaders perceived poverty as the fault and responsibility of the individual, and their programs were designed to help the individual correct the situation. They were opposed to monetary giving and to any public sector involvement in the relief of destitution; government was not to be trusted or to provide a "dole," which would encourage laziness and moral decay.

To accomplish this mission, the societies enlisted the aid of "friendly visitors"—the forerunner of the modern social worker—whose responsibilities were to seek out the poor, investigate their need, and certify them as worthy for private help. They were to provide a role model, advice, and moral instruction to the poor so that the latter could rid themselves of poverty. These ideas had a profound influence on the orientation of the early social workers in the family service field.

However, what the friendly visitors discovered was that much poverty was the result of societal forces far beyond the individual's control. Many children were destitute not because their parents were lazy or immoral, but because jobs were not available, breadwinners were incapacitated by industrial accidents, or parents had died. Although the friendly visitors continued to minister to the poor on a case-by-case basis, their recognition of the social roots of poverty converged with the philosophy underlying the establishment of the first settlement houses at the end of the nineteenth century.

The Settlement House movement was a middle-class movement designed to humanize the cities. It emphasized total life involvement, decentralization, experimental modes of intervention, and learning by doing. Although the early leaders shared the Charity Organization Societies' suspicion of public institutions, they were influenced by the concepts of philosophical idealism and pragmatism that shaped the Progressive Era. Consequently, they had a more communal orientation, were concerned about environmental as well as individual change, and placed a strong priority on empirical investigation of social conditions. Their programs included "developmental" services, such as language classes, day-care centers, playgrounds, and family life education. Convinced of the worth of the individuals and immigrant groups they served and the importance of cultural pluralism in America, they saw the causes of many social problems in the environment and sought regulations to improve them.

Thus, by the end of the nineteenth century, services were expanded to protect children and provide for some of their developmental needs within their own homes and communities. Such services were further developed and expanded in the twentieth century.

Administration of Services

By the last quarter of the nineteenth century, two distinct systems of out-of-home care for children had evolved to replace the care of children in mixed almshouses: free foster homes and children's institutions. Four different models were eventually adopted to administer these systems, each typified by the respective provisions of the laws enacted in Massachusetts, New York, Michigan, and Ohio (Abbott 1938).

In Massachusetts, almshouse care for children was abolished in 1879, and legislation was passed in 1887 requiring that city overseers place dependent children in private homes. If cities failed to comply, the State Board of Charities was authorized to place them at the expense of the local communities. Although some private institutions had been established in the state earlier in the century, there was little public subsidy for these facilities. Hence, the Massachusetts solution was primarily a system of state and locally funded foster home care for dependent children (Abbott 1938).

A very different approach was followed in New York State after the care of children in almshouses was prohibited in 1875. Local communities were given the responsibility of planning for these children and had the option of providing either subsidies to private agencies or developing a county-based system of public care. However, an earlier law required that children be placed in facilities under the auspices of the same religious faith as their parents, and sectarian agencies were pressing hard for subsidy. Consequently, a system developed whereby local communities paid a per capita subsidy to voluntary, primarily sectarian, agencies for the care of dependent children (Abbott 1938).

Michigan adopted still another approach after almshouse care for children was prohibited in 1881. A state school for dependent children had been established in 1871, which included a program to investigate and supervise foster homes for children placed by the school. This facility became the major resource for dependent children, although local counties were permitted to provide their own care and a few elected to do so (Abbott 1938).

Finally, instead of developing a state program of care as Michigan did, the Ohio legislature authorized the establishment of children's homes or orphanages in each local county (Abbott 1938).

Each of the remaining states adopted a slightly different model of care following the abolition of almshouse care for children. However, these tended to cluster around the example of one of the four state plans described above, and remnants of these patterns of service provision can be seen in the ways child welfare services are organized in different states today. The major distinctions are related to the allocation of responsibility between state, county, and local governmental units; the relative emphasis given to foster home vs. institutional care; and the degree of public reliance on and subsidy of voluntary agency services.

Related to the development of state systems of child care was the introduction of state policies and procedures for licensing and regulating child care facilities. As Grace Abbott (1938: 15) noted in her classic documentary history, *The Child and the State:*

Most of the states drifted into the policy of aiding private institutions because they were unwilling to accept responsibility for the care of the dependent, and because it seemed to be cheaper to grant some aid to private institutions than for the state to provide public care. . . . Private agencies increased and expanded when public funds became available, and as the money was easily obtained, they accepted children without sufficient investigation of the family needs and resources and kept them permanently or long after they could have been released to their families. This was costly to the taxpayer, but even more important, large numbers of children were deprived of normal home life by this reckless policy.

Later she goes on to say (Abbott 1938:17–18):

> The responsibility of the state to know how its dependent children are cared for was not recognized and was little discussed until the end of the nineteenth century. . . .
>
> At the meetings of the National Conference of Charities and Correction, discussion of the need and the results that might be expected from state supervision of child caring agencies began during the nineties. The case for state responsibility was well put at that time although the administrators' problems were not fully appreciated. . . . It was pointed out that the state should know where its dependent children are, its agents should visit and inspect institutions and agencies at regular intervals—including local public as well as all private agencies—and both should be required to make full reports to the State. Usually welcomed and even demanded by the best private agencies, state supervision was opposed by the poorer agencies and by many individuals who thought a private charity sponsored by a church or one which included the names of leading citizens on the list of board members was, of course, well-administered.

What is important about these comments from a historical perspective is that by the turn of the nineteenth century, leaders in the child welfare field had begun to recognize (1) the state's responsibility for all dependent children; (2) the potential conflict between agencies' needs for ongoing funding and support and children's needs for permanency planning; and (3) the importance of instituting strong regulatory systems, including licensing, service monitoring, and case accountability to protect the interests of children in the child care system.

Thus, by the end of the nineteenth century, the roots had been laid for a complex system of child care. Dependent children were cared for by one group of agencies providing institutional and foster care services. Child offenders were being cared for in a different system. And a third set of agencies, characterized by the Charity Organization Societies and the settlement houses, had started to care for children in their "own homes" in organized ways.

Twentieth Century

The developments at the end of the nineteenth century set the stage for what were to become the hallmarks of the child welfare field during the twentieth century: bureaucratization, professionalization, and expanded state intervention in the lives of families and children. The social status of children was elevated, but this came at the price of some loss of individual freedom and some diminution of voluntary involvement and community control. Bremner (1970–1974:117) notes:

> As the state intervened more frequently and effectively in the relations between parent and child in order to protect children against parental mismanagement, the state also forced children to conform to public norms of behavior and obligation. Thus the child did not escape control; rather he experienced a partial exchange of masters in which the ignorance, neglect, and exploitation of some parents were replaced by presumably fair and uniform treatment at the hands of public authorities and agencies. The transfer of responsibilities required an elaboration of administration and judicial techniques of investigation, decision, and supervision.

Some of the very factors contributing to the current dilemmas in child welfare are directly related to these shifts in responsibility (table 1).

Children's Bureau

The first major event affecting the development of child welfare services in this century was the establishment of the U.S. Children's Bureau in 1912, 3 years after the first White House Conference on Children. The movement to create a federal agency representing

TABLE 1. *Time Line: Evolving Federal Role in Children, Youth, and Family Services*

Year	Event
1909	First White House Conference on Children
1912	Creation of U.S. Children's Bureau
1935	Social Security Act, Title IV, ADC; and Title V, Child Welfare Services Program
1961	Social Security Amendment, AFDC (foster care)
1962	Social Security Amendment (75%/25% match for funding social services for current, former, and potential welfare recipients)
1967	Social Security Amendments: Title IV-B (Child Welfare Services Program, originally authorized under Title V); authorized use of Title IV-A funds for purchase of service from voluntary agencies
1974	Child Abuse Prevention and Treatment Act, P.L. 93-247 (amended in 1978, 1984, 1988, 1992, 1996, and 2003)
1975	Title XX of the Social Security Act
1978	Indian Child Welfare Act, P.L. 95-608
1980	Adoption Assistance and Child Welfare Act, P.L. 96-272 (Title IV-E)
1993	Family Preservation and Support Services Program (enacted as part of the Omnibus Budget Reconciliation Act, P.L. 103-66 and amended Title IV-B)
1994	Multiethnic Placement Act, P.L. 103-382, Title V-E
1996	Personal Responsibility and Work Opportunities Act, P.L. 104-193 (eliminated financial assistance entitlement under AFDC and replaced this with TANF)
1997	Adoption and Safe Families Act (ASFA), P.L. 105-89 (amended Title IV-E)
1999	Foster Care Independence Act, P.L. 106-169
2000	Child Abuse Prevention and Enforcement Act, P.L. 106-177
2001	Promoting Safe and Stable Families Amendment (amended Title IV-B), P.L. 107-133

children's interests was led by Jane Addams and Lillian Wald and included a coalition of leaders from the state boards of charities and corrections, voluntary social service agencies, settlement houses, labor and women's groups, and the National Child Labor Committee. Although the initial funding for the Children's Bureau was very small, restricting the number and range of activities it could undertake, it was given a very broad mandate to (U.S. Statutes 1912, as cited in Parker and Carpenter 1981:62):

> Investigate and report . . . upon all matters pertaining to the welfare of children and child life among all classes of our people, and . . . investigate the questions of infant mortality, the birth rate, orphanage, juvenile courts, desertion, dangerous occupations, accidents and diseases of children, employment, legislation affecting children in the several states and territories.

What was most significant about the passage of this law was that it represented the first congressional recognition that the federal government has a responsibility for the welfare of children. It also introduced the concept of public responsibility for all children, not just the groups of poor, neglected, disturbed, and delinquent children served by public and private agencies. Julia Lathrop was appointed the first chief of the Children's Bureau, and under her skilled leadership, the office gained widespread public support and multiplied its annual budget rapidly, enabling its staff to undertake a wide range of investigatory, reporting, and educational activities (for a detailed discussion, see Lathrop 1919, June 1–8). The Sheppard-Towner Act of 1921 gave the bureau responsibility for administering grants-in-aid to the states for maternal and child health programs, thereby expanding its influence even further and introducing the concept of federal payment for direct service provision.

The entry of the federal government into the field of child welfare did not occur without conflict. The initial bill authorizing the establishment of the bureau was opposed by some of the leaders in the voluntary social welfare sector who feared governmental monitoring and scrutiny, and by others who viewed the creation of such a federal agency as an unnecessary intrusion on states' rights. The debate on the Sheppard-Towner Act was more vitriolic, perhaps because of the early successes of the Children's Bureau, and perhaps because by 1921, the country had again entered a more conservative social era. For example, a senator from Kansas commented (Congressional Record 1921, as cited in Bremner 1970–1974:1017–1018):

> Fundamentally the scheme of the bill amounts to this: We are asked to select from all the millions of women of the United States four or five spinsters, whose unofficial advice would probably not be sought by a single mother in the land . . . we are asked to confer upon these inexperienced ladies a title and salary, whereupon it is assumed they will immediately become endowed with wisdom and be qualified to instruct the mother, who has been with her baby before it was born and after it was born, how to take care of that baby. Also it is assumed that this band of lady officials can perform that function in the homes of a hundred and ten million people.
>
> To what purpose do we make this revolutionary change? Why do we create this new army of government employees? . . . If it is claimed that the Children's Bureau is to devote its attention chiefly to the poor, my answer is that the poor are entitled to the best as well as the rich. . . . But this is not the purpose of the bill. I repeat that its basic idea is that the American people do not know how to take care of themselves; and that the state must force its official nose into the private homes of the people; that a system of espionage must be established over every woman about to give birth to a child and over the child, at least until it arrives at school age.

Despite periodic attacks such as these, the Children's Bureau continued to serve as the primary governmental agency representing the interests of children for many years. The activities of the Children's Bureau changed considerably over the years as the leadership shifted from those concerned with broad economic and social issues affecting the welfare of children to those who focused more narrowly on issues and problems in the child welfare field. But despite differing emphases and varying levels of influence, it has continued to carry out its primary functions of investigation, advocacy, standard setting, public education, research, and demonstration. Presently the Children's Bureau is a division of the Administration for Children and Families, a subdivision of the U.S. Department of Health and Human Services (HHS; see www.acf.hhs.gov/programs/cb/ for information about the Children's Bureau).

Early Developments in the Organization and Provision of Services

During the first three decades of the twentieth century, many of the trends in child welfare initiated during the late nineteenth century continued. In part because of the leadership of the Children's Bureau, notable progress was made during the early part of the century in improving the administration of child welfare services. An increased number of public child welfare agencies was established, and separate children's bureaus or divisions within the department of public welfare were created in some of the more progressive states. Many states moved to county-based rather than local systems of service provision, and state departments of welfare assumed increased responsibility for setting standards, licensing, and regulation of public and voluntary child care facilities.

Before 1935, the states had little leverage for influencing service provision at the local or county level, but Alabama assumed the lead in developing a coordinated system of state and county child welfare services, in part via the use of state grants-in-aid to counties for administration of the state truancy law. As additional state grants-in-aid were made available, other states followed this model.

Significant progress was also made in establishing civil service standards for the hiring and promotion of personnel in child welfare positions, insuring that more qualified persons were available to carry out what were increasingly being recognized as professional tasks (Abbott 1938).

Two major national voluntary organizations concerned with standard setting, coordination, agency accreditation, research, and knowledge dissemination in the field of family and children's services were established during this period: the American Association for Organizing Family Social Work (later, the Family Service Association of America) in 1919 and the Child Welfare League of America in 1920. Both of these organizations have had a long and continuing record of influence on the nature of family and child welfare services, especially in relation to the role of the social work profession in this service arena.

Also during this era, the long, rather notable history of child welfare research was initiated with the publication in 1924 of Sophie Van Theis's (1924) outcome study of 910 children placed in foster care by the New York State Charities Aid Association. Although it is never certain what combination of facts, values, and external social circumstances contribute to the shaping of public policy in a specific service domain, it is clear that the extensive research on child welfare services conducted since this first study has contributed greatly to the various ongoing debates regarding the goals and models of service provision.

The scope and level of juvenile court activities also increased considerably during this period, in spite of the concerns expressed by some immigrant and minority groups about excessive state intervention in their children's lives. By 1919, all but three states had passed juvenile court legislation, and the jurisdiction of the court had been extended in many locations (Abbott 1938). Also related to increased court intervention in family life were the expansion of court services, the assignment of the work of the courts to specialists trained in social investigation, the establishment of the first court clinic in Chicago in 1909 by psychologist William Healy, and the initiation of the child guidance movement a few years later with the founding of the Judge Baker Clinic in Boston. These developments both reflected and con-

tributed to a different understanding of the causes and solutions for juvenile delinquency, leading to a greater emphasis on individual treatment of children in the community and a blurring of the distinctions between delinquent, disturbed, and dependent youth.

Protective services for children were also expanded during this period, especially after 1912, when public agencies began to be charged with responsibility for this population (Bremner 1970–1974). These agencies gradually moved away from their earlier emphasis on law enforcement, focusing on providing casework services to parents to permit children to remain in their own homes.

At the same time, foster boarding homes and child care institutions for dependent children continued to expand. And the debate regarding the relative merits of foster homes vs. institutions, a debate that traditionally had strong religious overtones because of the lack of sufficient foster homes for Roman Catholic and Jewish children, continued well into the 1920s (Bremner 1970–1974).

Another significant development of the 1920s was the establishment of adoption as a child welfare service. Informal adoptions had, of course, occurred since early colonial days, and laws providing for public record of the legal transfer of parental rights from biological parents to adoptive parents were passed in the mid-nineteenth century in a number of states. But public recognition of the need to protect the interests of children in these transactions did not develop until the early twentieth century. Minnesota in 1917 was the first state to pass a law requiring that judges refer nonrelative adoption cases to a voluntary or public welfare agency for investigation prior to approval of the petition to adopt; by 1938, 24 states had passed similar legislation (Abbott 1938:64–66).

Note that although these investigations were designed to insure that the biological family ties had been appropriately terminated and that the adopting parents could provide adequate care and would accept full parental responsibilities, adoption at the time was viewed primarily as a service for couples unable to have children of their own, not as a service for dependent children in need of care. Adoption was provided only for young, healthy, white children, most of whom were born out of wedlock to middle-class women. This service was seldom planned for children of the poor. Moreover, although public agencies carried out many of the court-ordered investigations of adoptive parents, separate adoption services were established only under voluntary auspices. Adoption was not considered a right or even a need of dependent children in care of public agencies (Billingsley & Giovannoni 1972).

Expansion of In-Home Services

In reviewing various developments in the organization and provision of children's services during the early twentieth century, special emphasis must be given to Bremner's comment (1970–1974:247–248): "The great discovery of the era was that the best place for normal children was in their own homes. This idea conflicted with the widespread dislike of public relief but coincided with the philanthropic desire to preserve the integrity of the family." Delegates to the first White House Conference on Children in 1909 went on record as supporting the following principles (Letter to the President 1900, as cited in Bremner 1970–1974:365):

1. Home life is the highest and finest product of civilization.... Children should not be deprived of it except for urgent and compelling reasons. Children of parents of working character, suffering from temporary misfortune, and children of reasonably efficient and deserving mothers who are without the support of the normal breadwinners should as a rule be kept with their parents, such aid being given as may be necessary to maintain suitable homes for the rearing of the children.
2. The most important and valuable philanthropic work is not the curative, but the preventive; to check dependency by a thorough study of its

causes and by effectively remedying or eradicating them should be the constant aim of society.

Progress was made in the succeeding years toward the goal of maintaining children in their own homes by the institution of mothers' pensions or public aid to dependent children in their own homes. Illinois provided leadership in this direction by passing a Fund to Parents Act in 1911, and 20 other states passed similar legislation within the next two years. By 1935, all but two states had passed some type of mothers' aid laws (Abbott 1938). These funds were provided on a very limited and somewhat arbitrary basis. But even this small improvement in public assistance provisions for children in their own homes did not take place without controversy. For example, in 1912, Mary Richmond, author of the first basic text on social casework, is quoted as saying (Almy 1912, as cited in Abbott 1938:232):

So far from being a forward step, "funds to parents" is a backward one—public funds not to widows only, mark you, but to private families, funds to the families of those who have deserted and are going to desert.

Edward Devine, director of the New York School of Social Work, took a similar position, challenging the proposal for mothers' pensions (Devine 1913, as cited in Abbott 1938:232):

as having no claim to the name of pension and no place in a rational scheme or social legislation; as embodying no element of prevention or radical cure for any recognized social evil; as an insidious attack upon the family, inimical to the welfare of children and injurious to the character of parents.

However, other leading social reformers and social workers of the time vigorously supported the concept of maintaining children in their own families, and by 1923, "the number of dependent children being maintained in their own homes was approaching the number of those in institutions and far in excess of those in foster homes" (Bremner 1970–1974:248). A statement from the annual report of the New York Children's Aid Society for 1923 conveys the consensus that was gradually emerging among professional child welfare workers (New York Children's Aid Society 1923, as cited in Thurston 1930:138):

> There is a well-established conviction on the part of social workers that no child should be taken from his natural parents until everything possible has been done to build up the home into what an American home should be. Even after a child has been removed, every effort should be continued to rehabilitate the home and when success crowns one's efforts, the child should be returned. In other words, every social agency should be a "home builder" and not a "home breaker."

The nature of services provided to dependent children was modified still further during the 1920s by the growing preoccupation of leading social work educators with psychoanalytic theory and individual treatment. In conjunction with an expanded professional knowledge base about the developmental needs of children and adolescents, this trend led to widespread adoption of the goal of providing individualized services to dependent children and attending to their emotional needs, as well as to their needs for economic security. For example, Henry Thurston (1930:199) commented:

> What religion and theology have told us of the further needs of children to whom bread alone has been given, we have often failed to understand; but we are slowly learning to understand it as it is being restated for us in terms of the new psychology of the emotions and of behaviors. Dr. Herman Adler, of the Juvenile Psychopathic Institute of Chicago . . . says that to answer the question fully as to what a child needs, we must understand "a total personality in a total situation."

This expanded understanding of children's emotional needs contributed greatly to the development of improved child welfare services, but it had two unfortunate consequences. First, it led to increased emphasis on individual psychopathology rather than on social conditions as the source of family and child dysfunction and hence to the expansion of psychological rather than environmental services in the voluntary child care sector. Second, it contributed to the increased separation of voluntary family service and child welfare agencies, as the former were more likely to be staffed by professional workers interested in providing pure "casework," that is, counseling, whereas workers in the latter were required to provide a broader range of services.

These early twentieth-century developments in the field of family and children's services had a major impact on the nature and scope of programs designed to help American families cope with the economic and social problems experienced in the aftermath of the depression that began in 1929. The trends that had special significance for subsequent policy and program development were:

- Expansion of public sector involvement in the lives of families and children;
- Intensification of the traditional separation between the public and voluntary service sectors, especially in the eastern and midwestern states, where the voluntary agencies were firmly entrenched;
- Increasing preoccupation with psychological modes of treatment, especially among professional workers in the voluntary sector as they relinquished responsibility for traditional forms of alms giving and concrete service provision; and
- Crystallization of the boundaries between voluntary child welfare and family service fields due to increasing emphasis on specialization in out-of-home vs. in-home treatment.

Special Arrangements for the Care of Black Children

The history of child welfare services prior to the passage of the Social Security Act in 1935 is essentially a history of services for white children. Standard texts on the history of child welfare provide little information on services for black children; in fact, because of the middle-class white bias that has pervaded most studies of American history, relatively little was known about services for black families and children until the publication in 1972 of a text by Billingsley and Giovannoni (1972) on black children and American child welfare.

Because black children were systematically excluded from the child welfare services that developed for white children in the late nineteenth and early twentieth centuries—sometimes by explicit exclusionary clauses, sometimes by more subtle forms of discrimination—the black community developed what was essentially a separate system of care for their dependent children. During the period after the Civil War, black children were cared for through a variety of informal helping arrangements and a range of orphanages, homes for old folks and children, day nurseries, and homes for working girls (Billingsley & Giovannoni 1972; see also Peebles-Wilkins 1995).

This picture remained relatively constant until the 1920s, when several converging factors led to changes in the child welfare system's response to black children. One was the establishment in 1910 of the National Urban League, an organization that took a vocal, active role in pressing for more equitable distribution of child welfare services as part of its broader mission to achieve freedom and equality for all blacks. Another major impetus for change was the large-scale migration of blacks to urban areas during and after World War I, a development that forced increased recognition of the needs of black children. Finally, the changes taking place in the child welfare system itself created greater openness to black children: the number of public facilities increased; many of the voluntary agencies changed their exclusionary intake policies; and the shift from institution to foster home as the predominate form of care permitted agencies to recruit black foster homes for black children, thereby avoid-

ing potential racial tensions (Billingsley & Giovannoni 1972).

Thus by 1930, there was a general expectation, strongly supported by the participants at the White House Conference on Children, that black children were entitled to the same standards of care as white children and that they should generally be served through the existing child welfare system. This changed perception of the needs of black children had obvious benefits in relation to the goal of racial integration. But it also had several unfortunate consequences, as it halted the growth of the black child care system, limited the possibility of blacks assuming leadership roles in agencies caring for black children, and served to hide some of the subtler but ongoing forms of discriminatory treatment of black children in the child welfare system (Billingsley & Giovannoni 1972).

Passage of the Social Security Act

It has often been suggested that the legislation introduced in the first 100 days of the Roosevelt administration in 1933 changed the entire social fabric of the country by redefining the role of the federal government in addressing social welfare problems and moving the United States reluctantly, but inexorably, toward becoming a welfare state. Certainly the Social Security Act, passed in 1935, had a major impact on the structure and financing of child welfare services; in fact, some of the deficiencies in the current service system can be traced directly to the provisions of this law (see the introduction to Section I by Mallon and Hess). Yet the roots of many of the current policy dilemmas and service delivery problems were present before the passage of this law.

To summarize, the emerging issues in the child welfare field prior to 1935 can be characterized as follows:

1. The goals of child welfare services had begun to shift, in principle, from rescuing the children of poor families and providing them a

minimal level of sustenance, moral guidance, and work training via the provision of substitute care to providing the supports necessary to enable parents to care adequately for children in their own homes, arranging substitute care only on the basis of individualized assessment of case need.

2. The concept of state intervention in family life to protect the interests of children was gaining increased acceptance, and efforts had been made to expand societal provisions and protections for all children via the establishment of free compulsory education, child labor protections, the development of limited homemaker services, day nurseries, maternal and child health programs, mothers' pensions, and child guidance clinics.

3. As a consequence of the establishment of the juvenile court, juvenile offenders were receiving more individualized treatment, a larger number of youths were coming under the purview of the legal system, and the boundaries between the child welfare and criminal justice systems were becoming blurred.

4. The increasing bureaucratization and professionalization of the child welfare field, although improving standards for service and highlighting the goal of providing equal treatment to all, also functioned to increase the social distance between service providers and consumers and to deepen the gap between the goals and realities of service provision.

5. Large numbers of children continued to be placed in substitute care arrangements with little individualized case planning.

6. Black children continued to receive inferior, more punitive treatment than did whites; and poor families and children served through the public sector were less likely to receive the intensive individualized treatment available to those served by some of the voluntary, primarily sectarian, agencies.

7. Adoption was viewed as a service designed primarily for adoptive parents, and white,

healthy infants of middle-class unmarried mothers were the only children likely to be placed in adoptive homes.

Two components of the Social Security Act of 1935, both stemming in large measure from the recommendation of the Children's Bureau, had a significant impact on the subsequent development of child welfare services. Title IV, Grants to States for Aid to Dependent Children, sought to extend the concept of mothers' pensions by providing federal matching funds for grants to fatherless families, requiring a single state agency to administer the program, and mandating coverage of all political subdivisions in each state. It was designed as a federal grant-in-aid program and permitted state autonomy in setting eligibility standards, determining payment levels, and developing administrative and operational procedures. The program, later named Aid to Families of Dependent Children (AFDC), was eventually extended to families with a permanently and totally disabled parent, and, at state option, to families with an unemployed parent. Although the AFDC program became increasingly expensive and controversial, it undoubtedly contributed more than any other social program to the goal of enabling children at risk of placement to remain with their own families.

The other major component of the Social Security Act affecting the provision of child welfare services was Title V, Part 3, Child Welfare Services. This program was designed not only to help children in their own families, but also to benefit those in substitute care by "enabling the United States, through the Children's Bureau, to cooperate with State public welfare agencies in establishing, extending, and strengthening, especially in predominantly rural areas, public welfare services . . . or the protection and care of homeless, dependent, and neglected children, and children in danger of becoming delinquent" (Title V, Social Security Act 1935, as cited in Bremner 1970–1974: 615). Although the funding for this program was quite modest, states quickly took advantage of this relatively permissive legislation to obtain federal funding for child welfare services. To illustrate, prior to the passage of the Social Security Act, the organization of child welfare services at the state and county was in relative disarray in most jurisdictions. However, by 1938, all but one state had submitted a plan for the coordinated delivery of child welfare services (Bremner 1970 1974). This component of the Social Security Act, later subsumed under Title V-B, has had continuing influence on the development of child welfare services.

The Decades from 1940 to 1960

The period from the late 1930s to the late 1950s was a time of relative quiet, consolidation, and gain for the child welfare field. The total number and rate of children placed in foster homes and institutional care declined substantially after 1933 (Low 1966, as cited in Bremner 1970–1974), whereas the proportion of children receiving services in their own homes, the total public expenditures for child welfare, and the total number of professionals in public child welfare increased significantly during this period (Bremner 1970–1974; Richan 1978). Major strides were made by the Children's Bureau and the Child Welfare League of America in formulating and monitoring standards for service provision. Every state made significant progress in developing comprehensive, coordinated public child welfare services, insuring equal access to children of different social, economic, and ethnic backgrounds, and expanding professional educational opportunities for child welfare staff (Bremner 1970–1974). And because of the growing emphasis in the social work profession on the development of clinical knowledge and skills, the quality of individual services provided to families and children was greatly enhanced during this period.

The only significant shifts in service provision during these years took place in the voluntary sector, partly as a consequence of the public sector's assumption of many of the functions formerly assumed by private agencies and partly as the result of demographic changes. The Child Welfare League of America published its first standards for adoption practice in 1938, and many agencies initiated and expanded adoption services in the years after World War II. More elaborate procedures were instituted for studying potential adoptive couples, "matching" children and families, and monitoring the adoptive families during the period preceding legal adoption. Adoption studies were frequently assigned to the most experienced staff, and adoption workers began to acquire special status in the child welfare field. Although the emphasis shifted from viewing adoption primarily as a service for parents to seeing the child as the primary client, in most settings, healthy white infants continued to be considered the only real candidates for adoption. However, as the number of adoptive applicants increased, a few agencies began to experiment with intercountry and interracial adoptions. Also, the National Urban League sponsored a major project on foster care and adoption of black children from 1953 to 1958, and a 5-year interagency demonstration adoption project was established by 13 adoption agencies in the New York City area in 1955 to develop and implement methods of recruiting adoptive families for black and Puerto Rican children (Billingsley & Giovannoni 1972).

During the 1940s and 1950s, increased emphasis was also given to services for unmarried mothers. Although illegitimacy is a centuries-old social problem and special programs for unwed mothers were developed in this country early in the twentieth century, the historical concern was for the protection of the child and the punishment of the mother. It was not until the late 1930s that social workers started to focus attention on the needs of the unmarried mother. During the next two decades, there was a great upsurge in social work publications on such issues as the psychodynamic causes of unwed motherhood, the meaning and potential benefits of surrendering a child for adoption, and the role of the caseworker in working with unmarried mothers (see Bernstein 1960; Young 1954). As the illegitimate birth rate began to increase following World War II, many voluntary child welfare agencies established special services for unwed parents incorporating these new theoretical insights (Costin 1969).

During the same period, there was also a marked shift in the types of institutional care provided to dependent youth, as many of the traditional child care facilities began to be converted into various types of residential treatment centers. For example, in 1950, 45% of the white children in residential care were in institutions for dependent children, and 25% were in institutions for the mentally disabled. By 1960 only 29% were in child care institutions, and 36% were in facilities for the mentally disabled. Although the distribution of nonwhite children showed a similar trend, in 1960, over half of the nonwhite children (54%) were confined in correctional facilities compared to only 25% of the white children (Billingsley & Giovannoni 1972:89), suggesting that the trend toward individualized treatment planning was not strong enough to counter patterns of racially discriminatory treatment.

The relatively slow pace of change in the child welfare field during the 1940s and 1950s can be explained in part by the need for social workers to deal with other, more pressing problems—the aftermath of the depression and World War II. They then needed time to implement, refine, and expand existing services before turning their attention to new service requirements. Much professional energy during this period was also devoted to exploring psychological problems, improving casework methods, and enhancing professional status by providing service to clients above the poverty line. Most child welfare workers during this period tended to view the provision of individual casework services as the most prestigious and critical of their professional tasks. Having been relieved of their earlier public assistance

functions, social workers were endeavoring to provide high-quality therapeutic services to the clients who requested help from their agencies. They raised few questions about what was happening to the families and children not referred for casework services or to those who were unable to benefit from the types of service offered in the established family service and child welfare agencies.

Although the problems of the poor were brought to the attention of the profession again in the 1950s with the publication of several studies discussing efforts to work with "multiproblem," "disorganized," and "hard-to-reach" families (See Buell 1973; Geisman & Ayers 1952; New York City Youth Board 1958), these developments served primarily to stimulate workers to seek more effective ways of providing existing modes of casework service to this population. Even though it was clear that this subgroup of poor families was demanding a disproportionate amount of attention from public assistance, family service, child welfare, and public health agencies, direct service providers gave relatively little thought to their inability to work effectively with this population. Questions that should have been raised about the organization of services and the effectiveness of prevailing intervention strategies were rarely discussed.

The 1960s

Early in the 1960s, child welfare agencies began to be severely criticized for their failure to attend to the changing needs of the child welfare population. The first major challenge to the field was the publication of Maas and Engler's (1959) study, *Children in Need of Parents*. This study of children in foster care in nine communities posed many of the questions raised repeatedly since that time about children in "limbo": children who had drifted into foster care, had no permanent family ties, and were not being prepared for adoptive placement. The field has been attacked repeatedly in succeeding years—both from within and without—for failure to insure permanency planning, inability to prevent placement, failure to place children in need of protection, inherent racism and classism, antifamily bias, violation of parents' and children's rights, arbitrary decisionmaking procedures, incompetency and inefficiency of its staff, high costs, and mismanagement (see, e.g., Bernstein, Snider, & Meezan 1975; U.S. Department of Health, Education, and Welfare 1976; Gruber 1978; Knitzer, Allen, & McGowan 1978; Persico 1979; Strauss 1977; Temporary State Commission on Child Welfare 1975; Vasaly 1976).

The juvenile court has also come under attack. Several recent histories of American child welfare have challenged the traditional view of the juvenile court as protecting the interests of children and representing a radical change in their treatment. For example, in their analysis of the impact of the American child welfare system on black children, Billingsley and Giovannoni (1972) suggest that the labeling process by which black youth were described as "delinquent" in order to remove them from what were considered the less acceptable nineteenth-century forms of child care forced them to accept a more socially deviant label and to enter a less desirable system of care than that available to white youth. And Anthony Platt (1969:176–177) concludes his study of the movement to create the juvenile court in the late nineteenth century as follows:

> The child savers should in no sense be considered libertarians or humanists. . . . The child-saving movement was not so much a break with the past as an affirmation of faith in certain aspects of the past. Parental authority, home education, domesticity, and rural values were emphasized because they were in decline as institutions at this time. . . . In a rapidly changing and increasingly complex urban society, the child-saving philosophy represented a defense against "foreign" ideologies and a preservation of cherished values.

These attacks have done much to refocus attention on the problems in the field and to set a number of internal reform processes in motion. But the more significant determinant of changes in the child welfare field during the two decades prior to 1960 had been the external environment: political events and the changes in demographics, economic and social conditions, interest groups, and belief systems that shape the context in which child welfare services operate.

The inauguration of the Kennedy administration in 1961 ushered in an era of tremendous social ferment and change. The major issues and themes of the subsequent two decades are probably well known to the reader, at least in broad strokes. But to recap briefly, in the 1960s, we witnessed the rediscovery of poverty as a public issue; the ill-fated War on Poverty under the Johnson administration; the expansion of the Civil Rights movement, leading to the passage of the 1964 Civil Rights Act and the subsequent shocking realization that the guarantee of civil rights alone could not insure justice; the emergence of the concept of black power and the racial conflicts of the late 1960s; the development of the Welfare Rights movement and the establishment of other related types of clients' rights groups; the burgeoning of a youth culture that symbolized many challenges to traditional American values and mores; and the perpetuation of an unpopular war that contributed to the growing distrust and alienation of large segments of the population from governmental institutions (Ryan & Morris 1967).

The child welfare field of the early 1960s was a relatively small, self-contained service system with limited staff and resources. It maintained rather rigid system boundaries, making it difficult for many children and families to gain access to services and equally difficult for other clients to be discharged from care. Quality and coverage were very uneven; whereas some agencies, primarily in the voluntary sector, were providing intensive, highly specialized, professional services to a small number of select clients, other public and voluntary agencies struggled to provide minimum care and protection to large numbers of needy youngsters. Services were geared almost entirely toward placement, and individual casework was the primary intervention modality. Concepts of community control and clients' rights were essentially nonexistent (for a review of this period, see Kahn 1969).

Although the Children's Bureau attempted to provide leadership and direction via the promulgation of standards and the administration of small research and demonstration grants, until the late 1960s, overall federal participation in the child welfare field was minimal. Organizational and funding arrangements varied from state to state, but some combination of state and local responsibility for service provision was utilized in most areas. The participation of the public sector in the financing and direct provision of child care services had increased steadily since the turn of the century, but control of program planning and development, service priorities and policies, and program monitoring and evaluation remained primarily in the voluntary sector, under the auspices of local coordinating councils and welfare planning bodies. Consequently, there were minimal efforts to insure case integration or program coordination within the child welfare system, boundaries and linkages between child welfare and other social service systems were frequently haphazard and often dysfunctional, and agency accountability mechanisms were minimal.

The findings of a study by Ryan and Morris (1967) of the child welfare networks in metropolitan Boston in 1964 illustrate quite graphically the nature of the child welfare services in this era. Although there were obviously some idiosyncratic factors in the way services were organized in Boston, the consequences for families and children seeking help within the existing service network were not atypical of the experiences of similar clients in other areas of the country at the time. The study consisted of an examination for five weeks in 1964 of the total intake ($N = 683$) of thirteen public, voluntary, and sectarian agencies constituting the basic child welfare network for the metropolitan area and an intensive case reading analysis of the 265 cases ultimately accepted for service (Ryan & Morris 1967).

The study revealed that the child welfare network consisted of two relatively independent systems, one serving the suburban, white-collar, unmarried mother–adoptive family population; and the other, the urban-poor "child-in-family-in-trouble" population. Approximately 29% of the service inquiries could be categorized as unmarried mothers, 21% as child problems, and 50% as parenting problems. The agencies responded very differently to the requests for help, accepting about 65% of the unmarried mother cases, 34% of the child problem cases, and 29% of the parental problem situations. Moreover, the data suggest that intake decisions were made on a very stereotypical basis, largely unrelated to individual case need (Ryan & Morris 1967).

The agency network dealing with the unmarried mother population seemed to provide relatively efficient and effective services, helping women to plan for the birth of their children and arranging a significant number of adoptions. However, this population represented only about one-third of the total number of illegitimate births in the metropolitan area that year; little was known about the much larger number of unmarried mothers who did not approach the child welfare network for help and/or were not accepted for service if they did request assistance (Ryan & Morris 1967).

The other child welfare network attempted to serve a very different population of parents and children, many of whom were low-income urban residents, had long-standing familial difficulties, and presented a range of environmental, parent-child relationship, and mental health problems. For these clients, the child welfare system was clearly viewed as the end of the line. They were usually referred by the community after other attempts at service provision had failed and placement was seen as the only solution. Yet only about one-third of these cases were actually accepted for services. Little is known about what happened to the other potential clients, all of whom were apparently in need of intensive child welfare services (Ryan & Morris 1967).

Based on their findings, the authors concluded that the concept of a comprehensive child welfare service network in metropolitan Boston was essentially a myth. The lack of flexibility in intake policies and decisionmaking processes, combined with the lack of resources necessary to deal with the magnitude of the problem, made it impossible for the participating agencies to accept and serve many of the clients appropriately referred for services. Ryan and Morris's recommendations reflected the thinking of many other leaders in the field at the time: the development of a comprehensive, public family and children's service system; joint planning between the public and voluntary child welfare sectors; development of rational policies on specialization by voluntary agencies; expanding resources, financing, and staff; development of joint planning, coordinating, and accountability mechanisms for subsystems within the child welfare network; decentralization of program operations; closer coordination at the local level with other major public service systems; and expansion of preventive service and social action efforts.

The study has been described in some detail because it conveys clearly the nature of concern about family and children's services in the early 1960s that precipitated and accompanied many of the subsequent changes in the organization and delivery of social services. Forces for reform were in ascendancy again during these years, and several advisory committees and task forces composed of leading social welfare experts and key policymakers in the Kennedy and Johnson administrations were formed to study public welfare policy and consider needed changes in public assistance and social service programs. The 1962 and 1967 amendments to the Social Security Act reflected the recommendations of these advisory bodies, particularly in relation to the expansion of provisions for public social services, and set a policy framework for subsequent developments in this sphere (Lindhorst & Leighninger 2003).

What is important from a historical perspective is that the clear intention of the social welfare leaders involved in the deliberations that resulted in these Social Security Act amendments was to develop a comprehensive public service system that would meet the needs of low-income families. Futhermore, it was their intention in passing these amendments to diminish the dysfunctional separation between child welfare and family service programs and to guarantee children in families receiving AFDC the services and benefits available to children in foster care. In other words, it was hoped that the development of comprehensive public social services for families and children would help to alleviate many service delivery problems and inequities.

Unfortunately, this goal was essentially doomed from the start because of the unrealistic expectations and conflicting objectives, hopes, and fears that quickly developed among advocates and skeptics alike around the concept of expanded public social services. Social welfare leaders, envisioning a grand new scheme of service provision, failed to anticipate the degree to which legislative intent and rational social planning could be undermined by restrictive federal and state administrative regulations; political, bureaucratic, and staffing constraints within the public sector; and the intransigence of established interest groups in the family and children's service field. Political and civic leaders, concerned about the escalating costs of public assistance, supported the concept of expanded social services on the assumption that they would help to reduce welfare rolls. They were then sorely disillusioned when welfare costs continued to multiply as a consequence of changing demographic patterns, relaxed eligibility requirements, and increased "take-up" among potential AFDC recipients. Direct service providers and consumers were led to believe that the expansion of public funding would enhance the quality and quantity of service provision, and they were frequently frustrated, often enraged, when these expectations were not fulfilled. Civil rights and consumer groups, concerned about the potential for social control and invasion of privacy inherent in any effort to tie public assistance to service provision, became increasingly wary of efforts to expand state intervention in family life, no matter how well intentioned the motivation. And welfare rights activists and leaders of the War on Poverty, committed to the concept of maximum feasible participation of the poor, disparaged the so-called "service strategy" as a naïve attempt to solve the problems of poverty via the provision of casework services; instead, they argued that organizing efforts should be directed toward placing more resources in the hands of the poor, deprofessionalizing services, and challenging the policies and practices of established agencies (Wickenden 1976).

Despite this tremendous ambivalence about the potential costs and benefits of an expanded role for the public sector in the provision of services to families and children, federal and state investments in social services escalated rapidly during the 1960s, especially after the 1967 amendments to the Social Security Act, which permitted the purchase of service from voluntary agencies. Community and professional expectations regarding the social good and social reform that might be achieved through these investments expanded equally rapidly.

Many established child welfare agencies responded readily to the demands and opportunities posed by this changing perception of public responsibility for service provision. They expanded their range of service provision, increased efforts to insure better coordination of services, initiated demonstration projects aimed

at reaching newly defined populations at risk, developed more specialized foster home and group care facilities, and invested heavily in efforts to enhance the general level of staff training and program administration. But during the very period that the field was attempting to improve the quantity and quality of its service provision, it was also being exposed to new challenges and expectations.

Foster parent and adoptive parent groups began to organize, demanding more equitable treatment for themselves and the development of new types of adoption and foster care programs for children with "special needs" within the existing child welfare population. The movement toward de-institutionalization of youngsters confined in correctional facilities, mental hospitals, and schools for the retarded yielded whole new populations of children and youth that child welfare agencies were expected to serve. The emergence of the child advocacy movement in the late 1960s created pressure for child welfare workers to engage in social action efforts aimed at improving the quality of services provided by schools, hospitals, mental health facilities, and other community agencies impinging on the lives of children. Legal reformers concerned about parents' and children's rights began to challenge established agency policies and procedures regarding the movement of children in and out of care, as well as the quality, accessibility, and appropriateness of substitute care provisions. And renewed concern about the problems of child abuse and neglect led to the passage of state mandatory reporting laws, a dramatic increase in the number of cases of alleged child abuse and neglect that agencies were required to investigate, and expanded requests for assistance from police and hospital personnel attempting to provide protective services to children who were being defined as a new population at risk.

As a consequence of these various forces emerging in the late 1960s and early 1970s, the child welfare field was pressured to expand its boundaries in three basic directions: (1) to en-hance and expand in-home services for families and children, especially for those of low-income, minority backgrounds; (2) to establish more specialized substitute care resources for children formerly channeled to other service systems; and (3) to develop opportunities for adoptive placement of the formerly "unadoptable" spe-cial needs children in long-term foster care.

Yet these demands were exploding at a time when established child welfare agencies were losing their preeminence in the social welfare field; social work, long the dominant profes-sion in the welfare field, was under attack for its failure to solve the problems of poverty; the medical and legal professions were redefining critical policy and service delivery issues in the children's field; and community groups were demanding increased consumer participation in agency decisionmaking. In addition, agencies were being expected to develop new funding sources and new patterns of service coordina-tion; and the distribution of power among voluntary, state, and local service planners was shifting. Finally, the Child Welfare League of America, the primary research, standard-setting, and accrediting body in the voluntary sector, was being challenged for defining its organization's priority as membership services, not social action (Steiner 1976); and the Chil-dren's Bureau, the only federal agency with an established record of commitment to improv-ing the delivery of child welfare services, was decimated by the reorganization of the De-partment of Health, Education and Welfare in 1969. In other words, the child welfare field was attempting to respond to new demands and ex-pectations by expanding its service boundaries and resources at the same time that the very underpinnings of the field were under attack. The result was an inevitable system overload.

The 1970s and 1980s

The forces for change began to shift slightly in the 1970s. The women's liberation movement exploded on the American scene; blacks and other minority groups organized to develop political and economic power; the call for affir-mative action and equal treatment replaced the push for civil rights and equal opportunities; self-help and advocacy groups representing a wide range of interests, such as children, pris-oners, homosexuals, mental patients, physically disabled and retarded citizens, and single par-ents began to recognize the sources of their constituencies' oppressions and to organize more effectively to secure their rights. Quite inevitably, "middle America" began to react. Concern was growing about the national econ-omy, rampant inflation, and unemployment; the United States seemed to be losing its status as a world power and leader of the forces for good; fear of crime was becoming universal; the role of the churches was declining; the problems of divorce, delinquency, illegitimacy, and drug abuse could no longer be viewed solely as the province of the poor; historical allocations of power and resources were chang-ing; and traditional values, beliefs, and modes of behavior no longer seemed to bring the promised results.

In some ways, all of these pressures seem very far removed from recent developments in the child welfare field, but unfortunately, they are intimately related. The children served by this system—poor, often minority, neglected, dependent, abused, delinquent, and disturbed —constitute the very populations that should have benefited most from the broad social re-form efforts since the 1960s. Yet these young-sters and their families continue to be trouble-some to the larger community, and their very visibility and vulnerability make them conven-ient scapegoats for the inadequacies and fail-ures of these recent reform efforts and for the discomfort and alienation experienced by so many families today.

Child Abuse Prevention and Treatment Act. The first important federal legislative action of the 1970s in relation to child welfare services was passage of the Child Abuse Prevention and Treatment Act of 1974 (CAPTA). This law (which was revised in 1996, 2002, and 2003) provided a small amount of funding to states for research and demonstration projects dealing with child maltreatment. The law stipulated that to qualify for funding, states had to pass child abuse and neglect laws requiring mandated reporting of suspected and known cases of maltreatment, immunity for reporters, confidentiality, and a number of other minor provisions. Unfortunately, the law did not specify how child abuse and/or neglect was to be defined or operationalized. This lack of clear operational definitions has created innumerable problems over time for clients as well as for social service and court personnel. The law has served to focus enormous public attention on problems of child abuse and led every state to pass a mandatory child abuse reporting law. However, CAPTA has consistently been funded at low levels, leading to many unfulfilled expectations; and despite the title of the law, its focus has consistently been child abuse reporting, not child abuse prevention or treatment.

In addition to the mandates imposed by CAPTA, emerging directions in social service provision during the 1970s began to create still different expectations for child welfare services. As Wickenden (1976:581) has suggested, "it is difficult to fix an exact year or month when the goal of a 'comprehensive public welfare system' . . . began to be replaced by its opposite, the ideal of separation of services and money payments." Nor is it possible to determine precisely when the basic concepts underlying the structure of service provision in this country began to be reformulated. But early in the 1970s, it was clear that the winds of change had again arrived. Congress imposed a $2.5 billion ceiling on funding for social services in 1972, and Title XX of the Social Security Act was passed in 1975, redefining historical concepts regarding the appropriate decisionmaking responsibility, objectives, intervention strategies, and organi-

zational and funding patterns for social services in this country.

The basic shifts in the policies and patterns of service provisions reflected in this legislation can be summarized as:

- Greater state responsibility for social service planning and program development;
- Public participation in service needs assessment and review;
- Sharp reduction in the range and extent of federal regulations governing service provision;
- Development of comprehensive, integrated service plans;
- Creation of complex and varied funding packages among the various levels of government and public and private provider agencies;
- Diversification of the range of service provision;
- Diminished provisions for categorical programs aimed at special populations at risk;
- Expansion of joint public-voluntary programs;
- Increased emphasis on the objectives vs. the process of service delivery;
- Diminished role for social workers in the administration and delivery of services;
- Expansion of opportunities for provision of services to families above the poverty line;
- Democratization and decentralization of funding decisions and allocations; and
- Increased emphasis on fiscal and program accountability.

Commenting on the implications of Title XX for social services, Austin (1980:19) suggested that "the financing, regulation and management of human service programs has become a major domestic policy issue in the United States." This development had enormous implications for the child welfare field because it placed on the public agenda the issue of appropriate responsibility and care for dependent, neglected, troubled, and troublesome children.

It transferred the awesome responsibility for shaping the lives of children—a responsibility formerly entrusted only to parents and/or persons with professional expertise in child welfare—to contending forces in the political arena, and it created increased emphasis on rationality, efficiency, and control in the exercise of that trust (see also Gilbert 1971; Miller 1978; Schram 1981; Urban and Social Change Review 1980).

In the 1970s, child welfare agencies started to be attacked for their failure to keep children out of placement, minimize costs while maintaining appropriate resources for children who must be placed in temporary substitute care, and move children back into their own families or into permanent adoptive homes as quickly as possible (e.g., see Bernstein, Snider, & Meezan 1975; Billingsley & Giovannoni 1970, 1972, 1975; Fanshel & Shinn 1972; Knitzer, Allen, & McGowan 1978; Persico 1979; Strauss 1977). The tenor of these critiques contrasted markedly with the concerns raised by earlier commentators regarding the need to broaden the base of service delivery, reach underserved populations, and expand economic and social supports for all families (Billingsley & Giovannoni 1972; Kenniston 1977; Schorr 1974). In essence, earlier visions of using public funding to stimulate the development of child welfare services designed to enhance the development of all children at risk were replaced by the expectation that the child welfare field should serve only those children for whom state intervention is essential to insure a minimal level of care and protection. In addition, it was assumed that these children should be cared for in as rational, time-limited, and cost-efficient a manner as possible.

This redefinition of the expectations and potentials of the child welfare system significantly diminished the priority given to children's services within the human service sector and led to some marked changes in the way child welfare services are organized and delivered. To illustrate, a study of child welfare in 25 states provided some interesting insights regarding changing patterns of service provisions in the 1970s (U.S. Department of Health, Education, and Welfare 1976). The researchers observed that the development of child welfare service delivery systems in various states was very uneven and that the structures and organization of these delivery systems were constantly changing. As a consequence of widespread reorganization of state human services departments and frequent redefinitions of the client groups and services falling within the province of "child welfare," child welfare services seemed to be losing their organizational visibility and coherence.

Another concern raised by this study and echoed in the findings of a related study focused on clients seeking services from public social service agencies was the competency of staff now providing child welfare services (Jenkins 1981). The merger of public welfare and child welfare staff in many states, combined with the general trend toward lower educational and experience requirements for social service personnel and reduced opportunities for workers to receive advanced training and specialized consultation, resulted in a gradual deprofessionalization of child welfare services. This raised serious question about the capacity of staff to provide the quality and range of services required by the families and children entering the child welfare system.

Despite the concerns raised about organizational viability and staff competency, efforts to reform the delivery of child welfare services during this period were directed primarily toward revising the statutory base governing state intervention in family life and increasing the requirements for public accountability of service providers. For example, by 1977, 20 states plus the District of Columbia had instituted some type of formal judicial, court-administered, or citizen review (Chappell & Hevener 1977). Many others states followed, and the trend toward developing increasingly complex systems for internal case monitoring and program review became virtually universal.

Three other developments of the late 1970s also contributed the major shift in child welfare policy that occurred in 1980.

The first was one of the most significant legislative events of the 1970s, the passage of the Indian Child Welfare Act (ICWA) of 1978. The ICWA described the role that Native American families and tribal governments must play in decisions about the protection and placement of their children. It strengthened the role of tribal governments in determining the custody of Native American children and specified that preference should be given first to placements with extended family, then to Native American foster homes. The law mandated that state courts act to preserve the integrity and unity of Native American families.

The second was a new focus on the concept of permanency planning, precipitated by the theoretical writings of Goldstein, Solnit, Goldstein, and Freud (1973, 1979) on the concept of psychological parenting and the reports of successful demonstration projects designed to prevent placement and/or promote permanence for children in foster care through reunification or adoption was a major theoretical and practice shift in the field of children, youth, and family services (Burt and Balyeat 1974; Emlen, L'Ahti, & Downs 1978; Pike 1976; Pike, Downs, & Emlen 1977).

The third significant development was a series of Senate subcommittee hearings focused first on issues of adoption, and later, on broader foster care issues (Allen & Knitzer 1983:119).

The concerns embodied in the reform efforts discussed above were translated into explicit public policy with passage of the Adoption Assistance and Child Welfare Reform Act of 1980. Had this act been adequately funded and properly implemented, it had the potential for greatly enhancing the quality of traditional child welfare services. It essentially reversed the trend toward a diminished role for the federal government in the funding and structuring of social service provision, and it addressed directly many of the most frequently documented problems in the child welfare system. However, it sharply underlined the thrust toward viewing the child welfare system itself, rather than the children and families this field was developed to serve, as the primary object of concern—the essential target for social reform.

Adoption Assistance and Child Welfare Act. Hailed as the most important piece of child welfare legislation enacted in three decades, the Adoption Assistance and Child Welfare Act of 1980 (P.L. 96-272) required states to establish programs and make procedural reforms to serve children in their own homes, prevent out-of-home placement, and facilitate family reunification following placement. The Adoption Assistance and Child Welfare Reform Act officially introduced the concept of permanency planning as a primary objective of federal child welfare policy. The specific components of the bill were aimed at redirecting funds from foster care to preventive and adoption services, providing due process for all individuals involved, decreasing the time children spend in foster care, insuring placement for children in the least detrimental alternative setting, and insuring state planning and accountability. Perhaps most important for later developments in child welfare services was the law's requirement that states make "reasonable efforts" to prevent children from entering foster placements. The bill adopted what has been termed a "carrot and stick" approach (Allen and Knitzer 1983) by:

1. Amending Title IV-B to create new funding for preventive services;
2. Setting a cap on funding for foster care services that was to become effective once funding for Title IV-B reached a specified level;
3. Requiring state inventories of all children in foster care longer than 6 months;
4. Requiring development of state plans for foster care and adoption services and routine collection of aggregate and case data

to monitor implementation of these state plans;

5. Requiring individual case reviews of all children in placement after 6 months and judicial reviews of all children in care longer than 18 months; and

6. Providing open-ended funding for adoption subsidies for children defined as "hard to place."

No effort was made in this legislation to address inherent conflicts with the provisions of CAPTA.

After President Reagan was inaugurated in 1981, there were a number of congressional battles to eliminate funding for the CAPTA and to fold funding for the Adoption Assistance and Child Welfare Act into a block grant for social services. These efforts failed, but the effects of the conservative Reagan administration were felt in other ways in the child welfare arena. In 1981, Congress passed a social services block grant as part of the Omnibus Budget Reconciliation Bill of 1981. This bill compounded all the drawbacks of Title XX by decreasing social service funding, federal monitoring and regulation, reducing service standards, and decreasing emphasis on equity within and across state lines. The cut-backs in federal funding for social services did not impact directly on child welfare because funding for the Adoption Assistance and Child Welfare Act was kept out of the block grant. However, child welfare agencies experienced serious indirect results related to an increased need for services among families at risk and to increased family poverty created by cut-backs in such entitlement programs as AFDC and Medicaid. States, localities, and voluntary agencies struggled to respond to these needs, primarily by emphasizing provision of last-ditch, crisis services. Consequently, families at risk tended to defer routine, early intervention services and to present at child welfare agencies in greater need than they might have in earlier years.

Although the number of children in foster care leveled off briefly after passage of the Adoption Assistance and Child Welfare Act, reports of child abuse and neglect increased markedly, as did foster placements, during the later 1980s. There is no consensus as to the reasons for these trends. Some argued that these increases were the result of increased reporting, suggesting that there was no real increase in the problem of child maltreatment, simply an increase in the degree to which suspected cases were reported. Others attributed these trends to increases in maternal substance abuse, family homelessness, or poverty. Still others blamed the dramatic increase in kinship foster care that occurred following the U.S. Supreme Court decision in *Miller vs. Youakim* (1979), stating that children living in relatives' homes are entitled to the same level of foster care payments as children living with non-kin.

Despite these increases in child abuse reporting and foster placement, a number of programs were initiated during this period designed to demonstrate "reasonable efforts" to prevent placement of children in foster care. There were many variations in the type and duration of family-centered services offered, but they all were generally described as family preservation services. Homebuilders, started by the Behavioral Sciences Institute in Tacoma, Washington, was the program that ultimately received the most attention. The Edna McConnell Clark Foundation became very invested in this program model, called "intensive family preservation services," and formed a loose coalition of national organizations to work on developing materials that would assist in policy implementation at the state level. The foundation provided funding in the late 1980s for a group of states to engage in strategic implementation of Homebuilder-type services.

The 1990s

By 1992, this group of states had made progress in implementing intensive family preservation services as a significant aspect of state child welfare policy and had generated widespread support among professionals, state administrators, and legislators for family preservation as an important component of child welfare policy. Thus, a significant coalition of national organizations was ready to advocate federal legislation that would provide federal support for intensive family preservation services (Farrow 2001).

Family Preservation and Support Services Program. In 1993, Congress passed the Family Preservation and Support Services Program (FPSSP; P.L. 103-66), which earmarked federal funds for family support services and increased the funds available for family preservation services. The intent of this law was to help communities build a system of family support services to assist vulnerable children and families in an effort to prevent child maltreatment. Family preservation services were designed to help families experiencing crises that might lead to the placement of their children in foster care.

This law provided some funding for family preservation and family support services, officially recognizing the practice of family preservation, although the implementing regulations defined family preservation much more broadly than did the original model of Homebuilders-type services. States were to use the new funds to integrate preventive services into treatment-oriented child welfare systems, to improve service coordination within and across state service agencies, and to engage broad segments of the community in program planning at the state and local levels.

More importantly, the FPSSP stipulated that the planning process should include parents and consumers of services, community-based service providers, representatives of professional and advocacy organizations, and child welfare agency line staff, administrators, and supervisors. The intent was to make child welfare systems more responsive to families and communities by involving a broad range of stakeholders. Although family preservation programs

continued to expand during the 1990s, providing many high-risk families with the help they needed to maintain their children at home, several forces converged to raise concern about the value of these services (McGowan & Walsh 2000). These included, first, the continued rise in child abuse and neglect complaints, leading to increased foster care placements. Second, in contrast to earlier reports of the success of intensive family preservation services, carefully designed studies began to document some of the limitations of this model of service (Nelson 1997; Schuerman, Rzepnicki, & Littell 1994). Third, conservative lay commentators began to stir public anger about the dramatic rise in kinship foster care and the possibility of relatives of "bad" parents receiving money from the state to care for the children of their relatives (MacDonald 1999; Weisman 1994). Fourth, the resurgence of the conservative political forces began to legitimize public attacks on families in poverty dependent on AFDC who may have difficulty providing proper care for their children (MacDonald 1994). Finally, public exposés about a few isolated cases in which children in families that received family preservation services were later abused by their parents precipitated widespread debate about the relative value of family preservation vs. child protection and the need to give priority to children's safety (Farrow 2001).

The legislation that followed passage of the FPSSP in 1993 essentially reflected this shift away from the concept of preserving families toward protecting children.

Multiethnic Placement Act and Interethnic Placement Act. The Multiethnic Placement Act (MEPA; P.L. 103-382) also known as the "Howard M. Metzenbaum Multiethnic Placement Act of 1994," prohibited delaying or denying the placement of any child on the basis of race, color, or national origin. MEPA required states to diligently recruit prospective adoptive and foster care families that reflect the ethnic and racial diversity of children in need of foster and adoptive homes and required the federal government to impose fiscal penalties for states not in compliance with the anti-discrimination provision.

MEPA was designed to decrease the length of time that children wait to be adopted; prevent discrimination in the placement of children on the basis of race, color, or national origin; and facilitate the identification and recruitment of foster and adoptive families who can meet children's needs.

MEPA was amended in 1996 by the Inter-ethnic Placement Act (P.L. 104-10). This legislation strengthened the provisions of MEPA to insure that adoption and foster placements were not delayed or denied on the basis of race, color, or national origin.

Many child welfare practitioners and policy-makers (Brooks, Barth, Bussiere, & Patterson 1999) have expressed concern that the policies of racial matching and the ethics of transracial adoptions were indeed controversial; however, the passage of this legislation has done little to reduce the controversy (for a more detailed discussion, see the chapter by Groza, Houlihan, and Wood on adoption).

Personal Responsibility and Work Opportunity Reconciliation Act. The Personal Responsibility and Work Opportunity Reconciliation Act of 1996 (P.L. 104-193), commonly known as the "welfare reform law," eliminated the concept of financial entitlement under AFDC and replaced this with the Temporary Assistance for Needy Families (TANF) program. Passed with no real consideration of its potential impact on families in need of child welfare services, the law has a number of provisions that may make it more difficult for high-risk families in poverty to maintain their children safely at home. As Courtney (1997) commented, "the passage of P.L.104-193 marks the first time in U.S. history when federal law mandates efforts to protect children from maltreatment, but makes no guarantee of basic economic supports for children." To illustrate, the law imposes a 5-year lifetime

limit on receipt of TANF funds, imposes strict work requirements on parents receiving TANF, prohibits individuals convicted of drug-related offenses after passage of the law from receiving TANF or Food Stamp benefits for life, and permits states to establish a family cap that denies cash benefits to children born into families already receiving TANF.

Adoption and Safe Families Act. The most significant change in child welfare policy since the Adoption Assistance and Child Welfare Reform Act of 1980 is the passage of the Adoption and Safe Families Act of 1997 (ASFA; P.L. 105-89), which amends Title IV-E of the Social Security Act. ASFA requires that child safety be the paramount concern in making service provision, placement, and permanency planning decisions. Reflecting some of the same conservative sentiments that led to the passage of the welfare reform act the preceding year, the enactment of this law makes the safety of children the priority in all decisionmaking, diminishes the emphasis on family preservation, and promotes speedy termination of parental rights and adoptive placement when parents cannot quickly resolve the problems that led to placement. Although the law reaffirms the concept of permanency planning and reauthorizes the FPSSP, renaming it the "Safe and Stable Families Program," it specifies a number of circumstances under which states are not required to make "reasonable effort" to preserve or reunify families. It mandates a permanency hearing after a child has been in care for 12 months and every 12 months thereafter and requires states, with certain exceptions, to file a termination of parental rights petition in cases in which a child has been in care for 15 of the past 22 months. Thus parents who cannot resolve the problems that led to placement and may require longer treatment (e.g., substance abusers) are at risk of having their rights terminated, no matter what the age of the child or the degree of parent-child attachment.

In some ways, this law seemed designed primarily to promote adoptions, providing additional funding for states that increase their number of completed adoption and authorizing HHS to provide technical assistance to states and localities to help them reach their adoption targets. As Halpern (1998) commented, this law indicates that "Congress believes adoption is the new panacea for the problems of foster care." States that do not comply with its provisions risk losing a portion of their Title IV-E and Title IV-B funds.

On a positive note, ASFA signals a willingness to increase the federal role in child welfare services and to demand state accountability by mandating HHS to develop outcome measures to monitor state performance. The department, in response, developed national standards with benchmark indicators of success to measure performance on six statewide data indicators. These standards are identified as recurrence of maltreatment, incidence of child abuse and/or neglect in foster care, foster care re-entries, stability of foster care placements, length of time to achieve reunification, and length of time to achieve adoption.

The law reaffirms the importance of making reasonable efforts to preserve and reunify families, but also specifies that states are not required to make efforts to keep children with their parents when doing so places a child's safety in jeopardy. ASFA includes provisions that shorten the time frame for making permanency planning decisions and establishes a time frame for initiating proceedings to terminate parental rights. This law also requires a focus on results and accountability and makes it clear that it is no longer enough to insure that procedural safeguards are met. It is critical that child welfare services lead to positive outcomes for children.

John H. Chafee Foster Care Independence Program. The John H. Chafee Foster Care Independence Program (CFCIP), Title I of the Foster Care Independence Act of 1999 (P.L. 106-169), provides funds to states to assist youth and young adults (up to age 21) in the foster care component of the child welfare system in making a smoother, more successful transition to adulthood. This program replaces and expands Section 477 of the Social Security Act and allows states to use these funds for a broader array of services to youth "aging out" of the foster care system, including room and board. This legislation revises the program of grants to states and expands opportunities for independent living programs, providing education, training, and employment services, and financial support for foster youth to prepare for living on their own. The legislation requires the development of outcome measures to assess state performance in operating independent living programs and mandates a national data collection on services, the individuals served, and outcomes. In addition, the legislation provides states with the option to extend Medicaid coverage to 18- to 21-year-olds who have been emancipated from foster care. CFCIP emphasizes permanence for youth and increased funding for adoption incentive payments.

Most importantly, CFCIP enables states to expand the scope and improve the quality of educational, vocational, practical, and emotional supports in their programs for adolescents in foster care and for young adults who have recently left foster care.

Twenty-First Century
Child Abuse Prevention and Enforcement Act
As an outgrowth of the concern about inadequate responses to reports of child maltreatment, the Child Abuse Prevention and Enforcement Act (P.L. 106-77) was enacted at the start of the twenty-first century. This legislation authorizes the use of federal law enforcement funds by states to improve the criminal justice system. The intention was to provide timely, accurate, and complete criminal history record information to child welfare agencies, organizations, and programs that are engaged in the assessment of activities related to the protection of children, including protection against child sexual abuse, and placement of children

in foster care. It allows the use of federal grants by law enforcement to:

- Enforce child abuse and neglect laws, including laws protecting against child sexual abuse;
- Promote programs designed to prevent child abuse and neglect; and
- Establish or support cooperative programs between law enforcement and media organizations to collect, record, retain, and disseminate information useful in the identification and apprehension of suspected criminal offenders.

Intercountry Adoption Act

In response to the need to ratify the Hague Convention on Protection of Children and Cooperation in Respect to Intercountry Adoption, the U.S. Congress enacted the Intercountry Adoption Act of 2000 (P.L. 106-279). As background history, the Hague Convention set minimum standards and procedures for adoptions between implementing countries that prevent abuses, such as abduction or sale of children; ensured proper consent for the adoption; allowed for the child's transfer to the receiving country; and established the adopted child's status in the receiving country. This legislation makes clear that the U.S. central authority is established within the Department of State with general responsibility for U.S. implementation of the Hague Convention and annual reports to Congress. The State Department is responsible for:

- Monitoring each accrediting entity's performance of its duties and their compliance with the Hague Convention, the Intercountry Adoption Act (IAA), and applicable regulations; and
- Issuing certificates to cover Hague Convention adoptions/placements for adoption made in the United States necessary for their recognition, so long as the department has received appropriate documentation to establish that the requirements of the Convention, IAA, and other regula-

tions have been met. In addition, the Immigration and Nationality Act is to be amended to provide for a new category of children adopted under the Hague Convention and designed to meet other requirements to qualify for immigrant visas.

Promoting Safe and Stable Families Amendments

Promoting Safe and Stable Families Amendments were passed in 2001 (P.L. 107-133), in an effort to:

- Encourage and enable states to develop or expand programs of family preservation services, community-based family support services, adoption promotion and support services, and time-limited family reunification services;
- Reduce high-risk behavior by children with incarcerated parents by providing one-on-one relationships with adult mentors; and
- Continue improvements in state court systems, as required by ASFA.

The most significant part of this legislation is the amendment of the definition of family preservation services to include infant safe haven programs. The legislation added strengthening parental relationships and promoting healthy marriages to the list of allowable activities. There was a new focus added to the research, evaluation, and technical assistance activities. The legislation additionally created a matching grant program to support mentoring networks for children of prisoners, reauthorized funds for the Court Improvement Program, and authorized a vocational/education voucher program as part of the CFCIP.

Child and Family Services Reviews

Although the Child and Family Services Reviews (CFSR) actually began in 2000, Congress directed HHS in 1994 to develop regulations for reviewing state CFSR programs administered under Titles IV-B and IV-E of the Social Security Act. Prior federal reviews proved to be disappointing for both the states and the federal government, which at least in part led to the passage of the legislation. Although previous reviews had been effective in promoting state accountability for meeting requirements associated with state foster care programs, they were less worthwhile in insuring positive outcomes for the children and families served by state child welfare agencies, especially those outside the foster care program.

In consultation with the experts in the child welfare field, the Administration for Children and Families (ACF) within HHS developed and field-tested the new CFSRs in 14 states prior to implementing the reviews officially in FY2000. Using the statutory and regulatory underpinnings of the Title IV-B Child and Family Services Plan, including the principles that guided the development of the plan, ACF developed measures that reflect the substance and intent of those requirements through actual casework with children and families.

The CFSRs have as a goal to examine child welfare practices at the ground level, capturing the actual practice among caseworkers, children and families, and service providers, and determining the effects of those interactions on the children and families involved. The emphasis is on child welfare practice, based on a belief that, although certain policies and procedures are essential to an agency's capacity to support positive outcomes, it is the day-to-day casework practices and their underlying values that most influence such outcomes.

The CFSRs are also a primary mechanism for promoting the federal governments' agenda of change and improvement in services to children, youth, and families nationally. With a clear focus on program improvement planning, these CFSRs aim to provide an opportunity for the states and the federal government jointly to implement reforms at a systemic level that will realize and sustain improved outcomes for children, youth, and families. Furthermore, the CFSRs offer opportunities to frame policy and practice solutions clearly within the context of child welfare practice principles that reflect the mission and intent of federally funded CFS programs and state-of-the-art thinking on the most effective approaches to serving children and families.

As of 2004, ACF had conducted 52 CFSRs of state performance based on the national child welfare outcome standards (U.S. Department of Health and Human Services 2004b). Although an admirable start to improving outcomes for children, youth, and families, as the reviewers from HHS concluded in their Annual Report to Congress in 2004, "there is much room for improvement with regard to State performance on the seven national child welfare outcomes" (U.S. Department of Health and Human Services 2004a:21).

Other recent investigators and observers of the child welfare system have arrived at similar conclusions. To illustrate, in their report released on January 28, 2004, the U.S. General Accounting Office (2004:2) concluded that "child welfare agencies face a number of challenges related to staffing and data management that hinder their ability to protect children from abuse and neglect." More specifically, the report notes that low salaries hinder staff recruitment and retention, and lack of adequate numbers of trained staff limit the capacity of remaining staff to develop relationships with families and make decisions that insure safe and stable placements for children.

A report issued by Fostering Results, a nonpartisan group of child welfare experts, raised serious question about the ways in which federal financing rules stifle innovation and restrict funding of programs that could reduce the number of children in foster care. Based on an analysis of data from the state performance reviews as well as from the 39 states that had completed CFSRs at the time the study was conducted, the authors concluded that "every state failed to achieve substantial conformity in enough areas to demonstrate compliance with federally mandated performance expectations" (McDonald, Salyers, & Shaver 2004:221). As a means to improve state performance, Fostering Results argues that states must be allowed to move out of the "straightjacket" created by federal financing rules that prohibit use of federal funds designated for foster care on the services that could give children safer, more permanent homes. The report indicates that some states that have received waivers to use federal Title IV-E funds for purposes other than foster care have demonstrated improved performance on critical indicators. Therefore, this group recommends that HHS be permitted to give more state waivers to insure more flexible state use of federal funding.

The Pew Commission, another national, nonpartisan group of child welfare experts, reached similar, troubling conclusions after a year of study (Pew Commission 2004). The chair, a 20-year veteran of Congress, is quoted as saying, "The nation's foster care system is unquestionably broken." To address the many problems identified, the commission made strong recommendations designed to strengthen accountability in the child welfare agencies and the juvenile courts. More specifically, the commission highlights the ways in which current federal funding mechanisms encourage an overreliance on foster care and recommends giving states more flexibility in the use of federal monies to insure that they can offer a range of service options that might encourage maintaining children at home safely or facilitate swifter adoption or legal guardianship. To strengthen the performance of courts in child welfare decisionmaking and case review, the Pew Commission recommends a series of court performance measures and incentives for effective collaboration between juvenile courts and child welfare agencies (Pew Commission on Children in Foster Care 2004b).

Two long-time scholars of child welfare (Whittaker & Maluccio 2002:108) have recently written about "the troubled state of current child welfare services," pointing out that many of the leaders in the field have begun to call for radical change. These include Waldfogel's (1998) recommendations for redesigning child protective services, the Annie E. Casey Foundation's support of family-to-family initiatives and community partnerships, and their own recommendations for blurring the boundaries between in-home and placement services by offering respite care, whole-family group care, multiple forms of kinship care, and so forth (Whittaker & Maluccio 2002:127–128). These are all promising practice approaches, and the reports cited above suggest promising policy directions. However, it would be a mistake to think that any of these initiatives will "fix" all the current problems in the child welfare system. As I first wrote over 20 years ago (McGowan 1983:44):

> We are writing in the midst of a rapidly changing social climate. It would be foolhardy, if not impossible, to predict the ultimate impact of current political forces on reform efforts in the child welfare system. But the history of American child welfare suggests that many of the dilemmas confronting the field today reflect the solutions devised to address the problems of the past, and we can anticipate that although current proposals for change will resolve some issues, they will create still others. Henry Thurston (1930), writing fifty years ago about the history of child welfare, quoted Lowell's couplet:
>
> New occasions teach new duties;
> Time makes ancient good uncouth.

Certainly these comments are equally applicable today. Only a few lessons seem clear from the child welfare history reviewed in this chapter:

- Child welfare services are shaped primarily by social forces and trends in the larger society;
- Individuals and groups engaged in the design and provision of child welfare service can contribute—modestly and imperfectly,

but consistently—to improving the quality of life for children;

- The inherent tensions between the interest of children, parents, and the community at large can never be perfectly resolved;
- American society's willingness to invest in programs designed to enhance the welfare

of families and children is meager and begrudging at best; and

- The nature and definition of children's needs may shift over time, but social responsibility for the provision of supports and services responsive to these needs remains constant.

REFERENCES

Abbott, G. (1938). *The child and the state*, vols. 1–2. Chicago: University of Chicago Press.

Adoption and Safe Families Act. (1997). P.L. 105-89.

Adoption Assistance and Child Welfare Act. (1980). P.L. 96-272.

Allen, M. L., & Knitzer, J. (1983). Child welfare: Examining the policy framework. In B. G. McGowan & W. Meezan (eds.), *Child welfare: Current dilemmas, future directions*, pp. 93–141. Itasca, IL: Peacock Publishers.

Austin, D. M. (1980). Title XX and the future of social services. *The Urban and Social Change Review, 13*, 15–21.

Bernstein, B., Snider, D., & Meezan, W. (1975). *Foster care needs and alternatives to placement*. Albany: New York State Board of Social Welfare.

Bernstein, R. (1960). Are we still stereotyping the unmarried mother? *Social Work, 5*(July), 22–28.

Billingsley, A., & Giovannoni, J. (1970). *The children of the storm: A dream deferred*. New York: Citizens' Committee for Children.

Billingsley, A., & Giovannoni, J. (1972). *Children of the storm: Black children and American child welfare*. New York: Harcourt Brace Jovanovich.

Billingsley, A., & Giovannoni, J. (1975). *The children of the storm: A dream still deferred*. New York: Citizens' Committee for Children.

Bremner, R. H. (ed.). (1970–1974). *Children and youth in America: A documentary history*, vols. 1–3. Cambridge, MA: Harvard University Press.

Brooks, D., Barth, R. P., Bussiere, A., & Patterson, G. (1999). Adoption and race: Implementing the Multiethnic Placement Act and the Interethnic Adoptions Provisions. *Social Work, 44*, 167–178.

Buell, B. (1973). *Community planning for human services*. Westport, CT: Greenwood Press.

Burt, M., & Balyeat, R. (1974). A new system for improving care of neglected and abused children. *Child Welfare, 53*, 167–179.

Chappell, B., & Hevener, B. (1977). Periodic review of children in foster care: Mechanisms for reviews. Paper prepared for the Child Service Association, Newark, NJ.

Child Abuse Prevention and Enforcement Act. (2000). P.L. 106-177.

Costin, L. (1969). *Child welfare: Policies and practices*, second ed. New York: McGraw-Hill.

Courtney, M. E. (1997). Welfare reform and child welfare services. In S. B. Kamerman & A. J. Kahn (eds.), *Child welfare in the context of "welfare reform,"* pp. 1–35. New York: Cross-National Studies Research Program, Columbia University School of Social Work.

Emlen, A. C., L'Ahti, J., & Downs, S. W. (1978). *Overcoming barriers to planning for children in foster care*. Washington, DC: U.S. Government Printing Office.

Family Preservation and Support Services Program. (1993). P.L. 103-66.

Farrow, F. (2001). *The shifting policy impact of intensive family preservation services*. Chicago: Chapin Hall Center for Children at the University of Chicago.

Folks, H. (1978). *The care of destitute, neglected and delinquent children*, classic ed. New York: National Association of Social Workers.

Foster Care Independence Act. (1999). P.L. 106-169.

Gilbert, N. (1971). The transformation of social services. *Social Service Review, 51*, 624–641.

Goldstein, J., Solnit, A. J., Goldstein, S., & Freud, A. (1973). *Beyond the best interests of the child*. New York: Free Press.

Goldstein, J., Solnit, A. J., Goldstein, S., & Freud, A. (1979). *Beyond the best interests of the child*, second ed. New York: Free Press.

Gruber, A. (1978). Children in foster care: Destitute, neglected, betrayed. New York: Human Sciences Press.

Halpern, M. (1998). Abandoning family preservation in a rush to adoption. *Interdisciplinary Report on At-Risk Children & Families, 1*(1), 1, 10–11.

Indian Child Welfare Act. (1978). P.L. 95-608.

Jenkins, S. (1981). *Beyond intake: The first ninety days*. Washington, DC: U.S. Department of Health and Human Services.

Kahn, A. J. (1969). *Studies in social policy and planning*. New York: Russell Sage Foundation.

Kenniston, K. (1977). *All our children*. New York: Harcourt Brace Jovanovich.

Knitzer, J., Allen, M. L., & McGowan, B. (1978). *Children without homes*. Washington, DC: Children's Defense Fund.

Lathrop, J. (1919). Presidential address—Child welfare standards: A test of democracy. In *Proceedings of the*

National Conference of Social Work, pp. 5–41. Atlantic City, NJ, June 1–8, 1919.

Lindhorst, T., & Leighninger, L. (2003). "Ending welfare as we know it" in 1960: Louisiana's Suitable Home Law. *Social Service Review, 77,* 564–584.

Maas, H., & Engler, R., (1959). *Children in need of parents.* New York: Columbia University Press.

MacDonald, H. (1994). The ideology of family preservation. *The Public Interest, 115,* 45–60.

MacDonald, H. (1999). Foster care's underworld. *City Journal, 9*(Winter), 44–53.

McDonald, J., Salyers, N., & Shaver, M. (2004*). The foster care straitjacket: Innovation, federal financing & accountability in state foster care reform.* Chicago: Fostering Results.

McGowan, B. G. (1983). Historical evolution of child welfare services. In B. G. McGowan & W. Meezan (eds.), *Child welfare: Current dilemmas, future directions,* pp. 44–90. Itasca, IL: Peacock Publishers.

McGowan, B. G., & Walsh, E. M. (2000). Policy challenges for child welfare in the new century. *Child Welfare, 79,* 11–27.

Miller, D. (1978). Children's services and Title XX from a national perspective. *Child Welfare, 57,* 134–139.

Miller vs. Youakim. (1979). 440 U.S.

Multiethnic Placement Act. (1994). P.L. 103-382.

Nelson, K. E. (1997). Family preservation—What is it? *Children and Youth Services Review, 19,* 101–118.

New York City Youth Board (1958). *Reaching the unreached family.* Youth Board Monograph no. 5. New York: New York City Youth Board.

O'Connor, S. (2001). *Orphan trains: The story of Charles Loring Brace and the children he saved and failed.* Boston: Houghton Mifflin.

Parker, J. K., & Carpenter, E. M. (1981). Julia Lathrop and the Children's Bureau: The emergence of an institution. *Social Service Review 55,* 62–71.

Peebles-Wilkins, W. (1995). Janie Porter Barrett and The Virginia Industrial School for Colored Girls: Community response to the needs of African American children. *Child Welfare, 74,* 143–161.

Persico, J. (1979). *Who knows? Who cares?: Forgotten children in foster care.* New York: National Commission on Children in Need of Parents.

Personal Responsibility and Work Opportunities Act. (1996). P.L. 104-193.

Pew Commission on Children in Foster Care. (2004a). Voices from the inside, executive summary. Retrieved June 25, 2004, from pewfostercare.org.

Pew Commission on Children in Foster Care. (2004b). Pew Commission on Children in Foster Care releases sweeping recommendations to overhaul nation's foster care system. Washington, DC: Pew Foundation.

Pike, V. (1976). Permanent planning for foster children: The Oregon Project. *Children Today, 6,* 22–41.

Pike, V., Downs, S. W., & Emlen, A. C. (1977*). Permanent planning for children in foster care: A Handbook for social workers.* DHEW publication no. (OHDS)

77-30124. Washington, DC: U.S. Government Printing Office.

Platt, A. (1969). *The child savers: The invention of delinquency.* Chicago: University of Chicago Press.

Promoting Safe and Stable Families Amendment. (2001). P.L. 107-133.

Richan, W. C. (1978). *Personnel issues in child welfare services.* Washington, DC: U.S. Department of Health, Education and Welfare.

Rodham, H. (1973). Children under the law. *Harvard Educational Review, 43*(November), 489.

Ryan, W., & Morris, L. (1967). *Child welfare: Problems and potentials.* Boston: Massachusetts Committee on Children and Youth.

Schorr, A. (ed.). (1974). *Children and decent people.* New York: Basic Books.

Schram, S. (1981). Politics, professionalism and the changing federalism. *Social Service Review, 55,* 78–92.

Schuerman, J. R., Rzepnicki, T. L., & Littell, J. H. (1994*). Putting families first; An experiment in family preservation.* New York: Aldine de Gruyter.

Steiner, G. (1976). *The children's cause.* Washington, DC: Brookings Institution.

Strauss, G. (1977). The children are waiting: The failure to achieve permanent homes for foster children in New York City. New York: New York City Comptroller's Office.

Temporary State Commission on Child Welfare. (1975). *The children and the state: A time for change in child welfare.* Albany: State University of New York.

Thurston, H. W. (1930). *The dependent child.* New York: Columbia University Press.

Urban and Social Change Review. Special issue on public social services: From Title IVA to Title XX. (1980). *The Urban and Social Change Review, 13*(Summer).

U.S. Department of Health and Human Services. (2004a). *Findings from the Initial Child and Family Services Reviews 2001–2004.* Washington, DC: U.S. Department of Health and Human Services, Administration for Children and Families.

U.S. Department of Health and Human Services. (2004b). *Child welfare outcomes 2001: Annual report to Congress, executive summary.* Washington, DC: U.S. Department of Health and Human Services, Administration for Children and Families.

U.S. Department of Health, Education and Welfare. (1976). *Child welfare in 25 states: An overview.* Washington, DC: U.S. Department of Health, Education and Welfare.

U.S. General Accounting Office. (2004). *Child welfare: Improved federal oversight could assist states in overcoming key challenges.* GAO-04-418T. Washington, DC: U.S. General Accounting Office.

Van Theis, S. (1924). *How foster children turn out.* New York: Charities Aid Association.

Vasaly, S. (1976). *Foster care in five states.* Washington, DC: U.S. Department of Health, Education and Welfare.

Waldfogel, J. (1998). Rethinking the paradigm for child protection. *The Future of Children, 8*(10), 104–119.

Weisman, M. L. (1994). When parents are not in the best interests of the child. *Atlantic Monthly,* (July), 43–63.

Whittaker, J. K., & Maluccio, A. N. (2002). Rethinking "child placement": A reflective essay. *Social Service Review, 76,* 108–134.

Wickenden, E. (1976). A perspective on social services: An essay review. *Social Service Review, 50,* 574–588.

Young, L. (1954). *Out of wedlock.* New York: McGraw-Hill.

SECTION I
Child and
Adolescent
Well-Being

❖   ❖   ❖   ❖   ❖   ❖   ❖

Overview

Child welfare has traditionally been concerned with the safety and permanency of children. However, the Adoption and Safe Families Act of 1997 (ASFA; P.L. 105-89) mandates that specific and focused attention be given to the well-being of children and youth. However, without doubt, well-being is the most ambiguous of the ASFA trinity of safety, permanency, and well-being. Although safety is given prominence in ASFA legislation and language, we focus on child and adolescent well-being issues near the start of this volume. Philosophically, we believe that without adequate attention to well-being, there is a weakening of the foundation for both safety and permanency and important developmental issues are disregarded (fig. 1).

As outlined in the outcomes for the Child and Family Services Review process, there are three well-being variables; in actuality, the first of these is the most prevalent and the most wide ranging. The three well-being variables conceptualized under this framework are:

- Well-Being 1: Families have enhanced capacity to provide for their children's needs. This concept includes consideration of the needs of and services to children, parents, and foster parents and the involvement of children, youth, and families in case planning. In the federally derived framework, Well-Being 1 also includes the important area of worker visits with children and with parents. This area is critical, because the completed federal reviews in 52 states and territories have found a strong, statistically significant positive relationship between caseworker visits with children and other safety and permanency outcomes. In a study conducted by the Children's Bureau, there was a "strength" rating for caseworker visits with a child that was significantly associated with "substantially achieved" ratings for five of the seven outcomes (www. acf.hhs.gov/programs/cb, retrieved September 28, 2004).
- Well-Being 2: Children and youth receive appropriate services to meet their educational needs.
- Well-Being 3: Children and youth receive adequate services to meet their physical and mental health needs.

In insuring the well-being of children or youth, there are numerous issues that a child welfare professional should attend to. Among these are:

- Assessing the situation from the young person's perspective and either safely serving children and youth while they live with their families or preparing them for reunification, foster care placement, or adoption.
- Supporting the child or youth's adjustment to temporary placement in foster care homes and/or facilities, placement with an adoptive family, or reunification.
- Supporting the child or youth in dealing with feelings of loss, depression, and anxiety due to separation from parents and siblings.
- Supporting birth families, foster families, and the child or youth during the process.

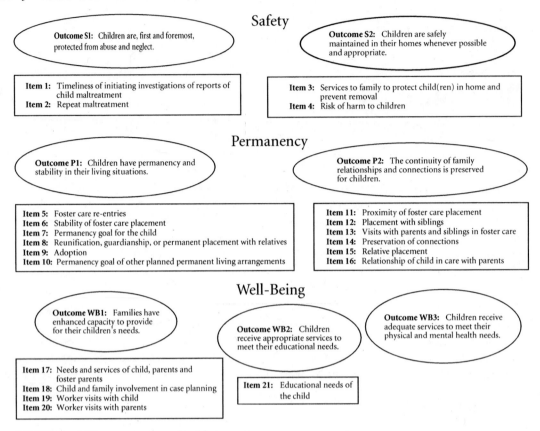

FIGURE 1. Safety, permanency, and well-being outcomes.

- Including the birth family (including fathers and paternal resources), foster parents, and the young person in case planning.
- Considering the preferences, norms, culture, and experiences of the child or youth and family when making the placement selection.
- Helping the child or youth maintain relationships with the birth family, relatives, informal support systems, and the community. This means children must be placed geographically in a community that facilitates maintaining family relationships through frequent parental visitation and that prevents unnecessary changes for children in school enrollment.
- Using frequent worker-parent/child visits to facilitate permanency plans.

- Insuring that the plan for the child or youth includes all domains of development (e.g., school performance, health, physical and emotional well-being).

In the first chapter in this section, Fraser and Terzian review the critical concepts and issues relevant to understanding risk and resilience in child development. From a strengths perspective, their focus on practice principles and strategies that support resilience frameworks resonates with the overarching philosophy that all families, despite the presence of some risk factors, possess factors that promote resilience and therefore, those strengths can be utilized to enhance their capacity to provide for their children's or youth's needs. These authors emphasize that the identification of and attempt to disrupt risk mechanisms is important in using the resilience perspective. An understanding of risk and resilience concepts and their application in practice is essential for child welfare practitioners.

In the four chapters that follow (Altman; Cohen, Hornsby, and Priester; Kemp, Allen-Eckard, Ackroyd, Becker, and Burke; and Chahine and Higgins), the authors focus on several key factors in working with families and supporting the well-being of children and youth: assessment; engagement of children, youth, and families; and engagement of families and communities using family team conferences. Philosophically, we believe that the approach to engagement influences the effectiveness of the assessment, which in turn, determines the appropriateness of the case plan and service implementation and ultimately the outcomes for children, youth, and families.

Engagement

Engaging families in the planning and service delivery early and in a focused way is essential for achieving the best possible outcomes for children and their families. The goal of engagement is to develop and maintain a mutually beneficial partnership with the family that will sustain the family's interest in and commitment to change. Frontline workers must find ways to engage families that protect the children and support maximum family involvement in defining needs and identifying solutions. During the first contact with the family, the child welfare worker must engage the family around the concern for the child's or youth's safety. Once the parents understand the safety concerns, attention can be given to what it will take for the family to protect the child and create the safe, stable, nurturing home environment that provides for the child's or youth's needs. As trust builds over time, the multiple issues that families may be struggling with emerge as the family and frontline worker frankly discuss the relevant issues and the urgency for addressing them.

Engagement must continue throughout the life of the case. Skilled workers will engage and reengage families in the change process, even following a "relapse." The caseworker may consider focusing on an issue that is of immediate interest to the family and communicating a concern for or appreciation of it. For example, engaging the family around the child's developmental needs and sense of time will make clear that reunification will happen when families can provide a nurturing environment. Acknowledging explicitly and often the demonstrable signs of progress while continuing to discuss safety and service planning can also facilitate continued engagement.

A worker's ability to engage families is significantly affected by the families' perception of the process—parents often perceive this process as an intrusion into the privacy and integrity of their families. Whatever the cause of the initial intervention, frontline workers, as Altman stresses in her chapter, must be cognizant of the family's feelings toward the system and find effective ways to engage families while protecting the children and helping a family identify needs and solutions.

Understanding cultural differences is also crucial to the staff's ability to engage the family and build relationships. Misinterpretation of culture can result in miscommunication and inappropriate or inaccurate interpretations and judgments that can negatively impact the agency-family relationship and case decisions.

Engagement with other professionals, extended family members, and caregivers also becomes critical. This engagement should promote focused assessment and decisionmaking and encourage everyone involved—agencies, extended families, birth families, and foster/adoptive families—to work together to identify and resolve the problems that brought children into care.

Assessment

The goal of assessment is to gather and analyze information that will support sound decisionmaking regarding the safety, permanency, and well-being of the child or youth and to determine appropriate services for the family. Assessment is based on the principle that all families have strengths that must be used to resolve the issues of concern; therefore, assessment provides an opportunity for families and workers to review family concerns, strengths, and resources together. Assessment includes an evaluation of family functioning and service needs based on information obtained from the family and other sources, such as schools, healthcare providers, and community agencies. Assessment thus provides the information that lays the foundation for subsequent implementation of services and strategies aimed at problem resolution. Assessment that engages relevant staff from related child- and family-serving agencies helps to highlight the comprehensive needs of the child and family and begins to identify how the multiple agencies can support the family. Assessment must be an ongoing process and should be conducted throughout the agency's involvement with the family.

With the implementation of ASFA and its emphasis on the timely achievement of permanency for children in the child welfare system, the assessment of families and children takes on renewed importance. To make realistic decisions about child safety, family preservation, reunification, and termination of parental rights, increased attention must be given to the appropriate assessment of the family's strengths and needs, and to the length of time required for the family to provide a safe, stable home environment.

An important challenge facing frontline workers is to take a comprehensive, ecological view of families' situations and to understand the contributions of various problematic behaviors to child maltreatment. Child maltreatment is complicated by personal health and substance abuse, as well as environmental, social, and economic factors. No less complex than the problems of their parents are the needs of

the children. Research literature indicates that maltreated children are at higher risk for a variety of poor developmental outcomes. To enhance the accuracy and utility of the assessment, the process should involve members of the immediate and extended family, others identified by the family, and professionals with expertise relevant to the issues of concern.

Case Planning and Implementation

The goal of case and/or service planning is to develop an individualized, strength-based, needs-driven case plan that addresses the unique needs of children and their families as identified through the assessment that, at the same time, meets the standards of professional social work practice and the safety, well-being, and permanency requirements of federal and state mandates.

Service implementation involves providing ongoing support for the family and children through brokering, facilitating, monitoring, coordinating, connecting, developing, and/or providing services identified in the case plan, as well as reporting to the courts and working with administrative reviewers.

A family-centered and strength-based approach to planning and implementation results in approaches that will best enhance the safety, permanency, and well-being of individual children, youth, and their families. The child's needs —which inevitably change over time—are always the frame of reference during planning and implementation. As discussed by the authors who have contributed to this section of the text, child welfare agency staff and biological and foster/adoptive families must be constantly mindful of the wide range of children's needs. The need for comprehensive assessment at the start of the case and services that support families provided in a community setting is clearly conceptualized and explored in the chapter by Kemp, Allen-Eckard, Ackroyd, Becker, and Burke and from a different perspective in the chapter by Chahine and Higgins. Both focus on the use of community family support meetings and family team conferences to promote the well-being of children and youth.

The Well-Being 2 variable of children and youth receiving appropriate educational services is covered in two chapters in this section. In the first of these, Elze, Auslander, Stiffman, and McMillen review the literature on the educational aspirations, academic achievement, and other educational experiences of youths in out-of-home care. They present findings from two studies that were conducted by research teams at the George Warren Brown School of Social Work at Washington University in St. Louis. Both studies, the Bridges to Life Options Study and the Youth Services Project, included adolescents involved in the child welfare system and gathered data on the youths' educational experiences, mental health problems, and family and peer environments. The chapter concludes by discussing the implications of the research for social work practice and describes some programmatic innovations to enhance the educational attainment of youths in care.

The second chapter focusing on educational aspects of children's well-being, by Walsh, spotlights a program model that promotes a community-based educational program. The Liberty Partnership program, created as a governor's initiative during the Decade of the Child, has as its goal the promise of a college education at New York State for students who graduate from high school and meet financial eligibility requirements. These community-based programs provide the comprehensive academic, cultural, recreational, and counseling supports necessary to enhance students' school performance and to motivate them to stay in school. Offering culturally competent services at a bilingual junior high school in East Harlem for more than a decade, the program primarily serves youth who are newer immigrants. All those served come from low-income families, including youth in foster care or at risk of out-of-home placements.

The Well-Being 3 variable concerning the degree to which children and youth receive adequate services to meet their physical and mental health needs is addressed in three chapters in this section of the volume. Insuring that the healthcare needs of children and youth in the child welfare system are met is the responsibility of many individuals, including their families, the child welfare agency, the healthcare system, the mental health system, and the court system. Children's and youth's health outcomes, as well as their chances for having permanent, safe, and secure homes, can be improved with access to a comprehensive healthcare system and adequate support for their families.

In the first chapter addressing this well-being variable, McCarthy and Woolverton present an overview of issues that impact the health of children and youth who are involved with the child welfare system. The authors discuss the health status and special healthcare needs of these young people, the child welfare system's responsibility to forge linkages with other systems and with families to insure that these needs are met, and the challenges faced in doing so. McCarthy and Woolverton also present a framework of critical components around which to develop approaches for overcoming the myriad challenges to providing children and youth with access to appropriate healthcare services. Taken together, the components of this framework describe a comprehensive, community-based healthcare system designed to meet the needs of the children, youth, and families served by the child welfare system. They also discuss important ethical issues and dilemmas related to the implementation of various approaches, as well as the knowledge and skills that social workers need to coordinate healthcare services for children and youth.

Utilizing case examples that are threaded throughout her chapter to illustrate salient points, Dore addresses child and adolescent mental health issues. The chapter explores the current understanding of the etiology of mental health problems in children and adolescents. It then examines the processes available for identifying and classifying disorders in childhood, as well as the types of disorders most often observed in young people and their prevalence across various domains. Current treatments are discussed, particularly those that are evidence-based (i.e., have strong empirical support for their effectiveness). Finally, Dore looks at the system-of-care concept that currently drives provision of children's mental health services in the United States, where those services are provided, and the public policies, including funding structures, that support or present barriers to provision of mental health care to children and youth today.

The chapter by Weaver, Keller, and Loyek on children and adolescents with disabilities rounds out this well-being section. These authors examine the needs and experiences of children with disabilities in the child welfare system at the start of the twenty-first century. Among the issues discussed are the interdependence of disability and maltreatment; how physical abuse may result in a disability; why children with disabilities are at risk for abuse; and foster care and adoption for children with disabilities. A review of the key aspects of resiliencies and protective factors that shape social work practice with this population is provided. The chapter concludes with an examination of the role of the social worker in practice with this population.

The final three chapters in this section (Salzburg; Staller; and Hawkins) do not fit neatly into any of the identified well-being variables as outlined in the Child and Family Services Review process. However, the experiences of children and youth in these areas can support or undermine their well-being.

Envisioning adolescence through the lens of being gay and lesbian entails deconstructing socially stigmatizing connotations and recontextualizing the experience for family units. In her chapter, Salzburg presents a model of promising practice for co-constructing adolescence for these youths and their families and proposes the creation of a more inclusive view of adolescence by considering the intersection of the family life-stage at adolescence with sons and daughters coming out as gay or lesbian. Consistent with the framework of this section, the discussion is situated within the theoretical constructs of risk and protective factors from the child welfare literature.

Hawkins's chapter presents an overview of important considerations for spiritually sensitive practice in a child welfare context. Positing that spirituality is sustaining and nurturing for many families, this author identifies what spirituality is and why it is relevant to practice, as well as the ongoing arguments against its inclusion. Hawkins also examines personal, familial, cultural, and societal aspects of spirituality and discusses how these impact clients. In addition, the chapter explores worker-related issues and how the interaction of practitioners' own personal and professional belief systems can influence effective and ethical practice. Finally, the author illustrates this content through a case example drawn from child welfare practice.

The well-being section concludes with a chapter by Staller that highlights a highly undesirable experience in its effects upon children's and youth's well-being—homelessness. With a focus on runaway and homeless youth, who are at great risk for involvement in the child welfare system, Staller addresses both policy and services as they relate to these populations. This chapter provides a comprehensive overview of the issues that affect these young people who are frequently overlooked by the traditional domains of child welfare.

MARK W. FRASER
MARY A. TERZIAN

Risk and Resilience in Child Development

Principles and Strategies of Practice

With no evidence of [my dream] ever being possible, I clung to that preposterous vision and, with the force of those dreams, willed it and made it happen. . . . I needed the world that made me feel uninvited to be wrong. So I imagined myself free. I imagined myself loved. I imagined myself as somebody.

Fisher (2001:330)

In his poignant memoir and award-winning screenplay, *Finding Fish*, Antwone Fisher (2001) skillfully expresses the hurt, disappointment, and longing that many children in foster care feel, knowing that they may never reunite with their biological families. Adapted into film by actor/director Denzel Washington and co-produced by Fisher himself, *Finding Fish* is an account of an African American boy's journey through foster care and his success at surmounting incredible odds. Discussing his motivation to write the memoir, Fisher (2004:3) remarks, "I wanted to tell my story because . . . I was told that I could not do it. It reminded me of how I was always told . . . that I was worthless, and that I would never accomplish anything in life." As driving forces in his life, Fisher alludes throughout his story to an indomitable sense of self-determination and his desire to prove others wrong. Fisher also attributes his success to the support of caring adults. He particularly acknowledges (2001:284) the contribution of his Navy psychiatrist, stating, "I could . . . see that he was listening to me intently. By listening, he was giving me, as the Indians say, 'Big Medicine.' . . . He was someone with whom I could share my accomplishments, someone

who knew enough about the distance I'd traveled to be impressed." In the popular and the scientific literatures, people who, like Fisher, overcome the odds are often called "resilient."

As portrayed in *Finding Fish*, resilience is the capacity to maintain or regain adaptive functioning in the face of adverse conditions. Early writings on resilience used the term "resilient" to describe individuals who seemed to have characteristics or traits—perseverance, creativity, intelligence, and humor—that allowed them to surmount difficulties that most people might find insurmountable (Garmezy, Masten, & Tellegen 1984; Rutter 1985). Inner city children, for example, who excelled in academics were described as "invulnerable" to the effects of stress (Anthony 1974; Garmezy 1971). This conceptualization of resilience (i.e., that some children have an inherent capacity to triumph over adversity regardless of the harsh conditions in which they live) is a particularly compelling idea in the United States, where the "American Dream" of overcoming obstacles to achieve social and economic success has particular mass appeal and cultural salience.

However, the notion that resilience connotes an invulnerability to stress has fallen out of favor, in light of empirical evidence that nearly all children who are exposed to adversity experience at least some negative effects (Garmezy 1993; Pollard, Hawkins, & Arthur 1999). It has been replaced in part by the idea that responses to stress vary by the level of risk exposure and the availability of socioenvironmental assets. That is, adaptation is a function of both the relative exposure to adversity and the character of personal and environmental resources (Luthar & Zigler 1991; Rutter 1985).

From this perspective, resilience is an apparent "self-righting" capacity that arises from dynamic, transactional processes involving an interplay between the person and environment (Luthar, Cicchetti, & Becker 2000; Werner 1989). Accordingly, the ability to reorganize after experiencing a trauma or to maintain an effort in the face of challenge is thought to vary by the degree of adversity children experience and the nature of the resources that they can marshal in times of need (Masten et al. 1999). For example, experiencing a stressful life event may not significantly affect functioning when low levels of stress have preceded it. However, combined with a history of chronic stress or with other risk factors that contribute to cumulative exposure, the same stressful event may be sufficient to produce a tipping point at which adaptation declines markedly. Identifying the numerous ways in which individual characteristics and environmental conditions interact to produce psychosocial functioning has shaped a growing body of research studies on resilience. The purpose of this chapter is to briefly summarize this fascinating, complicated literature and to distill from it implications for practice with children and adolescents.

Concept of Risk

Broadly defined, the term "risk factor" relates to any event, condition, or experience that increases the probability that a problem will be formed, maintained, or exacerbated. Risk factors may be problem-specific or nonspecific. Nonspecific risk factors are not related to particular disorders or problems; rather, they have the potential to lead to a variety of maladaptive emotional and behavioral outcomes (Greenberg, Domitrovich, & Bumbarger 1999). Child maltreatment, for example, is a nonspecific risk factor. It is associated with a variety of negative life course outcomes—delinquency, depression, post-traumatic stress disorder, drug use, and

difficulty forming close relationships with others (Jonson-Reid & Barth 2000; Maxfield & Widom 1996; Stewart, Dennison, & Waterson 2002; Zingraff, Leiter, Meyers, & Johnsen 1993). Similarly, poverty is a nonspecific risk factor. It affects the resources available to families and the level of threat in the environment (ranging from dangerous neighborhoods to poor housing and exposure to toxic chemicals). Poverty complicates parenting and, because it is correlated with poor nutrition and healthcare, it directly affects the cognitive, motor, and academic development of children (Duncan & Brooks-Gunn 2000; McLoyd 1998). It has a broad range of poor developmental outcomes. In contrast, specific risk factors increase the likelihood of a specific problem condition. For example, among sexually active adolescents, failure to use such protective measures as condoms results in higher risk for sexually transmitted diseases (STDs), but it does not affect the risk for delinquency (Rounds 2004). It is a specific risk factor for STDs. Some risk factors are implicated in many social problems, and other risk factors seem to play more circumscribed roles.

Individual Characteristics

Risk factors can be conceptualized as falling into three major categories: individual characteristics, contextual characteristics, and stressful life events (Fraser, Kirby, & Smokowski 2004). Sometimes called "risk traits," individual characteristics are biological and psychological predispositions that increase a child's chances for developing problem conditions (Pellegrini 1990). Some psychiatric disorders appear to be heritable (Rutter 1997). Parental schizophrenia, for example, is a risk factor for schizophrenia (Mowbray & Gioia-Hasick 2004), and parental depression is a risk factor for depression (Oyserman 2004). This does not mean that children whose parents have schizophrenia or depression will develop the disorder; but it does mean that children whose parents have the disorder have a higher likelihood of developing the disorder than do children whose parents do not have the disorder. In addition to such genetic liabilities, individual risk characteristics include cognitive deficits, such as poor concentration; affective problems, such as low emotional regulation; behavioral characteristics, such as impulsivity; and general biological sensitivities.

Biological risk factors increase vulnerability to adversity in different ways. For example, individuals with higher physiological thresholds for arousal may engage in risky behavior to fulfill a need for stimulation, or they may accidentally become involved in risky situations because their hypothalamic-pituitary-adrenal (HPA) axes do not properly activate in response to stress. Activation of the HPA axis is a critical survival mechanism because it alerts us to danger. Recent studies have shown that children who are exposed in early childhood to significant trauma (e.g., child maltreatment) may experience HPA mobilization so frequently that neurons become damaged and responsiveness to stress is diminished over time. In the same vein, a host of other cognitive or physiological conditions with roots in developmental disabilities and biological insult, such as fetal alcohol syndrome, affect developmental outcomes (for a review, see Curtis & Cicchetti 2003).

Individual risk factors clearly hold the potential to affect adaptation, but they do not appear to be immutable causes of poor developmental outcomes. Indeed, recent research suggests that many biological risk factors are experience-dependent. Historically thought to be fixed in nature and unchanging over time, physiological risk factors appear to have great plasticity over the life course, responding to the social environment and to psychopharmacological interventions (Curtis & Cicchetti 2003; Davidson 2000). As opposed to the mere presence of a biological or other individual risk factor, it is the interaction of individual and contextual characteristics that appears to affect vulnerability for developmental outcomes (Rutter 1997).

Contextual Characteristics

Contextual risk factors originate outside the individual, within the family, school, peer group, neighborhood, community, or society. Within the family context, maternal smoking, family stress, social isolation, parent-child conflict, and harsh and inconsistent discipline have been found to escalate risk for antisocial behavior (Loeber & Stouthamer-Loeber 1986; Wills, Sandy, Yaeger, & Shinar 2001). School factors associated with increased risk for delinquency include large school size, limited resources, high staff turnover, and inconsistent classroom management (Hawkins, Doueck, & Lishner 1998). Peer group factors, such as rejection by peers and association with delinquent peers, have been shown to increase risk for psychopathology (Coie et al. 1993) and antisocial behavior (Fraser 1996; Kauffman 1997; Patterson, Reid, & Dishion 1992). In one longitudinal study, for example, peer rejection amplified risk for aggression in boys (Coie, Terry, Lenox, Lochman, & Hyman 1995). Compared to boys who were either aggressive or rejected, boys who were both rejected and aggressive in third grade were more likely to engage in problematic behaviors from sixth to tenth grade (see also Miller-Johnson, Coie, Maumary-Gremaud, Bierman, & Conduct Problems Prevention Research Group 2002; Schwartz et al. 1998). Beyond the peer group, other contextual factors affect developmental outcomes. For example, such neighborhood characteristics as low collective efficacy (i.e., low social cohesion among neighbors with little sense of shared responsibility to intervene on behalf of the common good) have been associated with high crime rates (Sampson, Raudenbush, & Earls 1997). Finally, the context can be thought of as a social structure that provides both prosocial (e.g., work in legitimate businesses) and antisocial (e.g., work in illicit businesses) opportunities. Limited or blocked opportunities associated with poverty, racism, and discrimination create incentives for involvement in drug, gun, sex, fencing, and other illicit marketplaces (Cloward

& Ohlin 1960; McLoyd 1998). Like other risk factors, the influences of the social and physical environment vary across the course of child development, particularly social development (Hawkins, Catalano, & Miller 1992).

Stressful Life Events
Whereas some risk factors tend to affect behavior over a period of time, other risk factors, such as stressful life events, are more episodic in nature. These include (1) life events, such as divorce and loss; (2) traumatic experiences, such as abuse, neglect, rape, and natural disasters; (3) interpersonal problems, such as peer victimization; (4) familial factors, such as interparental conflict; and (5) neighborhood events, such as witnessing street violence. Stressful events include major turning points that produce marked disruption in child development and daily hassles that are characterized by frequent annoying or denigrating experiences. Turning point effects result from pivotal life events that dramatically alter risk statuses. Although there is variation in responses to life events, common turning points include an accident that produces disfigurement, arrest that leads to incarceration, and the death of, say, a parent that leads to a decline in family resources (Fraser 2004). In contrast, daily hassles relate to experiences that produce mild but recurrent and cumulative frustration (Von Weiss et al. 2002). For children, these hassles include avoiding bullies on the playground and taking the long route home so as to bypass a crack house; for parents, they may involve dealing daily with the discriminatory practices of store clerks, with inadequate child care, or with incompetent teachers.

Conceptual Models of Resilience
Scholars widely agree that resilience is defined as successful adaptation in the presence of adversity (Arrington & Wilson 2000; Luthar, Cicchetti, & Becker 2000; Olsson, Bond, Burns, Vella-Brodrick, & Sawyer 2003). Often it is further described as (1) overcoming the odds—

escaping the negative effects of risk; (2) sustaining competence under stress—maintaining positive functioning in response to stress; and (3) recovering from trauma—being able to regain normal functioning after suffering negative effects of trauma (Garmezy 1986; Garmezy, Masten, & Tellegen 1984). Although these definitions differ, each implies successful organization of resources and problem solving when confronted with adversity. However, research suggests that the degree of adaptation is related to the amount of risk exposure (in terms of its frequency, duration, and relative toxicity). When exposure is high, few children appear to emerge unscathed (Cicchetti & Rogosch 1997; Pollard, Hawkins, & Arthur 1999).

Based on the idea that children respond differentially to adversity, different models of resilience are beginning to emerge. Borrowing from statistical methods, the terms "additive" and "interactive" are used to distinguish models of resilience. In additive models, resilience is viewed as the "main effects" of factors where risk and protection are conceptualized as opposite ends of the same dimension (e.g., low social support vs. high social support). From this perspective, risk directly increases the probability of poor adaptation, and protection directly increases the probability of positive adaptation (Masten 1987). Thus, developmental outcomes and adaptation to stress are predicted by the relative balance of risk-producing and protection-producing influences in a child's life.

Alternately, in interactive models, resilience is conceptualized as the result of the interplay between protective factors and differing levels of risk. From this perspective, forces that increase vulnerability interact nonlinearly with forces that decrease vulnerability. Protective factors may have no effect in benign circumstances for which risk is low, but they may have great effect when conditioned on high risk (Fraser, Richman, & Galinsky 1999).

To make conceptual distinctions between the main and interactive effects of protection, some have used the terms "promotive factor" to relate to resources that exert positive effects irrespective of risk and "protective factor" to refer to resources that have little to no effect under conditions of low risk but a positive impact under conditions of high risk (Sameroff 1999; Sameroff & Gutman 2004). Scientists describe the direct effects of promotive factors as "main effects" and the buffering or moderating effects of protective factors as "interaction effects" (Roosa 2000).

Distinguishing Promotive from Protective Factors

Promotive factors are defined as those individual and contextual influences that exert direct positive effects on developmental outcomes, irrespective of level of risk (Sameroff & Fiese 2000). For instance, whereas low intelligence has been cited as a risk factor for antisocial behavior (Maguin & Loeber 1996), high intelligence may be viewed as a factor that promotes prosocial behavior (Masten 1994). Intelligence, then, can be conceptualized as a factor that promotes positive behavioral outcomes in all children. Compared to common risk factors, it is unclear whether promotive factors exert an equivalently strong effect on developmental outcomes. The poles of socioeconomic status (SES), for example, may not have equivalently deleterious and salutary effects. That is, although low SES—a common risk factor—is associated with many negative outcomes, high SES—the equivalent promotive factor—may not exert a comparably strong direct effect on positive developmental outcomes for youth.

To date, a small number of studies has compared risk and promotive effects. In a study of children in Philadelphia, for instance, Sameroff and his colleagues (Sameroff, Bartko, Baldwin, Baldwin, & Seifer 1999) created 20 promotive and 20 risk factors by defining a promotive factor as the top quartile of a distribution and a risk factor as the bottom quartile of the same distribution. A score in the bottom quartile of "family climate," for example, was called a risk factor, whereas a score in the top quartile was

called a promotive factor. In the analyses, cumulative promotive factors were about as efficient in predicting five social and behavioral outcomes as cumulative risk factors. Thus, in this dataset, risk and promotive factors were linearly related. They had mirror image effects, and one was about as informative as the other.

Understanding resilience in child development requires distinguishing promotive from protective effects. As noted earlier in this chapter, we use the term "protective factor" to refer to those factors that exert positive effects in the context of risk. Thus resilience is more than the absence of risk, as implied in the promotive vs. risk factor dichotomy. Instead, resilience occurs at the nexus of risk and adaptation, where children at high risk observe unexpectedly positive outcomes. This view of resilience is based on interactions, and research supporting it is only now emerging.

In recent years, for example, researchers have begun to turn from studying peer rejection as a risk factor to studying peer acceptance as a potential promotive and protective factor. In a longitudinal study of 585 families with children in kindergarten through second grade, Criss, Pettit, Bates, Dodge, and Lapp (2002) found peer acceptance to moderate the impact of low SES and harsh discipline on externalizing behavior (e.g., "gets in many fights"). In separate regression analyses for SES and harsh discipline, combinations of peer acceptance, SES, and harsh discipline were significantly correlated with behavior (i.e., they had main or promotive effects). Moreover, interaction terms with peer acceptance were significant (i.e., they had interactive or protective effects). In these analyses, peer acceptance exerted both promotive and protective influences on behavior. The findings suggest that peer acceptance predicts prosocial behavior among all children, and among children exposed to low SES or harsh discipline, it exerts an added protective effect (Criss, Pettit, Bates, Dodge, & Lapp 2002).

In a similar vein, an interaction model of resilience was supported—arguably—in work by

Prelow and Loukas (2003), who explored the relationship between four potentially protective factors and school achievement for 549 low-income, 10- to 14-year-old Latino youths. Maternal school involvement, parental monitoring, and the socioemotional competence of children plus their involvement in extracurricular activities were correlated positively with math and language achievement, over and above a measure of cumulative risk that included five familial and structural risk factors. In such studies, an intriguing question often emerges: are these effects protective or promotive? There are two ways to think about it. On one hand, because these four factors exerted main effects, they might be viewed as promotive. On the other hand, because the sample is only low income, they might be seen as interacting and protective. One would need a sample of all risk levels to sort this out.

Distinguishing between promotive and protective factors is complicated. In introducing the term "promotive effects," Sameroff and his colleagues appear to have made a useful distinction between main (i.e., promotive influences that affect all children) and interactive (i.e., protective influences that differentially affect children at risk) effects. But even though the terms "risk," "promotive," and "protective effects" now afford greater precision in discussing the influence of individual characteristics, contextual characteristics, and stressful events on child development, research distinguishing promotive from protective factors is nascent at best.

Protective Factors: Buffering, Interrupting, and Blocking Risk

When individual and environmental resources operate in the presence of risk to produce successful adaptation, those resources are said to operate protectively. Distinct from assets and strengths, protective factors activate in the context of risk (Rutter 1987). For example, whereas having health insurance does not confer good health, it serves a protective role if a child needs medical care as a result of an illness or accident. In the presence of adversity (a medical condition), it reduces vulnerability, and it improves the chances for recovery to good health. It is a protective factor. Although some researchers make a distinction between internal and external sources of protection, we define protective factors as any resources—individual or environmental—that minimize the impact of risk (Fraser et al. 2004).

Using an interaction model of resilience, protective factors serve three related functions. First, they act to reduce or buffer the impact of risk. In a 2-year longitudinal study comparing children exposed to violence with children having no exposure to violence, school support significantly decreased the likelihood that victimized children engaged in school misconduct and drug use, but it had a minimal effect on children who had not been victimized (O'Donnell, Schwab-Stone, & Muyeed 2002). School support, in this case, had a differential and positive effect for victimized children. Second, protective factors may interrupt a chain of risk, and thereby lessen the probability of further exposure to risk or, in the long run, the development of significant social or health problems. Drug abuse and delinquency prevention programs seek to achieve this goal. For example, a classroom-centered intervention implemented in the Baltimore public schools was designed to change the contingencies that occur in the peer group. It sought to increase prosocial behavior and peer acceptance, thus disrupting a risk chain in which peer rejection leads to association with delinquent peers (Ialongo et al. 1999). Finally, protective factors may prevent or block the onset of a risk factor. Social competence in making friends, solving social problems, and deflecting teasing or taunting appears to protect some children who are at risk for developing behavior problems (Criss, Pettit, Bates, Dodge, & Lapp 2002).

Seeking to understand how children from disadvantaged circumstances understand their own resilience, 86 youths in a stratified random sample of inner city Chicago youth were asked to tell the stories of their lives (Smokowski, Reynolds, & Bezruczko 1999). As in *Finding Fish*, important themes emerged. Youths emphasized the centrality of relationships with family, friends, and teachers—a protective factor identified in a number of studies of resilience (Pianta, Steinberg, & Rollins 1995). They told of strongly held values and beliefs, and of motivational support from others. One male student wrote (Smokowski, Reynolds, & Bezruczko 1999:440), "My mother, everything I do, she influences it. She helps me with everything I do. She always is open with conversation with me and she asks me my opinion of things and she gives me the right to voice my own ideas, not forcefully." The relational supports in these children's lives represent all three elements of protection—buffering risk, interrupting risk chains, and preventing the initial exposure to risk.

Sources of Resilience

Underlying the widespread fascination with resilience is a pivotal question: why do some children prevail over challenging circumstances? Numerous studies have attempted to identify the processes latent in resilience. Older studies tend to confound promotive factors with protective factors, ignoring interaction effects. More recent studies, however, are beginning to make the distinction. To briefly summarize the factors that appear to disrupt risk processes, we describe below the extant and emerging knowledge on sources of resilience, categorizing sources into individual, familial, and extrafamilial domains (Garmezy 1985; Rutter 1979, 1987, 2000; Werner & Smith 1992).

Individual Factors Associated with Resilience

Studies have identified a number of individual factors that contribute to resilience. These factors include constitutional and psychological attributes, such as temperament and sociability (Shaw, Bell, & Gilliom 2000; Werner & Smith 1992), internal locus of control, sense of optimism, skillful use of humor (Grossman et al. 1992; Masten & Reed 2002; Seligman 1992), and self-efficacy (Bandura, Caprara, Barbaranelli, Gerbino, & Pastorelli 2003; Davidson 2000). Social competence is often related to successful adaptation (Davidson 2000; Hubbard 2001). It involves many skills, including "social-cognitive capabilities and emotion regulation skills that permit children to select and engage in social behaviors sensitively and appropriately in different situations" (Bierman 2004:79). Similarly, social-cognitive factors, such as intelligence, the ability to work collaboratively with others, and the capacity to focus in the face of distraction, appear related both to academic achievement and to social success (Masten 1994).

Although self-efficacy may be as much an outcome of successful adaptation as a predictor of it, it includes constructs—social skill, self control, and resolve—that the popular literature often identifies as ingredients of resilience (Masten & Reed 2002). Recently, Bandura and his colleagues (Bandura, Caprara, Barbaranelli, Gerbino, & Pastorelli 2003) examined the relationship between affective, self-regulatory efficacy (i.e., ability to understand emotions in oneself and others and to regulate arousal) and behavioral functioning (i.e., prosocial vs. delinquent behavior). The researchers collected self-report assessments of efficacy and behavior from 464 adolescents, between the ages of 14 and 19, in an ethnically homogenous, socioeconomically diverse Italian community. Empathic efficacy (i.e., ability to identify and respond to the emotions of others) was negatively associated with delinquent behavior and positively associated with prosocial behavior. In addition, self-regulatory efficacy (i.e., being able to resist peer influences) was negatively associated with delinquent behavior. This study and others like it are part of a growing body of literature that suggests encoding social cues, interpreting cues in others, setting relational goals, and skillfully implementing a socially appropriate strategy are critical elements of successful adaptation (Crick & Dodge 1994; Dodge et al. 2003).

*Familial Factors Associated
with Resilience*

Both the structural and process characteristics of families have been shown to affect child outcomes. Processes within the family, such as those reflected in positive parent-child relations (Egeland, Carlson, & Sroufe 1993; Rutter 1987), low interparental conflict (McCloskey & Stuewig 2001), and effective parenting (Mistry, Vandewater, Huston, & McLoyd 2002; Tebes, Kaufman, Adnopoz, & Racusin 2001) appear to mediate developmental outcomes for all children. Compared to family processes, family characteristics, such as size, structure, and income, appear to have more modest effects, but they are nonetheless associated with a variety of developmental outcomes (Conrad & Hammen 1993; Linver, Fuligni, Hernandez, & Brooks-Gunn 2004; Werner 1993). Suggesting that structural characteristics affect family processes, which in turn influence child behavior, Mistry, Vandewater, Huston, and McLoyd (2002) recently found that parental distress, responsiveness, and disciplinary efficacy mediated the impact of economic hardship on children's social competence, prosocial behavior, and disruptive behavior. Across such family processes as communication and problem solving, parenting skills in discipline and supervision of children appear to be particularly important in mediating the effects of poverty. Similarly, Tebes, Kaufman, Adnopoz, and Racusin (2001) studied the impact of socioeconomic conditions and family processes (e.g., economic disadvantage, social network constriction, familial stress, parenting performance) on children's social, psychological, and academic functioning. In a sample of 177 low-income children and adolescents aged 2–17, effective parenting was consistently more predictive of child adaptation than parental psychopathology and family stress. The findings from this study suggest that promoting effective parenting may be especially important in producing positive outcomes for higher-risk youth.

*Extrafamilial Factors Associated
with Resilience*

A number of extrafamilial factors have been associated with resilience. From an ecological perspective, these factors may be conceptualized as belonging to three domains: school, neighborhood, and community or society. At the school level, school support, positive relationships with teachers (Meehan, Hughes, & Cavell 2003), and school bonding appear to promote successful adaptation (Hawkins & Lishner 1987; Morrison, Robertson, Laurie, & Kelly 2002). On the neighborhood level, where social interaction can be defined by geographic boundaries, factors that describe social cohesion and informal social control are associated with lower levels of crime. Extending Bandura's (1997) notion of self-efficacy, neighborhoods are sometimes said to have a collective capacity to influence outcomes. Collective neighborhood efficacy appears to be negatively related to neighborhood indicators of antisocial behavior and maladjustment (Nash & Bowen 1999; Sampson, Raudenbush, & Earls 1997). Similarly, community activities, such as belonging to a church or community center (Werner 1993) and receiving social support as a result of membership in organizations or groups (Dubow, Tisak, Causey, Hryshko, & Reid 1991; Wolkow & Ferguson 2001) are sometimes conceptualized as community factors. These factors appear related to resilience. However, unlike neighborhood factors, they do not describe features of communities. Rather, they describe individual participation in social processes afforded through societal resources.

Principles of Practice from a Resilience Perspective

Understanding the complex chain reactions through which individual and environmental factors interact to promote positive adaptation is a critical task if research on resilience is to inform practice (Rutter 1990). Historically, researchers focused on the negative impact of risk, without exploring the moderating role of protective factors. As a result, we know less about how protective factors buffer, interrupt, and prevent exposure to risk. More recently, researchers have attempted to focus on successful adaptation in an attempt to fill this gap in the literature. But to differentiate risk, promotive, and protective effects from one another, longitudinal studies must include samples of high- and low-risk children, and analyses must probe for the nonlinear effects that emerge in interactions. It is a tall order.

Notwithstanding the difficulty of the challenges that lie ahead, several important findings have already emerged from the study of resilience. These findings are beginning to give shape to three core practice principles regarding the design of interventions. Described below, they are: (1) strengthen protection and reduce risk; (2) understand the effect of the context; and (3) identify and disrupt risk mechanisms.

Strengthen Protection and Reduce Risk

One set of findings relates to the operation of cumulative protection vis-à-vis cumulative risk. Studies suggest that actual vulnerability has an exponential (as opposed to a simple linear) relationship to risk exposure (Sameroff, Seifer, Barocas, Zax, & Greenspan 1987). Accordingly, some researchers view the presence of three or more risk factors as a threshold that denotes high-risk status (Sameroff 1985). In addition, research suggests that certain risks are more likely to be accompanied by other, related risk factors. This finding has led to the idea that risk may be "bundled" or that exposure to one type of risk is highly correlated with exposure to other types (Rutter 2000). Poverty is often cited as an example of bundling, because it is typically accompanied by a host of other risk factors, such as single parenthood, low maternal education, parental substance abuse, low-status parental occupation, and large family size (Duncan & Brooks-Gunn 1997; Kauffman 1997). Because high levels of cumulative risk are associated with low levels of protection (Pollard, Hawkins, & Arthur 1999), there is a tipping point at which risk overcomes protection for many children and adolescents. Perhaps the most important conclusion from this stream of research is that a focus on assets, strengths, or protection alone will not produce positive outcomes for the highest-risk children. A core principle of a resilience orientation in practice is that protection must be strengthened and risk must be reduced.

Understand the Effect of the Context on Protection and Risk

A second set of findings has emerged from studies of individual and contextual factors that affect adaptation and developmental outcomes. It appears, for instance, that family-related conditions and processes exert great impact during childhood, whereas peer and school conditions and processes have great impact during adolescence (Fraser et al. 1999). Illustrating this point, a study investigating predictors of antisocial behavior found that association with delinquent peers did not predict problem behavior in childhood, but it did predict problem behavior in adolescence (Lipsey & Derzon 1998). Risk factors and—although we know less about them—protective factors appear to differ across child development.

As scholars begin to understand how risk varies in the context of child development, they are also giving more attention to broader environmental resources and conditions. The importance of the social and physical environment has been underestimated. When environmental disadvantage was statistically controlled in a longitudinal study of children in Rochester, New York, Sameroff, Bartko, Baldwin, Baldwin, and Seifer (1999) found an unexpected relationship across individual risk factors (e.g., mental health status, intelligence), environmental risk factors (e.g., neighborhood crime, poverty), and two developmental outcomes (academic achievement and social competence). Bright, resourceful children in high-risk settings experienced poorer social and academic outcomes than less bright and less resourceful children in low-risk settings. Compared to individual factors, contextual factors appear to have exerted relatively more influence on adaptational outcomes.

Indeed, contextual factors appear to so condition relationships that the same behavior may promote positive outcomes in one setting and elevate risk for poor outcomes in another (for a discussion, see Kaplan 1999). Showing gang colors or acting tough, for example, may reduce risk in one part of the city, but it may increase risk in another part of the city. Similarly, sociocultural factors, such as gender, race, ethnicity, and culture appear to condition the operation of risk and protection (Arrington & Wilson 2000). For example, compared to white children, children of color often experience higher rates of poverty, discrimination, and racism. But they may also have relatively higher cultural resources that hold the potential to buffer or block risk. Research suggests that, when the social environment nurtures it, a positive racial identity serves a protective function for African American children (Miller 1999) and, similarly, that environments that produce biculturalism (i.e., behavioral competence in both dominant and ethnic minority cultures) encourage resilience in immigrant youth (Barbarin, McCandies, Coleman, & Atkinson 2004; LaFromboise, Coleman, & Gerton 1993). So a second core principle of a resilience orientation to practice is protection and risk vary based on the social and developmental context.

Identify and Disrupt Risk Mechanisms

A third set of studies focuses on risk mechanisms. The term "risk mechanism" describes "the process whereby a risk factor contributes over time to heightened vulnerability" (Fraser et al. 2004:21). Understanding risk mechanisms is essential. Researchers have begun to more clearly define these risk chains or mechanisms. For example, child management by parents is a

commonly identified risk factor for delinquency (Loeber, Farrington, Stouthamer-Loeber, & Van-Kammen 1998). Child management consists of parenting skills in problem-solving, discipline, and communication. Patterson (1982) described a risk mechanism by which children develop antisocial behavior via parental child management. In this risk chain, children are negatively reinforced to engage in aggressive, defiant behavior when parents fail to set and consistently enforce family rules. According to what has become known as "coercion theory" (Reid, Patterson, & Snyder 2002), some children, when confronted with a parental request (e.g., "Turn off the television"), engage in aversive behavior (e.g., whining, arguing, confrontation) to avoid compliance. When parents acquiesce in the face of a child's opposition (and thus fail to address the escalated behavior), children escape the contingency. In essence, a child's aversive behavior is rewarded by parental acquiescence, and coercive escalation becomes an element in the child's repertoire of skills for solving social problems. As children employ this style of coercive interaction with others, it often ignites a devastating chain of relational risks involving weakened parent-child bonds of attachment, alienation from teachers, rejection by peers, poor achievement in school and other settings, and association with delinquent peers (Reid, Patterson, & Snyder 2002).

Perhaps the greatest challenge in using the resilience perspective is the specification of risk mechanisms. A resilience-based orientation is rooted in understanding the sequencing of events that elevate risk, including environmental contingencies and constrained opportunities. Thus the third core principle of a resilience orientation to practice is identify and attempt to disrupt risk mechanisms.

A Social-Cognitive Perspective on Resilience

Consistent with social process theories of human behavior (e.g., Catalano & Hawkins 1996; Hirschi 1969; Reid, Patterson, & Snyder

2002), recent studies suggest that resilience emerges in the context of interpersonal attachments that reward sustained effort in the face of adversity (Werner 1993; Werner & Smith 1992). From a social development perspective, attachments are conceptualized as a key element of a "social bond" to family, school, and society, and commitment is thought to derive from attachment and involvement with supportive others (e.g., see Guo, Hill, Hawkins, Catalano, & Abbott 2002; Herrenkohl, Hill, Chung, Guo, Abbott, & Hawkins 2003; Herrenkohl, Huang, Kosterman, Hawkins, Catalano, & Smith 2001). In a recent study of 289 fifth- and sixth-grade children, Murray and Greenberg (2001) found that positive relationships with teachers and bonding to school were associated with high levels of social and emotional adjustment in students with severe emotional disturbance and mild mental retardation. Other studies have found involvement with friends and neighbors to be tied to positive developmental outcomes for children and adolescents (Costello & Vowell 1999; De Li 1999). From the research, a relational perspective is emerging in which resilience is conceptualized as a product of social ties that provide support and reinforcement.

However, although children who are resilient often have relational supports and sustaining beliefs that provide motivation and commitment, there appears to be no single pathway or combination of protective factors that produces resilience. Instead, resilient children appear to have a self-righting capacity that arises from the confluence of a variety of biological, cognitive, and social environmental factors (Werner 1989). They have a skill at self-organization that allows them to encounter stress, reorganize resources, and press ahead. The ability to do this is characterized not by a specific set of protective factors but rather by a more general involvement with others, which is distinguished by attachments that lead in turn to opportunities and commitments.

From this perspective, children who are resilient often have both opportunities for involvement with supportive others and a range of cognitive-organizational skills that allow them to leverage benefit from social involvement. These opportunities and skills appear to arise from differential association with parents, uncles, aunts, coaches, teachers, and others whose behaviors are learned in the context of strong relational ties (Pianta, Steinberg, & Rollins 1995). Thus a simple and compelling idea is beginning to take shape regarding the many different pathways through which children seem to become resilient: across protective factors related to childhood problems, successful adaptation is a function of social-cognitive skill in organizing and using resources, opportunities for involvement with others (who assist in providing resources), and relational contingencies or environmental support for sustained effort.

Practice Strategies from a Social-Cognitive Perspective

Extending the three core principles of a resilience orientation to practice (i.e., strengthen protection and reduce risk, understand the effect of the context, and disrupt risk mechanisms), three additional practice strategies are implied from this social-cognitive perspective on resilience. Interventions should strengthen social-cognitive skills, create opportunities for involvement, and alter contingencies in the social environment (Catalano & Hawkins 1996).

Social-cognitive skills appear to contribute to the maintenance of social ties and the capacity of children to respond to trauma. Resilient children and youths seem to have a capacity to regulate emotions, reassess situations, reconceptualize goals, and adjust problem-solving strategies (Davidson 2000). The mix of skills and environmental supports that produce this reorganizing behavior is probably quite variable, but it includes at least the capacity to control arousal, encode cues in the environment, assess assets, and reformulate plans. A resilience orientation to practice focuses in part on enhancing these skills (for an application, see

Fraser, Day, Galinsky, Hodges, & Smokowski, 2004).

While enhancing social-cognitive skills, intervention should also create new opportunities for prosocial involvement. It should expose children to their peers who are committed to school (or other prosocial activities) and provide opportunities to build bonds of attachment to adults who may serve as mentors, role models, and friends. Changing the opportunity structure involves changing the social network. The goal is to create a matrix of new relational resources that increase access to conventional activities. It is through social ties that efforts are sustained and resolve emerges in the presence of challenge. Successful adaptation is a function in part of strong social ties and the opportunities that often emerge from them.

Finally, in the context of strengthening skills and providing opportunities, contingencies in the social environment must be developed to reward persistence in the face of adversity. Although the word "contingency" usually refers to rewards and punishments for behavior, we use the term here to describe the milieu of material and social reinforcements or supports that are necessary to maintain an exceptional effort when confronted with hardship. Resilience appears to arise from the chemistry of skills, opportunities, and rewarding relationships. It is less a personal trait than a pattern of responses that has high environmental dependence. These responses are a function of personal and environmental resources in which at least one person—a parent, teacher, social worker, religious leader, or someone else—develops a bond of attachment to a child and, through that bond, provides encouragement and support to overcome challenges (Doll & Lyon 1998). Behind success is almost always a relationship that provides a set of social contingencies. The commitments that accrue through strong relationships sculpt beliefs, shape behavior, and sustain efforts.

Tailoring Interventions

This perspective on resilience is based on understanding the dependence of successful adaptation on social-cognitive skills, environmental opportunities, and relational contingencies; however, interventions must always be tailored to fit both local conditions and sociocultural influences that nuance child development (Fraser & Galinsky 2004). To the extent that the risk mechanisms for particular social and health problems vary across settings and peoples, interventions must be fine-tuned to disrupt risk processes related to culture, gender, religion, sexual preference, and other aspects of diversity. This requires clearly specifying relevant risk and protective factors, assessing individual sensitivity to risk, and developing a strategy to interrupt risk chains. Recent research suggests, for example, that some aspects of substance abuse vary by gender, race/ethnicity, and immigrant status (Amaro, Blake, Schwartz, & Flinchbaugh 2001). So, to optimize the potential to prevent drug dependence, an intervention should be tailored such that activities have gender and cultural relevance. Developing a greater understanding of the influences of culture, gender, religion, and sexual orientation on risk factors is crucial in developing more effective interventions (e.g., see American Bar Association and National Bar Association 2001; Blake, Amaro, Schwartz, & Flinchbaugh 2001; Guthrie & Low 2000).

Conclusion

Resilience emerges from a dynamic, transactional process of interaction between personal characteristics and the environment. Like most apparent mysteries, there is behind the initial paradox of resilience an increasingly clear explanation. The capacity to reorganize subsequent to a trauma or to maintain one's level of functioning in the face of difficulty develops from the combined effects of social-cognitive skills, opportunities for involvement, and relational supports. Resilience is a regrouping, self-righting capacity that occurs as a result of personal and environmentally supported efforts to marshal and remarshal resources in the presence of challenge. When children prevail over adversity, we usually find relational resources that assist them in regulating emotions, assessing conditions, accessing opportunities, and sustaining efforts. As in *Finding Fish* (Fisher 2001), the social processes associated with resilience often involve someone in a child's life who, like Fisher's Navy psychiatrist, did not give up.

Conditioned on sobering findings that the capacity to respond successfully to adversity weakens with increased exposure to risk (Cicchetti & Rogosch 1997; Pollard, Hawkins, & Arthur 1999), a message of hope emerges from research on resilience. Biological risk factors, including gene expression and brain abnormalities, are not immutable traits (Curtis & Cicchetti 2003). Indeed, they appear to be highly plastic and dependent on the social environment (Davidson 2000; Johnson 1999). Similarly, factors such as social-cognitive skills and environmental conditions also appear to be plastic and dependent on the social environment. Biological, material, and social risk factors are subject to change across the life span. From individual and environmental change perspectives, there appear to be many points of potential intervention. The patina of hopefulness that characterizes research on resilience comes from uplifting stories of success like that of Antwone Fisher, from emerging knowledge of human behavior that is latent in these stories, and from promising practice strategies—rooted in our growing understanding of adaptation in the face of adversity—that hold the potential to change the life course trajectories of many children.

REFERENCES

Amaro, H., Blake, S. M., Schwartz, P. M., & Flinchbaugh, L. J. (2001). Developing theory-based substance abuse prevention programs for young adolescent girls. *Journal of Early Adolescence, 21,* 256–293.

American Bar Association and National Bar Association (2001). *Justice by gender: The lack of appropriate prevention, diversion, and treatment alternatives for girls in the justice system.* Washington, DC: American Bar Association and the National Bar Association. Retrieved October 13, 2003, from www.abanet.org/crimjust/juvjus/girls.html.

Anthony, E. J. (1974). The syndrome of the psychologically invulnerable child. In E. J. Anthony & C. Koupernik (eds.), *The child in his family: Children at psychiatric risk,* pp. 529–544. New York: Wiley.

Arrington, E. G., & Wilson, M. N. (2000). A reexamination of risk and resilience during adolescence: Incorporating culture and diversity. *Journal of Child and Family Studies, 9,* 221–230.

Bandura, A. (1997). *Self-efficacy: The exercise of control.* New York: Worth Publishers.

Bandura, A., Caprara, G. V., Barbaranelli, C., Gerbino, M., & Pastorelli, C. (2003). Role of affective self-regulatory efficacy in diverse spheres of psychosocial functioning. *Child Development, 74,* 769–782.

Barbarin, O., McCandies, T., Coleman, C., & Atkinson, T. (2004). Ethnicity and culture. In P. Allen-Meares & M. W. Fraser (eds.), *Intervention with children and adolescents: An interdisciplinary perspective,* pp. 27–53. Boston: Allyn and Bacon.

Bierman, K. L. (2004). *Peer rejection: Developmental processes and intervention strategies.* New York: Guilford Press.

Blake, S. M., Amaro, H., Schwartz, P. M., & Flinchbaugh, L. J. (2001). A review of substance abuse prevention interventions for young adolescent girls. *Journal of Early Adolescence, 21,* 294–324.

Catalano, R. F., & Hawkins, J. D. (1996). The Social Development Model: A theory of antisocial behavior. In J. D. Hawkins (ed.), *Delinquency and crime: Current theories,* pp. 149–197. Cambridge, UK: Cambridge University Press.

Cicchetti, D., & Rogosch, F. A. (1997). The role of self-organization in the promotion of resilience in maltreated children. *Development and Psychopathology, 9,* 797–815.

Cloward, R. A., & Ohlin, L. E. (1960). *Delinquency and opportunity: A theory of delinquent gangs.* New York: Free Press.

Coie, J. D., Terry, R., Lenox, K. F., Lochman, J. E., & Hyman, C. (1995). Childhood peer rejection and aggression as predictors of stable patterns of adolescent disorder. *Development and Psychopathology, 7,* 697–713.

Coie, J. D., Watt, N. F., West, S. G., Hawkins, J. D., Asarnow, J. R., Markman, H. J., et al. (1993). The science of prevention: A conceptual framework and some directions for a national research program. *American Psychologist, 48,* 1013–1022.

Conrad, M., & Hammen, C. (1993). Protective and resource factors in high and low risk children: A comparison of children with unipolar, bipolar, medically ill, and normal mothers. *Development and Psychopathology, 5,* 593–607.

Costello, B. J., & Vowell, P. R. (1999). Testing control theory and differential association: A re-analysis of the Richmond Youth Project Data. *Criminology, 37,* 815–842.

Crick, N. R., & Dodge, K. A. (1994). A review and reformulation of social information processing mechanisms in children's social adjustment. *Psychological Bulletin, 115,* 74–101.

Criss, M. M., Pettit, G. S., Bates, J. E., Dodge, K. A., & Lapp, A. L. (2002). Family adversity, positive peer relationships, and children's externalizing behavior: A longitudinal perspective on risk and resilience. *Child Development, 73,* 1220–1237.

Curtis, W. J., & Cicchetti, D. (2003). Moving research on resilience into the 21st century: Theoretical and methodological considerations in examining the biological contributors to resilience. *Development and Psychopathology, 15,* 773–810.

Davidson, R. J. (2000). Affective style, psychopathology, and resilience: Brain mechanisms and plasticity. *American Psychologist, 55,* 1196–1214.

De Li, S. (1999). Social control, delinquency, and youth status achievement: A developmental approach. *Sociological Perspectives, 42,* 305–324.

Dodge, K. A., Lansford, J. E., Burks, V. S., Bates, J. E., Pettit, G. S., et al. (2003). Peer rejection and social information-processing factors in the development of aggressive behavior problems in children. *Child Development, 74,* 374–393.

Doll, B., & Lyon, M. A. (1998). Risk and resilience: Implications for the delivery of educational and mental health services in the schools. *School Psychology Review, 27,* 348–363.

Dubow, E. F., Tisak, J., Causey, D., Hryshko, A., & Reid, G. (1991). A two-year longitudinal study of stressful life events, social support, and social problem-solving skills: Contributions to children's behavioral and academic adjustment. *Child Development, 62,* 583–599.

Duncan, G. J., & Brooks-Gunn, J. (1997). *Consequences of growing up poor.* New York: Russell Sage Foundation.

Duncan, G. J., & Brooks-Gunn, J. (2000). Family poverty, welfare reform, and child development. *Child Development, 71,* 188–196.

Egeland, B., Carlson, E., & Sroufe, L. A. (1993). Resilience as process. *Development and Psychopathology, 5,* 517–528.

Fisher, A. Q. (2001). *Finding fish: A memoir.* New York: Perennial.

Fisher, A. Q. (2004). *Antwone Fisher.* Retrieved on December 1, 2003, from www.foxsearchlight.com/filmmakers/fisher/.

Fraser, M. W. (1996). Aggressive behavior in childhood and early adolescence: An ecological developmental perspective on youth violence. *Social Work, 41,* 347–361.

Fraser, M. W. (ed.) (2004). *Risk and resilience in childhood: An ecological perspective,* second ed. Washington, DC: National Association of Social Workers Press.

Fraser, M. W., Day, S. H., Galinsky, M. J., Hodges, V. G., & Smokowski, P. R. (2004). Conduct problems and peer rejection in childhood: A randomized trial of the Making Choices and Strong Families programs. *Research on Social Work Practice, 14,* 313–324.

Fraser, M. W., & Galinsky, M. J. (2004). Risk and resilience in childhood: Toward an evidence-based model of practice. In M. W. Fraser (ed.), *Risk and resilience in childhood: An ecological perspective,* second ed., pp. 385–402. Washington, DC: National Association of Social Workers Press.

Fraser, M. W., Kirby, L. D., & Smokowski, P. R. (2004). Risk and resilience in childhood. In M. W. Fraser (ed.), *Risk and resilience in childhood: An ecological perspective,* second ed., pp. 13–66. Washington, DC: National Association of Social Workers Press.

Fraser, M. W., Richman, J. M., & Galinsky, M. J. (1999). Risk, protection, and resilience: Towards a conceptual framework for social work practice. *Social Work Research, 23,* 131–144.

Garmezy, N. (1971). Vulnerability research and the issue of primary prevention. *American Journal of Orthopsychiatry, 41,* 101–116.

Garmezy, N. (1985). Effects of residential treatment on adjudicated delinquents: A meta-analysis. *Journal of Research in Crime and Delinquency, 22,* 287–308.

Garmezy, N. (1986). On measures, methods, and models. *Journal of the American Academy of Child and Adolescent Psychiatry, 25,* 727–729.

Garmezy, N. (1993). Children in poverty: Resilience despite risk. *Psychiatry, 56,* 127–136.

Garmezy, N., Masten, A., & Tellegen, A. (1984). The study of stress and competence in children: Building blocks for developmental psychopathology. *Child Development, 55,* 97–110.

Greenberg, M. T., Domitrovich, C., & Bumbarger, B. (1999). *The prevention of mental disorders in school-aged children: A review of the effectiveness of prevention programs.* CMHS Publication. Washington, DC: U.S. Department of Health and Human Services. Retrieved September 30, 2002, from www. prevention. psu.edu/CMHS.html.

Grossman, F. K., Beinashowitz, J., Anderson, L., Sakurai, M., Finnin, L., & Flaherty, M. (1992). Risk and resilience in young adults. *Journal of Youth and Adolescence, 21,* 1–22.

Guo, J., Hill, K. G., Hawkins, J. D., Catalano, R. F., & Abbott, R. D. (2002). A developmental analysis of sociodemographic, family, and peer effects on adolescent illicit drug initiation. *Journal of the American*

Academy of Child and Adolescent Psychiatry, 41, 838–845.

Guthrie, B. J., & Low, L. K. (2000). A substance abuse prevention framework: Considering the social context for African American girls. *Public Health Nursing, 17,* 363–373.

Hawkins, J. D., Catalano, R. F., & Miller, J. Y. (1992). Risk and protective factors for alcohol and other drug problems in adolescence and early adulthood: Implications for substance abuse prevention. *Psychological Bulletin, 112,* 64–105.

Hawkins, J. D., Doueck, H. J., & Lishner, D. M. (1998). Changing teaching practices in mainstream classrooms to improve bonding and behavior of low achievers. *American Educational Research Journal, 25,* 31–50.

Hawkins, J. D., & Lishner, D. M. (1987). Etiology and prevention of antisocial behavior in children and adolescents. In D. H. Crowell & I. M. Evans (eds.), *Childhood aggression and violence: Sources of influence, prevention, and control. Applied clinical psychology,* pp. 263–282. New York: Plenum Press.

Herrenkohl, T. I., Hill, K. G., Chung, I. J., Guo, J., Abbott, R. D., & Hawkins, J. D. (2003). Protective factors against serious violent behavior in adolescence: A prospective study of aggressive children. *Social Work Research, 27,* 179–191.

Herrenkohl, T. I., Huang, B., Kosterman, R., Hawkins, J. D., Catalano, R. F., & Smith, B. H. (2001). A comparison of social development processes leading to violent behavior in late adolescence for childhood initiators and adolescent initiators of violence. *Journal of Research in Crime and Delinquency, 38,* 45–63.

Hirschi, T. (1969). *The causes of delinquency.* Berkeley: University of California Press.

Hubbard, J. A. (2001). Emotion expression processes in children's peer interaction: The role of peer rejection, aggression, and gender. *Child Development, 72,* 1426–1438.

Ialongo, N., Werthamer, L., Kellam, S. G., Brown, C. H., Wang, S., & Lin, Y. (1999). The proximal impact of two first-grade preventive interventions on the early risk behaviors for later substance abuse, depression, and antisocial behavior. *American Journal of Community Psychology, 27,* 599–641.

Johnson, M. (1999). Cortical plasticity in normal and abnormal development: Evidence and working hypotheses. *Development and Psychopathology, 11,* 395–411.

Jonson-Reid, M., & Barth, R. P. (2000). From maltreatment report to juvenile incarceration: The role of child welfare services. *Child Abuse and Neglect, 24,* 505–520.

Kaplan, H. B. (1999). Toward an understanding of resilience: A critical review of definitions and models. In M. D. Glantz & J. L. Johnson (eds.), *Resilience and development: Positive life adaptations,* pp. 17–83. New York: Kluwer Academic and Plenum Press.

Kauffman, J. K. (1997). *Characteristics of emotional and behavioral disorders of children and youth,* sixth ed. Upper Saddle River, NJ: Prentice Hall.

LaFromboise, T., Coleman, H. L., & Gerton, J. (1993). Psychological impact of biculturalism: Evidence and theory. *Psychological Bulletin, 114,* 395–412.

Linver, M. R., Fuligni, A. S., Hernandez, M., & Brooks-Gunn, J. (2004). Poverty and child development: Promising interventions. In P. Allen-Meares & M. W. Fraser (eds.), *Intervention with children and adolescents: An interdisciplinary perspective,* pp. 106–129. Boston: Allyn and Bacon.

Lipsey, M. W., & Derzon, J. H. (1998). Predictors of violent and serious delinquency in adolescence and early adulthood: A synthesis of longitudinal research. In R. Loeber & D. P. Farrington (eds.), *Serious and violent juvenile offenders: Risk factors and successful interventions,* pp. 86–105. Thousand Oaks, CA: Sage.

Loeber, R., Farrington, D. P., Stouthamer-Loeber, M., & Van Kammen, W. B. (1998). *Antisocial behavior and mental health: Explanatory factors in childhood and adolescence.* Mahwah, NJ: Lawrence Erlbaum Associates.

Loeber, R., & Stouthamer-Loeber, M. (1986). Family factors as correlates and predictors of juvenile conduct problems and delinquency. In M. Tonry & N. Morris (eds.), *Crime and justice: An annual review of research,* vol. 7, pp. 29–149. Chicago: University of Chicago Press.

Luthar, S. S., Cicchetti, D., & Becker, B. (2000). The construct of resilience: A critical evaluation and guidelines for future work. *Child Development, 71,* 543–562.

Luthar, S. S., & Zigler, E. (1991). Vulnerability and competence: A review of research on resilience in childhood. *American Journal of Orthopsychiatry, 61,* 6–22.

Maguin, E., & Loeber, R. (1996). Academic performance and delinquency. In M. Tomry (ed.), *Crime and Justice: A Review of Research,* vol. 20, pp. 145–264. Chicago: University of Chicago Press.

Masten, A. (1987). Resilience in development: Implications of the study of successful adaptation for developmental psychopathology. In D. Cicchetti (ed.), *The emergence of a discipline: Rochester Symposium on Developmental Psychopathology,* pp. 261–294. Hillsdale, NJ: Lawrence Erlbaum Associates.

Masten, A. (1994). Resilience in individual development: Successful adaptation despite risk and adversity. In M. C. Wang & E. W. Gordon (eds.), *Educational resilience in inner-city America: Challenges and prospects,* pp. 3–26. Hillsdale, NJ: Lawrence Erlbaum Associates.

Masten, A., Hubbard, J., Gest, S., Tellegen, A., Garmezy, N., & Ramirez, M. (1999). Competence in the context of adversity: Pathways to resilience and maladaptation from childhood to late adolescence. *Development and Psychopathology, 11,* 143–169.

Masten, A., & Reed, M. G. (2002). Resilience in development. In S. R. Snyder & S. J. Lopez (eds.), *The handbook of positive psychology*, pp. 74–88. Oxford: Oxford University Press.

Maxfield, M., & Widom, C. (1996). The cycle of violence: Revisited six years later. *Archives of Pediatric Adolescent Medicine, 150*, 390–395.

McCloskey, L. A., & Stuewig, J. (2001). The quality of peer relationships among children exposed to family violence. *Development and Psychopathology, 13*, 83–96.

McLoyd, V. C. (1998). Socioeconomic disadvantage and child development. *American Psychologist, 53*, 185–204.

Meehan, B. T., Hughes, J. N., & Cavell, T. A. (2003). Teacher-student relationships as compensatory resources for aggressive children. *Child Development, 74*, 1145–1157.

Miller, D. B. (1999). Racial socialization and racial identity: Can they promote resiliency for African American adolescents? *Adolescence, 34*, 493–501.

Miller-Johnson, S., Coie, J. D., Maumary-Gremaud, A., Bierman, K., & Conduct Problems Prevention Research Group (2002). Peer rejection and early starter models of conduct disorder. *Journal of Abnormal Child Psychology, 30*, 217–231.

Mistry, R., Vandewater, E., Huston, A. C., & McLoyd, V. C. (2002). Economic well-being and children's social adjustment: The role of family process in an ethnically diverse low-income sample. *Child Development, 73*, 935–951.

Morrison, G. M., Robertson, L., Laurie, B., & Kelly, J. (2002). Protective factors related to antisocial behavior trajectories. *Journal of Clinical Psychology, 58*, 277–290.

Mowbray, C. T., & Gioia-Hasick, D. (2004). Treatment and early intervention for schizophrenia. In P. Allen-Meares & M. W. Fraser (eds.), *Intervention with children and adolescents: An interdisciplinary perspective*, pp. 229–263. Boston: Allyn and Bacon.

Murray, C., & Greenberg, M. (2001). Relationships with teachers and bonds with school: Social and emotional adjustment correlates for children with and without disabilities. *Psychology in the Schools, 38*, 25–41.

Nash, J. K., & Bowen, G. L. (1999). Perceived crime and informal social control in the neighborhood as a context for adolescent behavior: A risk and resilience perspective. *Social Work Research, 23*, 171–187.

O'Donnell, D. A., Schwab-Stone, M. E., & Muyeed, A. Z. (2002). Multidimensional resilience in urban children exposed to community violence. *Child Development, 73*, 1265–1282.

Olsson, C. A., Bond, L., Burns, J. M., Vella-Brodrick, D. A., & Sawyer, S. M. (2003). Adolescent resilience: A concept analysis. *Journal of Adolescence, 26*, 1–11.

Oyserman, D. (2004). Depression during the school-aged years. In P. Allen-Meares & M. W. Fraser (eds.), *Intervention with children and adolescents: An interdisciplinary perspective*, pp. 264–281. Boston: Allyn and Bacon.

Patterson, G. R. (1982). *Coercive family process.* Eugene, OR: Castalia Publishing.

Patterson, G. R., Reid, J.B., & Dishion, T. J. (1992). *Antisocial boys.* Eugene, OR: Castalia Publishing.

Pellegrini, D. S. (1990). Psychosocial risk and protective factors in childhood. *Developmental and Behavioral Pediatrics, 11*, 201–209.

Pianta, R. C., Steinberg, M., & Rollins, K. (1995). The first two years of school: Teacher-student relationships and deflections in children's classroom adjustment. *Development and Psychopathology, 7*, 295–312.

Pollard, J. A., Hawkins, J. D., & Arthur, M. W. (1999). Risk and protection: Are both necessary to understand diverse behavioral outcomes in adolescence? *Social Work Research, 23*, 145–158.

Prelow, H. M., & Loukas, A. (2003). The role of resource, protective, and risk factors on academic achievement-related outcomes of economically disadvantaged Latino youth. *Journal of Community Psychology, 31*, 513–530.

Reid, J. B., Patterson, G. R., & Snyder, J. (2002). *Antisocial behavior in children and adolescents.* Washington, DC: American Psychological Association.

Roosa, M. W. (2000). Some thoughts about resilience versus positive development, main effects versus interaction effects and the value of resilience. *Child Development, 71*, 567–569.

Rounds, K. A. (2004). Preventing sexually transmitted infections among adolescents. In M. W. Fraser (ed.), *Risk and resilience in childhood: An ecological perspective*, second ed., pp. 251–279. Washington, DC: National Association of Social Workers Press.

Rutter, M. (1979). Protective factors in children's responses to stress and disadvantage. In M. W. Kent & J. E. Rolf (eds.), *Primary prevention of psychopathology: Social competence in children*, vol. 3, pp. 49–74. Hanover, NH: University Press of New England.

Rutter, M. (1985). Resilience in the face of adversity—Protective factors and resistance to psychiatric disorder. *British Journal of Psychiatry, 147*, 598–611.

Rutter, M. (1987). Psychosocial resilience and protective mechanisms. *American Journal of Orthopsychiatry, 57*, 316–331.

Rutter, M. (1990). Psychosocial resilience and protective mechanisms. In J. Rolf, A. S. Masten, D. Cicchetti, K. Neucherlein, & S. Weintraub (eds.), *Risk and protective factors in the development of psychopathology*, pp. 181–214. New York: Cambridge University Press.

Rutter, M. (1997). Nature-nurture integration: The example of antisocial behavior. *American Psychologist, 52*, 390–398.

Rutter, M. (2000). Resilience reconsidered: Conceptual considerations, empirical findings, and policy implications. In J. P. Shonkoff & S. J. Meisels (eds.), *Handbook of early childhood intervention*, second ed., pp. 651–682. New York: Cambridge University Press.

Sameroff, A. J. (1985). Environmental factors in the early screening of children at risk. In W. Frankenburg, W. R. Emde, and J. Sullivan (eds.), *Early identification of children at risk: An international perspective*, pp. 21–44. New York: Plenum Press.

Sameroff, A. J. (1999). Ecological perspectives on developmental risk. In J. D. Osofsky & H. E. Fitzgerald (eds.), *WAIMH handbook of infant mental health: Infant mental health groups at risk,* vol. 4, pp. 223–248. New York: Wiley.

Sameroff, A. J., Bartko, W. T., Baldwin, A., Baldwin, C., & Seifer, R. (1999). Family and social influences on the development of child competence. In M. Lewis & C. Feiring (eds.), *Families, risk, and competence,* pp. 161–186. Mahwah, NJ: Lawrence Erlbaum Associates.

Sameroff, A. J., & Fiese, B. H. (2000). Transactional regulation: The developmental ecology of early intervention. In J. P. Shonkoff & S. J. Meisels (eds.), *Handbook of early childhood intervention,* second ed., pp. 135–159. New York: Cambridge University Press.

Sameroff, A. J., & Gutman, L. M. (2004). Contributions of risk research to the design of successful interventions. In P. Allen-Meares & M. W. Fraser (eds.), *Intervention with children and adolescents: An interdisciplinary perspective,* pp. 9–12. Boston: Allyn and Bacon.

Sameroff, A. J., Seifer, R., Barocas, R., Zax, M., & Greenspan, S. (1987). Intelligence quotient scores of 4-year-old children: Socio-environmental risk factors. *Pediatrics, 79,* 343–350.

Sampson, R. J., Raudenbush, S. W., & Earls, F. (1997). Neighborhoods and violent crime: A multilevel study of collective efficacy. *Science, 277,* 918–924.

Schwartz, D., Dodge, K. A., Coie, J. D., Hubbard, J. A., Cillessen, A. H., et al. (1998). Behavioral and social-cognitive correlates of aggression and victimization in boys' play groups. *Journal of Abnormal Child Psychology, 26,* 431–440.

Seligman, M. (1992). *Learned optimism: How to change your mind and your life.* New York: Pocket Books.

Shaw, D. S., Bell, R. Q., & Gilliom, M. (2000). A truly early starter model of antisocial behavior revisited. *Clinical Child and Family Psychology Review, 3,* 155–172.

Smokowski, P. R., Reynolds, A. J., & Bezruczko, N. (1999). Resilience and protective factors in adolescence: An autobiographical perspective from disadvantaged youth. *Journal of School Psychology, 37,* 425–448.

Stewart, A., Dennison, S., & Waterson, E. (2002). Pathways from child maltreatment to juvenile offending. *Trends and Issues in Crime and Criminal Justice, 241,* 1–6.

Tebes, J. K., Kaufman, J. S., Adnopoz, J., & Racusin, G. (2001). Resilience and family psychosocial processes among children of parents with serious mental disorders. *Journal of Child and Family Studies, 10,* 115–136.

Von Weiss, R. T., Rapoff, M. A., Varni, J. W., Lindsley, C. B., Olson, N. Y., et al. (2002). Daily hassles and social support as predictors of adjustment in children with pediatric rheumatic disease. *Journal of Pediatric Psychology, 27,* 155–165.

Werner, E. E. (1989). High risk children in adulthood: A longitudinal study from birth to 32 years. *American Journal of Orthopsychiatry, 59,* 72–81.

Werner, E. E. (1993). Risk, resilience, and recovery: Perspectives from the Kauai longitudinal study. *Development and Psychopathology, 5,* 503–515.

Werner, E. E., & Smith, R. S. (1992). *Overcoming the odds: High risk children from birth to adulthood.* Ithaca, NY: Cornell University Press.

Wills, T. A., Sandy, J. M., Yaeger, A., & Shinar, O. (2001). Family risk factors and adolescent substance use: Moderation effects for temperament dimensions. *Developmental Psychology, 37,* 283–297.

Wolkow, K. E., & Ferguson, H. B. (2001). Community factors in the development of resiliency: Considerations and future directions. *Community Mental Health Journal, 37,* 489–498.

Zingraff, M. T., Leiter, J., Myers, K. A., & Johnson, M. C. (1993). Child maltreatment and youthful problem behavior. *Criminology, 31,* 173–202.

JULIE C. ALTMAN

Engagement in Children, Youth, and Family Services

Current Research and Promising Approaches

ngaging clients is the most fundamental step in the helping process, a key prerequisite for client change. Yet for all its importance, we know very little about how, when, or why it happens, and how it may be related to further change processes.

Recent pressures hasten our need to know the answers to some of these questions in the field of child welfare. The 1997 Adoption and Safe Families Act (P.L. 105-89) has shortened the timeline workers have to achieve family reunification with the families of children who have been placed in out-of-home care. Findings from the recent federal Child and Family Services Reviews indicate that no state currently meets the standards for family involvement in services, an unacceptable norm in the field of child welfare, and one that must be remedied.

This chapter reviews contemporary knowledge of engagement in child welfare services and offers the findings of current research to guide practice. It defines client engagement in services and explains its importance, supplies the context for and current conceptualizations of client engagement in services, and discusses promising approaches and new research on engagement. The knowledge, skills, and abilities that workers need to engage children, youth, and families in services are then discussed, as well as the ethical and value dilemmas inherent in this process.

We begin, however, with a case example, drawn from my current research (Altman 2004).

Through the experiences and words of one parent, the inherent difficulties and challenges of engagement in child welfare services emerge.

Ms. Fox

Ms. Fox is a 38-year-old African American woman with a childhood history of involvement in child welfare who lives in an impoverished urban neighborhood. Her daughter, Connie, aged 7, was removed from her care 3 months ago. Ms. Fox had been working as a postal employee prior to her daughter's removal; since then, she has been too upset to return to work.

Ms. Fox has three daughters. The oldest is 22, a college graduate, and currently the kinship caretaker of Connie. Her second daughter is 21 and currently stationed overseas in the Air Force. Ms. Fox admits that she and her older daughters, who were born to her when she was a young teen, were "basically raised like sisters." She considers Connie the only child that has been truly "hers."

She is in a long-term relationship with Connie's father, with whom she has frequent "bouts of domestic violence." On at least one occasion, Ms. Fox was jailed for assaulting him. Both she and her partner have problems with alcohol. Since Connie's removal, the two have lived apart. Ms. Fox worries that she will lose her public housing now that she has lost his income. She is managing, in part, by going to a food pantry.

Connie was removed from Ms. Fox's care after numerous child welfare reports had been made for educational and physical neglect and concerns about inadequate supervision and parental capacity to care for Connie. These concerns included alcohol abuse and domestic violence.

What follows are excerpts from an interview with Ms. Fox regarding her relationship with her child welfare worker, what she considers important at this stage of work, and what she believes engagement with a worker in the context of child welfare service delivery should entail.

Caseworker's and Client's Impressions of One Another

Although Ms. Fox believes the worker is trying her best, she struggles with the worker's differential sense of urgency. She is also concerned that the worker does not have a good handle on the most appropriate and effective resources for her, and she considers her unreliable:

And I don't want to say she don't do her job because maybe she's trying to do what she has to do but in my concern I think she need to follow up more. You know she says she gonna do something but she sent it in the mail. It never comes. You know she sent me to one place and these people tell me I'm ineligible for the program and then she don't send me nowhere else. And we have a finite amount of time for me to get my child back.

Ms. Fox expressed a strong desire for her worker to clarify her expectations:

Just tell me what to do. Tell me time, place, when, where, what—tell me. That's all she got to do. She leave things vague. You know, just meet me here. Just be here. I don't want to be here and just looking around like blah, you know, come on, tell me what floor you going to be on. Who's the name of this person you want me to see? What room she in? What floor? What's her name? Come on, give me something to work with, you know.

Ms. Fox related her concerns regarding the age and race of the worker and how these im-

pacted her perception of the worker's empathy and capacity to individualize:

This is a heavy responsibility of a job. I'm surprised they got somebody that young working here. You know this is a lot of responsibility, especially you're dealing with angry parents because I'm an angry parent right now, you know, and I don't want to take it out on her. You know she's basically a kid to me, you know, . . . If I had an older one, maybe they understand more. I don't even know if she got kids. . . . I don't think she has no idea of what I'm going through. No idea whatsoever.

She is Puerto Rican . . . and she probably deals with, sees these things, you know in her neighborhood, you know she's probably use to these drug addicts and she probably feel that they need their kids taken away. I'm not no damn crackhead in the street. Don't treat me like a crackhead.

Relationship with Worker

Ms. Fox struggled to characterize her relationship with her worker. Desiring more than just a friendly relationship, Ms. Fox expressed the need for instrumental help:

And she's very nice and she's, you know, sits and stays with us and she joins in like a family, you know . . . but that ain't helping me get her [my daughter] back, you know, sitting here clicking it, you know, we hanging out.

Ms. Fox indicates the need for her worker to be honest with her and to follow through consistently—"to say what she means, and mean what she says":

It's, it's really, I don't believe anything that she says basically. You know I don't get mad at her but don't tell me a lie. I know you don't know what to do with these people or this case or she's probably got a million like this. But don't tell me that you're going to come to my house and don't show up. Don't tell me that you're going to send me some mail and don't send it. Don't tell me that. If you, if you forgot then just act like, I rather have her play stupid and act like she don't know nothing than tell me something and lie about it. That's the worse thing you can do. You know 'cause I don't know what to do and then I think I'm getting somewhere.

Despite her reservations about the worker's skills and abilities as a change agent, Ms. Fox is inclined to reframe it in terms of organizational constraints and demands:

So sometimes I get irked because it's like you know I like her as a person, she's you know, I've got to get to know her. I did get to know her and she seems like she's very harried; she has a lot of kids to work with and everything and that's why I really don't try to pressure her too much, you know, about the situation.

Later in the interview, she acknowledged that she really wished the worker had more time for her:

I know she's busy, you know, and she's like she's got a million things to do but we're engaging because she does listen to me when I'm here. You know, if I could catch her face-to-face then we could talk....

This is a very serious situation and I know I'm just another caseload to you but this is serious shit to me. I need my child back, you know, don't just brush me off like that.

Desire for Change/Matching Needs and Services

Throughout the discussion, Ms. Fox emphasized her desire to do "whatever it takes" to insure that Connie will be returned to her care, yet remains unsure how skilled the worker is in helping her with this goal:

I'm ready to piss them a river. They keep accusing me and it's not fair. I said I'm not going to start doing drugs just so I can get in this program. Listen, they going to drive me to drink. I'm ineligible for this program if I don't have a dirty urine sample. I said I'm not going to do drugs just so I can get into this place. So you either send me somewhere else . . . or take your urine, maybe that's what she

need to do, she need . . . that's my main argument right there. Take my urine, please, somebody.

In this passage, Ms. Fox again expressed her desire for clear direction with respect to service referral and provision:

You know, I don't care, I'll do it. Whatever I've got to do. I really don't mind. But tell me. Don't just tell me the name of it like I know, anger management. Where can I go get some anger management? It's not like I'm shopping for it at Home Depot, you know what I'm saying? I don't know what to do or where to get it from.

Client Engagement

Client engagement in services can be viewed as both a process and a product. Engagement as a product is the outcome of beginning work with clients that is thought to be a necessary but not sufficient prerequisite to the middle or change phase of treatment. As a process, engagement is a complex and multilevel phenomenon that involves the establishment of a helping relationship between worker and client so that active work toward change can begin.

From one perspective, engagement can then be seen as the degree to which a given client is committed to collaboratively working with a social worker to address the issues that led them to the agency. From another perspective, it can be seen as the process whereby the social worker creates an environment of warmth, empathy, and genuineness that enables a client to enter into a helping relationship and actively work toward change. It is a dynamic, two-way process.

Yatchmenoff and her colleagues (2001:4). define client engagement as "positive involvement in the helping process." Prinz and Miller (1996:162) define it as "the participation necessary to obtain optimal benefits from an intervention." Compton and Galaway (1999) see engagement as an interactional process of communication, beginning when workers establish communication with a potential client and ending when there is a preliminary agreement to work together.

Key components, predictors, and related variables are still not entirely understood. Although the relationship between engagement in services and outcomes of those services may be reciprocal, we understand little about their interaction. How the client responds during the early phase of treatment may be based on client beliefs, goals, external constraints, and experiences in treatment, all of which could potentially be targeted for intervention. Engagement both precedes and contributes to formation of a helping relationship and is an ongoing challenge as the change process unfolds. This relationship, "the marrow of most mental health services for children," has not received enough attention in the research literature (Alexander & Dore 1999:256). Therefore, it is important to understand it better.

Importance of Client Engagement in Children, Youth, and Family Services

Client engagement is critical to progress in all helping relationships, but especially so in child welfare. To insure child protection, enhance planning for permanency, or expedite reunification, engagement with the client family is essential. With the passage of the Adoption and Safe Families Act (P.L. 105-89), which requires that decisions about termination of parental rights be made within a limited time, the urgency with which family engagement must be realized is even more critical.

Empirical evidence validates the importance of engaging with child welfare clients. Parents who cooperate are less likely to be referred to court (Karski 1999). Uncooperative parents may not be offered needed services (Jones 1993). Active participation in services enhances parents' willingness and ability to persevere with the work when it becomes difficult (Hess, McGowan, & Botsko 2003) and reduces the chances that parents will lose custody of their children (Atkinson & Butler 1996). There is also evidence to suggest that greater parental involvement in treatment planning results in fewer subsequent reports of child maltreatment (At-

kinson & Butler 1996). Research on intensive family preservation programs found effectiveness to be predicted by a family's early cooperation and engagement in services (Kinney, Haapala, & Booth 1991).

However valuable, empirical evidence suggests that worker-parent engagement in child welfare services, as a product, is elusive. A recent panel evaluating New York City's child welfare services noted that "the most significant challenge facing this system is to make further, critically needed improvements with regard to permanency," the heart of which should be a "re-thinking of the role of parents, around the primary themes of enhanced respect, engagement and partnership" (Special Child Welfare Advisory Panel 2001).

Recent results of the federal Child and Family Service Reviews (U.S. Department of Health and Human Services, Children's Bureau 2004) are no less discouraging. The findings of the 52 reviews conducted during FY2001–2004 yield a dismal pattern of parent engagement in child welfare services. Not a single state met the specific well-being outcome criteria for "Family Involvement in Case Planning" and "Caseworker Visits with Parents" (U.S. Department of Health and Human Services, Children's Bureau 2004:24). In fact, of the seven safety, permanency, and well-being outcomes studied in the Service Reviews, the weakest was found to be "families have enhanced capacity to provide for their children's needs." This finding supports concerns that child welfare work has, over time, been more heavily invested in providing quality supervision, care, and services for the children in placement than in working to engage with and meet the needs of the families from whom children and youth were removed.

Engagement

The potential benefits of early engagement with families entering the child welfare system are many. Early engagement improves workers' abilities to communicate with families. Engaging with families helps workers recognize the family's strengths earlier in the helping process, which can then facilitate middle-phase, problem-focused work. Engagement with families whose children are in foster care helps insure the preservation of the bond between parents and children. Recognizing that their parents are working for reunification gives children a sense of security. Sound engagement helps motivate families to work toward change, expediting permanency for their children.

In summary, there is evidence that successfully engaging clients in the change process is associated with successful treatment outcomes, but ironically, engagement happens all too rarely in child welfare. One factor affecting engagement is the context of the client-practitioner relationship.

Context for Client Engagement

Consideration of engagement in context requires a look at the involuntary nature of the intervention process in child welfare practice, the role of workers, the importance of cultural and family values, the use of power and authority, and the concepts of resistance and reactance.

When Is a Client a Client?

Nearly all child welfare clients, and most children referred for social services, can be considered involuntary or nonvoluntary clients (Rooney 1992:5). These individuals frequently have not asked for—nor do they want—services, and most do not see the need and/or value of the service for their families (Ivanoff, Blythe, & Tripodi 1994). They come to the attention of child protection through a judgment of their failures as parents, with goals selected and imposed on them by the child welfare system. Parents become clients when they decide that it is possible to accept the terms of the help offered. This may involve a considerable loss of self-esteem, and sometimes leads to desperate attempts to preserve a sense of adequacy (Compton & Galaway 1999). Parents often enter into the relationship with feelings of anger, anxiety, vulnerability, shame, fear, confusion, hos-

tility, and suspicion. Children in placement may bring similarly conflicted or even openly hostile feelings.

Engaging clients who do not come as voluntary clients requires more work. Guilt, anger, shame, and depression may lead them to appear reluctant, unmotivated, or unwilling. Unfortunately, clients' expressions of outrage at the child welfare system and at the worker as its representative can be so off-putting and personal that the worker withdraws from the relationship and client-worker engagement never takes place.

Moving between emotional and cognitive content in the engagement process can be useful. Practitioners need to recognize the circumstances under which clients have entered the child welfare system, allow them to tell their story, and share their feelings of these events. Only then will clients feel sufficiently well understood and comfortable to think about engaging with the worker to effect the necessary changes.

Workers, Workers, and More Workers

The high rate of worker turnover is a reality of the child welfare system. The problem of transferring cases frequently makes engagement with difficult-to-reach clients even more challenging. Asking clients to repeat their "stories" to every new worker they may be assigned can be very demoralizing, traumatizing, and frustrating, causing clients to rebel and disengage, thereby appearing recalcitrant.

Culture and Values

Engagement with clients requires critical worker skills and effort to reduce the distance of differences (Abney 2000). African Americans, Asian Americans, Latino Americans, and Native Americans are more likely to drop out of treatment sooner than non-Hispanic Caucasians (Sue, Zane, & Young 1994). Being aware of one's own individual and cultural values, biases, attitudes, and beliefs is an important step in providing culturally competent practice. Differences in the way people see and behave in the world abound. Knowing something about the client's worldview and having some useful strategies when attempting to engage them can help (Lum 1992; Winton & Mara 2001). In child welfare, it takes a skilled worker to work out compromises between client cultural values and legal standards of child and family caretaking. When clients perceive that their cultural values are not respected, their resistance can be great. Establishing a working alliance with clients cross-culturally requires careful attention to traditional notions and impacts of empathy, mutuality, power and authority, use of self, and communication (Shonfeld-Ringel 2001). Cultural and family values and childhood experiences provide very powerful reinforcements for existing behavior; families may well resent intervention and focus only on ways to escape from child welfare scrutiny.

Power and Authority

Most social work practice assumes a collaborative but inherently unequal relationship between worker and client (Alexander & Dore 1999). In child welfare practice, in particular, in which the use of power and authority are inherent, the worker-client relationship is fraught with inequality and the collaborative ideal is difficult to achieve (Rooney 2002). Yet the more clients feel that power and authority are shared, the more likely they are to form a positive working relationship, leading to better outcomes (Hess, McGowan, & Botsko 2003; Horvath & Luborsky 1993). Effective collaboration rests on creative ways to develop and balance a sense of reciprocity, shared power, and responsibility (DeChillo, Koren, & Schultze 1994).

Resistance vs. Reactance

Resistance is a much debated and misunderstood concept in social work. Many clients have been mislabeled as resistant, reluctant, unmotivated, and hostile, when in fact they never chose to become clients (Rooney 2002). Resistance may occur when the goals and services of the agency do not fit the client's needs, or when the client's definition of the problem is at odds with the agency's definition. These two situations frequently occur in child welfare settings. Resistant behavior can be reframed as a symptom of ambivalence, a sign that the worker is pushing beyond the client's readiness for change, or as an indication that the agency's services are ineffectual.

Changing is difficult. For clients not involved in a cooperative arrangement, it can be an antagonistic experience. Involuntary clients may not recognize the importance or necessity for change. They may be required by the agency or court to see workers against their will and may believe that the system is not just or fair. They may see the child welfare agency and its workers as unwanted intrusions into their lives and the remedies recommended to them as meaningless or harmful (Miller 1991). In the process of engagement, workers cross intimate personal boundaries of their clients. It is important to be sensitive and respectful, working to understand the significance of such intrusions from the client's point of view.

Rooney (1992) believes resistance should be reframed as reactance, the normal response to one or more personal freedoms being threatened (Brehm 1976). What workers can do to reduce reactance is, first, not expect it to go away on its own. Direct aid can be given by (1) restoring the freedom, such as giving clients some choice they can make; (2) contracting with them to restore the freedom, such as agreeing to give them unsupervised visits if they meet specific requirements; (3) supporting the choices and emphasizing the freedoms clients still have; (4) planning small, feasible steps toward the goal while rewarding efforts and progress along the way; and (5) understanding clients' perspectives on their situation and avoiding labeling (Rooney 1992).

Current Conceptualizations of Client Engagement in Services

Client engagement is important at every level of service with children, youth, and families.

Current conceptualizations of engagement as they pertain to a range of child welfare services are presented in this section.

Preventive Services

I have studied how potential child welfare clients decide whether to engage in agency-initiated, preventive services (Altman 2003). The families studied were known to be high risk for child abuse and neglect and were offered early intervention home visit services. The aim of the research was to understand, from the client's point of view, what mattered most to them as they contemplated engaging in a working relationship with an intervention program. Using qualitative methods, five themes were uncovered in the data: (1) how clients viewed their own need for the service offered; (2) how they understood the potential of the service to match those needs; (3) how effective they believed the potential service might be for them; (4) what the service would cost in exchange for the benefit they estimated it to have on their lives; and (5) how much choice they thought they had in freely deciding whether to accept or decline the services offered. These findings should be helpful to child welfare workers as they struggle to empathize with their clients and attempt to engage clients in services.

Protective Services

Yatchmenoff (2001) and her colleagues at Portland State University studied the engagement process of parents who had recently become child welfare protective service clients. Defining client engagement as "positive involvement in the helping process," they developed a measure that quantified its five major dimensions: receptivity, or a client's openness to receiving help; expectancy, or the perception of future benefit clients see; investment, or client commitment to the helping process; working relationship, or the quality of the interpersonal relationship between worker and client; and mistrust, the belief that the agency and/or worker is manipulative or malicious.

Intensive Family Preservation Services

Littell and her colleagues have devoted much time and effort on the study of client participation (a term some use synonymously with engagement) in intensive family preservation services (IFPS) (Littell 2001; Littell, Alexander, Girvin, & Reynolds 2001; Littell & Tajima 2000). They identify two components of parent participation in IFPS: collaboration in treatment planning and compliance with program expectations (Littell & Tajima 2000). Parental substance abuse, mental health problems, severe child care deficits, chronic child neglect, inadequate housing, minority status, and lack of extended family support predicted lower levels of participation in IFPS. Strong deficit orientations of workers in IFPS were linked to lower levels of collaboration and compliance in clients. Workers' perceptions of job clarity, quality of supervision, and worker autonomy were associated with enhanced client participation. Programs that provided a wide array of concrete services and emphasized advocacy were linked to high levels of collaboration. Figure 3 in Littell and Tajima (2000) represents their multilevel model of client participation in IFPS.

Promising Approaches and New Research

Current approaches to engaging children, youth, and families in services are being developed as the knowledge base regarding such processes increases. New research and promising approaches to engagement are presented here, including the working alliance, motivation, readiness and the transtheoretical model of change, self-efficacy, and other treatment innovations.

The Working Alliance

The concept of the working alliance is interwoven with the concept of engagement. Knowledge of and research into the concept of the working alliance is well developed in the field of psychotherapy and substance abuse, and has recently been applied to the field of child and family services (Alexander & Dore 1999; Altman

2004; Dore & Alexander 1996; Littell, Alexander, & Reynolds 2001).

The therapeutic, helping, or working alliance denotes the ability of the worker and client to work together in a realistic, collaborative relationship based on mutual respect, liking, trust, and commitment to the work of treatment. Bordin (1979) suggests three components of the alliance: (1) mutuality of agreement on treatment goals (goal); (2) agreement regarding the tasks and responsibilities of helper and client (task); and (3) the personal, affective bond felt between the two (bond). A "good enough" alliance is thought to be necessary before treatment can proceed. Horvath and Greenberg (1994) conceptualize alliance development as a series of windows of opportunity, decreasing in size with each session, thus further emphasizing the critical importance of early engagement. The quality of the initial contact between practitioner and client is considered instrumental to building a working alliance. Building trust, allaying fears and suspicions, demonstrating acceptance and empathy, and affirming client competence are all powerful and important early messages to convey (Dore & Alexander 1996).

Motivation, Readiness to Change, and the Transtheoretical Model

The transtheoretical model of change developed by Prochaska and DiClemente (1984) has been a useful one for practitioners in substance abuse and other fields. Its relevance to child welfare is as yet unknown, although a number of social work researchers have begun to explore its utility (Gelles 1998; Littell, Alexander, Girvin, & Reynolds 2001). Its contribution is the notion that change proceeds as a dynamic spiral, with distinct phases of precontemplation, contemplation, preparation, action, and maintenance. Appropriate engagement and treatment strategies are linked to each stage.

I recently explored the motivation and readiness of parents in the child welfare system (Altman, under review). Parents identified three prerequisite components to successful change efforts: readiness for change, having the capacity for change, and possessing a belief that change will help. Such knowledge contributes to our capacity to target interventions designed to enhance engagement. One application of these findings is encouraging clinicians to explore client beliefs that engaging in a helping process will aid in ameliorating the conditions that led to their identification as high risk.

Research on Common Elements of Engagement

In a study (Altman 2004) of the process of engagement between workers and parents in neighborhood-based foster care services, seven themes were found to be important by workers, parents, foster parents, and supervisors:

1. The need for parents and workers to set common and clear goals together;
2. The need for parents and workers to maintain a sense of hopefulness during the change process;
3. The need for parents to be aware, to acknowledge, and to understand their situations accurately;
4. The need for parents to be consistently motivated in their efforts to change;
5. The need for workers to identify, understand, and respect cultural issues in their relationships with families;
6. The need for workers to communicate truthfully, honestly, and respectfully; and
7. The need for workers to be persistent, diligent, and timely in their efforts to help families.

Self-Efficacy

Bandura's (1997) recent work on self-efficacy has the potential to impact how we engage children, youth, and families in the work we do with them. Self-efficacy, or people's beliefs about their ability to engage in or modify particular behaviors, is thought to be related to the goals they set in treatment, the expectations they bring, and their relative achievement of each (Longo, Lent, & Brown 1996). Atkinson & Butler (1996), for example, have documented the link between giving clients opportuntities to express their points of view, self-efficacy, and internal motivation.

Other Treatment Innovations

Intensive family preservation services. IFPS seek to engage families at high risk for having their children removed and placed into care. These services attempt to instill the belief that positive change can occur. IFPS emphasize provision of concrete resources that can be offered flexibly, according to the unique and individual needs of families (Dawson & Berry 2002). This flexibility helps to establish rapport, and applying a direct and real solution is thought to facilitate a level of engagement between worker and client that allows them to address more difficult problems.

Family group conferencing. This is a recent treatment innovation many child welfare agencies have adopted to engage families as collaborative partners in the treatment process. Aimed at bringing key treatment providers and family members together to collaboratively develop individualized treatment goals and plans, it has been touted as a significant way to start positive family change. Engagement in family group conferencing emphasizes inclusion and promotes decisionmaking based on the strengths and needs of families, building on the cooperative efforts of parents and workers for families in child welfare settings (Jackson & Morris 1999; Sieppert, Hudon, & Unrau 2000; Thomas 2000).

Neighborhood-based services. Neighborhood-based services are currently in vogue in public child welfare settings across the country. This service philosophy rests on the assumption that closer proximity between children, families, and service providers yields earlier, easier, more sustained, and more effective contact and service use among parties. Increased expectations

of collaboration and commitment are thought to impact the rates of engagement in services for clients in this model of service delivery.

Inclusive child welfare practice. This practice is an innovation that encourages or requires birthparents to participate in the direct care of children in foster care whenever and as soon as possible (Leathers 2002). It includes sustained contact and frequent visits, taking the children clothes shopping, to doctor appointments, and the like (Hess & Proch 1988).

Visiting. Early and frequent contact between children who have been placed in foster care and their families has long been linked to increased rates of reunification (Fanshel 1975). Visiting has also been linked to reduced length of time in placement (Davis, Landsverk, Newton, & Granger 1996), longer lasting reunification (Farmer 1996), and improved child well-being (Borgman 1985).

Further refinement and development of visiting as a vehicle for family engagement and for positive change in the field of foster care has been spearheaded by Hess (1987, 1988, 2003) and others who effectively articulate its importance to key outcome measures. Often referred to as the "heart of reunification" (Hess & Proch 1988, 1993), visiting provides workers with an accurate demonstration of parental capacity and motivation, gives children and families a chance to maintain important emotional bonds, and finally, reduces the sense of abandonment that children often feel with placement. Visit time can reinforce parental motivation to engage in needed services and can become an opportunity for clear communication of support and instrumental assistance for families.

Caseworker visits. Recent findings of the Child and Family Service Reviews document the importance of caseworker visits to children. Of the 52 most recently reviewed states, a clear correlation was found between caseworker visits with children and (1) maintaining the child's relationship with parents; (2) assessing needs and providing services to children and families; (3) involving children and parents in case planning; and (4) encouraging caseworker visits with parents (see also Morse & Hurwitz 2004).

Engaging Clients: Knowledge, Skills, and Abilities

Workers attempting to engage children, youth, and families in services must work hard to motivate clients to accept treatment and facilitate their initial efforts. In this section, an overview of knowledge and skills that successful workers possess is offered.

Knowledge for Practice

Knowing oneself is perhaps the most important but difficult challenge when trying to engage families in child welfare. Clearly facing one's own beliefs, values, and feelings about clients and their behavior is key. Workers must check tendencies to blame or punish parents for their deficits and incapacities, while realizing that failure to engage is not necessarily evidence of parents' inability to parent. They, too, need to remember that it is not the responsibility of the client to show readiness for treatment or "prove their love" for their children by engaging in services. Foster care is not a punishment for a parent who will then "learn a lesson." Although working in a straightforward and nonaccusatory way is difficult for workers and clients, workers should try to deal openly, realistically, and compassionately with family members and their emotions.

Assumptions that can be helpful to workers beginning work with child welfare clients include (Kadushin & Martin 1988; Kinney, Haapala, & Booth 1991):

1. Parents are not deliberately willful in their behavior, but rather are doing the best they can in response to the social and/or personal difficulties they face;
2. Parents are unhappy about the situation, even though defensive, and really do care about their families;

3. Families, given the opportunity, will demonstrate their strengths and positive attributes;
4. People are more alike than different;
5. Parents are the primary influence in the lives of their children;
6. The first and best effort should be made to help insure adequate care and protection of children in their own homes;
7. Families today experience multiple and complex demands in their daily life; and
8. Change is possible.

It is important to convey to clients that they are wanted and needed in the service planning. Workers should anticipate that this might not be easy for parents to believe and should consider the client's perspective. Motivating clients to comply and collaborate in the helping process should be an ongoing goal of the work. It is key to start where the client is.

Mutuality is critical in the beginning working relationship between client and worker. Acknowledging client expertise, strengths, and the mutuality already established on an ongoing basis is imperative. Contracting—that is, the series of shared decisions about responsibilities and services that the worker and client are continuously negotiating (Seabury 1985)— should be seen as an ongoing process, not a product. Client-driven goals should be given primacy while clarifying each partner's roles and expectations. Concerns should be presented as problems to be solved collaboratively.

Developmental knowledge of the population and substantive knowledge of the community and its resources within which one is working is essential. Engagement strategies vary, given the different developmental capacities and needs of the client. Assuring preschoolers of their safety by "throwing monsters out the window," for example, can be an effective engagement strategy (Harden 2000). Knowing community resources well and delivering assistance in accessing them is a strategy that can facilitate engagement with families who may be unsure or distrustful of what workers can do for them.

Skills and Abilities

Core conditions of helping include the therapist's characteristics of empathy, composure, readiness to discuss everything, encouragement, and purposefulness (Perlman 1986). Each characteristic communicates to clients that they are understood, that they will not be judged, and that the worker is eager and hopeful about offering needed help.

Empathy is communicating to clients that the essence of their experience and feelings is understood. When practitioners relate empathically, clients are more likely to continue contact than when little empathy is conveyed (Truax & Carkhuff 1967). Working to capture the essence of clients' experiences and their sense of being in the world is critical; recognizing and responding to the poignant parts of clients' narratives about their experiences has great value. Expressing empathy for the pressures that the client is currently experiencing can be facilitative.

Communication skills are critical. Conversations should be framed wisely, always letting clients know the purpose and reason for questions. Detecting hidden messages that underlie the words clients are saying and responding to these messages can let clients know that they are being heard and understood. Clients should be treated as experts on themselves and their families—as valuable, capable persons. Discussions should be as concrete as possible, with workers insuring that the client receives the message they were trying to send. Workers should be clear, simple, and direct regarding nonnegotiable parts of the intervention.

Honesty is vital to the success of interpersonal relationships and a precondition to reducing mistrust and thwarted expectations. Workers need to be honest and clear about their purpose, role, and authority. They need to do what they say, and say what they do. Clients want honest assessment and feedback, even if unpleasant, uncomfortable, difficult, or tense.

Hopefulness as a construct, and its role in the helping process, deserves further study. Mahoney (1979) defines a construct similar to hope, which he calls "participatory vitalism," as "an expectation of or trust in the satisfactory value of future experience" and considers it a key variable in the success of interpersonal intervention. In my recent study (Altman 2004), hope on the part of clients was significantly correlated with the working alliances they established with their workers, especially in the first 3 months of their work together. Workers should be helped to recognize the potential value of clients' hopefulness regarding future functioning, and strategies to support and build on it should be developed.

Regard and respect conveyed to clients at all stages in the helping process is important. Sensitivity to cultural, racial, religious, or developmental differences is essential. Workers need to be sure to allow for a wide range of meanings and interpretations that each individual involved in the helping relationship may place on experiences, communications, or actions.

Building on client strengths can make the engagement process easier, more positive, and more effective. When possible, amplifying opportunities for clients to think of a different, more satisfying future sets the stage for co-constructing cooperation (DeJong & Berg 2001). Affirming the client's struggle and asking questions about how he or she manages to cope in such difficult circumstances is another positive strategy.

Motivational congruence suggests that outcomes are more likely to be successful if there is some overlap between the client's and agency's perceptions of the situation (Reid & Hanrahan 1982; Rooney 1992, 2000; Videka-Sherman 1985). Worker's capacity to hear the client's story carefully and convey empathically that it is understood helps achieve such congruence. By building on one agreed-upon goal at a time, congruence grows. The fit between client motivation and the services that the worker tries to provide can also be improved by emphasizing client choice when possible, keeping clients informed about what to expect, and fostering client participation throughout the treatment process.

A focus on solutions often helps to get engagement on track (DeJong & Berg 2001). Helping clients immediately with individually identified needs and wants shows that the worker cares and is competent. Workers should break down complex problems into their components; start slowly; and work toward small, distinct goals, using positive reinforcement with every step. They should be careful not to blame or label clients as resistant, or to send a message that they are giving up. Workers should strive to get clients' views of what brought them to this situation, and find common themes that both can agree on to start the helping process.

Facilitate client comfort in the process of engagement. Visiting clients in their homes often makes it easier for them to feel at ease and more equal in the helping relationship. In one agency familiar to me, someone is responsible for baking cookies each morning, so that the environment has a welcoming smell, demonstrating a nurturing approach to help.

Ethical and Value Dilemmas in Engagement

Ethical and value dilemmas in the engagement process in child welfare abound. Because so many of these clients are apt to be involuntary or nonvoluntary (Rooney 1992), issues of client self-determination and paternalism are most salient.

Client Self-Determination

Self-determination is defined as the rights clients have to make their own decisions regarding social work treatment, to actively participate in the helping process, and to lead a life of their own choosing (Weick & Pope 1988). The assertion that the child welfare system knows what is best for them is a difficult one for clients. Weick and Pope (1988) suggest working to understand the meaning child welfare workers' involvement in their lives holds for clients, and facilitating clients' own knowledge of what is best for them. Self-determination recognizes and respects that a clients' "knowing" what is best for them is often dynamic, new, and uncertain. The role of the worker in these cases should be to support the awakening and development of client self-determination by creating a safe and comfortable climate for the client, and to develop opportunities for its full expression wherever possible.

Paternalism

Paternalism is a critical problem experienced when the rights of one person conflict with the rights of another, as is often the case in child welfare (Reamer 1987). In child welfare settings, workers act in the best interests of the child, by definition sometimes interfering with the rights of their parents to raise their children free from oversight or intervention. Opposing client wishes happens routinely when we remove a child from the care of a parent, against the parents' will, but in the best interests of the child. It often feels like an illusion of free choice we give to child welfare clients, when clearly, the goals and mandates have been imposed on them. The balance between alienating families due to overintrusion into their lives and neglecting them due to underinvolvement is a difficult one to achieve and is critical to the successful achievement of engaging them in services. There is no easy answer or clear right or wrong with regard to these dilemmas. Careful analysis of the policy and practice we engage in with families in the beginning stages of practice is key. Self-awareness, reflection, and good supervision can assist in this process.

Discussion

The case presented at the outset of this chapter illustrates a number of the difficulties inherent in engaging clients in child welfare treatment settings and provides stark reminders of where worker knowledge, skill, and ability could have been improved. Through an honest appraisal of her worker's attempts to help, Ms. Fox highlights a number of important practice principles in engaging families in child welfare. First, it is imperative that workers know the resources that they refer clients to, and are sure that they match the client's needs sufficiently prior to the referral. Going the extra step in clarifying the referral agency's location, requirements, and even accompanying a client to a first appointment could facilitate engagement in that service.

Second, Ms. Fox highlighted the importance of workers saying what they mean, and meaning what they say. If a worker makes a plan, she needs to be reliable in following through. Following up and staying with the client is a need expressed by most child welfare clients. Clarifying expectations and being concrete in the communications with clients is often necessary.

Third, the need for instrumental help, not just empathy, is vital. Clients want more than just to be listened to or understood; they want action.

Fourth, and the most compelling message sent by Ms. Fox, is the differential sense of urgency she and her worker had regarding the effort to be made toward reunification. Practitioners need to be empathic to this, take the impact on the child in these situations into clear consideration, and strive to adjust their treatment timeline accordingly.

Fifth, the importance of individualizing client's needs and capacities was emphasized. Understanding and building on Ms. Fox's strengths, in particular, might in this case have been an effective engagement strategy.

Finally, although Ms. Fox was very understanding of the context of the worker's practice and willing to endure the organizational and structural barriers that impacted the service she received, one might legitimately question whether this is a fair position for the client to assume. All social workers should engage continually in efforts to change organizational structure and culture to allow for more responsive and effective practice.

Conclusion

Engaging clients in child welfare services is a challenging but critical step in the process of change. To insure child protection, enhance planning for permanency, or expedite reunification, engagement with the client family is essential. The involuntary nature of clients in the child welfare system, the role of workers, the importance of cultural and family values, the use of power and authority, and the concepts of resistance and reactance are issues central to the process of engagement.

There is evidence that the ability to successfully engage clients in the change process is associated with successful treatment outcomes. Current approaches to engaging children, youth, and families in services are being developed as the knowledge base regarding such processes in various client populations increases. New research and promising approaches to engagement can be found in such areas as the working alliance, motivation, readiness and the transtheoretical model of change, self-efficacy, and other treatment innovations.

Practitioner knowledge for successful client engagement includes knowing oneself, knowing some core assumptions about families and change, understanding the client's need to feel wanted and needed, and supporting mutuality and human development. Skills and abilities critical to engagement include such core conditions as empathy, honesty, and good communication, the ability to offer clients regard and respect, hopefulness, the ability to use clients' strengths and to enhance engagement through motivational congruence, adoption of a solution focus, and the skill to facilitate client comfort.

REFERENCES

Abney, V. D. (2000). What principles and approaches can I use to engage clients across cultures? In H. Dubowitz & D. DePanfilis (eds.), *Handbook for child protection practice*, pp. 223–261. Thousand Oaks, CA: Sage.

Adoption and Safe Families Act. (1997). P.L. 105-89.

Alexander, L. B., & Dore, M. M. (1999). Making the parents as partners principle a reality: The role of the alliance. *Journal of Child and Family Studies, 8,* 255–270.

Altman, J. C. (2003). A qualitative examination of client participation in agency-initiated services. *Families in Society, 84,* 471–479.

Altman, J. C. (2004). *Engagement in neighborhood-based child welfare services.* Final report. Garden City, NY: Adelphi University School of Social Work.

Altman, J. C. (under review). Child welfare client perceptions of motivation and change.

Atkinson, L., & Butler, S. (1996). Court-ordered assessment: Impact of maternal noncompliance in child maltreatment cases. *Child Abuse and Neglect, 20,* 185–190.

Bandura, A. (1997). *Self-efficacy: The exercise of control.* New York: Worth Publishers.

Bordin, E. S. (1979). The generalizability of the psychoanalytic concept of the working alliance. *Psychotherapy: Theory, Research & Practice, 16,* 252–259.

Borgman, B. (1985). The influence of family visiting upon boys' behavior in a juvenile correctional institution. *Child Welfare, 64,* 629–638.

Brehm, J. (1976). *A theory of psychological reactance.* New York: Academic Press.

Compton, B., & Galaway, B. (1999). *Social work processes,* sixth ed. Belmont, CA: Wadsworth.

Davis, I., Landsverk, J., Newton, R., & Granger, W. (1996). Parental visiting and foster care reunification. *Children and Youth Services Review, 18,* 363–382.

Dawson, K., & Berry, M. (2002). Engaging families in child welfare services: An evidence-based approach to best practice. *Child Welfare, 81,* 293–317.

DeChillo, N., Koren, P. E., & Schultze, K. H. (1994). From paternalism to partnership: Family and professional collaboration in children's mental health. *American Journal of Orthopsychiatry, 64,* 564–576.

DeJong, P., & Berg, I. S. (2001). Co-constructing cooperation with mandated clients. *Social Work, 46,* 361–374.

Dore, M. M., & Alexander, L. B. (1996). Preserving families at risk of child abuse and neglect: The role of the helping alliance. *Child Abuse and Neglect, 20,* 349–361.

Fanshel, D. (1975). Parental visiting of children in foster care: Key to discharge? *Social Service Review, 49,* 493–514.

Farmer, E. (1996). Family reunification with high risk children: Lessons from research. *Children and Youth Services Review, 18,* 287–305.

Gelles, R. J. (1998). Treatment-resistant families. In R. M. Reece (ed.), *Treatment of child abuse,* pp. 304–312. Baltimore: Johns Hopkins University Press.

Harden, R. M. (2000). Assessment of clinical competence using an objective structured clinical examination. *Medical Education, 13,* 41–54.

Hess, P. (1987). Parental visiting of children in foster care: Current knowledge and research agenda. *Children and Youth Services Review, 9,* 29–50.

Hess, P. (1988). Case and context: Determinants of planned visit frequency in foster family care. *Child Welfare, 67,* 311–326.

Hess, P. (2003). *Visiting between children in care and their families: A look at current policy.* New York: National Resource Center for Foster Care & Permanency Planning, Hunter College School of Social Work.

Hess, P., McGowan, B., & Botsko, M. (2003). *Nurturing the one, supporting the many: The Center for Family Life in Sunset Park, Brooklyn.* New York: Columbia University Press.

Hess, P., & Proch, K. (1988). *Family visiting in out-of-home care: A practical guide.* Washington, DC: Child Welfare League of America.

Hess, P., & Proch, K. (1993). Visiting: The heart of reunification. In B. Pine, R. Warsh, & A. Maluccio (eds.), *Together again: Family reunification in foster care,* pp. 119–139. Washington, DC: Child Welfare League of America.

Horvath, A. O., & Greenberg, L. S. (1994). *The working alliance: Theory, research, and practice.* New York: Wiley & Sons.

Horvath, A. O., & Luborsky, L. (1993). The role of the therapeutic alliance in psychotherapy. *Journal of Consulting and Clinical Psychology, 61,* 561–573.

Ivanoff, A., Blythe, B., & Tripodi, T. (1994). *Involuntary clients in social work practice: A research-based approach.* Hawthorne, NY: Aldine de Gruyter.

Jackson, S., & Morris, K. (1999). Family group conferences: User empowerment or family self-reliance? *British Journal of Social Work, 29,* 621–630.

Jones, L. (1993). Decision-making in child welfare: A critical review of the literature. *Child and Adolescent Social Work, 10,* 241–262.

Kadushin, A., & Martin, J. (1988). *Child welfare services,* fourth ed. Pacific Grove, CA: Brooks/Cole.

Karski, R. L. (1999). Key decisions in child protective services: Report investigation and court referral. *Children and Youth Services Review, 21,* 643–656.

Kinney, J., Haapala, D. A., & Booth, C. (1991). *Keeping families together: The Homebuilders model.* Hawthorne, NY: Aldine de Gruyter.

Leathers, S. (2002). Parental visiting and family reunification: Could inclusive practice make a difference? *Child Welfare, 81,* 595–616.

Littell, J. H. (2001). Client participation and outcomes of intensive family preservation services. *Social Work Research, 25,* 103–114.

Littell, J. H., Alexander, L. B., Girvin, H., & Reynolds, W. (2001). Readiness for change and alliance formation: Results of a longitudinal study of home-based services in child welfare. Presentation given at the Society for Social Work and Research Meeting, Atlanta, GA, January 2001.

Littell, J. H., Alexander, L. B., & Reynolds, W. W. (2001). Client participation: Central and underinvestigated elements of intervention. *Social Service Review, 75,* 1.

Littell, J. H., & Tajima, E. (2000). A multilevel model of client participation in intensive family preservation services. *Social Service Review, 74,* 405–435.

Longo, D. A., Lent, W. K., & Brown, S. D. (1996). Social cognitive variables in the prediction of client motivation and attrition. *Journal of Counseling Psychology, 39,* 447–452.

Lum, D. (1992). *Social work practice with people of color.* Monterey, CA: Brooks/Cole.

Mahoney, M. J. (1979). Psychology of the scientist: An evaluative review. *Social Studies of Science, 9,* 349–375.

Miller, G. (1991). *Enforcing the work ethic: Rhetoric and everyday life in a work incentive program.* Albany: State University of New York Press.

Morse, J., & Hurwitz, A. (2004). *A training curriculum for child welfare professionals—Facilitating caseworker-parent and caseworker-child visiting.* New York: National Resource Center for Family-Centered Practice and Permanency Planning.

Perlman, D. (1986). The therapist as attachment figure. *Psychotherapy, 32,* 296–322.

Prinz, R. J. & Miller, G. E. (1996). Parental engagement in interventions for children at risk for conduct disorder. In R. D. V. Peters & R. J. McMahon (eds.), *Preventing childhood disorders, substance abuse and delinquency,* pp. 161–183. Thousand Oaks, CA: Sage.

Prochaska, J., & DiClemente, C. (1984). *The transtheoretical approach: Crossing traditional boundaries of change.* Homewood, IL: Dow Jones/Irwin.

Reamer, F. (1987). The concept of paternalism in social work. *Social Service Review, 57,* 255–260.

Reid, W., & Hanrahan, P. (1982). Recent evaluations of social work: Grounds for optimism. *Social Work, 27,* 331–339.

Rooney, R. (1992). *Strategies for work with involuntary clients.* New York: Columbia University Press.

Rooney, R. (2000). How can I use authority effectively and engage family members? In H. Dubowitz &

D. DePanfilis (eds.), *Handbook for child protection practice.* Thousand Oaks, CA: Sage.

Rooney, R. (2002). Working with involuntary clients. In A. Roberts & G. Greene (eds.), *Social workers' desk reference.* Oxford: Oxford University Press.

Seabury, B. A. (1985). The beginning phase. Engagement, initial assessment, and contracting. In J. Laird & A. Hartman (eds.), *A handbook of child welfare: Context, knowledge, and practice,* pp. 335–359. New York: Free Press.

Shonfeld-Ringel, S. (2001). A reconceptualization of the working alliance in cross-cultural practice with non-western clients: Integrating relational perspectives and multicultural theories. *Clinical Social Work Journal, 29,* 1.

Sieppert, A., Hudon, P. E., & Unrau, J. (2000). Family group conferencing in child welfare: Lessons from a demonstration project. *Families in Society, 81,* 382–391.

Sue, S., Zane, N., & Young, K. (1994). Research on psychotherapy with culturally diverse populations. In A. Bergin & S. Garfield (eds.), *Handbook of psychotherapy and behavior change,* fourth ed., pp. 783–817. Toronto: John Wiley & Sons.

Thomas, N. (2000). Putting the family in the driving seat: Aspects of the development of family group conferences in England and Wales. *Social Work and Social Sciences Review, 8,* 101–115.

Truax, C., & Carkhuff, R. (1967). *Toward effective counseling and psychotherapy: Training and practice.* Chicago: Aldine-Atherton.

U.S. Department of Health and Human Services, Children's Bureau (2004). Key findings from the CFSR— 52 Reviews. Washington, DC: U.S. Department of Health and Human Services.

Videka-Sherman, L. (1985). Barlett Practice Effectiveness Project: Report to National Association of Social Workers Board of Directors. Washington, DC: National Association of Social Workers.

Weick, A., & Pope, J. (1988). Knowing what's best: A new look at client self-determination. *Social Casework, 66,* 10–16.

Winton, M., & Mara, B. (2001). *Child abuse and neglect.* Needham Heights, MA: Allyn & Bacon.

Yatchmenoff, D. (2001). *Measuring client engagement in non-voluntary child protective services.* Doctoral dissertation, Portland State University, Portland, OR.

ELENA COHEN
DONNA T. HORNSBY
STEVEN PRIESTER

Assessment of Children, Youth, and Families in the Child Welfare System

This chapter defines and describes an approach to comprehensive, family-centered assessment in child welfare. It identifies the elements in the domains of safety; risk; parental, caregiver, and environmental protective capacity; and child well-being that encompass the assessment of families—including children and youth—in the child welfare system. In addition, the chapter sets forth the expected outcomes and key decisions at each stage of the casework process and offers practice guidelines that agencies can follow to plan and implement a comprehensive, family-centered assessment.

Demographic Patterns for Children, Youth, and Families and Populations Affected

Widespread agreement exists that the public child welfare system must produce more satisfactory outcomes for children and families. By all accounts, many of the families that come in contact with the child welfare system are faring poorly. In 2001, five million children and youth were reported as abused and neglected, and 903,000 of these reports were substantiated (57% were reports of neglect). More than 1,000 of the children died as a result of the abuse or neglect inflicted by family members, and many others bear the physical and mental scars from the maltreatment they have experienced (U.S. Department of Health and Human Services 2002).

Although abuse and neglect appear to affect children of all racial and ethnic origins, an analysis of national, state, and county data of the ethnicity of children in the child welfare system reveals that, compared with their presence in the general population, children and youth of color are involved disproportionately in the public child welfare system. This disproportionate involvement has long concerned agencies, workers, researchers, government, and community groups. However, few research studies have investigated the factors associated with this disproportionality. It appears that although the families belonging to each of the minority groups (i.e., African American, Latino/Hispanic, Native American, and Asian American/Pacific Islander) present unique and diverse profiles, families within each of these groups are extremely vulnerable (Casey Family Programs 2002:5). Once in the child welfare system, children of the four racial and ethnic groups follow different pathways and experiences as well as different outcomes (Child Welfare Research Team 2002:iii).

Rationale for Redesigning the Assessment Process in Child Welfare

An accurate and ongoing assessment of children and families from the point of referral to case closure provides the foundation for determining which children and youth the child welfare system will serve, the type and intensity of interventions and supports to be provided, and how these services are affecting the children, youth, and families served. An accurate assessment also determines which children and youth can stay safely at home; which need to be removed for safety; and when to reunify families, terminate parental rights, secure a different permanent family for a child or youth, and close cases. Therefore, to improve the outcomes of safety, permanency, and well-being, assessment is one of the most critical processes that requires review. Furthermore, under the Adoption and Safe Families Act (ASFA) of 1997, which emphasizes shortening foster care timeframes, achieving permanency for children, and accountability for results, the assessment of families takes on renewed importance.

In child welfare, assessment has generally been used to describe the process by which information is gathered to inform decisionmaking about a child or youth and family. Often, however, no explicit connection exists between the agency's assessment policies and:

- Goals of the agency's intervention (i.e., benefits children and families reap from their involvement with the agency);
- Role of the frontline worker (e.g., case manager, service provider, change agent);
- Goals of contact with the frontline worker (i.e., ensuring child safety, addressing causal factors by matching the assessment results to services, preventing future child abuse or neglect);
- Capacity of workers to conduct family-centered assessments (i.e., skills, necessary time, number of families workers can serve at a given time); or
- Management information systems (MIS), quality assurance (QA) mechanisms, and supervisory practices to support quality practices.

Increasingly, state child welfare agencies are using safety or risk instruments to help workers assess safety and risk factors for children. Safety and risk assessment tools can prove helpful in focusing workers' attention on current and future harm to the child or youth and in providing structure to the assessment. But, used alone, these tools fail to provide a comprehensive picture of the family or help engage them in problem solving. Neither are the tools ongoing, nor, importantly, are they connected with service planning, progress monitoring, or other decisionmaking. In other jurisdictions, assessment is used synonymously with safety or risk assessment and is isolated from investigation or family assessment. At other times, agencies are unclear about the difference between assessment and an evaluation, which usually refers to an appraisal done by a specialized professional (i.e., psychologists, substance abuse professionals) (Day, Robison, & Sheik 1998:13).

Definition of Comprehensive, Family-Centered Assessment

Comprehensive, family-centered assessment is the ongoing practice in child welfare of identifying, considering, and weighing factors that impact children and youth who enter the child welfare system. These factors encompass:

- Being safe;
- Being supported and cared for either while the family receives services with the child in the home or while moving to a permanent arrangement;
- Moving safely back home, when appropriate, as soon as possible;
- Achieving permanence with a caring, permanent family (i.e., family preservation, family reunification, adoption, guardianship); and
- Developing to their fullest potential in all domains.

Assessment is always conducted as a means to an end (i.e., a process to identify issues the family is facing and design a plan and provide services that will assist in resolving the issues identified).

Key Principles Underlying Comprehensive, Family-Centered Assessment

The following principles are based on the belief that family-centered practice advances the overall objectives of establishing safe, stable, and permanent families to promote the well-being of their members within the context of the authority and responsibility of state child welfare agencies:

- The safety, permanency, and well-being of children and youth constitute the leading criteria for decisionmaking;
- Whenever possible, families are seen as providing the best care and protection for their children and adolescents;
- The family as a unit, as well as its individual members, represents the focus of the child welfare casework process (i.e., intake, assessment, planning, service provision, monitoring of progress, and closure);
- Family members (including, as age appropriate, children and youth) must be actively involved in the development, implementation, and monitoring of the family service plan and services provision;
- Respect for families' racial and ethnic backgrounds, values, and customs is built into the organizational structures and services delivery system; and
- Successful outcomes of the interventions in child welfare are demonstrated in the child's developmental progress and well-being, increased capacity of the parents to nurture and protect their children and adolescents, and children's and youth's achieving timely permanency.

Domains and Elements of Comprehensive, Family-Centered Assessment

A comprehensive, family-centered assessment involves a series of direct contacts with the household family, other family members, and collateral contacts to evaluate and support a family in creating long-term solutions for identifying and addressing the safety and risk factors and underlying conditions that led or contributed to the maltreatment. A comprehensive, family-centered assessment must address the four domains discussed in the following sections.

Safety

A safety assessment is the systematic collection of information on current, significant, and clearly observable threats to the safety of the child or youth and of threatening family conditions to determine the degree to which the child or youth is likely to suffer maltreatment in the immediate future. Most safety assessment models use standardized criteria for assessing safety. All safety models have a list of threats of danger, defined as a specific family situation, emotion, motive, perception, or capacity of a family member that is out of control, imminent, and likely to exert severe effects on a vulnerable child (Action for Child Protection 2003:2). To determine safety, a worker:

- Collects relevant information on behaviors and conditions that constitute a threat to child and youth safety; and
- Identifies behaviors and conditions in the family that might offset the threat to child and youth safety.

Risk

Risk assessment is the collection and analysis of information to determine the degree to which key factors are present in a family situation that increase the likelihood of future maltreatment to a child or adolescent. The factors that contribute to and mitigate child maltreatment are related to the psychological status of parents; behavior of parents and caregivers; effects of environmental conditions on parents, children, and youth; and constitutional makeup of family members. These factors are often difficult to quantify and their interrelationships are sometimes misunderstood. Therefore, the factors frequently fail to lend themselves easily to the assessment of future maltreatment. The focus of risk assessment might change at specific decision points, such as:

- The report from the community represents a concern for potential risk;
- During investigation, the worker is assessing the origin and extent of the risk;
- At the planning stage, the worker uses the results of the risk assessment to develop strategies to respond to and reduce risk;
- During service implementation, the worker assesses the progress of families in reducing the risks identified and in monitoring changes in the family situation; and
- During case reviews and planning for closure, the worker is assessing the conditions that suggest risk is being reduced or has been sufficiently reduced to warrant case closure.

Parental Protective Capacity

A comprehensive, family-centered assessment must assess the inherent capacity of the family —or the resources that can be mobilized—to provide for the ongoing protection of the child or youth as well as assess the parents' motivation to change. When assessing parental protective capacity, the worker identifies and analyzes the presence and extent of relevant protective factors (either present or potential), behaviors, or dynamics. Protective capacity elements are those that help eliminate conditions that increase risk (not simply the absence of destructive behaviors) and strengthen the conditions that support healthy family interaction and child development. To assume, however, that identifying and building on capacities can alone prevent or mitigate maltreatment is dangerous. Workers cannot ignore the reality that some families who maltreat their children have serious difficulties, such as mental illness or substance abuse, and/or contextual deficits (e.g., poverty, unemployment). Nevertheless, they must also remember that many families who live in continually stressful, even dire, circumstances never intentionally harm their children.

Child Well-Being

A comprehensive, family-centered assessment also includes assessing the child and youth's ability to grow and develop to his or her fullest potential in all life domains. Most children and youth involved with the child welfare system have experienced abuse, neglect, separation from their parents, and other trauma that might lead to a variety of physical, cognitive, emotional, and behavioral problems. Additionally, these children and youth come from and are sometimes placed in high-risk environments characterized by poverty, instability, and parents or caregivers with mental health issues. These factors are usually associated with poor child developmental outcomes. To link a child or youth with appropriate services and make mental, educational, and health services available when needed, a comprehensive, family-centered assessment must assess his or her development in key areas.

Case Study: The Langer Family
Description of the Langer Family Situation at the Time of Intake

Doris Langer, 24, is the single mother of Duane, 8, and Noni, 4. She is receiving some Temporary Aid to Needy Families (TANF) benefits and works 30 hours a week in a child care center. She has a boyfriend, Mike Russey, who has been living with her and her children for the past 6 months; he is unemployed.

The public child welfare agency had received two previous reports about the Langer family, alleging neglect. One was for lack of appropriate clothes for winter (3 years ago), and one was for leaving Duane (6 at the time) alone while Ms. Langer filled in an evening shift for a co-worker. Both reports were substantiated. Since Ms. Langer understood the problems and agreed to not repeat them and there were no repeat neglect reports or observations of neglect by the worker, the agency closed the case after 6 months of visits with the mother and children.

Assessment at Intake/Report

The agency received a new report from Duane's school: he came to school with a large bruise on his right cheek. A medical examination also revealed several bruises on his back that appeared to have been caused by belt slaps.

At the time of intake/report, the hotline worker needs to (1) determine whether the report, if substantiated, meets the state's statutory criteria for abuse/neglect; (2) determine how urgent is the need for face-to-face contact with the child and family; and (3) review agency records to gather collateral information and determine if previous contact with the family occurred.

In this instance, the hotline worker took the report, found and reviewed the two previous substantiated neglect reports, determined that the report, if substantiated, would meet the state's statutory criteria for abuse, and determined that there was urgent need for face-to-face contact with the child and family. The hotline worker's supervisor authorized an investigation and required a face-to-face meeting with the child and family within 24 hours.

Assessment during the First Face-to-Face Encounter

At the time of the first meeting with the child and the family, the investigating worker needs to fully disclose to the family the reasons for his or her visit and help the family realize how their involvement can help resolve this matter; determine the child's safety or level of risk, identify child development issues; document facts surrounding the maltreatment; and identify kin resources and community linkages.

A visit to the home by the investigator found that there was quite an antagonistic relationship between Duane and Mr. Russey. Duane resented Mr. Russey's recent move into the home and his domineering behavior. Mr. Russey stated that when Ms. Langer is out of the home and he is providing child care, he expects Duane to obey, and if he does not, he will be punished. Mr. Russey stated that there was nothing wrong with spankings, including using a belt. Ms. Langer agreed that Duane could be difficult, and she did not object to Mr. Russey spanking Duane "if he needed it." All four people in the household agreed that Noni and Mr. Russey had a good relationship and that she never received any corporal punishment.

The investigating social worker also learned that Duane had dropped in academic performance since Mr. Russey moved into the house. The social worker was told that Ms. Langer has a mother and two sisters living in the same city, and that Ms. Langer was close with her oldest sister, Sonya Buford, who is married and has two children. The worker visited with Ms. Buford, who also agreed that Duane was not safe at home, but that Noni was. Ms. Buford offered to take Duane into her home if that became necessary because she did not want to see him "lose his family."

Assessment for Placement and for Developing the Service Plan

At the time of the assessment for placement, the child welfare worker needs to determine whether out-of-home placement is necessary and, if so, arrange for, work with, and support the placement of the child in an appropriate home other than the child's home. To do that, the worker will have to determine what type of placement is required and what is the plan for the child's permanency. To accomplish this, the worker needs to involve the family in planning for the child's appropriate placement in another home; develop a permanency plan with goals, visitation, timeframes for evaluation, and services to be provided to the biological and foster families; and develop a concurrent plan in the event reunification becomes impossible.

Having substantiated the physical abuse, the child welfare agency opened the case. Because Ms. Langer and Mr. Russey believed that physical punishment of the kind inflicted on Duane by Mr. Russey was acceptable, the investigator believed that Duane could not remain safely in the home at this time. In addition, Ms. Langer stated that she finally felt she had "found her man" and she did not want to jeopardize her relationship with Mr. Russey by disagreeing with his disciplining of Duane.

The case was referred to the child welfare agency's ongoing family services division, and the case assigned to a social worker. The social worker, with the assistance of Ms. Langer, planned a family meeting, consisting of the four members of the household, Ms. Langer's older sister, Ms. Buford, and Ms. Langer's mother. Duane's teacher was also invited because of the child's recent academic setbacks.

At the meeting, several decisions were made:

- Duane is going to live temporarily with Ms. Buford and her family while his family works on making the home safe for him. The permanency goal is reunification.
- There will be weekly, supervised visits.
- Mr. Russey agreed to join a stepfather's group at the local mental health clinic to learn more effective ways of parenting.
- He also agreed to check out job training at AmeriCorp.
- Duane will be able to continue in his school while he lives with his aunt's family. Ms. Lockard, following instructions from Duane's teacher, will tutor Duane three times a week at her sister's home.
- The social worker will visit with Duane and with Ms. Langer and Mr. Russey at least once a month.
- Ms. Lockard and Mr. Russey agreed to meet weekly with a family therapist to work conjointly on parenting skills in preparation for Duane's return.
- Should the plan for reunification not prove to be feasible, the Buford family would consider assuming guardianship of Duane.

The social worker agreed with these decisions in part because it appeared that Ms. Lockard and Mr. Russey are serious about their rela-

tionship and want to have a future together. Therefore, it would be in everyone's best interest if Mr. Russey could assume an appropriate and safe parenting role with the children.

Assessment during Monitoring

During progress monitoring, the worker must assess the child's or youth's circumstances for continuing threats to safety as well as progress toward achieving the family service plan goals, decreasing risks to parental protective capacity identified previously, and insuring that the child's or youth's well-being is improving.

A family meeting was held each month for 3 months. The same people participated in the meetings with the exception of the teacher, who attended only the first of these three meetings. During the meetings, it was learned that Duane's school performance was improving, and Ms. Langer and Mr. Russey were participating in the services they had agreed to. The social worker used these meetings to assess with the family the relationship between Mr. Russey and Duane, and probed to determine whether Mr. Russey was learning more appropriate parenting approaches. Verbally, Mr. Russey was able to express regret for hitting Duane and talked about some things he was learning in his stepfathers' group. At the third family meeting, the group planned with Mr. Russey an outing that he and Duane would have together.

A fourth family meeting was held to plan Duane's return to his home. Mr. Russey and Duane reported that they had fun on their outing, and both stated they were looking forward to Duane's return home. At this meeting, the family team worked together to develop a discipline plan that Mr. Russey would use with Duane when he was providing child care. It was a system of rewards and consequences for both good and unacceptable behavior. Ms. Langer also agreed to use this plan. Mr. Russey also discussed his own personal plan for "cooling down" if he found himself angry with Duane. The social worker planned to make a home visit during the first week of Duane's return home, and bi-weekly after that for a period of time. Ms. Langer and Mr. Russey agreed to call the social worker if they felt they were having problems in disciplining Duane.

Assessment during Closure
Closure is defined as the point at which the agency no longer maintains an active relationship with the family. It typically occurs when the family is stable following reunification. A decision to discontinue agency involvement with the family results when evidence exists that safety is attained and risk is manageable, reunification is achieved, a crisis or aftercare plan is in place and the family has been linked with supports that will promote child safety and well-being.

After several months of home visits, the social worker, in consultation with her supervisor, decided to close the case. Prior to closure, the worker and the family developed a crisis plan: if the parents felt stressed to the point that they feared they might strike Duane, they would ask for a family meeting with Ms. Langer's mother and her sister, Ms. Buford.

In a final home visit, the family team had a party to celebrate their achievements.

When, What, and How to Assess
Assessment is conducted at all stages of the casework process in child welfare. As the workers receive a report and investigate, open a case, plan and provide or refer to services, and review and terminate services, they are assessing safety; extent, duration, and severity of risk; protective capacity of the parents and the environment; and well-being of children and youth. Throughout this ongoing process of assessment and planning and delivery of services, workers must:

- Engage the family, as fully as possible, in becoming active participants in the assessment process;
- Clarify the agency's role (i.e., reason for the family-centered assessment, the state's concerns and expectations);

- Learn about the family's history and current conditions that might be affecting the safety, risk, and well-being of the child and the parental and environmental protective capacities;
- Listen respectfully, without judging, trying to understand the family's perception of childrearing, family relations, and help-seeking interventions; and
- Use their authority judiciously and avoid, as much as possible, power struggles.

Assessment at Intake
During intake, the child welfare worker needs to determine the response to the referral, the child's status in relation to the Indian Child Welfare Act, and the initial risk level.

Areas to be assessed. During intake, the agency conducts a preliminary assessment of safety elements as the information is received from the reporter.

Expected outcome. At the end of the intake process, the agency should have formed a rationale for a child welfare response.

Key decisions. During the intake process, the agency should make key decisions regarding the validity of the report:

- Does the report meet statutory criteria?
- If so, how urgent is the need for face-to-face contact?

Practice guidelines. The worker supports and encourages the reporter by:

- Explaining the purpose of Child Protective Services (CPS).
- Addressing fears and concerns the reporter might have, including confidentiality mandates.
- Asking about his or her relationship to the family and perception of family needs and strengths; the basis for his or her concerns; facts that might indicate the child has been harmed or is at risk; factors that might make

the child more vulnerable (e.g., difficult temperament, disabilities); location of the child, parent, and caregivers; and the names and locations of other people who can help understand what is happening in the family.
- Reviewing agency records to gather collateral information and determine if previous contact with the family occurred.
- Determining whether the allegation is within CPS mandates, whether the family should be referred to other community resources, and what level and type of response the agency should render.

Assessment during the First Face-to-Face Encounter

During the initial face-to-face encounter with the family, the worker should fully disclose to the family the reasons for his or her visit and help family members realize how their involvement can assist in achieving a clear understanding of the safety and risk issues for the child or youth, resulting in the development of an appropriate plan that will meet the needs of various members of the child family.

Areas to be assessed. When the agency determines that the family must be investigated, the worker visits the family and conducts an in-depth assessment of all safety elements and a preliminary assessment of risk factors, parental protective capacity, and child well-being to evaluate whether a child or youth is at risk of future maltreatment. This family review is best done in the home and the child's natural environment (e.g., childcare center, school).

Expected outcomes. At the end of the family review, the worker should have:

- Determined the child's or youth's safety or level of risk;
- Identified child development needs and issues;
- Documented facts surrounding maltreatment (e.g., indicators of substance abuse, domestic violence, mental health);

- Identified kin resources and community linkages; and
- Referred the family to resources.

Key decisions. During the family review, the worker should make key decisions about safety, risk, and child well-being:

- Is the child or youth safe?
- If not, what is needed to protect the child or youth in the home, with kin, or in out-of-home care?
- Are there aggravated circumstances? Should reasonable efforts be waived?
- Who should be involved as safeguards and safety mechanisms?
- What is the level of risk for future maltreatment?
- How should the agency respond to the risk factors identified?

Practice guidelines. The worker establishes the agency's credibility with the family by:

- Explaining the agency's mandates and the reason for involvement;
- Thoroughly reviewing previous records and information gathered at intake and from other professionals working with the family;
- Helping the family clearly understand the safety and risk factors for the child or youth; and
- Engaging the family by trying to reach an agreement on family needs and needs for the child's or youth's safety.

The worker gathers information about safety by:

- Observing the home environment and the family's interactions;
- Talking with each member of the family (including all children and youth, birth parents, and other adults in the home) to learn about needs and strengths;
- Talking with individuals (e.g., extended family, friends, neighbors, teachers) who might have knowledge of risk to the child

or youth and of the family members' needs and strengths;

- Screening for family behaviors and conditions that increase concern for child maltreatment (e.g., substance use, domestic violence, mental illness);
- Working with the family to determine the services needed to enhance their capacity to protect and care for the child or youth; and
- Asking the family about their capacity and willingness to accept intervention at the level needed to protect the child or youth.

The worker also reviews and analyzes information about risk, parental protective factors, and child well-being to determine:

- Potential risk factors and level of risk;
- Protective capacity of the family and community support systems to address safety concerns without agency intervention;
- Health, mental health, educational, and developmental needs and issues of children and youth that must be addressed;
- Contact information for maternal and paternal relatives who can protect the child or youth and support the family; and
- Available and appropriate services and resources that can immediately insure the child safety and the needs of the family.

If the child or youth must be placed outside the home to ensure safety, the worker reviews whether relatives or close friends should take temporary custody of the child.

Assessment for Placement

If placement is necessary, the child welfare worker should arrange for, work with, and support the placement of children and youth in an approved home or facility other than their own home. To do that, the worker will have to determine what type of placement is required and what is the reunification plan.

Areas to be assessed. When the agency determines that out-of-home placement is necessary, the worker must assess safety, risk, and caregiver protective capacity as well as child well-being on an ongoing basis.

Expected outcomes. At the end of the assessment for placement, the worker should have:

- Involved the family in planning the child for placement and established evidence of their involvement;
- Developed a permanency plan with goals, visitation, timeframes for evaluation, and services to be provided to biological and kin or foster families;
- Developed a concurrent plan in the event reunification becomes impossible; and
- Helped the family prepare the child or youth for placement and established evidence that the child has been prepared.

Key decisions. During the assessment for placement, the worker should make key decisions about the child's placement:

- What is the best (i.e., least restrictive), most family-like out-of-home placement (e.g., kinship care, family foster care, therapeutic foster care)?
- Can siblings be placed together?
- How can the connections with the family and community (e.g., placement proximity, parent-child visits, sibling visits, worker visits with parents and child, continuation in the same school) be maintained?
- What is a realistic permanency goal for the child or youth (e.g., reunification with parents and relatives, adoption, other permanent arrangements)?
- What are the timeframes for reevaluation?
- What services and supports will increase the likelihood of expedited permanency for each child or youth transitioning to independence?

Practice guidelines. The worker begins planning placement by:

- Identifying and evaluating both maternal and paternal family members for possible kinship placement and visitation;

- Gathering recommendations from parents about relatives, family friends, or both, as possible placement options; and
- Identifying noncustodial parents and their family members early and exploring their willingness and capabilities to meet the child's or youth's needs and protect him or her from future maltreatment.

Concurrently with the family review, the worker evaluates:

- Child well-being elements to determine how emotional, physical, and developmental needs will be met;
- Least disruptive (to the child's life) placement options, including proximity to parents and siblings for visitation;
- Visiting plan that will help increase parental protective capacity and reunification goals;
- Best possible permanency option if the child cannot be reunited with his or her parents;
- Parents' assessment of the best path to permanency, including alternatives to termination of parental rights, parental relinquishment, or guardianship; and
- Best strategies to prepare the child for placement.

Assessment for and during Planning

The goal of service planning is to develop an individualized, strength-based, needs-driven framework that addresses the unique needs of each child or youth and family.

Areas to be assessed. The family and child should be actively involved in preparing the service plan, during which there must be an in-depth exploration of the underlying origin and extent of the safety concerns and risk factors impacting parental protective capacity and child well-being. Again, assessing family members in their home usually results in a much better outcome, although assessment of parental protective capacity can be done in any environment where the family feels comfortable.

Expected outcomes. At the end of the assessment for and during planning, the worker should have:

- Identified and described the factors that must change (e.g., child or youth, parents, family, other supports) and why they must change to insure safety and reduce or mitigate risk of maltreatment as well as support child well-being;
- Developed an individualized, outcomes-oriented family service plan addressing all family members' needs;
- Insured that the family members understands the plan, their responsibilities, and potential consequences; and
- Developed a list of measurable, realistic, achievable goals and steps that include outcomes anticipated from the services and supports to be provided, benchmarks, and timeframes.

Key decisions. During this phase, the worker should make key decisions about planning for risk reduction, appropriate interventions, and services delivery:

- What factors must change to reduce or mitigate risk of maltreatment and enhance parental protective capacity to promote child well-being?
- What are the family outcomes that, when achieved, will indicate risks have been reduced and effects of maltreatment successfully addressed?
- What are the specific goals, timeframes, and responsibilities of the family, child welfare system, service agencies, and others for delivering services and tracking progress that will assist in achieving the outcomes?
- What intervention approaches are needed to address issues related to the underlying causes of the maltreatment?
- What are the potential obstacles to services delivery? How can these obstacles be addressed?

Practice guidelines. The worker collaborates with the family, when appropriate, by:

- Offering family members the opportunity to identify what they perceive as their strengths.
- Reviewing safety, risk, parental protective capacity, and child well-being factors by asking about the family's history and current conditions, family dynamics, disciplinary styles, and perception of help-seeking interventions.
- Identifying potential underlying causes of the maltreatment. He or she gathers evidence to demonstrate if and how these underlying causes are impacting protective capacity and identifies what must change for risk to decrease, reunification to occur, or both, as well as the services and supports needed to effect these changes.
- Analyzing information from, and making necessary referrals to, specialized assessments in areas of substance abuse, domestic violence, mental health, and developmental disabilities, including mental retardation.
- Using information gathered and analyzed to develop an individualized, outcomes-oriented family service plan with goals that are immediate, achievable, measurable, and time limited. The worker specifies who must provide what services, for how long, and with what frequency.

The worker plans for child well-being by:

- Reviewing the child's history and identifying his or her needs with the family;
- Talking with individuals who know the family and child (e.g., schoolteacher, physician, other family members);
- Observing and asking about the child's or youth's attachment to various family members and relationship to the parent or parents absent from the home;
- Observing the child or youth in different environments and in different contexts to identify his or her strengths and specific needs in each context, including the family context;
- Assessing the effects of the maltreatment on developmental needs of the child or youth (i.e., sensory-motor and language development, school readiness, social skills, and cognitive development);
- Analyzing all the information gathered to determine the best plan to support the child's or youth's needs; and
- Referring for further specialized professional evaluations the child or adolescent who has been sexually abused or demonstrates developmental delays or severe behavioral or mental health issues.

Assessment during Monitoring

Monitoring of progress insures that the agency's case plan maintains its relevance, integrity, and appropriateness, as well as achieves its outcomes.

Areas to be assessed. During progress monitoring, the worker must assess the child's or youth's circumstances for continuing threats to safety as well as progress toward the family service plan goals, decreasing risks to parental protective capacity identified previously, and ensuring that child well-being is improving.

Expected outcomes. During progress monitoring, the worker should:

- Check that safety is maintained and risks are managed;
- Verify progress toward or achievement of family service plan outcomes, goals, and benchmarks in all domains (i.e., safety, risk, parental protective capacity, and child well-being);
- Activate a concurrent plan, if necessary; and
- Verify that goals of permanency are achieved.

Key decisions. During progress monitoring, the worker should make key decisions regarding use of services, safety, and parental protective capacity:

- Are parents and the child or youth accessing, participating, and satisfied with services?
- Is the child or youth safe? What must be done to insure the child's continued safety?
- What changes have occurred in the conditions and behaviors contributing to the risk of maltreatment?
- What are the indicators that the family is progressing toward or has reached the desired plan outcomes?
- Is the visiting plan increasing parental protective capacity? Should the plan be modified?
- If placement is involved, are timetables for permanency on target?

Practice guidelines. The worker facilitates progress by:

- Eliciting the family's view of their own progress and discussing the agency's view of the family's progress;
- Reviewing the family's progress with other service providers and with the court, when the latter is involved;
- Insuring compliance with federal and other mandates (e.g., criminal record checks, drug and alcohol intervention, child health insurance); and
- Using timeframes and benchmarks established in the family service plan to assess child safety, family change, child well-being, and family thoughts about services received.

The worker assesses and responds to child and youth safety needs by:

- Continuing to review and address safety issues, accessing emergency services if the child is in danger;
- Analyzing information on indicators about the presence of factors affecting child and youth safety (outcome compliance);

- Determining whether a safety plan can be implemented to keep the child or youth safe when he or she returns home;
- Determining the extent to which activities set forth in the family service plan are being carried out (process compliance) and the obstacles the family members are confronting; and
- Reassessing the family's prognosis for reunification. If it remains or becomes poor, the agency places the child or youth with a family who will both support reunification and adoption or take guardianship should reunification become impossible.

Assessment during Closure
Closure is defined as the point at which the agency no longer maintains an active relationship with the family. It typically occurs when the family is stable following reunification or when the child or youth has been adopted and child welfare or post-adoption services are no longer needed.

Areas to be assessed. The decision that the agency will no longer be actively involved with the family must be based on an assessment of safety and risk to the child or youth. The agency can support the family's right to self-determination by ending services when the child or youth is safe and family members believe they no longer need services.

Expected outcomes. A decision to discontinue agency involvement with the family results when:

- Evidence exists that safety is attained and risk is manageable;
- Reunification or an alternate permanency plan is achieved;
- A crisis or aftercare plan is in place; and
- The family has been linked with community services that will support child safety and well-being.

Key decisions. In determining whether to discontinue agency involvement with the family, the worker should have made key decisions regarding child safety and agency and family plans to insure safety:

- Is the child or youth safe?
- If so, what is the best way to provide ongoing support to the family to help secure stability of changes and parental protective capacity?
- If not, does a need to modify the family service plan exist?
- Does the family know what to do in case of emergency to ensure child safety?

Practice guidelines. The worker verifies child or youth safety and well-being, risk reduction, and adequate parental protective capacity by meeting with family members, others important to the child, and representatives of other agencies providing services to the child or youth to assess progress toward family service plan goals and assess the family's ability to maintain stability without child welfare involvement.

Promising Approaches in Comprehensive, Family-Centered Assessment

A number of trends and promising approaches are emerging around the country to reform the child protection system. The following approaches represent rethinking of the assessment process to insure the safety of children and respond to the needs of families.

Concurrent Planning

Prior to the passage of ASFA, most states had developed a sequential approach to permanency planning. First, workers actively pursued the child's or youth's reunification with his or her biological family; then, if all hope of reunification was ruled out, workers explored other permanence options, such as adoption or guardianship. Although this sequential approach emphasizes the primacy of family reunification as a permanency option, it had an unintended negative consequence. Children and youth who could not return home often lingered in foster care for many years. To address this concern, practitioners have sought an alternative practice model—known as "concurrent

planning"—that allows placement in permanent homes more quickly.

The National Resource Center for Foster Care and Permanency Planning defines concurrent planning as a process of working toward reunification while establishing an alternative contingency backup plan (Greenblatt 1997:3). Concurrent planning represents a promising practice in assessment and service planning in that it supports, intensifies, and expedites efforts to achieve permanence in a child's life. Effective implementation of concurrent planning is based on a comprehensive and early assessment of families' strengths, needs, and current and past problems that assists the social worker in determining the risk of foster care drift and the need to place the child or youth with a permanency planning resource family (i.e., a family who can actively engage in supporting family reunification efforts and also commit to providing an alternate permanent home if reunification is impossible).

Involvement of Families in Decisionmaking

Some states are implementing new approaches to working with families based on forming a different type of relationship with the families they serve. These approaches, which go by different names, such as "family unity," "family conferencing," or "family group decisionmaking," have their roots in a New Zealand model in which child protective agencies bring together family and extended family members, involved neighbors, and community members in a structured meeting where family issues and strengths are identified collectively and the plan is crafted jointly. Family decisionmaking models allow the family (which is broadly defined) to participate in assessment and in a broad range of decisions about impact on child safety, permanence, and well-being (Merkel-Holguin 2003:1).

Differential Response

Some jurisdictions are developing more flexible child protective service systems in which low-risk or unsubstantiated cases are referred to early intervention or community resources while CPS focuses on more serious cases in which abuse and neglect are confirmed. By restricting the responsibilities of the public agency, it is hoped that limited child welfare resources can be targeted more effectively. This differential response approach (also called "assessment track," "dual track," "multiple track," or "alternative response") recognizes the variations in reports and the need for different approaches when handling dissimilar cases.

To implement a differential response approach, states have had to redesign their assessment practices (e.g., home conditions must be assessed along with the family's strengths and needs before appropriate services are provided) (Schene 2001:4). In addition, different jurisdictions have developed assessment tools to help differentiate families into the different tracks (Schene 2001:4).

Community Partnerships for the Protection of Children

Several communities and states are working to prevent maltreatment and safely divert low-risk cases from child protection agencies to a strong network of both informal and formal community resources that provide supports and services for vulnerable children, youth, and families. They do so by involving citizens and local organizations, identifying and building collaboration with informal support networks and local organizations, enhancing cross-system efforts, and developing new services when needed. Because the responsibilities of child protective services systems have become decentralized, communities are developing assessment processes that respond to this new way of engaging families, agencies, and communities to protect children and youth and support families (National Child Welfare Resource Center for Family-Centered Practice 2003:2).

Solution-Focused Approach to Child Welfare

A solution-focused approach to working with families in public child welfare takes the concept of family empowerment from rhetoric to reality. It does so, in part, by toppling the professional hierarchy that allowed therapists and professionals to exercise control over families in their role as experts on family problems. Instead, within the solution-focused paradigm, family service practitioners become consultants or assistants to the family. They work with a family, as equals, on what a family does right and how to do it right more often (Berg & Kelly 2000:45). Based on their approach to working with families, states implementing solution-focused approaches have developed a list of assessment protocols for frontline workers (De Jong, Berg, & Kelly 2002:3).

Proactive Supervision: Leading the Way

Several jurisdictions are revisiting and enhancing the role of supervisors in child welfare. The supervision approach provides highly structured, rigorous, objective supervision to frontline workers during the involvement of families with the agency. The supervisor is trained to direct the worker to insure that the agency remains in full partnership with families, natural helpers, and service providers when conducting the family assessment and to allow for timely outcomes of safety and permanency. The supervisor reinforces the use of a structured format for all family meetings whereby the parents, extended family, natural helpers, and service providers discuss safety, risk factors, and strengths and supports for safety (Smith 2002:1).

Agency Implementation of a Comprehensive, Family-Centered Assessment

The National Child Welfare Resource Center for Family-Centered Practice suggests the following steps for addressing critical planning issues and developing a comprehensive, family-centered assessment process:

- Describe the state's vision and identify the principles that assessment practice must reflect.

- Analyze the strengths and weaknesses of the state's current assessment practices by reviewing current policy, procedures, and practices; assessment tools; MIS; time involved in conducting assessments; training curricula; guidelines for supervisors; and QA procedures.
- Decide how assessment will be conducted to meet the requirements for a comprehensive, family-centered assessment discussed in this chapter (i.e., safety, risks, parental protective capacities, and child well-being).
- Develop a realistic implementation plan to redesign policy, procedures, assessment tools, time involved in conducting assessments, training, guidelines, supervisors, and QA procedures used to determine if and how family assessments are being conducted.
- Determine how the plan will be implemented (e.g., decide whether to start with a pilot of the new assessment process and evaluate the outcomes before beginning a statewide rollout of the new assessment process).

REFERENCES

Action for Child Protection. (2003). The difference between risk and safety. Monthly article (January) available at www.actionchildprotection.org/archive/article0103.htm.

Berg, I. K., & Kelly, S. (2000). *Building solutions in child protective services.* New York: W. W. Norton.

Casey Family Programs. (2002). *Understanding the difference between overrepresentation and disproportionate representation.* Paper presented at the Race Matters II Forum, Chicago, March 9–11, 2002.

Child Welfare Research Team. (2002). *An evaluation of factors related to the disproportionate representation of children of color in Santa Clara County's child welfare system: Child and family characteristics and pathways through the systems.* San Jose, CA: College of Social Work, San Jose State University.

Day, P., Robison, S., & Sheik, L. (1998). *Ours to keep: A guide for building a community assessment strategy for child protection.* Washington, DC: Child Welfare League of America.

De Jong, P., Berg, I. K., & Kelly, S. (2002). *Strengths-based interviewing protocols for CPS investigations and safety/service planning and for CPS follow-up contacts.* Detroit: State of Michigan Family Independence Agency, Children's Protective Services.

Greenblatt, S. (1997). The Adoption and Safe Families Act of 1997: A quick look and implications for practice. In *Permanency Planning Today,* p. 1. New York: National Resource Center for Foster Care and Permanency Planning, Hunter College School of Social Work.

Merkel-Holguin, L. (2003). *Putting families back into the child protection partnership: Family group decision-making.* Chicago: American Humane Association.

National Child Welfare Resource Center for Family-Centered Practice. (2000). *Rethinking child welfare practice under the Adoption and Safe Families Act.* Washington, DC: National Child Welfare Resource Center for Family-Centered Practice.

Schene, P. (2001). *Meeting each family's needs: Using differential response in reports of child abuse and neglect.* Washington, DC: National Child Welfare Resource Center for Family-Centered Practice.

Smith, C. (2002). *Public child welfare supervision: Guidebook for supervisors.* Washington, DC: National Resource Center for Family-Centered Practice.

U.S. Department of Health and Human Services. (2002). *Child maltreatment 2001.* Washington, DC: Children's Bureau.

SUSAN P. KEMP
KARA ALLEN-ECKARD
AMY ACKROYD
MELISSA F. BECKER
TRACEY K. BURKE

Community Family Support Meetings

Connecting Families, Public Child Welfare, and Community Resources

In this chapter, we examine supportive child welfare practice through the lens of one promising approach, the Community Family Support Meeting (CFSM). This emergent intervention uses participatory family decision-making methods to connect families with informal community resources and community-based social service professionals at times of crisis and transition. It thus provides a useful example of a practice method that adapts principles and perspectives drawn from community-based family support services for use within the mandate and realities of contemporary child welfare practice. The pilot project we describe here was developed in the context of an existing partnership between a state child welfare agency and several of its constituent communities.

Community-based family support programs typically focus on preventive services that support and strengthen family and parental functioning. Most programs have an open-door policy and, unlike child welfare services, parental participation is voluntary rather than mandated. Although a diverse array of programs and ser-

vices clusters under the family support umbrella (Pecora, Whittaker, Maluccio, & Barth 2000), they are unified by their investment in a common set of practice principles that have fundamental implications for the shape and content of family support services. These principles affirm that the need for support is a normal part of family life; all families have strengths as well as needs; and the essential elements of support include meaningful connections to neighborhood and community resources, both formal and informal, as well as to family and friends (Dunst 1996; Family Resource Coalition 1996; Hess, McGowan, & Botsko 2003). Ideally, supportive services are family-centered, focused on empowering parents and families to define their needs and enhance their capabilities, and acknowledge parents as the experts on their children and family (Dunst & Trivette 1994; Lightburn & Kemp 1994). They are committed to building relationships with family members based on equality and respect, affirming and enhancing families' cultural strengths and identities, and partnering with families to identify and prioritize needs and access relevant services and resources (Family Resource Coalition 1996). Strengthening individual and family functioning through empowering and collaborative services is thus a primary aim of family support efforts (Dunst & Trivette 1994).

The Community Family Partnership Project and its evaluation were made possible with funding from the Stuart Foundation and with the support of the Washington State Department of Child and Family Services. The opinions expressed herein, are, however, those of the authors.

Although these principles have long been embraced by community-based family support programs, they have been incorporated less readily into public child welfare services, which in the United States are organized primarily around a public mandate to protect children from abuse and neglect (Cameron & Vanderwoerd 1997; McCroskey & Meezan 1998). In recent years, public concern over high-profile incidents of child maltreatment has given even more weight to this historic commitment to child protection, with the result that in many child welfare jurisdictions, particularly given current fiscal constraints, the state's duty to protect children takes precedence over its parallel investment in supporting and maintaining families. Efforts to position family members as essential partners in child welfare decisionmaking, for example, face a range of counterpressures—from public demands for high levels of professional accountability for child welfare outcomes to the investment in hierarchical, professional-centered decisionmaking approaches that is deeply ingrained in public child welfare systems (Keys & Rockhill 2000; Nixon 2000; Pennell & Weil 2000; Turnell & Edwards 1999). Not surprisingly, these competing priorities make for complicated relationships between child welfare services and the families they serve, as social workers struggle to balance commitments to child safety, parental autonomy, and family integrity.

Despite the historically ambivalent and poorly defined place of supportive family services in public child welfare, there have always been practitioners, policymakers, and child welfare scholars who have considered the provision of supports for vulnerable families to be an important element of effective and ethical child welfare practice. We thus begin the chapter with a brief review of the nature and role of supportive services within the purview of public child welfare. We then provide an overview of the CFSM intervention, including its theoretical and practice foundations. We conclude with reflections on the challenges and oppor-

tunities inherent in implementing supportive interventions, such as CFSMs, in the complex and constrained environment that is contemporary public child welfare practice.

Supportive Services in Public Child Welfare

Supportive services have a mixed history in child protective services. Although, as Cameron and Vanderwoerd (1997) point out, interventions designed to support families and those designed to protect children are, in many respects, more similar than they are different, these foci tend to be represented as separate and sometimes antithetical. From the almshouses and indentured servitude of colonial America to the nineteenth-century child rescue societies and thence to contemporary permanency planning, the relative emphasis placed on child protection or family support has ebbed and flowed in relation to shifting understandings of child maltreatment and its causes (whether it is seen as an outcome of social-structural pressures on vulnerable families, or, conversely, as the result of individual- and family-level pathology) (Schene 1998). In the 1980s and early 1990s, efforts to support and preserve families were an important focus of public child welfare legislation (in the Adoption Assistance and Child Welfare Act of 1980 and particularly, the Family Preservation and Support Initiative of 1993), as they had been (at least in principle) in the child welfare provisions of the Social Security Act of 1935, which first established child welfare as a public institution. By the turn of the twenty-first century, however, in the wake of a series of highly publicized child deaths and in the face of increasing fiscal pressures, child welfare discourse shifted once again to a more narrowly constructed concern with children's safety and well-being. Embodying this shift was the Adoption and Safe Families Act of 1997, which prioritizes child safety over family preservation, refocuses funding for supportive services to include time-limited reunification services and adoption services, mandates the achievement of permanency outcomes within timelines that militate against the provision of open-ended supportive services to birth families, and increases the likelihood that parental rights will be terminated and children placed for adoption.

Although provisions for supportive services continue to be a component in child welfare policy, in practice these services tend to be separated from the "investigation, apprehension, litigation, care" nexus (Cameron & Vanderwoerd 1997:115) that forms the core of mandated child protection services. This separation takes several, interlocking forms. At the very front end of the child welfare system are many families in trouble who need help but are not yet on public child welfare caseloads, either because their problems do not fit with public agency mandates or because the issues that bring them to notice fall below the risk thresholds for public agency intervention. If the needs of these families for supportive interventions are not met in other ways—and often they are not—they either fall through the cracks or become the concern and responsibility of increasingly overwhelmed parallel service systems, particularly, the public schools. As problems escalate, families whose initial needs are for supportive services become increasingly stressed. Protective services then intervene, often with the result that children are removed from the family.

When families do become public agency clients, the daily practices of workers revolve around the needs of the child, with supports to families typically provided on a corollary basis, often by workers and agencies external to the public child welfare system. Family preservation programs, for example, which are a primary mechanism for providing supportive services to families already involved with child protective services, tend to be provided on a contractual basis by agencies separate from the public child welfare system. Although many child welfare systems have embraced family-centered practice (McCroskey & Meezan 1998), public

agency workers rarely have the time and resources to give priority to supportive services in their daily practice. Nor is there clarity (or agreement) about the function and value of family support interventions in child protective services. In reality, family support is thus largely the domain of community-based agencies and resources, compounding the larger separation of public child welfare as a social institution from the web of community-based agencies, resources, and networks that, together with families themselves, constitute "the ultimate child welfare system" (Schorr 1997:214).

This multilayered separation of supportive from protective services mirrors a larger debate on the mandate and function of public child welfare. In one view, scholars such as Bartholet (1999) and Gelles (1996) consider the provision of supportive services to be an important social investment but one that lies outside the purview of mandated child protective services (and indeed, as one that if incorporated into child welfare services risks actively undermining the system's charge to protect children). Not only do these arguments clearly dichotomize family support and child protection, but they suggest that family support is synonymous with family preservation, a conflation that muddies the waters when it comes to considering the long-term support needs of vulnerable families.

An alternative view proposes an integrative rather than dichotomous approach to the question of protecting children and/or supporting their families. From this perspective, which clearly we endorse in our own work, supportive services are envisioned as a core element of an expanded helping repertoire in public child welfare. This repertoire balances child welfare's protective and supportive functions; incorporates informal and formal resources; connects children and families to neighborhood and community supports; enhances social inclusion and social integration; and, at the programmatic level, reduces the structural isolation of public child welfare from community-based agencies and services. Efforts to refocus child welfare policy and practice in this direction have been a hallmark of recent efforts in the United Kingdom (Garrett 2003). In the United States, Waldfogel (1998, 2000) has proposed a differential response child protection system, organized such that a range of formal and informal services and resources are available to respond to families on a customized basis. Other influential advocates of a fully ramified and supportive child welfare system include Schorr (1997), the Edna McConnell Clark Foundation, and the Annie E. Casey Foundation, whose Family to Family Program (Omang & Bonk 1999) provides a blueprint for child welfare services that build networks of supports for families in their neighborhoods and communities. Writing from a Canadian perspective, Cameron and Vanderwoerd (1997) have likewise presented an eloquent argument for child welfare practice that transcends the family support/child protection dichotomy and thus more effectively responds to the particular and individualized needs of children and families.

The integrative model that Waldfogel (1998) and others propose represents a goal that may or may not be realized by child welfare systems struggling to balance multiple responsibilities in the face of fiscal constraints, intense public scrutiny, and ambivalence as to whether such an approach is appropriate for child protective services. Yet the support needs of multiply vulnerable families continue once they become child welfare clients. Indeed, as McCroskey and Meezan (1998:66) point out, for many such families, "the protective services system is the door through which families who may need help can access services." The provision of supports to families involved in child welfare is thus inescapably an issue for child welfare services.

Contemporary efforts to incorporate supportive principles and interventions in public child welfare practice cluster in two domains: (1) family preservation programs, and (2) participatory approaches that engage families in decisionmaking and strengthen connections

to kin networks and community resources. Both fall under the broader umbrella of family-centered services, in that they "share a guiding philosophy and emphasis on responding to family needs and strengths" (McCroskey & Meezan 1998:55). Family preservation programs, which embody many principles and practices from family support programs, typically are targeted at high-risk families, either those at imminent risk of losing children to placement or those working on reunification of child with the family (McCroskey & Meezan 1998). Typically time-limited, they focus on skill building and enhancement of supports. Often, as we noted above, family preservation services are provided on a contractual basis by agencies external to the child welfare system.

More salient to the model we present here is the fairly recent line of supportive practice that has emerged under the general umbrella of family decisionmaking. The New Zealand Children, Young Persons and Their Families Act (1989) provided a groundbreaking model for public child welfare legislation and practice that bridges the gap between family support principles and practice, which are inherently focused on building on family and community strengths, and child welfare practice, with its inevitable concern with issues of safety and risk. Embedded in this legislation is a statutory commitment to involving families fully in child welfare decisionmaking. Since their initial implementation in New Zealand, family group decisionmaking approaches have become an important element of international child welfare practice (Nixon, Merkel-Holguin, Sivak, & Gunderson 2000). Although diverse in form, these models hold in common the belief that efforts to insure child safety, permanency, and well-being require partnerships between family networks and child welfare services, and that a fundamental element of such partnerships is the involvement of families in decisionmaking (Burford 2000; Graber, Keys, & White 1996; Hassall 1996; Keys 1996; Merkel-Holguin 1996).

For all their intuitive relevance to the realities of many families involved in child welfare, and despite promising developments in several states, supportive practices have had a piecemeal and somewhat precarious existence in the U.S. public child welfare system. Because they focus more on chronic hassles than on the acute or crisis conditions that typically mobilize child welfare attention and involvement, they are both lower in priority and more prone to being cut when funding is tight than are services directed to child protection. As Whittaker and Maluccio (2002) have noted, they tend to be a "mixed bag," in the sense that they are diverse in form and neither well specified or clearly supported by empirical evidence. Nor, as we have pointed out, are they well integrated into public child welfare practice. This tendency to hold supportive services at arm's length embodies the "chronic ambivalence" (Halpern 1999:189) public child welfare evidences regarding the proper calibration between services focused on children and those addressed to their families.

For those of us who share with Whittaker and Maluccio (2002) a desire to reconnect family support and child protection, several challenges thus present themselves. First, there is a need to close the gap between public child welfare services and community-based family support services. Second, there clearly is work still to be done to design and test supportive services that fit well with the goals and responsibilities of public child welfare, and to build a solid evidentiary base for their use. Third, efforts to take these to scale need to be lodged within a larger investment in supportive philosophy and practice.

The intervention we present here, CFSM, represents only a very small step in these directions. It provides, however, a useful example of child welfare practice that brings together family support philosophy, family decisionmaking models, and recent work in community-centered child welfare practice.

Community Family Partnership Project

CFSMs are a central component of the Community Family Partnership Program (CFPP), which was developed by the Washington State Division of Children and Family Services in 1998 with support from the Stuart Foundation. The program has been implemented in three rural and two suburban communities. CFPP evolved from a growing recognition, stimulated by the staff's experience with family group decisionmaking programs, that public child welfare services, working in isolation, could not adequately serve families. Inspired by Annie E. Casey Foundation's Family to Family Program model (Omang & Bonk 1999), CFPP aimed to expand the boundaries of contemporary child welfare practice to more fully include both family and community resources, build strong public agency/community partnerships, and encompass family supportive principles.

Key elements of CFPP programming include the development of community foster care resources, supports for foster parents, and community supports and connections for families with few resources available at times of crisis. Although the mix of services looks different in each participating community, the program has five essential elements: the development of a network of community foster homes; local foster parent support groups; a Time Dollars program, which allows the business community to contribute to foster parent recruitment and support; education and outreach by public child welfare workers in project communities; and CFSMs, which extend family group decisionmaking models by including community representatives. To insure community leadership and representation in the development of program services, the project team hired five "Community Partners": individuals who are actively involved in each of the participating communities. The Community Partners include foster parents, a relative caregiver, a Head Start social worker, and a family support program director. They have worked closely with program staff to develop program services relevant to their particular communities. The collaboration between the Community Partners and the office staff has been a highlight of the CFPP, and has created new linkages among Division of Children and Family Services (DCFS), community service providers, and the project communities.

CFSMs: Practice Foundations

CFSMs are voluntary meetings that provide the opportunity for families involved with public child welfare services to develop plans for their family and children that incorporate community connections and resources along with support from extended family and friends. CFSMs encompass (1) an explicit focus on supportive services in the context of community-centered child welfare practice; (2) a related commitment to family *and* community participation in planning and decisionmaking; and (3) the provision of supportive services across the continuum of a child and family's involvement with child welfare services.

Supporting Families in Their Communities

The CFSM model shares with community-based family support programs an emphasis on the central role of social support, including community supports, in family well-being. Although, as Thompson (1995) rightly points out, social support plays a complicated role in the etiology and remediation of child maltreatment, it is also clear that many families that are involved with child welfare services lack positive and supportive connections in their communities. This seems particularly to be the case with neglectful families. Child neglect has many dimensions, but there is a consensus that neglectful families tend to struggle with a toxic and cascading mix of economic stress, social isolation, lack of social supports, and family issues, which in concert overtake already fragile parental and family coping systems (Berry, Charlson, & Dawson 2003). Although effective

interventions with such multiply vulnerable families typically need to be multifaceted (Halpern 1997), efforts to build connections to "social nurturance" (Garbarino 1987)—informal networks and community institutions that can support the family in the long run—are a central element.

This focus on community is consistent with social work's historic commitment to understanding and working with people in the context of the supports and challenges present in their neighborhoods and communities (Kemp, Whittaker, & Tracy 1997). It also builds on the premises and principles of family support practice (Dunst 1996; Family Resource Coalition 1996), which emphasize both the embeddedness of families in their communities and the importance of supportive personal and community connections to healthy child and family development (see also Goetz & Peck 1994; Hess, McGowan, & Botsko 2003; Hewlett & West 1998; Kagan & Seitz 1988). By linking families with community supports *and* providing opportunities for new and strengthened partnerships among community stakeholders, CFSMs not only support families but also provide a tangible forum for promoting community interconnectedness and investment in local families (Halpern 1999; Pennell & Weil 2000; Schorr 1997).

Collaborative Planning and Decisionmaking

The CFSM approach is designed to build on the actual and potential capacities of families, support family self-determination, and encourage mutual aid and support among family members and informal community resources. It incorporates an explicit commitment to building relationships with families and community members based on inclusion, equality, and respect. This philosophy reflects the model's foundations in family support principles (Dunst 1996; Dunst & Trivette 1994; Family Resource Coalition 1996; Goetz & Peck 1994), its strong base in strengths-based and empowering social work practice, and, most directly, its roots in family group decisionmaking models that emphasize decisions made in partnership with families rather than solely by professionals (Burford 2000; Connolly & McKenzie 1999; Keys 1996; Lohrbach 2003; Merkel-Holguin 1996; Pennell & Burford 1994). These models give families a key role in problem solving and the development of plans that are relevant to their current situations, needs, and abilities (Nixon 2000; Pranis 2000). In the continuum of family decisionmaking models, CFSMs have their roots in the Oregon Family Unity Meetings, strengths-based decisionmaking meetings in which child welfare workers partner with family members to develop support plans (Graber, Keys, & White 1996; Keys 1996).

The CFSM approach goes beyond many family decisionmaking models, however, in its emphasis on including community resources and partners. CFSMs aim to build partnerships between public and community agencies, community members, and families that reduce the burden on any one system and give all parties an opportunity not only to provide input but to share responsibility for supporting positive family outcomes. Such collaborations help families not only to meet personal goals and/or agency and court mandates, but also to develop relationships with resources in their natural environment that will help them to weather future crises. This development is especially important for those families with fewer connections (either physically or emotionally) to extended family or kin networks and less access to supportive relationships in general.

The model also reflects the growing body of evidence that identifies the salience of respectful, engaged relationships between parents and child welfare workers to the process of child welfare involvement and thus to child and family outcomes (McCroskey & Meezan 1998). In a large study of parenting in poverty in the United Kingdom (Ghate & Hazel 2002:251), for example, parents emphasized their desire to feel "in control of decisions and what happened

to them and their families" and to have their views and preferences respected. They stressed the importance of services that have practical value, meet parents' self-defined needs (e.g., one father said that in a time of crisis, help from social services was like someone offering to redecorate the house when what he really needed was help with moving the furniture) and are available when needed. Drawing on these findings, Ghate and Hazel suggest that support must be varied to meet the diversity of need, and to incorporate formal, semiformal, and informal aspects. They also emphasize the key, but often overlooked, point that support can be experienced negatively—as interference, burden, demands, or obligations—and that care must therefore be taken to insure that the support being offered is actually perceived as such by the family (on this point, see also Lincoln 2000).

Multiple Points of Supportive Intervention

In contrast to the tendency in child welfare to focus interventions at particular points in the continuum of child welfare involvement, the CFSM model assumes that supportive services can and should be provided to families across the spectrum of their contact with child welfare services. At the front end of the system, CFSMs provide a forum for public child welfare workers to partner with local communities and families in distress to prevent escalating problems and further involvement with mandated services. For families who are formally involved with child protective services, CFSMs are equally useful whether the focus of work is on preventing out-of-home placement or on planning for permanency. Meetings are also very useful in relation to key transitions, such as when children are being returned home or, as we note below, when youth are preparing for independent living.

CFSMs: Practice

In this section, we provide a general (and necessarily brief) overview of the CFSM model, including meeting coordination, who attends meetings, meeting goals, the process of a meeting, and the planning stage. Benefits, for the families themselves and for other meeting participants, are then highlighted. We conclude with a brief outline of promising applications of the model that emerged during the team's work on the project.

The following example is a composite of several family cases.

BUILDING A FAMILY SUPPORT NETWORK
A 64-year-old grandmother contacts Children's Services, indicating that her 31-year-old daughter has left her three grandchildren in her care for the past 2 months. Despite periodically checking in and promising to return, her daughter has not done so. One of the children has been sick, and the grandmother has used all of her sick leave as well as paid doctor bills out of pocket because she cannot access her daughter's medical coverage. She is concerned that she can no longer afford to care for the children, and that if she misses more work she will lose her job, which is her only source of financial support.

Children's Services tells the grandmother that the agency can do little to support her unless they petition the courts for custody of the children based on the mother's abandonment. The grandmother is very uncomfortable with charging her daughter but feels that she has few alternatives. The Children's Services worker then offers the grandmother the opportunity to participate in a CFSM with the goal of identifying potential resources and supports to enable her to continue to care for her grandchildren. She agrees to participate in a meeting.

When the CFSM facilitator meets with the grandmother, she identifies her immediate needs as medical coverage for the children, childcare/respite, and the establishment of some legal authority so that she can appropriately respond to the children's educational and medical needs if she is unable to locate their mother. Together, the meeting facilitator and the grandmother decide who should be invited to the meeting, including people who may be able to provide medical and financial resources, as well as legal options. They also invite the children's school counselors to help build a plan of support for the children. Finally, the grandmother identifies several family and community members who have offered to provide support in the past. It is determined that every effort will be made to include the mother, but that rather than addressing concerns about the mother's behavior, the primary focus of the meeting will be to support the care of the children with their grandmother.

A CFSM is held and a plan is developed. A participant from the welfare office is able to provide resources and complete applications to transfer medical coverage and financial benefits to the grandmother and to make her eligible for occasional child care respite. Family members and a family friend agree to provide occasional child care as well. The school counselors agree to check in with the grandmother and the children on a regular basis. Finally, the Children's Services worker and the family court representative help the grandmother weigh the pros and cons of formal court involvement. Ultimately, the grandmother chooses to petition for temporary guardianship through Family Court.

Although most of the supports developed at the meeting were available to the grandmother without her participation in a CFSM, her access to resources was fragmented and complicated. Furthermore, the onus was on her to locate and navigate these formal and informal systems. The participants in the CFSM were determined on the basis of the family's current needs, and they were invited to share resources and information that they were already poised to offer. Beyond the 2-hour time commitment asked for the meeting, all parties were able to offer support that was a natural fit for them or their agency. In the end, the inclusive plan provided this grandmother with the support she needed to continue to care for her grandchildren.

Meeting Coordination and Participation
A central role in CFSMs is that of the meeting facilitator, who is responsible for insuring that all aspects of the process—from setting up the meeting through facilitating it and preparing the plan—support the empowerment of the family and shared ownership of the plan. The

facilitator is trained in the use of the CFSM model, and his or her role with the family is related only to the meetings.

During the planning process, the primary family member and the facilitator jointly decide when and where the meeting will be held and who will be invited. In consultation with family members, the facilitator spends time before the meeting inviting participants and helping them understand the meeting process and goals. The facilitator's role continues after the meeting, as she or he draws up the plan, makes sure that the family members are in agreement with it, and distributes it to all meeting participants. Ideally, the facilitator will also do some level of follow-up to monitor the implementation of the plan and prepare for a follow-up CFSM if this is indicated.

Along with immediate and extended family members and representatives of those social service agencies who typically constitute the frontline of support to vulnerable families, CFSMs can include community members who seem likely to be able to support a family's particular needs. The CFPP Community Partners have an important role in seeking out linkages and connections to various supports in their community, from informal community members to more formal service providers, and are in a good position to suggest potential community participants in areas of need identified by family members. From school teachers and community agency staff members to the owner of the local automobile agency, community participants reflect the diversity of supports that are typically available to families in their local communities, but from which vulnerable families frequently are disconnected. Often, the partners also are invited to the meetings as participants involved in and knowledgeable about specific communities. Meeting participants are asked to come to the table with the expectation that they will partner with the family in developing and then implementing a support plan. Before any community resources are invited to the meeting, however, the primary family member is consulted to insure that these are seen as likely to be supportive and that they are a good fit with family needs. Research suggests that consulting family members about potential resources is likely to increase the chances that they will be perceived as useful (Nixon 2000).

The goals of the meeting vary, depending on the needs of individual families, but span the spectrum of child welfare involvement, from developing supports to prevent placement, to reunification or planning for permanent out-of-home care. Support may be focused on a parent, a relative or foster caregiver, or a youth in transition or crisis. The goals are clearly defined prior to the meeting, in consultation with both the primary family member and the person who has referred the family for the meeting, and are reviewed at the beginning of the meeting to insure that they are understood by all meeting participants.

Meeting Process and Plan

In CFSMs, as in the Oregon Family Unity Meetings, and in contrast to Family Group Conferences, workers, family members, and community participants remain together throughout the meeting and process of decisionmaking. The meeting comprises three phases. As there may be community members previously unknown to the family, it opens with introductions, a review of the process, and a discussion of goals identified by the family and referring caseworker. The second phase provides an opportunity to recognize family strengths and capacities to help move them toward their goal. Time is also spent on concerns—both those that initiated child welfare referral/involvement and any that have not been formally recognized.

After strengths and concerns have been discussed, the participants begin the third phase and collaborate on creating a plan to address the family's goals and needs. All participants are invited to offer resources and ideas and to participate fully in the process of the meeting. As Gaudin (1993:34) states, "successful mobilization of outside resources to meet the family's identified priorities helps to overcome the family's . . . distrust of professional helpers." Suggestions are incorporated into the plan only if the primary family member is in agreement. The goal of this portion of the meeting is to provide options and resources to the family; professionals can participate in this process as resources, but are not there to direct the family or tell them what is best for them.

Promising Applications of the CFSM Model

As CFPP has unfolded, the project team has taken the opportunity to extend the program model to practice needs and issues beyond its initial focus. Addressing two issues—the support needs of relative caregivers and of youth who will be emancipating from child welfare care—seem particularly promising.

In a child welfare context characterized by growing use of relative placements, including many with families whose own resources are limited, there is a need for interventions that address the additional support needs of relative caregivers. CFSMs can provide a roundtable for traditional and nontraditional relative resources to come together with public agency and community representatives. Often, relative caregivers are unaware of the resources available to them and are fearful that accessing formal resources may bring to the attention of authorities the fact that the parent is unavailable to care for the child. Thus relative caregivers remain an undersupported yet vital group in the patchwork of family structures.

CFSMs can also be an appropriate intervention in relation to youth emancipating from foster care. In these cases, the youth is instrumental in the planning process as the primary decisionmaker, and is given power regarding who attends the meeting and what the goals of the meeting are. Community members, identified based on the youth's goals, are invited to be part of a supportive network to the youth as she or he prepares to enter the community as an adult. These supports come from a pool of community participants varying from college recruiters and independent living case managers to former foster parents.

Potential Benefits to Families and Other Participants

Like the intervention itself, the potential benefits of CFSMs are multilayered. For families, these benefits include opportunities to become more active participants in defining their situations, needs, strengths, and capacities; to play a more active role in generating solutions; to develop more productive partnerships with agency and community professionals; and to make connections with local resources that can provide open ended and normative supports. Importantly, these connections can be tailored to a family's particular needs, in contrast to the "one size fits all" approach to service provision that is more common in child welfare services (Waldfogel 1998).

Embedded in this family-centered approach are potential benefits to community participants as well. In conventional child welfare planning meetings, the role of community members often seems perfunctory. Furthermore, as Pranis (2000) points out, differences in values and perspectives between community stakeholders and child welfare staff may create even more difficulties for the families who are the subject of decisionmaking processes. CFSMs have the potential both to involve community members more fully and to recognize their values and perspectives. In addition, they give community stakeholders an opportunity to better understand the role (and limitations) of the child welfare system in their families' and communities' lives and make connections with one another that strengthen networks of support for all families in the community. Not least, families and community members can communicate directly, rather than the child welfare agency being the conduit for community expectations.

From the public agency perspective, meetings can be used to provide additional layers of support to families whose level of need is worrisome but not of sufficient magnitude to qualify them for public agency involvement. As we noted earlier, this often occurs either before families meet thresholds for child welfare involvement, or as they are moving off public agency caseloads. The lack of ongoing supports for families who have been reunified with their children, for example, leaves families (and workers) vulnerable to the safety concerns that brought the family to child welfare attention in the first place. Not only do CFSMs provide the opportunity to link such families to ongoing supports, they also serve as a mechanism for building connections between public child welfare and community-based supports for children and families.

Viewed on all these levels, this relatively low-key intervention takes on new dimensions: as a mechanism for engaging and empowering families; as a mediating structure between families and their community networks; as a forum with the potential (over series of meetings) to enhance community social capital through the development of more ramified community networks; and as one medium for integrating public and community-based resources on behalf of families. As with all new models being introduced into established service delivery systems, however, our experience with implementing CFSMs has taught us much about the rewards and challenges inherent in the process of infusing family support principles into public child welfare practice.

An evaluation of the CFPP has been conducted concurrent with project implementation. The focus of the CFSM component of the evaluation is the meeting process—how meetings work, and what people's perceptions, opinions, and insights are regarding the meetings. Data sources for this component include post-meeting interviews with participants (parents, family members, friends, community service providers, and caseworkers), as well as surveys from facilitators. Other data include the plans that came out of the CFSMs and selected case record data from some families in the evaluation. In addition, researchers interviewed the project team, Community Partners, and other caseworkers and administrators in the public child welfare office, focusing on the process of day-to-day project administration, and the reach of the project through the office and the five project communities. Specific to our focus in this chapter, the process interviews included questions regarding how the CFSM component was being implemented. In the section that follows, we draw on information from the project evaluation to reflect on three areas that, as we noted above, are central to the model's supportive goals: (1) the process of the meetings; (2) the role of meetings in connecting families to community resources and supports; and (3) the development of community partnerships.

Points for Reflection

Meetings as Collaborative Spaces

What stands out from post-meeting interviews is the overall satisfaction of CFSM participants with the actual meetings. Almost everyone involved comes away with a positive outlook on the process of the meeting and on its value as a supportive intervention in its own right. In particular, the meetings clearly are powerful events for the families engaged in them: families feel included, heard, and value the opportunity to connect with needed supports and resources. One mother noted that the meeting was helpful "because it made us understand that we're not alone . . . that there were people who could help." A family network member commented that "I was . . . actually pleased that there were so many different agencies and different people involved in the life of this child. I thought it was actually quite awesome." As another mother said, "it was a big relief to have everybody show up and know that I had all this support going and to hear the things that people said, that they were cheering me on. And they were there for me, so it was really encouraging." There is a sense that everyone is brought to the table because they have something to offer, and the focus on family strengths gives a positive feel to the meeting. A mother said of her meeting, "several people said how proud they were of me. My CPS worker was really encouraging, saying that I've accomplished so much, and that things are happening because of . . . the work that I've put in. So, it made me feel good about myself."

Connecting Families to Community Resources and Supports

Overall, meeting participants have positive feedback on the involvement of community service providers in the meetings. People thought that the attendance of community providers is helpful to the individual families in terms of the potential support and resources they can provide. Expanding the meetings to include community participants is seen as a useful way to introduce families to local services, and respondents note that families leave the meeting with more knowledge regarding services that are available in their communities.

Getting the right community participants to the table, with the information they need to be maximally helpful to families, is, however, more challenging. Some community providers commented, for example, that they were unsure as to their role in the meeting, particularly those who had not previously worked with a specific family. Also challenging is the question of how to generalize the supportive connections made in the meeting to the work that follows. Despite plans that capture the agreements made in the meeting, our data suggest that for some families, the level of felt support and the number of community links post-meeting are not greatly changed. Several community service providers also noted that although the CFSM they attended had the potential to link families to their communities in new ways, they were less sure that the families would be able to capitalize on those links, given all that was going on in their lives. It seems, therefore, as though the possibility of developing relevant, ongoing links to community supports is there, but that these may not always be fully realized in the work that goes on beyond the meeting.

Community Partnerships

The professionals we interviewed agree that CFSMs are a useful way of increasing collaboration among service providers and between community agencies and DCFS. In particular, workers report that they like being able to develop partnerships with other providers who may work in the same community, and that CFSMs provide a good networking opportunity. In addition, several professionals commented on how helpful it is to work with other professionals on providing services and supports to families. Data from the process evaluation also underscore the increasingly salient role of the Community Partners in the project, who clearly are a very important element of the project and its efforts to provide community-centered services.

Conclusion

Our preliminary findings indicate that CFSMs are experienced by families and other meeting participants as affirming, empowering, and inherently supportive. By shifting the focus from client problems to the collaborative identification of concerns and solutions, CFSMs create additional possibilities for shared commitments to engagement and action (Pennell & Weil 2000; Pranis 2000). They provide families with an opportunity to articulate their needs and priorities and to connect these to relevant community resources and supports. They also offer a public forum for developing conversations and partnerships between families, public child welfare agencies, and community resources.

More difficult to realize fully is the next step: the translation of the supportive connections developed in the meetings into more tangible form, with the "legs" to carry these preliminary linkages beyond the meetings and into families' ongoing daily lives. We are not surprised by this finding—indeed, the difficulties inherent in generalizing what happens in the meeting to the work that families, community providers, and the child welfare agency do together beyond the meeting reflect, on a different level, the challenges inherent in bringing supportive practices fully to life in everyday child welfare practice.

Our pilot project is only a first step in fully specifying the CFSM intervention and in determining how communities and public child welfare agencies can best use it to partner with families. Although CFPP frames family building and community building as a paired and mutually reinforcing agenda, in practice, as our evaluation data point out, CFSMs are a necessary but not a sufficient step in the larger task of connecting families with multiple needs to community resources. We conclude, therefore, with some general thoughts, based in our practical experience with implementing the model. We also discuss what we have learned about issues that must be addressed to place supportive and participatory practice approaches on a more solid footing in public child welfare practice.

Ideally, interventions such as CFSMs represent one part of a larger commitment to embedding supportive, family- and community-centered approaches in all areas of child welfare practice, and to strengthening the connections between public agencies and formal and informal community stakeholders. As we learned in this project, realizing this agenda requires action on multiple levels, beginning with frontline workers, who need both space and tools if they are to integrate supportive interventions into their practice. As with any child welfare intervention, the choice to undertake a CFSM needs to be grounded in careful, differential assessment of family needs and issues. In particular, workers need guidance on how to balance participatory and supportive interventions with the assessment of risks to children and interventions directed primarily to child protection. Once a decision has been made that a supportive approach is appropriate, choosing which

intervention best fits a particular family is an important next step. In the realm of family decisionmaking models, for example, several approaches may coexist in one child welfare system. More work thus needs to be done to develop a well-calibrated continuum of supportive interventions grounded in good evidence for their differential use, and to develop in workers the commitment and capacity to use them well (Thomlison 2003).

Supportive interventions are defined as much by their grounding in family support principles as by the nature of the work that is done. To use such interventions as CFSMs appropriately, workers need training not only in the intervention, but also in the philosophy of practice that it reflects. Indeed, there is a need for education at all levels—to instill family support principles, to teach supportive interventions and their differential application, and to quell fears that families in crisis and the informal community networks in which they are embedded cannot be good resources for vulnerable children. Given the very real burdens on public agency social workers, a focus on worker empowerment, support, and encouragement is also essential—mirroring, in fact, the empowerment philosophy that is at the core of this practice model.

To fully realize the potential in the model and move it beyond the public child welfare agency, trainings should also be offered to the community professionals (e.g., school personnel, local mental health clinicians, after-school program workers) who constitute the informal child welfare system and who will be participating in meetings along with local families. In many ways, community-centered programs, such as CFPP, require the type of relationship building seen in traditional community development work (Pennell & Weil 2000; Wharf 2002), and the same persistent attention to building community capacity on behalf of children and families.

Many challenges inherent in bringing family support principles more fully into child welfare practice lie in the enduring gap that exists between the rhetoric of best practice and the reality of its implementation in what Donald Schön (1983) has aptly termed the "swampy lowland" of everyday practice. In the face of multiple demands on workers, fiscal constraints, liability concerns, institutional rigidities, and public expectations that child safety is a priority concern, many promising practices flourish only within the protective boundaries of research demonstration projects. To realize these commitments more broadly will thus require several levels of institutional scaffolding. Most fundamentally, administrators and supervisors need to be convinced of the salience of supportive practices to child welfare practice. Building such a base will require not only the development of a confirming body of evidence, but high-level institutional investment in supportive practice as an integral element of child welfare practice. It will also require the continued development of public-private partnerships (e.g., those already in place with the Annie E. Casey Foundation) with the capacity to take promising interventions to a larger scale.

Counterintuitively, in the context of systems with considerable investment in better specifying and standardizing practice, supportive interventions also require diligent attention to maintaining family-centered practices that in essence are deeply individualized. Our perspective on this conundrum is that legislators and child welfare administrators should be fully invested in the system-wide adoption of evidence-based family- and community-centered practices. At the same time, they must recognize that, at the level of everyday implementation, these practices must be flexible and able to respond to particular community and family needs (Keys & Rockhill 2000). In the case of the CFSMs, the voluntary nature of the meetings, their focus on strengths, and the underlying respect for the family should not be lost in the midst of efforts to promote them as a best practice.

Without a thorough institutional investment in supportive, community-centered practices, such interventions as CFSMs risk being no more than signal events in a larger pattern of service centered more on categorical rather than integrative approaches to the multidimensional needs of overwhelmed families and their children, and on managing rather than empowering these families. We are deeply mindful, as Nixon (2000) has cautioned, of the tendency for innovations in child welfare to operate as "parallel systems," running alongside business as usual but not quite connecting with or transforming the inner core of child protective practice. Getting beyond this structural separation, in our experience, involves dogged attention to the principles at the heart of supportive practice, and particularly to bringing family and community to the table as true partners with a shared commitment to solutions. Truly, as Halpern (1999:258) has aptly observed, "there are no shortcuts to strengthening supportive services for poor families."

REFERENCES

Adoption and Safe Families Act. (1997). P.L. 105-89.

Adoption Assistance and Child Welfare Act. (1980). P.L. 96-272.

Bartholet, E. (1999). *Nobody's children: Abuse and neglect, foster drift, and the adoption alternative.* Boston: Beacon Press.

Berry, M., Charlson, R., & Dawson, K. (2003). Promising practices in understanding and treating child neglect. *Child and Family Social Work, 8,* 13–24.

Burford, G. (2000). Advancing innovations: Family group decision making as community-centered child and family work. *Protecting Children, 16*(3), 4–20.

Cameron, G., & Vanderwoerd, J. (1997). *Protecting children and supporting families: Promising programs and organizational realities.* Hawthorne, NY: Aldine de Gruyter.

Connolly, M., & McKenzie, M. (1999). *Effective participatory practice: Family group conferencing in child protection.* Hawthorne, NY: Aldine de Gruyter.

Dunst, C. J. (1996). *Key characteristics and features of community-based family support programs. Guidelines for effective practice,* series monograph 11. Chicago: Family Resource Coalition.

Dunst, C. J., & Trivette, C. M. (1994). Aims and principles of family support programs. In C. J. Dunst, C. M. Trivette, & A. G. Deal (eds.), *Supporting and strengthening families: Methods, strategies, and practices,* pp. 30–48. Cambridge, MA: Brookline Books.

Family Preservation and Support Initiative. (1993). P.L. 103-66.

Family Resource Coalition. (1996). *Guidelines for family support practice.* Chicago: Family Resource Coalition.

Garbarino, J. (1987). Family support and the prevention of child maltreatment. In S. L. Kagan, D. R. Powell, B. Weissbourd, & E. F. Zigler (eds.), *America's family support programs: Perspectives and prospects,* pp. 99–114. New Haven, CT: Yale University Press.

Garrett, P. M. (2003). Swimming with dolphins: The assessment framework, New Labour, and new tools for social work with children and families. *British Journal of Social Work, 33,* 441–463.

Gaudin, J. (1993). *Child neglect: A guide for intervention (The User Manual Series).* Washington, DC: U.S. Department of Health and Human Services.

Gelles, R. J. (1996). *The book of David—How preserving families can cost children's lives.* New York: Basic Books.

Ghate, D., & Hazel, N. (2002). *Parenting in poor environments: Stress, support, and coping.* Philadelphia: Jessica Kingsley Publishers.

Goetz, K., & Peck, S. (1994). What is family support? In K. Goetz & S. Peck (eds.), *The basics of family support: A guide for state planners (and others),* pp. 1–2. Chicago: Family Resource Coalition.

Graber, L., Keys, T., & White, J. (1996). Family group decision making in the United States: The case of Oregon. In J. Hudson, A. Morris, G. Maxwell, & B. Galaway (eds.), *Family group conferences: Perspectives on policy and practice.* Sydney: Federation Press.

Halpern, R. (1997). Good practice with multiply vulnerable families: Challenges and principles. *Children and Youth Services Review, 19,* 253–275.

Halpern, R. (1999). *Fragile families, fragile solutions: A history of supportive services for families in poverty.* New York: Columbia University Press.

Hassall, I. (1996). Origin and development of family group conferences. In J. Hudson, A. Morris, G. Maxwell, & B. Galaway (eds.), *Family group conferences: Perspectives on policy and practice.* Sydney: Federation Press.

Hess, P. M., McGowan, B. G., & Botsko, M. (2003). *Nurturing the one, supporting the many: The Center for Family Life in Sunset Park, Brooklyn.* New York: Columbia University Press.

Hewlett, S. A., & West, C. (1998). *The war against parents: What we can do for America's beleaguered moms and dads.* Boston: Houghton Mifflin.

Kagan, S. L., & Seitz, V. (1988). Family support programs for new parents. In G. U. Michaels & W. A. Goldberg (eds.), *The transition to parenthood: Current theory and research,* pp. 311–341. New York: Cambridge University Press.

Kemp, S. P., Whittaker, J. K., & Tracy, E. M. (1997). *Person-environment practice: The social ecology of interpersonal helping.* Hawthorne, NY: Aldine de Gruyter.

Keys, T. (1996). Family decision making in Oregon. *Protecting Children, 12*(3), 11–14.

Keys, T., & Rockhill, A. (2000). Family group decision-making in Oregon. In G. Burford & J. Hudson (eds.), *Family group conferencing: New directions in community-centered child & family practice,* pp. 271–277. Hawthorne, NY: Aldine de Gruyter.

Lightburn, A., & Kemp, S. P. (1994). Family-support programs: Opportunities for community-based practice. *Families in Society, 75,* 16–26.

Lincoln, K. D. (2000). Social support, negative social interactions, and psychological well-being. *Social Service Review, 70,* 231–252.

Lohrbach, S. (2003). Family group decision making: A process reflecting partnership-based practice. *Protecting Children, 18*(4), 12–15.

McCroskey, K., & Meezan, W. (1998). Family-centered services: Approaches and effectiveness. *Future of Children, 8*(1), 54–71.

Merkel-Holguin, L. (1996). Putting families back into the child protection partnership: Family group decision making. *Protecting Children, 12*(3), 4–7.

Nixon, P. (2000). Family group conference connections: Shared problems and solutions. In G. Burford & J. Hudson (eds.), *Family group conferencing: New directions in community-centered child & family practice,* pp. 93–104. Hawthorne, NY: Aldine de Gruyter.

Nixon, P., Merkel-Holguin, L., Sivak, P., & Gunderson, K. (2000). How can family group conferences become family-driven? Some dilemmas and possibilities. *Protecting Children, 16*(3), 22–33.

Omang, J., & Bonk, K. (1999). Family to Family: Building bridges for child welfare with families, neighborhoods, and communities. *Policy and Practice, 12,* 15–21.

Pecora, P. J., Whittaker, J. K., Maluccio, A., & Barth, R. P. (2000). *The child welfare challenge: Policy, practice, and research,* second ed. Hawthorne, NY: Aldine de Gruyter.

Pennell, J., & Burford, G. (1994). Widening the circle: Family group decision making. *Journal of Child and Youth Care, 9*(1), 1–11.

Pennell, J., & Weil, M. (2000). Initiating conferencing: Community practice issues. In G. Burford & J. Hudson (eds.), *Family group conferencing: New directions in community-centered child & family practice,* pp. 253–261. Hawthorne, NY: Aldine de Gruyter.

Pranis, K. (2000). Conferencing and the community. In G. Burford & J. Hudson (eds.), *Family group conferencing: New directions in community-centered child & family practice,* pp. 40–48. Hawthorne, NY: Aldine de Gruyter.

Schene, P. A. (1998). Past, present, and future roles of child protective services. *Future of Children, 8*(1), 23–38.

Schön, D. A. (1983). *The reflective practitioner: How professionals think in action.* New York: Basic Books.

Schorr, L. (1997). *Common purpose: Strengthening families and neighborhoods to rebuild America.* New York: Doubleday.

Thomlison, B. (2003). Characteristics of evidence-based child maltreatment programs. *Child Welfare, 82,* 541–569.

Thompson, R. A. (1995). *Preventing child maltreatment through social support: A critical analysis.* Thousand Oaks, CA: Sage.

Turnell, A., & Edwards, S. (1999). *Signs of safety: A solution and safety oriented approach to child protection.* New York: Norton.

Waldfogel, J. (1998). *The future of child protection: How to break the cycle of child abuse and neglect.* Cambridge, MA: Harvard University Press.

Waldfogel, J. (2000). Reforming child protective services. *Child Welfare, 79,* 43–57.

Wharf, B. (ed.) (2002). *Community work approaches to child welfare.* Peterborough, Ontario: Broadview Press.

Whittaker, J. K., & Maluccio, A. N. (2002). Rethinking child placement: A "reflective" essay. *Social Service Review, 72,* 108–134.

ZEINAB CHAHINE
SELINA HIGGINS

Engaging Families and Communities

The Use of Family Team Conferences to Promote Safety, Permanency, and Well-Being in Child Welfare Services

New York City's public child welfare agency underwent a comprehensive reform in 1996. Renamed the Administration for Children's Services (ACS), the agency published *Protecting the children of New York: A plan of action* (1996), an innovative strategic plan that implemented progressive changes in core areas of child protection and family permanency.

The plan described a "mechanism [which] will promote a partnership of each community with ACS to secure the safety and well-being of every child brought to ACS' attention" (Administration for Children's Services 1996:111). The underlying intent of the mechanism concerned remediation for the lack of an "organized process for protective workers to consult the people who have the most knowledge of children and families who come into ACS" (Administration for Children's Services 1996: 111). The proposed process concerned the implementation of expedited case conferences at critical decisionmaking points to prevent potential child removals, accelerate planning subsequent to removals, and help families achieve successful outcomes. Additionally, the process would help to expedite fulfillment of the safety, permanency, and well-being mandates of the Adoptions and Safe Families Act (ASFA) of New York State (1999). ASFA stipulates that child welfare agencies must prioritize the health and safety of children in foster care and includes requirements concerning reasonable efforts to prevent placement, to reunify families following placement, and to arrange and finalize a new permanent home if reunification is no longer the goal. Hence, ACS developed and instituted Family Team Conferences (FTCs).

The ACS FTC model provides a continuum of information-sharing and decisionmaking forums that extend over the life of a family's involvement with child welfare, until a safe, permanent living arrangement is achieved for all children in the family. The philosophical premise behind the conferences stems from intrinsic social work values that require that service providers treat clients with respect and dignity, develop trusting work relationships, respect confidentiality, and provide families with individualized services that meet their unique needs. Although New York City's FTC model draws on elements from other conferencing models, such as Family Group Decision Making (Graber, Keys, & White 1996; Ribich 1998), Family Group Conferencing (Marsh & Crow 1998), and Team Decisionmaking (DeMuro 1999), the ACS model has been uniquely tailored to suit the needs of New York City's diverse population.

In so tailoring the model to best service the child welfare population of New York City, certain aspects of the traditional family conferencing models were modified. The period of preparation involved with the traditional conference was decreased to provide an expedited forum. Many jurisdictions utilize 20 to 30 hours or more of planning and preparation for each conference, the efforts of which can extend over a period of several weeks (Gunderson 1998; Hudson & Burford 2000). The purpose of such extensive planning is to shift from an "expert-based" process to a "family-based" process, which results in the ability of the family to use the proffered professional information to develop their own service plan. The extended preparation period thereby results in a high family attendance rate, the ability to resolve potential disruptions prior to the conference, and the creation of service plans acceptable to both family and court (Gunderson 1998:11).

In New York City, the initial FTC, known as the "72-hour child safety conference," (72-hour CSC) is held within 3 to 5 days of a child protective removal or a crisis-based referral. Focusing on the need to maintain children's attachments to their families, an accelerated conference provides expedited visits and service planning that may lead to a decrease in the length of stay of children in foster care. Although the amount of planning time is decreased in comparison to the traditional model, the 72-hour CSC itself is used for information gathering that will enhance subsequent meetings and service planning. The goal of the FTC model is to accelerate service connections that can assist with reunification or other applicable forms of permanency while still providing a high quality, strength-based forum for communication, relationship building, information sharing, and service planning.

FTCs involve parents, children (aged 10 or older), case managers and planners, extended family and other supports, involved community members, and service providers who have knowledge of and emotional investment in the family's well-being. The conferences are facilitated by trained MSW social workers. All participants are encouraged to work together to formulate safety, visiting, education, and permanency plans that insure positive outcomes for children and families.

Benefits of FTCs

The FTC model is beneficial to children and families who are, or will become involved with the child welfare system. Specific benefits of conferences include:

- Increased parent engagement, and the development of a greater investment by families in service planning due to partnership in decisionmaking and strength-focused plans;
- Increased understanding by the family members of their situation, and the impact of their own efforts to cope with stressors;
- Expedited stabilization of family crises through the swift development of a safety and permanency plan;
- An opportunity for the family's support network to be involved in planning;
- Facilitation of cooperation, communication, and teamwork among all stakeholders;
- An increased sense of shared responsibility for protecting children through community involvement in the conference process;
- A thorough assessment (using multidisciplinary information sharing) of family dynamics and underlying factors that threaten child safety;
- Access to appropriate services in a timely manner that can result in accelerated safety, stability, and permanency; and
- An obviated or expedited Family Court process through the involvement of parents in a service plan early in the child protective process.

Types of Conferences

Conferences are held at all critical decisionmaking points throughout the life of a case. The initial conferences in the continuum are the 72-hour CSC, held 3 to 5 days after a child protective removal, or after a referral for a family at elevated risk of removal; and the 30-day family permanency conference (FPC), held 30 to 35 days after the CSC, to refine and adjust the service plan, incorporate any recently discovered resources, and initiate permanency planning. Additional conferences in the FTC continuum include family service planning conferences, for families receiving court-ordered supervision; service plan reviews, held every 6 months by the case planning agency to assess and update the family's service plan; reunification/discharge conferences; independent living discharge conferences; and pre-adoption conferences.

Several types of 72-hour CSCs and 30-day FPCs are provided to families based on their individual strengths and safety needs. Elevated risk conferences are provided to families identified as being at increased risk for protective removal. These conferences provide an opportunity for families to work with service providers to reduce risk of harm by creating a community-based service plan to keep children safely at home.

Post-removal conferences are held with families within 3 to 5 days of a protective removal to minimize trauma, engage families in planning, expedite information sharing, identify prospective kinship resources, and create an individualized and comprehensive service plan that encapsulates safety, visiting, education, and permanency issues. The post-removal service plans also serve to fulfill the "reasonable efforts" to reunify families mandate required by the ASFA of New York State (1999).

Critical case conferences are held with families seeking voluntary placement of children into foster care. Many families are not aware that they can receive community-based services to help their children or do not know how to access these services. Critical case conferences provide an assessment of family strengths and needs and offer local service referrals to alleviate the need to place children in foster care (Administration for Children's Services 2003). Conferences are also held with families seeking help for youth aged 12 through 18, categorized as "persons in need of supervision." All FTCs help to engage families in decisionmaking and the implementation of an individualized service plan that promotes the safety, permanency, and well-being of children.

Conference Facilitation

CSCs and FPCs are facilitated by MSW social workers known as "child evaluation specialists" (CESs). "The Child Evaluation Specialist is a unique position at ACS, in that it fully integrates social work values into child welfare practice" (Higgins 1999:5). CES units are located in each of the 14 child protective field offices that serve the five boroughs of New York City. CESs continually receive specialized training to enhance their skills and expand their knowledge through attendance at a monthly postgraduate lecture series created especially for them. Many CESs have volunteered to become specialists in practice-applicable areas. They attend additional trainings and participate in work groups to provide feedback and share information. Current CES specialties and work groups include visiting, education, permanency, institutional placements, and family/community engagement. As social workers, CESs treat all conference participants with respect and dignity and use such social work skills as assessment, empathy, strength identification and affirmation, advocacy, and encouragement of self-determination. They engage family members and empower the latter's participation in the conference and in the service plan.

Strengths assessment is especially important in the conference process. CESs are trained to recognize that all individuals have strengths that can be harnessed toward improving the quality of life (Saleeby 1992). CESs actively seek to engage parents and children aged 10 or older in the planning process through the identification and affirmation of individual and aggregate strengths, which serve to empower parents and children and maintain their interest and participation in the planning process.

Engaging Families and Communities

As per the 2001 *A renewed plan of action for the administration for children's services:* "ACS believes the strengths found in every community must serve as a foundation to best serve children and families in a more closely integrated, culturally-competent neighborhood based service system" (Administration for Children's Services 2001:28). The Neighborhood Based Services initiative of ACS has therefore resulted in the development of "neighborhood networks," wherein local service providers and community members work in tandem to address and plan for changing child welfare needs. The ACS FTCs seek to create similar forums to draw on the strengths of communities to benefit individual families involved in the child welfare system.

Engagement of families and community participants is crucial to the success of FTCs. Insuring that family members are informed about the conferences and facilitating their participation can be challenging. Conflicting schedules and other obstacles make it difficult for some families to attend or to invite supports to the conferences. Families are encouraged to invite their informal community supports (friends, relatives, neighbors) to assist them with decisionmaking at the conference. Understandably, some parents are concerned about sharing their family problems and are reluctant to invite other individuals to the conferences. However, when extended family and community members attend the conferences, they can provide great support for parents during times of crisis and often become direct permanency resources. These supports can serve as a discharge resource for children or provide aid to the family, so children can remain safely at home or return home sooner.

ACS developed various strategies to overcome some of the barriers and to increase participation in conferences. Holding conferences in a familiar environment encourages increased participation by family members and by family and community supports. Conferences are also held in homes when parents are physically or emotionally unable to travel to another location; at foster care agencies, to facilitate family visits before or after the conferences; and in hospitals, to incorporate the participation of hospitalized parents or children and medical and/or psychiatric staff.

In addition, the CES program has developed an ongoing collaboration with ACS's Children of Incarcerated Parents program (CHIPP) to provide parental engagement and conferences at penal facilities or through teleconferencing for parents in the custody of the criminal justice system. Each incarcerated parent case is directly referred by CES to CHIPP to arrange for visiting and to help schedule a conference at the correctional facility. Incarcerated parent outreach and engagement is vital, because many of these parents do not have any other way to maintain contact with and plan for their children.

A contracted translation and interpretation service permits parental and family resource participation for persons with limited ability to speak English. The service provides translation and interpretation for more than 100 languages, including American Sign Language. Conference resource materials have been, or are currently being, translated into the six languages currently most in demand: Spanish, Creole, Russian, Arabic, Chinese, and Korean. These efforts have increased the ability of ACS to engage with New York City's diverse families and communities.

Individualized Services and Permanency Plans

Traditionally, child welfare professionals developed service plans and made decisions in isolation, based on their determination of the family's needs, without involving the family in the creation of an individualized, strength-based plan. Changing these practices has required a cultural shift for the child welfare system in New York City. The FTC model requires that families be engaged as partners in the decisionmaking process. The CES social workers who facilitate these conferences are trained to advocate for and to develop individualized visiting, education and permanency plans, based upon each family's unique strengths and needs. Visiting plans focus on maintaining the attachments between children and parents, which are necessary for healthy child development and the reduction of trauma (Haight, Kagle, & Black 2003; Hess 1982). ACS encourages a minimum of weekly visits. Moreover, plans often specify for visits to be held in nontraditional, neighborhood-based locations, such as restaurants, playgrounds, roller skating rinks, and parks. ACS is currently developing a link with the New York City Department of Parks and Recreation to provide special entrée to community-based gardens located throughout the city to provide a safe environment for visits between children in care and their families. Children and parents will be able to visit in the gardens, enjoy planting flowers together, and take part in arts events held therein. Holiday visits are also encouraged, many of which pertain to religious, ethnic, or cultural celebrations. These visits can also be held in the community, in the relevant house of worship, cultural center, or neighborhood that relates to the family's ethnicity. This approach to visiting represents a radical departure from the traditional practice of biweekly visits at the foster care agency. Changing practice on a large scale involving thousands of child welfare staff in New York City takes time and requires continuous reinforcement. The FTC model and the CES social work facilitators are playing a critical role in helping to transform the system.

ACS contracts for foster care services through many not-for-profit agencies. Foster care agency support of the enhanced visiting initiative has varied. Many agencies have recognized the attachment and motivational benefits of quality visiting plans and have been compliant with the design and implementation of the plans. Some agencies have not been as supportive, citing insufficient staff, insufficient hours of operation to permit evening and/or weekend visiting, and a resistance to unsupervised and/or community-based visits in situations for which no safety issues or court orders prohibiting unsupervised visiting exist. Through FTCs, CESs have become great advocates for high-quality, comprehensive visiting plans, and encourage the use of empathy by agency staff in helping families maintain connections during separation.

In the past, when children were removed from their homes, they often changed schools, due to placement outside of their communities of origin. Lack of communication with the new school often resulted in interruptions in their educational plans. Since the ACS reform effort also implemented a neighborhood placement approach, children are increasingly more likely to be placed in their borough and community, and therefore are more likely to remain in the same school. FTCs serve as another vehicle to insure that individualized education plans are developed quickly, so that children can maintain connections to their schools and communities of origin. Every FTC service plan incorporates an education plan for all school-aged children, whether remaining in the home or entering foster care. Education plans document a careful consideration of the optimal school environment and services, whether school transfers are necessary or evaluations are required, and whether students are receiving any mandated services. This is especially relevant to insuring adequate services for children receiving special education. "Family Team Conferences are a critical time to gather information regarding a child's educational needs . . . [and] can help to identify outstanding educational concerns, and develop a service plan that ensures the continuity of educational services for children who have become involved with the child welfare system" (Legal Aid Society 2002:12). Education plans developed at conferences must be accompanied by work with schools to insure the appropriateness of service provision as specified in the plan.

FTCs can also be helpful in preventing foster care placements and avoiding Family Court involvement. Elevated risk conferences are held with families identified as being at increased risk for protective removal. The goal of the elevated risk 72-hour conference is to keep children safe at home. This conference provides an opportunity for family engagement and the development of a community-based service plan that attempts to stabilize crises and avert court involvement. The 30-day conference serves as a follow-up, and if the family has stabilized through the use of appropriate services, Family Court involvement becomes unnecessary.

When a child's life or health is deemed to be at imminent risk, the need to insure safety becomes a necessary intervention. However, when the children cannot be maintained safely in the community, FTCs also have the potential for expediting Family Court involvement in child protective cases (Chahine 2003:7–8). Taking children into protective custody triggers the need to file a petition in Family Court (Family Court Act 1962). Within 3 to 5 days after the protective removal, an agency-based service plan is created at the post-removal 72-hour conference. If the family agrees with the plan, it can be shared with ACS, the parent's and the children's attorneys. If the attorneys do not object to the plan, it can be submitted to the court at the next hearing to expedite permanency for the children. Subsequent plans, developed at the 30-day conference, and at the semiannual service plan reviews can be submitted to the court to provide relevant information for dispositional determination. By working together with the legal community to expedite safety and permanency for children, the process becomes less adversarial, and a mutually acceptable disposition may be accelerated.

The Honorable Judge Sara Schechter (2001: 438), who presides over New York City's Manhattan Model Court Part, also known as the "Special Expedited Permanency Part," described the value of FTCs:

When the court was told that an ACS conference was about to occur, the court conference, or review was usually scheduled to follow the confer-ence. When a productive ACS conference had taken place, the court's preliminary conference was shorter, richer, and more productive, and fewer follow-up court conferences were required.

Incorporating FTC plans within court orders may therefore serve to reinforce service and timeframe compliance, thereby expediting permanency for families with children in foster care under ASFA.

Ongoing Challenges: From Implementation to Current Practice

FTCs, as with any revolutionary practice change, have experienced many implementation challenges. Besides the logistical problems of coordinating schedules and getting all participants to come to the table, one of the greatest challenges concerned the need for buy-in by child welfare staff and other stakeholders. Child protective staff initially perceived FTCs as adding to their workload. Although great effort went into explaining how the model could potentially help their work become more efficient and effective, buy-in occurred only after staff members experienced the model and were able to see the benefits directly. Thus the initial reluctance has been replaced by enhanced working relationships between ACS, agency staff, and families.

Foster care agency buy-in to conference attendance and service plan participation has also been challenging. Unlike many other jurisdictions, New York City has a contracted system of foster care service provision, in which ACS retains case management, but the contracted agencies provide the day-to-day monitoring and case planning services. Agencies are notified of conferences by the CESs and are expected to attend, engage with parents, participate in service planning, and arrange for a visit to be held either before or after the conference. In the case of the 72-hour conference, this event may be the agency's initial contact with the parent, as well as the first visit held since the protective removal.

Initial resistance by foster care agencies concerning the time for travel and participation has since been worked through, resulting in greater agency attendance. In some circumstances, the community-based location in which the conference is held occurs at the foster care agency to facilitate staff attendance. Although agency conference attendance has been tracked aggregately, ACS is currently implementing a plan to track individual agency attendance rates. The resultant individual tracking will reflect on agency scores in the ACS evaluation and quality improvement protocol, the mechanism that assesses and reports process, quality, and outcome measures for foster care agency service provision (Giuliani & Scoppetta 2001:113).

Because ACS FTCs exclude attorneys (to keep the focus on service planning and prevent the conference from becoming another adversarial legal forum), the legal community has yet to take full advantage of these conferences. Although some judges and other members of the legal community have recognized the benefit of the FTCs, using the service plans that are developed at the FTCs to expedite the Family Court process remains a challenge in New York City. The legal process remains very adversarial, and the FTC model continues to seek the engagement of attorneys and the court as partners in the process. Uncertainty on the part of children's law guardians about the conferences has been alleviated by extending conference invitations to their affiliated social workers to insure best-interest representation for children and the acceptance of and advocacy for service plans in Family Court. Efforts are underway to further convince parents' attorneys and Family Court judges of the usefulness of FTCs and the resultant service plans.

One of the most critical challenges to implementing the FTC model concerns parental engagement. Family participation is essential to holding a *family* team conference. Because conferencing is based on the social work values of social justice, strengths affirmation, and self-determination (National Association of Social Workers 1996), without the acceptance and involvement of family members, the entire concept of family conferencing is moot. Great efforts have been made to bring parents and other family members to the conference table. An initial analysis of parent engagement rates highlighted those CES units with rates higher than the citywide mean. Subsequent exploration revealed that several of these units exist within field offices that service some of the most high-risk and high-removal areas of New York City. Focus groups were held with the CESs from these offices to discern exactly how they were able to successfully engage with a generally difficult-to-reach child welfare population. The results of the groups were then shared with CESs assigned to other offices, which resulted in an increase in the rate of parent engagement citywide.

Another strategy utilized to increase parent engagement has been collaboration between CESs and the ACS Parent Advisory Work Group. This work group is comprised of parents who experienced the removal of a child, successfully negotiated the child welfare system, and subsequent to familial reunification, were hired as parent advocates or parent specialists by their former foster care providers or related agencies. The work group has been essential in providing feedback from a first-person perspective and family advocacy at some of the conferences, thus helping CESs and other ACS staff to better work with parents, caregivers, and other family members.

Great emphasis has also been placed on strengths identification and affirmation, which can be a very difficult process when working in a system that has traditionally focused on deficits. CESs therefore receive continual training on strengths identification to be able to recognize both the concrete and the abstract strengths (i.e., hopes, dreams, aspirations) that can serve to engage, affirm, and encourage family members.

Total: 27, 959

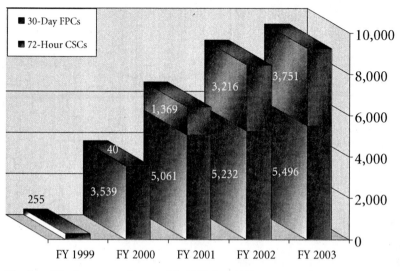

FIGURE 1. Number of family team conferences, July 1998–June 2003.

Community support is "crucial for over-coming systemic barriers likely to block the success of conferencing with families" (Macgowan & Pennell 2001:71). The best-intended service plan is of little or no value if the services are not available to the family. In years past, many neighborhoods, especially those with lower economic status, did not have the necessary resources to provide the wraparound services (Burchard & Burchard 2000) necessary for families to keep children safely at home or provide essential support to reunified families. To insure the availability of service provision, ACS has developed a Neighborhood Network model (Farrow & Executive Session on Child Protection 1997; Giuliani & Scoppetta 2001) to work with community planners and providers in developing a wide-ranging system to provide safety and support services to families.

Results

Since the first conference held in July 1998, through June 2003, the ACS Division of Child Protection has held 27,959 CSCs and FPCs (fig. 1). The scope and scale of conferences ex-

ceed those of any other jurisdiction. According to the independent New York City Child Welfare Advisory Panel (2003:23) "the implementation of family case conferencing (by ACS), on a scale unmatched by any other child welfare system in the United States, has been an impressive achievement." ACS has consistently provided 97% of removal cases with a 72-hour CSC. In FY2003 alone, ACS provided 2,821 post-removal, 2,074 elevated risk, and 601 non-removal placement CSCs. Although participation in the FTC process is completely voluntary, during FY2003, 78% of parents/caregivers chose to participate in their 72-hour CSCs, and 64% in their 30-day conferences. Of the conferences attended by parents/caregivers, attending parties achieved consensus on a service plan in the majority of conferences.

Assessment surveys, available in eight languages in addition to English (Spanish, French, Russian, Arabic, Italian, Creole, Chinese, Korean), are provided to parents/caregivers and participants at the end of each conference. Of the parents and participants who completed the surveys for January–June 2003, 88% of parents,

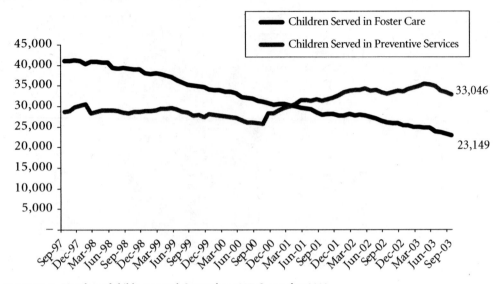

FIGURE 2. Number of children served, September 1997–September 2003.

98% of non-ACS service providers, and 100% of ACS staff stated that they felt the 72-hour CSC was useful to the family. Ninety-six percent of parents, 100% of non-ACS service providers, and 86% of ACS staff stated that they felt the 30-day FPC was useful to the family.

The results of family engagement efforts have been publicly recognized. A recent *New York Times* article (Kaufman 2004:B10) noted FTCs as "the official structure by which families meet."

Conclusion

FTCs have proven to be highly successful in engaging families and communities to develop individualized, strength-based service plans that promote safety and permanency for children. Due to diligent reform efforts, ACS has experienced a decrease in foster care placements and an increase in the number of children receiving preventive service over the past 6 years. As displayed in fig. 2, the number of foster care placements decreased from 41,215 in August 1997 to 21,829 in December 2003, and the use of preventive services increased

from 29,138 cases in August 1997 to 33,737 in December 2003. Although the total number of FTCs has increased every year, the decrease in post-removal conferences and the increase in elevated risk conferences correlates with the decrease in placements and increase in community-based preventive services experienced by ACS. Fig. 3 displays the change in conference usage between FY2002 and FY2003. The number of 72-hour post-removal conferences decreased from 3,282 in FY2002, to 2,821 in FY2003. The number of 72-hour elevated risk conferences held increased from 1,307 in FY2002 to 2,074 in FY2003. Fig. 4 also displays a similar change, with the number of 30-day post-removal conferences decreasing from 2,772 in FY2002 to 2,509 in FY2003. The number of 30-day elevated risk conferences increased from 190 in FY2002 to 908 in FY2003.

The quality of the conferences has been widely acclaimed by families, service providers, and independent agencies. As per the spring 2004 volume of *Voices* (Metzger 2004:19): "It is envisioned that the Family Team Conferences

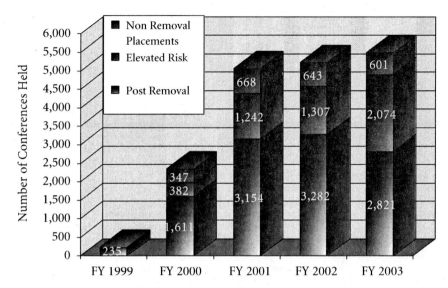

FIGURE 3. Number of 72-hour child safety conferences, July 1998–June 2003.

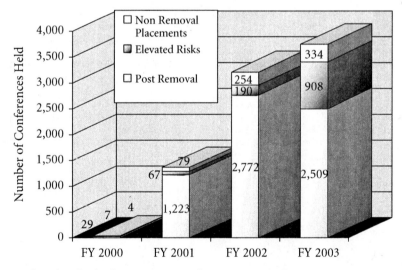

FIGURE 4. Number of 30-day family permanency conferences, May 1999–June 2003.

will connect youth with a parent, relative, adoptive parent or with a significant adult willing and capable to make a lifelong, legally binding commitment to a youth about to be discharged from care." Over all, FTCs provide families with an opportunity for self-determination and support in creating a roadmap to safety, permanency, and an enhanced quality of life.

REFERENCES

Administration for Children's Services. (1996). *Protecting the children of New York: A plan of action.* New York: Administration for Children's Services.

Administration for Children's Services. (2001). *A renewed plan of action for the Administration for Children's Services.* New York: Administration for Children's Services.

Administration for Children's Services. (2003). *Voluntary placement agreement protocol.* New York: Administration for Children's Services.

Burchard, J. D., & Burchard, S. N. (2000). The wraparound process with children and families. In G. Burford & J. Hudson (eds.), *Family group conferencing: New directions in community-centered child & family practice,* pp. 140–152. Hawthorne, NY: Aldine De Gruyter.

Chahine, Z. (2003). New York City Administration for Children's Services Division of Child Protection family team conferences. In R. Richter (chair), *Sixth annual Children's Law Institute, Litigation and Administrative Practice series handbook,* C-195, pp. 7–13. New York: Practising Law Institute.

DeMuro, P. (1999). *Team decisionmaking: Involving the family and community in child welfare decisions.* Baltimore: Annie E. Casey Foundation.

Family Court Act of the State of New York. (1962). *State of New York Statutes,* art. 10, sec. 1021–1024.

Farrow, F., & Executive Session on Child Protection. (1997). *Child protection: Building community partnerships.* Boston: The President and Fellows of Harvard University.

Giuliani, R. W., & Scoppetta, N. (2001). *A renewed plan of action for the Administration for Children's Services.* New York: Administration for Children's Services.

Graber, L., Keys, T., & White, J. (1996). Family group decision-making in the United States: The case of Oregon. In J. Hudson, B. Galaway, A. Morris, & G. Maxwell (eds.), *Family group conferences: Perspectives on policy & practice.* Monsey, NY: Willow Tree Press.

Gunderson, K. (1998). Pre-conferencing preparation: An investment in success. *Protecting Children, 14*(4), 11–12.

Haight, W. L., Kagle, J. D., & Black, J. E. (2003). Understanding and supporting parent-child relationships during foster care visits: Attachment theory and research. *Social Work, 48*(2), 195–207.

Hess, P. (1982). Parent-child attachment concept: Crucial for permanency planning. *Social Casework, 63,* 594–604.

Higgins, S. J. (1999). Practice for the real world: Imbuing child welfare practice with social work values. *Currents, 42*(3), 5, 9.

Hudson, J., & Burford, G. (2000). Introduction: Comparative practices. In G. Burford & J. Hudson (eds.), *Family group conferencing: New directions in community-centered child & family practice,* pp. 187–192. Hawthorne, NY: Aldine De Gruyter.

Kaufman, L. (2004). Birth parents retaining a voice in New York foster care model. *New York Times,* (June 3), pp. A1, B10.

Legal Aid Society. (2002). *Identifying and addressing educational problems in family team conferences.* New York: Legal Aid Society.

Macgowan, M. J., & Pennell, J. (2001). Building social responsibility through family group conferencing. *Social Work with Groups, 24*(3/4), 67–87.

Marsh, P., & Crow, G. (1998). *Family group conferencing in child welfare.* Oxford: Blackwell Sciences. Retrieved June 22, 2004, from emedia.netlibrary.com/reader/reader.asp?product_id=51735.

Metzger, S. (2004). Permanency for teens: New York City's emerging policy. *Voices, 5*(2), 18–19.

National Association of Social Workers. (1996). *Code of ethics.* Washington, DC: National Association of Social Workers.

New York City Child Welfare Advisory Panel. (2003). *Report on family engagement.* New York: New York City Child Welfare Advisory Panel.

Ribich, K. (1998). Origins of family decision making: Indigenous roots in New Zealand. *Protecting Children, 14*(4), 21–22.

Saleeby, D. (1992). *The strengths perspective in social work practice.* New York: Longman.

Schechter, S. P. (2001). Symposium: Family Court case conferencing and post-dispositional tracking: Tools for achieving justice for parents in the child welfare system. *Fordham Law Review, 42*(4), 427–439.

JAN McCARTHY
MARIA WOOLVERTON

Healthcare Needs of Children and Youth in Foster Care

nsuring that the healthcare needs of children and youth in the child welfare system are met is the responsibility of many, including their families, the child welfare agency, their out-of-home caregivers, the healthcare system, the mental health system, and the court system. Children and youth's health outcomes as well as their chances for having permanent, safe, and secure homes can be improved with access to a comprehensive healthcare system and adequate support for their families. In this chapter, we use the term "comprehensive healthcare" to refer to strategies and services for meeting the physical, dental, mental, emotional, and/or developmental needs of children and youth. It includes primary, tertiary, and specialty healthcare. We recognize the importance of meeting the emotional and behavioral needs of children and youth and the impact that involvement with the child welfare system can have on a child's emotional health; however, because the chapter by Dore provides an in-depth discussion of child and adolescent mental health, we do not discuss mental health issues in detail here.

Historically, the primary focus of the child welfare system has been to keep children and youth safe and to find permanent homes for them. This mission has involved protecting children from abuse and neglect. The system also strives to provide children with stable, permanent living situations, life-long relationships with nurturing caregivers, and continuous relationships with family members. More recently, however, the system has recognized the importance of focusing on a child's total well-being—insuring that children and youth receive adequate services to meet their physical health, mental health, and educational needs. This concept of well-being is stressed in the Adoption and Safe Families Act of 1997 (ASFA; P.L. 105-89) and is used in the Child and Family Services Reviews, a statewide level review process conducted by the Children's Bureau. To help children and youth achieve well-being, the child welfare system also focuses on enhancing the capacity of parents and guardians to provide for their children's needs.

In this chapter, we present an overview of issues that impact the health of children and youth who are involved with the child welfare system. We discuss the health status and special healthcare needs of these young people, the child welfare system's responsibility to forge linkages with other systems and with families to insure that these needs are met, and the challenges faced in doing so. We present a framework of critical components around which to develop approaches for overcoming the myriad challenges and provide children with access to appropriate healthcare services. Taken together, the components of this framework describe a comprehensive, community-based healthcare system designed to meet the needs of children and families served by the child welfare system. The comprehensive, community-based healthcare system described in this chapter and many of the findings presented here are based on a 3-year study done by the Georgetown University Child Development Center (see McCarthy & Woolverton 2002 for more detailed information on this study). We also discuss important ethical issues and dilemmas related to the implementation of various approaches, as well as the knowledge and skills that social workers need to coordinate healthcare services for children and youth. The chapter concludes with a summary analysis.

Because much of the research literature (as well as state efforts at system improvement to date) have focused on the needs of children who are in out-of-home care, our review of the current state of knowledge and practice in the field will, by necessity, cover this population more extensively than that of children and youth who are not in state custody. However, insuring the well-being, including healthy development, of all children and youth touched by the child welfare system remains the ultimate goal.

Data from federal reviews of the child welfare systems of 52 states and territories conducted from 2001 to 2004 revealed that less than 50% of states were considered to have substantially met the physical and mental health needs of children and youth (U.S. Department of Health and Human Services 2004).

Background

Until recently, there have been no efforts on a nationwide basis to track the health status of children and adolescents served by the child welfare system. Findings from the National Survey of Child and Adolescent Well-Being (NSCAW) are being reported currently. The Children's Bureau has undertaken NSCAW to learn about the experiences of children, youth, and families who come in contact with the child welfare system. NSCAW is gathering information associated with more than 6,200 children from public child welfare agencies in a stratified random sample of 92 localities across the United States. The first national longitudinal study of its kind, NSCAW is examining the characteristics, needs, experiences, and outcomes for these children, youth, and families. The study, authorized under the Personal Responsibility and

Work Opportunity Reconciliation Act of 1996, also will provide information about crucial program, policy, and practice issues of concern to the federal government, state and local governments, and child welfare agencies (Administration for Children and Families 2003). Other studies, conducted over the past decade in a number of states and localities, have examined a variety of health indicators and repeatedly documented that this population of children and youth has many unmet health needs. The vast majority of research studies have focused on children and youth in out-of-home foster care placements. Far less is known about the health status of children who come to the attention of the child welfare system but remain in their own homes or those who are in kinship care placements, although there is increasing evidence that these children and youth are at risk for poor health outcomes as well (e.g., see Leslie, Gordon, Ganger, & Gist 2002). (Final results from the NSCAW, not yet available, will provide longitudinal data on a national sample of children and youth who are in their own homes as well as in foster care.)

Children and youth in their own homes tend to receive fewer health and mental healthcare services than do those who are in foster care. Results from Child and Family Services Reviews in 35 states from 2002 to 2004 indicated that 85% of children in foster care received services to meet their physical health needs compared to 78% of those in their own homes. Also, 80% of children in foster care received mental health services to meet their needs compared to 65% of those in their own homes (Administration for Children and Families 2004). A U.S. General Accounting Office (1995) report found that young people placed with relatives received fewer health-related services of all kinds than did their peers placed with non-relative foster parents, as relatives received less monitoring and assistance from caseworkers.

Concern about the poor health status of children and youth in foster care led both the

Child Welfare League of America and the American Academy of Pediatrics to issue healthcare standards for children and youth in out-of-home care (American Academy of Pediatrics 1994, 2000; Child Welfare League of America 1988). These standards address policies and procedures for, among other things, assessing health needs, providing health services, and training caregivers and caseworkers. However, the standards have not been widely implemented among states and communities. In a recent nationwide survey (Halfon et al. 2002), only one-third of state child welfare agencies responding to the survey reported having adopted Child Welfare League of America/American Academy of Pediatrics standards. Instead, changes in the delivery of health services have been largely driven by lawsuits resulting in consent decrees (Halfon & Klee 1991).

Data from the federal reviews of 52 child welfare systems revealed that states are performing better on systemic factors than they are on improving actual child and family outcomes, including well-being outcomes. Systemic factors reviewed included statewide information system; service array; quality assurance system; case review system; agency responsiveness to the community; staff training; and foster and adoptive parent licensing, recruitment, and retention. The reviews examined the records of a sample of 50 children in each state and talked with the children, caregivers, and other stakeholders. The reviews determined whether states met (obtained "substantial conformity" on) a number of outcome indicators. To obtain substantial conformity, the state had to achieve the outcome for 90% of the individuals in the sample. Only one of the 32 states reviewed in the initial group of reviews was considered to have substantially met the physical and mental health needs of children and youth. This result has further reinforced the need for local, state, and federal agencies to focus on improving healthcare services for children in care.

Healthcare Needs of Children in the Child Welfare System

Most children involved in the child welfare system have certain risks to their health and development by virtue of the conditions that brought them to the system's attention. These conditions include physical, sexual, or emotional abuse, neglect, prenatal drug exposure, domestic violence, unstable living arrangements, and poverty. Children who are separated from their families and placed in state protective custody have additional vulnerabilities and needs related to placement itself. For these young people, existing risk factors may be exacerbated due to the trauma of separation from their families and by frequent placement changes. Silver, Amster, and Haecker (1999) describe how these effects can be particularly profound for very young children who are placed in foster care, whose health and development may be undermined by a lack of secure and stable attachments.

An additional health concern posed by entry into foster care is that many children come into the system with very little information about their birth and their developmental or health history. Child welfare workers often cite difficulty in obtaining this information at the time a child is removed from the home. This lack of information can lead to delays in provision of appropriate health services and can pose a safety issue for children with unknown health conditions, such as allergies, asthma, or seizure disorder, and for those who are on medications.

During the 1990s, there was increased attention to the needs and health issues for children in foster care. A 1994 policy statement by the American Academy of Pediatrics (1994) revealed that children and youth in foster care suffer much higher rates of serious emotional and behavioral problems, birth defects, chronic physical disabilities, developmental delays, and poor school achievement compared to those from similar socioeconomic backgrounds that were not in foster care. Similarly, a U.S. General Accounting Office (1995) report claimed that foster children are among the most vulnerable individuals in the welfare population and as a group, they are sicker than children and youth who are homeless and those living in the poorest sections of inner cities. A study of healthcare issues for California's foster care population (Institute for Research on Women and Families 1998) found that 40% to 76% of children in the state's foster care system had chronic medical conditions, and 50% to 60% had moderate-to-severe mental health problems. More recently, NSCAW found that more than 25% of the 700 children in the One-Year-in-Foster-Care sample have some type of recurring physical or mental health problem. NSCAW also assessed children's functioning on developmental measures and found that those in out-of-home care tended to fall marginally below the norm compared with the general population on nearly every measure, including measures of cognitive capacities, language development, behavioral problems, and academic achievement (Administration for Children and Families 2003).

These and other studies reveal that not only do children enter the child welfare system at greater risk for poor health outcomes, but on the whole, current systems are also not adequately addressing the complex healthcare needs of these youngsters in state protective custody. Particularly prominent gaps exist in access to needed dental services, mental health services, substance abuse services, and adolescent health services, including reproductive health services (e.g., see McCarthy 2002).

For any youth, adolescence is a journey between the ages of 10 and 18. During these years, youth experience enormous physical, mental, emotional, social, behavioral, and sexual changes, with many ups and downs, periods of turmoil and tranquility, and periods of transition and transformation (Howze 2002:1). Those youth in the child welfare system experience even greater disruption than do others. Everyone involved with adolescents, including

their social workers, must be ready for the ride and willing to include youth as central actors in planning for their own futures. One young woman, who was in foster care from age 11 through 18, poignantly describes what it felt like, at 15, to be left out of the planning process:

> My case review was scheduled for the middle of the afternoon. I had to get permission to leave school and go to the agency office. I arrived a little late, and the review had already started. They talked about my grades, my foster parents, and my birth mom. I listened to the conversation. Near the end, my social worker presented the plan for me to sign. I looked at it and discovered that in the health section, it said, "Begin taking birth control pills." I was astonished. At that point in my life, I had never had sex, I had no boyfriend, and I did not need birth control pills. I asked why this was part of the plan. My worker said that they wanted to be sure that I didn't get pregnant. It really upset me that everyone at the table assumed that I was sexually active, and that no one knew me well enough to know how I felt about my own sexuality. I refused to sign the plan.

Challenges to Meeting the Healthcare Needs of Children in the Child Welfare System

Even in a perfect system, the extent and complexity of the healthcare needs of children in the child welfare system would present challenges to providing appropriate care. The challenges to providing healthcare both for young people in state custody and those living in their own homes arise from impediments in the child welfare and healthcare systems and from difficulties coordinating care across systems.

Challenges in the Child Welfare System

Many child welfare agencies face system-wide problems, such as high caseloads, limited resources, and high rates of turnover in social workers, attorneys, and foster parents. These problems affect their ability to insure comprehensive healthcare for the children they serve.

In addition, specific healthcare-related barriers experienced in the child welfare system include:

- Confusion about who is responsible for consenting to evaluation and treatment of children in foster care and difficulty in obtaining that consent;
- Poor integration of healthcare plans and permanency plans (e.g., a reluctance to make healthcare and health plans a priority, viewing permanency and safety goals as separate and more critical than health and well-being);
- Lack of knowledge about healthcare issues among some social workers and caregivers;
- Missing information about child and family health history and inadequate strategies for gathering this information from parents or other caregivers;
- Inconsistent efforts to include birth parents in the healthcare of their children and youth; and
- Lack of transition supports and continuity of care when a child returns home, changes placements, is adopted, or moves into the adult system.

Challenges in the Healthcare System

The principal funding source for both health and behavioral health services for children in the child welfare system is Medicaid. In most states, close to 100% of children in foster care are eligible for publicly funded health insurance through Medicaid. Many publicly funded healthcare systems face challenges serving their constituencies. These difficulties are compounded for children in the child welfare system who need access to providers who understand and can meet their intensive and multilayered needs. Some specific challenges include:

- Insufficient service capacity and access to care (e.g., a lack of qualified providers to serve children and families on Medicaid; a shortage of dentists who accept Medic-

aid; long waiting lists for mental health services);
- Low reimbursement rates for Medicaid providers;
- Delays in obtaining Medicaid coverage when children enter foster care; and
- Loss of coverage at transition points, such as exiting foster care or placement changes.

In addition, healthcare systems are traditionally administered separately from child welfare systems, and healthcare providers do not have ready access to information about how the child welfare system works. Providers frequently are confused about the roles of foster and birth parents, as well as about issues regarding consent for treatment and the role of the court in ordering and monitoring healthcare services.

In most states and communities, Medicaid recipients receive healthcare services in managed care systems that are intended to promote access to needed services and improve quality while controlling costs and reducing overutilization of services. Managed care may pose unique barriers for children in the child welfare system, particularly if the managed care is not designed to accommodate the complex healthcare needs of this population.

Cross-System Challenges

Creating a comprehensive system for meeting the healthcare needs of children in the child welfare system requires multiple systems to work together. Cross-system challenges in working with the courts, child welfare, and health and mental healthcare systems include:

- Clarifying among systems the roles and responsibilities for health and mental health service provision;
- Strengthening communication between healthcare providers and child welfare workers;
- Integrating physical health and mental healthcare;
- Persuading courts to discuss child and family health needs during court proceedings;

- Navigating complicated management information systems and sharing incompatible data formats across systems;
- Addressing confidentiality issues about access to data;
- Working with inflexible funding sources; and
- Overcoming the lack of consistent cross-system training and education.

Forging Links across Systems to Meet the Healthcare Needs of Young People in the Child Welfare System

Although child welfare is the system responsible for insuring the safety, permanency, and well-being of its charges, it must forge links with families and with other systems to accomplish these goals. As the primary caregiver, a child's family (birth, relative, foster, or adoptive) can make or break a well-thought-out health plan. Families provide daily care; they observe and understand their children's strengths and needs, and they are responsible for insuring that their children have regularly scheduled appointments with healthcare providers. Without support for and from the family, it is difficult to guarantee that a child's healthcare needs will be met.

Most of the healthcare services needed by those served in the child welfare system are available through the healthcare system, not from the child welfare agency itself. As the challenges listed above indicate, barriers to comprehensive healthcare are a cross-system problem. Improving access to quality services requires a cross-system approach involving at a minimum the child welfare, health, mental health, substance abuse, early intervention, education, juvenile justice, and court systems.

The judicial role in decisionmaking for children in the child welfare system is unique as the courts are actively involved in planning for such children. In most states, judges have the final authority to make decisions about the need for placement of a child, and they are charged with approving plans for a child's care when the child is under protective supervision. In some states, this authority extends to ordering or approving healthcare services for the child or the child's parents (Battistelli 1996). Every court proceeding presents an opportunity to inquire about a child's health needs and order appropriate health services (New York State Permanent Judicial Commission on Justice for Children 1999).

Framework for a Comprehensive Approach to Healthcare

As discussed earlier in this chapter, children in the child welfare system have multiple and complex health and developmental needs. Attending fully to their needs requires the creation of a comprehensive, community-based healthcare system that includes a number of specific components. In *Meeting the health care needs of children in the foster care system,* McCarthy (2002) defines the components needed in a comprehensive system, as discussed below. This framework reflects practices and strategies offered in many states and communities; national healthcare standards such as those developed by the Child Welfare League of America (1989) and the American Academy of Pediatrics (1994); and the values embraced by community-based systems of care that serve children with mental health needs (Pires 2002; Stroul & Friedman 1994). A system of care incorporates a broad array of services and supports that is organized into a coordinated network, integrates care planning and management across multiple levels, is culturally and linguistically competent, and builds meaningful partnerships with families and youth at service delivery and policy levels.

Critical Components

The critical components of the comprehensive approach include:

- Initial screening and comprehensive health assessment;
- Access to healthcare services and treatment;

- Management of healthcare data and information;
- Coordination of care;
- Collaboration among systems;
- Family participation;
- Attention to cultural issues;
- Monitoring and evaluation;
- Training and education;
- Funding strategies; and
- Tailoring of managed care to fit the needs of the child welfare population.

The framework highlights the kinds of issues to consider when designing a comprehensive approach to healthcare for children in the child welfare system. It is used by states and communities to assess their healthcare systems, prioritize the steps involved in transformation, and envision what a comprehensive, well-functioning system should look like. The comprehensive framework is not a prescription for change, but rather a catalyst to prompt and guide discussion and planning. Provided below are definitions of each component, as well as features, characteristics, and some strategies that are effective in implementing the components.

Initial Screening and Comprehensive Health Assessment

In the comprehensive framework, initial health screenings and comprehensive health assessments are provided, as needed, for any child in the child welfare system. All children who enter foster care receive an initial health screening upon entry to identify health problems that require immediate attention. Comprehensive health assessments of those in foster care are conducted shortly after placement, at regular intervals during their stay in out-of-home placement, and as they reunify with their families or move to another placement.

Both screenings and assessments are conducted by qualified providers, in comfortable, accessible settings and are appropriate to a child's age, culture, and individual situation.

Comprehensive assessments are more extensive than initial screens and address a child's physical, dental, mental/emotional, and developmental strengths and needs. They focus on the child, the family, and the environment in which the child lives. Initial screens and comprehensive assessments often confirm suspicions and provide valuable information to help parents, caregivers, schools, judges, social service workers, and heathcare providers understand the child better and meet the child's healthcare needs more appropriately. Key features and characteristics of this component include:

- Implementing a strategy for obtaining child and family health history;
- Implementing a system to identify and refer all children and youth who enter out-of-home care;
- Providing accessible screening and assessment sites (i.e., within a reasonable distance of the child's home and open for extended hours);
- Minimizing the trauma a child is experiencing by making the screening and assessment as comfortable as possible;
- Involving informed adult participants who know the child well to provide needed information and comfort the child;
- Individualizing each assessment, and insuring that assessment tools are culturally appropriate;
- Recognizing the unique needs of adolescents in the child welfare system;
- Using providers with the experience, knowledge, and skill to work with children and youth in the child welfare system;
- Sharing results with the child or youth, family, out-of-home caregivers, other providers, social services, and the court when appropriate;
- Following up systematically on recommended care;
- Assessing the strengths, needs, and medical histories of other members of the child's family;

- Reassessing at strategic intervals, such as when youth leave foster care to live independently and when children or youth return home or change placements;
- Presuming that every child who enters foster care will be eligible for Medicaid, which allows for immediate screening, assessment, and emergency services; and
- Adhering to Medicaid's Early and Periodic Screening, Diagnosis, and Treatment program (EPSDT) standards.

The importance of gathering health history and family medical history prior to or at the time of a child's placement and immediately providing this information to a child's caregivers cannot be overstated. Without this information, both the child's caregivers and healthcare providers are forced to manage a child's routine and emergency healthcare "in the dark." The safety of children cannot be guaranteed if their medical history is unknown when they move into out-of-home placements. The following case example of a 3-year-old child, Tamika, illustrates this point (adapted from Silver, Amster, & Haecker 1999).

TAMIKA

Tamika was brought to the emergency room by ambulance, having just had a seizure in her foster parent's home. Ms. Bordon, the foster mother, although visibly shaken, tried to answer the questions of the medical staff. However, she did not know if Tamika had a history of seizures, whether she was allergic to anything, or whether she was on medication. There had been an unmarked bottle of pills given to Ms. Bordon when Tamika was placed with her, but she had been afraid to administer them because she did not know what they were or how they were to be taken. No medical information had accompanied Tamika when she had been placed 1 week before. Tamika had seemed well, although she did not talk as much as Ms. Bordon's own children at this age. The seizure had come on suddenly and lasted 15 to 20 minutes.

Access to Healthcare Services and Treatment

In the comprehensive framework, children are able to access both primary and specialty healthcare services. Strategies to insure access are addressed (i.e., immediate eligibility for Medicaid, transportation, no waiting lists, availability of providers who know and understand the needs of children and youth in the child welfare system, location of healthcare services, levels of care to meet specific needs, and payment sources for services).

In addition, emphasis is on providing a comprehensive array of healthcare services, from prevention to intensive intervention, that address the special physical, dental, emotional, and developmental healthcare needs of children in the child welfare system. Family support services that enable caregivers to attend to a child's healthcare needs also are available.

Different strategies exist to help children and youth in the child welfare system access appropriate services. In some locales, agency social workers have this responsibility; in others, healthcare consultants are available to assist child welfare staff or there are healthcare providers on site at the child welfare agency. Children may receive healthcare services from individual providers in the community, through foster care clinics, through community-based clinics, or through special networks of healthcare providers created to serve young people in the child welfare system. Key features and characteristics of this component include:

- An established system for accessing care. Procedures are in place for access to primary care physicians, regular well-child exams, immunizations, specialty care, and consultation with medical experts. These procedures are applicable for all children in the system. The system supports individual social workers, parents, and caregivers so that they do not have to establish procedures on a case-by-case basis.

- Strategies for recruiting and training qualified providers who are located near the children, their families, and their out-of-home caregivers. These include incentives for providers to participate and established qualifications for those who do participate. Such strategies expand the array of services available.
- Established protocols for emergency response, so that families and out-of-home caregivers have uninterrupted access to staff and providers on call.
- Community liaisons, such as public health nurses and mental health clinicians knowledgeable about community resources, to facilitate access to services. These liaisons are often located in the child welfare agency.

It is important that all children, including those in out-of-home placements, have an established relationship with a healthcare practitioner who knows and understands their needs. This practitioner can also serve as a resource for social workers when health issues need to be considered in the service planning process. The following comment from a child's foster care worker illustrates the benefits of establishing such ongoing relationships with healthcare providers:

> I work with a child, Reggie, who is medically fragile, and so have requested help from the pediatrician at the foster care clinic on numerous occasions. The pediatrician has been able to offer her invaluable opinion on the skills that foster parents need to care for Reggie. Another time, I asked the clinic to call the hospital when I felt that the hospital was going to release Reggie too soon. I feel that he would not have received the attention he needed if this had not been done. The pediatrician has also written letters to the court for me at trial time, so that the judge would have a better understanding of Reggie's special needs.

Management of Healthcare Data and Information

The framework insures that information about a child's healthcare and health status is gathered, organized, retained, and shared in a way that assures the information is complete, updated regularly, and available to persons closely involved with the care of the child.

Healthcare history information about the child and family is gathered at the time of the initial contact. Relevant information about healthcare is transferred when children enter or leave the child welfare system. An organized method for documenting, storing, updating, and sharing health information about each individual child (e.g., through a health passport or a computerized information system) is in place. Health data related to individual children can be aggregated to determine system-wide needs, gaps in services, outcomes, and policies. For children in foster care, one method for managing their healthcare records is by using "health passports" (known in some communities as "medical passports"). Passports usually include medical history, demographic information, immunization records, healthcare visit summaries, medications, test results, growth information, insurance information, and other special health, mental health, and developmental information. Some passports include educational information and a child's placement history. The passport is designed to move with the child from placement to placement and to be given to birth or adoptive parents when a child leaves the foster care system (Woolverton 2002). Although passports are commonly used, there are a number of barriers to using them successfully. Paper passports can be lost when children move, and it is difficult to insure that they will be completed regularly and kept up to date. Using electronic passports requires extensive clerical support, often not available in child welfare agencies.

In addition to healthcare passports, other data management methods include using standardized health forms, using computerized management information systems, integrating healthcare data in service planning, and aggregating healthcare data. Key features and characteristics important to implementing these data management strategies include the following.

Healthcare passports. Determine whether manual (paper) or electronic passports are most useful; decide who will be responsible for creating and updating the passport; establish procedures for gathering child and family health history information at the time of placement; decide who will hold the record; provide incentives for providers and foster parents to use and complete the passports, insure adequate clerical support, and guarantee that the passport accompanies children and youth when they move.

Standardized health forms. Use these forms to record the results of children and youth's health exams and doctor visits, insure that children receive healthcare according to EPSDT standards, and provide a permanent, uniform, centralized healthcare data record for each child.

Computerized management information systems. Use them to track and monitor services provided for each child, as a tickler system to identify when medical appointments are to occur, and to share healthcare information online among social workers, providers, and care coordinators.

Integration of healthcare data in service planning. Review healthcare summaries on individual children during administrative case review processes, court hearings, in child and family team meetings, and during home visits with the caretakers.

Aggregation/analysis of healthcare data. Identify emerging health issues for children, service gaps, and resource needs by aggregating healthcare data collected on individual children utilize data to assist in making appropriate policy and practice decisions and to determine trends, such as whether children with certain health problems remain in the system or experience more placements.

Coordination of Care

In the comprehensive framework, responsibility for coordination of healthcare is assigned to a specific person (e.g., care coordinator, medical case manager) or unit (e.g., healthcare management unit, liaison office). An individualized child health plan that documents healthcare needs and services provided is developed and maintained for each child.

Coordination of a child's healthcare by a person or specified unit is extremely important to insure that the child's healthcare needs will be met. Many states and communities rely on nurses to fill the role of care coordinators and to develop healthcare plans for their patients in the child welfare system. Key features that contribute to effective care coordination include:

- The organizational structure supports assignment of healthcare coordination responsibilities to one or more persons. Sufficient time and resources are committed to care coordination. Care coordinators are trained both in healthcare and in understanding how the child welfare system works. Care coordinators have manageable caseloads.

- Healthcare coordinators insure that each child has a medical home. "Medical home" refers to a specific entity responsible for continuous management of a child's healthcare. The American Academy of Pediatrics supports a medical home approach for children with special healthcare needs. This approach is family-centered (i.e., recognizing the family as principal caregiver and pediatricians as partners with parents), continuous (the pediatrician is available through a child's life and transitions), coordinated, comprehensive, and culturally competent. The medical home might be a community-based primary-care physician or pediatrician, a foster care clinic, or a community-based clinic (Parent Educational Advocacy Training Center n.d.). In addition, healthcare coordinators insure that each child has an individualized healthcare plan that is integrated with his or her permanency plan. The healthcare coordinator supports integration of the child's physical and mental healthcare, follow-through on recommendations made by providers, and discussion of the child's health needs in all case reviews and court hearings. The care coordinator often serves as a bridge between the healthcare system, the child welfare system, and children's families and out-of-home caregivers.

Collaboration among Systems

Health, mental health, child welfare, juvenile justice, courts, education, and other systems serving children; providers; families; out-of-home caregivers; and community organizations collaborate to meet the healthcare needs of children in the child welfare system in a comprehensive framework approach. This collaboration may be approached in a variety of ways through co-location of staff, sharing of financial resources, cross-system training, inter-agency collaborative service and/or planning teams, advisory boards that are representative of the collaborators, or formal interagency agreements.

As stated before, the child welfare agency cannot establish a comprehensive framework for children's healthcare alone. Providing appropriate healthcare requires a cross-systems approach for individual children and families as well as for system-level reform. Features that facilitate cross-system collaboration include:

- Devising strategies for consistent informal and formal communication across systems, such as interagency team meetings, memoranda of understanding and inter-agency agreements, designated liaisons, sharing office space, cross-system training on healthcare issues, and formal contracts;

- Facilitating participation of community-based agencies, such as local health departments and clinics;
- Providing courts with healthcare information about individual children so that they can make informed decisions; and
- Harnessing the influence of the courts to order needed services.

Family Participation

From the comprehensive framework perspective, families—birth, relative, foster, and adoptive—are viewed as partners in providing healthcare. They are involved as vital sources of information about the child's healthcare history, needs, and ongoing care, and to insure continuity of care in the transition from out-of-home care to permanent placements. A child's healthcare is addressed in the context of his or her family's strengths, needs, culture, beliefs, and environment. Families receive support services that will enhance their capacity to provide for their children's healthcare needs. Families also are included at the system level in planning, implementing, and evaluating strategies for providing healthcare.

Children in the child welfare system may be included in several types of family. They may live with, or be working toward reunification with, their birth parents. They may live with extended family members who serve as their guardians, an arrangement often called "kinship care." They may live with foster families, and those who cannot return to their birth families may be adopted. Insuring family participation entails listening to, involving, and addressing the needs of all of these families. However, this ideal is not always realized. As mentioned previously, findings from the federal review of 52 child welfare systems demonstrated that children living in their own homes are less likely to receive adequate physical and mental health services than are those in foster care (Administration for Children and Families 2004). Even though approximately 70% of children in the system are reunified with their birth parents or other relatives, efforts in many states and communities to include families in planning for their children's healthcare focus more on foster parents than on a child's birth parents or relatives (McCarthy, 2002). Families are a wonderful resource for system-level planning. They are the ones with the expertise to pinpoint needed resources and recommend policy changes. However, many communities find it difficult to create a structure or systematic strategies to reach out to families from the child welfare system and request their input.

In spite of these continuing challenges, some key features for promoting family participation include:

- Family-friendly strategies for gathering health history and consent from parents when children are placed in foster care;
- Participation of parents and out-of-home caregivers in their children and youth's healthcare visits;
- Home visits by nurses to provide specialized training about a child's specific healthcare needs and to support parents and other caregivers in obtaining follow-up care;
- Provision of needed healthcare for other family members; and
- Focus groups with families and evaluation of family satisfaction with healthcare services.

Attention to Cultural Issues

A knowledge of the diverse cultures represented among the children and families served by the child welfare system influences program development in a comprehensive framework for children's healthcare. This knowledge is used in the creation of the provider network, during staff training, and in the design and delivery of healthcare services to meet the needs of individuals from these different cultures.

The system incorporates an understanding of how people's cultures and beliefs shape their view of health and illness. Traditional and non-traditional approaches to healthcare are offered. The system is responsive to diverse children, youth, and families, including those with limited English proficiency, low literacy skills, and/or disabilities.

Providing culturally competent healthcare services for children in the child welfare system is a challenge in many communities. A 3-year study by the Georgetown University Child Development Center (McCarthy 2002) found that many communities in the study did not collect data to substantiate the number of children and families served from various cultures. They identified challenges more easily than strengths related to providing culturally competent healthcare services. Challenges included:

- Assessment tools that are not adapted for different cultures;
- Assessment teams that are primarily white working with children who are primarily of color;
- Pediatricians who have difficulty working with families of different cultures;
- Difficulty finding providers who speak the language of the children served; and
- Written reports that are not translated into a family's native language.

Characteristics that do facilitate the delivery of culturally competent healthcare for children and youth in the child welfare system include:

- Recruiting culturally and linguistically diverse providers who reflect the population being served;
- Developing community-based provider networks and locating clinics in the neighborhoods where children live;
- Making health passports and other written materials available in the child's or family's primary language;
- Implementing cultural competence training for child welfare and healthcare staff;
- Implementing therapeutic interventions based in the child's culture; and
- Using trained medical interpreters.

Families are usually the best resources for information about their children's healthcare needs, but some social workers, and frequently the "system" itself, do not take advantage of their knowledge, as illustrated in the following case example (McCarthy et al. 2003:25).

JOYCE

Joyce, the parent of two young children, put it this way, "At first, it was hard to work on the plan. I didn't feel like I was a member of the team; most of them were strangers. I wasn't really involved in the plan, but I still showed up for every meeting. I heard harsh things about what they said that I had done and what I had not done for my children."

"In the beginning, it felt like they were talking over my head. My mother and sister were taking care of my kids. Catena was 4 weeks old when I left her with my mother. She was born drug affected. They talked more to my mother than they did to me. I was doing what I was supposed to do. I had gone to treatment and was 90 days sober, but they still didn't talk to me. I knew something about my children—things that only a mother knows. I wanted to tell them that Catena was colicky and Tyrone had the shakes, but they asked my mother about this, instead of me."

"I put my hand on the table and said, 'Please talk to me.' When the team couldn't hear what I was saying, I wrote a personal letter for my worker to read to the team. She read it at the meeting. This really helped. It was the icebreaker for me."

Monitoring and Evaluation

Monitoring and evaluation in a comprehensive framework for children's healthcare insures that the healthcare procedures developed for children are actually being followed. Health outcomes for children are tracked; family, child, and provider satisfaction are assessed; and cost effectiveness is examined. Improvements are made based on the results of this monitoring system.

Many states and communities find it difficult to determine and track individual child health outcomes. They are more likely to assess whether healthcare procedures are being followed than to ascertain change in the children's health status. This tendency is due to a lack of resources and funding devoted to assessing health outcomes and to the short duration of involvement of many children with the child welfare system. The more common types of monitoring and evaluation activities include:

- Measurement of adherence to procedural requirements (e.g., tracking the number of children and youth who receive initial health screenings and comprehensive assessments, the percentage of children and youth who are assigned a primary care physician, the percentage of children and youth with up-to-date immunizations);
- Follow-up care compliance (e.g., tracking whether the recommendations made in assessments are actually followed, tracking whether children with special healthcare needs receive appropriate services, determining whether children who meet the criteria for enrollment in early intervention services through Part C of Individuals with Disabilities Education Act [P.L. 105-17] actually enrolled);
- Monitoring provider performance;
- Measuring child and family satisfaction; and
- Tracking achievement of service plan goals.

Training and Education

As one component of establishing a comprehensive healthcare approach, training is offered to parents, caregivers, healthcare providers, child welfare staff, and other stakeholders. Training is individualized to fit the audience and may focus on such issues as general health and developmental information, special healthcare needs of children and adolescents in the child welfare system, access to resources and services, healthcare policies and procedures, and operation of the child welfare system.

Parents, youth, and caregivers participate as cotrainers, helping others to learn from their experiences. Specific training about how to meet an individual child's special healthcare needs is provided for caregivers. Cross-system training is a vehicle for helping the child welfare and healthcare systems work well together.

Features that facilitate training about healthcare for children and youth in the child welfare system include:

- Institutionalizing training about healthcare issues for children and adolescents in the child welfare system at all levels (e.g., as part of new-worker training, in-service training, core training for new foster parents, ongoing training for experienced foster parents);
- Providing hands-on training for families whose children have special medical needs (provided by nurses in the families' homes);
- Conducting informal consultation that occurs when healthcare and child welfare staff are located in the same office, when nurses are included in multidisciplinary team meetings, and when parents and foster parents make clinic and doctor visits with their children;
- Providing cross-system training (i.e., new social work staff and new foster care nurses participate in the same orientation sessions); and
- Providing training for students and interns (e.g., rotations in foster care clinics that are part of teaching hospitals).

Funding Strategies

State and community leaders understand how to use a variety of funding resources that are targeted for different aspects of healthcare (e.g., treatment services, care coordination, data management, administration, training). Flexibility in funding strategies is encouraged, waivers are requested, and different Medicaid options are pursued when necessary to insure comprehensive healthcare services for children and youth in the child welfare system. Child-serving agencies enter into interagency agreements around the transfer of funds from one agency to another when needed to maximize funding resources.

Medicaid and state funds are the primary funding sources for health and mental health services for children in the child welfare system; however, other sources are also used. Strategies for funding comprehensive healthcare services for children and youth in the child welfare system include:

- Using Medicaid funds strategically to cover administrative costs, case management, and clinical services;
- Offering enhanced Medicaid rates for screening and assessing children in foster care;
- Creating mechanisms to cover administrative costs (e.g., using special state budget allocations to cover administrative costs that are not funded through Medicaid, through a contracted arrangement with an organization that manages the system);
- Pursuing funding from different sources and sharing the cost of services among the different systems (e.g., if a parent or a family member other than the identified child is not eligible for Medicaid, the child welfare agency may pay for healthcare services for these family members); and
- Using incentives to encourage provider involvement and the provision of special services (e.g., fiscal incentives to motivate providers to complete health passports, patient management fees to help recruit pediatricians for long-term service).

Tailoring Managed Care

When children in the child welfare system are included in publicly funded managed care plans, the comprehensive approach insures that their special needs are addressed in the design of the managed care system, contracts, the setting of capitation and case rates, the makeup of provider networks, and development of special provisions. Special provisions might relate to eligibility, enrollment, authorization of services, medical necessity criteria, the available service array, data collection, provider rates, and tracking outcomes.

Mechanisms exist to solve problems that arise from managed care and to insure access, continuity of care (especially when children change placements), services for family members (in addition to the identified child), and understanding of the unique needs of this population. Training and ongoing support are offered to families to assist them in navigating the managed care system.

Most states and communities now offer publicly funded healthcare services through some form of managed care. A national survey conducted in 2003 confirmed that 74% of the managed care systems responding to the survey cover children and youth in the child welfare system that are eligible for Medicaid. Sixty-six percent of the managed care systems cover children in state custody. In 90% of these systems, the enrollment of children in custody is mandatory rather than voluntary, and 42% of the systems covering these children are responsible for screening them as they enter custody to identify mental health problems and treatment needs (Stroul, Pires, & Armstrong 2004).

Many parents who experience the multiple stresses that lead to involvement with the child welfare system need health, mental health, and substance abuse services and supports that are offered through managed care systems. If their needs are not identified and addressed by the managed care system, it will be more difficult to insure the safety, permanency, and well-being of their children (McCarthy & McCullough 2003).

Features that contribute to making managed care work for children and families in the child welfare system include:

- Participation by the child welfare system in the design, implementation, and evaluation of the managed care system, and a commitment by the managed care organizations to serving children and families served by the child welfare system;
- Institutionalized problem-solving strategies and communication structures between the managed care and child welfare systems to address problems that inevitably occur (i.e., special liaisons or units in the child welfare agency who work closely with the managed care organization); and
- An established process to assist families and social workers in understanding and navigating the managed care system.

Ethical Issues and Values Dilemmas

As states and communities develop strategies for insuring that children and youth in the child welfare system have access to appropriate healthcare services, they grapple with a number of complex issues. It is important to recognize that in implementing any specific approach, there will be necessary trade-offs that need to be considered from multiple perspectives in advance of implementation. Consider the five examples discussed below.

Location of Initial Screening Sites

Communities seeking to provide screenings for all young people who are removed from their homes will likely seek to have screenings take place as soon as possible and in nearby locations. Thus some children are taken to hospital emergency rooms or are screened in emergency receiving centers. However, in setting up screening systems, the perspective of the child must be considered as well. Children and youth enter foster care in the midst of a crisis. Their comfort and state of mind should be considered as factors in selecting screening locations and procedures. Screening personnel must be sensitive to the child's situation, and utilize the screening as an opportunity to address how the child is coping with the crisis. Child Welfare League of America (1988:5) standards specify that screenings be conducted in the least traumatic way possible, and that "recognition must be given to the traumatic circumstances surrounding the child's entry into care."

Centralized vs. Community-Based Services

In terms of insuring that children and youth in care have continuity in the provision of their primary healthcare, it may be more efficient and effective to centralize care—for example, by establishing a specialized foster care clinic. Indeed, there is evidence to support that the presence of a foster care clinic in a community can improve immunization rates, reduce emergency hospitalizations, and improve placement stability for children with complex medical needs. Horowitz, Owens, and Simms (2000) found that children seen in a specialized foster care clinic were more likely to receive recommended follow-up services and to have developmental and mental health problems identified. Despite these advantages, children and families sometimes complain that centralized clinics limit choices for foster families that might wish to obtain care in their own communities, or to utilize providers who care for other members of the family. Some adolescents may also not wish to obtain healthcare in a setting associated with being in foster care, preferring to have their own provider.

Computerized Information Systems

We have stated earlier that coordinating healthcare across the many different systems requires the exchange of information and compatibility of data systems. This increased access to information needs to be balanced with confidentiality issues for the child and family. Protocols may need to be established to address the handling of confidential information, such as results of mental health assessments or HIV tests.

Parental Consent

Child welfare workers and healthcare providers are frequently frustrated by delays in procuring assessments and treatment for children. Such delays are often caused by confusion over who has the authority to consent for these services. In developing strategies to expedite issues of consent, it is important to involve birth parents in the process and educate them about the need for certain types of consent as it relates to their child's healthcare, as well as their rights to provide or deny consent. Youth in care who are over the age of 18 may consent to their own treatment.

Using Resources Fairly

Insuring that the same level of healthcare services is available to all children in the child welfare system—not just those in formal foster care—is a significant problem. The child welfare system is legally responsible (and under public scrutiny) for the care of those in its custody. It is also responsible for appropriate decisionmaking and services for children who live in their own homes and receive child protective services. In an era of scarce resources, it can be difficult to find strategies to insure equitable treatment of all clients of the child welfare system with respect to their healthcare needs.

Knowledge, Skills, and Attitudes

Child welfare stakeholders must be prepared to fill many different roles (e.g., direct service, management, administration) when designing, implementing, and participating in a system of healthcare services for children and their families. To effectively fulfill these roles requires certain knowledge, skills, and attitudes. The requisite knowledge includes understanding:

- Basic healthcare issues for any child (e.g., screening and assessment, check-ups, symptoms and treatments of common childhood diseases, immunization schedules and side effects);
- Child development and the characteristics of a variety of developmental disabilities (typical and atypical behaviors);
- Community healthcare resources;
- Legislation that guarantees care and services for certain children and youth (e.g., the Individuals with Disabilities Education Act);
- How Medicaid works;
- Principles, practice, and technology of managed care;
- Impact that a child's disabilities and special healthcare needs may have on his or her family; and
- Issues related to attachment and separation.

In addition, caseworkers must have the skills to be able to:

- Collaborate with healthcare providers, families, and schools;
- Interview children, youth, families, and healthcare providers—knowing the pertinent questions to ask;
- Determine when more information about specific healthcare issues is needed and to seek out the information;
- Navigate healthcare and managed care systems;
- Help families navigate the systems;
- Strategically access resources;
- Observe and recognize the warning signs of developmental delays, disabilities, and special healthcare needs;
- Make referrals for care;
- Follow up appropriately on recommendations;
- Monitor one's caseload to insure that no child falls through the cracks; and
- Integrate safety, permanency, and well-being in planning with the child and family, without sacrificing one goal for another.

Attitudes that frame an effective approach to a healthcare system include:

- Strength-based approach to service delivery;
- Belief in collaborative processes;
- Commitment to services that are provided within the context of the family and the community in which a child lives;
- Acknowledgment that a child's health and development influences his or her chance for safety, permanency, and well-being;
- Strong belief in partnering with families, including all families involved with the child;
- Support for a community-based approach in which the locus of services and the management and decisionmaking rest at the community level; and
- Respect for and attention to cultural diversity.

Conclusion

In this chapter, we have discussed the complex healthcare needs of children in the child welfare system and the enormous challenge this poses to communities to strengthen service capacity and create a comprehensive healthcare system that integrates health and social services for each child and family. In a comprehensive healthcare system, each child's physical health, mental health, and developmental needs should be identified and then addressed. The child welfare system should see that these tasks are performed in a predictable, timely, and thorough fashion. A designated person should be responsible for coordinating each child's care. Providers of services should be skilled, knowledgeable, and have sufficient time to devote to each child's needs, as well as the needs of parents and caregivers. Preventative healthcare should be instituted and maintained. Each child's progress should be monitored. Caregivers and birth parents should be fully informed and consulted about their children's healthcare. Intervention should be changed as circumstances change. All information should be documented and should follow each child in a seamless fashion.

Needless to say, achieving this goal of a comprehensive healthcare system entails a commitment of time and resources that may be scarce in the current environment. Many communities have been successful in developing and implementing promising approaches around one or more of the critical system components we have described. However, it is rare to find that any one community has fully addressed all of the components. In a time of scarce resources, it is even more crucial to demonstrate the value of a comprehensive healthcare system in terms of the outcomes achieved for children and families.

A comprehensive healthcare system enhances the ability of a state or community to achieve the three major goals of the child welfare system: safety, permanency, and well-being. For example, a child's safety cannot be insured if he or she requires medication that the family cannot afford, if an untreated medical condition creates undue stress in the family and the potential for abuse, or if his or her medical history is unknown when the child is placed in foster care. Foster parents who are unaware of a child's allergies or medical conditions (e.g., asthma) are not prepared to respond appropriately in a healthcare emergency. To insure a child's safety and avoid life-threatening situations, parents, caregivers, agency social workers, and providers must have a clear understanding of a child's healthcare needs and the services and supports required to meet those needs.

Improving access to healthcare enhances a child's chance for permanency. Access to adequate healthcare information assists parents, agencies, and courts in making appropriate placement decisions. Receiving appropriate healthcare services and supports increases the likelihood that a child's placement (temporary or permanent) will succeed and remain stable.

For a child or youth to achieve well-being, his or her issues of physical and mental health must be addressed and the developmental and educational needs of the child or youth must be met. In addition, parents must receive the services they need to enhance their capacity to provide for their children. Early and comprehensive care enhances a child's chance for healthy development, provides supports for caregivers, can reverse bleak prognoses, and can strengthen families and enhance permanency (New York State Permanent Judicial Commission on Justice for Children 1999). Whether the goal is reunification with their birth families or another permanent plan, such as adoption, legal guardianship, or independent living, children and youth benefit from appropriate healthcare services, and parents benefit from education and support services related to their children's care.

REFERENCES

Administration for Children and Families. (2003). *National survey of child and adolescent well-being—Baseline report for one-year-in-foster-care sample*. Retrieved June 30, 2004, from www.acf.hhs.gov/programs/core/ongoing_research/afc/wellbeing_reports.html#wave.

Administration for Children and Families. (2004). *Key findings from the initial Child and Family Service Reviews 2001 to 2004*. Retrieved October 30, 2004, from www.acf.hhs.gov/programs/cb/cwrp/results/index.htm.

Adoption and Safe Families Act. (1997). P.L. 105-89.

American Academy of Pediatrics. (1994). Health care of children in foster care. *Pediatrics, 93*(2), 335–338.

American Academy of Pediatrics. (2000). Developmental issues for young children in foster care. *Pediatrics, 106*(5), 1145–1150.

Battistelli, E. (1996). *Making managed health care work for kids in foster care: A guide to purchasing services.* Washington, DC: CWLA Press.

Child Welfare League of America. (1988*). Standards for health care services for children in out-of-home care.* Washington, DC: Child Welfare League of America.

Halfon, N., Inkelas, M., Flint, R., Shoaf, K., Zepeda, A., & Franke, T. (2002). *Assessment of factors influencing the adequacy of health care services to children in foster care.* Los Angeles: UCLA Center for Healthier Children, Families and Communities.

Halfon, N., & Klee, L. (1991). Health and development services for children with multiple needs. *Yale Law Policy Review, 9,* 71–96.

Horowitz, S. M., Owens, P., & Simms, M. D. (2000). Specialized assessments for children in foster care. *Pediatrics, 106,* 59–66.

Howze, K. (2002). *Health for teens in care—A judge's guide.* Washington, DC: American Bar Association.

Individuals with Disabilities Education Act. (1997). P.L. 105-17.

Institute for Research on Women and Families, California Foster Children's Health Project. (1998). *Code blue: Health services for children in foster care.* Sacramento: Center for California Studies, California State University.

Leslie, L. K., Gordon, J. N., Ganger, W., & Gist, K. (2002). Developmental delay in young children in child welfare by initial placement type. *Infant Mental Health Journal, 23,* 496–516.

McCarthy, J. (2002). *Meeting the health care needs of children in the foster care system: Summary of state and community efforts.* Washington, DC: Georgetown University Child Development Center.

McCarthy, J., Marshall, A., Collins, J., Arganza, G., Deserly, K., & Milon, J. (2003). *A family's guide to the child welfare system.* Washington, DC: Georgetown University Center for Child and Human Development.

McCarthy, J., & McCullough, C. (2003). *Promising approaches for behavioral health services to children and* adolescents and their families in managed care systems: A view from the child welfare system. Washington, DC: Georgetown University Center for Child and Human Development.

New York State Permanent Judicial Commission on Justice for Children. (1999). Ensuring the healthy development of foster children: A guide for judges, advocates, and child welfare professionals. White Plains: New York State Permanent Judicial Commission on Justice for Children.

Parent Educational Advocacy Training Center. (n.d.). A system of caregivers—Caring for children's health. Retrieved June 30, 2004, from www.peatc.org/FosterCare/children's_health_2.htm.

Personal Responsibility and Work Opportunities Act. (1996). P.L. 104-193.

Pires, S. (2002). Building systems of care: A primer. Washington, DC: National Technical Assistance Center for Children's Mental Health, Georgetown University Child Development Center.

Silver, J. A., Amster, B. J., & Haecker, T. (1999). Young children and foster care: A guide for professionals. Baltimore: Brookes Publishing.

Stroul, B. A., & Friedman, R. M. (1994). A system of care for children and youth with severe emotional distur-

bances, revised ed. Washington, DC: Georgetown University Child Development Center, Child and Adolescent Service System Program (CASSP) Technical Assistance Center.

Stroul, B. A., Pires, S. A., & Armstrong, M. I. (2004). Health care reform tracking project: Tracking state health care reforms as they affect children and adolescents with behavioral health disorders and their families—2003 state survey. Tampa: Research and Training Center for Children's Mental Health, Department of Child and Family Studies, Division of State and Local Support, Louis de la Parte Florida Mental Health Institute, University of South Florida.

U.S. Department of Health and Human Services. (2004). Summary results of the 52 CFSR reviews. Retrieved October 1, 2004, from www.acf.hhs.gov/programs/cb/cwrp/52results.

U.S. General Accounting Office. (1995). Foster care health needs of many young children are unknown and unmet. GAO/HEHS-95-114. Washington, DC: U.S. General Accounting Office.

Woolverton, M. (2002). Meeting the health care needs of children in the foster care system: Strategies for implementation. Washington, DC: Georgetown University Child Development Center.

MARTHA M. DORE

Child and Adolescent Mental Health

Lexy is the single parent of Patti, 14, Julie, 11, and Tommy, 8. Tommy has pervasive developmental disorder and requires 24-hour-a-day special care. Each morning, Lexy gets up at 5 A.M. to begin preparing for her day. She throws a load of wash into the washing machine and feeds the cats before she showers and dresses, hoping against hope that Tommy will not wake up until she finishes putting on her makeup. The moment Tommy awakens, the turmoil begins. He calls out for her and if she does not appear immediately, he begins a high-pitched wail that quickly awakens Patti and Julie, sleeping in the next room. Next he begins banging his forehead on the wall, unless Lexy can quickly put his helmet on him to discourage this behavior. Then Lexy tries to persuade Tommy to use the bathroom and get dressed. Often, this results in a physical altercation with Tommy running out of the room and Lexy chasing him around the house to get him dressed. As he grows larger and larger, the effort increasingly leaves Lexy exhausted and disheveled by the time the van arrives at 8:00 A.M. to pick Tommy up for his day treatment program. On several occasions during the morning effort to get him ready for school, Tommy has run out of the house and into the street, with Lexy grabbing him and physically dragging him back into the house. She can only imagine what the neighbors are saying about her failures as a single parent.

Nancy and Bob Elliot dread the ringing of the telephone between the hours of nine and ten in the morning, the time the school calls to tell them that their 13-year-old daughter Annalee has left school again. Often, Nancy has barely removed her coat from driving Annalee to school and delivering her to the door of her homeroom when the call comes. Nancy gets back in the car and heads downtown to "the strip," an arcade that is the local hangout for high school dropouts, unemployed older men, and teenagers who have decided to cut school that day. She usually stops to pick up Bob at his office, as alone she cannot manage Annalee and, anyway, she tells herself, Annalee listens better to her father's booming directives. If they are lucky, Nancy and Bob will quickly spot Annalee's spikey dyed purple hair in the crowded arcade. Their daughter is usually hanging over the back of some leather jacketed, heavily tattooed older teenager, seated at one of the many video games, all of which seem to involve killing and destruction.

After a scene, which often includes a gathering crowd of threatening-looking teens who curse and shout comments at Nancy and Bob, drawing the attention of the arcade security guard, who asks all three of them to leave, the Elliots manage to get Annalee into the car and drive home, all the while listening to a diatribe from their daughter, telling them how much she hates them and threatening yet another suicide attempt (there have been three, all of which have resulted in brief psychiatric hospitalizations), or to run away from home and live on the streets like some of her friends on the strip. By the time they arrive home, Nancy is usually in tears, Bob is in a silent fury, and Annalee slams out of the car and locks herself in her room, refusing even to come out for dinner. On several occasions, the Elliots thought they detected the sweet smell of marijuana smoke drifting from under the locked door of Annalee's room.

Esther and Kevin Ross were thrilled when their caseworker with the public child welfare agency told them they had been approved as adoptive parents for 3-year-old Sammy, their foster son. They knew that Sammy had been born with crack in his system, and that he had spent the first 18 months of his life living with his homeless, crack-addicted mother who moved from man to man and place to place, occasionally landing in a homeless shelter where the staff would observe her harsh and careless treatment of her little boy. Finally, after several reports to protective services, as a result of which nothing was done, Sammy's mother left him in the care of a fellow homeless shelter resident to run to the store for milk and never returned. Sammy was taken into foster care and placed with the Rosses, a middle-aged couple whose own children were grown. The Rosses quickly fell in love with Sammy, who seemed to need them desperately, crying hysterically when either one of them left his sight for even a few minutes. Because the child welfare agency could not locate Sammy's mother, and had no identity for his father, the agency moved quickly to terminate parental rights and free Sammy for adoption by the eager Rosses.

After a very rocky first year of tantrums, night terrors, and eating and soiling problems, Sammy seemed to settle in to his adoptive home. It was not until he started preschool that the Rosses began to get complaints from the teachers and other parents that Sammy was hitting and biting other children, especially the boys, and was caught repeatedly trying to put his hands down little girls' pants. The Rosses two older children, who are both married with young children of their own, dropped by their parents' home less and less often. Their younger daughter finally confessed that she had caught Sammy lying on top of her 2-year-old daughter making sexual movements and that she and her sister were afraid that Sammy would physically harm their children. The Rosses contacted the child welfare agency that had placed Sammy with them for some direction and guidance, only to be told that once the child was adopted, because he was not identified as a special needs child, the agency's responsibility had ended.

In each of the situations described above, parents are struggling to manage the behavior of children with serious emotional and be-

havioral disturbances. Scenarios like these are repeated hundreds of times daily all over the United States. Current epidemiological studies estimate that 18% to 22% of children and adolescents suffer from serious difficulty in psychosocial functioning at any given time in this country, and that 5% to 8% of these children have problems severe enough to qualify as a mental illness (Brandenburg, Friedman, & Silver 1990; Costello, Messer, Bird, Cohen, & Reinherz 1998; Costello et al. 1996; Lavigne et al. 1996; Reinherz, Giaconia, Lefkowitz, Pakiz, & Frost 1993). These percentages translate into over four million young people in the United States who are currently in need of mental health services and treatment.

As the stories of Tommy, Annalee, and Sammy illustrate, mental health problems in children and adolescents can manifest themselves at any age, even in very young children, are more common in boys in the preteen years and in girls at adolescence, and negatively impact not only the child but other individuals in the child's environment as well, including parents, siblings, teachers, peers, and even neighbors. Since the early 1980s, the mental health community in the United States has continually sought ways to respond more effectively to the emotional and behavioral problems of children. There has been a series of federal studies of this issue, including the recently issued *Report of the Surgeon General's Conference on Children's Mental Health: A national action agenda* (U.S. Department of Health and Human Services 2000). Each of these studies has documented the extensive service needs in this area and the lack of access to services for a large portion of affected children, youth, and their families. Recent figures indicate that only about one in five children who need mental health services actually receives them (U.S. Department of Health and Human Services 1999). Among those living in poverty, in rural communities, and those who are members of minority groups, these figures are much lower (Flisher et al. 1997; Halfon, Inkelas, & Wood 1995; Owens et al.

2002). Schools are the entry point to the mental health system for the majority of children and adolescents, with the mental health and general healthcare systems a close second (Farmer, Burns, Phillips, Angold, & Costello 2003). Children's emotional and, especially, behavioral disorders are most often first identified in an educational setting, where teachers quickly become aware when a child's problems in functioning negatively impact the classroom as a whole, as did Sammy's.

Pediatricians and other healthcare providers are common sources of identification of serious problems in functioning in infants and toddlers. In Tommy's case, his mother, who had two older children, noticed when he was just a baby that Tommy did not respond to her as her girls had done as infants. His tiny body stiffened when she held him and, when she tried to make eye contact with Tommy as she nursed him, he looked away as though avoiding her gaze. Tommy also rarely slept more than 30 minutes at a time, even at night, and seemed to startle and become frantic at the slightest noise. When she expressed her concerns to her pediatrician, he suggested that Tommy should be assessed when he was a little older, about 12 months or so, by a specialist in childhood developmental disorders.

For older children and adolescents, entry into the juvenile justice system is another point at which serious emotional or behavioral health problems may be identified (Farmer, Burns, Phillips, Angold, & Costello 2003). Adolescents like Annalee, whose problems are manifested in acting out behaviors, such as skipping school, staying out late at night past curfew, hanging out in unsavory areas of town, using illegal or controlled substances, and running away from home may find themselves reported to the juvenile authorities and detained as ungovernable in the local juvenile home or detention center. Many state juvenile justice systems now routinely screen all detained youth for mental health problems as well as indications of danger to themselves or others (Grisso & Under-

wood 2003; Nordness et al. 2002). A growing body of research is demonstrating that a high percentage of delinquent youth has one or more diagnosable mental disorders. A recent study of nearly 2,000 youths in an Illinois detention facility corroborated earlier estimates that approximately 60% of youthful offenders meet diagnostic criteria for at least one psychiatric disorder (Teplin, Abram, McClelland, Dulcan, & Mericle 2002). In the Illinois study, 56.5% of female juvenile detainees and 45.9% of male detainees met criteria for two or more disorders. The most common co-occurring disorders were substance use, oppositional disorders, and conduct disorders.

Children like Sammy, who come to the attention of child welfare authorities because of parental maltreatment, are at particularly high risk of mental health problems. Recent studies suggest that up to 80% of children entering foster care have significant mental health problems (Clausen, Landsverk, Ganger, Chadwick, & Litrownik 1998; Simms, Dubowitz, & Szilagyi 2000). This contrasts with 18% to 22% of children in the general population (Costello et al. 1996; Roberts, Attkisson, & Rosenblatt 1998). A recent national study by the Urban Institute found that, compared with other children, foster children had higher levels of emotional and behavior problems, more often had physical, learning, or mental health conditions that limited their psychosocial functioning, and were less engaged in school and more likely to have been expelled (Kortenkamp & Earle 2002). Even compared with children from similar socioeconomic and demographic backgrounds, those in foster care are at greatly increased risk for psychopathology (Halfon, Berkowitz, & Klee 1992; Landsverk & Garland 1999).

Despite research documenting the pervasive mental health needs of children and adolescents in the child welfare system, there is evidence that these needs are seldom adequately met (Blumberg, Landsverk, Ellis-MacLeod, Ganger, & Culver 1996; Halfon, Zepeda, & Inkelas 2002). A recent national study of children in foster care found that just 23% of those in care for at least 12 months received any mental health services (National Survey of Child and Adolescent Well-Being 2003). The Child and Family Service Reviews conducted by the Administration for Children and Families on child welfare case practice in 50 states, the District of Columbia, and Puerto Rico during 2001–2004 found that only four states were in substantial conformity with the federal mandate that children and adolescents in the care of the child welfare system should receive adequate services to meet their physical and mental health needs (Administration for Children and Families 2002). When this finding was separated into physical and mental health care, 46 states were found to need improvement in meeting the mental health needs of children in their care, whereas just four of the 50 states demonstrated some strength in this area. There are clearly significant problems in the ability of state child welfare agencies to address the extensive mental health needs of maltreated children like Sammy who enter their care.

Once mental health problems are identified in children and adolescents by any of these mechanisms, the question becomes one of cause and response: what combination of factors in the child and in the child's environment is contributing to maladaptive functioning and what can be done about it? In this chapter, I begin by exploring current understanding of the etiology of mental health problems in children and adolescents. I then discuss the processes available for identifying and classifying disorders in childhood, as well as the types of disorders most often observed in young people and their prevalence across various domains. Current treatments are identified, particularly those that are evidence-based or have strong empirical support for their effectiveness. Finally, I look at the system-of-care concept that currently drives provision of children's mental health services in the United States, where those services are provided, and the public policies, including funding structures, that support or present barriers to provision of mental health care to children and youth today.

Etiology of Emotional and Behavioral Disorders in Children and Adolescents

Although historically the debate over the causes of serious emotional and behavior disorders in children centered on the relative contributions of nature or heredity vs. nurture or environment, currently the focus is on the processes by which nature and nurture interact to result in psychopathology (Perry 2002; Rutter et al. 1997). Several notable longitudinal studies, including the work of Emmy Werner and her colleagues in Hawaii (Werner 1993), Michael Rutter in England (Rutter, Tizard, Yule, Graham, & Whitmore 1977), David Offord and others in Ontario, Canada (Offord, Boyle, Fleming, Blum, & Rae-Grant 1989), and Helen Reinherz at the School of Social Work at Simmons College in Boston (Reinherz, Giaconia, Lefkowitz, Pakiz, & Frost 1993) have followed the development of cohorts of children into adulthood and begun to identify those factors that seem to place children at risk of serious problems in their psychosocial development, as well as factors that appear to prevent dysfunction and foster resilience (Reinherz, Giaconia, Carmola Hauf, Wasserman, & Paradis 2000; Rutter 1985; Werner 1986). These studies have highlighted the complex underlying processes and pathways that account for childhood disorders and helped the field move beyond simplistic efforts at nosology and classification.

The concept of a normal developmental process that contains wide individual variations is a central aspect of current understanding of child psychopathology (Sroufe 1990). That is, the normal behaviors of children at all ages vary considerably; however, at each developmental stage, there are certain behaviors that are outside the boundaries of what is considered normal functioning (Cummings, Davies, & Campbell 2000). Thus for an 8-year-old like Tommy, repetitive rocking, head banging, screaming when mother does not appear promptly, running outdoors to avoid getting dressed for school, are all behaviors that are clearly outside normal expectations for a child of that age. For Sammy and Annalee, their deviations from developmental norms are somewhat less clear. For a child of 3 to bite and scratch his schoolmates is verging on abnormal, although one might give a child like Sammy, who had little appropriate socialization in his early years, some latitude to see if he responds to the clear boundaries set by the classroom teachers. Similarly, Annalee, who is 13 and in the throes of early adolescence, is exhibiting, in extreme form, some of the developmental tasks of separation and individuation that are revisited at puberty. Her behavior could be better understood if viewed in context: Is this new behavior for this child? Or does she have a history of opposition and defiance across previous developmental stages?

In this current interpretation of childhood disorders, there is an assumption that a child's psychosocial development represents a series of adaptations or, occasionally, maladaptations to new experiences or changing situations, determined by biological capacity, previous life experiences, and current environmental demands. Some children who function within the boundaries of normalcy at one developmental stage may be cognitively, emotionally, or behaviorally ill-equipped to manage the demands of the next one. Sammy, for example, may have functioned normally as a toddler at home with his adoptive parents, where the environment was familiar and highly structured, and novel stimuli were limited. However, when he started preschool with new demands for modulating his own behavior, heightened stimulation from the noise and excitement of other children, new surroundings, and a new routine, Sammy was unable to function within normative expectations for that environment and reverted to an earlier, more primitive level of functioning, biting, and hitting other children. Adaptive and maladaptive behaviors overlap. They are inextricably linked, and to recognize the latter, it is important to understand the former. As

Achenbach (1990:4) states, "many problems for which help is sought are quantitative variations on characteristics that may normally be evident at other developmental periods, in less intense degree, in fewer situations, or in ways that do not impair developmental progress."

Recent research on brain development, particularly in children who in early life have suffered physical and sexual abuse and/or physical and emotional neglect, is beginning to help us understand the psychosocial functioning of children like Sammy. It appears that abuse and neglect in infancy have effects on the developing brain that have a long-term detrimental impact on a child's emotional, behavioral, cognitive, and social functioning (Perry & Pollard 1998). Traumatic events in infancy disrupt homeostasis in multiple areas of the brain that organize to respond to threats. Clinical studies of severely maltreated children have identified symptoms of various mental and physical responses to trauma, including hyperarousal and dissociation. From a neurodevelopmental perspective, continuous arousal of these responses in infancy, when the brain is very malleable, floods the brain with certain chemicals, shaping its physical structure in particular ways and leading to sensitization, exaggerated responses to various stimuli, and, eventually, maladaptive personality traits (Perry, Pollard, Blakely, Baker, & Vigilante 1995; Teicher, Andersen, Polcari, Anderson, & Navalta 2002). Altered cardiovascular system regulation, affective lability, behavioral impulsivity, increased anxiety, increased startle response, and sleep abnormalities are observed sequelae of early childhood trauma thought to result from distortions in brain function (Perry, Pollard, Blakely, Baker, & Vigilante 1995). Perry and his colleagues believe, based on magnetic resonance imaging of the brains of abused and neglected children, that trauma in infancy has the effect of stunting development of areas of the brain that govern advanced cognitive functions, such as cause-and-effect reasoning and problem-solving. As a result, severely traumatized children may respond in primitive ways to stressful situations and to developmental demands. Because the brain is still developing rapidly up until about age 3, the effects of trauma on the brain can be ameliorated somewhat during that period; however, after that age, these effects become a more permanent part of the child's psychosocial functioning (Perry, Pollard, Blakely, Baker, & Vigilante 1995).

Another area of research that has informed current understanding of the etiology of severe emotional and behavioral problems in children like Sammy is the study of infant/caregiver attachment. According to attachment theory, the nurturing relationships that an infant experiences with its earliest caregivers set the stage for the child's ability to relate to others throughout life. Attachment is constructed through day-to-day interactions between caregiver and child, the product of a process of mutuality driven by qualities in both the infant and the caregiver. The security children feel in these caregiving relationships allows them to venture forth to explore their environment, expanding their understanding and awareness of the world, and thereby promoting cognitive and social development. In cognitive terms, the quality of attachment enables the young child to develop an internal representational model of himself/herself in relation to others and the expected responses of others (Main, Kaplan, & Cassidy 1985).

The current understanding of attachment is the result of years of observational studies of parent-infant interaction in natural settings across various cultures (Ainsworth 1969; Ainsworth, Blehar, Waters, & Wall 1978; Egeland & Farber 1984). These studies have categorized types of attachment into three primary groupings—secure, anxious, and avoidant—which describe how the infant responds to the caregiver (usually the mother) in a stressful situation. More recent studies of infants raised by rejecting or maltreating parents have added a fourth category, termed "disorganized/disoriented attachment" (Main & Solomon

1990). In this form of attachment, the child has no organized pattern or coherent strategy for responding to stressful situations, unlike children in the other three groups (Carlson, Cicchetti, Barnett, & Braunwald 1989).

Whether these patterns of attachment established in infancy are lifelong is open to question. There is evidence that even secure attachments can be disrupted by subsequent stressful life events in childhood. One recent longitudinal study found no relationship between the type of attachment at 1 year of age and at 18 years, although there was a relationship between type of attachment at 18 years and psychosocial adjustment at that age (Lewis, Fiering, & Rosenthal 2000). Other studies have found a closer relationship between type of early attachment and psychosocial functioning at older ages (Carlson 1998; Carlson & Sroufe 1995; Lyons-Ruth, Alpern, & Repacholi 1993). Carlson (1998) found clear associations between disorganized/disoriented attachment in infancy, the mother-child relationship in the preschool years, and disorders in behavioral functioning throughout childhood. It is currently believed by scholars that early attachment is not directly predictive of later functioning, but indicates the presence of a set of conditions that are associated with particular developmental paths for children (Sroufe, Carlson, Levy, & Egeland 1999). Developmental scientists now see attachment as "the dominant approach to understanding early socioemotional and personality development" (Thompson 2000:148).

As noted earlier in this chapter, longitudinal studies of children's development over time began the process of identifying specific factors that appear to place children at high risk of difficulties in psychosocial functioning. These risk factors may be located in the child, the family system, or the environment within which the family and child reside. Werner's (1986, 1993) studies of the developmental life course of children on the Hawaiian island of Kauai identified poverty, limited parental education, parental alcoholism, and parental mental illness as factors in the family system that present high risks to a child's adaptive development. Other studies have identified additional family factors, such as large family size with closely spaced births, parent involvement in criminal behavior, loss of a parent through death or divorce, and severe marital discord as having negative consequences for children's development (Egeland, Carlson, & Sroufe 1993; Luthar & Ziegler 1993; Rutter 1993). Child-specific risk factors identified in various studies include premature birth, difficult temperament, male gender, low intelligence, and physical disability (Garmezy & Masten 1991; Luthar 1991). Community-level risk factors include high rates of interpersonal violence, crime, and drug trafficking; deteriorated housing stock; inadequate community institutions, such as schools, parks, and recreation facilities; and low levels of social supports for families (Coulton 1996; Ernst 2001; Furstenberg 1993).

Those researchers who study factors that place children at high risk stress that such risk factors are not predictive of psychopathology, but, instead, contribute to processes that may result in dysfunctional outcomes (Cowan, Cowan, & Schultz 1996). Furthermore, the effects of risks are not uniform across different situations or among different people. Some researchers believe that there is a multiplicative effect of risk factors, such that the co-occurrence of two or more such factors exponentially increases the likelihood of maladaptive functioning in children (Rae-Grant, Thomas, Offord, & Boyle 1989; Rutter et al. 1977). Unfortunately, risk factors do tend to co-occur. Poverty, for example, is often accompanied by other factors, such as limited parent education, large family size, single parenthood, parent mental health and substance abuse, residence in economically disadvantaged neighborhoods with high rates of crime and violence, and few family supports. The National Survey of America's Families, conducted in 1997, found that about 8% of children younger than 18 reside in families with multiple risk factors that significantly increase the likelihood

of poor developmental outcomes (Moore, Vandivere, & Ehrle 2000). This survey found that 18% of children aged 6 to 11 and 25% of youth aged 12 to 17 living in high-risk situations demonstrated significant mental health problems, and 31% of high-risk children had been suspended from school, compared with 12% of other children in the survey (Moore, Vandivere, & Ehrle 2000).

Although much is now known about individual risk factors, less is understood about the processes by which risk factors operate to produce poor outcomes for children. Certain risk factors, such as severe child abuse, appear to have a direct precipitating impact on the development of child psychopathology (Cichetti & Toth 1995), whereas other factors, such as male gender or parental depression, contribute to dysfunctional outcomes only in conjunction with other, direct effect factors. If we were to look closely at the Elliot family over time, we might note a history of marital problems, paternal aggression, and maternal depression going back to Annalee's birth. If Annalee was a baby with a difficult temperament—fussy, colicky, and difficult to soothe—with a mother who was struggling to connect emotionally with her newborn and to please a loud, demanding, and threatening husband, the stage would have been set for problems in attachment between Annalee and her mother, which may have resulted in ongoing developmental vulnerability in Annalee and manifested in early adolescence with struggles in autonomy and identity.

"Resilient" is a term that is used to characterize individuals, children included, who exhibit positive psychosocial functioning despite the presence of significant risk factors and/or stressful events in their lives. Those researchers interested in preventing mental health problems in children and youth have sought ways to increase resilience by identifying factors that appear to offer some protection against risks. Like risk factors, protective factors are located in the child, the family, and the larger environmental context (Luthar & Ziegler 1993; Rutter 1985).

Child attributes include an easy-going temperament, positive self-esteem, female gender, and internal locus of control. Family characteristics include family cohesion and warmth, a positive parent-child relationship, and marital harmony; protective factors in the larger environmental context include the availability of a positive adult figure (e.g., teacher, coach); academic success; relationships with prosocial peers; and a safe, supportive neighborhood. Newer approaches to the primary and secondary prevention of mental health problems in children focus on identifying and reducing factors that place children at high risk for psychopathology, as well as locating and enhancing factors that offer protection and increase resilience (Smokowski 1998; Wyman, Sandler, Wolchick, & Nelson 2000).

Mental Disorders in Children and Adolescents

Types of Disorders and Their Prevalence

Epidemiological studies of nonclinical community samples have provided an increasingly clear picture of the prevalence of severe emotional and behavioral disorders among children and youth in the United States. A recent secondary analysis of seven datasets containing diagnostic data on nearly 3,000 children, ranging in age from 7 to 19, examined two key components defining serious emotional disturbance: psychiatric diagnosis and impairment in psychosocial functioning (Costello, Messer, Bird, Cohen, & Reinherz 1998). Psychiatric diagnoses were made using the Diagnostic and Statistical Manual (DSM) III or DSM III-Revised criteria. Impairment in functioning was defined and analyzed in two ways: (1) global impairment across all areas of functioning; and (2) impairment in one or more of three specific areas of functioning—family and friends, school, and community activities. Analyses looked at overall incidence of disorder; disorder by race and ethnicity, gender, and age; and the relationship between DSM diagnosis and functional impairment in one or more areas.

In this sample, the overall rate of disorder (a DSM Axis I diagnosis), irrespective of functioning level, was 23.6%. The most prevalent Axis I diagnoses were anxiety disorder (14.5%), simple phobia (8.6%), conduct disorder/oppositional disorder (8.3%), attention deficit disorder/hyperactive type (ADHD; 3.3%), depressive disorder (3.1%), and substance abuse disorder (1.5%). Slightly more than 5% of the nearly 3,000 children (5.4%) in this analysis were found to be globally impaired in their psychosocial functioning; that is, they were impaired in all three areas of functioning: family and friends, school, and community. For children with specific Axis I diagnoses, higher percentages of those with substance abuse disorders (46.7%), ADHD (30.3%), conduct and oppositional disorders (30.1%), and depressive disorders (22.5%) were considered to be impaired in all areas of psychosocial functioning.

In this analysis, age was correlated with emotional disorder; the older the child, the more likely he or she was to have a serious emotional disturbance. There were no differences across race or ethnic groups, or by gender. The greatest predictor of serious emotional disorder among the children in this study was family income level; the prevalence of disorder was almost twice as high among children from low-income families as among those from families with higher incomes. These findings are consistent with studies of the incidence and prevalence of mental illness in the adult population, which consistently demonstrate a relationship between poverty and mental illness. Overall, this study concluded that about one in 20 U.S. children between the ages of 9 and 17 has a significant emotional disorder that impairs his or her functioning in all aspects of living. This figure increases to one in 13 children if impaired functioning in just one of the three areas of living is considered (Costello, Messer, Bird, Cohen, & Reinderz 1998).

Findings from this secondary data analysis are consistent with findings from other epidemiological studies regarding the prevalence of mental disorders in children and youth. The importance of this study is its emphasis on clarifying the relationship between psychiatric diagnosis and psychosocial functioning. Although an anxiety disorder or a simple phobia may be limiting to a child and frustrating to the immediate family, this study suggests that it is the externalizing disorders—substance abuse, conduct disorders, oppositional disorders, and ADHD—that have the most effect on a child's functioning in all areas of his or her life. As we shall see later in this chapter, with perhaps the exception of ADHD, these are also the disorders that are least likely to be effectively treated in school settings, where most early problem identification takes place. Educational services mandated under the Individuals with Disabilities Education Act (IDEA; P.L.105-17) may not be very accessible to children with externalizing disorders because of the exclusionary provision for children deemed "socially maladjusted." Although the term is not further defined in the IDEA legislation, children who are oppositional, who intentionally break rules, or otherwise display problems in conduct, are differentiated from those with mental and emotional disorders and are excluded from special educational services under IDEA (Forness, Kavale, & Lopez 1993). Furthermore, there have recently been efforts to amend IDEA to allow schools to exclude from the classroom mentally or emotionally disabled students who are disruptive, including those whose diagnostic symptoms include behavioral difficulties (American Academy of Child and Adolescent Psychiatry 2002b).

Annalee's parents have tried repeatedly to access special services for their daughter to make it possible for her to function academically. They are convinced that, with the right psychological supports and behavioral treatment plan, Annalee could succeed in junior high school. But, instead of responding to their pleas for a meeting to discuss her special educational needs, school personnel insist that Annalee's only special needs are to come to school every day and stay there. The school principal recently notified the Elliots that if their daughter missed as few as 4 more school days during the year, she would fail all of her subjects and be retained in her current grade for the following school year. The Elliots know if that happens, Annalee will drop out of school altogether and they will lose her completely to the streets.

Assessment and Diagnosis of Mental Disorders in Children and Adolescents

The purpose of assessment and diagnosis of mental disorders in children and adolescents is twofold: (1) to understand the unique dimensions of individual biopsychosocial functioning, and (2) to identify signs and symptoms of specific diagnostic categories. Thus the focus is on both understanding the individual child within its biopsychosocial context and fitting that child into a nosological scheme that can inform interpretation and aid treatment of a particular disorder. The DSM of the American Psychiatric Association, which first added specific child-related classifications in 1980, has undergone several revisions over the past 25 years to better reflect current research and clinical knowledge regarding childhood disorders. Diagnostic criteria are increasingly specific to insure reliability in diagnosis. Despite these efforts, assigning diagnostic labels to children is more challenging than with adults because the expression, manifestation, and course of disorders in children is less clear than it is in adults and is often age and development specific. For example, the diagnostic significance of biting in young children changes radically over a period of just months. When an 18-month-old bites the arm of another child, we are not especially alarmed about the biter's psychosocial functioning; infants and toddlers use their mouths in a variety of ways to express themselves and explore the world. However, when Sammy at age 3 bites his classmates, particularly as one of a constellation of aggressive behaviors, it is cause for concern. Or consider Annalee's oppositional defiant behavior, which, although of concern because of its potential for placing her in high-risk situations with long-term negative consequences, is not uncommon and unexpected in an adolescent girl of 13 in the throes of puberty. If Annalee were a few years older and still engaging in this behavior, it would have very different diagnostic implications and be of much greater concern regarding the prognosis for a stable adulthood. Developing a clearer understanding of Annalee's difficulties requires a more nuanced picture of her present and past biopsychosocial functioning and stressful life events than simply knowledge of her current symptoms.

Contextualized understanding of a child's functioning requires assessing multiple domains of the child's life. This understanding involves gathering information from a diverse array of informants: parents or other caregivers (grandparents, foster parents, older siblings); daycare staff, classroom teachers and other school personnel, such as guidance counselors or school social workers who may have had contact with the child; pediatricians or other healthcare providers who have observed the child over time; and religious leaders, coaches, and others in the community who may have played a significant role in the child's life. As the quotation from Achenbach and the analysis of domain-specific functional impairment by Costello and her colleagues described above suggest, maladaptive behavior in children may be limited to one venue, such as home or school, or it may be pervasive across all areas of a child's life. Assessing the child's ability to function in each domain allows for a more complete and complex understanding of the level and type of disturbance and treatment possibilities. Labeling a child like Tommy as having a pervasive developmental disorder only describes a child with a set of limiting conditions, not an individual with strengths and potential.

Developing an understanding of an individual child's potential, as well as his limitations, is crucial in assessment and treatment planning. Partnering with parents and other family members in this process, as now called for in most mental health legislation, helps clinicians focus on a child's or an adolescent's strengths, as most parents, even those worn out with caring for a difficult child, such as Tommy's mother, Lexy, see their child as more than his special needs. Lexy and Tommy's sisters Patti and Julie notice Tommy's small achievements, like putting on his socks with the heels in the right place, or spreading peanut butter on bread without covering the table with it; they smile at his delight in the dolphins cavorting at the zoo or at the ants that busily scurry across the garden path. Assessment of a child or adolescent with an emotional or behavior disorder is a narrative of who that child currently is and who he or she can become. This narrative should encompass more than disability; it should also include possibility—for the child and for the family.

Treatment of Mental Disorders in Children and Adolescents

Until recently, the range of treatments for childhood mental disorders was relatively limited; play and talk therapies, milieu therapy, recreation therapy, and behavioral interventions based on social learning theory represented the extent of the clinical repertoire. Over the past two decades, with extensive funding support from the National Institute of Mental Health, there has been an explosion in the development and testing of new models of treatment for children and adolescents, both psychopharmacological and psychosocial. The current focus is on the use of treatments that are evidence-based; that is, treatments whose effectiveness with a particular population and diagnosis or condition has been demonstrated through rigorous scientific research and whose application is well defined and replicable (Brestan & Eyberg 1998; Burns, Hoagwood, & Mrazek 1999; Kazdin 2003; McClellan & Werry 2003).

In response to federal mandates to demonstrate the effectiveness of various approaches to treating serious emotional and behavioral disturbances in children and youth, as well as to pressure from managed care companies to contain healthcare costs, efforts in the psychiatric community have increasingly focused on classifying childhood disorders and specifying targeted treatments, particularly psychopharmacological interventions. A recent article on effective mental health treatments for children written by the head of the Child and Adolescent Treatment and Preventive Intervention Research Branch of the National Institute of Mental Health focused almost exclusively on the use of psychotropic medications for a range of childhood disorders, including depression and anxiety, ADHD, autism, and schizophrenia (Vitiello 2002). Although both the National Institutes of Health and the American Academy of Child and Adolescent Psychiatry have issued psychosocial treatment recommendations (American Academy of Child and Adolescent Psychiatry 2001; National Institutes of Health 2000), this article acknowledged that research on psychosocial interventions for children is hampered by an inability to garner private sources of research funding, compared to the resources studies of pharmacotherapy received from the pharmaceutical industry. The April 2000 issue of the newsletter of the Leonard Davis Institute at the University of Pennsylvania, Philadelphia, summarized the findings of the Children's Mental Health Alliance Project that sought to identify current treatment concerns. Among the project's findings was the dramatic growth in the use of psychotropic medications in children, even in preschoolers, for whom the developmental effects of such use are as yet undetermined. The institute newsletter (Leonard Davis Institute 2000:2) cites findings from a study published in the *AMA Journal* that "found that the number of preschoolers taking stimulants more than doubled between 1991 and 1995, and the number of children taking antidepressants increased 200 [percent]." Much of the application of psychopharmacological treatments in children is based on the use of these medications in adults. The underlying assumption is one of continuity in mental disorders throughout the life span; however, there is limited research supporting this belief. Symptoms of mental illnesses in children are generally more global and less categorical than in adults. Because of their limited cognitive development and abbreviated range of behavioral responses, a specific symptom in a child may indicate a variety of problems. For example, early morning wakefulness, which, in adults, is often a symptom of depression, may, depending on a child's developmental stage, signify a still-unregulated biological clock; a nightmare; hunger; a wet diaper; or a response to a change in environment or routine, such as a move to a new house; or entry into a new developmental stage, such as beginning kindergarten. For some adult mental illnesses, such as bipolar disorder, which is increasingly diagnosed in children, there is even a question whether they can actually occur in children because of the underdevelopment of certain parts of the brain until late adolescence (Geller & Luby 1997; National Institute of Mental Health 2001).

Psychopharmacological Interventions with Children

There is no question that some medications are strikingly effective in treating certain childhood disorders. For example, the effectiveness of such stimulants as Ritalin for the treatment of ADHD is well established (Greenhill, Halperin, & Abikoff 1999). Randomized clinical trials, the gold standard for establishing evidence-based treatments, have repeatedly demonstrated that stimulant medications are effective in managing core ADHD symptoms of inattentiveness, distractibility, and agitation, as well as increasing compliance and reducing aggression in children 3 years of age and older (American Academy of Child and Adolescent Psychiatry 2002a; McClellan & Werry 2003). There is also good clinical evidence supporting the use of selective serotonin reuptake inhibitors (SSRIs) and clomipramine for obsessive-compulsive disorder in children (Emslie, Walkup, Pliszka, & Ernst 1999). The U.S. Food and Drug Administration's approval was granted for the use of these medications in children as young as 6 almost 20 years ago. According to one review of evidence-based treatments, there are studies that support the use of SSRIs with other anxiety disorders in children as well (McClellan & Werry 2003).

Treatment guidelines established by the American Academy of Child and Adolescent Psychiatry (1998) suggest that the effectiveness of antidepressants to treat affective disorders in children has yet to be established. Some controlled studies have shown positive results, whereas others have not (McClellan & Werry 2003). Consequently, questions have been raised as to whether there are developmental differences in responses to these medications, or whether major depression in childhood is a different syndrome altogether from that found in adults. Similarly, neuroleptic or antipsychotic medications, frequently used in adults with schizophrenia spectrum disorders, have not been extensively studied in treating early-onset psychotic disorders in young people, although such medications have been found effective in controlling aggression and self-injurious behaviors associated with autism and other pervasive developmental disorders (McCracken et al. 2002).

Other psychopharmacological treatments of childhood disorders are generally based on very limited studies or have been extrapolated from adult use. Such issues as small sample sizes, problems with diagnostic inclusion criteria, high placebo response rates, and short treatment duration have limited the number of well-designed and executed studies that can establish the effectiveness of psychopharmacological treatments in children. Furthermore, there are almost no studies establishing the long-term physiological effects of such treatments over time. Some drugs, particularly some of the neuroleptics, are known to have serious, permanent side effects in adults; how these will affect the developing organism in a child is unknown. Thus, in addition to evidence-based psychopharmacological treatments and instead of unproven ones, children's mental health experts advocate using psychosocial interventions with proven effectiveness (Burns, Hoagwood, & Mrazek 1999).

Evidence-Based Psychosocial Interventions for Children and Adolescents

Historically, individual psychotherapy has been the treatment of choice for older children, whereas play therapy is used to treat emotional and behavior problems in younger children. Traditional forms of psychotherapy include supportive, psychodynamic, cognitive-behavioral, and interpersonal therapies, as well as those based on family systems theories. However, recent outcome studies have questioned psychotherapy's effectiveness in the treatment of children (Weiss, Catron, Harris, & Phung 1999; Weisz & Jensen 1999; Weisz, Weiss, Han, Granger, & Morton 1995), despite small sample sizes; difficulty in randomization; confounding intervening variables, such as parent mental illness and outside treatment of the control group; unacknowledged attrition; and lack of treatment fidelity (Weisz, Donenberg, Han, & Weiss 1995).

One form of psychotherapy for which there is significant evidentiary support is cognitive-behavioral treatment. This treatment has proven effective for a variety of emotional and behavior disorders exhibited by children and adolescents, including anxiety and depression, adjustment disorders, eating disorders, and conduct disorders (Asarnow, Jaycox, & Thompson 2001; Brestan & Eyberg 1998; Kazdin 2003; Kendall, Aschenbrand, & Hudson 2003; Ollendick & King 1998). Cognitive distortions are believed to play a major role in affective disorders in children, because their immature cognitive development heightens the possibility of misinterpreting or misperceiving situations or events. The focus of treatment is on (1) changing cognitive distortions that contribute to the child's anxiety or depression; (2) learning new behaviors and skills for coping with anxiety-provoking situations; (3) testing newly acquired skills in novel situations; and, (4) processing their outcomes with the therapist. Such cognitive strategies as self-talk are taught to the child to help mediate anxiety. Cognitive-behavioral therapies are usually time-limited, often lasting for 16 to 20 individual sessions with the child. Supplementary meetings are held with parents or other caregivers to teach them the basic principles of the approach, so that they can reinforce its continued use after treatment ends.

Another form of evidence-based treatment for children and youth with oppositional and aggressive behaviors is parent management training (Brestan & Eyberg 1998; Kazdin 1997; McClellan & Werry 2003; Webster-Stratton 1998). Parent management training is based on research that shows that parents or caregivers unintentionally reward a child's bad behavior by overresponding to the child when such behavior occurs and, at the same time, ignoring the child when his or her behavior is positive (Patterson 1982; Patterson, Reid, & Dishion 1992). The child's bad behavior is reinforced by the parents' attention even when the attention is negative, such as yelling, name-calling, threats, or physical aggression. This type of interaction between parent and child is termed the "coercive family process" and is thought to contribute to development of oppositional and conduct disorders in children (Patterson 1982).

The focus of parent management training is on teaching parents to alter this coercive interaction pattern by not responding to their child's provocative behaviors, by attending to and rewarding positive or desired behavior, and by ignoring or delivering mild forms of punishment to extinguish bad behavior. Parents are helped to set clear rules and expectations for their child to follow and taught how to negotiate and compromise with their child to achieve desired outcomes. Treatment sessions are held primarily with parents to allow them to review and practice their newly learned skills, to role play situations in which they apply the principles they are learning, and to review the behavior change program they are implementing

at home. Treatment is relatively short-term, the length depending on the extent of the child's difficulty and the parents' ability to grasp and apply the program's principles—from 4 to 8 weeks for parents of young children, and somewhat longer, 12 to 25 weeks, for parents of adolescents with serious conduct disorders (Kazdin 2003).

Parent management training has been extensively studied and is well supported by empirical research (Brestan & Eyberg 1998; Kazdin 1997). The model has been applied in diverse settings (home, school, community, institutions) with a range of age groups and across cultures (Kazdin 2003). Improvements observed in child behavior have been maintained for as long as 10 to 14 years (Long, Forehand, Wierson, & Morgan 1994). Adaptations of this model using videotapes with groups of parents of young children with conduct problems have received strong empirical support as well (Brestan & Eyberg 1998; Webster-Stratton 1998).

Disruptive behavior like Sammy's, which can range from relatively minor actions (e.g., talking back) to more severe forms of aggression (e.g., hitting, biting) is the most common reason for referral of preschool-aged children for mental health services. One evidence-based treatment designed to assist children like Sammy and their parents is parent-child interaction therapy (PCIT; Brinkmeyer & Eyberg 2003). This intervention focuses on strengthening the attachment between parent and child, essential for a child like Sammy with an early history of disordered/disorganized attachment resulting from maltreatment, as well as separation and loss of his birth parent. PCIT posits that "a secure, nurturing relationship is a necessary foundation for establishing effective limit setting and consistency in discipline that will achieve lasing change in the behaviors of parent and child" (Brinkmeyer & Eyberg 2003: 205). There are two phases to PCIT. The first phase focuses on developing the parent-child relationship, and the goal of the second phase is to improve parents' ability to set limits and apply consistent discipline. The effectiveness of PCIT in reducing children's disruptive behavior and increasing parenting competency has been demonstrated in a number of controlled studies comparing outcomes for families receiving PCIT to those for families on a treatment wait-list (Schuhmann, Foote, Eyberg, Boggs, & Algina 1998). Intervention with young behaviorally disordered children like Sammy is essential, because studies have shown that children with severe disruptive behaviors in the preschool years are at great risk for antisocial behavior and criminal involvement as adolescents and young adults (Loeber et al. 1993).

Given the current understanding of children's mental disorders as having multiple causes, it follows that several of the treatments that have positive empirical support focus on the multiple systems that interact to support or ameliorate a child's problematic functioning. For youth with conduct disorder and associated comorbid disorders, such as substance abuse, there are several family- and community-based approaches that have been shown to be effective in multiple outcome studies. These include multisystemic family therapy (MST), which works simultaneously with the family, youth, peers, and school to identify and address obstacles and establish supports for the child and family in their quest for change (Henggeler, Schoenwald, Borduin, Rowland, & Cunningham 1998). The developers of MST have worked to insure treatment fidelity by tailoring the intervention's application to antisocial behavior and serious emotional disturbances, and by licensing the intervention and mandating training and consultation from MST Services, Inc. The model has been empirically tested in a wide variety of studies, including a number of randomized controlled trials (Borduin et al. 1995; Henggeler, Melton, Smith, Schoenwald, & Hanley 1993). A recent metaanalysis of MST study outcomes has raised questions regarding claims of effectiveness, because of researchers' failure to include families who dropped out of treatment in the analyses of treatment results

(Littell 2003). However, Brestan and Eyberg (1998), who conducted a thorough review of the evidence base for psychosocial treatments of conduct-disordered children and adolescents, termed MST "probably efficacious." A review of evidence-based practice in child and adolescent mental health (Hoagwood, Burns, Kiser, Ringelsen, & Schoenwald 2001) cited MST as having among the strongest empirical support of any children's treatment. These authors note that studies of MST suggest that supervision and training of clinical staff and institutional support are critical to successful outcomes.

Other family-based treatment models with empirical support include multidimensional family therapy (MDFT; Liddle et al. 2001). Originally developed to treat adolescent substance abuse and associated behavior problems, MDFT has been empirically tested in multiple studies with ethnically diverse populations and a range of problem severities. Similarly, the family-based model developed in Pennsylvania under that state's Child and Adolescent Service System Program (CASSP) initiative was found to be effective in a study of nearly 2,000 participating families in preventing crisis hospitalization of severely emotionally disturbed children and stabilizing such children in their families and communities (Lindblad-Goldberg, Dore, & Stern 1998; Lindblad-Goldberg, Jones, & Dore 2004). CASSP is based on ecosystemic and structural family therapy principles. The Pennsylvania study highlights the multidetermined nature of children's mental health problems with its finding that about one-third of treated families were known to multiple service systems, including child welfare, substance abuse, adult mental health, and criminal justice.

A family-based treatment designed specifically for conduct-disordered and substance-abusing Hispanic youth and their families is brief strategic family therapy (BSFT), developed at the Center for Family Studies at the University of Miami (Robbins et al. 2003; Szapocznik & Williams 2000). According to its authors, BSFT was developed from a Hispanic perspective, recognizing and addressing cultural factors, particularly those stemming from different rates of acculturation between parents and children, which contribute to the development and maintenance of serious conduct problems in youth. BSFT is highly structured, problem-focused, and directive; it is intended to provide parents with practical experiences in effecting changes in their child's functioning (Robbins et al. 2003).

Each of these family-based treatments views the child or adolescent with severe emotional and behavior problems as embedded in a context described by family, school, community, and a peer network, all of which must be engaged to support improved psychosocial functioning in the child. Even those family-based treatments that initially drew primarily on family systems theory to inform their interventions have expanded their purview beyond the family to target the youth's social ecology, including peers, school personnel, other relevant service systems, and the family's support network (Szapocznik & Williams 2000).

In Annalee's case, a family-based approach might begin working with Annalee and her parents together to assess the situation and develop a clearer understanding of the history of the problems and each family member's commitment to changing the situation. Individual treatment with Annalee might focus on her hopes and dreams for herself and her current struggles to adjust to adolescence. Treatment with Annalee's parents together would draw on principles of parent management training to help Nancy and Bob Elliot learn new ways of responding to and managing their daughter's behavior. Psychoeducation would also help the Elliots develop a new understanding of the struggles a young girl experiences in today's culture in her efforts to become a woman. Intervention with Annalee's school would focus on getting an educational assessment to determine if there are any undiagnosed learning differences and identifying the services and supports she would need to succeed in junior high school. Community resources would also be engaged to help Annalee find satisfying and sustaining supports outside the family as she seeks to loosen family ties in more prosocial ways. For example, young teens like Annalee can often be engaged in volunteer activities that help to build a sense of self-efficacy and self-esteem by giving to others. Helping Annalee engage with prosocial peers would also be a focus of a family-based approach. Connecting with activities that interest a young adolescent girl, such as an art class, a modeling class, or a theater group, where other teenagers with similar interests can be found, is an essential component of a multidimensional treatment approach.

Mental Health Services for Children and Youth

Prior to the 1980s, mental health services for children consisted primarily of two types of care: (1) long-term care in inpatient settings, such as residential treatment centers and state psychiatric hospitals; and (2) outpatient treatment in a mental health center, psychiatrist's office, or child guidance clinic. Partial hospital or day-treatment programs, usually affiliated with an inpatient psychiatric hospital or residential treatment center, were available in some urban communities, as were treatment foster homes or group homes for seriously emotionally disturbed youth, often run by voluntary sectarian or nonsectarian child welfare organizations. Mental health care of children during this time was dominated by psychodynamic theories of the origins of children's mental disorders that frequently saw the family, particularly the mother, as the primary causal agent in the child's difficulties. Separating the child from the family was the preferred course of treatment. In some facilities, such as Bruno Bettelheim's children's residential treatment program, located on the University of Chicago campus, parents were not allowed contact with their child for as long as a year because of beliefs about their lethality to the child's recovery process.

Many social factors converged to bring about a sea change in children's mental health services during the 1970s and early 1980s. The family therapy movement, which began in the late 1950s and gathered strength during the 1960s and 1970s, strongly rejected psychodynamic interpretations of children's emotional and behavior problems. It focused instead on the functioning of the family system as a whole and on the role played by the child's symptoms in maintaining a dysfunctional system. In the view of family therapists, it was a mistake to treat a child apart from the family, as systems theory suggested that removal of one family member's symptoms would simply result in another family member becoming symptomatic and assuming the role of identified patient to maintain the system's functioning. Although this approach helped remove parents as the focus of blame and engaged them as partners with their children in the therapeutic process, the most prominent early family therapists, many of whom were male psychiatrists, continued the traditional medical role of expert authority. It was another, parallel movement that gave parents a true voice in the treatment of their children.

During the late 1960s and early 1970s, a series of lawsuits brought by social activists and parents whose children were residing in state-run facilities for the mentally and emotionally handicapped called into question the level of care provided to residents of these institutions. Graphic court testimony about the abuse and neglect perpetrated on hapless and helpless residents led to a series of legal decisions requiring states to provide adequate care for all those with handicapping conditions in the least restrictive, most normal settings possible. As a result, large state institutions downsized dramatically or closed their doors completely, releasing residents, including many children with serious emotional and behavior disorders, back into their families and communities. Parents, who had become activists in working for institutional reform, now turned their attention to insuring that community institutions, such as schools and mental health facilities, provided the services their children required.

In 1982, Knitzer documented the consequences of failing to provide adequate mental health services. In response to Knitzer's (1982) findings and to pressure from parent advocacy groups, the federal government initiated CASSP, designed to assist the states in developing a continuum of mental health care for children (Pumariega, Winters, & Huffine 2003). The CASSP initiative incorporated a set of principles intended to inform creation of a "system-of-care" for children's mental health services. These principles, articulated by Stroul and Friedman (1986), have become the central organizing force shaping the development of children's mental health services in the United States today. System-of-care principles include: (1) attention to the individual needs, preferences, and cultural characteristics of the child and family; (2) use of a strengths-based, rather than deficits-based, perspective; (3) involvement of families in their children's care and in program and system development; (4) cross-agency coordination and collaboration in service system management and service delivery; and (5) use of the least restrictive service setting that is clinically appropriate. With their recognition of the importance of family involvement in treatment planning and in helping to develop service systems, and their call for culturally competent service delivery and individualized treatment planning, the system-of-care principles initiated a radical change in how children's mental health services have been developed and delivered over the past 20 years.

Along with the CASSP initiative, a second piece of federal legislation significantly reshaped community-based care of children with mental disorders. In 1987, Congress passed the Education for All Handicapped Children Act (P.L. 94-142). This law mandated that children with special educational needs, including those with mental disorders, would be served in their community schools, mainstreamed in regular classes with support when possible and in self-contained classrooms when necessary. P.L. 94-142, as it was known, required that all children with special educational needs have an individualized education plan (IEP) that specified how the school would meet the child's particular learning needs. According to the law, parents were to be partners in developing this plan and were required to sign off on its provisions. Schools were mandated to provide whatever services the child needed to succeed academically, including, among others, psychological services, transportation, social work services, therapeutic recreation, and even a fulltime classroom aide.

IDEA, passed by Congress in 1990 and revised in 1997, supplanted P.L. 94-142, while retaining many of its provisions. Under IDEA, schools may classify a child with a mental disorder either as emotionally disturbed (ED) or as other health impairment (OHI). To qualify as ED under IDEA, a child must exhibit one or more of the following conditions: (1) an inability to learn that is not explained by intellectual, health, or sensory factors; (2) an inability to build or maintain satisfactory interpersonal relationships with peers or teachers; (3) inappropriate types of behavior or feelings under normal circumstances; and (4) a tendency to develop physical symptoms or fears associated with personal or school problems (Roberts, Jacobs, Puddy, Nyre, & Vernberg 2003). These qualifying conditions are determined by school personnel based on observation and experience with the child in the academic setting. When there is a DSM Axis I diagnosis by an outside mental health professional, the child may qualify for special educational services under the OHI designation if the symptoms interfere with the child's educational process, not simply on the basis of the DSM diagnosis.

Despite federal mandates directing schools to provide the services required for a child to function academically, it is estimated that less than 2% of children with serious emotional and behavioral disturbances actually receive appropriate educational services (U. S. Department of Health and Human Services 1999). Differential demand for and availability of services,

disagreements over responsibility for funding and providing such services, and conflicting legal interpretations regarding mandated services and educational needs have resulted in vastly differing service delivery across school districts (Palfrey, Singer, Raphael, & Walker 1990; Terman, Larner, Stevenson, & Behrman 1996). One of the difficulties in providing educational support services for children with serious psychiatric disorders is the lack of well-defined boundaries between educationally related services mandated under IDEA and services that are rehabilitative in nature. When is psychological treatment necessary to enable a child to form the interpersonal relationships with peers and teachers that facilitate learning, and when is it intended to restore a child's overall psychosocial functioning? In the first instance, the school district would be responsible for providing and paying for such treatment under IDEA; in the second instance, it would not. These kinds of distinctions have been the subject of an increasing volume of litigation, as parents and school districts square off in court to determine legal responsibility for funding the services needed to support a child's educational performance (Terman, Larner, Stevenson, & Behrman 1996).

In 1992, building on the CASSP foundation, the federal government initiated the Comprehensive Community Mental Health Services for Children and Their Families program to expand the availability of community-based mental health services for families and children by developing 67 local systems-of-care across the United States. The local systems-of-care sites funded by this initiative were quite varied, including whole states, such as Vermont and Rhode Island; inner-city neighborhoods, such as East Baltimore and the Mott Haven neighborhood in the Bronx; entire counties, such as Stark County, Ohio, and Ventura and San Mateo counties, California; and one American Indian tribe, the Navajo Nation, which spans several states. By 1999, more than 40,000 children and their families had received services from sites funded under this initiative (Holden, Friedman, & Santiago 2001). A 5-year evaluation of the first 22 sites funded under the Comprehensive Community Mental Health program found that, in comparison with sites providing children's mental health services using a traditional service delivery model, services within the system-of-care sites were more child- and family-centered, community-based, and culturally-competent (Hernandez et al. 2001). According to the evaluators, their findings indicate that the system-of-care philosophy is influencing mental health practice at the clinical level, not simply at the larger systems level. As a result of these and other evaluation findings, the Surgeon General's Report on Mental Health (U.S. Department of Health and Human Services 1999) incorporates the system-of-care philosophy in its recommendations for service system reform and delivery of mental health services to children and their families.

Two forms of community-based services that have developed from the system-of-care philosophy designed to support and sustain children with severe emotional and behavior disorders in their families and communities are intensive case management (ICM) and wrap-around services. ICM was modeled on adult mental health services for individuals who are chronically mentally ill and who require on-going support and assistance to remain stable in the community. Children's ICM works with families to coordinate provision of the array of community services needed to maintain the child in the least restrictive setting possible. Depending on the ICM model employed, the case manager plays a wide variety of roles—assessor of service need, service broker, purchaser of services, and provider of clinical services. Studies have shown that children receiving ICM services spend fewer days in psychiatric inpatient settings and more days in community settings with longer periods between hospitalizations (Evans, Armstrong, & Kuppinger 1996).

"Wrap-around services" is a term used to describe a model of community-based care that literally wraps individualized services around a specific child to maintain that child in a community setting. Wrap-around services reflect a philosophy of care that advocates doing whatever it takes to stabilize a child in all domains of functioning—home, school, and community —and to prevent placement in more intensive levels of care, such as psychiatric hospitals and residential treatment centers (VanDenBerg & Grealish 1996). Unlike ICM, which is provided by an individual case manager, wrap-around services are usually identified and developed by a team that includes the child and his parents, a care manager, other community partners, school personnel, and mental health clinicians. This team identifies goals for the child, then develops a plan of wrap-around services designed to achieve those goals.

Wrap-around services have proven effective in preventing out-of-home care of children with severe emotional and behavior disorders like Tommy's (Clark et al. 1998). A wrap-around program might provide an early-morning aide, who would come to Tommy's home to assist his mother in getting Tommy ready for school. The aide would also help Lexy design and implement a behavior modification plan that would help Tommy learn to get ready for school in such a way that eventually the aide's help would no longer be needed. Similarly, when Tommy is ready to be mainstreamed into a regular public school classroom, wrap-around services could provide a classroom aide who would remain at Tommy's side throughout the day to assist him in managing the academic and social demands of the classroom until he is able to do so with less intensive support. Wrap-around services might also include weekend respite services, so that Lexy and her daughters could enjoy some time together, a carpenter to modify the front door of the house so that Tommy cannot escape at will into the street, and even a evening get-together for Lexy's neighbors with Tommy's care manager, so that they can be helped to understand Tommy's special needs and the parenting demands on Lexy. Huffine (2002:809) describes these as "practical accommodations." With wrap-around services in place, it is likely that Lexy and her children would experience a more stable, less stressful, and more satisfying family life.

Access to Mental Health Care for Children and Youth

As noted previously, it is currently estimated that only about one in five children who need it actually receives mental health care (Kataoka, Zhang, & Wells 2002; Owens et al. 2002). Despite efforts by NIMH to expand access to mental health care for children through the initiatives described above, other social and economic factors have resulted in changes in mental health service availability such that the majority of funding is currently directed at those with severe, pervasive, and/or chronic disorders. Preventive services and those aimed at children and adolescents whose emotional and behavioral difficulties are not yet severe enough to cause disruption to the systems with which they interact are extremely limited. The introduction of managed care, cost containment, and benefit limits in private insurance, along with expanded drug benefits, have reshaped the delivery of mental health services in the private sector. Child psychiatry is now focused almost entirely on the management of psychotropic medications, rather than delivery of psychosocial interventions.

Medicaid, a jointly funded, federal-state program that provides health coverage to low-income individuals, is the largest provider of mental health services for children in the United States, especially for children in foster care. However, modest provider reimbursement and bureaucratic inefficiencies have resulted in few providers accepting this form of payment. Even providers who do accept Medicaid are restricted in the amount of treatment time that will be reimbursable, depending on state guidelines (U.S. Department of Health and Human Services 2000). Medicaid funds inpatient psychiatric hospitalization, residential treatment, and group home care for children and youth with mental disorders. To fund home- and community-based treatment programs, such as MST, states must apply for waivers to the usual reimbursement for out-of-home care. Medicaid also funds the Early and Periodic Screening, Diagnosis, and Treatment (EPSDT) program, which provides periodic screening of Medicaid-eligible children for physical, dental, vision, and hearing problems. EPSDT also covers medically necessary services designed to correct physical and mental conditions; however, few states include screening for mental health problems in their EPSDT programs, although they can do so under the legislation. Thus mental conditions whose treatments are covered under this program are seldom identified. The federal government also provides supplemental insurance under the State Children's Health Insurance Program (SCHIP) for working families whose income is too high to qualify for Medicaid coverage but is too low to afford private health insurance. States can choose to expand Medicaid to cover these children, to insure them through a separate program, or some combination of the two options. Children insured under an expanded Medicaid program are entitled to EPSDT screening and services; however, mental health coverage under the separate program provision is quite variable (Szilagyi et al. 2000).

A significant change in public mental health policy for children over the past few years is the substantial increase in funding to schools to address mental health and psychosocial concerns. There has also been a trend toward school-community collaboration in meeting the mental health needs of young people. Recent studies have shown that as many as three-fourths of children who receive any mental health services receive them in school settings (Wu et al. 1999). For most of these children, school-based services were the only mental health care they received (Leaf et al. 1996).

Mental health service use also varies by type of disorder and ethnicity. A recent study of mental health service utilization by children with disruptive and depressive disorders found that those with disruptive disorders are much more likely to be identified as needing services and to be referred for those services than those with depressive disorders (Wu et al. 1999). Similarly, a study of service use by ethnicity and funding source found that Hispanic youth were least likely to receive needed services, whereas youth with publicly-funded health insurance received more mental health care than either children with private health insurance or children with no health insurance at all (Kataoka, Zhang, & Wells 2002). Despite these findings of differential access to care, the most common finding across all studies is the low level of service access by children in need of mental health care.

Conclusion

In this chapter, I have examined child mental health: the origins of mental health problems in children and youth, the types and prevalence of these problems in children and adolescents across the United States today, how these problems are currently assessed and treated, and the service system that supports these treatments. We have seen how mental health problems are manifested in children and adolescents by viewing the experiences of three families struggling to meet the caregiving demands of children at different developmental stages with varying forms of maladaptive behavior. Their life experiences and the unique symptoms of their disorders suggest differing dynamic processes of nature and nurture, as manifested in Tommy, Sammy, and Annalee. It is likely that Tommy's current psychosocial functioning, reflective of pervasive developmental disorder, is primarily the result of a biological process, perhaps genetic in origin. Although positive nurturing by Lexy and others in his environment can help to modify the negative effects of Tommy's disorder and enhance positive aspects of his functioning, this case illustrates the limitations of nurture when nature has played a crippling hand.

Sammy, however, represents a child whose maladaptive functioning displays the effects of inadequate nurturing and traumatic early life experiences. Although he may have been biologically vulnerable because of the prenatal assault on his fetal development by his mother's drug use and accompanying lack of adequate nutrition, his physical and emotional neglect as a newborn, as well as the physical and sexual abuse he is said to have suffered at the hands of his mother's male partners, make Sammy a child whose personality and functioning were formed more by nurture than nature.

Annalee, our third case study, represents a young adolescent whose current emotional and behavioral difficulties suggest developmental vulnerability resulting from the interaction of nature and nurture over the course of her childhood. She was a sensitive, somewhat fussy infant cared for by a mother who was struggling with her own mental health problems and marital difficulties, thus setting the stage for heightened reactivity to the biological changes and psychosocial demands of puberty.

We have also explored the application of various evidence-based interventions with Tommy, Sammy, and Annalee and their families. We saw that wrap-around services, designed in collaboration with Lexy and others involved in Tommy's life, would provide the range of supports needed to maintain Tommy in his family, school, and community, and to maximize the possibilities for realizing his fullest potential.

We noted that PCIT, designed to help youngsters like Sammy—with problems in attachment and disturbances in their psychosocial functioning—experience the kind of positive nurturing relationship that will form the basis for authoritative caregiving by his loving adoptive parents. PCIT will teach the Rosses how to set clear limits with Sammy and to shape his behavior in ways that were not necessary with their own children, who never suffered the traumatic early abuse and neglect that Sammy did. The Rosses will learn the importance of consistent early intervention with children like

Sammy, whose aggressive behavior can be predictive of lifelong disturbance in psychosocial functioning.

Finally, we identified family-based therapy as the treatment of choice for Annalee and her family, who are challenged to cope with her oppositional and defiant behavior in transition to adolescence. The chaos she is creating for the family is reawakening her mother's depression and triggering her emotional withdrawal from her daughter, as well as exacerbating her father's tendency to become rigid and authoritarian.

Neither of these emotional responses will aid Annalee in resolving her developmental struggles. Family-based treatment will help this family regain its emotional balance by addressing the immediate crisis in ways that allows for growth and change in all family members.

These three narratives of Tommy, Sammy, and Annalee highlight the varied mental health needs of children and their families and reflect the importance of further development of the system-of-care that informs provision of mental health services in the United States today.

REFERENCES

Achenbach, T. M. (1990). Conceptualization of developmental psychopathology. In M. Lewis & S. M. Miller (eds.), *Handbook of developmental psychopathology*, pp. 3–14. New York: Plenum Press.

Administration for Children and Families (2002). *Summary results of the 2001 and 2002 Child and Family Service Reviews.* Retrieved from www.acf.hhs.gov/programs/cb/cwrp/2002cfsrresults.htm.

Ainsworth, M. D. (1969). Object relations, dependency, and attachment: A theoretical review of the infant-mother attachment relationship. *Child Development, 40,* 969–1025.

Ainsworth, M. D., Blehar, M. C., Waters, E., & Wall, S. (1978). *Patterns of attachment: A psychological study of the "strangesSituation."* Hillsdale, NJ: Lawrence Erlbaum Associates.

American Academy of Child and Adolescent Psychiatry. (1998). *Practice parameters for the assessment and treatment of children and adolescents with depressive disorders.* Washington, DC: American Academy of Child and Adolescent Psychiatry.

American Academy of Child and Adolescent Psychiatry. (2001). Practice parameters for the assessment and treatment of children and adolescents with schizophrenia. *Journal of the American Academy of Child and Adolescent Psychiatry, 40*(suppl.), 4S–23S.

American Academy of Child and Adolescent Psychiatry. (2002a). Practice parameters for the use of stimulant medications in the treatment of children, adolescents, and adults. *Journal of the American Academy of Child and Adolescent Psychiatry, 41*(suppl.), 26S–49S.

American Academy of Child and Adolescent Psychiatry. (2002b). *Statement from the American Academy of Child and Adolescent Psychiatry for the Senate Health, Education, Labor and Pensions Committee Hearing on IDEA Enforcement.* Washington, DC: American Academy of Child and Adolescent Psychiatry.

Asarnow, J. R., Jaycox, L. H., & Thompson, M. C. (2001). Depression in youth: Psychosocial interventions. *Journal of Clinical Child Psychology, 30,* 33–47.

Blumberg, E., Landsverk, J., Ellis-MacLeod, E., Gander, W., & Culver, S. (1996). Use of the public mental health system by children in foster care: Client characteristics and service use patterns. *Journal of Mental Health Administration, 23*(4), 389–405.

Borduin, C. M., Mann, B. J., Cone, L. T., Henggeler, S. W., Fucci, B. R., et al. (1995). Multisystemic treatment of serious juvenile offenders: Long-term prevention of criminology and violence. *Journal of Consulting and Clinical Psychology, 63,* 569–578.

Brandenburg, N. A., Friedman, R. M., & Silver, S. E. (1990). The epidemiology of childhood psychiatric disorders: Prevalence findings from recent studies. *Journal of the American Academy of Child and Adolescent Psychiatry, 29*(1), 76–83.

Brestan, E. V., & Eyberg, S. M. (1998). Effective psychosocial treatments of conduct-disordered children and adolescents: 29 years, 82 studies, and 5,272 kids. *Journal of Clinical Child Psychology, 27*(2), 180–189.

Brinkmeyer, M. Y., & Eyberg, S. M. (2003). Parent-child interaction therapy for oppositional children. In A. E. Kazdin & J. R. Weisz (eds.), *Evidence-based psychotherapies for children and adolescents*, pp. 204–223. New York: Guilford.

Burns, B. J., Hoagwood, K., & Mrazek, P. J. (1999). Effective treatment for mental disorders in children and adolescents. *Clinical Child and Family Psychology Review, 2,* 199–254.

Carlson, E. A. (1998). A prospective longitudinal study of attachment disorganization/disorientation. *Child Development, 69,* 1107–1128.

Carlson, E. A., & Sroufe, L. A. (1995). Contribution of attachment theory to developmental psychopathology. In D. Cicchetti & D. Cohen (eds.), *Developmental psychopathology: Theory and methods*, vol. I, pp. 581–617. New York: Wiley.

Carlson, V., Cicchetti, D., Barnett, D., & Braunwald, K. (1989). Disorganized/disoriented attachment relationships in maltreated infants. *Developmental Psychopathology, 25,* 525–531.

Cichetti, D., & Toth, S. (1995). Developmental psychopathology perspective on child abuse and neglect. *Journal of the American Academy of Child and Adolescent Psychiatry, 34,* 541–565.

Clark, H., Prange, M., Lee, B., Stewart, E., McDonald, B., & Boyd, L. (1998). An individualized wraparound process for children in foster care with emotional/behavioral disturbances: Follow-up findings and implications from a controlled study. In M. Epstein, K. Kutash, & A. Duchnowski (eds.), *Outcomes for children and youth with behavioral and emotional disorders and their families: Programs and evaluation best practices.* pp. 513–542. Austin, TX: Pro-Ed Publishing.

Clausen, J. M., Landsverk, J., Ganger, W., Chadwick, D., & Litrownik, A. (1998). Mental health problems of children in foster care. *Journal of Child and Family Studies, 7,* 283–296.

Costello, E. J., Angold, A., Burns, B. J., Stangl, D. K., Tweed, D. L., et al. (1996). The Great Smoky Mountains Study of Youth: Goals, design, methods, and the prevalence of DSM-III-R disorders. *Archives of General Psychiatry, 53,* 1129–1136.

Costello, E. J., Messer, S. C., Bird, H. R., Cohen, P., & Reinherz, H. Z. (1998). The prevalence of serious emotional disturbance: A re-analysis of community studies. *Journal of Child and Family Studies, 7,* 411–432.

Coulton, C. C. (1996). Effects of neighborhoods on families and children: Implications for services. In A. J. Kahn & S. B. Kamerman (eds.), *Children and their families in big cities,* pp. 87–120. New York: Cross-National Studies Research Program, Columbia University School of Social Work.

Cowan, P. A., Cowan, C. P., & Schultz, M. S. (1996). Thinking about risk and resilience in families. In E. M. Hetherington & E. Blechman (eds.), *Risk and resilience: Advances in family research,* vol. 5, pp. 1–38. Hillsdale, NJ: Lawrence Earlbaum Associates.

Cummings, E. M., Davies, P. T., & Campbell, S. (2000). *Developmental psychopathology and family process.* New York: Guilford.

Education for All Handicapped Children Act. (1987). P.L. 94-142.

Egeland, B., Carlson, E., & Sroufe, L. A. (1993). Resilience as process. *Development and Psychopathology, 5,* 517–528.

Egeland, B., & Farber, E. (1984). Infant-mother attachment: Factors related to its development and changes over time. *Child Development, 55,* 753–771.

Emslie, G. J., Walkup, J. T., Pliszka, S. R., & Ernst, M. (1999). Nontricyclic antidepressants: Current trends in children and adolescents. *Journal of the American Academy of Child and Adolescent Psychiatry, 38,* 517–528.

Ernst, J. S. (2001). Community-level factors and child maltreatment in a suburban community. *Social Work Research, 25,* 133–142.

Evans, M., Armstrong, M., & Kuppinger, A. (1996). Family-centered intensive case management: A step toward understanding individualized care. *Journal of Child and Family Studies, 5,* 55–65.

Farmer, E. M. Z., Burns, B. J., Phillips, S. D., Angold, A., & Costello, E. J. (2003). Pathways into and through mental health services for children and adolescents. *Psychiatric Services, 54*(1), 60–66.

Flisher, A. J., Kramer, R. A., Grosser, R. C., Alegría, M., Bird, H. R., et al. (1997). Correlates of unmet need for mental health services by children and adolescents. *Psychological Medicine, 27,* 1145–1154.

Forness, S. R, Kavale, K. A., & Lopez, M. (1993). Conduct disorders in the schools: Special education eligibility and comorbidity. *Journal of Emotional and Behavioral Disorders, 1,* 101–108.

Furstenberg, F. F. (1993). How families manage risk and opportunity in dangerous neighborhoods. In W. J. Wilson (ed.), *Sociology and the public agenda,* pp. 231–258. Newbury Park, CA: Sage Publications.

Garmezy, N., & Masten, A. (1991). The protective role of competence indicators in children at risk. In E. M. Cummings, A. L. Greene, & K. K. Karraker (eds.), *Life-span developmental psychology: Perspectives on stress and coping,* pp. 151–176. Hillsdale, NJ: Lawrence Earlbaum Associates.

Geller, B., & Luby, J. (1997). Child and adolescent bipolar disorder: A review of the past 10 years. *Journal of the American Academy of Child and Adolescent Psychiatry, 39*(9), 1168–1176.

Greenhill, L. L., Halperin, J. M., & Abikoff, H. (1999). Stimulant medications. *Journal of the American Academy of Child and Adolescent Psychiatry, 38,* 503–512.

Grisso, T., & Underwood, L. (2003). *Screening and assessing mental health and substance use disorders among youth in the juvenile justice system. Research and program brief.* Washington, DC: National Center for Mental Health and Juvenile Justice.

Halfon, N., Berkowitz, G., & Klee, L. (1992). Children in foster care in California: An examination of Medicaid reimbursed health services utilization. *Pediatrics, 89*(6 pt. 2), 1230–1237.

Halfon, N., Inkelas, M., & Wood, D. (1995). Nonfinancial barriers to care for children and youth. *Annual Review of Public Health, 16,* 447–472.

Halfon, N., Zepeda, A., & Inkelas, M. (2002). *Mental health services for children in foster care. Policy statement #4. Center for Healthier Children, Families and Communities.* Los Angeles: University of California at Los Angeles.

Henggeler, S. W., Melton, G. B., Smith, L. A., Schoenwald, J. K., & Hanley, J. (1993). Family preservation using multisystemic treatment: Long-term follow-up to a clinical trial with serious juvenile offenders. *Journal of Child and Family Studies, 2,* 283–293.

Henggeler, S. W., Schoenwald, S. K., Borduin, C. M., Rowland, M. D., & Cunningham, P. B. (1998). *Multisystemic treatment of antisocial behavior in children and adolescents.* New York: Guilford.

Hernandez, M., Gomez, A., Lipien, L., Greenbaum, P. E., Armstrong, K. H., & Gonzalez, P. (2001). Use of the system-of-care practice review in the national evaluation: Evaluating the fidelity of practice to system-of-care principles. *Journal of Emotional and Behavioral Disorders, 9*(1), 43–52.

Hoagwood, K., Burns, B. J., Kiser, L., Ringelsen, H., & Schoenwald, S. K. (2001). Evidence-based practice in child and adolescent mental health services. *Psychiatric Services, 52*(9), 1179–1188.

Holden, E. W., Friedman, R. M., & Santiago, R. L. (2001). Overview of the National Evaluation of the Comprehensive Community Mental Health Services for Children and Their Families program. *Journal of Emotional and Behavioral Disorders, 9*(1), 4–12.

Huffine, C. (2002). Child and adolescent psychiatry: Current trends in the community treatment of seriously emotionally disturbed youth. *Psychiatric Services, 53,* 809–811.

Individuals with Disabilities Education Act. (1997). P.L. 105-17.

Kataoka, S. H., Zhang, L., & Wells, K. B. (2002). Unmet need for mental health care among U.S. children: Variation by ethnicity and insurance status. *American Journal of Psychiatry, 159*(9), 1548–1555.

Kazdin, A. E. (1997). Parent management training: Evidence, outcomes, and issues. *Journal of the American Academy of Child and Adolescent Psychiatry, 36,* 1349–1356.

Kazdin, A. E. (2003). Psychotherapy for children and adolescents. *Annual Review of Psychology, 54,* 253–276.

Kendall, P. C., Aschenbrand, S. G., & Hudson, J. L. (2003). Child-focused treatment of anxiety. In A. E. Kazdin & J. R. Weisz (eds.), *Evidence-based psychotherapies for children and adolescents,* pp. 81–99. New York: Guilford.

Knitzer, J. (1982). *Unclaimed children: The failure of public responsibility to children and adolescents in need of mental health services.* Washington, DC: Children's Defense Fund.

Kortenkamp, K., & Ehrle, J. (2002). *The well-being of children involved with the child welfare system: A national overview.* Washington, DC: Urban Institute.

Landsverk, J., & Garland, A. F. (1999). Foster care and pathways to mental health services. In P. A. Curtis, G. Dale, Jr., & J. C. Kendall (eds.), *The foster care crisis: Translating research into policy and practice,* pp. 193–210. Lincoln: University of Nebraska Press.

Lavigne, J. V., Gibbons, R. D., Cristoffel, K. K., Arend, R., Rosenbaum, D., et al. (1996). Prevalence rates and correlates of psychiatric disorders among preschool children. *Journal of the American Academy of Child and Adolescent Psychiatry, 35*(2), 204–214.

Leaf, P. J., Alegria, M., Cohen, P., Goodman, S. H., Horwitz, S. M., et al. (1996). Mental health service use in the community and schools: Results from the four-community MECA study. *Journal of the American Academy of Child and Adolescent Psychiatry, 35,* 889–897.

Leonard Davis Institute (2000). Children's mental health: Recommendations for research, practice and policy. *LDI Issue Brief, 5*(7), 1–4.

Lewis, M., Fiering, C., & Rosenthal, S. (2000). Attachment over time. *Child Development, 71,* 707–720.

Liddle, H., Dakof, G., Parker, K., Diamond, G., Barrett, K., & Tejeda, M. (2001). Multidimensional family therapy for adolescent drug abuse: Results of a randomized clinical trial. *American Journal of Drug and Alcohol Abuse, 27,* 651–688.

Lindblad-Goldberg, M., Dore, M. M., & Stern, L. (1998). *Creating competence from chaos.* New York: Norton.

Lindblad-Goldberg, M., Jones, C. W., & Dore, M. M. (2004). Effective family-based mental health service for youth with serious emotional disturbance in Pennsylvania: The Ecosystemic Structural Family Therapy model. CASSP discussion paper. Harrisburg, PA: CAASP Training Center.

Littell, J. H. (2003). Systematic and nonsystematic reviews of research on the outcomes of multisystemic treatment. Paper presented at the Society for Social Work Research annual conference, New Orleans, LA, January 15–18, 2004.

Loeber, R., Wung, P., Keenan, K., Giroux, B., Stouthamer-Loeber, M. et al. (1993). Developmental pathways in disruptive child behavior. *Developmental Psychopathology, 5,* 103–133.

Long, P., Forehand, R., Wierson, M., & Morgan, A. (1994). Does parent training with young noncompliant children have long-term effects? *Behavioral Research Therapy, 32,* 101–107.

Luthar, S. S. (1991). Vulnerability and resilience: A study of high risk adolescents. *Child Development, 66,* 416–429.

Luthar, S. S., & Ziegler, E. (1993). Vulnerability and competence: A review of research on resilience in childhood. In M. E. Hertzig & E. A. Farber (eds.), *Annual progress in child psychiatry and child development, 1992,* pp. 232–255. New York: Brunner/Mazel.

Lyons-Ruth, K., Alpern, L., & Repacholi, G. (1993). Disorganized attachment classification and maternal psychosocial problems as predictors of hostile-aggressive behavior in the pre-school classroom. *Child Development, 64,* 572–585.

Main, M., Kaplan, N., & Cassidy, J. C. (1985). Security in infancy, childhood, and adulthood: A move to the level of representation. In I. Bretherton & E. Walters (eds.), Growing points of attachment theory and research. *Monographs of the Society for Research in Child Development, 50*(1–2), 66–104.

Main, M., & Solomon, J. (1990). Procedures for identifying infants as disorganized/disoriented during the Ainsworth Strange Situation. In M. T. Greenberg, D. Cicchetti, & E. M. Cummings (eds.), *Attachment in the preschool years: Theory, research, and intervention,* pp. 121–160. Chicago: University of Chicago Press.

McClellan, J. M., & Werry, J. S. (2003). Evidence-based treatments in child and adolescent psychiatry: An inventory. *Journal of the American Academy of Child and Adolescent Psychiatry, 42*(12), 1388–4000.

McCracken, J. T., McGough, J., Shah, B., Cronin, P., Hong, D., et al. (2002). Risperidone in children with autism and serious behavioral problems. *New England Journal of Medicine, 347,* 314–321.

Moore, K. A., Vandivere, S., & Ehrle, J. (2000). Sociodemographic risk and child well-being. *Assessing the New Federalism,* series B, no. B-18. Washington, DC: Urban Institute.

National Institute of Mental Health. (2001). National Institute of Mental Health research roundtable on prepubertal bipolar disorder. *Journal of the American Academy of Child and Adolescent Psychiatry, 40,* 871–878.

National Institutes of Health. (2000). National Institutes of Health consensus development statement: Diagnosis and treatment of attention-deficit/hyperactivity disorder (ADHD). *Journal of the American Academy of Child and Adolescent Psychiatry, 39*(2), 182–193.

National Survey of Child and Adolescent Well-Being (2003). *Baseline report for one-year-in-foster-care sample.* Retrieved June 30, 2004, from www.acf.hhs.gov/programs/core/ongoing_research/afc/well-being_reports.html.

Nordess, P. D., Grummert, M., Banks, D., Schindler, M. L., Moss, M. M. et al. (2002). Screening the mental health needs of youth in juvenile detention. *Juvenile and Family Court Journal, 53,* 43–50.

Offord, D., Boyle, M. H., Fleming, J., Blum, H. M., & Rae-Grant, N. (1989). Ontario Child Health Study: Summary of selected results. *Canada Journal of Psychiatry, 34,* 483–491.

Ollendick, T. H., & King, N. J. (1998). Empirically supported treatments for children with phobic and anxiety disorders: Current status. *Journal of Clinical Child Psychology, 27,* 156–167.

Owens, P. L., Hoagwood, K., Horwitz, S. J., Leaf, P. J., Poduska, J. M. et al. (2002). Barriers to children's mental health services. *Journal of the American Academy of Child and Adolescent Psychiatry, 41*(6), 731–738.

Palfrey, J. S., Singer, J. D., Raphael, E. S., & Walker, D. K. (1990). Providing therapeutic services to children in special educational placements: An analysis of the related services provisions of Public Law 94-142 in five urban school districts. *Pediatrics, 85,* 518–525.

Patterson, G. R. (1982). *Coercive family process.* Eugene, OR: Castalia.

Patterson, G. R., Reid, J. B., & Dishion, T. J. (1992). *Antisocial boys.* Eugene, OR: Castalia.

Perry, B. D. (2002). Childhood experience and the expression of genetic potential: What childhood neglect tells us about nature and nurture. *Brain and Mind, 3*(1), 79–100.

Perry, B. D., & Pollard, R. (1998). Homeostasis, stress, trauma, and adaptation: A neurodevelopmental view of childhood trauma. *Child and Adolescent Psychiatric Clinics of North America, 7*(1), 33–51.

Perry, B. D., Pollard, R. A., Blakely, T. L., Baker, W. L., & Vigilante, D. (1995). Childhood trauma, the neurobiology of adaptation, and "use-dependent" development of the brain: How "states" become "traits." *Infant Mental Health Journal, 16*(4), 271–291.

Pumariega, A. J., Winters, N. C., & Huffine, C. (2003). The evolution of systems of care for children's mental health: Forty years of community child and adolescent psychiatry. *Community Mental Health Journal, 39*(5), 399–425.

Rae-Grant, N., Thomas, B. J., Offord, D. R., & Boyle, M. H. (1989). Risk, protective factors, and prevalence of behavioral and emotional disorders in children and adolescents. *Journal of the American Academy of Child and Adolescent Psychiatry, 28,* 262–268.

Reinherz, H. A., Giaconia, R. M., Carmola Hauf, A. M., Wasserman, M. S., & Paradis, A. D. (2000). General and specific childhood risk factors for depression and drug disorders by early adulthood. *Journal of the American Academy of Child and Adolescent Psychiatry, 39,* 223–231.

Reinherz, H. Z., Giaconia, R. M., Lefkowitz, E. S., Pakiz, B., & Frost, A. K. (1993). Prevalence of psychiatric disorders in a community population of older adolescents. *Journal of the American Academy of Child and Adolescent Psychiatry, 32,* 369–377.

Robbins, M. S., Szapocznik, J., Santisteban, D. A., Hervis, O. E., Mitrani, V. B., & Schwartz, S. J. (2003). Brief strategic family therapy for Hispanic youth. In A. E. Kazdin & J. R. Weisz (eds.), *Evidence-based psychotherapies for children and adolescents,* pp. 407–424. New York: Guilford.

Roberts, M. C., Jacobs, A. K., Puddy, R. W., Nyre, J. E., & Vernberg, E. M. (2003). Treating children with serious emotional disturbances in schools and community: The Intensive Mental Health program. *Professional Psychology: Research and Practice, 34*(5), 519–526.

Roberts, R. E., Attkisson, C. C., & Rosenblatt, A. (1998). Prevalence of psychopathology among children and adolescents. *American Journal of Psychiatry, 155*(6), 715–725.

Rutter, M. (1985). Resilience in the face of adversity. *Psychiatry, 147,* 598–611.

Rutter, M. (1993). Resilience: Some conceptual considerations. *Journal of Adolescent Health, 14,* 626–631.

Rutter, M., Dunn, J., Plomin, R., Simonoff, E., Pickles, A. et al. (1997). Integrating nature and nurture:

Implications of person-environment correlations and interactions for developmental psychopathology. *Development and Psychopathology, 9,* 335–364.

Rutter, M., Tizard, J., Yule, W., Graham, P., & Whitmore, K. (1977). Research report: Isle of Wight studies, 1964–1974. *Psychological Medicine, 6,* 313–332.

Schuhmann, E. M., Foote, R., Eyberg, S. M., Boggs, S., & Algina, J. (1998). Parent-child interaction therapy: Interim report of a randomized trial with short-term maintenance. *Journal of Clinical Child Psychology, 27,* 34–35.

Simms, M. D., Dubowitz, H., & Szilagyi, M. A. (2000). Health care needs of children in the foster care system. *Pediatrics, 106*(4 suppl.), 909–918.

Smokowski, P. R. (1998). Prevention and intervention strategies for promoting resilience in disadvantaged children. *Social Service Review, 72,* 280–292.

Sroufe, L. A. (1990). Considering normal and abnormal together: The essence of developmental psychopathology. *Development and Psychopathology, 2,* 335–347.

Sroufe, L. A., Carlson, E. A., Levy, A. K., & Egeland, B. (1999). Implications of attachment theory for developmental psychopathology. *Development and Psychopathology, 11,* 1–13.

Stroul, B. A., & Friedman, R. (1986). *A system of care for severely emotionally disturbed children and youth.* Washington, DC: CASSP Technical Assistance Center.

Szapocznik, J., & Williams, R. A. (2000). Brief strategic family therapy: Twenty-five years of interplay among theory, research and practice in adolescent behavior problems and drug abuse. *Clinical Child and Family Psychology Review, 3,* 117–135.

Szilagyi, P. G., Holl, J. L., Rodewald, L. E., Pollard Shone, L., Zwanziger, J., et al. (2000). Evaluation of children's health insurance: From New York State's Child Health Plus to SCHIP. *Pediatrics, 105*(3 suppl. E), 687–691.

Teicher, M. H., Andersen, S. L., Polcari, A., Anderson, C. M., & Navalta, C. P. (2002). Developmental neurobiology of childhood stress and trauma. *Psychiatric Clinics of North America, 25*(2), 397–426.

Teplin, L. A., Abram, K. M., McClelland, G. M., Dulcan, M. K., & Mericle, A. A. (2002). Psychiatric disorders in youth in juvenile detention. *Archives of General Psychiatry, 59*(12), 1133–1143.

Terman, D. L., Larner, M. G., Stevenson, C. S., & Behrman, R. E. (1996). Special education for children with disabilities: Analysis and recommendations. *Future Child, 6,* 4–24.

Thompson, R. A. (2000). Legacy of early attachment. *Child Development, 71,* 145–152.

U.S. Department of Health and Human Services. (1999). *Mental health: A report of the Surgeon General.* Rock-

ville, MD: U.S. Department of Health and Human Services.

U.S. Department of Health and Human Services. (2000). *Report of the Surgeon General's Conference on Children's Mental Health: A national action agenda.* Rockville, MD: U.S. Department of Health and Human Services.

VanDenBerg, J., & Grealish, M. (1996). Individualized services and supports through the wraparound process: Philosophy and procedures. *Journal of Child and Family Studies, 5,* 7–21.

Vitiello, B. (2002). Current research on mental health treatments for children and adolescents. *Emotional & Behavioral Disorders in Youth, 2*(4), 87–88, 99.

Webster-Stratton, C. (1998). Preventing conduct problems in Head Start children: Strengthening parenting competencies. *Journal of Consulting and Clinical Psychology, 66,* 715–730.

Weiss, B., Catron, T., Harris, V., & Phung, T. J. (1999). The effectiveness of traditional child psychotherapy. *Journal of Consulting and Clinical Psychology, 67*(1), 82–94.

Weisz, J. R., Donenberg, G. R., Han, S. S., & Weiss, B. (1995). Bridging the gap between laboratory and clinic in child and adolescent psychotherapy. *Journal of Consulting and Clinical Psychology, 63,* 688–701.

Weisz, J. R., & Jensen, P. S. (1999). Efficacy and effectiveness of child and adolescent psychotherapy and pharmacotherapy. *Mental Health Services Research, 1,* 125–157.

Weisz, J. R., Weiss, B., Han, S. S., Granger, D. A., & Morton, T. (1995). Effects of psychotherapy with children and adolescents revisited: A meta-analysis of treatment outcome studies. *Psychological Bulletin, 117,* 450–468.

Werner, E. E. (1986). Resilient offspring of alcoholics: A longitudinal study from birth to age 18. *Journal of Studies on Alcohol, 47,* 34–40.

Werner, E. E. (1993). Risk, resilience, and recovery: Perspectives from the Kauai longitudinal study. *Development and Psychopathology, 5,* 503–515.

Wu, P., Hoven, C. W., Bird, H. R., Moore, R., Cohen, P., & Alegría, M. (1999). Depressive and disruptive disorders and mental health service utilization in children and adolescents. *Journal of the American Academy of Child and Adolescent Psychiatry, 38,* 1081–1090.

Wyman, P. A., Sandler, I., Wolchik, S., & Nelson, K. (2000). Resilience as cumulative competence promotion and stress protection: Theory and intervention. In D. Cicchetti, J. Rappaport, I. Sandler, & R. P. Weissberg (eds.), *The promotion of wellness in children and adolescents,* pp. 133–184. Washington, DC: Child Welfare League of America.

CYNTHIA J. WEAVER
DIANE W. KELLER
ANN H. LOYEK

Children with Disabilities in the Child Welfare System

On a continuum of vulnerability, children are indeed a vulnerable population. When a child or adolescent has a disability, whether diagnosed at the time of birth or later, the level of vulnerability is increased. Depending on the severity of the disability and the family environment, a variety of services may be required to insure a quality life for the child. In a functional, healthy family, a net of safety and support is developed for the child. The bond of parent to child is the foundation for creating and sustaining the net of safety, enabling the child to form an attachment for healthy development. The collaborative efforts of medical, educational, and social service professionals enhance the family safety net of care.

If a child with a disability is abused or neglected and enters the child welfare system, this safety net is stretched and sometimes torn beyond repair. Often parents' abilities to meet their child's needs is profoundly challenged, and the child welfare worker must direct a family to educational and supportive resources to sustain the family unit and allow the child to thrive. The role of the child welfare worker is central to the coordination of care and services for this vulnerable group of children.

In the event that out-of-home placement is required, medical, educational, and social services for a child with a disability are often put "on hold." A lapse in care may result while records are gathered, a placement is secured, and services are identified, often in a new geographic area. When the child with a disability enters the new environment, unique medical needs may be misunderstood, foster families may be ill-prepared for the combined medical and emotional needs, and the risk of frequent replacements may become a reality. Ultimately, the child's physical, emotional, and developmental health may be compromised. When children who have been placed in out-of-home care cannot be safely returned to their families, advocacy, sensitivity, and creativity are skills and qualities necessary to secure effective services and placements that will be of the highest caliber. Permanent placements must be sought that will provide children the ability to form an attachment to their caregiver equal to that of a healthy parental bond.

Social workers who can maintain compassion for the child with a disability and at the same time strongly advocate within somewhat impersonal systems and abusive family settings are needed in the child welfare field. The child welfare worker needs stamina to address the maltreatment inflicted on a child by the parent or caregiver, maltreatment that can cause permanent disabilities and possibly, death. The ability of the child welfare worker to balance emotions in order to provide effective interventions will indeed be challenged. Training within agencies or social work programs often does not prepare social workers for the overwhelming tasks and skills needed to interface with children with disabilities, the abuser, family members, and other service providers. Child welfare workers' reactions will frequently be polarized into a "fight or flight" response, either using harshness to protect their own feelings of helplessness, trauma, and/or counter-transference, or removing themselves from this population through shifts in job responsibilities or termination of employment.

However, for children with disabilities to develop to their fullest potential, medical, educational, and family support and therapeutic services must be provided in their biological, foster, or adoptive families (Hughes & Rycus 1998). Therefore, the child welfare worker has a key role in identifying and accessing appropriate services for children with disabilities and their families in the child welfare system and in the medical, social service, mental retardation, mental health, and educational systems.

In this chapter, we examine children with disabilities in the child welfare system at the start of the twenty-first century. Among the issues discussed are the interdependence of disability and maltreatment, how physical abuse can result in a disability, why children with disabilities are at risk for abuse, and special aspects of foster care and adoption for children with disabilities. We also review key aspects of resiliencies and protective factors that shape social work practice with this population. The chapter concludes with an examination of the role of the social worker in practice with this population. We focus primarily on physical disabilities; for a full discussion of mental health disabilities, see the chapter by Dore in this volume.

Case examples are threaded throughout the chapter to illustrate practice with children with disabilities. The graphic nature of the case examples, which are composites of actual cases, is not to shock the reader, but rather to help the reader understand the tragedy of abuse that results in permanent disabilities and possible death for helpless children. Social workers entering this field must have a clear picture of the children and the systems with which they will be working, as well as of the appropriate skills and training required. This preparation will foster the emotional resiliency, professional attitudes, and creative approaches needed for enduring and effective work with this group of children and their families.

Interdependence of Disability and Maltreatment

Services to children with disabilities and their families have traditionally been separated from child welfare services at the federal, state, and local levels. The focus of services, philosophical approaches to families, and legislative mandates often create service delivery systems with boundaries that are difficult to cross. Although age has been consistently identified as a factor related to specific types of abuse (National Clearinghouse on Child Abuse and Neglect Information 2004a), studies suggest that many children with developmental disabilities receive or are at risk for receiving services in the child welfare system (Goldson 1998; Patterson & Kratz 2002; Sullivan & Knutson 1998, 2000; Westat 1993). In addition, a large percentage of runaway youth has been identified as having a history of both maltreatment and a disability (Sullivan & Knutson 2000). This relationship between maltreatment and disability is also identified in the areas of foster care and adoption. Children who enter foster care as a result of maltreatment often have some type of disability (Harden 2004). Finally, the National Adoption Information Clearinghouse (1999) estimated that approximately one-half of children available for adoption had an identified developmental disability, with 21% of special needs adoptions identified as children with medical needs or physical, mental, or emotional disabilities.

Developmental Disability

The functional definition of a developmental disability was adopted by the federal government in 1978 and, with minor adaptations, is used to guide federal and state mandates relating to children with disabilities. A broad definition is: a developmental disability is a condition or disorder—physical, cognitive, or emotional —that has the potential to significantly affect the typical progress of a child's growth and development or substantially limit three or more major life activities, including self-care, language, learning, mobility, self-direction, capacity for independent living, and/or economic self-sufficiency (Developmental Disabilities Act 1984). A developmental disability may be congenital, or identified or acquired prior to the age of 22. Although the etiology of a disability often cannot be identified, many factors are associated with developmental disabilities.

Biological factors resulting in developmental disabilities include genetic or chromosomal abnormalities, such as Phenylketonuria (PKU), Tay Sachs, or Down Syndrome. Prenatal exposure to toxic substances can seriously affect normal fetal growth and development. Alcohol, tobacco, prescription drugs, street drugs, exposure to radiation, and the ingestion of certain chemicals as well as harmful chemical fumes can result in developmental disabilities. Complications of pregnancy and delivery and prenatal exposure to viral and bacterial infections (e.g., German measles) are related to various degrees of developmental disability. Characteristics related to the mother's age and health, as well as prematurity or abnormal growth rate of the fetus, are also factors related to developmental disability.

Fetal alcohol syndrome (FAS) is a preventable cause of mental retardation and developmental delay caused by prenatal alcohol consumption. Often children with FAS or fetal alcohol spectrum disorder (FASD) are in the child welfare system due to issues related to the drug and alcohol use of their parents. Children with FAS usually have some level of mental retardation or neurological disorder, including learning disabilities and behavior disorders. In the United States, it is estimated that approximately 12,000 children with FAS are born each year. In addition, the National Organization for Fetal Alcohol Syndrome (2004) estimates that

three times that many children have FASD. Children with FASD often present with a variety of issues, including low birth weight, irritability, feeding and sleep disturbances, developmental delays, academic problems, and behavior problems.

Postnatal factors (chronic diseases, injuries, and infectious diseases) are often preventable and account for 3% to 15% of identified developmental disabilities (Lipkin 1991). In a study conducted by the Communicable Disease Centers (1991), bacterial meningitis and child abuse were the leading causes of postnatal developmental disabilities in children aged 3 to 10. Auto accidents, drowning, and diving accidents often result in acquired disabilities for older children and adolescents.

CASE EXAMPLE 1

Believing that he was a "bad boy" and would be punished for the slightest infraction in behavior, Billy tried desperately to stay beyond his father's reach. Billy was never certain exactly what he did wrong, but he understood fully the form of discipline he would receive. Beatings with a belt were the norm. As young as he could remember, Billy knew his father was to be feared and that his mother was helpless to intervene. He often fled to the safety of a closet when his father beat his mother.

This day his mother's beating was savage, with his father cutting his mother with a kitchen knife. In fear for his mother's life, Billy moved from the safety of the closet to protect his mother. The anger of his father was heightened to think that his seven-year-old son would attempt to intervene. The father moved from the dying woman, grabbed Billy, and with repeated blows hit Billy in the head. A neighbor's concerned call to the authorities was the intervention that saved Billy's life.

Following Billy's recovery in the children's hospital, an alternative home was sought. With the funeral for Billy's mother that week, his father sentenced to life imprisonment, and no other relatives to provide his care, Billy was placed under the care of the county child welfare system. Yet, where would they find a home for a child with irreversible brain damage and the emotional needs of a one traumatized by the death of his mother, the incarceration of his father, and a history of physical abuse? Finding foster homes for children with both medical and emotional needs is extremely difficult, but not impossible.

Abuse May Result in Disability

Several long-term consequences of abuse and neglect have been identified in the literature, including developmental disability or delay (National Clearinghouse on Child Abuse and Neglect Information 2004b). A national study (National Center on Child Abuse and Neglect 1993) found that as many as 36% of the abused children in the sample sustained a disability as a result of abuse. Neglect in the form of inadequate supervision, nutrition, nurturing, or enrichment during the early years also can affect a child's development. Although the effects are sometimes temporary, Baladerian (1994) reports that permanent disabilities, such as mental retardation and learning disabilities, can result from neglect as well as from physical abuse.

One of the leading forms of fatal child abuse is shaken baby syndrome. When an angry or frustrated adult shakes an infant, the trauma can be similar to severe whiplash, often causing brain injury. Head trauma can result in cerebral palsy, mental retardation, developmental delays, and other neurological problems. At least 25% of the infants diagnosed with shaken baby syndrome die as a result of the abuse (Prevent Child Abuse America 2002). It is extremely important that parents be provided with the supports, education, and resources necessary to assist them in developing good parenting skills and in managing their emotions and reactions to their child caring responsibilities.

Children with Disabilities at Risk for Abuse

All children depend on their caregivers for safety, emotional support, education, and physical care. Because of their physical and/or cognitive needs, children with disabilities often require more intense care than do children without disabilities (Goldson 1998), placing them at greater risk for maltreatment (National Clearinghouse on Child Abuse and Neglect Information 2001).

Researchers have difficulty estimating rates of maltreatment among children with disabilities (National Clearinghouse on Child Abuse and Neglect Information 2001). In the only national study reported to date, Crosse, Kaye, and Ratnofsky (1993) found that children with disabilities were 1.7 times more likely to be maltreated than were children without disabilities.

However, a study conducted in 1997 in Omaha, Nebraska, found that children with disabilities were more than three times more likely to be maltreated than were children without disabilities (Sullivan & Knutson 2000). In addition, the study concluded that neglect was the most prevalent type of maltreatment of children with and without disabilities. Although this was not a national study, the finding demonstrates the need for further research to determine the true extent of abuse among this population. Reported rates of maltreatment for children with special needs are likely to be low for several reasons. Currently, there is no consistent procedure for reporting abuse of children in specific categories. In 1982, 50% of the states included information on disability in annual reports. In 1997, 38% reported that they identify children as having preexisting disabilities in their annual reports, and only 13% of states reported that specific disabilities are documented. In addition, only 4% of states identify children who have a developmental disability as a result of child maltreatment (Bonner & Crow 1997).

Sullivan and Knutson (1998) concluded that child protective workers fail to identify or document disabilities in the many children under their care. As a result, child welfare workers as well as foster and adoptive families may be involved with children that have not been identified as having a special need or as being eligible for supportive services. Foster and/or adoptive families need information, preparation, and access to resources to increase the probability of consistent placement or permanency. In addition, this lack of identification and subsequent documentation contributes to the underrepresentation of children with disabilities in national statistics. It is imperative that child welfare workers be knowledgeable about the warning signs of developmental delay and the symptoms of developmental disabilities and assist families in accessing appropriate services. National criteria and consistent documentation are needed to fully understand the scope of this issue.

The conceptualization of risk for maltreatment can be placed in an ecological context (Patterson & Kratz 2002; Sobsey 1994), identifying the multidirectional effects of the environment on the individual, as well as those of the individual on the environment. Although certain factors, such as parental substance abuse (Sobsey 1994) and history of violence (Ammerman & Baladerian 1993), are related to risk of maltreatment for all children, some factors are more strongly related to children with disabilities.

Even though a child is never to be perceived as the cause of maltreatment, characteristics of the child's disability may increase the potential for risk. A child with difficult behavior patterns and self-regulatory disorders may be at increased risk for maltreatment (Prevent Child Abuse America 2002). In addition, risk for harm increases when children with a disability do not understand what adult behaviors may be harmful to them or how to communicate to others about the abuse. Children with cognitive or language disabilities may be viewed by a perpetrator as "safe victims" (National Clearinghouse on Child Abuse and Neglect Information 2001) because the child's limited ability to communicate reduces the likelihood of the perpetrator being caught or successfully prosecuted.

Children with moderate-to-severe disabilities requiring long-term assistance with activities of daily living may also be at increased risk for abuse by caretakers (Ammerman & Baladerian 1993; Rogow & Hass 1999). Long-term care can negatively impact family relationships, increase caregiver stress, and reduce financial resources, thus increasing the risk for caregivers to abuse and/or neglect a child.

Family problems and dysfunction, including economic hardships, domestic violence, parental mental health problems, substance abuse, lack of social support, and inaccessible or unavailable services may also be factors contributing to risk of maltreatment (Sobsey 1994; Steinberg & Hylton 1998). In some cases, lack of knowledge about caring for a child with disabilities can be a factor in a parent's ability to cope with the child's needs. This lack of knowledge can lead to unrealistic expectations as well as stress related to having a child with a disability. A combination of these factors can result in increased potential for neglect or abuse (Prevent Child Abuse America 2002).

Respite Care

Although many situations warrant separation of a child from his or her birth family, others present the need for more proactive, preventive interventions. Respite services are designed to provide temporary relief for parents who begin to feel overwhelmed by the demands of daily caregiving. In a recent study involving families of children with developmental disabilities (Cowen & Reed 2002), stress related both to parental and child characteristics was decreased following respite care intervention. Respite services are often available in the child welfare system or in the mental health–mental retardation system. Both planned and crisis respite have become a part of the continuum of family services intended to reduce family stress, support family stability, and prevent abuse and neglect. A number of models have been developed and include both in-home and out-of-home models (Cernoch 1994).

CASE EXAMPLE 2

Mr. and Mrs. Johnson had cared for Carla at home since birth, even when doctors encouraged them to institutionalize her as an infant because of Carla's profound mental retardation and physical abnormalities. They had been diligent and resourceful in securing services and, although not wealthy, had provided a caring and nurturing environment for Carla. Now, aged 12, Carla was living longer than doctors had predicted.

Within the last year, life in the Johnson home had dramatically changed. Mr. Johnson died suddenly from a heart attack, and Mrs. Johnson, who had previously cared for Carla at home, needed to find work outside the home to support herself and Carla. Not having advanced educational training or prior work experience, Mrs. Johnson's employment options were limited, and she took a job that paid minimum wage. Mr. Johnson's life insurance policy and some savings offset costs for a time, but Mrs. Johnson knew that she would need to secure a higher paying position in the near future. Carla's physical care was now entrusted to strangers, as Mrs. Johnson worked outside the home to earn a living. This was a difficult transition for both Mrs. Johnson and Carla. Carla's behavior was adding a new dimension to her care; she had limited understanding about the recent death of her father and her mother's sudden exit from her daily care. Often in-home providers canceled shifts because of illness, weather, or the labor-intensive nature of Carla's care. At such times, Mrs. Johnson had to choose between working outside the home and remaining home to care for Carla. Mrs. Johnson's employment changed a number of times to accommodate her daughter's needs and she was dismissed because of repeated work absences. Extended family members, community resources, and funding streams were accessible for a time, but were soon depleted and no longer available.

Mrs. Johnson explored institutional care for Carla, something she had resisted since Carla's birth. With Carla's increased behavioral acting-out, her involved physical care, and adolescent development, a team approach to her care appeared to be the viable option. Visits to residential facilities revealed that Mrs. Johnson's limited income would not be sufficient to provide a setting for the level of care Carla required.

As a result of the recent physical and emotional upheavals in her life, Carla became ill and was hospitalized for an extended period of time. For the first time since before her husband died, Mrs. Johnson experienced extended respite and uninterrupted employment. Mrs. Johnson began to dread Carla's return home and the endless coordination of necessary services. Mrs. Johnson's guilt was unbearable, yet she knew from numerous previous attempts she would be unable to maintain their basic needs for long before declaring bankruptcy or going on welfare.

Mrs. Johnson never came to the hospital to take Carla home. Mrs. Johnson packed up her few belongings, left town, and traveled across country to begin a new life, hopeful that the County Department of Children and Youth Services would find Carla a better home than she could now provide. The abandonment of her vulnerable child would haunt her forever, and her remorse would spiral her into a deep depression. Carla, as well, moved into a severe depression, self-mutilating behaviors, and grieved loss of her parents. The child welfare supervisor was at a loss as to which worker to assign this case.

Foster Care and Adoption of Children with Disabilities

When abuse is investigated and child protective service workers determine that the appropriate intervention is to separate a child from his or her family, foster families can provide a safe, nurturing environment while a permanency plan is formulated. Reunification with the child's parents is ideal. However, when parents consistently fall short of demonstrating adequate parenting abilities, such alternatives as adoption or legal guardianship become the goal (Bass, Shields, & Behrman 2004).

More than 800,000 children spend some time in the foster care system each year (U.S. Department of Health and Human Services 2005) and about 45% to 50% of those children have a chronic health problem or disability (American Humane Association 2000). The needs of children with disabilities are often great, and successful foster placements demand attention to those needs. Foremost, foster caregivers must have the skills and resources to meet a child's special needs (Hughes & Rycus 1998). Foster parents of children with disabilities are expected to respond to physical, mental, emotional, behavioral, and medical needs, and navigate the legal and educational systems as required. Chipungu and Bent-Goodley (2004: 83) state, "given these high demands, it is not surprising that child welfare agencies often experience difficulty recruiting and retaining foster parents. Moreover, once recruited, foster parents face additional challenges as they endeavor to care for children with complex needs." Access to education, training, resources, and support services becomes critical to placement stability and the well-being of each child.

The child welfare system recognizes the benefit of family stability and consistent care for children with disabilities. Family stability can have positive effects on a child's health, academic performance, and social and emotional functioning (Harden 2004). Training and support for foster families must include resources relating to each child's specific disability, as well as the continued collaboration with medical, psychological, educational, and social service professionals. The risk of multiple placements is minimized if foster families are surrounded with an environment of comprehensive care (Chipungu & Bent-Goodley 2004).

CASE EXAMPLE 3

Jamal recently turned 15 and had spent most of his life in foster care. Periodically he had returned home to a father, now deceased, and then to an aunt, who—after Jamal set a fire in her garage—refused to have any contact with him. Jamal prided himself in the ability not to form attachments to his caregivers, for if your mother abandons you as an infant, your father dies from drugs, and family members will not come forward to provide care, then why risk forming attachments to strangers? When one foster home became unacceptable to Jamal, he knew the specific behavior that would cause the foster parent(s) to ask for his removal. Jamal lived in a variety of foster homes and settings; urban, rural, African American, Caucasian, single, heterosexual, and lesbian or gay parental systems. Jamal viewed himself as a "sur-

vivor" and would boast that life after placement would be a "breeze," counting the days until he would be 18 and "on his own."

Today, however, the news from the specialist at the children's hospital would not enable Jamal to be on his own in the future. Cancer was the diagnosis and the prognosis was not good. Over the next 2 years, Jamal experienced multiple hospitalizations, resulting in amputation of his leg, removal of a portion of his lung, multiple chemotherapy treatments, and a bone marrow transplant. Eventually Jamal was moved to a skilled nursing facility, still under the care of child welfare, but without a permanent birth or foster family member to provide care or visit during his final days of life.

Adoption Subsidy

Families who consider adopting children with disabilities require comparable ongoing support. In addition, "financial assistance is available [which] can include monthly cash payments, medical costs, some specialized services and adoption-related expenses" (National Adoption Information Clearinghouse 1999:6). Assistance provided through the federal Title IV-E adoption assistance program, or the adoption subsidy, can continue until the child becomes 18 years of age, or until age 21, if deemed necessary by the state. For children who are not eligible for the Title IV-E program, states provide various forms of adoption subsidies, depending on each child's specific needs. Title IV-E serves as a support for families in their efforts to meet the unique needs of their adopted children (National Adoption Information Clearinghouse 2000).

Quality interventions involving both children and families are critical to the success of special needs adoptions (Mack & Boehm 2002). Programs that incorporate collaboration, communication, and attention to the individual's needs show the most promise for favorable outcomes in the lives of children with disabilities.

Pennsylvania's Statewide Adoption Network (SWAN) is an example of an effective system designed to reduce the number of children waiting for permanent homes. Since 1992, about 14,000 children in Pennsylvania found permanent homes with the assistance of this adoption network. SWAN finalized 2,020 adoptions in FY2002–2003 alone. Children with disabilities are among those served by SWAN and its affiliated agencies.

SWAN is a partnership among Pennsylvania's Department of Public Welfare, the Pennsylvania Adoption Exchange, public and private adoption agencies, organizations, advocates, judges, the legal community, and foster and adoptive parents (Pennsylvania Adoption Exchange 2003). This collaboration allows professionals to locate potential homes for special needs children and communicate throughout the entire process, insuring a successful, supported placement.

Detailed child profiles are produced by county agencies that obtain custody when a child is abused or neglected. Profiles are also produced by adoption agencies for each family interested in pursuing adoption. Constant communication between all of Pennsylvania's 67 counties and both public and private adoption agencies expedites the process of identifying a match between families and children. SWAN-affiliated agencies insure that children and families have adequate preparation for the careful integration of the child into the family. When a placement is successful, SWAN workers assist the family throughout the adoption proceedings and remain in contact for further support and assistance during the challenges of parenting a child with special needs.

New York City is home to New Alternatives for Children (NAC), an effective program that specializes in serving children with disabilities, supporting medically fragile children and those transitioning from lengthy hospital stays into a home (Mack and Boehm 2002). NAC matches children with foster and adoptive families, and successfully reunites children with their natural families. The program administers 34 groups for children that involve music, art, tutoring,

and specialized support groups. Families have access to material resources (food, clothing, cash assistance) as well as emotional and educational support "tailored to each child and family's specific needs" (Mack & Boehm 2002). This individualized approach accounts for NAC's success in effectively identifying and fulfilling the unique needs of each child.

In 1989, a program to specifically address the needs of children with disabilities and those who were terminally ill was incorporated into a child welfare agency in the private sector (Weaver 1999). The dual training that one author of this chapter possessed in both social work and theology led to the development and inclusion of a chaplain in the social service agency. The chaplain provided services of a religious and/or spiritual nature, both for the children and their families (biological and foster). Frequently the spiritual needs of children in child welfare settings are overlooked, when, in fact, spirituality can often provide a strong place of comfort and resiliency for a child with disabilities and/or who is dying (see the chapter by Hawkins). Children and their caregivers will ask questions of a spiritual nature surrounding a disability and/or terminal illness. The chaplain can work closely with social workers to provide end-of-life care and funeral arrangements at the time of the child's death. Canda and Furman (1999) speak to the importance of providing a spiritually sensitive social work practice with a variety of populations and needs.

CASE EXAMPLE 4

Now 12 years of age, Mary is beginning to understand the nature of her living environment and why she has spent her educational life in special education classes. Mary also understands more clearly why her brother continues to experience multiple bouts of pneumonia and hospitalizations. Although relieved that she did not contract the AIDS virus, as did her younger brother, she is angered at her mother for the drug and alcohol abuse during the pregnancy that resulted in Mary's premature birth and subsequent developmental delays. Mary and her brother spent almost the first year of their lives in the hospital being treated for drug withdrawal, HIV/AIDS, and developmental delay. They were then placed in separate foster homes, each equipped to meet their individual, special needs. Visits between the siblings occur on a regular basis, although not frequently enough for two children with no other biological family but each other. As they age together in the foster care system and are now adolescents, Mary and her brother frequently discuss spiritual issues, such as: Why did God let this happen to our family? Is our mother in Heaven even though she did drugs? What will happen to us after death?

Resiliencies and Protective Factors

Children with special needs are highly diverse by virtue of age, individual history, type of abuse and the extent of its effects, and other distinct factors (Sullivan & Freundlich 1999). Needs vary according to each child's physical disability, as well as his or her mental and emotional health. Child welfare workers must consider such differences and identify those factors that have sustained each child for many years.

Resiliency in abused children involves the development of a variety of coping behaviors, which are the strengths that enable them to survive in their unsafe environments (Henry 1999). Studies have identified behaviors and personality traits that contribute to resilience in maltreated children. Among them are child IQ, temperament and health, optimism, sense of adventure, courage, self-understanding, humor, the ability to work hard and express emotions, risk-taking, flexibility, confidence, competence, and confidence in internal and external resources (Harden 2004; Henry 1999). In a recent study of adolescents with a history of physical abuse (Perkins & Jones 2004), the protective factors of positive school climate, spirituality, adult and family support, view of the future, and involvement in extracurricular activities contributed to the youth's resiliency and the

ability to limit risk-taking behaviors. Children with increased risk factors, such as poverty, abuse, and separation from family, seem to respond with more positive outcomes if they are provided safe and stable homes and opportunities to engage with a nurturing adult (Harden 2004).

Children who endure the challenges of a disability and neglect or abuse require some level of resiliency to survive physically and emotionally. For many children, sustaining life depends on such resiliency. Child welfare social workers, administrators, and foster parents can strengthen the child's resiliency by providing supportive and protective factors. Of utmost importance is the development of a permanency plan so that few if any re-placements are necessary.

Role of the Social Worker

There is an increased need for competent, knowledgeable professionals who can serve and advocate for children with disabilities and their families. Workers need to be familiar with legislation and policies in the medical, disability, and educational arena that guide services for their clients. Children with developmental disabilities are eligible for preschool and school-aged services under the Individuals with Disabilities Act (1997). In addition, many states provide early intervention services for children birth to 3 years of age (Education of the Handicapped Act Amendments of 1986; P.L. 99-457). Early Head Start and Head Start programs are good resources for children with disabilities and their families. According to program eligibility requirements, at least 10% of the children in Head Start programs must have a disability or developmental delay. Early Head Start, not available in every community, provides parent-infant support and education for infants younger than age 3 and their parents.

Additional training in the areas of mental retardation, medical social work, developmental delay, and early intervention will better assist the child welfare worker who has the responsibility of finding and supporting appropriate placements for children with disabilities. A number of training materials have been published for child welfare workers related to children with disabilities and their families. The topics include collaboration among parents, child welfare workers, and educators (O'Neill 2002), and training in developmental disabilities (Steinberg & Hylton 1998; Sullivan & Cork 1996).

Child welfare workers need to be able to identify the warning signs of developmental delays, understand the scope of various developmental disabilities, help families identify the strengths and needs of the child and family, assist families in adaptation of environments and expectations as appropriate, and act as mentors in assisting them to advocate for their child. Trained workers understand the challenges that face these families and can assist them in securing resources and communicating their needs. Effective training needs to be more comprehensive than traditional competency training for child welfare workers. According to Bonner and Crow (1997) only 7% of states mandate that child welfare workers receive training related to disabilities. The literature supports the adoption of policies that would require more specific training related to children with developmental disabilities and their families (Ammerman & Baladerian 1993; National Center on Child Abuse and Neglect 1993; Orelove, Hollahan, & Myles 2000).

Conclusion

The oversight of children and adolescents with disabilities in the child welfare system requires strong accountability by social workers, agencies, and legislators for the best interests of this population to be met. Training and networking with medical, educational, mental health/retardation, and community resources are necessary prerequisites for effective care for children with disabilities in the child welfare system. Caseloads including children with disabilities should be small, so that sufficient time and energies can be spent in securing additional training, supporting families, and networking with other agency resources. Agencies should provide the expertise, resources, supervision, and support that would strengthen the interventions provided by the social worker to families caring for children and youth with disabilities. Such incentives as small caseloads, specialized training, increased salary, and leave time surrounding the death of a child would provide longevity to the social worker's employment with this population of vulnerable children. Professionals desiring to work with these special children should have access to the tools and supports required to effectively meet the children's special needs and to care for themselves. The fragility and vulnerability of this population of children require the utmost of our sensitivity, advocacy, expertise, and creativity.

REFERENCES

American Humane Association. (2000). Meeting the needs of young children in foster care. Retrieved May 23, 2004, from www.americanhumane.org.

Ammerman, R. T., & Baladerian, N. J. (1993). *Maltreatment of children with disabilities.* Chicago: National Committee to Prevent Child Abuse.

Baladerian, N. J. (1994). Abuse and neglect of children with disabilities. ARCH National Respite Network and Resource Center factsheet no. 36. Retrieved June 24, 2003, from http://www.archrespite.org/archfs36.htm.

Bass, S., Shields, M. K., & Behrman, R. E. (2004). Children, families, and foster care: Analysis and recommendations. *The Future of Children, 14*(1), 5–29.

Bonner, B. L., & Crow, S. M. (1997). State efforts to identify maltreatment of children with disabilities: A follow-up study. *Child Maltreatment, 2*(1), 52–61.

Canda, E. R., & Furman, L. D. (1999). *Spiritual diversity in social work practice: The heart of helping.* New York: Free Press.

Cernoch, J. M. (1994). Respite for children with disabilities and chronic or terminal illness. ARCH National Respite Network and Resource Center factsheet no. 2. Retrieved June 24, 2003, from www.archrespite.org/archfs02.htm.

Chipungu, S. S., & Bent-Goodley, T. B. (2004). Meeting the challenges of contemporary foster care. Children, families, and foster care. *The Future of Children, 14*(1), 75–93.

Communicable Disease Centers. (1991). Postnatal causes of developmental disabilities in children aged 3–10 years. Retrieved June 24, 2004, from www.cdc.gov/mmwr/preview/mmwrhtml/00040247.htm.

Cowen P. S., & Reed, D. A. (2002). Effects of respite care for children with developmental disabilities: Evaluation of an intervention for at-risk families. *Public Health Nursing 19*(4), 272–283.

Crosse, S. B., Kaye, E., & Ratnofsky, A. C. (1993). *A report of the maltreatment of children with disabilities.* Washington, DC: U.S. Department of Health and Human Services.

Developmental Disabilities Act of 1984. (1984). P.L. 98-527.

Education of the Handicapped Act. (1986). P.L. 99-457.

Goldson, E. (1998). Children with disabilities and child maltreatment. *Child Abuse and Neglect, 22,* 663–667.

Harden, B. J. (2004). Safety and stability for foster children: A developmental perspective. *Children, Families and Foster Care, 14*(1), 31–47.

Henry, D. L. (1999). Resilience in maltreated children: Implications for special needs adoption. *Child Welfare, 78,* 519–540.

Hughes, R. C., & Rycus, J. S. (1998). *Developmental disabilities and child welfare.* Washington, DC: CWLA Press.

Individuals with Disabilities Education Act. (1997). P.L. 105-17.

Lipkin, P. H. (1991). Epidemiology of developmental disabilities. In A. J. Capute & P. J. Accardo (eds.), *Developmental disabilities in infancy & childhood,* pp. 43–61. Baltimore: Paul H. Brookes.

Mack, K., & Boehm, S. (2002). Serving children with disabilities. Retrieved June 16, 2003, from www.cwla.org/articles/cv0209serving.htm.

National Adoption Information Clearinghouse. (1999). Adopting children with developmental disabilities. Retrieved June 16, 2003, from naic.acf.hhs.gov/pubs/f_devdis.cfm.

National Adoption Information Clearinghouse. (2000). Adopting a child with special needs. Retrieved June 16, 2003, from naic.acf.hhs.gov/pubs/f_specne.cfm.

National Center on Child Abuse and Neglect (1993). A report on the maltreatment of children with disabilities. Washington, DC: U.S. Department of Health and Human Services.

National Clearinghouse on Child Abuse and Neglect Information. (2001). In focus: The risk and prevention of maltreatment of children with disabilities. Retrieved June 16, 2003, from nccanch.acf.hhs.gov/pubs/prevenres/focus.

National Clearinghouse on Child Abuse and Neglect Information. (2004a). Child maltreatment 2002 report. Retrieved June 16, 2003, from www.acf.hhs.gov/programs/cb/publications/cmreports.htm.

National Clearinghouse on Child Abuse and Neglect Information (2004b). Long-term consequences of child abuse and neglect. Retrieved May 25, 2004, from nccanch.acf.hhs.gov/pubs/factsheets/long_term_consequences.cfm.

National Organization for Fetal Alcohol Syndrome FAS/FASD/ARND/ARBD. Retrieved May 25, 2004, from www.nofas.org/healthcare/indicators.aspx.

O'Neill, P. (2002). *Abuse and neglect of children with disabilities: A collaborative response.* Richmond: Virginia Institute for Developmental Disabilities, Virginia Commonwealth University.

Orelove, F. P., Hollahan, D. J., & Myles, K. T. (2000). Maltreatment of children with disabilities: Training needs for a collaborative response. *Child Abuse and Neglect, 24,* 185–194.

Patterson, J. M., & Kratz, B. (2002). Child maltreatment among children with chronic illnesses and disabilities. Retrieved May 22, 2003, from fsos.che.umn.edu/kouneski/ChildDisabilities.ppt.

Pennsylvania Adoption Exchange. (2003). Statewide Adoption Network (SWAN). Retrieved July 31, 2003, from www.adoptpakids.org/paeswan.asp.

Perkins, D. F., & Jones, K. R. (2004). Risk behaviors and resiliency within physically abused adolescents. *Child Abuse and Neglect, 28,* 547–564.

Prevent Child Abuse America. (2002). Fact sheet: Maltreatment of children with disabilities. Atlanta, GA: National Resource Center on Child Abuse and Neglect.

Rogow, P., & Hass, J. (1999). *The person within: Preventing abuse of children and young people with disabilities.* Vancouver: British Columbia Institute Against Family Violence.

Sobsey, D. (1994). *Violence and abuse in the lives of people with disabilities: The end of silent acceptance?* Baltimore: Paul H. Brookes.

Steinberg, R., & Hylton, L. (1998). *Responding to maltreatment of children with disabilities: A trainer's guide.* Portland: Oregon Institute on Disability and Development and Oregon Health Sciences University.

Sullivan, A., & Freundlich, M. (1999). Achieving excellence in special needs adoption. *Child Welfare, 78,* 507–517.

Sullivan, P. M., & Cork, P. M. (1996). *Developmental disabilities training project.* Omaha, NE: Boys' Town National Research Hospital, Center for Abused Children with Disabilities.

Sullivan, P. M., & Knutson, J. F. (1998). The association between child maltreatment and disabilities in a hospital-based epidemiological study. *Child Abuse and Neglect, 22,* 271–288.

Sullivan, P. M., & Knutson, J. F. (2000). The prevalence of disabilities and maltreatment among runaway children. *Child Abuse and Neglect, 24,* 1275–1288.

U.S. Department of Health and Human Services. (2005). *Adoption and Foster Care Analysis and Reporting System. National adoption and foster care statistics.* Retrieved January 30, 2005, from www.acf.hhs.gov/programs/cb/dis/afcars9/publications/afcars.htm.

Weaver, C. J. (1999). Supporting the spirituality of children in foster care and their caregivers. In J. A. Silver, B. J. Amster, & T. Haecher (eds.), *Young children and foster care: A guide for professionals,* pp. 145–161. Baltimore: Paul H. Brookes.

Westat Corporation (1993). The incidence of maltreatment among children with disabilities. Washington, DC: National Clearinghouse on Child Abuse and Neglect.

DIANE E. ELZE
WENDY F. AUSLANDER
ARLENE STIFFMAN
CURTIS McMILLEN

Educational Needs of Youth in Foster Care

National statistics tell us that they [our youth] are educationally deprived, that they are behind and they need some time to catch up. Under the best of circumstances, our youths are getting high school educations at the age of 17 or 18. Foster youths are not, and if they don't finish high school by the time they leave care, they usually won't finish high school. That is not the path to independence.

Lyman and colleagues (1995:47)

Approximately 20,000 youths aged 18 to 21 emancipate or age out of foster care annually (U.S. Department of Health and Human Services 1999). Over a decade ago, the Panel on High-Risk Youth of the National Research Council's Commission on Behavioral and Social Sciences and Education (1993) determined that adolescents involved with the child welfare system were at high risk of educational failure and other deleterious outcomes. Despite the delivery of independent living program (ILP) services to more youths in foster care following the passage of the Title IV-E Independent Living Initiative of 1986 (P.L. 99-272), research findings continued to indicate that older adolescents exiting care were ill-prepared to live independently and self-sufficiently, in part due to low educational attainment (e.g., Barth 1990; Cook, Fleishman, & Grimes 1991; Courtney, Piliavin, Grogan-Kaylor, & Nesmith 2001; McMillen & Tucker 1998; Nixon 1998).

Persistent advocacy on the part of policymakers, child welfare professionals, youth advocates, and young people (Pizzigati 2001) gave rise to the Foster Care Independence Act of 1999 (P.L. 106-109), which established the John H. Chafee Foster Care Independence Program (CFCIP). This legislation doubled federal spending on ILP services, broadened eligibility, provided states with greater flexibility in their use of federal ILP funds, and required greater accountability for comprehensive planning, program performance, and outcomes (U.S. Department of Health and Human Services 2001). States can now provide a broader array of ILP services to current and former foster care youths up to age 21. Additionally, under the Promoting Safe and Stable Families Amendments of 2001 (P.L. 107-133), educational and training vouchers can be provided to young people until they reach, in some cases, the age of 23 (Kessler 2004). Although research has yet to determine the effectiveness of these initiatives in improving outcomes for youth exiting foster care, the educational attainment of youth in care is the focus of renewed interest from policymakers, sponsors of ILPs, youth advocates, child welfare professionals, and educators.

In this chapter, we review the literature on the educational aspirations, academic achievement, and other educational experiences of youths in out-of-home care, and present findings from two studies that were conducted by research teams at the George Warren Brown School of Social Work at Washington University in St. Louis. Both studies, the Bridges to Life Options Study and the Youth Services Project (YSP), included adolescents involved in the child welfare system and gathered data on their educational experiences, mental health problems, and family and peer environments. Finally, we discuss the implications of the research for social work practice and describe some programmatic innovations to enhance the educational attainment of youth in care.

Significance of the Issue

The Child Welfare League of America (1989) has long recommended that youth in out-of-home care receive an array of educational services. Why are the educational needs of youth in care of such importance?

Educational attainment is a strong predictor of adolescent well-being (Redd, Brooks, & McGarvey 2002) and adult functioning and self-sufficiency (Cook, Fleishman, & Grimes 1991; McDonald, Allen, Westerfelt, & Piliavin 1996). Educational deficits diminish the life chances of many youths exiting the child welfare system (Cook 1994; DeWoody, Ceja, & Sylvester 1993), particularly in a job market increasingly divided into low wage, entry-level jobs and high-wage positions requiring advanced training (Workforce Strategy Center 2000).

The educational histories of many youths in foster care are marked by grade retentions (Sawyer & Dubowitz 1994), placements in special education (Goerge, Voorhis, Grant, Casey, & Robinson 1992; Sawyer & Dubowitz 1994), poor academic achievement (Fanshel, Finch, & Grundey 1990; Festinger 1983; Pecora et al. 2003; Sawyer & Dubowitz 1994), multiple school changes (Blome 1997; Courtney, Piliavin, Grogan-Kaylor, & Nesmith 2001; Festinger 1983; Pecora et al. 2003), school behavior problems (Benedict, Zuravin, & Stallings 1996; Blome 1997; McMillen, Auslander, Elze, White, & Thompson 2003), and school attendance problems (Benedict, Zuravin, & Stallings 1996; Conger & Rebeck 2001; McMillen, Auslander, Elze, White, & Thompson 2003).

A disproportionate number of youths in foster care receive special education services, ranging from 30% to 40% (Courtney, Piliavin,

Grogan-Kaylor, & Nesmith 2001; English, Kouidou-Giles, & Plocke 1994; Evans 2004; Goerge, Voorhis, Grant, Casey, & Robinson 1992; Pecora et al. 2003; Sawyer & Dubowitz 1994). Even with these high prevalence rates, evidence exists that the special education needs of many youth in foster care remain unidentified (Goerge, Voorhis, Grant, Casey, & Robinson 1992). Many children enter foster care behind in their educational achievement and fail to catch up while in care (Conger & Rebeck 2001; McDonald, Allen, Westerfelt, & Piliavin 1996). Multiple school changes impede their educational progress and increase their risk of dropping out (Pecora et al. 2003; Teachman, Paasch, & Carver 1996). Among older adolescents in care, one study found that 50% reported four or more school changes (Courtney, Piliavin, Grogan-Kaylor, & Nesmith 2001), and another reported that 63% experienced at least one mid-year school change since seventh grade (McMillen, Auslander, Elze, White, & Thompson 2003). School dropout rates among youths leaving out-of-home care exceed the national average (Cook 1994; Mech 1994). Failure to obtain a high school diploma and/or postsecondary education may condemn these young people to poverty-level wages (Mech 1994).

Considering the critical role educational attainment plays in adult productivity, and that the federal ILP was enacted almost 30 years ago, existing studies, although important, reflect a dearth of research. Little is known about the educational trajectories of youths in out-of-home care and the factors that influence the course of their trajectories. Few program evaluations have been conducted on independent living services (Sheehy et al. 2000; U.S. General Accounting Office 1999). Most outcome studies on youths discharged from foster care report high school completion rates, but little else about their educational lives. Furthermore, these studies have often underestimated educational attainment because the data were collected only at discharge (McMillen & Tucker 1998). Even fewer studies have examined risk and protective factors associated with the educational aspirations, academic achievement, and school problems of youth in out-of-home care.

Youth in foster care often present with multiple psychosocial problems, including histories of physical and sexual abuse, family instability and disruption, health problems, multiple placements, substance abuse, delinquent behaviors, and mental health problems (Barth 1990; Jonson-Reid & Barth 2000; Rosenfeld et al. 1997). These risk factors may impinge on their ability to achieve independence and self-sufficiency. Educational success, however, may attenuate the adverse effects of such psychosocial risks on future well-being, making educational needs a priority area for intervention. Understanding the risk and protective factors associated with the educational experiences of foster care youth may suggest points of intervention for the professionals and families involved with these youths to maximize their educational attainment.

Review of the Literature

Educational Achievement

Since the 1960s, multiple studies have pointed to the persistence of educational achievement problems among youth in foster care (McDonald, Allen, Westerfelt, & Piliavin 1996). It should be noted that the majority of these studies used data collected from young people discharged from care before the passage of the Title IV-E Independent Living Initiative of 1986 (P.L. 99-272) (e.g., Blome 1997; Fanshel, Finch, & Grundy 1990; Festinger 1983; Jones & Moses 1984; Zimmerman 1982), and/or within 2 years of its passage when, for some states, independent living services were fairly new (e.g., Barth 1990; Benedict, Zuravin, & Stallings 1996; Buehler, Orme, Post, & Patterson 2000; Cook, Fleishman, & Grimes 1991). However, even more recent studies point to poor educational outcomes for youth in care (e.g., Courtney, Piliavin, Grogan-Kaylor, & Nesmith 2001; McMillen, Auslander, Elze, White, & Thompson 2003).

A national evaluation of ILPs, conducted in the 1980s by Westat, Inc. (Cook, Fleishman, & Grimes 1991), described a range of educational challenges among youth discharged from out-of-home care, including histories of grade retentions, placements in special education, and long absences from school. Despite these multiple problems, less than one-half of the youths received educational planning services (De-Woody, Ceja, & Sylvester 1993).

A substantial proportion of youths in care function below grade level; estimated rates range from 24% (English, Kouidou-Giles, & Plocke 1994) to 37% (Iglehart 1994). In a sample of predominantly African American children aged 5 to 19 in kinship care and attending Baltimore schools, Sawyer and Dubowitz (1994) found that their reading, math, language, and cognitive skills were significantly below those of other children in their schools. The Foster Youth Transitions to Adulthood study (Courtney, Piliavin, Grogan-Kaylor, & Nesmith, 2001) followed 141 17- and 18-year-olds that exited Wisconsin's foster care system in 1995 and 1996 after spending at least 18 months in care. Nearly two-thirds of these individuals scored at or below an eighth grade reading level (Courtney, Piliavin, Grogan-Kaylor, & Nesmith 2001). Mc-Millen, Auslander, Elze, White, and Thompson (2003) reported that 25% of the ILP youths had failed a class in the previous year.

Grade retention appears to be a common phenomenon among school-aged children in out-of-home settings. Sawyer and Dubowitz (1994) found that 41% of all such children and nearly two-thirds (63%) of the secondary school students had been retained at least once. Another Baltimore study of youth in care found that 38% had repeated a grade (Benedict, Zuravin, & Stallings 1996). Evans (2004) reported that of 392 school-aged children in Arkansas that entered foster care between July 1997 and May 2002, and reentered later on, 32% had been retained before their initial placement and 40% by reentry, an underestimation because the grade retention status of many was unknown.

Retention rates of 25% (McMillen, Auslander, Elze, White, & Thompson 2003) and 30% (Courtney, Piliavin, Grogan-Kaylor, & Nesmith 2001) were reported in two other studies with older adolescents in care.

Research consistently indicates that many youths in the foster care system fail to graduate from high school or secure a General Equivalency Diploma credential (GED), posing a serious barrier to their achievement of economic self-sufficiency and employment stability (Mech 1994). Reported high school or GED completion rates among youth formerly in care typically vary between 45% (Barth 1990) and 65% (Festinger 1983).

The Westat evaluation found that only 54% of the 18- to 24-year-olds had completed high school 2.5 to 4 years after discharge from out-of-home care, a rate comparable to that of youth living below the poverty level, but far below that (78%) of similarly aged young adults in the general population (Cook 1994). Aggregated data from four follow-up studies (including Westat's) on former foster care youth indicated that only 58% had obtained a high school diploma or GED by early adulthood, compared to 84% of 20- to 24-year-olds nationally (Mech & Fung 1994). Benedict, Zuravin, and Stallings (1996) found that 58% of their adult sample had completed high school or obtained a GED, with no significant difference between those that had been in kinship care (56%) versus non-relative family foster care (61%) as children. Eighty percent of the 141 17- and 18-year-olds in the Wisconsin foster care study were re-interviewed 12 to 18 months after leaving care, at which time, 37% had not yet completed high school or obtained a GED (Courtney, Piliavin, Grogan-Kaylor, & Nesmith 2001).

Notable exceptions to these low graduation rates have been reported in the literature, usually among youth who stayed in care longer (Casey Family Services 2001; Mallon 1998) or were followed for a longer period of time post-discharge (Blome 1997). Nearly three-quarters (74%) of youth discharged from Green Chimneys Children's Services in New York City left care with a high school diploma or a GED (Mallon 1998). A study of Casey Family Services (2001) alumni found that 73% had obtained a high school diploma or GED, with the rate significantly higher among youth who had been adopted or remained in care into early adulthood, compared to those who had exited care at age 18 or younger. Blome (1997) found over twice the dropout rate among high school sophomores in foster care compared to a group that was living with parents and matched on age, race, and gender (37% vs. 16%). However, 77% of youth formerly in out-of-home care had obtained a high school diploma or a GED 5 years later, although they were still more likely than their peers to be without a degree (23% vs. 7%).

Outcome data from Casey Family Programs point to the organization's success in facilitating high school completion rates comparable to those found in the general population, and significantly higher for African American and Latino alumni than for those groups in the general population. According to Pecora et al. (2003), educational advocacy, the integration of social work and education case management, and close monitoring of educational outcomes are among the distinguishing characteristics of Casey Family Programs. The recent Casey National Alumni study, which examined outcomes for more than 1,000 alumni aged 20 to 51 and served by Casey Family Programs between 1966 and 1998, found that 86% had completed high school or obtained a GED, with 72.5% accomplishing that milestone by the time their case closed. Among African American alumni, 91% secured a diploma or a GED, compared to 79% in the general population, and 88% of Latino alumni, compared to 57% in the general population (Pecora et al. 2003).

Evidence of higher educational attainment among a few youths exiting foster care pales in significance, however, next to the larger picture. A recent review of outcome data on youth served by the federal ILP between 1987 and 1996 provides reason for continued concern (U.S. Department of Health and Human Services 1999). Aggregated data from the 16 states that provided 1996 educational information, collected either 90 days after youths completed the ILP or exited foster care, showed that only 31% of the youths were either in high school or had received a diploma or GED, and another 3% were enrolled in college. Given that nearly two-thirds (65%) of all the youths were only 16 or 17 at the time of data collection, and another 22% were 18, the data suggest that many school-aged youths had dropped out by the time they completed the ILP or exited foster care.

Furthermore, most studies that report high school completion rates for youth currently or formerly in foster care combine GED recipients and high school graduates, obscuring the social and economic disparities between these two groups in their life outcomes. This is not surprising, given that the National Center for Education Statistics fails to report high school completers separately from GED recipients, even though GED recipients have dropped out of high school (Greene & Forster 2003). The Casey National Alumni study is the only major study that provided separate figures on high school completers (67.4% of the alumni) and GED recipients (18.6% of the alumni), but no investigation of differences in the outcomes between the two groups has been reported (Pecora et al. 2003).

The Child and Family Service Reviews (CFSR), conducted by the Children's Bureau and the Administration for Children and Families, provide additional data that point to unmet educational needs among youth in foster care. The reviews assess a state's performance in meeting national standards on child welfare outcomes related to safety, permanency, and child and family well-being, and are accomplished through an appraisal of statewide aggregate data, on-site examination of case records, and interviews with key stakeholders (U.S. Department of Health and Human Services 2000). Among the well-being outcomes evaluated is whether children receiving child welfare services will obtain appropriate services to meet their educational needs. Of the 32 states reviewed in 2001 and 2002, over three-quarters (78%) did not achieve substantial conformity to the educational outcome, meaning that less than 90% of the cases reviewed met the outcome (U.S. Department of Health and Human Services 2003).

Behavioral Problems in School

Few studies have reported on the school behavior problems of youth in care. McMillen, Auslander, Elze, White, & Thompson (2003) found that nearly three-quarters of their adolescent sample reported at least one suspension since seventh grade, and over one-quarter had physically fought with other students (29%) and/or verbally fought with teachers (28%) in the past year. Evidence exists that youth in care exhibit higher rates of behavioral problems in school (Seyfried, Pecora, Downs, Levine, & Emerson 2000) and are more likely to be suspended than their peers (Blome 1997).

Educational Aspirations

Postsecondary education or training is necessary to achieve higher wage jobs and economic self-sufficiency (Mech 1994; Workforce Strategy Center 2000). Alarmingly, a review of several ILPs indicated that the majority viewed GED attainment as the primary educational goal for youth in foster care (Workforce Strategy Center 2000). The U.S. General Accounting Office (1999) found that 34% of the states were not providing any postsecondary educational services to youth in foster care in 1998, more than a decade after the inception of the federal ILP. New Jersey's Garden State Coalition for Youth and Family Concerns reported that only 18% of the state's ILPs provided tuition assistance for postsecondary education, and only

6% helped youths with college applications, not unlike the situation elsewhere in the country (Mendel 2001).

Not surprisingly, youth in out-of-home care are less likely to attend college than the general population. Using data from the 1988 National Survey of Families and Households, Buehler and colleagues (2000) found that only 29% of the adults who had lived in family foster care as children or adolescents reported some formal education beyond high school, compared to 43% of the adults in a randomly selected comparison group. The Westat evaluation determined that 30% of youth discharged from foster care continued their education beyond high school. Of youth that had not completed college, 74% identified finances as a major deterrent (Cook, Fleishman, & Grimes 1991). Using linked administrative databases, an investigation of 11,408 youths who emancipated from child welfare in California between 1992 and 1997 determined that 55% attended a community college, but only 60% of those youths earned any credits, and less than 2% achieved their goal of obtaining a 2-year degree and transferring to a 4-year college (Needell, Cucaro-Alamin, Brookhart, Jackman, & Shlonsky 2002). The college completion rate appears low even among Casey alumni, despite Casey's strengths in educational advocacy, case management, and monitoring. Although 49% of the alumni had attended at least some college, a rate comparable to the 51.7% of the general population, only 9% had completed college, compared to 24.4% of the general population (Pecora et al. 2003).

Several studies provide evidence of high, but potentially frustrated, educational aspirations among youth in care. Although 50% of the foster care youth in Blome's (1997) study desired to graduate from college, and 45% had taken at least one college course, only 35% expected to attain a college degree, compared to 49% of a group matched on race, age, and gender. While still in care, 79% of the Wisconsin youths wanted to attend college, and 63% to complete college, but only 9% had entered college 12 to 18 months post-discharge (Courtney, Piliavin, Grogan-Kaylor, & Nesmith 2001). McMillen, Auslander, Elze, White, and Thompson (2003) found high educational aspirations among foster care youth with multiple academic and behavioral problems (i.e., 70% aspired to attend college), suggesting the need for thoughtful career counseling that would support their motivation and help them develop a realistic educational and vocational plan.

Risk and Protective Factors Associated with Educational Experiences

Little is known about the risk and protective factors associated with the educational experiences of youth in foster care. Prior research provides disparate findings on the relationship between placement characteristics and educational experiences. Type of placement was found to be associated with serious school behavioral problems in one study (Benedict, Zuravin, & Stallings 1996) but not in another, although the amount of time in placement was a significant factor (Zima et al. 2000).

Several studies found a relationship between placement restrictiveness and educational deficiencies. Among emancipated, or nearly emancipated, 21-year-olds from the Illinois foster care system, youths placed in less restrictive placements, such as transitional apartments or family-type living arrangements, progressed further educationally than did those in more restrictive settings (Mech & Fung 1994). McMillen and Tucker (1998) found that placement in an inpatient mental health facility decreased the likelihood of youths completing high school or attaining a GED. New York City foster children placed in congregate care settings showed a decline in school attendance and poorer attendance rates than those residing in either foster homes or kinship care (Conger & Rebeck 2001).

Studies have shown that entering care at a younger age, living with more children while in care (Sawyer & Dubowitz 1994), and experiencing a greater number of foster home placements (Zima et al. 2000) are associated with poorer academic achievement. The Casey Alumni study found that greater placement stability and a positive relationship with the last or longest foster family were among the strongest predictors of high school or GED completion (Pecora et al. 2003). Among adults raised in either foster homes or kinship care, no differences were found in their high school or GED completion rates, but a return to family from out-of-home care decreased the likelihood of completion (Benedict, Zuravin, & Stallings 1996).

Few studies have examined correlates of youths' educational experiences beyond placement characteristics. Externalizing problems have been implicated in lower educational attainment (Benedict, Zuravin, & Stallings 1996) and higher rates of behavioral problems in school (McMillen, Auslander, Elze, White, & Thompson 2003), including suspensions or expulsions (Zima et al. 2000). School behavioral problems were also found to be associated with marijuana use (McMillen, Auslander, Elze, White, & Thompson 2003); more specifically, suspensions were associated with age and male gender (Zima et al. 2000). Higher educational aspirations have been associated with better HIV-related knowledge, safer attitudes and intentions, and fewer risky sexual behaviors among youth living in residential centers (Slonim-Nevo, Auslander, & Ozawa 1995). Studies have shown high school or GED completion to be positively associated with age and being female (Benedict, Zuravin, & Stallings 1996), and negatively associated with running away while in care, mental retardation (McMillen & Tucker 1998), and grade retention (Benedict, Zuravin, & Stallings 1996). More intensive training for independent living and employment experience were found to predict high school or GED completion among Casey alumni (Pecora et al. 2003). Research has also identified frequent alcohol use (McMillen, Auslander, Elze, White, & Thompson 2003) and

being African American (Zima et al. 2000) as correlates of poorer academic achievement.

Bridges to Life Options Study and the YSP

Here we report on the educational experiences of youth that participated in the Bridges to Life Options study and the YSP, and the risk and protective factors associated with their educational achievement, school problems, and educational aspirations. Both studies used highly structured interview protocols, which included standardized instruments, to assess mental health problems; cognitive factors; family and peer environments; and educational status, aspirations, and achievement. For detailed descriptions of the samples, procedures, and measures, see prior work from the Bridges to Life Options study (Auslander et al. 2002; Edmond, Auslander, Elze, McMillen, & Thompson 2002; Elze, Auslander, McMillen, Edmond, & Thompson 2001; McMillen, Auslander, Elze, White, & Thompson 2003) and the YSP (Stiffman, Chen, Elze, Dore, & Cheng 1997; Stiffman, Hadley-Ives, Elze, Johnson, & Dore 1999).

The Bridges to Life Options study was a controlled evaluation of an HIV prevention program for youth in foster care that integrated HIV content and individualized educational planning sessions into an 8-month ILP. Youths were referred to the study by caseworkers from the Missouri Division of Family Services, group home workers, foster or biological parents, and self-referral. Youths were eligible for the program if they were aged 15 to 18 and were currently or recently had been in out-of-home care. The findings reported here are based on baseline data collected during four waves of interviews (1998–2002), building on our previous work that reported on the first three waves of study participants (McMillen, Auslander, Elze, White, & Thompson 2003).

The YSP examined adolescent mental health needs and use of mental health services over a 2-year period (1994–1996) among youth from the city of St. Louis who were recruited from four public service sectors that operate as gateways to mental health services: child welfare, education, juvenile justice, and primary health care. Because YSP reinterviewed youths 2 years after the initial interview, we report on changes that occurred in the their educational status and aspirations, and the risk and protective factors predicting school dropout that occurred after the first interview.

Bridges to Life Options Study

The sample consisted of 351 youths aged 15 to 19 (mean [M], 16.33; standard deviation [SD], .85), who were involved in the foster care system and participating in a life skills training program. Approximately one-half (54%) of the youths were female and 69% were persons of color, mostly African American. Nearly one-quarter (23%) lived with a relative, 18% resided in a family foster home, 53% lived in a group home or other residential facility, 3% were in an inpatient psychiatric facility at the time of the interview, and 4% lived in other situations.

Many youths reported multiple placements during their time in foster care. Over one-half (59%) had lived in their current placement less than 12 months, and these youths averaged three different placements during the past year. Those individuals who had ever lived in a foster home (55%) or congregate care facility (81%) reported a median of two foster home and three group home or residential treatment placements.

Educational status and aspirations. The majority of the youths (78%) were in school at the time of the baseline assessment. Of those not in school, 65% (*n* = 47) had dropped out; 18% (*n* = 18) had dropped out but obtained a GED; 11% (*n* = 8) had been expelled; and 6% (*n* = 4) had graduated. All but two individuals planned to either finish high school or obtain a GED, and nearly all the young people endorsed post-secondary educational plans, regardless of their current status. Over one-half (55%) planned to pursue a 2- or 4-year college degree; 17%, graduate school; 13%, vocational, technical, or

job training; and 10% planned to enter the military.

Educational instability. Many youths reported unstable educational histories. Over three-quarters of them (78%) had changed school districts two or more times since seventh grade (M, 2.99; SD, 2.15). Nearly two-thirds (64%) reported at least one mid-year school change, with more than one-third (37%) reporting two or more mid-year changes, most often due to changes in placement (48%) or moves by family (34%).

Educational achievement and learning problems. Achievement problems were common among these young people. Fifty-eight percent reported failing at least one class in the past year, the majority (67%) of which failed two or more classes (M, 2.89; SD, 2.16). Nearly one-quarter of the youths (24%; *n* = 83) had been retained at least once since the seventh grade, and 13 individuals reported two or more grade retentions. More than one-third (35%) had been told they had a learning problem, and 44% received special help in their last year of schooling. However, no special educational assistance was received by more than one-quarter (27%) of the youths with learning problems.

Behavioral problems in school. The youths reported frequent behavioral problems at school. Nearly three-quarters (72%) had been suspended at least once since seventh grade, and over one-half (58%) reported two or more suspensions (M, 6.30; SD, 11.97). Chi-square analyses showed that boys were significantly more likely to be suspended than girls (82% vs. 66%; $\chi^2 = 11.24$; $df = 1$; $p \leq .001$). More than one-quarter of the youths (29%) had a verbal fight with a teacher in the past year and 28% reported at least one physical fight with another student at school, 45% of whom had two or more fights. Seven youths reported physically fighting with a teacher in the past year. Nearly one-half (47%) had skipped school without permission in the past year, and 38% had skipped school more than once (M, 8.10; SD, 24.17).

TABLE 1. *Bivariate Relationships between Risk and Protective Factors and Youths' Educational Aspirations, School Behavior Problems, and Educational Achievement Problems: Bridges to Life Options Study*

Variable	Educational Aspirations[1]	School Behavior Problems[1]	Failed Classes in Past Year[1]	Grade Retention Since Seventh Grade[2]	School Dropout[2]
Demographic factors					
Age	−.15**	−.02	−.06	.07	.42++
Race (0 = white; 1 = youths of color)	.08	−.13**	−.17**	−.10	−.22**
Gender (0 = male; 1 = female)	.12*	.00	−.03	−.07	−.03
Educational parameters					
Educational instability	−.02	.03	.05	.18**	.17*
Learning problem	−.24++	.03	.04	.19**	−.10
School behavior problems	−.03	—	.22++	.10	.20**
Educational aspirations	—	−.03	−.07	−.20**	−.07
Mental health problems and substance use					
Internalizing problems	−.02	.05	.08	.19**	−.04
Externalizing problems	−.11*	.38++	.17+	.20**	.00
Alcohol use	−.03	.25++	.21++	.13*	.18*
Marijuana use	−.09	.35++	.18+	.15*	.10
Maltreatment history					
Emotional neglect	−.05	.07	.08	.11	.03
Emotional abuse	−.05	.10	.14**	.19**	.08
Physical abuse	−.04	.08	.05	.17**	.10
Physical neglect	−.05	−.04	.08	.19**	.12
Social context					
Negative peer behaviors	−.18+	.28++	.04	.23+	.21**
Placements in last year	−.11*	.22++	.02	.11	.26+
Lifetime placements	−.13**	.22++	.13**	.15*	.19*
Living in congregate care (0 = no; 1 = yes)	−.02	.12	−.02	−.00	−.15
Cognitive factors					
Future orientation	.18+	−.07	−.14**	−.14*	−.08

Notes: n = 351; —, data not available; *p ≤ .05; **p ≤ .01; +p ≤ .001; ++p ≤ .0001.
[1]Pearson product moment correlation coefficients.
[2]Standardized logistic regression coefficients.

Factors associated with educational aspirations, academic problems, and school dropout. As shown in table 1, those youth with higher educational aspirations were female, younger, and reported fewer externalizing problems, less involvement with negative peers, fewer placement changes while in foster care, no learning problems, and greater future orientation. White youths reported more school-based behavioral problems than did youths of color. Individuals with more school behavioral problems reported more externalizing problems, more frequent alcohol and marijuana use, greater involvement with negative peers, and a greater number of placement changes. The severity of mal-

treatment histories and school-based behavioral problems was not related to the educational aspirations of these youths; nor were maltreatment histories related to their behavioral problems in school.

White youths reported more failed classes in their last year of schooling than did African American youths. Those who experienced more failures reported a greater number of foster care placements, more problem behaviors, more severe histories of emotional abuse, and less future orientation. Grade retention was significantly related to mental health problems and substance abuse; greater childhood trauma; learning problems; more involvement with negative peers; greater school and placement instability; and lower educational aspirations and future orientation. School dropout was more likely to occur among white youths than those of color. Individuals who had dropped out were also older and reported more educational instability, behavioral problems in school, more frequent alcohol use, greater involvement with negative peers, and a greater number of foster care placements than did youths who stayed in school.

Multiple regression analyses were performed to determine the strongest predictors of educational aspirations and problems. The analyses revealed that higher aspirations were associated with being younger ($\beta = -.12$; $t = -2.24$; $p \leq .05$) more future-oriented ($\beta = .12$; $t = 2.22$; $p \leq .05$), and having no history of learning problems ($\beta = -.17$; $t = -3.13$; $p \leq .01$). Externalizing problems ($\beta = .28$; $t = 5.08$; $p \leq .0001$), marijuana use ($\beta = .23$; $t = 3.61$; $p \leq .001$), and the number of recent out-of-home placements ($\beta = .11$; $t = 2.06$; $p \leq .05$) were most strongly associated with the youths' school behavior problems.

Failing more classes was significantly associated with race ($\beta = -.12$; $t = -2.18$; $p \leq .05$), school behavior problems ($\beta = .14$; $t = 2.36$; $p \leq .05$), and alcohol use ($\beta = .15$; $t = 2.69$; $p \leq .01$). Only educational instability was associated with grade retention in the multiple regression analysis ($\beta = .16$; odds ratio [OR], 1.08; $p \leq .05$). Finally, being older ($\beta = .45$; OR, 2.63; $p \leq .0001$) and experiencing more out-of-home placements within the past year ($\beta = .25$; OR, 1.45; $p \leq .01$) were associated with youths dropping out of school.

YSP

A total of 792 youths were interviewed in 1994, with 85% ($n = 675$) successfully followed and reinterviewed in 1996. One-quarter (24.7%) of those interviewed were from the child welfare system. Because these data provide information on the youths' educational status over a 2-year period, we based our analyses on the 167 youths

from the child welfare system who completed both interviews. At time 1, the youths were between 14 and 18 years of age (M, 15.2; SD, 1.28). The majority of the sample was female (62%) and African American (88%).

At the time of their first interview, 50.3% of the youths lived with a parent or other relative, 39% lived in a group home or other residential facility, 8.4% resided in a family foster home, and 2.3% lived in other situations. Nearly two-thirds (64.7%) had lived in a foster home or residential facility at some point in their lives. The median time spent in out-of-home placements was 21 months. By the time of their second interview, 33.5% of the youths had changed foster homes or residential facilities at least once, of whom 45% had changed placements more than once (M, 2.19; SD, 1.79).

Educational status and school dropout behavior. A significant number of individuals prematurely exited from school between their two interviews. Although 91.6% ($n = 153$) of the youths were in school in 1994, 24% of them had dropped out by 1996. This dropout rate approximates the dropout rate in the city of St. Louis, which was 23.2% aggregated over 2 school years (1993–1995) (Citizens for Missouri's Children 1996). More than one-third (38.3%) of the youths who dropped out did so prior to the tenth grade, 29.8% reported completing the tenth grade before dropping out, and nearly one-third (31.9%) exited school after completing their junior year.

Of the 14 youths that had already dropped out at the time 1 interview, most reported, 2 years later, that they were pursuing some type of education. However, only one had returned to high school, one was in college, and another was in vocational training. Fifty percent said they were working on their GED, but only one had actually obtained a GED. Three were not in any educational program.

Educational aspirations. A pattern of diminishing aspirations emerged among the youths between time 1 and time 2. The majority of them reported high educational aspirations at time 1: 82% planned to attend college, 8% wanted to pursue vocational training, and 10% planned to finish high school or obtain a GED. However, by time 2, those aspiring to attend college dropped to 59% of the sample. Although the percentage of youths planning to pursue vocational training increased to 21%, 15% of those who formerly desired postsecondary education or training lowered their expectations to the achievement of a high school diploma or GED.

Educational achievement and learning problems. Achievement problems were common among these young people. At time 1, 16% reported receiving mostly Fs and Ds in their last semester, and an additional 45% received mostly Cs; they reported similar grades at time 2.

Nineteen percent had been told they had a learning problem, but 43% of them reported receiving no school-based services, such as special academic help or counseling, between time 1 and time 2. Forty-one percent had repeated a grade, with 13 youths reporting two or more retentions. Of the 16 youths who repeated a grade after their first interview, four had dropped out of school.

Factors associated with educational aspirations, academic problems, and school dropout. Bivariate analyses demonstrated that multiple factors were significantly associated with educational aspirations and academic achievement (see table 2). Youths reporting higher aspirations and better grades were from a higher socioeconomic class, less involved with negative peers, and less likely to have a child. Grade retention

TABLE 2. *Bivariate Relationships between Risk and Protective Factors and Youths' Educational Aspirations, School Behavior Problems, and Educational Achievement Problems at Time 2: Youth Services Project*

Variable	Educational Aspirations T_2[1]	Grades in School T_2[1]	Ever Retained[2]	Dropout between T_1 and T_2[2,3]
Demographic factors				
Age	−.10	−.05	.33[++]	.28[**]
Race (0 = white; 1 = youths of color)	−.11	−.03	.10	−.09
Gender (0 = male; 1 = female)	.07	−.10	−.24[**]	.19
Socioeconomic status	.24[**]	.18[*]	−.17	−.32[**]
Educational parameters				
Learning problem	.08	−.13	.26[**]	.12
Educational aspirations	.27[+,4]	.18[*]	.06	.06
Grades in school	.18[*]	.25[+,4]	−.15	−.19
Mental health problems and substance use				
Depression symptoms	−.04	−.06	.27[**]	.23[*]
Conduct disorder symptoms	.00	−.14	.17[*]	.14
Substance use symptoms	−.04	−.14	.07	.14
Social context				
Having a child	−.26[++]	−.17[*]	−.09	.19
Family support	.05	.07	.00	−.25[**]
Time in foster home	−.08	−.09	−.12	.02
Lived in congregate care (0 = no; 1 = yes)	.02	.03	.13	−.04
Family instability	−.04	−.00	.18[*]	.13
Participation in social activities	.14	.20[**]	−.02	−.16
Negative peer behaviors	−.25[++]	−.29[++]	.14	.33[**]

Notes: n = 167; —, data not available; *$p \le .05$; **$p \le .01$; †$p \le .001$; ††$p \le .0001$.
[1]Pearson product moment correlation coefficients.
[2]Standardized logistic regression coefficients.
[3]n = 153; 116 youths remained in or completed school; 37 dropped out between T_1 and T_2.
[4]Correlation between the variables at T_1 and T_2.

and school dropout were positively associated with age and more symptoms of depression. Youths who had been retained also reported past learning problems, greater family instability, and more conduct disorder symptoms. Those who had dropped out between time 1 and time 2 reported greater involvement with negative peers, less family support, and lower socioeconomic status than did the youths who remained in or completed school.

Chi-square analyses revealed that youths who left school prematurely were more likely to meet criteria for major mental health diagnoses and to report three or more significant symptoms of mental health problems at time 1 than did those who remained in or completed school. Youths who dropped out reported over twice the rate of major depressive disorder (24% vs. 11%; $\chi^2 = 3.92$; $df = 1$; $p \leq .05$), and they were much more likely to report serious behavior problems (73% vs. 46%; $\chi^2 = 7.86$; $df = 1$; $p \leq .01$), along with the youths who had been retained (65% vs. 45%; $\chi^2 = 6.65$; $df = 1$; $p \leq .01$).

Multiple regression results demonstrated that higher educational aspirations at time 1 ($\beta = .17$; $t = 2.20$; $p \leq .05$), having a child ($\beta = -.16$; $t = -2.11$; $p \leq .05$), involvement with negative peers ($\beta = -.21$; $t = 2.62$; $p \leq .01$), and socioeconomic status ($\beta = .16$; $t = -2.09$; $p \leq .05$) were the strongest predictors of educational aspirations at time 2. Past grades ($\beta = .22$; $t = 2.88$; $p \leq .01$) and negative peer behaviors ($\beta = -.22$; $t = -2.76$; $p \leq .01$) were significantly associated with more recent grades. Age ($\beta = 0.31$; OR, =1.6; $p \leq .01$), gender ($\beta = -.25$; OR, .37; $p \leq .01$), and learning problems ($\beta = 0.20$; OR, 2.4; $p \leq .05$) predicted grade retention. Finally, age ($\beta = 0.27$; OR, 1.5; $p \leq .05$) and socioeconomic status ($\beta = -.32$; OR, .60; $p \leq .05$) were most strongly associated with school dropout.

Discussion of the Bridges and YSP Findings

The results of the Bridges to Life Options and YSP studies shed light on individual and environmental factors related to the educational aspirations and academic achievement of youths involved with the child welfare system. The Bridges study reveals an alarming number of school problems among the ILP participants, including multiple school changes, learning problems, grade retentions, failed classes, multiple suspensions, and other behavioral problems in school. A startling proportion of the YSP participants had dropped out, been retained, and lowered their educational aspirations.

For older adolescents in foster care, the Bridges findings provide empirical support for a direct relationship between their premature exits from secondary education and the instability of their living situations. Prior research with adolescents shows that changing schools interferes with educational progress and predicts school dropout (Teachman, Paasch, & Carver 1996). For youths in foster care, their school changes are often precipitated by placement changes, which may account, among other factors, for their high dropout rates. Among the Bridges participants, multiple school changes were among the strongest predictors of grade retention and behavioral problems in school. Furthermore, the more out-of-home placements they experienced in the last year, the greater their likelihood of dropping out. Although younger children's academic achievement appears to be compromised by a greater number of lifetime placements (Zima et al. 2000), our findings suggest that more recent placement changes may derail the educational trajectories of older adolescents in care. Young children lack the power to leave school, as their age keeps them under adult control. However, older adolescents in foster care, after years of educational stress, may decide to quit when confronted with yet another placement change and its subsequent challenges, in what should be their final years of secondary education.

Socioeconomic status emerged as the strongest predictor of school dropout among the YSP youth, a result consistent with earlier research (Cairns, Cairns, & Neckerman 1989). Interestingly, in the Bridges and YSP studies, no association was found between educational aspirations and dropout status. These young people dropped out regardless of their educational dreams. Particularly disturbing is the pattern of diminishing educational aspirations that emerged among the YSP youth, and that the younger adolescents in the Bridges study endorsed higher aspirations than did the older ones.

Further research is needed to uncover the reasons behind such declines in the aspirations of youths in out-of-home care and to evaluate strategies aimed at maintaining high aspirations or increasing low aspirations. Youth advocates and researchers have suggested that many youths in care lack educational planning services; knowledge about educational options and resources; financial assistance for post-secondary education; and adults in their lives who monitor homework, hold out high expectations, and mentor them concerning their educational goals (Sheehy et al. 2000). Lacking these or other supports, they may feel overwhelmed by present circumstances, perceive insurmountable barriers between their immediate situations and a college education, or they may simply not know how to proceed.

With two exceptions, there were no differences in educational problems across gender and race. The young men in the Bridges program did report a greater likelihood of being suspended, compared to the young women, a finding consistent with previous research on behavioral problems among school-aged children in foster care (Zima et al. 2000). Although racial disparities in academic achievement and educational status are well documented in the St. Louis region, with poorer outcomes found among African American youths compared to white youths (FOCUS St. Louis 2001), white youths in the Bridges study were more likely to report failed classes. This finding may be partially explained by the unique characteristics of adolescents in the foster care system. Evidence exists that white youths in foster care may present with more serious emotional and behavioral problems than do African American youths, (Auslander et al. 2002; Landsverk, Davis, Ganger, Nwton, & Johnson 1996), which may compromise their educational achievement.

Implications for Social Work Practice

The serious educational deficiencies among youth in foster care point to the critical need for intensive remedial education and tutoring services to help them achieve grade level skills, and educational advocates to help arrange for and monitor the provision of appropriate educational programming. Recent initiatives funded by the Annie E. Casey Foundation identified these interventions, among others, as best practices to prepare youth for successful transitions from out-of-home care (Sheehy et al. 2000; Workforce Strategy Center 2000). Comprehensive strategies are urgently needed to increase the literacy of youth in care, prepare them to meet college entry standards, and access the necessary educational resources to meet their educational needs (Workforce Strategy Center 2000).

The educational and residential instability reported by youths in the Bridges and YSP studies and in prior research underscore the important role educational advocates can play in the lives of youths in out-of-home care. Ideally, educational advocates would follow their assigned youths through school and placement changes, and manage their educational information, facilitate timely transfers of educational records, and monitor the delivery of educational services (Ayasse 1995; Sheehy et al. 2000). The Foster Youth Services (FYS) programs in California, some in operation since 1972, provide youths in foster care with tutoring, counseling, mentoring, and case management services. Educational liaisons insure timely transfer of records among schools and expeditious placement of children in educational programs. Students receiving FYS services have shown significant improvement in their educational performance, including higher rates of high school completion, better in-school behavior, and higher academic achievement (Ayasse 1995).

Youths in care attribute their educational difficulties to behavioral problems, worries and concerns about their families-of-origin, frequent absences from school, anxiety about their future, and other issues related to their out-of-home status that distract them from schoolwork and impede their educational performance (Finkelstein, Wamsley, & Miranda 2002). Fearing stigmatization, many youths wish to hide their foster care status from their peers and may limit their interactions with other children to avoid unintentional disclosures (Finkelstein, Wamsley, & Miranda 2002). Additionally, it is not uncommon for young people and their foster parents to experience negative biases from school personnel (Powers & Stotland 2002).

School social workers can sensitize teachers and administrators to the challenges facing those foster care youths who may be struggling to perform academically. These students can often benefit from school-based individual and group counseling (Altshuler 1997). The Vera Institute of Justice operated a demonstration project for New York City's Administration for Children's Services that placed child welfare workers in five Bronx middle schools to offer intensive support to foster children (Finkelstein, Wamsley, & Miranda 2002). The participants exhibited improved attendance rates and modest academic gains, and their foster parents increased their involvement in the children's education (Vera Institute of Justice 2004).

Youths in foster care with high aspirations and college-ready educational skills pose a different set of professional challenges. Currently, states vary widely on the nature and scope of services offered to promote postsecondary education among youths in care (U.S. Department of Health and Human Services 1999; U.S. General Accounting Office 1999; Workforce Strategy Center 2000). Even model ILP programs report frustration in their attempts to increase college enrollment rates (Kellam 2001). According to the Workforce Strategy Center (2000), youths in care must be set on a trajectory to high-wage careers through extensive educational and career preparation joined with the requisite social and financial supports. They should receive college preparatory assistance, such as help with high school course selections, college planning, and college application processes. Tutoring programs must help them meet college entry standards. Youths in care should also be provided with educational mentors, tuition waivers for state universities and colleges, and other forms of financial aid for postsecondary education (Sheehy et al. 2000; Workforce Strategy Center 2000). Since 2000, the Silicon Valley Children's Fund has awarded over 60 Youth Education Scholarships™ to students aging out of the child welfare system (Silicon Valley Children's Fund 2004).

ILPs should develop strong linkages with community colleges and other postsecondary institutions. The California Community College Foundation is a model initiative that attempts to maximize the connection between youths in foster care and community colleges. All independent living classes are held on the community college campuses, and youths also attend college classes that promote college preparation and readiness (Workforce Strategy Center 2000). Greater interagency coordination and collaboration can maximize access to financial aid and other supports for postsecondary education and training (Massinga & Pecora 2004).

Foster parents can be instrumental in facilitating the educational progress of youths in their care (Zanghi, Detgen, Jordan, Ansell, & Kessler 2001). They can help young people develop educational and career goals, structure study time, participate in Individualized Education Program (IEP) meetings, advocate with schools to insure appropriate service delivery, and encourage youths to explore postsecondary education. A partnership between the Illinois Department of Children and Family Services and Northern Illinois University trains foster parents in educational advocacy (Vera Institute of Justice 2004).

Overcoming Systemic Barriers

Key stakeholders point to multiple systemic barriers that interfere with the school attendance of youths in foster care (Advocates for Children 2000; Powers & Stotland 2002). School enrollment requirements vary widely among the states and from district to district. A school district may require all prior educational and medical records as a condition for school admission, resulting in long delays in enrolling some youths, yet not provide interim educational programming (Powers & Stotland 2002). Delays in transferring records between schools often results in children's long absences from school, inappropriate educational placements, and denials of credit for completed schoolwork (Advocates for Children 2000). Interviews with 70 youths in care determined that nearly 42% had experienced delays in school enrollment, often due to lost or misplaced records, with more than one-half reporting absences from school for 2 to 4 weeks (Advocates for Children 2000). State laws and regulations may prohibit school districts from denying youths immediate admission if records are unavailable, but these directives may be unknown to caseworkers and foster parents (Advocates for Children 2000; Powers & Stotland 2002). A lack of collaboration and communication among child welfare agencies, local school districts, foster parents or congregate care staff, and biological parents may also interfere with timely enrollment in school, placement in appropriate special education programs, and overall educational progress (Altshuler 1997; Mullen 2004; Powers & Stotland 2002). Biological parents may be inappropriately (and illegally) excluded from educational decision-making, and caseworkers, school personnel, and caretakers may lack clarity around who should sign educational forms and initiate special education evaluations and IEP meetings (Advocates for Children 2000). Child welfare caseworkers are often confused about their responsibilities related to the educational progress of their clients, and should receive training that clearly delineates their obligations.

Multiple strategies are required to eliminate these systemic barriers and facilitate the educational progress of youths in foster care. Keen interest in the educational attainment of youths in care is coming from many directions. Recent legislation enacted in California (i.e., Assembly Bill 490) was designed to promote educational stability, timely transfer of records, and more sensitive treatment of youths in care by educational and child welfare institutions (see fig. 1). Under the law, every district must designate a staff person to act as an educational liaison for youths in care. Child welfare placement decisions must take into consideration children's educational stability. School districts must allow children in out-of-home placements to remain in their school of origin for the remainder of the academic year, and children cannot be penalized for missing school due to placement changes or court appearances (Children's Law Center of Los Angeles 2004).

Court Appointed Special Advocate (CASA) programs are increasing their capacity to address the educational needs of the children they serve. CASA: Advocates for Children of New York State and the Permanent Judicial Commission for Justice for Children are collaborating to develop workshops and written guidelines for CASA volunteers for meeting the educational needs of their clients. National CASA is incorporating educational issues into new training curricula. CASA in the state of Washington is encouraging its volunteers to incorporate education-related concerns into court reports. CASA of Humboldt County in California has developed a manual devoted to educational advocacy, *Working Together: A Guide to Educational Advocacy,* that is available on its Web site (Mullen 2004).

The centerpiece of the Jim Casey Youth Opportunities Initiative, a national foundation focused on improving outcomes for youths exiting foster care, is the opportunity passport, comprised of three components: (1) an individual development account for asset building; (2) a personal debit account for immediate

Effective January 1, 2004, AB 490 (Steinberg), Chapter 862, imposes new duties and rights related to the education of dependents and wards in foster care. The Act's key provisions are:

- Establishes legislative intent that foster youth are insured access to the **same opportunities** to meet academic achievement standards to which all students are held, maintain stable school placements, be placed in the least restrictive educational placement and have access to the same academic resources, services, and extracurricular and enrichment activities as all other children. Makes clear that **education and school placement decisions** are to be dictated by the **best interest** of the child.
- Creates **school stability** for foster children by allowing them to remain in their school of origin for the duration of the school year when their **placement changes** and remaining in the same school is in the child's best interests.
- Requires county placing agencies to promote educational stability by considering in **placement decisions** the child's school attendance area.
- Requires Local Educational Agencies (LEAs) to designate a staff person as a **foster care education liaison** to ensure proper placement, transfer, and enrollment in school for foster youth.
- Makes LEAs and county social workers or probation officers jointly responsible for the **timely transfer of students** and their **records** when a change of schools occurs.
- Requires that a **comprehensive public school** be considered as the first **school placement option** for foster youth.
- Provides that a foster child has the right to remain enrolled in and attend his/her school of origin pending resolution of school placement **disputes**.
- Allows a foster child to be **immediately enrolled** in school even if all typically required school records, immunizations, or school uniforms are not available.
- Requires an LEA to deliver the pupil's **education information and records** to the next educational placement within 2 days of receiving a transfer request from a county placing agency.
- Requires school districts to calculate and accept **credit for full or partial coursework** satisfactorily completed by the student and earned while attending a public school, juvenile court school, or nonpublic, nonsectarian school.
- Authorizes the **release of educational records** of foster youth to the county placing agency, for purpose of compliance with WIC 16010, case management responsibilities required by the Juvenile Court or law, or to assist with transfer or enrollment of a pupil.
- Insures that foster youth will not be penalized for **absences** due to placement changes, court appearances, or related court ordered activities.

FIGURE 1. Insuring educational rights and stability for foster youth.

needs; and (3) "door openers," a variety of benefits that could include college registration fees, access to job training, and preapproval for tuition waivers or subsidized housing (Massinga & Pecora 2004).

What Can Child Welfare Caseworkers Do?

Child welfare caseworkers are well positioned to help youths on their caseload access educational services. Under CFCIP, services may include assistance with high school or GED completion; tutoring; postsecondary educational planning; assistance with SAT and ACT assessments, admissions and financial aid applications, and setting up college visits; college tuition assistance; and expenses for textbooks, fees, and room and board. For youths who have aged out of foster care and are under 21, the

CFCIP allows states to grant up to $5,000 for postsecondary education. The National Foster Parent Association and the Orphan Foundation of America offer college and vocational scholarships to youths in foster care. Youths in care are also eligible for federal financial aid, such as Pell Grants, Supplemental Educational Opportunity Grants, and federal loans. Some states waive tuition at community colleges and public universities for youths in foster care (Mullen 2004; Workforce Strategy Center 2000).

Child welfare caseworkers should be knowledgeable about federal and state laws and regulations protecting children's educational rights and have available a list of educational advocacy organizations. For children in foster care who need special education services, federal and state laws and regulations require the appointment of educational surrogates, or "surrogate parents," to make educational decisions on the child's behalf. Unless parental rights are terminated, biological parents retain the right to make educational decisions for their children. Surrogate parents possess all the rights of a parent in the special education process, including requesting testing and evaluation, signing consent forms, participating in IEP meetings, approving special education services, and requesting due process proceedings. However, states vary in the eligibility criteria and appointment process for surrogate parents. It is not uncommon for children in foster care to slip through the cracks and experience delays in the assignment of a surrogate parent (Powers & Stotland 2002). Child welfare caseworkers may be in the best position to insure that such assignments are made for the children with special needs on their caseloads.

Child welfare workers should be familiar with the performance indicators for the child welfare outcomes that are assessed in CFSRs. An examination of the indicators for the educational outcome shows that child welfare caseworkers have responsibility for case managing their client's educational needs and documenting educational assessment, planning, and services provision in case records. Through on-site case record reviews and interviews with caseworkers, parents, foster parents, and children, the CSFR team investigates the following core educational issues (U.S. Department of Health and Human Services 2000):

- Determination of whether the child experienced multiple school changes due to being in foster care;
- Identification of special education needs through appropriate testing and evaluation, and the provision of services to meet those needs;
- Provision of early intervention services for preschool children with developmental delays;
- Inclusion of school records in case files;

- Advocacy by the child welfare agency with the educational system to obtain necessary educational services for clients;
- Attention to education in case planning; and
- Provision of education records to foster parents.

Conclusion

Transitioning to adulthood can be difficult even for young people growing up in supportive families, schools, and communities. Older youths in the foster care system present child welfare and education systems with serious challenges. Although many youths in foster care successfully transition to a productive and self-sufficient adulthood, too many are held back by educational deficits and poor job readiness skills. With these limitations, exacerbated by mental and physical health problems, a lack of social support, and inadequate life skills preparation, they risk a life of poverty-level wages, homelessness, and incarceration.

Exciting and innovative programs are emerging across the country to enhance the educational and career opportunities for youths aging out of foster care. Much remains to be accomplished, however, as available funds are insufficient to meet the needs of this population and states vary widely in the services provided. Programs should be rigorously evaluated so that monies can be directed at program models that improve youths' outcomes. With such shared concern about the future well-being of youths currently in care, the time is ripe for new and creative collaborations among policymakers, child welfare professionals and educators, independent living specialists, youth advocates, young people, and their families and other caretakers.

Acknowledgments

This work was supported by Grant No. RO1 HD35445 from the National Institute of Child Health and Human Development and the Annie E. Casey Foundation to the George Warren

Brown School of Social Work at Washington University (Bridges to Life Options Program); and Grant No. 5R24MH50857 from the National Institute of Mental Health (Youth Services Project). The authors acknowledge the

many contributions of Tracy Drufke, Bridges to Life Options project director, Washington University, and the staff of the Missouri Division of Family Services, St. Louis County Office.

REFERENCES

Advocates for Children of New York. (2000). *Educational neglect: The delivery of educational services to children in New York City's foster care system.* New York: Advocates for Children of New York.

Altshuler, S. J. (1997). A reveille for school social workers: Children in foster care need our help! *Social Work in Education, 19,* 121–127.

Auslander, W. F., McMillen, J. C., Elze, D., Thompson, R., Jonson-Reid, M., & Stiffman, A. (2002). Mental health problems and sexual abuse among adolescents in foster care: Relationship to HIV risk behaviors and intentions. *AIDS and Behavior, 6,* 351–359.

Ayasse, R. H. (1995). Addressing the needs of foster children: The Foster Youth Services Program. *Social Work in Education, 17,* 207–215.

Barth, R. (1990). On their own: The experiences of youth after foster care. *Child and Adolescent Social Work Journal, 7,* 419–440.

Benedict, M. I., Zuravin, S., & Stallings, R. Y. (1996). Adult functioning of children who lived in kin versus nonrelative family foster homes. *Child Welfare, 75,* 529–549.

Bernstein, D. P., & Fink, L. (1998). *The Childhood Trauma Questionnaire: A retrospective self-report.* San Antonio: Psychological Corporation and Harcourt Brace & Company.

Blome, W. W. (1997). What happens to foster kids: Educational experiences of a random sample of foster youth and a matched group of non-foster youth. *Child and Adolescent Social Work Journal, 14,* 41–53.

Buehler, C., Orme, J. G., Post, J., & Patterson, D. A. (2000). The long-term correlates of family foster care. *Children and Youth Services Review, 22,* 595–625.

Cairns, R. B., Cairns, B. D., & Neckerman, H. J. (1989). Early school dropout: Configurations and determinants. *Child Development, 60,* 1437–1452.

Casey Family Services. (2001). *The road to independence: Transitioning youth in foster care to independence.* New Haven: Casey Family Services.

Children's Law Center of Los Angeles. (2004). AB 490 Overview. Retrieved July 22, 2004, from www.youthlaw.org/ab490.htm.

Child Welfare League of America. (1989). *Child Welfare League of America standards for independent-living services.* Washington, DC: Child Welfare League of America.

Citizens for Missouri's Children. (1996). *1996, Missouri kids count.* St. Louis, MO: Citizens for Missouri's Children.

Conger, D., & Rebeck, A. (2001). *How children's foster care experiences affect their education.* New York: Vera Institute of Justice.

Cook, R. (1994). Are we helping foster youth prepare for their future? *Children and Youth Services Review, 16,* 213–229.

Cook, R., Fleishman, E., & Grimes, V. (1991). *A national evaluation of Title IV-E foster care independent living programs for youth: Phase 2, final report,* vols. 1, 2. Rockville, MD: Westat.

Courtney, M. E., Piliavin, I., Grogan-Kaylor, A., & Nesmith, A. (2001). Foster youth transitions to adulthood: A longitudinal view of youth leaving care. *Child Welfare, 80,* 685–717.

DeWoody, M., Ceja, K., & Sylvester, M. (1993). *Independent living services for youths in out-of-home care.* Washington, DC: Child Welfare League of America.

Edmond, T., Auslander, W., Elze, D., McMillen, C., & Thompson, R. (2002). Differences between sexually abused and non-sexually abused adolescent females in foster care: Implications for treatment. *Journal of Child Sexual Abuse, 11,* 73–99.

Elze, D. E., Auslander, W., McMillen, C., Edmond, T., & Thompson, R. (2001). Untangling the impact of sexual abuse on HIV risk behaviors among youths in foster care. *AIDS Education and Prevention, 13,* 377–389.

English, D. J., Kouidou-Giles, S., & Plocke, M. (1994). Readiness for independence: A study of youth in foster care. *Children and Youth Services Review, 16,* 147–158.

Evans, L. D. (2004). Academic achievement of students in foster care: Impeded or improved? *Psychology in the Schools, 41,* 527–535.

Fanshel, D., Finch, S., & Grundy, J. (1990). *Foster children in a life course perspective: The Casey Family Program experience.* New York: Columbia University Press.

Festinger, T. (1983). *No one ever asked us: A postscript to foster care.* New York: Columbia University Press.

Finkelstein, M., Wamsley, M., & Miranda, D. (2002). *What keeps children in foster care from succeeding in school? Views of early adolescents and the adults in their lives.* New York: Vera Institute of Justice.

FOCUS St. Louis. (2001). *Racial equality in the St. Louis region: A community call to action.* St. Louis, MO: FOCUS St. Louis.

Foster Care Independence Act. (1999). P.L. 106-109.

Goerge, R., Voorhis, J., Grant, S., Casey, K., & Robinson, M. (1992). Special education experiences of foster children: An empirical study. *Child Welfare, 71,* 419–437.

Greene, J. P., & Forster, G. (2003). *Public high school graduation and college readiness rates in the United States.* Education Working Papers no. 3. New York: Center for Civic Innovation, Manhattan Institute.

Iglehart, A. P. (1994). Adolescents in foster care: Predicting readiness for independent living. *Children and Youth Services Review, 16,* 159–169.

Independent Living Initiative. (1986). P.L. 99-272.

Jones, M. A., & Moses, B. (1984). *West Virginia's former foster children: Their experience in care and their lives as young adults.* New York: Child Welfare League of America.

Jonson-Reid, M., & Barth, R. (2000). From placement to prison: The path to adolescent incarceration from child welfare supervised foster or group care. *Children and Youth Services Review, 22,* 493–516.

Kellam, S. (2001). An unfinished bridge to independence. *Advocasey.* Retrieved June 5, 2004, from www.aecf.org/publications/advocasey/fall2001/index.htm.

Kessler, M. (2004). *The John H. Chafee Foster Care Independence Program—The transition years: Serving current and former foster youth ages eighteen to twenty-one.* Tulsa: National Resource Center for Youth Services, University of Oklahoma.

Landsverk, J., Davis, I., Ganger, W., Nwton, R., & Johnson, I. (1996). Impact of child psychosocial functioning on reunification from out-of-home placement. *Children and Youth Services Review, 18,* 447–462.

Lyman, S., Banks, A., Hahn, A., Harding, J., Keenan, L., Ludy-Dobson, C., Phillips, S., & Smit, M. (1995). In E. V. Mech & J. R. Rycraft (eds.), *Preparing foster youths for adult living: Proceedings from an invitational research conference,* pp. 45–51. Washington, DC: Child Welfare League of America.

Mallon, G. P. (1998). After care, then what? Outcomes from a study of an independent living program. *Child Welfare, 77,* 61–78.

Massinga, R., & Pecora, P. J. (2004). Providing better opportunities for older children in the child welfare system. *The Future of Children, 14,* 151–173.

McDonald, T. P., Allen, R. I., Westerfelt, A., & Piliavin, I. (1996). *Assessing the long-term effects of foster care: A research synthesis.* Washington, DC: Child Welfare League of America.

McMillen, C., Auslander, W., Elze, D., White, T., & Thompson, R. (2003). Educational experiences and aspirations of older youth in the foster care system. *Child Welfare 72,* 475–495.

McMillen, J. C., & Tucker, J. (1998). The status of older adolescents at exit from out-of-home care. *Child Welfare, 78,* 339–360.

Mech, E. V. (1994). Foster youths in transition: Research perspectives on preparation for independent living. *Child Welfare, 73,* 603–623.

Mech, E. V., & Fung, C. C. (1994). Placement restrictiveness and educational achievement among emancipated foster youth. *Research on Social Work Practice, 9,* 213–228.

Mendel, D. (2001). Fostered or forgotten? *Advocasey.* Retrieved June 5, 2004, from www.aecf.org/publications/advocasey/fall2001/index.htm.

Mullen, L. (2004). Supporting the educational needs of children and youth in care. *The Connection, 20*(2), 6–9.

National Research Council, Commission on Behavioral and Social Sciences Education, Panel on High-Risk Youth. (1993). *Losing generations: Adolescents in high-risk settings.* Washington, DC: National Academy Press.

Needell, B., Cuccaro-Alamin, S., Brookhart, A., Jackman, W., & Shlonsky, A. (2002). Youth emancipating from foster care in California: Findings using linked administrative data. Berkeley: University of California, Center for Social Services Research.

Nixon, R. (1998). *Improving economic opportunity for youth formerly served by the foster care system: Identifying the support network's strengths and needs: Final report.* Washington, DC: Child Welfare League of America.

Pecora, P. J., Williams, J., Kessler, R. C., Downs, A. C., O'Brien, K., Hiripi, E., & Morello, S. (2003). Assessing the effects of foster care: Early results from the Casey National Alumni Study. Retrieved July 23, 2004, from www.casey.org/Resources/Publications/NationalAlumniStudy.htm.

Pizzigati, K. (2001). Public policy to help youth leaving foster care achieve independence: Where are we going? How do we get there? In K. A. Nollan & A. C. Downs (eds.), *Preparing youth for long-term success: Proceedings from the Casey Family Program National Independent Living Forum,* pp. 15–25. Washington, DC: Child Welfare League of America.

Powers, P., & Stotland, J. F. (2002). "Lost in the shuffle revisited": The Education Law Center's Report on the education of children in foster care in Pennsylvania. Philadelphia: Education Law Center.

Promoting Safe and Stable Families. (2001). P.L. 107-133.

Redd, Z., Brooks, J., & McGarvey, A. M. (2002). Educating America's youth: What makes a difference? Retrieved July 22, 2004, from www.childtrends.org.

Rosenfeld, A. A., Pilowsky, D. J., Find, P., Thorpe, M., Fein, E., et al. (1997). Foster care: An update. *Journal of the American Academy of Child and Adolescent Psychiatry, 36,* 448–457.

Sawyer, R. J., & Dubowitz, H. (1994). School performance of children in kinship care. *Child Abuse and Neglect, 18,* 587–597.

Seyfried, S., Pecora, P. J., Downs, A. C., Levine, P., & Emerson, J. (2000). Assessing the educational outcomes of children in long-term foster care: First findings. *School Social Work Journal, 24*(2), 68–88.

Sheehy, A. M., Oldham, E., Zanghi, M., Ansell, D., Correia, P., & Copeland, R. (2000). *Promising practices: Supporting transition of youth served by the foster care system.* Tulsa: National Resource Center for Youth Services, University of Oklahoma.

Silicon Valley Children's Fund. (2004). Youth Education Scholarship.™ Retrieved July 22, 2004, from www.svcf.org/kidsfirstprogram/youtheducationscholarship.html.

Slonim-Nevo, V., Auslander, W. F., & Ozawa, M. N. (1995). Educational options and AIDS-related behaviors among troubled adolescents. *Journal of Pediatric Psychology, 20,* 41–60.

Stiffman, A. R., Chen, Y. W., Elze, D., Dore, P., & Cheng, L. C. (1997). Adolescents' and providers' perspectives on the need for and use of mental health services. *Journal of Adolescent Health, 21,* 335–342.

Stiffman, A. R., Hadley-Ives, E., Elze, D., Johnson, S., & Dore, P. (1999). Impact of environment on adolescent mental health and behavior: Structural equation modeling. *American Journal of Orthopsychiatry, 69,* 73–86.

Teachman, J. D., Paasch, K., & Carver, K. (1996). Social capital and dropping out of school early. *Journal of Marriage and the Family, 58,* 773–783.

U.S. Department of Health and Human Services. (1999). *Title IV-E independent living programs: A decade in review.* Washington, DC: U.S. Government Printing Office.

U.S. Department of Health and Human Services. (2000) *Child and Family Services Reviews Procedures Manual.* Washington, DC: U.S. Department of Health and Human Services.

U.S. Department of Health and Human Services. (2001). *Report to the Congress: Developing a system of program accountability under the John H. Chafee Foster Care Independence Program.* Washington, DC: U.S. Department of Health and Human Services.

U.S. Department of Health and Human Services. (2003). Summary of the results of the 2001 and 2002 Child and Family Services Reviews. Retrieved July 15, 2004, from www.acf.hhs.gov/programs/cb/cwrp/2002cfsrresults.pdf.

U.S. General Accounting Office. (1999). *Foster care: Effectiveness of independent living services unknown.* Washington, DC: U.S. General Accounting Office.

Vera Institute of Justice. (2004). *Foster children & education: How you can create a positive educational experience for the foster child.* New York: Vera Institute of Justice.

Workforce Strategy Center. (2000). *Promising practices: School to career and postsecondary education for foster care youth.* Baltimore: Annie E. Casey Foundation.

Zanghi, M., Detgen, A., Jordan, P. A., Ansell, D., & Kessler, M. L. (2001). *Promising practices: How foster parents can support the successful transition of youth from foster care to self-sufficiency.* Portland: University of Southern Maine, Edmund S. Muskie School of Public Service, Institute for Public Sector Innovation.

Zima, B. T., Bussing, R., Freeman, S., Yang, X., Belin, T. R., & Forness, S. R. (2000). Behavior problems, academic skill delays and school failure among school-aged children in foster care: Their relationship to placement characteristics. *Journal of Child and Family Studies, 9,* 87–103.

Zimmerman, R. B. (1982). *Foster care in retrospect.* New Orleans: Tulane University Press.

ELAINE M. WALSH

A University Program to Serve Youth in the School Setting

The Hunter College Liberty Partnership

chools are increasingly acknowledged as a natural point of entry for service provision to students and their families because they reach all youth and convey no stigma. Social workers operating on-site at schools can develop preventive services for students and influence the environment of the school itself, opportunities seldom offered in other settings. In this chapter, I describe a program, the Hunter College Liberty Partnership program (HCLPP), which is a comprehensive educational and social service program created in 1988. Funded by the State Education Department of New York, it is one of more than 50 Liberty Partnership programs in the state, all of which were mandated to reflect collaboration among a college or university, a community-based organization, and a local junior high or high school.

The request for proposals for the Liberty Partnership programs was issued in 1988 in response to New York Governor Cuomo's initiative during the Decade of the Child. Originally, the goal was to promise college education to New York State students who graduated from high school and met financial eligibility requirements. Recognizing that only 70% of all high school students graduate, the New York State Legislature initiated and appropriated funds for the Liberty Partnership programs. These programs were to provide the comprehensive academic, cultural/recreational, and counseling supports necessary to enhance the school performance of students and motivate them to stay in school. The challenge set before

these programs was to improve school attendance and performance, increase school completion rates, and enable youngsters to become contributing members of society. The education department did not outline program parameters, leaving grant-seekers to propose various models of service delivery.

HCLPP is a comprehensive dropout prevention and educational enhancement services program. The goal of HCLPP is to confront issues that might interfere with the academic success of youngsters at risk. HCLPP extends counseling services, tutoring, mentoring, recreational and enrichment activities, special academic classes, social activities, and an after-school program to prepare students for either postsecondary education or meaningful employment.

HCLPP has offered services at a bilingual junior high school in East Harlem since 1990. The school enrolls approximately 200 youths each year in the seventh and eighth grades. Ninety-eight percent of the students in the school are Hispanic. Many have recently arrived from Mexico, South America, or the Caribbean, and some are undocumented citizens. All are low-income. This school was chosen as an appropriate site for a dropout prevention program because repeated studies have demonstrated that disproportionate numbers of Hispanic students drop out of school before graduation. Furthermore, Hispanic clients in particular seem to view the school as an accessible environment that is less threatening than highly structured conventional clinics and agencies.

Because all the youngsters in this school have limited English proficiency, they all fall under the grant's guidelines of service delivery to a population at risk of dropping out.

Because all the youth in this school are at risk, Hunter College was able to propose a universal program, which looks at the total school as the unit of intervention (Garbarino 1992). Recognizing that identifying specific youngsters in a school as those at-risk can create another risk factor for youth so identified, the proposal was clear in its intent to deliver services universally. To guide the development of the HCLPP service delivery model, the principal investigator turned to the School Development program (SDP). SDP, developed by James Comer (1988) in the New Haven, Connecticut, schools, focuses on the mental health of the students attending the school.

Two questions underlie all program development and refinement in the HCLPP: What conditions (both external and internal) interfere with the education of the students as a whole and of any particular student? And what enrichment opportunities will enable the students to join the American mainstream? Although the program's core components have remained relatively constant over time, the Hunter College program has been modified somewhat since it began; knowledge, program evaluations, and consumer feedback have provided a context for making some changes annually. The current program has three major components: social services; after-school services; and high school follow-up.

Social Service Component

Social services to this junior high school include counseling; life skills training; referral to outside sources; linkage to needed medical and legal assistance; advocacy with housing, welfare, and child welfare authorities; and intervention with the school and family systems when necessary for the well-being of the child.

At the beginning of the school year, each seventh-grade student is asked to fill out a form with questions about the youngster's history, current living arrangements, how long they have been in the United States, and whether they are most comfortable talking in English or Spanish. It also asks whether they have any school-related concerns and whether they would like to speak to a counselor.

Within the first 2 weeks of school, a member of the social work staff, which is made up of six or seven social work interns and a clinical supervisor, meets with each of the youngsters, who, based on their autobiographical statements, either want or need to be seen quickly. Following these initial interviews, all remaining youngsters are seen individually in the first 2 months of the school year. From these interviews emerges a caseload of students who need to be seen regularly.

School staff members also refer youngsters whose attendance is problematic, whose school performance is far below expectations, or who are known to be undergoing a personal private crisis. Case conferences are held to determine what kinds of group services are needed and who should be seen in individual or group counseling.

The youngsters in need of counseling services are seen on an ongoing basis in the school during school hours. It is often difficult to convince schoolteachers and administrators to let the students out of class for counseling. To insure that students do not have to be excused from the same class regularly, individual and group counseling sessions are scheduled on different days of the week and on a rotating class basis. This system recognizes the importance of regular school attendance while also emphasizing the importance of the program as a factor in the students' academic success.

Although some youth attend the after-school program, counseling sessions after school hours are limited because many students have family and employment obligations, or because their families insist that the youngsters come straight home for safety reasons. Many of the students themselves are afraid to stay after school because they fear for their own safety. Staying for counseling after school would entail venturing out onto the streets without the strength in numbers provided by a cohort, such as participants in the after-school program have.

Each social work intern is assigned to a homeroom and is viewed as the case manager for the students in that classroom. To develop a greater familiarity with the youngsters, social work interns regularly attend morning and afternoon homeroom sessions. This allows them the added benefit of seeing the youngsters in context rather than only in the confines of counseling sessions. A multifaceted understanding of their clients' lives emerges. This enables more sophisticated and focused interventions, no matter whether with the child, the family, the school, or all three.

Because the interns become such an integral part of the students' lives, the students themselves often go directly to the interns for help. Students often tell of petty altercations with fellow students that they would like to have help in resolving; they share information about violence and gang activity that is to happen; they express sadness that a father has left the home or a mother is in the hospital; they inform the social work intern that there is no food in the house or there is no heat. Functioning as case managers, the interns work according to their assessment of the situation, the problems, and available resources.

The interns also work closely with the homeroom teachers. Weekly meetings are held with the homeroom teacher, the social work intern, and the clinical supervisor. This provides an opportunity for the teacher to discuss emerging issues, apprise the intern of any schedule changes, and make suggestions regarding program development. It allows the intern to inform the teacher about referrals he or she has made without giving details that would violate the students' confidentiality. Together, they often plan seasonally appropriate celebrations or activities for the class. For example, when students were preparing to make their high school selections, the teachers together with the social work interns created a forum in which alumni were invited to tell the students about their high school experiences. These teacher-intern meetings are crucial for the smooth running of all program components, because teachers often view social work interns as a threat. They often see social workers as separate from both the classroom and the school and can undermine a program if they do not feel included in it. Teacher input is a valuable source of information and insight for the interns. Regularly scheduled weekly meetings avoid breakdowns in communication and contribute to an essential collaboration.

Another part of the social service program entails administering a life skills training unit for all eighth-grade students, which is offered as part of their homeroom health curriculum. For this training, the students are formed into small groups. Life skills groups are essentially a preventive measure. As delineated by Gilchrist and Schinke (1984), the intention is to empower the approximately 20% of the student population committed to prosocial behavior regarding sexual activity and substance abuse. Furthermore, this approach seeks to convince the middle 60% who are wavering to adhere to prosocial behavior. Life skills training admittedly does little for the 20% who are already involved in high-risk behaviors. Other, more focused interventions are necessary to deal with such problems (Gilchrist & Schinke 1984).

Members of life skills groups, together with the interns, choose the group's curriculum. Over time, group members have selected such topics as sex education, violence in the community, self-esteem, parents' unwillingness to accept their children's "Americanization," prejudice among students, coping mechanisms to enhance academic success, substance abuse and the family, and parental discipline vs. child abuse.

One of the major focuses of these groups is the empowerment of individual students. Recognizing that not all youngsters are willing or able to discuss their problems in a group, interns encourage the development of alternative help-seeking behavior. To that end, the interns write phone numbers and addresses on the blackboard. These include information about health clinics where the students can get information on birth control, agencies they can call for help in abuse situations, and clinics for abuse counseling. This enables youngsters to seek help on their own without program staff intervention.

After-School Program

Because of the population served, the majority of the students need academic assistance, athletic opportunities, and cultural enrichment. Many students also need help with learning the social skills that will help them gain entry to mainstream society. To serve these needs, HCLPP offers a comprehensive after-school program 3 days a week. Although the social work interns regularly encourage the students to participate in the after-school activities and have input into the program's design, initially, they were not the primary service providers in this program, which is administered by other staff members and Hunter College undergraduates. Over time, however, the interns have become involved in supervising the college students and tutoring, which helped them to develop relationships with the students starting where the students are. The trust gained when an adolescent is helped in a concrete way (e.g., improving math skills) has enabled social work interns to form solid clinical relationships.

After-school program activities are important for this population because adolescents often become involved in illegal or status-offending activities in the unsupervised hours between 3:00 and 5:00 P.M. Just providing supervision during those crucial hours is a means to reduce antisocial behavior among adolescents (Carnegie 1992). Youth development theory has been used to create a multifaceted after-school enrichment program.

The school's teachers and administration offer suggestions as to academic enhancement needs. HCLPP offers homework assistance as well as additional English and math classes during the after-school program. Initially teachers from the school were hired to teach the classes; however, due to funding constraints and complications related to having issues from the school day carry over into the after-school experience, the use of teachers was eliminated. Hunter College undergraduate student volunteers provide homework help and receive course credit for their services.

In addition, enrichment programs in computer skills, art, dance, and sports are offered on alternate days. The after-school program provides the youngsters with extracurricular opportunities that their more financially privileged counterparts receive through private lessons. The program also offers them the chance to develop needed social skills as they learn to interact appropriately with one another and with the Hunter undergraduates. These social skills and cultural activities are seen as essential components that contribute to their continued school attendance and completion (Comer 1988).

Many of the students are hesitant to leave their Spanish-speaking community for fear that they will feel estranged and threatened in the English-dominant communities of New York City. To help familiarize them with New York's endless opportunities and train them to utilize public transportation, many trips are scheduled. Over time, the program has taken participants to visit the Statue of Liberty, Ellis Island, several museums, and libraries; to ice skate in Rockefeller Center; and to fish in Central Park. The youngsters are also brought to Hunter College to use the library and sports facilities and to participate in computer classes. In this way, the students receive the exposure necessary for broadening their horizons. The program also includes working with a community-based organization. Since its inception, HCLPP has collaborated with a number of community-based organizations that can provide opportunities that the program itself cannot offer. These have included a theater company and a beacon program that offered night programs, English as a second language classes, and GED services for parents and teens in the program.

High School Follow-up

The New York State Department of Education mandates that as a condition of the Liberty Partnership grants, programs follow and serve participants until they graduate from high school. Unfortunately, this is a much more complicated mandate in New York City than in small upstate communities. The ninth- through twelfth-grade students who participated in the HCLPP enroll in more than 40 high schools throughout the city. The State Department of Education did not anticipate this problem and cannot provide sufficient funding to enable the individual follow-up realistically required to track every eighth-grade graduate through high school. In an effort to serve the high school students who participated in HCLPP in junior high, we have initiated four different follow-up approaches, each of which includes opportunities for counseling, mentoring by Hunter College students, academic assistance, help with high school adjustment, college, and work preparation, and exposure to college life.

One follow-up approach has been to develop on-site services at the few high schools that have a significant number of program graduates and are willing to collaborate. This approach has been very difficult to implement because of lack of space for additional programming at the high schools and the difficulties inherent in trying to pull students out of regularly scheduled classes to meet with HCLLP staff for counseling or academic assistance. Teachers are very reluctant to have students leave class for any reason.

A second follow-up strategy has been to offer programming at the college, including counseling, tutoring, preparation for SATs, employment preparation, and recreation. In addition, the HCLPP students are encouraged to use many of the facilities at the college, including the library and computer labs, and to just "hang out" in some of the lounges, meeting with their mentors or one another. This approach has been very successful with some of the graduates, who seem to enjoy using the college as sort of a drop in center.

A third follow-up approach has been to offer special programs for the graduates after school at the junior high school. Some graduates have become engaged in these and have enjoyed tutoring the junior high students. However, most do not want to return to their old school. Finally, efforts have been made to work with local community-based organizations, encouraging the development of special programs for this population. Unfortunately, this approach has also been underutilized, perhaps in large measure because so many of the youths want and need to find jobs after school.

In sum, there has been no effective solution found to the challenge of following up with HCLPP participants through high school. Each of our follow-up strategies has been effective with some of the students, but none has reached all. Many youths do return to program staff at the junior high school or the college when they are reaching the end of their high school years to ask for help with completing college or job applications, preparing for standardized tests, or simply examining their options. Still others visit when they have dropped out of high school and want help in getting back on track. Although we have no way of determining precisely what percentage do return, our best estimate is that we see about 70% of the junior high graduates at some time during their high school careers.

Transactions with the Child Welfare System

As a universal program, HCLPP must inevitably address the needs of students and families who are engaged with a range of specialized service systems (e.g., healthcare, income maintenance, housing/homelessness, juvenile justice). However, youths involved with the child welfare system present special challenges. First, if a youth is in foster care, it is assumed that the foster care agency should be the primary service provider, but it is extremely difficult to obtain needed information from the child welfare worker or the foster parent or to engage them in any type of collaborative planning. Second, like all children who enter school after the year has started, it is often very hard for children in foster care to adjust to a new school. Third, school personnel do not know how to work with the child welfare system and get very frustrated when they call and do not obtain immediate cooperation from the child welfare agency. Hence, they often look for help from our staff in interacting with the child welfare agency. Fourth, school administrators prefer to control all calls to the child abuse hotline and are upset if one of the program staff members makes a call. They do not accept the status of the social workers as mandated reporters. Finally, issues of confidentiality are a constant struggle because school personnel and the child welfare workers, if they become engaged, persistently attempt to get our workers and student interns to reveal confidential information about their cases.

These struggles create excellent learning opportunities for our student interns. Unfortunately, interns tend to develop negative views of the child welfare system as a consequence of frequently unhelpful interactions with child welfare workers.

Conclusion

The social services of HCLPP, in combination with its after-school activities, provide extensive wrap-around services to the students in the junior high school. One program component still awaiting further development is increased participation of the parents.

Comer (1988) recognized early on that the culture of the school and of the parents could

be perceived as antagonistic and that this, in turn, could affect the child's school performance. We have reached out to parents not just individually but also programmatically. After conducting a needs assessment, English classes were offered and child care was provided to enable parents to attend. Well-attended seminars occur when they are focused on issues that concern parents and guardians. Seminar topics have included dealing with adolescents, immigration, the rights of parents in school, and advocating for the child's education. Although there is parent participation, it is not at the level that it could be. This could be due to the parents' heavy work schedules and the reluctance of the school to encourage parent involvement except in an ancillary way. Much work in this area remains.

Extensive records of school attendance and performance in junior high are maintained. As indicated above, the program has been able to maintain contact with only about three-quarters of the high school students who participated. Factors related to this include school dropout, relocation, change of student identification numbers over time, New York City discharge policies, and student disinterest. Based on internal program evaluations, it has been documented that extended participation in the program leads to increased attendance at junior high school. The effects on grades are less clear. Psychosocial gains have been documented. Regular program participants demonstrate increased self-confidence and internalized locus of control.

Although a program such as HCLPP clearly is not a panacea for the social and environmental ills facing these youngsters, it is an opportunity to intervene in an institution central to the lives of the children. If the hours spent in school can be made more effective and rewarding both academically and socially, a great deal has been accomplished. And if after-school opportunities contribute to students' expanded sense of life's possibilities, they may gain the resilience needed to overcome many adverse circumstances. Such programs as Liberty Partnership have demonstrated that when resources are provided in a nonstigmatized way, they are well received. Yet the reality is that the resources needed to provide the academic and social foundation that immigrant youths need to succeed is not yet a priority for this country.

REFERENCES

Carnegie Council on Adolescent Development. (1992). *A matter of time: Risk and opportunity in the non-school hours.* New York: Carnegie.

Comer, J. (1988). Educating poor minority children. *Scientific American, 259*(5), 42–48.

Garbarino, J. (1992). *Children and families in the social environment,* second ed. Hawthorne, NY: Aldine de Gruyter.

Gilchrist, L. D., & Schinke, S. P. (1984). *Life skills counseling with adolescents.* Austin: Pro-Ed.

SUSAN SALTZBURG

Co-Constructing Adolescence for Gay and Lesbian Youth and Their Families

Informed by a constructionist sensitivity, we are challenged to step out of the realities we have created, and to ask significant questions—what are the repercussions of [our] ways of talking, who gains, who is hurt, who is silenced, what traditions are sustained, which are undermined?

Gergen (1994:63)

Coming of age can be a difficult and heart-wrenching process for gay and lesbian young people because so much of their time and emotional energy is dominated by trying to manage the hostile social environment and the fears and repercussions of coming-out to (or being "found out" by) family and peers. Despite the increased exposure of gay and lesbian issues in the media, the portrayal of gay and lesbian lives as a normative variance of our human experience is often overshadowed by the disparaging imagery attached to homosexuality. For adolescents who are just realizing their gay and lesbian affectional and sexual orientation, these stigmatizing attitudes serve to bear down on their spirits, stifle their voices, and obstruct their developmental pathways through adolescence.

As gay and lesbian youths look out into the world searching for images of adolescence that might confirm and resonate with their circumstances, they are further silenced by the emptiness that stands before them. The absence of cultural blueprints recognizing and explicating the stories of these young people reflects the overall omission of gay and lesbian children and families from the infrastructures of our societal institutions (Mallon 2002). It is important for all persons (especially developing youths) to see aspects of their personhood reflected in the world that surrounds them. This mirrored reflection serves as a source of validation and a framework for all the possibilities of "to be" and "to become." When adolescents cannot find their social reflection in the faces of friends, lyrics of a song, images on the screen, or in the language constituting day-to-day life, there emerges a sense of existential irrelevance. For gay and lesbian youths, this translates as "not existing" except as a socially constructed aberrance of "what is" and "what should be."

As a result, gay and lesbian adolescents step into their gay identity without the resources to provide a social context for growing up gay, loving in gay relationships, and developing resiliency in the face of homophobia. For many, there are no opportunities for acquaintance-ship with other gay and lesbian peers and their families, mentorship by gay adults who can serve as role models (e.g., teachers, coaches, camp counselors) or access to an active and affirming gay community.

Analogous to the circumstances encountered by youths, parents of adolescent sons and daughters who are just coming-out face many of the same challenges and uncertainties as their offspring (Boxer, Cook, & Herdt 1991; Saltzburg 2004). Still immersed in their active parenting roles, parents are naturally drawn into the coming-out of their adolescent children. The day-to-day circumstances and activities viewed (through a heterosexist lens) as "normal" and routine for adolescents—based on the parents' experiences with their other children or memories of their own adolescence—begin to look different because of their child's emerging gay or lesbian identity. Without a set of normative parental expectancies (Menaghan 1989; Silverberg 1996; Silverberg & Steinberg 1990) and no visible images of other parents guiding their children through gay adolescence, this cohort of parents feels existentially alone, socially isolated, and estranged from their children by having no frame of reference (Saltzburg 2004).

Although there has been increased media coverage of gay men and lesbians in recent years, none of it has resulted in normalizing, ritualizing, or celebrating gay adolescence. For the family, the underlying gay identity formation of the youth permeates all levels of the child's existence and restructures his or her adolescence and the family's participation in it, in unfamiliar ways. Prevailing heterosexist traditions and presumed social norms have concealed the vicissitudes of gay adolescence, leaving the landscape of this life stage to be socially constructed as the phenomenon unfolds for individual families (Saltzburg 2004).

In this chapter, I highlight the importance of creating a more inclusive view of adolescence by considering the intersection of the family life stage at adolescence (Carter & McGoldrick 1999; Garcia-Preto 1985) with sons and daughters coming-out as gay or lesbian. In doing so, I present a promising model of practice for co-constructing adolescence for these youths and their families. Envisioning adolescence through the lens of being gay and lesbian entails deconstructing socially stigmatizing connotations and recontextualizing the experience for family units. This enhanced version of adolescence provides gay and lesbian youths and their parents with opportunities to thrive and grow in self-affirming directions by integrating the gay identity into their overall sense of selves. In keeping with the framework of this text, the discussion is situated within the theoretical constructs of risk and protective factors from the child welfare literature.

Demographic Patterns

It is only in recent years with the heightened presence of gay and lesbian activism that young people are coming-out in the earlier years of adolescence. Exact figures representing the numbers of gay and lesbian young people are difficult to determine, as many youths are still questioning and coming to terms with their gay identities throughout their adolescence, and others remain tightly closeted in their gay identities to thwart off the risks of exposure. Identifying parents of gay and lesbian young people is a relatively new occurrence as well, coinciding with the advent of sons' and daughters' coming-out at adolescence (in the past, parents often did not learn of their children's gay identities until they were launched from the home as young adults). These parents for the most part still remain a silent and invisible group.

As critical information about gay and lesbian youth has gradually begun to permeate our collective social consciousness over the past decade, recognition of the unique and high-risk circumstances surrounding their lives becomes part of the public record. Because sexual orientation is not something that is identified on birth certificates, school records, or death certificates, and because it is not a characteristic readily visible to the eye, the numbers of gay and lesbian youth are probably much higher than what has been surmised. Although determining exact figures may be difficult, an increase in the reports of serious incidents affecting the lives of gay and lesbian young people has begun to be recognized.

Following a report released from the U.S. Department of Health and Human Services (1989) that estimated gay and lesbian youth to represent more than 30% of all adolescent suicides, concerned activists from across the broad landscape of the gay, lesbian, bisexual, and transgendered (GLBT) community began to form coalitions to address this issue. Although the rigor of the research methodology of this report was challenged (McDaniel, Purcell, & D'Augelli 2001), the emergent information played an important role in heightening public awareness and served as a springboard for further research in this area.

A number of studies has emerged corroborating the suicide risks of gay and lesbian adolescents. Hunter (1990) found a correlation between youths who were the victims of peer violence (resulting from their perceived gay status) and suicide attempts or ideation in 41% of male respondents and 34% of female respondents; Remafedi, Farrow, and Deisher (1991) found that one-third of the gay adolescent participants in their study reported having attempted suicide as a result of social isolation, family ejection, and self-devaluation; Proctor and Groze (1994) indicated that 40.3% of the gay and lesbian youth they studied had attempted suicide and 25.8% had considered suicide; and Remafedi, French, Story, Resnick, and Blum (1998) reported a correlation between sexual orientation and risk for suicide, with 28% of the gay adolescents in the study reporting at least one suicide attempt compared to 4% of the heterosexual male respondents and 20% of the lesbian youths reporting a suicide attempt compared to 14% of the straight female respondents.

Further linking the suicide concerns for gay and lesbian youths with environmental factors, a 1999 national survey of GLBT and questioning youth revealed that 46% reported verbal harassment, 36.4% reported sexual harassment, and 12.1% reported physical assault in their school settings. Of those reporting harassment at school, more than one-third of the youths stated that no one intervened on their behalf when homophobic remarks were heard. A total of 69% of the youths studied reported experiencing some form of blatant harassment or violence (Gay, Lesbian, Straight, Educators Network 1999).

Similar findings were found in a study of high school students in Massachusetts (Garofalo, Cameron-Wolf, Kessel, Palfrey, & Durant 1998), which revealed that gay, lesbian, and bisexual youth were more than four times as likely than heterosexual students to experience being threatened with a weapon on school grounds and five times as likely to skip school because of fears regarding personal safety. This same research indicated that gay and lesbian youths were more than three times as likely to have attempted suicide. Of 4,000 Massachusetts high school students studied (Healy 2001), almost 40% of the gay and bisexual students attempted suicide compared to 10% of their heterosexual peers. As the scope of research reaches out to include larger numbers of adolescents and as gay and lesbian students feel more secure in revealing their sexual orientation, there is the likelihood that the figures representing youth experiencing these life-compromising and life-threatening problems will increase.

Societal Context

Serving as the moral triad for existentially situating homosexuality in our society, the effects of homophobia, social stigmatization (Martin & Hetrick 1988), and heterosexist privilege permeate the infrastructure of our societal institutions, saturating social attitudes, families' belief systems, and individuals' self-images. In the face of intolerance, oppression, and marginalization, the trickle-down effects impacting families are devastating and the risks for adolescents coming-out as gay and lesbian extremely high.

The exclusion of gay and lesbian adolescence from the chronicles of our everyday lives reflects the blatant absence of laws, social policies, social services, school-based programs, and educational curriculum specifically recognizing the lives of these youths. Growing up in a society that asks for service in its military, but disencourages disclosure of their identity ("don't ask, don't tell"); requires payment of taxes, but denies them the spiritual, emotional, and financial benefits (e.g., healthcare benefits, spousal social security benefits) of having a legally recognized marriage or life union; demands obedience to its laws, but blocks the passage of hate-crime laws; and encourages gainful employment, but permits employment discrimination teaches gay and lesbian young people that their lives do not carry the same value as those of the heterosexual population. It is an oppressive message that envelops these youths and weighs heavily on their developing psyches and day-to-day survival.

Establishing a visible presence and equitable services for gay and lesbian adolescents requires investment and participation across all levels of our societal institutions. Because mainstream society remains historically locked in a pejorative view about homosexuality, our societal institutions have not been organized with the vision or language that recognizes the co-existence of gay and lesbian youths; nor have programs relevant to their needs been initiated. The dearth of institutional mechanisms for taking into account the lives of these young people leaves them without access to resources and devoid of opportunities for the normative activities of adolescence. Adapting our social environment and societal institutions to the broad spectrum of strengths and needs of gay and lesbian adolescents entails restructuring our social consciousness to include images of families with gay and lesbian children and understanding the issues surrounding their lives.

Vulnerabilities and Risk Factors

The montage of homophobic stories that has been documented (e.g., see Dane Bauer 1995; Monette 1992) as the knowledge base relating to the lives of gay and lesbian persons continues to be passed down from one generation to the next. Deprecating images that represent predatory inclinations, an undue emphasis on sexualized behaviors, and psychological-sociological pathology permeate societal institutions and family

belief systems, becoming incorporated into the evolving identities of gay and lesbian youths (Savin-Williams 1994). These internalized messages erode self-esteem, hopes for the future, and the confidence of establishing solidarity with parents. As the realization of what being gay signifies to the greater world cognitively crystallizes for these youngsters, they struggle to manage the fears of being found out, the decision of whether to disclose, and the anticipated or actual response of family, peers, and esteemed others (teachers, counselors, coaches) in their lives. The outcome of these critical others' responses to their coming-out plays a determining role in the hierarchy of risk factors potentially facing these vulnerable youths.

Family-Based Risk Factors

Given the developmental vulnerabilities of adolescence, it is during the family crisis following coming-out (Borhek 1988; Griffin, Wirth, & Wirth 1996; Herdt & Koff 2000; Saltzburg 2004) that gay and lesbian youths are most susceptible to a number of critical environmental risk factors. Whereas parents of other socially oppressed groups are viewed as essential for cushioning their children from the harsh blows of external stressors and preparing them for living in the face of persecution (Uribe & Harbeck 1992), parents of gay and lesbian adolescents are often unaware of their children's new status, do not yet possess the first-hand knowledge for understanding their children's circumstances, or are struggling themselves with the advent of their own oppressed status (as parents of gay and lesbian young people). Having no point of reference for what it means to be gay or lesbian, parents of adolescents just coming-out may initially feel displaced from their children's lives and inept in their parenting roles, leading to withdrawal from active parenting (Saltzburg 2004).

Because family support is a critical predictor of adolescent health and adjustment (Morano, Cisler, & Lemerond 1993) the perceived or actual shifts in parental support, involvement, and investment following adolescent coming-out pose a significant threat to the healthy functioning and survival of the adolescent in the family system (Saltzburg 1996; Savin-Williams 1989). While gay and lesbian youngsters are looking for parental understanding and assurance following disclosure, the disorganizing effects of internalized homophobia and feelings of displacement from their child's life may envelop the parents, resulting in emotional distancing between them and their children (Saltzburg 2004). Self-reports from youth further corroborate incidents of withdrawal of resources, ejection from the home, or familial abuse as common aspects of their experience following disclosure (Hammelman 1993; Hunter & Schaecher 1987; Kournay 1987; Martin & Hetrick 1988).

Environmental and Social Isolation
Risk Factors

As adolescents struggle with their parents' response to their coming-out, they are also immersed in assessing the response of their immediate social environment—especially with regard to peer acceptance. Fears of exposure, feelings of estrangement (because of perceived differences), or actual peer rejection produce a state of withdrawal or alienation from those who have served as their social cohort. Because the assault on their self-esteem is so great, many come to believe that their lives have no worth. Without a network of others to fill the void of reference-group membership, emotional intimacy with close friends and confidants, and recreational companionship, the young person becomes socially isolated, leading to loneliness, despondence, and hopelessness.

Corresponding to the despondence that these youths feel without the ready availability of an accepting peer group, they experience a sense of devastation when they lose (or perceive themselves to lose) the visible support of adults outside of the family who have come to represent significant others in their lives, such as teachers, coaches, neighbors, scout leaders, and ministers. Emotional well-being and psychosocial development are compromised when there are no opportunities for having normative adolescent peer friendships and recreational activities, adult role models to look up to and emulate, and adult mentors who demonstrate caring and investment.

Mosaic of Risk Factors

Tied into the sadness of becoming aware of others' negative attitudes and opinions about homosexuality is the sense of aloneness stemming from the lack of readily accessible resources. When the social systems that should serve as the organizing and protective structures for the health, growth, and well-being of children fail to recognize and meet their needs, the systems themselves become part of the risk factors (Lawson & Anderson-Butcher 2001). Risk factors for gay and lesbian youths (as for all children) may present themselves in sequential order, resulting in a domino effect on the life and resources of the adolescent (Lawson & Anderson-Butcher 2001).

Confronted with the toxic effects of homophobia that permeate all levels of one's immediate social environment, including parents, family, friends, school, and community, gay and lesbian youths are in jeopardy of an array of risk factors:

- Compartmentalizing their sexual identity by "passing" as straight (Hetrick & Martin 1987; Savin-Williams 1994, Troiden 1989), leading to anonymous gay sex or heterosexual acting-out (Hetrick & Martin 1987);
- Parental distancing (Saltzburg 2004);
- Ejection from the home (Hammelman 1993; Hunter & Schaecher 1987; Martin & Hetrick 1988; Savin-Williams 1989, 1994);
- Emotional abuse, physical violence (Hetrick & Martin 1987; Uribe & Harbeck 1992), and sexual abuse (Martin & Hectrick 1998);

- Running away and homelessness (Martin & Hetrick 1988; Remafedi 1990; Sanford 1989; Savin-Williams 1994); and
- Harassment at school, leading to truancy, poor achievement, and school drop-out (Hunter & Schaecher 1987; Martin & Hetrick 1988; Sanford 1989; Savin-Williams 1994; Uribe & Harbeck 1992).

Further compounding their risks in these life-compromising circumstances, many of these youths turn to drugs, alcohol, and sexual encounters as a means to escape their fears and loneliness (Martin & Hetrick 1988; Savin-Williams 1994; Whitlock 1989). All of these risk factors are associated with diminished self-esteem.

In addition, without the safety net of the family home and support of family members, young people are particularly vulnerable to a set of risk factors that come with living on the streets (often a result of family ejection, rejection, and abuse), including becoming victims of violence (e.g., rape, physical assaults, murder; Hunter & Schaecher 1987; Martin & Hetrick 1988; Uribe & Harbeck 1992); turning to prostitution, drug trafficking, and delinquent behaviors to survive (Martin & Hetrick 1988; Savon-Williams 1994; Uribe & Harbeck 1992; Whitlock 1989); and becoming susceptible to an array of health problems (e.g., sexually transmitted diseases, HIV, drug abuse, unwanted pregnancy; Ryan & Futterman 1998).

The emotional and physical devastation tied to the broad spectrum of risk factors associated with the lives of gay and lesbian youths leads to a high incidence of depression, anxiety, and suicidality (D'Augelli 1993; Fikar 1992; Hammelman 1993; Hershberger & D'Augelli 1995; Hetrick & Martin 1987; Hunter & Schaecher 1987; Kournay 1997; Morrison & L'Heareux 2001; Proctor & Groze 1994; Remafedi, Farrow, & Deisher 1991; Remafedi, French, Story, Resnick, & Blum 1998; Sanford 1989; Sears 1991).

Although Robinson, Walters, & Skeen (1989) and Holtzen and Agriesti (1990) found that, in time, most parents adjust to their adult children's gay or lesbian status, family life-cycle literature (Carter & McGoldrick 1999; Garcia-Prieto 1985) suggests that the unique features of adolescence place children and parents at greater risk when children come out during adolescence compared to when they come out as adults (Saltzburg 2004). It is during the small window of time following disclosure, when children are despairing for parents' and others' acceptance and parents are frantically trying to situate this phenomenon in their lives, that gay and lesbian adolescents fall prey to environmental risks, depression, and suicidality.

Resilience and Protective Factors

As is the case with all children, parent investment, family support, peer group acceptance, and societal affirmation constitute the pathways to successful outcomes in the lives of gay and lesbian youngsters (Kirby & Fraser 1997).

Serving as the anchor for adolescent stability and wellness (Walsh 1993), parent (or caregiver) involvement and investment fortifies the young person for successfully maneuvering through adolescence. Predictable consistency of parental presence and parent-role functioning in a youngster's life instills a sense of safety, stability, and self-worth (Collins & Luebker 1994; Grovetant & Cooper 1986), allowing the adolescent to reach out and explore his or her environment while still relying on the safety net of parents for support, protection, and comfort. Furthermore, parents who are able to maintain active participation and involvement in children's lives in the face of problems project investment, enduring affection, and hope for their offspring, which models adaptation and instills resilience (Kinard 1995; Thomlison 1997).

Given that so many of the essential developmental tasks of adolescence find their resolution in the context of attachment and family relationships (Rice 1990), it is essential to their welfare that adolescents believe that the attachment figures understand their situation and are responsive to their emotional needs. Because parent response is a predictor for gay and lesbian adolescent self-esteem and stability (Savin-Williams 1990), we must find ways to keep parents connected to their children throughout the coming-out process. To help parents sustain the previously held thoughts about their child as a positive and hopeful extension of themselves (fortifying parenting investment; Cohen & Weissman 1984), the protective work focuses on dispelling the disparaging societal messages attached to homosexuality and replacing them with positive, affirmative images.

Opening up pathways for parents to gain more knowledge and exposure about being gay and lesbian (and the challenges for youth) will positively support their adjustment in several important ways: (1) it helps them understand how to support their children; (2) it keeps them involved in their adolescents' lives; (3) it contributes to normalizing the experience for the family; and (4) it psychologically reestablishes their role as their children's buffer and protector from harsh external influences. By empowering parents with information and familiarity, we can reestablish their confidence in their parenting role and reassure them of their value and permanence in their children's lives (Saltzburg 1996).

Paving the way for strengthening the parenting connection following adolescent coming-out occurs at three levels of restructuring the parental vision: the first entails revisioning their son or daughter as a gay or lesbian person; the second, revisioning themselves as parents of a gay or lesbian child; and the third, revisioning the adolescent experience to reflect the activities, traditions, and spirit of gay and lesbian young people (Saltzburg 2004). Preparing the professionals who work with adolescents and families to support parents through this adaptation process lies at the crux of services to youths and families.

Creating a Normative Social Environment for Adolescents

To create and nurture a normative experience of adolescence for gay and lesbian young people

further entails making available age-appropriate social, educational, and recreational opportunities and establishing traditions that memorialize this special period in their lives (Saltzburg 1996). Socially acknowledging their coming-of-age stories and ritualizing the corresponding developmental milestones will normalize their lives for parents and families as well.

When significant adults in the lives of young people (e.g., parents, friends, teachers, neighbors, social workers, mentors, ministers) offer availability, caring, empathy, and guidance (Finkelhor & Berliner 1995), they contribute to easing the psychosocial challenges of adolescents and strengthening their resilience. Gay and lesbian youths, in particular, are in need of adult support to shelter them from the harsh, homophobic attitudes and actions perpetrated in society, bolster their self-confidence, and applaud their transition into their gay identity.

Designing programs and activities specifically geared for the needs of gay and lesbian youths must draw from the sociological aspects of their unique circumstances, as well as from developmental literature on adolescence. This integrated understanding lends itself to recognizing the key aspects of adolescents' lives and incorporating them into programmatic planning. Giving these young people opportunities to try out primary areas of adolescent functioning normalizes their experience and promotes development. Such opportunities include:

- Socialization activities (e.g., coffeehouse get-togethers, dances, picnics, sleepovers), as their pool of peers is often small or nonexistent;
- Recreational activities corresponding to the interests of gay and lesbian youths (interests that often cross over gender role prescriptions) and provide the opportunity for infusion of gay themes;
- Peer leadership training (focused on strengthening self-esteem, coping with social stigma, and tying their gay identity to a community of others); and

- Health education (including safe sex and HIV awareness, alcohol and drug abuse prevention).

Working on the timely tasks of normative adolescence and learning to manage the unique challenges of being gay are important elements for successful outcomes for gay and lesbian youths.

Co-Constructing Protective Factors across Societal Institutions

Protecting gay and lesbian youths from the vast array of risk factors that impinge on their lives calls for a united response across societal institutions, situating the lives of these young people within the same socially valued context as their heterosexual counterparts. Such a response requires first, problem recognition and second, collaboration. The latter involves establishing a network of socially instituted structures whose aim is to reconstruct the socially disparaging meaning attached to being gay and lesbian, safeguard the lives of gay and lesbian young people, and provide for their developmental needs (e.g., parent/family involvement, socialization, education, recreation, health care). Developing these protective structures entails putting in place a set of interrelated strategies across systems:

- Developing affirming, inclusive language across societal institutions pertaining to gay and lesbian persons;
- Reaching out to parents, caregivers, and families to provide information, support, and resources;
- Providing cultural competency education and training pertaining to working with gay and lesbian individuals, and particularly, the circumstances of gay and lesbian youths (to human services professionals, educators, juvenile justice professionals, youth development programs, and healthcare professionals);
- Designing protocols for foster care, residential settings, homeless shelters, and court-

involved placements for gay and lesbian youth that take into consideration their sexual orientation, vulnerabilities, and special needs;
- Establishing policies in school systems that acknowledge, support, protect, mentor, and advocate for gay and lesbian students;
- Incorporating program initiatives into youth development programs that are welcoming and inclusive of gay and lesbian adolescents and their interests;
- Creating youth development programs that are specifically designed for the outreach, support, socialization, leadership training, recreation, and advocacy of gay and lesbian adolescents; and
- Establishing accessible healthcare services that are knowledgeable, respectful, and proactive of the health issues of gay and lesbian youths.

Promising Approaches

Drawing on the documented merits, fundamental tenets, and conceptual design of support group structures, youth development programs, and mentoring relationships, a Massachusetts statewide group network of alliances of gay and lesbian youth was conceived. The organizing goal for the start-up and maintenance of this multigroup affiliation rested in the commitment to serve as a catalyst in the community to protect the lives of gay and lesbian youth and normalize their adolescent experience by providing opportunities to participate in customary adolescent socialization activities. Although there have been other support groups and drop-in center initiatives for gay and lesbian youth, the design of a statewide affiliation of community groups was new and offered unique possibilities.

State Network of Affiliated Groups for Youth Outreach

In 1992, in response to the U.S. Department of Health and Human Services report (1989) on youth suicide documenting the highest percentage of youth suicide and family ejection in families with gay and lesbian children, the Commonwealth of Massachusetts authorized the formation of the first Governor's Commission on Gay and Lesbian Youth in the nation (Massachusetts Governor's Commission on Gay and Lesbian Youth 1994). This marked an unprecedented interest in the plight of these young people demonstrated by state leaders. As institutional consciousness was being raised with respect to the health, safety, and educational issues of gay and lesbian young people, a group of GLBT adult volunteers from across the state (who were, independently of one another, involved in providing social outreach and support to GLBT youths) came together to lay out the framework for a statewide association of community groups for gay and lesbian adolescents. Safeguarding and normalizing the adolescent experience for gay and lesbian youth was at the core of the network's mission.

Celebrating the Lives of GLBT Youth

Born of the collective vision of those volunteers forming the statewide group network of Alliances for Gay and Lesbian Youth (AGLY) and their collegial support and mentorship to one another, smaller groups in the network started to expand and new groups began to emerge. In pursuing my ongoing commitment to working with gay and lesbian youths and their families, I, in my capacity of clinical social worker, became a participating member of the AGLY network when I joined a newly formed AGLY group in the southeastern region of the state in 1994 as one of the two adult advisors. Those beginning years were ones of carving out the role and responsibilities of the network while establishing and fortifying the evolving context of the individual community youth alliances. Unique to the structure of these affiliated, freestanding groups was the sense of allegiance, connection, and accountability to the larger network. We (the GLBT adult advisors) came together to meet as a group network for one full day a month for sharing stories, presenting

new ideas, developing policy, formulating funding strategies, and seeking fortification and renewal from one another. In many ways, we were replicating the enriching elements of the youth group process in our adult network group.

A broad-spectrum approach to programming was identified as essential for breaking down the socially imposed barriers that were impeding the social and emotional development of these youths and placing them at risk. At the same time, there was a strong commitment to honoring and celebrating the lives of GLBT young people by creating normative experiences for them and providing them with the support and tools for coping with societal bias. The unlimited possibilities for developing social activities, peer leadership programs, and pride-building experiences with large numbers of diverse youths was a unique advantage of the formalized network of community-based groups. This is particularly important for socialization among GLBT adolescents, as their pool of "known" peers is typically small. The network has participated in such annual statewide functions as youth pride events, a weekend youth retreat, a statewide prom (hosted by an AGLY group), and a GLBT youth conference.

A Mentoring Resource

Taking on a more prominent role in the community (both as a statewide network and as individual youth alliances) called for increased policy formulation, grant writing, public relations exposure, and structures of accountability. The vision of the network members began to crystallize into the promising possibility of serving as a mentoring resource for GLBT young people, as well as for the significant others who were in close contact with these youths, including parents, families, educators, human services professionals, and health professionals. The far-reaching impact of our mentorship was subsumed under the weekly meetings and activities with youths, consultation and trainings with community organizations and schools, psychoeducational groups for parents and family members, and the cosponsorship of community-building events.

Instituting strategies to counteract the environmental risks for gay and lesbian youth may be conceptualized as a form of mentorship. With respect to the AGLY network, the mentoring construct served as an organizing structure that encompassed three levels of intervention: (1) mentoring of gay and lesbian adolescents; (2) mentoring of parents (and families) of adolescent sons and daughters who are coming-out; and (3) mentoring of those providing services to these youths and their families. For youth, the AGLY groups become the ideal context for adult mentors to work side-by-side with young people in an array of roles that restore and strengthen the adolescent experience. Reflective of the mentoring relationship described in the literature (Einolf 1995; McPartland & Nettles 1991; Smink 1990; Yancey 1998), the adult advisors serve a number of important roles with respect to the youth and parents in the community, such as role models, advocates, teachers, coaches, and counselors. The third level of mentoring intervention, which in some ways is the underlying structure for the first two, broadens the concept to include mentoring those persons who are instrumental in the program design and service delivery for children and families in our communities. In this light, the mentoring construct becomes a vehicle for training others about cultural competency for working with the GLBT population and their families.

Research Support

There is recent research dealing with the problems encountered by gay and lesbian youths, including coming-out to parents and others from the youth's perspective (see the detailed listing in section on risk factors), gay and lesbian youth identity formation (Plummer 1989; Trioden 1989), response to the needs of gay and lesbian students in school settings (Hunter & Schaecher 1987; Sears 1992; Uribe & Harbeck 1992), issues pertaining to child welfare initiatives and per-

manency planning for GLBT youths (Mallon 1998, 2002), and the initial responses of parents learning that their adolescent is gay or lesbian (Saltzburg 2004). However, there has been minimal research looking at normalizing adolescence for gay and lesbian young people and their families. Establishing programs for these youths and evaluating their effectiveness is still an area of research that needs development.

Assessments and Interventions

To develop relevant policies and institute meaningful programming, professionals providing services to youth must possess a broad knowledge base with respect to the cultural implications, unique differences, and social issues that currently define the lives of gay and lesbian young people and their families. As with other culturally different groups, expectations for culturally competent practice is imperative to successful intervention outcomes.

To achieve diversity and relevance across institutional programming and insure cultural competency in direct practice with gay and lesbian youths, training modules may be broken down into strategic areas of focus:

- Raising awareness of the historical oppression and current social injustices perpetrated against GLBT persons;
- Creating the opportunity for self-awareness regarding one's own values and beliefs about homosexuality;
- Providing specialized information with respect to gay identity formation, unique characteristics of gay and lesbian families, and family adjustment to a member coming out;
- Delineating environmental risk factors for gay and lesbian adolescents;
- Illuminating the critical elements of adolescent development and coming-out as gay or lesbian for youths, parents, and caregivers; and
- Expediting exposure to the GLBT community and culture.

Ethical Issues

Constructing a social reality that includes the "everyday phenomenon" that some of humankind is gay and lesbian might suggest examining what this means relative to our society's beliefs about social justice and human rights. Although we purport to venerate the ideals of social justice and human rights, these values are not always reflected in our institutional frameworks. When gay-straight families interface with a world that behaves as if such families do not or should not exist, a set of pejorative values is reinforced that diminishes the importance of some people and some children; this process translates as an absence of societal investment and a refusal to allocate public funds.

The question underscoring society's responsibility to gay and lesbian youths can be stated as: how can gay and lesbian adolescents draw on the resources of family and societal institutions to support identity development, positive life experiences, and self-affirming life contributions? It is a question whose roots lie in the power differentials existing in a heterosexist society that marginalizes gay and lesbian persons. Formulating a response is beyond the capacities of the individual adolescent and family unit; it is lodged in the ideological infrastructure of the larger social systems. These organizing structures cradle the dominant values and beliefs that determine the worth of one set of people above another, and in turn, set the direction of policy, programs, and services.

Although child welfare advocates have touted their pledge for insuring the welfare of all children and families, until recently, the needs of gay and lesbian children have been largely overlooked. To create humane, empowering, life-affirming situations for all youths, we must insure nurturing conditions for living in which all children fare well (Gil 1985). Linking gay and lesbian youths and families to the same community resources that support overall adolescent development and well-being lies at the heart of the problem. This access to resources (Rappaport, Reischl, & Zimmerman 1992) rep-resents an act of empowerment, and will be implemented through laws, social policy, and human rights.

Case Examples and Discussion

When young people do not fit the accepted social molds for "normative adolescence," it may leave them feeling detached from others and without images from which to draw examples for their lives. For gay or lesbian youths living without the opportunity to realize their many possibilities, identity formation draws solely from the known heterosexist culture and stereotyping of gay and lesbian persons. The empty images leave these young people feeling empty as well. For instance, gay and lesbian youths are frequently deprived of the very rudimentary experiences of everyday adolescence, such as relating to a popular song whose words reflect their current or future lives (as gay men or lesbians), going to a school dance with a special romantic interest, participating in school team sports without the risk of locker-room harassment, or planning "sleepovers" with peers (being excluded from those of nongay peers because of homophobia and being denied hosting "gay sleepovers" due to parents' discomfort and concerns) (Saltzburg 2001).

The network of AGLY groups serves as an organizing structure for creating a social environment inclusive of all GLBT youth. Reintroducing the stabilizing force of the peer group back into the lives of GLBT young people reestablishes the resources of emotional intimacy, social cohorts, and a peer reference group. Without the benefit of intervening protective factors, gay and lesbian youths become drawn into the pejorative perception of homosexuality that has been historically relegated to gay men and lesbians.

Closeted Gay Identity

When the routine exploration of romance and sexuality for gay and lesbian adolescents is cast in a socially deviant light and when sexual acts (behaviors) are the only aspects of being gay that they have the opportunity to know, then these sexual behaviors, veiled in secrecy and shame, may come to exist in isolation from the rest of their personhood (Martin 1982; Martin & Hetrick 1988; Savin-Williams 1996). In contextualizing this, we find gay and lesbian adolescents looking for human connection and self-affirmation through sexual acts; this often places them in secretive, unsafe, and compromised situations (e.g., indiscriminate, anonymous, or unsafe sex; sex while consuming alcohol or taking drugs; sex with older adults; prostitution). The shame and sadness generated from such situational behaviors may lead to self-hatred and hopelessness. The story of one such youth is Patrick.

PATRICK'S STORY

Seventeen-year-old Patrick was terrified that his family or friends might discover that he was gay. He had been struggling with how to integrate his emerging sexuality with the rest of who he was as a person since he was 12 years old. Active in high school sports, well liked by peers, and romantically sought after by female friends, there seemed to be no place in Patrick's life for realizing his homosexuality. Coming-out for Patrick represented the anticipated loss of friendships, peer status, an esteemed position as a student athlete, and a source of pride for his parents. Confiding in no one and personally not acquainted with anyone else who was gay (or who was "out"), he silently endured endless episodes of derisive and prejudicial jokes and comments pertaining to gay men and lesbians by family and peers. The latter further reinforced his need to hide his sexual orientation.

As the physiological feelings, affectional ties, and cognitive synthesis related to same-sex attraction engulfed him, Patrick turned to the Internet for connecting with other gay males. The anonymity created by these contacts frequently lead to in-person meetings with men much older than himself and incidents of indiscriminate, unsafe, and impersonal sex. Recurrent, secretive rendezvous without any interpersonal connection or sense of caring on the other's part, combined with his constant fears of being "found out," left Patrick overwhelmed with shame, self-recrimination, and loneliness. Patrick gradually

slipped into a clinical depression and tried to kill himself.

Patrick was referred to an AGLY group by the psychiatrist treating his depression. As he slowly became immersed in the socializing experience, had the opportunity to learn about the societal contributions of gay and lesbian individuals, and had access to adult role models, the despair and hopelessness began to lift. Realizing his gay identity beyond the sexual acts provided a sense of connection and relativity to his overall identity formation, strengthening his self-esteem and self-worth. In time, Patrick worked with adult advisors and group peers to begin a dialog with his parents and his straight friends. The various socializing components of the AGLY network groups became the vehicle for modeling the hopeful possibilities for growing up as a gay man.

Adolescent Identity Exploration

To discover the inroads to their own individualized identities, adolescents need to have opportunities for exploration and experimentation. One important aspect of this experimenting lies in personal style as the building blocks for self-definition. Extremes in clothes, hairstyles, and personal accessories are generally tolerated in consonance with recognizing the important function of exploration for identity development. However, the same degree of experimentation by gay and lesbian youths is often met with intolerance, resistance, and family or social sanctions. By denying adolescents opportunities to pursue creative outlets for carving out identities, we may further reinforce their sense of personal detachment.

As many gay and lesbian youths courageously step into their gay identity, there is the tentative, yet purposeful, attempt at wanting to "look gay" by wearing labeling insignia (e.g., the diversity rainbow design, the upside-down pink triangle, cross-gendered clothing, hair styles attributed to gay men and lesbians) that serve as a badge of membership in this subculture and provide a sense of belonging and validation for the adolescents. One such example is a 15-year-old youth named Kenny.

KENNY'S STORY

The more Kenny's father chastised him for dressing in the flamboyant clothes that he found self-affirming and self-defining, the more Kenny felt cut off from himself and others. With the support and encouragement of friends in the AGLY youth group, Kenny began to experiment with pieces of dress apparel that put him in touch with this inner sense of self, and at the same time were not overly offensive to his father. This creative compromise materialized in the form of a pink silk scarf. Kenny explained that as he slipped on this symbol of personal identity, the shackles of pretense and intrapersonal dissonance slipped away. No matter where he was or what he was doing, the rich silk scarf contextualized his experience as a young gay male.

Adolescent Experimentation and Peer Acceptance

While thousands of students each year prepare for their high school prom, gay and lesbian adolescents stress over whether they should attend with a friend of the opposite gender to conform to the socially prescribed protocol, or not attend at all. To further complicate their dilemma, there are the decisions of what to wear to this momentous event that will bring pleasure and pride to the young person and further memorialize the occasion. If the traditional prom gown holds little meaning for a young woman's burgeoning lesbian identity and represents the prevailing heterosexist gender prescriptions, wearing this attire offers little self-affirmation and self-satisfaction for the youth. Redefining normative situations for adolescents across sexual orientation and gender opens up possibilities for personal growth and enhanced self-esteem. One such possibility is seen with a gay youth named Tommy.

TOMMY'S STORY

Tommy was one of the youths participating in the Youth Pride celebrations in Boston. The morning of Youth Pride, a community group of GLBT adolescents gathered for brunch and socialization prior to the GLBT Youth Prom that evening. When Tommy arrived to the gathering, he asked with an inviting smile if we wanted to see what his mother had bought for him to wear to the prom; as we nodded our heads yes, he removed from his backpack a new pair of dark brown dress slacks and a brown silk shirt. While his peers were admiring these new clothes, Tommy broke into laughter as he then announced, "Now, do you want to see what I am *really wearing* to the prom?" With that he pulled out a black velvet dress, fish net stockings, and high heels. After a moment of hesitation to process the significance of Tommy's disclosure, there was the roar of laughter and cheers. For Tommy, there was the excitement and jubilation of being able to be himself in an accepting environment.

Mentoring a Parent

Many gay and lesbian young people are asked to compromise their sense of identity to accommodate societal and familial norms. They speak of having to dismantle their rooms or change their clothes when extended family members are in the home or when they might be seen out in the community, so as to keep the secret or not offend anyone.

One parent of a gay youth spoke of her fears of how others might react to what she termed her son's "more effeminate dress style." She worried how his outward signs of being gay might affect attitudes toward him in school and their family's acceptance in the community (Saltzburg 2001). Although perceiving herself as a loving parent who had come to accept her son's gay sexual orientation, she viewed his public display of being gay as something to be monitored and censored to protect him and their family and to avoid imposing his "gay lifestyle" on others. She cited "being around young children" (Saltzburg 2001:112) as an example of such a circumstance—reinforcing the connotation of deviancy that has been historically ascribed to homosexuality.

The turning point for this parent began when she met an AGLY adult advisor who came to be a trusted mentor. There was finally someone who knew first-hand what it was like to grow up as a gay male, and could provide the missing pieces of information that were fueling her fears and biases about homosexuality. The AGLY mentor played a critical role in helping this parent come to understand that negating the value of her son's life by asking him to compartmentalize himself into separate entities of private, secretive "gay" self (shame) and public "passing straight" self (pride), she was contributing to his sense of inner fragmentation and the internalization of self-hatred. The face-to-face encounter with someone this mother came to respect and look to as a friend revealed the possibilities for understanding her child's circumstances, reestablishing her place in his life, and envisioning her son's future.

Conclusion

Examining the lives of gay and lesbian young people as they step into their parallel coexistence with others situated at the adolescent stage of development carries relevance for human services professionals providing services to these youths and their families. This coexistence calls for a recasting of adolescence, as we have come to know it through the heterosexist lens, to accommodate the needs of gay and lesbian youths. Until recently, we have assigned them the daunting task of being adolescent without the supportive structures of a safe, friendly, and empowering social environment.

Consistent with the pervasive omission of gay and lesbian culture from the historical development of our societal institutions, we have not traditionally allocated funds and programming for gay and lesbian youths; healthcare services, youth development programs, and foster care programs have all evolved outside the consideration of this minority population. Incorporating their presence into our current public systems would invite a broad spectrum of societal investments and spark a realignment of public attitudes and resources.

Adapting our social environment and societal institutions to the developmental strengths, issues, and needs of gay and lesbian youths entails restructuring our social consciousness to include images of families with gay and lesbian children. This inclusive reimaging serves to support parents in revisualizing their children as gay and lesbian, provide opportunities for developmental identity exploration and socialization for gay and lesbian youths, and protect children and families from the devastating effects of social marginalization.

REFERENCES

Borhek, M. V. (1988). Helping gay and lesbian adolescents and their families. *Journal of Adolescent Health Care, 9,* 123–138.

Boxer, A. M., Cook, J. A., & Herdt, G. (1991). Double jeopardy: Identity transitions and parent-child relations among gay and lesbian youth. In K. Pillemer & K. McCartney (eds), *Parent-child relations throughout life.* Mahwah, NJ: Lawrence Erlbaum Associates.

Carter, B., & McGoldrick, M. (1999). The changing family life cycle: A framework for family therapy. In B. Carter & M. McGoldrick (eds.), *The changing family life cycle,* third ed., pp. 3–28. Boston: Allyn and Bacon.

Cohen, R. S., & Weissman, S. (1984). The parenting alliance. In R. S. Cohen, B. J. Cohler, & S. Weissman, (eds.), *Parenthood: A psychodamic perspective,* pp. 33–49. New York: Guilford.

Collins, W. A., & Luebker, C. (1994). Parent and adolescent expectancies: Individual and relational signifi-cance. In J. G. Smetana (ed.), *Beliefs about parenting: Origins and developmental implications.* San Francisco: Jossey-Bass.

Dane Bauer, M. (1995). *Am I Blue?: Coming out from the silence.* New York: HarperTrophy.

D'Augelli, A. R. (1993). Preventing mental health problems among lesbian and gay college students. *Journal of Primary Prevention, 13*(4), 1–17.

Einolf, L. H. (1995). Mentoring to prevent school drop outs. *Journal of Behavioral Education, 5*(4), 447–459.

Fikar, C. R. (1992). Gay teens and suicide. *Pediatrics, 89,* 519–520.

Finkelhor, D., & Berliner, L. (1995). Research on the treatment of sexually abused children: A review and recommendations. *Journal of the American Academy of Child and Adolescent Psychiatry, 34,* 1–16.

Garcia Preto, N. (1985). The adolescent phase of the family life cycle. In M. Mirkin & S. Koman (eds.), *Handbook of adolescents and family therapy,* pp. 21–38. New York: Gardner Press.

Garofalo, R., Cameron-Wolf, R., Kessel, S., Palfrey, J., & DuRant, R. H. (1998). The association between health risk behaviors and sexual orientation among a school-based sample of adolescents. *Pediatrics, 101,* 895–902.

Gay, Lesbian, Straight Educators Network (1999). *GLSEN 1999 School climate survey.* New York: GLSEN.

Gergen, K. J. (1994). *An invitation to social construction.* Thousand Oaks, CA: Sage.

Gil, D. (1985). The ideological context of child welfare. In J. Laird & A. Hartman (eds.), *A handbook of child welfare,* pp. 11–33. New York: Free Press.

Griffin, E. W., Wirth, J. W., & Wirth, A. G. (1996). *Beyond acceptance: Parents of lesbians and gays talk about their experiences.* Englewood Cliffs, NJ: Prentice-Hall.

Grovetant, H. D., & Cooper, C. R. (1986). Individuation in family relationships. *Human Development, 29,* 82–100.

Hammelman, T. L. (1993). Gay and lesbian youth: Contributing factors to serious attempts or considerations of suicide, *Journal of Gay & Lesbian Psychotherapy, 2,* 77–89.

Healy, P. (2001). Suicides in state top homicides. *Boston Globe,* (February 28), p. 22.

Herdt, G., & Koff, B. (2000). *Something to tell you.* New York: Columbia University Press.

Hershberger, S. L., & D'Augelli, A. R. (1995). The impact of victimization on the mental health and suicidality of lesbian, gay and bisexual youths. *Developmental Psychology, 31,* 65–78.

Hetrick, E., & Martin, A. D. (1987). Developmental issues and their resolution for gay and lesbian adolescents. *Journal of Homosexuality, 13,* 25–43.

Holtzen, D. W., & Agriesti, A. A. (1990). Parental responses to gay and lesbian children: Differences in homophobia, self-esteem, and sex-role stereotyping. *Journal of Social and Clinical Psychology, 9,* 390–399.

Hunter, J. (1990). Violence against lesbian and gay male youths. *Journal of Interpersonal Violence, 5,* 295–300.

Hunter, J., & Schaecher, R. (1987). Stresses on lesbian and gay adolescents in schools. *Social Work in Education, 9,* 180–184.

Kinard, M. (1995). Assessing resilience in abused children. Paper presented at the Fourth International Family Violence Research Conference, Durham, NH, July 26–29, 1995.

Kirby, L. D., & Fraser, M. W. (1997). Risk and resilience in childhood. In M. Fraser (ed.), *Risk and resilience in childhood: An ecological perspective,* pp. 10–33. Washington, DC: National Association of Social Workers Press.

Kournay, R. F. (1987). Suicide among homosexual adolescents. *Journal of Homosexuality, 15,* 163–182.

Lawson, H. A., & Anderson-Butcher, D. (2001). In the best interests of the child: Youth development as a child welfare support and resource. In A. L. Sallee, H. A. Lawson, & K. Briar-Lawson (eds.), *Innovative practices with vulnerable children and families,* pp. 291–321. Dubuque, IA: Eddie Bowers.

Mallon, G. (1998). *We don't exactly get the Welcome Wagon: The experience of gay and lesbian adolescents in child welfare systems.* New York: Columbia University Press.

Mallon, G. (2002). There's no place like home: Achieving safety, permanency, and well-being for lesbian and gay adolescents in out-of-home care settings. *Child Welfare, 81,* 407–439.

Martin, A. D. (1982). Learning to hide: The socialization of the gay adolescent. In S. C. Feinstein, J. G. Looney, A. Schartzberg, & A. Sorosky (eds.), *Adolescent psychiatry: Developmental and clinical studies,* pp. 52–65. Chicago: University of Chicago Press.

Martin, A. D., & Hetrick, E. S. (1988). The stigmatization of the gay and lesbian adolescent. *Journal of Homosexuality, 15,* 163–183.

Massachusetts Governor's Commission on Gay and Lesbian Youth. (1994). *Prevention of health problems among gay and lesbian youth: Making health and human services accessible and effective for gay and lesbian youth.* Boston: Governor's Office.

McDaniel, S., Purcell, D., & D'Augelli, A. (2001). The relationship between sexual orientation and suicide: Research findings and future directions for research and prevention. *Suicide and Life-Threatening Behavior, 31*(1 suppl.), 84–105.

McPartland, J. M., & Nettles, S. M. (1991). Using community adults as advocates or mentors for at-risk middle school students: A two-year evaluation of Project RAISE. *American Journal of Education,* (August), 568–586.

Menaghan, E. G. (1989). Psychological well-being among parents and non-parents: The importance of normative expectedness. *Journal of Family Issues, 10,* 547–565.

Monette, P. (1992). *Becoming a man: Half a life story.* New York: Harcourt Brace Jovanovich.

Morano, C. D., Cisler, R. A., & Lemerond, J. (1993). Risk factors for adolescent suicidal behavior loss, insufficient familial support, and hopelessness. *Adolescence, 28,* 851–865.

Morrison, L. L., & L'Heareux, J. (2001). Suicide and gay/lesbian/bisexual youth: Implications for clinicians. *Journal of Adolescence, 24,* 39–49.

Plummer, K. (1989). Lesbian and gay youth in England. *Journal of Homosexuality, 17,* 195–223.

Proctor, C. D., & Groze, V. (1994). Risk factors for suicide among gay, lesbian, and bisexual youths. *Social Work, 39,* 504–512.

Rappaport, J., Reischl, T., & Zimmerman, M. (1992). Mutual help mechanisms in the empowerment of former mental patients. In D. Saleebey (ed.), *The strengths perspective in social work practice,* pp. 84–97. White Plains, NY: Longman.

Remafedi, G. (1990). Study group report on the impact of television portrayals of gender roles on youth. *Journal of Adolescent Health Care, 11,* 59–61.

Remafedi, G., Farrow, J. A., & Deisher, R. W. (1991). Risk factors of attempted suicide in gay and bisexual youth. *Pediatrics, 87,* 869–875.

Remafedi, G, French, S., Story, M., Resnick, M. D., & Blum, R. (1998). The relationship between suicide risk and sexual orientation: Results of a population-based survey. *American Journal of Public Health, 88,* 57–60.

Rice, K. G. (1990). Attachment in adolescence: A narrative and meta-analytic review. *Journal of Youth and Adolescence, 19*(5), 511–538.

Robinson, B., Walters, L., & Skeen, P. (1989). Response of parents to learning that their child is homosexual and concern over AIDS: A national study. *Journal of Homosexuality, 18,* 59–79.

Ryan, C., & Futterman, D. (1998). *Lesbian and gay youth.* New York: Columbia University Press.

Saltzburg, S. (1996). Family therapy and the disclosure of adolescent homosexuality. *Journal of Family Psychotherapy, 7*(4), 1–18.

Saltzburg, S. (2001). Learning that an adolescent son or daughter is gay or lesbian: The parent experience. *Dissertation Abstracts International,* section A (*Humanities & Social Sciences*), *62*(9-A), 3190.

Saltzburg, S. (2004). Learning that an adolescent is gay or lesbian: The parent experience. *Social Work, 49,* 109–118.

Sanford, N. D. (1989). Providing sensitive health care to gay and lesbian youth. *Nurse Practitioner, 14*(5), 30–47.

Savin-Williams, R. C. (1989). Coming out to parents and self-esteem among gay and lesbian youths. *Journal of Homosexuality, 18,* 1–35.

Savin-Williams, R. C. (1990). *Gay and lesbian youth: Expressions of identity.* Washington, DC: Hemisphere.

Savin-Williams, R. C. (1994). Verbal and physical abuse as stressors in the lives of lesbian, gay male and bi-sexual youths: Associations with school problems, running away, substance abuse, prostitution, suicide. *Journal of Consulting and Clinical Practice, 62,* 261–269.

Savin-Williams, R. C. (1996). Self-labeling and disclosure among gay, lesbian, and bisexual youths. In J. Laird & R. J. Green (eds.), *Lesbians and gays in couples and families,* pp. 153–182. San Francisco: Jossey-Bass.

Sears, J. T. (1991). *Growing up gay in the South: Race, gender, and journeys of the spirit.* New York: Harrington Park Press.

Sears, J. T. (1992). Educators, homosexuality, and homosexual students: Are personal feelings related to professional beliefs? *Journal of Homosexuality, 22,* 29–48.

Silverberg, S. B. (1996). Parents' well-being at their children's transition to adolescence. In C. D. Ryff & M. M. Seltzer (eds.), *The parental experience in midlife.* Chicago: University of Chicago Press.

Smink, J. (1990). Mentoring programs for at-risk youth: A dropout prevention research report. Clemson, SC: National Dropout Prevention Center.

Uribe, V., & Harbeck, K. M. (1992). Addressing the needs of lesbian, gay, and bisexual youth: The origins of PROJECT 10 and school-based intervention. *Journal of Homosexuality, 22,* 9–28.

U.S. Department of Health and Human Services. (1989). *Report of the secretary's Task Force on Youth Suicide,* vol. 3: *Prevention and interventions in youth suicide.* DHHD publication ADM 89-1622. Washington, DC: U.S. Government Printing Office.

Walsh, F. (1993). Conceptualization of normal family processes. In F. Walsh (ed.), *Normal family processes,* pp. 3–69. New York: Guilford Press.

Whitlock, K. (1989). *Bridges of respect: Creating support of lesbian and gay youth,* second ed. Philadephia: American Friends Service Committee.

Yancey, A. K. (1998). Building positive self-image in adolescents in foster care: The use of role models in an interactive group approach. *Adolescence, 33,* 253–267.

KAREN M. STALLER

Runaway and Homeless Youth

Policy and Services

Inasmuch as services for runaway and homeless youth fall outside of the domain of traditionally defined child welfare services (Fitzgerald 1996), runaway and homeless youth have always been present in all U.S. populations. Although the labels used to describe them have changed, social reformers, child advocates, jurists, historians, and others have documented their existence over the centuries (Brace 1872; Mayhew 1861; Miller 1991; Riis 1892a,b; Rothman 1991; Staller 1999). In the mid-nineteenth century, they were called "waifs," "orphans," "half-orphans," "temporarily homeless," "outcasts," "maladjusted," "destitute," "indigent," "wayward," "wanderers," "incorrigibles," "child street vendors," "newsies," "little laborers," "morally depraved," "fallen," and "friendless." In the 1960s, we talked about "status offenders," as well as "hippies," "flower children," and "love children." More recently, we have called them "runaways," "homeless," "throwaways," "castaways," "shoveouts," and "street kids."

Although these labels are not completely interchangeable, they have tended to describe youth who share some characteristics. In general, they are teenagers who have left their families or other legal caretakers, either voluntarily or involuntarily, for some amount of time. Perhaps the single unifying characteristic is that they make decisions and act outside the governance of their legal custodians at a point in life when we generally find such independence socially unacceptable or at least questionable. Whitbeck and Hoyt have called this "precocious independence" (1999:10).

In an attempt to address the extensive topics of "runaway and homeless youth" and "policy and services" in this chapter, I:

- Examine the historical and societal context for our most recent discussions on "runaway" youth;
- Consider the policy and program responses that emerged in light of these discussions, as well as trace the expansion of programs since their inception;
- Examine the challenging and complicated problem of defining "runaway" youth;
- Look at the demographic patterns and characteristics associated with runaway and homeless youth;
- Examine the current social science literature on vulnerabilities and risks associated with running away and with the runaway youth population;
- Look at the small but growing literature on resilience and protective factors exhibited by runaway youth;
- Outline the range of programs that serve these youth and examine their effectiveness; and
- Identify some of the major ethical and value dilemmas associated with working with this population.

Finally, I close the chapter with some concluding issues for the reader's consideration.

Historical and Societal Context
The most recent incarnation of the runaway and homeless youth problem arguably emerged

in the mid-1960s. Several societal factors contributed to shaping our current understanding of the runaway problem, runaway youth policies, and services. First, in the early 1960s, states began to separate "status offenses" from other legal interventions targeted at youth. As a matter of public policy in the late 1960s and early 1970s, policymakers diverted and deinstitutionalized status offenders from restrictive facilities, and alternative services for runaway youth began to emerge as grassroots, community-based efforts to meet the needs of drifting and wandering youth. One alternative service was the "runaway shelter," which supplemented and supplanted the "crash pads" of the 1960s counterculture; another was the runaway hotline, which grew out of concern for the safety of runaway youth. Both models are still offered as core services under current federal legislation found in the Runaway and Homeless Youth Act (RHYA).

Status Offenses

In the early 1960s, many states began conceptually separating status offenses from "abused and neglected" youth and "juvenile delinquents." Status offenses, also known as "in need of supervision" cases, covered habitual behaviors that were regulated only because of the youth's status as a minor. (In addition to running away, these behaviors included truancy, violating curfews, being ungovernable or incorrigible, and the like.) In general, abused and neglected youth were referred to the child welfare system and juvenile delinquents (children who committed acts that would be criminal if they were adults) were referred to the juvenile justice system. Status offenders did not have an obvious institutional home. Although communities developed programs for dealing with them, in general, they did not fit neatly within the existing systems.

Diversion and Deinstitutionalization

Policymakers and service providers in the 1960s and 1970s argued that such behaviors as running away did not warrant incarceration or other restrictive measures associated with the juvenile justice system. In 1967, President Lyndon Johnson's Commission on Law Enforcement and the Administration of Justice produced a report on juvenile delinquency and its prevention. Among other things, it recommended that status offenses be decriminalized, offenders be deinstitutionalized, and these youth be diverted from the juvenile justice system to community-based alternatives (Siegel & Senna 2000). Taken together, these policy priorities reflected a growing sense that runaway youth should be diverted to community-based alternative programs rather than dealt with through law enforcement and juvenile delinquency mechanisms. Given this political and social context, the question was: what invention model or models would best serve runaway youth?

The 1967 "Summer of Love" and Huckleberry House

During the mid-1960s, hippies and other free spirits gathered in identifiable counterculture areas, such as Haight-Ashbury in San Francisco and the East Village in New York City. The crash pads, communes, and other shared living opportunities in these communities were mostly operated by young adults, but younger, drifting teenagers were rarely turned away.

In 1967, Haight-Ashbury hosted a media-touted "Summer of Love," meant to be a celebratory gathering of youth. However, local residents worried that many of the arriving love pilgrims would be younger, more vulnerable youth. This concern gave rise to an experimental program called Huckleberry House (Beggs 1969; Staller 1999), one of the first runaway youth shelters of the era. Soon other communities were creating similar alternative runaway programs, including Covenant House in New York City, Ozone House in Ann Arbor, Looking Glass in Chicago, and Bridge over Troubled Water in Boston.

Initially, these community-based, privately funded, experimental agencies ran afoul of parents, police, and traditional service providers because they offered a new brand of service. Youth autonomy and self-determination were at the core of their service philosophy. Young people were not "ordered" or "placed" into the programs by courts through the juvenile justice or child welfare systems. Instead, youth often self-referred and sought out these services on their own. Furthermore, although the programs generally required parental notification at some point (to avoid violating custodial interference laws), in general, providers would not return an unwilling child home or report a child to authorities. This made the programs attractive to precociously independent youth.

Corll Murders, Runaway Safety, and Runaway Hotlines

In 1973, the gruesome activities of Dean Corll, an unassuming candy-store owner in Houston, came to national attention. For several years, Corll had been inviting boys, mostly runaways, to parties at his house. He sexually assaulted, tortured, and then murdered them. He even hired two teenagers, Wayne Henley and David Brooks, to procure runaways for him, paying them $100 for this service. When Corll threatened Henley, Henley murdered Corll and led police to the bodies of 27 boys. At that point, it was the largest serial murder in U.S. history. Concerned about the safety of runaway youth, the Houston community organized the first runaway hotline, Operation Peace of Mind (OPM), designed to allow runaways to obtain information on safe shelters and to convey messages to their worried parents. OPM quickly got a WATTS number, making it accessible to runaways nationwide. From this tragedy emerged a second service approach to runaway youth: the runaway hotline.

Policy Response and Programs

Runaway Youth Act of 1974

In 1974, with Houston fresh in the public mind, Congress enacted the Runaway Youth Act (RYA).

Significantly, the RYA was contained within the Juvenile Justice Delinquency and Prevention Act and characterized as a delinquency-prevention measure. The RYA provided grants to local runaway youth shelters and to a Chicago-based runaway hotline that evolved into The National Runaway Switchboard (800-621-4000; www. nrscrisisline.org).

The RYA seemed to wed all the societal interests of the day. It dealt with runaways outside the system of law enforcement and juvenile justice, thus diverting them from public systems of care. It supported community-based alternatives that promised to prevent delinquency and/or save these youths from exploitation. It favored youth autonomy (in keeping with increasingly protected constitutional rights of young people). It provided grants to experienced runaway programs. In short, it was a nice fit on all fronts.

Expansion of the RYA

Since 1974, the RYA legislation has been amended and expanded, helping to define the scope of the public problem and to fund services targeting the runaway and homeless youth population. In 1980, the legislation was renamed the RHYA and the focus population expanded to include homeless as well as runaway youth. Currently, the populations of youth identified and covered under the act include homeless youth, street youth, and home-based youth, as well as runaways.

Services funded under the RHYA are also increasingly diverse and now include crisis shelters, transitional living, street outreach, after care, prevention, and the runaway hotline. The Department of Health and Human Services, through the Family and Youth Services Bureau (FYSP), administers and coordinates the three primary programs funded under the RHYA: the Basic Centers programs (emergency shelters), Traditional Living programs (TLP), and Street Outreach programs.

Basic Center program services may include food, clothing, shelter, and medical care referrals, as well as counseling and recreational programs. In FY2003, 345 basic centers received funding. TLPs were designed for those youth aged 16–21 who could not return home and needed longer-term assistance—up to 18 months—than short-term emergency crisis shelters could provide. These programs could be structured as group homes, supervised apartments, or placements with host families. Among other services, TLPs provided stable living accommodations, basic life skills classes (e.g., budgeting, food preparation, housekeeping), GED preparation, and job preparation. In 2003, this section of the RHYA was amended (P.L. 108-96) to include maternity group homes, which provide transitional living for pregnant and parenting young people that include classes in parenting, child development, health, nutrition, family budgeting, and other topics specific to young parents. Street Outreach programs target youth deemed to be at-risk for sexual abuse and/or exploitation. Street-based projects include crisis intervention and counseling; housing information and referral; transitional living; and healthcare service referrals; as well as advocacy, education, and prevention services for alcohol and drug abuse, sexually transmitted diseases (including HIV/AIDS), and physical and sexual assault. For updated information on these programs, see the FYSP website at www.acf.hhs.gov/programs/fysb.

In addition to expanded services for maternity group homes, the latest amendment to the RHYA of October 2003 included reference to providing "linguistically appropriate" services, suggesting that Congress is increasingly aware of the diversity of youth seeking services.

Taken together, this package of services (i.e., crisis care; outreach intervention; education and advocacy concerning safe sex, health, and housing needs; home-based counseling; and transitional living) is the range of programs theoretically available to runaway and homeless youth, although actual service offerings vary dramatically from community to community.

Population Definitions

Federal officials, private social service providers, and social science researchers often disagree on the proper typology for use when dealing with the population. The U.S. General Accounting Office (1989:13) has defined a runaway as "a situation in which a youth is absent from his or her home or place of legal residence at least overnight without permission." The RYHA has defined homeless youth and street youth as follows:

Homeless youth is any individual

- who is not less than 16 years of age and not more than 21 years of age;
- for whom it is not possible to live in a safe environment with a relative; and
- who has no other safe alternative living arrangement (1980:5714-1(b)(1)).

Street youth is a juvenile who spends a significant amount of time on the street or in other areas of exposure to encounters that may lead to sexual abuse (1980:5712d (d)).

Perhaps the most controversial definitions involve youth who have been excluded intentionally from their family homes by their adult caretakers. The Office of Juvenile Justice and Delinquency Prevention (OJJDP), for example, rejected the term "throwaway" commonly used by social scientists and youth advocates and replaced it with, "thrownaway," because it "unambiguously conveys what has been done to the child" rather than a "quality of the child" (Sweet 1990:3).

More recently "runaway" and "thrownaway" have been collapsed into one "runaway/thrownaway" category for reporting purposes because researchers found that the distinction between the two was less than clear-cut (Hammer, Finkelhor, & Sedlak 2002). In this study a runaway episode was defined as:

- A child leaves home without permission and stays away overnight;
- A child 14 years old or younger (or older, but who is mentally incompetent) who is

away from home chooses not to come home when expected to and stays away overnight; or

- A child 15 years old or older who is away from home chooses not to come home and stays away two nights.

A thrownaway episode is defined as:

- A child is asked or told to leave home by a parent or other household adult, no adequate alternative care is arranged for the child by a household adult, and the child is out of the household overnight; or
- A child who is away from home is prevented from returning by a parent or other household adult, no adequate alternative care is arranged for the child by a household adult, and the child is out of the household overnight.

The exercise of considering these various definitions and the implications that can be drawn from them is illuminating. It is clear that youth leave home for different reasons, for different amounts of time, and that they have different opportunities for returning. Characteristics at issue include the age of the child, his or her mental capacity, time away, estrangement from home, and the like. Younger youth —who leave for shorter periods of time, travel shorter distances, and are more likely to return home at the end of the episode—are most often labeled "runaways," whereas older youth—who live on their own for extended periods of time, may be more street-acculturated, and are less likely to return to their families—are more often called "homeless" or "street youth." As a result, the service needs of these various youth differ quite dramatically. Whereas runaways may need crisis intervention (e.g., food and shelter for a night), those gone for longer periods may require extensive transitional help.

Given the variety of definitions used, students are warned to consider carefully how terms are defined when they read reports, study findings, program evaluations, newspaper articles, or statistics about the population's size or characteristics. The various portraits painted in such documents reflect how the population is being conceptualized.

Demographic Patterns

Given the struggle over definitions, it is not surprising that the size of the runaway and homeless youth population and its basic characteristics vary dramatically from study to study. Researchers attempting to estimate the number of runaway youth are plagued by many of the methodological and logistical problems faced by those enumerating other hard-to-reach subcultures, such as the adult homeless. Furthermore, within the runaway and homeless youth population, such subgroups as lesbian, gay, bisexual, transgender, or questioning (LGBTQ) youth, or undocumented aliens may be still harder to reach.

An oft-repeated figure presented by the National Network for Youth estimates that between 1.0 and 1.3 million youths run away from home each year. Recently, Hammer, Finkelhor, and Sedlak (2002) conducted an extensive second-wave research project called the National Incidence Studies of Missing, Abducted, Runaway, and Thrownaway Children (NISMART-2) for the OJJDP (see their Web site at www.ojjdp. ncjrs.org/pubs/missing). These data were drawn from three sources: household surveys of adult caretakers, household surveys of youth, and a study of juvenile facilities. It is the most comprehensive examination to date of the scope of the runaway and homeless youth problem, although there are obvious limitations to what parents and/or youth might report in a survey. Hammer and colleagues determined that 1,682,900 youth had experienced a runaway/ thrownaway incident in 1999, and 71% of those were endangered during the incident.

Characteristics of the Runaway and Homeless Youth Population

Current incidence studies find that girls and boys experience runaway/thrownaway episodes in equal numbers (Hammer, Finkelhor, & Sedlak 2002). However, their treatment outside the home and/or their usage of services may reflect gender differences. For example, the National Runaway Switchboard reported that 75.5% of its calls in 2002 came from girls. In 1990, OJJDP (Sickmund 1990:1) reported that "girls, whites, and youth 14 through 16 years old were more likely than other youth to be referred to court for running away." FBI statistics indicate that 59.4% of the national runaway arrests in 2001 were of girls (U.S. Federal Bureau of Investigation 2002). Researchers have reported that boys are more likely to be older and to be classified as homeless or throwaway than are girls (Kufeldt, Durieux, & Nimmo 1992; Kurtz, Lindsey, Jarvis, & Nackerud 2000; Thompson, Pollio, & Bitner 2002; U.S. General Accounting Office 1989). Taken together, these findings suggest the need to be attentive to service use and institutional responses based on gender.

It is a bit difficult to report threshold or average ages that youth run away from home, in part because data collected reflect institutional realities and agency constraints. For example, state and local arrests of runaways compiled by the FBI are used as an indicator of the size and characteristics of the population. Its data indicate that approximately 80% of all runaway arrests in 2001 occurred between the ages of 13 and 16, and, of those, 36.8% occurred between 13 and 14 (U.S. Federal Bureau of Investigation 2002). However, these statistics also reflect jurisdictional age limits. For example, New York State defined runaways as below the age of 16 until 2002, when it moved the age up to 18 years old. Researchers frequently rely on the age guidelines of the agencies or outreach programs that they use to conduct their studies. Edelbrock (1980) included children and youth in his study between the ages of 4 and 16 years, whereas Unger and colleagues (1997) included adolescents and young adults from ages 13 to 23. This range, from 4 to 23, hints at the numerous practical problems and various developmental issues associated with serving youth

lumped together under the runaway and homeless categories.

The current incidence study on runaway/ thrownaway youth found that they "did not come disproportionately from any of the major racial and ethnic groups" (Hammer, Finkelhor, & Sedlak 2002). Other studies have reported that youth of color are represented disproportionately in the homeless youth population compared to the runaway youth population (U.S. General Accounting Office 1989). Some researchers have found that runaway or homeless youth come from families of lower-middle socioeconomic status (Adams, Gullotta, & Clancy 1985; Englander 1984) or from families with long-term economic problems (Bass 1992; Janus, Burgess, & McCormack 1987). These data ought to be viewed cautiously. Many researchers collect financial information directly from youth, which raises questions about the reliability and validity of the data and the overall accuracy of the findings.

At the time the RYA was enacted, Congress expressed concern for the interstate nature of the runaway problem. However, it appears from current data that the majority of runaways/ thrownaways stay relatively close to home and usually within their home state. Hammer, Finkelhor, and Sedlak (2002) report that about 38% of the runaways/thrownaways travel less than 10 miles from home. Thirty-one percent travel between 10 and 50 miles and another 23% travel more than 50 miles. Eighty-three percent did not leave the state. Most left home for less than a week (76%) and of those, 18% were gone less than 24 hours. Significantly, however, 15% left for more than a week but less than a month, and another 7% left for more than a month. In general, relatively few youth travel long distances and/or are away from home for long periods of time. Nonetheless, these youth are likely to have the most pressing service needs and be most at risk for negative outcomes.

The sexual orientation profile of the runaway and homeless youth population is a subject of debate. Whitbeck and Hoyt (1999) found that 94% of the boys and 95% of the girls in their study identified as heterosexual. However, researchers and clinicians who specialize in work with gay and lesbian youth are quick to point out that "they are socialized to hide," making it difficult to quantify their numbers and making "service provision indisputably more complex" (Mallon 1999:129). Kruks (1991) noted that nonheterosexual orientations are likely underreported in street youth and that young lesbian street youth are even harder to identify than gay street youth.

Many providers believe that gay and lesbian youth are overrepresented in the street youth population. Estimated rates of LGBTQ youth among the homeless population have ranged from 6% to 42% (Cochran, Stewart, Ginzler, & Cauce 2002; Mallon 1999). Mallon reported on a survey conducted by Streetworks Project—an outreach and drop-in program in New York City—which found that 42% of the youth identified as gay, lesbian, or bisexual. This wide range in estimates may reflect genuine geographic differences in rates (for example, LGBTQ youth may drift to geographic areas that they find more tolerant); however, the differential rates may also reflect varying comfort levels of youth in disclosing their preferences to researchers.

Vulnerabilities and Risks

It is fairly safe to assume that runaway and homeless youth do not leave blissfully happy family situations. Furthermore, the existing research (as well as common sense) supports the contention that extended or repeated absences from home are correlated with a host of poor outcomes that jeopardize the futures, and sometimes the lives, of adolescents. Our portrait of runaway and homeless youth is bleak, in part, because much of our research draws study samples from relatively high-risk environments, such as street-based programs, drop-in clinics, and runaway and homeless youth shelters. Nonetheless, for the youth who end up in these situations, there are some serious and

troubling correlates and consequences. Even worse, for those who leave home for extended periods of time, there is evidence that the cumulative effect of multiple risk factors seriously jeopardize their long-term well-being.

Family Composition and Home Environment

There are several reasons why youth leave home, but family tension is often a primary factor, stemming from family recomposition, allegations of physical and/or sexual abuse, or other family problems.

As increasing numbers of American children and youth are being raised in reconstituted and blended families, an OJJDP study found that runaways came "disproportionately from stepparent-type households" compared to the general population (Finkelhor, Hotaling, & Sedlak 1990:11). A 1991 nationwide survey of runaway and homeless youth programs in the United States found that 45% of the youth lacked a father at home (Bass 1992). In a large-scale study of homeless youth, Shane (1991) found that roughly 63% came from single-parent families; 20% came from reconstituted families; and less than 20% of the population was living in traditional two-parent families (with both biological and/or adoptive parents present). Children report problems with abuse (sexual, physical, and emotional) by stepparents, tension with new parental figures and stepsiblings, as well as increased tension with the biological parent over the new family constellation.

In a study comparing stress and coping patterns among adolescent runaways (from a private counseling agency) and nonrunaways (from a high school), Roberts (1982) found that six stress-producing events were reported only by runaways. He concluded (1982:25) that "parent-youth conflict, physical abuse, and school problems continue to emerge as situational variables which are associated with adolescent runaway behavior."

Janus, Burgess, and McCormack (1987) found that 71.5% of shelter-based youth reported physical abuse and 38.2% reported having been raped or attacked. Male runaways in a shelter-based population exhibited "dramatically higher rates of sexual abuse than did those of randomly sampled populations" (1987:410). Using a home-based sample rather than a shelter-based one, Hammer, Finkelhor, and Sedlak (2002:8) reported that 21% of the runaway/thrownaway population had been "physically or sexually abused at home in the year prior to the episode or was afraid of abuse upon return."

Cochran, Stewart, Ginzler, and Cauce (2002) found that although LGBTQ youth left home for many of the same reasons as their heterosexual counterparts, the former were at greater risk for actually leaving home than were youth identifying as heterosexual. Others assert that LGBTQ youth are particularly susceptible to being asked or forced to leave home (Kruks 1991; Mallon 1999).

Data from the National Runaway Switchboard in 2002 indicate that a substantial number of callers identify "family dynamics" as the problem (41.4%); significantly fewer discuss alcohol/drug use (3.6%), physical abuse (3.6%), emotional/verbal abuse (3.0%), neglect (1.6%), and sexual abuse or sexual assault (1.15%). These discrepancies among studies make sense, given the source and type of information collected; however, in their totality, they point to family troubles and tensions as a significant factor in the lives of runaway and homeless youth.

Of note, many of the studies of family characteristics rely on self-report data from youth and thus raise issues of validity. Whitbeck, Hoyt, and Ackley (1997) compared the reports of adolescents and their parents and found that although there were significant differences between them, the reports presented similar portraits. They concluded that runaway and homeless youth depicted their family environments accurately.

Public Care Instability

Disturbingly high rates of runaway and homeless youth report involvement in the foster care and/or juvenile justice systems. In fact, sometimes these youth are dubbed "system kids" or "doubly homeless." In a nationwide survey of 360 runaway youth programs, agency staff reported that one out of five youths who arrived at shelters came directly from a foster home or group home; 38% had been in foster care at some time during the previous year and another 27% had been in "trouble with juvenile justice system" (Bass 1992:9). Mallon (1998) reports that gay and lesbian youth are more likely than other youth to flee the foster care for safety reasons and can end up on the street. Janus, Burgess, and McCormack (1987) reported over half (57%) of their study population had been arrested and had been involved with the juvenile justice system. OJJDP found that 15% of its thrownaway subjects had been in a juvenile detention center (Finkelhor, Hotaling, & Sedlak 1990). Furthermore, OJJDP estimated that 12,800 youths ran away from juvenile facilities including group foster homes, residential treatment centers, and other mental health facilities in 1988 (Office of Juvenile Justice and Deliquency Prevention 1989). According to this report, these children tended to have even more serious runaway episodes and almost half left the state. Thus it is clear that runaway and homeless youth travel between and among public and private institutional settings during their journeys.

School

In addition to problems at home, researchers have found that runaway and homeless youth have problems at school (Brennan, Huizinga, & Elliot 1978; Thompson, Safyer, & Pollio 2001). Shane (1991) found that nearly half his sample had "education/school problems" and Bass (1992) found that 53% of her national sample of service providers reported that their clients had problems with school, making it the highest-ranking factor influencing runaway behavior in her study. In a government study on homeless youth (U.S. General Accounting Office 1989: 16), 50% of the population had "dropped out or been expelled from school." The report noted this was significantly higher than the 14–29% estimated nationwide.

Shelter-based studies confirm what seems intuitively obvious—that the longer the youth was away from home, the lower the youth's school attendance (U.S. General Accounting Office 1989). In a shelter-based regional study, Kurtz, Jarvis, and Kurtz (1991:311) found that homeless youth were "significantly less likely than non-homeless youth to attend school regularly and more likely to be dropouts." These findings are troubling, particularly when considering the long-term employment prospects for homeless youth.

Lack of Life Skills

Taken together, early and repeated flights from troubled homes or foster care placements coupled with failures in school suggest that runaway and homeless youth will have difficulty surviving on their own. Securing basic resources (e.g., food, shelter, clothing) can be difficult for several reasons. Such policies as compulsory education, truancy statutes, and child labor laws are obviously—and reasonably—geared toward keeping youth in school and out of the work force. Furthermore, for youth under the age of majority (usually 18 years old), many activities of adulthood (e.g., signing a lease, loan, or employment contract) require the signature of a legal custodian. For older youth, limited education further reduces employment opportunities, so runaway and homeless youth face serious constraints in trying to secure resources independently.

Policymakers and service providers worry that because youth have limited resources, they will either make poor life decisions (thereby endangering themselves) or be forced into dangerous situations. For example, the public worries about youth being driven to "survival sex" (prostitution or bartering sex for shelter), being exploited and victimized (e.g., by pimps, johns, drug dealers), or engaging in criminal activities (e.g., petty theft, trespassing) to meet their basic needs.

Sexual Risk Behaviors and "Survival Sex"

Although adolescence is a time of sexual development and exploration, researchers have documented several sexual risk behaviors associated with runaway and homeless youth that give cause for concern. Among them are early onset of sexual behavior (Rotheram-Borus et al. 1992); multiple sexual partners (Cochran, Stewart, Ginzler, & Cauce 2002; Forst 1994; Pennbridge, Freese, & MacKenzie 1992; Rotheram-Borus & Koopman 1991; Rotheram-Borus et al. 1992); alcohol and drug use (Kipke, Montgomery, & MacKenzie 1997; Koopman, Rosario, & Rothman-Borus 1994; Pennbridge, Freese, & MacKenzie et al. 1992); unsafe sex practices, including inconsistent condom use (Forst 1994; MacKellar et al. 2000; Pennbridge, Freese, & MacKenzie et al. 1992; Rotheram-Borus et al. 1992).

Seroprevalence rates for HIV among the runaway and homeless youth population are reported to be high, particularly in such urban areas as New York City, Los Angeles, and San Francisco (Athey 1991; Stricof, Kennedy, Nattell, Weisfuse, & Novick 1991). Some researchers report minority and gay youth to be at even higher risk for HIV infection (Rotheram-Borus et al. 1992; Rotheram-Borus, Rosario, & Koopman 1991). Furthermore, Greene and Ringwalt (1998) found that lifetime pregnancy rates for adolescent girls (aged 14–17) who had lived on the streets were 48% and for those who had resided in a runaway shelter, 33%.

Much has been written about survival sex and homeless youth. Survival sex refers to bartering sex for money, drugs, or shelter to meet basic needs, or to involvement in the sex industry (e.g., pornography, performing in nightclubs) because of limited legitimate employment opportunities. Several researchers have explored the extent to which runaway and homeless youth are driven to these activities out of need (Forst 1994; Greene, Ennett, & Ringwalt 1999; Luna 1991; Pennbridge, Freese, & MacKenzie 1992; Rotheram-Borus et al. 1992; Yates, MacKenzie, Pennbridge, & Swofford 1991). Greene, Ennett, and Ringwalt (1999) found that 28% of street youth and 10% of shelter-based youth in their representative samples had engaged in survival sex. Youth who engage in prostitution are at greater risk for many health-related problems and are more than five times as likely to report their sexual identity as homosexual or bisexual (Yates, MacKenzie, Pennbridge, & Swofford 1991).

Some researchers have documented the sugar daddy or kept youth phenomena, in which youth barter sexual favors in exchange for shelter and/or food (Kruks 1991; Luna 1991). Kruks (1991:518) argues that these relationships are damaging for several reasons, among them because promises of love and nurturing are "compelling," even though the sugar daddy relationships "in many ways have similar dynamics to incest." Other researchers note that youth do not see these exchanges for drugs, food, or shelter as exploitative but rather as the "beginning of a potential relationship" (Whitbeck & Hoyt 1999:86). In fact, Whitbeck and Hoyt found that one of the strongest predictors of engaging in survival sex was a prior history of sexual abuse by adult caretakers. Thus, youth may not be driven to it suddenly out of desperation, but may be acting on familiar behavior and relationship patterns. Thus there is some debate in the literature on how to characterize these relationships and from whose perspective. What is clear is that the accumulation of such sexual risk factors as multiple partners, unprotected sex, drug and alcohol use, and lack of resources places runaway and homeless adolescents at higher risk for health-related problems.

Physical and Mental Health Risk Factors

Homeless street youth are at high risk for poor physical and mental health outcomes (Ensign

1998; see also West Coast Scientific Symposium on Health Care of Runaway Street Youth 1991). Researchers (Wright 1991:31) have found that homeless youth exhibited a package of acute disorders (including upper respiratory infections, skin ailments, lice infestations, and trauma of all sorts) and chronic disorders (including peripheral vascular disease, tuberculosis, gastrointestinal disorders, poor dentition, nutritional deficiency disorders, and for girls, pregnancy-related problems) directly and immediately associated with a homeless existence. Wright (1991:30) concluded that "nearly one homeless teen in five is afflicted with some infectious or communicable disorder that poses a potential threat to the public health."

Mental health problems associated with runaway and homeless youth include depression (Maxwell 1992; Smart & Walsh 1993; Unger, Kipke, Simon, Montgomery, & Johnson 1997), low self-esteem (Maxwell 1992; Unger, Kipke, Simon, Montgomery, & Johnson 1997), suicide ideation, suicide attempts, and self-injurious behavior that includes self-mutilation (Leslie, Stein, & Rotheram-Borus 2002; Molnar, Shade, Kral, Booth, & Watters 1998; Rotheram-Borus 1993; Stiffman 1989; Teare, Authier, & Peterson 1994; Thompson, Pollio, Constantine, Reid, & Nebbitt 2002; Tyler, Whitbeck, Hoyt, & Johnson 2003; Unger, Kipke, Simon, Montgomery, & Johnson 1997; Yoder, Hoyt, & Whitbeck 1998) and other psychotic symptoms (Mundy, Robertson, Robertson, & Greenblatt 1990). Runaway and homeless youth have higher rates of abusive family histories (sexual and physical), and studies have found that a history of abuse is a predictor of mental health problems (especially depression, suicide ideation, and suicide attempts) in the homeless youth population (Molnar, Shade, Kral, Booth, & Watters 1998; Unger, Kipke, Simon, Montgomery, & Johnson 1997; Yoder et al. 2003).

Furthermore, runaway and homeless street youth have difficulty obtaining health and mental health services (Council on Scientific Affairs

1989; Kennedy 1991; Shane 1991; Stiffman 1989). Therefore, their ailments are likely to be undertreated or untreated. In addition, geographic differences are evident. Homeless and runaway youth in Los Angeles were "almost twice as likely to report that they were tested for HIV than were youth in San Diego" (De Rosa, Montgomery, Hyde, Iverson, & Kipke 2001: 144). Differential access to health care is likely to contribute to differential treatment. Studies suggest that it is also critical to attend to youth's perceptions of health information and their access to health care (Ensign & Gittelsohn 1998; Sobo, Zimet, Zimmerman, & Cecil 1997). For example, Sobo, Zimet, Zimmerman, and Cecil found that many runaway and homeless youth doubted experts providing information on HIV/AIDS.

Most of these studies were conducted in major metropolitan areas on the East or West coasts of the United States. Some researchers have challenged these findings as not representative of youth in other parts of the country. Zimet and colleagues (1995) studied runaway youth in Cleveland and found lower than average drug use, sexual risk behaviors, and other health-compromising behaviors than were reported in studies conducted elsewhere in the country. This work is a clear warning not to generalize study results too broadly, particularly when the dire findings come from unique urban areas such as New York City or Los Angeles.

Substance Use and Abuse Risk Factors

Studies have found that runaway and homeless youth use tobacco, alcohol, and other drugs at substantially higher rates than does the general population of nonrunaway and nonhomeless youth (Greene, Ennett, & Ringwalt 1997). Hammer, Finkelhor, and Sedlak (2002) report relatively high percentages of involvement with drugs (19% of the children were reportedly substance dependent, 18% were in the company of someone known to be abusing drugs, 17% were reportedly using hard drugs). Thompson, Pollio, Constantine, Reid, and Nebbit (2002)

found that 94% of their shelter sample had used marijuana. Frequently, substance abuse has been studied in association with risk factors, such as mental health problems (Smart & Walsh 1993; Stiffman 1989; Unger, Kipke, Simon, Montgomery, & Johnson 1997) and sexual behavior (Pennbridge, Freese, & MacKenzie 1992; Zimet et al. 1995).

Criminal Activity and Delinquency
Risk Factors

Hagan and McCarthy (1997:200) studied extensively the relationship between street youth and crime in two Canadian cities and in their own words, paint "a mostly grim picture of the daily lives of urban street youth." Using the theoretical notions of criminal embeddedness, capital, and social learning, they develop the concept of "criminal capital," which helps explain how and why youth get entrenched in a street-based lifestyle (McCarthy & Hagan 1995: 63). They find that street youth spend a "large part of the time looking for food, shelter, and money" and "hanging out, panhandling, partying, and foraging in the shadow economy of the street" (Hagan & McCarthy 1997:200). They conclude that the outlook for most of them is bleak. Other researchers report on the struggles that homeless adolescents face in making money to pay for their basic needs and note the insecurity that accompanies such a lifestyle (Dachner & Tarasuk 2002; Gaetz & O'Grady 2002). Using qualitative research methods and storied representation, Finley and Finley (1999) provide a fascinating account of the flavor of life on the streets for homeless youth that vividly captures some of these struggles.

Baron and Hartnagel (1997) found that homelessness, drug and alcohol use, having peers who engage in criminal behavior, and lack of income all contributed to increased criminality in street youth. They also found that there was an increased risk for violent behavior for youth who were in the long-term homeless category when they had minimal economic resources and perceived lack of opportunity, and when they had a history of victimization on the street or a history of physical abuse at home. Childhood victimization and running away were found to increase the risk of arrest as juveniles (Kaufman & Widom 1999).

Cumulative Risk Factors

There is a growing body of literature on the longitudinal trajectory of runaway and homeless youth development, thanks to the work of Whitbeck and colleagues. They have developed and utilized a risk amplification model for use in examining the pathways through which "street experiences amplify negative developmental effects originating in the family" (Whitbeck, Hoyt, & Yoder 1999:274). In other words, they consider the cumulative effect of early family experiences (e.g., abuse, victimization) coupled with additional street-based experiences (e.g., affiliation with high-risk peers, risky sexual behavior, deviant survival strategies, substance use) as a part of the youth's overall life development. The researchers have explored a number of different associations among childhood and family background and street risk factors. For example, childhood victimization was found to increase the likelihood of later victimization on the streets (Hoyt, Ryan, & Cauce 1999; Tyler, Hoyt, Whitbeck, & Cauce 2001); familial and street risk factors were associated with alcohol abuse (McMorris, Tyler, Whitbeck, & Hoyt 2002) and gang membership (Yoder, Whitbeck, & Hoyt 2003). Furthermore, Simons and Whitbeck (1991) found support for their hypothesis that chronic runaways were at risk for adult homelessness.

These studies are important for many reasons. First, they attempt to examine the longitudinal development of youth (although they use cross-sectional data to do so). Second, they examine the cumulative effect of life experiences—or chain of events—rather than studying isolated incidents. Finally, they offer a theoretical framework to help understand the connection between family-based experiences, street-based experiences, and adult outcomes (absent intervention). This work begins to piece together an important but often neglected longitudinal picture.

Resilience and Protective Factors

As suggested above, the runaway and homeless youth literature is replete with studies of bad outcomes; not enough has been done on the resilience or protective factors associated with running away. It is time to add positively framed questions to the repertoire of research questions, such as: which runaway and homeless youth make successful transitions to adulthood and how?

The work of Lindsey, Kurtz, Jarvis, and Nackerud starts down this path. This research team has applied a strengths-based approach to looking at how runaway youth successfully navigate the troubled waters between adolescence and adulthood. Specifically, they looked at the role of formal and informal helpers (Kurtz, Lindsey, Jarvis, & Nackerud 2000) and at personal strengths and resources (Lindsey, Kurtz, Jarvis, Williams, & Nackerud 2000). In the former study, they found that youth identified family, friends, and professional helpers as important, and that their help fell into five categories: caring, trustworthiness, setting boundaries and holding youth accountable, concrete assistance, and counseling. In the latter study, former runaway youth identified learning new attitudes and behaviors, personal attributes, and spirituality as helping them to make successful transitions to adulthood.

In a pilot study on "successful runaways," informants were recruited at a competitive and prestigious university using an advertisement in a student newspaper that asked for volunteers in good academic standing with histories of running away as teenagers (K. M. Staller, pers. obs.). Students who responded were doing extremely well, both personally and academically. They offer a very different picture of their experience than the one painted by drawing from our best empirical evidence to date. In this pilot study, most of these subjects disliked the label "runaway," which they felt—not unreasonably—had negative connotations. When asked for a substitute description, to paraphrase one, he had merely taken a short vacation from home to get away from bickering, out-of-control parents, seeking refuge in the more tranquil home offered by a friend's family. Leaving home briefly was a very good thing for him. In addition, running away empowered some of these youth to have important conversations with their parents that they had been unable to initiate. In this study, youth made safe and wise decisions, in part because they had other resources at their disposal (including success in school and the support of friends, teachers, or coaches). This pilot study —along with data from NISMART-2, which indicated that most runaway youth return home —suggests that if we want to understand how running away is used by youth, it is necessary to consider seriously the full range of their behaviors. The bias in the literature toward homeless and street youth may do a disservice to social work practitioners who are called on to deal with various runaway episodes that may expose youth to fewer life-threatening risks but may, nonetheless, have important developmental consequences.

Programs and Program Effectiveness

Further research is also necessary in the areas of outcome studies, program effectiveness, and policy evaluation. Given that runaway and homeless youth shelters have been in use since the late 1960s, remarkably little has been written evaluating their effectiveness or examining the outcomes for youth who use such services. Work has begun in this area with the research efforts of Thompson, Pollio, and others (Pollio, Thompson, & North 2000; Teare, Authier, & Peterson 1994; Thompson, Pollio, & Bitner 2000; Thompson, Pollio, Constantine, Reid, & Nebbit 2002; Thompson, Safyer, & Pollio 2001). In general, they have found that various subgroups of shelter users were discharged to home environments at differential rates, that those

who go home do better than those discharged elsewhere, and that this improvement is sustained in the short term.

The discharge rates to home from shelters vary dramatically, based on the characterization of the youth and his or her relationship to family. Thompson, Safyer, and Pollio (2001) distinguished between runaway-homeless, throwaway, and independent youth and found significant differences in the characteristics of these subgroups and the likelihood of their returning home. Kurtz, Jarvis, and Kurtz (1991) found that although 53% of their sample defined as nonhomeless returned home, only 30% of the homeless youth did. Teare, Authier, and Peterson (1994) found that more than half their sample of shelter residents returned home, but others were discharged to residential treatment facilities, medical hospitals, drug programs, detention centers, and mental hospitals.

It is difficult, but not impossible, to track crisis shelter consumers after their discharge (Pollio, Thompson, & North 2000). Thompson, Pollio, and Bitner (2000) found that youth who return home after a brief shelter stay reported more positive outcomes on several measures than did youth discharged to other settings. Although findings are preliminary, they appear promising. Thompson, Pollio, Constantine, Reid, and Nebbit (2002) found that the short-term outcomes for youth, measured at 6 weeks postdischarge, indicated improvement compared to intake assessments. These improvements included increased feelings of support from family, better relationships with schools, higher rates of employment, diminished sexual activity, and higher self-esteem. Less is known about the outcome of youth discharged from shelters to nonhome environments. It is essential to continue to investigate the effectiveness of runaway and homeless services—both short and long term—as well as the outcomes for youth discharged from shelters to a variety of different settings.

In addition to the paucity of studies on the effectiveness of the runaway shelter as an overall intervention, there are very few studies evaluating the efficacy of targeted services delivered within shelters. One of them, conducted by Rotheram-Borus and colleagues (2003), examined an HIV-prevention program called "Street Smart" at two runaway shelters and compared the results to youth at two control shelters. Among other findings, they determined that girls who had participated in an intensive HIV intervention program significantly reduced their unprotected sexual acts and drug use over the long-term. Thus it is equally important to examine the package of services offered to youth at crisis shelters and transitional living facilities.

Ethical Issues and Value Dilemmas

For service providers (e.g., social workers, doctors, lawyers), working with runaway and homeless youth can be problematic because parental consent is generally necessary to serve underaged clients. Although the youths may be quick to declare themselves "emancipated" from their legal custodians and insist on their independence, in most states, emancipation proceedings require affirmative and formal legal action. Furthermore, most states have laws making it criminal to interfere with the custodial rights of parents, harbor a minor, contribute to the delinquency of a minor, or threaten the welfare of a minor.

At the heart of most of the ethical issues and value dilemmas is the question of how much autonomy (or self-determination) ought to be afforded these precociously independent youth (Staller & Kirk 1997). When should a youth's civil rights be protected, even if that means protecting the right to engage in behavior that might be harmful to him or her? When should a youth's decisions give way to parental or state authority? When should the state intervene, for what purpose, and to what extent?

Self-Determination

Should runaway and homeless youth have a protected liberty interest in making bad deci-

sions? Who determines that the decisions are "bad"? For example, if a 16-year-old boy is living on the street and engaging in high-risk sexual behavior, what should we do? Let him continue because it is his choice? Intervene to save him because he is putting himself at risk? Intervene to protect the public from him because his behavior is a public health risk? If we choose intervention, how coercive should it be? Should we counsel him and hope he makes wiser decisions in the future? Should we send him to a restrictive facility so that he is prohibited from engaging in this behavior until he has reached the legal age of adulthood? These questions can, and should, be debated at length.

Parental Consent

Parental consent is always an issue when working with runaway and homeless minors. By definition, these youth are in conflicted relationships with their legal caretakers. The question then becomes when and for what kinds of services should, or must, parental consent be obtained? For example, must parents give permission for a youth to sleep at a runaway shelter for the night? What about getting medical attention (including pregnancy or HIV testing, drug treatment, and contraception)? What about parental participation in developing a case plan for an adolescent who refuses to return home? What if parents are not available? The answers to these questions will vary, depending on the age and circumstances of the youth and his or her family. Nonetheless, they involve an array of ethical and legal complexities that make working with this population a challenge.

Confidentiality

Most runaway shelters, hotlines, and other services promise confidentiality to clients in an effort to gain their trust and entice them into services. What if the social worker learns that the youth has committed a crime, has an outstanding warrant, is a drug dealer, is suicidal, or is engaged in activities that place his or her sexual partners at high risk? When must information be shared, when would it be helpful to share, and from whose perspective should that determination be made?

Mandated Reporting

Social work practitioners are mandated to report child abuse and neglect. Although the legal rules may seem clear about when they should make such a report, as a practical matter when dealing with runaway and homeless adolescents, these rules can be very difficult to apply. First, unlike younger youth, where blame for neglect is easily placed with parents, in the case of adolescents, parental neglect arguments are sometimes complicated by the youth's own "bad" behavior. Are parents neglectful or are adolescents defiant and ungovernable? Second, many runaway and homeless youth have already taken leave of foster care (sometimes for good reason). Is there any point trying to return them to a system or program that has not worked? Finally, as a purely practical matter, foster care services are scarce for older adolescents, particularly those with many problems (e.g., mental health issues, substance abuse, sexual acting out). In short, balancing the abstract reporting requirements of the state with real-world limitations and consequences for adolescent clients is challenging. Should social workers report older adolescent cases when they know no services are available?

Conclusion

The runaway and homeless youth literature has grown substantially since 1974, when the RYA was enacted, but there remains much to do. Several broad areas merit particular attention. First, we must learn more about the dynamic nature of runaway behavior. We need to learn how and why youth move between and among systems of care; closely associated to that is the need to continue developing the longitudinal picture for these youth. However, this picture should include those individuals who do well in addition to those who do not. If we learn what distinguishes one from the other, we may learn how to increase positive outcomes for all at-risk youth. We need to develop theoretical frameworks with which to integrate the existing knowledge on runaway and homeless youth. How can we make sense of what we know? How can we put the pieces together in a comprehensive picture to better understand and serve these youth? Finally, we need further work on program and policy evaluation to determine the effectiveness of our interventions, which will require defining meaningful short- and long-term outcome measures. Developing these lines of inquiry should help us design better overall service strategies for the runaway and homeless youth population.

Although early studies of shelter service outcomes are promising (Thompson, Pollio, Constantine, Reid, & Nebbit 2002), there is still cause to be concerned as we piece together a comprehensive picture. For example, the sequence of amendments to the RYA should raise concern (Staller 2004). First, increasingly troubled and socially estranged youth are being served (runaways, homeless, street youth). Second, responsibility for these youth is being shifted away from public entities to the voluntary sector (schools, mental health, law enforcement, foster care, juvenile justice). This incremental legislative tinkering suggests that "runaway" policy is expanding in two directions —population expansion and system diversion. Taken together, these two legislative trends are troubling. On the surface, they seem to excuse, or partially excuse, an expanding array of public systems from care, discipline, treatment, education, and socialization of increasingly troubled youth. This is of particular concern when one considers the research findings that indicate so many youth arrive at runaway shelters directly from foster care, have been expelled from school, and have serious mental health problems. It raises a fundamental question: is this really an alternative for those youth who need it because they do not succeed in our public systems or are we allowing public systems to abandon the most challenging and difficult kids, without proper support and guidance, at younger ages? If future research finds the increasing array of programs under the RHYA is providing an effective alternative for some youth, then the programs are serving a necessary niche. However, to the extent that alternative services permit public entities to marginalize youth further from their systems of care, such services may hurt the very youth they are designed to help.

REFERENCES

Adams, G. R., Gullotta, T., & Clancy, M. A. (1985). Homeless adolescents: A descriptive study of similarities and differences between runaways and throwaways. *Adolescence, 2*(79), 715–724.

Athey, J. L. (1991). HIV infection and homeless adolescents. *Child Welfare, 70,* 517–538.

Baron, S. W., & Hartnagel, T. F. (1997). Attributions, affect, and crime: Street youths' reactions to unemployment. *Criminology, 35*(3), 409–434.

Bass, D. (1992). *Helping homeless youths: Runaway & homeless adolescents in the United States.* Washington, DC: National Association of Social Workers Press.

Beggs, L. (1969). *Huckleberry's for runaways.* New York: Ballantine Books.

Brace, C. L. (1872). *The dangerous classes of New York and twenty years' work among them.* New York: Wynkoop & Hallenbeck.

Brennan, T., Huizinga, D., & Elliot, D. (1978). *The social psychology of runaways.* Lexington, MA: Lexington Books.

Cochran, B. N., Stewart, A. J., Ginzler, J. A., & Cauce, A. M. (2002). Challenges faced by homeless sexual minorities: Comparison of gay, lesbian, bisexual, and transgender homeless adolescents with their heterosexual counterparts. *American Journal of Public Health, 92*(5), 773–777.

Council on Scientific Affairs. (1989). Health care needs of homeless and runaway youths. *Journal of the American Medical Association, 262,* 1358–1361.

Dachner, N., & Tarasuk, V. (2002). Homeless "squeegee kids": Food insecurity and daily survival. *Social Science and Medicine, 54,* 1039–1049.

De Rosa, C. J., Montgomery, S. B., Hyde, J., Iverson, E., & Kipke, M. D. (2001). HIV risk behavior and HIV testing: A comparison of rates and associated factors among homeless and runaway adolescents in two cities. *AIDS Education and Prevention, 13*(2), 131–148.

Edelbrock, C. (1980). Running away from home: Incidence and correlates among children referred for mental health services. *Journal of Family Issues, 1*(2), 210–228.

Englander, S. (1984). Some self-reported correlates of runaway behavior in adolescent females. *Journal of Consulting and Clinical Psychology, 52,* 484–485.

Ensign, J. (1998). Health issues of homeless youth. *Journal of Social Distress and the Homeless, 7*(3), 159–174.

Ensign, J., & Gittelsohn, J. (1998). Health access to care: Perspectives of homeless youth in Baltimore City, U.S.A. *Social Science & Medicine, 47,* 2087–2099.

Finkelhor, D., Hotaling, G., & Sedlak, A. (1990). *Missing, abducted, runaway and throwaway children in America: First report: Numbers and characteristics. National incidence studies.* Executive summary. No. 87-MC-CX-K069. Washington, DC: Office of Juvenile Justice and Delinquency Prevention and Westat.

Finley, S., & Finley, M. (1999). Sp'ange: A research story. *Qualitative Inquiry, 5*(3), 313–337.

Fitzgerald, M. D. (1996). Homeless youths and the child welfare system: Implications for policy and service. *Child Welfare, 75,* 717–730.

Forst, M. L. (1994). Sexual risk profiles of delinquent and homeless youths. *Journal of Community Health, 19,* 101–114.

Gaetz, S., & O'Grady, B. (2002). Making money: Exploring the economy of youth homeless workers. *Work, Employment and Society, 16*(3), 433–456.

Greene, J. M., Ennett, S. T., & Ringwalt, C. L. (1997). Substance use among runaway and homeless youth in three national samples. *American Journal of Public Health, 87*(2), 229–235.

Greene, J. M., Ennett, S. T., & Ringwalt, C. L. (1999). Prevalence and correlates of survival sex among runaway and homeless youths. *American Journal of Public Health, 89*(9), 1406–1409.

Greene, J. M., & Ringwalt, C. L. (1998). Pregnancy among three national samples of runaway and homeless youth. *Journal of Adolescent Health, 23,* 370–377.

Hagan, J., & McCarthy, B. (1997). *Mean street: Youth crime and homelessness.* Cambridge, England: Cambridge University Press.

Hammer, H., Finkelhor, D., & Sedlak, A. J. (2002). NISMART: Runaway/Thrownaway Children: National Estimates and Characteristics. OJJDP. Grant Number 95-MC-CX-K004. Retrieved October 2002 from www.ojjdp.ncjrs.org/pubs/missing.

Hoyt, D. R., Ryan, K. D., & Cauce, A. M. (1999). Personal victimization in a high-risk environment: Homeless and runaway adolescents. *Journal of Research in Crime and Delinquency, 36*(4), 371–392.

Janus, M., Burgess, A., & McCormack, A. (1987). Histories of sexual abuse in adolescent male runaways. *Adolescence, 22*(86), 405–417.

Juvenile Justice Delinquency and Prevention Act. (2002). 42 USC 5601.

Kaufman, J. G., & Widom, C. S. (1999). Childhood victimization, running away, and delinquency. *Journal of Research in Crime and Delinquency, 36*(4), 347–370.

Kennedy, M. R. (1991). Homeless and runaway youth mental health issues: No access to the system. *Journal of Adolescent Health, 12,* 576–570.

Kipke, M., Montgomery, S., & MacKenzie, R. (1997). Homeless youth: Drug use patterns and HIV risk profiles according to peer group affiliation. *AIDS and Behavior, 1,* 247–259.

Koopman, C., Rosario, M., & Rothman-Borus, M. (1994). Alcohol and drug use and sexual behaviors placing runaways at risk for HIV infection. *Addictive Behaviors, 19,* 95–103.

Kruks, G. (1991). Gay and lesbian homeless/street youth: Special issues and concerns. *Journal of Adolescent Health, 12*(7), 515–518.

Kufeldt, K., Durieux, M., & Nimmo, M. (1992). Providing shelter for street youth: Are we reaching those in need? *Child Abuse and Neglect, 16,* 187–199.

Kurtz, P. D., Jarvis, S. V., & Kurtz, G. L. (1991). Problems of homeless youths: Empirical findings and human services issues. *Social Work, 36,* 309–314.

Kurtz, P. D., Lindsey, E. W., Jarvis, S., & Nackerud, L. (2000). How runaway and homeless youth navigate troubled waters: The role of formal and informal helpers. *Child and Adolescent Social Work Journal, 17*(5), 381–402.

Leslie, M. B., Stein, J. A., & Rotheram-Borus, M. J. (2002). Sex-specific predictors of suicidality among runaway youth. *Journal of Clinical Child and Adolescent Psychology, 31*(1), 27–40.

Lindsey, E. W., Kurtz, P. D., Jarvis, S., Williams, N. R., & Nackerud, L. (2000). How runaway and homeless youth navigate troubled waters: Personal strengths and resources. *Child and Adolescent Social Work Journal, 17*(2), 115–140.

Luna, G. C. (1991). Street youth: Adaptation and survival in the AIDS decade. *Journal of Adolescent Health, 12*(7), 511–514.

MacKellar, D. A., Valleroy, L. A., Hoffmann, J. P., Glebatis, D., LaLota, M., et al. (2000). Gender differences in sexual behaviors and factors associated with non-use of condoms among homeless and runaway youth. *AIDS Education and Prevention, 12*(6), 477–491.

Mallon, G. P. (1998). *We don't exactly get the welcome wagon: The experience of gay and lesbian adolescents in child welfare systems.* New York: Columbia University Press.

Mallon, G. P. (1999). *Let's get this straight.* New York: Columbia University Press.

Maxwell, B. E. (1992). Hostility, depression, and self-esteem among troubled and homeless adolescents in crisis. *Journal of Youth and Adolescence, 21*(2), 139–150.

Mayhew, H. (1861, reprinted 1968). *London labour and the London poor.* Toronto: Dover.

McCarthy, B., & Hagan, J. (1995). Getting into street crime: The structure and process of criminal embeddedness. *Social Science Research, 24,* 63–95.

McMorris, B., Tyler, K., Whitbeck, L., & Hoyt, D. (2002). Familial and on the street risk factors associated with alcohol use among homeless and runaway adolescents. *Journal of Alcohol Studies, 6,* 34–43.

Miller, H. (1991). *On the fringe: The dispossessed in America.* Lanham, MD: Lexington Books.

Molnar, B. E., Shade, S. B., Kral, A. H., Booth, R. E., & Watters, J. K. (1998). Suicidal behavior and sexual/physical abuse among street youth. *Child Abuse and Neglect, 22,* 213–222.

Mundy, P., Robertson, M., Robertson, J., & Greenblatt, M. (1990). The prevalence of psychotic symptoms in homeless adolescents. *Journal of the American Academy of Child and Adolescent Psychiatry, 29,* 724–731.

National Runaway Switchboard. (2002). NRS annual report—2002. Chicago: National Runaway Switchboard.

Office of Juvenile Justice and Delinquency Prevention. (1989). *Annual report on missing children.* Washington, DC: U.S. Department of Justice, Office of Justice Programs.

Pennbridge, J. N., Freese, T. E., & MacKenzie, R. G. (1992). High-risk behaviors among male street youth in Hollywood, California. *AIDS Education and Prevention,* (fall suppl.), 24–33.

Pollio, D. E., Thompson, S. J., & North, C. S. (2000). Agency-based tracking of difficult-to-follow populations: Runaway and homeless youth programs in St. Louis, MO. *Community Mental Health Journal, 36*(3), 247–258.

Riis, J. A. (1892a). *The children of the poor.* New York: Charles Scribner's Sons.

Riis, J. A. (1892b, reprinted in 1971). *How the other half lives.* New York: Dover.

Roberts, A. R. (1982). Stress and coping patterns among adolescent runaways. *Journal of Social Service Research, 5*(1/2), 15–27.

Rotheram-Borus, M. J. (1993). Suicidal behavior and risk factors among runaway youths. *American Journal of Psychiatry, 150*(1), 103–107.

Rotheram-Borus, M. J., & Koopman, C. (1991). Sexual risk behaviors, AIDS knowledge, and beliefs about AIDS among runaways. *American Journal of Public Health, 81*(2), 208–210.

Rotheram-Borus, M. J., Meyer-Bahlburg, H. F. L., Koopman, C., Rosario, M., Exner, T. M., et al. (1992). Lifetime sexual behaviors among runaway males and females. *Journal of Sex Research, 29*(1), 15–29.

Rotheram-Borus, M. J., Rosario, M., & Koopman, C. (1991). Minority youth at high risk: Gay males and runaways. In S. Gore & M. Colton (eds.), *Adolescent stress: Courses and consequences,* pp. 181–200. Hawthorne, NY: Aldine de Gruyter.

Rotheram-Borus, M. J., Song, J., Gwadz, M., Lee, M., Van Rossem, R., & Koopman, C. (2003). Reductions in HIV risk among runaway youth. *Prevention Science, 4*(3), 173–187.

Rothman, J. (1991). *Runaway and homeless youth: Strengthening services to families and children.* White Plains, NY: Longman.

Runaway and Homeless Youth Act. (1987). P.L. 100-17.

Runaway Youth Act. (1974). P.L. 93-415.

Shane, P. G. (1991). An invisible health and social policy issue: Homeless/runaway youth, *Journal of Health & Social Policy, 2*(4), 3–14.

Sickmund, M. (1990). *Runaways in juvenile courts. OJJDP update on statistics.* Washington, DC: Office of Juvenile Justice and Delinquency Prevention.

Siegel, L., & Senna, J. (2000). *Juvenile delinquency: Theory, practice and law,* seventh ed. Belmont, CA: Wadsworth/Thomson Learning.

Simons, R. L., & Whitbeck, L. B. (1991). Running away during adolescence as a precursor to adult homelessness. *Social Service Review, 65,* 224–247.

Smart, R. G., & Walsh, G. W. (1993). Predictors of depression in street youth. *Adolescence, 28*(109), 41–53.

Sobo, E. J., Zimet, G. D., Zimmerman, T., & Cecil, H. (1997). Doubting the experts: AIDS misconceptions among runaway youth. *Human Organization, 56*(3), 311–320.

Staller, K. M. (1999). *Runaway youth: Contending cultural voices and policy responses, 1960–1978.* Doctoral dissertation, Columbia University, New York.

Staller, K. M. (2004). Runaway youth system dynamics: A theoretical framework for analyzing runaway and homeless youth policy. *Families in Society, 85,* 379–390.

Staller, K. M., & Kirk, S. A. (1997). Unjust freedom: The ethics of client self-determination in runaway and homeless youth shelters. *Child and Adolescent Social Work Journal, 14*(3), 223–242.

Stiffman, A. R. (1989). Suicide attempts in runaway youths. *Suicide and Life-Threatening Behavior, 19*(2), 147–159.

Stricof, R. L., Kennedy, J. T., Nattell, T. C., Weisfuse, I. B., & Novick, L. F. (1991). HIV seroprevalence in a facility for runaway and homeless adolescents. *American Journal of Public Health, 81*(supp.), 50–53.

Sweet, R. W. (1990). *"Missing children": Found facts. OJJDP: Juvenile Justice Bulletin.* Reprinted from NIJ Reports no. 224. Washington, DC: Office of Juvenile Justice and Delinquency Prevention.

Teare, J. F., Authier, K., & Peterson, R. (1994). Differential patterns of post-shelter placement as a function of problem type and severity. *Journal of Child and Family Studies, 3,* 7–22.

Thompson, S. J., Pollio, D. E., & Bitner, L. (2000). Outcomes for adolescents using runaway and homeless youth services. *Journal of Human Behavior and the Social Environment, 3*(1), 79–87.

Thompson, S. J., Pollio, D. E., Constantine, J., Reid, D., & Nebbitt, V. (2002). Short-term outcomes for youth receiving runaway and homeless shelter services. *Research on Social Work Practice, 12,* 589–603.

Thompson, S. J., Safyer, A., & Pollio, D. E., (2001). Differences and predictors of family reunification among subgroups of runaway youths using shelter services. *Social Work Research, 25*(3), 163–172.

Tyler, K. A., Hoyt, D. R., Whitbeck, L. B., & Cauce, A. M. (2001). The impact of childhood sexual abuse on later sexual victimization. *Journal of Research on Adolescence, 11*(2), 151–176.

Tyler, K. A., Whitbeck, L. B., Hoyt, D. R., & Johnson, K. D. (2003). Self-mutilation and homeless youth: The role of family abuse, street experiences, and mental disorders. *Journal of Research on Adolescence, 13*(4), 457–474.

Unger, J. B., Kipke, M. D., Simon, T. R., Montgomery, J. B., & Johnson, C. J. (1997). Homeless youths and young adults in Los Angeles: Prevalence of mental health problems and the relationship between mental health and substance abuse disorders. *American Journal of Community Psychology, 25,* 371–394.

U.S. Federal Bureau of Investigation. (2002). *Uniform crime reports (UCR),* pp. 244–248. Washington, DC: U.S. Department of Justice.

U.S. General Accounting Office. (1989). *Homelessness: Homeless and runaway youth receiving services at federally funded shelters.* GAO/HRD-90-45. Washington, DC: U.S. General Accounting Office.

West Coast Scientific Symposium on Health Care of Runaway Street Youth. (1991). Proceedings of the West Coast Scientific Symposium on Health Care of Runaway Street Youth. *Journal of Adolescent Health, 12*(7).

Whitbeck, L. B., & Hoyt, D. R. (1999). *Nowhere to grow: Homeless and runaway adolescents and their families.* Hawthorne, NY: Aldine de Gruyter.

Whitbeck, L. B., Hoyt, D. R., & Ackley, K. A. (1997). Families of homeless and runaway adolescents: A comparison of parent/caretaker and adolescent perspectives on parenting, family violence, and adolescent conduct. *Child Abuse and Neglect, 21,* 517–528.

Whitbeck, L. B., Hoyt, D. R., & Yoder, K. A. (1999). A risk-amplification model of victimization and depressive symptoms among runaway and homeless adolescents. *American Journal of Community Psychology, 27*(2), 273–296.

Wright, J. D. (1991). Health and homeless teenagers: Evidence from the National Health Care for the Homeless Program. *Journal of Health & Social Policy, 2*(4), 15–35.

Yates, G. L, MacKenzie, R. G., Pennbridge, J., & Swofford, A. (1991). A risk profile comparison of homeless youth involved in prostitution and homeless youth not involved. *Journal of Adolescent Health, 12*(7), 545–548.

Yoder, K. A., Hoyt, D. R., & Whitbeck, L. B. (1998). Suicidal behavior among homeless and runaway adolescents. *Journal of Youth and Adolescence, 27*(6), 753–771.

Yoder, K. A., Whitbeck, L. B., & Hoyt, D. R. (2003). Gang involvement and membership among homeless and runaway youth. *Youth and Society, 34*(4), 441–467.

Zimet, G. D., Sobo, E. J., Zimmerman, T., Jackson, J., Mortimer, J., et al. (1995). Sexual behavior, drug use, and AIDS knowledge among Midwestern runaways. *Youth and Society, 26*(4), 450–462.

CATHERINE A. HAWKINS

Spiritually Sensitive Practice with Children, Youth, and Families

At the beginning of the twenty-first century in America, we find ourselves living in a highly complex, rapidly changing, and increasingly multicultural society. The literature on spirituality and social work practice strongly suggests that we are in the midst of a paradigm shift. Kilpatrick (1999) describes this shift as characterized by "secular spirituality" (the quest for meaning outside of organized religion), globalization, and spiritual pluralism. Frame (2003) talks about the move from modernism toward postmodernism and social constructivism, in which truth is relative and there are no absolutes. Sherwood (1998) also acknowledges the importance that postmodernism places on "meaning making" and how, from this perspective, we "co-author our stories." Canda and Furman (1999) contend that existentialism and transpersonal theory have emerged from dissatisfaction with "dehumanizing" aspects of society, including positivism and religious exclusivity.

It is not surprising that our constantly evolving profession would be engaged in this societal paradigm shift. Social work education has broadened its scope to include both a spiritual and postmodernist perspective. A recent article in the *Chronicle of Higher Education* observed that social work programs are embracing the teaching of spirituality (Miller 2001). The 1994 Council on Social Work Education (CSWE) Curriculum Policy Statement mandates that religious and spiritual content be taught in both diversity and practice areas, whereas the 2002 CSWE Educational Policy and Accreditation Standards (Council on Social Work Education 2002) requires spiritual development content to be covered in the Human Behavior and the Social Environment area. The emerging emphasis on spirituality as an important aspect of social work is also evident by the proliferation of presentations at professional conferences and the expanding scholarly literature on this topic.

Spirituality is a well-established aspect in many fields of practice, such as addiction, counseling, and healthcare. A perusal of major child welfare texts and journals, however, indicates a virtual absence of content on spirituality, except as a clearly recognized component of culture. Yet spirituality is experienced much more broadly than by cultural affiliation alone; it is also an intensely personal experience that is regarded as a common drive in all people. In addition, there are considerable variations within cultural groups in terms of spiritual beliefs and practices. Inclusion of this content in the child welfare literature would be consistent with the profession's long tradition of respect for diversity, recognition of a strengths-based approach, and advocacy for a holistic model of practice.

In this chapter, I present an overview of important considerations for spiritually sensitive practice. The chapter includes a discussion of what spirituality is and why it is relevant to practice, as well as ongoing arguments against its inclusion. It also examines personal, familial, cultural, and societal aspects of spirituality and how these impact clients, and discusses effective and ethical practice, focusing on holistic assessment and intervention. In addition, I explore worker-related issues and how the interaction of practitioners' own personal and professional belief systems can influence practice. Finally, I illustrate this content through a case example drawn from child welfare practice.

Why Spiritually Sensitive Practice?

Despite the profession's early roots in a Judeo-Christian worldview, social work has developed a strong secular tradition. There are many reasons for this, such as the cultural belief in separation of church and state, the antagonism of psychoanalysis toward religion, the pursuit of professional status, and adherence to a positivist tradition (Bullis 1996; Russel 1998). These are powerful forces that still exert a strong influence over our profession today. As a result, the argument for including a spiritual perspective in practice is not universally accepted, and spirituality continues to be a controversial topic.

In the past, if religious or spiritual concerns surfaced in a practice situation, one approach was to actively discourage discussion. It was as if the deepest, most profound meaning for the client was not relevant to the work at hand. If the spiritual concerns could not be avoided, another approach was to refer clients to clergy for guidance. Thus spiritual issues were to be separated from other related issues, similar to the dichotomy that once existed between physical and emotional health. Another approach to dealing with spiritual concerns was to attempt to treat them as if they were purely psychological problems. There are, however, inherent differences between the psychological and the spiritual, and psychotherapy is not an appropriate modality for all people or all problems. Today, adherents of spiritual sensitivity would argue that these approaches are both simplistic and insensitive.

An ongoing difficulty in integrating spirituality into practice is that most social workers do not receive adequate training in this area. In a large national survey of social work practitioners, Canda and Furman (1999:13) found that "over 73% of respondents indicated that they did not receive any instruction in spiritu-

ality or religion in their social work education. Even in courses dealing with human diversity, only about 13% received such content." There are other training opportunities in addition to formal education. Nonacademic training may include supervision, peer consultation, professional development workshops and conferences, personal psychotherapy, and other growth experiences. Practitioners typically undergo sufficient self-examination of their own biases to work competently with diverse clients. Such efforts at professional preparedness and personal self-awareness will not only enhance effectiveness, but may also reduce the likelihood of ethical impropriety (Fukuyama & Sevig 1999).

Defining Spirituality

Although the concept of spirituality is often given a religious or supernatural connotation, it is a far broader concept. "Spirit" is defined most simply as "the activating or essential principle influencing a person" (Webster's Dictionary). It is derived from the Latin "spirare," meaning "to breathe." It is generally described as an innate tendency that gives meaning, value, and purpose to life. It lies at the very core of our identity (who we are), our personality (how we think and feel), and our behavior (what we do). It encompasses relatedness, wholeness, openness to self and others, and a connectedness or transcendence to something greater than ourselves. Although most definitions of spirituality imply a theist orientation (i.e., belief in a supreme being), this is not a necessary component (e.g., some people find art or nature to be transcendent). What is critical in defining "spirituality" is the transformative nature of a belief or experience to take us to a higher level of functioning, beyond a focus on the self or the mundane. This transcendence is often described as love, compassion, hope, or forgiveness.

Spirituality should be distinguished from religion. Spirituality is viewed as intrinsic—an inner journey or search for meaning and purpose. Religion, in contrast, is viewed as extrinsic —an outer expression of faith and behavior.

Religion is characterized by adherence to a formal set of beliefs within an organized structure or institution, specific doctrine or dogma, and clearly defined rituals. Smith (1994) identifies the following eight major religious traditions in the world: Buddhism, Christianity, Confucianism, Hinduism, Islam, Judaism, Native, and Taoism. In addition, there are numerous sects within each of these traditions.

The relationship between religion and spirituality can be complex. Ressler's (1998a) typology, as presented by Sherwood (1998), can be helpful in distinguishing these two concepts. It posits four possible patterns in how people express this relationship: spiritual and religious, spiritual and nonreligious, religious and nonspiritual, and nonspiritual and nonreligious. The language used is very much a matter of personal choice. In this chapter, I emphasize the more inclusive and typically less emotionally charged term "spirituality."

Debate about Inclusion

Although in this chapter I clearly favor incorporating a spiritual perspective into practice, there is ongoing debate about the issue. Numerous authors have explored why this practice is controversial (Cornett 1992; Frame 2003; Prest & Keller 1993). Canda (1998) conducted a content analysis of 30 social work publications between 1988 and 1998 and found that only three citations overtly opposed a spiritual perspective. This finding cannot be viewed as overwhelming support for including spiritual content in professional practice, however, as it only reflects one measurement. Opponents to this position may express it in ways other than through publications.

The following arguments have been advanced for not including a spiritual perspective in practice. First, a spiritual dimension is seen as too subjective, in that it is not quantifiable or observable. Second, there is concern about practitioners failing to distinguish between religion and spirituality and, as a result, proselytizing or imposing their values on clients. Third, spiritu-

ality is viewed as encompassing private information; discussion of spirituality in practice is regarded as a violation of personal boundaries. Fourth, spirituality is perceived as contrary to the problem-solving perspective that is geared toward helping individuals to master the environment and control outcomes. Fifth, religion is often regarded as intolerant, narrow-minded, oppressive, and the source of difficulties due to rigid, conservative, and fundamentalist dogma. And finally, social workers frequently interpret social and economic justice in terms of discrimination and oppression (e.g., involving real, concrete, and pressing needs imposed on individuals by a hostile environment) rather than in terms of personal, interpersonal, or transpersonal distress.

Each of these concerns, however, can be answered with a counterargument. First, many theoretical constructs that are accepted as valid (such as "ego") cannot be well defined or measured, yet they are still valued for enriching practice. Second, it is recognized that no therapeutic approach is value-free and that conscientious practitioners will engage in ongoing self-monitoring to avoid imposing any beliefs onto a client. Third, most social work relationships are intrusive to some degree, yet personal concerns must still be addressed, albeit in a respectful way. Fourth, all people operate from a fundamental belief system and the position that there are no limits to adaptation or problem-solving ability is, itself, a spiritual belief. Fifth, although history is replete with the misuse of religion to divide and discriminate, such dogma is antithetical to a truly spiritual perspective. Finally, social justice is not limited to rectifying clearly identifiable inequities, but is also inclusive of helping people with profound life issues, such as hope, purpose, and self-worth.

There are other compelling reasons to include spirituality in practice or at least to be aware of its significance. The presenting problem may have an overtly spiritual aspect to it. In addition, even if spirituality is not directly relevant to the problem (and some people argue that all problems are spiritual), it is part of a holistic approach that is closely tied to personal and cultural variables. It enhances our understanding and empathy for the client's worldview (i.e., how he or she understands, interprets, or attaches meaning to experiences). And, from a strengths perspective, it is important to be open to spirituality because a considerable body of research literature links the practice of spirituality with positive mental and physical health (Van Hook, Hugen, & Aguilar 2001; Young, Cashwell, & Shcherbakova 2000).

Social work and spirituality are highly compatible. Although acknowledging the traditional antagonism between the spiritual and the scientific, Richards and Bergin (1997:9) argue for the need to integrate both domains if practitioners are to have a full and accurate picture of clients' lives: "spiritual questions deserve thoughtful, deliberate, and authentic responses." Bullis (1996) presents several ways that spirituality and social work are related, noting that they are connected historically and philosophically in that both promote social progress and self-respect. Each contributes to the other's effectiveness (i.e., social, political, and economic change and personal transformation). And spirituality and social work both aim to understand and empathize with the other person's cosmology, which may be a necessary component of healing.

Diversity and Demographics

Social work has long advocated an appreciation of diversity. Inclusivity based on spirituality is perhaps the richest expression of this value, as it cuts across all diverse groups. In fact, most definitions of diversity have traditionally included religious affiliation. Furthermore, the definition of culture usually includes religion. Therefore, it is incumbent upon every practitioner to be familiar with religious traditions, particularly with regard to how they influence clients and shape communities. (See Van Hook, Hugen, & Aguilar 2001 for an overview of religious traditions.)

However, it is equally important to avoid stereotyping specific cultural groups as strictly identifying with particular religious traditions. As the world becomes increasingly globalized, the familiar patterns of "who belongs to what tradition" are quickly evaporating. Fukuyama and Sevig (1997) observe that some regard spirituality as a function of culture, whereas others view it as a universal drive experienced uniquely by each person and influenced by culture. Constantine (1999) notes that clients of color may view counselors as unwilling to explore these issues and, therefore, as less able to meet their needs effectively, even though spiritual issues often underlie the concerns that bring them in for assistance. (See Cascio 1999; Fukuyama and Sevig 1999; Ortiz, Villereal, & Engel 2000 for further information on diversity, spirituality, and multicultural counseling.)

Members of several diverse groups have been oppressed by fundamentalist or dogmatic religion and may need opportunities to explore their identity and self-worth. Fukuyama and Sevig (1999) explore cultural-specific spirituality (noting Native American, Afrocentric, and women's worldviews specifically). Frame (2003) presents a multistage process model developed by Hickson and Phelps (1997) for women's spiritual development that entails the sequential themes of exploration, interdependence, balance, transformation, and wholeness. Frame (2003) also identifies unique challenges faced by gay and lesbian people (e.g., integrating multiple identities, facing judgmental attitudes from their families, coping with the impact of AIDS) and provides guidelines for working with this population. Frame also notes that other groups present special needs for spiritually sensitive practice, including children and adolescents, the elderly, and those experiencing death or loss.

Spirituality is not only relevant from a holistic, diversity, and strengths-based perspective, it is a sustaining force in American culture. Hugen (2001) presents data collected from national surveys (Gallup 1996, 1998) that illustrate the extent of religious pluralism in America. Some key findings are: 96% of participants report that they believe in God or a universal spirit, 90% pray (the majority at least daily), 90% identify with a specific religion, and 43% attend religious services at least weekly. Furthermore, 85% of Americans identify themselves as Christian (57% Protestant and 26% Catholic) and 15% are non-Christian. Of non-Christians, 2% are Jewish and 1% each follow Islam, Hinduism, and Buddhism. Hispanics are predominately Catholic, but 25% are Protestant. African Americans are 73% Protestant, 10% Catholic, and a growing number are Muslim. There are a greater number of Muslims than of either Episcopalians or Presbyterians. Of Arab Americans, 33% are Muslim.

It is clear that our society has become cross-cultural. Immigration from throughout the world has significantly changed the religious composition of the United States. In addition, there is a trend across all groups toward more individualism and personal autonomy in religious expression. Another trend is what Bullis (1996) refers to as the process of "spiritual democratization" or the freeing of spiritual traditions from their cultural contexts. This process makes different traditions more accessible to all persons. It also opens the authority role to non-clerical professionals (including social workers) and laypersons. This can have the benefit of cultural enrichment; however, it can also carry with it the risk of distorting or even trivializing the tradition.

Developmental Models

Two different theoretical perspectives are particularly germane to this discussion: life-span development and spiritual development (Canda & Furman 1999; Frame 2003). Life-span developmental models explicate the emergence and evolution of spirituality in the context of the larger life cycle. The most familiar of these is Erikson's psychosocial developmental theory, in which spirituality is a significant (although not always explicit) factor in each developmental stage. In contrast, spiritual development refers to a more precise and focused process.

From a psychosocial perspective, spirituality is a universal construct that is woven throughout the life span, although it is expressed in individual ways. The major themes of spirituality typically pertain to identity formation and interpersonal intimacy. They can play out in productive or destructive ways. Kelly (1995:69) notes that Erikson identified the important roles that religion plays in human development:

(1) fostering a faith that supports a child's sense of trust and hope, in contrast to religious faith that instills fear; (2) building up a system (ideology) of values, sometimes manifested in religious tradition, that adolescents may relate to in their expanding search for personal identity; (3) promoting a sense of universalism to undergird the generative care of adulthood; [and] (4) contributing to older adults' formulation of a mature sense of the meaningful and integral wholeness of life.

Pellebon and Anderson (1999) remark that spirituality operates much like culture in the underlying influence it has on the development process of a family and how members attach meaning to socialization experiences involving significant life events (e.g., childbirth) or different life stages (e.g., parent-adolescent conflict).

Such roles can obviously have significant implications for spiritually sensitive practice with children, youth, and families. In children and adolescents, spiritual conceptualization is closely linked to cognitive development. The spiritual needs of children may go unacknowledged because of the misguided notion that they cannot grasp philosophical or theological concepts. However, for many children, spirituality is highly relevant when discussed in age-appropriate ways. As adolescents expand their cognitive abilities and become capable of abstract thinking, they are deeply concerned with the search for personal identity and meaning. Given the issues of abuse and neglect that many children and adolescents in the child welfare system have experienced, it is important to address these concerns. Young adults may be struggling with individuating from family spiritual beliefs or practices and establishing their own worldview. As they progress through adulthood, people face unavoidable disappointments and often grapple with the most fundamental questions of meaning and purpose. They may need an outlet for exploring unresolved trauma from the past or crises in the present. Many middle-aged or elderly adults find themselves caring for young children through kinship arrangements at a stage of life when this is not developmentally expected. They may be facing parenting issues while contending with multiple stressors related to poor health or financial problems, as well as confronting their own mortality. Spirituality is an important resource as the elderly adjust to the inevitable process of loss and death.

There are numerous developmental models that describe how people "grow and change" within a strictly spiritual framework. Although many of these models are tied to age ranges, they are distinctly separate from psychosocial theory. Perhaps the most comprehensive is Fowler's (1981) faith development theory, which proposes a seven-stage model progressing from primitive faith to universal faith. Encompassing the entire life span, each stage is characterized by particular quality or spiritual capacity. All of the models have been criticized as being too hierarchical, stage specific, and Eurocentric. However, they can be useful to practitioners in gaining a better understanding of spirituality, enhancing empathy with particular clients, and increasing self-awareness. (See Canda and Furman 1999; Frame 2003; and Kelly 1995 for more detailed discussions of the different models of spiritual development.)

Overview of Practice

Many authors argue that the very nature of social work practice is spiritual and the need is not so much for inclusion of spiritual content as for the recognition that it has always been present. The question then becomes not whether one should incorporate spirituality into practice, but how best to do so. The goal of advocating for a spiritual perspective is to make social workers more aware of this innate aspect of practice so they can, in turn, make it more accessible for clients (Canda & Furman 1999). Derrickson (1996) distinguishes between spiritual guidance (which should be the purview of clergy or pastoral counselors) vs. spiritual care (how we respond to our clients) and spiritual work (how we pursue our own growth). Although awareness of spirituality is germane to almost all client concerns, the problem-solving approach can create confusion in this regard. "Spiritual issues are better thought of as dilemmas or difficulties that need to be tended, rather than problems that need to be solved. . . . The search for meaning may not lend itself to measurable outcomes or concrete solutions; it simply is. It is part of the struggle or process of the search itself, which holds the meaning" (Graham, Kaiser, & Garrett 1998:54). Thus a spiritual perspective, properly applied, is not intended to persuade or advise, but rather to explore and clarify, maximizing clients' potential within their own chosen framework.

As with all social work practice, in spiritually sensitive practice, one should place the greatest emphasis on the importance of the helping relationship. Canda and Furman (1999:186) state that "spiritually sensitive practice is not merely a matter of discussing religion or spirituality with clients. It is a way of being and relating throughout the entire helping process." They identify the following five guiding principles: Value clarity, respect, client centeredness, inclusivity, and creativity. Faiver, Ingersoll, O'Brien, and McNalley (2001) also provide five general guidelines for spiritually sensitive practice. First is strengthening the therapeutic alliance, affirming the importance of a person's religious/ spiritual worldview, and conveying empathic understanding of the importance it has for them (regardless of how helpful or harmful it may appear to you). Second is enhancing empathic communication by choosing vocabulary and images that are congruent with the client's worldview. Third is a willingness to consult with "healers" or "friendly clergy" in the person's life to gain deeper insight into the client's worldview and to strengthen the therapeutic alliance. Fourth is discerning the client's cognitive, moral, or faith-oriented developmental level, using one of the accepted models. And their fifth guideline is distinguishing healthy from unhealthy practices and considering whether there are pathological elements to the client's belief system, recognizing that this requires considerable experience, sincerity, and caution.

Canda and Furman (1999) conceptualize a holistic model of spirituality, noting that spirituality consists of three metaphors: spirituality as the center of the person, as one aspect of the person, and as the wholeness of the person. They contend that the most familiar and accepted approach is to view spirituality as one aspect of the person (the bio-psycho-socio-spiritual quaternity of functioning), albeit the one that infuses and impels the other aspects. The other two metaphors are indirectly relevant to practice. Spirituality as the center of the person pertains to our fundamental humanity and is expressed through the core values of unconditional positive regard and the belief that all people should be treated with respect and dignity. Spirituality as wholeness of the person refers to a highly integrated individuals who have moved beyond a focus on the self as a separate entity and instead pursue unity with self, others, and "the All."

Graham, Kaiser, and Garrett (1998) propose that there are essentially two ways that social workers engage clients in a spiritual process. The first is through the helping relationship and the second is through reframing problems as spiritual issues. "Addressing spiritual issues ideally occurs on two levels: first, it is useful to simply name the issue as such. . . . Secondly, the social work relationship itself can become a medium for addressing spiritual issues" (1998: 58). They identify four dimensions for "naming the spiritual": belonging and alienation, faith

and doubt, hope and despair, and suffering and joy. Thus within a trusting relationship, the worker can incorporate the spiritual aspect into any problem through helping clients to recognize and acknowledge the underlying spiritual concern that they are facing. Helminiak (2001) identifies three appropriate responses to a client's spiritual issues: validation, reinterpretation (or refocusing), and rejection. Rejecting aspects of spirituality would be indicated if the client espoused beliefs indicating satanic control or hexes, prohibitions against being angry with God or against questioning, and equating inner peace with the will of God (and thus ignoring reality or responsibilities). Faiver, Ingersoll, O'Brien, and McNalley (2001) note that a spiritual approach is contraindicated if a client expressly states a desire not to explore spiritual issues, if a client is clearly emotionally or mentally unstable, or if spirituality has no relevance to the presenting problem.

The Association for Spiritual, Ethical, and Religious Values in Counseling has identified core spiritual competencies. A list of these nine competencies can be found on their website (www.aservic.org). They are summarized as:

1. Explain the relationship between religion and spirituality;
2. Describe religious and/or spiritual beliefs and practices in a cultural context;
3. Engage in self-exploration of one's own religious and/or spiritual beliefs;
4. Describe one's religious and/or spiritual belief system and explain various models of religious and/or spiritual development across the life span;
5. Demonstrate sensitivity and acceptance of a variety of religious and/or spiritual expressions in the client's communication;
6. Identify the limits of one's understanding of a client's religious and/or spiritual expression and demonstrate appropriate referral skills;
7. Assess the relevance of the religious and/or spiritual domains in the client's therapeutic issues;

8. Be both sensitive and receptive to the religious and/or spiritual themes in the counseling process as they fit the client's expressed preferences; and

9. Use the client's religious and/or spiritual beliefs in the pursuit of therapeutic goals as they fit the client's expressed preferences.

Assessment

It is crucial to include spirituality in assessment if the social worker is to fully understand a client's functioning within his/her environmental context. There are two types of spiritual assessment: a broader, more general framework for practice in which spirituality is one aspect of overall assessment, or a narrower, more focused framework specifically targeting spiritual functioning. This section addresses general assessment issues. (See Faiver, Ingersoll, O'Brien, & McNalley 2001; Frame 2003; and Richards & Bergin 1997 for discussions of conducting an extensive, in-depth spiritual assessment.) Note that "assessment" is also used in the literature in reference to scales that quantifiably measure some dimension of a client's spiritual experience or beliefs (e.g., see Frame 2003).

Even if approached in very general terms, spirituality is such a complex, multifaceted, and personal experience that data collection can seem quite daunting to the practitioner. As in broaching any potentially sensitive topic, the social worker should explain the reason for introducing it (especially the benefits to the client) and secure the client's consent to proceed. The worker should ask the client whether he or she is comfortable discussing this topic and, if indicated, explain the distinction between spirituality and religiosity. The worker should pay close attention to nonverbal communication and present the material in a nonjudgmental and open-minded way. For many clients, the practitioner's exploration of this topic will indicate cultural sensitivity, as it may be central to a client's heritage. The practitioner's comfort in discussing such matters may encourage clients to share their worldview. (See Faiver, Ingersoll,

O'Brien, & McNalley 2001, for a sample intake form and Bullis 1996 for a "spiritual history" format.)

Faiver, Ingersoll, O'Brien, and McNalley (2001:93) identify guidelines concerning incorporating spirituality into assessment by maintaining a "concurrent awareness of religious/spiritual factors that may be contributing to client problems and their potential resolution." Their guidelines include asking about clients' present belief systems (including the lack of one); inquiring how beliefs affect their current functioning; exploring their history regarding denomination or faith (if any) in which they were raised and how this influenced them; and exploring how deeply clients are invested in this area. Significant differences between past and present beliefs or practices might indicate potential areas of conflict. They suggest that slightly altering Adler's question ("What would be different in your life if you didn't have this problem?") can help identify core spiritual concerns (e.g., "What would be different in your life if you didn't have this religion or spirituality?").

Faiver, Ingersoll, O'Brien, and McNalley (2001) provide recommendations for focusing on cognitive, affective, and behavioral aspects of spirituality. For example, cognitively, it is important to explore any manifestations of guilt, shame, or distorted thinking. In terms of affect, one can examine how the belief system has a positive or negative impact on the client, and especially how it might be related to feelings of depression, anxiety, or labile mood. With regard to behaviors, one can examine rituals or routines, being alert to indicators of excessive religiosity or inappropriate habits or gestures. They caution that, in assessing religious or spiritual functioning, it is critical to distinguish between integrative spiritual experiences and disintegrating psychotic ones.

In this regard, it is often necessary to assess pathology. Frame (2003) and Richards and Bergin (1997) distinguish between healthy and unhealthy beliefs or practices. Psychotic, delusional, or obsessive-compulsive beliefs or practices are deemed unhealthy. If appropriate, the *Diagnostic and Statistical Manual of Mental Disorders* (DSM)-IV includes "religious or spiritual problem" as a diagnostic category apart from mental or emotional disorders. Some clients will not be aware of their beliefs and underlying values and how these shape their feelings, thoughts, and behaviors, whereas others will consciously recognize their beliefs as a protective or risk factor. In child welfare practice, assessing spirituality should not only include unhealthy or pathological functioning of an individual client, but also the potential of harm to others.

Intervention

As with assessment, the literature can be divided into two types of approaches to intervention. On the one hand, intervention can be viewed within a broader, more general framework in which spirituality is one aspect of overall treatment (see the section giving an overview of practice). This approach, which applies to most social work practice, is based on preexisting secular therapeutic models, which do not expressly address religious and/or spiritual aspects. Thus intervention is geared toward integrating a spiritual component into secular models. On the other hand, intervention can be viewed within a narrow, more focused framework specifically directed at spiritual functioning. Frame (2003) refers to this dichotomy as implicit (utilizing therapeutic strategies within existing frameworks) vs. explicit (utilizing expressly religious or spiritual strategies). Guidelines for incorporating religious or spiritual issues into traditional models (e.g., psychodynamic, humanistic, cognitive behavioral) are not well articulated in the literature.

Richards and Bergin (1997) identify five categories of spiritual interventions for counselors to consider whether operating from a secular (implicit) or a spiritual (explicit) perspective. First, intervention can occur either in-session or out-of-session (i.e., pray with client during

session or for client outside of session). Second, interventions can be labeled as either "religious" (utilizing some aspect of client's overt religious belief or practice; e.g., references to scripture) or "spiritual" (focusing on the client's inner, subjective meaning and experience). Third, interventions that are designated as religious can be either denominational (entailing client's specific theology) or ecumenical (more universal and not identifiable with a particular theology). Fourth, interventions are viewed as either transcendent or nontranscendent. In the former case, the client and counselor share a common worldview and spiritually based strategies can be used (e.g., calling on a higher power for assistance). In the latter, the client and the counselor do not share a worldview and interventions that are not of a religious/spiritual nature are pursued. Fifth, spiritual interventions, as any other, can be regarded as based primarily in an affective, behavioral, cognitive, or interpersonal theoretical perspective.

Frame (2003) notes that it is important to evaluate the fit between clients and their faith community. Given a client's view, involvement with a faith community may be an important aspect of intervention. Some clients need to search for a more accepting or supportive group, whereas others may need to consider rejoining or enhancing involvement with a positive group. It may be helpful to suggest that clients consult with a religious or spiritual leader to clarify mistaken beliefs. Under some circumstances, with the client's permission, it may be indicated that the social worker pursues such consultation on the client's behalf. Bullis (1996) discusses strategies for collaborating with clergy and also indicates when this would not be appropriate: either the client or the social worker is ambivalent, the social worker determines that the community has renounced the leader, the social worker's role is not clearly defined, or the community does not recognize the social worker's role.

Frame (2003) further identifies three thorny issues that are often encountered in spiritually sensitive practice. These are handling therapist self-disclosure, dealing with client's religious or spiritual authorities, and managing harmful beliefs or practices. First, regarding self-disclosure, clients might ask about a social worker's beliefs because they fear being judged or misunderstood. Although the degree of appropriate self-disclosure is debatable in any situation, Kelly (1995) recommends a "middle way," in which the worker defers a direct answer and explores the underlying concern implied by the question or reassures the client that his or her beliefs will be respected. If the client persists, however, a direct answer is preferable to evasion. Second, it may be helpful to assist clients in clarifying the extent to which religious authority influences their lives. One technique, for example, is to ask clients to identify all of the sources of authority in their lives and to rank them in order of importance. This may lead to greater awareness of how they make choices. The more closely a client adheres to religious authority, the less likely they are to be influenced by the practitioner. Third, client beliefs that are perceived as harmful can lead to a serious value conflict. The social worker may be required to take steps to protect the client or others. Once safety concerns have been resolved, numerous approaches can be used. For example, cognitive therapy can be employed to modify distorted thinking or to understand the roots of a dysfunctional belief system with the goal of developing a healthier perspective.

An important consideration in intervention is the need to assess clients for alcoholism, addiction, and other compulsive behaviors. This is particularly pertinent to child welfare practice given the pervasiveness of these problems in troubled families. Faiver, Ingersoll, O'Brien, and McNalley (2001) and Okundaye, Smith, and Lawrence-Webb (2001) have concise discussions of spirituality and the 12 steps of recovery.

Another important consideration in working with families, especially distressed ones, is resilience. This is a well-known concept at the individual level that is becoming more promi-

nent at the family level (Hawley & DeHaan 1996; Walsh 1996). Hawley (2000:104) characterizes resilience as "the ability to withstand and grow under stressful conditions, an emphasis on strengths and resources, the importance of positive perceptions about adversity, and a recognition that social and developmental contexts shape resilience in families." Helping a family to utilize their spiritual strengths, such as affirming belief systems and identifying community resources, can foster family resilience.

Explicit intervention strategies reach beyond the usual domain of practice, which is a source of the controversy concerning the spiritual perspective. These include prayer, meditation, journaling, bibliotherapy, and authorative writings. Faiver, Ingersoll, O'Brien, and McNalley (2001) give a lengthy list of specific spiritual interventions, including (but not limited to) blessing, confessing, forgiving, and guiding. Explicit spiritual interventions may be controversial and pose ethical dilemmas in social work practice. Caution is warranted here, particularly in working with children and adolescents, which would require parental or guardian consent before proceeding. Frame (2003) recommends that practitioners follow specific guidelines if explicit strategies are employed. These include obtaining informed consent, determining appropriateness given the norms of the setting, monitoring one's own self-awareness and personal insight, assessing the connection between client beliefs and problems, establishing a trusting and respectful relationship, working within client values, maintaining peer support, and utilizing client sources of support. An explicit approach should not be used when it is inconsistent with agency policy, the client is not interested or is psychotic or delusional, it is not relevant, permission is not given by the guardian, or there is no strong therapeutic relationship.

Values, Ethics, and Worker Issues

Contemporary social work values are based on secular humanism. Despite their earliest roots in charitable work, current professional values attempt to draw a clear line between the sacred and the secular. Many social workers doubtless have strong religious values, which may greatly influence their approach to practice even if generally accepted professional guidelines discourage them from acknowledging it. Lowenberg (1988) points out the fallacy of the value-neutral stance, which evolved in reaction to the "paternalistic moralism" of the early charity workers. Lowenberg (1988:96) writes "Value neutrality is itself a value, a value that may be more insidious because it does not appear openly as a value" and contends that this espoused nonjudgmental stance is unrealistic because all people operate from a belief system and make judgments. Instead, he cautions against the more damaging stance of "unrestrained judgmentalism." He recommends several strategies to avoid this extreme: evaluating behavior (rather than the person), suspending judgment, equalizing power, and respecting the "divine spark" in every human being.

Aponte (1995:168) contends that values are of special importance to low income and minority families: "We can talk all we want about empowering poor and minority families, but unless we strengthen their values, culture, and transcendent purpose in life, they will not know their own power." He identifies three problems experienced by families with "underdeveloped" values systems: they lack a strong sense of identity, self worth, and life purpose; they are more vulnerable to imposition of values by agency workers; and they have less ability to direct their lives and solve problems. Practitioners can help families to strengthen their value system through discussing and clarifying, offering alternative viewpoints, or influencing them (e.g., prohibiting abuse).

In discussing the importance of client-worker match in terms of religious beliefs, Lowenberg (1988:94) speculates that the lack of "spiritual sharing" may be a source of great difficulty in social work: "Social workers in the mismatched combinations must accept responsibility for

making certain that the value discrepancy will not interfere unduly with the helping process." Any combination of religiosity in either the client or worker can pose particular problems (i.e., even if both are highly religious, they may differ in their beliefs).

One of the fundamental precepts emphasized throughout the literature is the need for social workers to be aware of their own personal values and how these influence professional relationships and behaviors. There are several ways to enhance self-awareness in the area of spirituality. One is to gain increased knowledge about the relationship between spirituality and values (Hall 1996). Another is to use spiritual assessment tools, paying close attention to questions that elicit strong feelings. As discussed previously, these tools are typically thought of as client-focused, although practitioners can also use them to gain a better understanding of themselves. Faiver, Ingersoll, O'Brien, and Mc-Nally (2001) supply an extensive, open-ended format for evaluating one's own belief system. A third is to explore one's own family of origin's spirituality and how this shapes one's personal and professional values (Frame 2003). Finally, as in any clinical situation, value difficulties may best be resolved through supervision, peer consultation, personal counseling or pastoral support, or referral of the client to a more appropriate resource.

Most authors advocating in favor of a spiritual perspective in practice contend that it is completely compatible with social work ethics. Canda and Furman (1999:262) state: "we agree that it is very important to use explicit spiritually based practices on the basis of careful ethical reflection, but we do not see this as fundamentally different from ethical decisions making about other practice activities." In fact, one could assert that to not include spirituality is inconsistent with professional values and ethics, as this approach does not foster empowerment through self-determination or recognition of cultural diversity. Benningfield (1998) posits that all of the potential problems of addressing spirituality and religion in therapy fall under two main categories: dealing with the subject inappropriately or avoiding it inappropriately. Bullis (1996) notes that social workers need to know the legal consequences of spiritual behavior, as well as the cultural practices associated with personal healing. Due to the religious clause of the First Amendment, it is improper and possibly unconstitutional to prevent or discourage clients from pursuing religious or spiritual practices of their choosing (Ressler 1998b). Furthermore, such practice could be unethical according to the National Association of Social Worker's Code of Ethics (National Association of Social Workers 1999), which directs social workers to foster maximum self-determination for clients and prohibits discrimination based on religion.

Incorporating spirituality into child welfare practice may present additional ethical challenges. For example, clients are often involuntary, possess limited insight or motivation to change, and face tremendous social and economic adversity. Child welfare systems are notoriously bureaucratic and underfunded, such that caseworkers or social workers are overworked and underpaid. Thus they may not have the time or inclination to engage clients in a discussion of their spirituality. Agency policies on this topic may be vague or nonexistent and may offer limited guidance. For example, I contacted a supervisor at Child Protective Services in a large city in Texas for her anecdotal impressions. She knew of no policy prohibiting discussion of religion or spirituality with clients. The statewide intake form asks only for religious affiliation or denomination. The one relevant policy guideline pertains to placement decisions in terms of protecting the child's ethnic identity. Foster parents are expected to provide religious training consistent with that of the birth parents, although this may not always be pursued. Clients are encouraged to use their support system, including religious institutions. Nevertheless, policy and agency factors combined can have a cumulative effect that might make spiritually sensitive child welfare practice quite daunting.

The standards of excellence for family foster care services published by the Child Welfare League of America (1995:64–65) states that "the family foster care agency and the foster parents, with the parents whenever feasible, should collaborate to provide the children in their care with opportunities for spiritual development, in accordance with the wishes of the child and the child's parents." The guidance (1995:65) continues:

> To the extent possible, the child should attend his or her own church, synagogue, or other place of worship. The plan should include how best to meet the spiritual development of the child when the religious affiliation or wishes of the parents and other family members are not known, or the wishes of the parents or their religious affiliations are different from those of the foster family.

The following case example illustrates the wisdom of this practice standard and the use of spiritually sensitive practice in addressing a former foster child's experience in which attention to her spiritual development was not provided.

CASE EXAMPLE

Adrienne is a 27-year-old African American single mother of three children: Kevin (aged 10), Monica (aged 5), and Thomas (aged 2). She has never married; her two younger children have the same father (Charles). She does not get child support from either man; she does not know where Kevin's father is. Although Charles lives in Austin, he is only sporadically involved with his children. Adrienne has a high school diploma. She is employed part-time as a grocery store cashier; she does not receive benefits. She lives in Austin, a mid-sized metropolitan area in central Texas with a depressed economy due to a lingering downturn in the high tech industry.

Kevin and Monica attend the local elementary school. Thomas stays with Adrienne's neighbor, Velma, a 65-year-old retired teacher. Velma enjoys caring for Thomas. She does not charge Adrienne and only asks her to provide snacks and diapers for the baby. However, 2 weeks ago, Velma fell and broke her hip and is no longer able to care for Thomas. Adrienne has missed work to stay home with Thomas, and because she works evenings, has often left Thomas in Kevin's care. She also has been late for work several times and was told that she would be fired if this continues.

Adrienne does not have a support system beyond Velma. She was removed from her own biological family due to sexual abuse. She does not maintain contact with either her foster family or her biological family. She does not use alcohol or drugs when she is alone with the children. When Charles makes one of his occasional visits, she has sent them to stay with Velma. At these times, he and Adrienne drank excessively and they often have had loud, lengthy arguments that Velma said were very upsetting to the children. Adrienne does not have any close female friends; she says that she does not have the time or energy.

Thomas has a history of chronic ear infections and is in danger of loosing his hearing unless he has surgery for drainage tubes. With Velma's help, Adrienne was always able to take him to the doctor and give him medicine. Now he is ill with another infection. She knows that she can get free treatment at the public hospital; however, she is reluctant to pursue this route because she is afraid that the authorities will take him from her the way that she was removed from her own family.

Last week a teacher made a referral to Child Protection Services because she was concerned about Kevin. He had always been a cooperative and hard-working student. She noticed that he has recently been coming to school in dirty clothes and falling asleep in class. He seemed to be increasingly irritable and aggressive and precipitated a fight with a classmate. When she talked to him about it, he reported that he is worried about his mother, overwhelmed with caring for his younger siblings, unable to sleep, and has been leaving the house at night to "hang out" on the street with the older boys.

Following the telephone intake, an investigative worker visited the home and conducted an initial assessment. In consultation with the supervisor, she made a determination that neglect had occurred, specifically citing Thomas' medical condition. Adrienne was referred to intensive Family Based Safety Services (commonly known as "family preservation") and Esperanza Gomez, a recent MSW graduate, was assigned to be her caseworker. Upon meeting with Adrienne, Esperanza concluded that, despite her current difficulties, Adrienne had numerous strengths that would help her overcome her current crisis. Most notably, she been able to adequately provide for her children, did not have a serious substance abuse problem or other mental health concerns, and showed a stable living and work history. Adrienne was offered agency services to assist with parenting needs and financial problems and psychotherapy.

Esperanza's first priority was medical care for Thomas, and an appointment was arranged for the next day. However, when Esperanza arrived to take them to the appointment, she found Adrienne lying in bed and the older children trying to console the crying baby. She quickly determined that Adrienne was having an acute depressive episode and immediately implemented a crisis intervention. The children were removed to an emergency shelter. Upon further evaluation, it was determined that Adrienne was experiencing a major depression and temporary foster care was arranged for the children until her condition improved. The children were assigned to their own caseworker, who coordinated their care, especially Thomas' medical needs.

Meanwhile, Adrienne received mental health services, including medication, cognitive behavioral therapy, and supportive life skills training. She had biweekly supervised visits with the children. Within 8 weeks, Adrienne's depression had improved to the point that the children were returned to her. Thomas' ear infection was under control and Kevin's school behavior was improving. She was once again deemed appropriate for intensive family based safety services and Esperanza began to work with her again.

Esperanza and Adrienne developed a joint family service plan. It addressed the multiple needs facing Adrienne and her family, including medical treatment, child care, employment, parenting, depression, and substance abuse. Esperanza visited Adrienne and her children at least twice a week for 4 to 6 hours a day to teach in-home parenting skills and provide emotional support. Adrienne continued in individual therapy; she and the two older children participated in family therapy.

Adrienne and Esperanza developed a strong relationship. When asked how her therapy was going, she told Esperanza that she had mentioned to her therapist that she used to go to church with her biological family (Southern Baptist) but that stopped when she entered foster care at age 12. She has never gone back to church but has been thinking a lot about it lately. She said that her therapist seemed unwilling to discuss this with her and asked Esperanza about her religious beliefs. Esperanza indicated that she thought this was an important topic and that she would like to hear more about Adrienne's spirituality. She explained about spiritual assessment. They discussed what Adrienne's prior experience had been and what she felt that she was currently missing in her life. Esperanza's accepting attitude and willingness to listen seemed to encourage Adrienne to continue and this initiated an ongoing discussion.

She recalled feeling welcomed and supported in the church that she attended as a child, saying that "it felt like a family." As she spoke, she connected several losses: the move to foster care, no longer going to this church, and the removal of her children. She noted that Kevin was at the same age that she was when she was placed. Esperanza asked if she wanted to build the church experience back into her life. Adrienne knew that Velma liked her church (and noted that church members were helping her with the recovery from her fall). Esperanza encouraged her to talk to Velma about her experiences. Within a few weeks, Adrienne began to accompany Velma to her local church. She and Esperanza continued to discuss her spiritual beliefs and experiences. It seemed to her that the church was a functional potential resource. Esperanza asked if she could speak with the pastor. Fortunately, the church had a child care facility that Adrienne could use until Velma fully recovered.

Esperanza monitored Adrienne's compliance with the family service plan and was able to observe that she actually applied her new skills at home with the children. Adrienne was able to find a retail position at a department store that offered regular hours, benefits, and discounts. She is now home in the evenings so she can supervise and care for the children. Her children now attend Sunday school and weekly Bible study classes. The church has an active youth ministry, with after-school programs, field trips, and life skills training. One of the male leaders serves as a mentor for Kevin. Adrienne continued to make steady progress in psychotherapy, especially in terms of healing the trauma of her sexual abuse. One sign of increased autonomy was that Adrienne also set limits on visits from Charles until he agrees not to bring alcohol into her home.

Esperanza worked with Adrienne for 9 months. As their work continued, the frequency of their contact diminished. However, Esperanza continued to encourage her to talk about her spiritual feelings. One interesting discussion pertained to their cultural experiences with religion. Adrienne spoke about her guilt and shame and was able to ask God for forgiveness. At one point, Esperanza felt uncomfortable about the word "God" but realized this was her own bias. She was careful not to play the role of spiritual leader or psychotherapist. She encouraged and supported strengths that enhanced client sense of self-determination and empowerment, including her spirituality. At their last contact, Adrienne was optimistic about her future and confident about her abilities as a parent, feeling that she now had renewed faith on which to build a positive life for herself and her children.

Conclusion

It is perhaps the spiritual dimension that prompted many social workers to enter a field of service dedicated to helping others, especially the poor and vulnerable. There is a growing, if not fully accepted, movement to incorporate this perspective into social work practice. This chapter has presented an overview of important considerations for spiritually sensitive practice with children, youth, and families. Fortunately, spiritual practice is about love, compassion, forgiveness, hope, growth, recovery, strength, support, dignity, worth, meaning, resilience, and optimism—not only for our clients, but also for ourselves.

Acknowledgment

The case example was developed with the assistance of Angela Ausbrooks, MSW.

REFERENCES

Aponte, H. (1995). *Bread and spirit: Therapy with the new poor.* New York: W. W. Norton.

Benningfield, M. F. (1997). Addressing spiritual/religious issues in therapy: Potential problems and complications. *Journal of Family Social Work, 24*(4), 25–42.

Bullis, R. K. (1996). *Spirituality in social work practice.* Washington, DC: Taylor & Francis.

Canda, E. R. (ed.). (1998). *Spirituality in social work: New directions.* Binghamton, NY: Hayworth Pastoral.

Canda, E. R., & Furman, L. D. (1999). *Spiritual diversity in social work practice: The heart of helping.* New York: Free Press.

Cascio, T. (1999). Religion and spirituality: Diversity issues for the future. *Journal of Multicultural Social Work, 7*(3/4), 129–145.

Child Welfare League of America. (1995). *Standards of excellence for family foster care services,* revised ed. Washington, DC: Child Welfare League of America.

Constantine, M. G. (1999). Spiritual and religious issues in counseling racial and ethnic minority populations: An introduction to the special issue. *Journal of Multi-Cultural Counseling and Development, 27*(4), 179–182.

Cornett, C. (1992). Toward a more comprehensive personology: Integrating a spiritual perspective into social work practice. *Social Work, 37,* 101–102.

Council on Social Work Education. (2002). *Educational policy and accreditation standards.* Alexandria, VA: Council on Social Work Education.

Derrickson, B. (1996). The spiritual work of dying: A framework and case studies. *Hospice Journal, 2*(2), 11–30.

Fabricatore, A. N., Handal, P. J., & Fenzel, L. M. (2000). Personal spirituality as a moderator of the relationship between stressors and subjective well-being. *Journal of Psychology and Theology, 28*(3), 221–228.

Faiver, C., Ingersoll, R. S., O'Brien, E., & McNalley, C. (2001). *Explorations in counseling and spirituality: Philosophical, practical, and personal reflections.* Pacific Grove, CA: Brooks/Cole.

Fowler, J. W. (1981). *Stages of faith.* New York: Harper and Row.

Frame, M. W. (2003). *Integrating religion and spirituality into counseling: A comprehensive approach.* Pacific Grove, CA: Brooks/Cole.

Fukuyama, M., & Sevig, T. (1997). Spiritual issues in counseling: A new course. *Counselor Education and Supervision, 36,* 224–232.

Fukuyama, M., & Sevig, T. (1999). *Integrating spirituality into multicultural counseling.* Thousand Oaks, CA: Sage.

Gallup, G. H., Jr. (1996). *Religion in America.* Princeton: Princeton Religious Research Center.

Gallup, G. H., Jr. (1998). *Newsletter of the Princeton Religious Research Center.* Princeton: Princeton Religious Research Center.

Graham, M. A., Kaiser, T., & Garrett, K. J. (1998). Naming the spiritual: The hidden dimensions of helping. *Social Thought, 18*(4), 49–61.

Hall, C. M. (1996). *Identity, religion, and values: Implications for practice.* Washington, DC: Taylor & Francis.

Hawley, D. (2000). Clinical implications of family resilience. *American Journal of Family Therapy, 28*(2), 101–116.

Hawley, D., & DeHann, L. (1996). Toward a definition of family resilience: Integrating life-span and family perspectives. *Family Process, 35,* 283–298.

Helminiak, D. A. (2001). Treating spiritual issues in secular psychotherapy. *Counseling and Values, 45*(3), 163–200.

Hickson, J., & Phelps, A. (1997). Women's spirituality: A proposed practice model. *Journal of Family Social Work, 2,* 43–57.

Hugen, B. (2001). Introduction. In M. Van Hook, B. Hugen, & M. Aguilar, *Spirituality within religious traditions in social work practice.* Pacific Grove, CA: Brooks/Cole.

Kelly, E. W. (1995). *Spirituality and religion in counseling and psychotherapy: Diversity in theory and practice.* Alexandria, VA: American Counseling Association.

Kilpatrick, A. (1999). Ethical issues and spiritual dimensions. In A. Kilpatrick & T. Holland, *Working with families: An integrative model by level of need,* pp. 50–63. Boston: Allyn and Bacon.

Lowenberg, F. (1988). *Religion and social work practice in contemporary American society.* New York: Columbia University Press.

Miller, D. W. (2001). Programs in social work embrace the teaching of spirituality. *Chronicle of Higher Education.* Retrieved May 18, 2001, from chronicle.com.

National Association of Social Workers. (1999). *Code of ethics of the National Association of Social Workers.*

Washington, DC: National Association of Social Workers Press.

Okundaye, J. N., Smith, P., & Lawrence, W. C. (2001). Incorporating spirituality and the strengths perspective into social work practice with addicted individuals. *Journal of Social Work Practice in the Addictions, 1*(1), 65–82.

Ortiz, L., Villereal, S., & Engel, M. (2000). Culture and spirituality: A review of the literature. *Social Thought, 19*(4), 21–36.

Pellebon, D. A., & Anderson, S. C. (1999). Understanding the life issues of spiritually-based clients. *Families in Society: The Journal of Contemporary Social Work, 80*, 229–239.

Prest, L. A., & Keller, J. F. (1993). Spirituality and family therapy: Spiritual beliefs, myths, and metaphors. *Journal of Marital and Family Therapy, 19*, 137–148.

Ressler, L. E. (1998a). When social work and Christianity conflict. In B. Hugen (ed.), *Christianity and social work: Readings on the integration of Christian faith and social work practice,* pp. 165–186. Botsford, CT: National Association of Christian Social Workers.

Ressler, L. E. (1998b). The relation between church and state: Issues in social work and the law. In E. R. Canda (ed.), *Spirituality in social work: New directions,* pp. 81–95. Binghampton, NY: Hayworth Pastoral.

Richards, P. S., & Bergin, A. E. (1997). *A spiritual strategy for counseling and psychotherapy.* Washington, DC: American Psychological Association.

Russel, R. (1998). Spirituality and religion in graduate social work education. In E. R. Canda (ed.), *Spirituality and social work: New directions.* Hazeldon, PA: Haworth.

Sherwood, D. A. (1998). Spiritual assessment as a normal part of social work practice: Power to help and power to harm. *Social Work and Christianity, 25*(2), 80–90.

Smith, H. (1994). *The illustrated world's religions: A guide to our wisdom traditions.* San Francisco: Harper.

Van Hook, M., Hugen, B., & Aguilar, M. (2001). *Spirituality within religious traditions in social work practice.* Pacific Grove, CA: Brooks/Cole.

Walsh, F. (1996). The concept of family resilience: Crisis and challenge. *Family Process, 35,* 261–281.

Young, J. S., Cashwell, C. S., & Shcherbakova, J. (2000). The moderating relationship of spirituality on negative life events and psychological adjustment. *Counseling and Values, 45*(1), 49–58.

SECTION II
Child and
Adolescent Safety

❖   ❖   ❖   ❖   ❖   ❖   ❖

Overview

Underscored by the mandate that "the safety of children is the paramount concern that must guide all child welfare services," the passage of the Adoption and Safe Families Act (ASFA) of 1997 (P.L. 105-89:1145) affirmed that child welfare agencies have a primary responsibility for insuring that children and youth are safe from abuse and neglect (U.S. Department of Health and Human Services 2000).

Prevention of Neglect and Abuse

The abuse and neglect of children and youth pose a grave hazard to their overall health and well-being, with both immediate and life-long physical, psychological, and social consequences. The presence of child abuse and neglect constitutes the primary reason that most children and adolescents come to the attention of the child welfare services system in the United States. As traditionally constituted, services aimed at protecting children and youth who have been identified as abused or neglected have been of paramount importance to the field of children, youth, and family services. However, a more recent and growing movement in the United States is represented by strategies and programs that aim to prevent child abuse before it has the chance to occur and that thereby aim to avert the frequently damaging consequences of such maltreatment for children, their families, and the wider social fabric. We begin this section on safety with a chapter that examines what it known about the prevention of child abuse and neglect by Guterman and Taylor. These authors provide the rationale for child abuse and neglect prevention and present the possibilities as well as the challenges and dilemmas facing the field of prevention as it advances in the twenty-first century.

Child Protective Services

To emphasize the importance of safety, ASFA legislation:

- States explicitly that child safety is the paramount consideration in decisionmaking regarding service provision, placement, and permanency planning for children; and
- Clarifies the reasonable efforts requirements related to preserving and reunifying families by reaffirming the importance of reasonable efforts, yet identifying those dangerous circumstances in which states are not required to make such efforts to keep the child with the parents.

Furthermore, in the Children and Family Service Reviews process, the safety variables, which are considered first, are summarized and evaluated in two areas:

- Safety 1: Children and youth are, first and foremost, to be protected from abuse and neglect. One aspect of this variable is timeliness of initiating investigations of reports of child maltreatment; the second is the prevention of repeated maltreatment.
- Safety 2: Children and youth are safely maintained in their own homes whenever possible and appropriate. The primary aspect of this variable is the provision of services to families to protect children and

youth in their homes and to prevent removal and risk of harm to children or youth.

In the child welfare system, the initial attention to the safety of children and youth is located with Child Protective Services (CPS) programs. CPS is the core program in all child welfare agencies and, in collaboration with other community agencies and organizations, such as schools, leads the efforts to insure child safety. More broadly, CPS refers to a highly specialized set of laws, funding mechanisms, and agencies that together constitute the government's response to reports of child abuse and neglect (Waldfogel 1998:105). The authority for CPS programs stems from laws established in each state that define child abuse and neglect and specify how CPS agencies should respond to reports of child maltreatment. Caseworkers in CPS agencies have the responsibility to address the effects of child maltreatment, implement service responses that will keep children and youth safe from abuse and neglect, and work with families to prevent the likelihood of child maltreatment in the future (DePanfilis & Salus 2003). DePanfilis, in her chapter on child protection, traces the path of child abuse and neglect reports from the point of referral through the process of providing ongoing services to children, youth, and families involved in the child protection system. After first describing the philosophy and policy context for child protection programs and describing the nature and extent of child abuse and neglect in the United States, the author addresses the purposes of these. Finally, information on the effectiveness of CPS programs is provided followed by a brief summary of CPS reforms being implemented across the United States.

Risk Assessment

In their chapter on child and adolescent risk assessment, Shlonsky and Gambrill remind the reader that child welfare staff members make many decisions about child safety based on judgments. Life-changing decisions are made in a context of uncertainty. Caseworkers must distinguish between child neglect, poor parenting, and the effects of poverty, and they must do this without the aid of accurate assessment tools. One such judgment concerns risk assessment. The child welfare professional must ask him- or herself a series of questions that will lead to a reasoned assessment of risk, among them being: Will this parent abuse or reabuse his or her child in the near future? What is the probability that she or he will do so? Risk assessment requires the integration of various kinds of data (e.g., self-report, observation, agency protocol) that differ in their accuracy, complexity, and subsequent value when making key decisions. Risk assessment is subject to a host of errors, including overestimating or underestimating the true probability of risk to a child. Such errors may result in failing to protect children from harm or imposing unneeded services that increase rather than decrease risk, such as unwarranted placement of the children in foster care. Efforts to improve decisionmaking in child welfare have typically focused on the development of risk assessment tools. Although sometimes a flawed process, steps must be taken to protect children from abuse while maximizing the decisionmaking freedom of parents.

Family Preservation: Both a Goal and a Form of Service

When children have suffered maltreatment or lack of protection at the hands of their families, a common emotional and professional response has been to remove the children from harm's way, separating children and their parents and/or siblings. For many years, this had been the first response, with the number of children and youth placed into alternative or foster homes growing throughout the 1970s. Berry, in her chapter on family preservation, reminds readers that "family preservation" is a widely used term in services to children and families, and it represents both a goal of services (preserving the connection between children and their parents and extended family), and also a specific form of services, often called "intensive family preservation services" (IFPS). The distinction between the goal of family preservation and the specific means by which to achieve it is an important one; agencies and practitioners can agree on the goal while employing different methods to achieve the preservation of family relationships.

Family preservation services, notes Berry, should not be confused with family support services, but often are. Family support programs (addressed in the well-being section of this volume) are typically less intensive and more widely available to a range of families in need. Families do not have to be experiencing substantiated child maltreatment to access family support services; they are generally available to all who seek them. Family preservation services, in contrast, are provided to families that are involved in the public child welfare system for substantiated child maltreatment. Such families are usually mandated to participate in these services or lose their children to foster care.

Berry's chapter discusses the evolution of family preservation and presents the basic tenets and components of family preservation service models. After descriptions of two major service models, the chapter provides detail about promising approaches that are empirically supported. Special attention is also given to the assumptions and values underlying the goal of family preservation and method of working with families. The chapter concludes with a discussion of the values, skills, and training that are helpful for those seeking to work to preserve families at risk of disintegration.

Substance Abuse

Maltreatment is rarely the only issue for families that enter into the child welfare system. Substance abuse and other addictions, serious physical or mental illness, domestic violence, and HIV/AIDS are often critical factors. Poverty is pervasive, and inadequate or unsafe housing are also significant problems. These serious dif-

ficulties can result in extremely complex family situations that need multiple and coordinated services.

In her chapter on substance abuse issues in the family, Fenster estimated that 9% (six million) of American children live with a substance-abusing parent (Office of Applied Studies 2003). Fenster's chapter focuses on the impact of alcohol and other drug (AOD) abuse on four subpopulations within the family: (1) AOD-abusing parents, (2) pregnant AOD-addicted mothers and their offspring, (3) children of AOD-abusing parents, and (4) adolescent AOD abusers. For each group, demographic patterns and risk factors are outlined and where applicable, protective factors and child welfare policy related to substance abuse are summarized. Fenster uses a case example to provide readers with assessment guidelines and treatment strategies and reviews innovative programs. Ethical issues that may arise when working with substance abuse in the family are also considered.

Numerous studies show that drug abuse is common among families coming to the attention of the child welfare system. Maluccio and Ainsworth's chapter offers a different focus on substance abuse issues, as they discuss family reunification practice with parents who abuse drugs. Citing a survey by the Child Welfare League of America (1998) that found that at least 50% of substantiated child maltreatment reports involved parental abuse of alcohol or other drugs, the authors note that children from families with parents who abuse drugs are almost three times more likely to be physically or sexually assaulted and four times more likely to be neglected than are children from non-substance-abusing families (National Center on Addictions and Substance Abuse at Columbia University 1998).

Domestic Violence

The overlap of domestic violence with child abuse and the concern about the impact of domestic violence on the lives of children are not new concerns. Over the past 25 years, researchers, child advocates, battered women advocates, and policymakers have grappled with how best to keep families safe while protecting the adult and child victims of violence. Unanswered questions surround who should be held accountable for the exposure to domestic violence—the mother, the usual caregiver, who is unable to protect her children; or the father, most often the abuser of the mother but frequently an invisible member of a child welfare case plan (Edleson 1998). How should child welfare systems respond to families with domestic violence? Does exposure to domestic violence indicate child maltreatment? Does the role of child welfare systems include removing children for their own protection and to break the cycle of violence?

In her chapter on this topic, Postmus discusses the answers to these questions by reviewing the research, including studies concerning the number of children impacted by domestic violence and the consequences faced when children are exposed. She follows with a discussion of the philosophical challenges facing the child welfare system and domestic violence service providers, along with the barriers and assumptions encountered when attempting to address these challenges. A brief description of state and local initiatives is also presented, along with some practical guidelines for screening, assessing, and intervening with children from families with domestic violence. The chapter concludes with practice, policy, and research implications for addressing this complex problem when children are exposed to domestic violence.

Practice Issues

Throughout this section, a number of practice issues relevant to the protection of children are identified. ASFA emphasizes the importance of maintaining children and youth safely in their own homes. Among the practice activities in relation to child/youth safety is the development and implementation of a plan that insures safety. Child/youth safety must be the first con-

sideration during planning and implementation of services (while the child/youth remains in the home or during the processes of selection of placement resources, arranging visits, reunification, and termination of services). Another critical task aimed at insuring the safety of the child or youth in placement is the completion of substitute caregiver criminal background checks, the review of licensing or certification files, and the assessment of the physical environment.

Because parents must demonstrate safe parenting before a child or youth may be reunified, parental compliance with the plan for services alone is not sufficient to justify reunification. Practitioners must assess whether sufficient changes have taken place in the problems that contributed to the child's placement to insure that the child can safely return home.

One of the challenges of child welfare practice is the integration of family-centered practice with protective authority. An important factor in achieving this balance is the involvement of children, youth, and parents or other primary caregivers, including fathers and paternal resources, in all aspects of planning and implementation to the degree that they are able and to the extent permitted by any outstanding orders of the court. The use of family resources (including extended family, fictive kin, and paternal resources) should first be considered when creating a safety plan, and the use of family preservation practices should be considered when appropriate to safely maintain a child or youth in his or her own home. Community members—such as neighbors and community groups—should also be considered as resources, whereas agency intervention—such as out-of-home placement—should be the last option.

It is critical that practitioners clarify what is and is not negotiable about the case plan and family overall involvement with the child welfare system (e.g., court orders, safety considerations). Options and alternatives should be considered with the family should reunification not appear immediately possible (e.g., voluntary surrender, directed consent, kinship care, guardianship). In every phase of services, safety planning is a priority; safety planning is not a one-time activity that occurs and can then be forgotten.

REFERENCES

Adoption and Safe Families Act. (1997). P.L. 105-89.

Child Welfare League of America. (1998). *Alcohol and other drug survey of state child welfare agencies.* Washington, DC: Child Welfare League of America.

DePanfilis, D., & Salus, M. (2003). *Child Protective Services: A guide for caseworkers.* Washington, DC: U.S. Department of Health and Human Services.

Edleson, J. L. (1998). Responsible mothers and invisible men. *Journal of Interpersonal Violence, 13*(2), 294–298.

National Center on Addiction and Substance Abuse at Columbia University. (1998). *No safe haven: Children of substance-abusing parents.* New York: Columbia University.

Office of Applied Studies. (2003). *Children living with substance-abusing or substance-dependent parents.* Rockville, MD: Substance Abuse and Mental Health Services Administration. Retrieved June 30, 2003, from www.DrugAbuseStatistics.samhsa.gov.

U.S. Department of Health and Human Services. (2000). *Rethinking child welfare practice under the Adoption and Safe Families Act of 1997.* Washington, DC: U.S. Government Printing Office.

Waldfogel, J. (1998). Rethinking the paradigm for child protection. Protecting Children from abuse and neglect. *The Future of Children, 8*(1), 104–119.

NEIL B. GUTERMAN
CATHERINE A. TAYLOR

Prevention of Physical Child Abuse and Neglect

The physical abuse and neglect of children pose a grave threat to their overall health and well-being, with both immediate and longer-term biological, psychological, and social consequences. The presence of child abuse and neglect constitutes the primary reason that most children encounter the child welfare services system in the United States. As traditionally constituted, child protective services (CPS) aim to protect children who have been identified as abused or neglected. However, a more recent and growing movement in the United States is represented by strategies and programs that aim to prevent child abuse before it has the chance to occur, and thereby attempt to avert the frequently damaging consequences of such maltreatment for children, their families, and the wider social fabric. In this chapter, we examine physical child abuse and neglect and its prevention, the rationale and support for prevention, and some of the present challenges and dilemmas facing the field of prevention as it advances. We maintain a specific focus on the interrelated problems of physical abuse and neglect, involved in approximately 80% of child maltreatment cases reported to CPS systems in the United States (U.S. Department of Health and Human Services 2003); we do not address the important problems of child sexual abuse or emotional abuse/neglect.

Physical Abuse and Neglect: A Threat to Child Health and Development

Although the effects of maltreatment may vary according to the child's age, the nature of the maltreatment, available supports and resources for the child and family, and other ongoing environmental stressors, an array of developmental consequences have been consistently linked with exposure to child abuse and neglect. Medical consequences of physical child maltreatment may include physical injuries, such as traumatic brain injury, retinal hemorrhages, burns, bone fractures, neurological damage, and delayed physical growth (Bonnier, Nassogne, & Evrard 1995; Drotar 1992; Dykes 1986; Lancon, Haines, & Parent 1998; Lewis 1992; Libby, Sills, Thurston, & Orton 2003; Money 1977; Perry & Pollard 1997; Perry, Pollard, Blakley, Baker, & Vigilante 1995). Children who are the victims of physical abuse and/or neglect are also at increased risk for having cognitive and language deficits (Allen & Oliver 1982; Allen & Wasserman 1985; Azar, Barnes, & Twentyman 1988; Cicchetti & Beeghly 1987; Fantuzzo 1990; Hoffmanplotkin & Twentyman 1984; Kolko 1992; Perry, Doran, & Wells 1983), as well as a host of emotional problems, including increased anxiety, depression, post-traumatic stress, low self-esteem, suicidal ideation and behavior, and problems with self-regulation of emotions (Allen & Tarnowski 1989; Cicchetti & Lynch 1993; Diaz, Simantov, & Rickert 2002; Dykman 1997; Gaensbauer & Mrazek 1981; Kazdin, Moser, Colbus, & Bell 1985; Lansford et al. 2002; Oates, Forrest, & Peacock 1985; Shields, Cicchetti, & Ryan 1994; Silverman, Reinherz, & Giaconia 1996). Abused or neglected children are also at heightened risk for developing multiple sociobehavioral problems, including difficulties with social relationships and developing trust and attachments (Carlson, Cicchetti, Barnett, & Braunwald 1989; Cohn 1979; Dodge, Pettit, & Bates 1994; Egeland & Sroufe 1981; Kaufman & Cicchetti 1989; Kinard 1979; Lansford et al. 2002; Main 1986), increased aggression, and externalizing behavior. Later in life abused and neglected children face increased chances of involvement in criminal activities (Aber, Allen, Carlson, & Cicchetti 1990; Cummings, Hennessey, Rabideau, & Cicchetti 1994; Dykman et al. 1997; Hoffmanplotkin & Twentyman 1984; Lansford et al. 2002; Maxfield & Widom 1996; Polansky, Chalmers, Buttenwieser, & Williams 1981; Salzinger, Kaplan, Pelcovitz, Samit, & Krieger 1984; Widom & Maxfield 2001) and substance and/or alcohol abuse (Diaz, Simantov, & Rickert 2002; Malinosky-Rummell & Hansen 1993; Widom & White 1997).

Unfortunately, the consequences of physical abuse and neglect are likely to be most devastating for the youngest victims. In addition to facing heightened risk for fatality (e.g., see U.S. Department of Health and Human Services 2004), very young children who are maltreated are at inordinate risk for nonorganic failure to thrive, shaken baby syndrome, mental retardation, impaired growth and dwarfism, brain injuries, blindness, or severe injuries to other parts of the body (Frank, Zimmerman, & Leeds 1985; Mrazek 1993; National Research Council 1993). A variety of neurological sequelae that may have profound implications for later life have been increasingly documented as consequences of physical child maltreatment, including brain contusions, intracranial hemorrhages, brain atrophy, and alterations in the development of the limbic system of the brain linked with memory, emotions, and basic drives (Cheah, Kasim, Shafie, & Khoo 1994; Frank, Zimmerman, & Leeds 1985; Ito, Teicher, Glod, & Harper 1993; Teicher, Ito, Glod, Schiffer, & Gelbard 1996). Given the broad array of consequences associated with childhood physical abuse and neglect, it is not surprising that such experiences increasingly appear to form one of

the central taproots for some of the most intractable social and adult mental health problems facing the American public, including violence and crime, substance and alcohol abuse, and depression (National Research Council 1993).

Although there remains a lack of consensus concerning what precisely constitutes an incident of physical child abuse and neglect, given variations in legal, practical, scholarly, and contextually informed points of view, practitioners and scholars most often adopt as a working definition those acts of commission or omission by parents or responsible caregivers that result in or pose substantial risk of injury or harm to a child (DePanfilis & Salus 1992; Dubowitz & Guterman, in press). Drawing from such a definition, the problem of physical child abuse and neglect is extensive. Having so far reviewed the substantial risks that maltreatment poses to children, in the remainder of this chapter, we focus on the incidence of the problem, its etiology, and emerging prevention efforts that appear most promising (home visitation, social support services, and universal efforts), as well as challenges and dilemmas that need to be addressed as the prevention field advances.

Incidence of Physical Child Abuse and Neglect

The problem of physical child abuse and neglect has remained a remarkably persistent one in the United States. Indeed, from the 1960s onward, reported incidents of child maltreatment continued to climb sharply upward until just the past several years, when reports of child maltreatment appear to have leveled off. Although part of the rapid increase was likely due to increased public awareness and motivation to identify the problem to authorities, it is also likely that these numbers reflected an actual increase in the problem of physical child abuse and neglect in the United States over the past several decades (see Guterman 2001a). For every 1,000 children in the United States, about 36 are reported as victims of maltreatment to protective services each year (U.S. Department of Health and Human Services 2004).

Although a variety of child maltreatment forms are reported to the nation's CPS system, cases of neglect (61%) and physical abuse (19%) constitute 80% of the reports made in the United States (U.S. Department of Health and Human Services 2004). Of these forms of child maltreatment, most data sources indicate that the younger the child, the higher the risk of victimization, particularly in its most severe forms. For example, nearly eight out of ten child maltreatment fatalities (76%) occur in children younger than 4 years old, and 41% of all child maltreatment related fatalities occur during the first year of life (U.S. Department of Health and Human Services 2004); moreover, infants face the highest risk of homicide during their first week of life (Paulozzi & Sells 2002).

Etiology of Physical Child Abuse and Neglect

Evidence from several decades of research has identified a wide array of factors that appear to contribute to the likelihood that a child will be physically abused and/or neglected, and therefore suggest a variety of pathways for prevention. These factors have commonly been organized according to a multileveled rubric, often using what has been termed an "ecological" or "ecological developmental" framework (e.g., Belsky 1980; Cicchetti & Lynch 1993; Garbarino 1977). This framework highlights that physically abusive and/or neglectful behavior derives from the complex set of transactions within and between:

- The microsystem representing the parent, child, and their interactions;
- The meso- and exosystems in which the parent-child dyad are embedded, including the settings, networks of relationships, and institutions in which the parent and child socialize and are sustained; and

- The macrosystem made up of overarching social structural elements within which the meso- and exosystems are themselves lodged (Badr 2001; Belsky 1980; Bronfenbrenner 1977; Garbarino 1977, 1980).

Although it is beyond the scope of this chapter to comprehensively present the known etiological findings related to physical child abuse and neglect, we do highlight some of the clearest themes in the existing etiological research. For a more in-depth discussion of the etiology of physical child abuse and neglect, see National Research Council (1993), Guterman (2001a,b), and Trickett and Schellenbach (1998).

In the parent-child microsystem, the primary attachments that parents have formed during childhood in their own families of origin appears as a key etiological factor, particularly the degree to which parents themselves experienced abuse or neglect (e.g., Egeland, Jacovitz, & Sroufe 1988; George 1996; Widom 1989; Zuravin, McMillen, DePanfilis, & Risley-Curtiss 1996). Although little evidence supports the popular assumption that the presence of parental mental illness, in a general sense, is associated with maltreatment risk, several specific problematic aspects of parents' socio-emotional functioning have been linked with physical maltreatment risk. Parents at risk of physical abuse and neglect often exhibit depression and low self-esteem (e.g., Chaffin, Kelleher, & Hollenberg 1996; Christensen, Brayden, Dietrich, & McLaughlin 1994; Culp, Culp, Soulis, & Letts 1989; Ethier, Lacharite, & Couture 1995; Kotch, Browne, Ringwalt, & Stewart 1995; Nair et al. 1997). Problems with the abuse of alcohol or other psychoactive substances have also been specifically linked with maltreatment risk (Chaffin, Kelleher, & Hollenberg 1996; U.S. Department of Health and Human Services 1999), especially during the early childhood years. For example, children 4 years of age or younger are the victims in approximately half of all substantiated cases of child maltreatment involving substance or alcohol abuse (National Center on Child Abuse and Neglect 1993). Maltreating parents have often been observed to have specific deficits in social coping skills, including a hyper-responsivity to child-related stimuli and deficits in interpreting and responding to social cues (e.g., Milner & Crouch 1998; Pruitt & Erickson 1985). Maltreating parents often also report feeling "out of control" in their lives and frequently hold an external locus of control orientation (Ellis & Milner 1981; Gynn-Orenstein 1981; Nurius, Lovell, & Maggie 1988; Stringer & Lagreca 1985; Wiehe 1992).

Work by Bugental and colleagues (Bugental, Blue, & Cruzcosa 1989; Bugental, Lyon, Lin, McGrath, & Bimbela 1999) and Patterson and colleagues (Patterson 1982; Reid 1989) has demonstrated that abusive or neglectful parent-child interactions can, in part, be understood as resulting from a cyclical pattern in which a child's behavior is perceived as difficult or stressful by a parent and responded to in a coercive or insecure fashion, provoking still further difficult or stressful behaviors from the child, promoting a potential downward cyclical spiral toward abusive parental behaviors. In addition (and consistent with the learned helplessness theory of Seligman 1975), parents may respond to child behaviors perceived as difficult or stressful by withdrawing, becoming depressed, and showing decreased responsiveness and sensitivity to their children's cues (e.g., Donovan, Leavitt, & Walsh 1998; Murray, Fiori-Crowley, Hooper, & Cooper 1996). It has been shown that children responded to in such ways tend to display dysregulated behavioral patterns through excessively demanding behaviors, excessive crying, or by exhibiting their own depressive behavior patterns (Cox, Puckering, Pound, & Mills 1987; Field 1992, 1998). Such dyadic interaction processes may spiral downward over time into neglectful parenting behaviors. Importantly, findings by Field (1998) indicate that a dyadic depressive, potentially neglectful interaction may be linked with the

presence of biochemical substrates, which may appear at birth or even in utero.

Beyond stressful interactions with their children, parents at risk for abuse and neglect face an array of life stressors both within the family and in the mesosystem in which parent-child interactions are embedded (e.g., Browne 1988; Hillson & Kupier 1994; Kolko, Kazdin, Thomas, & Day 1993; Kotch, Browne, Dufort, & Winsor 1999; Nair, Schuler, Blacka, Kettinger, & Harrington 2003; Rodriguez & Green 1997). Studies have documented that such parental stressors as material deprivation, unemployment, low educational attainment, and multiple life events or geographic moves are associated with heightened risk for child maltreatment (e.g., Chan 1994; Justice & Justice 1985; Murphey & Braner 2000; Straus & Kantor 1987).

Given that more than twice as many female-headed as male-headed single parent households live below the poverty line (34% vs. 16%), the role of fathers in child maltreatment is an important factor (Fields & Casper 2001). Higher maltreatment rates are common in single-parent, female-headed homes, likely due to multiple mechanisms, such as fewer emotional and economic resources for the mother (e.g., Gelles 1989; Giovannoni & Billingsley 1970; Seagull 1987). Furthermore, fathers and male partners, when present, are highly over-represented as perpetrators in cases of severe and even fatal child abuse (Brewster et al. 1998; Krugman 1985; Margolin 1992). A growing body of evidence indicates that, in particular, fathers suffering such economic hardships as unemployment and those who abuse alcohol and other substances are more likely to abuse their children (Ammerman, Kolko, Kirisci, Blackson, & Dawes 1999; Jones 1990). Furthermore, the quality of the relationship between the mother and her partner can play an important role in parent-child relationships (c.f. Belsky 1979; Brunelli, Wasserman, Rauh, Alvarado, & Caraballo 1995).

Although a positive relationship between parents may serve as a buffer against abuse and neglect, a negative or unsupportive one may heighten risk. The presence of domestic violence between partners can be particularly foreboding. Domestic violence co-occurs at high rates with physical child abuse and neglect, especially in its most severe forms. Studies of children suspected of being maltreated who were seen in hospital settings have reported that between 45% and 59% of mothers showed evidence of being battered by their partners (MacLeod & Nelson 2000; McKibben, De Vos, & Newberger 1991; Stark & Flitcraft 1988), and domestic violence has been shown to be present in more than 40% of child maltreatment fatalities (Child Fatality Review Panel 1993; Felix & McCarthy 1995; Oregon Children's Services Division, 1993). Perhaps most importantly, a study of more than 2,500 at-risk mothers involved in a home visiting program found that not only does domestic violence often co-occur with child maltreatment, but it also frequently predates it, raising the odds of child abuse within the family by three-fold (McGuigan & Pratt 2001). Thus domestic violence appears to be a potent predictor of child maltreatment.

Just as parental relationships may have a positive or negative impact on risk for abuse and neglect, so may the broader social networks and characteristics of the communities in which families live. In particular, social networks may alter the relationship between parents' perceived stresses (e.g., those that are socioeconomically derived) and their parenting behaviors. Research spanning three decades has consistently discerned important links between problematic aspects of families' social networks and heightened child maltreatment risk (e.g., Adamakos et al. 1986; Chan 1994; Coohey 1996; Gaudin, Polansky, Kilpatrick, & Shilton 1993; Gracia & Musitu 2003; Salzinger, Kaplan, & Artemyeff 1983; Straus & Smith 1992). Studies have tended to report that, compared with nonmaltreating families, maltreat-

ing families have smaller, less dense social networks with whom they carry out less contact and reciprocal exchanges (e.g., Course, Schmidt, & Trickett 1990; Crittenden 1985; Elmer 1967; Kotelchuck 1982; Lovell 1988; Salzinger et al. 1983; Young 1964). It has also been reported that maltreatment risk is higher for families living in community settings characterized by a lack of cohesion and in which community life is unstable, disorganized, and highly violent (Coulton, Korbin, Su, & Chow 1995; Korbin 1994; Osofsky, Wewers, Hann, & Fick 1993; Richters & Martinez 1993).

One of the central stressors identified in maltreatment risk is that of family poverty. Studies have found that families reported to child protective service systems are more likely to have single mothers, unemployed fathers, receive public assistance, and/or live in poor neighborhoods (e.g., Ards 1989; Coulton, Korbin, Su, & Chow 1995; Drake & Pandey 1996; Hampton & Newberger 1985; Lindsey 1994; Zuravin 1989). As summarized by Pelton (1994:166–167), "there is overwhelming and remarkably consistent evidence . . . that poverty and low income are strongly related to child abuse and neglect and to the severity of child maltreatment." However, the vast majority of impoverished families are never identified as maltreating (e.g., Sedlack & Broadhurst 1996). Although economic impoverishment is one of the most consistently observed predictors of physical child abuse and neglect, it must be considered in combination with other risk and protective factors that may modify the risk (c.f. Sameroff & Gutman 2004).

Finally, although a highly complex issue, cultural influences have been considered for some time as factors that may protect against or shape the risk for child maltreatment. The role of culture has most frequently been considered as the means by which cultural messages convey norms of parenting behavior, along with sanctions and allowances for a variety of parenting practices (Finkelhor & Korbin 1988; Korbin 1987, 1994). Wide variation has been noted across cultural contexts regarding culturally accepted and normative supervisory arrangements, the number and nature of caregivers, and disciplinary and indigenous medical practices employed with children (e.g., Fischler 1985; Korbin 1994; Ritchie & Ritchie 1981). Corporal punishment that may appear to be physical abuse in some cultural contexts may be wholly acceptable and defined as normative in other contexts (Solheim 1982). Given this variation, what may be accepted as normative child rearing patterns in a specific cultural context may be misconstrued across cultural boundaries as child maltreatment, especially in situations in which professionals must enact child protection laws and policies derived from a majority cultural value system (e.g., Gray & Cosgrove 1985). It has been argued that these reasons provide a partial explanation for an overrepresentation of minority group families in studies using official CPS data (e.g., Jason, Amereuh, Marks, & Tyler 1982; Lauderdale, Valiunas, & Anderson 1980; Spearly & Lauderdale 1983). Although a great many questions still remain unanswered in our understanding of the many dynamics that influence and lead to physical child abuse and neglect, we nonetheless have developed a substantial body of knowledge that can be drawn from when considering efforts to prevent and treat physical child abuse and neglect.

Emerging Interventions in Child Abuse Prevention

Organized efforts to address the problem of physical child abuse and neglect have been identifiable for more than a century in the United States; however, it was not until the latter half of the twentieth century that professionalized and clinical intervention was initiated to address the problem. The "discovery" of the battered child syndrome in the 1950s and early 1960s has long been credited with the initiation of a national movement that spurred the development of federal and state policies, programs, and clinical interventions aimed at

preventing and treating the problem of child maltreatment in the United States (see Lindsey 1994). During this time, the nation's CPS system was established and institutionalized, and several major policy initiatives established a legal and programmatic framework in which the problem of child maltreatment is presently addressed. However, it is only in the past two decades that efforts to prevent child abuse have become prominent.

Home Visitation Services

The dominant preventive service strategy employed across a wide variety of communities in the United States is the home visitation approach. Home visitation services typically identify families through a universal service system, most frequently via the healthcare system, at the point of birth of a child, or even before. Once identified and determined to face some future risk of physical child abuse and/or neglect (either by demographic means or individual psychosocial screening), families are voluntarily offered the services of a home visitor, who travels to the home to provide parenting guidance and case management services to link up families with necessary supports and resources. Home visitors often provide parenting guidance from structured parenting curricula and can address a range of topics with parents, such as learning how to breastfeed, responding to their baby's crying, and coping skills during the stressful postnatal period and first years of the child's life. Although home visitation programs vary across program models, personnel employed, and communities in which they are anchored, all aim to foster the parent-child attachment and mobilize supports for the parent during the highly vulnerable and sensitive perinatal period and shortly after. The programs typically provide for weekly home visits in the early months, and often taper off after 2 or more years.

Several broad historical developments have been credited for the recent growth of early home visitation services specifically concerned with the problem of child abuse and neglect. These include deinstitutionalization in children's services, in acknowledgment of the detrimental effects of separating children from their parents and of the benefits of supporting the parent-child attachment (e.g., Bowlby 1951; Goldfarb 1945; Spitz 1945; Yarrow 1961). Accompanying this was an increasing scholarly emphasis on attachment theory (Bowlby 1969) and an ecological model of child development and maltreatment (Belsky 1980; Bronfenbrenner 1977; Garbarino 1977), which provided the initial intellectual underpinning for early intervention services provided in the home.

In the context of these developments, Kempe (1976) first proposed and later tested a "health visitor" program in the United States as a preventive measure specifically for the problem of child abuse and neglect. Kempe was well aware of promising findings reported in allied early intervention studies and the increasing emphasis on the parent-infant bonding process. At the same time, he recognized that the most families at risk were accessible before maltreatment took place via healthcare settings at the point of birth or during prenatal medical visits. Gray, Cutler, Dean, and Kempe (1979) first studied in a controlled fashion early home visitation aimed at reducing future maltreatment risk and reported hopeful findings linked with a possible reduction of severity of maltreatment related injuries, although their overall findings were not reported as statistically significant.

Hawaii's Healthy Start program. Influenced by the findings of Gray, Kempe, and colleagues, Calvin Sia, a pediatrician and member of Hawaii's CPS advisory committee, invited Kempe to plan child abuse prevention activities for families in Hawaii. Dr. Sia and the director of the Family Stress Center, Gail Breakey, obtained a grant from the National Center for Prevention and Treatment of Child Abuse and Neglect to implement a pilot home visitation program developed by Kempe and a CPS advisory committee in 1975 (Breakey & Pratt

1991; Earle 1995). In 1985, Healthy Start began as a state-funded demonstration program in Oahu serving a high-risk population. Hawaii's Healthy Start model was explicitly developed with the aim of preventing child abuse and neglect by achieving the following interrelated goals: (1) improving family coping, (2) promoting positive parenting, (3) facilitating parent-child attachment, (4) promoting optimal child development, and (5) improving the use of community resources, particularly ongoing access to a "medical home" for the family (Breakey & Pratt 1991; Daro, McCurdy, & Harding 1998). The program has drawn its theoretical basis from the work of Helfer (1987) and Fraiberg (1980) and from social learning theory (Bandura 1986), emphasizing the need to "reparent the parent" to break the cycle of abuse and neglect.

A glowing informal evaluation conducted after 3 years of services received great national attention, reporting that "not a single case of abuse among the project's 241 high-risk families had been reported [to CPS] since the demonstration began" (Breakey & Pratt 1991: 18:122). Several more carefully controlled examinations of the model have since been reported (Duggan et al. 1999, 2004). Although continuing to show promise, these evaluations have also reported less glowing findings than did the initial evaluation, allowing researchers to examine aspects of the program that may need to be extended or modified (Daro & Harding 1999). Findings from a randomized trial have prompted more careful consideration of the engagement and retention process, given that 50% of families across sites dropped out of the program within the first year (Duggan et al. 1999). The Hawaiian program now also provides ongoing support until the child reaches 3 or 4 years of age rather than the original prototype program, which served families until the child reached kindergarten (Windham 1998). Nonetheless, the model presently continues to enjoy perhaps the widest emulation of any early home visitation program specifically targeting child maltreatment in the United States.

Initiation of Healthy Families America. Aware of the growing evidence base in home visitation services, the U.S. Advisory Board on Child Abuse and Neglect issued a report in 1991 recommending "the replacement of the existing child protection system with a new, national, child-centered, neighborhood-based child protection strategy." Within this approach, the board singled out as its most important recommendation the immediate phasing in of "universal voluntary neonatal home visitation system" of services (U.S. Advisory Board on Child Abuse and Neglect 1991:ix, xlvii). All 15 board members unanimously supported this recommendation, as home visitation services were viewed as one of the most hopeful strategies to stem the tide of maltreatment. The advisory board (1991:xlvii) emphasized that "complex problems like child maltreatment do not have simple solutions. While *not a panacea,* the board believes that *no other single intervention* has the promise that home visitation has" (emphasis in original). Such a recommendation served to undergird perhaps the largest-scale efforts at advancing early home visitation services designed to prevent maltreatment across the United States.

On the heels of the advisory board's recommendation, Prevent Child Abuse America (PCA America; formerly the National Committee to Prevent Child Abuse) launched a national initiative to promote the development of early home visitation programs in communities across the United States. PCA America found the Hawaiian Healthy Start program a fitting model from which to advance this development. The Healthy Start model had been the most comprehensively disseminated program at the statewide level, proving to be an approach that could be scaled up: expanding from a program to a statewide system of services. Furthermore, the Healthy Start model matched PCA America's view that child abuse stems from a complex and diverse set of causes, and thus the ideal programmatic approach would be one that served to build on and coordinate existing community supports and services, individualizing services in ways that matched the unique needs of the family. The Healthy Start model was viewed as a linchpin program around which other community-based family supports could be orchestrated at the case level (Daro & Harding 1999; Daro & Winje 1998; Mitchel & Cohn-Donnelly 1993). The initiative was launched in January 1992 and rapidly expanded from the initial dozen new sites per year to more than 70 new sites per year in 1995 and 1996 (Daro & Winje 1998). By 2002, more than 450 programs linked with the Healthy Families America initiative were identified as in operation, representing almost a forty-fold increase in the number of programs in just 10 years (Daro & Winje 1998; Prevent Child Abuse America 1999, 2002).

Nurse Home Visitation program. For the past 25 years, in parallel with the abovementioned program developments, Olds and colleagues have been studying and developing the Nurse Home Visitation program (earlier dubbed the "Prenatal/Early Infancy project"), a program that has proved to be a milestone in the advancement of early home visitation services in the United States (Olds 1982; Olds, Henderson, Chamberlin, & Tatelbaum 1986; Olds, Henderson, Tatelbaum, & Chamberlin 1986). The Nurse Home Visitation program was designed to address broad areas of maternal and child development, specifically to improve the outcomes of pregnancy, the quality of maternal caregiving, child health and development, and maternal life course development (Kitzman et al. 1997; Olds et al. 1997). Guided by research and grounded in theories of human ecology (Bronfenbrenner 1979), human attachment (Bowlby 1969), and self-efficacy (Bandura 1977), the program has been refined over 20 years with detailed visit-by-visit protocols developed to guide nurse home visitors. Randomized clinical trials of the program have been conducted in Elmira, New York; Memphis, Tennessee; and Denver, Colorado with a specific focus on primiparous, low-income mothers (Olds 2002).

The initial evaluation study, conducted in Elmira between 1978 and 1982, reported a select but broad array of positive outcomes in the domains of pregnancy (e.g., increased birthweight, decreased maternal smoking), child development (e.g., infants' cognitive development in smoking mothers), and maternal life course (e.g., fewer subsequent pregnancies, fewer months on welfare) (Olds, Henderson, Tatelbaum, & Chamberlin 1986; Olds et al., 1999). And especially promising for maltreatment prevention, during the first 2 years of life, only one case of low-income unmarried teen mothers who received nurse home visitation was substantiated for maltreatment (4%), compared to eight cases of low-income unmarried teens not receiving home visitation (19%) (Olds, Henderson, Chamberlin, & Tatelbaum 1986). In addition, the infants of women visited by nurses were seen in the hospital emergency room fewer times than those of controls, and low-income teens who were nurse-visited punished and restricted their children less frequently and provided their children with a larger number of appropriate play materials (Olds, Henderson, Chamberlin, & Tatelbaum 1986). Because of the careful research design executed in the Elmira trial, the positive outcomes of Nurse Home Visitation program were touted as the first hard evidence that early home visitation services, if designed and implemented appropriately, could indeed reduce child maltreatment risk before-the-fact.

As the outcomes in the Elmira trial were reported on a sample of largely white mothers in a semirural setting, Olds and colleagues sought to replicate the study and its findings in a sample of primarily African American women in Memphis. Although this study did not report protective service data and the gains observed were on the whole less comprehensive than those attained in the Elmira study, the Memphis trial demonstrated that home-visited families had fewer and less severe child hospitalizations, improved child rearing attitudes, and more supportive home environments for the children's development (Kitzman et al. 1997). These findings have importance because they demonstrate that the Nurse Home Visitation program's effects are potentially transferable to other community contexts.

Perhaps most exciting are the follow-up studies from the original Elmira trial that have documented positive outcomes of the program 15 years after its implementation. At this follow-up, home-visited unmarried low socioeconomic status mothers had fewer subsequent births that were spaced further apart, were on public assistance for a shorter length of time, reported fewer problems with substance or alcohol abuse, and had less criminal involvement than did control group mothers (Olds et al. 1997). In addition, the children of these mothers, compared with those from the control group, had significantly fewer incidents of running away, arrests, and criminal convictions; they were more likely to have lifetime sex partners and were less likely to be involved in drugs and smoking (Olds et al. 1998), behaviors often associated with a history of child maltreatment. Further work has also demonstrated that home visits can moderate the established link between child maltreatment and the early onset of such problematic behaviors, as no such association was present for those children from home-visited families, ostensibly because the frequency of maltreatment had been reduced due to the program (Eckenrode et al. 2001). Such significant findings 15 years after the initiation of perinatal home visitation services continue to be pivotal in propelling early home visitation forward as a hopeful solution to the problem of child maltreatment and its consequences.

In a comprehensive review of the broadening field of home visitation services to prevent child maltreatment, the Centers for Disease Control and Prevention's Task Force on Community Preventive Services (Hahn et al. 2003:5,7) found "strong evidence of effectiveness" for home visitation services in preventing child maltreatment, with a median reduction in child abuse or neglect of 40%, and suggested that their report could be used to "support, expand, and improve existing home visitation programs, and to initiate new ones." With the promise of home visiting services firmly established, various types of enhancements to such services are now also being examined for their effectiveness. The addition of a cognitive appraisal component to home visiting services, for example, aimed at altering perceptions of parental competence, has been associated with a significantly lowered occurrence of physical child abuse (Bugental et al. 2002). Social support group enhancements to home visitation have also shown promise, as discussed in the next section.

Social Support Interventions
Home visiting interventions, although promising, are also, by design, limited in their capacity to address some of the more potent etiological influences identified in physical child abuse and neglect, particularly those derived from socioecological stresses. Several social support intervention models have received preliminary support in addressing some of these broader contextual challenges by helping at-risk parents overcome social isolation and more effectively tap informal support networks for material, emotional, and informational support. For example, after participating in a social support skills training group, pregnant and parenting teens demonstrated improvements in social skills and social supports (Barth & Schinke 1984; Schinke, Schilling, Barth, Gilchrist, & Maxwell 1986). Likewise, the Social Network Intervention project (SNIP) engaged parents at risk of child neglect in social skills training and linked them with mutual aid groups and neighborhood helpers. Parents receiving SNIP services reported improvements in their social

networks and in a broad range of parenting attitudes linked with child neglect (Gaudin, Wodarski, Arkinson, & Avery 1990–1991).

Group enhancements to home visitation programs have also specifically been linked with positive parenting outcomes. One such program, focused on improving parent-child attachment, was associated with greater participation in home visiting services and a trend toward improved parental perceptions regarding infants' needs (Constantino et al. 2001). Similarly, Guterman (2001a,b) has reported promising preliminary outcomes linked with parental involvement in a social networking group intervention for high-risk parents, including positive changes in parents' social networks, reported stresses, sense of control, and child behavior problems. A second pilot test of this model examined an improved and expanded version that was integrated with home visitation services. Once again, improvements were demonstrated in both the quality and quantity of mothers' social network ties, perceived family resources, and parenting stress; in addition, mothers in this second pilot also showed a decrease in child abuse potential (Guterman 2003).

Perhaps the largest-scale social support intervention in practice aiming to prevent child abuse is Parents Anonymous, a self-help group model that integrates professional clinical guidance indirectly but is run by parents who have identified themselves as at risk for abusing their children. Initially founded in 1970, Parents Anonymous groups have expanded across the United States and provide support to an estimated 100,000 parents per year (Rafael & Pion-Berlin 1999). Participants in Parents Anonymous groups set their own agendas, often addressing parenting and family communication skills, and are encouraged to be in contact with one another outside the group meetings for support and to begin to take leadership and responsibility in the group functioning. Significantly, Parents Anonymous has developed into a national movement and organization providing technical assistance and advocacy, seeking to foster changes in the policies and programming that may aid in addressing the problem of child abuse on a larger scale. As with other self-help movements in the United States, there is a paucity of carefully controlled outcome data on the effectiveness of Parents Anonymous. An initial evaluation found that participating parents self-reported changes in parenting behaviors, more appropriate child developmental expectations, and reduced incidence of child abuse (Rafael & Pion-Berlin 1999). Recently, the U.S. Office of Juvenile Justice and Delinquency Prevention initiated an effort to study Parents Anonymous under more carefully controlled conditions, and such findings will be instructive to the widening interest in socially supportive preventive strategies.

Universal Prevention Strategies

Universal preventive strategies addressing the problem of physical child abuse and neglect are analogous to other universal preventive health strategies, such as child immunization or water fluoridation, in that they seek to intervene with an entire population, regardless of identified risk. Universal interventions avoid the potential stigma that may accompany the targeting and associated labeling of at-risk groups. Although some efforts have been made to engage in broad-based public campaigns to prevent child maltreatment—for example, through the distribution of educational magazines for parents of infants (Laurendeau, Gagnon, Desjardins, Perreault, & Kischuk 1991) or by providing all new parents with educational materials about the risks of shaking babies (e.g., Showers 1992)—very little empirical evidence is available that sheds light on the efficacy of such universal strategies. Given the expense of such broad strategies and the high societal value in the United States on protecting individual liberties and privacy, universal prevention strategies have received less attention to date, and efforts to enact broad policies, such as "no

spanking zones" in communities, have not fared well (e.g., Wong 1999). Although far from conclusive, the available evidence for such a ban on corporal punishment, enacted in Sweden in 1979, suggests that such strategies hold the potential to substantially influence public attitudes and behaviors regarding physical abuse or neglect (e.g., Durrant 1999).

Challenges and Dilemmas in Child Abuse Prevention

Although the reviewed programs and strategies offer much hope in the prevention of child abuse and neglect, multiple challenges associated with the complexity of this issue have yet to be fully addressed. According to Daro and Donnelly (2002), the field has made such mistakes as oversimplifying the issue, ignoring crucial connections with CPS, ignoring the need to shore up political will through multiple mechanisms, sacrificing the quality of programs for increased availability of services, and overstating the promise of known solutions. Here we also emphasize several additional challenges facing the field of physical child abuse and neglect prevention.

Population Focus: Issues of Targeting and Screening

Although some prevention programs have sought to serve all families giving birth to a child within an identified healthcare system (universal strategy), the majority of programs limit services to families believed to be at higher risk for future maltreatment, in an effort to allocate resources most judiciously (targeted strategy) (Gomby 2000). Therefore, an important precursory challenge for most maltreatment prevention approaches is to first appropriately identify families that would most benefit from intervention, and then to configure the intervention to best meet their needs. Although screening and risk assessment of families appear sensible from an economic standpoint, they raise a host of complicated and problematic issues with important implications for the future of maltreatment prevention. Risk screening for maltreatment, for example, raises issues of additional costs, the potential stigma associated with being positively screened, and most troubling, the many persistent problems with the accuracy of such screens (c.f. Caldwell, Bogat, & Davidson 1988; McDonald & Marks 1991). Screening processes can also drive the nature of services delivered by determining the pool of served families and their attendant service needs (see Guterman 1999). Even though it is beyond the scope of this chapter to thoroughly examine the difficulties associated with risk screening, it is important to recognize that sound targeting strategies must be closely integrated with the services delivered. Without such integration, even the most rigorously designed and tested preventive interventions are likely to be mismatched with the population served, and therefore ineffective (see Guterman 2001a for further discussion).

Engagement and Retention in Services

Assuming that families have been appropriately targeted and matched with intervention services, a second ongoing challenge faced by early prevention strategies is how to engage and retain targeted families in services—a persistent concern, as the impact of a program is likely to be compromised for families that leave services prematurely (Gomby 2000). Fortunately, a growing body of empirical findings is providing some guidance with respect to factors that are linked with successful engagement and retention of families in such programs.

Studies have linked variability in program participation rates with multiple family, program, provider, and community characteristics. Mothers who are young, poorly educated, and with high risk at birth infants were found to have higher rates of engagement (Duggan et al. 2000), whereas those who were white and socially isolated had lower engagement rates (McGuigan, Katzev, & Pratt 2003a). In recent

studies, higher retention rates have been found for mothers who are older, nonwhite, married, unemployed, nonsmoking, who enrolled during their first or second trimester of pregnancy, and who had need for greater social support (Daro, McCurdy, Falconnier, & Stojanovic 2003; McCurdy, Gannon, & Daro 2003; McGuigan, Katzev, & Pratt 2003b; Navaie-Waliser et al. 2000); however, the role of maternal age, ethnicity, and social support status appears equivocal (Herzog, Cherniss, & Menzel 1986; Luker & Chalmers 1990; Olds & Kitzman 1993). The characteristics of the home visitor also play a role, with higher retention rates found for home visitors who are younger, African American, and who receive more supervision; programs that have lower caseloads and match participants and providers based on both parenting status and ethnicity also had higher retention rates (Daro, McCurdy, Falconnier, & Stojanovic 2003; McGuigan, Katzev, & Pratt 2003b). Finally, community-level factors have also proved significant, with lower rates of engagement and retention found for mothers in communities with lower overall health indicators and higher rates of community violence, respectively (Daro, McCurdy, Falconnier, & Stojanovic 2003; McGuigan, Katzev, & Pratt 2003a). Because the effectiveness of a program strongly depends on the engagement and retention of participants in services, factors that influence these rates should be carefully considered during program development and prior to implementation.

Implementation Challenges

Not all child abuse prevention programs are created or implemented equally. Programs may vary by the components they employ, the professionals or nonprofessionals they use, the service dosage delivered, the populations served, and the specific outcomes or mediating factors they hope to address. Controversy remains regarding the optimal service providers for home visitation programs, with some evidence suggesting that health professionals, such as nurses or mental health professionals, demonstrate more favorable outcomes over paraprofessionals, at least in shorter-term programs (Hahn et al. 2003). However, some researchers have argued that the evidence base does not yet clarify who the optimal service deliverers are or what their professional backgrounds should be (Guterman, Anisfeld, & McCord 2003).

Furthermore, evidence is beginning to accumulate that preventive strategies, such as home visiting, may work for some populations but have reduced effectiveness on others. For example, the presence of domestic violence appears to diminish the impact of the Nurse Home Visitation program, as child maltreatment reports did not differ between control and program groups when there was there was a high incidence of domestic violence in the home (Eckenrode et al. 2000). Such emerging evaluations of programs signal the need for more careful consideration of precisely what components of various programs are most successful, under what conditions, and for which populations. Only with these advances in the knowledge base will the field most likely assure that only the most effective strategies will be advanced, resulting in a greater preventive impact on a wider scale.

Conclusion

It must be recognized that although professionals have made important headway in addressing the problem of physical child abuse and neglect in the past half-century, we are presently in the early stages of establishing a rigorous knowledge base from which to guide our prevention and treatment efforts. Major gaps remain in understanding, for example, how to prevent physical abuse and neglect in substance-abusing or domestically violent families, and perhaps most troublingly, how to prevent maltreatment-related child fatalities. The field presently has highly promising knowledge about intervention models that address the problem of physical child abuse and neglect in a broad way. However, important gaps still exist in the knowledge base that might assist us to tailor intervention strategies to the specific needs of individual families and risk subgroups, whether these are families having specific mental health issues, suffering from impoverishment, or enduring social isolation. We must recognize that ongoing large-scale efforts are required in the practice arena to prevent physical abuse and neglect and to develop a systematic knowledge base that can guide our practices in sound and reliable ways.

REFERENCES

Aber, J. L., Allen, J. P., Carlson, V., & Cicchetti, D. (1990). The effects of maltreatment on development during early childhood: Recent studies and their theoretical, clinical, and policy implementations. In V. C. D. Cicchetti (ed.), *Child maltreatment: Theory and research on causes and consequences*, pp. 576–619. New York: Cambridge University Press.

Adamakos, H., Ryan, K., Ullman, D. G., Pascoe, J., Diaz, R., & Chessare, J. (1986). Maternal social support as a predictor of mother-child stress and stimulation. *Child Abuse and Neglect, 10*, 463–470.

Allen, D. M., & Tarnowski, K. J. (1989). Depressive characteristics of physically abused children. *Journal of Abnormal Child Psychology, 17*(1), 1–11.

Allen, R., & Oliver, J. M. (1982). The effects of child maltreatment on long-term development. *Child Abuse and Neglect, 6*, 299–305.

Allen, R., & Wasserman, G. A. (1985). Origins of language delay in abused infants. *Child Abuse and Neglect, 9*, 335–340.

Ammerman, R. T., Kolko, D. J., Kirisci, L., Blackson, T. C., & Dawes, M. A. (1999). Child abuse potential in parents with histories of substance use disorder. *Child Abuse and Neglect, 23*, 1225–1238.

Ards, S. (1989). Estimating local child abuse. *Evaluation Review, 13*, 484–515.

Azar, S. T., Barnes, K. T., & Twentyman, C. T. (1988). Developmental outcomes in abused children: Consequences of parental abuse or a more general breakdown in caregiver behavior? *Behavior Therapist, 11*, 27–32.

Badr, L. K. (2001). Quantitative and qualitative predictors of development for low-birth weight infants of Latino background. *Applied Nursing Research, 14*(3), 125–135.

Bandura, A. (1977). Self-efficacy: Toward a unifying theory of behavior change. *Psychological Review, 84,* 191–215.

Bandura, A. (1986). *Social foundations of thought and action: A social cognitive theory. Prentice-Hall series in social learning theory.* Englewood Cliffs, NJ: Prentice-Hall.

Barth, R. P., & Schinke, S. P. (1984). Enhancing the social supports of teenage mothers. *Social Casework—Journal of Contemporary Social Work, 65,* 523–531.

Belsky, J. (1979). Interrelation of parental and spousal behavior during infancy in traditional nuclear families—Exploratory analysis. *Journal of Marriage and the Family, 41,* 749–755.

Belsky, J. (1980). Child maltreatment: An ecological integration. *American Psychologist, 35*(4), 320–335.

Bonnier, C., Nassogne, M. C., & Evrard, P. (1995). Outcome and prognosis of whiplash shaken infant syndrome; late consequences after a symptom-free interval. *Developmental Medicine & Child Neurology, 37,* 943–956.

Bowlby, J. (1951). Maternal Care and Mental Health. Geneva: World Health Organization.

Bowlby, J. (1969). *Attachment and loss.* New York: Basic Books.

Breakey, G., & Pratt, B. (1991). Healthy growth for Hawaii's "Healthy Start": Toward a systematic statewide approach to the prevention of child abuse and neglect. *Zero to Three, 11*(4), 16–22.

Brewster, A. L., Nelson, J. P., Hymel, K. P., Colby, D. R., Lucas, D. R., et al. (1998). Victim, perpetrator, family, and incident characteristics of 32 infant maltreatment deaths in the United States Air Force. *Child Abuse and Neglect, 22,* 92–101.

Bronfenbrenner, U. (1977). *Toward an experimental ecology of human development.* Cambridge, MA: Harvard University Press.

Bronfenbrenner, U. (1979). *The ecology of human development: Experiments by nature and design.* Cambridge, MA: Harvard University Press.

Browne, D. II. (1988). The role of stress in the commission of subsequent acts of child abuse and neglect. *Early Child Development & Care, 31*(1–4), 27–33.

Brunelli, S. A., Wasserman, G. A., Rauh, V. A., Alvarado, L. E., & Caraballo, L. R. (1995). Mothers reports of paternal support—Associations with maternal child-rearing attitudes. *Merrill-Palmer Quarterly—Journal of Developmental Psychology, 41,* 152–171.

Bugental, D. B., Blue, J., & Cruzcosa, M. (1989). Perceived control over caregiving outcomes: Implications for child abuse. *Developmental Psychology, 25,* 532–539.

Bugental, D. B., Ellerson, P. C., Lin, E. K., Rainey, B., Kokotovic, A., & O'Hara, N. (2002). A cognitive approach to child abuse prevention. *Journal of Family Psychology, 16*(3), 243–258.

Bugental, D. B., Lyon, J. E., Lin, E. K., McGrath, E., & Bimbela, A. (1999). Children "tune out" in response to the ambiguous communication style of powerless adults. *Child Development, 70*(1), 214–230.

Caldwell, R. A., Bogat, G. A., & Davidson, W. S. (1988). The assessment of child abuse potential and the prevention of child abuse and neglect: A policy analysis. *American Journal of Community Psychology, 16,* 609–624.

Carlson, V., Cicchetti, D., Barnett, D., & Braunwald, K. (1989). Disorganized disoriented attachment relationships in maltreated infants. *Developmental Psychology, 25,* 525–531.

Chaffin, M., Kelleher, K., & Hollenberg, J. (1996). Onset of physical abuse and neglect: Psychiatric, substance abuse, and social risk factors from prospective community data. *Child Abuse and Neglect, 20,* 191–203.

Chan, Y. C. (1994). Parenting stress and social support of mothers who physically abuse their children in Hong Kong. *Child Abuse and Neglect, 18,* 261–269.

Cheah, I. G., Kasim, M. S., Shafie, H. M., & Khoo, T. H. (1994). Intracranial haemorrhage and child abuse. *Annals of Tropical Paediatrics, 14*(4), 325–328.

Child Fatality Review Panel. (1993). *Child Fatality Review Panel annual report for 1993.* New York: New York City Human Resources Administration.

Christensen, M. J., Brayden, R. M., Dietrich, M. S., & McLaughlin, F. (1994). The prospective assessment of self-concept in neglectful and physically abusive low-income mothers. *Child Abuse and Neglect, 18,* 225–232.

Cicchetti, D., & Beeghly, M. (1987). Symbolic development in maltreated youngsters: An organizational perspective. *New Directions for Child Development, 36,* 213–233.

Cicchetti, D., & Lynch, M. (1993). Toward an ecological transactional model of community violence and child maltreatment—Consequences for children's development. *Psychiatry—Interpersonal and Biological Processes, 56*(1), 96–118.

Cohn, A. H. (1979). Effective treatment of child-abuse and neglect. *Social Work, 24,* 513–519.

Constantino, J. N., Hashemi, N., Solis, E., Alon, T., Haley, S., et al. (2001). Supplementation of urban home visitation with a series of group meetings for parents and infants: Results of a "real-world" randomized, controlled trial. *Child Abuse and Neglect, 25,* 1571–1581.

Coohey, C. (1996). Child maltreatment: Testing the social isolation hypothesis. *Child Abuse and Neglect, 20,* 241–254.

Coulton, C. J., Korbin, J. E., Su, M., & Chow, J. (1995). Community-level factors and child maltreatment rates. *Child Development, 66,* 1262–1276.

Course, S. J., Schmidt, S. K., & Trickett, P. K. (1990). Social network characteristics of mothers in abusing and nonabusing families and their relationships to parenting beliefs. *Journal of Community Psychology, 18*(1), 44–59.

Cox, A. D., Puckering, C., Pound, A., & Mills, M. (1987). The impact of maternal depression in young children. *Journal of Child Psychology, Psychiatry and Allied Disciplines, 28,* 917–928.

Crittenden, P. M. (1985). Social networks, quality of child rearing, and child development. *Child Development, 56,* 1299–1313.

Culp, R. E., Culp, A. M., Soulis, J., & Letts, D. (1989). Self-esteem and depression in abusive, neglecting, and nonmaltreating mothers. *Infant Mental Health Journal, 10*(4), 243–251.

Cummings, E. M., Hennessy, K. D., Rabideau, G. J., & Cicchetti, D. (1994). Responses of physically abused boys to interadult anger involving their mother. *Development and Psychopathology, 6,* 31–41.

Daro, D., & Donnelly, A. C. (2002). Charting the waves of prevention: Two steps forward, one step back. *Child Abuse and Neglect, 26,* 731–742.

Daro, D., & Harding, K. A. (1999). Healthy Families America: Using research to enhance practice. *Future of Children, 9*(1), 152–176.

Daro, D., McCurdy, K., Falconnier, L., & Stojanovic, D. (2003). Sustaining new parents in home visitation services: Key participant and program factors. *Child Abuse and Neglect, 27,* 1101–1125.

Daro, D., McCurdy, K., & Harding, K. (1998). *The role of home visiting in preventing child abuse: An evaluation of the Hawaii Healthy Start program.* Chicago: National Committee to Prevent Child Abuse.

Daro, D., & Winje, C. (1998). *Healthy Families America: Profiles of pilot sites, Center on Child Abuse Prevention Research.* Chicago: National Committee to Prevent Child Abuse.

DePanfilis, D., & Salus, M. K. (1992). *Child protective services: A guide for caseworkers,* vol. 6. Washington, DC: U.S. Department of Health and Human Services.

Diaz, A., Simantov, E., & Rickert, V. I. (2002). Effect of abuse on health—Results of a national survey. *Archives of Pediatrics & Adolescent Medicine, 156,* 811–817.

Dodge, K. A., Pettit, G. S., & Bates, J. E. (1994). Effects of physical maltreatment on the development of peer relations. *Development and Psychopathology, 6*(1), 43–55.

Donovan, W. L., Leavitt, L. A., & Walsh, R. O. (1998). Conflict and depression predict maternal sensitivity to infant cries. *Infant Behavior and Development, 21,* 505–507.

Drake, B., & Pandey, S. (1996). Understanding the relationship between neighborhood poverty and specific types of child maltreatment. *Child Abuse and Neglect, 20,* 1003–1018.

Drotar, D. (1992). Prevention of neglect and nonorganic failure to thrive. In D. J. Willis, E. W. Holden, & M. S. Rosenberg (eds.), *Prevention of child maltreatment : Developmental and ecological perspectives,* pp. 115–149. New York: Wiley.

Dubowitz, H., & Guterman, N. B. (in press). Preventing child neglect and physical abuse. In A. Giardino (ed.), *Child maltreatment—A clinical guide and reference.* Maryland Heights, MO: GW Medical Publishing.

Duggan, A. K., McFarlane, E., Fuddy, L., Burrell, L., Higman, S. M., et al. (2004). Randomized trial of a statewide home visiting program: Impact in preventing child abuse and neglect. *Child Abuse and Neglect, 28,* 597–622.

Duggan, A. K., McFarlane, E. C., Windham, A. M., Rohde, C. A., Salkever, D. S., et al. (1999). Evaluation of Hawaii's Healthy Start Program. *Future of Children, 9*(1), 66–90.

Duggan, A. K., Windham, A., McFarlane, E., Fuddy, L., Rohde, C., et al. (2000). Hawaii's Healthy Start program of home visiting for at-risk families: Evaluation of family identification, family engagement, and service delivery. *Pediatrics, 105*(1), 250–259.

Durrant, J. E. (1999). Evaluating the success of Sweden's corporal punishment ban. *Child Abuse and Neglect, 23,* 435–448.

Dykes, L. (1986). The whiplash shaken infant syndrome: What has been learned? *Child Abuse and Neglect, 10,* 211–221.

Dykman, R. A., McPherson, B., Ackerman, P. T., Newton, J. E., Mooney, D. M., et al. (1997). Internalizing and externalizing characteristics of sexually and/or physically abused children. *Integrative Physiological & Behavioral Science, 32*(1), 62–74.

Earle, R. B. (1995). *Helping to prevent child abuse—And future criminal consequences: Hawaii Healthy Start.* Washington, DC: National Institute of Justice.

Eckenrode, J., Ganzel, B., Henderson, C. R., Smith, E., Olds, D., et al. (2000). Preventing child abuse and neglect with a program of nurse home visitation—The limiting effects of domestic violence. *Journal of the American Medical Association, 284,* 1385–1391.

Eckenrode, J., Zielinski, D., Smith, E., Marcynyszyn, L. A., Henderson, C. R., et al. (2001). Child maltreatment and the early onset of problem behaviors: Can a program of nurse home visitation break the link? *Development and Psychopathology, 13,* 873–890.

Egeland, B., Jacovitz, D., & Sroufe, L. A. (1988). Breaking the cycle of abuse. *Child Development, 59,* 1080–1088.

Egeland, B., & Sroufe, L. A. (1981). Attachment and early maltreatment. *Child Development, 52,* 44–52.

Ellis, R. H., & Milner, J. S. (1981). Child abuse and locus of control. *Psychological Reports, 48*(2), 507–510.

Elmer, E. (1967). *Children in jeopardy.* Pittsburgh: University of Pittsburgh Press.

Ethier, L. S., Lacharite, C., & Couture, G. (1995). Childhood adversity, parental stress, and depression of negligent mothers. *Child Abuse and Neglect, 19,* 619–632.

Fantuzzo, J. W. (1990). Behavioral treatment of the victims of child abuse and neglect. *Behavior Modification, 14,* 316–339.

Felix, A. C., & McCarthy, K. F. (1995). An analysis of child fatalities, 1992. Boston: Commonwealth of Massachusetts Department of Social Services.

Field, T. (1992). Infants of depressed mothers. *Development and Psychopathology, 4*(1), 49–66.

Field, T. (1998). Maternal depression: Effects on infants and early intervention. *Preventive Medicine, 27*, 200–203.

Fields, J., & Casper, L. M. (2001). America's families and living arrangements: March 2000. *Current Population Reports 25*, pp. 20–53. Washington, DC: U.S. Census Bureau.

Finkelhor, D., & Korbin, J. (1988). Child abuse as an international issue. *Child Abuse and Neglect, 12*, 3–23.

Fischler, R. S. (1985). Child abuse and neglect in American Indian communities. *Child Abuse and Neglect, 9*, 95–106.

Fraiberg, S. (1980). *Studies in infant mental health: The first year of life*. New York: Basic Books.

Frank, Y., Zimmerman, R., & Leeds, N. M. (1985). Neurological manifestations in abused children who have been shaken. *Developmental Medicine & Child Neurology, 27*(3), 312–316.

Gaensbauer, T. J., & Mrazek, D. A. (1981). Differences in the patterning of affective expression in infants. *Journal of the American Academy of Child and Adolescent Psychiatry, 20*, 673–691.

Garbarino, J. (1977). The human ecology of child maltreatment: A conceptual model for research. *Journal of Marriage and the Family, 24*, 721–735.

Garbarino, J. (1980). *Protecting children from abuse and neglect: Developing and maintaining effective support systems for families*. San Francisco: Jossey-Bass.

Gaudin, J. M., Polansky, N. A., Kilpatrick, A. C., & Shilton, P. (1993). Loneliness, depression, stress, and social supports in neglectful families. *American Journal of Orthopsychiatry, 63*, 597–605.

Gaudin, J. M., Wodarski, J. S., Arkinson, M. K., & Avery, L. S. (1990–1991). Remedying child neglect: Effectiveness of social network interventions. *Journal of Applied Social Sciences, 15*, 97–123.

Gelles, R. J. (1989). Child abuse and violence in single-parent families—Parent absence and economic deprivation. *American Journal of Orthopsychiatry, 59*, 492–501.

George, C. (1996). A representational perspective of child abuse and prevention: Internal working models of attachment and caregiving. *Child Abuse and Neglect, 20*, 411–424.

Giovannoni, J. M., & Billingsley, A. (1970). Child neglect among the poor—Study of parental adequacy in families of 3 ethnic groups. *Child Welfare, 49*, 196–204.

Goldfarb, W. (1945). Psychological privation in infancy and subsequent adjustment. *American Journal of Orthopsychiatry, 15*, 247–255.

Gomby, D. S. (2000). Promise and limitations of home visitation. *Journal of the American Medical Association, 284*, 1430–1431.

Gracia, E., & Musitu, G. (2003). Social isolation from communities and child maltreatment: A cross-cultural comparison. *Child Abuse and Neglect, 27*, 153–168.

Gray, E., & Cosgrove, J. (1985). Ethnocentric perception of childrearing practices in protective services. *Child Abuse and Neglect, 9*, 389–396.

Gray, J., Cutler, C., Dean, J., & Kempe, C. H. (1979). Prediction and prevention of child abuse and neglect. *Journal of Social Issues, 35*(2), 127–139.

Guterman, N. B. (1999). Enrollment strategies in early home visitation to prevent physical child abuse and neglect and the "universal versus targeted" debate: A meta-analysis of population-based and screening-based programs. *Child Abuse and Neglect, 23*, 863–890.

Guterman, N. B. (2001a). *Stopping child maltreatment before it starts: Emerging horizons in early home visitation services*. Thousand Oaks, CA: Sage.

Guterman, N. B. (2001b). *Strengthening early home visitation through parental empowerment and informal network development*. Paper presented at the Eighth Annual Colloquium of the American Professional Society on the Abuse of Children, Washington, DC, June 15–18, 2001.

Guterman, N. B. (2003). *Tapping parent's informal social networks to strengthen the preventive impact of home visitation*. Paper presented at the Department of Defense Joint Services New Parent Support Conference, New Orleans, July 2003.

Guterman, N. B., Anisfeld, E., & McCord, M. (2003). Home visiting. *Pediatrics, 111*, 1491–1492.

Hahn, R. A., Bilukha, O. O., Crosby, A., Fullilove, M. T., Moscicki, E. K., et al. (2003). First reports evaluating the effectiveness of strategies for preventing violence: Early childhood home visitation and firearms laws. *Findings from the Task Force on Community Preventive Services, 52*(RR-14), 1–20.

Hampton, R. L., & Newberger, E. H. (1985). Child abuse incidence and reporting by hospitals: Significance of severity, class, and race. *American Journal of Public Health, 75*(1), 56–60.

Helfer, R. E. (1987). The developmental basis of child abuse and neglect: An epidemiological approach. In R. E. Kempe & R. D. Krugman (eds.), *The battered child*, fourth ed., pp. 60–80. Chicago: University of Chicago Press.

Herzog, E. P., Cherniss, D. S., & Menzel, B. J. (1986). Issues in engaging high-risk adolescent mothers in supportive work. *Infant Mental Health Journal, 7*, 59–68.

Hillson, J. M. C., & Kupier, N. A. (1994). A stress and coping model of child maltreatment. *Clinical Psychology Review, 14*(4), 261–285.

Hoffmanplotkin, D., & Twentyman, C. T. (1984). A multimodal assessment of behavioral and cognitive deficits in abused and neglected preschoolers. *Child Development, 55*, 794–802.

Ito, Y., Teicher, M. H., Glod, C. A., & Harper, D. (1993). Increased prevalence of electrophysiological abnormalities in children with psychological, physical, and sexual abuse. *Journal of Neuropsychiatry and Clinical Neurosciences, 5*, 401–408.

Jason, J., Amereuh, N., Marks, J., & Tyler, C. (1982). Child abuse in Georgia: A method to evaluate risk factors and reporting bias. *American Journal of Public Health, 72,* 1353–1358.

Jones, L. (1990). Unemployment and child abuse. *Families in Society—The Journal of Contemporary Human Services, 71,* 579–588.

Justice, B., Calvert, A., & Justice, R. (1985). Factors mediating child abuse as a response to stress. *Child Abuse and Neglect, 9,* 359–363.

Kaufman, J., & Cicchetti, D. (1989). The effects of maltreatment on school-aged children's socioemotional development: Assessments in a day camp setting. *Developmental Psychology, 15,* 516–524.

Kazdin, A., Moser, J., Colbus, D., & Bell, R. (1985). Depressive symptoms among physically abused and psychiatrically disturbed children. *Journal of Abnormal Psychology, 94,* 298–307.

Kempe, C. H. (1976). Approaches to preventing child abuse: The health visitor concept. *American Journal of Diseases of Children, 130,* 941–947.

Kinard, E. M. (1979). Psychological consequences of abuse for the child. *Journal of Social Issues, 35(2),* 82–100.

Kitzman, H., Olds, D., Henderson, C. R., Hanks, C., Cole, R., et al. (1997). Effect of prenatal and infancy home visitation by nurses on pregnancy outcomes, childhood injuries, and repeated childbearing. *Journal of the American Medical Association, 278,* 644–652.

Kolko, D. J. (1992). Characteristics of child victims of physical violence—Research findings and clinical implications. *Journal of Interpersonal Violence, 7(2),* 244–276.

Kolko, D. J., Kazdin, A. E., Thomas, A. M., & Day, B. (1993). Heightened child physical abuse potential: Child, parent, and family dysfunction. *Journal of Interpersonal Violence, 8(2),* 169–192.

Korbin, J. (1987). Child maltreatment in cross-cultural perspective: Vulnerable children and circumstances. In R. Gelles & J. Lanchaster (eds.), *Child abuse and neglect: Biosocial dimensions,* pp. 31–55. Hawthorne, NY: Aldine de Gruyter.

Korbin, J. (1994). Sociocultural factors in child maltreatment. In G. B. Melton & F. D. Berry (eds.), *Protecting children from abuse and neglect: Foundations for a new national strategy,* pp. 182–223. New York: Guilford.

Kotch, J. B., Browne, D. C., Dufort, V., & Winsor, J. (1999). Predicting child maltreatment in the first 4 years of life from characteristics assessed in the neonatal period. *Child Abuse and Neglect, 23,* 305–319.

Kotch, J. B., Browne, D. C., Ringwalt, C. L., & Stewart, P. W. (1995). Risk of child abuse or neglect in a cohort of low-income children. *Child Abuse and Neglect, 19,* 1115–1130.

Kotelchuck, M. (1982). Child abuse and neglect: Prediction and misclassification. In R. Starr (ed.), *Child abuse prediction: Policy implications.* Cambridge, MA: Ballinger.

Krugman, R. D. (1985). Fatal child abuse: Analysis of 24 cases. *Pediatrician, 12,* 68–72.

Lancon, J. A., Haines, D. E., & Parent, A. D. (1998). Anatomy of the shaken baby syndrome. *Anatomical Record, 253(1),* 13–18.

Lansford, J. E., Dodge, K. A., Pettit, G. S., Bates, J. E., Crozier, J., & Kaplow, J. (2002). A 12-year prospective study of the long-term effects of early child physical maltreatment on psychological, behavioral, and academic problems in adolescence. *Archives of Pediatrics & Adolescent Medicine, 156,* 824–830.

Lauderdale, M., Valiunas, A., & Anderson, R. (1980). Race, ethnicity, and child maltreatment, An empirical analysis. *Child Abuse and Neglect, 4,* 163–169.

Laurendeau, M., Gagnon, G., Desjardins, M., Perreault, R., & Kischuk, N. (1991). Evaluation of an early, mass media parental support intervention. *Journal of Primary Prevention, 11(3),* 207–225.

Lewis, D. O. (1992). From abuse to violence—Psychophysiological consequences of maltreatment. *Journal of the American Academy of Child and Adolescent Psychiatry, 31,* 383–391.

Libby, A. M., Sills, M. R., Thurston, M. K., & Orton, H. D. (2003). Costs of childhood physical abuse: Comparing inflicted and unintentional traumatic brain injuries. *Pediatrics, 112,* 58–65.

Lindsey, D. (1994). *The welfare of children.* New York: Oxford University Press.

Lovell, M. L., & Arnott, R. D. (1988). An evaluation of a group intervention to increase the personal social networks of abusive mothers. *Children and Youth Services Review, 10,* 175–188.

Luker, K. A., & Chalmers, K. I. (1990). Gaining access to clients—The case of health visiting. *Journal of Advanced Nursing, 15(1),* 74–82.

MacLeod, J., & Nelson, G. (2000). Programs for the promotion of family wellness and the prevention of child maltreatment: A meta-analytic review. *Child Abuse and Neglect, 24,* 1127–1149.

Main, M., & Solomon, C. (1986). Discovery of a new insecure-disorganized, disoriented attachment pattern. In T. B. B. M. Yogman (ed.), *Affective development in infancy.* Norwood, NJ: Ablex.

Malinosky-Rummell, R., & Hansen, D. J. (1993). Long-term consequences of childhood physical abuse. *Psychological Bulletin, 114(1),* 68–79.

Margolin, L. (1992). Child abuse by mothers' boyfriends: Why the overrepresentation? *Child Abuse and Neglect, 16,* 541–551.

Maxfield, M. G., & Widom, C. S. (1996). The cycle of violence—Revisited 6 years later. *Archives of Pediatrics & Adolescent Medicine, 150,* 390–395.

McCurdy, K., Gannon, R. A., & Daro, D. (2003). Participation patterns in home-based family support programs: Ethnic variations. *Family Relations, 52(1),* 3–11.

McDonald, T. P., & Marks, J. (1991). A review of risk factors assessed in child protective services. *Social Services Review, 65,* 112–132.

McGuigan, W. M., Katzev, A. R., & Pratt, C. C. (2003a). Multi-level determinants of mothers' engagement in home visitation services. *Family Relations, 52*(3), 271–278.

McGuigan, W. M., Katzev, A. R., & Pratt, C. C. (2003b). Multi-level determinants of retention in a home-visiting child abuse prevention program. *Child Abuse and Neglect, 27,* 363–380.

McGuigan, W. M., & Pratt, C. C. (2001). The predictive impact of domestic violence on three types of child maltreatment. *Child Abuse and Neglect, 25,* 869–883.

McKibben, L., De Vos, E., & Newberger, E. H. (1991). Victimization of mothers of abused children: A controlled study. In R. L. Hampton (ed.), *Black family violence,* pp. 75–83. Lexington, MA: Lexington Books.

Milner, J. S., & Crouch, J. L. (1998). Physical child abuse: Theory and research. In R. Hampton (ed.), *Family violence prevention and treatment.* Newbury Park, CA: Sage.

Mitchel, L., & Cohn-Donnelly, A. (1993). Healthy Families America: Building a national system. *The APSAC Advisor, 6*(4), 9–27.

Money, J. (1977). Syndrome of abuse dwarfism (psychosocial dwarfism or reversible hyposomatotropism) —behavioral data and case report. *American Journal of Diseases of Children, 131,* 508–513.

Mrazek, P. J. (1993). Maltreatment and infant development. In J. C. H. Zeanah (ed.), *Handbook of infant mental health,* pp. 159–170. New York: Guilford.

Murphey, D. A., & Braner, M. (2000). Linking child maltreatment retrospectively to birth and home visit records: An initial examination. *Child Welfare, 79,* 711–728.

Murray, L., Fiori-Crowley, A., Hooper, R., & Cooper, P. (1996). The impact of postnatal depression and associated adversity on early mother-infant interactions and later infant outcomes. *Child Development, 67,* 2512–2526.

Nair, P., Black, M. M., Schuler, M., Keane, V., Snow, L., et al. (1997). Risk factors for disruption in primary caregiving among infants of substance-abusing women. *Child Abuse and Neglect, 21,* 1039–1051.

Nair, P., Schuler, M. E., Blacka, M. M., Kettinger, L., & Harrington, D. (2003). Cumulative environmental risk in substance-abusing women: Early intervention, parenting stress, child abuse potential and child development. *Child Abuse and Neglect, 27,* 997–1017.

National Center on Child Abuse and Neglect. (1993). *A report to Congress: Study of child maltreatment in alcohol abusing families.* Washington, DC: U.S. Department of Health and Human Services.

National Research Council. (1993). *Understanding child abuse and neglect.* Washington, DC: National Academy Press.

Navaie-Waliser, M., Martin, S. L., Campbell, M. K., Tessaro, I., Kotelchuck, M., & Cross, A. W. (2000). Factors predicting completion of a home visitation program by high-risk pregnant women: The North Carolina Maternal Outreach Worker program. *American Journal of Public Health, 90,* 121–124.

Nurius, P. S., Lovell, M., & Maggie, E. (1988). Self-appraisals of abusive parents: A contextual approach to study and treatment. *Journal of Interpersonal Violence, 3*(4), 458–467.

Oates, R. K., Forrest, D., & Peacock, A. (1985). Self-esteem of abused children. *Child Abuse and Neglect, 9,* 159–163.

Olds, D. (1982). The prenatal/early infancy project: An ecological approach to prevention. In J. Belsky (ed.), *In the beginning: Readings in infancy,* pp. 270–285. New York: Columbia University Press.

Olds, D. (2002). Prenatal and infancy home visiting by nurses: From randomized trials to community replication. *Prevention Science, 3*(3), 153–172.

Olds, D., Eckenrode, J., Henderson, C., Kitzman, H., Powers, J., et al. (1997). Long-term effects of home visitation on maternal life course and child abuse and neglect: Fifteen year follow-up of a randomized trial. *Journal of the American Medical Association, 278,* 637–643.

Olds, D., Henderson, C., Chamberlin, R., & Tatelbaum, R. (1986). Preventing child abuse and neglect —A randomized trial of nurse home visitation. *Pediatrics, 78,* 65–78.

Olds, D., Henderson, C., Cole, R., Eckenrode, J., Kitzman, H., et al. (1998). Long-term effects of nurse home visitation on children's criminal and antisocial behavior—15-year follow-up of a randomized controlled trial. *Journal of the American Medical Association, 280,* 1238–1244.

Olds, D., Henderson, C., Kitzman, H., Eckenrode, J. J., Cole, R. E., & Tatelbaum, R. C. (1999). Prenatal and infancy home visitation by nurses: Recent findings. *Future of Children, 9*(1), 44–65.

Olds, D., Henderson, C., Tatelbaum, R., & Chamberlin, R. (1986). Improving the delivery of prenatal care and outcomes of pregnancy: A randomized trial of nurse home visitation. *Pediatrics, 77,* 16–28.

Olds, D., & Kitzman, H. (1993). Review of research on home visiting for pregnant women and parents of young children. *Future of Children, 3*(3), 53–92.

Oregon Children's Services Division. (1993). *Task force report on child fatalities and critical injuries due to abuse and neglect.* Salem: Oregon Department of Human Resources.

Osofsky, J. D., Wewers, S., Hann, D. M., & Fick, A. C. (1993). Chronic community violence—What is happening to our children? *Psychiatry—Interpersonal and Biological Processes, 56*(1), 36–45.

Patterson, G. (1982). *Coercive family process.* Eugene, OR: Castalia.

Paulozzi, L., & Sells, M. (2002). Variation in homicide risk during infancy—United States, 1989–1998. *Morbidity and Mortality Weekly Report, 51*(9), 187–189.

Pelton, L. (1994). The role of material factors in child abuse and neglect. In G. B. Melton & F. D. Berry (eds.), *Protecting children from abuse and neglect: Foundations for a new national strategy,* pp. 131–181. New York: Guilford.

Perry, B. D., & Pollard, R. (1997). *Altered brain development following global neglect in childhood.* Paper presented at the Society for Neuroscience Annual Meeting, New Orleans, May 22-26, 1997.

Perry, B. D., Pollard, R. A., Blakley, T. L., Baker, W. L., & Vigilante, D. (1995). Childhood trauma, the neurobiology of adaptation, and "use-dependent" development of the brain: How "states" become "traits." *Infant Mental Health Journal, 16*(4), 271–291.

Perry, M. A., Doran, L. D., & Wells, E. A. (1983). Developmental and behavioral characteristics of the physically abused child. *Journal of Clinical Child Psychology, 12,* 320–324.

Polansky, N. A., Chalmers, M. A., Buttenwieser, E., & Williams, D. P. (1981). *Damaged parents: An anatomy of child neglect.* Chicago: University of Chicago Press.

Prevent Child Abuse America. (1999). *Healthy Families America: A snapshot view.* Chicago: Prevent Child Abuse America.

Prevent Child Abuse America. (2002). *Healthy Families America: A distinctive approach to home visiting.* Chicago: Prevent Child Abuse America.

Pruitt, D. L., & Erickson, M. R. (1985). The child abuse potential inventory: A study of concurrent validity. *Journal of Clinical Psychology, 41,* 104–111.

Rafael, T., & Pion-Berlin, L. (1999). *Parents Anonymous: Strengthening families.* Juvenile Justice Bulletin 29. Washington, DC: Office of Juvenile Justice and Delinquency Prevention.

Reid, J. B., & Gallagher, P. R. (1989). The development of antisocial behaviour patterns in childhood and adolescence. *European Journal of Personality, 3*(2), 107–119.

Richters, J. E., & Martinez, P. (1993). The NIMH Community Violence Project: I. Children as victims and witnesses to violence. *Psychiatry, 56,* 7–21.

Ritchie, J., & Ritchie, J. (1981). Child rearing and child abuse: The Polynesian context. In J. Korbin (ed.), *Child abuse and neglect: Cross-cultural perspectives.* Berkeley: University of California Press.

Rodriguez, C. M., & Green, A. J. (1997). Parenting stress and anger expression as predictors of child abuse potential. *Child Abuse and Neglect, 21,* 367–377.

Salzinger, S., Kaplan, S., & Artemyeff, C. (1983). Mothers' personal social networks and child maltreatment. *Journal of Abnormal Psychology, 92*(1), 68–76.

Salzinger, S., Kaplan, S., Pelcovitz, D., Samit, C., & Krieger, R. (1984). Parent and teacher assessment of children's behavior in child-maltreating families.

Journal of the American Academy of Child Psychiatry, 23, 458–464.

Sameroff, A., & Gutman, L. M. (2004). Contributions of risk research to the design of successful interventions. In P. Allen-Meares & M. W. Fraser (eds.), *Intervention with children and adolescents: An interdisciplinary perspective,* pp. 9–26. Boston: Pearson Education.

Schinke, S. P., Schilling, R. F., Barth, R. P., Gilchrist, L. D., & Maxwell, J. S. (1986). Stress-management intervention to prevent family violence. *Journal of Family Violence, 1*(1), 13–26.

Seagull, E. A. W. (1987). Social support and child maltreatment—A review of the evidence. *Child Abuse and Neglect, 11,* 41–52.

Sedlack, A. J., & Broadhurst, D. D. (1996). *Third national incidence study of child abuse and neglect.* Final report. Washington, DC: U. S. Department of Health and Human Services.

Seligman, M. E. P. (1975). *Helplessness: On depression, development, and death.* San Francisco: W.H. Freeman.

Shields, A. M., Cicchetti, D., & Ryan, R. M. (1994). The development of emotional and behavioral self-regulation and social competence among maltreated school-age children. *Development and Psychopathology, 6,* 57–75.

Showers, J. (1992). "Don't shake the baby": The effectiveness of a prevention program. *Child Abuse and Neglect, 16,* 11–18.

Silverman, A. B., Reinherz, H. Z., & Giaconia, R. M. (1996). The long-term sequelae of child and adolescent abuse: A longitudinal community study. *Child Abuse and Neglect, 20,* 709–723.

Solheim, J. S. (1982). A cross-cultural examination of the use of corporal punishment on children: A focus on Sweden and the United States. *Child Abuse and Neglect, 6,* 147–154.

Spearly, J., & Lauderdale, M. (1983). Community characteristics and ethnicity in the prediction of child maltreatment rates. *Child Abuse and Neglect, 7,* 91–105.

Spitz, R. A. (1945). Hospitalism: An inquiry into the genesis of psychiatric conditions in early childhood. *Psychoanalytic Study of the Child, 1,* 53–74.

Stark, E., & Flitcraft, A. H. (1988). Women and children at risk: A feminist perspective on child abuse. *International Journal of Health Services, 18,* 97–118.

Straus, M. A., & Kantor, G. (1987). Stress and child abuse. In R. S. K. R. Helfer (ed.), *The battered child,* fourth ed., pp. 42–59. Chicago: University of Chicago Press.

Straus, M. A., & Smith, C. (1992). Family patterns and child abuse. In M. A. Straus & R. J. Gelles (eds.), *Physical violence in American families,* pp. 245–262. New Brunswick, NJ: Transaction Publishers.

Stringer, S. A., & Lagreca, A. M. (1985). Correlates of child-abuse potential. *Journal of Abnormal Child Psychology, 13,* 217–226.

Teicher, M. H., Ito, Y., Glod, C. A., Schiffer, F., & Gelbard, H. A. (1996). Neurophysiological mechanisms of stress response in children. In C. R. Pfeffer (ed.), *Severe stress and mental disturbance in children*, pp. 59–84. Washington, DC: American Psychiatric Press.

Trickett, P. K., & Schellenbach, C. J. (1998). *Violence against children in the family and the community.* Washington, DC: American Psychological Association.

U.S. Advisory Board on Child Abuse and Neglect. (1991). *Creating caring communities: Blueprint for an effective federal policy on child abuse and neglect.* Washington, DC: U.S. Government Printing Office.

U.S. Department of Health and Human Services. (1999). *Blending perspectives and building common ground: A report to Congress on substance abuse and child protection.* Washington, DC: U.S. Government Printing Office.

U.S. Department of Health and Human Services. (2004). *Child maltreatment, 2002.* Washington, DC: U.S. Government Printing Office.

Widom, C. S. (1989). The cycle of violence. *Science, 244,* 160–166.

Widom, C. S., & Maxfield, M. G. (2001). *An update on the "cycle of violence" research in brief.* Vol. NCJ 184894. Washington, DC: U.S. Department of Justice.

Widom, C. S., & White, H. R. (1997). Problem behaviors in abused and neglected children grown up: Prevalence and co-occurrence of substance abuse, crime and violence. *Criminal Behaviour & Mental Health, 7*(4), 287–310.

Wiehe, V. (1992). Empathy and locus of control in child abusers. *Journal of Social Service Research, 9*(2–3), 17–30.

Windham, A. (1998). *Comprehensive evaluation of the Hawaii Healthy Start program: Maternal outcomes at year 1.* Paper presented at the Seventh Healthy Families America Research Network Meeting, Chicago, May 11, 1998.

Wong, E. (1999). Oakland panel rejects no-spanking proposal. *Los Angeles Times,* (January 27), A3.

Yarrow, L. J. (1961). Maternal deprivation: Toward an empirical and conceptual re-evaluation. *Psychological Bulletin, 58,* 459–490.

Young, L. (1964). *Wednesday's children: A study of child neglect and abuse.* New York: McGraw-Hill.

Zuravin, S., McMillen, C., DePanfilis, D., & Risley-Curtiss, C. (1996). The intergenerational cycle of child maltreatment: Continuity versus discontinuity. *Journal of Interpersonal Violence, 11*(3), 315–334.

Zuravin, S. J. (1989). The ecology of child abuse and neglect: Review of the literature and presentation of data. *Violence and Victims, 4*(2), 102–120.

DIANE DEPANFILIS

Child Protective Services

The passage of the Adoption and Safe Families Act (ASFA) of 1997 (P.L. 105-89) affirmed that child welfare agencies have a primary responsibility for insuring that children and youth are safe from abuse and neglect (U.S. Department of Health and Human Services 2000). The Child Protective Services (CPS) program, a core program in all child welfare agencies, leads efforts to insure child safety in collaboration with community agencies. More broadly, CPS "refers to a highly specialized set of laws, funding mechanisms, and agencies that together constitute the government's response to reports of child abuse and neglect" (Waldfogel 1998a:105). The basis for CPS programs stems from laws established in each state that define child abuse and neglect and specify how CPS agencies should respond to reports of child maltreatment. Social workers in CPS agencies have the responsibility to address the effects of child maltreatment, implement service responses that will keep children and youth safe from abuse and neglect, and work with families to prevent the likelihood of child maltreatment in the future (DePanfilis & Salus 2003; U.S. Department of Health and Human Services 1988).

According to the National Association of Public Child Welfare Administrators (1999), the mission of the CPS agency is to: (1) assess the safety of children and youth; (2) intervene to protect children and youth from harm; (3) strengthen the ability of families to protect their children, or (4) provide an alternative safe family for the child or adolescent. The Child Welfare League of America also affirms this mission by suggesting that the CPS agency assess the risk to, and safety of, children and youth and provide or arrange for services to achieve safe, permanent families for children and youth who have been abused or neglected or who are at risk of abuse or neglect. The CPS agency also facilitates community collaborations and engages formal and informal community partners to support families and protect children from abuse and neglect (Child Welfare League of America 1999). The purpose of this chapter is to trace the path of child abuse and neglect reports from the point of referral through the process of providing ongoing services to children, youth, and families involved in the child protection system. Before doing this, I describe the philosophy and policy context for CPS programs and the nature and extent of child abuse and neglect in the United States. Finally, I describe the limited information available on the effectiveness of CPS programs, and then supply a brief summary of CPS reforms being implemented across the United States.

Philosophy of CPS

CPS agencies operate on the philosophical belief that every child has a right to adequate care and supervision and to be free from abuse, neglect, and exploitation. Laws to protect children and youth assume that it is the responsibility of parents to see that the physical, mental, emotional, educational, and medical needs of their children are met adequately. Further assumptions are that CPS should intervene only when parents request assistance or fail, by their acts or omissions, to adequately meet their children's basic needs and keep them safe from abuse or neglect, as defined by state civil laws (DePanfilis & Salus 2003).

When there is a need to intervene following a report of abuse or neglect, CPS agencies do so on the belief that most parents want to be good parents and have the strength and capacity, when adequately supported by CPS and the community, to care for their children and youth and keep them safe. Intervention proceeds on the assumption that most children are best cared for in their own families. Therefore CPS focuses on strengths and provides the assistance needed for families to keep their children and adolescent safe so that the family may stay together. Only when safety cannot be assured are actions taken to protect children by placing them in out-of-home care.

When children and youth are placed in out-of-home care because their safety cannot be insured, the preferred CPS plan is to reunify children with their families, as it is believed that children and adolescents do best with families where there has been a foundation of love, trust, safety, and security. Thus work with the family focuses on ways that families may make changes to reduce the risk of future maltreatment. Only when a successful reunification cannot occur are other, more permanent options, such as adoption, considered for children and youth.

Legal Basis for CPS

The legal framework regarding the parent-child relationship, referred to as "Parens Patriae," has traditionally balanced the rights and responsibilities among parent, child, and state. It has long been recognized that parents in this society have a fundamental liberty interest, protected by the Constitution, to raise their children as they see fit. This parent-child relationship grants certain rights, duties, and obligations to both parent and child, including the responsibility

of the parent to protect the child's safety and well-being. If a parent, however, is unable to meet this responsibility, the state has the power and authority to protect a child or youth from significant harm, and this authority is enacted through the CPS agency (Goldman & Salus 2003). CPS agencies operate under civil laws that guide reporting of child abuse and neglect and dictate the basis for intervening in family life when a child or youth may have been abused or neglected. This is in contrast to criminal laws that guide intervention by law enforcement agencies.

Federal Laws

Most historians point to the establishment of the Children's Bureau in 1912 as the first significant federal involvement in child welfare and child protection, but it was not until some time later that the first federal laws related to child abuse and neglect were established. The chapter by McGowan in this volume provides a substantive review of the laws and policies affecting services to children, youth, and families. Here, I provide a brief overview of six federal laws that relate to child abuse and neglect and CPS.

Adoption Assistance and Child Welfare Act. This law (1980; P.L. 96-272) requires states to establish programs, procedures, and services to protect maltreated children in their own homes whenever possible, and to facilitate family reunification if placement in out-of-home settings is necessary (Goldman & Salus 2003).

Adoption and Safe Families Act. ASFA (1997; P.L. 105-89) builds on earlier child welfare legislation and was designed to insure child safety, decrease the time required to reach permanent placements when children have been placed in out-of-home care, increase the number of adoption and other permanent options, and enhance state capacity and accountability for reaching these goals (U.S. Department of Health and Human Services 2000).

Child Abuse Prevention and Treatment Act (CAPTA). As amended in 1978, 1984, 1988, 1992, 1996, and 2003, CAPTA (1974; P.L. 93-247) was established to (1) set standards and provide vehicles for funding to insure that states accept and respond to reports of child abuse and neglect and (2) monitor research and compile and publish materials for persons working in the field (National Clearinghouse on Child Abuse and Neglect Information 2003a).

Family Preservation and Support Services program. Enacted as part of the Omnibus Budget Reconciliation Act (1993; P.L. 103-66), this law provides funding for prevention and support services for families at risk of maltreatment and family preservation services for families experiencing crises that might lead to out-of-home placement (Goldman & Salus 2003).

Promoting Safe and Stable Families program reauthorization. This law (2001; P.L. 107-133) builds on principles established in ASFA by encouraging states to develop or expand programs of family preservation services, community-based family support services, adoption promotion and support services, and time-limited family reunification services and extends funding for the Promoting Safe and Stable Families Program for an additional 5 years (National Clearinghouse on Child Abuse and Neglect Information 2003b).

Strengthening Abuse and Neglect Courts Act. This act (2000; P.L. 106-314) was designed to improve the efficiency and effectiveness of the courts' handling of abuse and neglect cases.

State Laws

State child abuse and neglect reporting laws have been enacted in all 50 states, the District of Columbia, and the U.S. territories. These statutes specify procedures that a mandatory reporter must follow when making a report of child abuse or neglect. In most states, the statutes require mandated reporters to make a report immediately upon any suspicion of abusive or neglectful situations (National Clearinghouse on Child Abuse and Neglect Information 2003a). Although there are variations, most state laws identify professionals, such as social workers, as mandated reporters and require reporting when these individuals come in contact with children who they suspect may have been maltreated according to the definitions in state law. In all jurisdictions, the initial report may be made orally to either the CPS agency or to a law enforcement agency. These reporting laws also provide definitions of child abuse and neglect, structure the requirements for investigation or assessment of reports, and may further delineate the purposes of CPS and other service responses.

In addition to child abuse and neglect reporting laws, states also have laws that define the basis for intervention to protect children and youth and the circumstances under which CPS agencies may petition the juvenile or family court to intervene on behalf of victimized children (Feller, Davidson, Hardin, & Horowitz 1992). According to Davidson (1997:483), "a civil child protection action—also commonly referred to as care, protection, endangerment, dependency, abuse, or neglect proceeding—is the most frequent judicial response to child maltreatment." In civil child protection cases, the decision to go to court is usually made by the CPS worker when the assessment suggests that the child or youth will not be safe without court intervention. Family and juvenile courts have the authority to make decisions about what happens to a child or youth after he or she has been identified as in need of the court's protection (Goldman & Salus 2003). Social workers who practice in CPS and other child welfare service programs must be comfortable with their roles in presenting information to the court (see the chapter by Hardin), as approximately 20% of all substantiated reports of child abuse and neglect result in petitions to the court to arrange for the safety of the child (U.S. Department of Health and Human Services 2004b).

Definitions of Child Abuse and Neglect

Definitions of child maltreatment (i.e., physical abuse, sexual abuse, neglect, psychological abuse, or neglect) in each state law provide the legal basis for intervening by CPS agencies. Criminal definitions establish when acts or omissions may be considered criminal offenses. And researchers may define abuse or neglect in other ways to evaluate the effectiveness of an intervention or identify the relationship between certain characteristics and child maltreatment. For states to receive federal funds through CAPTA, the federal government (U.S. Department of Health and Human Services 2003:44) sets minimum standards that must be incorporated in the definitions of child maltreatment in state laws: "The term 'child abuse and neglect' means, at a minimum, any recent act or failure to act on the part of a parent or caretaker, which results in death, serious physical or emotional harm, sexual abuse or exploitation, or an act or failure to act which presents an imminent risk of serious harm." Sample definitions that may guide CPS intervention for each of the four types of child abuse and neglect are given here.

Neglect may be defined as omissions in care by a person responsible for the child's care (e.g., parent or other caregiver), resulting in significant harm or the risk of significant harm to the child or youth (Dubowitz 2000a). Neglect may further be defined as failure to meet children's basic needs for physical care, supervision and protection, nurturance, education, and healthcare.

Physical abuse may be defined as an inflicted act by a person responsible for the child's or youth's care, resulting in significant physical injury or the risk of such injury (Dubowitz 2000b). Examples of inflicted acts include punching; beating; kicking; biting; shaking; throwing; stabbing; choking; burning; or hitting with a hand, stick, strap, or other object (Goldman & Salus 2003).

Sexual abuse may be defined by nonconsensual sexual acts, sexually motivated behaviors involving children and youth, or sexual exploitation of children (Berliner 2000) by a person responsible for the child's care. Child sexual abuse includes a wide rage of behaviors, such as oral, anal, or genital penile penetration; anal or genital digital or other penetration; genital contact with no intrusion; fondling of a child's breasts or buttocks; indecent exposure; inadequate or inappropriate supervision of a child's voluntary sexual activities; and use of a child or adolescent in prostitution, pornography, internet crimes, or other sexually exploitative activities (Goldman & Salus 2003).

Psychological maltreatment may be defined as a repeated pattern of behavior or extreme incident by persons responsible for the child's care that conveys to the child that he or she is worthless, flawed, unloved, unwanted, endangered, or only of value in meeting another's needs by a person responsible for the child's care (American Professional Society on the Abuse of Children 1995). Psychological maltreatment includes both abusive acts against a child or youth and omissions of care. Forms of psychological maltreatment include spurning (e.g., hostile rejecting and degrading behavior); terrorizing (e.g., threats to harm a child or someone important to a child); exploiting or corrupting (e.g., encouraging the child or youth to participate in self-destructive or criminal behaviors); denying emotional responsiveness (e.g., ignoring or failing to express affection); and isolating (e.g., confining a child from experiencing developmentally appropriate experiences) (Brassard & Hart 2000).

Incidence of Child Abuse and Neglect

In 2002, state CPS agencies received 2.6 million referrals alleging maltreatment related to 4.5 million children and youth. This is estimated to be a rate of 35.9 referrals to 1,000 children, based on data from 39 states that had sufficient information available (U.S. Department of Health and Human Services 2004a). However, as illustrated in fig. 1, CPS agencies provide services in response to only a small percentage of these referrals.

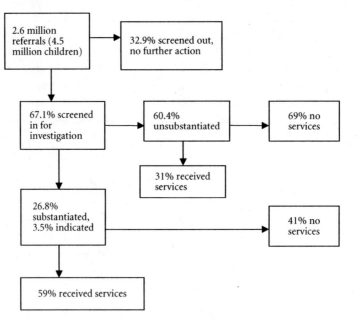

FIGURE 1. CPS screening and response to child abuse and neglect reports in 2002. Based on data from U.S. Department of Health and Human Services (2004a).

Once received, states screen out an average of 32.9% of child abuse and neglect referrals from receiving any investigation or assessment. Screening rates vary substantially among states, from a low of 1.7% in Alabama to a high of 72.3% in Maine. Of the referrals accepted as a report and investigated, more than half (60.4%) led to a finding of "unsubstantiated," suggesting that sufficient evidence of child abuse or neglect was not found by the CPS worker. In contrast, an estimated 896,000 children were determined to be victims of child abuse or neglect in 2002, based on determining that a report was substantiated or indicated. The rate of victimization per 1,000 children in the national population has dropped from 13.4 children in 1990 to 12.3 children in 2002.

In 2002, more than 60% of child and youth victims experienced neglect, approximately 20% were physically abused; 10% were sexually abused; and 7% were emotionally maltreated. In addition, almost 20% were associated with other types of maltreatment based on specific state laws and policies. Some children and youth experienced more than one type of maltreatment, so the total adds up to more than 100%.

Receipt of Services Following a Report of Child Abuse or Neglect

According to state statistics in 2002, approximately 59% of victims and 31% of nonvictims, such as siblings, received services as a result of a CPS investigation or assessment. Additional analyses indicated that children and youth who were prior victims of maltreatment were more than 80% more likely to receive services than were first-time victims, and children and youth with multiple types of maltreatment were more than 80% more likely to receive services than those with only one type of recorded maltreatment. Approximately 80% of victims were provided in-home services and 20% were provided foster care services. In addition, approximately 4% of nonvictims also experienced a removal —usually a short-term placement during the course of the investigation (National Clearinghouse on Child Abuse and Neglect Information 2004).

CPS Case Process

Receiving Reports of Child Abuse or Neglect

Mandatory child maltreatment reporting statutes (civil laws) provide definitions of child abuse and neglect to guide those individuals mandated to identify and report suspected child abuse and neglect. These reports activate the child protection process. When a CPS worker receives a report alleging child abuse or neglect, a decision is made about whether to accept the report for an investigation or initial assessment. This decision is usually made depending on whether the circumstances being alleged (if true) would meet the definition of child abuse or neglect in the state statute. In some states, concern that a child may be at risk for child abuse or neglect is sufficient reason for the CPS agency to respond, often in collaboration with a community agency.

Stages of the Child Protective Services Process[1]

To fulfill the purposes previously described, CPS receives reports of suspected child maltreatment; assesses the risk to, and safety of, children and youth; and provides or arranges for services to increase safety and well-being of children and youth who have been abused or neglected or who are at risk of abuse or neglect. Each situation proceeds through one or more of a series of CPS process stages: (1) intake; (2) initial assessment/investigation; (3) family assessment; (4) intervention planning; (5) service provision; (6) evaluation of case progress; and (7) case closure. Key decisions vary at each of these process stages (DePanfilis & Salus 2003).

Intake. CPS is responsible for receiving and responding to reports of suspected child abuse and neglect. Key decisions at this stage are: (1) to determine if the reported information meets the statutory and agency guidelines for child maltreatment and should therefore result in a face-to-face contact with the child or

[1]This section is drawn from DePanfilis & Salus (2003).

youth and family and, if so, (2) to determine the urgency with which the agency must respond to the report. Intake workers interview persons calling with concerns about a report of suspected child abuse or neglect to make these decisions. In some states, there is a statewide hotline for making reports. In other states, reports are made to the local CPS agency.

Initial assessment. After receiving a report, CPS conducts an initial assessment/investigation by interviewing the child or youth, siblings, parents or other caregivers, and other individuals who may have information concerning the alleged maltreatment. If the referral information suggests that a crime may have been committed, these contacts by CPS are usually coordinated with law enforcement. Two key assessments that are conducted at this stage are an assessment of the safety of the child (i.e., whether there is imminent risk of severe harm) and an assessment of the risk of maltreatment (i.e., the likelihood of future child maltreatment). Key decisions at this stage are to determine: (1) whether child maltreatment occurred as defined by state law; (2) whether the child's or youth's immediate safety is a concern and, if it is, the interventions that will insure the child's protection; (3) whether there is a risk of future maltreatment and the level of that risk; and (4) whether continuing agency services are needed to help the family keep the child safe, reduce the risks of future maltreatment, and address any effects of child maltreatment. Some cases are closed at this stage if there is no basis to provide services to the child or youth and family.

Family assessment. The goal for all assessments in CPS is to gather and analyze information that will support sound decisionmaking regarding the safety, permanency, and well-being of the child or youth. Once a determination of child abuse and neglect has been made and the child's immediate safety has been insured, the next step is to conduct a family assessment. The family assessment is a comprehensive process for identifying, considering, and weighing factors that affect the child's or youth's safety, permanency, and well-being. The goal of this assessment is to develop, in partnership with the family, the plans and services needed to assure the child's safety, permanency, and well-being (U.S. Department of Health and Human Services 2000). During this stage, the CPS worker engages family members in a process to understand their strengths, risks, and intervention needs. Key decisions at this stage are to determine: (1) the risk factors creating concern that the child may be maltreated in the future; (2) the protective factors or strengths that may reduce the likelihood of future maltreatment; (3) the effects of maltreatment observed in the child and/or other family members; and (4) the level of motivation or readiness of family members to participate in intervention that will reduce the risk of maltreatment and address any effects of maltreatment.

Intervention planning. To achieve the programmatic outcomes of CPS (i.e., child safety, child permanency, child well-being, and family well-being), intervention must be planned and purposeful. These outcomes are achieved through three types of plans: (1) a safety plan, which is developed whenever it is determined that the child is at risk of imminent severe harm; (2) a case plan, which follows the family assessment and sets forth outcomes and goals and describes how the family will work toward these outcomes; and (3) if a child or youth has been placed in out-of-home care, a concurrent case plan, which identifies alternative forms of permanency and addresses both how reunification can be achieved and how legal permanency with a new parent can be achieved if efforts to reunify fail. Key decisions at the case planning stage are to determine: (1) the case outcomes, which will be the target of intervention (e.g., enhanced family functioning, behavioral control of emotions, enhanced self-esteem, enhanced parent-child interaction); (2) the case goals that will help family members achieve these outcomes; (3) the interventions that will best

support the achievement of these goals and outcomes; and (4) the best provider of these interventions.

Service provision. This is the stage at which the case plan is implemented. It is the role of the CPS worker to arrange for, provide, and/or coordinate the delivery of services to maltreated children, their parents or other caregivers, and the family. The services that are selected to help families achieve outcomes and goals are based on an appropriate match of services to goals and on best practice principles. Other chapters in this volume provide examples of the types of services and treatment that might be employed by CPS workers to help reduce the risk of child maltreatment and/or help a child or other family member address the effects of maltreatment. Key decisions at this stage include: (1) identifying the specific services that will be delivered, and the intensity and duration of the services; (2) determining who is best positioned to deliver these services; (3) determining appropriate intervals for evaluating family progress; and (4) specifying mechanisms for coordinating among service providers (e.g., developing and sharing information, schedule of team meetings).

Evaluation of progress. Assessment is an ongoing process that begins with the first client contact and continues throughout the life of the case. Progress toward achievement of outcomes and goals should be formally evaluated at least every 3 months. Key decisions that must be made during this stage of the process include assessing: (1) the current safety status of the child or youth; (2) level of achievement of family-level outcomes; (3) level of achievement of goals and tasks in the case plan; (4) changes in the risk and protective factors previously identified; and (5) level of success in addressing any of the effects of maltreatment on the child or youth and other family members.

Case closure. The process of ending the relationship between the CPS worker and the family involves a mutual review of progress and includes a review of the beginning, middle, and end of the helping relationship. Optimally cases are closed when families have achieved their outcomes and goals, children or youth are safe, and the risk of maltreatment has been reduced or eliminated. Cases are sometimes closed, however, when families still need assistance. When needs are still apparent that go outside the scope of the CPS system, every effort is made to help the family receive services through appropriate community agencies. Some closings occur because the client discontinues services and the agency does not have a sufficient basis to refer the situation to juvenile or family court. When this happens, the caseworker will carefully document what risks may still be present so that this information is available should the family be referred to the agency at a later time.

Outcomes of CPS

With the passage of ASFA in 1997, CPS agencies are required to design their intervention systems to measure the achievement of outcomes (see the chapter by Sahonchik, Frizsell, & O'Brien). There has been consensus that child welfare outcomes at the program level, may be organized around four domains: child safety, child permanence, child well-being, and family well-being. Although all four are important, federal and state laws emphasize child safety and permanence, and these two outcomes are often used in global evaluation of agency or system performance. In contrast, at the individual case level, caseworkers usually attempt to achieve child safety and permanence through efforts to insure child and family well-being (Courtney 2000).

Child and Youth Safety

The safety of children and youth is the paramount concern that guides CPS practice. Children and youth are safe when they are first and foremost protected from abuse and neglect and safely maintained in their own homes when-

ever possible (U.S. Department of Health and Human Services 2000). When safety is assessed, caseworkers are determining the degree to which a child or youth is secure from the threat of danger, harm, or loss. In many states, the evaluation of child safety is equivalent to the determination that the child is at imminent risk of serious harm (DePanfilis 1997). Safety is the overarching consideration in casework decisionmaking, service provision, placement, and planning for permanency (U.S. Department of Health and Human Services 2000).

Child and Youth Permanence

Permanency focuses primarily on insuring that children and youth have stability in their living situations and the continuity of family relationships and connections is preserved for children (U.S. Department of Health and Human Services 2000). Creating permanent living arrangements and emotional attachments for children and youth is a primary CPS outcome, particularly when they have been placed in out-of-home care due to abuse or neglect. This goal is based on the assumption that stable, caring relationships in a family setting are essential for the healthy growth and development of the child. The emphasis is on the provision of reasonable efforts to prevent removal and reunify families, and on promoting the timely adoption of children and youth who cannot return safely to their own homes (Courtney 2000; U.S. Department of Health and Human Services 2000).

Child and Youth Well-Being

Although CPS practice focuses primarily on safety and permanency for children and youth, the general well-being of children and youth who come in contact with the system must also be addressed. In particular, the CPS worker is concerned that any effects of child maltreatment on the child's or youth's physical, emotional, behavioral, and cognitive development be identified. This requires that children's and youth's physical and mental health, educational, and other needs are assessed and that preventive or treatment services are provided or arranged for, when warranted (Courtney 2000).

Family Well-Being

Families must function at some basic level to provide a safe and permanent environment for raising children and adolescents. This includes demonstrating financial, emotional, and social self-sufficiency; providing age-appropriate supervision; and developing and sustaining nurturing parent-child relationships. Caseworkers are expected to facilitate change in the family so that the family can meet the basic needs of its members and insure their protection. Interventions are geared to maximize family strengths and reduce risks.

Effectiveness of CPS

Since passage of ASFA in 1997, the U.S. Department of Health and Human Services (DHHS) has been charged to determine the extent to which states are successful in attaining targeted outcomes and identify areas where assistance is needed (see the chapter by Milner, Mitchell, & Hornsby). One way that DHHS fulfills this mandate is by producing an annual report to Congress related to state performance on seven national child welfare outcomes (U.S. Department of Health and Human Services 2004b). Data for this report are based both on self-assessments and on-site Child and Family Service Reviews (CFSRs). One outcome area related to child safety that most directly relates to the performance of CPS programs addresses the recurrence of child maltreatment (U.S. Department of Health and Human Services 2004b:252):

> Outcomes Report Measure 1.1—Maltreatment recurrence. CFSR National Standard: Of all children who were victims of substantiated or indicated child abuse and/or neglect during the first 6 months of the period under review, 6.1% or fewer children had another substantiated or indicated report within 6 months of the first report.

In 2001, 40 states reported sufficient data to the National Child Abuse and Neglect Data System to calculate outcome measure 1.1. Analyses of these data suggested differences between states, as the percentages of maltreatment recurrence within a 6-month period ranged from 1.8 to 14.1, with a median of 8.0 (U.S. Department of Health and Human Services 2004a). Thirteen states (32.5%) met the national standard for this measure of 6.1% or less. Those states in rank order from lowest percentage of recurrences to highest were: Virginia, Pennsylvania, Delaware, South Carolina, Michigan, Arizona, Texas, Minnesota, Nebraska, West Virginia, Maine, Wyoming, and Arkansas. In 10 states (25%), maltreatment recurrence within 6 months was greater than 10.0% (California, Connecticut, Illinois, Iowa, Massachusetts, Missouri, Montana, New York, Rhode Island, and Washington). In four states (10%), maltreatment recurrence within 6 months was less than 4.0% (Delaware, Michigan, Pennsylvania, and South Carolina). A comparison between 1999 and 2001 is depicted in table 1.

TABLE 1. *Contrast of State Performance on the Recurrence of Child Abuse and Neglect between 1999 and 2001*

	Year			National
Outcome Measure	1999	2000	2001	Standard (%)
Percentage of children who were victims of substantiated or indicated child abuse and/or neglect during the first 6 months of reporting period and who had another substantiated or indicated report within a 6-month period	8.5 ($n = 29$)	8.6 ($n = 34$)	8.9 ($n = 40$)	≤6.1

Source: U.S. Department of Health and Human Services (2004b).

Contrasting the findings with respect to outcome measure 1.1, DHHS used information from completed CFSRs (U.S. Department of Health and Human Services 2004b) to speculate on the reasons for poor performance related to the recurrence of child abuse and neglect. Information from the analysis of data from the CFSR final reports suggests that the difficulties states experience in preventing maltreatment recurrence may be due to one or more of the following:

- Risk assessments that are inadequate with respect to identifying underlying family issues, such as substance abuse and domestic violence;
- Services that do not sufficiently address risk issues, such as providing parenting education services when parents have domestic violence problems; and
- Monitoring of families that is insufficient to assess service participation and change in risk factors in cases in which children remain in their homes.

CPS Reforms

In 1993, the U.S. Advisory Board on Child Abuse and Neglect noted that child protection systems in this country were in a state of emergency and called for a new national neighborhood-based strategy for protecting children. Since that time, results of the Harvard Executive Session, a task force that studied the child protection system, suggested that the CPS system problems could be categorized into five primary criticisms (Waldfogel 1998b).

- *Overinclusion.* Some families are referred to CPS who should not be. Families may have other problems that warrant intervention by other service systems but reporting sources contact CPS out of ignorance. Referral may also occur for malicious reasons. In either case, families come in contact with the CPS system inappropriately.
- *Capacity.* The number of families referred to the system exceeds the system's ability to

respond effectively. The resources devoted to support CPS systems have not kept pace with the demands on the systems to accept and respond to reports of child maltreatment effectively.
- *Underinclusion.* Some families who should be referred to CPS are not. It is well documented that many more children are suspected to be victims of child maltreatment than are actually reported to CPS (Sedlak & Broadhurst 1993).
- *Service orientation.* The authoritative approach of some CPS systems is not appropriate for many of the families referred to it. Because child abuse and neglect is the consequence of the complex interplay between risk and protective factors, families are identified with problems at all stages of problem development. Not all families will benefit from an investigative response.
- *Service delivery.* Many families do not receive the services they need. As reflected in fig. 1, many families referred with problems caring for their children are not provided services through our current CPS system.

During the past 10 years, there has been a growing consensus that states and communities need to change the way they protect children and youth, and many states have taken the lead to make the protection of children a community responsibility. The U.S. Advisory Board on Child Abuse and Neglect (1993) based their recommendations on the idea that the local neighborhood or community can assist in the identification and prevention of conditions that lead to child maltreatment. Other experts (Waldfogel 1998a,b) have also suggested that it may be time to rethink the manner in which our CPS systems are structured. One type of reform to CPS systems, called "differential response systems," have implemented nonadversarial, flexible responses to family circumstances. Systems are redesigned to deliver quality supportive services the first time red flags are identified instead of waiting for children and youth to experience serious and sometimes fatal injuries from neglect or abuse. Community agencies in partnership with CPS work to triage services so that together the community can help families meet the basic needs of their children and keep them safe. A national study of child welfare reforms (U.S. Department of Health and Human Services 2003) identified 20 states that offer one or more alternatives to the traditional CPS investigative response. In policy, the overall goals of the alternative response systems identified by this study were to provide a response option to those families whose situations did not meet the mandate or criteria for CPS involvement, to serve low-risk or low-severity situations, and/or to ameliorate family situations. State policies emphasized overlapping but slightly different purposes of alternative response options. Eleven states (55.0%) identified child safety as a purpose of the alternative response; nine states (45.0%) identified family preservation or strengthening as a purpose of the response; and four states (20.0%) identified preventing child abuse and neglect as a purpose. Although most evaluations of these efforts are at preliminary stages, some early results look promising (Institute of Applied Research 1998, 2003; Texas Department of Protective and Regulatory Services 1999; Virginia Department of Social Services 1999).

Summary

CPS is the central agency responding to reports of child abuse and neglect and intervening to increase the safety of children and youth, reduce the risk of future maltreatment, and address the effects of child abuse and neglect. To be truly successful, CPS intervention must be coordinated with other community agencies at each stage of the CPS process. At intake, CPS depends on other professionals, community providers, and the general public to identify children and youth who may be at risk of child abuse or neglect. At initial assessment, CPS often coordinates the initial assessment with law enforcement's investigation. During family assessment, the CPS worker depends on assessments provided by mental health professionals and addictions specialists to truly understand the strengths and needs of all family members. During service provision, the CPS worker may coordinate services provided by other community service providers who may be in the best position to respond to the complex treatment needs of the child or youth and other family members. Finally, evaluating family progress and deciding when services are no longer necessary are best accomplished in collaboration with the family and all members of the intervention team. Ultimately, the protection of children and youth is a community responsibility.

REFERENCES

Adoption and Safe Families Act. (1997). P.L. 105-89.

Adoption Assistance and Child Welfare Act. (1980). P.L. 96-272.

American Professional Society on the Abuse of Children. (1995). Practice guidelines on the psychosocial evaluation of suspected psychological maltreatment in children and adolescents. Chicago: American Professional Society on the Abuse of Children.

Berliner, L. (2000). What is sexual abuse? In H. Dubowitz & D. DePanfilis (eds.), *Handbook for child protection practice*, pp. 18–22. Thousand Oaks, CA: Sage.

Brassard, M. R., & Hart, S. (2000). What is psychological maltreatment? In H. Dubowitz & D. DePanfilis (eds.), *Handbook for child protection practice*, pp. 23–27. Thousand Oaks, CA: Sage.

Child Abuse Prevention and Treatment Act. (1974). P.L. 93-247.

Child Welfare League of America. (1999). *CWLA standards of excellence for services for abused or neglected children and their families*, revised ed. Washington, DC: Child Welfare League of America.

Courtney, M. (2000). What outcomes are relevant for intervention. In H. Dubowitz & D. DePanfilis (eds.), *Handbook for child protection practice*, pp. 373–383. Thousand Oaks, CA: Sage.

Davidson, H. A. (1997). The courts and child maltreatment. In M. E. Helfer, R. S. Kempe, & R. D. Krugman (eds.), *The battered child*, fifth ed., pp. 482–499. Chicago: University of Chicago Press.

DePanfilis, D. (1997). Is the child safe? How do we respond to safety concerns? In T. Morton & W. Holder (eds.), *Decision making in children's protective ser-*

vices, pp. 121–142. Atlanta: National Resource Center on Child Maltreatment.

DePanfilis, D., & Salus, M. (2003). *Child protective services: A guide for caseworkers.* Washington, DC: U.S. Department of Health and Human Services. Retrieved June 3, 2004, from nccanch.acf.hhs.gov/profess/tools/usermanual.cfm.

Dubowitz, H. (2000a). What is child neglect? In H. Dubowitz & D. DePanfilis (eds.), *Handbook for child protection practice*, pp. 10–14. Thousand Oaks, CA: Sage.

Dubowitz, H. (2000b). What is physical abuse? In H. Dubowitz & D. DePanfilis (eds.), *Handbook for child protection practice*, pp. 15–17. Thousand Oaks, CA: Sage.

Feller, J. N., Davidson, H. A., Hardin, M., & Horowitz, R. M. (1992). *Working with the courts in child protection.* Washington, DC: National Center on Child Abuse and Neglect. Retrieved June 3, 2004, from nccanch.acf.hhs.gov/pubs/usermanuals/courts/courts.pdf.

Goldman, J., & Salus, M. K. (2003). *A coordinated response to child abuse and neglect: The foundation for practice.* Washington, DC: Department of Health and Human Services. Retrieved June 3, 2004, from nccanch.acf.hhs.gov/profess/tools/usermanual.cfm.

Institute of Applied Research. (1998). *Missouri child protection services family assessment and response demonstration impact evaluation: Digest of findings and conclusions.* St. Louis, MO: Institute of Applied Research.

Institute of Applied Research. (2003). *Minnesota alternative response evaluation second annual report: Executive summary.* St. Louis, MO: Institute of Applied Research.

National Association of Public Child Welfare Administrators. (1999). *Guidelines for a model system of protective services for abused and neglected children and their families.* Washington, DC: American Public Human Services Association.

National Clearinghouse on Child Abuse and Neglect Information. (2003a). *Child abuse and neglect state statutes series statues-at-a-glance reporting procedures.* Retrieved June 3, 2004, from nccanch.acf.hhs.gov/general/legal/statutes/sag/repproc.cfm.

National Clearinghouse on Child Abuse and Neglect Information. (2003b). *Major federal legislation concerned with child protection, child welfare, and adoption.* Retrieved June 3, 2004, from nccanch.acf.hhs.gov/pubs/otherpubs/majorfedlegis.cfm.

National Clearinghouse on Child Abuse and Neglect Information. (2004). *Child maltreatment 2002: Summary of key findings.* Retrieved June 3, 2004, from nccanch.acf.hhs.gov/pubs/factsheets/canstats.cfm#2.

Omnibus Budget Reconciliation Act. (1993). P.L. 103-66.

Sedlak, A., & Broadhurst, D. (1993). *Third national incidence study of child abuse and neglect.* Washington, DC: U.S. Department of Health and Human Services.

Strengthening Abuse and Neglect Courts Act. (2000). P.L. 106-314.

Texas Department of Protective and Regulatory Services. (1999). *Flexible response evaluation.* Austin: Texas Department of Protective and Regulatory Services.

U.S. Advisory Board on Child Abuse and Neglect. (1993). *Neighbors helping neighbors: A new national strategy for the protection of children.* Washington, DC: Department of Health and Human Services.

U.S. Department of Health and Human Services. (1988). *Study findings: Study of national incidence and prevalence of child abuse and neglect: 1988.* Washington, DC: U. S. Government Printing Office.

U.S. Department of Health and Human Services. (2000). *Rethinking child welfare practice under the Adoption and Safe Families Act of 1997.* Washington, DC: U.S. Government Printing Office.

U.S. Department of Health and Human Services. (2003). *National study of child protective services systems and reform efforts review of state CPS policy.* Washington, DC: U.S. Department of Health and Human Services. Retrieved June 6, 2004, from aspe.hhs.gov/hsp/cps-status03/state-policy03/.

U.S. Department of Health and Human Services. (2004a). *Child maltreatment 2002: Reports from the states to the national Child Abuse and Neglect Data System.* Washington, DC: U.S. Government Printing Office. Retrieved June 3, 2004, from www.acf.hhs.gov/programs/cb/publications/cmreports.htm.

U.S. Department of Health and Human Services. (2004b). *Child welfare outcomes 2001: Annual report to Congress.* Washington, DC: U.S. Department of Health and Human Services. Retrieved June 6, 2004, from www.acf.hhs.gov/programs/cb/publications/cwo01/.

Virginia Department of Social Services. (1999). *Final report on the multiple response system for child protective services in Virginia.* Richmond: Virginia Department of Social Services.

Waldfogel, J. (1998a). Rethinking the paradigm for child protection. *Protecting Children from Abuse and Neglect*, 8(1), 104–119.

Waldfogel, J. (1998b). *The future of child protection.* Cambridge, MA: Harvard University Press.

ARON SHLONSKY
EILEEN D. GAMBRILL

Risk Assessment in Child Welfare

Challenges and Opportunities

Child welfare staff members make many decisions based on judgments. One concerns risk assessment: will this parent abuse or reabuse his or her child in the near future? What is the probability that she or he will do so? Risk assessment requires the integration of various kinds of data (e.g., self-report, observation, agency protocol) that differ in their accuracy, complexity, and subsequent value when making key decisions. Risk assessment is subject to a host of errors, including overestimating or underestimating the true probability of risk to a child. Such errors may result in failing to protect children from harm or imposing unneeded services that increase rather than decrease risk, such as unwarranted placement of the children in foster care. Efforts to improve decisionmaking in child welfare have typically focused on the development of risk assessment tools. As of 1996, at least 76% of U.S. states used some type of risk assessment measure as a decision aid in child welfare cases (Tatara 1994); however, most have questionable reliability and/or validity (Camasso & Jagannathan 2000; Lyons, Doueck, & Wodarski 1996; Wald & Woolverton 1990). More recent actuarial instruments developed by the Children's Research Center have the potential to lessen some of these concerns (Baird, Wagner, Healy, & Johnson 1999; Baird & Wagner 2000), yet other issues remain.

The Decisionmaking Context

Decisions are made in a context of uncertainty. Caseworkers must distinguish between child neglect, bad parenting, and the effect of poverty, and they must do this without the aid of accurate assessment tools. Both personal and environmental factors influence decisions. Barriers to accurate decisions include (1) limited knowledge; (2) limited information processing capacities; (3) personal obstacles, such as lack of perseverance, reliance on ineffective problem-solving strategies, and lack of familiarity with problem-related knowledge; and (4) the task environment. Problems that confront clients are often difficult, challenging even the most skilled staff. Predictions must be made under considerable uncertainty in terms of the relationship between the information at hand (predictor variables) and service outcome. Rarely is all relevant material available, hampering problem-solving efforts. Even when a great deal is known, this knowledge is usually in the form of statistical associations that cannot readily be calculated without assistance (Dawes 1998). Competing social values may also influence error. For example, steps must be taken to protect children from abuse while maximizing the decisionmaking freedom of parents.

Although the strategies practitioners use to simplify judgmental tasks and decrease effort may often help in making accurate judgments, at other times, they may result in errors. Preconceptions may get in the way, as well as day-to-day mood changes that influence judgment. Not only are initial beliefs resistant to new evidence, they also are remarkably resistant to challenges of the evidence that led to them (see Gambrill 1990; Hastie & Dawes 2001). Practi-

302

tioners are subject to a number of confirmation biases. For example, they disregard data that do not support their preferred beliefs and assign exaggerated importance to data that do support their beliefs (for a review, see Klayman 1995). The fundamental attribution error is common, in which causes are mistakenly attributed to dispositional characteristics of the person (e.g., impulsivity) and environmental variables (e.g., poor quality housing) are overlooked. These cognitive biases highlight the importance of developing risk assessment measures that minimize their influence. Misunderstandings regarding probabilities can result in faulty problem solving. Child protection services (CPS) workers are not generally taught how to think statistically, instead relying on a combination of experience, intuition, and individual heuristics. Common errors in assessing how closely two or more events are related include ignoring nonoccurrences, preconceptions about which events are related, and attempted proof by selected instances (attending to observed rather than relative frequency).

Environmental characteristics also influence decisions. Decisions made in child welfare are affected by the values and policies of agencies and the broader community (Costin, Karger, & Stoesz 1996; Margolin 1997; Pelton 1989). Time pressures and distractions may encourage a mindless, mechanical approach in which decisions are made with little care. Pressure to conform may result in poor decisions, as illustrated by the play of "group think" in case conferences (Dingwall, Eekelaar, & Murray 1983; Janis 1982). Group think refers to neglecting alternative views in a group focused on attaining agreement with one particular view (e.g., see Janis 1982).

Actuarial vs. Clinical Decisionmaking

The many sources of bias suggest the need for procedures that minimize them. Actuarial models are designed to address some of these biases (see Gambrill & Shlonsky 2000). They are based on empirical relationships between certain pre-dicted variables and outcomes. Actuarial models can be contrasted to consensus-based systems in which practitioners assess selected characteristics identified by agreement among experts, and then make their own judgment about an outcome, such as risk. Both can be contrasted to clinical intuition, which is not informed by expert consensus. To date, more than 130 studies have found actuarial models to be superior to clinical prediction in a variety of complex circumstances (Dawes, Faust, & Meehl 1989; Grove & Meehl 1996). Risk assessment models in child welfare are, essentially, lists of variables (e.g., caregiver and child characteristics or attributes, abuse circumstances, environmental circumstances) that have been found to predict an outcome of interest (e.g., the initial occurrence or the recurrence of abuse). Concerns about actuarial processes raised by Wald and Woolverton (1990) nearly a decade ago remain (see the section on methodological challenges).

Decisionmaking in child welfare has been consistently characterized by low reliability (Lindsey 1992). Reliability refers to the degree to which different workers make the same placement decisions when presented with the same data. Lindsey (1992) generously estimates the reliability of placement decisions to be .25 and, using figures derived from a nationwide survey (Lindsey 1991) estimates that, even with perfect validity (the degree to which a measure actually predicts an event), the actual "hit rate" (number of correctly classified cases) with this reliability can only reach 72%. According to Lindsey, this finding means that, overall, 48% of placements were unnecessary and 45% of the children needing placement remained at home. Following up on Lindsey's work, Ruscio (1998) showed that the hit rate assuming zero validity (completely random) is 58%. Thus the actual hit rate probably lies between 58% and 78%, indicating that there is a high error rate in child protective services placement decisions. More recently, Baird and Wagner (2000) found that an actuarial model (the Michigan Family Risk model) had far greater predictive validity compared to two consensual models (the Washington and California models), yet the hit rate is still low enough to be of concern.

Methodological Challenges

Although actuarial models out-predict clinical decisions, they are limited in their predictive capacity by many factors. Other tools may be useful for different types of case decisions, but suffer from many of the same factors.

Definitional Dilemmas

Predicting child abuse and neglect is made more difficult by the vague definitions of outcome measures. The criteria defining maltreatment are diffuse across studies, making metaanalysis impossible (Wald & Woolverton 1990). Although neglect is the most common form of child maltreatment, with a nationwide occurrence estimated at 59% of investigated referrals (U.S. Department of Health and Human Services 2003), its definition is characterized by subjectivity (Rose & Meezan 1996), decreasing the likelihood of accurate assessment. For example, Zuravin (1999) reviewed all empirical studies with findings regarding child neglect in a major child maltreatment journal between 1992 and 1996. Out of 25 articles, only two used the same operational definition. (It should be noted that the estimate of 59% is based on incomplete data—not all states submitted information—and children could have been counted more than once if more than one report was filed during the reporting period. The University of California–Berkeley Center for Social Services Research [Needell et al. 2004] calculates the percentage of substantiated or indicated maltreatment referrals of children in California using unduplicated counts. They find that 52% of substantiated referrals are for neglect, although this is likely an underestimate, as neglect is only counted in the absence of physical or sexual abuse.)

To date, actuarial tools in child welfare use substantiation (social work finding that maltreatment has occurred) as their outcome variable measuring the recurrence of abuse, and this is usually done retrospectively. However, substantiation may not be the most valid measure of recurrence (Drake 1996; Wolock, Sherman, Feldman, & Metzger 2001). The use of the instrument itself must also be considered. Is the tool being used to assess risk initially, to assess whether a child should be returned to their biological parents, or at some other point in the life of the case?

Concerns about Reliability and Validity

Although the distinctions mentioned in the preceding section have varying types of risk associated with varying sets of predictors, the same risk assessment instrument may be used by agencies at different points in time, resulting in varying degrees of reliability and validity (Camasso & Jagannathan 2000; Wald & Woolverton 1990). Reliability refers to the consistency in use of a measure: does a measure yield the same results at different times or with different raters? Validity refers to whether a measure actually measures what it was designed to. A variety of other factors, such as changes in risk over time and lack of baserate data (see sections that follow), may also compromise reliability. In addition, research concerning risk assessment often makes use of previously constructed measures (see English & Graham 2000); some portion of them, essentially establishing a new measure (see Wolock, Sherman, Feldman, & Metzger 2001); or creates a new measure. Examples include measures of social isolation, family conflict, parenting skills, and depression. There is a lack of attention to and concern with reliability and validity of measures used (e.g., of parenting skills, child behavior).

Changes in Risk over Time or in the Stages of Development

Risk may change over time (DePanfilis & Zuravin 1998) and protective services workers may be unaware of the point in the cycle at which they are intervening. This has implications for prediction. If escalation is always assumed at the point of risk assessment, the false positive rate might be very high (low specificity). If escalation is not assumed, the number of false negatives might be high (low sensitivity). CPS workers may get some of the more obvious serious cases at a certain stage in the process (high escalation) and encounter a certain number of low risk cases with the potential to escalate, only they do not know how to identify them.

Absence of Baserate Data

The risk of recurrence cannot be explored in the absence of intervention by child protective service agencies (Wald & Woolverton 1990). For instance, researchers in the field cannot know the real rates of recurrence of the most obvious and severe maltreatment because children experiencing such abuse are most likely removed from the homes of their abusers or major steps are taken to insure their safety. Therefore, those in the field are mostly limited to knowing the rates of recurrence among parents or caregivers who committed less serious offenses, those for whom the discovery of the extent of maltreatment was limited, or for whom the maltreatment is in the beginning stages of a more severe progression. Given these limitations, obtaining an accurate baserate of maltreatment is probably impossible. Researchers can only measure the effectiveness of one predictive tool against the other. Furthermore, discovering the false positive rate is almost impossible. Once the risk has been responded to (i.e., child welfare services are provided), the likelihood of recurrence of abuse in the absence of intervention cannot be determined. Child abuse investigation is, by definition, a reactive process.

Predicting for Individuals

Although an instrument may have high overall predictive validity, the predictive capacity for an individual is lower because of the wide variation among individuals. Thus, even though using a good assessment instrument can im-

prove the overall rate of correct predictions over time, predictions for specific individuals are less certain.

Severity as a Problem

Although severity of abuse is listed in almost every consensus-based and actuarial model, there is little or no indication that it is related to recurrence of abuse (Camasso & Jagannathan 2000; Wald & Woolverton 1990). This may be in part because of the high likelihood that the most severe cases result in the most severe interventions (placement), thereby eliminating the possibility of future harm (again, we come back to the intervention effect). If this is the case, severity of abuse should be left out of the model once intervention has occurred. An examination of the severity of reabuse (as opposed to severity of initial abuse) may be more fruitful. When examining recurrence, however, severity of abuse is not usually addressed. Most studies use rate of re-report, rate of resubstantiation, and rate of reentry to foster care as indicators of reabuse. These measures do not address severity. A notable exception is Children's Research Center's models of reabuse resulting in injury or hospitalization (Johnson 2004; Wagner, Johnson, & Johnson 1998). These measures, although promising, are still limited by the low baserate of occurrence of injury.

Sensitivity and Specificity

Despite being an improvement over clinical and consensus-based models, actuarial models are rarely able to predict reabuse at acceptable levels of sensitivity (correctly classifying those children who will be reabused). There is an inverse relationship between sensitivity and specificity (correctly classifying those children who will not be reabused). That is, as the sensitivity of an instrument is increased, its specificity decreases. High sensitivity results in a high percentage of true positives (children identified as high risk who subsequently experience reabuse), as well as a high percentage of false positives (children identified as high risk who do not subsequently experience reabuse). High specificity results in a high percentage of true negatives (children identified as low risk who do not subsequently experience reabuse), as well as a high percentage of false negatives (children identified as low risk who subsequently experience reabuse). The baserate of reabuse will influence the percentage of false positives and false negatives (see Munro, in press). Assigning risk involves establishing cut points—values at which different decisions are made above and below the value. Media coverage surrounding a child abuse fatality might prompt a shift to "conservative" policies (lowering of cut points), resulting in an increase in the number of false positives. However, attending to false positives and false negatives may not be the best way to assess the efficacy of risk assessment tools. Instead, a graduated classification scheme has been proposed and is being used as a decision aid that identifies those children at ever-increasing risk of reabuse (Baird & Wagner 2000). That is, rather than rely on a binary prediction (reabuse/ no reabuse), an actuarial classification scheme categorizes people into varying degrees of risk (e.g., low, medium, high, very high). Thus, although the hit rate will be similar, the user gets a more nuanced sense of the degree of risk.

Implications for the Design and Use of Risk Assessment Tools

Collaborative efforts on the part of researchers, child welfare administrators, and line staff will be required to address challenges to the development of valid risk assessment tools.

Increasing Reliability

Researchers, while leaving room for innovation, should standardize the operational definitions of key variables included in studies of risk. Many individual risk items are open to interpretation and are based on clinical decisions. Each interpretation and action is subject to error. Individual risk measures, such as level of social or familial support, seriousness of injury, and severity of abuse, require judgments that

may be influenced by the availability of services and representative heuristics. In addition, protective service workers make decisions about the authenticity of claims made by parents, family members, abuse reporters, and others as they input items into the risk assessment instrument. Once risk has been estimated, clinical skills are used to conduct an in-depth assessment, select and carry out service plans, identify other needs, and evaluate progress. These tasks create other sources of risk.

Description of Reliability and Validity

Authors should clearly describe the reliability and validity of measures they use and inform readers when the measures used are of unknown reliability and validity. The aim is to provide sufficient information so that readers can review the status of the reliability and validity of the scales used.

Consideration of Baserates

Consideration of the baserates of relevant events in the general population should be incorporated into risk assessment models. For instance, child injuries occur in families not involved with CPS, and the rate of occurrence in the child welfare population is misleading if a comparable rate of occurrence in the noninvolved population is not considered in statistical calculations (see Munro 2002).

Temporal Considerations

Simply taking a cross section of child welfare cases, random or otherwise, counting the numbers of children who are reabused, and comparing risk factors can lead to inaccurate results as a consequence of sampling bias. Families involved in the child welfare system for longer periods of time would have a greater probability of study inclusion than would families entering and exiting care more quickly, yet these two types of families may be very different.

Attending to Strengths

Although there is a great deal of emphasis on family strengths in the child welfare literature, this emphasis is often lost in risk assessment models. Protective influences may interact with identified risk factors to minimize the likelihood of negative events (Macdonald & Macdonald 1998). Furthermore, risk may not be additive (i.e., adding deficits and subtracting strengths), but multiplicative (i.e., a specific combination of risk factors modifies their individual effect, increasing or decreasing risk in different ways) or have some other nonlinear effect (for a good discussion, see Selvin 1996). To incorporate strengths into a statistical model, detailed information about family strengths must be present in the case file (Wagner 2003). Otherwise, deficits will continue to predominate simply for lack of better information.

Establishing Clinical Overrides

Overrides should be tracked to establish their reliability and validity in comparison with the model as part of the model improvement process. However, the actuarial classification should only be overridden when the known probability of the outcome is close to zero. Otherwise, there will be a tendency to make more errors in the opposite direction and the two will not balance out (Grove & Meehl 1996).

Statistical Concerns

Although certain variables may be significant when considered individually, they may be highly correlated, and significance may fade when they are included in a multivariate analysis. Statistical bias is also a concern. For example, although relative risk between groups can be estimated using logistic regression, results are reported in terms of relative odds ratios (e.g., "the odds are 4 to 1 that a child will be re-abused given this set of characteristics"). Relative odds ratios, however, always overestimate relative risk if the true relative risk is less than 1 (less likely) or greater than 1 (more likely). These terms are only equivalent when there is no association (true relative risk = 1). In addition, relative risk is not the same as absolute risk. That is, a comparison of the risk for two groups

is not the same as the overall likelihood that an event will occur for either group. Both measures of risk are essential.

Implementation Concerns

A clumsy implementation process unattuned to the culture of the agency may undermine a tool's use, despite its ability to predict well. Risk assessment tools should be implemented only after careful evaluation, including review of the fidelity of the implementation process. All staff should be trained in the proper use of the tool, and proficiency tests should be given to check the effectiveness of training (e.g., in enhancing reliability). Risk assessment tools should be developed and implemented in an environment that supports consistency, constructive criticism, and accountability at all staff levels for in-house as well as contracted service providers, to increase safety and reduce risk to the children, families, child welfare staff, and agencies involved (see Gambrill & Shlonsky 2001).

Need for Systemic Risk Management Programs

Risk assessment in child welfare has largely focused on identifying individual or family risk factors associated with future harm or on the value of various assessment tools constructed of such factors, paying scant attention to risks posed by the system and its larger context. The term "risk assessment" implies that there is an effort to assess risk to children when, if one examines what is done, only some potential sources of risk are addressed (e.g., risk of biological parents to their children). A narrow approach has been taken to assessing risk to children who are potentially or actually involved in the child welfare system: developing risk assessment instruments to predict which children should come into care and which should not. This narrow approach ignores a host of other factors that may influence risk to children, including quality of assessment and services provided to children and families and the validity of evaluation methods. If we are concerned about risk to children, we should make efforts to identify and minimize *all* sources of avoidable risk. Research regarding risks suggests that this effort will require systemic risk management programs that attend to multiple sources of risk to children, including staff and management practices and policies that contribute to risk.

Ideally, risk management should minimize risk from all sources that contribute to unwanted outcomes (e.g., harm to children), not only those risks posed by parents to their children, but also risks posed by child welfare staff and service providers to clients. Procedures to decrease both types of risk should be put in place. Risks may be avoidable or unavoidable. We suggest that avoidable risks now taken in child welfare include incomplete assessment, referring clients to agencies offering ineffective services, and the pursuit of vague outcomes. Unnecessarily risky decisions during early phases influence risk during later phases. For example, if assessment is fragmented and incomplete, ineffective or harmful services may be selected. Agency administrators and practitioners can draw on practice-related research to identify practices and policies that minimize risk.

Unnecessary risks may result from the use of invalid risk assessment instruments and the misuse of valid measures. Research by Munro (1999) suggests that assessments of risk made by child welfare staff are based on a narrow range of evidence. A key avoidable risk to children may be the lack of an individualized assessment that permits judicious selection of service plans most likely to maximize positive outcomes. Approaches to assessment that pose unnecessary risk to children and families include using invalid measures (e.g., of parenting skills), describing outcomes vaguely, pathologizing clients, and overlooking assets.

It does little good to spend money to develop actuarial prediction methods if agencies then fail to provide appropriate services. Combining accurate assessment with high-quality services is essential for risk management (Moss 1995). Combining accurate risk assessment and evidence-based selection of services is a key step in minimizing risk to children, parents, social workers, and agencies. Currently, there is little clear description of variations in services (e.g., substance abuse, parenting programs) and their outcomes. For instance, parents are referred to many different parent training programs. Are they all equally effective? Are any effective? Are certain types of parent training programs better for certain types of parenting problems? At present, there is little clear information about what services are offered to what effect. For example, there is little information about the extent to which current parent training programs offered in child welfare take advantage of information available about the effectiveness of such programs and the barriers to their implementation (e.g., see Barlow 1997). Program evaluators and researchers should describe variations in services and their outcomes, including clear descriptions of services used (e.g., number of sessions, format used, duration of each session); outcomes sought, including intermediate steps; criteria used to evaluate whether each is attained; and the degree to which service components are empirically based (i.e., have survived critical tests of their effectiveness in relation to the desired outcomes). Other important questions include: How effective are these services for families identified by actuarial tools as high risk? Low risk? Are follow-up data available? What arrangements are made for generalization and maintenance of gains? How long do gains last?

Purchasing ineffective or harmful services increases the risk to children by losing opportunities to alter factors related to child maltreatment. For any service provider, the referring child welfare agency should examine the gap between those services they provide to referred clients, the services that should be provided based on related research findings, and those services that the client would find acceptable. For each service purchased, agency administrators, supervisors, and practitioners should ask: Is anything known about its effectiveness? If so, what? Does it do more good than harm? Or more harm than good? Is it of unknown effect (not being evaluated in a research setting or being evaluated poorly)? Or of unknown effect, but now being evaluated in a good research program? Vague agreements between child welfare agencies and referral agencies pose another unnecessary risk to children. Unless service agreements are clear regarding what is expected, providers cannot be held responsible for meeting desired outcomes, such as timely reports.

Providing services without carefully evaluating their impact opens the door to the wishful thinking that services will be successful when, in fact, there may be no progress or effects are harmful, ultimately increasing rather than decreasing risk. In addition, risk management requires an organizational culture and climate that facilitates and maintains related components (e.g., see Helmreich & Merritt 1998). Reason (1997:195, 196) suggests that a safety culture is composed of four critical components:

1. A reporting culture, defined as "an organizational climate in which people are prepared to report their errors and near misses";
2. A just culture, described as "an atmosphere of trust in which people are encouraged, even rewarded, for providing essential safety-related information—but in which they are also clear about where the line must be drawn between acceptable and unacceptable behavior";
3. A flexible culture—for example, shifting from a hierarchal mode of taking charge "to a flatter professional structure, where control passes to the task experts on the spot"; and
4. A learning culture, which involves the "willingness and the competence to draw the right conclusion from its safety information system, and the will to implement major reforms when their need is indicated."

Agencies should undertake an assessment to identify opportunities to shape their culture for effective management programs that minimize risk. An effective risk management program will require careful attention to contingencies in effect at an agency: What behaviors are reinforced, punished, or ignored? Are behaviors that contribute to risk management reinforced? Are tools and cues arranged that increase the likelihood that they occur? To change old norms or develop new culture, meaningful incentives will have to be provided to establish and maintain behaviors that minimize risk.

Yet another way to minimize risk is to track errors, accidents, and mistakes (both avoidable and unavoidable), and use this feedback to minimize those that are avoidable before a breach in the system occurs. Studies of risk and error reveal a systemic process that typically involves a number of "latent causes" (i.e., those that precede the point at which an error is made) that contribute to "manifest causes" (i.e., the point at which a mistake occurs) (Reason 1997, 2001; Vincent 2001). Examples of latent causes in child welfare include policies regarding caseworker home visits and caseload size. For instance, due to high caseloads (latent cause), a worker may fail to visit a child or not spend enough time with the child's family to adequately assess risk (manifest cause), and a parent may later abuse that child. Inappropriate blame and subsequent organizational response may stem from hindsight bias. Macdonald and Macdonald (1998:3) define this basic error in risk assessment as regarding "the outcome as evidence of the prior existence of a risk at a sufficiently high probability to justify intervention." They view hindsight bias as a misunderstanding of risk, not as excessive attention to outcome. The field should also distinguish between errors and moral lapses. The former are made in a context of good intentions. The latter are characterized by indifference to the rights of clients and the potential harms they may suffer. An environment must be created in which an open and informed analysis of individual and organizational errors, both latent and manifest, can occur. Open systems characterized by free flow of information and clear documentation should permit greater error recognition and encourage the adoption of promising systemic innovations.

Reviewing complaints made by clients provides information about how services can be improved. Ignoring or neglecting to harvest them poses another source of avoidable risk to children. A quality improvement program that includes an ongoing audit of key indicators is an integral part of an overall risk management program. Moss (1995:97) suggests that the essential features of quality improvement are that it is "reflective and not punitive or defensive; that it relies on learning and improving; and that it is based on an understanding of the needs of the customer [client] and on good evidence."

Thus we suggest that staff at all levels have responsibilities in relation to risk management. Administrators have a responsibility to arrange policies, audit systems, and contingency systems that minimize risks to children, while also attending to safeguarding the assets of the organization. They should be integrally involved in establishing effective risk management systems, critically reviewing the quality of these programs, arranging required training, and improving the program based on continuous feedback. Supervisors have the responsibility to see that agency policies are implemented effectively. Line staff members have a responsibility to report errors and maintain a level of expertise regarding agency procedures, measures used, and effective interventions for the clients they serve. Line staff should also be involved in maintaining and upgrading the system, as well as promoting a culture conducive to risk management.

Barriers to Systemic Risk Management Programs

Risk management programs highlight the uncertainty involved in making decisions. This may be an unpleasant topic for clients and social workers who search for certainty. Risk management programs cast the searchlight on staff and policy at all levels regarding what is done to what effect, not just on clients. Implementing such programs calls for an openness to criticism—in fact, a welcoming of criticism as a way to enhance the quality of services. These criticisms include a candid discussion of how much risk can be attenuated without altering basic structural arrangements (e.g., political and economic realities) that contribute to the likelihood of risk (see Halpern 1990). This broader view may be threatening, particularly in cultures in which mistakes are not viewed as opportunities for improvement, authoritarian policy reigns and clients have little say, and there is reluctance to alter broad structural arrangements.

The management of risk is closely connected to the knowledge the field seeks, the knowledge it ignores, and what those in the field do with what is learned, all of which is related to cognitive biases and risk-taking styles (e.g., see Mullen & Roth 1991). Decisions about what knowledge to seek, use, and disseminate influence risk to all parties involved in the child welfare systems: clients, staff, politicians, and taxpayers. Many decisions prevent the discovery of knowledge. We suggest that knowledge that helps to minimize the risk and increase the safety of children in the child welfare system includes:

1. A clear description of the reliability and validity of assessment methods used;
2. A description of what services are used to what effect;
3. A candid recognition of uncertainties involved in child welfare practice;
4. A description of avoidable and unavoidable errors, including their rates and contexts; and
5. Clear descriptions of the gaps between methods used and what research suggests is most likely to result in desired outcomes.

This call for transparency of what is done and to what effect will be threatening to many child welfare agency staff at all levels, but should be pursued nonetheless. Those in the field can draw on literature regarding innovation to design programs that increase the likelihood that valid assessment, intervention, and evaluation methods will be adopted and used appropriately (e.g., see Rogers 1995).

Factors that Encourage Implementation of Systematic Risk Management Programs

Several interrelated developments encourage the implementation of systemic risk management systems in child welfare. These developments include increased attention to the possibility of doing harm in the name of helping in the professions, consideration of mistakes and their systemic nature, and research describing the influences of organizational culture and climate on employee behavior (Reason 1997, 2001; Vincent 2001). Another key advance is the evidence-based practice movement, which draws on rigorous reviews of practice-related claims (e.g., see Oxman & Guyatt 1993), attends to ethical issues (e.g., involves clients as informed participants), and helps both professionals and clients gain access to practice- and/or policy-related research findings and critically appraise what they find.

Evidence-Based Practice

Evidence-based medicine (EBM) arose as an alternative to authority-based medicine in which decisions are based on such criteria as consensus, anecdotal experience, or tradition (see Chalmers 1983; Sackett, Richardson, Rosenberg, & Haynes 1997; Sackett, Straus, Richardson, Rosenberg, & Haynes 2000). Evidence-based practice (EBP) involves "the conscientious, explicit and judicious use of current best evidence in making decisions about the care of individual [clients]" (Sackett, Richardson, Rosenberg, & Haynes 1997:2). It consists of "integrating individual clinical expertise with the best available external clinical evidence

from systematic research concerning the efficacy and safety of therapeutic, rehabilitative, and preventive regimens" (1997:2). Clinical expertise is used to integrate information from diverse sources (Haynes, Devereaux, & Guyatt 2002). Sackett and colleagues (Sackett, Straus, Richardson, Rosenberg, & Haynes 2000:3–4) describe five steps in evidence-based practice:

1. Converting information needs related to practice decisions (e.g., about prevention, diagnosis, prognosis, therapy, causation) into answerable questions.
2. Tracking down with maximum effectiveness the best evidence with which to answer these questions.
3. Critically appraising that evidence for its validity (accuracy), impact (size of the effect), and applicability (usefulness in practice).
4. Applying the results of this appraisal to practice and policy decisions. This step involves deciding whether the evidence found (if any) applies to the decision at hand and considering client values and preferences in making decisions, as well as other applicability concerns.
5. Evaluating the effectiveness and efficiency in carrying out the previous steps and seeking ways to improve them in the future.

Advantages of EBP include:

- Enabling staff and clients to make decisions based on the best available evidence (e.g., helping practitioners to keep up-to-date with current research findings related to important decisions that affect children and their families);
- Encouraging participation in evidence-based continuing education programs that contribute to high-quality practice;
- Honoring ethical obligations to clients (e.g., to offer competent services, to fully inform clients); and
- Clearly describing outcomes sought and progress indicators, and tracking these on an ongoing basis.

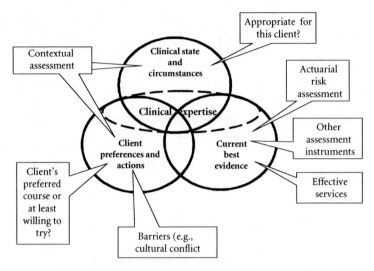

FIGURE 1. The process of EBP using risk assessment. From Haynes, Devereaux, and Guyatt (2002).

Hallmarks of EBP are transparency of what is done and to what effect, and a consideration of the values and expectations of clients, including involving clients as informed participants in decisions made. The transparency of what is done and to what effect should encourage risk management programs that minimize errors, mistakes, and harm and maximize the use of services found to help clients achieve valued outcomes. Increased attention to errors, mistakes, and harm in the helping professions and recognition of limited resources should also encourage risk management programs. These trends will increase accessibility of information related to important decisions for both clients and professionals.

The relationship of EBP to risk assessment is suggested in fig. 1. Using current best evidence as an entry point, an actuarial assessment of risk can target scarce resources to clients at highest risk. Relevant data sources on current best evidence include the Cochrane and Campbell Collaboration databases. A contextual assessment is needed to identify strengths and needs, as well as client preferences. At this point, current best evidence is again sought regarding

assessment tools, such as depression inventories and child behavioral indicators, and the effectiveness of service options, such as parenting classes. The result is integrated with client circumstances and characteristics, including client preferences, and clinical expertise is used to integrate data from diverse sources. Both risk assessment using an actuarial tool and contextual assessment are decision aids in evidence-based practice. To be viable, both aids must be supported by child welfare agencies. Such support requires an agency in which the values of EBP are incorporated, including transparency concerning what is done and to what effect. The agency must also integrate research with practice, involve clients as informed participants, and address application barriers.

Effective services should be identified and made available for locally prevalent problems. For instance, using data from actuarial and contextual assessment tools, each agency should identify interventions that are most successful with high-risk families. Such tailoring of services requires an ongoing effort to evaluate the impact of services. The use of high-quality experimental and quasi-experimental designs that incorporate intent-to-treat analyses, where appropriate, can be used to explore the effectiveness of interventions for clients at various risk levels. Administrative data are valuable for monitoring broad trends and suggesting future directions for services. In addition, those involved in developing risk assessment tools should take advantage of helpful guidelines for communicating and understanding risk (e.g., Gigerenzer & Edwards 2003) and attend carefully to involved parties' interests and background beliefs about risk, so that appropriate risk communicative tools are created (Morgan, Fischoff, Bostrom, & Atman 2002).

EBP and Risk Assessment:
An Abbreviated Example

To illustrate how risk assessment, EBP, and elements of risk management can be used at the client level, suppose an investigative CPS worker is presented with the following client scenario. A referral comes in from the local clinic stating that Mary, a single mother (aged 22) has continually failed to provide medical care for her only child, David (aged 5 months). Specifically, Mary has not followed through with treatment for David's chronic skin condition (not life threatening), the child appears dirty and unkempt, and Mary refuses to have her son immunized. Mary and David live with Mary's mother Joan (aged 50) in public housing. On investigation, the caseworker observes that the child does, indeed, have an apparently untreated skin condition, has been in the same dirty diaper for quite some time, and the house is not "infant safe" (i.e., small ingestible items, many sharp edges, heavy objects on unstable platforms, accessible harmful chemicals, exposed wiring, and other safety hazards abound).

A safety plan is developed in which immediate hazards are rectified and the child remains in the care of his mother. During the course of the investigation, the caseworker conducts a contextual assessment (Gambrill 1997, 2005) outlining the strengths and needs of this family. Some highlights include:

- Mary's mother (Joan) is a source of emotional and financial support, as is a network of relatives and friends;
- Mary provides for her child to the best of her current ability and is very strong in her conviction that she can take care of her child;
- Mary lacks some of the skills necessary to effectively and safely parent this child (she is unaware of many of David's developmental needs, has unrealistic developmental expectations, and her disciplinary skills are largely limited to yelling and angry protests); and
- There are some concerns that Mary suffers from depression (a BDI-2 was scored well above the clinical cut point).

At the close of investigation, a risk assessment instrument was completed (California Family Risk Assessment; see fig. 2), finding this family to have a moderate degree of risk of having a recurrence of maltreatment in the next 18 to 24 months (the family received a score of 4 out of a possible 10 on the neglect subscale of the instrument). If unsafe housing conditions had not been corrected, the score would have been 5, placing the family in the high-risk category. Prior to the close of the investigation, the caseworker began developing a case plan using the process of EBP (Sackett 2003) as highlighted in Gibbs (2003). A searchable effectiveness question was posed (for depressed single mothers of infants with a substantiated allegation of child neglect, what intervention is most likely to prevent further incidents of maltreatment, including population, problem, intervention, and outcome), a search was conducted using the Cochrane Collaboration databases, Medline, and PsycInfo incorporating methodologic filters, and findings were evaluated for rigor (see Gibbs 2003). This process revealed that home visiting by

CALIFORNIA FAMILY RISK ASSESSMENT

Case Name: _____ Case #: _____ Date: ___/___/_____

County Name: _____ Worker Name: _____ Worker ID#: _____

NEGLECT	Score	ABUSE	Score

N1. Current Complaint is for Neglect

    a. No.. 0

    b. Yes .... 1 _____

A1. Current Complaint is for Abuse

    a. No.. 0

    b. Yes .... 1 _____

N2. Prior Investigations (assign highest score that applies)

    a. None.. 0

    b. One or more, *abuse* only 1

    c. One or two for *neglect* 2

    d. Three or more for *neglect* .... 3 _____

A2. Number of Prior Abuse Investigations (number:)

    a. None.. 0

    b. One.. 1

    c. Two or more .... 2 _____

N3. Household has Previously Received CPS (voluntary/court-ordered)

    a. No.. 0

    b. Yes .... 1 _____

A3. Household has Previously Received CPS (voluntary/court-ordered)

    a. No.. 0

    b. Yes .... 1 _____

N4. Number of Children Involved in the CA/N Incident

    a. One, two, or three............................... 0

    b. Four or more .... 1 _____

A4. Prior Injury to a Child Resulting from CA/N

    a. No.. 0

    b. Yes .... 1 _____

N5. Age of Youngest Child in the Home

    a. Two or older 0

    b. Under two... 1

A5. Primary Caretaker's Assessment of Incident (check applicable items and add for score)

    a. Not applicable....................................... 0

    b. Blames child.. 1 _____

    c. Justifies maltreatment of a child......... 2 _____

N6. Primary Caretaker Provides Physical Care Inconsistent with Child Needs

    a. No.. 0

    b. Yes .... 1 _____

A6. Domestic Violence in the Household in the Past Year

    a. No.. 0

    b. Yes .... 2 _____

N7. Primary Caretaker has a Past or Current Mental Health Problem

    a. No.. 0

    b. Yes 1

A7. Primary Caretaker Characteristics (check applicable items and add for score)

    a. Not applicable 0

    b. Provides insufficient emotional/ .... psychological support .... 1 _____

    c. Employs excessive/inappropriate discipline... 1

    d. Domineering parent .... 1 _____

N8. Primary Caretaker has Historic or Current Alcohol or Drug Problem (Check applicable items and add for score)

    a. Not applicable 0

    b. Alcohol (current or historic) 1

    c. Drug (current or historic) .... 1 _____

A8. Primary Caretaker has a History of Abuse or Neglect as a Child

    a. No.. 0

    b. Yes .... 1 _____

N9.	Characteristics of Children in Household (Check applicable items and add for score)		A9.	Secondary Caretaker has Historic or Current Alcohol or Drug Problem

N9. Characteristics of Children in Household
(Check applicable items and add for score)

    a. Not applicable 0
    b. Medically fragile/failure to thrive 1
    c. Developmental or physical disability... 1
    d. Positive toxicology screen at birth...... 1 _____

A9. Secondary Caretaker has Historic or Current
Alcohol or Drug Problem

    a. No.. 0
    b. Yes, alcohol and/or drug (check all applicable)
       ___ Alcohol ___ Drug .... 1 _____

N10. Housing (check applicable items and add for score)

    a. Not applicable 0
    b. Current housing is physically unsafe ... 1
    c. Homeless at time of investigation ...... 2 _____

A10. Characteristics of Children in Household
(check appropriate items and add for score)

    a. Not applicable 0
    b. Delinquency history............................ 1
    c. Developmental disability 1
    d. Mental health/behavioral problem..... 1 _____

TOTAL NEGLECT RISK SCORE _____

TOTAL ABUSE RISK SCORE _____

SCORED RISK LEVEL. Assign the family's scored risk level based on the highest score on either the neglect or abuse instrument, using the following chart:

Neglect Score		Abuse Score		Scored Risk Level
0–1	_____	0–1	_____	Low
2–4	_____	2–4	_____	Moderate
5–8	_____	5–7	_____	High
9+	_____	8+	_____	Very High

POLICY OVERRIDES. Circle *yes* if a condition shown below is applicable in this case. If *any* condition is applicable, override final risk level to *very high.*

Yes   No   1. Sexual abuse case AND the perpetrator is likely to have access to the child victim.

Yes   No   2. Non-accidental injury to a child under age two.

Yes   No   3. Severe non-accidental injury.

Yes   No   4. Parent/caretaker action or inaction resulted in death of a child due to abuse or neglect (previous or current).

DISCRETIONARY OVERRIDE. If a discretionary override is made, circle yes, circle override risk level, and indicate reason. Risk level may be overridden one level higher.

Yes   No   5. If *yes,* override risk level (circle one):   Low   Moderate   High   Very High

Discretionary override reason:

Supervisor's Review/Approval of Discretionary Override: _____   Date: ___/___/_____

FINAL RISK LEVEL (circle final level assigned):   Low   Moderate   High   Very High

National Council on Crime and Delinquency/Children's Research Center, 426 South Yellowstone Drive, Suite 250, Madison, WI 53719. Phone (608) 831-1180. Reprinted with permission. Please do not use or distribute without approval.

FIGURE 2. California family risk assessment form.

nurses may have some success at preventing child abuse and is effective at decreasing accidental injury in high-risk cases (Han et al. 2003), although it should be noted that most families' involvement in studies preceded any contact with child protective services. The caseworker found that nurses were more effective than paraprofessionals (Olds et al. 2002) and that the presence of domestic violence in the home might compromise the benefits of the service (Eckenrode et al. 2000).

Based on the risk rating and the nature of the challenges faced by the family, the decision was made to open the case for in-home services. The results of the search were discussed with the client and she was amenable to nurse home-visiting services. She stated that she preferred nurses to doctors, indicating that she felt she would be more likely to listen to a nurse about how to best meet her child's needs. As a result of the agency's ongoing commitment to finding and obtaining high-quality services with evidence of effectiveness, home-visiting services had already been developed and were available through the county department of health. A referral was made and services were initiated promptly. The continuing social worker on the case proceeded to address Mary's depression using the same EBP process.

Conclusion

Risk assessment in child welfare is a necessary but uncertain endeavor, compromised by the lack of information needed to develop valid risk assessment tools (e.g., provision of services, which hinders knowledge regarding what would have happened without them). Actuarial models of risk assessment tools have the best batting average, but are limited in their capabilities. For example, they do not provide an individualized assessment that may be required to plan services. Methodological challenges to assessing risk include the lack of reliability and

validity of measures, definitional dilemmas, temporal issues (including changes in risk over time), the absence of baserate data, difficulties predicting for individuals, and the lack of sensitivity and specificity of measures. In addition, there are many sources of risk, including the risk to children of harm by their biological parents. These multiple sources of risk (typically ignored to date) include services provided to children and families that have little or no evidence of effectiveness, lack of careful assessment of service needs, an agency culture that is reactive rather than proactive in its pursuit of risk reduction, and irrelevant professional education programs. EBP is designed to integrate evidentiary (e.g., do services do more good than harm?), ethical (e.g., are staff competent to provide expected services?), and application concerns (e.g., are resources adequate?) (Gambrill 2003). It offers an opportunity to enhance the adequacy of risk assessment and to maximize opportunities to protect children from harm and increase their safety.

The quality of decisions in child welfare is influenced by the validity of risk assessment tools used, as well as by the quality of risk management programs (if any) in effect. The increased interest in EBP and its emphasis on a rigorous search for and critical appraisal of practice- and/or policy-related claims, involvement of clients as informed participants, and transparency of what is done and to what effect, should contribute to enhancing the quality of services provided to children and families. For implementation of EBP to occur, research suggests that changes in agency culture will be required, as well as changes in the culture of professional education. Methodological problems are also significant and must be addressed. Yet the children and families we serve deserve no less than our best in addressing these challenges.

REFERENCES

Baird, S. C., and Wagner, D. (2000). The relative validity of actuarial and consensus-based risk assessment systems. *Children and Youth Services Review, 22,* 839–871.

Baird, S. C., Wagner, D., Healy, T., & Johnson, K. (1999). Risk assessment in child protective services: Consensus and actuarial model reliability. *Child Welfare, 78,* 723–748.

Barlow, J. (1997). *Systematic review of the effectiveness of parent-training programmes in improving behaviour problems in children aged 3–10 years.* Oxford: Health Services Research Unit, Department of Public Health, Oxford University.

Camasso, M. J., & Jagannathan, R. (2000). Modeling the reliability and predictive validity of risk assessment in child protective services. *Children and Youth Services Review, 22,* 873–895.

Chalmers, I. (1983). Scientific inquiry and authoritarianism in perinatal care and education. *Birth, 10*(3), 151–166.

Costin, L. B., Karger, H. J., & Stoesz, D. (1996). *The politics of child abuse in America.* New York: Oxford University Press.

Dawes, R. M. (1998). Behavioral decision making, judgment, and inference. In D. Gilbert, S. Fiske, & G. Lindzey (eds.), *The Handbook of Social Psychology,* pp. 589–597. Boston: McGraw-Hill.

Dawes, R. M., Faust, D., & Meehl, P. E. (1989). Clinical versus actuarial judgment. *Science, 243,* 1668–1674.

DePanfilis, D., & Zuravin, S. J. (1998). Rates, patterns, and frequency of child maltreatment recurrences among families known to CPS. *Child Maltreatment, 3*(1), 27–42.

Dingwall, R., Eekelaar, J., & Murray, T. (1983). *The protection of children: State intervention and family life.* Oxford, UK: B. Blackwell.

Drake, B. (1996). Predictors of preventive services provision among unsubstantiated cases. *Child Maltreatment, 1*(2), 168–175.

Eckenrode, J., Ganzel, B., Henderson, C. R., Smith, E., Olds, D. L., et al. (2000). Preventing child abuse and neglect with a program of nurse home visitation: The limiting effects of domestic violence. *Journal of the American Medical Association, 284,* 1385–1391.

English, D. J., & Graham, J. C. (2000). An examination of relationships between children's protective services social worker assessment of risk and independent LONGSCAN measures of risk constructs. *Children and Youth Services Review, 22,* 897–933.

Gambrill, E. (1990). *Critical thinking in clinical practice.* San Francisco: Jossey-Bass.

Gambrill, E. (1997). *Social work practice: A critical thinker's guide.* New York: Oxford University Press.

Gambrill, E. (2003). Evidence-based practice: Implications for knowledge development and use in social work. In A. Rosen and E. K. Proctor (eds.), *Developing practice guidelines for social work intervention.* New York: Columbia University Press.

Gambrill, E. (2005). *Social work practice: A critical thinker's guide,* second ed. New York: Oxford University Press.

Gambrill, E., & Shlonsky, A. (2000). Risk assessment in context. *Children and Youth Services Review, 22,* 813–837.

Gambrill, E., & Shlonsky, A. (2001). The need for comprehensive risk management systems in child welfare. *Children and Youth Services Review, 23,* 79–107.

Gibbs, L. (2003). *Evidenced-based practice for the helping professionals.* Pacific Grove, CA: Brooks/Cole-Thompson.

Gigerenzer, G., & Edwards, A. (2003). Simple tools for understanding risks: From innumeracy to insight. *British Medical Journal, 327,* 741–744.

Grove, W. M., & Meehl, P. E. (1996). Comparative efficiency of informal (subjective, impressionistic) and formal (mechanical, algorithmic) prediction procedures. *Psychology, Public Policy, and Law, 2,* 293–323.

Hahn, R. A., Bilukha, O. O., Crosby, A., Fullilove, M. T., Liberman, A., et al. (2003). First reports evaluating the effectiveness of strategies for preventing violence: Early childhood home visitation. Findings from the Task Force on Community Preventive Services. *Morbidity & Mortality Weekly Report. Recommendations & Reports, 52*(RR-14), 1–9.

Halpern, R. (1990). Fragile families, fragile solutions: An essay review. *Social Service Review, 64,* 637–648.

Hastie, R., & Dawes, R. M. (2001). *Rational choice in an uncertain world: The psychology of judgment and decision making.* Thousand Oaks, CA: Sage.

Haynes, R. B., Devereaux, P. J., & Guyatt, G. H. (2002). Clinical expertise in the era of evidence-based medicine and patient choice. *American College of Physicians —ACP Journal Club, 13*(March/April), 189–193.

Helmreich, R. L., & Merritt, A. C. (1998). *Culture at work in aviation and medicine: National, organizational, and professional influences.* Brookfield, VT: Ashgate.

Janis, I. L. (1982). *Groupthink: Psychological studies of policy decisions and fiascoes,* second ed. Boston: Houghton Mifflin.

Johnson, W. (2004). *Effectiveness of California's child welfare structured decision-making (SDM) model: A prospective study of the validity of the California Family Risk Assessment.* Oakland, CA: Alameda County Social Services Agency.

Klayman, J. (1995). Varieties of confirmation bias. In J. R. Busemeyer, R. Hastie, and D. L. Medin (eds.), *Decision making from a cognitive perspective,* pp. 156–171. New York: Academic Press.

Lindsey, D. (1991). Factors affecting the foster care placement decision: An analysis of national survey data. *American Journal of Orthopsychiatry, 61,* 272–281.

Lindsey, D. (1992). Reliability of the foster care placement decision: A review. *Research on Social Work Practice, 2*(1), 65–80.

Lyons, P., Doueck, H. J., & Wodarski, J. S. (1996). Risk assessment for child protective services: A review of the empirical literature on instrument performance. *Social Work Research, 20*(3), 143–155.

Macdonald, K. I., & Macdonald, G. M. (1998). Perceptions of risk. In P. Parsloe (ed.), *Risk assessment in social care and social work: Research highlights,* pp. 17–52. London: Jessica Kingley Publishers.

Margolin, L. (1997). *Under the cover of kindness: The invention of social work.* Charlottesville: University of Virginia Press.

Morgan, M. G., Fischoff, B., Bostrom, A., & Atman, C. J. (2002). *Risk communication.* New York: Cambridge University Press.

Moss, F. (1995). Risk management and quality of care. In C. Vincent (ed.), *Clinical risk management,* pp. 88–102. London: British Medical Journals.

Mullen, J. D., & Roth, B. M. (1991). *Decision-making: Its logic and practice.* Savage, MD: Rowman & Littlefield.

Munro, E. (1999). Common errors of reasoning in child protection work. *Child Abuse and Neglect, 23,* 745–758.

Munro, E. (2002*). Effective child protection.* Thousand Oaks, CA: Sage.

Munro, E. (in press). A simpler way to understand the results of risk assessment instruments. *Children and Youth Services Review.*

Needell, B., Webster, D., Cuccaro-Alamin, S., Armijo, M., Lee, S., et al. (2004). *Child welfare services reports for California.* Retrieved June 30, 2004, from cssr.berkeley.edu/CWSCMSreports.

Olds, D., Robinson, J., O'Brien, R., Luckey, D. W., Pettitt L. M., et al. (2002). Home visiting by paraprofessionals and by nurses: A randomized, controlled trial. *Pediatrics, 110,* 486–496.

Oxman, A. D., & Guyatt, G. H. (1993). The science of reviewing research. In K. S. Warren & F. Mosteller (eds.), *Doing more good than harm: The evaluation of health care interventions,* pp. 125–134. New York: New York Academy of Sciences.

Pelton, L. (1989). *For reasons of poverty: A critical analysis of the public child welfare system in the United States.* New York: Praeger.

Reason, J. T. (1997). *Managing the risks of organizational accidents.* Aldershot, UK: Ashgate.

Reason, J. T. (2001). Understanding adverse events: The human factor. In C. Vincent (ed.), *Clinical risk management,* second ed., pp. 9–30. London: British Medical Journals.

Rogers, E. M. (1995). *Diffusion of innovation,* fourth ed. New York: Free Press.

Rose, S. J., & Meezan, W. (1996). Variations in perceptions of child neglect. *Child Welfare, 75,* 139–160.

Ruscio, J. (1998). Information integration in child welfare cases: An introduction to statistical decision-making. *Child Maltreatment, 3,* 143–156.

Sackett, D. L. (2003). Pose a specific question of importance to your client's welfare. In L. Gibbs (ed.), *Evidence based practice for the helping professions,* pp. 122–142. Pacific Grove, CA: Brooks/Cole-Thompson.

Sackett, D. L., Richardson, W. S., Rosenberg, W., & Haynes, R. B. (1997). *Evidence-based medicine: How to practice and teach EBM.* New York: Churchill Livingstone.

Sackett, D. L., Straus, S. E., Richardson, W. S., Rosenberg, W., & Haynes, R. B. (2000). *Evidence-based medicine: How to practice and teach EBM,* second ed. New York: Churchill Livingstone.

Selvin, S. (1996). *Statistical analysis of epidemiologic data,* second ed. New York: Oxford University Press.

Tatara, T. (1994). Some additional explanations for the recent rise in the U.S. child substitute care population: An analysis of national child substitute care flow data and future research questions. In R. Barth, J. D. Berrick, & N. Gilbert (eds.), *Child welfare research review,* vol. 1, pp. 126–145. New York: Columbia University Press.

U.S. Department of Health and Human Services. (2003). *Child maltreatment 2001.* Washington, DC: U.S. Department of Health and Human Services.

Vincent, D. (ed.). (2001). *Clinical risk management: Enhancing patient safety,* second ed. London: British Medical Journals.

Wagner, D. (2003). Discussion at the Symposium on Decision Making in Child Welfare. University of California, Berkeley, December 4, 2003.

Wagner, D., Johnson, K., & Johnson, W. (1998). *Using actuarial risk assessment to target service interventions in pilot California counties.* Paper presented at the 13th National Roundtable on CPS Risk Assessment, San Francisco, May 15–18, 1998.

Wald, M. S., & Woolverton, M. (1990). Risk assessment: The emperor's new clothes? *Child Welfare, 69,* 483–511.

Wolock, I., Sherman, P., Feldman, L. H., & Metzger, B. (2001). Child abuse and neglect referral patterns: A longitudinal study. *Children and Youth Services Review, 23,* 21–47.

Zuravin, S. (1999). Child neglect: A review of definitions and measurement research. In H. Dubowitz (ed.), *Neglected children: Research, practice, and policy,* pp. 24–46. Thousand Oaks: Sage.

MARIANNE BERRY

Overview of Family Preservation

"Family preservation" is a widely used term in services to children and families, and it represents both a goal of services (preserving the connection between children and their parents and extended family), and also a specific form of services, often called "intensive family preservation services," (IFPS). The distinction between the goal of family preservation and the specific means by which to achieve it is an important one; agencies and practitioners can agree on the goal while employing different methods to preserve family relationships.

Family preservation services should not be confused with family support services, but they often are. Family support programs are less intensive and more widely available to a range of families in need. Families do not have to be experiencing substantiated child maltreatment to access family support services; they are generally available to all who seek them. Family preservation services, in contrast, are provided to families that are involved in the public child welfare system for substantiated child maltreatment. Such families are usually mandated to participate in these services or lose their children to foster care.

In this chapter, I discuss the evolution of family preservation as a goal and present the basic tenets and components of family preservation service models. Special attention is paid to the assumptions and values underlying this goal and method of working with families. After a basic description of two major service models, I provide some detail about promising approaches that are empirically supported. I then discuss the difficulty of conducting definitive research in an area in which practice models are intended to be as applied, creative, and individualized as IFPS. Finally, the chapter ends with a discussion of the values, skills, and training that are helpful for those seeking to work to preserve families at risk of disintegration.

Family Preservation as a Goal

When children have suffered maltreatment or lack of protection at the hands of their families, a common emotional and professional response is to remove those children from harm's way and to separate children and their parents and/or siblings. For many years, this was the first response, with the number of children and youth placed into alternative or foster homes growing throughout the 1970s. In 1980, in response to the increasing number of children growing up in these alternative homes, a federal law, the Adoption Assistance and Child Welfare Act of 1980, was passed. This act mandated that, for states to receive their full share of foster care payments from the federal government, they had to show that they had first made reasonable efforts to keep children and youth with their families by reducing the risk of harm to those children. The goal of family preservation was thus enacted into federal (and subsequently, state) laws in the early 1980s.

Following that legislation, individual states were compelled to determine how to show that they had made reasonable efforts to preserve the family before they could legally place the child into foster care with another family, and perhaps even move toward adoption of that child by another family. Even while the child was in another home, the first goal of business for agencies was to try to improve the conditions at home, so that the child could safely return to his primary or extended family. Only states that could show they made reasonable efforts to preserve families and family ties could receive their full share of foster care funding for the children and youth who were temporarily separated or who could not return home. This requirement of making reasonable efforts toward preserving families led to an increased call for programs and practice models that could satisfy the requirement that reasonable efforts to preserve families had been made.

Family Preservation as a Service or Practice Model

During the 1980s, following the Adoption Assistance and Child Welfare Act of 1980, there occurred rapid growth of programs that promised to reasonably and effectively keep a large proportion of maltreated and troubled children safe at home with their families. Often purported to have begun with the Homebuilders™ program in California and then Washington State, these programs quickly spread across the country and the world. Their growth in the United States was driven by early reports of effectiveness with child welfare populations (AuClaire & Schwartz 1987; Bribitzer & Verdieck 1988; Kinney, Madsen, Fleming, & Haapala 1977) and the need for state programs to show their legislatures and the federal government that they were indeed making credible efforts toward the goal of family preservation.

To meet the requirement for making reasonable efforts to preserve families, states, counties, and child service agencies turned toward IFPS. The first service model adopted by many had been developed and tested by the Homebuilders™ agency beginning in the 1970s, so this model was largely functional when the demand for distribution grew. Since the introduction of the Homebuilders™ model, other programs have proliferated. These have been primarily modifications on the same theme. Here I discuss the original model and the modifications to it and their contributions to preserving families.

Homebuilders™

In the 1980s, creators of Homebuilders™ were very clear that there are several tenets of their IFPS model that are critical to the integrity and success of the model (Kinney, Haapala, & Booth 1991). First of all, the model is indeed intensive. Caseworkers carry a caseload of two families at one time, but serve each family in 6 weeks or less. The theoretical basis of the intervention is cognitive-behavioral, with families learning techniques of praise, rewarding positive behavior, keeping charts of positive and negative child behaviors, learning nonpunitive punishment techniques, and the like. Much less emphasis is put on understanding the origins of problematic interactions than on solutions to problems occurring at the moment.

The model emphasizes the importance of serving the family in its own home, where problems are occurring and where a more accurate assessment of family interactions, problems, and assets can be gained (Kinney, Haapala, & Booth 1991). Interventions are based on an individualized assessment of family strengths and needs. Caseworkers are trained extensively in cognitive-behavioral techniques and in serving as a model of positive parent-child interaction and problem solving. Caseworkers are encouraged to spend as much time as possible with the family in the environment when and where problems occur (e.g., at home around the dinner table, after school during homework time, at school with teachers). Caseworkers are also given great autonomy and creativity in solving problems, congruent with the individualized approach to treating families. There are no standard requirements for number of work hours spent in the office or on certain activities.

One of the most important tenets of the Intensive Family Preservation model created by

1. In most cases, it is best for children to grow up with their natural families.
2. One cannot easily determine which types of families are "hopeless," and which will benefit from intervention.
3. It is our job to instill hope.
4. Clients are our colleagues.
5. People are doing the best they can do.
6. We can do harm as well as good; we must be careful.

FIGURE 1. Values of the Homebuilders™ Family Preservation model.

the Homebuilders™ team is the combination of both soft and concrete services in the strengthening of families (Kinney, Haapala, & Booth 1991). In working with families during the 1970s, Homebuilders™ staff and supervisors realized that most families who were reported to the agency for parent-child interaction problems, such as maltreatment or troubled adolescents, also had such basic needs as safe housing, adequate food, space for privacy within the home, and paid utilities. Attempting to work with families to achieve calm and positive social interaction patterns when children were hungry or there was no heat in the home was doomed to failure.

Services therefore became very concrete in the early stages of each case. What distinguishes the Intensive Family Preservation model and its skill-based orientation is that caseworkers do not arrange for landlords or community agencies to provide these ancillary resources. Instead, the caseworker becomes a teacher of how to do modest home repair, how to economically shop for nutritious meals for the family, and how to negotiate with landlords and others for household or community improvements. These hands-on interactions become "teaching moments" for problem-solving; helping families work together; and building patience, hope, and a sense of mastery.

Although families are encouraged to learn the skills to solve their own problems, the Homebuilders™ creators also recognize that no intervention of 4 to 6 weeks will bring all families to complete safety and positive interaction. Therefore, an important part of intervention is

also introducing families to the formal and informal community resources that can continue to support the family once the short-term service has ended.

Finally, and perhaps most importantly, the Homebuilders™ founders created a list of value statements about the work of family preservation that have influenced at least two generations of family-centered services, both intensive and generic (fig. 1). Reflected in the value statements are the beliefs that the caseworker may have expertise about problem solving and other positive techniques, but that the family also has an expertise: about its history, its view of its strengths and problems, and the way its members would like things to improve. This leveling and sharing of authority and responsibility for change is reflected in both big and small interactions between caseworker and family members. The use of caseworker authority and coercion is held to a minimum; the constant tenor of the caseworker is to build and maintain hope that the family can make positive changes and the home can be a safe place for everyone to live.

Modifications and New Models of Family Preservation Services

Family preservation programs can also focus on family systems and social network interventions, enhancing and enlarging a family's relationships and social networks as a safety net and supportive circle (Bitonti 2002; Mosier et al. 2001; Nelson, Landsman, & Dentelbaum 1990). The growth of family preservation programs that seek to enhance social networks is a logical result of the evolution in family services to community-based networks and systems of care. Social network interventions utilize a case-management role of the social worker in which linkages between agencies are dependent on good communication and collaboration on behalf of the family.

A new and widely adopted model of family preservation has recently emerged from the University of South Carolina and Scott Henggeler, called "Multi-Systemic Therapy"™ (MST™; Henggeler, Melton, Smith, Schoenwald, & Hanley 1993; Henggeler, Schoenwald, & Pickrel 1995). This model of service was initially focused on the prevention and reduction of serious chronic delinquent and criminal behavior by adolescents. Following an extensive review of the empirical literature on the contributing factors to delinquency and promising approaches, the MST™ model was developed to work with the adolescent and the multiple systems in which the adolescent is embedded (family, friends, school, and neighborhood).

Highly trained therapists work intensively with the adolescent and the multiple systems to end or reduce negative relationships, learn problem solving and positive activities, and ultimately decrease or eliminate delinquent and criminal behavior. Often the therapeutic work takes place in a clinical setting rather than at the home. This tenet is based on the dedication of MST™ developers to controlling extraneous influences on the therapeutic process. Researchers also have an enhanced ability to monitor treatment fidelity when work takes place in a clinical setting (Henggeler, Schoenwald, & Pickrel 1995).

Similarities and Differences among Family Preservation Programs

The MST™ and other models are consistent with the original Homebuilders™ principles and structures in that treatment is focused on the present, is action oriented, uses cognitive-behavioral approaches to skill building, is embedded in the home and community, and includes family members as active participants and planners in the intervention. Treatment is planned to be intensive, and caseworkers have low caseloads so that they can spend the time required to produce important changes in the skills and relationships in the family. Treatment is also planned to be relatively short term, based on the cognitive-behavioral tenet that learning new skills does not require long-term uncovering of historical development of the problem or slow and gradual insight into current patterns of behavior.

The two models diverge, however, in that MST™ founders are much more dedicated to monitoring and insuring treatment fidelity and measuring therapists' adherence to the model (Henggeler, Schoenwald, & Pickrel 1995). This commitment to monitoring treatment fidelity has enabled model proponents to identify the circumstances under which the model is effective. The inability to do this has been a critical shortcoming for the Homebuilders™ model. Although the MST™ model has been more rigorously monitored and evaluated, the population served by MST™ is much more narrow, primarily limited to juvenile offenders or youth with serious emotional disturbances or antisocial behavior. Although a few pilot expansions of the model with populations of abused and neglected children have reported negligible results (Brunk, Henggeler, & Whelan 1987), the model has continued to be utilized with antisocial and emotionally disturbed adolescent populations.

Context Surrounding Family Preservation Programs

Family Preservation and Child Maltreatment
IFPS are embedded in the child welfare service array, which contains many services, including prevention of child maltreatment, investigation of allegations of child maltreatment, family support services, placement prevention, foster care, adoption, community-based mental health services, and juvenile justice services. IFPS are typically among those services provided to families who have been investigated and sub-

stantiated for child maltreatment to try to reduce or eliminate the maltreatment behaviors and prevent the need for the out-of-home placement of the child. This service model is but one component of a full range of service options for families with differing needs.

Thus in the child welfare arena, IFPS are provided to families experiencing child maltreatment—physical child abuse, child neglect, sexual abuse, or a combination of these problems. In most cases, sexual abuse cases are not served by family preservation programs, because the most common response in such cases is to remove the perpetrator from the home. If this is not possible, then the child is usually removed from the perpetrator (placed into foster care) for his or her own protection, and thus family preservation is not the service of choice.

Note that, among the child welfare population of families, child neglect is much more common than abuse (Sedlak & Broadhurst 1996). Child neglect, or the inability or unwillingness to meet a child's basic needs, is often associated with material poverty, as poor families often cannot adequately feed, clothe, and medically care for their children, regardless of their intent. Child welfare agencies are therefore required to serve as a general financial safety net for families in poverty, once it has been determined that the children are neglected. Services for these families can largely consist of securing the financial and material resources not provided to the population of families receiving general assistance. Indeed, it is anticipated that many families who have exceeded their eligibility for Temporary Assistance for Needy Families will become clients of the child welfare system when their general benefits run out (Loprest 1999).

There are substantial differences in the nature of the two forms of maltreatment, abuse and neglect. Child neglect is an act of omission, in which children are chronically deprived of basic needs, such as food, clothing, adequate shelter, and adequate parenting practices, including hygiene, health care, supervision, safety precautions, and minimal nurturing and attention. In contrast, child abuse is an act of commission, in which parents or others act violently or cruelly toward the child, including spontaneous physically injurious acts and habitual use of severe disciplinary practices.

Abuse and neglect can happen to children of any age. Infants are particularly susceptible to neglect, because of their inability to meet their own needs. As children grow older, physical abuse can increase, until children learn ways to escape it or protect themselves (often by using their own forms of violence). Both forms of maltreatment can exist in the same family and happen to the same child.

What is largely common to all forms of child maltreatment is the environmental context in which it occurs. Families who abuse or neglect their children are often overwhelmed by living in an environment bombarded by stress of all kinds. Maltreating families often have few financial resources; live in dangerous or impoverished neighborhoods; have few or stressful social relationships, including adult relationships; and little awareness of or access to formal supports, such as child care, respite from parenting, recreational opportunities, or education. Although not all families who experience these stressors subsequently abuse or neglect their children, the presence of these conditions can exacerbate parenting practices that are already ineffectual.

Further contributing to child maltreatment, drug and alcohol use are a common coping mechanism for overwhelmed parents. The U.S. Department of Health and Human Services (1999) estimates that 675,000 children are seriously mistreated each year by an alcoholic or drug-abusing caretaker. Furthermore, it has been found that drug and alcohol is involved or implicated in as many as 80% of foster care placements in the United States (Chasnoff 1998).

Finally, although poverty can be a significant contributor to familial stress and child maltreatment, abuse and neglect do not only occur in poor communities or populations in poverty. Child maltreatment can occur in families of any social status. However, those families with greater financial resources are less likely to be reported to child welfare agencies by hospital personnel who examine children for suspicious injuries or illnesses (DePanfilis 1997; Lindsey 1994), and those who are reported often have the material resources needed for legal representation or other alternatives to child welfare involvement. Poverty and its concomitant demons are significant factors for those families served by child welfare agencies, and must therefore be concretely addressed in any attempts to reduce ongoing maltreatment.

Societal Context for Family Preservation

IFPS are a response to two important and alarming trends in the United States (and other countries around the world). First, the incidence of maltreatment to children is increasing. A total of 1.5 million children was known to be abused or neglected in the United States in 1993 (U.S. Department of Health and Human Services 1996). The Third National Incidence Study of Child Abuse and Neglect (NIS-3), conducted nationally in 1993–1994, found that child maltreatment had increased since the second such study in 1986 by 66%. The number of children either seriously injured or in danger of maltreatment quadrupled during that time. Beyond those children known to be maltreated in that time frame, the NIS estimates that much larger numbers of children were maltreated but unreported.

Child welfare agencies can only serve those families who come to their attention, however. Of those families who are investigated for child maltreatment, a minority actually receive child welfare services, and the 1996 NIS-3 study found that the percentage served by child welfare is actually decreasing (U.S. Department of Health and Human Services 1996). About one-third of incidents reported to NIS monitors and meeting maltreatment criteria were investigated by child protective services (CPS). Although the proportion of cases investigated has decreased over time, the actual number of investigations has remained steady, suggesting that the investigative capacity of CPS is at its limit.

At the same time, the number of children going into foster care in the United States has also increased. Currently, there are more than 500,000 children in foster care in the United States (Denby & Curtis 2003). Several societal and systemic factors have contributed to this increase. First, as the number of families reported for child maltreatment have increased, the demand for the system to protect these children has become critical. Second, other societal trends that exacerbate familial stress have also increased in the past decade. Unemployment rates have increased, as have rates of poverty for several segments of society. Increases in drug and alcohol use and abuse have been substantial in the past decade, and drugs and alcohol are implicated in the majority of child maltreatment reports (Chasnoff 1998). These societal conditions are not easily improved, especially by an overwhelmed and underresourced child welfare system. The services and resources needed to address poverty, unemployment, and drug and alcohol abuse are expensive and often politically unpopular. Therefore, child welfare services and particularly "family preservation services are expected to solve major social problems, one family at a time" (Schuerman, Rzepnicki, & Littell 1994:241). It is no wonder that child welfare systems are often pressed to place children into foster care when they cannot solve or ameliorate these larger problems.

Policy Context for Family Preservation

Beyond their community and social contexts, family preservation services are also embedded in the policies and structures required by federal and state child welfare policy. As mentioned previously, the Adoption Assistance and Child Welfare Act of 1980 had significant and far-reaching effects on the demand for child welfare agencies to work to preserve families and provide services that could accomplish this goal in a short period of time. The act mandated that family preservation be accomplished in 2 years, or to move to terminate parental rights and find a permanent adoptive home for the child.

In 1997, new federal legislation was enacted —the Adoption and Safe Families Act. In this legislation, the timeframe for family preservation attempts was shortened to 12 months. In other words, child welfare agencies have 12 months to show that children have been safely maintained in their own homes and that the family can make it on their own, or agencies must move toward termination of parental rights and adoption of the child. Family preservation services are now faced with significantly compressed timeframes in which to accomplish the remediation of significant personal, family, and community problems.

Characteristics of Families Receiving Family Preservation Services

Although there is no typical family in the child welfare service system or a family preservation program, there are common risk factors and vulnerabilities observed in this population. The parent or associated adult has usually been found to have physically abused or neglected their child. Often, the family is headed by a single parent (usually the mother), who has multiple children younger than school age, who are therefore in need of all-day attention. She is usually young, often less than 30 years old, and has little education beyond high school. The parenting problems center around inconsistent attention to, or discipline of, the children; low patience or tolerance of frustration; and inappropriate knowledge or expectations of children's behavior. These parental problems are intensified if the parent(s) is developmentally delayed or impaired by drug or alcohol use.

Given their history of neglect and/or abuse, the children are likely to have behavior problems. Due to poor access to health care in poor communities, they are also likely to have medical, physical, developmental, or learning disabilities that have often gone undetected by the medical community. Because the children are likely to be less than 6 years old, they require constant and diligent attention, which overwhelmed mothers or fathers can seldom sustain. The more special needs that a child has, the higher the likelihood of abuse and/or neglect, and family preservation programs are therefore highly likely to serve this special-needs population, which expands the range of services necessary.

Environmentally, the family is often living in substandard housing and communities with poor resources. As mentioned previously, material poverty is a frequent contributor to the family stress that leads to child maltreatment. For families living in rural areas, public transportation and employment opportunities can be rare or nonexistent. The availability of such community services as mental health centers, drug and alcohol treatment centers, and day care can vary widely from community to community, but is particularly salient for families who are experiencing child maltreatment and familial stress.

Resilience and Protective Factors

The families served by family preservation programs also have strengths. Because IFPS are reserved for those families who are at the greatest risk of losing their children to foster care, families in these programs are often highly motivated to change. When parents are introduced to the program, they are made to understand that this may be their last, best hope to remain a family, and this realization can jolt parents into action, even though previous services of a more general or conventional nature have failed to work.

Most family preservation programs operate from a strengths perspective, which posits that all families have strengths, including their expertise about how their family works and behaves, what their own hopes and dreams are for themselves and their members, and what has worked and failed in the past. Family preservation caseworkers use this expert knowledge of the family to help them craft a plan for change, including strategies to not repeat mistakes of the past, to build on past and current successes and resources, and to make sure that the plan is congruent with the hopes and dreams of the family members.

The most critical element of success for any plan for family change, including family preservation program plans, is the engagement of family members in that plan. Therefore, family preservation caseworkers use an arsenal of techniques to assess and utilize the strengths of family members; use nonblaming and nonshaming language and practices; and constantly affirm, praise, and support members' attempts at change and the learning of new skills. These techniques are built on recognition of the strengths and capacities of family members for change and hope, the most important assets in any family.

Promising Approaches

Research on formal IFPS has been performed for almost 30 years. The results have been mixed and quite controversial. Many studies have been done, plagued by the problems of questionable methodologies, comparisons of a variety of types of family preservation programs with questionable fidelity to program models, and application to a plethora of families and problems (Berry, Bussey, & Cash 2001; Rossi 1992). Large evaluations of family preservation programs have in general found placement rates to be identical between treatment and comparison groups (Heneghan, Horwitz, & Leventhal 1996). On close review of evaluation methodologies, one finds that the treatment and comparison groups are sometimes not equivalent, despite the best efforts to achieve random assignment (Schuerman, Rzepnicki, & Littell 1994; U.S. Department of Health and Human Services 2001), and that samples are too small to detect treatment effects (Fraser, Nelson, & Rivard 1997; Rossi 1992).

Critics have lamented the fallibility of using child placement as an outcome measure when it is also an intervention (Berry 1992; Rossi 1992; Schuerman, Rzepnicki, & Littell 1994). They have called for additional and more clinically meaningful outcome measures, including the recurrence of maltreatment and other measures of child and family well-being (Meezan & McCroskey 1996). Others (Besharov 1994; Gelles 1996) have blasted the wholesale adoption of such an untested or unproven approach as political ideology and cost-cutting run amok.

Child welfare programs are an applied field of study: one cannot select a sample of abused and neglected children and randomly deny services to half of the group, so as to determine the effect of some treatment on the other half. States and agencies are federally and morally mandated to intervene in all known cases of child maltreatment. Therefore, true experimental designs in the study of family preservation services are rare. Researchers and evaluators have tried creative and elaborate methods to tease out the effects of family preservation services compared to "conventional" child welfare services (which are more ill-defined than family preservation services), and to perhaps further isolate the effects of the specific components of the service. Here I review the findings of the most recent and important research in the study of intensive family preservation programs.

Effectiveness of Family Preservation Programs

Is intensive family preservation successful in preserving families and keeping their members safe? After receiving the service:

- Are families more likely than controls to be preserved?
- Are families less likely to abuse or neglect their children (because preserving well-being is at least as important as preserving family ties)?
- Are families more likely than controls to be better off, in terms of improved skills, conditions, and relationships?

Effectiveness in Preserving Families

Despite the myriad complications in the morass of program evaluations in this field, certain specific studies and methodologies are helping tease out whether these programs are effective and, more importantly, what components of these programs seem to be most critical (Kirk & Griffith 2004; McCroskey & Meezan 1997; Schuerman, Rzepnicki, & Littell 1994). The most recent and sophisticated study of IFPS has been conducted in North Carolina (Kirk & Griffith 2004). In this study, the authors examined the archival records of all families at high risk of child placement by the state's child welfare system over a 6-year period. The authors compared results for families who received IFPS with those who received conventional child welfare services. They measured whether IFPS providers were indeed faithful to the model, in terms of an immediate response, short-term service, higher intensity of service in the initial weeks, and the direct provision of services between caseworker and family. They also measured whether those families receiving IFPS were indeed high risk. The IFPS families had younger parents, children with more serious injuries, more prior substantiated reports of maltreatment, and more prior placements in foster care. Thus the families receiving IFPS were a much higher risk group, for both subsequent reports of maltreatment and subsequent placement.

Including only those cases demonstrating fidelity to the IFPS model, the authors found no significant difference in placement rate at 1 year following intake, which most past studies would have concluded as evidence of the ineffectiveness or lack of improvement of IFPS over conventional services. However, given the much higher risk present in these families, the similar placement rates are quite remarkable. Using event history analysis to control for the risk factors, the study found a significant positive effect for IFPS. As Kirk and Griffith (2004:9) put it, "when risk factors were controlled during the analysis in both treatment and comparison cases, IFPS significantly outperformed traditional child welfare services in every comparison by preventing or delaying out of home placement."

Who is most likely to stay out of placement or keep their children at home? The best predictor of success in family preservation services is the engagement of families (Berry, Cash, & Brook 2000; Bitonti 2002; Lewis 1991; Littell & Schuerman 2002; Littell and Tajima 2000). When families are asked what caseworker behaviors most contributed to their engagement and cooperation, they are likely to mention the early provision of concrete resources and services (e.g., household repairs, payment of utility bills, location of respite and day care). Families are also likely to remark that family preservation caseworkers listen to them in ways that other caseworkers have not (Lewis 1991). This is assumed to be a reflection of the emphasis in family preservation services on individualized treatment, empowerment of family members to participate in case planning and goal setting, and the intensity and duration of time spent in direct contact with the family. Placement rates are lower when families say they can trust their caseworker and feel that they are treated fairly (Fraser, Pecora, & Haapala 1991).

Consistent across most research of family preservation programs, families who are most successful in avoiding placement during and following family preservation are those with acute rather than chronic problems. Acute physical abuse is more likely to be successfully treated than is chronic child neglect or caretaking by developmentally delayed parents (Berry 1997; Berry, Cash, & Brook 2000; Chaffin, Bonner, & Hill 2001; McCroskey & Meezan 1997). Placement is also particularly likely when parents have not learned consistent parenting techniques during treatment (Berry, Cash, & Brook 2000). Drug-addicted parents are particularly difficult to treat in this short-term program, largely due to the incongruency of embedding long-term drug treatment in a short-term family preservation case plan. These parents have the poorest outcomes in family preservation services (Littell & Schuerman 2002). Parents of a lower socioeconomic status were also found in one study to have poorer outcomes (MacLeod & Nelson 2000).

What kinds of children are least likely to benefit from IFPS? Children with acting-out or aggressive behavior problems are the most likely to be placed into foster care, despite having received IFPS (Bitonti 2002; McCroskey & Meezan 1997). In addition, children who have been in foster care in the past are likely to be replaced into foster care, regardless of the services they receive (Maluccio 2000; McCroskey & Meezan 1997). Children are more likely to go into foster care from family preservation services if they are African American, poor, and/or have an incarcerated family member (Denby & Curtis 2003; McCroskey & Meezan 1997).

The characteristics of the services most associated with placement prevention are certainly important to identify. Consistently, researchers have noted the significant contribution of concrete services to placement prevention rates (Berry 1997; Chaffin, Bonner, & Hill 2001). Programs that can help meet the basic needs of families ameliorate compounded stressors. Such programs reduce the financial stress of meeting children's basic needs and the likelihood that social workers and family court judges will assess the parents as unfit providers. In addition, the provision of concrete help early in treatment helps to show the family that the caseworker "means business" and can get things done.

Findings regarding the structure of family preservation services are mixed. Some studies have found outcomes are the same regardless of whether services are delivered in 3 months or 6 months (Chaffin, Bonner, & Hill 2001). Some researchers have found that successful families are those who have received more direct service time with their caseworker (Berry, Cash, & Brook 2000), whereas others find that the longer the service is provided, the more likely the outcome will be poor (perhaps reflecting more severe problems, or ineffective services) (Berry, Cash, & Brook 2000). Other research has found no effect of service duration or intensity (Chaffin, Bonner, & Hill 2001; Littell & Schuerman 2002).

Effectiveness in Increasing Safety

Many evaluations of IFPS have gone beyond measuring whether families have remained intact and have examined whether children remained safe at home. Keeping children home while in continued danger of maltreatment has never been a goal of family preservation programs. Using subsequent reports of child maltreatment as the marker of service failure, results are mixed as to the ability of family preservation to prevent further abuse.

In a statewide study of IFPS in Illinois in the late 1990s, Schuerman, Rzepnicki, and Littell (1994) reported that 30% of all cases had a report of child maltreatment subsequent to receiving IFPS. New reports of abuse were particularly likely when the family members were experiencing cocaine addiction or housing problems. No characteristics concerning the intensity or duration of the service had any effect on either child placement or continued abuse; in other words, reabuse was no less likely whether the family had received shorter term service or lower amounts of visits/time from their caseworker. Littell and Schuerman (2002) note cocaine addiction and housing problems as substantial "marker variables" that significantly test the ability of a short-term family preservation intervention to produce positive effects.

Several studies of outcomes in child welfare services, not only those of family preservation programs, have found that good services cannot rush good outcomes (Barth & Berry 1994). Although expedience is a factor that is in the best interest of children (by reducing the harm to their sense of continuity and permanence), outcomes are less than satisfactory when services and preparations of children and families are rushed or incomplete. Studies of intensive family reunification programs (programs to support families in reunifying with their children in foster care) have found that reabuse is more likely when children are returned before spending 6 months in care (Courtney 1995).

Effectiveness in Enhancing Parent, Child, and Family Well-Being

Very few studies have had the resources and wisdom to measure improvements in family functioning beyond the prevention of placement and reabuse. Asking caseworkers and families to rate family well-being at multiple points throughout the life of a case and locating field instruments sensitive enough to detect change in families within a 2- to 3-month timeframe are daunting tasks in a clinical setting, much less in the world of highly stressed families and their caseworkers.

One study that has measured gains in well-being among a child welfare population was conducted in Los Angeles by McCroskey and Meezan (1997). While participating in a family preservation program for an average of 19 weeks, families and caseworkers rated families on a number of measures of well-being. By the end of treatment, and at follow-up points, families participating in the intensive program had made significant improvements. For example, infants and toddlers had improved in their emotional and verbal responsiveness, and preschoolers showed improvement in learning. Children of all ages displayed reduced acting-out behaviors, but these improvements were lost by 1 year posttreatment. Parents showed few improvements in their mental health but showed significant improvements in their living conditions and financial stability.

A multiple regression analysis (McCroskey & Meezan 1997:208) found that those families who were most likely to improve in parent-child relations following family preservation services had "parents with less severe problems at case opening who were more emotionally unstable, less likely to use good judgment, and who received help handling their financial matters." When asked to rate what worked with each family, caseworkers attributed the success of the program in most cases to parental cooperation, direct service time (rather than work with collaterals), using teaching skills rather than counseling skills, and the provision of financial and housing assistance.

Lessons Learned

Note that many studies have identified the contribution of direct service time with the caseworker as a critical correlate of successes, including placement prevention, prevention of reabuse, and improvement in family skills and relations. This finding lends support to the conceptualization of IFPS as a home-based, intensive, hands-on form of service, in which caseworker and family members work in partnership toward mutually agreed-upon goals. Families who receive more direct service time with their caseworker say they are more cooperative and have more trust in their caseworker, and outcomes are better when families are cooperative (Littell 2001).

The question remains, however, as to the benefit of short-term services. The rationale for a short-term model is the decades of research demonstrating that cognitive-behavioral techniques so critical to producing behavior change can produce results in a short period of time when intensively and consistently applied (Halliday-Boykins & Henggeler 2001). For this reason, IFPS can be very effective when the problems are of an acute nature and center on parenting practices or interactions among family members.

However, as noted previously, most of the families served by the child welfare system for child maltreatment are also besieged by more intractable problems, including poverty, unemployment, low education, mental illness, and substance abuse. These are conditions not easily solved by learning new behavior patterns within 8 weeks, or even 6 months. As Halpern (1990: 647) states:

Services cannot alter the social conditions that produce or exacerbate, and ultimately reproduce, individual and family problems ... good services are not everything. But given our continuing reluctance to alter basic social arrangements and priorities that cause damage to so many children and families, we should at least commit ourselves to the objective of assuring them good quality services.

Limitations of the Research

One important caveat is critical when interpreting research findings about placement prevention. Those personnel and programs who deliver family preservation services are usually not the ones responsible for the primary outcome: the decision of whether children are ultimately removed and placed into foster care. Family court judges and review panels are the ultimate arbiters of any foster care removal, and although they may take agency recommendations on family progress and safety into account in their decision to remove, they can also diverge from this recommendation. As the number of investigations of maltreatment have increased and the severity of injuries and neglectful conditions have worsened (Sedlak & Broadhurst 1996), many courts are exercising greater caution and placing children out of the home as a safety precaution. In these cases, family preservation agencies and caseworkers may feel that families have shown adequate progress in skills and safety among their members, but the families suffer the consequences of case failure and child placement.

The Problem of Treatment Infidelity

The program structure and content of family preservation programs are fairly well specified, and can be expensive. For example, both Homebuilders™ and MST™ recommend low caseloads and experienced and well-trained staff. The cost of serving low caseloads can be offset by the short timeframe that each family is served (e.g., a caseworker can equally serve four families every 3 months or 16 families for a year with the same level of effort). But if agencies demand higher productivity, it is difficult to hold caseloads to a low level. Similarly, both the Homebuilders™ and MST™ models require significant time spent in direct contact between caseworker and family, which can be difficult if agencies require in-office supervision, staffing, court appointments, and the like. For this reason, there have been widespread modifications of the original models to fit the realities of child welfare.

These modifications have driven evaluators and policymakers to distraction. Programs have reported their placement prevention rates and their prevention of reabuse as attributed to their family preservation program, but without specific information on the structure and nature of the program. Assumptions are made about the effectiveness of family preservation programs, even though the service that was provided could be significantly watered down or no longer recognizable as IFPS. Let the buyer —or reader of these program evaluations or newspaper editorials—beware.

For example, the MST™ model has been adopted by many agencies, some licensed to practice the model and some adopting the principles of the model without intensive training in it. In this respect, the MST™ model is experiencing much the same proliferation and unmonitored modification as did the Homebuilders™ program in the 1980s. The MST™ model has been found by its developers to be ineffective with child welfare populations experiencing child abuse and neglect (Brunk, Henggeler, & Whelan 1987), but has been applied to this population nonetheless. Just as for the Homebuilders™ model, as the MST™ model has gained notoriety and offered evidence of effectiveness, aspects of the model have been adopted and adapted for use in a variety of populations, without the treatment fidelity emphasized by its founders.

Straying from the Model

Therefore, let us consider program modifications that are *not* supported, or are at least questioned, by the findings of research and evaluation to date. Most notably, the research findings reviewed above point to the importance of low caseloads for family preservation work. The critical service component of large amounts of time spent on direct service and the teaching of skills, which leads to better client engagement, cooperation, and trust, appears to be the bedrock of efforts to prevent abuse, prevent placement, and improve family skills and relations. The types of changes warranted for families who abuse their children do not occur easily or in partnership with strangers.

The kinds of changes required of abusive or neglectful parents also do not occur in classrooms. The findings of research on family preservation and on parenting programs in general find that didactic teaching of skills, where teachers teach and parents listen, are wholly ineffective at producing lasting behavior change (Macdonald 2001). For parents to learn new skills, they need the ability to practice those skills with their children in the settings in which parenting challenges occur—the home, the car, the grocery store. For this reason, it is unwise for family preservation programs to modify their structure to include multiple referrals to didactic instruction, such as anger management or parent training classes. Given what parents say about the importance of a trusting relationship with their caseworker, it appears important that these skills are taught and modeled by the family preservation caseworker. Once family preservation work moves to a model of case management, the central behavioral tenets, supported by research to be critical to success, have evaporated.

Assessments and Interventions

The empirical research reviewed above provides many insights and recommendations to those contemplating working in family preservation services or with families who abuse or neglect their children. First and foremost, it is critical that caseworkers and therapists conduct a thorough and contextual assessment of the family—one that captures a family's strengths and needs. Although most instruments currently in use focus on problems and on the parent-child relationship alone, there are some instruments more appropriate to family preservation work. The North Carolina Family Assessment Scale (Kirk & Reed-Ashcraft 1998) was developed specifically for use with family preservation and family reunification work and captures the strengths and needs in the domains of environment, social support, parenting skills and conditions, and child well-being. It has high reliability and validity, and caseworkers like it (Berry, Cash, & Mathiesen 2003).

A second, critical, lesson learned from the empirical research on family preservation programs is the importance of using hands-on cognitive-behavioral methods, applied and modeled in the home with the family. Caseworkers cannot expect to be effective in changing long-standing patterns of maladaptive behavior by referring families to a myriad of agencies and counselors who may or may not provide congruent advice or techniques. Given the empirical evidence for the effectiveness of cognitive-behavioral techniques in changing the behaviors of maltreating parents, these are the techniques that should be applied for change to occur in a short timeframe. With federal mandates for the termination of parental rights unless behavior changes within 12 months, using proven methods of change is the only practice for caseworkers and therapists that is ethical with this population.

The third lesson that informs effective family preservation practice is the provision of concrete supports to families, and provided in such a way that caseworkers and families develop concrete skills beyond learning to dial the phone for help. As discussed earlier, families and caseworkers benefit in many ways from the partnership involved in securing and using concrete supports to reduce stress in families. This calls for agencies and administrators to support caseworkers in their need for concrete resources for and concrete skills with families, which may demand additional training and funding.

Family preservation work is necessarily creative and sometimes odd. For caseworkers to individualize the treatment approaches and resources to the family's need, there must be some level of autonomy and flexibility afforded the caseworker. For caseworkers to be in the home when problems are occurring, their work hours will primarily be after hours and on weekends, in the homes and communities where families live. The resources and materials deemed relevant to family goals may be unorthodox, but when past methods and resources have not been effective, it is time to try new approaches.

Finally, family preservation work cannot and should not be provided as a case management model. The intensity and creativity demanded, as well as the constant modeling of positive patterns of interaction between family members, calls for a hands-on approach by a dedicated caseworker or team. Asking families to attend multiple services at multiple agencies around the community violates many assumptions and proven tenets of the family preservation model. This type of case management approach may be effective with families with fewer needs or those who are suffering fewer stressors related to imminent child removal, but will not work to preserve and strengthen families at this level of need.

Ethical Issues and Value Dilemmas

Is family preservation in the best interest of the child? Not always. As mentioned earlier, IFPS are but one program in the entire array of child welfare services available to families, and should not be provided to all families entering the child welfare system. There are children for whom immediate removal and placement into foster care is the correct decision—children who are not safe at home and cannot be made safe at home in the near future. There are families for whom less intensive, less expensive service options are appropriate, such as those families

who do not need the intensity or intrusion of a home-based practitioner following them to the kitchen or grocery store to model new patterns of behavior.

Given the proven ineffectiveness of family preservation models with parental drug addiction and homelessness, it is time to rethink the approach to these families when maltreatment is the presenting issue. Short-term solutions have not been shown to be effective, regardless of the intensity. Problems of addiction, mental illness, and poverty are chronic conditions, not maladaptive behavior patterns easily overcome by learning new behavior responses to stress. The child welfare system is challenged to develop new responses to these problems that will not result in the wholesale removal of children from large segments of the population. This is already occurring in several neighborhoods of New York City, where as many as 12% of all infants are removed from their families in their first year (Wulczyn 1991).

So when and how do we decide to move toward the termination of parental rights? Is parental drug involvement the death knell for a child's connection to his family? Under current federal legislation, it is. Can we find new homes, even kinship homes, for all the children affected by parental drug abuse? What about chronic neglect, often accompanied by parental mental delay or illness, particularly depression? Children are slated to be placed in a new family if their parents cannot overcome these problems within 12 months. Can intensive family preservation programs treat mental illness and developmental delays of parents in such a short time frame? If not, are we cheating children by delaying their inevitable removal? These are the thorny questions facing advocates for children and families who are trying to find sturdy solutions for these fragile families (Halpern 1990).

Conclusion

Family preservation is an individualized model of services that specifies the use of particular skills and techniques. It is not merely a goal or a wish that families can remain safely together when experiencing child maltreatment. Practicing a family preservation approach means that agencies and caseworkers have low caseloads, work intensively with families in the setting in which problems are occurring, and use cognitive-behavioral techniques to produce behavior change in a short timeframe. In addition, the caseworkers access community resources to support families who experience more than the usual familial stresses, and work creatively with each family to craft a plan that addresses their specific challenges and uses their particular strengths.

All of these tenets of the model are jeopardized by a political arena that is not family-friendly, particularly to families with problems with drugs, mental illness, or other long-term problems. IFPS can only be one approach, reserved for those families who can benefit from short-term cognitive-behavioral home-based treatment. For families with these more chronic, intractable problems, it is imperative that longer-term and broader societal solutions be identified and implemented. Current legislative mandates that terminate parental rights to children in short order may be seen as in the best interests of children's need for safety, but the severing of that connection between parent and child, physical and emotional, is not to be taken lightly. Family relationships are basic, complicated, and enigmatic: this is no place for a rush to judgment.

REFERENCES

Adoption and Safe Families Act. (1997). P.L. 105-89.

Adoption Assistance and Child Welfare Act. (1980). P.L. 96-272.

AuClaire, P., & Schwartz, I. M. (1987). Are home-based services effective? A public child welfare agency's experiment. *Children Today, 16,* 6–9.

Barth, R. P., & Berry, M. (1994). Implications of research for the welfare of children under permanency planning. In R. Barth, J. D. Berrick, & N. Gilbert (eds.), *Child welfare research review,* vol. 1. New York: Columbia University Press.

Berry, M. (1992). An evaluation of family preservation services: Fitting agency services to family needs. *Social Work, 37,* 314–321.

Berry, M. (1997). *The family at risk: Issues and trends in family preservation services.* Columbia: University of South Carolina Press.

Berry, M., Bussey, M., & Cash, S. J. (2001). Evaluation in a dynamic environment: Assessing change when nothing is constant. In E. Walton, P. Sandau-Beckler, & M. Mannes (eds.) *Balancing family-centered services and child well-being.* New York: Columbia University Press.

Berry, M., Cash, S. J., & Brook, J. P. (2000). Intensive family preservation services: An examination of critical service components. *Child and Family Social Work, 5,* 191–203.

Berry, M., Cash, S. J., & Mathiesen, S. G. (2003). Validation of the strengths and stressors tracking device with a child welfare population. *Child Welfare, 82,* 293–318.

Besharov, D. J. (1994). Looking beyond 30, 60, 90 days. *Children and Youth Services Review, 16,* 445–452.

Bitonti, C. (2002). Formative evaluation in family preservation: Lessons from Nevada. *Children and Youth Services Review, 24,* 653–672.

Bribitzer, M. P., & Verdieck, M. J. (1988). Home-based, family-centered intervention: Evaluation of a foster care prevention program. *Child Welfare, 67,* 255–266.

Brunk, M., Henggeler, S. W., & Whelan, J. P. (1987). A comparison of multisystemic therapy and parent training in the brief treatment of child abuse and neglect. *Journal of Consulting and Clinical Psychology, 55,* 311–318.

Chaffin, M., Bonner, B. L., & Hill, R. F. (2001). Family preservation and family support programs: Child maltreatment outcomes across client risk levels and program types. *Child Abuse and Neglect, 25,* 1269–1289.

Chasnoff, I. J. (1998). Silent violence: Is prevention a moral obligation? *Pediatrics, 102,* 145–148.

Courtney, M. E. (1995). Reentry to foster care of children returned to their families. *Social Service Review, 69,* 226–241.

Denby, R. W., & Curtis, C. M. (2003). Why special populations are not the target of family preservation services: A case for program reform. *Journal of Sociology and Social Welfare, 30*(2), 149–174.

DePanfilis, D. (1997). Intervening with families when children are neglected. In H. Dubowitz (ed.) *Neglected children: Research, practice and policy.* Thousand Oaks, CA: Sage.

Fraser, M. W., Nelson, K. E., & Rivard, J. C. (1997). Effectiveness of family preservation services. *Social Work Research, 21,* 138–153.

Fraser, M. W., Pecora, P. J., & Haapala, D. A. (1991). *Families in crisis: The impact of intensive family preservation services.* Hawthorne, NY: Aldine de Gruyter.

Gelles, R. J. (1996). *The book of David: How preserving families can cost children's lives.* New York: Basic Books.

Halliday-Boykins, C. A., & Henggeler, S. W. (2001). Multisystemic therapy: Theory research and practice. In E. Walton, P. Sandan-Beckler, & M. Mannes (eds.), *Balancing family-centered services and child well-being.* New York: Columbia University Press.

Halpern, R. (1990). Fragile families, fragile solutions: An essay review. *Social Service Review, 64,* 637–648.

Heneghan, A. M., Horwitz, S. M., & Leventhal, J. M. (1996). Evaluating intensive family preservation services: A methodological review. *Pediatrics, 97,* 535–542.

Henggeler, S. W., Melton, G. B., Smith, L. A., Schoenwald, S. K., & Hanley, J. H. (1993). Family preservation using multisystemic treatment: Long-term follow-up to a clinical trial with serious juvenile offenders. *Journal of Child and Family Studies, 2*(4), 283–293.

Henggeler, S. W., Schoenwald, S. K., & Pickrel, S. G. (1995). Multisystemic therapy: Bridging the gap between university- and community-based treatment. *Journal of Consulting and Clinical Psychology, 63,* 709–717.

Kinney, J., Haapala, D. A., & Booth, C. (1991). *Keeping families together: The Homebuilders model.* Hawthorne, NY: Aldine de Gruyter.

Kinney, J., Madsen, B., Fleming, T., & Haapala, D. A. (1977). Homebuilders: Keeping families together. *Journal of Consulting and Clinical Psychology, 45,* 667–673.

Kirk, R. S., & Griffith, D. P. (2004). Intensive family preservation services: Demonstrating successful placement prevention using event history analysis. *Social Work Research, 28,* 5–15.

Kirk, R. S., & Reed-Ashcraft, K. (1998). *User's guide for the North Carolina Family Assessment Scale, version 2.0.* Chapel Hill: University of North Carolina School of Social Work, Jordan Institute for Families.

Lewis, R. E. (1991). What are the characteristics of intensive family preservation services? In M. W. Fraser, P. J. Pecora, & D. A. Haapala (eds.), *Families in crisis: The impact of intensive family preservation services.* Hawthorne, NY: Aldine de Gruyter.

Lindsey, D. (1994). *The welfare of children.* New York: Oxford University Press.

Littell, J. H. (2001). Client participation and outcomes of intensive family preservation services. *Social Work Research, 25,* 103–113.

Littell, J. H., & Schuerman, J. R. (2002). What works best for whom? A closer look at intensive family preservation services. *Children and Youth Services Review, 24,* 673–699.

Littell, J. H., & Tajima, E. A. (2000). A multilevel model of client participation in intensive family preservation services. *Social Service Review, 74,* 405–435.

Loprest, P. (1999). Families who left welfare: Who are they and how are they faring? *Assessing the New Federalism,* pp. 122–134. Washington, DC: Urban Institute.

Macdonald, G. (2001). *Effective interventions for child abuse and neglect.* Chichester, NY: Wiley.

MacLeod, J., & Nelson, G. (2000). Programs for the promotion of family wellness and the prevention of child maltreatment: A meta-analytic review. *Child Abuse and Neglect, 24,* 1127–1149.

Maluccio, A. N. (2000). Foster care and family reunification. In P. A. Curtis, G. Dale, & J. C. Kendall (eds.). *The foster care crisis: Translating research into policy and practice.* Lincoln: University of Nebraska Press.

McCroskey, J., & Meezan, W. (1997). *Family preservation and family functioning.* Washington, DC: Child Welfare League of America.

Meezan, W., & McCroskey, J. (1996). Improving family functioning through intensive family preservation services: Results of the Los Angeles experiment. *Family Preservation Journal, 1,* 9–31.

Mosier, J., Burlingame, G. M., Wells, M. G., Ferre, R., Latkowski, M., et al. (2001). In-home, family-centered psychiatric treatment for high-risk children and youth. *Children's Services: Social Policy, Research, and Practice, 4*(2), 51–68.

Nelson, K. E., Landsman, M. J., & Dentelbaum, W. (1990). Three models of family-centered placement prevention services. *Child Welfare, 71,* 177–188.

Rossi, P. H. (1992). Assessing family preservation programs. *Children and Youth Services Review, 14,* 77–97.

Schuerman, J., Rzepnicki, T., & Littell, J. (1994). *Putting families first.* Hawthorne, NY: Aldine de Gruyter.

Sedlak, A. J., & Broadhurst, D. D. (1996). *Executive summary of the Third National Incidence Study of Child Abuse and Neglect.* Washington, DC: National Clearinghouse on Child Abuse and Neglect.

U.S. Department of Health and Human Services. (1996). *National Incidence Study—3.* Washington, DC: U.S. Department of Health and Human Services.

U.S. Department of Health and Human Services. (1999). *Blending perspectives and building common ground: A report to Congress on substance abuse and child protection.* Washington, DC: U.S. Department of Health and Human Services.

U.S. Department of Health and Human Services. (2001). *Evaluation of family preservation and reunification programs.* Washington, DC: U.S. Department of Health and Human Services.

Wulczyn, F. (1991). *The community dimension of permanency planning.* New York: New York State Department of Social Services, Division of Family and Children Services.

JUDY FENSTER

Substance Abuse Issues in the Family

The abuse of alcohol, tobacco, and illicit drugs is the number one health problem in the United States, costing taxpayers billions of dollars annually and affecting millions of families (Schneider Institute 2001). In this chapter, I focus on the impact of alcohol and other drug (AOD) abuse on four subpopulations within the family: (1) AOD-abusing parents, (2) pregnant AOD-addicted mothers and their offspring, (3) children of AOD-abusing parents, and (4) adolescent AOD abusers. For each group, demographic patterns and risk factors are outlined. Where applicable, I summarize protective factors and child welfare policy related to substance abuse. Assessment guidelines, treatment strategies, and innovative programs are reviewed, and ethical issues that may arise when working with substance abuse in the family are considered. A case example is provided for discussion.

Parental Substance Abusers
Demographic Patterns, Vulnerabilities, and Risk Factors
It is estimated that 9% (6 million) of American children live with a substance-abusing parent (Office of Applied Studies 2003). A study by Columbia University's National Center on Addiction and Substance Abuse found AOD abuse to be a factor in seven out of 10 cases of child maltreatment (Reid & Macchetto 1999). In the 1990s, rising rates of illicit drug use were linked with increased rates of reported child abuse, as well as all types of domestic violence (Sedlak & Broadhurst 1996).

In a sample of child welfare cases open in 1994 involving substance abuse, the Children's Bureau found illicit drugs to be the problem for 40% of families, alcohol for 25%, and alcohol combined with other drugs for 35% of families. In this national study, substance abuse was found in equal amounts among white and African American families, with only 6% of substance-abusing families identifying themselves as Hispanic (U.S. Department of Health and Human Services 1999). Data from other national surveys indicate that the ethnic identification of the majority of parental substance abusers is white, followed by African American and Hispanic (U.S. Department of Health and Human Services 1999). Rates of substance use and abuse are higher among those with less education and the unemployed. Prevalence of substance abuse is highest among Native Americans and lowest among Asian/Pacific Islanders (National Institute on Alcohol Abuse and Alcoholism 2002).

Compared to men, women begin drinking later in life and have lower rates of alcohol use and misuse (Collins & McNair 2003). However, maternal AOD abuse has increased dramatically in the past two decades (Freundlich 2000). Women who continue drinking move more quickly from casual use to addiction, develop accompanying health problems more rapidly, present for services at later stages of dependency, have less family support for treatment, and attain lower treatment retention rates than do men (Blume 1990; Kane-Cavaiola & Rullo-Cooney 1991; U.S. Department of Health and

Human Services 1999). Women are also more likely than men to combine the use of alcohol with other drugs, especially prescription and over-the-counter drugs, thus increasing the danger of adverse consequences (Peterson, Nisenholz, & Robinson 2003).

Women are more apt than men to present their substance use as precipitated by a specific event or trauma and to resist labels such as "alcoholic." Even when they acknowledge heavy AOD use, they tend to identify other issues, such as marital tensions or life stressors, as their main concern and to see their drug use as a way of coping with life problems. Thus, when troubled, they are inclined to seek services other than substance abuse treatment (Kane-Cavaiola & Rullo-Cooney 1991; Thom 1986). Research on substance use patterns among women of color has highlighted shared sociocultural factors as determinants of AOD problems, including lower socioeconomic status, higher incidence of depression, and such negative life events as physical and sexual abuse (Collins & McNair 2003; Hesselbrock & Hesselbrock 1997; Wilsnack, Vogeltanz, Klassen, & Harris 1997).

When substance abuse co-occurs with psychopathology, risk to the child increases. Prevalence of lifetime comorbidity of substance abuse and mental illness in the general population has been estimated at ranging between 51% and 86%, with highest rates of comorbid mental disorder found among women and those whose drug of choice is alcohol (Kessler, Nelson, & McGonagle, 1996; Kessler et al. 1997).

Protective Factors
The biopsychosocial model, which posits the intermingling of biological, psychological, and cultural factors in the etiology of social problems and solutions, can be used to delineate various mechanisms that serve to protect against AOD abuse in the family. For example, those who participate in religious activities are more apt than the nonreligious individuals to abstain from alcohol (Herd & Grube 1996). This has

been hypothesized as a protective factor in African American communities, for which church affiliation is central to family life, and particularly among African American women, who tend to participate in church activities more than their male counterparts (Taylor, Mattis, & Chatters 1999).

Among Asian Americans, it has been estimated that up to 50% possess a gene affecting their ability to metabolize alcohol. The resulting facial flushing and other adverse physical reactions have been associated with higher rates of abstinence and lower rates of problem drinking in this group (Gilbert & Collins 1997; Higuchi, Parrish, & Dufour 1992). However, as individuals of Asian background remain in the United States and acculturate to American drinking norms, their rates of use and abuse increase, thus illustrating the interplay of biology and society in influencing substance use (Padilla, Sung, & Nam 1993).

Parental Substance Abuse and the Child Welfare System
In AOD-related cases, child maltreatment is likely to be more chronic and more severe, with neglect being the most common form of maltreatment reported, followed by physical abuse (U.S. Department of Health and Human Services 1999). Once referred to child welfare professionals, children of chemically addicted parents are more likely to be re-referred for child protective services, to be removed from the home, to stay longer in foster care, and to have parental rights terminated than are children of parents without substance abuse problems (English, Marshall, Brummel, & Orme 1999; Wolock & Magura 1996). Although parental substance abusers are equally likely to be male or female, substance-abusing mothers are more likely than fathers and African American mothers more likely than mothers of other races to be reported for child maltreatment (U.S. Department of Health and Human Services 1999).

In 1997, Congress implemented the Adoption and Safe Families Act (P.L. 105-89), intended to speed up permanency plans for children under the supervision of the child welfare system. As a result, child welfare professionals and court officials were placed on an accelerated schedule—usually 12 months—to determine whether the goal for permanency for a given child should be family reunification, adoption, or guardianship. The new law also required states to begin terminating parental rights for any child who has been in foster care for 15 out of the past 22 months.

Some states have responded to the need for faster permanency decisions by enacting statutes specifically to address foster care cases involving parental substance abuse. For example, in Illinois, if a mother has been offered treatment following the birth of an infant prenatally exposed to drugs, she can be declared an unfit mother if she later gives birth to another drug-exposed infant (Ross 1997). In California, agencies are not bound to offer family reunification services if a chronic history of parental substance abuse and treatment refusal has been documented. Thus far, 30 states have enacted laws identifying substance abuse as potential grounds for termination of parental rights (U.S. General Accounting Office 1998).

One challenge for child welfare staff investigating maltreatment has been recognizing and assessing parental substance abuse, as this has not historically been part of their training (Dore, Doris, & Wright 1995). Moreover, many workers do not know whether local laws require them to record the presence of substance abuse when investigating child maltreatment (National Center on Addiction and Substance Abuse 1998). The result is that they often fail to assess chemical dependency as a risk factor (English, Marshall, Brummel, & Orme 1999).

Pregnant Substance Abusers and Their Offspring
Demographic Patterns, Vulnerabilities, and Risk Factors
The percentage of children under age 4 who were reported to child welfare authorities due to in utero AOD exposure doubled between 1986 and 1991 (U.S. Department of Health and Human Services, National Center on Child Abuse and Neglect 1997). The relationship between alcohol consumption during pregnancy and fetal harm has been well documented in the past few decades. Jones and Smith first coined the phrase "fetal alcohol syndrome" (FAS) in 1973, to describe a pattern of facial and other physical deformities in newborns. Since then, labels such as "fetal alcohol effects" (FAE) and "alcohol-related neurodevelopmental disorder" (ARND) have been used to describe infants exposed to alcohol in utero who manifest identifiable problems, but who do not have all of the facial abnormalities or growth retardation of children classified as FAS (Conner & Streissguth 1996). Children with FAS, FAE, and ARND evidence learning, language, memory, motor, and accompanying emotional-behavioral difficulties lasting into adulthood (Mattson & Riley 1998; Zuckerman & Brown 1993). Most disturbing are statistics showing that 10% of mental retardation is caused by FAS, FAE, and ARND, making this constellation of disorders the most common known cause of mental retardation (National Center on Addiction and Substance Abuse 1996). The United States has the highest incidence of FAS in the world (Abel 1998).

Marijuana is the illicit drug used most often by pregnant mothers, followed by cocaine (U.S. Department of Health and Human Services 1999). Infants prenatally exposed to cocaine may suffer a range of neonatal consequences, including withdrawal symptoms, higher risk of sudden infant death syndrome, low birth weight, and abnormal head circumference (Chasnoff 1988; NAPARE 1992; Zuckerman 1993).

However, research on long-term developmental outcomes for drug-exposed children has been inconclusive. This result has led some experts to view prenatal illicit drug exposure as less damaging to child development than alcohol (U.S. Department of Health and Human

Services 1999) and others to suggest that mediating factors in the child's postnatal environment interact with biological influences to produce varying outcomes in this population (Zuckerman 1993).

Although numerous studies have documented such risks as low birthweight and growth retardation among neonates exposed prenatally to narcotics (e.g., heroin, methadone), no evidence of long-term deficits has been found (Hans 1989; Atkinson & Butler 1996). However, due to narcotic dependency that may develop in the womb, neonates may suffer withdrawal symptoms that increase the risk of postnatal medical complications. Withdrawal symptoms may comprise irritability, nausea, sweating, diarrhea, vomiting, and seizures, with severity of symptoms related to the dose received in utero (Zuckerman & Brown 1993).

Research on the effects of other illicit drugs on human fetuses is scarce; however, animal research has suggested risk factors for newer drugs such as MDMA (ecstasy). One such study found that rats exposed prenatally to MDMA suffered enduring memory and cognitive deficits (Broening et al. 2001).

Prenatal Substance Abuse and the Child Welfare System

Infants exposed to drugs during pregnancy represent a small proportion of children reported to the child welfare system. Most studies find that only 10% to 20% enter foster care at or soon after birth, although about one-third more enter the system within a few years (U.S. Department of Health and Human Services 1999).

Controversy abounds around how society should respond to the problem of drug-exposed infants. Unresolved policy issues include which mothers and neonates should be screened for drug use, how to conduct the screenings, whether child protective services should be involved, and whether infants who test positive should be removed from the home. Accordingly, the child welfare response to prenatal substance abuse varies widely across regions. Some states and localities test all pregnant women and neonates, whereas others screen intermittently (Birchfield, Scully, & Handler 1995; Chavkin, Breitbart, Ellman, & Wise 1998). Whereas some states mandate the reporting of AOD-exposed infants to child welfare authorities, others rely on the discretion of the medical team to make a referral. In some states, prenatal exposure in and of itself constitutes neglect and triggers an assessment for possible removal of the child from the custody of their parents (Ross 1997).

The court's desire to protect children from harm caused by substance-involved parents has at times collided with its duty to preserve individuals' constitutional rights. In New York State, for example, a judge barred a couple with a history of drug abuse and child neglect from procreating until they could prove they could care for the children they already had (Santora 2004). The fact that illicit drugs, found to be less damaging to the fetus than alcohol, are more likely to be picked up through current screening procedures raises the question of fairness in testing. In addition, the scarcity of treatment facilities for this population contributes to the likelihood of prenatal substance abuse—especially of illicit drugs—resulting in termination of parental rights.

Children of Substance Abusers

Demographic Patterns, Vulnerabilities, and Risk Factors

Although children living with substance-abusing parents are distributed evenly across the childhood age span, younger children are the most vulnerable to child maltreatment by a substance-abusing parent and most likely to come to the attention of child welfare agencies. In 1996, two-thirds of the 1,185 deaths attributed to child abuse and neglect were perpetrated by addicted parents on victims under the age of 5 (Reid & Macchetto 1999). This age group also represents the fastest growing population in out-of-home care.

Chemically addicted parents may neglect their children while seeking drugs; drain needed resources to purchase drugs; or risk their child's well-being while engaged in obtaining, selling, or other criminal activities related to drug use (U.S. General Accounting Office 1998). In terms of parenting styles, substance abusers may be overcontrolling, punitive, unresponsive, or otherwise emotionally unavailable to their children (Burns, Chetik, Burns, & Clark 1991). They may fail to maintain parent-child boundaries, treating their children as peers or expecting them to fulfill the role of the parent (Black 1995). Parents under the influence of drugs may experience lower frustration tolerance and easing of inhibitions that prevent violent behaviors, thus increasing the risk of child abuse (Kelly 2002).

Children and youth of substance-abusing parents are more likely than those from non-addicted families to have such problems as conduct disorder; delinquency; intellectual deficits; anxiety; depression; engaging in lying, stealing, and fighting; and lower confidence/self-esteem (Gfroerer & De La Rosa 1993; West & Prinz 1987). They are also at risk of developing substance abuse problems earlier, of escalating use more quickly, and of developing more serious dependency than are children and adolescents of nonaddicted parents (Kinney 2003).

Long-term effects of parental substance abuse on children vary and are confounded by other variables, such as family stability and poverty. Most longitudinal studies of children of alcoholics demonstrate that the majority does not develop serious problems. However, for those who do suffer negative consequences, effects are far-reaching. Adult children of alcoholics marry less often than those not raised in alcoholic homes; those who do marry are 30% to 40% more likely to divorce (Call 1998).

Protective Factors and Resilience
There is some evidence that maternal drug use affects children more than paternal drug use, and interacts with the mother's personality traits to produce behavioral outcomes in offspring. In one study, substance-abusing mothers who were more conventional, related well to their children, and were interpersonally more adept had toddlers who manifested lower levels of anxiety or regressive behavior than did the toddlers of substance-abusing mothers without these characteristics (Brook, Tseng, & Cohen 1996). Results also indicated that high maternal drug use could be offset by low paternal drug use. In families where both parents used drugs, toddlers demonstrated the most regressive behavior.

Studies of resilience in children of substance abusers have focused on shared characteristics that helped the children overcome adversity. In one study, children unimpaired by their parents' alcoholism had good communication skills, at least average intelligence, a caring attitude, a desire to achieve, and a belief in helping oneself. They were also good at seeking and getting attention from others (Werner & Smith 1989).

Adolescent Substance Abusers
Demographic Patterns, Risk Factors, and Protective Factors
Teenagers are more apt than any other age group to engage in risky behaviors of all kinds. Indeed, experimentation with addictive drugs usually begins in adolescence and has been seen as a correlate of adolescent novelty-seeking and impulsivity. Recent research has linked such traits to maturational changes in brain regions that occur during the teenage years, suggesting that immature inhibitory control systems contribute to impulsive actions in teens, including AOD use (Chambers, Taylor, & Potenza 2003).

National surveys reveal that approximately 46% of high school–aged youth drink alcohol (Barrett 2003). According to data from the 2003 Monitoring the Future survey, 77% of students have tried alcohol and 58% of twelfth graders have been drunk at least once in their lifetime (Johnston, O'Malley, & Bachman 2002). The decade between 1990 and 2000 saw a sharp rise in teenage use of illicit drugs, especially MDMA, LSD, and amphetamines. More recent data indicate a reduction since then in teenage usage of these drugs, as well as the use of marijuana and tranquilizers. Whereas in 2001, reported lifetime illicit drug use among teens was 41%, in 2003 it was 37.4%. Past-month usage of marijuana, the illicit drug most commonly used by youth, declined from 16.6% to 14.8% during the same period. However, the use of inhalants, Oxycontin™ and Vicodin™, increased slightly (National Institute on Drug Abuse 2004).

Rates of drug use—both licit and illicit—are generally lower among African American than among white youth (Johnston, O'Malley, & Bachman 2002). Adolescents in the United States have much higher rates of illicit drug use than do those in Europe, although they have lower rates of alcohol and tobacco use (Zernike 2001).

Although gender patterns of AOD use and abuse among adolescents mirror adult patterns, with prevalence higher among boys than girls, the gap is narrowing. According to the 2001 Monitoring the Future Study, 36% of twelfth grade boys and 24% of girls reported binge drinking (Johnston, O'Malley, & Bachman 2002). Adolescent girls appear to be more vulnerable, due to their tendency to get addicted more quickly using smaller amounts of drugs (Barrett 2003; Johnson, O'Malley, & Bachman 2002). Teenage girls who use drugs are also more susceptible to negative consequences, such as brain and liver damage, are more likely to abuse prescription drugs, and are more likely to be depressed or suicidal than are teenage boys who abuse substances (National Center on Addiction and Substance Abuse 2003).

After two decades of research, the National Institute on Drug Abuse (2002a) has identified the following risk factors that make AOD use more likely among youth and adolescents:

- Chaotic home environments;
- Parent who abuses substances or is mentally ill;
- Poor parent-child attachments;
- Shy or aggressive classroom behavior;
- Poor school performance;
- Affiliation with substance-using or deviant behavior-prone peers; and
- Perceptions of approval of drug-using behaviors among family, coworkers, or peers.

In the same study, the institute identified the following protective factors making AOD use less likely in this population:

- Strong family bonds;
- Parents who monitor activities and peers and are involved in their children's lives;
- Clear and enforced rules of conduct within the family;
- Good school performance; and
- Adoption of conventional norms about drug use.

Recently, researchers have cautioned against assuming that risk and protective factors observed among white youth apply to African American youth. For example, black youth are more likely than white youth to report having seen someone selling drugs in their community and to believe that obtaining illicit drugs would be easy (U.S. Department of Health and Human Services 1995). Yet some observers suggest that this greater exposure, contrary to the case for white youth, serves a protective function in that black youth are brought face-to-face with the negative consequences of drug use, resulting in lower rates of most illicit drug use among black teenagers (Wallace 1999).

Assessment and Intervention with AOD-Abusing Families

Assessment

Assessing families with AOD problems, whether the problem is with an adult, child, or adolescent, involves obtaining an in-depth drug-use history, including the quantity, frequency, onset, and consequences of use. Taking a psychosocial history, as well as conducting or referring clients for psychiatric and physical examinations, is also warranted. Screening instruments to detect AOD use—ranging from self-report questionnaires to urinalysis and other laboratory measures—are often employed when substance use is suspected but not fully acknowledged by the client. Additionally, understanding the meaning of the drug use to the user—what it does for as well as what it does to the individual—can help the worker identify underlying issues and unmet needs that may reinforce or interact with usage. Investigation may involve interviews with the family, school, and other professionals, as well as gathering data from prior assessments.

In addition to the information detailed above, assessment of parental substance abusers should include an evaluation of parenting skills and deficits, familial and other supports, childcare options, vocational background, legal status, involvement with child welfare and other social service agencies, reproductive and health status, and any history of violence. For maternal substance abusers, assessing relationship issues, taking a sexual history, including possible sexual abuse or dysfunction, and identifying potential barriers to treatment are important adjuncts.

When assessing children and adolescents, developmental issues should be considered, and the role of children within the various systems in which they interact explored. In addition to obtaining a developmental history, the worker should examine the child's level of functioning at school; quality of home life; relationship with parents, teachers, and peers; and participation in the community. Assessing children pre- or postnatally exposed to drugs should further involve examination of speech and language abilities, intellectual functioning, socioemotional development, and behavioral problems (Niccols 1994).

Regarding adolescent AOD abuse, it is also important to ascertain whether drug use is experimental, occasional, binge-related, or chronic, as different patterns of use yield different levels of negative consequences in teens. Thus a teenager who experiments with marijuana in a safe setting is at less risk than one who binges monthly on potentially lethal amounts of alcohol, or who uses regularly in response to external circumstances (e.g., peer pressure) or internal cues (e.g., depression, drug cravings).

Furthermore, assessing the level of impairment using such standard criteria as those from the Diagnostic and Statistical Manual of Mental Disorders (DSM) may present a challenge. Due to age and patterns of use, adolescents may not experience symptoms, such as tolerance and withdrawal, two DSM IV criteria for diagnosing substance abuse and dependence. Clinicians should instead look for behavior, cognitive, or mood disturbances that accompany drug abuse (Segal & Stewart 1996).

Intervention

Intervention with AOD-abusing families runs the gamut from self-referred preventive services, healthcare initiatives for pregnant mothers, school or community-based drug education, to court-ordered treatment in child protective cases. Treatment may occur in outpatient, inpatient, or residential settings, and may be augmented by 12-Step and other self-help or support groups. Chronic shortages of substance abuse treatment for those who need it have been reported in the past decade (Substance Abuse and Mental Health Services Administration 1998; U.S. Department of Health and Human Services 1999). Specifically, the demand for facilities that specialize in treating adolescents, maternal substance abusers, and the dual-diagnosed far exceeds the availability of such programs. This is unfortunate, as research supports the effectiveness of dedicated treatment for these groups (Drake et al. 2001; Hodgins, El Guebaly, & Addington 1997; National Institute on Drug Abuse 2002b).

Knowledge and skills needed by professionals working with substance abusing families may include the following.

Treatment planning. Good treatment planning consists of aiding the client in identifying

TABLE 1. *Web Resources for Further Information*

National Clearinghouse on Child Abuse and Neglect Information
www.nccanch.acf.hhs.gov

National Clearinghouse for Alcohol and Drug Information
www.health.org

National Clearinghouse on Families and Youth
www.ncfy.com

National Center on Substance Abuse and Child Welfare
www.ncsacw.samhsa.gov

National Institute on Drug Abuse
www.drugabuse.gov

Substance Abuse and Mental Health Services Administration
www.DrugAbuseStatistics.samhsa.gov

Center for Substance Abuse Prevention
www.samhsa.gov/csap

Drug Policy Research Institute
www.lindesmith.org

Child Welfare League of America
www.cwla.org

National Organization on Fetal Alcohol Syndrome
www.nofas.org

their needs and strengths, locating resources (see table 1), creating and carrying through a plan of action, and following up. Goals should be broad enough to encompass such concerns as housing, childcare, parenting, and legal issues. Close monitoring of progress in treatment is essential to determine whether and when family reunification can occur. After treatment is completed and a family reunified, aftercare services, such as ongoing caseworker visits and referral to Alcoholics Anonymous or similar self-help groups, can help prevent relapse.

Motivational interviewing. Motivating parents to address their substance abuse problems is crucial to intervention, as research shows lack of motivation to seek and remain in treatment is a major barrier for this population (Sheehan & Libby 1998; Zlotnick, Franshino, Clair, Cox, & St. John 1996). Motivational Enhancement, a form of brief therapy, was developed as a means of moving clients toward changing their addictive behaviors (Miller & Rollnick 1991). Using client-centered techniques, the counselor provides empathy to help clients explore and articulate their ambivalence about change and tip the balance toward taking action.

Staged interventions. Prochaska and Di Clemente (1986) have portrayed chemically addicted individuals as negotiating their way through various stages in their journey toward recovery. The Developmental Model (U.S. Department of Health and Human Services 1999) posits six stages that recovering individuals must undergo:

1. Transition: person realizes that he or she cannot safely use drugs;
2. Stabilization: person learns how to separate him- or herself from stimuli that promote drug usage;
3. Early recovery: person confronts the need to develop a drug-free lifestyle;
4. Middle recovery: person establishes such a lifestyle;
5. Late recovery: person faces up to self-distortions that led to dysfunction; and
6. Maintenance: person continues lifelong process of growth.

Working with substance abusers involves gearing treatment to the individual's stage of recovery. Thus in the early phase of treatment, the worker may be more directive, furnishing education about the impact of AOD abuse and the process of recovery. Later phases of recovery may focus on such topics as problem behaviors, relationships, social skills training, career goals, and relapse prevention.

Group work. Substance abuse treatment is often delivered in group modalities. There are several advantages for clients working in groups. Observing dysfunctional behaviors and attitudes in others can help clients acknowledge their own fallacies. Peers can model behaviors appropriate for recovery and can expose one another's "stinkin' thinkin'," a term coined by Albert Ellis to describe irrational and self-defeating beliefs that lead to emotional and behavioral disturbance (Ellis 1986). Many clients enjoy the attention and support provided in the group, as well as the opportunity to connect with and contribute to others. However, it should not be assumed that every individual will benefit from a group experience. Screening members for suitability and placement in a specific group is important to enhance success rates. The worker should look for a good fit in terms of the individual's type and level of psychopathology, stage of recovery, level of motivation, ability to tolerate frustration or conflict, and prior group experiences.

Family systems. Families may participate in various ways and at various stages of AOD treatment. Some families approach professionals for help in getting their loved ones into treatment. Others are involved collaterally during the treatment process, the goal being to support the client's sobriety. After the identified client has "graduated" from a substance abuse treatment program, the family may continue to need help in such areas as adjusting to new norms, experimenting with new roles, and changing dysfunctional patterns of behavior or communication.

Community building. Community-building efforts involve forming partnerships between local residents and organizations to reinforce sobriety and protect citizens from AOD abuse and its consequences. Community interventions have the advantage of offering the possibility for broader systems change (Young, Gardner, & Dennis 1998). In one model known as "Community Reinforcement," youth are linked through church, family, and friends with community activities, where they can have successful social interactions without using drugs or alcohol (Meyers, Smith, & Lash 2003).

Programs: Promising Approaches
Co-location Programs: Linking Foster Care Agencies and Drug Treatment Providers
Several states have begun piloting programs in which professionals from substance abuse facilities are co-located at child welfare agencies, working in tandem with child welfare staff. When a caseworker investigating maltreatment suspects familial substance abuse, they refer the case to the substance abuse counselor, who conducts an assessment and provides referral and monitoring as needed. In New Jersey, the Department of Youth and Family Services piloted a program that purchased the services of substance abuse counselors to augment the expertise of their child welfare staff. Cross-training of foster care workers and drug treatment staff members taught the former about chemical dependency and the latter about child welfare issues. Although outcome data on treatment completion and family reunification have not been reported to date, the program did achieve its goal of increasing the percentage of parents who entered substance abuse treatment (Young, Gardner, & Dennis 1998).

Family Drug Courts
Family drug courts have been characterized as "an effort by judges to impose accountability not only on substance abusing parents, but also on a social welfare system that is fragmented, uncoordinated, and generally ill-prepared for

the multiple, intertwined problems of families with substance abuse problems" (National Center on Addiction and Substance Abuse 1998:75). Family drug court programs target substance-abusing parents whose children have been or are in danger of being removed from the home due to maltreatment (U.S. General Accounting Office 1999). Parents deemed motivated are immediately referred for substance abuse treatment in lieu of punishment. A case manager is assigned to facilitate collaboration between the various agencies involved, monitor treatment, and link the parent with resources. Intermittent drug testing and regular meetings of the team assist professionals in making timely decisions regarding permanency. Although most programs have yet to conduct formal evaluations due to budgetary constrictions, preliminary data indicate that family drug courts produce parents who comply with court mandates (Atkinson & Butler 1996; Famularo, Kinsherf, & Fenton 1989).

Family-Centered Preventive Services

Family-centered programs are sometimes embedded in preventive services, such as intensive family preservation or early intervention programs. In this model, rather than being blamed for their substance use and its impact on their children, parents partner with case managers to develop the optimum treatment plan for the entire family. Based on the assumption that parents possess the capacity to nurture their offspring, the focus here is on parental strengths rather than inadequacies. Services attempt to respond to family needs, and one-stop shopping is prioritized. Family-oriented services show promise in that they enable parents to feel empowered (Trivette, Dunst, Boyd, & Hamby 1996; Thompson et al. 1997) and are valued by clients as helpful (Heneghan, Horwitz, & Leventhal 1996). In at least one study, family-centered intensive case management was associated with higher rates of family reunification (Evans et al. 1994).

Concurrent Planning

Concurrent planning (Katz 1999) involves working to reunify the AOD-involved family while simultaneously preparing another permanency plan should reunification efforts fail. The aim of concurrent planning is to allow the parent some leeway to engage in the process of recovery while reducing the amount of time it takes to achieve permanency for the child. As with co-location programs and family drug courts, there is no information available on long-term outcomes for children whose cases are handled through concurrent planning.

Ethical Issues and Values Dilemmas

Despite some of the innovations described above, challenges to reunifying AOD-involved families remain. One predicament has been characterized as the "conflicting time clocks" of the treatment, legal, and welfare systems. Under the law, children have the right to a permanent custody decision within 12 to 18 months. However, treatment providers tend to view addiction as a chronic biopsychosocial disease, for which treatment may be brief or may last several years. Accordingly, they view recovery as a lifelong process, and relapse not as a failure of treatment, but, rather, a part of the process—that is, an opportunity for clients to learn how to deal with triggers that threaten their sobriety. Such learning processes take time—time that vulnerable children on their own developmental trajectories do not have. Another time clock is that of the social welfare system, under which families receiving Temporary Aid to Needy Families benefits must find work within 24 months or lose their benefits. This adds another complication for addicted parents who are considering treatment.

The need for standard criteria to guide determination of when and under what circumstances families should be reunified has been noted, and efforts have been made to delineate and categorize indicators for safe reunification (Karrol & Poertner 2002). However, questions remain as to what outcomes are expected on what timelines and how to best measure "readiness" for safe return of the child. For example, is a child safe when a parent completes treatment? When a parent remains abstinent for a certain amount of time? If so, how much time? Likewise, what are grounds for termination of parental rights? Initial refusal to enroll or failure to complete a treatment program? Multiple failures to enroll or to complete treatment? Any reported use of a substance following treatment? Reported use of a substance combined with parental dysfunction? Deciding which client (the adult or the child) has precedence, which time clock to follow, and which criteria to use to judge success creates values dilemmas for caseworkers and court officials.

An ethical issue that has yet to be fully resolved has to do with confidentiality. Treatment facilities are required by law to protect the privacy of clients in their care. However, to make timely custody decisions, foster care agencies and courts need information about how parents are progressing in treatment. The resulting conflict of interest hinders mutual cooperation and collaboration between caseworkers and treatment staff. To overcome this obstacle, some child welfare agencies request that parents sign a consent form giving them the right to obtain information about their progress in treatment. Alternatively, federal law stipulates that a substance abuse facility may enter into a Qualified Service Organizational Agreement (QSOA) with a foster care agency, allowing both programs access to information regardless of client consent. However, to date, few child welfare and substance abuse agencies have established QSOAs (U.S. Department of Health & Human Services 1999).

MS. KENT

Ms. Kent was reported to child protective services by teachers concerned about the disheveled appearance and declining school performance of her daughter, Serina, 8. A child welfare worker was dispatched to the home to conduct an investigation. The caseworker waited 10 minutes for Ms. Kent to respond to the doorbell, a delay for which Ms. Kent offered no explanation. Once inside, the worker discovered no food in the home, but she did spot what appeared to be drug paraphernalia in the corner of a back room. When asked if she had the means to satisfy Serina's food and clothing needs, Ms. Kent responded that "Serina's a big girl—she knows how to take care of herself."

During the interview, Ms. Kent, a single mother working part-time as a waitress, appeared tired and distracted. Questioned about recent drug or alcohol use, Ms. Kent became irritable, stating that "that's nobody's business but my own." When the worker explained that substance abuse can lead to neglect of one's parental duties, Ms. Kent denied any substance use. However, concerned about possibly being judged an unfit mother and separated from Serina, Ms. Kent agreed to meet with an addiction counselor co-located at the child welfare agency for further evaluation. The substance abuse screening revealed that Ms. Kent did indeed have a drinking problem, exacerbated by occasional use of cocaine. The frequency, dosage, and date of onset suggested that the problem was at the level of abuse rather than dependency.

Working together, the substance abuse counselor and child welfare worker convinced Ms. Kent that it was in her best interest to enter substance abuse treatment, and scheduled an intake interview for the following day at an outpatient program, which would enable her to continue working part-time. Serina was temporarily placed in kinship foster care with her maternal grandmother, and was referred to a school-based group for latency-aged children of substance abusers. Ms. Kent's progress in treatment was closely monitored by protective services staff. After graduating from an 18-week substance abuse treatment program, completing parenting classes, and meeting other requirements for safeguarding Serina's welfare, Ms. Kent was reunited with her child.

This case illustrates several principles of assessment and treatment of AOD-affected families. The investigating child welfare worker noted signs of child neglect, including the lack of food in the home and Ms. Kent's unrealistic expectations that a child of Serina's age should "take care of herself." The worker also picked up on possible signs of substance use, including the presence of drug paraphernalia and Ms. Kent's sluggish and irritable behavior. Because her child welfare agency was piloting a co-location program, with an addiction expert on site, the caseworker was able to refer Ms. Kent for a substance abuse evaluation immediately. When the determination of polydrug abuse was made, the professionals worked in tandem to motivate Ms. Kent to take action. Having as-

sessed Ms. Kent's problem as one of substance abuse rather than dependence, the workers referred her for outpatient treatment, which represented the least restrictive option considering her needs. Knowing that a parent's resolve to enter treatment can quickly abate, they made an appointment for Ms. Kent at the treatment facility within 24 hours. The workers obtained a waiver from Ms. Kent that allowed them to obtain information regarding her progress from the substance abuse treatment facility. This helped guide them in making decisions regarding custody.

REFERENCES

Abel, E. (1998). Fetal alcohol syndrome: The "American paradox." *Alcohol & Alcoholism, 33*(3), 195–201.

Adoption and Safe Families Act. (1997). P.L. 105-89.

Atkinson, L., & Butler, S. (1996). Court-ordered assessments: Impact of maternal non-compliance in child maltreatment cases. *Child Abuse and Neglect, 20,* 185–190.

Barrett, D. (2003). Study: Girls more easily addicted to drugs. *Associated Press,* (February 5, 2003), p. 58.

Birchfield, M., Scully, J., & Handler, A. (1995). Perinatal screening for illicit drugs: Policies in hospitals in a large metropolitan area. *Journal of Perinatology, 15,* 208–214.

Black, C. (1995). *You can't go forward without finishing the past: Healing the pain of abandonment, fear and shame. Children of alcoholics: Selected readings.* Rockville, MD: National Association for Children of Alcoholics.

Blume, S. B. (1990). Chemical dependency in women: Important issues. *American Journal of Drug and Alcohol Abuse, 16*(3–4), 297–307.

Broening, H. W., Morford, L. L., Inman-Wood, S. L., Fukumura, M., & Vorhees, C. V. (2001). Methylenedioxymethamphetamine (ecstasy)-induced learning and memory impairments depend on the age of exposure during early development. *Journal of Neuroscience, 21,* 3228–3235.

Brook, J. S., Tseng, L., & Cohen, P. (1996). Toddler adjustment: Impact of parents' drug use, personality and parent-child relations. *Journal of Genetic Psychology, 157*(3), 281–295.

Burns, K., Chetik, L., Burns, W. J., & Clark, R. (1991). Dyadic disturbances in cocaine-abusing mothers and their infants. *Journal of Clinical Psychology, 47,* 316–319.

Call, J. (1998). Alcoholics' kids face marital woes. *Deseret News,* Provo, UT, (November 15, 1998), p. A12 .

Chambers, R. A., Taylor, J. R., & Potenza, M. N. (2003). Developmental neurocircuitry of motivation in adolescence: A critical period of addiction vulnerability. *American Journal of Psychiatry, 160,* 1041–1052.

Chasnoff, I. J. (1988). Cocaine use in pregnancy. *New England Journal of Medicine, 313,* 666–669.

Chavkin, W., Breitbart, V., Ellman, D., & Wise, P. H. (1998). National survey of the states: Policies and practices regarding drug-using pregnant women. *American Journal of Public Health, 88,* 117–119.

Collins, R. L., & McNair, L. D. (2003). *Minority women and alcohol use.* National Institute on Alcohol Abuse and Alcoholism. Retrieved June 30, 2004, from www.niaaa.nih.gov/publications.

Connor, P. D., & Streissguth, A. P. (1996). Effects of prenatal exposure to alcohol across the life span. *Alcohol Health and Research World, 20*(3), 170–175.

Dore, M. M., Doris, J., & Wright, P. (1995). Identifying substance abuse in maltreating families: A child welfare challenge. *Child Abuse and Neglect, 19,* 531–543.

Drake, R. E., Essock, S. M., Andrew, S., Carey, K., Minkoff, K., et al. (2001). Implementing dual diagnosis services for clients with severe mental illness. *Psychiatric Services, 52,* 469–476.

Ellis, A. (1986). Rational-emotive therapy. In I. L. Kutash & A. Wolf (eds.), *Psychotherapist's casebook.* San Francisco: Jossey-Bass.

English, D., Marshall, D., Brummel. S., & Orme, M. (1999). Characteristics of repeated referrals to child protective services in Washington State. *Child Maltreatment, 4,* 297–307.

Evans, M. E., Armstrong, M. I., Dollard, N., Kuppinger, A. D., Huz, S., & Wood, V. M. (1994). Development and evaluation of treatment foster care and family-centered intensive case management in New York. *Journal of Emotional and Behavioral Disorders, 2,* 228–239.

Famularo, R., Kinsherf, R., & Fenton, T. (1989). Post-traumatic stress disorder among maltreated children presenting to a juvenile court. *American Journal of Forensic Psychiatry, 10,* 33–39.

Freundlich, M. (2000). The impact of prenatal substance exposure: Research findings and their implications for adoption. In R. Barth, M. Freundlich, & D. Brodinsky (eds.), *Adoption and prenatal alcohol and drug exposure,* p. 1–21. Washington, DC: CWLA Press.

Gfroerer, J. C., & De La Rosa, M. (1993). Protective and risk factors associated with drug use among Hispanic youth. *Journal of Addictive Diseases, 12*(2), 87–107.

Gilbert, M. J., & Collins, R. L. (1997). Ethnic variation in women's and men's drinking. In R. W. Wilsnack & S. C. Wilsnack (eds), *Gender and alcohol,* pp. 357–378. New Brunswick, NJ: Rutgers Center of Alcohol Studies.

Hans, S. L. (1989). Developmental consequences of prenatal exposure to methadone. *Annals of the New York Academy of Science, 562,* 195–207.

Heneghan, A. M., Horwitz, S. M., & Leventhal, J. M. (1996). Evaluating intensive family preservation programs: A methodological review. *Pediatrics, 97,* 535–542.

Herd, D., & Grube, J. (1996). Black identity and drinking in the U.S.: A national study. *Addiction, 91,* 845–857.

Hesselbrock, M. N., & Hesselbrock, V. M. (1997). Gender, alcoholism and psychiatric comorbidity. In R. W. Wilsnack, & S. C. Wilsnack (eds), *Gender and alcohol,* pp. 49–71. New Brunswick, NJ: Rutgers Center of Alcohol Studies.

Higuchi, S., Parrish, K. M., & Dufour, M. C. (1992). The relationship between three subtypes of the flushing response and DSM-III alcohol abuse in Japanese. *Journal of Studies on Alcohol, 53,* 553–560.

Hodgins, D., El Guebaly, N., & Addington, J. (1997). Treatment of substance abusers: single or mixed gender programs? *Addiction, 92,* 805–812.

Johnston, L. D., O'Malley, P. M., & Bachman, J. G. (2002). *Monitoring the future: National survey results on drug use, 1975–2001.* Vol. I: *Secondary School Students.* NIH publication no. 02-51-6. Bethesda, MD: National Institute on Drug Abuse.

Kane-Cavaiola, C., & Rullo-Cooney, D. (1991). Addicted women: Their families' effect on treatment outcome. *Chemical Dependency: Theoretical Approaches and Strategies, 12,* 111–119.

Karoll, B. R., & Poertner, J. (2002). Judges', caseworkers' and substance abuse counselors' indicators of family reunification with substance-affected parents. *Child Welfare, 81,* 249–270.

Katz, L. (1999). Concurrent planning: benefits and pitfalls. *Child Welfare, 78,* 71–87.

Kelly, S. J. (2002). Child maltreatment in the context of substance abuse. In J. E. Meyers, L. Berliner, & C. T. Hendrix (eds.), *The APSAC handbook on child maltreatment,* second ed. Thousand Oaks, CA: Sage.

Kessler, R. C., Crum, R. M., Warner, L. S., Nelson, C. B., Schulenberg, J., & Anthony, J. C. (1997). Lifetime co-occurrence of DSM-II-R alcohol abuse and dependence with other psychiatric disorders in the National Comorbidity Survey. *Archives of General Psychiatry, 54,* 313–321.

Kessler, R. C., Nelson, C. B., & McGonagle, K. A. (1996). The epidemiology of co-occurring addictive and mental disorders: Implications for prevention and service utilization. *American Journal of Orthopsychiatry, 66,* 17–31.

Kinney, J. (2003). *Loosening the grip: A handbook of alcohol information,* seventh ed. New York: McGraw-Hill.

Mattson, S., & Riley, E. (1998). A review of the neurobehavioral deficits in children with fetal alcohol syndrome or prenatal exposure to alcohol. *Alcoholism: Clinical and Experimental Research, 22*(2), 279–294.

Meyers, R. J., Smith, J. E., & Lash, D. N. (2003). The community reinforcement approach. *Recent Developments in Alcohol Treatment, 16,* 183–195.

Miller, W. R., & Rollnick, S. (1991). *Motivational interviewing.* New York: Guilford.

NAPARE. (1992). NAPARE study indicates recovery possible for children. *Pediatrics, 89,* 231–244.

National Center on Addiction and Substance Abuse. (1996). *Substance abuse and the American woman.* New York: Columbia University.

National Center on Addiction and Substance Abuse. (1998). *No safe haven: Children of substance-abusing parents.* New York: National Center on Addiction and Substance Abuse. Retrieved March 22, 2002, from www.casacolumbia.org.

National Center on Addiction and Substance Abuse. (2003). *The formative years: Pathways to substance abuse among girls and young women ages 8–22.* New York: Columbia University.

National Institute on Alcohol Abuse and Alcoholism. (2002). *Alcohol and minorities: An update.* Alcohol Alert no. 55. Rockville, MD: National Institute on Alcohol Abuse and Alcoholism.

National Institute on Drug Abuse. (2002a). Risk and protective factors in drug abuse prevention. *NIDA Notes, 16*(6), 5.

National Institute on Drug Abuse. (2002b). Adolescent treatment programs reduce drug abuse, produce other improvements. *NIDA Notes, 17*(1), 11.

National Institute on Drug Abuse. (2004). Teens' drug use declines dramatically, according to MTF survey results. *NIDA Notes, 19*(1), 15.

Niccols, G. A. (1994). Fetal alcohol syndrome: Implications for psychologists. *Clinical Psychology Review, 14*(2), 91–111.

Office of Applied Studies. (2003). *Children living with substance-abusing or substance-dependent parents.* Rockville, MD: Substance Abuse and Mental Health

Services Administration. Retrieved June 30, 2004, from www.DrugAbuseStatistics.samhsa.gov.

Padilla, A. M., Sung, H., & Nam, T. V. (1993). Attitudes toward alcohol and drinking practices in two Vietnamese samples in Santa Clara County. *Horizon of Vietnamese Thought and Expression, 2,* 53–71.

Peterson, J. V., Nisenholz, B., & Robinson, G. (2003). *A nation under the influence: America's addiction to alcohol.* Boston: Allyn and Bacon.

Prochaska, J. O., & Di Clemente, C. C. (1986). The transtheoretical approach. In J. C. Norcross (ed.), *Handbook of eclectic psychotherapy.* New York: Bruner/Mazel.

Reid, J., & Macchetto, P. (1999). *No safe haven: Children of substance-abusing parents.* New York: National Center on Addiction and Substance Abuse, Columbia University.

Ross, J. (1997). *Parental substance abuse: Implications for children, the child welfare system, and foster care outcomes.* Statement to Congress by the director of Income Security Issues, Health, Education and Human Services Division, October 28, 1997. Report GAO/T-HEHS-98-40. Washington, DC: U.S. General Accounting Office.

Santora, M. (2004). Negligent upstate couple is told not to procreate. *New York Times,* (May 11, 2004), p. B6.

Schneider Institute for Health Policy. (2001). *Substance abuse, the nation's number one health problem.* Waltham, MA: Brandeis University.

Sedlak, S., & Broadhurst, D. D. (1996). *Executive summary of the third national incidence of child abuse and neglect (NIS-3).* Washington, DC: U.S. Department of Health and Human Services.

Segal, B. M., & Stewart, J. C. (1996). Substance use and abuse in adolescence: An overview. *Child Psychiatry and Human Development, 26*(4), 193.

Sheehan, J., & Libby, B. (1998). Project SAFE Substance Abuse Family Evaluation. Presentation at Between Two Worlds—Child Maltreatment and Substance Abuse Conference, Los Angeles, June 22–24, 1998.

Substance Abuse and Mental Health Services Administration. (1998). *Analyses of substance abuse and treatment need issues.* Rockville, MD: U.S. Department of Health and Human Services.

Taylor, R. J., Mattis, J., & Chatters, L. M. (1999). Subjective religiosity among African Americans: A synthesis of findings from five national samples. *Journal of Black Psychology, 25,* 524–543.

Thom, B. (1986). Sex differences in help-seeking for alcoholic problems. *British Journal of Addiction, 81,* 777–788.

Thompson, L., Lobb, C., Elling, R., Herman, S., Jurkeiwicz, T., & Hulleza, C. (1997). Pathways to family empowerment: Effects of family-centered delivery of early intervention services. *Exceptional Children, 64,* 93–113.

Trivette, C., Dunst, C., Boyd, K., & Hamby, D. (1996). Family-oriented program models, helpgiving practices, and parental control appraisals. *Exceptional Children, 62,* 237–248.

U.S. Department of Health and Human Services. (1995). *Drug use among racial/ethnic minorities.* Washington, DC: U.S. Government Printing Office.

U.S. Department of Health and Human Services. (1999). *Blending perspectives and building common ground: A report to Congress on substance abuse and child protection.* Washington, DC: U.S. Government Printing Office.

U.S. Department of Health and Human Services, National Center on Child Abuse and Neglect. (1997). Child maltreatment 1995: Reports from the states to the National Center on Child Abuse and Neglect. Washington, DC: U.S. Government Printing Office.

U.S. General Accounting Office. (1998). *Foster care: Agencies face challenges securing stable homes for children of substance abusers.* Report to the chairman, Committee on Finance, U.S. Senate. Department of Health and Human Services, September 1998. Report GAO/HEHS-98-182. Washington, DC: U.S. General Accounting Office.

Wallace, J. M., Jr. (1999). Explaining race differences in adolescent and young adult drug use: The role of radicalized social systems. *Drugs & Society, 13*(1–2), 21–36.

Werner, E., & Smith, R. (1989). Vulnerable but invincible: A longitudinal study from birth to age 18. *Journal of Studies on Alcohol, 47,* 34–40.

West, M. O., & Prinz, R. J. (1987). Parental alcoholism and childhood psychopathology. *Psychological Bulletin, 102,* 204–218.

Wilsnack, S. C., Vogeltanz, N. D., Klassen, A. D., & Harris, T. R. (1997). Childhood sexual abuse and women's substance abuse. *Journal of Studies on Alcohol, 58,* 264–271.

Wolock, I., & Magura, S. (1996). Parental substance abuse as a predictor of child maltreatment re-reports. *Child Abuse and Neglect, 20,* 1183–1193.

Young, N. K., Gardner, S. L., & Dennis, K. (1998). *Responding to alcohol and other drug problems in child welfare: Weaving together practice and policy.* Washington, DC: CWLA Press.

Zernike, K. (2001). Study finds teenage drug use higher in U.S. than in Europe. *New York Times,* (February 21, 2001), p. A10.

Zlotnick, C., Franshino, K., Clair, N., Cox, K., & St. John, M. (1996). The impact of outpatient drug services on abstinence among pregnant and parenting women. *Journal of Substance Abuse Treatment, 13*(3), 195–202.

Zuckerman, B. (1993). Effects on parents and children. In D. J. Bensen & K. W. Hanson (eds.), *When drug addicts have children,* pp. 112–131. Washington, DC: American Enterprise Institute/CWLA.

Zuckerman, B., & Brown, E. (1993). Maternal substance abuse and infant development. In C. H. Zeanah (ed.), *Handbook of infant mental health.* New York: Guilford.

ANTHONY N. MALUCCIO
FRANK AINSWORTH

Family Reunification Practice with Parents Who Abuse Drugs

Historically, family reunification practice in the United States and other countries, particularly Australia, has been based on the premise that children in foster or residential care should either be returned to their birth families as quickly as possible or placed permanently with their kin or another permanent family. This either-or orientation has been criticized as too simplistic and not in the best interests of the child (Warsh, Pine, & Maluccio 1996). Consequently, in the field as well as in the professional literature, there has been considerable rethinking of family reunification, with emphasis on a flexible approach to working with children in out-of-home care and their families to meet their unique needs and circumstances. Such rethinking has led Warsh, Pine, and Maluccio (1996:7) to the following expanded definition:

> Family reunification is the planned process of reconnecting children in out-of-home care with their families by means of a variety of services and supports to the children, their families, and their foster parents or other service providers. It aims to help each child and family to achieve and maintain, at any given time, their optimal level of reconnection—from full re-entry of the child into the family system to other forms of contact, such as visiting, that affirm the child's membership in the family.

Through this expanded definition, we view family reunification as a dynamic process that takes into account each child and family's changing qualities, needs, potential, and social situations. We also point to "the role of the biological family as the preferred child rearing unit; the potential of most families to care for their children, if properly assisted; and the value of involving, as appropriate, any and all members of the extended family" (Maluccio 2000:167). Our assumption is that, with appropriate services and supports, most families can get back together and be helped through the child welfare service delivery system to remain together. We recognize, however, that in certain situations, reunification is not possible or desirable; instead, termination of parental rights is warranted and children need to be placed with other permanent families.

In the process of assessing the family's readiness for reunification with their children, there may occur the challenge of understanding and dealing with the presence of drug abuse by parents. In recent years, there has been a significant increase in the numbers of children entering out-of-home care due to parental abuse and neglect associated with drug abuse by parents. As we have indicated elsewhere (Maluccio & Ainsworth 2003:511), these parents present a special challenge for agencies and practitioners. In particular: is it possible to insure a child's safety and future development if reunification is pursued when parental drug use is ongoing? To answer this question, we examine the incidence of drug abuse by birth parents and its

Sections of this chapter have been adapted from Maluccio (2000) and Warsh, Pine, and Maluccio (1996).

impact on family reunification practice and explore promising service models.

Substance Abuse by Birth Parents of Children in Out-of-Home Care

Numerous studies show that drug abuse is common among families coming to the attention of the child welfare system (for a review of selected studies, see Maluccio and Ainsworth 2003). For example, a survey by the Child Welfare League of America found that at least 50% of substantiated child maltreatment reports involved parental abuse of alcohol or other drugs (Child Welfare League of America 1998). Children from families with parents who abuse drugs are almost three times more likely to be physically or sexually assaulted and four times more likely to be neglected than are children from nonsubstance-abusing families (National Center on Addictions and Substance Abuse at Columbia University 1998). More than 15 years ago, the National Committee for Prevention of Child Abuse (1989) estimated that 9 to 10 million children are affected by substance-abusing parents and that 675,000 children are maltreated each year by an alcoholic or drug-addicted caretaker.

Similar findings have been noted in Australia. For example, in New South Wales, it is estimated that up to 80% of child abuse reports investigated by the Department of Community Services have concerns about drug- and alcohol-affected parents (New South Wales Department of Community Services 2002). In Victoria, approximately two-thirds of parents in substantiated cases of abuse and neglect have alcohol and other substance-abuse problems (Victoria Department of Human Services 2002).

Children of substance-abusing parents are often exposed to a number of additional risks in their family and social environment. These typically include (Tracy 1994):

- Chaotic and often dangerous neighborhoods;
- Poverty, homelessness, or unstable housing;
- Parents who lack an extended family and community support system;
- Mothers who have been victimized as children;
- Mothers who are in relationships characterized by domestic violence; and
- Parent or parents with poor parenting skills and few or no role models for effective coping.

As Cash (2003:392) found in an ecological study of maternal child abuse and child neglect, there is "an interplay among family history, interpersonal risk factors, current family functioning, and community networks." Such an interplay is particularly evident in the families of children in out-of-home care.

Parental Substance Abuse and Out-of-Home Care

Studies in the United States have also found that, for between one-third and two-thirds of children in out-of-home care, parental substance abuse is a contributing factor to their placement (Besinger, Garland, Litrownick, & Landsverk 1999; Landsverk & Garland 2000). Children whose parents have substance-abuse problems are younger than other children in the child welfare system (under 5 years) and more likely to be the victims of severe and chronic neglect (Semidei, Radel, & Nolan 2001). Children from these families are also more likely to be placed in out-of-home care than to be helped at home by such community-based services as child guidance clinics (U.S. Department of Health and Human Services 1999).

In an analysis of parental characteristics of children and young people in out-of-home care in the Australian state of Victoria, it was found that around half of the mothers were known to have issues with substance abuse, most commonly alcohol, followed by heroin, marijuana, and amphetamine use. The proportion of fathers known to have issues with substance use was around one-third of the population (Victoria Department of Human Services 2002).

Moreover, although 1% of the general population in Australia use heroin, in 22% of families with children and young people in foster care in Victoria, the birth mother was known to be using or had used heroin. In families with children in care with the fathers, 13% were using or had used heroin. Additionally, nearly one-third (31%) of Victorian families involved in the child protection system and experiencing substance abuse had 10 or more notifications of alleged child maltreatment and just over one-quarter had five or more notifications (Victoria Department of Human Services 2002).

Removing children from homes with substance-abusing parents does not necessarily reduce the risks to their growth and development and their safety. When these children enter out-of-home placement, they tend to remain in care for longer periods of time and are less frequently reunified with their biological parents or freed for adoption, compared with children placed for reasons unrelated to substance abuse (Walker, Zangrillo, & Smith 1991). In addition, the problems that precipitated the need for placement often remain largely unchanged, thus creating additional obstacles to family reunification (National Black Child Development Institute 1989).

Impact on Children in Out-of-Home Care

Although there is extensive research on family reunification in regard to such issues as patterns of exit from care and the role of parent-child visiting, there has been limited attention to family reunification in relation to parental substance abuse. One rare study was conducted by Frame, Berrick, and Brodowski (2000). These researchers focused on a random sample of 88 children who first entered care between 1990 and 1992 and had experienced a second spell of out-of-home care by 1996. The authors found that maternal substance abuse is associated with a manifold increase in the likelihood of a child's reentry to care, compared to situations in which substance abuse is absent.

Additional research is required to identify effective practice strategies and promote services that lead to positive outcomes. Toward this purpose, Thomlison, Maluccio, and Wright (1996:133) discuss the need to explore such issues as:

- What are the most effective strategies that practitioners can utilize in work with substance-abusing parents and their children?
- What intensity and duration of services are needed to produce positive outcomes?
- What services are required for these children and families following their reunification?

Continuing Relevance of Family Reunification Practice

Although further research is needed as outlined above, there is extensive theoretical and practical justification for emphasis on family reunification practice in cases involving parental substance abuse. Support for family reunification derives from various premises about the value of rearing children in a family setting, the primacy of parent-child attachment, and the role of the biological family in human connectedness. These premises are supported by child development theories, which emphasize the importance of the mother-child bond, stability in living arrangements, and continuity of parent-child relationships in the child's development and functioning.

Of course, drug abuse by a parent threatens her or his ability to provide stability in living arrangements and to maintain continuity of parent-child relationships. As a consequence of their drug use, parents may be physically or psychologically unavailable or unable to provide such essential needs as nurturance and comfort to their children. As a result, children are admitted into out-of-home care or are left in questionable living arrangements.

Findings from recent studies point to a range of implications for policy and practice in the area of family reunification:

- Intensive, family-centered services positively affect reunification rates, as there is emphasis on strong client–social worker alliance, skill training programs, meeting the concrete needs of family members, and enhancing social supports from kin and others in the family's networks (Fraser, Walton, Lewis, Pecora, & Walton 1996).
- Strategies for building parent-worker relationships and behavioral interventions, such as training parents in stress relief techniques, can facilitate reunification (Lewis, Walton, & Fraser 1995).
- Aggressive outreach is essential in provision of reunification services for children from racial minority groups: "African-American children are far less likely than Caucasian children to be reunified with their families" (Barth 1997:289, 294).
- Poverty and inadequate housing place children at risk of out-of-home care and reduce the success of reunification efforts (Jones 1998).
- The inclusion of relatives in decision-making around permanency planning contributes substantially to successful reunification (Burford, Pennell, MacLeod, Campbell, & Lyall 1997).

In particular, the above studies and other investigations (Maluccio 2000:167) support the conclusion that "it can be cost-effective as well as humane to support practitioners in efforts to create and use opportunities to work with families during foster home placement; provide supports to parents before and after reunification; and encourage and facilitate child-family visiting throughout the placement."

Enhanced Family Reunification Practice with Substance-Abusing Parents

New Service Models

In response to the impact of substance abuse on families and children traditionally served by the child welfare system, various service innovations have emerged. As documented in the report by the National Center on Addictions and Substance Abuse at Columbia University (1998), examples of such innovations include:

- Creating new diagnostic tools, such as the Substance Abuse Subtle Screening Instrument. Parents complete this instrument, and the results guide them and their caseworkers in determining the best treatment options. Selected parents are referred to support groups, which in initial studies has resulted in a decrease of 88% in drug and alcohol use over 3 months by parents who complete the program.
- Using certified drug and alcohol counselors, who collaborate with social workers dealing with parents, as well as with paraprofessionals who serve as home visitors. A prominent feature of this approach is that social workers are better able to assess the risk of child maltreatment and then develop appropriate case plans.
- Facilitating access to consultation, evaluation, and treatment of clients through a multipronged approach. This approach includes staff development, training, and skill building in relation to addiction; development of practice standards for assessment and quality assurance; and co-location of alcohol and drug abuse specialists with child welfare personnel.
- Training workers from public child welfare agencies in the areas of addiction and the process of recovery. Preferably the training is done through collaboration with a network of private providers.
- Locating substance abuse counselors in state child welfare offices. The counselors perform on-site substance abuse evaluations, identify treatment resources, and work with clients, particularly during the referral and engagement process.
- Facilitating the collaboration of child welfare agencies with the courts in planning and implementing judicially ordered treatment services for parents. This collab-

TABLE 1. *Three-Stage Model of Family Reunification*

Stage	Approach	Intervention	Agency Involvement
1	Persuasion/voluntary	Casework	State/NFP
2	Direction/required	Treatment/group program	State/NFP/DA
3	Compulsion/imposed	Court order	State/NFP/DA/court

Source: Adapted from Ainsworth and Summers (2001).
Notes: DA, Drug agency; NFP, Not-for-profit agency.

oration also facilitates access to housing, transportation, and medical services.

For a detailed description of these innovative programs, see the National Center on Addictions and Substance Abuse at Columbia University (1998:43–75).

Multiple Attempts at Reunification

A recurring issue is that of how many attempts at reunification should be allowed, in fairness to parents as well as the children. In response, Ainsworth and Maluccio (1998) have proposed a three-stage model of reunification practice, as depicted in table 1. The model builds on a study that the authors conducted for the Western Australia Department of Family and Children's Services.

The first stage is collaborative, as it emphasizes the caseworker's use of nondirective counseling techniques and other methods of influence and persuasion, along with the voluntary participation of parents. The second stage involves direction, through placing treatment requirements on the parents. For example, they must be willing to work to resolve drug use issues and be ready to utilize drug treatment services. This approach is confrontational, as it requires parents to deal with the issues that precipitated the child's entry into care and to engage in prosocial behavior, as well as improve their parenting practices. The third stage is characterized by compulsion, as treatment requirements are imposed on the parents through the use of the power of the law and legal sanctions. Parents are helped to understand that their rights will be terminated if they do not address the drug abuse issue.

In light of the evidence of developmental harm inflicted on children as a result of the impact of drug use by parents and the consequent exposure to abuse and neglect, there is considerable justification for the above three-stage, time-limited model, with no repetition of any of the stages. Without such protection, the child's opportunity to achieve an adequate level of behavioral and emotional functioning is severely compromised. However, in the event of a continuing failure of family reunification efforts following various attempts, in some carefully selected case situations in which parents maintain concern for the child and do not harm her or him, the parents might still be encouraged and supported to maintain optimal and safe contact with their children (Ainsworth & Maluccio 1998).

Conclusion

There is a need to rethink and enhance traditional approaches to family reunification practice with substance-abusing parents. In particular, specialized groups for recovering addicts can be used to teach them parenting skills, to help them become advocates for their children's needs in school settings as elsewhere, and to challenge parental behavior and motivate parents toward change.

The multifaceted treatment strategies delineated in this chapter illustrate the child care and protection responsibilities of agencies—governmental and voluntary—that provide child welfare and/or drug abuse services. Above all, such services can help to empower parents in their quest to cope with their ongoing problems and life challenges and to contribute—even if only minimally—to the development and well-being of their children.

REFERENCES

Ainsworth, F., & Maluccio, A. N. (1998). The policy and practice of family reunification. *Australian Social Work, 51*(1), 3–7.

Ainsworth, F., & Summers, A. (2001). *Family reunification and drug use by parents. Research report for the Care for Children Advisory Committee.* Perth, Australia: Western Australia Department of Family and Children's Services.

Barth, R. P. (1997). Effects of age and race on the odds of adoption versus remaining in long-term out-of-home care. *Child Welfare, 76*, 285–308.

Besinger, B. A., Garland, A. F., Litrownick, J., & Landsverk, J. (1999). Caregiver substance abuse among maltreated children in out-of-home care. *Child Welfare, 78*, 221–239.

Burford, G., Pennell, J., MacLeod, S., Campbell, S., & Lyall, G. (1997). Reunification as an extended family matter. *Community Alternatives: The International Journal of Family Care, 9*(2), 33–55.

Cash, S. J. (2003). An ecological model of maternal substance abuse and child neglect: Issues, analyses, and recommendations. *American Journal of Orthopsychiatry, 73*, 392–404.

Child Welfare League of America. (1998). *Alcohol and other drug survey of state child welfare agencies.* Washington, DC: Child Welfare League of America.

Frame, L., Berrick, J. D., & Brodowski, M. L. (2000). Understanding re-entry to out-of-home care for reunified infants. *Child Welfare, 79*, 339–369.

Fraser, M., Walton, E., Lewis, R. E., Pecora, P., & Walton, W. K. (1996). An experiment in family reunification: Correlates of outcomes at one-year follow up. *Children and Youth Services Review, 18*, 335–362.

Jones, L. (1998). The social and family correlates of successful reunification of children in foster care. *Children and Youth Services Review, 20*, 305–323.

Landsverk, J., & Garland, A. F. (2000). Foster care and pathways to mental health services. In P. A. Curtis, G. Dale, Jr., & J. C. Kendall (eds.), *The foster care crisis: Translating research into policy and practice,* pp. 193–210. Lincoln: University of Nebraska Press, in association with the Child Welfare League of America.

Lewis, R., Walton, E., & Fraser, M. W. (1995). Examining family reunification services: A process analysis of a successful experiment. *Research on Social Work Practice, 5*(3), 259–282.

Maluccio, A. N. (2000). What works in family reunification. In M. P. Kluger, G. Alexander, & P. A. Curtis (eds.), *What works in child welfare,* pp. 163–169. Washington, DC: CWLA Press.

Maluccio, A. N., & Ainsworth, F. (2003). Drug abuse by parents: A challenge for family reunification practice. *Children and Youth Services Review, 25*, 511–533.

National Black Child Development Institute. (1989). *Who will care when parents can't: A study of black children in foster care.* Washington, DC: National Black Child Development Institute.

National Center on Addiction and Substance Abuse at Columbia University. (1998). *No safe haven: Children of substance-abusing parents.* New York: Columbia University.

National Committee for Prevention of Child Abuse. (1989). *Fact sheet: Substance abuse and child abuse.* Chicago: National Committee for Prevention of Child Abuse.

New South Wales Department of Community Services. (2002). *Annual report.* Sydney: New South Wales Department of Community Services.

Plasse, B. R. (1995). Parenting groups for recovering addicts in a day treatment program. *Social Work, 40*, 65–75.

Semidei, J., Radel, L. F., & Nolan, C. (2001). Substance abuse and child welfare: Clear linkages and promising responses. *Child Welfare, 80*, 109–128.

Thomlison, B., Maluccio, A. N., & Wright, L. W. (1996). Protecting children by preserving their families: A selective research perspective on family reunification. *International Journal of Child and Family Welfare, 2*(2), 127–136.

Tracy, E. M. (1994). Maternal substance abuse: Protecting the child, preserving the family. *Social Work, 39*, 534–540.

U.S. Department of Health and Human Services. (1999). *The AFCARS report—Current estimates as of January 1999.* Washington, DC: U.S. Department of Health and Human Services.

Victoria Department of Human Services. (2002). *An integrated strategy for child protection and placement services.* Melbourne: Victoria Department of Human Services.

Walker, C., Zangrillo, P., & Smith, J. M. (1991). *Parental drug abuse and African American children in foster care: Issues and study findings.* Washington, DC: National Black Child Development Institute.

Warsh, R., Pine, B. A., & Maluccio, A. N. (1996). *Reconnecting families—A guide to strengthening family reunification services.* Washington, DC: CWLA Press.

JUDY L. POSTMUS

Domestic Violence in Child Welfare

The overlap of domestic violence with child abuse and the concern about the impact of domestic violence on the lives of children are not new concerns. Over the past 25 years, researchers, child advocates, battered women advocates, and policymakers have grappled with how best to keep families safe while protecting the adult and child victims of violence. Questions left unanswered surround who should be held accountable for the exposure to domestic violence—the mother, the usual caregiver who is unable to protect her children, or the father, most often the abuser of the mother but frequently an invisible member of a child welfare case plan (Edleson 1998). How should child welfare systems respond to families with domestic violence? Does exposure to domestic violence indicate child maltreatment? Does the role of child welfare systems include removing children for their own protection and to break the cycle of violence? My purpose in this chapter is to discuss the answers to these questions by reviewing the research, including the number of children impacted by domestic violence and the consequences faced when children are exposed. The review is followed by a discussion of the philosophical challenges that must be met by the child welfare system and domestic violence service providers, along with the barriers and assumptions faced when attempting to address these challenges. I also present a brief description of state and local initiatives, along with some practical guidelines for screening, assessing, and intervening with children from families with domestic violence. I conclude with practice, policy, and research implications for the future of addressing the complex problem of children exposed to domestic violence.

Domestic Violence Defined

Domestic violence is defined as a pattern of behavior in which the batterer intentionally attempts to physically, sexually, psychologically, emotionally, or economically harm the victim with whom there is an intimate relationship (Barnett, Miller-Perrin, & Perrin 1997; Browne 1993; Gelles & Harrop 1989). Physical violence may include pushing, shoving, grabbing, kicking, biting, hitting, choking, or threatening with a weapon (Straus, Hamby, Sugarman, & Boney-McCoy 1996). Psychological and emotional abuse may include humiliation, isolation, fear and intimidation, threats, emotional withholding, and verbal attacks (Marshall 1999; Okun, Melichar, & Hill 1990; Tolman 1992). Regardless of the type of abuse or the tactics employed, the goal of the abuser is to seek control over an intimate partner.

The National Violence against Women Survey conducted between 1995 and 1996 (Tjaden & Thoennes 1998) indicated that 1.4 million women are victims of violence each year, committed by an intimate partner, defined as current or former husband, cohabiting partner, or date. Additionally, Tjaden and Thoennes (1998) reported that women were at greater risk of violence than were men, and that as the seriousness of the violence and injuries increased, the number of female victims increased whereas the number of male victims decreased. The results also indicated that women were six times more likely to be injured by intimate partner violence than were men, and that the risk of serious or lethal violence increases when women leave the relationship. Their conclusions indicated that 52% of all women have experienced some form of physical or sexual violence during their lifetime—from intimate partners as well as strangers (Tjaden & Thoennes 1998).

Although the data indicate that most victims of domestic violence or intimate partner violence are women, men are also victims—but not as often and not as overwhelmingly as for women. In this chapter, I therefore refer to victims of domestic violence as women and batterers as men, recognizing that men can be victims and women can be batterers.

Understanding the Phenomenon of Children Exposed to Domestic Violence

Terms like "witnessing" or "observing" domestic violence have been replaced by the term "exposed" to domestic violence. Exposure to domestic violence can include watching or hearing violent events, being directly involved with the event, or experiencing the aftermath of the event (Fantuzzo & Mohr 1999). Exposure can also include being manipulated by the batterer to gain further control over his partner (Faller 2003). In this section, I review the impact of domestic violence on children who are directly or indirectly exposed to domestic violence.

Prevalence

Over the past 25 years, researchers have attempted to estimate both the number of children who are exposed to domestic violence and the rate of overlap between the occurrence of domestic violence and child abuse. The most commonly cited research concludes that 3.3 million (Carlson 1984) to 10 million children (Straus 1991) witness domestic violence each year. Other researchers estimate that 30% to 60% of families with domestic violence experience child abuse and vice versa (for a review, see Edleson 1999a).

There are several challenges to understanding the implication of the scope of the overlap of child abuse and domestic violence. First, most of the estimates given on the overlap of child abuse and domestic violence are primarily based on retrospective studies, in which identified adult victims of domestic violence are asked about their abuse experiences as children (Wolak & Finkelhor 1998). Other estimates have come from children of women residing in domestic violence shelters, most frequently used by women who experience severe and ongoing physical abuse (Gondolf, Fisher, & McFerron 1988). It is difficult to determine if the estimates are skewed to either inflate or deflate the amount of overlap (Wolak & Finkelhor 1998). Second, the exposure to domestic violence was simplified as dichotomous, yes/no answers and did not capture the severity or type of violence, proximity of the children to the violence, the age of the child at the time of exposure, or duration of the exposure (Groves 1999). Regardless, the estimates of the number of children exposed directly or indirectly to domestic violence make this a significant social problem to be understood and examined.

Consequences

Domestic violence affects children who may witness the actual violence, hear the sounds of the abuse, or see the aftermath of the violence, such as police involvement (Carlson 1984). Jaffe, Wolfe, and Wilson (1990) describe a model that outlines how children are directly and indirectly influenced by domestic violence in the home. Children who are influenced directly are those who see the violence and are hurt intentionally or accidentally during an attack on their mother as they attempt to intervene. Children may also suffer psychological damage, which can manifest through internal or external behaviors, including withdrawal, anxiety, aggressive tendencies, delinquency, sleep disturbances, and somatic problems (Edleson 1999a; Kernic et al. 2003). Indirectly, children may be affected by the lack of consistent parenting or by high levels of irritability and tension associated with violent homes (Wolak & Finkelhor 1998). During separation and divorce, children may also become part of the power and control of an abuser, who still seeks to manipulate the mother by abducting the children or grilling them for information about their mother (Hester & Radford 1992). Finally, children exposed to domestic violence are at risk of being abused themselves or being neglected (Norman 2000).

Although domestic violence can directly or indirectly influence children and youth, it is difficult to generalize about the type, duration, and severity of domestic violence and its influence on them (Wolak & Finkelhor 1998). Wolak and Finkelhor (1998) reviewed the research on the risk and protective factors that determine how a child perceives, responds to, and copes with being exposed to domestic violence in the home. For example, infants and toddlers may react differently to being exposed to domestic violence compared to school-aged children or teenagers; most of the differences rely on the developmental tasks that are interrupted when domestic violence is present. Another risk factor identified in the literature is gender, but the results are inconclusive. Some studies indicate that boys are more likely than girls to become more aggressive as a result of witnessing domestic violence (Jaffe, Wolfe, & Wilson 1990) whereas other studies found no significant differences between genders (Lehmann & Rabenstein 2002; Wolak & Finkelhor 1998). Other risk factors include the nature and severity of the violence observed, the nature of the social interventions and whether they were perceived as helpful, and the cumulative stress of experiencing violence and other problems in the home (for a reviews, see Wolak & Finkelhor 1998).

Despite the influence of risk factors on children who are exposed to domestic violence, children also have aspects of their lives that provide protection from the impact. These protective factors include the characteristics of the child, the quality of family support, and the quality of extrafamily support (Wolak & Finkelhor 1998). Although their study did not focus on domestic violence, Werner and Smith's (1992) longitudinal study of children in Hawaii found that even in the face of extreme poverty, neglect, and abuse, children can be resilient. After following 505 children for 40 years throughout childhood and into adulthood, the primary predictor of resilience in the aftermath of childhood maltreatment was the presence of a caring and supportive adult in childhood. The researchers conclude (1992:202): "Our findings and those by other American and European investigators with a life-span perspective suggest that these buffers (protective factors) make a more profound impact on the life course of children who grow up under adverse conditions than do specific risk factors or stressful life events." Thus children have both risk and protective factors that make it difficult, if not impossible, to predict the outcome of the exposure to domestic violence for individual children.

Although the current body of research sheds some light on the impact of exposure to domestic violence in the homes, the research thus far has limitations. Most of the reports on children's behaviors came from mothers residing in domestic violence shelters, a group of women who typically have experienced severe and prolonged violence and who may interpret behaviors differently from other adults and from the children themselves (Wolak & Finkelhor 1998). Additionally, children who are living in domestic violence shelters may have different behaviors than those who are not in shelter due to the disruptions and emotions from leaving home. Demographic factors, including age, gender, intellectual functioning, socioeconomic status, race, unemployment, age of parents, as well as "family factors known to affect children adversely, such as substance abuse by parents, paternal or maternal physical or mental health, pathology, and stress, parenting ability, and stability of the home environment" are often not taken into consideration when measuring the impact of witnessing domestic violence (Wolak & Finkelhor 1998:98).

The challenge, then, faced by child and battered women advocates is how best to intervene with families experiencing domestic violence while keeping children and their mothers safe from further abuse.

Philosophical Conflicts

Tense relationships often exist between child protection services (CPS) and domestic violence service providers. This tension primarily stems from a difference in philosophy and preferred approach to dealing with violence in the home. Typically, the CPS approach seeks to strengthen families, enable children to remain safe in their homes, or remove children (temporarily or permanently) who remain at risk (Aron & Olson 1997). The primary functions of CPS workers are to screen and investigate reports of child maltreatment to determine whether the report has merit. If the report is substanstiated, CPS workers must assess the risk of harm to the child and the needs of the family to determine whether interventions or services are necessary. Historically, CPS practices often include opening child abuse cases in the name of the primary caregiver, who is usually the mother. The CPS worker develops a service plan that focuses on the mother's ability to protect her children; if she continues to remain in an abusive home, CPS workers will often force a mother to leave an abuser or charge her with "failure to protect" her own children (Carter & Schechter 1997).

In contrast, the philosophy or approach of battered women advocates is to empower victims to reach their desired goals, which often include keeping victims and their children safe. Practitioners are keenly aware that for victims to reach safety, a time-consuming and frustrating process often occurs, with victims struggling with life-changing decisions about leaving their partners (Brown 1997). Thus domestic violence practitioners support and empower victims throughout the process of leaving—even protecting victims from CPS and other agencies that may not understand the needs of victims (Schechter & Edleson 1994).

Both of these approaches assume that the needs and goals of abused women and their children are in conflict. In the midst of this conflict, little attention is paid to the abuser (Edleson 1998). If the abuser is neither the legal guardian nor the biological parent, he is often missing in the case file and is not held accountable for stopping the abuse. Instead of blaming one another, the challenge for CPS and domestic violence practitioners is to shift the responsibility of the abuse to the abuser and work together to provide safety for both the mother and her children (Schechter & Edleson 1994).

Although it seems logical, then, that both CPS and domestic violence programs would have as goals the safety of battered women and their children, there are several obstacles that make it difficult for these groups to work together (Mills 1998a; Schechter & Edleson 1994). Historically, the relationship between these two groups of advocates has been described as adversarial and competitive, as both groups seek better funding, recognition, and policy changes to protect either the domestic violence victim or her children (Beeman, Hagemeister, & Edleson 1999; Mills 1998a). Most CPS services are court-ordered, whereas most domestic violence services are not (Carter, Weithorn, & Behrman 1999). Advocates of battered women have resisted the development of laws addressing the effects on children who witness domestic violence for fear that such laws could lead to mandatory reporting of child abuse in domestic violence cases. CPS workers often become frustrated with the long process needed for victims to achieve safety (Brown 1997); they may become more demanding and controlling over the decisions of victims (Wilson 1998). Additionally, structural barriers may impede collaboration, including computer systems that record the mother's name, thereby holding her accountable for the protection of her children (Edleson 1998) or the lack of legal clout that workers have to pursue the batterer and to hold him accountable (Beeman, Hagemeister,

& Edleson 1999). Thus by not focusing on holding the abuser accountable and keeping the mother and children safe, CPS and battered women advocates may unknowingly cause more problems and grief for domestic violence victims and their children.

Assumptions

The conflicts between the two fields and the corresponding services are often influenced by assumptions made by child welfare workers about domestic violence. The assumptions made impact the services received by mothers and their children. Assumptions not only drive the decisions and discretion afforded workers, but also influence the policies that determine service provision. Therefore, it is important to evaluate whether these assumptions are true, as indicated by the available research.

For example, in one recent study in England, Humphreys (1999) qualitatively analyzed child welfare case files and conducted semistructured interviews with caseworkers. Her findings suggest that caseworkers minimize domestic violence by not mentioning it in the file or identifying it, but by focusing instead on other problems, such as alcohol abuse, and by not including the fathers in their assessments. However, in situations in which either the mother or child was seriously injured, the caseworkers prioritized domestic violence and used it as the primary reason for setting up a child protection conference. Although the ability to generalize these findings to other communities or countries is limited, the results mirror anecdotal information that suggests that child welfare workers do not prioritize domestic violence in their assessments or case plans unless the violence is severe.

In another study, Beeman, Hagemeister, and Edleson (2001) reviewed police files that identified cases of domestic violence and child maltreatment and then compared these files to child welfare files of child maltreatment of the same time period. The final sample included 205 families, for which 104 files had dual violence and 101 had child maltreatment only. Their findings suggest that families with dual violence were assessed at higher risk and were more likely to be eligible for CPS, yet were less likely to receive services; instead, they were more likely to be referred to the county attorney (Beeman, Hagemeister, & Edleson 2001). These results indicate that CPS workers may not have the training or skills to work with families with domestic violence and instead are more comfortable referring such families to the criminal justice system.

In summary, the failure to prioritize domestic violence, failure to provide services, and the tendency to make automatic referrals to the criminal justice system indicate that the decisions made by child welfare workers can be influenced by their assumptions about domestic violence. Here I explore four different assumptions about children exposed to domestic violence that have historically guided the practices and policies of the child welfare system.

Assumption 1: Domestic violence is a form of child maltreatment. Research has shown that when domestic violence is present, so is child abuse and neglect and vice versa at a rate between 30% and 60% (Edleson 1999b). Research has also indicated that children exposed to domestic violence are at risk of being abused themselves or being neglected (Norman 2000). "The American Humane Association concluded that child abuse is at least 15 times more likely to occur in households where domestic violence is present than in those with adult violence" (Mills et al. 2000:317). Additionally, the United States Advisory Board on Child Abuse and Neglect found that domestic violence is linked to child deaths in the United States (Mills et al. 2000).

Many observers have argued that because of this high rate of overlap, all child welfare workers should include domestic violence as part of their assessment of risk factors (Norman

2000) particularly in view of the research on the impact of exposure to domestic violence, including the emotional, behavioral, and physical consequences, discussed earlier. No one argues that if a child is physically or sexually abused, appropriate action must be taken. However, it becomes less clear if there is no abuse but rather a witnessing or exposure to domestic violence. Is being exposed to domestic violence a form of child maltreatment?

The concern with this assumption is that "anxiety about children's safety and helplessness to intervene with violent men sometimes left workers blaming battered women for their abuse and taking actions which could be seen as punitive" (Mills et al. 2000:326). There has yet to be any research that shows a direct relationship between witnessing domestic violence and problems in child development (Edleson 1999b). Most researchers sampled child maltreatment cases to identify domestic violence or looked for evidence of child maltreatment in families in which domestic violence exists. The challenge with this sampling method is that only the most extreme cases of child maltreatment are reported, and not all battered women seek shelter or safety services (Edleson 1999b). Additionally, when looking at case records, researchers must rely on the ability and discretion of staff to screen for child maltreatment and domestic violence and to accurately document their findings (Edleson 1999b). "The fact that many studies have shown an association between witnessing domestic violence and negative behavioral and/or emotional responses does not mean that witnessing domestic violence causes these negative outcomes" (Magen 1999:129).

Additionally, if all cases of identified families with domestic violence are reported to child welfare systems, the systems would quickly become overburdened and unable to respond to cases of clearly identified abuse, an unintended consequence that occurred in Massachusetts (Aron & Olson 1997). Furthermore, battered women may be unwilling to disclose abuse to

professionals who are mandated reporters, for fear of getting CPS involved and possibly being separated from their children.

The problem lies with defining the phrase "witnessing domestic violence." Such factors as physical presence, type of violence, the duration and severity of the violence, and the amount of exposure all play a part in the impact of such violence on children. As discussed earlier, there are many risk and protective factors for children that mediate the impact of the exposure to domestic violence: being exposed to domestic violence does not automatically lead to negative outcomes (Magen 1999).

The determination of whether exposure to domestic violence is a form of maltreatment may lie with the theoretical perspectives on what causes domestic violence. If policymakers and child welfare workers believe in the social learning model in which children learn behaviors from their parents and transmit them intergenerationally (Bandura 1977), then it would make sense that any child exposed to domestic violence is at risk, regardless of any mediating factors. However, if one believes the feminist theory, wherein domestic violence is not a personal problem but a political one and a function of a patriarchal culture that allows and encourages males domination over females (Schechter 1982), then one may focus on holding the batterer accountable, empowering victims to have more control in their lives and in the lives of their children, and assessing each case according to the type, amount, and severity of the incidences. The challenge here is that research has not been able to conclusively determine what causes domestic violence. Hence, one's beliefs may influence how to intervene with families experiencing domestic violence.

Assumption 2: Children who witness domestic violence are more likely to become abusers or victims as adults. Researchers have concluded that being exposed to domestic violence as a child is positively correlated with involvement in a violent domestic relationship as an adult (Browne

& Saqi 1988; O'Keefe 1995; Rosenbaum & O'Leary 1981; Straus 1980). However, experiencing or witnessing domestic violence does not automatically lead to being involved in intimate partner violence—it is only a risk factor (Fisher 1999). This finding means that although not all children exposed to domestic violence become batterers or victims, many batterers and victims were exposed to domestic violence as children. The key to properly interpreting the statistics lies in examining the sampling methods; researchers have asked adult batterers and victims to retrospectively report on their exposure to domestic violence as children. Thus exposure is a risk factor, but other mediating factors exist, including protective factors that may influence the outcomes for children. Yet this assumption is widely held by policymakers and child welfare workers. It makes sense to want to protect children from domestic violence to stop the cycle of violence, but without assessing other mediating factors, CPS workers may unwittingly make decisions that negatively impact the children and their mothers.

Assumption 3: Victimized mothers often abuse or neglect their children. Although we know that there are similarities found in homes in which domestic violence and child abuse exist, the challenge is to determine who is the abuser of the children. Some theories posit that battered women may abuse their children "to prevent the child from creating an excuse for the batterer to batter . . . and to keep the children in line to prevent the batterer from abusing both the mother and the child" (Mills et al. 2000: 308). Additionally, battered women may abuse their children as an outlet for their frustration at being abused themselves (Mills 1998a). Other anecdotal reports suggest that battered women face problems with parenting, such as blaming the children for their abuse, not realizing the impact of the abuse on the children, and being unaware of the emotional bond between the children and the father (Kaufman-Kantor & Little 2003).

Other common perceptions of battered women are that they are more likely to "demonstrate emotional unavailability and impaired parenting toward their children" (Sullivan, Nguyen, Allen, Bybee, & Juras 2000:52). To challenge this perception, Sullivan and her colleagues examined how women's victimization relates to their parenting stress and in turn, how the parenting relates to their children's adjustment. The results indicate that most of the battered women enjoyed their role as parent and that "while mothers had experienced substantial levels of physical abuse in the four months preceding the first interview, findings indicated they continued to be emotionally available to their children" (2000:61). The study also found that battered women were more likely to use nonviolent forms of discipline, including declaring time outs, removing privileges, or grounding their children. Finally, all of their results were confirmed by the children regarding the availability of the mothers to them and their methods of discipline.

Batterers also abuse their children as a means of controlling or hurting their adult partners. For example, a batterer may use the children to spy on the mother's movements and relationships (Zorza 1995). Additionally, although less than half of the reported child abusers are male, men are most often the perpetrators in the most severe forms of child abuse (Edleson 1999b; Stark & Flitcraft 1988). Interestingly, the male abuser is frequently missing or invisible in child welfare case files and often left untouched by any court-ordered interventions (Edleson 1998).

Finally, children can be hurt accidentally by getting in the middle of a violent episode either intentionally, as an attempt to protect the mother, or unintentionally because they happen to be in the same room (Mills et al. 2000). In one study of battered women in shelter, the children surveyed reported that 44% of them attempted to protect their mothers, and of these, 37% were hit in the process (Mills et al. 2000).

Can battered women become abusers themselves? Absolutely. However, one must look beyond the physical and emotional abuse of children to see the role the batterer takes in the abuse—either directly or indirectly. As Stark and Flitcraft (1988:102) have observed:

> If violence is evoked by struggles around traditional sex roles, the practical result of reinforcing these roles may be to restrict a woman's perceived options, increase her vulnerability to violence, decrease her capacity to protect her children from violence, exacerbate her own frustration and anger, and increase the probability that she will be destructive to self and others, including her children.

Assumption 4: Battered women must leave the abusive relationship to keep themselves and their children safe. The common reaction of most service providers, including child welfare and battered women advocates, is to separate the abuser from the victim as a way to protect the victim from further harm. This tactic of removing a family member for his or her protection is a common intervention used in child welfare agencies. Yet child welfare agencies in most states can provide protective services to only those children and families who have suffered the greatest harm, and in many cases, remove the child from his or her family for reasons of safety. This removal and long-term separation can produce injuries and experiences to the child that far outweigh and outlast the initial maltreatment. Longitudinal research has shown that living in multiple homes (often in foster care) is more predictive of poor outcomes in adulthood than is the original maltreatment (McDonald, Allen, Westerfelt, & Piliavin 1996).

This concept of removing individuals from their home also was and is used by the domestic violence movement through the creation of shelters, restraining orders, and criminal laws to jail batterers—all with the intent of keeping victims safe from further abuse. Yet how is safety defined and who defines it? Ellen Pence, author of the Duluth Model and the Safety and Accountability Audit, states that individuals define safety based on their own peace of mind. She further states that it is the government's

responsibility—specifically, state governments' —to insure the safety of its citizens (Pence & Lizdas 1998). This responsibility gives states the authority to protect their citizens by having law enforcement, child welfare systems, and the criminal justice system hold criminals responsible and protect individuals from further harm. What happens, however, when the state's responsibility of safety conflicts with a battered woman's views of safety?

Unfortunately, the remedies to keep women and children safe have not yet been proven by research as being effective and helpful for all parties involved—the individuals, the service providers, and the state. The limited research done thus far has concluded that restraining orders are inconsistently enforced (Finn & Colson 1990) and have no effect on stopping abuse for women with severe injuries (Grau, Fagan, & Wexler 1985). The research findings on mandatory arrest and prosecution policies are at best mixed as to the effectiveness of these policies (Mills 1998b). Finally, little research exists evaluating the effectiveness of domestic violence shelters (Davis & Srinivasan 1995).

In the meantime, while service professionals —including child welfare and battered women advocates—are encouraging women to leave, research indicates that some women are more likely to be seriously injured or killed by their abusive partners when they leave the relationship, not when they stay in it (Tjaden & Thoennes 1998). Thus the assumption that battered women must leave the relationship to remain safe may put them and their children at greater risk of further abuse.

Unintended consequences. One unintended consequence of these four assumptions is that states have passed laws requiring professionals to report children who witnessed domestic violence to the state's abuse hotlines. For example, California, Oregon, Utah, and Washington have all included the exposure to domestic violence as a form of child neglect (Magen 1999). Additionally, Utah has made the unreported witnessing of domestic violence two or more times a misdemeanor (Edleson 1999b).

Although some states have clear guidelines for mandated reporting, others have ambiguous policies that leave the decision to report up to the individual. This leaves caseworkers a wide range of discretion on whether to assess for and include domestic violence in their findings, and whether to substantiate a finding of neglect (Norman 2000). Faced with ambiguous policies, a wide range of discretion, frustrations or fear of working with batterers, and pressures to resolve the report in a timely fashion, caseworkers may fall back on the mandate to protect children from harm and place the blame on the mother for not protecting her children from exposure to domestic violence.

Thus, another unintended consequence of the assumptions is that CPS workers have been removing children for witnessing domestic violence. In one study, Stark and Flitcraft (1988) found that children of battered women were more likely to be removed from the home compared with those of nonabused women (Stark & Flitcraft 1988). "However, to define witnessing domestic violence as a form of child neglect may be dangerous for battered women; doing so ignores important findings from research on witnessing domestic violence and may reflect poor practice on the part of the systems that have been developed to protect children" (Magen 1999:128).

This practice of removing children when exposed to domestic violence led to the class action lawsuit in 2002 in New York City, Nicholson vs. Scoppetta. Judge Weinstein ruled in his findings (Carter 2002:3) that "government may not penalize a mother, not otherwise unfit, who is battered by her partner, by separating her from her children; nor may children be separated from the mother, in effect visiting upon them the sins of their mother's batterer." The judge further stated that reasonable efforts, a term not unfamiliar to child welfare agencies, must be made to separate the batterer from the victim and her children while providing reason-

able, adequate protection, such as assisting in helping the family find shelter or other safe accommodations and filing a protective order against the batterer. Additionally, the judge stated that mothers are to be informed of their rights and those of their children prior to child welfare systems taking any actions to removing children and that these rights be provided in both English and Spanish. Finally, the judge ordered that training and supervision be given to child welfare workers and contractors, a domestic violence specialist be hired as part of a clinical consultant team, and a review committee be established to enforce the terms of the findings, which must provide the court and all other interested parties with monthly reports (Carter 2002).

The findings from this lawsuit have had a ripple effect across the country. Child welfare agencies began examining their strategies when intervening with families experiencing domestic violence. Some states had already established practices, whereas others are still examining how to best serve families that experience domestic violence. In the following sections, I review the current practices of local and state initiatives.

Current Practices

Although researchers have noted the interaction of domestic violence and child maltreatment, the responses of state agencies, domestic violence programs, and communities have not taken this observation into account (Carter & Schechter 1997). Few states have developed strategies to address the interaction, with even fewer generating evaluation data to determine whether their strategies are working.

Several states have attempted to include screening and services for children as part of the child welfare system. These efforts have included collaborating with other agencies, such as probation or the courts, as well as providing training to child welfare workers to screen and intervene with families experiencing domestic violence. The following review of these efforts includes those with promising ideas as well as those that are empirically supported.

Massachusetts

Massachusetts has a long history of addressing the challenges of helping children who are exposed to domestic violence. In their evaluation of case files, the Department of Social Services (DSS) discovered that 70% of cases referred for intensive services also had domestic violence, but that the investigative worker identified domestic violence in less than half the cases (Aron & Olson 1997). Initially, DSS piloted a project that required professionals to report child abuse and initiate an investigation if a child was exposed to domestic violence. The consequences of that project resulted in a large number of reports made without additional funds or staff to handle the reports and in women not disclosing their abuse to professionals for fear of losing custody of their children to DSS. As a result, DSS scrapped the pilot project and instead created a domestic violence unit staffed by advocates or specialists from the domestic violence field. The purpose of this unit was to provide training and consultation to child protective staff, to offer education, training, and collaboration with other community agencies (including shelters), and to provide direct services to battered women who were identified by the child welfare system.

Six months after the implementation of the domestic violence unit, a study was conducted to evaluate the effectiveness of co-locating a battered women advocate with child welfare workers. More than 70% of all DSS cases were referred to the unit for domestic violence services, a significant increase compared to the number of identified cases prior to having the specialized unit (Mills et al. 2000).

Michigan

Similar to Massachusetts, Michigan has a long history of addressing the challenges faced when CPS serves families experiencing domestic violence. In the mid-1990s, Michigan established the Domestic Violence Prevention and Treatment Board, a statewide coordinated effort to end domestic violence. The mandate of the board included CPS collaboration with family preservation services and domestic violence programs to enhance the safety of children. The collaboration resulted in the development of the Families First program, a program that recognized that the safety for children can best be accomplished by insuring the safety and self-sufficiency of their mothers (Aron & Olson 1997; Saunders & Anderson 2000). The focus of Families First was to provide cross-training on domestic violence for all program managers, supervisors, and caseworkers, as well as battered women advocates and domestic violence shelter staff. The biggest change in services occurred with allowing shelter staff to make direct referrals to the Families First program instead of the traditional approach of CPS initiating the referral to the program.

Through the collaboration of battered women advocates and staff from Families First, training is mandated for all child welfare workers focusing on batterers, the criminal and civil laws pertaining to domestic violence, and community resources. Additionally, the training covers such topics as substance abuse, sexual abuse, parenting, and child development. The results from the collaborative efforts and the training found that workers decreased their rate of holding victims responsible for their children's safety from 54% to 40% and decreased their referrals to couples counseling from 74% to 46%. Additionally, the training results found more child welfare workers empathizing with battered women (an increase from 74% to 84%) and less emphasis on ending the relationship (down from 40% to 28%) (Saunders & Anderson 2000).

Oregon

A review of case files in Oregon determined that agency staff, even without any domestic violence training or formal assessment procedures, had found that 26% of families with children entering foster care were exposed to domestic violence. Additionally, domestic violence was a factor that distinguished severe physical abuse cases from those of moderate or mild abuse, whereas only 2% of all families were offered domestic violence services (Aron & Olson 1997). As a result, several communities within the state received funding to develop training, encourage collaboration among community organizations, and implement a pilot project in which an advocate for battered women would be co-located in a CPS office. Unfortunately, limited evaluation exists of their efforts (Aron & Olson 1997). Oregon has recently looked at case practice at a state level and is involved in an effort to change the child welfare system, provide consistent and mandatory training, and encourage collaborative efforts. No research exists to determine the scope or effectiveness of these changes.

San Diego, California

Although San Diego also has a track record of addressing the problem of domestic violence in the community, the link between domestic violence and child protection was not addressed until the early 1990s, when a mother and her child were murdered by the mother's boyfriend, who had been on probation. The mother had been referred to the Children's Services Bureau (CSB) for voluntary services and the caseworker was not aware of the boyfriend's probationary status. After running a cross check on other cases, CSB saw a large overlap between the two systems and decided that changes were needed. Thus the Family Violence project was created to better protect victims of domestic violence by coordinating case management activities between probation and the CSB staff (Aron & Olson 1997). This project provides an administrative and technological bridge between the two agencies with the intent of holding batterers accountable and increasing the awareness of both agencies' staffs about domestic violence and child abuse. Limited evaluation of the project exists; early data indicated prob-

lems with the CSB computer system. The system allows caseworkers to list only one problem to be coded, resulting in the listing of domestic violence only when it is the sole problem faced by the family (Aron & Olson 1997).

Hawaii

In Hawaii, the primary linkage between domestic violence and child welfare services lies with the criminal justice system. Child welfare workers have access to the criminal histories of batterers, as well as to any restraining orders, permanent or temporary. Additionally, the family court judge presides over all child abuse and neglect cases and over all petitions for restraining orders; hence, the judge can cross-reference restraining-order cases, directly question families about the safety of their children, and make referrals to CPS. Although this ability to cross-reference cases in the criminal justice and child welfare system is a step forward, there still is a lack of available services for families experiencing domestic violence (Aron & Olson 1997).

Greenbook Initiative

The National Council of Juvenile and Family Court Judges commissioned an advisory committee to develop recommendations on how best to work with families with children who are exposed to domestic violence. The committee produced the Effective Intervention in Domestic Violence and Child Maltreatment Cases: Guidelines for Policy and Practice (Schechter & Edleson 1999), commonly referred to as the "Greenbook." In an effort to provide a seamless service delivery system, in early 1991 the U.S. Department of Justice and the Health and Human Services funded six sites across the United States to implement the Greenbook and focus on coordinating efforts between the courts, child welfare agencies, domestic violence shelters, and other professional groups (e.g., law enforcement, medical providers, schools) involved with families experiencing domestic violence. These sites include El Paso County, Colorado; Grafton County, New Hampshire;

Lane County, Oregon; St. Louis County, Missouri; Santa Clara County, California; and San Francisco County, California.

Early reports indicate some success as well as some obstacles with the Greenbook initiative (Caliber 2004). These obstacles include a lack of trust among participating organizations, which hindered their ability to overcome any ideological differences; inadequate resources, which undermined collaboration among organizations; and limited ability for the organizations to collaborate, because the inclusion of some members hurt the effort (Caliber 2004). The results are preliminary; more time and evaluation are needed to determine if this promising initiative will help or cause more problems for organizations working with families experiencing domestic violence and child maltreatment.

Other Communities

Other local communities have attempted different strategies to address the overlap of domestic violence and child abuse. For example, a pilot project in New Haven and Hartford, Connecticut, included mental-health specialists available 24 hours a day to respond to police who call when children are present during a domestic violence incident. The on-call therapist may either go to the scene or provide mental health services or referrals within 72 hours of the incident. This project emphasizes the collaboration between police and mental health specialists addressing the realization that dealing with domestic violence is not relegated to one professional group (Anderson & Cramer-Benjamin 1999).

Another program in Los Angeles brings together elementary teachers, mental health specialists, law enforcement, the district attorney's office, and probation departments to work with children exposed to domestic violence. Therapy, mentoring, and educational programs, all intended to help children cope with the violence they have witnessed, provide opportunities for children to interact with professionals from different backgrounds who may be involved with their families (Murphy, Pynoos, & James 1997).

Other community-based programs, such as those of Boston and New Orleans, focus on training law enforcement and teachers on child development and the impact of witnessing domestic violence, setting up 24-hour hotlines for information, education, and referrals for children, and education and information for physicians, especially pediatricians, to better inform them about the impact of domestic violence on children and the best way to screen for such impact (Groves & Zuckerman 1997; Osofsky 1997).

Responding to the Problem

In addition to interagency training, collaboration, and coordination initiatives, the literature identifies methods for screening and assessing domestic violence and responding with appropriate interventions for all family members involved—the children, the victims, and the batterers. Given the dynamics of domestic violence, including fear, isolation, secrecy, and control, domestic violence is often not detected by child welfare agency staff members (McKay 1994). In addition, due to the fear of having their children removed from their custody and their perceptions of professionals as blaming them for the abuse battered women are reluctant to report domestic violence (Davis 1984).

Screening and Assessing

Screening procedures should routinely include direct and indirect questions regarding the existence of abuse in the family. Direct inquiry includes such questions as "Have you ever been hit, slapped, poked, or pushed by an intimate partner?" Indirect inquiry includes such questions as "Many women today are physically and emotionally abused by their significant others. Has this ever happened to you?"

When screening for domestic violence, such questions should always be asked in private, out of the hearing of the potential batterer (Carter

& Schechter 1997). If the batterer refuses to allow the worker to meet privately with the mother and/or the children, the worker should set up a time when he or she can meet privately and should make routine statements that insist on the privacy of the questions, such as "agency rules dictate that I must meet individually and privately with every member of the family."

In New York City, an intake questionnaire was developed by the Family Violence Prevention project, a program designed to address the coexistence of domestic violence and child maltreatment (Magen, Conroy, & Tufo 2000). The questionnaire had five sections, including a face sheet, interview questions, the extent of domestic violence, caseworker's assessment, and applicant's evaluation. The face sheet included basic demographic information about individuals in the house. The interview questions helped the caseworker ask about conduct ranging from "normal" marital conflict and arguments to actual abusive behavior using questions from the Revised Conflict Tactics Scale (Straus, Hamby, Sugarman, & Boney-McCoy 1996). If the interview questions revealed the presence of domestic violence, then the worker was instructed to determine the extent of the domestic violence by completing a section designed to collect specific information on the type and frequency of abuse and the protective measures used by the victim to keep herself and her children safe. The fourth section included a caseworker's assessment, including current and past abuse and the action steps taken by the worker to help the client deal with the abuse. The final section of the questionnaire, the applicant's evaluation, contained consumer satisfaction questions about the perceived helpfulness of the questionnaire. The evaluation of the implementation of this questionnaire showed some positive results. First, the questionnaire led to a 300% increase in the number of women identified as victims (Magen, Conroy, & Tufo 2000). The data generated also indicated that many of the women were victims of severe and life-threatening violence, had reported taken

some form of action to stop the abuse, and responded positively to the caseworker's interventions. Finally, the majority of women expressed favorable perceptions to having been asked about domestic violence by their caseworkers (Magen, Conroy, & Tufo 2000).

Fleck-Henderson (2000) interviewed DSS supervisors as part of a needs assessment, asking them about challenges when working with families with domestic violence. The challenges they listed include 10 concerns: (1) assessing dangerousness; (2) assessing kids to determine the impact of domestic violence on them and deciding whether to keep a case open; (3) understanding risk if abuse is minimized; (4) knowing responsibilities when dealing with batterers; (5) knowing when focusing on safety actually increases the risk of violence and knowing what to do; (6) collaborating with other agencies and maintaining confidentiality; (7) knowing where to find more resources for all family members, including children, victims, and batterers; (8) considering cultural differences; (9) taking care of their own and workers' safety and liability; and (10) managing their and their workers' frustrations and feelings of powerlessness. The challenges listed by the supervisors were used to develop training to address these challenges.

The results of these studies indicate the need for screening and assessing for domestic violence among families involved with the child welfare system. Assessments should take into account the frequency and severity of domestic violence, any parental or child injury, the parental ability to nurture, and any actual or attempted actions mothers take to protect themselves and their children from further abuse (Kaufman-Kantor & Little 2003). Additionally, caseworkers should assess multiple forms of victimization that mothers have experienced, including physical, sexual, emotional, psychological, and economic abuse in the current relationship, past relationships, and as a child (Kaufman-Kantor & Little 2003). Once domestic violence has been identified, workers should evaluate the danger posed to the children and the mother, the physical, emotional, and developmental impact of domestic violence on the children, and the strategies used by the mother to protect herself and her children in the past (Carter & Schechter 1997).

Interventions

After screening and assessing for domestic violence, the worker is then challenged to provide appropriate and sensitive interventions. The values supporting effective interventions include recognition that protecting the battered woman will also protect the child, that individualizing services will help the worker realize that not every case of family violence is the same, and that holding the batterer accountable for the abuse and not blaming the mother will help protect her children (Goodmark 2001). The child welfare worker should attempt to meet three goals with all domestic violence cases: protect the child; help the abused mother protect herself and her children using noncoercive and supportive interventions; and hold the batterer accountable and responsible for stopping the abusive behavior (Carter & Schechter 1997).

Wolak and Finkelhor (1998) suggest guidelines for practitioners when working with children either in a crisis or noncrisis situation. In a crisis situation, such as when the police have been called or the mother is fleeing the home, practitioners should focus on helping the mother and her children to complete a safety plan, including plans on what to do if the violence recurs. In a noncrisis situation, practitioners should be developmentally and culturally appropriate when encouraging children to reveal their exposure to the abuse. Practitioners should also coordinate their efforts with other professionals, including battered women advocates and teachers. Finally, workers should be aware of any custody issues (Wolak & Finkelhor 1998).

When working with children exposed to domestic violence, the goals of intervention should include the promotion of an open discussion of the children's experiences, helping children understand and cope with their emotions while producing positive behaviors, reducing the symptoms experienced as a result of the violence, and helping the family create a safe, stable, and nurturing environment for the child (Groves 1999). When interviewing children to determine whether domestic violence is present in the home, Faller (2003) suggests using cognitive interviewing and narrative elaboration. Cognitive interviewing, for example, would prompt the worker to discuss everything about the domestic violence event to reconstruct the context of the abuse. Narrative elaboration techniques are useful for school-aged children and include the use of cue cards to serve as triggers of the violent event. Different types of questions should be used: general questions, focused questions, invitational questions, or multiple choice questions (Faller 2003). Little has been written on individual therapy given to children exposed to domestic violence; more research is needed in this area.

Implications and Conclusion

Does exposure to domestic violence indicate child maltreatment? How should child welfare systems respond to families with domestic violence? In this chapter I attempted to answer these complicated questions by reviewing the research, including the number of children impacted by domestic violence and the consequences when they are exposed. The philosophical challenges between the child welfare system and domestic violence shelters have been identified, along with the barriers and assumptions faced when attempting to address these challenges. State and local initiatives were presented, as well as practical guidelines for screening, assessing, and intervening with children from families with domestic violence. The literature and research review prompts a summary of the implications for those involved with families experiencing domestic violence including training, practice, policy, and research implications.

Implications for Training

Training of child welfare workers must focus on teaching them skills in interviewing children, battered women, and perpetrators in a sensitive manner, knowledge about resources in the community, and information about legal resources—criminal and civil—available to battered women (Fleck-Henderson 2000). In recent years, domestic violence training for child welfare workers has been evaluated to determine whether training influences workers' responses to families experiencing domestic violence. The results indicate that training does bring about changes in attitudes about, assessment of, and interventions for domestic violence (Magen & Conroy 1998; Mills & Yoshihama 2002; Saunders & Anderson 2000).

Although training has been helpful for child welfare workers, it is not a panacea. The issues related to serving battered women and their children are often complex and cannot be solved through training alone (Fleck-Henderson 2000). Such issues as poverty, substance abuse, and mental health may complicate plans to keep women and children safe from further abuse. Additionally, the attitudes and beliefs of child welfare workers may also impact the decisions they make with regards to assessing for and intervening with domestic violence (Postmus & Ortega 2004).

Implications for Practice

Successful practice with families experiencing domestic violence, as suggested in the literature, establishes and achieves the goals of holding the batterer accountable, supporting the battered woman and her children, and keeping the family safe from further harm (Edleson 1998). Collaboration among all interested organizations and agencies is also crucial when working with these families (Schechter & Edleson 1999). The Greenbook initiative is a solid first step in encouraging communities to work together to keep families safe, but much more work and evaluation is needed. Workers must take the initiative to learn about domestic violence and work closely with different professionals with a common commitment to keep families safe without blaming the mother and leaving the abuser unaccountable for his actions. Finally, workers must be patient; system change, community change, and individual change do not occur overnight. Nonjudgmental support is essential to working with others, whether professionals or battered women and their children.

Implications for Policy

Child welfare agencies and domestic violence service providers must evaluate current policies and practices to determine what does and does not work when it comes to keeping women and children safe from abuse. Without statewide policy shifts, reallocation of resources, changes in agency philosophy, and the development of standard procedures for screening, protective investigations, and case management, workers will be left frustrated not only in their dealings with battered women but also with their place of employment.

For example, during a recent training session I conducted on domestic violence, child welfare supervisors expressed their frustrations of wanting to give women time to go through the process of leaving an abusive relationship yet being forced to maintain the deadlines dictated by the Adoption and Safe Families Act. Additionally, supervisors expressed frustrations with local law enforcement's inability to hold batterers accountable—especially those that violated restraining orders. Although their frustrations were only anecdotal, more work is needed to examine how both child welfare and criminal justice policies may hinder child welfare workers as they attempt to be supportive of battered women.

Implications for Research

A review of the literature indicates that it is imperative that further research be conducted to evaluate current practices and initiatives to determine the effectiveness of various policies, programs, and practices. States must be encouraged to open their case files for researchers to review and to offer suggestions on ways to improve services without condemning or blaming agencies or individual workers. To illustrate, in 2003, the Department of Children and Families in the state of Kansas authorized the Kansas Coalition Against Sexual and Domestic Violence to conduct a Safety and Accountability Audit (Pence & Lizdas 1998) with the goal of assessing the system's response to families involved with the child welfare system who also are experiencing domestic violence. The forthcoming results will provide a blueprint for the state to examine its policies and practices, as well as a model for other states to emulate as they consider evaluating their own child welfare systems.

Finally, researchers must not lose sight of battered victims themselves as the former develop methodologies and sampling plans when evaluating policies or practices. Too often, the voices of these victims are not heard when it comes to policy or program evaluation (Nichols-Casebolt & Spakes 1995).

REFERENCES

Adoption and Safe Families Act. (1997). P.L. 105-89.

Anderson, S. A., & Cramer-Benjamin, D. B. (1999). The impact of couple violence on parenting and children: An overview and clinical implications. *American Journal of Family Therapy, 27*, 1–19.

Aron, L. Y., & Olson, K. K. (1997). *Effort by child welfare agencies to address domestic violence: The experiences of five communities.* Urban Institute. Retrieved July 10, 1999, from www.urban.org/welfare/ARON3.htm.

Bandura, A. (1977). *Social learning theory.* Englewood Cliffs, NJ: Prentice-Hall.

Barnett, O. W., Miller-Perrin, C. L., & Perrin, R. D. (1997). *Family violence across the lifespan: An introduction.* Thousand Oaks, CA: Sage.

Beeman, S. K., Hagemeister, A. K., & Edleson, J. L. (1999). Child protection and battered women's services: From conflict to collaboration. *Child Maltreatment, 4*(2), 116–126.

Beeman, S. K., Hagemeister, A. K., & Edleson, J. L. (2001). Case assessment and service receipt in families experiencing both child maltreatment and woman battering. *Journal of Interpersonal Violence, 16*, 437–458.

Brown, J. (1997). Working toward freedom from violence. *Violence Against Women, 3*(1), 5–26.

Browne, A. (1993). Violence against women by male partners: Prevalence, outcomes, and policy implications. *American Psychologist, 48*(10), 1077–1087.

Browne, K., & Saqi, S. (1988). Approaches to screening for child abuse and neglect. In K. Browne, C. Davies, & P. Stratton (eds.), *Early prediction and prevention of child abuse,* pp. 57–85. New York: Wiley.

Caliber. (2004). *The Greenbook Demonstration Initiative: Process evaluation report, Phase I (January 2001–June 2002).* Retrieved July 8, 2004, from www.thegreenbook. info.

Carlson, B. E. (1984). Children's observations of interparental violence. In A. R. Roberts (ed.), *Battered women and their families,* pp. 147–167. New York: Springer.

Carter, J. (2002). *Policy talks.* Washington, DC: Family Violence Prevention Fund.

Carter, J., & Schechter, S. (1997). *Child abuse and domestic violence: Creating community partnerships.* Retrieved July 9, 1999, from www.igc.org/fund/materials/ speakup/child_abuse.html.

Carter, L. S., Weithorn, L. A., & Behrman, R. E. (1999). Domestic violence and children: Analysis and recommendations. *Future of Children, 9*(3), 4–21.

Davis, L. V. (1984). Beliefs of service providers about abused women and abusing men. *Social Work, 29,* 243–250.

Davis, L. V., & Srinivasan, M. (1995). Listening to the voices of battered women: What helps them escape violence. *Affilia, 10*(1), 49–69.

Edleson, J. L. (1998). Responsible mothers and invisible men. *Journal of Interpersonal Violence, 13,* 294–298.

Edleson, J. L. (1999a). Children's witnessing of adult domestic violence. *Journal of Interpersonal Violence, 14,* 839–870.

Edleson, J. L. (1999b). The overlap between child maltreatment and woman battering. *Violence Against Women, 5*(2), 134–154.

Faller, K. C. (2003). Research and practice in child interviewing: Implications for children exposed to domestic violence. *Journal of Interpersonal Violence, 18,* 377–389.

Fantuzzo, J. W., & Mohr, W. K. (1999). Prevalence and effects of child exposure to domestic violence. *Future of Children, 9*(3), 21–33.

Finn, P., & Colson, S. (1990). *Civil protection orders: Legislation, current court practice, and enforcement.* OJP-86-C-002. Washington, DC: National Institute of Justice.

Fisher, D. (1999). Preventing childhood trauma resulting from exposure to domestic violence. *Preventing School Failure, 44*(1), 25–34.

Fleck-Henderson, A. (2000). Domestic violence in the child protection system: Seeing double. *Children and Youth Services Review, 22,* 333–354.

Gelles, R. J., & Harrop, J. W. (1989). Violence, battering, and psychological distress among women. *Journal of Interpersonal Violence, 4,* 400–420.

Gondolf, E. W., Fisher, E., & McFerron, J. R. (1988). Racial differences among shelter residents: A comparison of Anglo, black, and Hispanic battered women. *Journal of Family Violence, 3*(1), 39–51.

Goodmark, L. (2001). A balanced approach to handling domestic violence in child welfare cases. *ABA Child Law Practice, 20*(5), 49–58.

Grau, J., Fagan, J., & Wexler, S. (1985). Restraining orders for battered women: Issues of access and efficacy. *Women & Politics, 4*(3), 13–28.

Groves, B. M. (1999). Mental health services for children who witness domestic violence. *Future of Children, 9*(3), 122–133.

Groves, B. M., & Zuckerman, B. (1997). Interventions with parents and caregivers of children who are exposed to violence. In J. D. Osofsky (ed.), *Children in a violent society,* pp. 183–201. New York: Guilford.

Hester, M., & Radford, L. (1992). Domestic violence and access arrangements for children in Denmark and Britain. *Journal of Social Work and Family Law, 15,* 57–70.

Humphreys, C. (1999). Avoidance and confrontation: Social work practice in relation to domestic violence and child abuse. *Child And Family Social Work, 4,* 77–87.

Jaffe, P., Wolfe, D., & Wilson, S. (1990). *Children of battered women.* Newbury Park, CA: Sage.

Kaufman-Kantor, G., & Little, L. (2003). Defining the boundaries of child neglect: When does domestic violence equate with parental failure to protect? *Journal of Interpersonal Violence, 18,* 338–355.

Kernic, M. A., Wolf, M. E., Holt, V. L., McKnight, B., Huebner, C. E., & Rivara, F. P. (2003). Behavioral problems among children whose mothers are abused by an intimate partner. *Child Abuse and Neglect, 27,* 1231–1246.

Lehmann, P., & Rabenstein, S. (2002). Children exposed to domestic violence: The role of impact, assessment, and treatment. In A. Roberts (ed.), *Handbook of domestic violence intervention strategies,* pp. 333–395. Oxford: Oxford University Press.

Magen, R. H. (1999). In the best interests of battered women: Reconceptualizing allegations of failure to protect. *Child Maltreatment, 4*(2), 127–135.

Magen, R. H., & Conroy, K. (1998). *Training child welfare workers on domestic violence: Final report.* New York: Columbia University, School of Social Work.

Magen, R. H., Conroy, K., & Tufo, A. D. (2000). Domestic violence in child welfare preventative services: Results from an intake screening questionnaire. *Children and Youth Services Review, 22,* 251–274.

Marshall, L. L. (1999). Effects of men's subtle and overt psychological abuse on low-income women. *Violence & Victims, 14*(1), 69–88.

McDonald, T. P., Allen, R. I., Westerfelt, A., & Piliavin, I. (1996). *Assessing the long-term effects of foster care.* Washington, DC: Child Welfare League of America.

McKay, M. M. (1994). The link between domestic violence and child abuse: Assessment and treatment considerations. *Child Welfare, 73,* 29–39.

Mills, L. (1998a). Integrating domestic violence assessment into child protective services intervention: Policy and practice implications. In A. R. Roberts (ed.), *Battered women and their families: Interventions, strategies, and treatment programs,* second ed., pp. 129–158. New York: Springer.

Mills, L. (1998b). Mandatory arrest and prosecution policies for domestic violence: A critical literature review and the case for more research to test victim empowerment approaches. *Criminal Justice and Behavior, 25*(3), 306–318.

Mills, L., Friend, C., Conroy, K., Fleck-Henderson, A., Krug, S., et al. (2000). Child protection and domestic violence: Training, practice, and policy issues. *Child and Youth Services Review, 22,* 315–332.

Mills, L., & Yoshihama, M. (2002). Training children's service workers in domestic violence assessment and intervention: Research findings and implications for practice. *Children and Youth Services Review, 24,* 561–581.

Murphy, L., Pynoos, R. S., & James, C. B. (1997). The trauma/grief-focused group psychotherapy module of an elementary school–based violence prevention/intervention program. In J. D. Osofsky (ed.), *Children in a violent society,* pp. 223–255. New York: Guilford.

Nichols-Casebolt, A., & Spakes, P. (1995). Policy research and the voices of women. *Social Work Research, 19*(1), 49–55.

Norman, J. (2000). Should children's protective services intervene when children witness domestic violence? *Trauma, Violence and Abuse, 1*(3), 291–293.

O'Keefe, M. (1995). Predictors of child abuse in maritally violent families. *Journal of Interpersonal Violence, 10,* 3–25.

Okun, M. A., Melichar, J. F., & Hill, M. D. (1990). Negative daily events, positive and negative social ties, and psychological distress among older adults. *Gerontologist, 30*(2), 193–199.

Osofsky, J. D. (1997). Prevention and intervention programs for children exposed to violence. In J. Osofsky (ed.), *Children in a violent society.* New York: Guilford.

Pence, E., & Lizdas, K. (1998). *The Duluth Safety and Accountability Audit: A Guide to assessing institutional responses to domestic violence.* Duluth, MN: City of Duluth.

Postmus, J. L., & Ortega, D. (2004). Serving two masters: When domestic violence and child abuse overlap. Unpublished paper.

Rosenbaum, A., & O'Leary, K. D. (1981). Marital violence: Characteristics of abusive couples. *Journal of Consulting and Clinical Psychology, 49*(1), 63–71.

Saunders, D. G., & Anderson, D. (2000). Evaluation of domestic violence training for child protection workers and supervisors: Initial report. *Children and Youth Services Review, 22,* 375–398.

Schechter, S. (1982). *Women and male violence.* Boston: South End Press.

Schechter, S., & Edleson, J. L. (1994). *In the best interest of women and children: A call for collaboration between child welfare and domestic violence constituencies.* Paper presented at the Conference on Domestic Violence and Child Welfare: Integrating Policy and Practice for Families, Racine, WI, June 8–10, 1994.

Schechter, S., & Edleson, J. L. (1999). *Effective intervention in domestic violence & child maltreatment cases: Guidelines for policy and practice.* Reno, NV: National Council of Juvenile and Family Court Judges.

Stark, E., & Flitcraft, A. H. (1988). Women and children at risk: A feminist perspective on child abuse. *International Journal of Health Services, 18*(1), 97–118.

Straus, M. A. (1980). Social stress and marital violence in a national sample of American families. *Annals of the New York Academy of Sciences, 347,* 229–250.

Straus, M. A. (1991). *Children as witness to marital violence: A risk factor for life-long problems among a nationally representative sample of American men and women.* Paper presented at the Ross Roundtable on Children and Violence, Washington, DC, September 12–16, 1991.

Straus, M. A., Hamby, S. L., Sugarman, D. B., & Boney-McCoy, S. (1996). The Revised Conflict Tactics Scales (CTS2): Development and preliminary psychometric data. *Journal of Family Issues, 17*(3), 283–316.

Sullivan, C. M., Nguyen, H., Allen, N. E., Bybee, D. I., & Juras, J. (2000). Beyond searching for deficits: Evidence that physically and emotionally abused women are nurturing parents. *Journal of Emotional Abuse, 2*(1), 51–71.

Tjaden, P., & Thoennes, N. (1998). *Prevalence, incidence, and consequences of violence against women: Findings from the national violence against women survey.* Washington, DC: National Institute of Justice.

Tolman, R. M. (1992). Psychological abuse of women. In R. T. Ammerman & M. Hersen (eds.), *Assessment of family violence: A clinical and legal sourcebook,* pp. 26–46. New York: John Wiley & Sons.

Werner, E. E., & Smith, R. (1992). *Overcoming the odds: High risk children from birth to adulthood.* Ithaca, NY: Cornell University Press.

Wilson, C. (1998). Are battered women responsible for protection of their children in domestic violence cases? *Journal of Interpersonal Violence, 13,* 289–293.

Wolak, J., & Finkelhor, D. (1998). Children exposed to partner violence. In J. L. Jasinski & L. M. Williams (eds.), *Partner violence: A comprehensive review of 20 years of research,* pp. 73–112. Thousand Oaks, CA: Sage.

Zorza, J. (1995). How abused women can use the law to help protect their children. In E. Peled, P. Jaffe, & J. L. Edleson (eds.), *Ending the cycle of violence: Community response to children of battered women,* pp. 147–169. Thousand Oaks, CA: Sage.

SECTION III
Permanency for Children and Youth

❖   ❖   ❖   ❖   ❖   ❖   ❖

Overview

With the passage of the Adoption Assistance and Child Welfare Act over two decades ago and the more recent enactment of the Adoption and Safe Families Act of 1997, permanency planning has served as the broad practice and legal umbrella for the provision of the continuum of child welfare services. Building on the knowledge derived from a number of demonstration and research projects (see Gambrill & Stein 1994; Pecora, Whitaker, Maluccio, Barth, & Plotnick 2000), permanency planning involves a mix of family-centered, child-focused, and culturally relevant philosophies, management and program components, and practice strategies designed to help children and youth live in families that offer a continuity of relationships with nurturing parents or caregivers and the opportunity to establish lifetime relationships (Maluccio & Fein 1993).

Because it is widely acknowledged that separation, loss, and unresolved grief—as well as the uncertain and often long-term nature of the foster care experience—can have a negative impact on children's overall sense of belonging, identity formation, and emotional well-being, the process and outcomes of permanency planning are intended to safely limit entry into placement, and failing that, to limit the time children and youth spend in care. Thus, planning for children's permanency as well as their safety and developmental well-being should begin when a family first comes in contact with the child welfare agency. From this initial contact, permanency efforts are supported by actively including families and children/youth in individualized case planning; by insuring that workers visit both the child and parents frequently; and by coordinating service delivery and competent decisionmaking, including legal entities, about where children and youth will grow up. Permanency planning requires that case-by-case assessments (which integrate a safety or risk assessment) and interventions balance the time needed for a family to make necessary changes with a young person's need for continuity of relationships and secure attachments and his or her ability to tolerate separation and loss.

As explored in depth in this section of the text, permanency planning involves a mix of family-centered casework and legal strategies designed to insure that children and youth have safe, caring, stable, and lifetime families in which to grow up. According to the National Resource Center for Foster Care and Permanency Planning at the Hunter College School of Social Work (1999), these strategies include:

- Targeted and appropriate efforts to protect safety, achieve permanence, and strengthen family and child well-being;
- Early intervention and prevention, with reasonable efforts to prevent unnecessary out-of-home care when safety can be assured;
- Safety as a paramount concern throughout the life of the case, with the identification of those aggravated circumstances in which reasonable efforts to preserve or reunify families may not be required;
- Appropriate least restrictive out-of-home placements within family, culture, and

community, with comprehensive family and child assessments, written case plans, goal-oriented practice, and concurrent permanency plans required;

- Reasonable efforts to reunify families and maintain family connections and continuity in children's relationships when safety can be assured;
- Reasonable efforts to find alternative permanency options through adoption, legal guardianship, or in special circumstances, another planned alternative permanent living arrangement outside the child welfare system when children cannot return to their parents;
- Filing of termination of parental rights petitions 15 months after placement when this action is in best interests of the child and exceptions do not apply;
- Collaborative case activity—establishing partnerships among birth parents, foster parents, agency staff, court and legal staff, and community service providers;
- Frequent, high-quality parent-child visits, as well as worker-child and worker-parent visits; and
- Timely case reviews, permanency hearings, and decisionmaking about where children will grow up, taking into account the child's sense of time.

In the Child and Family Services Review process, the permanency variables have been conceptualized in two broad areas:

—Outcome Permanency 1: Children have permanency and stability in their living situations through:
- Decreasing foster care re-entries;
- Achieving the stability of foster care placement;
- Establishing a permanency goal for the child;
- Accomplishing reunification, guardianship, or permanent placement with relatives;
- Adoption; or

- Permanency goal of other planned permanent living arrangements.
—Outcome Permanency 2: The continuity of family relationships and connections is preserved for children through:
- Proximity of the child's foster care placement to the parents' home;
- Placement with siblings also in care;
- Visits with parents and siblings in foster care;
- Preservation of connections;
- Placement with a relative; and
- Maintaining a relationship between the child in care and his/her parents.

An array of permanency outcomes (each discussed in this section) is desirable for children and youth, with priority given to those that maintain the child's existing family and kin relationships and connections. Therefore, achieving permanency calls for initially attempting to keep children and youth at home safely with their parents to prevent the trauma of unnecessary separation and placement or, failing that, placing children with relatives when possible and with other siblings entering care. These issues are fully explored in Hegar and Scannapieco's chapter on preservation of the extended family–kinship care and in Hegar's chapter exploring the importance of maintaining sibling connections.

For children and youth who cannot safely remain with their families and for whom placement in family foster care is therefore necessary, numerous issues must be considered. These are discussed in Barbell and Freundlich's overview of family foster care and in Bullard and Johnson's examination of group care settings. For the majority of children and youth, family reunification (see the chapter by Pine, Spath, and Gosteli), is the preferred permanency option. Cordero and Epstein explore a technique for refining the practice of reunification in their chapter, which discusses a project involving "mining" successful foster care records of substance-abusing families. Parent-child visiting, at the heart of reunification, is explored by co-editor Hess in her chapter.

When children and youth cannot return home within the federally mandated timeframe of 12 to 15 months, alternative permanency options should be pursued, including adoption by relatives, foster parents, or a new family (Groza, Houlihan, and Wood explore these issues in their chapter); customary adoption in Indian communities (see the chapter by Cross and Fox); legal guardianship with relatives, foster parents, or another caring adult (see the chapter by Testa and Miller); and in special circumstances, another planned alternative living arrangement with relatives, foster parents (considered by Renne and co-editor Mallon in their chapter), or a small community-based group or residential setting—each with attention to lifetime family connections that can be nurtured and preserved.

Increasingly, child welfare practitioners understand that their work, even when reunification is not possible, must also involve birth families (see Hollingsworth's chapter on birthmothers whose parental rights are terminated and Cooper Heitzman's chapter focusing on a birth mother–child reunion story). Practitioners must also consider the effects of permanency efforts that may not be positive (see Festinger's chapter on adoption disruption). In their chapter, Wright and Freundlich review the salient issues concerning post-permanency services that support families in achieving continued permanence and stability.

Permanency planning balances the rights and needs of children, youth, and parents with the harm that can be brought by the passage of time and delays in decisionmaking. Although there is no one correct outcome for achieving permanency for all children and youth, the challenge is to arrive in a timely manner at the permanency outcome that offers the greatest measure of emotional and legal permanency for each child or youth. The unique circumstances for youth in foster care are considered in a chapter focusing on youth development and independent living services by Nixon.

Fulfilling the promise of permanency requires that children, youth, and family service practitioners are aware of the need to include the following elements in their practice:

- Family-centered and strengths/needs-based practice;
- Community-based service delivery;
- Cultural competence and respect for diversity;
- Open and inclusive practice;
- Nonadversarial approaches to problem solving and service delivery; and
- Concurrent rather than sequential consideration of all permanency options.

The chapters in this section of the text address a broad range of issues. Furthermore, since they are written by academics, practitioners, and others with a wide range of experiences in the field, the reader will also find diverse opinions and perspectives concerning permanency planning and, in some cases, about child welfare in general.

REFERENCES

Adoption and Safe Families Act. (1997). P.L. 105-89.

Adoption Assistance and Child Welfare Act. (1980). P.L. 96-272.

Gambrill, E., & Stein, T. (1994). *Controversial issues in child welfare.* Englewood, NJ: Prentice-Hall.

Maluccio, A. N., & Fein, E. (1993). Permanency planning: A redefinition. *Child Welfare, 62,* 195–201.

National Resource Center for Foster Care and Permanency Planning. (1999). *Handouts on concurrent permanency planning.* New York: National Resource Center for Foster Care and Permanency Planning, Hunter College School of Social Work.

Pecora, P., Whitaker, J. K., Maluccio, A. N., Barth, R. P., & Plotnick, R. D. (2000). *The child welfare challenge: Policy, practice, and research,* second ed. Hawthorne, NY: Aldine de Gruyter.

BARBARA A. PINE
ROBIN SPATH
STEPHANIE GOSTELI

Defining and Achieving Family Reunification

In this chapter, we focus on an important aspect of child welfare practice—family reunification. The chapter begins with national statistics on the number of children in foster care in the United States, and presents a brief overview of the policy context of family reunification. The discussion outlines a broader definition of positive outcomes in family reunification and provides information on the risk and protective factors of families working toward reunification. Promising research-based practice approaches, the skills and values needed for effective practice in family reunification, and ethical aspects of practice are discussed. Case examples are provided throughout to illustrate practice principles for working with children in out-of-home care and their families.

Children in Out-of-Home Care

In response to child maltreatment, state child protective service agencies often remove children from their homes and place them in foster care. In 2001, approximately 903,000 children were victims of abuse and neglect in the United States (U.S. Department of Health and Human Services 2003b), and 542,000 children were in the foster care system because of maltreatment (U.S. Department of Health and Human Services 2003a).

Demographic Characteristics

What were the characteristics of these children who were separated from their birth families?

Girls were almost as likely as boys to be in out-of-home care: 48% of children in care are girls. In terms of age, there is a nearly equal division of younger and older children. Those between the ages of 1 and 10 make up 46% of the foster care population, whereas children aged 11 to 17 represent 40%. The largest group, representing 29% of children in care, are between the ages of 11 and 15. Thirteen percent of children are less than 1 year old; fewer than 1% are 19 or older, reflecting most state policies of aging children out of care at age 18. The race of three-quarters of children in care is also nearly equally divided between black non-Hispanic (38%) and white non-Hispanic (37%). The remaining quarter of the children are Hispanic (17%), American Indian, Asian, Alaska Native, or their race/ethnicity is unknown (U.S. Department of Health and Human Services 2003a). As these figures clearly show, children of color are greatly overrepresented in the population of children who are separated from their families and placed in foster care.

Placement Settings and Service Goals

Almost half of the children in care (48%) were placed in nonrelative foster family homes, and almost one-quarter (24%) were in kinship care placements. Ten percent of children were placed in an institution, and 8% were in a group home. The remaining 10% had run away, were in preadoptive homes or supervised independent living, or had been returned to their homes for a trial visit (U.S. Department of Health and Human Services 2003a). According to these government statistics, reunification is the case goal for almost half of the children in care (44%); during the 2001 fiscal year, 57% of children who exited foster care were reunified with their parent(s) or primary caretaker(s). This outcome—going back home to children's birth families—has typically been viewed as the goal of foster care practice. More recently, however, as discussed below, this limited view of positive outcomes for children has been challenged and new objectives have emerged in both policy and practice.

Defining Family Reunification

The Adoption Assistance and Child Welfare Act (P.L. 96-272), passed in 1980 amid growing concern about the length of time children spent in foster care, emphasized placement prevention and family reunification. When children could not return to their family of origin, new permanent families, chiefly through adoption, were to be found. The law also demanded greater accountability from state child welfare agencies in achieving policy goals (Pine 1986). As a result of this landmark legislation in permanency planning, agencies placed renewed emphasis on reunification. Outcomes were view dichotomously —either children were returned home or they were not. This view did not seem to fit with the needs of many families who were receiving child welfare services, however, and some observers (Maluccio, Warsh, & Pine 1993:5–6) began to question its usefulness:

> It is time to challenge this all-or-nothing premise as too simplistic, and to view family reunification as a flexible, dynamic approach to meeting the needs of children and their families in an individualized and carefully thought-through way—as a response to the unique qualities, needs, and situations of each child and family.

In response, Maluccio, Warsh, & Pine (1993: 6) developed a new definition of family reunification:

Family reunification is the planned process of reconnecting children in out-of-home care with their families by means of a variety of services and supports to the children, their families, and their foster parents or other service providers. It aims to help each child and family to achieve and maintain, at any given time, their optimal level of reconnection—from full reentry of the child into the family system to other forms of contact, such as visiting, that affirm the child's membership in the family.

Moreover, the child welfare field often uses the terms "reunification" and "reintegration" interchangeably. However, Petr and Entriken (1995:525) note that it is important to make a distinction between the two terms: "reintegration refers to the physical reintegration of children with their families and reunification is a more encompassing term that includes reintegration as one component." This definition views reunification outcomes on a continuum, rather than as a dichotomy. Not every parent can care for her child on a daily, full-time basis. However, with this expanded view of reunification, which includes reintegration, the parent-child bond can still exist and be maintained through other types of connections, as the following case example illustrates.

MARIA, ANGEL, AND JESSICA GONZALEZ

Maria Gonzalez was an 18-year-old mother of two. Both of her children were removed from her care due to severe neglect. She was committed to both of her children, but had been a single parent since the age of 15. Having been a foster child herself, Maria did not have an extended family that could provide her with the support she needed to parent success fully. Maria's oldest child, Angel, was 3 at the time she was placed in foster care; her younger daughter, Jessica, was 18 months old. The siblings were placed together in a two parent foster home with three older birth children.

Shortly after being placed, it became clear that Angel was presenting with severe behavioral problems, including impulsivity that could potentially place her in harm's way. Angel appeared to have a fascination with hot things and would attempt to touch the hot stove or hot water if it was running. She would run into the street, and at times attempted to climb out of windows. All of the members of Angel's foster family actively participated in watching Angel to make sure she remained safe. Angel's mother, Maria, agreed that she had had similar problems keeping Angel safe, and had frequently used corporal punishment as a way to try to stop the behavior. Maria was also able to acknowledge that Angel may have experienced sexual abuse at the hands of one of her relatives. Angel received early intervention through the school system, as well as therapy, but continued to present as a very loving, but challenging child.

Maria worked diligently with a private nonprofit reunification program and with the foster parents and was able to make significant gains in her parenting abilities. During this time, Maria also became involved with Juan, and when they began to live together, Juan participated in reunification services. Together they began to build a stable family unit, which included the birth of their own child. Due to the newfound stability and improved parenting skills, they were able to have Jessica reunified with them. However, when Maria became pregnant again, they realized that they would not be able to meet the challenges of parenting Angel. At this point, both Maria and Juan had developed a strong relationship with the foster family and realized that Angel would continue to receive the care she needed if she remained with that family. Both families agreed to an open adoption, so that Angel will remain with a family who is committed to her, but will also maintain ties to her birth family.

New Policy Developments

Family reunification has taken on a special significance in child welfare practice since the passage of the Adoption and Safe Families Act (ASFA) in 1997 (P.L. 105-89). This federal legislation revised and clarified many of the policies established under the Adoption Assistance and Child Welfare Act of 1980. Congress had several goals when it passed these revisions, including improvement in child safety and the promotion of permanency for children through adoption and other permanent plans, as well as reunification. ASFA establishes new guidelines for the amount of time children should spend in out-of-home care before a petition to terminate their parents' rights is filed. Under ASFA, states are required to develop a concurrent plan while working toward reunification. They must file for termination of parental rights and implement the concurrent plan for cases in which a child has been in care 15 months out of the most recent 22 months, if family reunification is not possible during this period. There are some exceptions to this timeline for families facing extremely challenging issues (Child Welfare League of America n.d.-b). However, the establishment of these timelines places a renewed emphasis on family reunification practice, and ASFA specifically provides funding for intensive reunification services (National Family Preservation Network 2003). ASFA also clarifies a key part of the previous legislation, outlining the exceptions allowed to states for making reasonable efforts to preserve and reunify families.

Vulnerabilities and Strengths of Families Receiving Reunification Services

Characteristics of the families and their children who are to be reunified as well as elements in the family's environment have been found to influence the prospects of reunification. Some parents are incarcerated, which makes visiting —a key intervention in family reunification— challenging if not impossible (see the chapter by Hess on visiting). The length of a parent's prison sentence may not fit with the timelines for reunification. Families dealing with domestic violence issues also face unique obstacles to reunification. Different intervention models guide the various systems that may be working with the family, such as the judicial, social service, or healthcare systems. Therefore, there may be incompatible priorities and goals for the family that create conflict (Adler, Hax, Stanley, & Zhou 2000). Substance abuse is also a significant risk factor for families working toward reunification (Frame, Berrick, & Brodowski 2000; Hoffman & Rosenheck 2001; Hohman & Butt 2001; Karoll & Poertner 2002; Richie 2001), as are children's difficulties. Landsverk, Litrownik, Newton, Granger, and Remmer (1996) found that children who had emotional or behavioral problems were only half as likely to be reunified with their families as were children without these problems. In another study that examined likelihood of reunification, Nugent, Carpenter, and Parks (1993) considered adolescent status offenders (mostly runaways) and found that older youths, those not currently in school, those for whom child abuse was the presenting problem, and those involved in either the juvenile justice or the child welfare systems were the least likely to be reunified with their families.

Poverty and the challenges resulting from poverty are also major risk factors for separated families. Several factors related to poverty can impact reunification efforts, including a low level of education, work in low or unskilled jobs, and unstable housing (Landy & Munro 1998). Jones (1998:320) notes that "poverty and economic deprivation, as expressed by inadequate housing, may be the greatest risk from the social environment for successful reunification." In addition, the service system can create barriers to reunification by not focusing enough attention on the reunification goals, placing children in foster care far from their family and community, allowing the juvenile justice system to take on a primary and guiding role, failing to provide a community-based system of services, or failing to collaborate with and involve the family in the reunification process (Petr & Entriken 1995). Moreover, being forced to exchange welfare payments for work due to benefit time limits can greatly impede reunification. Wells, Guo, and Li (2000), in a study of welfare leavers in one Ohio county, found that as many as 75% of their children in foster care remained there after 18 months, compared to 4% of children whose mothers continued to receive benefits.

Many children in care represent one or more failed reunification efforts (Maluccio, Abramczyk, & Thomlison 1996). Estimates of recidivism range from 20% to 40% (Maluccio, Fein, & Davis 1994; Rzepnicki, Schuerman, & Johnson 1997; Tatara 1993; Terling 1999). However, few studies have examined factors associated with reentry into foster care or developed profiles of families least likely to be reunified in the first place. A study of reentry by Terling (1999) showed a high correlation between parental substance abuse and a child's return to care. Terling (1999) also found that parental competence was a factor in reentry. When parents were unable to provide an environment that complied with child protection standards because they either could not comprehend or accept the agency's negative assessment of it, their children were more likely to return to out-of-home care. When Festinger (1996) compared a group of children who returned to care with a similar group that did not, she found that lower ratings of parental skills, fewer social supports, and the number and severity of the children's problems were all predictors of reentry within 2 years of their original discharge from foster care. Jones (1998) found that in families that are experiencing economic deprivation or who have children with medical or behavioral issues, there is a greater likelihood of reentering the foster care system. The same study (Jones 1998: 321) noted that neglect "predicted re-referral but not re-entry" into the child welfare system. A third study (Hess, Folaron, & Jefferson 1992; Hess & Folaron 1991) examined 62 children's unsuccessful reunification with their families and their reentry into care. The most frequent contributor to placement reentry was nonresolution of the parent problem(s) that precipitated placement. Multiple service delivery system problems, including high caseload size, staff turnover, and insufficient regulation of reunification practice interacted with the serious nature of families' problems to reduce the chances for successful reunification. In addition, Hess and Folaron (1991:404) reported that in more than half of the first 40 cases examined,

> the parent's ambivalent attitude [about reunification] was found to contribute specifically and directly to placement reentry . . . it would appear that it would have been an appropriate service goal to aid the parents in becoming less ambivalent and either more committed to reunification or clearer about their disinterest in parenting and therefore more able to work toward another permanency goal.

Despite the challenges they face, many families whose children have been removed due to abuse and neglect have some protective factors that increase the likelihood of reunification. One of the most important factors related to successful reunification is economic status. Caregivers with higher levels of income and greater job stability are more likely to be reunified with their children. Another factor that is related to economic status is housing. Families with stable, safe housing are more likely to be reunified. The size and quality of the families' social support network also has shown to be positively correlated with reunification (Festinger 1996; Fraser, Walton, Lewis, & Pecora 1996). It is critical that any intervention with families focus on finding and using these protective factors and family strengths, as in the following practice example.

One private nonprofit child welfare agency providing reunification services to families whose children have been removed by the local child welfare department uses such a "strengths perspective." As part of the program intake, a comprehensive assessment that focuses on the family strengths is completed. This strengths perspective is important to both the engagement with the family and service goal planning, which frequently uses the strengths a family has

as a means to accomplish the goals that they, together with their assigned worker, agree to work toward. During the assessment phase, agency practitioners identify family strengths by interviewing family members, collaborating with family members and important others, working with the family to complete a family genogram and/or ecomap, and collaborating with other service providers and personnel in children's schools. Investing the time to complete a comprehensive assessment that includes information from an array of professional and nonprofessional sources at the outset of work with a family is vital to having a solid foundation on which to build the subsequent work.

The benefit of this approach to assessment is aptly demonstrated in the following example of a family successfully reunified.

THE SANCHEZ FAMILY

Understanding a family's culture is always a vital part of any assessment process. When working with the Sanchez family, state child welfare workers who did not speak Spanish made the decision to remove the 12-year-old son after his father had hit him in the face. The child had come to school with a bruised cheek, and after some prodding had stated that his father was responsible for the injury.

Although there is clearly no justification for injuring a child, during intake into a specialized family reunification program, the social worker ascertained that the father had lost his temper when his son arrived home after midnight having been out driving around in a car with a 14-year-old friend. This was an intact family originally from Puerto Rico that had moved to the United States to provide more opportunities to their five children. The parents were now struggling with the influences that their urban living environment was having on their sons. Information from the school system and community partners validated that this father had no previous history of violent episodes and maintained an otherwise strong and positive presence in his children's lives. Once the father's position as the respected head of his household had been restored, this family was open to services and to addressing the tensions in the family that led to the outburst and subsequent injury. The local child welfare department was able to advocate for the family to obtain a Section 8 housing voucher, which allowed them to move to a better neighborhood and into a house with enough room for everyone.

A focus on strengths is at the core of new practice approaches to reunifying families described below.

Promising Practices in Family Reunification

Most studies of family reunification have looked at what facilitates family reunification. These studies have focused mainly on the importance of such factors as service variables and child and family characteristics. For example, a study by Fraser and his colleagues (Fraser, Walton, Lewis, & Pecora, 1996; Lewis 1994; Walton, Fraser, Lewis, & Pecora 1993) achieved significant success using a 90-day intensive family preservation model with separated families, achieving a 93% reunification rate with the 57 children whose families were involved in the program. Success was attributed to service variables such as the provision of concrete services, the establishment of strong worker-family relationships, and the provision of skills training to parents. Staff and Fein (1994), reporting on another experimental family reunification program, also found that concrete assistance to the families involved promoted reunification. Nugent, Carpenter, and Parks (1993) found that adolescents and their families who participated in family therapy and completed all of the services planned for the family were more likely to be reunified than those who did not. Finally, Courtney and Wong (1996) showed that the earlier youths exited from care, the more likely they were to be reunified with their families, a finding that supports early and intensive intervention.

Visiting

One service variable—visiting—has received the most attention in the research. Between 1978 and 1993, there were at least 12 studies that examined the impact of parent-child visiting on reunification (Hess 1999). Most of this research supports the view that visiting is good for parents and children. In fact, visiting has been called the heart of family reunification (Hess & Proch 1993). As these authors indicate, visiting helps maintain family ties, provides reassurance to children and parents, and provides opportunities to assess parent-child interaction and the development of new skills. In their study of 925 children, Davis, Landsverk, Newton, & Granger (1996) found that visits were the key to discharge from care. When visit plans were developed, the likelihood of visits was increased; most children who visited with their parents at the level recommended by the courts were reunified with their families.

Family-Centered Practice

Programs designed to reunify children with their families should come from a family-centered practice orientation. The Child Welfare League of America (n.d.-a) describes family centered practice as "A way of working with families, both formally and informally, across service systems to enhance the capacity of families to care for and protect their children." A key component of this approach is recognizing and building on the strengths of families and family relationships and meeting a variety of their needs to achieve optimal outcomes. This approach may benefit families dealing with many challenges, including eviction, family violence, child maltreatment, substance abuse, lack of food, incarcerated parents, and physical or mental health issues (Child Welfare League of America 1989). The following case history illustrates the family-centered approach to reunification practice.

THE WALKER FAMILY

Ms. Walker, a 35-year-old mother of three children, Steven aged 13, Susan aged 10, and Dani aged 8, had a history of severe depression with psychotic features and substance abuse. Ms. Walker had been involved with the local child welfare department for a number of years, and they had provided assistance with mental health and drug treatment, as well as shelter housing. Ms. Walker had a supportive family network that included her mother and sister, who both lived locally. The combined efforts of family members and a committed child welfare worker had previously been able to prevent placement of the children. However, when Ms. Walker's continued substance abuse led to further allegations of neglect and eviction from her state-subsidized housing, all three children were removed from her care. Ms. Walker's family rallied once again, and her sisters were able to take the children. One sister took the two oldest children, Steven and Susan, and another sister took the youngest, Dani. Ms. Walker herself went to live with her mother.

Ms. Walker entered a dual diagnosis treatment program, received intensive outpatient services, and worked with an intensive family reunification program for more than a year. Despite the concentration of the services and collaboration between service providers, Ms. Walker was not able to maintain her treatment and provide a home for her children and herself. The demands of both were simply too much, and Ms. Walker was supported in her decision to commit to her own continued recovery, so that she could be a positive addition to her children's lives. Ms. Walker's family was initially very angry with her, and accused her of abandoning her children. By making use of the Family Conferencing Model (see Waites, Macgowan, Pennell, Carlton-LaNey, & Weil 2004), the family was able to work through their anger and agree to a plan, whereby all the children were reunified under the care of Ms. Walker's older sister, with Ms. Walker continuing to be an important visiting resource for the children. Ms. Walker was committed to her children; however, her own severe mental illness prevented her from being a full-time parent. The solution created by her family and service providers allowed her to remain an important part of her children's lives.

Intensive Family Reunification Services
Intensive family reunification services (Fraser, Walton, Lewis, & Pecora 1996; Pierce & Geremia

1999; Walton 1998) is a promising program model that follows the family-centered intervention approach. The National Family Preservation Network (2003:34) defines these services as "short-term, intensive, family-based [programs that are] designed to reunite families when children are likely to remain in out-of-home placement for longer than six months without this intervention." Therefore, intensive services are not appropriate or necessary for families that are likely to be reunified after a brief time in foster care—ideally within 2 or 3 months from the time of removal. The National Family Preservation Network (2003) has outlined basic standards for intensive family reunification services:

- Staff availability on 24-hour basis, every day of the week;
- Small caseloads for staff—ideally two to four families;
- One-on-one contact with the family immediately after a referral is made—ideally within 72 hours;
- Predominantly home-based services that are intensive—between 5 and 20 hours a week;
- Programming that includes weekend and evening services; and
- Time-limited services—ideally between 60 and 90 days.

Use of Assessment Tools
Because families often face many challenges that could be barriers to reunification, a wide array of services may be needed in addition to assistance that addresses the jeopardy issue(s) that resulted in the child being removed from the home and placed in out-of-home care. It is essential that a comprehensive assessment be conducted with the family to determine the services needed. A number of new assessment tools are available. One of these is the North Carolina Family Assessment Scale for Reunification (NCFAS-R). Initial studies using the NCFAS-R indicate that this is a promising in-

strument for use in reunification practice. It has been adopted by several state and private nonprofit child welfare agencies (Colorado Department of Human Services 2003; Kirk 2002). NCFAS-R is designed to assess families in seven key areas or domains: environment, parental capabilities, family interactions, family safety, child well-being, caregiver/child ambivalence, and readiness for reunification. These domains reflect the major areas that practitioners should consider when working with families toward an optimal level of family functioning that insures child safety and well-being. Using an intensive family reunification services program model, NCFAS-R could be useful in determining if a family needs services in any one of the following areas (National Family Preservation Network 2003):

- Parent training;
- Family communication building;
- Behavior management;
- Marital counseling;
- Life skills training;
- Self-management of moods/behavior;
- School interventions;
- Safety planning;
- Relapse prevention;
- Concrete and advocacy services; and
- Other services, as needed.

Social Work Staff with Specialized Competencies

Pine, Warsh, and Maluccio (1993) delineate five competency areas for social workers involved in family reunification practice: valuing families; assessing readiness for reunification; establishing goals for reunification; implementing the reunification plan; and maintaining the reunification and ending the service.

Valuing families relates to the values and attitudes that guide a social worker's practice, especially valuing the birth family as the preferred child-rearing unit, but also seeing family reunification as a process with a variety of possible outcomes over time. Social workers in this field of practice also benefit from understanding and valuing family diversity, including differences in family membership, lifestyles, and parenting methods.

Social workers also must have the skills necessary to assess the readiness of the family for reunification. Interactions with the family need to build trust and confidence. Without this trust, the ability to comprehensively assess the family may be compromised. Therefore it is important that the cultural and racial background of the family be considered when deciding what assessment approaches and tools to use with each family. In addition, recognizing barriers to reunification outside of the family system should be an integral part of the assessment process. Finally, the assessment should include both the strengths and challenges facing a family, rather than just the obstacles to reunification, because, as noted earlier, an understanding of family strengths is essential to success in reunification.

After a social worker has worked with a family and developed a comprehensive assessment, goals based on the strengths and challenges outlined in the assessment must be identified, and support provided to the family to help them reach these goals. Involving families in both assessment and goal planning is essential; if this partnership is not established and family members are not engaged, there may be many additional barriers to overcome when working toward reunification.

The achievement of the goals established by the social worker and family members requires that the plan for reunification services be individualized and implemented in a timely fashion. Great care must be given to insuring that the services offered and provided specifically address the needs and difficulties that have led to the child's placement. As indicated earlier, parent-child visits are a key component of such services. To develop and implement the service plan an understanding of parenting skills and theories—as well as of child development—is necessary for practitioners. Further, as Pine, Warsh, and Maluccio (1993:40) note, practitioners working with families toward re-unification require several additional areas of competencies, including "family therapy, child abuse, and legal issues in child welfare." In addition, it is important for them to have basic knowledge of substance abuse and the dynamics of recovery (McAlpine, Marshall, & Doran 2001). A comprehensive discussion of practice competencies in reunification can be found in Warsh, Maluccio, and Pine (1994).

Once a permanent plan has been put into place for a family, either reunification or another plan, it is important to provide post-reunification services to the family. The family may need continued services and supports during the adjustment phase. Additionally, the family should be prepared for the termination of services, which should include a closing session to outline the accomplishments and strengths of the family and to help them to establish priorities for reaching any goals that may remain. Finally, the social supports and community services currently in place should be reviewed, and any additional needed support put in place prior to termination.

Service Environment that Supports Competent Practice

Competent staff can only be effective in reunifying families if they work in an environment that supports their work. This support includes elements of the services system, such as the agency's mission, policies on reunification, attention to cultural competence, the design of reunification services; and elements of the work environment, such as workload, training, and supervision (Hess, Folaron, & Jefferson 1992). In addition, the agency's relationships with other organizations bears on effectiveness, including those with the court system, schools, law enforcement agencies, the media, and other governmental bodies (Warsh, Pine, & Maluccio 1996).

Information Not Yet Available

Much still remains unknown about both service variables and the characteristics of families that affect success in reunification. For example, it is not known whether culture or ethnicity influences outcomes or what service approaches are most effective with special populations (Maluccio, Abramczyk, & Thomlinson 1996). Nor is it known what role language may play in either service delivery or outcomes; an important consideration, given the growth of Spanish-speaking populations likely to be served by child welfare agencies. What is the impact on outcomes of social class, and social class differences between staff, caregivers, and families served? What outcomes besides a child's return home (e.g., family functioning, child development) are influenced by services? Given the extent of the problems that many children and families in the child welfare system face, do intensive, short-term services make a difference (Fraser, Nelson, & Rivard 1997)? What services are needed to achieve lasting gains for these families (Maluccio, Abramczyk, & Thomlinson 1996)? What other factors affect outcomes—for example, specialized training of family reunification practitioners and foster parents (Warsh, Maluccio, & Pine 1994; Warsh, Pine, & Maluccio 1996 ; Fraser, Nelson, & Rivard 1997)? And finally, studies of family preservation and reunification have yet to show the differential contribution of the core elements of a program to its outcomes (Fraser, Nelson, & Rivard 1997). Another area that needs further exploration is a key intervention in family reunification practice—visiting. Future research needs to study and clearly delineate "the black box" of services provided with parent-child visits (Davis, Landsverk, Newton, & Granger 1996; Hess 1987, 2003).

Ethical Issues in Reunification Practice

There are several major ethical dilemmas faced by social workers working with families toward family reunification. Protective services staff generally remove and place children in out-of-home care for a particular issue or event that has been reported to and investigated by the agency. However, once a family becomes involved with the child protection system, the assessment and treatment process may open a Pandora's box of other challenges facing the family. This type of situation presents several dilemmas for social workers. Should these newly discovered challenges facing the family, which are in addition to the jeopardy issue that brought the child into care, be included in the treatment goals that the family must address to be reunified? How does one define "good enough" parenting? What presents a greater risk to a child: remaining in foster care or returning home? When is removal of a child and the resulting trauma necessary? When a parent clearly displays deficits in his ability to keep his children safe, a dilemma occurs, illustrated by the following case example.

THE JONES FAMILY

The Jones family had their 10-year-old son removed from their care for unexplained injuries. The rest of the Jones children, five in all, remained in the care of their parents. The family had managed to obtain a Section 8 housing voucher that allowed them to live in a middle class suburban neighborhood with a very good school system. However, the Jones family home was infamous in the neighborhood, as it was in disrepair and frequently had large amounts of trash in the yard. Needless to say, the neighbors were suspicious about the care that the children received. In addition, the children would arrive at school looking unkempt and were frequently absent. When the Jones's 10-year-old son arrived at school with a gash near his eye, only 2 weeks after having arrived at school with his arm in a cast from being broken, the school became concerned and contacted the state child welfare department. As this child had a long history of injuries resulting from minor accidents, and as the parent's description of events was vague and appeared to blame the other children without taking any responsibility themselves, the state child welfare department decided to remove the child from the home.

Family reunification social workers assigned to this family found some quite unusual dynamics, in that Mr. Jones suffered from epileptic seizures as the re-

sult of a severe industrial accident. This accident had left the children's father with significant impairments that, in addition to the seizures, included at times slurred speech and tangential thought processes. Mr. Jones's interactions with his children appeared disjointed, and his statements to workers were frequently inappropriate. Mrs. Jones presented as the stabilizing force within the family, but she, too, had some serious medical conditions and frequently became overwhelmed with the demands of caring for five children and her husband. The family survived on the small disability pension that Mr. Jones received, as well as some side jobs he could get from time to time. The children's clothing was often obtained from donations or thrift stores; they were in stark contrast to the clothes of the more affluent students at the schools the children attended. The family members had clearly been stigmatized because of their significant and obvious class differences. The children recognized this and were embarrassed to go to school—the underlying cause of the frequent absences. Both Mr. and Mrs. Jones appeared unable to address this issue either with their children or with the school system. The ability of the parents to provide the necessary oversight for five active children also appeared compromised and had led to the many injuries incurred, especially by their one son.

Despite the many challenges this family faced, one of the unifying forces was the family members' love of baseball. All the children played and Mr. Jones coached their Little League teams. If Mr. Jones experienced a seizure, the children would work together to get him to the car so that Mrs. Jones could drive him home.

While in foster care, their 10-year-old son exhibited severe withdrawal and both eating and sleep disturbances. The child repeatedly requested that he be returned home and would pine between family visits. Through the weekly parent-child visits, the reunification practitioners were able to see a very close-knit, strong family unit. They discovered that the child in question was actually accident prone, although they also worked with both parents to recognize the steps they could take to keep him as safe as possible. By presenting this more complete picture of the many ways that Mr. Jones was, indeed, a "good enough" parent, a swift reunification was effected, with the focus of the work on planning and implementing post-reunification services. Family members were also supported in their efforts to advocate for their members in both the medical and educational systems they came into contact with.

Social workers also may face the conflicting goals of permanency and child safety. The very fact of involvement by child welfare authorities may threaten family integrity. Sometimes this involvement represents such an intrusion that the family has difficulty getting beyond it to work on the concerns that have been raised about them, as the following Smith family case illustrates. The case also underscores the ethical imperative of cultural competence in working with families toward reunification.

THE SMITH FAMILY

Ms. Smith, who was originally from Jamaica, had had her 9-year-old son Kenneth removed from her care for neglect. Kenneth had repeatedly arrived at school dirty and unkempt, and efforts to discuss the issue with his mother had been unsuccessful. Ms. Smith had presented as erratic and, at times, bizarre, leading to concerns around her mental health. On one particular day, Kenneth arrived at school in a particularly alarming state and also appeared to have bruises on his arms that he would not explain. The school contacted the local department of child welfare and made a report. When the child welfare worker attempted to question Ms. Smith, she refused to cooperate and took the position that what she did with her child was none of their business. Due to the lack of cooperation and concerns regarding Ms. Smith's mental health and the care that Kenneth received, he was removed from the home and placed in foster care. Ms. Smith's mother was ruled out as a resource, as Ms. Smith was currently residing with her and did not appear to have any other resources available.

When the reunification social worker began to work with Ms. Smith, it became clear that Ms. Smith was having great difficulty engaging in the work. She simply did not agree that there was any justification

to remove her son. Attempts to move beyond this point and focus on the steps necessary to have him returned were unsuccessful. In an effort to better understand Kenneth's family and the resources they represented for him, the social worker began to work with Ms. Smith on a family genogram. By actively engaging Ms. Smith in the creation of the family genogram and by reaffirming her position as an expert on her own family, the worker was able to understand the strengths available within the family system, as well as the family history. Through the use of the genogram narrative, Ms. Smith was able to explain that both she and her mother had struggled with bouts of severe depression throughout their lives. Ms. Smith, in fact, had an older son who had needed to be cared for by her cousin when he was younger. This shared caregiving within the family system was acceptable and had been supported by Ms. Smith's family and community, an experience that stood in stark contrast to the current situation in which the state had become involved. By reframing the current situation in terms of the past, Ms. Smith was able to acknowledge that her own mental health challenges made it difficult for her to parent her son all the time. By using the genogram as a means of exploring the family that was available to Kenneth, the worker was able to "discover" Ms. Smith's cousin, who had cared for her older son, and who continued to live next door. By bringing the problem solving back into the family, Kenneth was able to be placed with his mother's cousin, and Ms. Smith was more willing to address some of her own mental health needs.

What if a family self-refers to child protective services? This may occur when the family is looking for assistance because they do not have the resources to meet their basic needs, such as clean and safe housing. What if, as a result of the parents' self-referral, their children are removed? What criteria should be used for reunification in these cases?

Sometimes policy mandates, such as ASFA's strict timelines for reunification, can cause problems for parents. Social workers have ethical obligations to advocate for needed services, but how can they deal with a criminal justice system in which so many of the families they work with have one or more incarcerated parents? Do their agencies have in place visiting programs for these parents? Are workloads structured in such a way as to enable social workers to drive long distances to arrange parent-child visits? Do agencies advocate against public housing policies that prohibit residence based on criminal records, thus making it difficult for parents to comply with child welfare requirements of safe and stable housing? The following case illustrates these dilemmas and the realities of the challenges in reunification practice.

MR. COOPER AND HIS SON JIMMY

Mr. Cooper was an incarcerated 22-year-old father of two when his 2-year-old son Jimmy was removed from his mother's care and placed in foster care. By the time that Mr. Cooper was released from jail, his son had been in foster care for more than 8 months.

On his release, Mr. Cooper immediately contacted the state child welfare department and informed them of his wish to be reunified with Jimmy. Mr. Cooper was asked to provide information regarding his compliance with his parole, as well as proof of stable housing. He was able to provide both, and weekly parent-child visits were instituted. Mr. Cooper clearly loved his son and their interactions were extremely positive. Mr. Cooper planned to have his son live with him in the home of his current girlfriend, who was also mother to his younger daughter.

Due to the seriousness of Mr. Cooper's past crimes, the state child welfare department required him to demonstrate his ability to provide a stable and safe environment for his son and to complete mandatory treatment programs prior to any reunification. During the time frame in which this work was scheduled to occur, Mr. Cooper began to experience difficulties with his current relationship. His girlfriend, who had four children of her own, appeared less than willing to undergo the requirements to have his son reunified to their home. Mr. Cooper then lost his employment and was thus unable to obtain any independent housing.

Initially, Mr. Cooper continued to visit with his son, but gradually, as it became clear that he would not be able to provide for his son's needs, these visits became too painful and they became less frequent. Mr. Cooper had formed a relationship with his son's foster parent. He continues to sporadically check in to see how his son is doing, but reunification is no longer something he discusses. The plan at this time is for the foster parent to adopt Jimmy.

Conclusion

As this chapter makes clear, work with families already separated by out-of-home placement is one of the most challenging practice areas in child welfare. These families may face many challenges—child abuse and neglect, poverty, homelessness, substance abuse, domestic violence, mental illness—in the struggle to be together again. Recent and renewed attention to family reunification has produced some promising practice approaches and new thinking about family connectedness and permanency for children. At the core of successful family reunification practice is a belief in "the essential bonds of the family, in the family's ability to make change, and in the importance of focusing on a family's strengths to achieve (and maintain) reunification" (Zamosky, Sparks, Hatt, & Sharman 1993:174) and a commitment to providing the services and supports that each family and child needs.

REFERENCES

Adler, M. A., Hax, H., Stanley, J., & Zhou, W. (2000). *Coordinated community responses to domestic violence in three Maryland communities*. Mississippi State, MS: Southern Sociological Society.

Adoption and Safe Families Act. (1997). P.L. 105-89.

Adoption Assistance and Child Welfare Act. (1980). P.L. 96-272.

Child Welfare League of America. (1989). *Standards for services to strengthen and preserve families with children*. Washington, DC: Child Welfare League of America.

Child Welfare League of America. (n.d.-a). *Glossary of terms*. Retrieved April 1, 2004, from www.cwla.org/newsevents/terms.htm.

Child Welfare League of America. (n.d.-b). *Summary of the Adoption and Safe Families Act of 1997*. Retrieved April 3, 2004, from www.cwla.org/advocacy/asfapl105-89summary.htm.

Colorado Department of Human Services. (2003). *Child and Family Services Review: Program improvement plan*. Retrieved April 1, 2004, from www.cdhs.state.co.us/cyf/cwelfare/PIP%2010-13.pdf.

Courtney, M. E., & Wong, Y. I. (1996). Comparing the timing of exits from substitute care. *Children and Youth Services Review, 18*, 307–334.

Davis, I. P., Landsverk, J., Newton, R., & Ganger, W. (1996). Parental visiting and foster care reunification. *Children and Youth Services Review, 18*, 363–382.

Festinger, T. (1996). Going home and returning to foster care. *Children and Youth Services Review, 18*, 383–402.

Frame, L., Berrick, J. D., & Brodowski, M. L. (2000). Understanding reentry to out-of-home care for reunified infants. *Child Welfare, 79*, 339–369.

Fraser, M. W., Nelson, K. E., & Rivard, J. C. (1997). Effectiveness of family preservation services. *Social Work Research, 21*(3), 138–153.

Fraser, M. W., Walton, E., Lewis, R. E., & Pecora, P. J. (1996). An experiment in family reunification: Correlates of outcomes at one-year follow-up. *Children and Youth Services Review, 18*, 335–361.

Hess, P. (1987). Parental visiting of children in foster care: Current knowledge and a research agenda. *Children and Youth Services Review, 9*, 29–50.

Hess, P. (ed.). (1999). *Visitation: Promoting positive visitation practices for children and their families through leadership, teamwork, and collaboration*. Harrisburg, PA: Commonwealth of Pennsylvania, Department of Public Welfare.

Hess, P. (2003). *Visiting between children in care and their families: A look at current policy*. New York: National Resource Center for Foster Care and Permanency Planning.

Hess, P., & Folaron, G. (1991). Ambivalences: A challenge to permanency for children. *Child Welfare, 60*, 403–424.

Hess, P., Folaron, G., & Jefferson, A. B. (1992). Effectiveness of family reunification services: An innovative evaluative model. *Social Work, 37*, 304–311.

Hess, P., & Proch, K. (1993). Visiting: The heart of reunification. In B. A. Pine, R. Warsh, & A. N. Maluccio (eds.), *Together again: Family reunification in foster care*, pp. 3–19. Washington, DC: Child Welfare League of America.

Hoffman, D., & Rosenheck, R. (2001). Homeless mothers with severe mental illnesses and their children: Predictors of family reunification. *Psychiatric Rehabilitation Journal, 25*(2), 163–169.

Hohman, M. M., & Butt, R. L. (2001). How soon is too soon? Addiction recovery and family reunification. *Child Welfare, 80*, 53–67.

Jones, L. (1998). The social and family correlates of successful reunification of children in foster care. *Children and Youth Services Review, 20*, 305–323.

Karoll, B. R., & Poertner, J. (2002). Judges', caseworkers', and substance abuse counselors' indicators of family reunification with substance-affected parents. *Child Welfare, 81*, 249–269.

Kirk, R. (2002). *Final project report: Tailoring Intensive Family Preservation Services for family reunification cases*. Retrieved February 20, 2004, from www.nfpn.org/tools/articles/files/researchreport.doc.

Landsverk, J., Litrownik, A. J., Newton, R., Granger, W., & Remmer, J. (1996). *Psychological impact of child maltreatment*. Washington, DC: National Center on Child Abuse and Neglect.

Landy, S., & Munro, S. (1998). Shared parenting: Assessing the success of a foster parent program aimed at family reunification. *Child Abuse and Neglect, 22*, 305–318.

Lewis, R. E. (1994). Application and adaptation of intensive family preservation services to use for the reunification of foster children with their biological parents. *Children and Youth Services Review, 16*, 339–361.

Maluccio, A. N., Abramczyk, L. W., & Thomlison, B. (1996). Family reunification of children in out-of-home care: Research issues and perspectives. *Children and Youth Services Review, 18*, 287–305.

Maluccio, A. N., Fein, E., & Davis, I. P. (1994). Family reunification: Research findings, issues, and directions. *Child Welfare, 73*, 489–504.

Maluccio, A. N., Warsh, R., & Pine, B. A. (1993). Family reunification: An overview. In B. A. Pine, R. Warsh, & A. N. Maluccio (eds.), *Together again: Family reunification in foster care*, pp. 3–19. Washington, DC: Child Welfare League of America.

McAlpine, C., Marshall, C. C., & Doran, N. H. (2001). Combining child welfare and substance abuse services: A blended model of intervention. *Child Welfare, 80*, 129–149.

National Family Preservation Network. (2003). *Intensive family reunification services protocol*. Retrieved April 3, 2004, from www.nfpn.org/reunification/files/ifrs_protocol.pdf.

Nugent, W. R., Carpenter, D., & Parks, J. (1993). A statewide evaluation of family preservation and family reunification services. *Research on Social Work Practice, 3*, 40–65.

Petr, C. G., & Entriken, C. (1995). Services system barriers to reunification. *Families in Society, 76*, 523–533.

Pierce, L., & Geremia, V. (1999). Family reunion services: An examination of a process used to successfully reunite families. *Family Preservation Journal, 4*(1), 13–30.

Pine, B. (1986). Child welfare reform and the political process. *Social Services Review, 60,* 339–359.

Pine, B. A., Warsh, R., & Maluccio, A. N. (eds.). (1993). *Together again: Family reunification in foster care.* Washington, DC: Child Welfare League of America.

Richie, B. E. (2001). Challenges incarcerated women face as they return to their communities: Findings from life history interviews. *Crime and Delinquency, 47*(3), 368–389.

Rzepnicki, T. L., Schuerman, J. R., & Johnson, P. (1997). Facing uncertainty: Reuniting high-risk families. In J. D. Berrick, R. P. Barth, & N. Gilbert (eds.), *Child welfare research review,* vol. 2, pp. 229–251. New York: Columbia University Press.

Staff, I., & Fein, E. (1994). Inside the black box: An exploration of service delivery in a family reunification program. *Child Welfare, 73,* 195–211.

Tatara, T. (1993). *Characteristics of children in substitute and adoptive care: A statistical summary of the VCIS national child welfare data base.* Washington, DC: American Public Welfare Association.

Terling, T. (1999). The efficacy of family reunification practices: Reentry rates and correlates of reentry for abused and neglected children reunited with their families. *Child Abuse and Neglect, 23,* 1359–1370.

U.S. Department of Health and Human Services. (2003a). *The AFCARS Report: Preliminary FY 2001 estimates as of March 2003 (8).* Retrieved November 13, 2003, from www.acf.hhs.gov/programs/cb/publications/afcars/report8.pdf.

U.S. Department of Health and Human Services. (2003b). *Child maltreatment 2001.* Washington, DC: U.S. Government Printing Office.

Waites, C., Macgowan, M. J., Pennell, J., Carlton-LaNey, I., & Weil, M. (2004). Increasing the cultural responsiveness of family group conferencing. *Social Work, 49,* 291–300.

Walton, E. (1998). In-home family-focused reunification: A six-year follow-up of a successful experiment. *Social Work Research, 22*(4), 205–214.

Walton, E., Fraser, M. W., Lewis, R. E., & Pecora, P. J. (1993). In-home family-focused reunification: An experimental study. *Child Welfare, 72,* 473–487.

Warsh, R., Maluccio, A. N., & Pine, B. A. (1994). *Teaching family reunification: A sourcebook.* Washington, DC: Child Welfare League of America.

Warsh, R., Pine, B. A., & Maluccio, A. N. (1996). *Reconnecting families: A guide to strengthening family reunification services.* Washington, DC: Child Welfare League of America.

Wells, E. A., Guo, S., & Li, F. (2000). *Impact of welfare reform on foster care and child welfare in Cuyahoga County, Ohio: Interim report.* Cleveland, OH: Mandel School of Applied Social Sciences, Case Western Reserve.

Zamosky, J., Sparks, J., Hatt, R., & Sharman, J. (1993). Believing in families. In B. A. Pine, R. Warsh, & A. N. Maluccio (eds.), *Together again: Family reunification in foster care,* pp. 155–175. Washington, DC: Child Welfare League of America.

ANTONIA CORDERO
IRWIN EPSTEIN

Refining the Practice of Family Reunification

"Mining" Successful Foster Care Case Records of Substance-Abusing Families

In this chapter, we demonstrate how a qualitative, clinical data-mining approach to practice-based research can contribute to knowledge development in foster care practice. More particularly, findings concerning substance-abusing families are extracted from a broader retrospective study of families mandated into care for reasons of neglect, domestic violence, or substance abuse. The larger study surfaces, refines, and illustrates relationships between factors that precipitate placement and differential casework practices with children, families, and foster parents that are associated with positive reunification. This chapter focuses on successful reunification practice with families affected by substance abuse.

Substance Abuse Factors in Foster Care

Substance abuse is a factor in two-thirds of the cases of children in foster care (Barth 2001; DiLorenzo, Johnson, & Bussey 2001; Schuck & Widom 2001; U.S. Department of Health and Human Services 1999; U.S. House Ways and Means Committee 2000). The Adoption and Safe Families Act of 1997 welfare reform legislation has heightened the need to address parental abuse effectively because foster care time frames have been reduced to expedite permanency planning decisions. For substance-abusing parents to recover from addiction and improve parenting, child welfare practitioners must perform accurate assessments, provide timely services, and conduct effective case plan-

ning (Hanson 2001; McGowan & Walsh 2000; Tracy & Pine 2000). When placement is necessary, attention must shift to the potential for prompt and healthy reunification of children and their families.

Unfortunately, however, little systematic attention has been paid to evaluating effective family reunification services with substance-abusing families (Semidei, Radel, & Nolan 2001; Special Child Welfare Advisory Panel 2000). In this practice-research vacuum, foster care administrators and practitioners function without a set of empirically derived reunification principles and interventions. Consequently, research on social work practice needs to examine and explicate the link between substance-abusing client characteristics, casework interventions, and positive family reunification outcomes (Davis, English, & Landsverk 1995; Holman & Butt 2001; Jones 1993; Van Bergeijk & McGowan 2001). Out of this reflective process, hypotheses about effective practice can be derived and systematically tested (Epstein & Blumenfeld 2001; Klein & Bloom 1995).

Strengths Perspective in Foster Care

Historically, the profession of social work has carried primary responsibility for the provision of services in foster care (Laird & Hartman 1985). Despite the acknowledged limitations of the foster care system, social work practice principles in child welfare emphasize the strengthening of family bonds and role of extended families and communities (Early & GlenMaye 2000; Gitterman 2001; Maluccio, Pine, & Tracy 2002). The family-centered practice approach supports and builds on family strengths and resilience (Early & GlenMaye 2000; Gitterman 2001; Maluccio, Pine, & Tracey 2002; Saleebey 1996). The practice principles of this approach include: (1) placing primacy on assessment and support of family strengths; (2) recognition of the family's ability to assess and understand their problematic functioning and situations; and (3) collaboration, partnership, and empowerment of family members to design strategies that achieve desired goals and outcomes.

The family-centered approach links the well-being of the child with the welfare of the family, supporting interventions that involve all family members in service planning and decisionmaking and mobilizing community and family strengths (Maluccio, Pine, & Tracey 2002; Van Bergeijk & McGowan 2001; Videka-Sherman & Mancini 2001). Proponents exemplify Maluccio, Warsh, and Pine's (1993) conception of family reunification as the planned process of reconnecting children in out-of-home care with their families to help them achieve and maintain their optimal level of reconnection.

Although these principles are clearly stated, they have yet to be fully explicated. When articulated, they are rarely grounded in practice-based research findings. In this chapter, we illustrate how qualitative "clinical data-mining" (Epstein & Blumenfield 2001) of positive reunification outcomes can be employed to identify case characteristics and provide examples of strength-based foster care practices with substance-abusing parents.

Method

Our study was conducted at a private, non-sectarian child welfare agency in New York City. The agency exemplified a high-quality family-centered practice approach, serving 500 children and 1,000 families in foster and kinship care. Similar to comparable foster-care agencies, it prided itself on comprehensive documentation of its foster care practices. However, documentation was primarily used for quality assurance and supervision rather than for practice-research purposes. Like many other New York City agencies, its client base was comprised primarily of low-income African American (73%) and Latino (23%) families.

Design

Practice-based research is defined as "the use of research-inspired principles, designs and information gathering techniques within existing forms of practice to answer questions that emerge from practice in ways that inform practice" (Epstein 2001:17). Clinical data-mining (CDM) is a practice-based research strategy Epstein has most recently advocated. In this approach, available clinical information is used to create retrospective databases for practice-based studies. In quantitative CDM, quantitative data are retrieved as is, and qualitative information is converted into quantitative data. Ultimately, the quantitative data are analyzed by computer to deteremine client characteristics, practice interventions, and treatment outcomes, and to explore the associations among these sets of variables (Epstein & Blumenfield 2001).

Although Rehr (2001) suggests the utility of this approach in studying social work interventions in health and mental health, her point applies to child welfare work as well. Similarly, child welfare workers routinely record enormous amounts of information about their clients, their interventions, and their practice outcomes. This information can be unintrusively mined to generate reliable, valid, and generalizable knowledge regarding child welfare practice. A recent doctoral dissertation demonstrates this with regard to intensive family preservation (Hanssen 2003).

Nonetheless, most researchers rarely examine the available clinical information, dismissing it as unreliable and subjective (Kagle 1996). As a result, the truth value of such information remains unexplored, stored in filing cabinets and/or computerized files used only for supervisory and administrative purposes.

In this chapter, we illustrate the contribution that *qualitative* CDM can make in refining foster care practice knowledge. To this end, a retrospective case review of successful reunification cases is employed to examine (1) behavioral characteristics that are attendant during reunification of families affected by substance abuse; (2) casework practices unique to reunification of families affected by substance abuse; and (3) common, strength-based casework practices that emerge from all cases during the reunification process.

Case Selection

Because of the amount of information contained within each case record (placement stays for the study's families ranged between 2 and 10 years), the study was limited to 18 case records. To reduce sampling error, these 18 were selected by systematically sampling every fifth record of all such case records. "Success" was operationally defined as those closed cases in which children were returned to a biological parent or a kinship guardian. Of the total sample, half were mandated into care for substance abuse. To promote validity and reliability, the first author conducted qualitative coding of all the data.

The child in care, the foster parent, the reunified family, and the caseworker's interventions were the central units of the analysis of the study process. A minimum criterion of 1 year in care was used in selecting the cases because,

TABLE 1. *Study Subgroups*

| Families | Placement Precipitants | | |
	Neglect	Domestic Abuse	Substance Abuse
Foster care	2	3	4
Kinship care	2	2	5

Note: N = 18.

it was assumed that after a year, families were more likely to have been reunited as a result of casework services rather than independent court mandates. In the larger study, family subgroups (foster care and kinship) were conceptualized and analyzed by placement precipitant (i.e., neglect, domestic violence, or substance abuse; see table 1).

Data Collection

In the absence of empirically tested foster care casework criteria, we employed the Professional Review Action Group (PRAG) model (Hess, Folaron, & Jefferson 1992) for assessing the quality of foster care practice for placement reentry as a template for identifying positive reunification activities. Hence the PRAG model was employed deductively as a conceptual framework to organize and focus the data collection and promote reliability in the retrieval of reunification practice elements (table 2).

Data Analysis

In accordance with the overall aim of practice-based research, our analysis seeks to provide

TABLE 2. *PRAG Model Case Activity Criteria*

1. Accurately identifying and assessing, with the family, the problems and needs that require placement to protect the child
2. Developing quality case plans that reflect accurate assessment, changes required for the child to be safe with the parents, agency and parent responsibilities, the permanency planning goal, and services to support achievement of the permanency goal
3. Engaging family members in appropriate services that specifically target identified problems and needs
4. Coordinating the multiple services provided to all family members, including foster family care and parent-child visiting
5. Monitoring and assessing the family's adherence to the service plan and the degree of actual changed achieved
6. Assessing whether and when reunification should occur
7. Preparing all family members for the transition process of the child's return home, including the development of a specific plan for the child's protection
8. Coordinating the continuation of services to support family members following reunification
9. Closely monitoring the child's safety in the home until reunification has stabilized

foster care social workers with a greater understanding of their practice through another accepted social work framework; that is, psychosocial stages of the helping process. Accordingly, the study utilized Meyer and Palleja's (1995) delineation of the helping process (exploration, assessment, intervention, and termination) as a combined deductive-inductive framework to identify and describe stages of the reunification process.

However, as an example of practice-based research, this study makes no claim at producing cause-effect evidence of the effectiveness of social work interventions. Instead, our intention is to locate and refine our understanding of casework practices and describe their utilization in the context of foster care best practices.

Findings and Case Illustrations

In general, the findings of this study suggest that there are case characteristics and casework practices that are commonly found during the reunification process with successfully reunified families; that is, stages of the reunification process (fig. 1).

Exploration Stage

Placement precipitants and engagement. Among the families mandated for substance abuse, the placement precipitant was commonly attributed to neglect arising from maternal substance abuse. For example:

> BM [biological mother] relayed to me [caseworker] a lot of her history. She talked about the difficulty of having her youngest child taken right from hospital because of positive drug toxicology.

However, there was ample evidence of children also being at risk due to paternal substance abuse (five of the nine families mandated into care for substance abuse had drug addicted fathers).

Engagement efforts were also commonly documented among the families mandated for substance abuse. Accordingly, workers' engagement efforts were directed at strengthening and enhancing parental/foster care relations with children in care:

> Although BF [biological father] has stated that he would attempt to visit children regularly, he has failed to visit consistently. CW [caseworker]

Exploration ▶▶	Assessment ▶▶	Intervention ▶▶	Termination
1. Placement Precipitant ▼ ▼ 2. Engagement of Family in: ▼ ▼ a. Family Reunions ▼ b. Assessment of Family Relations and Dysfunctional Behavioral Patterns	1. Family Strengths ▼ ▼ a. Parent-Child/Sibling Bonds and Supportive Kinship/Foster Parent Relations b. Therapy Compliance 2. Reunification Barriers ▼ a. Compromised Parental/Child Relations b. Placement Separation Anxiety c. Domestic Violence d. Substance Abuse e. Unplanned Pregnancy	1. Repairing Compromised Parental–Child Relations 2. Allaying Placement Separation 3. Challenging Domestic Violence Barriers 4. Disrupting Inconsistent Substance Abuse Patterns 5. Interrupting Unplanned Pregnancy Patterns	1. Mitigating Reunification Ambivalence 2. Reviewing the Family Rehabilitation Process 3. Monitoring the Final Phase of Reunification

FIGURE 1. Stages of the reunification process.

will schedule home visit to encourage him to visit regularly and involve him in planning for children.

CW has made home visits and feels comfortable discussing childcare issues with FM [foster mother]. FM is open to suggestions and is candid in her approach to caring for child.

Maternal family relations and transmission of dysfunctional intergenerational patterns. For the families in the larger study, the assessment of maternal family relations and dysfunctional behavioral family patterns was commonly documented during the exploration stage. Among families mandated for drug abuse, there was recorded evidence of positive maternal family involvement and support for the children's return to their mother:

MGM and I [caseworker] had a discussion about the history of BM's drug problem. . . . BM used to bring the kids to stay with her [MGM] whenever she [BM] was busy trying to get drugs. Gradually, it became more and more frequent until at one point the kids were simply living with her [MGM]. She has been very supportive of BM's role as mother.

Sadly, all of the families mandated for substance abuse had documented evidence of intergenerational patterns of severe childhood trauma and/or substance abuse:

Children have been transferred from the KMA [kinship maternal aunt] home to foster care. . . . KMA has pleaded guilty to sexually abusing her 16-year-old god daughter. . . . Her biological son was temporarily removed pending an investigation that he was being exposed to marijuana use by his uncle and aunt.

Assessment Stage

The larger study found extensive documentation of both individual and familial strengths as well as limitations. Documented strengths fell into the categories: (1) parent-child bonds, (2) sibling bonds, (3) supportive kinship/foster parent relations, and (4) therapy compliance.

Family strengths and therapy compliance. All of the families affected by substance abuse exhibited strengths as well as limitations. During the reunification process, workers charted the children's renewed or enhanced affectional bonds between the child in placement and the biological parent(s):

BM has a loving and nurturing relationship with her children. She visits her children consistently and expresses concern about their well-being. . . . BM has great strengths, which we [agency] believe will help her enhance the functioning of her family. However, these strengths will take time for her to enhance and implement.

In instances in which parental-child bonds were tenuous, kinship family bonds served as temporary parental replacements until the affectional bond with parents could be strengthened:

BM continues inconsistent visits with [her] child. . . . Child communicates well with KMGM [kinship maternal grandmother], who provides stability. . . . KMGM has been very supportive of her daughter's [biological mother] role as mother. She has allowed BM to participate in the child care responsibilities (such as shopping with them and [attending] school conferences). This has resulted in providing a close mother-child relationship.

Sibling bonds were a significant resource as well, mitigating placement separation anxiety by serving as a surrogate affectional bond until the parental bond could be reestablished:

Child currently resides in same foster home with her younger sister. The siblings have a good relationship and gain strength from each other. Child is protective of younger sister and they look to each other for support. . . . Younger sib [in care] has strong attachment to her sister and she has placed her in a parental role in order to fill the void of an absent mother.

Therapy compliance and sustained treatment gains of the biological parents were evident in all of the reunited families. Unique to the families mandated for substance abuse, workers recorded initial parental resistance to attending family therapy, followed by parental sobriety and treatment compliance:

> BM and children are seen in separate sessions. BM's sessions have focused on family communications, readjusting to family life, alternative to punishment and the development and use of coping skills. . . . The focus during the children's sessions [has] been the issues of readjustment as a family unit, sharing, peer pressure, and the development and use of coping skills. The children appear to enjoy the counseling sessions. They report that they apply, although not consistently, what they have learned to their daily lives. The family also participates in a parent and child group. They actively participate in the group discussion and activities.

For these families, drug detoxification and rehabilitation appeared to be a prerequisite for the achievement of sustained family treatment gains.

Reunification barriers. Recurrent barriers noted among the families affected by substance were (1) compromised parental-child relations, (2) placement separation anxiety, (3) domestic violence, (4) recurrent substance abuse, and (5) unplanned pregnancies.

For all families in the study, compromised parent-child relations manifested themselves in abdication of the parental role and responsibilities, or difficulty in managing children's behavior. At times these patterns were clearly associated with parents' poor intergenerational family relations. Often the mother's problematic childhood attachment experiences affected her ability to attach to her children.

Of particular note among families mandated for substance abuse was the frequency with which their children were placed into care, the early placement of the children, the duration of the placement, and the high likelihood that their children were to be discharged to a kinship guardian rather than returned to a biological parent. These characteristics pertained even in successful reunification cases:

A permanency planning goal of discharge to relative is being sought in order to provide consistency, stability and permanency in child's life. BM seems to be having difficulty correcting problems in her life. She has been noncompliant with entering drug rehabilitation since child has been in foster care, for over 4 years.

Separation anxiety triggered by the placement experience was evident in all the families under study. All children, many parents, and even some foster parents in the larger study displayed placement separation anxiety, ranging from the child's initial placement reaction to separation reactions during family visits. In this regard, there appeared no differences between families mandated into care for substance abuse and families in placement for neglect and domestic violence:

> The sib's removal from his natural family and removal from different foster homes has had a debilitating affect. . . . He has made progress in making the transition from one foster home to another. . . . He has decreased acting out behavior. He has also discussed his feelings about reunification; however, he is still insecure about his future and stability as a result of [his] unstable past.

However, children placed with kinship families appeared to have a tempered separation reaction; often having spontaneous unsupervised visits with their biological parents in the kinship home:

> The child's trial discharge to her mother's custody has gone smoothly, primarily because her mother has moved permanently into MGM's home and child has not had to change households. Child's relationship with mother and MGM are very close, and the family functions smoothly.

Irrespective of the mandated reason for placement, among all of the clinical records of families in the larger study there was documentation of what Bennett (1995) terms a "coincidence" or association between drug abuse and domestic violence: when one existed, so did the other. Among all families that were mandated for drug abuse, however, two prominently recorded barriers to reunification were domestic violence and drug relapse. In other words, all had a coincidence of domestic violence and substance abuse, and five of the nine drug-abusing families had histories of intergenerational domestic violence and substance abuse patterns:

> According to MGM, MGF [maternal grandfather] abused drugs and was emotionally and physically abusive toward MGM. MGM and her children left husband and they moved in with MGM's father. It is during this time that MGM reports BM became "rebellious" and ran away from home. . . . MGM believes that BM became involved with drugs during this time.

Drug abuse relapse was a recurring barrier that generated risk factors for many of the children in care:

> The child expressed his feelings strongly (about his parents continued drug use). . . . He was at the blackboard. When I [caseworker] saw the blackboard, it read something like this, "The boy was angry at his parents because they did drugs and he asked them to stop. If they keep doing it, he will do drugs."

In sum, it was common among substance-abusing mothers to carry the primary responsibility for child care, be reared in families affected by substance abuse and family violence, employ drugs as a primary coping mechanism, and be involved with drug-using partners.

Unplanned pregnancies were recurrent barriers to reunification for all families in the larger study. Among the drug-abusing families, however, there was a remarkable pattern of unplanned pregnancies (eight of nine families). Of these eight families, four parents had unplanned pregnancies just prior to the discharge of their children in care, substantially impeding planning and/or delaying reunification:

> Agency is requesting another extension of placement for all foster children for a variety of rea-

sons. . . . Another consideration involves the upcoming birth and its effects on the family. Agency would like an opportunity to assess the newborn's safety in the home before placing the older children with their parents.

Additionally, unplanned pregnancies locked the parents in conflictual relationships with abusive or substance-abusing partners, impeding the dependent parent's ability to insure the child's safety upon discharge from the placement:

> BM is in her eighth month and reports no medical problems during her pregnancy. . . . BM has reported several incidents of conflict between herself and husband in the past years, some involving violence. . . . CW witnessed loud, angry arguments between the BPs [birth parents] during home visit, at which one of their children in care (who was on a supervised visit) was present and was very frightened and upset.

Intervention Stage

Meyer and Palleja (1995) assert that assessment and intervention should be closely linked. For all reunified cases, there is a substantial congruence documented between social work interventions and assessed reunification barriers. Although a wide range of interventive strategies is documented in the larger study, their complexity and variations—along with individual family dynamics and histories—render comparative analysis of all interventions across the two sets of family subgroups impossible. However, the successful efforts of caseworkers to address common reunification barriers among drug abusing families are noted here.

Repairing compromised parental-child relations. Among families mandated for substance abuse, workers employed various interventions to address poor parental-child relations. During family visits, workers supported and monitored parent-child interactions:

> BM is planning for return of her children. It appears that she will need additional parenting skills in light of her difficulty at disciplining. . . . The

visits between BM and children have helped strengthened their relationship. These visits have helped the children become accustomed to the new role that their mother plays in their lives; that is, they now view her as a full-time caretaker and disciplinarian rather than someone with whom they simply visit.

Workers also attempted to reconcile estranged family members by engaging them in the reunification process, supporting the mother's substance abuse recovery, and/or minimizing the child's placement separation reaction:

CW asked MGM [about her] interests in the child. MGM said that she loved the child very much and would love to have her back with her. MGM cared for child prior to BM abandoning her to a friend's care. . . . MGM often encourages BM to visit with the child and participate in childcare responsibility.

Allaying placement separation anxiety. As with compromised parental-child relations, social workers documented a range of interventive efforts directed at allaying placement separation fears:

FM [foster mother] shared that child is doing well until she sees natural family and returns to FM. CW acknowledged how difficult it must be for FM to see child become so anxious at separation. FM is able to express her despair at not knowing how to calm her. CW tried to help FM understand child's feelings and alternatives in helping child deal with separation. CW emphasized that child needed to ventilate and it was not realistic to expect her not to cry. CW assured FM that in time, the separation will be less difficult for everyone.

Remarkably, placement fears among kinship children were rarely recorded. As previously mentioned, it appears that by its very nature, placement of children in kinship care may diminish reactive placement separation fears. In an apparent effort to capitalize on this factor, workers often set up parent-child reunions in the kinship home rather than in the agency. This practice appears to reduce the need for

treatment interventions to alleviate the children's separation reaction.

Confronting domestic violence barriers. Domestic violence–related interventions were recorded among almost all families affected by substance abuse. Workers employed a dual interventive focus toward drug-related domestic violence; that is, engaging the biological parents in drug rehabilitation and domestic violence counseling:

CW and BM discussed the safety of her children, what she wants for them, and her ability to be the primary caretaker. . . . It appears that the BF has been physically abusive to her and that BM is ambivalent about their future together. CW has tried to be supportive. She explained to BPs that this situation must be resolved before the children can be returned to the home. . . . BPs have been referred for domestic violence counseling.

This consistent pattern suggests recognition by workers that, in addition to drug dependency, entrenched drug-dependent/conflictual patterns (at times intergenerational in nature) needed to be addressed:

BM has a childlike quality about her. . . . Apparently, her mother [maternal grandmother] has been aware of BM's inability to take care of herself but has not helped her to have a sense of herself. MGM seems to be dominating personality and BM gives in as easily to her as [to] the men in her life. CW continues to support and monitor BM's participation in [domestic violence] group counseling.

Disrupting inconsistent recovery from substance abuse. Inconsistent recovery from substance abuse (drug relapse) was the most challenging problem workers recorded when working with families mandated for substance abuse. Intervention efforts included assisting parents to identify elements in their environment that triggered their relapses and aiding them to find alternative nondestructive coping mechanisms:

CW confronted BM about her lack of consistent attendance at drug program. BM said she has been very upset and sad, because her friend has AIDS. . . . BM keeps all of her feelings inside—all her anger, sadness, frustration, etc. When they become too much for her, she tends to use drugs.

Intervention efforts may also include assisting parents to address their drug relapse while employing administrative limit setting (e.g., changing the permanency planning goal to adoption) to assist parents confront the consequences of their resistance to drug rehabilitation:

There has been no progress made toward achieving the permanency plan of return to parent. BM has not complied with services nor cooperated with drug rehabilitation or parenting skills classes. The goal was changed to discharge from parent to relative. . . . After many discussions with KMGM and BM, she [BM] agreed with plan and has signed a notarized letter that she would like KMGM to become child's legal guardian. She continues to visit child and has not given up hopes to have child live with her some day.

Interrupting unplanned pregnancy patterns. Efforts to address reunification barriers posed by unplanned pregnancy patterns, although evident, were the least documented interventions. Nonetheless, there was evidence of some efforts to interrupt the unplanned pregnancy patterns that delayed discharge:

Oldest sib was pushing a baby carriage when CW made home visit. . . . He continued to say he didn't want to be pushing any strollers like his sister and her boyfriend. He stated that he plans to be "safe." He related that he has a new girlfriend in the neighborhood. . . . CW took this opportunity to review safe sex and to emphasize how important it was to avoid contracting STD [sexually transmitted dieases], HIV, AIDS, etc.

Termination Stage

Ambivalence about reunification. Patterns for all families in the larger study substantiate Hess and Folaron's (1991) contention that effective permanency planning requires addressing normative reunification ambivalence prior to return of the children in care. For families mandated for drug abuse, there was extensive documented evidence of ambivalence expressed about reunification by the child, parent, and/or placement guardian; supporting Meyer and Palleja's (1995) suggestion that the ending of the helping process may generate fear or reactivate feelings of loss.

Among the children in care, there was recorded evidence of their ambivalence about returning linked to their fear of parental abuse and drug relapse:

She appears to be angry and saddened by her father's abuse and her mother's inability to protect her from her father. . . . She told CW "I don't want to live Mom, if her Dad's at home." . . . Child continues to express ambiguous feelings in her relationship with mother. She desires to return home to the mother she loves but is not certain that her mother can stay off drugs.

In the case of the recovering substance-abusing parent, the loss of a dependent addictive lifestyle often triggered regressive behavior, compelling the worker to address this reactive termination response:

Discharge plan has been interrupted because of BM's return to her relationship with abusive BF. Unsupervised visitation will resume following BM's termination of drug use and proven commitment to leaving BF.

Kinship/foster parental reunification ambivalence was also frequently recorded. However, unlike the response to separation reaction evidenced by some placement guardians, kinship/foster parent reunification ambivalence addressed in the final stage of intervention did not undermine the reunification process:

FM asked CW when BM would be taking the child [in care] for an overnight visit. She sounded like she had strong feelings about BM's progress and how it would affect the child. FM added that it was not only becoming difficult each day for her to imagine the child leaving her [foster home] but that it was difficult for FM's relatives as well.

Reviewing the recovery process. During evaluation of the termination stage, the study found indications of distinct modes of rehabilitation for each mandated subgroup. Within each case record, there was a documented review of a recovery course pattern that was related to the respective family subgroup. Accordingly, in families mandated for substance abuse, parental sobriety appeared to be facilitated by workers' recognition and support of the normative drug recovery process. This support included an understanding of drug relapses as part of the rehabilitation process and attainment of long-term sobriety, identification of environmental and coping stressors that lead to relapse, development of the addicted parent's self-resolve for recovery, and attainment of a social network to support their newly recovering status:

> BF spoke of his drug treatment, his recovery, and the difficulty staying "clean." He told me (CW) that two of his friends had left the program to get high. These two men, like him, had arrived at the last step of recovery. He said that it was difficult for him to see this happen. He added, however, that by witnessing this, he had been able to see what kind of situation/environment to stay away from to avoid "picking up." He stated, "It's all about people and places. If you're able to stay away from the people who are using drugs and the places in which they hang out, then that's the best way to avoid getting pulled in." BF appeared positive about his recovery.

Monitoring of the final reunification phase. Case records of families mandated for substance abuse documented evidence of workers' monitoring the period of unsupervised visiting/trial discharge and the provision of future preventive services:

> Agency is requesting permission to start weekend visits of the children with their BM. . . . BM has secured adequate housing and is visiting children consistently. . . . CW informed BM that she was proud of her accomplishments in completing drug program. But at present time, she needed to give her children priority in her life, not an abusive relationship. BM said she asked husband to leave at the end of the month. . . . Children are visiting weekends. . . . The goal is to enroll BM and children into family therapy. . . . Trial discharge has been requested. . . . CW sent BM [a] community referral for ongoing family therapy. . . . Preventive services will be requested for this family. Services will include individual counseling, family therapy, and random drug testing.

Implications

The study's examination of the case records of successfully reunified drug-abusing families documented the four stages of the reunification helping process. Accordingly, there are a number of practice implications that are consistent with and/or refine existing theory concerning work with families mandated for substance abuse. These implications are discussed here.

The evidence of positive parent/kinship-child and sibling bonds among successfully reunited families supports Videka-Sherman and Mancini's (2001) assertion about the importance of workers' assessing parental-child interaction patterns. In addition, the findings support Newcomb and Locke's (2001) proposition that there is a link between the parent's childhood maltreatment experiences and their manner of relating to their children. Consequently, caseworkers are encouraged to use family genograms to assess intergenerational strengths and dysfunctional family patterns.

The study findings suggest that participation in family therapy aids the process of repairing family relations. Although treatment courses varied in length and focus among the families, there was evidence that sustained treatment participation improved child and parental/extended family relations, underscoring the premise of Gitterman (2001) and Early and

GlenMaye (2000) of family resilience and suggesting that mental health intervention can interrupt dysfunctional family patterns.

As was evident in other studies (Hans 1999; Schuck & Widom 2001), childhood trauma and substance abuse were precipitating factors for the study's biological mothers, resulting in compromised integrity of the family system, dysfunctional behavioral patterns, and child neglect. This maternal pattern supports Jones, Hughes, and Unterstaller's (2001) call for gender differences in addiction and treatment approaches. Consequently, caseworkers are encouraged to follow the prescriptive advice of Holman and Butt (2001): understand the addiction process to help addicted mothers address unresolved childhood trauma; identify components of the environment that are stressors that trigger their substance use; and assist addicted mothers in developing and using effective, safe, and nondestructive alternative coping strategies. In short, by understanding the recovery process, workers can translate the essential components of recovery into an effective reunification plan.

Although half the study's 18 families were mandated into care for drug abuse, the case records documented that 14 of the 18 families were in some way affected by substance abuse. This finding corroborates Rittner and Dozier's (2000) contention that, although most child welfare professionals recognize the association of substance abuse and child welfare referrals, actual rates of child abusers who are substance abusers are unknown because not all investigated families are carefully screened for substance use. Therefore, with increasing numbers of child welfare families mandated into care, accurate assessments by child welfare workers of current and past family substance use for all families mandated into care is essential for effective case planning.

In conclusion, the findings suggest that child welfare curriculum should include (1) resilience theory in relation to attachment bonds; (2) acknowledgment of placement separation anxiety

and reunification ambivalence as a normative part of the foster care process; (3) assessment tools to identify family strengths and dysfunctional intergenerational patterns; and (4) knowledge of the essential components of the addiction/recovery process and to develop an effective reunification plan.

Limitations

Clearly, clinical data-mining studies have methodological limitations. In this instance, 18 carefully selected foster care case records represented the sole data source. Case records do reflect the worker's subjective view of the practice experience. Moreover, child welfare agencies are often constrained by structural service delivery limitations (e.g., high crisis-oriented service demands vs. fixed staff resources). At times, they may prioritize provision of crisis service over service documentation, affecting the integrity of service recording and, in turn, the validity of the findings of data-mining studies.

In addition, although the agency under study is typical of a private nonsectarian contracted agency, the use of only one agency in the study limits the generalizability of the findings. Even though unplanned pregnancy, domestic violence, substance abuse, and reunification ambivalence patterns were evident among virtually all of the larger study's families, the limited size of the total sample and subsamples requires that further research be undertaken to evaluate the extent to which these patterns are prevalent in the general foster care population and their effects on the reunification process.

Despite the aforementioned limitations, the illustrative richness and clear practice implications of the findings suggest that qualitative clinical data-mining can be a valuable tool in practice-based research.

Conclusion

Substance abuse compromises the integrity of the family system, in some cases leading to cyclical intergenerational behavioral patterns. As a result, the reunification process must engage and assess the drug-addicted parent in context of their strengths, reunification barriers, and the environment. Tracy and Farkas (1994) suggest the assessment should include family history and behavioral patterns (including kinship and foster care relations) that affect drug-abusing parents and the intergenerational risk factors to the children in care. In doing so, the worker can develop a comprehensive assessment and implement effective intervention strategies. In the termination stage, workers need to address reunification ambivalence as manifested by regressive parental behaviors, such as drug relapses, and reactive fears expressed by the children in care or by their placement guardians.

Family reunification is a challenging area of child welfare practice about which there is little evidence-based research. In this chapter, we have demonstrated the potential of qualitative clinical data-mining in refining foster care practice. Findings underscore the feasibility of this practice-based research approach for describing agency practice, refining training protocols, and enhancing social work curricula.

REFERENCES

Adoption and Safe Families Act. (1997). P.L. 105-89.

Barth, R. (2001). Research outcomes of prenatal substance exposure and the need to review policies and procedures regarding child abuse reporting. *Child Welfare, 80,* 275–295.

Bennett, L. (1995). Substance abuse and the domestic assault of women. *Social Work, 40,* 760–771.

Davis, I., English, D., & Landsverk, J. (1995). *Outcomes of permanency planning for 1166 foster children.* Study report for federal grant 90CW 1075. San Diego, CA: San Diego State University School of Social Work and San Diego County Department of Social Services.

DiLorenzo, P., Johnson, R., & Bussey, M. (2001). The role of spirituality in the recovery process. *Child Welfare, 80,* 257–273.

Early, T., & GlenMaye, L. (2000). Valuing families: Social work practice with families from a strengths perspective. *Social Work, 45,* 118–130.

Epstein, I. (2001). Using available clinical information in practice-based research: Mining for silver while dreaming of gold. In I. Epstein & S. Blumenstein (eds.), *Clinical data-mining in practice-based research: Social work in hospital settings,* pp. 15–31. Binghampton, NY: Haworth Press.

Epstein, I., & Blumenfield, S. (eds.). (2001). *Clinical data-mining in practice-based research: Social work in hospital settings.* Binghampton, NY: Haworth Press.

Gitterman, A. (ed.). (2001). *Handbook of social work practice with vulnerable and resilient populations.* New York: Columbia University Press.

Hans, S. (1999). Demographics and psychosocial characteristics of substance-abusing pregnant women. *Clinical Perinatology, 26,* 55–67.

Hanson, M. (2001). Alcoholism and other drug addictions. In A. Gitterman (ed.), *Handbook of social work practice with vulnerable and resilient populations,* pp. 64–96. New York: Columbia University Press.

Hanssen, D. (2003). *Looking inside the black box of intensive family preservation services.* Doctoral dissertation, City University of New York.

Hess, P., & Folaron, G. (1991). Ambivalence: A challenge to permanency for children. *Child Welfare, 70,* 402–425.

Hess, P., Folaron, G., & Jefferson, A. (1992). Effectiveness of family reunification services: An innovative evaluative model. *Social Work 37,* 304–309.

Holman, M., & Butt, R. (2001). How soon is too soon? Addiction recovery and family reunification. *Child Welfare, 80,* 54–67.

Jones, L. (1993). Decision making in child welfare: A critical review of the literature. *Child and Adolescent Social Work Journal, 10,* 241–262.

Jones, L., Hughes, M., & Unterstaller, U. (2001). Posttraumatic stress disorder (PSTD) in victims of domestic violence: A review of the research. *Trauma, Violence & Abuse, 2,* 99–119.

Kagle, J. D. (1996). *Social work records,* second edition. Prospect Heights, IL: Waveland Press.

Klein, W., & Bloom, M. (1995). Practice wisdom. *Social Work, 40,* 799–808.

Laird, J., & Hartman, A. (eds.). (1985). *A handbook of child welfare: Context, knowledge and practice.* New York: Free Press.

Maluccio, A., Pine, B., & Tracy, E. (2002). *Social work practice with families and children.* New York: Columbia University Press.

Maluccio, A., Warsh, R., & Pine, B. (1993). Family reunification: An overview. In B. Pine, R. Warsh, & A. Maluccio (eds.), *Together again: Family reunification in foster care,* pp. 3–19. Washington, DC: Child Welfare League of America.

McGowan, B., & Walsh, E. (2000). Policy challenges for child welfare in the new century. *Child Welfare, 29,* 11–27.

Meyer, C., & Palleja, J. (1995). Social work practice with individuals. In C. Meyer & M. Mattaini (eds.), *The foundation of social work practice,* pp. 105–125. Washington, DC: NASW Press.

Newcomb, M., & Locke, T. (2001). Intergenerational cycle of maltreatment: A popular concept obscured by methodological limitations. *Child Abuse, 25,* 1219–1240.

Rehr, H. (2001). Foreword. In I. Epstein & S. Blumenstein (eds.), *Clinical data-mining in practice-based research: Social work in hospital settings,* pp. xv–xxiv.
Binghampton, NY: Haworth Press.

Rittner, B., & Dozier, C. (2000). Effects of court-ordered
substance abuse treatment in child protective services case. *Social Work, 45,* 131–140.

Saleebey, D. (1996). The strength perspective in social
work practice. White Plains, NY: Longman.

Schuck, C., & Widom, C. (2001). Childhood victimization and alcohol symptoms in females: Causal inferences and hypothesized mediators. *Child Abuse and
Neglect, 25,* 1069–1092.

Semidei, J., Radel, L., & Nolan, C. (2001). Substance
abuse and child welfare: Clear linkages and promising
responses. *Child Welfare, 80,* 109–128.

Special Child Welfare Advisory Panel. (2000). Advisory
report on front line and supervisory practice. New
York: Special Child Welfare Advisory Panel.

Tracy, E., & Farkas, K. (1994). Preparing practitioners
for child welfare with substance-abusing families.
Child Welfare, 73, 57–67.

Tracy, E., & Pine, B. (2000). Child welfare education and
training: Future trends and influences. *Child Welfare,
79,* 93–113.

U.S. Department of Health and Human Services. (1999).
*Blending perspectives and building common ground. A
report to Congress on substance abuse and child protection.* Retrieved May 23, 2000, from aspe.hhs.gov/hsp/
subabuse99/subabuse.htm.

U.S. House Ways and Means Committee. (2000). Recent trends affecting child welfare populations and
programs. In *The 2001 green book,* section 11, pp. 106–
114. Washington, DC: U.S. Government Printing
Office. Retrieved March 5, 2003, from aspe.hhs.gov/
2000gb/sec11.txt.

Van Bergeijk, E., & McGowan, B. (2001). Children in
foster care, In A. Gitterman (ed.), *Handbook of social
work practice with vulnerable and resilient populations,*
pp. 399–434. New York: Columbia University Press.

Videka-Sherman, L., & Mancini, M. (2001). Children in
foster care. In A. Gitterman (ed.), *Handbook of social
work practice with vulnerable and resilient populations,*
pp. 367–398. New York: Columbia University Press.

MARK F. TESTA

JENNIFER MILLER

Evolution of Private Guardianship as a Child Welfare Resource

The right of every child to guardianship of the person (Smith 1955), either natural guardianship by birth or adoption, or legally appointed guardianship by the courts (Smith 1955; Weissman 1964), was first promulgated by child welfare professionals in the 1950s. The impetus was the discovery that many dependent and neglected children and child beneficiaries of federal cash assistance programs—veteran's pensions, survivor benefits, and aid to dependent children—lacked the protection of either a natural or legal guardian to safeguard the child's interests, make important decisions in the minor's life, and maintain a personal relationship with the child (Breckinridge & Stanton 1943; U.S. Department of Health and Human Services 1961). Consideration was given briefly in the 1960s to promoting private guardianship as a permanency option by offering subsidies to relatives and foster parents who assumed legal responsibility for foster children (Taylor 1966). But this approach was soon eclipsed by more aggressive efforts in the 1970s to conserve children's natural guardianship through family preservation and reunification, and when this was not possible, to secure its substitute through adoption.

Interest in subsidized guardianship rekindled in the 1980s for the thousands of neglected and abused children placed formally in foster

Portions of this chapter originally appeared in Testa, M. (2004), When children cannot return home: Adoption and guardianship, *Future of Children: Children, Families, and Foster Care*, 14(1), 115–130. Published by the David and Lucile Packard Foundation.

care with kin. States were searching for novel permanency options that were less disruptive of familial relationships than termination of parental rights and adoption. Finally, in the 1990s, the federal government acted on this interest by granting waivers to states to mount demonstrations in the use of Title IV-E funds to finance subsidized guardianship programs for foster children who otherwise would have remained in public custody.

In this chapter, we trace the evolution of private guardianship as a child welfare resource, starting with Hasseltine Taylor's (1935) *Law of Guardian and Ward*. Thirty years after her publication in 1935, she called for a federal demonstration to test the benefits and costs of providing financial subsidies to families who assume private guardianship of dependent and neglected children. Her plea went unheeded, however, as permanency planning advocates rallied around the passage of the Adoption Assistance and Child Welfare Act (AACWA) of 1980 (P.L. 96-272), which emphasized family reunification and adoption as solutions to "foster care drift." We analyze the waning enthusiasm over the act's capacity to deliver on its promise of permanence. Perceptions that professional resistance to transracial placement and an overemphasis on family preservation were working against adoption prompted passage of federal laws in the 1990s that outlawed the use of race in placement decisions and narrowed the circumstances in which reasonable efforts must be pursued to preserve the biological family. During this time, the growth of kinship foster care prompted reconsideration of subsidized guardianship as a permanency option and led to an increase in the number of states subsidizing guardianship through federal waivers, state funding, and the Temporary Assistance for Needy Families (TANF) block grant. The growth of subsidized guardianship initiatives has also led to an understanding of the components that contribute to guardianship arrangements that insure safety, stability, and permanence for children.

Since the passage of the Adoption and Safe Families Act (ASFA) of 1997 (P.L. 105-89), states have succeeded in making good on President Clinton's challenge of doubling the number of adoptions and guardianships over a 5-year period (McDonald, Salyers, & Testa 2003). Forecasts prepared by the Congressional Budget Office (1999) predict that the number of children in assisted permanent arrangements may soon surpass the number of children remaining in foster care. Now these successes are spawning their own counterreactions. Concern is mounting that relatives and foster parents are being pressured into making ill-considered commitments, which will result in thousands of children returning to public custody. Anticipation of these risks has sparked debate over whether private guardianship is sufficient for maintaining family commitments or whether termination of parental rights and adoption must be pursued to make these commitments legally binding. Whatever the outcome, there is growing consensus that postpermanency services and adequate financial subsidies must be supplied to adoptive and guardian families to preserve the stability of these living arrangements. The chapter concludes with a discussion of possible changes that may be in store for public child welfare as state and local systems adapt to the shifting balance between foster care and permanence in the care and protection of neglected and abused children.

Evolution of Private Guardianship as a Child Welfare Resource

The institution of guardianship was well established in American legal history prior to the law of adoption (Taylor 1966). Deriving from English Common Law (Weissman 1950), the law of guardian and ward was originally fashioned to safeguard the inheritance of orphaned children. For this reason, the authority to appoint guardians of the property and person of the child (also called "private guardianship") was lodged in probate courts.

State child welfare statutes later extended the law of guardian and ward beyond the protection of orphans to the guardianship of the persons of dependent, neglected, and abused children whose parents were unwilling or unable to exercise proper care and supervision. The transfer of guardianship of the persons of dependent, neglected, and abused children from the birth parent to an agency administrator, probation officer, or county or state department (also called "public guardianship") has become routine in most court-ordered child protection and foster care.

Despite its long history, it is only recently that child welfare authorities have seriously begun to explore the use of private guardianship as a way to provide children in foster care a route to permanency. The foundation for this thinking was laid down in the 1935 monograph by Hasseltine B. Taylor. She proposed that private guardianship be extended to all children, not only those with property, who lacked the natural guardianship of parents by reason of death, absence, neglect, or abuse. Her proposal encompassed children formally placed in foster care as well as children left informally by parents in the care of relatives, friends, and neighbors.

Responding to this proposal and related work by Breckinridge and her students (Breckinridge & Stanton 1943), the Children's Bureau sponsored a study of the need for guardianship in postwar America (Weissman 1964). The problem had grown more prominent as a result of war casualties; family disruption; and children's eligibility for social security, veteran's, and welfare benefits in cases for which there was no parent to oversee the expenditure of funds.

Despite the documented need, the federal study revealed that private and public guardianship were infrequently used as a child welfare resource.

The Children's Bureau report (Weissman 1964) recommended the development of procedures for finding and routinely reporting children in need of guardianship so that new guardians could be judicially appointed. It urged that such procedures also be used to regulate the passing along of children to the informal custody of relatives, friends, and neighbors. But it stopped short of recommending making such procedures mandatory. Although acknowledging that unlike birth or adoptive parents, guardians were not legally liable for the support of their wards, the report made no special recommendations regarding compensation of private guardians or the provision of public subsidies to offset the costs of guardianship. In subsequent work, Weissman (1950) acknowledged this omission but gave assurances that the Children's Bureau recognized the importance of adequate financial compensation for securing safe and stable homes for children under private guardianship.

The case for subsidized guardianship was first made in an article that Taylor (1966) published thirty years after her *Law of Guardian and Ward*. In it, she proposed a federal demonstration to test whether a permanent home with a court-appointed guardian was preferable to long-term foster care. She cited the lack of a publicly provided subsidy to children with nonrelated guardians (Aid to Families with Dependent Children [AFDC] was available to related guardians) as a major impediment to the wider use of private guardianship as an alternative to foster care. She suggested that a demonstration would not only help to assess the costs of expanding eligibility for public assistance beyond parents and related custodians but would also help deal with the uncertainty that some agencies and workers felt over whether guardianship added much value beyond what adoption or substitute care already provided.

Preference for Natural Guardianship by Birth or Adoption

Interest in private guardianship as a child welfare resource took a back seat in the 1970s as the nascent "permanency planning" movement gave new urgency to the principle of every child's right to natural guardianship through birth or adoption. Child advocates and policymakers had viewed with alarm the substantial numbers of children remaining in foster care for long periods, often until they reached adulthood (Pike, Downs, & Emlem 1977). Recognition of every child's need for permanence had been building since the problem of foster care drift was first documented in 1959 (Maas & Engler 1959). The permanency planning movement emphasized the psychological damage inflicted on foster children in allowing them to drift aimlessly in public custody without a plan for permanence. The incorporation of psychoanalytical concepts helped to legitimize the concern by underscoring the importance of permanent attachment relationships for healthy child development (Bowlby 1969; Goldstein, Freud, & Solnit 1973).

In the 1970s, the Children's Bureau funded a child welfare demonstration in the state of Oregon, which helped to popularize the concept of permanency planning. Its purpose was to test the feasibility of finding permanent homes for children who otherwise would have grown up in long-term foster care (Emlen, Lahti, & Downs 1978). Although the architects of the Oregon demonstration recognized legally appointed guardianship as a form of permanence, they placed primary emphasis on upholding natural guardianship through either reunification or adoption. As they explained, the customary way in which children's rights, welfare, and interests are protected in American society is by those adults whom the law holds to be their parents, either biological or adoptive (Emlen, Lahti, & Downs 1978). Termination of parental rights and adoption provide a legally binding means of establishing a substitute parental relationship when the dereliction of guardianship by biological parents is sufficiently egregious to warrant the child's permanent separation from them.

The preference for biological or adoptive parenthood over legal guardianship found expression in AACWA of 1980. That act required states to make "reasonable efforts" to preserve families prior to foster placement, or if the child must be removed, to make possible the child's timely return to the home. In situations in which reunification was judged not to be in the child's best interest, AACWA permitted states to make adoption assistance payments to adoptive parents of foster children with special needs. AACWA (1980:1114) defined "special needs" as:

> A specific factor or condition (such as the child's ethnic background, age, or membership in a minority or sibling group, or the presence of factors such as medical conditions or physical, mental, or emotional handicaps) because of which it is reasonable to conclude that such child cannot be placed with adoptive parents without providing adoption assistance.

Although AACWA also recognized legal guardianship as a permanency option, it made no special provision for guardianship assistance payments similar to the assistance available to adoptive parents of foster children.

Tilt Toward Termination of Parental Rights and Adoption

A decade after AACWA enunciated every child's right to natural guardianship by birth or adoption, optimism over the act's capacity to bring stability and security to the lives of foster children began to fade. Although reliable time series on foster care trends are lacking for the period immediately prior to AACWA's passage, some federal officials pieced together statistics from different sources to advance the claim that the number of children in out-of-home care had decreased dramatically as a result of AACWA— from an estimated half million in 1977 to less than one-quarter million in 1983. Other ob-

servers disputed this assertion (Steiner 1981), citing Title IV-E statistics that failed to show any such pattern consistent with so dramatic a change. Nonetheless, whatever gains may have been made care following AACWA's passage in reducing the numbers of children in out-of-home care, voluntary reporting of foster care statistics from the states showed that by the late 1980s, foster care caseloads were again on the rise.

Between FY1986 and FY1990, the size of the U.S. foster care population expanded by 45%: from 280,000 to 407,000 (Tatara 1991). Analysis of the "flow" of children into and out of the foster care system, as reported to the Voluntary Cooperative Information System (VCIS)[1] suggested that some of the rise could be attributed to the increased intake of children into foster care due to parental drug addiction, concentrated urban poverty, and the AIDS epidemic. However, in the opinion of the lead researcher at the American Public Welfare Association who maintained the VCIS archive (Tatara 1993), the size of the substitute care population had grown mainly because of a marked decline in the rate of exits from care, which contributed to the accumulation of children in long-term foster care.

One of the explanations Tatara (1993) offered for the accumulation was the apparent success of family preservation programs in keeping intact the natural guardianship of birth parents and preventing out-of-home placements. To the extent that family preservation programs are successful in preventing removal,

[1] VCIS was operated by the American Public Welfare Association and funded by the U.S. Department of Health and Human Services. It collected information voluntarily submitted by the states and compiled it in an annual report starting in FY1982. Prior to the development of the Adoption and Foster Care Analysis and Reporting System, VCIS was the primary source of data on the national child welfare system and the only source of comprehensive data estimates on the adoption of special needs children who at some time had been part of the substitute care system.

the residual group of children who ultimately are placed poses a greater challenge to ordinary reunification efforts because family preservation and in-home services have already been attempted and failed.

Even though experimental evaluations of family preservation programs repeatedly have demonstrated that the most expensive and intensive programs (e.g., Homebuilders™) are not worth the extra outlay, the success of many intact family services should not be overlooked. For example, the Illinois Family First Evaluation showed that at 1 year after service initiation, 27% of the families in the experimental group had at least one child removed from their custody (Schuerman, Rzepnicki, & Littell 1994). Among families receiving regular intact family services, the placement rate was 21% during the same time period. Thus although intensive family prevention proved less effective than regular intact family services in preventing placement, the fact still stands that more than two-thirds of families in both groups remained intact many months after the conclusion of services.

As the emphasis on intact family services restricted the flow of children into the public foster care system to only those with the most challenging family histories, child protection and adoption advocates began voicing concerns that states might be going too far in upholding the natural guardianship of birth parents. They found fault with both the courts and child welfare agencies for continuing to adhere to reasonable efforts requirements to return the child home many months after initial placement prevention efforts had failed. They charged that many states misinterpreted "reasonable efforts" to mean "every effort" and that AACWA perpetuated the malpractice of allowing children to spend too many years detached from their biological parents while preventing them from forming any new attachments to their foster homes, which often changed many times throughout the course of their foster care stays (O'Laughlin 1998).

As the gap between the numbers of exits from and entrants to the child welfare system widened, the size of the foster care population swelled during the early 1990s to more than 500,000 children—the highest ever reported by states up to that time. According to surveys collected by the Child Welfare League of America (1994), at least 100,000 of the 500,000 children in foster care were waiting for adoptive homes. Yet only 27,000 children were adopted from public foster care in the mid-1990s.

The disparity between the large number of children in foster care who needed permanent homes and the smaller number actually adopted prompted President Clinton in 1996 to direct the secretary of Health and Human Services to make specific recommendations for doubling, over the next 5 years, the annual number of foster children who are adopted or permanently placed. This resulted in Adoption 2002, an initiative to promote bipartisan federal leadership in adoption and other permanent placements for children in the public child welfare system (Duqette, Hardin, & Dean 1999). Shortly thereafter, Congress passed ASFA (in 1997).

The new law specifically addressed the concern that states had been misinterpreting "reasonable efforts" to mean every effort to prevent removal or return a child home. ASFA clarified that the child's health and safety shall be the paramount concern in making such efforts. It also identified a number of circumstances in which reasonable efforts would not be required. These included circumstances in which the parent had subjected the child to aggravated abuse and neglect, such as torture, sexual abuse, and abandonment, or when the parent had murdered or committed voluntary manslaughter of another child of the parent or if the rights of the parent to a sibling had been terminated previously.

ASFA once again recognized guardianship as a permanency option, but did not address the need for financial assistance to support guardianship families or acknowledge it as a potential remedy for helping children exit foster care.

Rather, ASFA endorsed adoption as the primary solution for the backlog of children in foster care who could not or should not return home. It sought to counter court inertia by tightening two important timelines for children regarding permanency hearings and the termination of parental rights. It requires a permanency hearing to be held within 12 months of the child's entering foster care. ASFA also requires that the state file or join a petition to terminate the parental rights of any child if he or she has been in foster care for 15 of the past 22 months. Exceptions to this requirement are: a relative is caring for the child, a compelling reason exists why termination would not be in the best interests of the child, or the state did not provide "reasonable efforts" for reunification, if necessary.

ASFA contains no special provisions to increase the supply of adoptive homes. But it did seek to lessen the financial disincentives to permanence by authorizing the payment of adoption bonuses to states, which can amount to as much as $6,000 per child adopted. Congress assumed that an adequate supply of homes existed but that resistance to transracial adoption and foot dragging by the states and the courts in terminating parental rights had interfered with the supply connecting up to the demand for permanent homes. While state and federal initiatives concentrated on the recruitment of new adoptive homes, however, a revolution in permanency planning with kin was quietly unfolding at the state level. The increasing recognition that kin were valuable permanency resources for children raised the potential for subsidized guardianship to a new level.

Growth of Kinship Foster Care

Innovations in permanency planning with kin were stimulated by the growing public reliance on relatives as foster parents in the late 1980s (U.S. Department of Health and Human Services 2000). Although relatives had always provided the first line of protection for children who could not live with their birth parents, most of this caregiving occurred informally, outside of the child welfare system. When grandparents, aunts, and uncles needed financial aid to care for their dependent kin, they were usually referred to state and federal public assistance programs rather than to the foster care system. Even when children were formally removed from parental custody and placed with kin, most public agencies continued to pay relatives the lower public assistance amount even if their home qualified for the higher licensed foster care subsidy (Testa 1997).

This practice of disparate treatment of kin and non-kin was struck down as unconstitutional by the 1979 Supreme Court decision, *Miller vs. Youakim*. This ruling stipulated that families who met the same foster home licensing standards as nonrelatives could not be denied federal foster care benefits for reasons of kinship alone.

The impact of *Miller vs. Youakim* on foster care caseloads was not fully felt until the mid-1980s. Between 1986 and 1990, the percentage of children placed in formal foster care with relatives rose from 18% to 31% of public placements in the 25 states that were able to supply such information to the U.S. Department of Health and Human Services (Spar 1993). During the same period, the absolute number of foster care placements grew nationally by 45% from 280,000 to 407,000 (Tatara 1993). By comparison, the population receiving federal public assistance under AFDC grew by only 6% and the U.S. child population by less than 1% (U.S. House Ways and Means Committee 1994).

The growth of kinship foster care after 1986 can be interpreted as a response to two developments. First, it was in response to growing concerns in many circles that the racial and ethnic heritage of children should be given primary consideration in placement decisions. This perspective had reached a pinnacle of support in 1979, with the passage of the Indian Child Welfare Act (ICWA), which deferred to the wishes of extended families and tribal communities in the placement of Native American children. ICWA gave tribes the authority to intervene in state courts, even against parental wishes, and to challenge the placement of children outside the Native American community. Claims to similar preferences for consideration of a child's extended family relationships grew in the wake of ICWA. This perspective is reflected in the statutory preferences for kinship placements, which many states passed in the late 1980s (Gleeson & Craig 1994).

Second, formal placement with kin was a reaction to the limited capacity of the child welfare system to recruit an adequate supply of licensable foster homes, particularly in inner city neighborhoods (Leos-Urbal, Bess, & Geen 2000). With the spike in foster care demand as a result of the spread of HIV, concentrated poverty, and cocaine and other drug addition, public welfare authorities increasingly turned to relatives to enforce state child protective laws.

As the national foster care population expanded from 400,000 foster children in 1990 to more than 500,000 children in 1995 (U.S. House Ways and Means Committee 2002), child welfare researchers began spotting connections between the caseload growth and the rise in kinship foster care. They noticed that although foster children living with kin tended to have more stable placements than did children living with non-kin (Iglehart 1994; Scannapieco, Hegar, & McAlpine 1997; Wulczyn & Goerge 1992), their rates of reunification and adoption were much lower (Berrick, Barth, & Needell 1994; Testa 1997; Thornton 1991), thereby contributing to the backlog of foster children in long-term care.

In an effort to resolve the anomaly of greater placement stability but diminished legal permanence, researchers initiated a number of studies on kinship care and permanence. Some of the early research suggested that although relatives were prepared to raise their dependent kin to adulthood, they were reluctant to adopt. For example, some scholars reported that most caregivers were resistant to the idea of adopting their own kin because their attachment was already sealed by blood ties (Thornton 1991). Other observers posited that African American customs worked against the formalization of kinship bonds through adoption (Burnette 1997). At the same time, awareness grew of the cultural resistance to termination of parental rights in the Native American community. The growth of "customary adoption" as a way to retain kinship ties and tribal identity was also a factor (Cross 2003).

Mindful of the long-standing African American tradition of informal adoption and Native American interest in customary adoption, both of which did not necessitate terminating parental rights, policy analysts began searching for alternative permanency options that were less disruptive of customary kinship norms than adoption. Time and again, the search led back to the guardianship discussions that the Children's Bureau had initiated in the aftermath of World War II.

Rediscovery of Private Guardianship as a Child Welfare Resource

Most child welfare advocates today accept the principle, as did Taylor decades ago, that adoption is clearly superior to guardianship and long-term foster care wherever it is both possible and appropriate. But the circumstances under which adoption is now viewed as both possible and appropriate have vastly changed since Taylor, Breckinridge, Weissman, and others first entertained the idea of private guardianship as a child welfare resource.

Most of these early champions of guardianship held fast to the conventional belief that adoption was primarily an alternative means of family formation. Adoption was perceived as largely for infertile married couples seeking to adopt infants who physically resembled them. Infants who were not healthy or did not match the physical characteristics of the majority of adoption seekers, who were white, were generally thought of as "unadoptable" (Smith 1997). So when Taylor (1935) enumerated the sorts of children she believed were likely candidates for private guardianship, she was working from a much longer list than would be recognized today as "unadoptable," including handicapped infants, older juveniles, and minority children. Furthermore, because adoption substituted all the rights and obligations of the birth parents, including the duty to support the child, conventional opinion at the time also countenanced the reluctance of some families to adopt and assume this additional financial responsibility. For this and other reasons, Taylor suggested that many persons might find the role of guardian more attractive than that of adoptive parent.

Since Taylor made her original case for subsidized guardianship in the 1960s, ideas about the adoptability of children and the motivations of adoptive parents have both evolved. Influenced by the permanency planning movement, definitions of adoptable children have broadened to include older juveniles, minority children, and children with special developmental, emotional, and behavioral needs. Paralleling this change has been a shift in the underlying motivations for adoptions from infertility to what some researchers call "preferential adoption" (Chandra, Abma, Maza, & Bachrach 1999). Families now also adopt to express humanitarian values, provide a permanent home for a foster child, and preserve a child's ties to a kinship, ethnic, or cultural group (Hoksbergen 1986). In addition, federal adoption subsidies under AACWA have expanded adoption opportunities to families who formerly would not have been able to afford the support of another child.

These changes in child adoptability, parental motivation, and adoption affordability have altered perceptions of the desirability of legal guardianship as a permanency option in two ways. First, the trend toward preferential adoption has expanded the circumstances in which adoption is deemed as appropriate or possible and narrowed the circumstances in which guardianship is viewed as the only practical alternative to long-term foster care. Second, the trend has also prompted practitioners to delineate

more precisely the conditions under which guardianship might be more appropriate than long-term foster care or adoption.

Leashore (1985) specified a number of conditions under which guardianship might better serve the interests of the child, birth parent, substitute caregiver, and the state than would either long-term foster care or adoption. In cases in which the legal grounds are insufficient to prove parental unfitness but reunification is still undesirable, private guardianship creates legal certainty and stability in the substitute care relationship that is lacking when the state retains legal custody of the child. Furthermore, transfer of guardianship makes the caregiver personally responsible for the welfare of the child and relieves the state of the civil liability for inadequate foster care. Guardianship also allows for the continued involvement of birth parents in the lives of their children, as parental rights are not terminated and the birth parents retain visitation rights. For this reason, guardianship might help to lessen the separation trauma, sense of loss, and identity conflicts that sometimes develop when children are adopted, particularly if they are old enough to remember their parents or cherish their heritage. Private guardianship is less expensive than foster care because the costs of casework services, public guardianship administration, foster home licensing, and judicial review are no longer incurred when the child welfare case is closed. Also the duty for child support remains with the birth parent, so the state could seek to recover some of the costs of the subsidy program through child support enforcement, which cannot be done with subsidized adoption because the support obligation transfers to the adoptive parent. Finally, as Leashore (1985) noted, private guardianship is more in keeping with the custom of informal adoption that has long been established in the African American community.

The custom of informal adoption has historical roots in African American adaptations to slavery and job migration patterns, which disproportionately deprived black children of regular parental care (Hill 1977). Grandparents, aunts, uncles, or other extended and "fictive" kin would take over childrearing responsibilities until the parents were able to resume custody or the children reached adulthood. This tradition continued in the urban North, where informal adoption helped to compensate for the discriminatory withholding of voluntary and statutory child welfare services from black neighborhoods (Billingsley & Giovannoni 1972). Although recent developments in the public child welfare system demonstrate that many of these informal adoptions can be transformed into formal adoptions (Testa, Kristen, Cohen, & Woods 1996) significant proportions of kin remain uncomfortable with this permanency option.

Thornton's (1991:112, 113) interviews with a small sample of kinship foster parents in New York City illustrate the sorts of reservations relatives usually express about adopting their own kin. Most of those interviewed felt adoption was unnecessary because they were already related by blood: "adopt my own grands! It doesn't make sense to the kids. To me, this would be confusing to them." Others expressed worries that adoption would cause conflict in their relationship with the birth parents: "I'm not trying to take over these children from their parents." Although Thorton concluded that kinship foster parents were overwhelmingly against the idea of adopting their related foster children, he observed that most of his respondents were prepared to raise their related foster children to adulthood: "These children are just like my own children. I will take care of them until they get out on their own." Thornton found merit in the idea of subsidized guardianship as an alternative to adoption. But he recommended that an experiment be conducted to assess the adequacy of care under different levels of post-guardianship support before withdrawing casework services altogether.

The concept of guardianship as a supplemental permanency option to adoption was also endorsed by Williams (1992), who later became associate commissioner of the Children's Bureau. Like other scholars, she recognized that guardianship complemented African American traditions of informal adoption, but unlike Thornton, she did not perceive the unique circumstances of kinship care as posing an insurmountable barrier to formal adoption by kin.

Williams (1992) acknowledged reunification and adoption as the preferred choices and recommended that guardianship be pursued only when adoption was inappropriate or unavailable as a permanency option. She stressed that the goal of guardianship, like adoption, ought to be the establishment of a substitute parent–child relationship that is continuous, protected from disruption, and conducive to the healthy development of the child. Toward this end, she urged that guardianship be granted only after a psychosocial study determined the significance of the bond between the child and the prospective guardian and the depth of the caregiver's commitment. Although she also acknowledged that private guardianship is designed to be self-sustaining, she allowed that access to post-guardianship services and guardian subsidies may be necessary to insure the stability of the relationship.

Support for the concept of subsidized guardianship as a supplementary permanency option, especially for children in long-term kinship care, grew during the 1990s. The idea was endorsed by nearly every "blue-ribbon" committee that was convened on the subject of kinship foster care (American Bar Association 1999; American Public Welfare Association 1997; Child Welfare League of America 1994; Mayor's Commission for the Foster Care of Children 1993). In its report, the Child Welfare League of America (1994:83) recommended "providing federal reimbursement to states for children in kinship care under a program similar to subsidized special needs adoption."

Although no specific legislative action was taken as a result of the report, the U.S. Department of Health and Human Services did invite states to submit applications for subsidized guardianship demonstrations "which would allow children to stay or be placed in a familial setting that is more cost effective than continuing them in foster care (Federal Register 1995: 31483). Five states—Delaware, Illinois, Maryland, North Carolina, and Oregon—initially received waivers to mount subsidized guardianship demonstrations. An additional four states —Minnesota, Montana, New Mexico, and Wisconsin—were approved between 1999 and 2004.

Subsidized Guardianship: IV-E Waiver Demonstrations, State, and TANF-Funded Programs

States' interest in waivers to use federal funds for guardianship subsidies is a clear indication of the growing consensus on the need for an alternative permanency option for relative caregivers. Although some states had long-standing subsidized guardianship programs on the books, few were subsidized adequately; in most states, the guardianship laws were infrequently applied for children in foster care. With the convergent forces of ASFA calling for more timely permanency decisions, relatives who did not want to adopt, and youth who did not want to break their bonds with birth parents, the viability of subsidized guardianship to serve as another choice for families was brought to the forefront.

With the advent of waiver authority, states had an option for funding subsidized guardianships that was not previously available. Subsidized guardianship rapidly became the most commonly sought waiver request out of a host of interventions for which states could use federal funds more flexibly. Although the federal government was committed to testing the efficacy of only a limited number of waivers until evaluations of the initial set were completed, the approval of the first six waivers raised the national discussion about its appropriateness as a permanency option to a new level. The waivers afforded states the opportunity to use federal funds to subsidize guardianship placements when return home and adoption were not possible. In many states, the waiver presented the best chance they had for garnering the resources necessary to subsidize guardianships at the foster care level, and therefore offer relative caregivers a real incentive to move the child from foster care to a permanent placement. Some of the waivers, such as those in Montana and New Mexico, also offered an alternative to adoption for tribal communities who do not recognize termination of parental rights as a viable option.

Although some states seized the waiver opportunity, others were reluctant to enter into a demonstration project that required them to conduct rigorous evaluations (Cornerstone Consulting Group 1999). This resistance to an experimental evaluation design, with control and experimental groups, emanated from the belief that all children in the state should be offered this alternative permanency option and that having a control group would deny some children this opportunity. Other states held back due to a concern about cost neutrality provisions, which require states to demonstrate that the waiver did not result in any additional federal expenditures beyond what would have been spent in the absence of the demonstration.

Another group of states continued to subsidize guardianship placements with state funds. By 2003, 17 states were offering guardianship subsidies to children in stable relative foster care placements, although many of these are funded at a level less than the foster care subsidy (Allen, Bissell, & Miller 2003). This inequality in the subsidy levels often acted as a disincentive to permanency for caregivers who needed the financial support to adequately care for the child.

Yet another group of states secured funding from the TANF block grant, which replaced the AFDC program in 1996. This flexible source of funding allowed 10 states to offer subsidies to caregivers, although four of these were for children discharged to the custody of relatives before they were placed into foster care. This option helped those states that secured the funding in the late 1990s, when they experienced a surplus in TANF funding. By 2001, TANF surpluses were hard to come by, due to the economic downturn, making it more difficult to use these funds for this effort.

By 2003, there were 34 states and the District of Columbia offering some level of guardianship subsidy (Allen, Bissell, & Miller 2003). As the collective wisdom about these programs was shared, a common set of elements needed to making guardianship a meaningful option for children also emerged. These elements were meant to insure that children in guardianship arrangements achieved optimal levels of safety, security, and permanence. They also served to deflect potential resistance to guardianship among those who considered it to be less desirable than adoption. Although not all states adopted all elements, some that were common across many states included:

- Ruling out reunification and adoption: insuring that children have every opportunity to return to birth parents or be adopted to achieve the highest forms of legal permanency was a high priority in many state subsidy programs and was written into the terms and conditions of every waiver state;
- Equalizing subsidies: providing a subsidy equal to that received by families through foster care (or would receive if they adopted the child) provided an added incentive to caregivers needing the financial support to make a permanent commitment to the child;
- Insuring safety and stability: several actions were instituted to insure that children were in safe and stable placements, including requiring that the children be in the home for a minimum amount of time—typically 1 year—before guardianship could be considered. Background and safety checks of relative caregivers, as well as assessments of the relative's commitment to the child were also required in many states; and

- Insuring eligibility for other services and supports: most states made provisions for children to continue receiving Medicaid, and some also recognized the need for older youth to continue receiving independent living services and educational benefits to help make the transition to adulthood.

The momentum for a more comprehensive federal policy governing guardianship continued to grow. In 2004, the bipartisan Pew Commission on Children in Foster Care released its recommendations for reforming federal child welfare financing and strengthening court oversight of children in foster care. One of its central recommendations was to provide "federal guardianship assistance to all children who leave foster care to live with a permanent, legal guardian" (2004:18).

Congressional momentum also began to build in 2004 with the introduction of the Kinship Caregiver and Support Act (S. 2607) by Senators Hillary Clinton (D-NY) and Olympia Snowe (R-ME). The legislation proposed to allow states to use Title IV-E child welfare funding to subsidize guardianship placements for children living with relatives. The legislation also recognizes the many relatives caring for children outside of the child welfare system by providing grants to states to connect them to services and supports in the community.

Competing Concepts of Permanence: Lasting or Binding

Despite the growing acknowledgement that guardianship might be more appropriate in certain circumstances than adoption, the concern still arises that the simpler judicial process of awarding guardianship might detract excessively from adoptions because of the additional legal step of terminating parental rights. Therefore as a precaution, all of the Title IV-E waiver terms and conditions, as well as many state laws, limit eligibility to children for whom family reunification and adoption have been ruled out as viable permanency options. However, there is the opposite concern that forcing all substitute care arrangements into the legal mold of adoption might cause more harm than good, especially among relatives who may wish to retain their identities as grandparents, aunts, and uncles and may be reluctant to participate in the termination of the parental rights of family members.

The experimental designs of the Title IV-E waivers permit the testing of whether the availability of subsidized guardianship truly helps to boost legal permanence over the levels that would have been attained if reunification and subsidized adoption were the only permanency options. Findings from the Illinois Subsidized Guardianship Waiver Demonstration support the efficacy of subsidized guardianship as a supplementary permanency option to reunification and subsidized adoption (Testa 2002). Comparison of the control and experimental groups as of June 1999 showed a 6.7% difference in permanency rates that is statistically significant at the .01 level (one-tail test). As key indicators from administrative and survey data show that statistical equivalence was successfully achieved through randomization (Westat 1999), the only substantive difference between the two groups is the intervention. Thus, the higher permanency rate in the experimental group may be attributed to the availability of subsidized guardianship.

However, this permanency boost does come with strings attached. Even though the Illinois demonstration finds a much greater selection of adoption by kin than prior literature indicated likely, the rising level of adoptions in the control group raises the possibility that some adoptions may have indeed been lost in the long run due to the availability of subsidized guardianship. It is estimated that of the 12% of children in the experimental group who moved to private guardianship in Illinois, as many as 45% might have instead been adopted in the absence of the waiver as of June 1999 (Testa 2002).

Is this trade-off of higher permanencies at the expense of fewer adoptions worth it? Some

might argue that the loss of adoptions reflects inadequate application of the "rule-out" procedures. Cases that should have moved to adoption were inappropriately taken into private guardianship. But others might say that the trade-off appropriately reflects the wider choice of permanency options that are offered to families in the experimental group but denied to the control group.

At the root of this disagreement are two alternative definitions of permanence: one as "lasting" and the other as "binding." One definition holds that the biological bonds and social attachments of kinship are sufficiently lasting to insure a family's intention to raise a foster child to adulthood. The other contends that the commitment must be made legally binding through formal adoption to enforce permanence.

Since its beginnings in the early 1970s, the permanency planning movement in the United States has promoted a concept of permanence as "lasting." The goal is to find a foster child a home that is intended to last indefinitely, in which the sense of belonging is rooted in cultural norms, has definitive legal status, and conveys a respected social identity (Emlen, Lahti, & Downs 1978). With the growing availability of subsidized guardianship and other permanent living arrangements with kin, however, some legal advocates have advanced the idea that the commitment also needs to be made legally "binding" to qualify as permanence (Bartholet 1999; Takas & Hegar 1999). This redefinition demotes guardianship as a permanency goal because it is more easily vacated by the caregiver and more vulnerable to legal challenge by birth parents than termination of parental rights and adoption.

This concept of permanence as legally binding is a recent innovation in permanency planning. Although it is widely accepted that permanency commitments should not be broken casually, there is a lack of agreement as to whether this newer concept confers much additional value above and beyond the original concept of permanence as lasting. Furthermore there is some concern that forcing all caregiving commitments into the nuclear family mold of adoption might cause more harm than good.

Some scholars point out that a "best interests of the child" analysis does not automatically support emphasis on termination of parental rights in favor of adoption (O'Laughlin 1998). These scholars are critical of the ASFA provision that replaces the "best interests of the child" analysis with an artificial one that assumes termination is in the child's best interests. A timeline termination policy of 15 out of 22 months implicitly assumes that a child needs a permanent home with a single set of parents without considering the harm that may result. For instance, the Illinois Supreme Court (2002: 112) recently declared the state's application of ASFA's timeline termination policy unconstitutional. It ruled that the passage of 15 months alone was not sufficient grounds for ruling unfitness on the assumption that "a fit parent does not allow his or her child to languish in foster care for 15 months." As a noted child psychologist (Jenkins 1981:55) observes, children can, in fact, experience "both psychological ties to biological parents and close attachments to caretakers."

The issue of whether a timeline termination policy makes sense can be considered separately from the question of whether there is an appropriate hierarchy of preferable permanency goals. As mentioned above, the Title IV-E guardianship waiver terms and conditions for each of the states and many state statutes restricted eligibility to children for whom family reunification and adoption have been ruled out as viable permanency options. In Illinois, this rule-out provision was written into statute: the legislation establishes a hierarchy of permanency goals that ranks private guardianship above the goal of independence but below the goals of reunification and adoption. In selecting any permanency goal, courts are instructed to indicate in writing the reasons a specific goal was selected and why the higher ranked goals were ruled out.

Acceptance of a hierarchy of preferable permanency goals still leaves open the question of who should have the final say about what form of legal permanence is in the best interests of the child. After the misinformation and myths about adoption are cleared away, a layer of resistance to kinship adoption still remains that is not so easily dismissed. Some relatives prefer to leave the rights of the biological parents undisturbed and to become instead the child's legal guardian. Even when parental rights are terminated, some relatives prefer to remain the child's custodian as grandmother, aunt, or cousin rather than become the child's adoptive parent. Still other families are willing to assume as the legal guardian some additional financial burden beyond the subsidy, but they are reluctant to assume the full child support obligation as an adoptive family. Should such family preferences be honored by child welfare agencies and the courts?

When this question was put to the test in Illinois, two opposing factions emerged. On the one side were mostly researchers and caseworkers, who believed that the extended family should have the decisive say over which permanency option to pursue. They argued that the kinship network was in the best position to determine whether adoption or guardianship was in keeping with their family's sense of belonging, cultural norms, and notions of a respected social identity. These sentiments were consistent with the original psychological definition of permanence as lasting. On the other side were mostly lawyers and judicial hearing officers, who argued that adoption must be ruled out by the courts beyond a shred of a doubt before guardianship could be offered as an option. In circumstances in which the child was still young and an unrelated family expressed a willingness to adopt, some argued that rule-out required removing the child from the stable care of a relative foster parent and placing the child in the unrelated adoptive home. When pressed for a justification, the explanation was offered that adoption is more binding than guardianship.

Whether the newer legal definition of permanence as binding supercedes the older psychological definition of permanence as lasting will depend to some extent on how important the obligatory aspects of caregiving relationships are judged relative to the familial aspects. Are the biological bonds and social attachments of kinship sufficiently lasting to insure a relative's intention of raising a child to adulthood? Or are the legal obligations of adoption necessary to give a child a lifelong family that will survive the vicissitudes of kinship, shared family experience, and common cultural identity? Longitudinal research is currently being conducted in the federal demonstration sites, which will hopefully answer these questions. For the moment, the best evidence about the stability of guardianship arrangements comes from a few cross-sectional surveys and follow-up studies that rely primarily on administrative data.

Stability of Guardianship and Adoption

The push for permanence through adoption and guardianship has recently begun to raise concerns that families are being forced into making ill-considered commitments that will result in placement disruptions or displacements from permanence after finalization. The term "disruptions" refers to ruptures of foster or pre-adoptive placements that occur prior to finalization of a permanency arrangement. "Displacements" refers to post-finalization ruptures of adoptive or guardian arrangements that may result in the child's return to the public foster care system. Lastly, "dissolutions" refers to adoptions or guardianships that have ended as a result of terminating the adoptive parent's rights or vacating the caregiver's rights of guardianship.

The evidence to date suggests that displacements from permanence are far fewer than observers may have feared. In Illinois, administrative records show that of the 6,820 cases that entered subsidized guardianship since 1997, 3.5% were no longer living in the home of the original guardian as of March 2002. Approxi-

mately one-third of the guardianship ruptures were attributable to the death or incapacitation of the guardian. The remaining two-thirds occurred because the caregiver no longer wanted to exercise parental authority and the guardianship was legally dissolved.

Focusing on these dissolutions in Illinois, 3.1% of the guardianships that were awarded in 1997 have been dissolved as of March 2002; 2.7% of the 1998 guardianships have been dissolved; and 3.5% of the 1999 guardianships have been dissolved. Of all the guardianships that have been dissolved or disrupted because of death and incapacitation, 49% necessitated the reappointment of the Illinois Department of Children and Family Services (IDCFS) as the public guardian of the child because there was no other family member available to become the child's private guardian. Altogether the reappointment of IDCFS accounts for only 2% of the subsidized guardianships awarded since 1997. Even though a longer period of observation is necessary to assess the overall stability of guardianship arrangements in Illinois, as of now, the rates of guardianship ruptures are similar to adoption ruptures, controlling for the differing ages at entry.

The Washington Guardianship study also found that, contrary to the concern that children were ill served in dependency guardianships, more than 80% of the children interviewed indicated they were happy with their guardianship (English, Ober, & Brummel 1999). Administrative data indicated that about 86% of the Washington children placed in guardianships remain with their guardians until they are 18 years old.

California's evaluation results from the first 2 years of implementation of their Kinship Guardianship Assistance program (Kin-GAP) also show promising results in relation to the stability of guardianship placements. Of the first 6,701 children placed in Kin-GAP between January 2000 and July 1, 2001, only 1.6% had substantiated referrals after exiting foster care to Kin-GAP. Of these, 25% of the referrals were for general neglect, including caretaker incapacity. Only 0.8% (55 children) reentered foster care, the largest proportion of which, 40%, also involved general neglect (Needell et al. 2002).

In spite of the greater stability of foster placements, legal guardianships, and adoptions among kin, it is important to recognize that kinship care is not an unconditional safety net. Research on the stability of kinship care in states without subsidized guardianship programs suggests that rates of disruption are sensitive to both the level of financial support and the availability of post-discharge services to the family. A study of disruption rates in Texas reports failure levels as high as 50% for children discharged from foster care to the physical custody of kin (Terling-Watt 2001). Many of the differences among the Illinois, Washington, and California experiences arise from the fact that Texas commonly discharges children to the physical custody of kin who must turn to TANF for financial support. Little in the way of post-discharge services is provided to deal with adolescent development, the special needs of children, and the age and health limitations of the caregivers. Furthermore, state oversight of these post-discharge arrangements continues. Unsupervised visits between parent and child are prohibited. When relatives allow it and are discovered, it usually results in the removal of the child.

Post-permanency Services and the Future of Foster Care

Congressional Budget Office projections show that in this decade, the number of children receiving federal adoption assistance payments will exceed the number of children in Title IV-E reimbursed foster care (Congressional Budget Office 1999). This important milestone has already been achieved in states like Illinois, where the number of children in subsidized adoptive and guardianship homes surpassed the total number of children in foster care in July 2000. This changing balance between children in permanent homes and children in foster care has

had a profound impact on the Illinois system and prefigures the possible challenges that other child welfare systems are likely to face in the future in serving a residual population of older foster children with special developmental, educational, and emotional needs.

To preserve the successes that the permanency planning movement achieved in overcoming adoption stereotypes and moving more children to permanent homes who formerly would have been consigned to long-term foster care requires adaptations of the service system. Agency involvement after adoption finalization was discouraged in earlier adoption practice (Howard & Smith 1995). However, the particular vulnerability of adolescents and the limitations of existing community resources to address the unique challenges of caring for adopted children with special needs means that public authorities must now take the leadership role for planning, coordinating, and funding post-permanency services (Watson 1992).

Surveys of adoptive families reveal common patterns of need for post-permanency services. Fortunately, most adoptive families (64%) report never experiencing an emergency or crisis concerning any of their adopted children. But many do. Most adoptive families facing an emergency or crisis usually turn first, like families in general, to informal systems of support—relatives, friends, neighbors, and other adoptive families (Hemmens, Hardina, Madsen, & Wiewel 1986). When these informal supports are exhausted, families will next turn to physicians, religious leaders, and then former adoption workers. The common types of post-permanency services that adoptive families request include respite care (weekend or short-term to alleviate parental stress), camp and other summer activities, support groups for adoptive parents and children, educational support (tutoring, testing, and advocacy), counseling, and assistance with finding and paying for residential treatment (Howard & Smith 1995). Even though post-guardianship services are of more recent vintage, guardians express many of the same needs, allowing for differences in attachment, loss, and grief when relatives become the permanent guardians.

The changing balance between foster care and legal permanence also has implications for the organization of services to children who stay in the foster care system. Just as the introduction of family preservation and support services increased the complexity of serving foster children by preventing the removal of less difficult children for brief episodes of care, permanency planning adds to this complexity by discharging foster children at younger ages to permanent homes who formerly would have grown up in the system. The net effect is that foster care providers will be dealing with a residual group of older wards with special developmental, emotional, and learning needs. This residual population will place additional demands on the system for mental health and remedial education services that can easily outstrip the capacity of regular foster care in the absence of special wrap-around and other supportive services. Services should also assist all older wards in making a successful transition to independent adulthood, regardless of whether they age out of the system or find permanence as adolescents with legal guardians or adoptive parents. The recent extension of federal college benefits to older wards adopted after age 16 offers a model for insuring that independence goals complement rather than substitute for permanency plans.

Half a century after the Children's Bureau enunciated every child's right to guardianship, achievement of this goal is in sight for the majority of children now entering the child welfare system. Foster care is fast transforming into the brief interlude between when children's natural guardianship with birth parents cannot be conserved and when permanence can be reestablished through adoption or legally appointed guardianship. However, the shifting balance between temporary foster care and legal permanence will challenge the current organization of the child welfare system for years to come.

REFERENCES

Adoption and Safe Families Act. (1997). P.L. 105-89.

Adoption Assistance and Child Welfare Act. (1980). P.L. 96-272.

Allen, M., Bissell, M., & Miller, J. (2003). *Expanding permanency options for children: A guide to subsidized guardianship programs.* Washington, DC: Children's Defense Fund and Cornerstone Consulting Group.

American Bar Association. (1999). *Guidelines for kinship placements.* Washington, DC: American Bar Association.

American Public Welfare Association. (1997). *Report of kinship care.* Washington, DC: American Public Welfare Association.

Bartholet, E. (1999). *Nobody's children: Abuse and neglect, foster drift, and the adoption alternative.* Boston: Beacon Press.

Berrick, J. D., Barth, R., & Needell, B. (1994). A comparison of kinship foster homes and foster family homes: Implications for kinship foster care as family preservation. *Children and Youth Services Review, 16,* 33–64.

Billingsley, A., & Giovannoni, J. M. (1972). *Children of the storm.* New York: Harcourt Brace Jovanovich.

Bowlby, J. (1969). *Attachment and loss.* New York: Basic Books.

Breckinridge, S. P., & Stanton, M. (1943). The law of guardian and ward with special reference to the children of veterans. *Social Service Review, 17,* 265–302.

Burnette, D. (1997). Grandparents raising grandchildren in the inner city. *Families in Society: The Journal of Contemporary Human Services, 23,* 489–501.

Chandra, A., Abma, J., Maza, P., & Bachrach, C. (1999). *Adoption, adoption seeking, and relinquishment for adoption in the United States.* Advance data from vital and health statistics no. 306. Hyattsville, MD: National Center for Health Statistics.

Child Welfare League of America. (1994). *Kinship care: A natural bridge.* Washington, DC: Child Welfare League of America.

Congressional Budget Office. (1999). *CBO baseline for foster care and adoption assistance.* Washington, DC: Human Resources Cost Estimate Unit.

Cornerstone Consulting Group. (1999). *Child welfare waivers: Promising directions, missed opportunities.* Houston: Cornerstone Consulting Group.

Cross, T. (2003). Guiding values and philosophy. In *Developing culturally based tribal adoption laws and customary adoption codes. A technical assistance manual and model code.* Portland, OR: National Indiana Child Welfare Association.

Duquette, D. N., Hardin, M., & Payne Dean, C. (1999). *Adoption 2002: The president's initiative on adoption and foster care.* Washington, DC: Children's Bureau, National Clearinghouse on Child Abuse and Neglect Information.

Emlen, A., Lahti, J., & Downs, S. (1978). *Overcoming barriers to planning for children in foster care.* DHEW Publication no. (OHDS) 78-30138. Washington, DC: U.S. Government Printing Office.

English, D. J., Ober, A. J., & Brummel, S. C. (1999). *Report on the Washington State guardianship study.* Olympia, WA: Office of Children's Administration Research, Washington State Department of Social and Health Services.

Federal Register. (1995). *The Federal Register.* Washington, DC: Office of the Federal Register, National Archives and Records Administration.

Gershenson, C. P. (1985). *Child welfare research notes #9.* Washington, DC: Department of Health and Human Services, Administration for Children, Youth, and Families.

Gleeson, J., & Craig, L. (1994). Kinship care in child welfare: An analysis of states' policies. *Children and Youth Services Review, 16,* 731.

Goldstein, J., Freud, A., & Solnit, A. J. (1973). *Beyond the best interests of the child.* New York: Free Press.

Hemmens, G., Hardina, D., Madsen, R., and Wiewel, W. (1986). *Changing needs and social services in three Chicago communities.* Vol. 4: *Hardship and support systems in Chicago.* Washington, DC: Urban Institute.

Hill, R. B. (1977). *Informal adoption among black families.* Washington DC: National Urban League Research Department.

Hoksbergen, R. A. (ed.). (1986). *Adoption in worldwide perspective.* Lisse, The Netherlands: Swets & Zeitlinger.

Howard, J. A., & Smith, S. (1995). *Adoption preservation in Illinois: Results of a four-year study.* Bloomington: Illinois State University.

Iglehart, A. P. (1994). Kinship foster care: Placement, service, and outcome issues. *Children and Youth Services Review, 16,* 107–122.

Illinois Supreme Court (2002). *People v. IDCFS.*

Jenkins, S. (1981). Book review. *Social Casework,* (May), p. 317.

Leashore, B. R. (1985). Demystifying legal guardianship: An unexplored option for dependent children. *Journal of Family Law, 23*(3), 391–400.

Leos-Urbel, J., Bess, R., & Geen, R. (2000). *State policies for assessing and supporting kinship foster parents.* Washington, DC: Urban Institute.

Maas, H. S., & Engler, R. E. (1959). *Children in need of parents.* New York: Columbia University Press.

Mayor's Committee for the Foster Care of Children. (1993). *Report from the Mayor's Committee for the Foster Care of Children in New York City.* New York: Office of the Mayor.

McDonald, J., Salyers, N., & Testa, M. (2003). *Nation's child welfare system doubles number of adoptions from foster care.* Chicago, IL: Fostering Results.

Needell, B., Shlonsky, A., Webseter, D.; Lee, S., Armijo, M., & Cuccaro-Alamin, S. (2002). *Report to the legislature on the Kinship Guardianship Assistance Payment (Kin-GAP) program.* Berkeley: University of California–Berkeley.

O'Laughlin, M. M. (1998). A theory of relativity: Kinship care may be the key to stopping the pendulum of terminations vs. reunifications. *Vanderbilt Law Review, 51,* 1427–1457.

Pew Commission on Children in Foster Care. (2004). *Fostering the future: Safety, permanence and well-being for children in foster care.* Washington, DC: Pew Commission on Children in Foster Care.

Pike, V., Downs, S., & Emlen, A. (1977). *Permanent planning for children in foster care; A handbook for social workers.* DHEW Publication no. (OHDS) 77-30124. Washington, DC: U.S. Government Printing Office.

Scannapieco, M., Hegar, R., & McAlpine, C. (1997). Kinship care and foster care: A comparison of characteristics and outcomes. *Families and Society, 78,* 480–488.

Schuerman, J. R., Rzepnicki, T. L., & Littell, J. H. (1994). *Putting famiies first: An experiment in family preservation.* Hawthorne, NY: Aldine de Gruyter.

Smith, A. D. (1955). *The right to life.* Chapel Hill: University of North Carolina Press.

Smith, J. (1997). *The realities of adoption.* New York: Madison Books.

Spar, K. (1993). *Kinship foster care: An emerging federal issue.* Washington, DC: Library of Congress, Congressional Research Service.

Steiner, G. Y. (1981). *The futility of family policy.* Washington, DC: Brookings Institution.

Takas, M., & Hegar, R. L. (1999). The case for kinship adoption laws. In R. L. Hegar & M. Scannapieco (eds.), *Kinship foster care: Policy, practice and research,* pp. 54–67. New York: Oxford University Press.

Tatara, T. (1991). Overview of child abuse and neglect. In J. E. Everett, S. S. Chipungu, & B. R. Leashore (eds.), *Child welfare: An Africentric perspective,* pp. 187–219. New Brunswick, NJ: Rutgers University Press.

Tatara, T. (1993). *Characteristics of children in substitute and adoptive care: A statistical summary of the VCIS National Child Welfare Data Base.* Washington, DC: American Public Welfare Association.

Taylor, H. B. (1935). *Law of guardian and ward.* Doctoral dissertation, University of Chicago School of Social Service Administration, Chicago.

Taylor, H. B. (1966). Guardianship or "permanent placement" of children. In J. Tenbroek & the California Law Review (eds.), *The law of the poor,* pp. 417–423. San Francisco: Chandler Publishing.

Terling-Watt, T. (2001). Permanence in kinship care: An exploration of disruption rates and factors associated with placement disruption. *Children and Youth Services Review, 23,* 111–126.

Testa, M. (1997). Kinship foster care in Illinois. In R. Barth, J. Berrick, & N. Gilbert (eds.), *Child welfare research,* vol. 2, pp. 103–126. New York: Columbia University Press.

Testa, M. (2002). Subsidized guardianship: Testing an idea whose time has finally come. *Social Work Research, 26*(3), 145–158.

Testa, M., Kristen, S., Cohen, L., & Woods, M. (1996). Permanency planning options for children in formal kinship care. *Child Welfare,* 75: 451–470.

Thornton, J. L. (1991). Permanency planning for children in kinship foster homes. *Child Welfare, 70,* 593–601.

U.S. Department of Health and Human Services. (1961). *Legislative guides for the termination of parental rights and responsibilities and the adoption of children.* No. 394. Washington, DC: Social Security Administration.

U.S. Department of Health and Human Services. (2000). *Report to Congress on kinship foster care.* Washington, DC: U.S. Department of Health and Human Services.

U.S. House Ways and Means Committee. (1994). *1994 green book.* Washington, DC: U.S. Government Printing Office.

U.S. House Ways and Means Committee. (2002). *2002 green book.* Washington, DC: U.S. Government Printing Office.

Watson, K. (1992). Providing services after adoption. *Public Welfare, 50,* 5–13.

Weissman, I. (1950). Legal guardianship of children? *Social Welfare Reform, 12,* 75–100.

Weissman, I. (1964). Guardianship: Every child's right. *Annals of the American Academcy of Political and Social Science, 355,* 134–139.

Westat. (1999*). Evaluation of the Illinois subsidized guardianship waiver demonstration. Preliminary findings.* Rockville, MD: Westat.

Williams, C. W. (1992). Expanding the options in the quest for permanence in child welfare. In J. Everett, B. Leshore, & S. Chipungu (eds.), *An Africentric perspective of child welfare,* pp. 113–129. New Brunswick, NJ: Rutgers University Press.

Wulczyn, F., & Goerge, R. M. (1992). Foster care in New York and Illinois: The challenge of rapid change. *Social Service Review, 66,* 278–294.

TERRY L. CROSS
KATHLEEN FOX

Customary Adoption as a Resource for American Indian and Alaska Native Children

For many of those who are sitting in the privacy of their offices or homes reading this . . . cultural extinction is not a thought that haunts them. Yet, cultural extinction is a very real nightmare for many . . . members of the tribal nations.

Madrigal (2001:103)

The issue of adoption of American Indian children has a long and complicated history fraught with trauma for Native Americans and their communities (Duran & Duran 1995; Locust 1998; Robin, Rasmussen, & Gonzalez-Santin 1999). Before the passage of the Indian Child Welfare Act of 1978 (ICWA), American Indian children were removed from their homes by the hundreds of thousands by child welfare professionals and agencies that believed American Indian homes were generally unfit. Widespread poverty and social problems on reservations were not addressed but were cited as reasons for the wholesale removal of children to non-Indian homes. Cultural differences also accounted for inappropriate removals. Foremost among these differences is the concept of "family" itself. Whereas in mainstream America, the individual's primary source of identity is the nuclear family, in many Indian communities, the individual is defined by his or her membership in the extended family, clan, and tribe. Extended families share responsibility for the welfare of all family members. This practice is reflected in the names applied to relatives. Terms such as "mother," "father,"

"aunt," and "uncle" are interchangeable for all relatives of a child of a certain age, and "brother" or "sister" apply to cousins as well as to siblings in some traditional Indian cultures (Swinomish Tribal Mental Health Project 1991). Often children are raised, temporarily or permanently, by relatives (placed informally or customarily). Mainstream child welfare workers sometimes mistook these arrangements for abandonment.

By the mid 1970s, the removal of Indian children from their homes and communities reached epidemic proportions. As stated by Pevar (2002:133):

Imagine the outcry if the government announced a plan to take one-fourth of all the white children in the country, separate them from their parents, and then place them in institutions or in foster care or adoptive homes. Until 1978, it was as if such a plan actually existed for reservation Indian children.

A survey of states with large Indian populations by the Association on American Indian Affairs between 1969 and 1974 found that 25% to 35% of all Indian children had been separated from their families and placed in foster care homes, adoptive homes, or institutions (Byler 1977; George 1997). Congressional hearings documented that most of these removals were inappropriate, unnecessary, and conducted without due process. The provisions of ICWA specifically address the abuses of the past by

423

creating legal requirements for state courts that wish to take Indian children into custody.

Among other provisions, ICWA makes the termination of parental rights in Indian families more difficult than in mainstream families, and, when a child is removed from his or her parents, provides explicit preferences for placing the child in an adoptive home: (1) with a member of the child's extended family, (2) with other members of the child's tribe, or (3) with other Indian families.

Before the passage of ICWA, Indian children were placed in foster care homes at rates as high as five to eight times that for other children (Byler 1977); after ICWA, they were placed in foster care at a rate 3.6 times higher than that for others (Plantz, Hubbell, Barrett, & Dobrec 1998). Although this decrease demonstrates progress, the rate of removal of Indian children from their homes is still alarmingly high. According to Plantz, Hubbell, Barrett, and Dobrec (1998), in the late 1980s, Indian children were .9% of the children's population but 3.1% of the total substitute care population.

SHANNON CROSSBEAR

The sounds of five young ones, running in and out, admonishments of "close the screen door" and "if you're coming in, you have to stay in, no more in and out" echo through the house. My grandchildren are here. There are five of them. Cory James, at 8, leads the cadre of children and is always at the edge of creating an adventure that the adults interpret as a "scheme." Allaura, at 6, has drama queen down to a fine art, baby blues, and a knack for sensitivity that substitutes on occasion for common sense. Brianna is a wise 5, with an intellect that matches her intensity. She is precocious and has a perfected pout that makes any attempt at discipline difficult. Chris is also 5 and constantly in the process of catching up with his older siblings. He has a sweet shyness and can retain a single focus while maintaining complete oblivion to what is going on around him. Rashone, at 2½, is like a bundle of curiosity, with an "on" button. The words "Run" and "Rashone" are interchangeable when it comes to this young one. When he wraps his arms around your knees, it doesn't matter that he has not yet mastered language and speech; he communicates with clarity his every need.

These are my grandchildren; C.J. with his clear voice, present at the drum, learning the songs and taking his place as a singer. Allaura with butterfly movements, a shawl dancer, that lives up to her name, Proud When She Dances. Brianna with her straight back, hands on hips, elbows out, in fluid motion as she dances the medicine dance of the jingle dress. Chris explodes with the action of the grass dancer, low-to-the-ground shimmer, a slight breeze moving through the fields of grass, then eruption into dancing, swirling, free and in flight. Rashone, intent on demonstrating his commitment to entering into the world of his brothers and his dad, alternates between picking up the drum stick and attempting the sounds of the songs, and dancing in full abandonment to the beat of the drum.

The thing is, that this family would be incomplete without anyone of them. It was not always so. You see, the two girls were biologically born to my son and daughter-in-law. The three boys were gifted to us in another way. This is a story about the Indian Child Welfare Act. It doesn't look like what happens in non-native communities. The three boys, along with their grandpa, were always present at the drum and dance group that my son and his family participated in. The girls played with the boys and other children attending the weekly social gatherings. Then after several weeks of not seeing the boys, they asked about them. What they heard next would change all our lives. The boys had been removed from the household. They were currently in a shelter, no blood family members were available or eligible to be considered for their care, and they would be separated, if and when they could find a placement. My son, Patrick, looked at Rachel and there was no question as to what would happen next. They spoke with the girls and all agreed that the boys would come to stay with them for whatever time was needed. They would do what ever it took to keep these boys in community, with relatives and raised as Ojibwa children.

It was not an easy or smooth path. There was the emergency placement, then the qualifying for foster care status. Then, after months of attempts at reunification, a determination regarding permanent placement occurred. Family contact was maintained, sometimes with challenging results, leading to jealousy and accusations in the community. Still, they continue in determining the boundaries and protocols that would allow for the best interest of the children.

The determination was such that Pat and Rachel would "adopt" the boys, raise them, nurture and protect them. Loving them was a given. Adoption, all the rights and responsibilities of parenting, while allowing their mother and father to not terminate their parental rights. This allowed for supports to be put in place for the continued care of the children, to address the needs as they arise, and not remove the possibility of reunification if future circumstances allow for a healthy relationship to be forged with the biological parents. Meanwhile, we welcome our expanded family while contributing to the cultural shield that leads to resilience as individuals and as a community.

This could not happen without the opportunities, supports, and protection of the Indian Child Welfare Act, without the special conditions allowed under nonrelinquishments of rights, and guardianships, and tribal and state agreements.

The three boys would be separated, most likely unconnected to family and culture, lost in a sea of foster families with the additional trauma inflicted by those losses. We pray that their parents will be able to someday find peace with those things that prevent them from fulfilling their parenting role but we are grateful to have the gift of these children in our lives to teach about our relationship to each other and us.

Perhaps the best demonstration is in the bonding of siblings. Recently, the young ones each received some money, which they decided, on their own, to pool and give to the oldest sibling with a new roach for his regalia. When asked why, they responded, "C.J. is our big brother and we want him to look good when he dances because he is part of our family and we love him."

These are OUR children and grandchildren and I am proud to be part of their family and I love them.

Yet clearly, there is still a need for the adoption of Native American children whose cur-

rent family situation is chaotic or dysfunctional. While in the old days these children would have been parceled out among other tribal members, preferably relatives, today they are likely to be removed by mainstream or even tribal child welfare workers. Frequently these workers are unable to find them permanent homes. Since the passage of ICWA, adoption rates of Indian children have plummeted. In 1996, MacEachron, Gustavsson, Cross, and Lewis reported that the adoption rate of American Indian children had dropped an estimated 93% between 1978 (the year ICWA was passed) and 1986. Thus the children being removed from American Indian families are more likely than ever to be placed in foster care or other nonpermanent situations, such as residential or institutional care.

Barth, Webster, and Lee (2002:155), in a study of 36,000 California children who entered out-of-home care from 1988 through 1992, concluded that "American Indian/Alaska Native children in California appear to have unique adoption patterns that emphasize adoption by kin and especially by aunts and uncles." However, they found that the rates of adoption vs. remaining in long-term care were substantially lower for American Indian children compared to white or Latino children, and that it was relatively rare for American Indian children in California to be adopted by American Indian couples. These results illustrate both the preferences of American Indians for placement with relatives, and the current difficulties associated with finding unrelated, permanent Indian homes. These difficulties include lack of resources, as well as lack of culturally relevant models of care for families who may be willing to adopt. For rural communities, which include Indian reservations, the problems of transportation and isolation exacerbate the difficulties of finding and maintaining both foster and permanent homes. In addition, such problems as fetal alcohol syndrome, prevalent in American Indian families, lead to unique challenges for adoptive children and parents (Dorris 1989).

Trends in Adoption/Child Welfare Policy and Practice

The Adoption and Safe Families Act of 1997 (ASFA), enacted almost 20 years after ICWA, compounded the problem of finding Indian homes for Indian children and youth. ASFA, with provisions heavily weighting permanency options toward termination of parental rights and adoption, did not specifically address how provisions that conflict with ICWA would be addressed (Simmons & Trope 1999). However, because ICWA is a specific law and ASFA more general, ICWA provisions still apply, despite ASFA. ASFA timelines and procedures, if followed without attention to ICWA, can create unnecessary conflicts. Although the Multiethnic Placement Act of 1994 (Curtis & Alexander 1996) also postdated ICWA, it clearly did not apply to children covered by the ICWA (Barth, Webster, & Lee 2002).

The National Indian Child Welfare Association (NICWA) and other associations and agencies that are committed to protecting Indian children and culture have been working with federal and state agencies to clarify some of the ASFA/ICWA overlap and conflict, while also working to improve practice.

Meanwhile, these organizations and agencies have been implementing ICWA with an overall goal of maintaining the integrity of tribal communities. Among the many initiatives undertaken, programs have been developed to assist American Indian children in finding culturally appropriate homes. The Indian Adoption program, sponsored by the Jewish Family & Children's Service of Phoenix, Arizona, was founded right after the passage of ICWA. It emphasized the recruitment of Indian parents for Indian children and the permanent placement of these children in stable, loving, Indian homes. Two years after ICWA, 100 children had been placed (Goodluck & Eckstein 1978; Goodluck & Short 1980).

The Indian Child and Family Consortium (ICFC), also founded shortly after the passage of ICWA, provides education for families, ther-

apy sessions for at-risk children and teens, activities and events to promote cultural values, and assistance in grant writing for preserving tribal culture. ICFC works with other local county programs to provide a support network for children in care. A special program assists families in transporting children to powwows, group therapy, theater, special tribal events, and other functions (Madrigal 2001).

These programs have just begun the work that needs to be accomplished to overcome four centuries of the destruction of Indian homes and communities.

Permanency Issues

Although permanency planning is a rather new development in the field of child welfare, the concept of belonging—the heart of permanency planning—is central to Indian culture. Tribal society is based first and foremost on the family. In Indian culture, family membership means much more than being the child of given parents. It means belonging to an extended family or interdependent, nurturing support network. In many tribes, these extended family networks are organized into larger groups or clans that offer individuals another point of reference in their sense of belonging. The tribe offers a formalized group recognition of belonging that goes beyond family and clan.

When these reference points are intact, they offer the individual a sense of trust over an extended period of time—a crucial aspect of permanency. The group, or interdependent, nature of Indian society offers the individual strength, a sense of purpose, and a sense of commonality with other members of the group. This sense of commonality promotes the individual's commitment to the group, as well as the group's commitment to the individual, and is reinforced by tribal custom and the oral tradition. It is unfortunate that over time, this cultural system has eroded somewhat and there are Indian families that have lost the ties that bind them to extended family, tribe, and culture.

Although not all Indian people are served by the cultural system in the way they were historically, it is also true that these reference points for belonging still exist and can be sought out and enhanced as resources, even for those individuals estranged from their culture. ICWA embodies this belief in its order of placement preferences. Permanency planning in Indian child welfare, therefore, has as much to do with maintaining a child's connection and sense of belonging to the extended family, clan, or tribe as it does with maintaining ties to the biological parents.

Termination of parental rights is valued as the method of choice to insure permanence in the mainstream child welfare system. However, in Indian child welfare, it has the potential of severing the child's connection to an extended family or tribe.

Tribes must ask themselves if termination of parental rights serves a viable function in an extended family system in which connectedness and belonging go far beyond emotional bonds with biological parents. Only careful community-based decisionmaking can answer this question. Although termination of parental rights may or may not be an acceptable option, permanence is a highly valued concept among Indian people, and alternative, culturally based methods to achieve it are necessary and legitimate.

Indian Traditional Adoptions

In many American Indian/Alaska Native communities, individuals are adopted formally or informally into an existing family. Adoptees include not only children, but also adults who have come to be associated with a family. Elders may adopt children who have few other family ties, and children or young people may adopt elders as grandparents. Family membership can be a way to define who is "in" or "out" of a social group (Swinomish 1991).

Historically, adoptions in American Indian tribes/nations were conducted with great ceremony, entailing the full, unqualified acceptance of a child or adult into not only the family but the tribe. Mary Jemison, adopted by the Seneca in 1755, reported "I was ever considered and treated by them as a real sister, the same as though I had been born of their mother" (Seaver 1991:61).

Traditional naming ceremonies for children born or adopted into a tribe not only "give children a path in life, they also build a spiritual network that organizes kinship obligations with respect to meeting physical, health, and emotional needs of children" (Red Horse 1997:246). Naming ceremonies are held for both birth children and adopted children or adults.

One of the most promising developments for Indian children incorporates traditional forms of adoption into customary adoption. This approach to permanency can be viewed as a midway point on a continuum between termination of parental rights and legal guardianship. Customary adoption promotes the use of American Indian traditions to guide the conduct of permanency, as opposed to formal adoption, which includes termination of parental rights. Customary adoption fits culturally with the extended family concept and it formalizes and protects ongoing care of the child by an extended family member or other recognized potential parents. It eliminates the philosophical barrier to adoption as conducted in mainstream society; namely, the abhorrence of termination of parental rights.

Customary Adoption

In many tribes, customary adoption is the process of creating relatives and joining individuals into family relationships. It expands family resources for a young person without terminating preexisting relationships. Customary adoption modifies the custodial and legal relationship of the birth parents with the child but does not terminate a birth parent's emotional relationship with the child, the child's relationships with the birth parent or extended birth family, or the extended family's relationship with the child.

Key Definitions of Customary Adoption

Several key definitions are central to this discussion and are essential to the formulation of legal elements of an emerging model currently being developed by NICWA and collaborators (Cross 2002).

"Adoption" means a tribal legal process pursuant to tribal law, including custom, which gives a child a legally recognized permanent parent-child relationship with a person other than the child's birth parent and severs or modifies the legal parent-child relationship between the child and the child's birth parent but does not sever the child's relationship with the child's clan or the child's birth or extended family (under certain circumstances). In the case of an adult adoptee, it is a tribal legal process pursuant to tribal law, including custom, which gives an adult a legally recognized permanent parent-child relationship with a person other than the adult's birth parent. "Custom" means a long-established, continued, reasonable, and certain practice considered by the tribal community to be binding, or a usage or practice common to many community members or to a particular place in the community that has not been developed by the tribal or any other government, and that the court or other appropriate entity can enforce. "Customary adoption" means a traditional tribal practice recognized by the community that gives a child a permanent parent-child relationship with someone other than the child's birth parent.

Recently NICWA has developed a culturally specific child welfare practice and judicial process for the recognition and certification of customary law regarding the adoption of American Indian children. Furthermore, it has set out a culturally based conceptual framework for tribes to conduct formal adoptions without termination of parental rights. Whether to formulate either or both of these concepts into law is a landmark policy decision for tribes and represents one of the most important exercises of sovereignty that a tribe can undertake.

This approach to permanency is but one potential solution to a complex set of problems affecting Indian children, families, and tribes today. Almost every tribe has customs associated with adoption, so it is not a foreign concept. In fact, in surveying tribes, NICWA has found none that did not have current or historical customary processes for adoption. Also, no tribes were found to have expressed customs equivalent to termination of parental rights. Although it is safe to assume that such things probably did happen, NICWA could not find ceremonies, rituals, or common practices that ended relationships between parents and children. In fact, many tribes actively abhor the idea and will not subject their children to this unthinkable act. Other means are seen as appropriate for achieving permanency.

It is true that there are many differences among tribes, both in their superficial circumstances and in the deepest foundations of their cultures and histories. There are also many similarities. In this context—the care of children and youth—it is possible to identify areas where cultural values play a particularly important role. Discussion of the exact meaning of the role of those values in policy should be left to each tribe. One of the similarities that impacts the current discussion is that in Indian tribal systems, a child is born into a particular family and from the moment of birth, that child's place in the world is defined by his or her relationships with his or her mother's and father's families. In a fundamental sense, a child's very definition as a human being is in the context of the family in which he or she is born.

Although historically a child might have been given to a member of the parent's family or clan for a variety of reasons, permission from an official agency or department was not envisioned or necessary. However, there are at least three concerns that may now compel a tribe to consider the need for official approval of customary adoption. First, federal law and policies are weighted heavily toward the termination of parental rights and require the implementation of permanency plans when children cannot return to birth families in a reasonable time frame. Second, important financial and programmatic resources, such as adoption assistance, are available only when a child is legally regarded as adopted. Third, legally recognized consents are necessary for education and medical treatment.

In addition, it is important to acknowledge that not all customary placements are voluntary. Family members may have to intervene and take a child into their control, pursuant to the customary responsibility afforded the family, when they see the child at risk. Legal processes may be necessary to forestall fighting and family "tugs-of-war" when families cannot resolve these issues on their own (Cross, McNevins, Grossman, Deloria, & Dorsay 2003).

Legal Basis for Tribal Adoption Laws

Because Indian tribes are governmental entities that predate the United States, they retain sovereign authority over a variety of areas. One of the tribe's basic sovereign rights is the right to decide the custody of its children. As part of its sovereign right, a tribe has the power and jurisdiction to articulate and formally certify through law its own customary practices concerning child custody and to create law based on its historical, customary, and current unique cultural interpretations of civil relationships. This power includes the power to enact formal adoption procedures and conduct adoption of children pursuant to custom or traditional law as part of tribal law, and formally certify, through its legal process, adoptions made pursuant to tribal custom.

In the exercise of their sovereignty, each tribal government must address the following questions: How do we handle these unique and complex relationships between children and youth, birth parents, extended family, and adoptive parents? In the context of federal policy that pressures us to change who we are, how do we form policy that protects children, preserves culture, and meets the needs of a diverse population? What if tradition says that it is the extended family whose "parental rights" cannot be culturally terminated? Only the extended family, not the tribe or governments, can limit or terminate the "rights" or responsibilities of the birth parents. Should tribal governments intervene and, if so, when? Answering these and other complex questions and implementing those answers in the form of code, policy, and programs is the essence of sovereignty.

Tribes can set policy and regulations that define adoption in all of its forms, its meaning in the tribal society, and the legal consequences of its conduct. In many tribes, customary adoption is the process of making relatives and joining individuals into family relationships. It represents expanding family resources for a child without terminating existing relationships. By most customs, adoption modifies the custodial and legal relationship of the birth parents with the child but does not terminate a birth parent's emotional relationship with the child or the child's relationships with the birth parent or extended family of birth, or the extended family's relationship with the child. By some customs, the rights of the birth parents are subordinate to the rights and responsibilities of the extended family and adoptive parents, and the best interests of the child guide the division of rights and responsibilities toward the child.

Historically, tribes had to deal with parental behavior that was so severe that relatives intervened to remove children, in some cases permanently. Thus, termination of parental rights may be culturally based in some tribal communities.

Despite having the authority to put customary practices into code, few tribes would choose to write the particulars of a ceremony, ritual, or traditional practice into code, thereby freezing it in time and making it public. It is, however, possible for a tribe to treat customary laws or practices in two ways for the purpose of writing laws. It can formally sanction a practice and affirm that the outcome of the practice has the force of law, and it could also use the underlying legal theories and premises of the customary practices to frame, codify, and support modern interpretations of historic practices. By choosing to certify a customary adoption as having the force of law, a tribe does not codify the practice. It does not describe it, freeze it in time, or even dictate what it is. It simply sets up a process whereby a specified individual, usually the adoptive parent, can petition the court to certify that the customary adoption occurred and that it meets the criteria set broadly by the code. In addition, the code can set out safeguards to insure the safety and well-being of the child or adolescent.

A customary adoption is a practice, ceremony, or process conducted in a manner that is long-established, continued, reasonable, and certain and considered by the people of a tribe to be binding or found by the court to be authentic, as a usage or practice common to many tribal members.

Conclusion

Tribal adoption law based in culture must consider that children cannot protect themselves and depend on adults to protect them, their

rights, and their resources. Neither can children insure that they have a family to grow up in and call their own. Tribes are developing and implementing customary adoption laws designed to insure permanency, as well as solve complex cross-jurisdictional and cross-cultural challenges. At the same time, these tribes are striving to protect the child's safety; preserve the child's sense of belonging; protect and preserve the child's identity, rights, and obligations as a member of his or her tribe, clan, and extended family; protect the child's assets, resources, and potential opportunities; and assist courts to make determinations in the best interests of the child when the parties cannot agree about placement decisions or when the court determines that the agreement is not in the child's best interest.

These are not small challenges but, as is often the case, tribes are turning to their culture for answers to complex problems and finding that the wisdom of established traditions is providing the guidance needed for today's world.

REFERENCES

Adoption and Safe Families Act. (1997). P.L. 105-89.

Barth, R., Webster, D., & Lee, S. (2002). Adoption of American Indian children: Implications for implementing the Indian Child Welfare and Adoption and Safe Family Acts. *Children and Youth Services Review, 24,* 139–158.

Byler, W. (1977). The destruction of American Indian families. In S. Unger (ed.), *The destruction of American Indian families,* pp. 1–11. New York: Association on American Indian Affairs.

Cross, T. L., McNevins, M., Grossman, T., Deloria, P. S., & Dorsay, C. (2003). *Developing culturally based tribal adoption laws and customary adoption codes: A technical assistance manual and model code.* Portland, OR: National Indian Child Welfare Association.

Cross, T. (2002). *Customary adoption; Making family.* Portland, OR: National Indian Child Welfare Association.

Curtis, C. M., & Alexander, R. (1996). The Multiethnic Placement Act: Implications for social work practice. *Child and Adolescent Social Work Journal, 13,* 401–410.

Dorris, M. (1989). *The broken cord.* New York: Harper & Row.

Duran, E., & Duran, B. (1995). *Native American postcolonial psychology.* Albany: State University of New York Press.

George, L. J. (1997). What the need for the Indian Child Welfare Act? *Journal of Multi-Cultural Social Work, 5,* 165–175.

Goodluck, C. T., & Eckstein, F. (1978). American Indian adoption program: An ethnic approach to child welfare. *White Cloud Journal, 1,* 3–6.

Goodluck, C. T., & Short, D. (1980). Working with American Indian parents: A cultural approach. *Social Casework, 61,* 472–475.

Indian Child Welfare Act. (1978). P.L. 95-608.

Locust, C. (1998). Split feathers: Adult American Indians who were placed in non-Indian families as children. *Pathways, 13,* 4–5.

MacEachron, A. E., Gustavsson, N. S., Cross, S., & Lewis, A. (1996). The effectiveness of the Indian Child Welfare Act. *Social Services Review, 70,* 451–463.

Madrigal, L. (2001) Indian Child Welfare Act: Partnership for preservation. *American Behavioral Scientist, 44,* 1505–1511.

Multiethnic Placement Act. (1994). P.L. 103-382.

Pevar, S. L. (2002). *The rights of Indians and tribes: The authoritative guide to Indian and Tribal rights,* third ed. Carbondale and Edwardsville: Southern Illinois University Press.

Plantz, M., Hubbell, R., Barrett, G. J., & Dobrec, A. (1998). *Indian child welfare: A status report of the survey of Indian child welfare and implementation of the Indian Child Welfare Act and section 428 of the Adoption Assistance and Child Welfare Act of 1980.* Washington DC: U.S. Department of Health and Human Services and U.S. Department of the Interior, Bureau of Indian Affairs.

Red Horse, J. (1997). Traditional American Indian family systems. *Families, Systems, and Health, 15,* 243–250.

Robin, R. W., Rasmussen, J. K., & Gonzalez-Santin, E. (1999). Impact of out-of-home placement on a South-western American Indian tribe. *Journal of Human Behavior in the Social Environment, 2,* 69–89.

Seaver, J. E. (1991). *The Life of Mary Jemison, Deh-he-wa-mis.* Baltimore, MD: Gateway Press.

Simmons, D., & Trope, J. (1999). *P.L. 105-89 Adoption and Safe Families Act of 1997: Issues for tribes and states serving Indian children.* Portland: National Resource Center for Organizational Improvement, Edmund S. Muskie School of Public Service, University of Southern Maine.

Swinomish Tribal Mental Health Project. (1991). *A gathering of wisdoms, tribal mental health: A cultural perspective.* LaConner, Washington: Swinomish Community.

VICTOR GROZA

LINDSEY HOULIHAN

ZOE BREEN WOOD

Overview of Adoption

According to the 2000 Census (U.S. Census Bureau 2003), 2.5% of all children in the United States are connected to a family through adoption. Thus there are more than 2 million adopted children. There are virtually no regional differences in the percentage of children adopted, with the exception of Alaska (which has a higher percentage), attributed to informal adoption practices that are common among Native American groups (see the chapter by Cross and Fox).

Adoption involves three major groups—the adoption triad of birth parents, adoptive parents, and adoptees—in a unique legal, social, and emotional arrangement. Regulating relationships among members of the adoption triad are laws, rules, and policies that affect how they come together and guide their relationship over time. However, the times have been changing, and there is reason to expect that more changes are in store. The Hague Convention is due to be implemented in the United States in 2005, and the state-by-state legal and policy changes regarding open adoption, access to birth records, and the right of adoptive parents to complete and accurate information on the children they adopt are systematically transforming adoption. This changing sociopolitical environment will bring challenges to the practitioner who tries to understand the clinical and practice issues encountered by birth parents, adoptive parents, and adoptees. It is clear that the issues of secrecy that plagued adoptive practice from the 1950s through the 1980s have been modified. In addition, the 1980s ushered

in a greater number of older children with traumatic histories being placed for adoption, and the 1990s was accompanied by a steady increase of international adoptees. So the issues encountered by child welfare practitioners will differ, depending on the type of the adoption, the member of the triad being considered, and the time period when the adoption occurred.

In this chapter, we provide an overview of adoption in the United States. We summarize major policies that affect different aspects of adoption, including a critique of the policies. We also outline major practice issues in adoption, including the strengths perspective, closed adoptions, older children from the public system, kinship adoption, sibling adoptions, and international adoptions. Case examples are used to highlight some points. The chapter highlights tools that are useful for working in adoption. It identifies gaps in the research about adoption and outlines an agenda for the future, including those areas not discussed in this chapter.

Adoption is not only multifaceted, it is also a mosaic. One group of adoptees, representing the biggest shift in adoption populations, consists of those who live with one birth parent and are subsequently adopted by that parent's spouse, who is not otherwise related to the child (a stepparent adoption). In most states, stepparent adoptions are the most common (Barth 1992), reflecting the general societal trend of stepfamilies replacing nuclear families as the dominant form of family life in the United States. Usually, stepparent adoptions involve stepfathers adopting a stepchild. This type of adoption has been classified as a related adoption and comprises about half of all adoptions in the United States (Stolley 1993).

A second group of adoptees consists of the healthy infants, who are predominantly placed with middle- and upper-middle–class families. About one-third of unrelated domestic adoptions are arranged independently (Stolley 1993), meaning that children are placed directly in adoptive families without agencies acting as intermediaries. In independent adoptions, the primary intermediaries are usually attorneys. Some observers estimate that infant adoptions account for approximately 15% of adoptions (Barth 1992; Stolley 1993). However, infant adoptions may actually comprise less than 5% of adoptions in the United States. The exact percentage is not known, but infant adoptions have decreased since the 1970s.

In 2002, about 20,000 children entered the United States from other countries. Over the past 10 years, there have been more than 100,000 children adopted from other countries. The 2000 Census estimates that 13% of children that have been adopted came from foreign countries (U.S. Census Bureau 2003). About half the children adopted since 1990 came from Asia, about one-third from Russia and other Eastern European countries, and less than 10% came from Central or South America. The children from Asia were mostly from China or South Korea, those from Eastern Europe were predominantly from Russia, and the children from Central or South America were primarily from Guatemala (U.S. Department of State 2004).

More girls than boys are adopted (U.S. Census Bureau 2003). This trend is a result of a number of factors, such as women preferring to adopt girls, single parents adopting mostly girls, and international adoptions comprising mostly girls. Although cultural attitudes traditionally favor male over female children, it is interesting to note that in the arena of adoption, girls are preferred over boys. One explanation is that women are the driving force in initiating adoption in married couples, and women pre-

fer to raise daughters. The increase of international adoption has also supported the increase of girls. The most recent statistics indicate that nearly 65% of children adopted internationally are female (U.S. Department of State 2004). An adjunct to explaining the preponderance of girls is that China, now the leading country in facilitating international adoptions, places mostly female children (more than 90%). A final factor in the gender imbalance is that adoption by single women has increased over time, and these women have a preference for female adoptees.

These general patterns describe the multiple facets of adoption in the United States. To some degree, social policies have both affected these patterns and responded to the patterns. It is important for any practitioner in adoption to understand the policy context of adoption.

Social Policies Affecting Adoption

The most influential federal law on adoption in the 1990s was the Adoption Assistance and Child Welfare Act of 1980. That law impacted adoption by:

- Requiring that states make reasonable efforts to prevent removal of children from their birth homes, and that they make reasonable efforts to reunify children who had been removed;
- Encouraging states to place for adoption children who had special needs (a child was determined to have special needs by virtue of her or his age, mental or physical impairment, membership in a sibling group, or belonging to a racial minority group); and
- Providing federal funds to help cover the cost of a maintenance subsidy for a child with special needs after she or he had been adopted.

By the mid-1990s, however, there was a growing dissatisfaction with efforts to achieve permanency for waiting children. On the one hand, the emphasis on preventing removal and working toward reunification in all instances had led to highly publicized instances in which agencies seemingly ignored the safety needs of vulnerable children with tragic results. On the other hand, increasing numbers of children remained trapped in the foster care system for longer periods of time. Furthermore, of those children who were waiting, a disproportionate number were found to be children of color. Federal legislative efforts aimed at correcting these problems resulted in the passage of the Adoption and Safe Families Act of 1997, the Multiethnic Placement Act of 1994 (P.L. 103-382), and the Interethnic Adoption Act in 1996 (P.L. 104-188).

Adoption and Safe Families Act

Major provisions of Adoption and Safe Families Act (ASFA; P.L. 105-89) center around the concepts of safety and permanency. Each of the main provisions of the act is discussed here.

Safety. The legislation stipulates that a child's health and safety are paramount in making decisions about removing or returning a child. ASFA specifies the situations in which the agency does not need to make reasonable efforts to reunify a child with his or her birth family (e.g., parental murder or manslaughter of another child, felony assault of a child, rights of a sibling terminated, other aggravated circumstances defined by state law). Criminal record checks became required for prospective foster and adoptive parents before final placement of a child (states, however, could opt of out of this provision).

Permanency. The law reinforces the concept that foster care must be seen as a temporary setting and not a place for a child to grow up. Agencies were encouraged to engage in concurrent planning—working simultaneously toward family reunification and adoption or another permanent alternative—for all children in care. The termination of parental rights petitions became required, unless an exception applied, when: the child had been in state foster care

for 15 of the past 22 months; a court had determined that a child was an abandoned infant under state law; or one of the reasons for not pursuing reasonable efforts had been established.

ASFA sought to reduce the use of long-term foster care by limiting permanency options at the 12-month hearing to return home (by a specified date), placement for adoption (with termination petition filed by a specified date), or establishment of legal guardianship (defined as a judicially created relationship between child and caretaker that is intended to be permanent and self-sustaining). The law established an abbreviated time frame for decisionmaking for every child who came into care.

Controversies surrounding ASFA. Since the passage of ASFA, the number of children served in foster care has stayed relatively stable. The Voluntary Cooperative Information System (VCIS) data are not very reliable before 1998 (P. Maza, pers. comm.). In 1998, 817,000 children were served in foster care, and in 2002 (the latest year data are available), 813,000 children were served in foster care (Adoption and Foster Care Analyis and Reporting System 2004), suggesting that the number of children entering care is stable. However, exits from care have varied over the same time period, with adoptions increasing. For example, in 1998, 257,000 exited care, or about 32% of the children served. In 2002, 303,000 children exited care, or about 37% of those served. Adoptions increased from 37,000 in 1998 (5% of the children served) to 53,000 in 2002 (7% of children served). A number of concerns have been expressed, however, about ASFA.

In some states, there has been an increasing backlog in the courts of cases for which termination petitions have been filed but overcrowded dockets result in continued delays. In other communities, the concern is expressed that if parental rights are terminated without an adoptive home identified, children become legal orphans for whom no one other than a public agency has responsibility. It is noted that some difficulties faced by families of children in care (e.g., substance abuse) cannot be easily remedied in a 12-month period, especially when treatment resources are severely limited. The rush toward termination of parental rights in those instances is thought to be a disincentive for parents to deal with their substance-abuse problems. At the same time, the lack of available adoptive placements for these children increases the risk that they will languish in a legal limbo. Finally, it is often difficult for a foster family to work toward reunification of the child with the birth family and to make a commitment to adopt the child if they cannot be reunified. The concern is that families may put less effort into supporting reunification as an outcome.

Multiethnic Placement Act and Interethnic Placement Act Adoption Provisions

Certain trends were brought to the forefront in the 1990s as the number of white infants who were awaiting adoptive placements continued to diminish. Children of color were disproportionately represented in the foster care system. Minority children make up about 39% of the U.S. population but approximately 59% of the children in the child welfare system (U.S. Department of Health and Human Services 2004). African American children are much more likely to enter care than are Hispanics and Asians (Garland, Ellis-Mclead, Landsverk, Ganger, & Johnson 1998) and tend to stay in care longer (Barth 1997; Hogan & Siu 1988; Jenkins & Diamond 1985; Olsen 1983). The African American child is twice as likely to remain in foster care than to be adopted (Barth 1997). Barth (1997:298) writes that "an African-American infant has nearly the same likelihood of being adopted as a Caucasian three- to five-year-old." Adoption policies and practices in this country favored placing children in same-race households. Given these factors, there was a concern that such racially matched placements impeded the achievement of permanence. Thus,

the Multiethnic Placement Act (MEPA) and the Interethnic Placement Act (IEPA) were enacted in two succeeding congressional sessions.

The stated intentions of these laws are threefold: To decrease the length of time that children wait to be adopted; to facilitate recruitment and retention of foster and adoptive parents who can meet the distinctive needs of the children awaiting placement; and to eliminate discrimination on the basis of the race, color, or national origin of the child or the prospective parent.

The basic provisions of MEPA and IEPA are that states or agencies receiving federal funding for foster care or adoption cannot delay or deny a child's placement on the basis of the child's race or the prospective parent's race, color, or national origin; states and agencies cannot deny the opportunity to become a foster/adoptive parent on the basis of the prospective parent's race, color, or national origin; and states must diligently recruit foster and adoptive parents who reflect the racial and ethnic diversity of the children in the state who need foster and adoptive homes to remain eligible for federal assistance for their child welfare programs.

Although many child welfare practitioners felt that policies of racial matching or the ethics of transracial adoptions were indeed controversial, the passage of this legislation has done little to lessen the controversy. By stating that an important goal of MEPA and IEPA is to reduce the time that children wait for adoptive placement, an assumption is that racial matching policies have had a substantial effect on delays or denials of adoption for many children (Brooks, Barth, Bussiere, & Patterson 1999). Adoptive placement decisions are much more complex, however, and no evidence has been presented that placing children in same-race homes had substantially impeded the placements of children of color.

The laws have done little to provide direction to child welfare workers about how to evaluate the importance of race in a child's life. In response, many states have interpreted MEPA and IEPA to say that race can never be considered when making placement decisions. This is contrary to what is known about the needs of some children for support in the development of racial or ethnic identity. Another area of controversy has been that of resources. The federal government did not provide additional funding for the implementation of this legislation and, with the addition of the interethnic provisions, stipulated that states could lose substantial funding for failure to comply with these laws. A key question is: how might this threatened or actual loss of funding impact the speed with which children achieve permanence? This question remains unanswered.

Safe Haven Laws

In contrast to the previous laws that were passed at the federal level, safe haven laws have been passed in 45 states in an attempt to address the problem of newborns that are abandoned in unsafe situations (e.g., trash cans, on a sidewalk) that could result in serious harm or death (National Conference of State Legislatures 2003). These laws cite examples of women or girls who leave their newborn to die rather than turn the baby over to responsible individuals who can care for the child.

Most such laws designate hospitals, emergency medical services, fire stations, and police stations as safe locations. Either immunity from prosecution is granted, or the law allows for an affirmative defense to prosecution for any individual who leaves an unharmed infant in a designated location. The maximum age of an eligible child also varies, often from 72 hours to 30 days. Another key provision of these laws is that they allow for the mother to leave the child anonymously, without being required to provide any medical or family history for the child.

For those states that are keeping records on the number of infants abandoned after passage of safe haven legislation, these laws are reported to have a limited effect in preventing infant abandonment (National Conference of State Legislatures 2003). Concern is expressed that this solution does not address the under-lying causes of the problem and that additional problems have been created as well. Two of the most frequently cited are the ability of the parent to leave the child without providing critical information about the child's medical and family history, and that the rights of biological fathers to make a decision about parenting the child are denied. Because these laws are relatively new, their impact is still being evaluated.

The Hague Convention

The Hague Convention on Intercountry Adoption is a multilateral treaty that was approved by 66 nations on May 29, 1993. This international legal document was operationalized from the U.N. Convention on the Rights of the Child (1989). The U.N. Convention broadened the rights of children more than any other legal document and directly created the groundwork for the Hague Convention. The purpose of the Hague Convention on Intercountry Adoptions is to set standards to protect the rights of the adopted child, as well as of birth and adoptive parents. Another purpose directly related to the treaty is the prevention of child trafficking internationally. Prior to the Hague Convention, international adoptions remained largely unregulated, as opposed to domestic adoptions, for which governing bodies oversee the adoption process. The lack of regulation related to international adoption has given rise to charges of setting program fees for child placement akin to a market value. The criticism of international adoption has been that it relegates children to be traded as commodities (Groza, Ileana, & Irwin 1999; Tessler, Gamache, & Liu 1999).

The Intercountry Adoption Act of 2000, which was the U.S. implementation of the Hague treaty, was passed by Congress and signed into law by President Clinton. In 2002, 46 countries had ratified the treaty and 13 had signed. However, the implementation of the Hague Convention provisions in the United States will occur only after the Immigration and Naturalization Service and the Department of State publish implementing regulations in the Federal Register. As of 2004, the United States was still in the process of developing the implementation policies, with expectation that they would be in place some time in 2005.

A summary of the Hague Convention is as follows. A child has the right to a family; however, the country of origin must first try to place the child or reunite the child with the biological parents. An intercountry adoption will take place if it is in the best interests of the child and consent to the adoption has been given freely. In addition, the receiving country must assess and determine that the prospective parents are suited to adopt. Adoptions can occur only from one Hague Convention country to another. Furthermore, each participating nation must establish a central authority to oversee the implementation of the convention. In the United States, the U.S. State Department will serve as the central authority. Adoption agencies and individual providers must be accredited to standards set up by the central authority. Although rare exceptions may be permitted, no contact will be made between the prospective parents and parent or institution where the child may temporarily reside until certain requirements have been satisfied.

Although the Hague Convention has many benefits in regards to providing legal provisions to discourage child trafficking and has supportive guidelines for regulation of international adoption, the treaty has not been without criticism. Some adoption agencies and professionals in the United States have questioned several aspects of the legislation. One criticism has been that the increased bureaucracy in the form of regulation and accreditation will increase costs incurred by adoptive parents. In addition, child placement and permanency will be delayed because of increased paperwork for both sending and receiving countries. A final criticism is that children must first be referred in-country, where in many developing nations the child welfare agencies are weak and cannot adequately support domestic adoption for the immediate placement and safety of waiting children. The result will be children waiting longer in poor circumstances that may compromise their health, development, and well-being. Because the law has not been implemented in the United States as of the writing of this chapter, the actual impact is still a matter of speculation.

Practice Issues in Adoption

Whereas the previous section identified the policy context of contemporary adoption practice, this section outlines practice issues in adoption.

Adoption from a Strengths Perspective

The strengths perspective is relevant to adoption practice in a number of ways. If there is an adoption in the client's background, asking about the positive aspects of adoption orients the practitioner to strengths. Strengths may then be used in the intervention. For example, nontraditional families may have more flexible and inclusive views of creating a family that may affect the experience of loss in adoption for adoptees. Adoptive families may also have personal and social resources that protect against negative adoption outcomes. These resources include such personal attributes as patience, a sense of humor, and the ability to enjoy small accomplishments. Social resources include good formal and informal social, emotional, and material support. These resources need to be identified, acknowledged, and used. An additional way to focus on strengths may be to stop considering the lack of a strong racial or ethnic identity as a deficit, but to consider having a strong identity as a strength. By framing adoption issues as the lack of identity, the orientation becomes one of deficit and pathology instead of successful adaptation in the absence of a strong racial or ethnic identity. Also, adoptive parents can be engaged more successfully to help build strengths in children rather than approached as if they lack something if they cannot or will not build a racial or ethnic identity in the adoptee. Finally, there is no evidence to suggest that white families cannot build the knowledge and skills needed to help their minority children navigate successfully in life and deal with discrimination and prejudice. They may struggle with how to teach such skills and may not want to address the problem when adoptees are older. However, without empirical evidence to the contrary, the strengths approach can be used to help families with minority children as they face challenges during the life cycle.

The strengths perspective can also be used in framing issues. Approaches to work with adoptive families that are problem-focused tend to rely on counseling and parenting techniques as the sole agents of change. Greater transformation in families can occur when parents discover that many of the challenges with which they are struggling are more endemic to children who are adopted, particularly those with problematic placement histories before adoption. Framing the issues as normative allows families to move beyond blaming and use their many strengths to manage the issues.

Adoption is a solution. There is no doubt that thousands of children will experience a better life through adoption and be spared circumstances that would compromise their health and development, if not scar them for life. When children cannot reside with their birth family, adoption offers the best opportunity for them. That does not mean that it works for all triad members or that clinical issues related to individual or family functioning or development do not emerge. It does mean that as part of a strengths orientation, practitioners must see adoption overall as a solution, even if there are specific cases for which this may be doubtful. Also, those individuals and families who are successful in adoption will not present themselves for services, and they represent the majority of triad members. It is easy to lose perspective in the helping professions because those seeking services are the families and individuals with difficulties.

Success in adoption is not only an outcome, but a journey. Navigating one issue successfully increases the likelihood that any member of the triad will be able to resolve other issues as they arise. Other issues manifest in different ways and at different times throughout the life cycle. If practitioners approach triad members as if many of the difficulties they experience are normative crises (Pavao 1992) to be expected, and without giving the message that successful resolution at one stage does not mean that the issue will remained resolved, then practice moves to a less pathology-focused orientation and toward a normative and strength orientation.

Vulnerabilities and Risks in Adoption

The strengths perspective does not require a practitioner to ignore real clinical issues. Rather, it is a framework for orienting assessment and intervention. This section highlights the vulnerabilities and risks in various types of adoption that are important considerations for adoption practice.

Infants Placed in Closed Adoptions

For many couples who experience infertility, adoption is considered the "next best" choice. Often such couples seek to adopt healthy infants and operate from the mistaken assumption that if the adoption is closed (i.e., the birth parent does not know the identity or location of the adoptive family and vice versa), there will be little chance that the birth parent will try to get the baby back. They seek to take the child home and raise him or her as if the baby had been born to them and may even deny that the child is adopted. Core issues that often must be resolved include secrecy, denial, loss, and shame (Rosenberg & Groze 1997; see the chapters by Cooper, Heitzman, and Hollingsworth).

This can lead to a number of risks for the child and the family. The lack of information about the birth family can interfere with the adoptee's identity development. No or inaccurate information about the reason for placement can lead to low self-esteem in the adoptee, and the development of rescue fantasies concerning the birth parent. Secrecy concerning the adoption can lead to a deep sense of betrayal when the adoptee learns that he or she has been deceived. The adoptive parent's silence concerning the adoption can lead the child to assume that he or she is part of a secret that is too horrible to discuss. Finally, lack of information about the birth family can deny the adoptee and his or her adoptive family access to vital information about medical history and health and psychological risks. All of these factors can interfere with the development of a strong and healthy bond between the adoptee and his or her adoptive family.

Best practice encourages the adoptive family and adoptee to grieve the losses (Rosenberg & Groze 1997) and explore the reasons that may have made them fearful of having contact with the birth family. Adoptive families do best when they neither deny nor insist on the differences between their families and families who have come together by birth (Kirk 1964). Healthy adoptive families acknowledge and are open to discussing adoption without dwelling on it. Finally, it is important to encourage families to consider a range of openness in adoption and to consider the child's best interest when determining the level of information and contact with members of the birth family. Openness ranges from completely open with ongoing contact to the traditional closed adoption, and the degree of openness may and often does change over the life cycle. Families considering adoption should be aware of all the options and variations in options that are available to them.

A number of practitioners have written about core clinical issues that may emerge for adoptees placed as infants. Some draw heavily on psychoanalytical orientations (Lifton 1988, 1994; Verrier 1993), others draw from psychological models (Brodzinsky 1990), and some blend orientations within a family-systems framework (Groza & Rosenberg 2001; Reitz & Watson 1992; Winkler, Brown, van Keppel, & Blanchard 1988). It is beyond the scope of this chapter to discuss fully all these models. Instead they are mentioned here to guide future reading in this area. The following case example highlights some of the issues mentioned here.

JOSHUA

Joshua was placed with Sarah and Andrew in a closed adoption at the age of 5 days. Although Joshua knew he was adopted, his parents spoke little about the circumstances surrounding the adoption and provided Joshua with no information about his birth history. As he was growing up, Joshua soon learned that asking questions about his birth family resulted in disapproval or anxiety from his parents. During his early years, Sarah and Andrew reported that Joshua was "extremely well adjusted" and "just like any other boy" who did well in school and was active in a traveling soccer team coached by his adoptive father. However, at about the age of 13, Joshua's grades declined, he changed his style of dress (from "preppy" to "Gothic"), and he terminated his involvement in sports. The more Sarah and Andrew encouraged their son to return to his previous ways, the more defiant Joshua became, with daily battles around whether Joshua was wearing black. His parents regularly followed him to school to make sure he turned in his homework. Frustrated and angry, Sarah and Andrew brought their son to a therapist for his "depression." In treatment, Joshua spoke of feeling "like an alien" who was nothing like his adoptive parents. The therapist helped Joshua and his parents search for his birth family. As they worked together on this quest, and discovered more information, the family found itself growing closer together. At 16, when he finally was able to meet his birth father, Joshua stopped wearing black.

Older Children from the Public Child Welfare System

With the increasing number of children entering the public system due to abuse; neglect; abandonment; or parental substance abuse, incarceration, or poverty, and the added emphases of federal and state laws on timely permanency, more and more older children are being placed in adoptive homes. Children who are adopted beyond infancy are seen as posing additional challenges. Even though adoption is considered to be a permanent and legally binding arrangement of bonding a child to a family, stories abound of adoptions disrupting (i.e., the parents asking to be relieved of their responsibility for the child before the adoption is legalized) or dissolving (i.e., parents petitioning the court to "give the child back" legally; see the chapter by Festinger). Disruption rates from 7% to 60% have been reported (Barth & Berry 1988; Groze 1986; Kagan & Reid 1986; Rosenthal, Schmidt, & Conner 1988); the range in rates is attributed to the age of the child, with older children who have behavioral and emotional problems experiencing higher rates of disruption. The most commonly used estimate is that about 15% of adoptions disrupt (Barth & Berry 1988), which means that most adoptions remain intact. Risk factors include the child's history of multiple separations and maltreatment; difficulties in attachment; the increased likelihood of medical or psychological conditions due to drug or alcohol exposure in utero or later; inadequate nutrition and physical care; delays in physical, psychological, or social development; and lack of preparation and postplacement support for adoptive families. It is important for social workers to insure that all of the available background information about the child and his or her birth family is gathered and reviewed to determine not only the child's current functioning but how his or her past is likely to impact future functioning. This information should be shared fully and truthfully with prospective adoptive parents to assist in making a realistic decision about placement.

In addition, it is crucial that adoptive parents be educated about lifelong adoption issues and the special vulnerabilities of older children from the public system. Ongoing support, including individual and family counseling; concrete services, such as postadoption services and adoption subsidies; access to support groups; and assistance with advocacy for the child's special needs in the educational system are all ways that the social worker can strengthen and support the adoptee and his or her family.

Several trends have developed of practice and research concerning the clinical issues that may emerge for adoptees placed as older children. Some approaches draw heavily on postpsychoanalytical orientations by focusing on attachment (Keck & Kupecky 1998, 2002; O'Connor & Zeanah 2003). Some researchers recommend controversial therapies, such as holding therapy (Keck & Kupecky 1998, 2002; Welch 1988); others draw from psychological models, such as cognitive-behavioral approaches (Beck 1995) and family systems models (Groze 1994, 1996; Groze & Rosenthal 1991a). There is increasing recognition that the clinical and practice issues for both infant and older adoptees are similar (Groza & Rosenberg 2001) and encourages use of the same interventions for both populations. The following is a case example that touches on these issues.

BRANDI

Brandi was adopted at the age of 13 after living in eight different foster homes. Her history included reports of physical and sexual abuse in her birth home (including having had her crib set on fire while she was asleep), numerous reports of acting out, poor school performance, and further sexual abuse in foster care. By the time she was adopted by Melissa, a single parent, Brandi had been diagnosed as mildly mentally retarded with reactive attachment disorder and attention deficit hyperactive disorder. Melissa took 2 months' maternity leave at the time of Brandi's placement and focused on helping Brandi feel safe. She noticed that Brandi soon followed her everywhere (even to the bathroom if allowed) and was most comfortable "snuggling" on the sofa. Brandi waged major tantrums around going to school and seemed to always get "sick" when she actually did go. Melissa relied on an adoptive parent support group to help her strategize ways to help Brandi increase her time at school and utilized special subsidies to help pay for specialized treatment. When the time came for Melissa to return to work, she was able to make special arrangements with her employer to allow her to bring Brandi with her at times and at other times to be able to work from home.

By the time Brandi reached age 18, mother and daughter proudly reported Brandi's graduation from high school and her obtaining a part time job in her mother's office.

Kinship Adoption

When children must come into the custody of child welfare agencies, recent federal laws, including the ASFA and the Personal Responsibility and Work Opportunity Act, view placing the child with kin as the first and best option. Kinship care offers several benefits to children, including providing familiar caregivers and continuity in familial patterns, reducing the trauma of separation, reinforcing children's sense of identity and self-esteem, offering more stability in placement, reducing the stigma of foster care, and promoting sibling relationships (Beeman & Boisen 1999; Berrick, Needell, Barth, & Jonson-Reid 1998; Lorkovich, Piccalo, Groza, Brindo, & Marks, in press; Wilson & Chipunga 1996). Approximately one-third of all children in custody are reported to be placed with relatives (Needell & Gilbert 1997), which makes kinship foster care the fastest growing out-of-home placement (Bonecutter & Gleeson 1997).

Although this form of placement provides many benefits, numerous challenges also exist. First and foremost is that the child welfare system itself was not originally developed to view kin as placement resources. There has been little recognition that kinship caregivers have their own special needs, including the tendency to be older, less educated, more likely to be living in poverty and having health problems (Bonecutter & Gleeson 1997; Scannapieco, Hegar, & McAlpine 1997). At the same time, children placed with relatives have the same needs as other children in the child welfare system who are placed with strangers. Yet studies show that kinship care families receive fewer services, experience more delays in receiving concrete services, and are monitored less frequently than are other families (Davidson 1997; Needell & Gilbert 1997). In addition to all of the issues that any foster or adoptive family faces, there are the additional issues of loss and stigma in knowing that the child has come into care because of the failing of a family member.

Placement of a relative's children can produce a great deal of stress on the kin family system. This often results in the need for a range of services from legal consultation, financial support, medical and mental health services, educational resources for the child, parent education and counseling, support group information, and/or other concrete services. Social opinion that relatives "should take care of their own" has led to fewer services and supports being available to kin families, putting them at higher risk for problems in the placement. Without these supports, children placed in relative's homes are at greater risk for return to the child welfare system. The following is an example of issues that emerge in kinship adoptions.

THE MORRISONS

The Morrison household underwent a drastic change when William and Monique adopted Monique's sister's children, aged 5, 7, and 8, after their mother was sentenced to 15 years on a felony drug charge. The family grew from three children—aged 3, 6, and 9—to six children under the age of 9. Monique had worked as a bank teller and had placed her youngest child in day care but found she needed to stop working to attend to the needs of her niece and nephews. The children had been left alone or with strangers and been severely neglected. They were behind in school and were reported to fight so frequently with the teachers and other children that Monique found herself being called to the school on a daily basis. They were delayed developmentally, with the youngest having acquired no speech. The Morrison's birth children reported feeling jealous and angry that their cousins were taking all of their parents' time and energy, and the Morrisons themselves reported that they were receiving no financial or emotional support from the agency that placed the children with them. They felt it was their obligation to take care of their family members but were so overwhelmed with the demands that they were considering placing the children back with the county.

International Adoption

Unlike the child welfare system in the United States, where children are placed in foster family care for temporary placement or adoption if they cannot remain with the biological family, the majority of children adopted internationally enter their adoptive families from orphanages or other child welfare institutions (Groze 1996). The regimentation and ritualization of institutional life do not provide children with the quality of life or the experiences they need to be healthy, happy, fully functioning adults. In group care, the child's needs are secondary to the requirements of the group's routine. Relationships between adults and children are usually superficial and brief, with little continuous warmth and affection. Institutional staff members do not connect emotionally or physically with children in the same way that families connect with children. Often, there are too many children and not enough staff, with the result that few children receive any individualized attention or care and so suffer emotional neglect (Miller 2000), if not physical neglect.

Institutionalized children, because of often-inadequate sanitation, nutrition, and medical care and an ineffective nurturing environment, are at high risk for impaired health, development difficulties, behavioral aberrations, and attachment problems (Miller 2000; Rutter et al. 1995). Children raised in institutions have fewer opportunities to develop selective attachments (Smyke, Dumitrescu, & Zeanah 2002) and institutional care is associated with attachment problems (Ames 1997; Chisholm 1998; Smyke, Dumitrescu, & Zeanah 2002).

However, the effects from institutionalization are not uniform. Although institutions compromise early development, not all children are treated equally in the same institution. Some children are prenatally exposed to risk factors that are exacerbated by institutional care. Prenatal medical care, nutrition, stress, exposure to toxic substances or environments, and genetics influence the developing neonate. Some children are born with a predisposition to be cranky, sickly, or colicky. Some are spontaneously responsive to any stimulus or person, whereas others are more lethargic or less responsive. Some children are physically more attractive than others. These factors influence how caregivers respond to these children. Children who are cranky, sickly, or colicky are challenging; they are usually ignored by staff or subjected to harsh treatment if they demand more time than caregivers can give. At the same time, if a child responds easily when spoken to or touched, and the caregiver gets some satisfaction from the response, the child receives more attention and responds even more positively. Finally, children who are physically attractive receive more attention than their less attractive counterparts. And children with obvious physical handicaps may receive less attention if they are placed with children who have no apparent handicaps.

The main reason children enter institutions is poverty. In a review of records of children presented to parents as candidates to adopt internationally, Jenista (2000) found that when parental issues were mentioned, poverty was the determining issue in 28% of the cases. However, about 25% of children enter the institution/orphanage due to parent abuse or neglect and 14% enter due to substance abuse. The conclusion is that many of the children adopted internationally have high medical and social risks that are often exacerbated by institutional care. This risk can be further compounded by abuse in the institutions. However, the incidence of physical and sexual abuse among institutionalized children is unknown (Miller 2000).

Families adopting internationally often need comprehensive services prior to and following adoptive placement. Aggressive gathering and full disclosure of all background information are critical components of effective practice. Comprehensive background information provides the starting point for preparing the family to anticipate their needs for services and support.

Findings from a study of Romanian adoptees (Groza & Ileana 1999), the first large wave of international adoptees after the fall of communism, suggest that various types of day care and respite care may be in great demand. Significant percentages of families desire additional help or counseling in various substantive areas (parenting skills, child development, and adoption issues). Continued development of such programs is recommended. Informal supports appear to be utilized and desired more often than formal, agency-related supports. Adoption workers may want to pay particular attention to social support systems in the home study phase, and, perhaps, more importantly, develop ways to extend greater support to families over the course of the adoption. Adoptive parent support groups provide formal and informal support, educate the parents about a myriad of issues, normalize the adoptive experience, and encourage families to advocate for their children.

Supporting Adoption: Promising Approaches

Sibling Adoption

For most individuals, the relationship with siblings is the longest relationship they will have in their lifetimes. Although the sibling relationship may be primary at some times in life and more distant at others, a person's identity is intricately interwoven with his or her siblings. Studies suggest that of children in foster care, 93% of the children had full, half, or step-siblings (Timberlake & Hamlin 1982) and up to 85% of children enter foster care with a sibling (Wedge & Mantle 1991). According to Hochman, Huston, and Feathers-Acuna (1992), 30% of the children entering foster care are part of sibling groups of four or more. A crucial question facing social workers when making decisions concerning foster or adoptive placement is whether it is better to place all brothers and sisters together, individually, or in subgroups.

Best practice in adoption begins with a belief that siblings should be kept together. Multi-dimensional assessments of the sibling relationship (see Groza, Maschmeier, Jamison, & Piccalo 2003) must occur prior to making placement decisions, and siblings should always be placed together unless an assessment produces compelling reasons to separate them. Although there may be many factors that complicate sibling placement, there are several strategies for keeping them together. These factors include clear agency policies concerning the value of sibling relations; making sibling groups a priority at the time that children enter placement; exploring extended family and kinship resources; and spending more effort recruiting, training, and retaining families that wish to adopt siblings. Other strategies include flexibility in licensing of foster and adoptive homes and visiting policies that encourage regular contact among siblings who are placed apart. It must be remembered that the job of placement professionals is to find families for children, not children for families. Thus efforts must be expended to fully assess the sibling relationship and prepare and support families who are open to taking sibling groups. Although loss is very much a part of adoption, the loss of one's siblings can be prevented by concerned and competent social workers.

MATTHEW, MARK, AND MAGDA

Matthew, Mark, and Magda are siblings. Matthew lives with his paternal grandmother in a rural area of West Virginia and has lived with her for 5 years. He is 10 years old. Mark, 7, and Magda, 5, had been living with their birth parents until a year ago. Their father went to prison for murdering another man in a drug deal. The mother abandoned the children with the maternal grandmother. The mother is a prostitute and drug addict, living on the streets in Las Vegas. Six months ago, parental rights were terminated. The maternal grandmother said she did not want to raise the kids. Three months ago, without the case worker knowing it, she had placed the two children in separate households. Mark went to family friends, a couple unable to have children and who were about the age as Mark's birth parents. The friends visited with the maternal grandmother about once a month, where Mark would see his sister. Mark liked the parents and the father, an athlete, often played sports with him. Magda went to a niece. The niece had a child 4 years ago, a girl, who died of leukemia 2 years ago. She and her husband suffered from secondary infertility. Magda is settled and happy in her placement. A family group conferencing therapist suggested that the county close the case because the family had made a placement decision. They should support the current placements for adoption. An attachment therapist reported that the children were very attached to one another, had never lived apart, wanted to be together, and that the lifelong relationship between the siblings was more important to maintain than the temporary attachments to the current placement.

International Adoption Centers

Due to the rapid increase in the number of international adoptions, which have more than tripled during the past 25 years, the need for specialized healthcare for adoptive families has increased. The creation of specialty international adoption clinics has provided full service medical consultation programs for families interested in adopting internationally. Many of the arriving adoptees face health challenges (e.g., infectious diseases, malnutrition, developmental delays, attachment disturbances) that the typical pediatrician has not treated.

The focus of international adoption clinics is to address health and medical issues related to international adoption, assess the effects of institutionalization on development and growth, and identify adoptees who are in need of early intervention or other services. The clinics work closely, and often collaboratively, with primary care providers, to prescribe and monitor care of children during the early phases of transition from institutional care to family care. The approximately 25 clinics located in the United States provide a range of services discussed below.

Pre-adoptive medical evaluation. A member of the clinic staff, usually a physician, will review referral materials. The doctor will offer a medical opinion about the health of the child that the family is considering adopting. In addition, he or she will offer information about the country of origin, questions to ask at the orphanage, common health problems, child and family preparation, and referral to support groups.

Postadoption health, developmental, and behavioral screenings. Visits are scheduled shortly after arrival in the United States. The children receive a comprehensive medical evaluation, often including a physical, developmental, behavioral, and growth evaluation.

Follow-up visits. Families bring their children for follow-up visits that focus on issues related to the first postadoption visit. These issues are primarily related to growth and development, speech and language development, infectious diseases, and attachment issues. Throughout the process, the staff members at the international adoption clinics work in conjunction with the primary care physicians to coordinate care.

Research. Many international adoption clinics initiate research projects to further the knowledge base in this area. Current research projects are often in areas in which little research has been conducted, such as infectious diseases, immunizations, and attachment.

Education. Many clinics offer a variety of services to the community. Prepareting classes help families to prepare for the realities of international adoption. Seminars, workshops, and lectures are also presented to educate adoptive families, adoption professionals, and health professionals.

These centers generate revenue by the services they provide. Some are attached to hospitals and some are located in university-affiliated hospitals. They charge fees for their various services. Some fees are covered by health insurance, whereas others are paid by the families. A few clinics provide on-line services, telephone consultation, and video conferencing. Given that the lives of many international adoptees are medically and developmentally complicated, these clinics have carved a niche in the service delivery system for meeting the needs of international adoptive families who have access to them.

Tools for Working in Adoption

The ability to put information about one's life into perspective is necessary to develop a good self-concept. For adoptees, there are often significant gaps in the information they have about their own history. Adoptees often do not have many details about their birth families, and what they do know is often only distorted facts or stories of dysfunctional episodes. The life book, ecomap, social network map, life map, and placement genogram (Aust 1981; Hartman 1984; McMillen & Groze 1994; Pinderhughes & Rosenberg 1990; Wheeler 1978; Young, Corcran-Rumppe, & Groze 1992) are particularly helpful tools for assessment and intervention with adoptees and adoptive families. These tools are discussed in more details below. There are also resource materials that examine the unique issues in the adoptive family life cycle (Rosenberg 1992), as well as practice techniques specifically for the adoptive family (Reitz & Watson 1992). Understanding and using these tools and being familiar with the growing body of literature about adoptive families can help practitioners work more skillfully and sensitively with these families.

Families must integrate the adoptive child or children into their family systems, which requires flexibility. As part of the home study process, families should be assessed in their level of adaptability. Less adaptable families should be seen as at risk. They should not be screened out of the adoption process, but they may need special assistance as part of their preparation for adoption and ongoing support to enhance their flexibility. After placement,

preventive models, such as the family-bonding model (Pinderhughes & Rosenberg 1990), offer a psychoeducational approach to assist with the issues the new adoptive family must resolve to promote integration.

Adopted families with adequate resources are stable and can manage the different stresses and difficulties they encounter. In the assessment of resources and stressors to the family, an ecomap (Hartman & Laird 1983) and social network map (Tracy & Whittaker 1990) can be helpful. The ecomap visually diagrams the resources and stressors in the life space of the family, and the social network map examines both the structure and function of social networks. Both can be used to assess family resources, gaps in resources, and stressors.

For older adopted children, two instruments that can help both parents and therapists in their cognitive work with children are the life book and the placement genogram. The life book (Aust 1981; Wheeler 1978) is a scrapbook that contains photos, drawings, and other mementoes from the child's life experiences. It is used to help children connect and integrate their past to the present and assist in planning for the future. If children do not have a life book when they enter adoptive placement, they can be assisted in developing one post-placement that can serve as a guide for addressing past relationship issues.

The placement genogram (Groze, Young, & Corcran-Rumppe 1991; McMillen & Groze 1994) is a diagramming technique that traces the child's placement history starting from birth and records pertinent information about each placement. For instance, the date of parental rights termination, allegations of abuse, and relationships with significant caregivers might be documented on the placement genogram. This information can help provide insight into the issues raised by adoptive families as they try to understand the child's behavior and its impact on their family (Hartman & Laird 1983). The placement genogram also helps the child to explore the meaning of relationships and how those relationships have influenced his or her life.

As a practitioner helps a child to unfold the life history, he or she can begin to explore the child's "working models" of relationships and help cognitively restructure the models to increase attachment in the adoptive home. Melina (1986) suggests that adoptive parents can facilitate attachment cognitively by assisting children in examining and understanding their past, giving them a vision for the future, and using appropriate and positive physical contact.

These are a few of the tools available for working with adoptive families. As adoption practice grows, more tools will be developed and existing ones modified. The most important aspect of working in adoption, regardless of the tools and techniques used, is building a relationship with the adoptive family. A practitioner has to be knowledgeable about the various aspects and issues in adoption, but knowledge will not substitute for good relationship-building skills. Once a practitioner has a good relationship, then knowledge and evidence-based practice will be critical to working in adoption.

Although the clinical literature on working in adoption has grown dramatically, empirical knowledge that is the hallmark of evidence-based practice has developed more slowly. The next section highlights the gaps in our research knowledge about adoption.

Identifying the Research Gaps

Research in adoption is still in its toddler stage. Even exploratory and descriptive studies on many topics are still lacking. For example, there is a dearth of research on stepparent adoption and a lack of empirical knowledge about the experiences, opinions, and attitudes about adoption in families of color.

Many available studies suffer from problems of sample size, sampling strategy that affects external validity, measurement, methodological issues (e.g., appropriate comparison groups),

and the overreliance on cross-section compared to longitudinal designs. Adoption research would benefit from more meta-analyses, such as those being published on early intervention (Bimmel, Juffer, van Ijzendoorn, & Bakermans-Kranenberg 2003) and on transracial adoption (Hollingsworth 1997).

The concepts of most interest to workers are often the most elusive to measure. For example, how do we measure attachment in older children? How do we capture the parent-child dynamic when measuring patterns of attachment? How do we define success in adoption? How can we understand the expectations of adopting parents and of adoptees and how do expectations affect adoption issues?

One thorny issue is what constitutes the best comparison group for adopted children. For children adopted as infants, should it be siblings that remained in the birth family, born before or after the adoption? Should it be children raised in foster care that were never adopted? For transracial adoptees, should it be a mixed-race child raised by the parent of a different race? Should it include both single parents and mixed-race families? For children adopted through the public system, should it be the children returned to birth families after foster care or children who never leave foster care? There are many confounding variables, regardless of the choices made.

Although workers in many countries are engaged in various types of adoption research, the results are often not widely disseminated. There is much that could be learned from this international literature, which offers diverse perspectives that can be used to build a better knowledge base about adoption.

In addition, there are many midrange theories and conceptual models specific to issues or specific groups of adoptees but no comprehensive framework for understanding individual and family adjustment. Even current models are limited by their failure to include a life-course perspective in adoption. For example, the clinical issues for a birth mother are different at the time she discovers she is pregnant, when she considers adoption, at relinquishing, immediately after relinquishment, and throughout her life course. Research from the perspective of all triad members, supplemented from views by professionals and disciplines encountered by triad members, is needed. Often the information available to practitioners to guide clinical interventions draws upon the perspective of only one member of the adoption triad.

Many questions are still unanswered. Although we know something about birth mothers who surrender children, we know little about birth fathers. Virtually nothing is known about birth parents whose parental rights were involuntarily terminated. Too little attention has been paid to the voice of the adoptee over the lifespan; for example, what do adoptees experience as they become parents themselves? How do adoptees think about adoption in old age? What wisdom can they impart, given their life experiences?

In an attempt to understand the group, we ignore the heterogeneity of adoption and the adoption experience. We need to look for the nuances in groups and issues that do not fit a linear model of understanding. Adoption experiences vary; individual, family, social, and temporal contexts must be considered in conceptualizing the adoption experience.

Finally, the historical reliance on a psychodynamic orientation and focus on risks and problems has undermined creativity in adoption research. It is only by moving beyond pathology paradigms and into those incorporating concepts of resilience, strength, and coping will adoption research, theory, and practice provide a better and more holistic view of adoption.

As social scientists are trained in triad research, the field of adoptive research will mature. However, such research needs better funding. The amount of money that has come from federal institutes is insignificant. An issue that directly affects 2.5% and indirectly affects more than 60% of the U.S. population (Evan B. Donaldson Adoption Institute 1997) merits much more generous funding to answer basic and advanced research questions.

The Future of Adoption

As discussed in this chapter, adoption has changed dramatically over time. New populations of adoptees have emerged, different policies have been enacted, and the practice thinking about the adoption process and issues continues to develop. In concluding this chapter, we briefly identify other important issues that were not covered but are essential for good adoption practice.

The first such issue is that of the ethics and standards in contemporary American adoption practice that affect infant, older child, and international adoptions. The work of Babb (1999, 2001), Fogg-Davis (2002), Freundlich (2000a,b), and Freundlich and Liberthal (2001) provide valuable readings in this area. Many ethical issues arise in the various forms of adoption. The following case highlights some issues that need attention in more complicated cases.

MS. GREEN
Ms. Green has been a foster mother for 5 years, working for a private foster care agency. For 4.5 of those 5 years, she has fostered three brothers aged 7, 6, and 5. In addition to her monthly stipend of $700 per child to foster a sibling group with special needs, she gets a medical card, reimbursement for travel, homemaker services, respite care, a yearly clothing allowance for each child, monthly foster care worker visits, case management services, and in-home family therapy and counseling. Recently, the parental rights of the boys have been terminated, and they are available for adoption. Ms. Green wants to adopt the boys but once she adopts them, she loses all the services she has had as a foster parent. Even though the typical monthly adoption subsidy is only $500, the local county child welfare office has offered her $800

per child per month. She does not think that she can live on this amount and purchase the services the children need. She has requested $1,200 per child per month. She says that she will relinquish the children back to the child welfare agency if the agency cannot offer her more money. The foster care worker and agency adoption worker have no other families interested in the boys and are committed to keeping them together. The judge who grants the adoption has some concerns about a single parent adopting.

A second set of issues concerns nontraditional families. In particular, single parents and gay and lesbian families are adoption resources. Although gay and lesbian parent adoptions are sometimes controversial in some states and with some groups, there is good cause to further explore gay and lesbian singles and couples as adoption resources (Mallon 2004; Ryan, Pearlmutter, & Groza 2004). Little research on single adoptive parents has been conducted in the past decade to further examine this adoption resource (Groze 1991; Groze & Rosenthal 1991b; Shireman 1988; Shireman & Johnson 1976, 1985, 1986). These resources need to be maximized for adoption.

New perspectives are gaining wider recognition as these relate to the issues in adoption. In general, behavior genetics attempts to deconstruct the influence of genetics from the influence of the family and social environment. The adoption study is considered the most powerful design for investigating environmental influences on behavior in humans (Plomin & DeFries 1985; Stoolmiller 1999). This approach will shape how adoption research will be conducted in the years to come. Hopefully, adoption researchers will guide such studies into areas of concern to child welfare.

As the world has become more globalized, information sharing has increased dramatically. Adoption research and practice from other countries will influence the United States and vice versa. In particular, innovative and compelling research is being conducted on adoption in England (O'Connor & Rutter 2000; Rutter & English and Romanian Adoptees Study Team 1998), the Netherlands (Juffer, Stams, & van Ijzendoorn 2004; Stams, Juffer, Rispens, & Hoksbergen 2000; Stams, Juffer, & van Ijzendoorn 2002), and Norway (Andresen 1992; Dalen 1995, 2001; Howell 2001, 2002, 2003). The future of adoption includes more international collaboration.

In addition, new adoption initiatives merit attention. The Adoption Opportunities program continues to fund innovative projects in adoption, increasing the length of projects in 2001 to 5 years of funding. The Collaboration to AdoptUSKids (www.adoptUSkids.org) is a project of The Children's Bureau. In October 2002, The Children's Bureau contracted with the Adoption Exchange Association and its partners to devise and implement a national adoptive family recruitment and retention strategy, operate the AdoptUSKids.org website, encourage and enhance adoptive family support organizations, and conduct a variety of adoption research projects. This initiative is at the forefront of the promotion of older children for adoption. Such initiatives and innovations will insure that children and youth have access to the families they deserve and adoptive families have the resources required to successfully provide for their care.

REFERENCES

Adoption and Foster Care Analyis and Reporting System. (2004). Administration for Children and Families, National Adoption and Foster Care Statistics. Washington, DC: Adoption and Foster Care Analysis and Reporting System.

Adoption and Safe Families Act. (1997). P.L. 105-89.

Adoption Assistance and Child Welfare Act. (1980). P.L. 96-272.

Ames, E. W. (1997). The development of Romanian orphanage children adopted to Canada. Burnaby, Canada: Simon Fraser University.

Andresen, I. K. (1992). Behavioural and school adjustment of 12–13-year-old internationally adopted children in Norway: A research note. *Journal Of Child Psychology and Psychiatry and Allied Disciplines, 33*(2), 427–439.

Aust, P. H. (1981). Using the life story book in treatment of children in placement. *Child Welfare, 40*(8), 535–560.

Babb, A. (2001). Ethics in contemporary American adoption practice. In V. Groza & K. Rosenberg (eds.), *Clinical and practice issues in adoption: Bridging the gap between adoptees placed as infants and as older children,* revised and expanded ed., pp. 105–155. Westport, CT: Bergen and Garvey.

Babb, L. A. (1999). *Ethics in American adoption.* Westport, CT: Bergin and Garvey.

Barth, R. P. (1992). Adoption. In P. J. Pecora, J. K. Whittaker, A. N. Maluccio, R. P. Barth, & R. D. Plotnick (eds.), *The child welfare challenge: Policy, practice, and research,* pp. 361–398. Hawthorne, NY: Aldine de Gruyter.

Barth, R. P. (1997). Effects of age and race on the odds of adoption versus remaining in long-term out-of-home care. *Child Welfare, 76,* 285–308.

Barth, R. P., & Berry, M. (1988). *Adoption and disruption: Rates, risks, and responses.* Hawthorne, NY: Aldine de Gruyter.

Beck, J. S. (1995). *Cognitive therapy: Basics and beyond.* New York: Guilford Press.

Beeman, S., & Boisen, L. (1999). Child welfare professional's attitudes towards kinship foster care. *Child Welfare 78,* 315–337.

Berrick, J. D., Needell, B., Barth, R., & Jonson-Reid, M. (1998). *The tender years: toward developmentally sensitive child welfare services for very young children.* New York: Oxford University Press.

Bimmel, N., Juffer, F., van Ijzendoorn, M. H., & Bakermans-Kranenberg, M. J. (2003). Problem behavior of internationally adopted adolescents: A review and meta-analysis. *Harvard Review of Psychiatry, 11*(2), 64–77.

Bonecutter, F. J., & Gleeson, J. P. (1997). Broadening our view: Lessons from kinship foster care. *Journal of Multicultural Social Work, 5*(1), 99–119.

Brodzinsky, D. (1990). A stress and coping model of adoption adjustment. In D. Brodzinsky & M. Schecter (eds.), *The psychology of adoption,* pp. 3–24. New York: Oxford University Press.

Brooks, D., Barth, R. P., Bussiere, A., & Patterson, G. (1999). Adoption and race: Implementing the Multiethnic Placement Act and the Interethnic Adoptions Provisions. *Social Work, 44,* 167–178.

Chisholm, K. (1998). A three year follow-up of attachment and indiscriminate friendliness in children adopted from Romanian orphanages. *Child Development, 69,* 1092–1106.

Dalen, M. (1995). Learning difficulties among intercountry adopted children. *Journal of Nordic Educational Research, 15*(4), 524–538.

Dalen, M. (2001). School performances among internationally adopted children in Norway. *Adoption Quarterly, 5*(2), 39–57.

Davidson, B. (1997). Service needs of relative caregivers: A qualitative analysis. *Families in Society, 78,* 502–510.

Evan B. Donaldson Adoption Institute. (1997). *Benchmark adoption survey: First public opinion survey on American attitudes toward adoption.* Retrieved June 30, 2004, from www.adoptioninstitute.org/survey/baexec.html.

Fogg-Davis, H. G. (2002). *The ethics of transracial adoption.* Ithaca, NY: Cornell University Press.

Freundlich, M. (2000a). *Adoption and ethics: The market forces in adoption.* Adoption and Ethics series. Washington, DC: Child Welfare League of America and Evan B. Donaldson Adoption Institute.

Freundlich, M. (2000b). *Adoption and ethics: The role of race, culture, and national origin in adoption.* Washington, DC: Child Welfare League of America and Evan B. Donaldson Adoption Institute.

Freundlich, M., & Liberthal, J. K. (2001). *Adoption and ethics: The impact of adoption on members of the triad.* Adoption and Ethics series. Washington, DC: Child Welfare League of America and Evan B. Donaldson Adoption Institute.

Garland, A. F., Ellis-Mclead, E., Landsverk, J. A., Ganger, W., & Johnson, I. (1998). Minority populations in the child welfare system: The visibility hypothesis reexamined. *American Journal of Orthopsychiatry, 68,* 142–146.

Groza, V., & Ileana, D. (1999). International adoption and adoption services. In T. Tepper & L. Hannon (eds.), *International adoption: Challenges and opportunities,* pp. 42–61. Pittsburg, PA: Parent Support Network for the Post Institutionalized Child.

Groza, V., Ileana, D., & Irwin, I. (1999). *A peacock or a crow? Stories, interviews and commentaries on Romanian adoptions.* South Euclid, OH: Willes e-press.

Groza, V., Maschmeier, C., Jamison, C., & Piccalo, T. (2003). Siblings and out-of-home placement: Best practices. *Families in Society, 84,* 480–490.

Groza, V., & Rosenberg, K. (eds.). (2001). *Clinical and practice issues in adoption: Bridging the gap between adoptees placed as infants and as older children,* revised and expanded ed. Westport, CT: Bergen and Garvey.

Groza, V. (1986). Special needs adoption. *Children and Youth Services Review, 8,* 363–373.

Groza, V. (1991). Adoption and single parents: A review. *Child Welfare, 70,* 321–332.

Groze, V. (1994). Clinical and nonclinical adoptive families of special needs children. *Families in Society, 75,* 90–104.

Groze, V. (1996). *Successful adoptive families: A longitudinal study of special needs adoption.* Westport, CT: Praeger.

Groze, V., & Rosenthal, J. A. (1991a). A structural analysis of families adopting special-needs children. *Families in Society, 72,* 469–481.

Groze, V., & Rosenthal, J. A. (1991b). Single parents and their adopted children: A psychosocial analysis. *Families in Society, 72,* 67–77.

Groze, V., Young, J., & Corcran-Rumppe, K. (1991). *Post Adoption Resources for Training, Networking and Evaluation Services (PARTNERS): Working with special needs adoptive families in stress.* Washington, DC: U.S. Department of Health and Human Services.

Hartman, A. (1984). *Working with adoptive families beyond placement.* New York: Child Welfare League of America.

Hartman, A., and Laird, J. (1983). *Family-centered social work practice.* New York: Free Press.

Hochman, G., Huston, A., & Feathers-Acuna, A. (1992). *The sibling bond: Its importance in foster care and adoptive placement.* Washington, DC: National Adoption Information Clearinghouse.

Hogan, P. T., & Siu, S. (1988). Minority children and the child welfare system: A historical perspective, *Social Work, 33,* 493–498.

Hollingsworth, L. D. (1997). Effect of transracial/transethnic adoption on children's racial and ethnic identity and self-esteem: A meta-analytic review. *Marriage and Family Review, 25,* 99–130.

Howell, S. (2001). Self-conscious kinship: Some contested values in Norwegian transnational adoption. In S. Franklin & S. McKinnon (eds.), *Relative values: Reconfiguring kinship studies,* pp. 203–223. Durham, NC: Duke University Press.

Howell, S. (2002). Community beyond place: Adoptive families in Norway. In V. Amit (ed.), *Realizing community: Concepts, social relationships and sentiments,* pp. 84–104. New York: Routledge-Taylor & Francis Group.

Howell, S. (2003). Kinning: The creation of life trajectories in transnational adoptive families. *Journal of the Royal Anthropological Institute, 9,* 465–484.

Intercountry Adoption Act. (2000). P.L. 106-279.

Interethnic Adoption Act [Removal of Barriers to Interethnic Adoption]. (1996). P.L. 104-188.

Jenista, J. (2000). Preadoption review of medical records. *Pediatric Annals, 29*(4), 212–215.

Jenkins, S., & Diamond, B. (1985). Ethnicity and foster care: Census data as predictors of placement variables. *American Journal of Orthopsychiatry, 55,* 267–276.

Juffer, F., Stams, G.-J. J. M., & van Ijzendoorn, M. H. (2004). Adopted children's problem behavior is significantly related to their ego resiliency, ego control, and sociometric status. *Journal of Child Psychology and Psychiatry, 45,* 697–706.

Kagan, R. M., & Reid, W. J. (1986). Critical factors in the adoption of emotionally disturbed youth. *Child Welfare, 65,* 63–73.

Keck, G. C., & Kupecky, R. M. (1998). *Adopting the hurt child: Hope for families with special-needs kids: A guide for parents and professionals.* Colorado Springs, CO: Pinion Press.

Keck, G. C., & Kupecky, R. M. (2002). *Parenting the hurt child: Helping adoptive families heal and grow.* Colorado Springs, CO: Pinion Press.

Kirk, D. (1964). *Shared fate: A theory of adoption and mental health.* London: Free Press of Glencoe.

Lifton, B. J. (1988). *Lost and found: The adoption experience.* New York: Harper & Row.

Lifton, B. J. (1994). *Journey of the adopted self.* New York: Basic Books.

Lorkovich, T. W., Piccalo, T., Groza, V., Brindo, M. E., & Marks, J. (In press). Kinship care and permanence: Guiding principles for policy and practice. *Families in Society.*

Mallon, G. P. (2004). Gay men choosing parenthood. New York: Columbia University Press.

McMillen, J. C., & Groze, V. (1994). Using placement genograms in child welfare practice. *Child Welfare, 73,* 307–318.

Melina, L. R. (1986). *Raising adopted children: A manual for adoptive parents.* New York: Harper & Row.

Miller, L. C. (2000). Initial assessment of growth, development, and the effects of institutionalization in internationally adopted children. *Pediatric Annals, 29*(4), 224–232.

Minis, H., & Keck, G. (2003). A clinical/research dialogue on reactive attachment disorder. *Attachment and Human Development, 5,* 297–301.

Multiethnic Placement Act. (1994). P.L. 103-382.

National Conference of State Legislatures. (2003). *Child Welfare Project. Update: Safe havens for abandoned infants. July 21, 2003.* Retrieved June 30, 2004, from www.ncsl.org/programs/cyf/ailaws.htm.

National Resource Center for Permanency Planning. (2000). *Legislative summary.* New York: National Resource Center for Permanency Planning.

Needell, B., & Gilbert, N. (1997). Child welfare and the extended family. In R. P. Barth, J. D. Berrick, & N. Gilbert (eds.), *Child welfare research review,* pp. 85–99. New York: Columbia University Press.

O'Connor, T. G., & Rutter, M. (2000). Attachment disorder behavior following severe deprivation: Extension and longitudinal follow-up. *Journal of the American Academy of Child and Adolescent Psychiatry, 39,* 703–712.

O'Connor, T. G., & Zeanah, C. H. (2003). Attachment disorders: Assessment strategies and treatment approaches. *Attachment and Human Development, 5,* 223–244.

Olsen, L. J. (1983). Predicting the permanency status of children in foster care. *Social Work Research and Abstracts, 18,* 9–20.

Pavao, J. (1992). Normative crises in the development of the adoptive family. *Adoption Therapist, 3*(2), 1–4

Personal Responsibility and Work Opportunity Act. (1996). P.L. 104-193.

Pinderhughes, E. E., & Rosenberg, K. (1990). Family bonding with high-risk placements: A therapy model that promotes the process of becoming a family. In L. M. Glidden (ed.), *Formed families: Adoption of children with handicaps*, pp. 261–282. Binghamton, NY: Haworth Press.

Plomin, R., & DeFries, J. C. (1985). *Origins of individual differences in infancy: The Colorado Adoption project.* Orlando, FL: Academic Press.

Reitz, M., & Watson, K. W. (1992). *Adoption and the family system: Strategies for treatment.* New York: Guilford Press.

Rosenberg, E. B. (1992). *The adoption life cycle: The children and their families through the years.* New York: Free Press.

Rosenberg, K. F., & Groze, V. (1997). The impact of secrecy and denial in adoption: Practice and treatment issues. *Families in Society, 78*, 522–530.

Rosenthal, J. A., Schmidt, D., & Conner, J. (1988). Predictors of special needs adoption disruption: An exploratory study. *Children and Youth Services Review, 10*, 101–117.

Rutter, M., & English and Romanian Adoptees Study Team. (1998). Developmental catch-up, and the deficit, following adoption after severe global early deprivation. *Journal of Child Psychology and Psychiatry, 39*, 465–476.

Rutter, M., Quinton, D., Hay, D., Dunn, J., O'Connor, T., & Marvin, R. (1995). *The social and intellectual development of children adopted into England from Romania.* Report prepared for the Department of Health, London.

Ryan, S., Pearlmutter, S., & Groza, V. (2004). Coming out of the closet: Opening agencies to gay and lesbian adoptive parents. *Social Work, 49*, 85–96.

Scannapieco, M., Hegar, R. L., & McAlpine, C. (1997). Kinship care and foster care: A comparison of characteristics and outcomes. *Families in Society, 78*, 480–488.

Shireman, J. F. (1988). *Growing up adopted: An examination of some major issues.* Chicago: Chicago Child Care Society.

Shireman, J. F., & Johnson, P. R. (1976). Single persons as adoptive parents. *Social Service Review, 50*, 103–116.

Shireman, J. F., & Johnson, P. R. (1985). Single-parent adoptions: A longitudinal study. *Children and Youth Services Review, 7*, 321–334.

Shireman, J. F., & Johnson, P. R. (1986). A longitudinal study of black adoptions: Single parent, transracial, and traditional. *Social Work, 31*, 172–176.

Smyke, A. T., Dumitrescu, A., & Zeanah, C. H. (2002). Attachment disturbances in young children. I: The continuum of caretaking casualty. *Journal of the American Academy of Child and Adolescent Psychiatry, 41*, 972–982.

Stams, G.-J. J. M., Juffer, F., & van Ijzendoorn, M. H. (2002). Maternal sensitivity, infant attachment, and temperament in early childhood predict adjustment in middle childhood: The case of adopted children and their biologically unrelated parents. *Developmental Psychology, 38*, 806–821.

Stams, G.-J. J. M., Juffer, F., Rispens, J., & Hoksbergen, R. A. C. (2000). The development and adjustment of 7-year-old children adopted in infancy. *Journal of Child Psychology and Psychiatry, 41*, 1025–1037.

Stolley, K. S. (1993). Statistics on adoption in the United States. In I. Schulman (ed.), *The future of children*, pp. 26–42. Los Altos, CA: Center for the Future of Children.

Stoolmiller, M. (1999). Implications of the restricted range of family environments for estimates of heritability and nonshared environment in behavior-genetic adoption studies. *Psychological Bulletin, 125*, 392–409.

Tessler, R., Gamache, G., & Liu, L. (1999). *West meets East: Americans adopt Chinese children.* Westport, CT: Bergin and Garvey

Timberlake, E. M., & Hamlin, E. R., II. (1982). The sibling group: A neglected dimension of placement. *Child Welfare, 61*, 545–552.

Tracy, E. M., & Whittaker, J. K. (1990). The social network map: Assessing social support in clinical practice. *Families in Society, 71*(8), 461–470.

U.S. Census Bureau. (2003). *Adopted children and stepchildren: 2000.* Washington, DC: U.S. Census Bureau.

U.S. Department of Health and Human Services. (2004). *Preliminary FY 2002 estimates as of Agusut 2004. The AFCARS Report.* Retrieved December 1, 2004, from www.acf.hhs.gov/programs/cb/publicaitons/afcars/report9.htm.

U.S. Department of State. (2004). Immigrant visas issued to orphans coming to the U.S. Retrieved June 30, 2004, from travel.state.gov/orphan_numbers.html.

Verrier, N. N. (1993). *The primal wound: Understanding the adopted child.* Baltimore, MD: Gateway Press.

Wedge, P., & Mantle, G. (1991). *Sibling groups and social work: A study of children referred for permanent substitute family placement.* Brookfield, MA: Avebury Press.

Welch, M. G. (1988). *Holding time.* New York: Simon & Schuster.

Wheeler, C. (1978). *Where am I going? Making a life story book.* Juneau, AK: Winking Owl Press.

Wilson, D. B., & Chipunga, S. S. (1996). Introduction to the kinship care special issue. *Child Welfare, 75*, 387–396.

Winkler, R., Brown, D., van Keppel, M., & Blanchard, A. (1988). *Clinical practice in adoption.* New York: Pergamon Press.

Young, J., Corcran-Rumppe, K., & Groze, V. (1992). Integrating special-needs adoption with residential treatment. *Child Welfare, 71*, 527–535.

TRUDY FESTINGER

Adoption Disruption

Rates, Correlates, and Service Needs

O ver the years, there have been widespread changes in the policies, practices, and attitudes toward foster child adoption in the United States. One of the more noticeable changes in recent years has been in the volume of adoptions. According to federal estimates, the number of adoptions of children in public out-of-home care between 1983 and 1995 remained quite flat, between 17,000 and 20,000 (Maza 2000). Since then, the numbers have increased considerably in response to various federal legislative initiatives. For example, the Adoption Assistance and Child Welfare Act of 1980 mandated permanency planning for all children in state custody. Courts and agencies were directed to pursue the goal of adoption for children who were unlikely to return to their birth families. The legislation also required states to establish an adoption subsidy program, and provided federal funds to be used as part of the state's subsidies for children adopted from foster care. The most recent rise in adoptions has been in response to the Adoption Incentive program (also known as the Adoption Bonus program) of the Adoption and Safe Families Act of 1997, which provided both policy and fiscal incentives to states for increasing the number of adoptions (U.S. General Accounting Office 2003). It was the first outcome-oriented incentive program (Maza 2000), as it authorized payments to states for increasing the number of children adopted from public out-of-home care. Thus by FY1998, roughly 36,000 adoptions had taken place (Maza 2000), and a FY2000 report (Children's Bureau 2002) estimates that 51,000 children

were adopted from the public child welfare system nationwide.

The national picture was paralleled in all the states, as well as in cities with large child welfare populations. For instance, New York City figures show a dramatic rise in finalized adoptions from 1,212 in 1990 to 3,735 adoptions completed in 1999, dipping somewhat to 2,777 finalized adoptions in 2002 (New York State Department of Social Services 1991, 2000, 2003).

The national increase in foster care adoptions has been accompanied by a rise in professional concerns that more adoptive placements would disrupt and more adoptions would fail. Before discussing the professional concerns, it is necessary to clarify these two situations. In the adoption literature, the term "disruption" has commonly referred to the removal of a child from an adoptive placement before the adoption has been legalized (Barth & Berry 1988; Festinger 1986, 1990). Situations in which a child has been returned to the custody of the child welfare system following legal adoption has been termed "dissolution," a term that was coined early on by professionals in the adoption field (Donley 1978) and continues to be used officially (National Adoption Information Clearinghouse 2002).

The concerns about adoption disruption and dissolution are not new. Years ago, they were fueled by the belief that disruptions and dissolutions were apt to increase dramatically as caseworkers sought adoptive homes for children who earlier had been considered unadoptable. More recently, the concerns have been intensified as a result of the focus on increasing adoptions and on speeding the adoption process. In fact, some observers in the past have suggested that efforts to promote adoptions might lead to more adoptions that end (Barth, Berry, Yoshikami, Goodfield, & Carson 1988). More recently, it has been noted that part of the concern has been based on the assumption that increases in adoptive placements and adoption would be a function of speedy and inadequate home selection (Barth & Miller 2000). Worries have also been kindled by guesses and rumors about high rates of disruption. Such concerns are not surprising, because disruptions are painful for all involved—the children, the adoptive parents, and the caseworkers.

Rumors and guesses sometimes fill the void when there is a dearth of knowledge. In this regard, however, there is quite a sizable empirical literature on rates of disruption, showing that it is not such a frequent occurrence. In contrast, very little is known about the frequency of dissolution following legal adoption because it is so difficult to obtain accurate data. The limited data that are available show dissolution to be a rather rare event (Festinger 2002).

In this chapter, I focus on disruption. I begin with a review of available research on rates of adoption disruption, followed by a summary of child, family, agency, and other factors related to disruption and a discussion of practice implications. Parts of this review rely heavily on a previous article (Festinger 1990) that dealt with both disruption rates and correlates.

Rates of Adoption Disruption

Past reports on rates of disruption are quite scattered. Until the early 1970s, adoption disruption was rarely mentioned, probably because the phenomenon occurred so infrequently. For instance, Kadushin (1980) cites nine studies, including one of his own (Kadushin & Seidl 1971), covering the period up to 1970. These studies were mainly concerned with children who were white, very young, and without known handicaps at placement. Although there were minor variations among the studies, of the more

than 34,000 adoptive placements of children that were monitored, only 1.9% disrupted.

More recent studies have increasingly focused on or included children who were older, from minority groups, or handicapped. These studies have reported higher rates of disruption. For example, Kadushin (U.S. Congress 1975) cites figures from a North Carolina agency that showed a disruption rate of 8% among 410 placements of children with special needs who were placed between 1967 and 1974. Statistics from California public agencies noted a disruption rate of 7.6% in 1973, a considerable increase over the 2.7% reported by the same agencies in 1970, apparently reflecting "the increasing number of older children being placed" (Bass 1975:115). A Michigan agency that specialized in the placement of children with special needs (Unger, Dwarshuis, & Johnson 1977) reported that of 199 children placed from 1968 through 1976, the rate of disruption was 10.6%. A Canadian report (Cohen 1981) cited an increase in annual adoption disruptions in Ontario from 4% to 7% between 1971 and 1978, noting that disruptions occurred with greater frequency among private and kin placements than in agency placements. Disruption figures were also reported by the evaluators of an effort to place 115 children with special needs from a number of New York State counties. Of the 41 adoptive placements between 1975 and 1977, 15% had disrupted by the time data collection stopped in 1977 (Welfare Research 1978).

Developmentally disabled children placed for adoption during a 12-month period between 1978 and 1979 were the subject of a report of a mail survey of agencies in the United States and Canada (Coyne & Brown 1985). The authors reported descriptive data on 693 children, over half of preschool age, placed in adoptive homes by 292 agencies. An overall disruption rate of 8.7% was reported, a conservative estimate, as it did not include information from workers who were no longer with an agency. Soon thereafter, a report from Connecticut (Fein, Davies, & Knight 1979) of a program serving emotionally disturbed children of "latency age" reported disruptions of placements for four of the 13 children placed in adoptive homes. At roughly the same time in Ohio, a report by Roberts (1980) of a demonstration project designed to expand adoption services to children with special needs noted a 13.6% rate of disruption for the 59 children placed, and a small study of children from a group care setting in North Carolina (Borgman 1981) reported that nine out of 19 initial adoptive placements did not hold.

In 1982, Lahti reported the results of a follow-up of cases from a demonstration project in Oregon. Of 107 children in adoptive placements with new or former foster parents, the placements of 5.6% had disrupted, with no differences apparent between these two sets of foster parents. Furthermore, no differences in rates of disruption were noted among cases assigned to workers who had been specially trained to work intensively with families and a comparison group receiving regular casework services.

Another agency study (Kagan & Reid 1986) of adoptive placements between 1974 and 1982 of 78 older youths with severe emotional and learning problems noted that roughly 53% had earlier been in at least one adoptive placement that disrupted. Unfortunately, such calculations, based on prior disruptions, are not comparable to other reports on rates. Roughly at the same time, Tremitiere (1984) distributed questionnaires to 116 agencies in Pennsylvania and 40 agencies serving children with special needs located outside that state. Based on usable responses received from 45 agencies, Tremetiere reports on the range of disruption proportions within various age groupings of children over a 5-year period. My calculations from her tables show that disruptions of placements among the youngest children (those under 6) were fairly level between 1979 (1.4%) and 1982–1983 (1.6%). For older children (those who were 6 to 18), however, the proportion of disruptions

rose from 7.2% in 1979 to roughly 12% in 1982–1983. Furthermore, a report from a New Jersey agency that specialized in adoptive placements of children with special needs showed that of 309 children, the adoptive placements of 21.4% had disrupted by the end of the data collection period in 1981 (Boyne, Denby, Kettenring, & Wheeler 1984).

Argent (1984) reported on the work of Parents for Children, a British agency dedicated to the adoptive placement of children with special needs. Between late 1976 and early 1983, the agency placed 75 children into 56 families. By May 1983, the placements of 14 children (18.7%) had disrupted. A few years later, Partridge, Hornby, and McDonald (1986) presented data on 235 placements of 212 children from six agencies in four northeastern states. Most of the children were white, nearly 8 years old on average at the time of adoptive placement, and almost all were considered to have special needs. Based on information about disruptions or dissolutions from 1982–1984, the investigators arrived at a disruption rate of 8.6%.

The problems of estimating rates of disruption are highlighted in another report that presented figures from five state agencies (Benton, Kaye, & Tipton 1985). In some instances, disruption rates were based on the ratio of disruptions (of placements that could have begun in prior years) to new placements in a given year, whereas in others, they were based on a cross-sectional sample of cases in adoptive home placements. In three state agencies, current disruptions were counted, whereas in two states, prior histories of disruptions of children in current adoptive placements were used. Data obtained from this mixture of approaches showed disruption rates for 1984–1985 ranging from 6.9% to 20%. In only one of the states, Virginia, was a sample tracked over time. This consisted of 53 children who were placed in adoptive homes in 1983. It is reported that 18 to 24 months later, by June 1985, 19% of these had one or more disruptions. Another study around this time (Groze 1986), based on data from a southwestern agency, reported a 14.9% rate of disruption among 91 cases examined.

A New York City study (Festinger 1986) used a longitudinal approach, following more than 900 children in adoptive placements in March 1983, who were ages 6 or older at the time of those placements. A large majority was designated black or Latino. During the first year, roughly 8.2% of all adoptive placements disrupted. There was a relatively steady trickle of disruptions during the second and third years of adoptive placement, so that the overall rate was estimated to fall between 12% and 14%. Age was a factor here, as the estimated rate of disruption for those who were 11 or older was roughly between 16% and 19%, whereas for those aged 6 to 10, the rate was a lower 8% to 11%.

Soon thereafter, a California study (Barth & Berry 1988; Barth, Berry, Yoshikami, Goodfield, & Carson 1988) reported on 926 children age 3 or older in adoptive placements between 1980 and mid-1984. Intake placement forms filed with the state were used to obtain data about adoptive placements, supplemented by information on case outcomes from adoption workers in 13 counties, as well as from a variety of interviews with a smaller subgroup of families. Most of the 926 children were white, placed with foster parents, placed alone rather than with siblings, and ranged in age from 3 to 17.9 years at the time of their adoptive placement. By 1986, roughly 10% of placements had disrupted, with a higher proportion (18.8%) of placements from 1980 than for subsequent placement years. Thus for placements of 1982, a lower rate (9.2%) had disrupted by 1986, this proportion dropping to 7.4% among placements of 1984. A related report (Berry & Barth 1990) focused on 99 adolescents aged 12 to 17 from the larger California study just mentioned. Among these teenagers, the rate of disruption was reported as 24.2%, with lower rates among Latino (10%) and black adolescents (14%) than

among whites (23%), who constituted most of the sample.

A few years later, a 1991 article (McDonald, Lieberman, Partridge, & Hornby 1991) reported on a study of 212 children representing 235 placements from six agencies between January 1982 and July 1984 (see also Partridge, Hornby, & McDonald 1986). Most were children with special needs, aged 3 and older, and white. Data were collected using content analyses of case records, augmented by agency statistics and interviews with agency administrators. All disruptions and dissolutions combined were compared to a randomly selected 25% sample of placements initiated between January 1982 and July 1984. The 212 children consisted of 54 whose placement had disrupted and 158 whose placements had not. Disruptions of greater than 20% are reported. But because the comparison group of 158 was based on a 25% sample, the overall rate of disruption for 686 children is, according to my calculations, roughly 8% (as also reported in the Partridge, Hornby, & McDonald 1986 report) rather than the much larger percentage reported in the 1991 published article.

The subject of disruption has been of interest in the United Kingdom as well. Thus a report from a city in the northeast of England (Holloway 1997) describes a retrospective 5-year cohort study of 129 children placed for adoption between January 1986 and December 1990. Almost all (95.3%) were aged 6 or younger at adoptive placement. In fact, more than half were under the age of 1 at the time. It is therefore not too surprising that only 2% of these placements disrupted. And in stark contrast, a 1998 report from the United States (Pinderhughes 1998) focused on families who adopted 53 children older than 5 through four agencies in New England and Ohio in the mid-1980s. The children were on average 10.8 years of age at adoptive placement. The placements of 13 children (24.5%) disrupted.

Finally, in an attempt to document the rate of disruption across all segments of an adoptive population, Goerge, Howard, Yu, and Radom-sky (1997) presented data from a multivariate, longitudinal analysis of children entering care in Illinois between 1976 and 1994. Among a total 4,840 cases of adoptive placement, 583 (12.1%) disrupted. Because this figure included some placements made near the end of data collection that might disrupt in time, a rate of 13.4% for placements prior to 1987 was considered more accurate, as it eliminated the problem of right-censored data. It is of interest that the authors report a decline in the disruption rate following the 1980 passage of the Adoption Assistance and Child Welfare Act to an average 9.9% between 1981 and 1987, a time when the rate of adoption was gradually increasing.

Before leaving the discussion of rates, a comment on adoptive or legal guardianship placements with kin is in order. Although kinship foster care placements during the first 3 years of care have been shown to be more stable than non-kin foster placements (Testa 2001), there is a dearth of data on disruption following adoptive placements among kin not traveling the legal guardianship route (Freundlich & Wright 2003). Although one study of kinship placements (Terling-Watt 2001) reported a rather high disruption rate among 875 kinship placements in Texas (29% in the first 6 months of placement), it is not clear whether these were adoptive placements; in addition, the definition of disruption used was very broad and therefore not comparable to other studies reported here. Studies of disruption cited earlier may have included, but not reported on, kinship placements. Most likely, kinship adoptive placement disruption is a rare phenomenon, as the placement would have deteriorated earlier and not become an adoptive (or guardianship) placement to begin with.

The variety of approaches used in these reports and studies attests to the difficulty faced when attempting to arrive at an accurate estimate of the rate of disruption. Some researchers focused on new adoptive placements, whereas others used all children already in an adoptive placement at a particular point in time (thus losing their history), following the children until an outcome was known. Most reports focused only on disruptions, but a few included dissolutions, which are impossible to disentangle. Some did not differentiate between single child and group sibling placements, although the inclusion of the latter can affect the rates reported and can result in problems of independence with respect to some data, such as the characteristics of the adoptive parents. Finally, with the exception of the Goerge, Howard, Yu, and Radomsky (1997) study, which used administrative data to track cases forward over an 18-year period, the studies have used shorter follow-up periods, thus probably missing some cases because of the right-censoring problem.

Nevertheless, what can one say about all of these results? For one, the figures show that the proportion of disruptions has increased since the 1970s. This trend appears to hold regardless of problems of methodology and precision and probable variations in the definitions used. The general rise in disruption rates is not terribly surprising, as adoptive homes were increasingly sought for older children and for those with other special needs (e.g., sibling groups; children with physical, educational, or emotional handicaps). It is also clear that disruption rates are not uniform. This must be kept in mind as one thinks about rates: a global rate is really a composite of many rates that may differ depending on which particular group or subgroup is examined. Furthermore, the focus on disruption, although dramatic, distorts the picture. When evaluating levels of disruption, it is best not to think of such rates in isolation, but to view them in conjunction with completed adoptions. Worries and rumors about disruption rates appear to have exaggerated the extent of the problem. It is indeed impressive that the rates reported since the mid-1980s, despite some variations here and there, do not differ substantially. Excluding studies that singled out small groups of older children, disruption rates have mostly varied from about 9% to 15%.

Among older children, the reported rate has reached roughly 25%. Such rates hardly need to arouse astonishment, or be viewed in a negative light. In the long run, the vast majority of children will have been adopted.

Correlates of Adoption Disruption

A focus on rates alone is not much use for practitioners, who, when working with a child and an adoptive family, are faced with numerous factors describing the child and his or her history, the adoptive family, and the services available, to mention a few. So let us turn to factors that have been reported as associated with adoptive disruption, when these have been compared to adoptions. Many of the studies already mentioned, in addition to some others, generated a plethora of factors, too many to report on here. Because many studies did not utilize multivariate analyses, it is often not even clear which factors are the strongest predictors of disruption. So I use a bit of poetic license to present some highlights in a summary that attempts to capture the flavor of what has been reported, while omitting many of the details. A cautionary note is in order, as various problems are overlooked, such as differences in the method of sampling and in the data gathering methods, the nature and wording of questions that may have been asked of workers and/or families, the depth of analyses, and even in the working definition of disruption. The reader also needs to be aware that different studies addressed different factors, so that when a particular factor is mentioned as a correlate of disruption in four studies, it is a mistake to assume that all the other studies examined that factor.

Children and Their Placement History

Most demographic characteristics of the children have no bearing on the outcome of adoptive placements. In most studies, the gender of the children made no difference. Among a few studies that showed gender to be a factor (Barth, Berry, Yoshikami, Goodfield, & Carson 1988; Barth & Berry 1988; Boneh 1979; Rosenthal, Schmidt, & Conner 1988; Schmidt 1986), males were overrepresented among disruptions. The race of children was rarely a factor, as was the case for religion.

In contrast, more than a dozen studies have shown age to be a consistent predictor of disruption (e.g., Barth & Berry 1988; Benton, Kaye, & Tipton 1985; Festinger 1986; Goerge, Howard, Yu, & Radomsky 1997; Groze 1986; Mac-Donald 1991). Whether one examines age at entry into foster care, age when the children became legally free for adoption, or age at the time of the adoptive placement, children whose placements disrupted were older than those who were adopted. In addition, a few researchers have reported that the disruption group took longer to become legally free than those whose placements held (Boneh 1979; Partridge, Hornby, & McDonald 1986), whereas others reported no time lag differential (Boyne, Denby, Kettenring, & Wheeler 1984; Festinger 1986). The total length of time in foster care prior to the adoptive placement has also yielded mixed results. Some data show that this time was longer for those whose placements eventually disrupted than for the adoptees (Boneh 1979; Partridge, Hornby, & McDonald 1986), whereas other data show no such connection (Festinger 1986; Groze 1996; Smith & Howard 1991) or indicate that the time was shorter (Berry & Barth 1990; Goerge, Howard, Yu, & Radomsky 1997; Zwimpfer 1983).

Several investigators have focused on the children's histories prior to their adoptive placements, noting that the histories of those whose placements disrupted showed a higher incidence of various kinds of abuse or neglect compared to children whose placements held (Partridge, Hornby, & McDonald 1986; Schmidt 1986), or were more likely to show a history of sexual acting out (Smith & Howard 1991). In addition, a prior removal from a foster home due to inadequate parenting has been cited as a factor in disruption (Boneh 1979).

The average number of placements in foster homes and group settings has been a fairly consistent predictor of disruption. These averages have been considerably higher for disruption than for adoption outcomes (Boneh 1979; Festinger 1986; McDonald, Lieberman, Partridge, & Hornby 1991; Schmidt 1986), although some observers have reported no differences (Groze 1986; Smith & Howard 1991). Previous disruptions of adoptive placements have also been cited (Barth & Berry 1988; Barth, Berry, Yoshikami, Goodfield, & Carson 1988; Boyne, Denby, Kettenring, & Wheeler 1984; Festinger 1986; Partridge, Hornby, & McDonald 1986). The nature of past placements also differed for the two outcomes. More of those whose placements eventually disrupted, when compared to the adoptees, had at some point resided in a group facility (Boneh 1979; Festinger 1986; Pinderhughes 1998).

Some of the children were placed together with their siblings, whereas others were placed singly. The data on whether this was a factor connected to the outcome are exceedingly mixed, with three studies showing that placements with siblings were overrepresented among disruption outcomes (Benton, Kaye, & Tipton 1985; Boneh 1979; Kadushin & Seidl 1971), three studies indicating that such placements were less likely to disrupt (Festinger 1986; Rosenthal, Schmidt, & Conner 1988; Schmidt 1986), and four studies showing no difference in the outcome (Barth, Berry, Yoshikami, Goodfield, & Carson 1988; Boyne, Denby, Kettenring, & Wheeler 1984; Groze 1986; Smith & Howard 1991). Such a mixture of results suggests that other factors related to sibling placements were at work.

In sum, compared to children who were adopted, those whose placements disrupted were older at all stages of the process. They had more placements of all sorts, had been placed in more families, and their longest stay there was more protracted. Furthermore, they were more apt to have had a previous adoptive placement, or a placement in a group setting. Prior histories of care were more problematic. Their more checkered placement history suggests that these children exhibited more problems early on or developed them during their stay in care. They entered into an adoptive relationship in the wake of a more varied placement history. Because that history included a longer family placement, one can imagine past disappointments when these relationships ended and perhaps greater wariness about subsequent placements. Because they were older, they brought with them a history of past experiences. It is plausible to assume that they were therefore less adaptable and had greater difficulties adapting to new situations in foster care. In short, they were more difficult to manage. One can speculate that the older children may have been faced with a conflict between their growing need for independence, in conjunction with a nonidealization of parents, and the attachment tasks inherent in adoption. These difficulties could have been exacerbated if adoptive parents lacked sufficient skills and the flexibility needed to bend with, and be responsive to, the ebb and flow of emotions of older children. It is also quite possible that because of their older age, more of these children had developed firmer psychological links to their families of origin and may even have viewed adoption as an act of disloyalty. All these elements combined are apt to have interfered with their assimilation into their adoptive families.

Adoptive Parents

The demographic characteristics of the adoptive parents—their age, race, education, and income—had either no bearing on (or mixed associations with) the outcome of adoptive placements. For instance, several studies showed higher education to be related to disruption (Barth, Berry, Yoshikami, Goodfield, & Carson 1988; Rosenthal, Schmidt, & Conner 1988), whereas more than seven studies showed education not to be a factor. The employment outside the home of either or both adoptive parents has also had no bearing on the outcome (Benton, Kaye, & Tipton 1985; Festinger 1986), although a father's lower occupational status has been linked to disruption (Westhues & Cohen 1990).

The couple or single status of the adoptive parents is unrelated to the outcome, with the exception of one study's finding single parents overrepresented among disruptions (Partridge, Hornby, & McDonald 1986; McDonald, Lieberman, Partridge, & Hornby 1991). Factors such as length of marriage and prior divorce, mentioned in a few studies, have either had mixed results or had no bearing on outcome. Social worker ratings of parental functioning and parenting skills have also been reported as strongly associated with intact, rather than disrupted, placements (Rosenthal, Schmidt, & Conner 1988). Unfortunately the raters knew the outcome, which no doubt influenced these ratings. The background of adoptive parents has received little attention. Two studies that dealt with this issue (Rosenthal, Schmidt, & Conner 1988; Schmidt 1986) found that parents in the disruption group came from families with fewer or no children.

More than six studies have examined whether the adoptive families were foster parents with whom the children had been living for some time, or were new families. It is hardly surprising that almost all of these studies report that among placements that disrupted, a larger proportion of the children were with new families rather than with foster families (e.g., Coyne & Brown 1985; Rosenthal, Schmidt, & Conner 1988; Schmidt 1986; Smith & Howard 1991). There has been very limited investigation of adoptive placements with relatives. One study that included a moderate number of such homes found that these placements were less likely to disrupt (Festinger 1986).

Parental preferences about the characteristics of children they want to adopt have also been examined by a few investigators. Among placements that disrupted when compared to those that did not, a larger proportion of adoptive parents were less flexible in their preferences or had more preferences. Clearly, such pickiness at the start did not augur well in the long run. Furthermore, disruptions were more likely when stated requests, for instance on age, were not met (Boneh 1979; Schmidt 1986).

Composition of the Home

Questions concerning a possible effect of the presence of biological children have generated considerable interest; hence, a number of studies have examined this issue with mixed results. For instance, four studies found no connection to outcome (Barth & Berry 1988; Boyne, Denby, Kettenring, & Wheeler 1984; Festinger 1986; Zwimpfer 1983), one study (Groze 1986) found the presence of other children in the home was associated with reduced risk, whereas two showed that disruption was more likely if biological children resided in the adoptive home (Boneh 1979; Kadushin & Seidl 1971). Kadushin and Seidl (1971) suggested, however, that this result was probably confounded. That is, adoptive parents with biological children were older, and were in turn offered older children for adoption, and it was the older age of the placed children that was linked to disruption. Using a somewhat different measure, Pinderhughes (1998) noted that adoption disruption was more likely among smaller families.

A number of other factors, such as the ages of other children, their gender, and the racial composition of the home, has also been examined. For instance, in one study, the difference in age between the children in the home was unrelated to outcome, but the age distribution was. Sample children who were in the middle position, flanked by both older and younger children who were not biological siblings of the sample children, were more vulnerable to disruption than were those who occupied the oldest or youngest position (Festinger 1986). However, another study noted that when the adoptive child assumed the position of eldest, disruption was more likely (Boneh 1979). Finally, the gender of other children in the home and the racial composition of the adoptive home have been examined in one study that showed these factors to be unconnected to the outcome (Festinger 1986).

In sum, most aspects of these households—the number of other children, their ages, sex, and race—were not linked to outcome. Here and there, elements distinguished between disruptions and adoptions. These are isolated findings, warranting replication. Overall, one is impressed by the limited significance of household composition in the outcome of adoptive placements.

Children's Problems

The number and severity of problems at the time of the adoptive placement has been a consistent predictor of disruption in more than 10 studies (e.g., Benton, Kaye, & Tipton 1985; McDonald, Lieberman, Partridge, & Hornby 1991; Rosenthal, Schmidt, & Conner 1988; Smith & Howard 1991). Usually these factors consist of one or a combination of emotional, cognitive, or physical problems. Smith and Howard (1991) examined rosters of potential behavioral and emotional problems following the adoptive placement and highlighted the prevalence of sexual acting out, vandalism, defiance, stealing, and lying as prevalent among the disrupted group. Other workers have noted that although various problems were linked to disruption, mental retardation (Boyne, Denby, Kettenring, & Wheeler 1984) and physical and/or intellectual handicaps were not (Benton, Kaye, and Tipton 1985; Smith & Howard 1991). The existence of specific problem behaviors prior to the adoptive placement has also been examined. Thus, in contrast to nondisruptions, a larger proportion of those whose placements disrupted exhibited such behaviors as serious eating problems, sexual promiscuity, stealing, suicidal behavior, fire setting, wetting or soiling, vandalism, or physical aggression toward others (Partridge, Hornby, & McDonald 1986). A more recent study (Smith & Howard 1991), however, found no such differences prior to adoptive placement, with the exception of sexual acting out, which was seen more frequently among children whose placement eventually disrupted. Finally, adoptive parents' capacity to deal or cope with the problems presented by the children has been examined. It is no surprise that disruption outcomes were linked to lower ratings of the parents than was the case among adoptions (Festinger 1986; Schmidt 1986).

Contact with Biological Parents and Others

That a child may have unresolved feelings about separation from past biological family members has been suggested as an important element in his or her ability to accept and attach to an adoptive family. Festinger (1986) approached this issue by collecting information about the timing of each child's last contact with biological parents. The recency of their contacts was immaterial to the outcome. However, children whose placements disrupted were older at the last contact than those who were adopted. This finding was in line with their older age at all stages of the process and suggested that more of those children whose placements disrupted had developed firmer psychological links to their families of origin than was true of youngsters who were adopted. Another study (Smith & Howard 1991) used case record information to rate attachment to birth parents, finding that although both adoption and disruption groups had weak attachments to birth parents, the placements of those who were rated strongly attached to their birth mothers were more likely to disrupt.

Motivation and Placement Risk

It comes as no surprise that lower ratings of the strength of motivation to adopt, or to be adopted, were linked to disruption (Festinger 1986). Furthermore, couples who share an equal commitment to the adoption were less likely to experience a disruption (Partridge, Hornby, & McDonald 1986), as was the case among families where fathers were affectively involved and played a sustaining role (Westhues & Cohen 1990).

A larger proportion of disruptions were thought to be risky situations at the time of the adoptive placement, compared to adoptions.

The ratings of motivation and risk, like some other ratings reported earlier, were undoubtedly influenced by the fact that they relied to some extent on inferences made after the outcome was known. Therefore the differences just discussed are probably exaggerated. In view of this likely distortion, it is noteworthy that in one study, roughly 42% of the children with disruption outcomes (Festinger 1986), and in another study more than 60% with that outcome (Zwimpfer 1983) were in placements that were not considered particularly risky. Apparently there were some surprises when trouble arose. In fact, one study reported that for nearly half the children whose placements disrupted, signals of trouble were never given or recognized, or were first noted only 4 or more months after the adoptive placement (Festinger 1986). Another study indicated that in 58% of cases of disruption, the worker did not learn of the problems until 2 months or less before the actual disruption (Partridge, Hornby, & McDonald 1986). A third study attempted, through a review of the records, to provide evidence of a "suspected tendency by social workers to ignore warning signals" and noted that less than 20% of cases of disruption "attracted any negative observations at all by the social workers during the supervision period" (Zwimpfer 1983: 172). The tendency not to recognize signs of trouble in adoptive placements has, in the past, been discussed by others as well (Brown 1963; Gochros 1967).

What was going on? Perhaps home visits were cursory because staff had too many other responsibilities. Perhaps signs of problems were overlooked because the implications of such recognition, that one may have made a mistake, are upsetting (Brown 1963). There may be an alternative interpretation. Let us look at the larger picture. Generally, the children whose placements disrupted were older, had been in foster care for some time, and most were thought to exhibit problems of one sort or another. Finding new families or encouraging foster families to adopt often could take con-

siderable effort. As has been stated by Meezan and Shireman (1982), this no doubt sometimes involved persuasion of people who were reluctant to take such a serious step, and at times led workers to oversell a child (Kadushin 1980). In recent years, pressures for the timely achievement of adoption goals possibly prompted workers to pressure people to avoid delays in making decisions. In the process, workers probably also persuaded themselves about the strengths of these placements. Thus it is plausible that once the goal of an adoptive placement was achieved, workers overvalued the families and exaggerated their desires and abilities to cope. Risks may have been inadequately assessed and signals of trouble not spotted or belatedly recognized. This is not to say that all disruptions could have been avoided, but to suggest that a more open and conscious recognition of practices that include persuasion, and the attendant effects on workers themselves, could be salutary. Such recognition would help workers to anticipate, and therefore increase their accuracy in assessing the weaknesses or potential areas of risk in many situations at an early stage. This greater accuracy could in turn lead workers to explore ways to counteract forces that contribute to the deterioration of placements.

Service Characteristics

Sometimes children were adoptively placed with families whose homes had been studied and approved by a different agency. This circumstance occurred more often among placements that disrupted than among adoptions (Boneh 1979; Festinger 1986; Partridge, Hornby, & McDonald 1986). It would be wrong to conclude that reliance on adoption studies completed by others is risky, because in most such instances, the children were placed with new families rather than with former foster families, and placements with new families were more apt to disrupt for reasons other than who had studied and approved the home.

Time spent in preparing the child for the adoptive placement has been found to be unrelated to the eventual outcome (Boneh 1979). Other researchers have shown that pre-placement meetings between the child or foster family and the adoptive parents were unrelated to the outcome (Boyne, Denby, Kettenring, & Wheeler 1984; Festinger 1986). Yet others have reported that group sessions with the current caregiver, once referred to as "the goodbye blessing" prior to the adoptive placement, reduced the likelihood of disruption (Partridge, Hornby, & McDonald 1986), or had no bearing on outcome (Schmidt 1986).

Although one study noted that the number of workers carrying a case was not associated with outcome (Smith & Howard 1991), staff discontinuities of a particular sort have been linked to disruption (Festinger 1986). That is, staffing patterns in which the same workers did not simultaneously prepare both a child and an adoptive family were disproportionately in evidence among placements that disrupted. Apparently, when different workers had responsibility for preparing children and their families, the risk of disruption increased, perhaps because disparate information was communicated to the child and family. Furthermore, situations in which the last worker who prepared the child did not go on to supervise the adoptive home were also more frequently seen among disruption than adoption outcomes. When preparation and supervision were carried out by different staff members, the child was not only faced by a new family but also by a new worker. It is also possible that the relationship between foster care and adoption staff members may sometimes have been strained (Donley 1978), which played a role in the clarity of what was communicated. All these things could have hindered a smooth transition into an adoptive placement.

During the period of supervision that followed the adoptive placement, worker contacts with adoptive families and children were, on the whole, more frequent for placements that disrupted than for those resulting in adoption (Festinger 1986; Partridge, Hornby, & Mc-

Donald 1986; Smith & Howard 1991). Worker time with the families and children, referrals for counseling and support groups, and the use of respite care clearly increased somewhat in response to serious problems in these placements.

Disruption Circumstances

Studies have reported on lengthy rosters of reasons given by workers for disruption, reflecting the complex nature of family-child interactions, as well as numerous, sometimes idiosyncratic, situational elements that were at play (Benton, Kaye, & Tipton 1985; Festinger 1986; Kadushin & Seidl 1971; Partridge, Hornby, & McDonald 1986; Smith & Howard 1991). In view of the variations in the categories used to classify these reasons, and variations across studies in the meaning of each category, I can only attempt a very crude summary. Nevertheless, there is general agreement that the largest group of reasons for disruption concerned the families' inabilities or reduced willingness to cope with the children's problems, demands, and behaviors, combined with unrealistic parental expectations. Various attachment difficulties were also mentioned. Reasons concerning the marital relationship or situational factors, such as illness of parents or financial stress, are much less frequently cited. Note that when adoptive parents were interviewed (Barth & Berry 1988; Benton, Kaye, & Tipton 1985; Partridge, Hornby, & McDonald 1986), although such interviews were few in number, many differences between their perceptions and those of workers emerged. For instance, with respect to the reasons for disruption, Benton, Kaye, and Tipton (1985) note that whereas workers emphasized a child's behavior, parents cited their lack of preparation for or knowledge of a child's problems, or felt they were misinformed about a child's prognosis. Furthermore, whereas workers spoke of a child's not meeting parental expectations or a failure to bond to the parent, parents emphasized a child's not wishing to be adopted or spoke of failure to bond to other siblings.

Some Thoughts about Correlates

It is difficult to arrive at a neat summary statement about factors that predict disruption because the picture is so complex, involving the children and their histories, the adoptive families and their circumstances, and service factors. Factors in all these areas have distinguished between placements that did or did not disrupt. Such a plethora of findings is partly a function of the limitations of univariate analyses among factors, many of which were probably correlated, and would have been reduced by using multivariate approaches. Findings were also often quite contradictory. This was apt to be in part a function of differences among samples and methodologies, but it also leads one to ask whether the group of disrupted placements is really composed of several subgroups that require separate analyses for clarity in prediction. For instance, there would be merit in separating the analyses of foster parent adoptive placements and new (sometimes called "legal risk" or "stranger") placements. The former, for example, has consistently been shown to have lower rates of disruption, most likely because the child and family have in many instances been together for some time. If problems in these placements arose, the placements would have "disrupted" before they became adoptive, and thus were not part of an adoption disruption group. The common prediction that foster parent placements are less likely to disrupt is in a sense an artifact of a select group of placement "remainers" that did not experience a prior replacement. But this conclusion, as Barth and Berry (1988) have also suggested, requires further study.

The other two factors that have most commonly been predictors of disruption are the older age of the child at adoptive placement (or at entry into foster care or legal freeing) and the psychological and behavior problems exhibited by the child. As already mentioned, older children bring more of a history of past experiences, possibly including more prior placements and more families, stronger psychological links to birth families, greater wariness about entering into new relationships, and perhaps less adaptability with respect to new family constellations and situations. The problems that some of these children exhibited were more difficult for families to manage and presented the adoptive families with major challenges to their patience and skills.

Interviews with adoptive parents (Barth & Berry 1988; Schmidt, Rosenthal, & Bombeck 1988; Valentine, Conway, & Randolph 1987) following disruption, although based on small samples of volunteers, provide some clues about their disappointments, sense of failure, guilt and sorrow, and perspective on what they felt went awry. Important themes concerned the attachment problems of the children and the parents' expectations for a less difficult child, a difference between what they imagined and the reality. Other themes concerned such things as children's difficulty "letting go" of birth families, and gaps in information about the child's background. Parents felt the information about the child was neither accurate nor complete, that they were given a sales pitch, and felt ill-prepared to handle the problems presented by the youths placed in their homes. Some felt the children were not ready to be adopted. They also spoke of little support from agencies following the placements.

Practice Implications

These studies point directly to the importance of extensive and accurate preparation of all parties—the children and the prospective adoptive parents—and the parents' recognition that children adopted when older have greater adjustment difficulties than do infants (Sharma, McGue, & Benson 1996). Prospective parents for older children may require help in moving beyond such recognition to an acceptance of that likely reality. Furthermore, prospective parents need to be given as much accurate information as possible about the children and their backgrounds to avoid being enticed into stretching beyond their comfort level with regard to the kind of child they had in mind (Nelson 1985).

At the same time, families may need help in altering idealistic notions that their love and acceptance are sufficient to overcome the children's sense of deprivation and loss. This is especially important because such beliefs can arouse considerable guilt if children begin to exhibit emotional and/or behavior problems. In this regard, adoptive parents can be helped to recognize that many children come from high-risk backgrounds that include genetic vulnerabilities in addition to adverse past environmental experiences (Cadoret 1990; Erich & Leung 2002; Rutter 2000). Individually, or in combination, these vulnerabilities are likely to have a bearing on the child's psychological makeup. However, adoptive parents should also be told that studies show there is much individual variation in children's responses to such past conditions, possibly due to various protective influences, including factors related to resilience.

Much has been written about the elements of thorough pre- and post-placement preparation, indicating that various supports that may be needed at different points in time (Barth & Berry 1988; Berry 1997; Groza & Rosenberg 2001; Laws 2001; Smith & Howard 1999). Unfortunately, all these recommendations have been set forth amid an absence of any evaluation of their effectiveness. For the child, the construction of a life book, establishment of the child's level of commitment to adoption, and contact with other adoptees individually as peer mentors or as a support group have been recommended. For the adoptive family, full disclosure of a child's background and difficulties, the availability of medical records of the birth parents, and the child's birth records are considered very important. Adoptive parents have also suggested that child-specific information from sessions with a child's current or previous caregiver can be very helpful.

Research has found large discrepancies between what information social workers stated

they gave and what the parents stated they received (Barth & Berry 1988). Although it is unclear which assessment is accurate, this difference does lead to the conclusion that it is important for social workers to insure that parents hear and understand the information provided. In this regard, it can be useful to ask families to predict possible child behaviors and have the family role play responses. This exercise can also provide the social worker an opportunity to discuss various parenting skills and strategies.

Support groups, including a "buddy" family as mentor and meetings with other adoptive families, warm lines (telephone support services), respite care, and on-line support groups, have been discussed in the literature. Also, assigned readings, providing factual information about adoption, and discussions regarding subsidy contract negotiations and relevant tax laws have been suggested. Furthermore, the availability of training in behavior management methods as a preventive approach, and of adoption preservation services, as well as help in advocating for the child in day care and school have been recommended (Laws 2001). Also, if the intended adoption is a so-called "open" one with some level of links maintained with the birth parents, there are additional considerations for support (Grotevant & McRoy 1998). For all adoptions, following the placement, social worker contact with the family is vital so that the family can discuss whatever questions and concerns may arise, and workers can assist families in developing plans and strategies or provide referrals, if needed. Finally, adoptive parents need information about accessing various community supports and services so that they know where to turn in case the need arises.

After Disruption

What happened to these children after their adoptive placements disrupted? This is a key question, for the answer is of utmost importance when considering adoption disruption. The focus here is on the number of these children who were ultimately adopted or were, at a minimum, in another adoptive placement awaiting legalization. Unfortunately, accurate figures are not available because the percentages reported are totally a function of when, after placements disrupted, the investigators asked the question. Therefore the figures underestimate the final outcome. Nevertheless, a brief review is useful. For example, Kadushin and Seidl (1971) indicated that about 50% of the children were adopted by other families, and that adoptive placements were planned for yet more. Unger, Dwarshuis, and Johnson (1977) reported that roughly 90% of the children were re-placed in other adoptive families. Donley (1978), based on accumulated information from a number of specialized adoption programs, noted that more than 75% were successfully re-placed. Boneh (1979) stated that nearly 40% of those whose placement disrupted had been legalized in another placement by the end of the study period. Boyne, Denby, Kettenring, and Wheeler (1984:159) reported that "many of those who disrupted" went on to a legalized adoption with other families. Benton, Kaye, and Tipton (1985) indicated that in one state for which information was usable, 41% of the children were subsequently residing in another adoptive home, and that others possibly would be so placed. Partridge, Hornby, and McDonald (1986) noted that 58% were placed again for adoption, but that 24% of the re-placed cases had again disrupted when case records were reviewed. Festinger (1986) found that within 6 to 18 months after a disruption, 42% had either been adopted or were in adoptive homes awaiting legalization, and adoption remained the plan for another 21%. Finally, Rosenthal, Schmidt, & Conner (1988) reported that 74% of those who had experienced a disrupted placement were successfully placed.

It is evident that disruptions, when they occur, are not the final blow to the children's adoption. Nor can it be said that these children could not make an adequate adjustment to an adoptive placement. The figures just cited show otherwise. In view of the emotional baggage that children bring to a placement, the multiplicity of factors in the home environment, and the flaws in our ability to predict their interaction, it is inevitable that some disruptions will occur. The point is that disruptions neither end the hope for, nor likelihood of, a later successful adoption. In the process, children, families, and workers can learn how to improve the chances that the next placement will hold.

The figures on re-placement suggest that in many cases, there may have been a mismatch, in the sense that the "chemistry" appeared to be wrong, or soured after a time. This is akin to what has been called a problem in the "goodness of fit" (Thomas & Chess 1984:1), when the properties of the environment, its expectations and demands, are not in accord with the child's "own capacities, motivations, and style of behaving." It is also possible that some of these families misjudged their own abilities or were encouraged or stretched to adopt children who were really more than they could handle. Whatever the reason, it is apparent that at this particular point in time "these specific children and these specific parents were a failing combination" (Kadushin & Seidl 1971:34).

It is apparent that some configurations of factors are more risky and require more concentrated service efforts, and that staff training needs and the problems posed by staff discontinuities require review. Adoption services need to consider ways to assist workers to recognize any tendency to ignore warning signals to help workers anticipate and assess vulnerability and areas of risk, so that early intervention is possible before a crisis erupts.

The wonder is that in the long run, most of these children do get adopted. That happy news is fast forgotten when disruptions occur. It is a jarring experience for all involved. Moves in foster care are handled with much more equanimity. The expectation that moves will not occur in adoptive placements all too often leads all parties to the adoption to feel they have failed. Debriefing sessions are needed to understand what was not working, so that the parents, the child, and the agency can learn from the experience. Furthermore, agencies can provide an open forum for discussion of these situations (Fitzgerald 1985) and foster an environment that avoids recrimination, blame, and defensiveness —one that moves "away from a model of practice based on success or failure" (Aldgate and Hawley 1986:45). Adoptive placements of older children and of children with problems oblige agencies to take risks. To do so implies that goals may not be reached. But not to do so also entails taking the risk of not giving children who are waiting the opportunity to grow up in families they can call their own.

REFERENCES

Adoption and Safe Families Act. (1997). P.L. 105-89.

Adoption Assistance and Child Welfare Act. (1980). P.L. 96-272.

Aldgate, J., & Hawley, D. (1986). Helping foster families through disruption. *Adoption and Fostering, 10,* 44–49.

Argent, H. (1984). *Find me a family.* London: Souvenir Press.

Barth, R. P., & Berry, M. (1988). *Adoption & disruption: Rates, risks and responses.* Hawthorne, NY: Aldine de Gruyter.

Barth, R. P., Berry, M., Yoshikami, R., Goodfield, R., & Carson, M. L. (1988). Predicting adoption disruption. *Social Work, 33,* 227–233.

Barth, R. P., & Miller, J. M. (2000). Building effective post-adoption services: What is the empirical foundation? *Family Relations, 49,* 447–455.

Bass, C. (1975). Matchmaker-matchmaker: Older-child adoption failures. *Child Welfare, 54,* 505–511.

Benton, B. B., Kaye, E., & Tipton, M. (1985). *Evaluation of state activities with regard to adoption disruption.* Washington, DC: Urban Systems Research and Engineering.

Berry, M. (1997). Adoption disruption. In R. Avery (ed.), *Adoption policy and special needs children,* pp. 77–106. Westport, CT: Auburn House.

Berry, M., & Barth, R. P. (1990). A study of disrupted adoptive placements of adolescents. *Child Welfare, 69,* 209–225.

Boneh, C. (1979). *Disruptions in adoptive placements: A research study.* Boston: Department of Public Welfare, Office of Research Evaluation.

Borgman, R. (1981). Antecedents and consequences of parental rights termination for abused and neglected children. *Child Welfare, 60,* 391–404.

Boyne, J., Denby, L., Kettenring, J. R., & Wheeler, W. (1984). *The shadow of success: A statistical analysis of outcomes of adoptions of hard-to-place children.* Westfield, NJ: Spaulding for Children.

Brown, F. (1963). Supervision of the child in the adoptive home. In I. E. Smith (ed.), *Readings in adoption,* pp. 332–342. New York: Philosophical Library.

Cadoret, R. J. (1990). Biologic perspectives of adoptee adjustment. In D. M. Brodzinsky & M. D. Schechter (eds.), *The psychology of adoption,* pp. 25–41. New York: Oxford University Press.

Children's Bureau. (2002). *The AFCARS report: Interim FY 2000 estimates as of August 2002.* Washington, DC: U.S. Department of Health and Human Services.

Cohen, J. S. (1981). *Adoption breakdown with older children.* Toronto: University of Toronto.

Coyne, A., & Brown, M. E. (1985). Developmentally disabled children can be adopted. *Child Welfare, 64,* 607–615.

Donley, K. S. (1978). The dynamics of disruption. *Adoption and Fostering, 92,* 34–39.

Erich, S., & Leung, P. (2002). The impact of previous type of abuse and sibling adoption upon adoptive families. *Child Abuse and Neglect, 26,* 1045–1058.

Fein, E., Davies, L. J., & Knight, G. (1979). Placement stability in foster care. *Social Work, 24,* 156–157.

Festinger, T. (1986). *Necessary risk: A study of adoptions and disrupted adoptive placements.* Washington, DC: Child Welfare League of America.

Festinger, T. (1990). Adoption disruption. In D. M. Brodzinsky & M. D. Schechter (eds.), *The psychology of adoption,* pp. 201–218. New York: Oxford University Press.

Festinger, T. (2002). After adoption: Dissolution or permanence? *Child Welfare, 81,* 515–525.

Fitzgerald, J. (1985). When adoption fails—Understanding disruption. *Journal of the Royal Society of Health, 4,* 133–138.

Freundlich, M., & Wright, L. (2003). *Post-permanency services.* Washington, DC: Casey Family Programs.

Gochros, H. (1967). Not parents yet: A study of the post-placement period in adoption. *Child Welfare, 46,* 317–349.

Goerge, R. M., Howard, E. C., Yu, D., & Radomsky, S. (1997). *Adoption, disruption, and displacement in the child welfare system, 1976–94.* Chicago: University of Chicago, Chapin Hall Center for Children.

Grotevant, H. D., & McRoy, R. G. (1998). *Openness in adoption: Exploring family connections.* Thousand Oaks, CA: Sage.

Groza, V., & Rosenberg, K. F. (2001). *Clinical and practice issues in adoption.* Westport, CT: Bergin & Garvey.

Groze, V. (1986). Special-needs adoption. *Children and Youth Services Review, 8,* 363–375.

Holloway, J. S. (1997). Outcome in placements for adoption or long-term fostering. *Archives of Disease in Childhood, 76*(3), 227–230.

Kadushin, A. (1980). *Child welfare services,* third ed. New York: MacMillan.

Kadushin, A., & Seidl, F. W. (1971). Adoption failure: A social work postmortem. *Social Work, 16,* 32–38.

Kagan, R. M., & Reid, W. J. (1986). Critical factors in the adoption of emotionally disturbed youths. *Child Welfare, 65,* 63–73.

Lahti, J. (1982). A follow-up study of foster children in permanent placements. *Social Service Review, 56,* 556–571.

Laws, R. (2001). The history, elements, and ongoing need for adoption support. In V. Groza & K. F. Rosenberg (eds.), *Clinical and practice issues in adoption: Bridging the gap between adoptees placed as infants and as older children,* pp. 81–103. Westport, CT: Bergin & Garvey.

Maza, P. (2000). Using administrative data to reward agency performance: The case of the federal adoption incentive program. *Child Welfare, 79,* 444–456.

McDonald, T. P., Lieberman, A.A., Partridge, S., & Hornby, H. (1991). Assessing the role of agency services in reducing adoption disruption. *Children and Youth Services Review, 13,* 425–438.

Meezan, W., & Shireman, J. F. (1982). Foster parent adoption: A literature review. *Child Welfare, 61,* 525–535.

National Adoption Information Clearinghouse. (2002). *Disruption and dissolution.* Washington, DC: U.S. Department of Health and Human Services.

Nelson, K. A. (1985). *On the frontier of adoption: A study of special-needs adoptive families.* New York: Child Welfare League of America.

New York State Department of Social Services. (1991). *Final annual summary of characteristics of children in foster care.* New York: New York State Department of Social Services.

New York State Department of Social Services. (2000). *Final annual summary of characteristics of children in foster care.* New York: New York State Department of Social Services.

New York State Department of Social Services. (2003). *Interim annual summary of characteristics of children in foster care.* New York: New York State Department of Social Services.

Partridge, S., Hornby, H., & McDonald, T. (1986). *Legacies of loss—Visions of gain: An inside look at adoption disruptions.* Portland: Center for Research and Advanced Study, University of Southern Maine.

Pinderhughes, E. E. (1998). Short-term placement outcomes for children adopted after age five. *Children and Youth Services Review, 20,* 223–249.

Roberts, B. (1980). *Adoption project for handicapped children: Ohio District 11.* Washington, DC: Office of Human Development Services.

Rosenthal, J. A., Schmidt, D., & Conner, J. (1988). Predictors of special needs adoption disruption: An exploratory study. *Children and Youth Services Review, 10,* 101–117.

Rutter, M. (2000). Children in substitute care: Some conceptual considerations and research implications. *Children and Youth Services Review, 22,* 685–703.

Schmidt, D. M. (1986). Presentation of research findings on prevention of adoption disruption. In D. M. Schmidt (ed), *Special needs adoption: A positive perspective,* pp. 124–132. Denver: Colorado State Department of Social Services.

Schmidt, D. M., Rosenthal, J. A., & Bombeck, B. (1988). Parents' views of adoption disruption. *Children and Youth Services Review, 10,* 119–130.

Sharma, A. R., McGue, M. K., & Benson, P. L. (1996). The emotional and behavioral adjustment of United States adopted adolescents: Part II. Age at adoption. *Children and Youth Services Review 18,* 101–114.

Smith, S. L., & Howard, J. A. (1991). A comparative study of successful and disrupted adoptions. *Social Service Review, 65,* 248–265.

Smith, S. L., & Howard, J. A. (1999). *Promoting successful adoptions—Practice with troubled families.* Thousand Oaks, CA: Sage.

Terling-Watt, T. (2001). Permanency in kinship care: An exploration of disruption rates and factors associated with placement disruption. *Children and Youth Services Review, 23,* 111–126.

Testa, M. F. (2001). Kinship care and permanency. *Journal of Social Service Research, 28*(1), 25–43.

Thomas, A., & Chess, S. (1984). Genesis and evolution of behavioral disorders: From infancy to early adult life. *American Journal of Psychiatry, 141,* 1–9.

Tremetiere, B. S. (1984). *Disruption: A break in commitment.* Presentation given at the Ninth North American Council of Adoptable Children Conference, Chicago, August 1–4, 1984.

Unger, C., Dwarshuis, G., & Johnson, E. (1977). *Chaos, madness, and unpredictability . . . Placing the child with ears like Uncle Harry's.* Ann Arbor, MI: Spaulding for Children.

U.S. Congress. (1975). *Adoption and foster care.* Hearings before the Senate Subcommittee on Children and Youth of the Committee on Labor and Public Welfare. Washington, DC: U.S. Government Printing Office.

U.S. General Accounting Office. (2003). *Foster care: States focusing on finding permanent homes for children, but long-standing barriers remain.* Testimony before the House Subcommittee on Human Resources, Committee on Ways and Means. Washington, DC: U.S. Government Printing Office.

Valentine, D., Conway, P., & Randolph, J. (1987). Place-ment disruptions: Perspectives of adoptive parents. In D. Valentine (ed), *Infertility and adoption: A guide for social work practice,* pp. 231–244. Binghamton, NY: Haworth Press.

Welfare Research. (1978). *Evaluation of the test of re-gional planning in adoption.* Albany, NY: Welfare Research.

Westhues, A., & Cohen, J. S. (1990). Preventing disrup-tion of special-needs adoption. *Child Welfare, 69,* 141–155.

Zwimpfer, D. M. (1983). Indicators of adoption break-down. *Social Casework: Journal of Contemporary Social Work, 64,* 169–177.

LESLIE DOTY HOLLINGSWORTH

Birth Mothers Whose Parental Rights Are Terminated

Implications for Services

Birth mothers who do not have custody of their children have been in large part either overlooked or downplayed in the child welfare literature. Women who relinquished their biological child for adoption were perceived as having made a mistake and were joined in a collective societal effort to forget the "mistake" and move on with their lives. As special needs adoptions of older children began to replace traditional infant adoptions, consideration was given to whether an adoption would be open to contact with the birth parent or closed to such contact, but with control often in the hands of the adoptive parents. More recently, birth parents have come into the social welfare system as perpetrators of child abuse or neglect, leaving them open to perceptions that they are undeserving of having their own needs and interests attended to, or undeserving of continuing to parent their children.

What is known about the effect of loss of custody on birth mothers has been derived primarily from studies of relinquishing mothers, particularly phenomenological studies. A list of these studies and their characteristics is provided in table 1.

Although knowledge gained from these studies has not extensively influenced social welfare policies and practice, the results suggest that parents who lose custody of their children may be left with significant health, mental health, substance abuse, and family problems. They may therefore make up a substantial pro-portion of persons needing and/or receiving services.

In this chapter, I use knowledge gained from studies of women who have relinquished to anticipate the experiences and service needs of birth mothers whose parental rights have been terminated involuntarily in the judicial system and to set forth a relevant research agenda for services and policies. Because such research is just beginning, the chapter is not based on empirical data. The one exception consists of excerpts from semistructured interviews with women with a serious mental illness who lost custody (L. D. Hollingsworth, unpub. data). Although additional factors play a part and must be considered, these case examples are useful in demonstrating how involuntary loss of custody may be experienced by birth mothers. I discuss the psychological, somatic, and family-related symptoms to which birth mothers who relinquish are vulnerable and the social attitudes and policies that affect non-custodial birth mothers' experiences.

Because a large proportion of women without custody are known to have a mental illness or substance abuse problem, particular attention is given to this population. In addition, because most studies of relinquishment or loss of custody have been limited to women and because women are heavily represented in the social welfare system, the focus of this chapter is on women. However, I limit this discussion even while recognizing that knowledge of the

TABLE 1. *Overview of Relinquishment Studies Reviewed*

Author	Year	Sample Size	Data Collection and Sample Characteristics
Pannor, Baran, & Sorosky[1]	1978	38	Interviews with participants who contacted the pilot project to study the effects of relinquishment. (Included two birth fathers.) Time since relinquishment: 1–33 years.
Burnell & Norfleet[1]	1979	80	Three hundred multiple-choice format questionnaires were mailed to a randomly selected sample of women who had placed their children through an agency. Time since relinquishment: 1.5–3 years for most participants.
Lamperelli & Smith[1]	1979	19	Interviews and observations of women throughout the pregnancy and postpartum period in a maternity home.
Rynearson[1]	1982	20	Psychiatric outpatients (none in psychiatric therapy specifically for issues related to relinquishment). Women with psychotic or schizophrenic disorders were excluded. Time since relinquishment: 15–21 years.
Deykin, Campbell, & Patti[1]	1984	334	Written questionnaire from members of a support group for relinquishing parents (321 birth mothers, 13 birth fathers).
Winkler & van Keppel	1984	213	Mailed questionnaire and personal interview with single women between 15 and 25 years old at relinquishment and who relinquished their first-born child within 3 months of birth. Time since relinquishment: 0–20 or more years.
Millen & Roll[1]	1985	22	Interviews with women receiving psychotherapy (two specifically for the issue of relinquishment). Time since relinquishment: 5–20 or more years.
Condon[1]	1986	20	Interviews with birth mothers attending a support group for women. Time since relinquishment: 1–35 years.
Tennyson[1]	1988	1	Case study in which the respondent was interviewed during the third trimester and at 48 hours and 1 month after birth.
Blanton & Descher[1]	1990	59	Interviews with women who had relinquished their infants in open or closed adoptions through one of four adoption agencies. Time since relinquishment: 1 year or more.
Faulkner	1991	3	One group interview lasting several hours. Time since relinquishment: 20–23 years.
Lancette & McClure[1]	1992	5	Interviews with mothers who had contacted a pregnancy help line. Time since relinquishment: less than 2 years.
Field	1992	444	Mailed survey comparing women in New Zealand who relinquished and had reunified and women who had not reunified. Time since relinquishment: 27–40 years.
Brodzinsky, A.[1]	1992	214	Mailed surveys to birth mothers recruited through letters from adoption agencies with which they had relinquished their first child. Time since relinquishment: 19.3 months on average.
McAdoo[1]	1992	41	Semistructured interviews with birth mothers recruited through personal familiarity with the research, an adoption search and support organization, and word of mouth.
Davis[1]	1994	14	Interviews with searching mothers. Time since relinquishment: 6–27 years.
Lauderdale & Boyle	1994	12	In-depth interviews with birth mothers recruited through search and support organizations and word of mouth. Relinquishment period: 1950–1969.
Weinreib & Konstam	1995	8	Interviews with white women recruited through support groups for women who had relinquished or through local newspapers, who were 18–28 years old at the time of relinquishment. Time since relinquishment: 16–35 years.
DeSimone	1996	264	Mailed questionnaire completed by mostly white birth mothers who had relinquished an infant for adoption and who were reunited from adoption organizations, word of mouth, or newspaper advertisements.
Logan	1996	30	Interviews using semistructured questionnaires with 29 birth mothers and two birth fathers in Manchester, England, who had relinquished at least one child when they were in their "low teens to late thirties."
Thomas, Tori, Wile, & Scheidt	1996	28	Reviews of medical records of women with histories of psychiatric hospitalizations, also including 22 women who had had abortions and 32 women with no children.
Thomas & Tori	1999	38	Structured interviews from the four locked psychiatric units at a large general hospital. Study was subsequently expanded to include 36 women who had had abortions and 45 women who had experienced both abortions and relinquishments.

Source: Based on Table 1 in Askren & Bloom (1999).
[1]Studies that were part of the original Askren & Bloom (1999) review.

well-being of birth fathers in the child welfare system also represents a serious gap.

Finally, the emphasis of the chapter on the well-being of birth mothers does not reduce the importance of the well-being of the children who have been victimized. The limits are placed only to allow attention to an inadequately addressed population in the social welfare system.

I have several important purposes in this chapter. First, I seek to close a gap in the assessment and interventions for persons seeking services in the social welfare system—that of overlooking the effect of the loss of custody of a child on a person's well-being and life outcomes. Studying the effect of loss of custody requires service providers to acknowledge such loss as a serious precipitant in psychosocial and somatic problems. Second, the chapter may provide direction for research on policies that lend future support for services to persons affected. Third, it may improve preventive efforts by raising the consciousness of service providers regarding the human qualities of persons whose behavior (of relinquishing for adoption or perpetrating child abuse or neglect) may be constructed as inhuman.

Demographic Patterns for Affected Children, Youth, and Families

Establishing accurate data on the total number of children relinquished for adoption has been hampered by data collection difficulties, particularly problems with underreporting (Bachrach, Stolley, & London 1992; Chandra, Abma, Maza, & Bachrach 1999). Historically, relinquishments have occurred among young, unmarried, white women from middle to higher socioeconomic backgrounds. In the period when relinquishments were highest, the percentage of children relinquished by never-married, white women less than 45 years of age was 19.3, compared to 1.5% of children of never-married African American women under 45 years old.

Bachrach, Stolley, and London (1992) analyzed data from the National Survey of Family Growth (U.S. Department of Health and Human Services 1995) involving 430 unintended pre-marital births to non-Hispanic white women. In a multivariate analysis in which a number of other variables were controlled, women were less likely to relinquish in later than in earlier years, when they were out of school before the pregnancy occurred, when they had worked or were working for pay, when they had had a prior birth, and when the child was male. The older a woman was and the more education her own mother had beyond high school (a proxy for socioeconomic status), the more likely she was to relinquish. (The finding regarding age was the reverse of what was expected and was believed explained by the association of age with other variables in the model.)

Because records tend to be kept in children's rather than parents' names, the number of parents who have had their parental rights terminated involuntarily is not known. However, of the 542,000 children who were in foster care on September 30, 2001, the parental rights of parents of 65,000 of them (12%) had been terminated (Adoption and Foster Care Analysis and Reporting System 2004).

Although we do not know for certain the demographic characteristics of these parents, we do know that child maltreatment is the primary reason parental rights are terminated. Such studies as the National Incidence Study of 1993 (Sedlak & Broadhurst 1996) demonstrate that almost 60% of cases of child maltreatment involve neglect and that poverty is implicated in child neglect. Children from families with incomes below $15,000 are 22 times more likely to experience maltreatment. Children of single parents have a 77% greater risk of physical abuse and an 87% greater risk of neglect than children from married couple homes. Whereas 21.6% of children under 6 years old in the United States live in poverty, 59.1% of children of the same age who live with a single parent are in poverty. Finally, children from families with large numbers of children are more likely to experience maltreatment than their counterparts from smaller families.

These findings indicate, first, that lower incomes, being in a single-parent family, and being in a family with a larger number of children are associated with child maltreatment. Second, the findings suggest that the women whose parental rights are terminated because of child maltreatment also tend to be single parents, and to have lower incomes and larger numbers of children compared to women whose parental rights are not terminated.

Children of color are consistently overrepresented in the foster care system. At the end of FY2001, 38% of children in foster care in the United States were black and non-Hispanic (Adoption and Foster Care Analysis and Reporting System 2004). In addition, 17% were Hispanic, 2% were non-Hispanic Native American or Alaska Native, 1% were non-Hispanic Asian, and 2% were biracial or of two or more non-Hispanic races. Again, if we assume that the race and ethnicity of children reflects the race and ethnicity of mothers in most cases, we reach the conclusion that close to 60% of the women whose parental rights are terminated are women of color. Although attention is generally called to the overrepresentation of children of color in foster care, it is important to note that 37% of the children were white, leading to the conclusion that the proportion of white women whose parental rights have been terminated approximates this same number. I address the importance of this observation in a later discussion of the vulnerabilities and risks confronting poor women in the child welfare system.

Women whose parental rights are terminated may also be more likely to have a psychiatric problem or diagnosis, a substance abuse problem, or both. Among the characteristics of 206 severely abused and/or neglected children brought to Boston Juvenile Court on care and protection orders (Jellinek, Bishop, Murphy, Biederman, & Rosenbaum 1992), 43% of parents were found to have a documented diagnosis of substance abuse and 31% had a documented psychiatric diagnosis (with an additional 11% having historical or behavioral evidence of a psychiatric diagnosis).

Societal Context

The relinquishment of children for adoption has been identified in much of the adoption and social welfare literature as a voluntary choice women made in the best interests of their children. However, phenomenological studies of these women, and writing by such scholars as Leroy Pelton (1989), make it clear that their actions were not voluntary. Instead, relinquishment occurred in the context of a society that ostracized women who became pregnant without being married, that blamed and shamed the woman while excusing or overlooking the male partner, and that threatened rejection of children born in such circumstances—all resulting in a lack of resources and support to make a decision to parent one's own child. Parents of these women were often victims of such a society, compelled to force their daughters into giving up their grandchildren by withholding support and resources for a decision to parent the child.

Repression and denial were part of the social context in which birth mothers relinquished their children. Women were typically not allowed to see their child or to give it a name, were discouraged from talking about her or him, and were encouraged to forget about the episode and get on with their lives. Birth certificates were altered to reflect the name of the adoptive parents.

A virtual elimination of relinquishments occurred by the mid-1990s. By the time of the release of the 1995 National Survey of Family Growth (U.S. Department of Health and Human Services 1995, representing data collected between 1989 and 1995), relinquishments had dropped from a high of 8.7% of children born to all never-married women under 45 years of age prior to 1973, to less than 1%. Among white women, relinquishments had decreased from 19.3% before 1973 to 1.7% in 1995 (Chandra, Abma, Maza, & Bachrach 1999). Prominent among the perceived reasons for these decreases were more accepting societal attitudes toward unmarried births. In addition, the availability of artificial birth control and legal abortions provided alternatives to unwanted pregnancies.

Interestingly, the same year relinquishments began their decline, the Child Abuse Prevention and Treatment Act of 1974 was passed. Although the need for improvements in the protection of children cannot be disputed, this legislation brought substantial numbers of children into the child welfare system. In 1976, approximately 669,000 children were reported to child protection agencies. By 1987, the number had increased to 2,178,000, and by 1997 to 2,923,374 (Pecora, Whittaker, Maluccio, & Barth 2000). Many child maltreatment reports are unsubstantiated, and when reports are substantiated, services may be provided to children and families in their own homes. However, many of the children involved are placed in out-of-home care, and of those children, many become eligible for adoption. By the end of FY2001, there were 542,000 children in foster care in the United States, and adoption was the goal for 22% of them. Children in the public child welfare system had begun to replace relinquished children as sources of adoption.

Other social policies may have made it easier to adopt while making it more difficult for birth parents to maintain custody of their children. For example, responding to the large number of nontraditional children (older children, members of minority groups or sibling groups, and children with disabilities) brought into the children's services system under the Child Abuse Prevention and Treatment Act, the Adoption Assistance and Child Welfare Act of 1980 (P.L. 96-272) provided subsidies to encourage the adoption of children with special needs. The Adoption Incentives provision associated with the Interethnic Adoption provision under the Small Business Job Protection Act (1996) provided tax credits to persons who adopted. The Adoption and Safe Families Act (1997) had a goal of freeing children for adoption more quickly and at an earlier age.

The Personal Responsibility and Work Opportunity Reconciliation Act of 1996 (frequently referred to as "welfare reform legislation") has been criticized by some observers as assisting adoptions while making it more difficult for birth parents to maintain custody. For example, prior to its passage, Olasky (1994) called for reform in what was perceived as a welfare program that supported unmarried births and the underlying immoral actions that writer believed were associated with them. Redirecting such support to adopters of hard-to-place children was the suggested alternative. Pollitt (1996), however, recognized the withdrawal of income support from biological mothers living in poverty (through welfare reform) while increasing support to economically advantaged adoptive parents (through adoption incentive provisions) as a trend. Although acknowledging the intense desire of adoptive parents to parent a child, Pollitt (1996:9) pointed out that "theirs is not a problem a teenager should be asked to solve."

Welfare reform has actually been accompanied by decreases in the number of women receiving income support. Decreases, although smaller in proportion, in children and families living in poverty have also been noted (Lindsey 2004). At the same time, foster care placements in a number of states have decreased (Lindsey 2004). Because there may be differences by state, and problematic data collection and analysis may affect outcomes, researchers have been encouraged to continue observing the relationship between welfare reform, poverty, and foster placements.

As a final example of the influence of social policies on the loss of custody, Collins (1997) has called attention to an emerging population policy in which certain women are qualified to play some roles but not others, a policy that is based in social advantage. In a plenary speech to attendees of an Annual Conference of the National Council on Family Relations, Collins described this emerging population policy as differentiating between "genetic mothers" (who contribute biologically to the genetic material of the nation's children), "gestational mothers" (who carry the developing fetus until birth), and "social mothers" (who care for the children who are actually born). Collins defined "population policy" as a constellation of social policies, institutional arrangements, and ideological constructs that shape the reproductive histories of different groups of women. Although traditional views presented white, middle class women as performing all three functions of motherhood well, assisted in their social mothering by working class white women and by African American women, issues around fertility and assisted reproductive technology have made it possible for each group of women to specialize in one of the three categories (i.e., genetic, gestational, and social motherhood). Collins further asserted that middle class and affluent white women, through their ability to transmit the national culture to the young, are seen as superior to all other groups in socializing white youths into naturalized hierarchies of race, gender, sexuality, and social class. She perceived this group of women as the mothers of the nation. Infertility among them is considered a national tragedy and such policies as workplace benefits that support the reproductive functions of these women (and, one might now add, that support the general adoption activities of the women and their partners) aim to increase their roles as the mothers of the nation.

Finally, Collins points out that from this emerging population policy, working class women are encouraged to become genetic and gestational mothers, but are increasingly not seen as fit to serve as the social mothers. Thus, they are increasingly encouraged to give up their children for adoption. She notes that changes in abortion policy, affirmative action, and welfare policies support such initiatives. Hollingsworth (2001) raised similar concerns related to the passage of the Adoption and Safe Families Act that, although directed at protecting the health and safety of children, made it easier for disadvantaged birth parents to lose custody and for advantaged persons to acquire infants and young children who were more desirable for adoption.

Policies in the judicial system have also had the potential for increasing terminations of parental rights. In large measure attributable to the "three strikes and you're out" rule (Casey & Wiatrowski 1996), it has been estimated that 75% of the women in U.S. prisons are mothers and the sole caretakers of their children. Approximately 25,700 inmates are said to have more than 56,000 children under the age of 18 at a given time and, although most of these children are likely placed with relatives during the mother's incarceration, close to 10% are placed in foster care or other institutions (Casey & Wiatrowski 1996).

Societal attitudes can also play a part in increasing terminations by the way perceptions of women in the child welfare system are constructed. Although writing from the standpoint of the Canadian child welfare system, Swift (1995) describes a system that produces the concept of "bad mothers" who do not care for their children and who are therefore unworthy of help. Instead, such women are considered to deserve only to have their children helped through exertion of a state authority over the family. Swift points out that this approach on the part of the state reproduces the conditions of poverty, marginalization, and violence in which these families live in the first place.

Pelton (1997) calls attention to the "rescuer" orientation toward families in the child welfare system. It is this orientation that frequently underlies decisions to remove children from their biological families as the solution to problems the family experiences. In summary, social policies and attitudes have in many instances combined to increase the potential for women in certain circumstances to lose custody of their children and may continue to do so.

Vulnerabilities and Risk Factors
Studies of birth mothers who relinquished children for adoption have consistently shown that these women develop certain psychological and somatic symptoms and that these symptoms persist years beyond the relinquishment, until reunion with the adoptee or throughout the birth mother's life. In this section, I present

the symptoms for which birth mothers who relinquished a child for adoption have been found to be vulnerable. I make a case for the development of similar symptoms among birth mothers whose parental rights are terminated involuntarily.

Symptoms of Relinquishing Birth Mothers

Long-term symptoms of women who have relinquished can be categorized into three types: psychological, psychosomatic, and marital/family. The symptoms represent those that have been identified in various studies of the experiences of birth mothers.

Psychologically, women who have relinquished have described or presented with symptoms of depression, social anxiety, agoraphobia, and other anxiety/phobic states; isolation and withdrawal; emotional numbing and dissociation; feelings of loss of self, inadequacy, or a damaged sense of self, coupled with self-mutilation and self-destructive behavior; guilt about having relinquished, made more intense because they, and others, feel they have only themselves to blame; anger at, and disillusionment with professionals, birth fathers, parents, and others who could have prevented the loss and did not; recurrent feelings of stress, alarm, and anguish; fantasies of reunion with the child and the birth father; and recurrent preoccupation with fear the child may be in danger or worry about the child's happiness, health, and well-being.

Of 20 women in one study who had relinquished children (Rynearson 1982), 12 had been diagnosed with dysthymic disorder and eight with generalized anxiety disorder, borderline personality disorder, or dependent personality disorder. Chemical dependency and eating disorders are noted in some women and may be used as coping mechanisms, along with numbing and repression. In one study (reviewed in Stiffler 1991), 49 of 64 relinquishing birth mothers studied had thought of committing suicide and 14 had attempted it.

Women who have relinquished a child for adoption may have health or psychosomatic symptoms. These problems have been found to include recurrent gynecologic infections, frequent or severe headaches, sexual dysfunction, secondary infertility, and other somatic symptoms (Askren & Bloom 1999).

Finally, the relinquishment of a child for adoption has been found to have an effect on a birth mother's marital and/or family relations much later. For example, a number of women do not become pregnant again (36% in one review; Stiffler 1991). Others are perfectionistic, possessive, and/or overprotective with subsequent children, or they may feel tense and uneasy around children in general. Sexual dysfunction is also reported by some women.

Although not all birth mothers who relinquish have all the symptoms mentioned here, no studies reported a total absence of symptoms. Studies of openness in adoption revealed mixed results (Askren & Bloom 1999). In some instances, particularly when birth mothers felt more control in placement decisions, pathologic symptoms were reduced. However, for other birth mothers, openness in adoption meant that the pain experienced with the loss was never-ending.

Symptoms experienced by relinquishing birth mothers as reactions to the loss of their child have been found in many instances to persist beyond the relinquishment itself, to recur particularly around key events, such as the child's birthday or the anniversary of the relinquishment, and to persist throughout the birth mother's life. In fact, one of the factors found to make the grief experience even more intense for birth mothers who relinquish than for those whose children have died is that the children are still alive and potentially accessible, yet inaccessible. The hope is always present that the decision can be or could have been reversed.

Implications for Presence in the Social Welfare System

The expectation that birth mothers who relinquished are in the social welfare services system currently is based on two realities: one, the period of time relinquishments were most prevalent, and two, the persistent nature of symptoms associated with relinquishment. Looking at the 20 years before 1973, when relinquishments began to decline, and using 15 years as the average maternal age at delivery, relinquishments would have been at their highest between 1952 and 1972, making these women between 48 and 68 years old in 2005. Remembering that relinquishments still made up 4.1% of children born to all never-married women under age 45 (7.5% for white women) between 1973 and 1981, in 2005, these women, having given birth at an average age of 15, would now be between 39 and 47 years of age. In one study (reviewed by Stiffler 1991), half of birth mothers reported much pain and suffering 40 years after the relinquishment; the average length of time birth mothers sought help after relinquishment was 14.7 years. Thus from an age standpoint, it seems reasonable to assume that a substantial proportion of these women could be receiving services.

Implications for Birth Mothers Whose Parental Rights Are Terminated Involuntarily
Is it reasonable to assume that birth mothers will respond to the involuntary termination of their parental rights in ways similar to the responses of birth mothers who relinquished their children for adoption? There are reasons to make such an assumption. First, both experiences involve loss. Crisis studies indicate that loss is accompanied by grief and longing for the return of the lost object, and that the grief may be pathological in lasting long beyond the period associated with more usual grief reactions. Second, the loss involves a child to whom one has given birth. Mantecon (1994:6–7), in her report of a study of the relinquishment experiences of six birth mothers, including her own experience, criticizes the inattention to motherhood in theory and research, writing that "what has [also] been lost to social consciousness (as a result) is the awareness and understanding that birth is a soul passage for the woman experiencing it, an archetypal shift occurring in a woman's soul when she bears a child." She

quotes several theorists in discussing the spiritual experiences of pregnancy and birth that link the birth mother and her offspring. There is no reason to think the birth experience would be any different for the birth mother whose parental rights are terminated by the state than those of the birth mother who relinquishes or who parents her child. Third, although early relinquishments were framed as voluntary, Pelton (1989) points out these voluntary decisions were usually made in the context of a lack of resources for support available to the relinquishing mother, making it an involuntary action.

Pathological reactions to terminations of parental rights may be more intense because they are framed not as an act of love but resulting from an act of harm toward one's children. Women whose parental rights are terminated not only blame themselves but also are blamed by society. In many instances, children of women whose parental rights have been terminated are being cared for by relatives, so that birth mothers are exposed to them regularly and to the reality that they have no right to them. Finally, contextual factors—poverty, single parenthood, large family size, race, and ethnicity—have been regularly implicated in the maltreatment that can result in the termination of parental rights.

Resilience and Protective Factors
Impressive among birth mothers who relinquished children for adoption is that they developed mechanisms for survival and coping and that, in relinquishing, they had what they felt were the child's best interests in mind. In recent years, birth mothers have taken a more activist role through such organizations as Concerned United Birthmothers, making it possible for birth mothers to obtain information about relinquished children, educating the public about the losses associated with relinquishment, and pursuing policies that support birth parents having the choice of parenting their children.

Little is known about how birth mothers cope with the termination of their parental rights. In semistructured interviews conducted recently with 82 women with a serious mental illness who had ever lost custody of their child or children temporarily or permanently (L. D. Hollingsworth, unpub. data), 56% of the women were able to acknowledge the helpfulness of the alternative placement for their own well-being.

One protective factor identified is the informal assistance provided by relatives and friends to birth mothers during their struggles to cope with active symptoms of serious mental illness while parenting their children. In the study just referred to, the largest proportion of persons providing help were sisters of the birth mother, followed by the birth mother's own mother and the children's biological father from whom the birth mother was estranged. Friendships were a noteworthy source of support.

Research

As reported earlier, both quantitative and qualitative data have been collected regarding the experiences of birth mothers who relinquished a child. Results have been surprisingly consistent. Phenomenological studies have the benefit of describing the lived experiences of these women.

The primary limitation in relinquishment research has been the relatively small sample sizes or the lack of nationally representative data. In the most recent National Survey of Family Growth (U.S. Department of Health and Human Services 1995), as in previous cycles, researchers sought information regarding relinquishments. A respondent was determined to have relinquished if she volunteered that a baby she gave birth to was unnamed and placed for adoption, or if she answered yes to a direct question regarding whether she had ever placed a child for adoption who was born to her. Of 10,846 women between the ages of 15 and 44 who participated, only 64 births to never-married women were relinquished (82 were relinquished altogether). Although underreporting is believed to be a factor, the results point to the difficulty in obtaining representative data. At the same time, several phenomenological studies have been done, most of them for doctoral dissertations. These studies have the benefit of allowing readers to share the lived experiences of women who have relinquished.

Research that focuses on the experiences of birth fathers relinquishing children for adoption is limited. Research is virtually nonexistent where court-ordered termination of parental rights is concerned. Studies are also needed on the attitudes that child welfare professionals hold regarding the maltreatment of children, the factors involved, and the people responsible.

There is a lack of research, either quantitative or qualitative, on the experiences of women whose parental rights have been terminated. Computerized searches turn up no studies of terminations per se. Research on child custody loss has been limited to descriptive studies or, recently, to parenting issues of women with serious mental illness. There is also a dearth of research on how the termination of parental rights influences women seeking or receiving social welfare services, particularly those for whom health, mental health, substance abuse, and family counseling are provided.

Assessments and Interventions

Studies of relinquishing birth mothers have prompted calls for including inquiry about relinquishment in assessment and interventions. In their review of relinquishment studies, Askren and Bloom (1999:396) write: "Health care providers need to focus on this neglected population in order to discover the most appropriate way to provide their care." They also summarize recommendations for interventions that have come out of other relinquishment studies. Recommended interventions include counseling, dream analysis, role playing, interviews with adoptive parents, anticipatory guidance for the grief reaction, and continuing support from a healthcare professional.

Service providers should include in any structured assessment procedure inquiries about whether a woman has ever lost a child—through death, relinquishment, a divorce action, or judicial termination. Interventions should be tested that provide birth mothers with support, an opportunity to talk about their experiences, and encouragement of the activist roles of birth mothers. Education can be provided to families and communities regarding the effects of this phenomenon.

Ethical Issues and Value Dilemmas

With regard to the termination of parental rights, ethical issues and value dilemmas may be observed in the circumstances that lead to the termination of women's parental rights and in the response—or absence of a response—to women whose rights have been terminated.

A major issue is the overlap between the existence of a market for adoptable children and the public responsibility to protect children. The Adoption and Safe Families Act has been criticized for its built-in potential for further disenfranchising disadvantaged birth families and further benefiting advantaged parents who wish to adopt a healthy infant (Hollingsworth 2001). Factors criticized include the provision for more rapid terminations in the absence of proven methods for parents to take corrective action within the time limits (e.g., recover from substance abuse problems); the prioritization of adoption over reunification through the provision of federal incentive payments to states and agencies that increase adoptions but not safe reunifications; and a system of "concurrent" planning, in which a plan for adoption coexists with efforts toward reunification in the context of incentives directed toward adoption.

In addition to these potential structural biases, values may abound in the media, in communities, and among child welfare professionals that adoption is the plan that is in the best interest of children. Child welfare professionals may find themselves wanting to adopt the children in their care or they may identify more with parents seeking to adopt than with the birth mother. In spite of evidence of the influence of social context and socially unjust circumstances that encouraged relinquishments for such a long period, and that continue to allow the large number of parental rights terminations,

social welfare professionals have been willing to proceed according to a medical model that has held birth mothers responsible for the outcomes of their children. The absence of appropriate research and of services responsive to birth parents perpetuates this phenomenon.

Case Examples

The following case examples demonstrate the lasting effects of the loss of custody on birth mothers.

BIRTH MOTHER A

The 47-year-old woman, diagnosed with major depression, had returned after spending 2 months on the East Coast, where her mother had died and she (the birth mother) had attempted to sort out her mother's legal affairs. Upon returning to southeastern Michigan, she found that her husband and three minor sons no longer lived where they had all lived together. Unable to locate them, she hired a private investigator. After a long legal battle, interspersed with psychiatric hospitalizations (one of which occurred during the time of the final divorce hearing, so that she was not present at the hearing), they were divorced, and her husband obtained full custody of the children. Asked during an interview whether she felt the loss had had an effect on her, she replied:

> I think it was unfair the way I lost them and it really has affected my life, worrying about them on a daily basis. Do they have enough food to eat? Are they being taken care of emotionally? How are they doing in school? And questions like that. . . . Yes, it has an effect on them because they are not—you know, how when you grow up you have a mother to teach you how to put your clothes away and do things like that. They don't have that kind of order. They have not developed that.

BIRTH MOTHER B

A 38-year-old mother with bipolar disorder and unspecified personality disorder lost custody of her 9- and 14-year-old children to relatives, with whom they remained until adulthood. The birth mother was under a court order not to visit the children. Asked whether she felt it had been helpful to her in any way for someone else to raise the children, she responded: "No, I still cry a lot about it. . . . I still scream at officials, and I still get politically involved with other families that have been tormented the way I've been tormented."

BIRTH MOTHER C

A 36-year-old woman, with major depression and living in southeast Michigan, reported that placements with her daughter began when the daughter was 2. Finally, after multiple hospitalizations and unsuccessful placements with relatives, the woman felt forced to give up custody to a couple, the woman of whom was the sports coach of her daughter (who was by then in high school).

> Interviewer: Okay. And you said that they now have guardianship over her?
> Respondent: Yes.
> Interviewer: Okay. How did that come about?
> Respondent: Well, since Mrs. _____ wanted to take care of her and she wanted to do it legally and not get in any trouble . . . we went down to the court downtown and she got guardianship, you know, legally. And I had to give up all my parental rights.
> Interviewer: Okay. How did you feel doing this?
> Respondent: I felt sad and I felt, like, betrayed, but that's what had to happen. So. . . .
> Interviewer: Tell me . . . you said you felt sad and betrayed. Tell me a little bit more about that.
> Respondent: Well, the initial date that it all happened, we went down to the court and Mrs. _____, she told me, she said, "I'm not taking Beth away from you. I'm not Beth's mom." That's what she said. And, you know, that hurt me, but that's something I have to live with.
> Interviewer: Because she told you she wasn't trying to take your place, but at the same time you felt low?
> Respondent: It was the system. It's been really hard, really hard. And they're a lot better off than I am. . . . He's a banker downtown and she's a teacher.

Services

Research outcomes reported with regard to the experiences of women who relinquish or lose custody of their children have resulted in some services that directly target the needs of these women. Different needs are targeted by different programs, depending on the philosophy and orientation of the program. Exemplars include the programs described below.

The Center for Family Connections in Cambridge, Massachusetts, under the direction of Dr. Joyce Maguire Pavao, functions according to a family systems model that considers adoption a life-long occurrence, marked by a series of "normative" developmental crises, and affecting all persons involved in any way in the adoption. Rather than being a placement agency, the center operates solely to provide services to those affected by and affecting adoption. Services are provided to birth parents, adopted persons, adoptive parents, and extended family members in individual, group, or family sessions. Openness in adoption is valued and services emphasize attention to the needs and perspectives of all individuals involved but with particular attention to the birth parents, with whom the adoption originated. The center also provides professional training and consultation to practitioners, policymakers, and other professionals involved in adoption. A book written by Pavao (1998) is very useful in providing information about the center's philosophy and practice methods and numerous examples. Two observations by Pavao have particular implications for practitioners providing services to birth mothers whose parental rights have been terminated. First, she observes that a large proportion of these women—80% or more— have backgrounds themselves that involved experiences of trauma. Thus interventions appropriate for persons with trauma issues may be considered. Second, because child abuse or neglect have often been involved, women who have had their parental rights terminated often must acknowledge their own role in the termination before they are able to move forward in their healing. Interventions that focus on micro-, meso-, and macrosystem issues are appropriate here.

Adoption Crossroads in New York City, under the direction of clinical social worker Joe Soll, provides support groups, advocacy, social action, and an innovative program called "Healing Weekends" for birth mothers of adopted persons. "Healing Weekends" are scheduled events open to a limited number of birth mothers and their offspring who have reunited. Soll was an organizer of the 1998 March on Washington, District of Columbia, for adoptee civil rights (2004). Although interventions include a micro- and meso-system focus, the Adoptions Crossroads program is unique in its emphasis on macrosystem factors surrounding the placement of children for adoption.

Catholic Human Services in Traverse City, Michigan, provides mostly preplacement services to birth mothers that are primarily microsystemic in nature. Services are provided to women faced with making a decision regarding their pregnancy. Whereas traditional services involved issues of shame and social stigma, services currently provided tend to be to single women facing the birth of a second, third, or fourth child and without the resources to provide for the child. In some instances, women, anticipating an automatic termination because of having had parental rights terminated previously (related to state policy), seek placement as a way of assuming some control over the decisionmaking regarding their child. Regardless of the surrounding circumstances, issues of ambivalence, grief, and regret surface and are addressed, along with needs for relationship counseling, housing, financial assistance, and legal services. In addition, planning and implementing an adoptive placement and decisions regarding the openness of the placement are considered. Adoptions supervisor Jim Gridder (1988) is the author of *Lifegivers: Framing the birthparent experience in open adoption.*

One final unique program is the Family & Children's Resource Program (2004) provided through the Jordan Institute for Families of the University of North Carolina School of Social Work, Chapel Hill. Through this program, training coordinator Amy Ramirez offers a 2-day, competency-based curriculum entitled "The emotional aspects of termination of parental rights." The training is offered to child welfare workers and focuses on such topics as the impact of termination of parental rights on birth parents as well as on children and on child welfare workers, and grief and loss issues for all involved in the adoption. Providing such training to child welfare workers can be expected to have an impact on the way they deliver services to birth parents and their children.

Conclusion

In this chapter, I have sought to make use of knowledge from studies of the experiences of relinquishing birth mothers. This knowledge is used to anticipate the reactions that may be experienced by birth mothers whose parental rights are terminated as a result of child maltreatment and to consider public policies and services that may be appropriate for study. I have called attention to the social context (the social structure, societal attitudes, and public policies), rather than individual deficiencies, as at least partial explanation for these experiences. What is most clear is that two types of services are needed. First, there is a need for services that assist birth mothers with the immediate and long-term effects—psychological, somatic, and relational—of the loss of their children. Second, interventions are needed that are aimed at changing the social structure that continues to perpetuate conditions under which these losses occur. Current services, although limited, tend to be of the first type. The results of these services are encouraging, but human services professionals should not lose sight of the need for more macrolevel emphasis.

REFERENCES

Adoption and Foster Care Analyis and Reporting System. (2004). *Administration for Children and Families, National Adoption and Foster Care Statistics.* Washington, DC: Adoption and Foster Care Analysis and Reporting System.

Adoption and Safe Families Act. (1997). P.L. 105-89.

Adoption Assistance and Child Welfare Act. (1980). P.L. 96-272.

Askren, H. A., & Bloom, K. C. (1999). Postadoptive reactions of the relinquishing mother: A review. *Journal of Obstetric, Gynecological, and Neonatal Nursing, 28,* 395–400.

Bachrach, C. A., Stolley, K. S., & London, K. A. (1992). Relinquishment of premarital births: Evidence from national survey data. *Family Planning Perspectives, 24,* 27–48.

Casey, K. A., & Wiatrowski, M. D. (1996). Women offenders and "Three strikes and you're out." In D. Shichor & D. K. Sechrest (eds.), *Three strikes and you're out: Vengeance as public policy,* pp. 222–243. Thousand Oaks, CA: Sage.

Chandra, A., Abma, J., Maza, P., & Bachrach, C. (1999). *Adoption, adoption seeking, and relinquishment for adoption in the United States.* Advance data from vital and health statistics no. 306. Hyattsville, MD: National Center for Health Statistics.

Child Abuse Prevention and Treatment Act. (1974). P.L. 93-247.Collins, P. H. (1997). *Producing the mothers of the nation: Race, class, and contemporary U.S. population policies.* Speech at the annual conference, National Council on Family Relations, Kansas City, MO, November 15–18, 1997.

DeSimone, M. (1996). Birth mother loss: Contributing factors to unresolved grief. *Clinical Social Work Journal, 24,* 65–76.

Faulkner, E. J. (1991). The birthmother: Her fantasies, feelings, and defenses. *Dissertation Abstracts International, 52*(4-B).

Field, J. (1992). Psychological adjustment of relinquishing mothers before and after reunion with their children. *Australian & New Zealand Journal of Psychiatry, 26,* 232–241.

Hollingsworth, L. S. (2001). Adoption policy in the U.S.: A word of caution. *Social Work, 45,* 183–186.

Jellinek, M. S., Bishop, S. J., Murphy, J. M., Biederman, J., & Rosenbaum, J. F. (1992). Screening for dysfunction in the children of outpatients at a psychopharmacology clinic. *American Journal of Psychiatry, 148,* 1031–1036.

Lauderdale, J. L., & Boyle, J. S. (1994). Infant relinquishment through adoption. *Image: Journal of Nursing Scholarship, 26*(3), 213–217.

Lindsey, D. (2004). *The welfare of children,* second ed. New York: Oxford University Press.

Logan, J. (1996). Birth mothers and their mental health: Unchartered territory. *British Journal of Social Work, 26,* 609–625

Mantecon, V. H. (1994). Re-membering broken bonds: An in-depth exploration of the phenomenology of child-surrender. Doctoral dissertation, Pacifica Graduate Institute, Pacific Oaks, CA (1990). UMI Dissertation Services no. LD03198.

Olasky, M. (1994). Adoption is an act of compassion. In A. Harnack (ed.), *Adoption: Opposing Viewpoints,* pp. 121–142. San Diego, CA: Greenhaven.

Pavao, J. M. (1998). *The family of adoption.* Boston: Beacon.

Pecora, P. J., Whittaker, J. K., Maluccio, A. N., & Barth, R. P. (2000). *The child welfare challenge,* second ed. Hawthorne, NY: Aldine de Gruyter.

Pelton, L. H. (1989). *For reasons of poverty: A critical analysis of the public child welfare system in the United States.* Westport, CT: Praeger.

Pelton, L. H. (1997). Child welfare policy and practice: The myth of classlessness. *American Journal of Orthopsychiatry, 67,* 545–553.

Personal Responsibility and Work Opportunity Reconciliation Act. (1996). P.L. 104-193.

Pollitt, K. (1996). Adoption fantasy. *Nation, 23*(July), 9.

Rynearson, E. K. (1982). Relinquishment and its maternal complications: A preliminary study. *American Journal of Psychiatry, 139,* 338–340.

Sedlak, A. J., & Broadhurst, D. D. (1996). *Executive summary of the Third National Incidence Study of Child Abuse and Neglect.* Retrieved November 30, 2004, from www.calib.com/nccanch/pubs/nix3.txt.

Small Business Job Protection Act. (1996). P.L. 104-188.

Stiffler, L. H. (1991). Adoption's impact on birthmothers: "Can a mother forget her child?" *Journal of Psychology & Christianity, 10,* 249–259.

Swift, K. J. (1995). *Manufacturing "bad mothers:" A critical perspective on child neglect.* Toronto: University of Toronto Press.

Thomas, T., & Tori, C. D. (1999). Sequela of abortion and child relinquishment among women with major psychiatric disorders. *Psychological Reports, 84,* 773–790.

Thomas, T., Tori, C. D., Wile, J. R., & Scheidt, S. D. (1996). Psychosocial characteristics of psychiatric inpatients with reproductive losses. *Journal of Health Care for the Poor and Underserved, 7*(1), 15–23.

U.S. Department of Health and Human Services. (1995). *National survey of family growth: Cycle 5.* Hyattsville, MD: U.S. Department of Health and Human Services.

Weinreb, M., & Konstam, V. (1996). Birthmothers: A retrospective analysis of the surrendering experience. *Psychotherapy in Private Practice, 15*(1), 59–70.

Winkler, R., & van Keppel, M. (1984). *Relinquishing mothers in adoption: Their long-term adjustment.* Melbourne: Institute of Family Studies.

JUDITH COOPER HEITZMAN

Epiphany

An Adoptee and Birth Mother's Reunion Story

With the adoption of my 8-week-old daughter in 1977, I was ecstatic. Growing up as the oldest of nine children, I had always loved children and looked forward to having my own. Yet by the age of 22, I had already had two miscarriages and was unable to have more children. The opportunity to mother an adopted child was a great gift to me.

First Steps

I remember so many things about the adoption. For one thing, it almost did not happen. We (my first husband and I) had been residents of Indianapolis, Indiana, when we initially applied for adoption in 1975. We had moved to Boise, Idaho, in August 1976. Shortly thereafter, I called the Boise agency to advise them of our new address. The director of adoptions told me that we were no longer eligible because we had moved out of the diocese. I was grief stricken and outraged. I told him we never would have accepted the transfer if we had known that. He called back the same day, and told me they had reconsidered. We were still on the list.

We continued our subjection to what seemed to be a grueling scrutiny of our parental fitness. We were approved as adoptive parents in February 1977. At that time, 15 months had already passed since we began the adoption process; it was taking 24 to 36 months from inception of the process to the placement of the infant child. We got a call on March 18, 1977, to come that very day and pick up our baby girl. We were far from ready! We had no furniture, clothing, baby paraphernalia. I had started crocheting a baby blanket, but was only about two-thirds finished. No matter! We ran out and bought the basics at the local discount department store. We did not even have a name picked out! We rushed from our home in Pocatello, Idaho, to pick up the child. We decided on the drive to Indianapolis to name her Jan Robin Pinkerton—Jan because it was uncommon at that time (or so we thought) and Robin for my maternal grandmother, Mary Robin McCauliff. We arrived at about 6:00 P.M. at the agency and picked up our new baby girl. What a moment of ecstasy! We stopped at my parents' home that same night and celebrated the first grandchild in the family. Many of my eight brothers and sisters were still at home. It was quite an eventful night. So much jubilation! When we arrived back in Pocatello, our neighborhood friends had scavenged their closets, set up a baby crib, and washed and folded enough diapers, blankets, and clothes to take us through the next 2 months. What a day!

It was another 9 months before the adoption was legally finalized. During this time, we waited for a home study from the local social worker. When at last we went to court in December 1977, it was another day of celebration. I suppose some folks fear that something might go wrong and the baby might be taken from you before the adoption is legally complete. I was no exception, and so breathed a sigh of relief when the court hearing was over and the adoption was final.

Interestingly, our daughter's birth name, "Patricia Jane Houseman," was left on the adoption papers in error. In those days, adoptions were closed, meaning the names of the birth and adoptive parents were not shared. So this was quite an error. We knew the birth mother was from Boise. Because I was born and raised in Boise, and my parents and siblings still lived there, it was easy for me to research the phone directory for the name "Houseman." There were only two listings in the Boise directory and both were on Old Oak Tree Road.

Longing for Roots

When Jan was 3 years old, her adoptive father and I divorced. I retained full custody. Raising her as a single parent was taxing at times, but still a joy. When Jan was 10 years old, I remarried. However, as the years passed, my daughter grew more despondent about being given away by her birth mother. Each year on Mother's Day, since she was about 5 years old, she would ask me, "Why did my mother give me up?" Each year, I would explain that although I had not spoken to her birth mother, women usually do this because they want a better life for their child. But that was not enough for my Jan.

As she grew older, I told her that on her eighteenth birthday, I would give her the birth name. And on that birthday, I kept my promise: she received a birthday card from me with her birth name inside. She was glad to have this information, along with snippets of details about her birth family she had learned over the years from me through the office that handled the adoption.

In December 1996, Jan had a baby girl of her own. Like her mother before her, she had a child out of wedlock at the age of 19. Like her mother before her, the birth father "disappeared" and had no contact with the baby. Jan's stepfather was aged 65 years at the time of Maggie's birth. Her mother's father was 64 years old when Jan was born. Jan began to see family patterns. As infants, Maggie and Jan are mirror images of one another. Jan and Maggie look identical in their respective baby pictures! But Jan still hungered for knowledge of her roots.

Reconnection

In July 1998, my husband and I were able to visit Ireland, the home of my ancestors. I was profoundly moved to experience this link with my past. I began to think of how significant this void was to Jan. So, in the fall of 1998, I asked her if she was still considering contacting her family of origin. She said yes, but was fearful about how to approach them and about the possible outcome. We discussed the matter, acknowledging that sometimes the outcome is not positive, but decided it was worth the risk. And so I wrote a letter on Jan's behalf to the two Houseman families on Old Oak Tree Road. To make matters easier, the neighbor who lived in the same block of Old Oak Tree Road was a friend I had known for 25 years. I called my friend and asked if I could use her as a reference, so the Houseman family would not think the letter was some kind of prank. She agreed, and I sent the letter from my office address, on October 18, 1998.

In about 10 days, I received a note from Mrs. Annie Houseman, Jan's maternal grandmother. She asked me to call for a private conversation. I called her that same day, and we talked for over an hour. She explained how the letter had been delayed because of an incorrect zip code. She told me how her daughter, Lorraine (Jan's birth mother), had been a joy to raise, how she loved animals, and some of her extraordinary actions, like bringing in a caterpillar to bathe when she was a tot. I told how Jan also loved crawly things as a child, and had held a slug at age 4 until I had to use a scouring pad to clean her hands. She told me how Lorraine had liked exotic pets like geckos. I marveled that Jan had always voiced a desire to own a gecko! She told of meeting with Lorraine and showing her my letter. She wanted to know why I was in favor of this meeting. I told her about my Ireland experience and my thoughts about Jan deserving to know her roots, too.

Annie said Lorraine wanted to approach this slowly and carefully because she has another daughter, age 12, who did not know anything about Jan. I assured Annie that I had known their name and address for 21 years, so she could be safe in knowing we would respect their privacy and wishes. Then I agreed to meet with Lorraine, by her request, at my office. We scheduled a time for a Saturday evening when her daughter, Sarah, would be gone to visit her own father (Lorraine had been divorced for about 5 years). We agreed to meet between 7:00 and 7:30 P.M. on November 14, 1998.

First Sight

I had told Jan nothing of these events because, like Lorraine, I was also feeling protective of my daughter. However, on Sunday, November 8, Jan asked if the Houseman family had responded to my letter. At that point, I acknowledged the correspondence and gave her a full report on the details to date. So she knew I was planning to meet with her birth mother on November 14.

The morning of November 14, 1998, I was so nervous that I awoke early and wrote poetry and prayers asking God for the gift of wisdom. There was another time in my life (unrelated to this story) that I had a golden opportunity to do something loving, but ran from it because of anxiety. I prayed to learn from that loss and have the courage to see this through. I went to my office that evening, jumpy as water on a hot griddle! Lorraine arrived at 7:05 P.M. We were both so tense at first, but quickly said so and that eased our discomfort. I offered her some refreshment, a soft drink or a beer. She chose the Mountain Dew®, without knowing that it is also Jan's favorite drink. We chatted for a few minutes. She told me why and how she made the decision to give up her child, and I told her snippets of history. Lorraine brought the birth certificate, the only evidence she had of Jan. I saw a little crooked foot like the one Jan had had as a tiny tot. Lorraine had never owned a photograph of Jan. She saw Jan's and Maggie's pictures in my office. She told me that Robin was her grandmother's name. I told her that Robin was my grandmother's name.

I thanked Lorraine and told her what a precious gift raising Jan had been to me. She said she could never have done that. After about 30 minutes together, I asked Lorraine why she wanted to meet me first. She said, "I didn't think I could take it if she hates me and tells me face to face." "Oh, she definitely doesn't hate you," I said, "but she does want to meet you. And I'm supposed to ask you if you want to meet her." Lorraine replied enthusiastically, "Oh, yes!" "When?" I asked. "Any time," she replied. "How about tonight?" I asked. "That would be good," Lorraine said. I called home and asked Jan if she wanted to meet Lorraine tonight. At first she did not answer the phone, a real first at our house! But when I reached her, she got really excited and said, "I've got to take a shower first! Give me about 30 minutes!" As my office is only about 5 minutes from my home, that was easy to do.

A Match

We arrived at our house at a little before 8:00 P.M. on November 14, 1998. Lorraine met Jan and Jan's 2-year-old daughter, Maggie. They were both excited, but obviously nervous. My husband, Tom Haller, had gone out and bought two dozen roses, one bouquet for me and one for Lorraine. He had taken two single buds and placed them each in a vase, one for Jan and one for Maggie. After a few minutes, we went to the family room to look at Jan's childhood pictures. Maggie had gone to bed, and we sat in the family room and told stories until after 1:00 A.M. During the evening, I noticed that Lorraine had long fingers like Jan. I asked, "can you do something weird with your fingers?" Lorraine indeed showed us that she could also bend her fingers backward in the same quirky manner as Jan! I squealed "it's a match!" and we all roared with laughter. Before Lorraine left, she affirmed Jan so beautifully. She also said, "when Sarah comes home tomorrow night, I'm going to tell her all about this. I'm really pumped about this!"

Lorraine left our home with a few pictures of Jan growing up and an armful of roses. After she had gone, I said to Jan, "After tonight, your life will never be the same again!" She answered brightly with a glowing smile, "I know!"

Extended Family

The following Tuesday, Lorraine called and left a message on my answering machine at work. She had told Sarah, who was "thrilled, and wants to meet her sister as soon as possible." So the following Friday, November 20, 1998, Jan met her sister. During the week we had scanned picture albums and collected a life history of Jan in photographs for Lorraine. Lorraine Scartelli (she told us her surname that night, and Jan told hers) brought baby pictures of Sarah, which looked almost identical to Jan's. Even though the girls have different fathers, they look identical. Jan's father was Hispanic, and Sarah's father was Italian, so we thought that perhaps the Mediterranean connection reinforced their look-alike factor. Lorraine and Jan exchanged home phone numbers.

The next weekend, Jan, Maggie, Tom, and I were invited to the home of Lorraine's parents on Old Oak Tree Road. On Saturday, Annie Houseman (maternal grandmother) called me to review her plans. "Now, I've decided to have food buffet style instead of a sit-down meal, so all my family won't be staring at Jan. I don't want them to make her uncomfortable. They will swarm her, I'm sure. Also, Barry [the maternal grandfather] wants to meet Tom, so we hope he will come along, even though this started out to be a hen party." I affirmed her plans. When I hung up, I shared this information with Jan. Jan started to cry (something she does not easily). I asked her what was wrong. "I never thought it would be like this," she answered. "I thought they wouldn't want me." She and her birth mother had experienced the same hopes and fears.

I woke up early on December 6 and told my husband, "this is really a red-letter day . . . St. Nicholas Day *and* the day we go to the home on Old Oak Tree Road that I have known about for 21 years!" It was delightful meeting Annie and Barry Houseman. Their hospitality was lovely, and they were so gracious and grateful. Annie even said, "thank you for giving her back!" We laughed and I said, "Let's be clear. I'm not giving her back, just helping her have what belongs to her."

Filling in the Blanks

Tom was escorted through the grounds of the Houseman place, several acres with small buildings behind the main house. Barry and Tom shared stories of Barry's father, "Grandpa" Houseman, and Tom's uncle, Chester Halbach, who had both raised carrier pigeons in World War II and had been in a "pigeon club" together in the 1940s. Barry told how Lorraine had spent long hours with Grandpa learning about the pigeons. Tom told how Jan had been to Uncle Charles' pigeon farm and museum.

Annie told me that she never influenced Lorraine's decision to give up her baby for adoption, but she was so disappointed that she plotted in her mind how to track us. The court had told Lorraine that after her termination of parental rights hearing, the next family in the courtroom would be the adoptive family. Annie had plotted to sneak down to the courthouse, watch who came in after Lorraine, and follow them to the parking lot and get their license number! She did not do it, though, because she did not want to upset her daughter and was unfamiliar with the courthouse. This was not at all accurate, as our hearing had been in Idaho some 9 months later, a fact that I shared with Annie and Lorraine.

Some of Annie's friends of 40 years came to the gathering. One woman said as she entered the room, "I don't have to ask which one it is . . . you look just like Lorraine. I saw you when you were just one hour old." Jan's face was so precious and bright as she drank in this history of her life. Annie and Lorraine presented us with three gifts: a birthday gift of stuffed animal puppies for Maggie, whose second birthday was coming up on December 13; five roses for Jan, one each to represent Lorraine, Sarah, Jan, Maggie, and me; and a red crystal angel for me, as a thank-you for writing the letter.

Creating a New Paradigm

The following Tuesday, Annie and I met for lunch. She said to me, "I don't know how to do this." I agreed that I was also unclear, but was willing to allow our revelations to unfold. Annie shared that her family did not want to make Jan uncomfortable. We talked about the decision to give up Lorraine's infant for adoption. Annie shared candidly. "It was like a death for me. I never thought I would see her again in my life. And when that letter came, it was a miracle."

The following Saturday, Lorraine and Annie came to Maggie's birthday celebration. Sarah was also invited but had other commitments. They met my parents, Carl and Marie Collogan. They also met some of our friends, including Janet Rend, who has long been Jan's dear friend and is Maggie's godmother; Don Maguire, Maggie's godfather; and some of Jan's friends from work.

Lorraine and Sarah accepted an invitation to our home for Christmas dinner. They joined our family of four and my brother. Later on Christmas day, Jan and Maggie went to the home of Barry and Annie Houseman on Old Oak Tree Road to meet Lorraine's sisters and their children and significant others.

On the Wednesday after Christmas, we four (Tom, Jan, Maggie, and I) were invited back to Annie and Barry's home. We met more of Lorraine's extended family. Barry and I played pool pitted against Jan and Tom. Lorraine watched her grandbaby Maggie. Sarah teased her sister.

Hearts Full of Gratitude

I am grateful for this most precious gift to our family. I have witnessed Jan's healing these past few months. It has been like watching an emo-

tional wound close. Jan has had more than her share of losses. Her adoptive parents divorced when she was 3. We never could manage to get along well. The animosity between families was a constant source of grief for Jan. She has a stepmother who had a daughter and a son. Jan was close to her stepbrother and stepsister as a child. Her stepbrother died of cancer when Jan was 17 years old. And her stepsister has often lived out of town and they have drifted apart. Since she met her birth family, Jan smiles all the time now. She and her sister are getting to know one another and are finding new ways to tease each other!

Many friends have told me that it was no accident that Jan's birth name was left on the adoption papers. I, too, believe that providence unfolds in due time. Others have told me their family adoption stories since this episode in our life began. Most of them have not been so pleasant. Within 3 weeks of November 14, I heard from three adoptive parents, two birth parents, and a woman who was adopted as an infant. Someone, usually the birth parents or the adoptive parents, gets in the way of a smooth meeting. Often, it is the adopted child who bears the brunt of the suffering. I am grateful that our search found a loving and warm family of origin for Jan.

Some friends have asked me if I am afraid that Jan will leave us and move in with her natural mother and sister. I believe that is Jan's choice as an adult if she so wishes. I know that my life has also been healed, having this opportunity to see my beloved daughter come to better know herself and her roots.

All of our family members, the Housemans, Hanovers, Scartelli, Overtons, and Collogans, are pioneering this new territory. Everyone seems to be respectful of one another's privacy, history, and choices. Lorraine has voiced her certainty that I am Jan's mother, and that she is grateful to have the chance to become friends with Jan. Sarah has voiced her understanding that Jan will be her sister "forever," even if her mother dies. Jan has expressed her gratitude to have this opportunity to know about herself, her roots, and her people. Annie has her miracle. I am seeing my daughter heal before my eyes, and I am grateful that Maggie will be able to grow up knowing all about herself.

Just before Christmas, all the roses had died except one. We kept that rose in a vase until it, too, was dead. However, as I went to toss it into the trash, I noticed that the dead rose (a cut flower) had grown three new shoots! So I kept that dried flower in water. And on January 5, 1999, it was still green and growing. This is not a phenomenon I have ever witnessed when dealing with cut flowers. Perhaps it is not unusual, but to me it appeared as another affirmation of the new growth in our family.

If you ask yourself, Who is the "real" family? The answer is: "All of us!" This has been the best Christmas present ever!

Afterword

It is the spring of 2004. It has been 5½ years since the reunion occurred. During this time, our whole family attended Sarah's graduation from middle school. Jan had another daughter in 1999. She moved into an apartment and then, 3 years ago, she purchased her first home. Lorraine helped her move. The two of them maintain a relationship. They enjoy one another's company. We have plans to be together this year, as we have since the reunion, on Mother's Day.

I continue to be grateful for the loving relationships among us. I am convinced that this arrangement is not unusual. It is an extraordinary gift to all of us. The hope of our family in publishing this story is to encourage professionals serving adoptive families and other families who come to this intersection in life to be open to it. The joys have far outweighed the fears.

JENNIFER RENNE
GERALD P. MALLON

Facilitating Permanency for Youth

The Overuse of Long-Term Foster Care and the Appropriate Use of Another Planned Permanent Living Arrangement as Options for Youth in Foster Care

HECTOR

Seventeen-year-old Hector has been in foster care since he was 8. His mother was a substance abuser, his father deceased. At age 9, upon entering the foster care system, Hector was placed in a foster home with Mrs. Ruiz, a single mother with grown children. Things went well in that home. Hector occasionally visited his birth mother, but his interactions with her were marred by her promise to "get and stay clean," a promise that she was unable to keep. Hector's permanency goal was reunification with a concurrent plan for adoption. Mrs. Ruiz had indicated that if Hector became freed for adoption, she would be a permanent resource for him. After 15 months of working toward reunification, Hector's social worker and the team decided to move toward the goal of adoption, as it was increasingly evident that Hector's birth mother could not be a permanent resource for him. The termination of parental rights process was initiated, but there were many procedural delays. After 3 years in the Ruiz foster home, Hector's mother's parental rights were still not terminated, and Mrs. Ruiz unexpectedly died. This was another difficult loss for Hector, who was devastated by the death of his "second Mom." Mrs. Ruiz's adult children lived in another state and did not feel that they could provide a home for Hector, now aged 11, and so the city child welfare agency began to consider other placement options for Hector. After many attempts at finding Hector the best, most nurturing family, Hector was placed in a foster home with Mr. Peterson and three other teenaged foster children. Hector's bereavement issues were never fully pro-

cessed by his social worker, but his law guardian and social worker worked together to try to assist him in obtaining counseling outside of the agency. Hector went for only one session and then refused to attend subsequently scheduled counseling sessions, saying "I'm not crazy, just sad."

After 1 year, the situation in the Peterson home deteriorated. Hector, now 12, had great difficulty getting along with two of the other young men placed in the home. After multiple attempts at trying to preserve this foster home placement, Hector, his social worker, and his law guardian made a plan for him to be placed temporarily in a community-based group home. At age 13, Hector was informed that his mother's parental rights had been terminated and he was free for adoption. But his social worker made it clear that finding an adoptive home for him would be very difficult, given his age. Hector gave up all hope of ever being adopted and no one ever asked him about whether he wanted to be adopted.

In the meantime, Hector's "temporary" group home placement now extended to more than 4 years. Hector's social worker and law guardian tried diligently to connect him to permanent resources in the community. One day, Hector's social worker found him a mentor, and this connection changed the course of Hector's life. In Hector's words:

I lived in a group home for 4 years, no family to speak of, no visits . . . nothing. . . . I was pretty much on my own. One day, my social worker got me this guy who they said was gonna be my mentor. I thought "Oh, yeah, same crap as always, some volunteer to work with the troubled teen for a couple of weeks and then I'll never see him again." But, I was wrong. Mike, my mentor, was a great guy, he became like family to me. In fact, after I left care, he was my biggest support. He is the person I could call at 2 A.M. or whenever I needed to talk with someone. He always remembers my birthday . . . I am at his house on Christmas . . . at Thanksgiving . . . he is my family. This past year, he and I decided that we should make our relationship permanent and legal. I was already free for adoption, so we decided to petition the court so that Mike could adopt me.

Facilitating permanency for youth in foster care can be very challenging work. As evidenced by the case example above, many teens who have been in the child welfare system have experienced multiple placements, multiple losses in their young lives, and are at a challenging crossroad between childhood and adulthood. Adults who work with such youth must help them identify caring, committed adults with whom the youth might be able to establish a life-long connection.

The policies and practices of the child welfare system maintain a very clear focus for younger children in need of permanency. However, its efforts toward facilitating permanency for adolescents have been less explicit. The practice and professional literature speaks to the importance of permanence for adolescents and how continued instability increases the long-term risks for teens, which may continue well into adulthood.

In this chapter, we explore the prominent issues regarding permanency for adolescents, but focus on why the permanency goal of long-term foster care (LTFC)—which was in fact deleted from the Adoption and Safe Families Act (ASFA)—or another planned permanent living arrangement (APPLA)—which is a permanency goal identified in ASFA legislation, but often misunderstood by child welfare professionals—are utilized as the default permanency plans for adolescents. Using the case

example at the start of the chapter, several questions about permanency for adolescents are explored and used to frame this discussion.

Questions

There are three questions that frame our discussion about the overutilization of LTFC or independent living and the inappropriate use of the designation "APPLA" as a permanency goal for adolescents. The first of the most critical questions that child welfare practitioners should consider is:

1. How can child welfare and legal professionals best achieve permanence for teens?

As if the main question itself were not complicated enough, two additional conundrums exist:

2. How has independent living, also known as LTFC, become the default plan for adolescents?
3. How have child welfare professionals come to view APPLA as the default permanency option for adolescents?

Overutilization of LTFC as a permanency goal for adolescents has emerged for several reasons. Contemporary child welfare, despite systemic reform efforts, has held firmly to a crisis orientation that tends to focus on younger children, whom the system views as a more vulnerable population in need of protection. In addition, the development of Title IV-E independent living as a separate program with a separate funding stream, combined with questions regarding adolescent adoptability and/or willingness to be adopted, have contributed to the system's further estrangement from its adolescent population, who often experience long lengths of stay in care. As such, although independent living is not, in fact, a permanency goal, but an array of services for older adolescents, independent living as shrouded in the mantle of LTFC has become for many workers the convenient default plan for adolescents in foster care.

All adolescents, even those who live with their birth families, require independent living skills—a set of self-sufficiency and transitional skills to assist them in transitioning toward independence. But all youth need stability and permanence in their lives as well. Even with solid life-skills training and practice, youth in foster care need a familial support system when they exit care that allows for life-long connections (see Muskie School of Public Service 2003). In addition to the challenge of defining what permanency means for adolescents, state agencies have struggled with how achieving permanency affects the independent living program.

In 1980 and 1997, the United States implemented large-scale child welfare improvement efforts; however, neither the Adoption Assistance and Child Welfare Act nor ASFA fully addressed the needs of older youth in care. Although the government created separate legislation to address the needs of this group, it did not chart a clear youth permanency pathway. (The John H. Chafee Foster Care Independence program was created with the passage of the Foster Care Independence Act in 1999. The Chafee Foster Care Independence program replaced the Title IV-E Independent Living initiative of 1986.)

The permanency needs of adolescents in foster care do not rest solely on a false dichotomy of independent living vs. adoption. Such "either/or" arguments suggest that much more work needs to be done with respect to defining youth permanency, examining the various pathways to permanency for adolescents, and moving toward integration of youth development strategies to assist young people in their transition from adolescence to young adulthood (for further discussion, see Framework and Measures for Youth Permanency 2004).

APPLA

ASFA (Adoption and Safe Families Act: 475(5)(C)) defines the term "APPLA" as "any permanent living arrangement not enumerated in the statute." As stated in the ASFA legislation, APPLA is a permanency goal for youth that may be used if compelling reasons are documented in the case record and in court. How-

ever, it is a goal that has become increasingly overused and inappropriately used as a default plan for many older adolescents in foster care.

There are several grounds, as outlined by Fiermonte and Renne (2002), for establishing compelling reasons to set a legitimate goal of APPLA: (1) an older teen who specifically requests that emancipation be established as his or her permanency plan; (2) the case of a parent and youth who have a significant bond, but the parent is unable to care for the youth because of an emotional or physical disability and the youth's foster parents have committed to raising him or her to the age of majority and to facilitate visits with the disabled parent; or (3) the tribe has identified another planned permanent living arrangement for the youth.

In many cases, the misuse of APPLA as a permanency goal has replaced what was formerly known as LTFC, which was clearly deleted from the statute. The preamble to the regulations further explains: "Far too many children and youth are given the permanency goal of long-term foster care, which is not a permanent living situation for a child" (ASFA).

Using APPLA, without providing supports to establishing permanency, as a replacement for LTFC is an unsuitable permanency goal because LTFC has seldom been stable, may disrupt often, and may lead to frequent moves for the youth. This is the antithesis of permanency. As such, APPLA, like independent living, has conveniently become for many, the "default" permanency goal for many adolescents in foster care.

The child welfare system must develop integrated strategies, approaches, and policies that assist agencies as they prepare to focus additional attention and provide leadership for the complex issues of facilitating permanency for older adolescents. The National Resource Center for Foster Care and Permanency Planning, the National Resource Center for Legal and Judicial Issues, the National Resource Center for Youth Development, the Child Welfare League of America, the National Resource Center for Special Needs Adoption, and other organizations have increasingly focused attention on the promotion of positive permanency outcomes for older adolescents in foster care (see Charles & Nelson 2000).

Meeting the Needs of Youth in Foster Care
ASFA requires child welfare agencies to focus more intently on an adolescent's need for safety, permanency, and well-being. An emphasis on effective casework and permanency planning that begins the moment a young person enters care is essential to meeting the accelerated time frames for achieving permanency as mandated by ASFA.

A concrete demographic portrait of adolescents in out-of-home care is needed to establish a clear picture of what this ASFA mandate means for child welfare agencies. Estimates from the Federal Adoption and Foster Care Analysis and Reporting System (2004) Interim Estimates for FY2001 as of March 2003 from all 50 states indicate, that on September 30, 2001, there were 542,000 children and youths in foster care aged 11 years and older. Youths account for 49% (260,475) of this total number. Gender is almost equally split, with males representing 52% of the population. Sixty percent of the children and youth in care are children and youth of color, with African Americans and Latinos representing the largest proportion at 38% and 17%, respectively.

Placement settings for all children and youth in care were: nonrelative foster family home (48%), relative foster family home (24%), institution (10%), group home (8%), pre-adoptive home (4%), and supervised independent living program (1%), with 3% on trial discharge to their families and 2% listed as runaways. Sixty-four percent of these children and youth had been in care more than 12 months, with 32% in care more than 3 years. Despite their reported length of time in care, the largest majority of these children and youth had a case goal of reunification, accounting for 44% of the total. Adoption was the second most frequent goal, at 22%. Even though it was stricken from ASFA,

long-term care was the goal for 8% (45,792) of these children and youth. Six percent (33,309) of the youth had a goal of emancipation.

In FY2001, 290,001 children and youths entered foster care. Of that number, 40% were between the ages of 11 and 18. During this same period, 263,000 children and youth exited foster care. The average length of stay of those who exited care during FY2001 was 22.1 months. The majority (57%; 148,606) of these children and youth were reunified with parents or caretakers. Eighteen percent (46,668) achieved a goal of adoption, and 7% were slated for emancipation (U.S. Department of Health and Human Services 2004).

These statistics provide some indication of the number and the demographic and case characteristics of the thousands of older foster youth in the child welfare system. It is generally agreed that between 20,000 and 25,000 youths age out of the system each year, many of whom are unprepared or marginally prepared to transition to adulthood. With these numbers as background, we now turn to an examination of the outcomes for older youth exiting the foster care system.

In recent years, a number of studies has examined outcomes for older youth as a result of the Title IV-E independent living program. This research has evaluated the impact of services for youth both before and after exiting care. There is a growing body of knowledge indicating that life-skills instruction has a positive impact on outcomes for older foster youth (Cook 1991, 1994); however, studies have also demonstrated these youth are still inadequately prepared to make the transition to adulthood (Courtney, Piliavin, & Grogan-Taylor 1995; Courtney, Piliavin, Grogan-Taylor, & Nesmith 1998, 2001).

Although much of this literature has been reviewed elsewhere, one point bears repeating here: Several studies (Barth 1986, 1990; Iglehart 1994) found that foster youth who have contact with their birth parents while in care have better outcomes than do youth who do not maintain these contacts. The importance of these relationships holds true even after youth leave the foster care system. These young people, many of whom have spent years in foster care, return to the very homes from which they were removed years before (Cook 1991; Courtney, Piliavin, Grogan-Taylor, & Nesmith 1998; Mallon 1998, 2004; Mech 1988a,b, 1994; McMillen & Tucker 1999). Youth also seek out relatives and remain connected to foster parents or others they met while in the foster care system. It is these relationships—these emotional connections—that will have the greatest impact on the young person's ability to navigate the difficult transitions into adulthood.

Although older foster youth benefit from the services they receive through the federal Independent Living program, these services are not in themselves adequate to prepare adolescents for the transition to adulthood. The potential benefit of families (or other permanent, lifelong connections, not just a "childhood family") to the development and emancipation of adolescents has been frequently overlooked or dismissed. Some service providers make the mistaken assumption that adolescents should "move on" or emotionally detach from families and other significant permanent connections. Others have promoted the concept of interdependence as opposed to independence, making the case that no one ever truly lives as independent. However, foster care youth need the same permanent family connections as youth in the general population. The system must do better in fostering and supporting these connections.

Array of Permanency Options

ASFA set out a hierarchical range of permanency options available to all children and youth in foster care:

- Youth are reunified safely with their parents or relatives;
- Youth are adopted by relatives or other families;
- Youth permanently reside with relatives or other families as legal guardians;
- Youth are connected to permanent resources via fictive kinship or customary adoption networks; or
- Youth are safely placed in APPLA, which is closely reviewed for appropriateness every 6 months.

Although each of these permanency options may be valid and appropriate for youth, in this chapter, we examine the final permanency goal of APPLA and discuss its appropriate application.

Planned Permanent Living Arrangements

The assignment of the permanency goal APPLA assumes that reunification, adoption, legal guardianship, and relative placement have been ruled out. ASFA revised the list of permanency goals for children and youth originally provided in the Adoption Assistance and Child Welfare Act and eliminated reference to LTFC as an option. ASFA, however, did define as a successful permanency outcome planned permanent living arrangements other than reunification or adoption. As noted previously, in 2000, 8% of the children in care had LTFC as a permanency goal (U.S. Department of Health and Human Services 2004). As the mandates of ASFA are fully implemented, fewer children will likely remain in foster care for extended periods of time, and LTFC will be used less frequently as the permanency goal for children. In many states, LTFC is currently used only in certain situations and, by policy, is permitted only for young people in care who are 12 or older. ASFA created APPLA as a final permanency option for children. Although ASFA is clear that APPLA is the least preferred permanency option, the term is somewhat ambiguous and has generated many questions in the child welfare community. Because this area is so confusing at times for many professionals and because it has such relevance for older adolescents in foster care, we supply more detail in this section on

APPLA. In previous work, Fiermonte and Renne (2002) have provided an excellent review of these issues. Their original work is summarized here.

What Is APPLA?

As defined by Fiermonte and Renne (2002: 26–27):

> APPLA is not a catchall for whatever temporary plan is needed when none of the preferred permanency plans are practical. Rather, APPLA is a truly permanent arrangement that is the goal for the child. The ASFA regulations define the term as any permanent living arrangement not enumerated in the statute. APPLA is intended to be planned and permanent. "Planned" means the arrangement is intended, designed, considered, premeditated, or deliberate. "Permanent" means enduring, lasting, or stable. In other words, the agency must provide reasons why the living arrangement is expected to endure. The term "living arrangement" includes not only the physical placement of the young person, but also the quality of care, supervision, and nurture that the young person will receive. Although "living arrangement" may not necessarily be a specific residence or facility, it does imply certain stabilizing features.

The preferred permanency plan for an adolescent involves a specific adult or couple (as opposed to an organization or agency) who will care for the young person, exercise certain powers and responsibilities, and most likely live with the young person. Furthermore, the caregiver's relationship with the youth will continue beyond the life of the dependency case. Therefore it follows that APPLA will either involve a permanent adult caregiver of the youth or at least adult parent figures playing permanent and important roles in the youth's life. Permanency plans should include services that meet the youth's immediate needs but should also focus on building relationships between the youth and those adults who will be a network of support for him or her. APPLA can certainly include family foster care, but it will usually be foster care with a particular family or individual.

What Does Not Qualify as APPLA?

LTFC. The statute explicitly prohibits LTFC as a permanency option. ASFA struck the term "LTFC" and the preamble to the ASFA regulations explained that far too many children are given the permanency goal of LTFC, which is not a permanent living situation for a youth. The requirement of compelling reason is in place to encourage states to move children from foster care into the most appropriate permanent situation available. LTFC is often not stable and may disrupt, leading to frequent placement moves for the youth and thus placement instability.

Emancipation. Emancipation is unfortunately what sometimes happens when young people leave foster care without a permanent plan. Emancipation and independent living are not permanency goals, they are services. As such, they lack certain permanency features as spelled out by APPLA. Emancipation certainly has specific relevance for some older children who are close to transitioning out of the foster care system, but it is not and should not be considered a permanency pathway for youth.

Efforts to finalize a permanency plan are assessed 12 months after foster care entry. The inquiry should include whether the agency conducted early assessment and planning when the youth was placed. Often children are placed on an emergency basis with foster parents who are not willing to adopt or commit to providing long-term care. There is sometimes a lack of conscious planning as the agency leaves the teen in an arrangement originally intended as an emergency placement.

Permanency planning may become more complicated as the young person becomes attached to the foster parents. For example, at the 12-month permanency hearing, when the agency may request approval of its APPLA and a finding that reasonable efforts to finalize the APPLA have been made, it might be discovered that the agency provided few services early in the case. Thus what might have been a successful reunification case, or relative placement case, has now become APPLA because the agency was delinquent in its initial efforts.

Earlier sections of this volume discussed the other permanency options under ASFA: reunification, adoption, legal guardianship, customary adoption, and permanent placement with relatives (see the chapters by Pine, Spath, and Gosteli; Groza, Houlihan, and Wood; Cross and Fox; Testa and Miller; Hegar and Scannapieco). At every permanency hearing and each 6-month review, workers should ask whether a more preferred permanency option is possible. Because circumstances change, a youth's permanency plan must be revisited at subsequent hearings. It is important to remember that when APPLA is selected as the permanency goal, it will sometimes turn out to be temporary, in spite of some efforts to make it permanent.

The permanency plan must be revisited at least annually at the required permanency hearing and may be reviewed more frequently. Circumstances change in a young person's life, and sometimes a more preferred permanency option can be achieved later in the case. For example, at one hearing, the plan might be APPLA but by the following hearing, a relative may have come forward and expressed a willingness to care for the youth on a long-term or permanent basis. A mentor relationship between a young person and an adult may initially be a guardianship plan and later may evolve into an adoption.

What Efforts Has the Agency Made to Identify and Recruit a Permanent Placement?

The worker should determine whether the agency has thoroughly searched for relatives. Has the agency asked current and former caregivers, including former foster parents, if they are willing to commit to providing long-term care for the youth? Are there any mentors, coaches, teachers, counselors, or employers who might be appropriate and willing to provide a permanent home for the youth?

What Are the Youth's Preferences?

Often the youth can identify a possible placement that the caseworker has not thought about. The youth can provide input not only on the issue of placement, but also can suggest who might be a good mentor or respite care provider. The notion of permanency should include cultivating life-long relationships, especially for older teenagers. Sometimes the youth uncovers resources other individuals have overlooked. An example is that of a 17-year-old youth who was placed with, and ultimately adopted by, the cafeteria supervisor at his group home.

The agency's reasonable efforts to secure APPLA should include ongoing discussions with the youth about who might provide long-term care or support and guidance. The judge hearing the case should consider hearing from the child on these issues as well.

What Are the Compelling Reasons Why a More Preferred Permanency Plan Is Not Being Selected?

If the agency concludes, after considering reunification, adoption, legal guardianship, or relative placement, that the most appropriate permanency plan is APPLA, the agency must document for the court the compelling reason for the alternate plan. The judge presiding over the case must evaluate the compelling reasons why a more preferred option is not being pursued. The term "compelling" means convincing and persuasive, and implies a strong burden of proof and persuasion.

The regulations give three examples of a compelling reason for establishing APPLA as a permanency plan: (1) an older teen who specifically requests that emancipation be established as his or her permanency plan; (2) a parent and youth who have a significant bond but the parent is unable to care for the youth because of an emotional or physical disability and the youth's foster parents have committed to raising the youth to the age of majority and to facilitate visitation with the disabled parent; or (3) an Indian tribe has identified APPLA.

The regulations clearly state that no permanency option should be ruled out for an entire group of the foster care population. Therefore these three examples are not meant to create broad categories to be generally applied. For instance, all 15-year-olds who are requesting emancipation cannot be treated the same. For one youth, APPLA might be appropriate, but for another, reunification might remain a possibility, or a relative willing to care for the youth may have recently been identified. The point is that permanency planning is based on the specific best interests, individual needs, and circumstances of each child or youth.

Is the Proposed Plan Actually a Permanent Living Arrangement?

Child welfare and legal professionals should ask how the proposed arrangement will be more stable and secure than ordinary foster care. Is this the most family-like arrangement for the youth? Which adults will maintain a continuing, close parent-child relationship with the young person? Permanent placement with foster parents who agree to care for the youth indefinitely is an acceptable APPLA, but permanent long-term placement in the foster care system without a specific family who will commit long-term to the youth is not an appropriate permanency plan for the youth and in fact may be harmful to the young person.

A family network may provide permanence and stability for a youth. For example, there might be long-distance relatives who want to share custody, or older relatives who do not want to assume custody alone because they fear they may not be alive much longer, so would prefer a shared custody arrangement.

What Support Structures Are in Place?

APPLA implies a permanency plan that is markedly more stable and family-like than a mere extension of foster care. Support structures that enhance the stability of a living arrangement are vital when a youth is not living with a specified adult. Independent living is often the permanency plan for older children. This is distinct from emancipation because independent living contemplates an arrangement that is stable and secure, with a focus on those features of the plan that enhance stability and permanency, whereas emancipation implies a discharge from foster care by virtue of the youth's age.

Often, independent living services focus on the youth's educational, vocational, or mental health needs, without identifying and working with adults with whom the young person can establish or strengthen a relationship. Consequently, many individuals 18 and older may leave foster care with no caregivers and no alternative homes or families. Moreover, in many instances, teens exit foster care with no ongoing relationships with adults who care about them and their futures. By considering alternative placements and services that allow them to maintain close ties with biological parents, relatives, foster parents, and perhaps even formal mentors, the agency locates potential supporters who can provide further assistance while the youth is in foster care and beyond.

The reasonable efforts by the agency that are described here could contribute to finalizing APPLA for older children. These elements do not necessarily make the placement APPLA, but they contribute to the stability and permanency of the living arrangement.

Mentoring. This arrangement provides adult supervision and guidance for the youth, and may include a formal, structured, subsidized arrangement. It allows shared parenting responsibilities when no single person can provide for them and is appropriate for some older children. The teenaged youth may even live independently. Formal mentoring from a network of adults gives the youth the support system needed to function during the transition to adulthood. Another strength of this arrangement is that it builds ties and relationships between the youth and mentors that last well beyond the dependency case. Mentors can provide educational or employment advice and assistance, and help prevent juvenile crime, unemployment, school dropout, and teen pregnancy. The child welfare system has not traditionally taken advantage of these programs, and resources for formal mentor programs are often lacking. In existence since 1902, the Big Brother/Big Sister program is an example of an effective mentoring program. Less formal arrangements can be achieved by looking to the adults already involved in the youth's life. These adults may include a foster parent of the youth's siblings, for example.

Community-Based programs. In some cultures, the community in which children are raised offers various services and plays a prominent role in children's upbringing. For example, much attention focuses on the disproportionate representation of African American children in foster care (see the chapter by McRoy). In crafting alternative permanency plans for African American children, the child welfare system could better use the informal, communal nature of extended families within the African American community. Some advocates, particularly in Indian communities, argue for a broader concept of parental rights that includes many community members beyond biological and foster parents (see the chapter by Cross and Fox). A network of supportive adults may be more valuable than a single supportive caregiver, especially as children age out of the system. Therefore it is sometimes necessary for the agency to explore and develop a network of community members to respond to the youth's needs.

One example of a community support network is a New York City independent living partnership in which young people and their adult mentors meet for weekend retreats and monthly support group sessions. The PRIDE (Personal and Racial/Ethnic Identity Development and Enhancement) program uses the time and talents of former foster children from the foster child's cultural background who act as mentors and positive role models.

Does the Youth Have Any Special Needs, and What Services Is the Agency Providing?

The agency must continue to provide for the youth's needs. Sometimes as the young person deals with mental health issues and makes behavioral and educational progress, prospective caregivers are more willing to commit to providing a permanent home for the youth. Such changing circumstances make it important to revisit the issue of compelling reasons at every permanency hearing for the youth.

For example, at the first permanency hearing, APPLA might be accepted as the permanency plan, based on the compelling reasons that there are no identifiable caregivers and that the youth needs residential treatment to address severe emotional problems associated with a history of sexual abuse. As the youth's special needs are met and treatment succeeds, the case might be up for review 12 months later, and the youth might have been discharged from residential treatment, living with a supportive aunt. APPLA would no longer be the appropriate permanency plan, as the agency could explore relative placement, legal guardianship, or even adoption with the aunt. To satisfy any permanency plan, including APPLA, workers must make sure the youth's special needs are being met.

What Efforts Has the Agency Made to Assess the Safety, Quality, and Stability of APPLA?

Once APPLA has been identified, the agency must ensure the youth will be safe and well cared for. This may involve a formal home study. Sometimes a provider is delivering independent living services, and the agency should verify that the living arrangements are safe and appropriate. Teenagers in foster care can be a challenging population to work with. Too often they are not provided proper care and supervision. Crafting a stable, planned, permanent arrangement can have a major impact on their future success. The agency should therefore regularly assess the degree to which the placement is safe and appropriate.

Can Group Care Be Considered APPLA?

Rarely is group care a living arrangement that is planned and permanent. Consider the following factors to determine if group care placement is a suitable APPLA.

Temporary vs. permanent. It is helpful to distinguish between a temporary group care arrangement and an APPLA. A youth can be placed in a group home temporarily without the placement constituting a permanency plan. For example, a youth temporarily placed in a group home may have a permanency plan of returning home.

Group care should not be considered APPLA if the youth's release from group care is reasonably likely during the youth's minority. Instead, group care is a step toward achieving the youth's permanency plan—be it adoption, reunification, or some other action. Group care as APPLA requires clear evidence that the young person will not be able to function in a family setting before reaching adulthood.

Stability, predictability, and continuity. The assumption that group care must last through a youth's minority is not sufficient to make group care APPLA. For reasons stated above, a plan for a single placement should not be considered necessary or sufficient to make group care a plan for permanence. After all, if a single group placement was enough, an orphanage would be considered APPLA. A plan to keep a youth in a specific facility or program might, however, be a factor—if it helps demonstrate the stability, predictability, and continuity of the arrangement.

Advocate or guardian. An individual designated as the youth's permanent advocate or guardian can help qualify a group care facility or program as APPLA. To make an advocate or guardian a factor, there should be reason to believe that such a person will play a major and enduring role in the youth's life. There must be (1) strong assurances that the advocate will continue indefinitely and (2) reasons to believe a close relationship exists between the advocate and youth. The adult should be committed to helping the youth through adulthood and, ultimately, until the youth leaves group care.

Designated contacts. What if there is a long-term plan, for "transfers up" within a facility, when the youth demonstrates progress in functioning in a family or in society? This condition alone should not qualify the group care as APPLA because it provides the youth with no stable and enduring relationship with an adult or couple. The analysis might depend on whether there is some assurance that the young person will have a continuing and specific set of persons to relate to and work with. Group care might, however, qualify as APPLA if there are designated contacts with specific individuals, such as relatives.

Seven Key Foundational Principles

A youth permanency framework is built on seven key foundational principles. These principles express the overarching values that must guide all policies, programs, practices, services, and supports for young people. They are interrelated and work together in a dynamic, synergistic way. Although these principles are numbered here, the sequence does not reflect a preferential order or each principle's respective worth or relevance. Each principle is critical and should be reflected in all policies, programs, practices, and supports of the agency, which should be developed and implemented in ways that:

1. Recognize that every young person is entitled to a permanent family relationship, demonstrate that the agency is committed to achieving that goal, and include multiple systems and the community at large in the effort to identify and support such relationships.

2. Are driven by the young people themselves, in full partnership with their families and the agency in all decisionmaking and planning for their futures, recognizing that young people are the best source of information about their own strengths and needs.

3. Acknowledge that permanence includes a stable, healthy, and lasting living situation in the context of a family relationship with at least one committed adult; reliable, continuous, and healthy connections with siblings, birth parents, extended family, and a network of other significant adults; and education and/or employment, life skills training, supports, and services.

4. Begin at first placement. Efforts to effect reunification with the young person's birth family must be made concurrently with immediate planning for other permanency options, insuring stability when out-of-home placement is needed.

5. Honor the cultural, racial, ethnic, linguistic, and religious/spiritual backgrounds of young people and their families and respect differences in gender and sexual orientation.

6. Recognize and build on the strengths and resilience of young people, their parents, their families, and other significant adults.

7. Insure that services and supports are provided in ways that are fair, responsive, and accountable to young people and their families and do not stigmatize them, their families, or their caregivers.

Component Areas

Clearly, issues pertaining to the overuse of LTFC and inappropriate application of APPLA have serious and long-term consequences for youth in foster care. Most policymakers and practitioners have long advocated for a reframing of the issues of permanency for youth. In June 2004, the National Resource Center for Foster Care and Permanency Planning at the Hunter College School of Social Work in New York and the Casey Center for Effective Child Welfare Practice of Casey Family Services in New Haven, Connecticut, brought together an impressive group of individuals to discuss permanency for young people. Comprised of youth in foster care, foster parents, birth parents, attorneys, representatives from the National Resource Centers, and state and private child welfare professionals, this group has offered an organizing framework that can be used by child welfare agencies across the country to help young people achieve and maintain permanence. It neither prescribes nor recommends best practice models, but instead identifies six key components that should be addressed so that public child welfare agencies can best identify and support permanence for young people in out-of-home care. It may also promote a viable alternative to the overuse of LFTC or the inappropriate designation of APPLA for youth in foster care.

The belief and value that every child and young person deserves a permanent family relationship is paramount in this work. Permanence is not a philosophical process, a plan, or a foster care placement; nor is it intended to be a family relationship that lasts only until the child turns 18. Instead, permanence is about locating and supporting a life-long family. For young people in out-of-home placement, planning for permanence should begin at entry into care and be youth-driven, family-focused, continuous, and approached with the highest degree of urgency. Child welfare agencies, in partnership with the larger community, have a moral and professional responsibility to find a permanent family relationship for each child and young person in foster care.

Permanence should bring physical, legal, and emotional safety and security in the context of a family relationship and allow multiple relationships with a variety of caring adults. At the same time, young people in out-of-home care must be given opportunities within the family and community environment to learn the array of life skills necessary to become independent and interdependent adults. Insuring that children have both permanent relationships *and* life skills for independence is critical to future well-being.

Permanence is achieved with a family relationship that offers safe, stable, and committed parenting, love, unconditional life-long support, and legal family membership status. Permanence can be the result of reunification with the birth family or legal guardianship or adoption by kin, fictive kin, or caring and committed others.

The seven key principles described above can be translated into practice through six component areas of the work of the agency. Work done in each component should reflect the core values defined by the key principles. To develop an effective and comprehensive system of permanence for young people, child welfare agencies should address all six of these components. Dramatic improvements in the overall system of identifying, supporting, and maintaining permanent family connections for young people in out-of-home placement will only occur when improvements in each of the six individual components are achieved.

1. Empower young people through information, support, and skills (including independent living skills) to be fully involved partners in directing their own permanency planning and decisionmaking.
   A. Staff value, support, and provide opportunities for young people to advocate for themselves; young people receive preparation that enables them to acquire the skills necessary to do so; and communication with them is honest, direct, and respects them as true partners.
   B. Agencies place young people in positions where they are in charge of driving discussions and options and they receive training, preparation, services, and support from child welfare agencies, multiple systems, and the community at large to enable them to do so.
   C. Staff are trained and supported in using specialized permanency planning skills that assist young people in addressing

their fears, feelings, family issues, hopes, dreams, and aspirations.

2. Empower a wide range of individuals to participate in permanency planning, beginning with birth family and including extended family; tribal members; past, present, and future caregivers; other adults who are significant to the young person; other systems with whom young people are involved; and other community members.
   A. Young people and individuals identified by them, including birth parents, extended family, caregivers, tribal members, and others who care about them are meaningfully included and supported in participating in all meetings, case planning, and decisionmaking as true partners.
   B. Agencies respect and accommodate the needs of young people and individuals identified by them, including birth parents, extended family, caregivers, tribal members, and others who care about them, to enable and support their participation as true partners.
   C. Young people are supported in maintaining, identifying, seeking out, and developing relationships with significant connections, including birth parents, siblings, both paternal and maternal kin, and other significant caring adults, including those that may have occurred earlier in life.
   D. Multiple systems within the community, including health, mental health, education, recreation, job training, juvenile justice, family court, faith-based organizations, and the business community are engaged in the permanency planning process, where appropriate, for individual young people.

3. Consider, explore and implement a full range of permanency options in a timely and continuous way.
   A. Agencies, young people, and their families together identify the range of actual

and available permanency options, beginning with an extensive identification of the family of origin.

B. Agencies articulate to young people, their families, and their caregivers the full range of actual and available permanency options and the implications of each.

C. All team members (including young people, family members, child welfare staff, staff of other systems with whom young people are involved, and other community stakeholders) receive training and support on the complete spectrum of options and are provided opportunities to express and work through their values related to permanency.

D. Concurrent planning for multiple options and relationships is employed early, regularly, and on an ongoing basis for all young people, integrating a plan for family permanency together with a plan for the development of life skills and the provision of supports and services.

E. The permanency option decided on together with each team (including young person, family members, and other significant adults) is based on the young person's individual situation, needs, and preferences; represents his or her best interest; and is reassessed regularly until a plan is achieved that includes a permanent family relationship as well as life skills, supports, and services.

F. Agency staff values and supports the consideration of all potential family permanency outcomes as they relate to meeting the best interests of the young person.

4. From the outset, continuously and concurrently employ a comprehensive range of recruitment options.

A. Recruitment can occur within existing connections and relationships.

1. Young people are asked regularly and systematically about people in their lives who could assist in helping them

plan for their future and/or serve as permanent resources.

2. Young people are provided with the skills and opportunities to interact with multiple systems and community members in ways that help build permanent relationships.

3. Multiple strategies are employed to identify potential permanent family resources and significant adult connections, including a review of the entire case file, as well as conversations with multiple sources, such as the young person, birth parents, siblings, extended family members, tribal members, former and current caregivers, teachers, and other individuals in the community who care about the young person.

4. Youth-specific recruitment strategies specific to each young person's network of relationships are used to simultaneously engage individuals identified by young people in a joint planning process and in a process of mutual exploration of the extent and level of permanent family commitment they could provide.

B. Recruitment can involve "new" resource families.

1. Youth-designed, self-promoting recruitment strategies and processes are employed, depending on the youth's preferences and level of comfort.

2. All recruitment messages are shaped by the voices of young people and families who have experienced the continuum of permanency relationships.

3. An array of methods and media are used to raise awareness about the needs of young people, as well as to communicate recruitment messages to the community.

4. A pool of potential permanency resource families who reflect the cul-

tural, racial, ethnic, linguistic, and religious/spiritual backgrounds of the young people needing placement exists and is continually replenished through targeted recruitment efforts.

5. A pool of potential permanency resource families who have a demonstrated knowledge of, commitment to, and concern for young people and can parent young people with the unique needs, characteristics, and issues represented in the population exists and is continually replenished through targeted recruitment efforts.

5. From the beginning of placement, provide services and supports to continuously insure that young people and their families have every opportunity to achieve and maintain physical, emotional, and legal permanence.

A. Young people and agencies, in partnership, make decisions about obtaining services and supports, which are made available through clearly established, consistent processes.

B. Birth family and tribal members, caregivers, and other significant adults in a young person's life are involved in decisions about obtaining services and supports, which are made available through clearly established, consistent processes.

C. Services and supports are provided to young people and their parents or their permanent families in ways that have the following characteristics.

1. Urgent: recognize the essential priority of assuring love and commitment to young people while meeting their well-being needs, including their educational needs.

2. Comprehensive: address all aspects of a young person's well-being, including life skills.

3. Continuous: are available from the day of entry into care to beyond the achievement of permanency goal, without age limitations.

4. Universally available: are available regardless of permanency goal, educational or employment choice, living arrangement, or permanency outcome.

5. Customized: meet the unique needs of young people, birth families, and permanent families and assessed and adjusted regularly to reflect progress and changes.

6. Culturally appropriate: value and honor the culture of the young person and his or her birth family and permanent family.

7. Accessible: provide access to the full range of services and supports in a timely and convenient manner.

D. The financial needs of young people and their families are recognized, sources of funding to meet their needs are identified, and assistance in accessing such funding is provided, regardless of legal status.

E. Community members and community agencies are involved in providing and advocating for supports and services to young people and their families.

6. Collaborate with other systems that serve young people and families to engage young people and families as true partners and to provide services, support, and opportunities during and after placement.

A. Agency staff and partners in other systems receive training, education, and support to address their fears, feelings, assumptions, and beliefs about permanency and positive youth development to support a culture of youth and family partnership.

B. Young people, their families, and others who care about young people are directly involved in the development and delivery of all agency and cross-system training and education about permanency and positive youth development to support a culture of youth and family partnership.

C. Young people, their families, and the systems that serve them (including courts and attorneys) have a common understanding, language, and set of beliefs about permanency definitions and work to expand permanency options with a focus on youth-defined options.

D. Agency staff, together with young people and families, engage both traditional and nontraditional partners in the community to broaden awareness and advocate for the need for life skills and permanence for young people in out-of-home care.

E. Young people and families are continuously involved in designing, implementing, and evaluating the systems that serve them.

F. Agency staff, together with young people and families, continuously identify and address critical system, cross-system, and policy changes needed to develop an effective and comprehensive system of permanence for young people.

This framework of youth permanency and the discussions that will emerge from it can assist the field of children, youth, and family services to move away from the destructive overuse of LFTC and the inappropriate use of APPLA and toward the promotion of more positive outcomes for youth in foster care.

REFERENCES

Adoption and Foster Care Analyis and Reporting System. (2004). *Administration for Children and Families, National Adoption and Foster Care Statistics.* Washington, DC: Adoption and Foster Care Analysis and Reporting System.

Adoption and Safe Families Act. (1997). P.L. 105-89.

Adoption Assistance Child Welfare Act. (1980). P.L. 96-272.

Barth, R. P. (1986). Emancipation services for adolescents in foster care. *Social Work, 67,* 165–171.

Barth, R. P. (1990). On their own. *Child and Adolescent Social Work, 7,* 419–440.

Charles, K., & Nelson, J. (2000). Permanency planning: Creating life-long connections—What does it mean for adolescents? Tulsa, OK: National Resource Center for Youth Development.

Cook, R. (1991). A national evaluation of Title IV-E foster care independent living programs for youth: Phase 2 final report. Rockville, MD: Westat.

Cook, R. (1994). Are we helping foster youth prepare for their future? *Children and Youth Services Review, 16,* 13–29.

Courtney, M. E., Piliavin, I., & A. Grogan-Taylor. (1995). *The Wisconsin study of youth aging out of out-of-home care: A portrait of children about to leave care.* Madison, WI: Institute for Research on Poverty.

Courtney, M. E., Piliavin, I., Grogan-Kaylor, A., & Nesmith, A. (1998). Foster youth transitions to adulthood: Outcomes 12 to 18 months after leaving out-of-home care. Madison: University of Wisconsin–Madison.

Courtney, M. E., Piliavin, I., Grogan-Kaylor, A., & Nesmith, A. (2001). Foster youth transitions to adulthood: A longitudinal view of youth leaving care. *Child Welfare, 80,* 685–687.

Fiermonte, C., & Renne, J. L. (2002). *Making it permanent: Reasonable efforts to finalize permanency plans for foster children.* Washington, DC: American Bar Association, Center on Children and the Law/National Resource Center on Legal and Judicial Issues.

Foster Care Independence Act. (1999). P.L. 106-169.

Iglehart, A. P. (1994). Adolescents in foster care: Predicting readiness for independent living. *Children and Youth Services Review, 16,* 159–169.

Mallon, G. P. (1998). After care, then where? Evaluating outcomes of an independent living program. *Child Welfare, 77,* 61–78.

Mallon, G. P. (2004). *Facilitating permanency for older adolescents: A toolbox for youth permanency.* Washington, DC: Child Welfare League of America.

McMillen, J. C., & Tucker, J. (1999). The status of older adolescents at exit from out-of-home care. *Child Welfare, 78,* 339–360.

Mech, E. V. (1988a). Preparing foster adolescents for self support: A new challenge for child welfare services. *Child Welfare, 67,* 487–495.

Mech, E. V. (ed.). (1988b). *Independent-living services for at-risk adolescents.* Washington, DC: Child Welfare League of America.

Mech, E. V. (1994). Preparing foster youth for adulthood: A knowledge-building perspective. *Children and Youth Services Review, 16,* 141–146.

Muskie School of Public Service. (2003). *Partnering with youth: Involving youth in child welfare training and curriculum development*. Portland: University of Southern Maine.

U.S. Department of Health and Human Services. (2004). *Adoption and Foster Care Analysis and Report*. Retrieved October 31, 2004, from www.acf.hhs.gov/programs/cb/publications/afcars/report9.htm.

KATHY BARBELL

MADELYN FREUNDLICH

Foster Care Today

Overview of Family Foster Care

Foster care is a complex service. It serves children who have experienced abuse or neglect, their biological parents and families, and their foster parents. Children in foster care may live with unrelated foster parents, relatives, or families who plan to adopt them, or in group homes or residential treatment centers. Because foster care is designed as a temporary service that responds to crises in the lives of children and their families, it is expected that children who enter care will either return to their parents as soon as possible, or be provided with safe, stable, and loving families through placement with relatives or adoption. Some children and youth, however, remain in foster care for extended periods, and many young people age out of the system and go on to live on their own. Over the past decade, the population of young people in foster care has grown dramatically, and the challenges associated with achieving permanency for them have mounted. As foster care faces new and increasing demands, policies and practice must respond in ways that insure that children, their families, and their caregivers receive the highest quality service possible. In this chapter, we examine foster care at the start of the twenty-first century: the population trends that currently shape foster care; the factors that affect the families and children served through foster care; and the key aspects of practice that shape foster care as it is currently provided. We conclude with a look at the future of foster care.

The Growing Foster Care Population

Although not the only factor affecting foster care services, the sheer volume of children in foster care has had a tremendous impact on the system's capacity. Federal data and other supplemental sources help to establish a clear picture of the increasing population of young people in foster care related to the increasing numbers of substantiated reports of child abuse and neglect; the higher rates of entry into foster care than of exit from care; the high rates of reentry into care; and the placement of children in foster care through other systems.

Child Abuse and Neglect

In 2002, the number of reports of child abuse and neglect was estimated at 1,800,000 (U.S. Department of Health and Human Services 2004). Of these reports, 896,000 were substantiated. Variations exist among states, but the overall percentage of children determined to be abused or neglected who were subsequently placed in foster care was 20% (approximately 265,000 individuals).

Entries, Exits, and Reentries

The number of children in foster care has steadily increased since the 1960s, with the exception of a few years in the early 1980s. In 1962, 272,000 children were in foster care; by 2001, the number had grown to 542,000 (U.S. Department of Health and Human Services 2003a).

Consistently more children enter foster care each year than exit. During FY2001, 290,000 individuals entered foster care and 263,000 exited care (U.S. Department of Health and Human Services 2003a). High reentry rates also contribute to the growing numbers of children in foster care. Nationally, in FY2000, approximately 10% of children entering foster care had previously been in care within the previous 12 months (U.S. Department of Health and Human Services 2003b).

Placements from Other Systems

The growing number of children in foster care is also related to placements from other systems; specifically, the mental health and juvenile justice systems. Landsverk and Garland (1999) estimate that between half and two-thirds of the children who enter foster care have behavioral or emotional problems that warrant mental health treatment. Similarly, Gilberti (1999) found that growing numbers of children and youth with serious emotional problems are being relinquished to child welfare agencies so that residential treatment can be arranged for them. Other observers point to the increasing trend of diverting youth into foster care from the juvenile and criminal justice systems (Hornby & Collins 1981; Timberlake & Verdieck 1987). Between 1984 and 1990, the number of individuals who entered foster care after committing status and delinquent offenses increased by 52% (Tatara 1993).

The 10% or higher annual growth rate of the population in foster care poses substantial practice and policy challenges related to case planning, decisionmaking, and service delivery. These challenges are likely to become even more significant in the future, should the population in foster care continue to grow at recent rates.

Factors Affecting Families and Children Served by Foster Care

Historically, broader economic and political realities have affected the welfare of families, children, and youth. These factors—poverty, homelessness, adolescent parenthood, and parental substance abuse—impact the overall functioning and well-being of families and consistently play a key role in the extent to which child abuse and neglect occur and foster care is needed.

Poverty

Poverty has always affected the well-being of children and families. Although the United States is one of the wealthiest nations in the world, it has high rates of poverty, particularly child poverty. In 1999, almost 17% of U.S. children (12.1 million) lived at or below the federally established poverty line (U.S. Census Bureau 1993, 2000b). Poverty in the United States disproportionately affects children of color and those of single parents. Fifteen percent of white children live at or below the poverty line, compared to 34% of Latino and almost 37% of African American children (U.S. Census Bureau 2000a). Poverty also disproportionately affects the growing population of children being raised by single parents. Children living with their mothers only (58%) are far more likely to live in a low-income family than are those living with their fathers only (34%) or with two parents (16%) (U.S Census Bureau 1993). In 1999, more than half (56%) of all African American children and almost one-third (32%) of their Latino peers lived in one-parent homes, compared to 23% of white children (Federal Interagency Forum on Child and Family Statistics 2000). The combination of race and single parenting place young people of color at an increased risk of poverty.

Poverty severely limits the ability of some families to provide basic necessities for their children, including food, shelter, clothing, healthcare, and transportation to school and needed services. Given the impact of poverty on the ability of many families to provide adequately for their dependents, it is not surprising that children living in poverty are far more likely to be reported to child protective services as victims of child neglect (Duncan & Brooks-

Gunn 1998). The extent to which determinations of child maltreatment lead to foster care placement also appears tied to poverty. Both Lindsey (1994) and Pelton (1989) found that the major determinant of children's removal from their parents' custody was not the severity of child maltreatment but the instability of parental income. Data from other sources confirm that a significant number of children and youth in foster care are from poor families. In 1999, more than half the children in foster care qualified for federally assisted foster care, which is tied to eligibility for welfare benefits (U.S. House of Representatives 2000).

Homelessness

Increasingly, the homeless population in the United States has come to include families with children. In 1999, such families represented more than one-third (37%) of the homeless population (U.S. Conference of Mayors 1999). In a growing number of cases, homelessness leads to involvement with the child welfare system and the subsequent entry of children into foster care. A 1994 national study found that children whose families had housing problems were almost twice as likely to be in foster care as those whose families did not (U.S. Department of Health and Human Services 1997a). Homelessness and unstable housing have continued to pose challenges to the reunification of children in foster care with their families (Child Welfare League of America 1990) and also has a significant impact on young people who leave foster care. As many as three in ten homeless adults were formerly in foster care (Roman & Wolfe 1995).

Adolescent Parenthood

Although the rate of births to adolescents has declined significantly since the early 1990s (from 62 per thousand births in 1991 to a record low of 49.6 births per thousand in 1998), close to half a million children had teenaged mothers in 1998 (Curtin & Martin 2000; U.S. Department of Health and Human Services 1993). Ado-

lescent parenting has been associated with increased rates of child maltreatment. In Illinois, researchers found that the age of the mother was associated with higher rates of abuse and neglect and foster care entry (Goerge & Lee 1996). Children born to teenaged mothers were twice as likely to be victims of abuse and neglect as those born to 20- or 21-year-old mothers (Goerge & Lee 1996). About one-fourth of the abuse and neglect reports involving adolescent mothers result in foster care placements, compared to one-fifth of those involving older mothers (Goerge & Lee 1996).

The realities that adolescent parents and their children face raise key questions about the extent to which services are available to young parents, whose ability to care for their offspring may be compromised by their own abilities. The same factors that heighten the risk of foster care entry for children of adolescent parents —factors related to maturity, sound decision-making, and ability to support a child—affect efforts to reunify children in foster care with their adolescent parents.

Parental Substance Abuse

Since the 1980s, parental substance abuse has increased markedly, with a significant growth in maternal drug use as a result of the crack cocaine epidemic (Freundlich 2000). Parental substance abuse has been associated directly with child abuse and neglect and foster care entry (North American Commission on Chemical Dependency and Child Welfare 1992; U.S. Department of Health and Human Services 1999). The U.S. Department of Health and Human Services (1999) found that parental substance abuse is a factor in between one- and two-thirds of all reports of child abuse or neglect. Children who enter foster care because of parental abuse of alcohol or other drugs tend to remain in foster care longer than those whose parents do not abuse substances. One study found that children whose parents abuse alcohol or other drugs remain in foster care an average of 11 months as opposed to 5 months for those with nonabusing parents; the former are also less likely to leave foster care within a year than the latter (55% vs. 70%) (U.S. Department of Health and Human Services 1999).

Mental health issues are also a reality for many children in foster care (see Dore's chapter in this text). The following vignette reflects some of the critical issues that families encounter when a child is psychiatrically hospitalized.

LEXIE

Lexie is 13 and had been in therapy for the past 7 years. He has a history of three suicide gestures; violent outbursts directed at his parents, siblings, and classmates; and, very recently, a suicide attempt. He has had three admissions to a private psychiatric hospital, including his current hospitalization following the suicide attempt.

The family's health insurance company has notified the hospital that the coverage has been exhausted and the costs must be assumed by Lexie's parents. The parents are both employed, have three other children, and no savings due to a high rent payment and debts incurred for Lexie's previous treatment stays and medication costs. They have applied for Medicaid and the Child Health Insurance Program in the past year, but their combined income makes them ineligible for assistance. The hospital has notified them that they must discharge Lexie immediately unless advance payments are received for his care.

The parents have safety concerns if Lexie returns home at this time. Their employers have been supportive of their need to take time off to meet Lexie's care needs, but their jobs are currently at risk if they need to take extended time off. The parents know from involvement in web chat rooms that other families have used the child welfare system as a way to continue mental health services in the hospital and community. They do what other families very reluctantly had to do to get these services; they tell the hospital that they will not take Lexie home.

The hospital files a child protective services report with the state child welfare agency alleging child neglect, which results in a court order to place Lexie in the custody of the agency while the neglect investigation is conducted. Lexie's hospital costs will now be covered by Medicaid. He remains in the hospital for another 2 weeks and is then discharged to a placement with a foster family that provides intensive treatment foster care services.

Foster Care Practice

Foster care practice at the beginning of the twenty-first century is affected by a number of factors: the diminished number of foster parents and the changes in the roles expected of them; the increased reliance on kin as caregivers; the use of concurrent planning; the use of an expanded array of permanency options; the increased use of specialized foster care placements; increased foster care accountability; and increased emphasis on the development and retention of qualified professional staff.

Availability of Foster Parents as Resources for Children

Increasingly in much of the United States, foster parents are in short supply, especially in large cities (Chamberlain, Moreland, & Reid 1992; Kahn & Kammerman 1990). In the 1970s and 1980s, unrelated foster families provided care for most of the children in foster care, but by 1999, the estimated 142,000 licensed foster families cared for less than half (48%) of those in care (Dougherty 2001; U.S. Department of Health and Human Services 2000a). Although the number of children in foster care increased by 68% between 1984 and 1995, the number of foster parents decreased by 4% (Child Welfare League of America 1997; U.S. House of Representatives 2000).

Recruitment and retention of foster parents have become critical issues. Broad social and economic changes, such as larger numbers of women working out of the home and an increase in single parent families, have made the recruitment of foster parents more challenging. Additionally, although many foster parents leave fostering because they age and retire, many others leave because they are dissatisfied with their experiences as foster parents.

Financial and systemic factors also challenge efforts to recruit and retain foster parents. Historically, foster parents have been reimbursed at low rates for the care they provide and have been expected to subsidize children's care with their own funds. In 1996, the average monthly foster care reimbursement rate was $356 for children aged 2, $373 for children aged 9, and $431 for youths aged 16 (U.S. House of Representatives 1998). These low rates often combine with the lower incomes of many foster parents who are single, older, and persons of color (Barbell, 1996; Fein, Kluger, & Maluccio 1990). Despite concerns to the contrary, few individuals choose to foster as a way to increase their incomes (only about 7%, according to James Bell Associates 1993). Instead, low-to-moderate–income families are often stressed financially by the need to continuously subsidize the care of the children whom they foster.

Looking for systemic factors affecting foster parent recruitment and retention, surveys of foster parents repeatedly find that the primary reason foster parents leave fostering is a lack of agency responsiveness, communication, and support. According to the National Commission on Family Foster Care (1991), as many as 60% of foster parents withdraw from the program within the first 12 months. As reasons, the foster parents often cited insufficient emergency, weekend, or vacation respite; inadequate consultation and support from social workers; poor agency response to crisis situations; disrespect for foster parents as partners and team members; difficulty obtaining liability insurance to protect them in the event that the children in their care cause harm to their or others' property; inadequate training; and few opportunities to provide input into training or services for foster parents.

These issues, which obviously affect retention, also impact recruitment. Consistently, those currently serving as foster parents have proven to be the most effective recruiters of new foster parents (Barbell & Sheikh 2000). Foster parents' attitudes about the agency with which they are affiliated—perspectives shaped to a great extent by agency responsiveness, communication, and support—affect not only their own participation but their willingness to assist agencies in bringing new foster parents into the program.

Changing Role of Foster Parents

Historically, foster parents have been viewed as temporary caregivers—"babysitters"—for children in foster care. Children have generally been placed and removed from foster parents' care with little regard to the latter's rights or feelings about their charges (Dougherty 2001). Traditionally, foster parents were not considered as potential adoptive parents for the children for whom they were caring, even when the latter had bonded deeply with them. In the 1980s, however, foster parents began to be viewed as more integral to the planning for their foster children. With the emphasis on permanency, agencies began to ask foster parents to become more involved with the birth parents and more frequently sought them out as adoptive parents (Dougherty 2001). Nonetheless, agencies typically have not clearly defined the roles that foster parents were expected to play and, to the extent that foster parents have been asked to take on new responsibilities, often have offered little training or support.

Currently, foster parents take on a number of roles. They nurture the children they foster; support their healthy development; provide guidance and discipline; advocate on behalf of the children with schools; mentor birth parents; support the relationship between offspring and birth parents; and recruit, train, and mentor new foster parents (Child Welfare League of America 1995; Dougherty 2001).

The roles of nurturing, promoting child development, and providing guidance and discipline are traditional foster parent responsibilities. As agencies move toward new models of permanency and recognize the strengths that foster parents bring beyond these traditional roles, many foster parents are assuming roles of advocacy, mentoring, facilitation, and re-cruitment and training of new foster parents (Doughtery 2001; Wasson & Hess 1989). In addition to serving in these new roles, a growing number of foster parents are adopting the children they have fostered. For example, in 2001, 59% of the children adopted from foster care were adopted by their former foster parents (U.S. Department of Health and Human Services 2003), a trend that is likely to continue as the use of concurrent planning (discussed later) increases.

Agencies today are also placing increased emphasis on foster parents as members of the permanency planning team. Under Adoption and Safe Families Act of 1997 (ASFA), foster parents must be given notice of and an opportunity to be heard in any court review or court hearing regarding a child in their care. This federally recognized legal right makes clear that foster parents should be valued as partners in assessing the needs of children, planning for permanency, and providing courts with key information (Center for Families, Children and the Courts 2000). Although at the practice level not all agencies have involved foster parents as partners and team members, many have worked to change agency culture to make it possible for foster parents to play a viable role—as full team members—in assessment, service planning, and decisionmaking. Training and support are essential to insure that foster parents have the tools they need to fully meet their responsibilities in this regard (Dougherty 2001).

In response to both the dwindling supply of foster parents and the increased expectations of foster parents, a trend to professionalize foster care has emerged (Miedema & Nason-Clark 1997). Professional foster parents are hired as members of the agency's professional staff to care for children with specialized behavioral, emotional, physical health, and developmental needs (Testa & Rolock 1999). As trained professional foster parents, these staff members are paid an annual salary at a rate that exceeds the monthly room-and-board payments that typi-cally are paid to other types of foster parents. Although professional foster care programs are associated with positive outcomes regarding stability, sibling placement, and community-based placements for children, the practice also raises questions in an era of welfare reform: are birth parents being penalized for remaining at home to care for their children while professional foster parents receive salaries to provide "stay-at-home" foster care? (Testa & Rolock 1999:123).

Increasing Reliance on Kin

Recent years have seen dramatic growth in the use of kinship care (sometimes referred to as "formal kinship care" or "relative foster care") as a resource for children served through the foster care system (U.S. House of Representatives 2000). In 1986, 18% of the children in foster care lived with relatives who were not their parents; by 2001, 24% of those in care lived with kin (Office of the Inspector General 1992; U.S. Department of Health and Human Services 2003). As a resource for children, kinship care occurs more often in urban settings; typically involves the care of young children; and is much more likely to be the caregiving arrangement for African American children. The latter, in one study, were found to be eight times as likely as other children to be in formal kinship care (U.S. Department of Health and Human Services 1997b).

Outside the formal child welfare system, in 1994 more than two million children lived with relatives without a parent being present (U.S. Department of Health and Human Services 1997b). By providing care for their relatives, these informal kin caregivers often make it possible to avoid placing the children in formal foster care. These caregivers, however, may face a range of stresses. Most informal kin caregivers are grandmothers; are more likely to be unmarried, poor, and unemployed; and tend to be less educated than those parents who care for their own offspring (U.S. Department of Health and Human Services 1997b).

Kinship care has come to be viewed as an essential option in the array of child welfare services, and in many states, it is expressly favored over care by nonrelatives (Child Welfare League of America 1999; U.S. Department of Health and Human Services 1998). States have had different policies regarding kinship caregivers, however, including how they define an eligible relative (Geen 2003; Malm & Geen 2003). Some states limit kinship care to biological relatives; others extend the definition of kin to neighbors, godparents, and other adults with a close but no biological relationship to the child (Boots & Geen 1999; Geen 2003). Licensing (and corresponding payment) policies also have varied. In January 2000, however, federal regulations were issued that now require states to use the same licensing or approval requirements for relative foster homes as they do for nonrelative homes (some exceptions are permitted for requirements not related to safety) to obtain Title IV-E reimbursement for the care of children formally placed with kin (U.S. House of Representatives 2000).

As kinship care has come to play an increasingly important role in foster care, attention has been directed to the principles that underlie this aspect of care. In 2000, the U.S. Department of Health and Human Services (2000b) provided Congress with a report on kinship care (as required by the ASFA). The report listed a number of principles as guidelines for ongoing discussions about the use of kinship care, including:

- Safety, permanency, and the well-being of children should continue to be the focus of the child welfare system;
- Best interest of the child should guide kinship placements;
- The child welfare system should not supplant families' own efforts or income assistance programs through foster care funding; and
- Although relatives should be viewed as resources, each situation should be individually assessed.

As these principles suggest, kinship care is a vital component of foster care today, but there is a need to continue to assess the decision-making processes involved in using kinship care and the supports and services that should be mobilized for kin (including financial resources).

Use of Concurrent Planning for Children and Youth in Foster Care

Since 1980, the primary focus in the provision of foster care services has been permanency planning; that is, providing services that will lead to children and youth's exit from foster care to safe and stable families as soon as possible. In relation to permanency planning, the foster care population can be conceptualized as two or more distinct populations. One subgroup fits the permanency model and moves through the system fairly rapidly, with most exits resulting in reunifications. However, other subgroups do not fit that model, and often stay in the system for a long time (Wulczyn, Harden, & Goerge 1997:64).

The children in this second group are principally those who entered foster care under the age of 1; are disproportionately African American, Native American, or Latino; and most often come from families who are dealing with chronic poverty, domestic violence, and substance abuse (Katz 1999).

For these children, concurrent planning— that is, work toward the reunification of the family while simultaneously developing an alternative plan for the child (Katz, Robinson, & Spoonemore 1994)—can be used to insure permanency. Concurrent planning incorporates a number of key components: differential diagnosis early in stays in foster care to identify families who are less likely to achieve reunification, timelines, visiting between children and parents, written agreements, and the development of a "Plan A" and a "Plan B" (Katz 1999: 80). In each case in which concurrent planning is undertaken, children are placed with a family —either foster parents or relatives—who are willing and able to work closely with the child's parents but who also are prepared to become the permanent family for the child should re-unification prove impossible. The birth parents are fully advised of both the concurrent plan-ning process and the nature of the child's place-ment (Mallon 2003).

Of critical importance in the concurrent planning process are foster parents who can in-corporate and balance the multiple roles that they are asked to play (Katz 1999). As concur-rent planning is implemented, several program-matic components must be in place to support caregivers throughout the process. Commu-nication is critical. Caregivers (whether foster parents or kin) must be given some assessment of the probabilities that the child will be re-united with his or her parents or freed for adoption (or some other alternative). At the same time, agencies must also clearly commu-nicate to caregivers that the level of "risk" is not quantifiable (Katz 1999:84). Specialized train-ing must be provided for caregivers to help them support the child's birth parents and the agency's plan to work toward reunification over a planned period of time. Finally, nonrelative caregivers must be given the opportunity to become personally acquainted with the birth parents and provided with support as they de-velop effective relationships with them (Schene & Sparks 2001).

Range of Permanency Alternatives

Reunification continues to be the principal per-manency goal for children in foster care. In 2001, 44% of children in care had a permanency goal of reunification, and 57% of those who left care in FY2001 were reunited with their birth parents (U.S. Department of Health and Human Services 2003). Adoption, however, has become the permanency goal for a growing number of children in care since the 1997 enactment of ASFA (U.S. Department of Health and Human Services 2000a, 2001). The number of children in foster care adopted each year has increased substantially (U.S. Department of Health and Human Services, 2000a, 2001c, 2003).

An emerging permanency option for children and youth in foster care is guardianship (see the chapter by Testa and Miller). For many kin, adoption is not a viable alternative because of hesitancy to change family relationships in a way that may undermine existing relationships; strong cultural resistance to the termination of parents' rights; or the desires of the child, par-ticularly adolescents, that adoption not be pursued (Cornerstone Consulting Group 2001). Guardianship is being increasingly considered as a permanency option for these kin and chil-dren. Some states have developed subsidized guardianship programs, which provide kin not only with the legal status of guardian but with financial support and access to follow-up ser-vices (Cornerstone Consulting Group 2001). Much remains to be learned about the out-comes of these relatively new programs, but early results show that for kin and children in guardianship arrangements, relationships are as stable and as permanent as those established through adoption (Westat 1999).

ASFA revised the list of permanency goals for children originally provided in the Adoption As-sistance and Child Welfare Act of 1980 and elim-inated reference to long-term foster care as an option. ASFA, however, did define as a successful permanency outcome permanent living arrange-ments other than reunification or adoption. In 2001, 8% of the children and in care had long-term foster care as a permanency goal (U.S. De-partment of Health and Human Services 2003). As the mandates of ASFA are fully implemented, fewer children will likely remain in foster care for extended periods of time, and long-term foster care will be used less frequently as a permanency goal. In many states, long-term foster care is cur-rently used in only certain situations and, by pol-icy, is permitted only for young people in care who are 12 or older (Children's Rights 2001).

Increased Use of Specialized Placements in Foster Care

Increasingly, the complex needs of children in foster care call for specialized placements that can provide them with the level of care and services that their needs require. Over the past decade, agencies have developed specialized foster care programs that offer a high level of care for children with significant behavioral, emotional, physical, health, and developmental needs (Barth, Courtney, Berrick, & Albert 1994). Specialized foster parents are recruited, trained, and paid higher monthly rates for the care that they provide children with special needs. Although these resources play a vital role in insuring that these needs are appropriately met (Testa & Rolock 1999), they raise questions about the use of specialized foster care. For example, foster care encompasses the concept of "step down"; that is, the placement of children at lower levels of services and at reduced reimbursement rates as their behavioral, emotional, physical, and developmental problems resolve. In some instances, children are "stepped down" through their removal from specialized foster families with whom they are doing well and progressing; in other cases, they are "stepped down" by reducing the services provided and the reimbursement rate given to their specialized foster parents. Both "step down" methods raise questions about the children's best interests and the incentives that such approaches create. Another set of questions relates to permanency planning for children in specialized foster care, and in particular, the impact of such placements on the use of adoption as the permanency plan.

The following vignette illustrates the complexity of the lives that are affected by the foster care system, including the devastating effects of multiple placements.

TAMARA

Tamara spent 8 years in foster care. She was originally placed in care at age 10 as a result of severe maltreatment by her parents, who had a history of substance abuse. While in care, she had 12 placements, including seven with foster families and five in different group homes. Tamara had to change schools many times because of these placement changes. She dropped out of school when she was 17 and in the ninth grade.

Tamara was discharged from foster care when she was 18 years old. She was living in a homeless shelter when she became pregnant. She was working at a minimum wage job and could not afford to rent an apartment on her own, so she moved in with the baby's father, who was dealing and using drugs. She too became involved with drug use. When Tamara's daughter, Saba, was 1, the child's father was arrested and sent to prison for a drug-related offense. Tamara struggled to maintain her job, pay the rent, and care for Saba. She had no support from her family, as she had lost all contact with them during her time in foster care. She was isolated and alone.

A report was made to Child Protective Services (CPS) when Tamara overdosed on drugs and was brought to the emergency room and later admitted to the hospital. The family court ordered Saba into the custody of the child welfare agency, which placed her with a foster family when no maternal or paternal kin could be located. The court also ordered services to Tamara so that she and her daughter could be reunified.

Tamara received substance abuse treatment at a community-based treatment center. She again lived in a shelter while she participated in the program. The foster family provided frequent visitation opportunities in their home between Saba and Tamara. Tamara and the foster mother developed a very supportive relationship, resulting in Tamara's enhancement of her parenting and social skills. She had been in recovery for a year, had a full-time job, and was working on her GED; housing, however, remained an issue that prevented implementation of the reunification plan.

Tamara's social worker helped Tamara get on the waiting list for the local housing authority's Family Unification Program that provided apartment rent subsidies. When Saba was 2.5 years old, Tamara received the subsidy and moved into her own apartment. The foster family's church program helped Tamara with furniture and household items and provided a scholarship for Saba's enrollment in the church-run child development center. After a series of overnight visits with Tamara, the agency recommended and the court approved the reunification plan and returned custody of Saba to Tamara. The foster family continues to be a part of their lives.

A growing number of children are also being served through group and residential care. In September 2001, more than 100,000 children in foster care lived in group homes and institutional settings (U.S. Department of Health and Human Services 2003). This figure represents a more than 50% increase since 1990 (Tatara 1993; U.S. Department of Health and Human Services 2003). Some children are placed in group or residential settings as soon as they enter foster care because of behavioral and emotional problems; others are eventually placed in group or residential care because of repeated placement failures in family settings. Of increasing concern has been the extent to which group and residential care is being or should be used for children in foster care. Among the issues that must be examined more closely are (1) the growing use of specialized foster care as a community-based alternative to institutional placements for children in foster care and (2) the earlier use of residential treatment for young people with serious behavioral and emotional problems so that they do not experience repeated placement failures before being deemed eligible for more intensive treatment services.

Increased Accountability

In 2001, the U.S. Department of Health and Human Services mandated that each state conduct periodic Child and Family Service Reviews of their federally funded child welfare services, including foster care. These reviews are designed to assess each state's performance on three key outcomes: child safety, permanence, and child and family well-being (U.S. House of Representatives 2000). Federal law and accompanying regulations identify seven criteria as indicators of state compliance with the standards set by law and regulations (see table 1). In addition, the federal government has seven specific national standards that states must meet. Of the seven standards, five relate to foster care:

1. The rate at which children re-enter foster care within 12 months of a previous stay in care;
2. The percentage of children with their parents in less than 12 months of entering foster care;
3. The percentage of children who were adopted and who left foster care within 24 months of foster care entry;
4. The percentage of children in foster care for less than 12 months who have two or fewer placements; and
5. The median length of time that children remain in care.

If a state is found to be in substantial nonconformity with the federal requirements, it must develop and implement a corrective action plan approved by the U.S. Department of Health and Human Services. Should the state fail to comply with the plan, the federal government may withhold federal funding as a penalty (U.S. House of Representatives 2000). The new

TABLE 1. *Child and Family Services Reviews: Outcomes and Indicators*

Outcome	Indicator
Child safety	Protection of children from abuse and neglect
	Safe maintenance of children in their own homes whenever possible
Permanence	Permanency and stability in children's living situations
	Preservation and continuity of family relationships and connections
Child and family well-being	Capacity of families to provide for children's needs
	Appropriate services to meet children's educational needs
	Adequate services to meet children's physical and mental health needs

federal review processes, the national outcome standards, and the penalties that may be assessed when states fail to provide child welfare services at an acceptable level signal a new level of accountability for foster care services. (An additional standard relates to the recurrence of maltreatment for children for whom there had been a substantiated or indicated report within the previous 6 months. The seventh standard, length of time in foster care, unlike the other six standards, has not as yet been assigned a performance target.)

Developing and Retaining Qualified Child Welfare Professionals

Of critical importance to quality foster care practice is an adequate number of qualified professional staff. This goal, however, has been difficult to achieve because of ever-expanding caseloads, high levels of staff turnover, and budget-driven staff reductions and decreases in such staff supports as training (Rycraft 1994). Rising demands for out-of-home care services have caused caseloads to expand, resulting in unmanageable workloads and, in many instances, low morale. One survey found that annual caseworker turnover rates ranged from 20% for public agencies to 40% for private agencies (Child Welfare League of America, American Public Human Services Association, & Alliance for Children and Families 2001). Although average caseload sizes vary, in numerous systems they far exceed those recommended by the Child Welfare League of America (Children Rights 2001). Under such conditions, social workers are unlikely to have frequent and consistent contact with birth parents, children, or foster parents, or to develop and implement effective permanency plans.

Caseworkers who provide foster care services often lack the education and experience they need to provide quality services. Only 25% to 27% of child welfare caseworkers who provide direct services have any social work training, and of these, only 9% to 10% have graduate degrees in social work (Child Welfare League of America 1996). Only 50% of caseworkers have experience in working with children and families in any human service field. Low salaries (the result of agency declassification of caseworker positions and deletion of requirements for professional social work education) contribute to the difficulties in attracting experienced and professionally trained staff (Rycraft 1994). At the same time, the deprofessionalization of child welfare has made the field less attractive to professionally trained social workers (McDonald & McCarthy 2000).

Given the educational backgrounds and experience levels of many foster care caseworkers, the need for ongoing staff training is critical. Although training programs have been developed over the past decade, programs often struggle with transmitting the requisite knowledge and skills that all levels of foster care staff must have to deliver effective foster care services. Particularly when staff turnover is high and caseloads are large, programs confront real challenges in achieving high competency levels among staff. Ongoing quality supervision becomes particularly important under such circumstances.

The Future of Foster Care

If foster care is to be most responsive to the needs of children and families, it must be shaped by five key principles (Dougherty 2001):

1. A family focus that views foster care as a service for the entire family, as opposed to a service for the child or for the parents only;
2. A child-centered orientation that places the needs of the individual child at the forefront of case planning;
3. The delivery of services from a community-based perspective so that children and youth remain in contact with the important people in their lives and live in a familiar environment;
4. Developmental appropriateness, so that the care and services that a child receives are responsive to the child's age and physical,

cognitive, behavioral, and emotional status; and

5. Cultural competence, so that the cultural strengths and values of all families are respected and accommodated.

As the practitioners of foster care look to the future, they must recognize that biological families will always play a key role in children's lives, irrespective of the permanency outcomes that are planned for them. Foster care must recognize the importance of these connections and their relationship to children's sense of self, ability to cope with and resolve loss, and ability to form new and more lasting attachments (Fahlberg 1991; Jewett 1982). Foster care also must fully implement practices that insure that children are placed with families within their own cultural groups, neighborhoods, and communities whenever possible. A community-

based approach to foster care broadens the definitions of "family" and "helping" to include a variety of individuals and organizations that can assist families and children in more inclusive and, often, less conventional ways.

Over the past decade, foster care increasingly has become the safety net for families in crisis. Foster care practice has responded in important ways—through, for example, expansions in the roles of foster parents, the greater involvement of kin, new permanency planning approaches, the development of new foster care resources, and greater foster care accountability. It, however, cannot on its own meet the full range of the complex needs of children and their families. As foster care looks to the future, community partners are critical to insuring the safety and well-being of children and youth as permanency is being planned and achieved.

REFERENCES

Adoption and Safe Families Act. (1997). P.L. 105-89.

Adoption Assistance and Child Welfare Act. (1980). P.L. 96-272.

Barbell, K. (1996). *Foster care today: National and South Carolina perspective.* Presentation at the South Carolina Council on Child Abuse and Neglect Annual Conference: Foster Parent Recruitment and Retention, Columbia, SC, June 23–26, 1996.

Barbell, K., & Sheikh, L. (2000). *A community outreach handbook for recruiting foster parents and volunteers.* Washington, DC: Child Welfare League of America.

Barth, R. P., Courtney, M. E., Berrick, J. D., & Albert, V. (1994). Specialized foster care. In R. P. Barth, M. E. Courtney, J. D. Berrick, & V. Albert (eds.), *From child abuse to permanency planning: Child welfare pathways and placements,* pp. 79–92. Hawthorne, NY: Aldine de Gruyter.

Boots, S. W., & Geen, R. (1999). *Family care or foster care: How state policies affect kinship care providers.* Series A, no. A-34. Washington, DC: Urban Institute.

Center for Families, Children and the Courts. (2000). *Caregivers and the courts: A primer on juvenile dependency proceedings for California foster parents and relative caregivers.* San Francisco: Center for Families, Children and the Courts.

Chamberlain, P., Moreland, S., & Reid, K. (1992). Enhanced services and stipends for foster parents: Effects on retention rates and outcomes for children. *Child Welfare, 71,* 387–401.

Children's Rights. (2001). *Winning for children: Using the courts to reform child welfare.* New York: Children Rights.

Child Welfare League of America. (1990). *Homelessness: The impact on child welfare in the 1990s.* Washington, DC: Child Welfare League of America.

Child Welfare League of America. (1995). *Standards of excellence for family foster care.* Washington, DC: Child Welfare League of America.

Child Welfare League of America. (1996). *1995 salary study.* Washington, DC: Child Welfare League of America.

Child Welfare League of America. (1997). *Child abuse and neglect: A look at the states.* Washington, DC: Child Welfare League of America.

Child Welfare League of America. (1999). *CWLA Standards of excellence for kinship care.* Washington, DC: Child Welfare League of America.

Child Welfare League of America, American Public Human Services Association, & Alliance for Children and Families. (2001). *The child welfare workforce challenge: Results from a preliminary study.* Boston: Walker Treischman Training Center.

Cornerstone Consulting Group. (2001). Guardianship: Another place called home. Houston: Cornerstone Consulting Group.

Curtin, S. C., & Martin, J. A. (2000). Births: Preliminary data for 1999. In *National vital statistics reports 48,* pp. 112–144. Hyattsville, MD: National Center for Health Statistics.

Dougherty, S. (2001). *Toolbox no. 2: Expanding the role of foster parents in achieving permanency*. Washington, DC: Child Welfare League of America.

Duncan, G. J., & Brooks-Gunn, J. (1998). Making welfare reform work for our youngest children. *Child Poverty News and Issues 8*(1). Retrieved May 31, 2001, from cpmcnet.columbia.edu/dept/nccp/news/spring98/3spring98.html.

Fahlberg, V. (1991). *A child's journey through placement*. Indianapolis, IN: Perspectives Press.

Federal Interagency Forum on Child and Family Statistics. (2000). *America's children: Key national indicators of well-being, 2000*. Washington, DC: U.S. Government Printing Office.

Fein, E., Kluger, M., & Maluccio, A. (1990). *No more partings: An examination of long-term foster family care*. Washington, DC: Child Welfare League of America.

Freundlich, M. (2000). The impact of prenatal substance exposure: Research findings and their implications for adoption. In R. P. Barth, M. Freundlich, & D. Brodzinsky (eds.), *Adoption and prenatal alcohol and drug exposure*, pp. 1–21. Washington, DC: CWLA Press.

Geen, R. (2003). *Finding Permanent Homes for Foster Children: Issues Raised by Kinship Care*. Washington, DC: Urban Institute.

Gilberti, M. T. (1999). *An analysis of litigation strategies to address custody relinquishment of children with serious emotional disturbance*. Washington, DC: Brazelon Center for Mental Health Law.

Goerge, R. M., & Lee, B. J. (1996). Abuse and neglect of the children. In R. A. Maynard (ed.), *Kids having kids: Economic costs and social consequences of teenage pregnancy*, pp. 205–230. Washington DC: Urban Institute Press.

Hornby, H., & Collins, M. (1981). Teenagers in foster care: The forgotten majority. *Children and Youth Services Review, 3*, 7–20.

James Bell Associates. (1993). *The national survey of current and former foster parents*. Washington, DC: U.S. Department of Health and Human Services.

Jewett, C. (1982). *Helping children cope with separation and loss*. Boston: Harvard Common Press.

Kahn, A. J., & Kammerman, S. B. (1990). Social services for children, youth, and families in the United States. *Children and Youth Services Review, 9*, 1–180.

Katz, L. (1999). Concurrent planning: Benefits and pitfalls. *Child Welfare, 78*, 71–87.

Katz, L., Robinson, C., & Spoonemore, N. (1994). *Concurrent planning: From permanency planning to permanency action*. Seattle, WA: Lutheran Social Services of Washington and Idaho.

Landsverk, J., & Garland, A. F. (1999). Foster care and pathways to mental health services. In P. A. Curtis, G. Dale, & J. C. Kendall (eds.), *The foster care crisis: Translating research into policy and practice*, pp. 193–210. Lincoln: University of Nebraska Press.

Lindsey, D. (1994). *The welfare of children*. New York: Oxford University Press.

Mallon, G. (2003). *Overcoming systemic barriers to concurrent planning*. Portland, ME: National Resource Center for Organizational Improvement.

Malm, K., & Geen, R. (2003). *When child welfare agencies rely on voluntary kinship placements*. Washington, DC: Urban Institute.

McDonald, J., & McCarthy, B. (2000). Effective partnership models between the state agencies, community, the university, and community service providers. In *Child Welfare Training Symposium: Changing paradigms of child welfare practice: Responding to opportunities and challenges, Washington, DC, June 28–29, 1999*, pp. 43–72. Washington, DC: Children's Bureau.

Miedema, B., & Nason-Clark, N. (1997). Foster care redesign: The dilemma contemporary foster families face. *Community Alternatives: International Journal of Family Care, 9*(2), 15–28.

National Commission on Family Foster Care. (1991). *A blueprint for fostering infants, children and youths in the 1990s*. Washington, DC: Child Welfare League of America.

North American Commission on Chemical Dependency and Child Welfare. (1992). *Children at the front: A different view of the war on alcohol and drugs*. Washington, DC: Child Welfare League of America.

Office of the Inspector General. (1992). *Using relatives for foster care*. OEI-06-09-02390. Washington, DC: U.S. Department of Health and Human Services.

Pelton, L. H. (1989). *For reasons of poverty*. New York: Praeger.

Roman, N. P., & Wolfe, P. (1995). *Web of failure: The relationship between foster care and homelessness*. Washington, DC: National Alliance to End Homelessness.

Rycraft, J. R. (1994). The party isn't over: The agency role in the retention of public child welfare caseworkers. *Social Work, 39*, 75–80.

Schene, P., & Sparks, B. (2001). Implementing concurrent planning: A handbook for child welfare professionals. Portland, ME: National Resource Center for Organizational Improvement.

Tatara, T. (1993). *Characteristics of children in substitute and adoptive care: A statistical summary of the VCIS National Child Welfare Data Base*. Washington, DC: American Public Welfare Association.

Testa, M. F., & Rolock, N. (1999). Professional foster care: A future worth pursuing? *Child Welfare, 78*, 108–124.

Timberlake, E., & Verdieck, M. (1987). Psychosocial functioning of adolescents in foster care. *Social Casework, 68*(4), 214–222.

U.S. Census Bureau. (1993). *We the American . . . children*. Washington, DC: U.S. Department of Commerce.

U.S. Census Bureau. (2000a). *Poverty in the United States: 1999*. Current Population Report series P60–210. Washington, DC: U.S. Government Printing Office.

U.S. Census Bureau. (2000b). *Press briefing on 1999 income and poverty estimates.* Washington, DC: U.S. Department of Commerce.

U.S. Conference of Mayors. (1999). *A status report on hunger and homelessness in America's cities: 1999.* Washington, DC: U.S. Conference of Mayors.

U.S. Department of Health and Human Services. (1993). Advance report of final natality statistics, 1991. *Monthly Vital Statistics Report, 42*(3), 1–6.

U.S. Department of Health and Human Services. (1997a). *National study of protective, preventive, and reunification services delivered to children and their families.* Washington, DC: U.S. Government Printing Office.

U.S. Department of Health and Human Services. (1997b). *Informal and formal kinship care.* Washington, DC: U.S. Department of Health and Human Services.

U.S. Department of Health and Human Services. (1998). *Children placed in foster care with relatives: A multi-state study.* Washington, DC: U.S. Department of Health and Human Services.

U.S. Department of Health and Human Services. (1999). *Blending perspectives and building common ground: A report to Congress on substance abuse and child protection.* Washington, DC: U.S. Government Printing Office.

U.S. Department of Health and Human Services. (2000a). *The AFCARS report: Interim estimates for fiscal year 1998.* Retrieved September 29, 2000, from www.acf.dhhs.gov/programs/cb/stats/tarreport/rpt04003/ar0400.htm.

U.S. Department of Health and Human Services. (2000b). *Report to the Congress on kinship foster care.* Washington, DC: U.S. Department of Health and Human Services.

U.S. Department of Health and Human Services. (2001). *AFCARS report #5.* Retrieved June 2, 2001, from www.acf.dhhs.gov/programs/cb/publications/afcars/apr2001.html.

U.S. Department of Health and Human Services. (2003a). *Child maltreatment 2002.* Washington, DC: U.S. Department of Health and Human Services.

U.S. Department of Health and Human Services. (2003b). *Child welfare outcomes 2000: Annual report.* Washington, DC: U.S. Department of Health and Human Services.

U.S. Department of Health and Human Services. (2004). *AFCARS report (preliminary estimates for FY 2001 as of March 2003).* Retrieved June 30, 2004, from www.acf.hhs.gov/programs/cb.

U.S. House Ways and Means Committee. (1998). *1998 green book: Overview of entitlement programs.* Washington, DC: U.S. Government Printing Office.

U.S. House Ways and Means Committee. (2000). *2000 green book: Overview of entitlement programs.* Washington, DC: U.S. Government Printing Office.

Wasson, D., & Hess, P. (1989). Foster parents as child welfare educators. *Public Welfare, 47,* 16–22.

Westat. (1999). *Evaluation of the Illinois subsidized guardianship waiver demonstration: Preliminary findings.* Rockville, MD: Westat.

Wulczyn, F. H., Harden, A. W., & Goerge, R. M. (1997). *An update from the multistate foster care data archive: Foster care dynamics 1983–1994.* Chicago: University of Chicago, Chapin Hall Center for Children.

REBECCA L. HEGAR
MARIA SCANNAPIECO

Kinship Care

Preservation of the Extended Family

Kinship foster care is the placement of children who are in state custody in the homes of their relatives (by birth, marriage, or adoption) or in the homes of other close family associates, such as godparents or fictive kin. Both in the United States and internationally, use of kinship foster homes for child placement has attracted considerable professional interest, particularly since about 1980 (Child Welfare League of America 2000; Greeff 1999; Hegar & Scannapieco 1999; Ryburn 1998). In the United States, the relatively high proportion of foster children who are placed with their kin by the state is part of a larger American demographic tableau: children living in the homes of relatives without state intervention. That pattern is referred to in this chapter as "kinship caregiving." We address both kinship caregiving and kinship foster care in this chapter, although the primary emphasis is on kinship foster care.

In this chapter, we first introduce the scope of kinship caregiving and kinship foster care by summarizing demographic trends and patterns. We also provide a brief historical overview and consider how governmental policy has shaped the evolution of kinship foster care. We review the research literature with regard to several topics: outcomes for children, youth, and families involved in kinship foster care; tools for those working in kinship care to provide assessment and interventions; and promising approaches and programs using kinship foster care and their evaluation. The chapter concludes with case studies, a discussion of value-based

and ethical issues, and an assessment of the role of kinship care in preserving extended families.

Demographic Patterns Involving Kinship Caregiving and Kinship Foster Care
Kinship Caregiving
The phenomenon of children living in households without either of their parents being present may have been more common earlier in our history, when premature adult death was much more frequent and successful single parenthood was less feasible because of the unavailability of day care and financial aid. However, by the middle of the twentieth century, that family pattern was very rare in the general U.S. population. Census data show that in 1960 and 1970, less than 2% of American children lived in households without either parent, and the proportion had risen only to 2.2% in the 1980s (Saluter 1989). Beginning in the later 1980s, there was a notable increase to 4.3% by 1995 (Saluter 1996). It now appears that this pattern has stabilized, and even perhaps declined slightly, to 4% of U.S. children in 2002 (Fields 2003). In perhaps the only national survey concerning kinship and non-kinship foster care, Ehrle and Geen (2002) estimate that the total number in kinship caregiving placements may approach 300,000 individuals.

Census data after 1990 make it possible to identify children in foster care and to separate them from others who do not co-reside with parents. When foster children are excluded, 3.9% of children lived in households without either parent in 1995 (Saluter 1996) and 3.7% did so in 2002 (U.S. Census Bureau 2003), although many foster children are also living with relatives, as discussed below.

The most recent U.S. Census data reveal much more than previous censuses about the children and families involved in kinship caregiving, particularly grandparent-headed families (U.S. Census Bureau 2003). For example, 44% of children who live with neither parent reside in the households of one or both sets of grandparents. Older youth are more likely to live with grandparents, and the age group least likely to do so is children under age 3. Interestingly, most children living with grandparents have brothers or sisters also living there, and the typical such sibling group has three children. As might be expected, households where both grandparents are present are substantially better off financially than those with single grandparents, particularly those headed by grandmothers. Although only 16% of caregiving two-grandparent homes and 19% of single grandfathers live below the federally defined poverty level, 46% of caregiving single grandmothers are officially poor (U.S. Census Bureau 2003). It is also noteworthy that the largest group (27%) of caregiving two-grandparent families lives outside of metropolitan areas, whereas the largest group (29%) of single-grandmother caregivers lives in the central cities of areas with at least a million inhabitants. Also, 36% of children living solely with grandparents lack health insurance (Fields 2003:8).

The picture sketched by U.S. Census data is consistent with findings from a national survey by Ehrle and Geen (2002), who report that, compared with children in non-kin foster care, those in kinship placements are more likely to be poor and to live with a single, unemployed caregiver who lacks a high school diploma and receives fewer social services. Research concerning caregiving grandmothers supports that lack of resources and health problems are related to psychological distress (Kelley, Whitley, Sipe, & Crofts Yorker 2000; Kolmer 2000; Minkler, Roe, & Price 1993).

Kinship caregiving in the United States has not been evenly distributed among racial and ethnic groups, and the most recent data confirm the continuation of this reality. For example, census data for both 1960 and 1980 reported more than 11% of African American children living in family settings without a parent (Saluter 1989). The proportion may have declined slightly during the 1990s (Saluter 1996); recent data show 8.2% of African American children living without parents (Fields 2003). This rate can be compared with 4.9% of Hispanic, 3.2% of Asian/Pacific Islander, and 3.1% of white children in family settings without a parent (Fields 2003). The most recent reports reflect increased rates for the Hispanic population, for which 4.4% of children were affected in 1995 (Saluter 1996). Reasons for the differences may be due to cultural patterns, differential rates of poverty and single parenthood, and the effects of discrimination that we and others have discussed in detail elsewhere (Barrio & Hughes 2000; Brown, Cohon, & Wheeler 2002; Burton 1992; Hegar 1999a,b; Hegar & Scannapieco 1995; Scannapieco & Jackson 1996). Black and Hispanic children living without parents in the homes of grandparents are highly likely to be poor. The percentages living in households with incomes less than the federal poverty level are 49.5% for African Americans and 51.2% for Hispanics (U.S. Census Bureau 2003).

Kinship Foster Care

The U.S. Census may well underrepresent many U.S. groups, such as homeless or undocumented children and families. It is interesting that recent data identify only 235,000 foster children (Fields 2003:2), although most other official reports are more than twice as high (Children's Bureau 2003). This finding suggests that families filling out census forms fail to identify many foster children as such, which may happen most often when a child also has another relationship with the head of the household, such as grandchild. It is therefore likely that many kinship foster children are indistinguishable in census data from the children and families discussed above under kinship caregiving. Furthermore, census data provide no specific information about those it identifies as foster children, and other national databases are also limited in detail.

What is known about the numbers and characteristics of children in kinship foster care comes primarily from limited national child welfare statistics (e.g., Children's Bureau 2000, 2003), a single national survey (Ehrle & Geen 2002), and research studies of state or local child welfare programs, which may not be representative of the country as a whole. For example, much of the available research has been done in relatively few states and urban areas, including jurisdictions in California, Illinois, and Maryland. Although the literature has been reviewed more thoroughly elsewhere (Children's Bureau 2000; Scannapieco 1999b), this section provides a brief overview and update.

Studies suggest that the children in kinship foster care are most likely to be grade school aged and that it is common for sibling groups to live together in kinship foster care (Berrick, Barth, & Needell 1994; Dubowitz, Feigelman, & Zuravin 1993; Grogan-Kaylor 2000; Scannapieco, Hegar, & McAlpine 1997; Welty, Geiger, & Magruder 1997). The most frequent reasons for placement are substance abuse (including prenatal drug exposure) and parental neglect (Beeman, Kim, & Bullerdick 2000; Berrick Barth, & Needell 1994; Dubowitz, Feigelman, & Zuravin 1993; Grogan-Kaylor 2000; Iglehart 1994; Scannapieco, Hegar, & McAlpine 1997; Thornton 1991). African American children are greatly overrepresented in the foster care population, and they are also disproportionately likely to be placed in kinship foster care rather than in traditional foster care (Beeman, Kim, & Bullerdick 2000; Berrick, Barth, & Needell 1994; Grogan-Kaylor 2000; Iglehart 1994; Scannapieco, Hegar, & McAlpine 1997).

Kinship foster care is typically provided by female relatives, most often the maternal grandmothers and aunts of the children (Dubowitz, Feigelman, & Zuravin 1993; Le Prohn & Pecora 1994; Scannapieco, Hegar, & McAlpine 1997; Thornton 1991). These relatives tend to be older than traditional foster parents; they are more likely to be single, have lower levels of education and income, and have poorer health (Berrick, Barth, & Needell 1994; Dubowitz, Feigelman, & Zuravin 1993; Gebel 1996; Le Prohn & Pecora 1994; Scannapieco, Hegar, & McAlpine 1997). It is apparent that the available research sketches a picture of kinship foster care that is similar to that suggested by the findings cited above concerning kinship caregiving.

Societal Context of Kinship Foster Care
History and the Role of Policy
Although kinship caregiving is a pattern found in virtually all of the world's cultures—with roots in biblical law, ancient literature, and medieval European courts—and in many traditional cultures—particularly those in the Pacific and African regions (Ernst 1999; Hegar 1999b)—the use of formal kinship foster care is quite a recent phenomenon. Indeed, any foster care involving payment for the child's board and lodging is only about 100 years old, having been advocated as the child welfare service of the future by Folks in 1902.

In Western society, kin have frequently had legal obligations to support one another in times of need. For example, the English Poor Law of 1601 required that grandparents and grandchildren, as well as parents and children, provide support and care for one another when necessary (Jansson 1997). In general, the cultural expectation has been that kin will provide for one another without being financially compensated. However, during the latter twentieth century, that assumption also began to change. The relative-payee Aid for Families with Dependent Children grant, which aided a family when a child came from an eligible household and was living in the home of a relative, was explicitly addressed in the Social Security amendments of 1962 (Axinn & Stern 2001). Relatives also qualified as providers of home health aid under Medicaid. Then in 1977, the Supreme Court ruled in *Miller vs. Youakim* that relatives who meet foster care licensing standards must be permitted to receive federal foster care funds. For years, many states were slow to add relatives to the foster care rolls, but additional policy on the federal level has helped create momentum for change.

The next federal impetus for kinship care came in 1978, with the Indian Child Welfare Act, which established a hierarchy of preferred placements for Native American children. Placement with extended family is the first preferred option. Then, in 1980, the Adoption Assistance and Child Welfare Act expressed a preference for the least restrictive, most family-like placement option, which may also have supported use of kinship foster care.

During the 1990s, legislation added additional impetus to the use of kinship foster care, beginning with the Social Security Act Amendments of 1994. Federal waivers were authorized for a limited number of states to use Title IV-B and IV-E monies in innovative ways, and several states designed programs to support kinship foster parents and offer some subsidized guardianships (Children's Bureau 2000). In addition, the Personal Responsibility and Work Opportunity Reconciliation Act of 1996 expressed a preference that states place children with relatives over nonrelatives, as long as the relatives meet state child protection standards. Finally, the Adoption and Safe Families Act of 1997 reiterated the preference for permanent placement with relatives and exempted kinship foster placements from a new requirement that termination of parental rights take place within a set time period. Despite the movement of federal policy to support kinship foster care, the legislation of the 1990s also gave states considerable latitude in implementation, part of the trend called the "new federalism." This devolution of authority to the states has led to extensive variation among states in funding and services for kinship foster care (Geen & Berrick 2002;

Gleeson 1996, 1999a; Gleeson & Craig 1994; Hegar & Scannapieco 2000; Leos-Urbel & Geen 2002).

Current State of Kinship Foster Care

Kinship placements are currently used in three ways that can be viewed in sequence as a child and family encounter the child welfare system (Scannapieco 1999a). First, a child or youth may be placed with relatives as a way to divert the family from the juvenile court and formal child placement. This is probably the most traditional approach, and it is used extensively in many jurisdictions, including some that do not report many children in formal kinship foster care. Services may be provided to the kinship caregivers on a voluntary basis for a period of time, and they may be eligible for a child-only Temporary Assistance for Needy Families (TANF) grant or, in a few states, for special funding for kinship caregivers. At least 39 states have reported diverting children from foster care by facilitating kinship placements for children (Leos-Urbel & Geen 2002), and the number of children affected may approach 200,000 (Ehrle & Geen 2002). These children and their relatives become informal kinship caregiving situations, as discussed above.

Second, a child or youth may be formally adjudicated and placed in foster care with a kinship home that meets either all state foster care standards or standards adapted specifically for kinship foster homes. In this case, the child and family receive child welfare services and either the full or a reduced state board payment, depending on state policy (Hegar & Scannapieco 2000).

The best current evidence suggests that about one-quarter of children in state custody are placed in kinship foster homes (Children's Bureau 2003), and that proportion has remained stable, or even declined somewhat, since the beginning of the 1990s (Beeman, Kim, & Bullerdick 2000; Geen & Berrick 2002). However, the proportion of foster children in kinship homes is significantly higher in some states and many urban areas. For example, researchers report 43% of foster children in California and 47% of those in Illinois in such arrangements (Beeman, Kim, & Bullerdick 2000; Needell et al. 2001; Testa 1997). Of children placed in 1998 in Illinois, 58% entered kinship foster care (Children's Bureau 2000; Child Welfare League of America 2000).

The third way in which kinship foster care is used in child placement is as a planned permanent home for a foster child. This placement can occur when a kinship foster home that has had the child in placement for some time agrees to accept guardianship or to pursue adoption. It may allow the state to cease providing financial support and services, although in many cases, transitional services would be provided, and several states are experimenting with subsidized guardianship that is similar to subsidized adoption. When either subsidized adoption or guardianship is possible, the state usually continues to provide medical coverage and may include a monthly subsidy. Permanent kinship placement also can occur when a relative home is located for a child who has been in traditional foster care. Relatives then sometimes assume custody or guardianship through the courts without first having been foster parents.

Recent federal reports reflect that either going to live with a relative or being placed in guardianship (almost always with a relative) was the case goal for 8% of the 542,000 children in foster care in 2001 (Children's Bureau 2003). Furthermore, of the 50,000 children estimated to have been adopted from public child welfare agencies in fiscal 2001, 23% were adopted by relatives. If this proportion holds in the future, almost one-quarter of the children for whom the long-term plan is adoption (22%) also may be placed permanently with relatives. These figures suggest that approximately 13% of foster children may ultimately leave state custody for placement in the homes of relatives through adoption, guardianship, or less formal kinship caregiving. In some states, the proportion is certainly much higher.

Outcomes, Risks, and Benefits Related to Kinship Foster Care

Outcome research on kinship foster care is inconclusive, making it difficult to know its strengths and challenges and how they affect families and children. However, there is a growing body of literature that provides some evidence of the risks and benefits related to kinship foster care. This section explores differences between children in kinship foster care and those in the general population, as well as those in non-kinship care. Variables that have been examined in the research literature are the duration and stability of placements, permanency-planning goals, child well-being, educational and health variables, and the kin caregivers' intentions concerning continued care.

Kinship foster care placements last longer than traditional foster home placements and reunification rates are lower (Berrick, Barth, & Needell 1994; Courtney & Needell 1997; Dubowitz et al. 1994; Scannapieco, Hegar, & McAlpine 1997; Testa 1997; Thornton 1991; Wulczyn & Goerge 1992; Wulczyn, Kogan, & Harden 2003). These conditions prevailed even before the enactment of Adoption and Safe Families Act of 1997, discussed above, the provisions of which can be expected to amplify this difference. Placements with relatives have been widely reported to be relatively stable (Berrick, Barth, & Needell 1994; Courtney & Needell 1997; Dubowitz et al. 1994; Iglehart 1994; Leslie, Landsverk, Horton, Ganger, & Newton 2000; Scannapieco, Hegar, & McAlpine 1997; Testa & Rolock 1999; Usher, Randolph, & Gogan 1999). However, the evidence is not entirely consistent. In a follow-up study of foster care that examines the differences between kinship and non-kinship placements, Benedict, Zuravin, and Stallings (1996) and Glisson, Bailey, and Post (2000) found no difference in length of stay in care, whereas Wells and Guo (1999) report no difference in reunification rates following kinship and non-kinship placements.

Testa (2002) found that reunification and stability in care were related to the kinship caregivers' perceptions of the parents' cooperativeness. Children whose parents were perceived by the caregivers as not participating in the case plan and not cooperating with visitation were less likely to be reunified and more likely to experience replacement in another home. Another factor that may influence both reunification and stability in care is financial reimbursement received by the kinship caregiver (Courtney & Needell 1997; Testa 2002). It is possible that receipt of welfare payments for relative children in care may reduce reunification rates (Courtney & Needell 1997). This possibility is supported by Testa (2002), who reports that, as payment decreases to kinship caregivers, re-placement of children increases, as does reunification.

Many kinship foster parents express commitment to the children in their care and indicate their willingness to care for them as long as needed (Berrick, Barth, & Needell 1994; Dubowitz et al. 1994; Gebel 1996; Gordon, McKinley, Satterfield, & Curtis 2003; Thornton 1991). In many studies, such relatives have expressed reluctance or unwillingness to adopt children who are already related to them (Berrick, Barth, & Needell 1994; Gleeson 1999b; Gordon, McKinley, Satterfield, & Curtis 2003; Thornton 1991), and they have historically been unlikely to assume legal guardianship of the children (Iglehart 1994). However, as already noted, 23% of recent public agency adoptions are by relatives (Children's Bureau 2003), and caseworkers believe relative adoption to be an appropriate and reasonable goal in most cases (Gleeson, O'Donnell, & Bonecutter 1997). Therefore, the assumption that relatives do not adopt may be changing. Even several years ago, Gebel (1996) found no difference between relatives and non-relatives, either in the length of time they were willing to care for children, or in their willingness to consider adopting children placed with them.

Studies vary widely concerning permanency planning goals for children in kinship care. For example, the proportion of cases with the

goal of independent living upon discharge ranges from 15% (Scannapieco, Hegar, & McAlpine 1997) to 88% (Thornton 1991). Return to parental custody is the reported goal in 33% (Dubowitz et al. 1994) to 43% of cases (Scannapieco, Hegar, & McAlpine 1997), which may be a lower rate than for non-relative care (Bonecutter 1999). However, Scannapieco, Hegar, and McAlpine (1997) found that children in kinship and traditional foster care do not differ with respect to agency permanency planning goals.

The benefits and risks to children in kinship foster care can be gauged by comparing their well-being with that of the general child population and with children who are in non-relative foster care. Reports about the physical health status of children appear to vary with the source of assessment. Based on medical evaluations, Dubowitz and colleagues (1992) found that only 10% of the children in kinship care are free of any medical problems. In contrast, Berrick, Barth, and Needell (1994) found that most children are assessed by the care provider to be in excellent or good health, even though 40% of the children had been exposed prenatally to drugs. Prenatal drug exposure for children in kinship care was related to increased health problems (Berrick, Barth, & Needell 1994; Keller et al. 2001; U.S. General Accounting Office 1999). Grogan-Kaylor (2000) reports that children with health problems are significantly less likely to be placed in kinship foster care.

Children in kinship care experience more behavioral problems than in both the general population (Dubowitz et al. 1994) and the foster care population (Berrick, Barth, & Needell 1994; Keller et al. 2001). Behavior in school is judged to be satisfactory for children in kinship care in approximately 60% of the cases (Berrick, Barth, & Needell 1994; Dubowitz et al. 1994; Iglehart 1994). However, with regard to scholastic performance, 36% (Iglehart 1994) to 50% (Dubowitz et al. 1994) of the kinship care children are performing below grade level compared to the general population, but they are less likely to repeat a grade than the rest of the foster care population (Benedict, Zuravin, Somerfield, & Brandt 1996; Brooks & Barth 1998).

When children in kinship foster care are compared with others using standardized instruments for assessing childhood behavior, the results are mixed. Berrick, Barth, and Needell (1994) found that children of all ages in kinship foster care score at least one standard deviation above the norm on the Behavior Problem index, and Dubowitz and colleagues (1994) found that 35% of the children have an overall Child Behavior Checklist score in the clinical range. However, it is noteworthy that Berrick, Barth, and Needell (1994) report that kinship foster children between the ages of 4 and 15 have fewer behavioral problems than do children in the same age group in traditional foster care. In the same vein, Iglehart (1994) reports that, although 33% of children in kinship care have behavioral problems serious enough to be noted in the case record, children in traditional foster care are even more likely to have adjustment problems. Benedict, Zuravin, and Stallings (1996) also report that children in relative care are less likely to have developmental or behavioral problems than do children in non-relative care. Gebel (1996) found that kinship foster parents rated more children as good-natured and fewer children as being difficult to handle than did unrelated foster parents. Finally, Shore, Sim, Le Prohn, and Keller (2002) report that teachers' perceptions of the behavior of youth in kinship and non-kinship foster care did not differ significantly. Neither group differed from the general population on most scales of the Teacher's Report form.

As mentioned above, very little research has compared the adult functioning of individuals who had been placed as children in relative versus non-relative care. In one such study (Zuravin, Benedict, & Stallings 1999), no difference was found in education, employment, income, or housing variables. Social support and experiences with life stressors were reported at similar levels for both groups. Differences were found, however, in the area of physical health: young people from non-relative care reported higher levels of hypertension than did young people from kinship care. And, although the rates of cocaine and marijuana use were similar between the groups, a greater number of young people who had been placed with kin reported using heroin at some time in their lives. Additionally, a significantly higher number of youth from kinship care reported trading sex for drugs (Zuravin, Benedict, & Stallings 1999).

Assessments and Interventions

As discussed above, kinship foster placements typically are quite stable. Some models of kinship foster care also require less rigorous training and offer less supervision of kinship homes than is true of traditional homes (Scannapieco & Hegar 1995). We previously have suggested that the stability and length of kinship placements, as well as the diminished supervision often offered to them, call for two kinds of screening (initial approval of the home and a permanency evaluation) before placement of children in kinship foster homes, except when the placement is made on a strictly emergency, time-limited basis (Scannapieco & Hegar 1996). This proposal directs attention to two sets of factors: those associated with the first use of any home for child placement (including parenting and family aspects, matters of safety and protection of the children, and physical environment), and those associated with selecting a permanent placement for particular children (including an assessment of what the home offers along the three dimensions of attachment, permanence, and kinship) (Hegar 1993). Across all of these factors, kinship placements raise issues that are substantially different from those encountered in traditional foster care, suggesting that each criterion for assessment must be adapted for use with kinship homes.

Shlonsky and Berrick (2001) have proposed a comprehensive framework for assessing and understanding the care children receive in kinship and non-kinship homes. They conceptualize the domains of quality of care as seven factors: child safety, educational support, mental health and behavioral support, developmental factors, furtherance of positive reciprocal attachment, characteristics of quality caregivers, and quality of life. These authors caution that, despite the legal and philosophical mandate for kinship care placement, assessment of the quality of care is essential in improving outcomes for children.

Jackson (1996, 1999) also discusses how the assessment process is unique when children are placed with relatives. She advocates a shift from assessing the dyad (parent and child) to assessing the triad of the child or children, parent, and extended family (Jackson 1996) and to providing services to the triad (Jackson 1999). Individualized assessment must focus on understanding the extended family system and the strengths and challenges the triad brings to the kinship foster placement (Jackson 1996; Shlonsky & Berrick 2001). According to Jackson (1996), the bases of an assessment framework for kinship foster care placements are an intergenerational perspective of the triad members; a multidimensional assessment of interpersonal, family, and environmental systems; and acknowledgment of cultural realities in extended families.

Another thoughtful approach to the assessment of kinship foster homes has been developed by Chipman, Wells, and Johnson (2002). Based on a qualitative study of caregivers, children, and agency staff, they suggest differences between kinship and non-kinship placements, review existing guidelines for evaluating kinship homes, and suggest additional factors to consider in the process of studying and approving kinship placements. Kinship home assessments clearly need to be approached differently than traditional foster home studies. The different strengths that families bring to kinship care need to be considered, and issues of permanency must be viewed from the perspective of the kinship network.

Kinship Foster Care Programs, Promising Approaches, and Their Evaluation

It is well documented that kinship caregivers and foster homes receive fewer resources, services, and training than do non-kinship foster homes (Berrick, Barth, & Needell 1994; Brooks & Barth 1998; Burnette 1999; Dubowitz et al. 1994; Ehrle & Geen 2002; Gebel 1996; Iglehart 1994; Scannapieco, Hegar, & McAlpine 1997; Thornton 1991; U.S. General Accounting Office 1999), yet they are in greater need of services and resources than are traditional foster parents (Berrick, Needell, & Barth 1999; Ehrle & Geen 2002). Kinship caregivers are often unprepared for taking on the responsibility of caring for one or more children, and they may experience substantial adjustment difficulties in their lives (Gleeson, O'Donnell, & Bonecutter 1997; Gordon, McKinley, Satterfield, & Curtis 2003; Minkler & Roe 1993; Osby 1999).

It would benefit the child welfare system to insure that kinship care families receive the needed services and supports that promote the safety, permanency, and well-being of the children in its care. Elsewhere we have discussed the array of support and intervention needs of kinship caregivers and foster parents (Scannapieco & Hegar 2002). In this chapter, we highlight some innovations and culturally sensitive approaches and programs designed to meet the needs of kinship caregivers or foster parents and the children in their homes.

Mediation through Family Group Conferencing

One of the most quickly proliferating practice concepts is family group decisionmaking to mediate the best placement decisions for children. Involving extended family members in the mediation planning process brings detailed knowledge and information about the kinship network and its strengths and challenges, and it empowers the family in the decisionmaking process (American Humane Association 1996; Berrick, Needell, & Barth 1995; Ryburn 1998; Wilcox et al. 1991). The key elements to family group conferencing are:

- Family meetings are called if a child welfare agency performs an initial assessment and determines a child is in need of care and protection;
- Family members who currently or potentially play a role in the child's life attend the meeting, including the child's parents, extended family members, close friends, godparents, and others whom the family defines as kin;
- Family members are prepared for the conference to clarify the process, tasks, and roles;
- Child welfare staff, teachers, psychologists, and other professionals who are working with the family also typically attend the meeting;
- Parents may limit participation by other family members;
- The meeting setting is amiable and in a neutral location, so that all participants feel comfortable about expressing their thoughts and feelings;
- The major underlying principle of family decisionmaking is the involvement of the extended family in brainstorming about options for the care and protection of the children;
- Children are given an opportunity to give input about where and with whom they would prefer to live; and
- Child welfare workers or designated professionals not involved in the case (professional mediators) mediate the decisionmaking process by helping the family develop a plan for the child or children.

Family meetings, no matter the configuration, generally produce a plan that is acceptable to professionals and includes placement within the kinship network (Ryburn 1998). Addition-ally, they have been found to reduce out-of-home placement and increase placement of children in their same ethnic, racial, and/or religious group (American Humane Association 1996). In that way, family group conferencing is culturally sensitive and is proving to be quite effective in addressing the goals of safety, permanency, and child well-being.

Subsidized Guardianship

Other innovations in kinship foster care concern financial benefits available to relatives. The child welfare system provides services to kinship families through one of two federally funded programs: TANF and the foster care program through Title IV-E funds. State kinship foster care programs can be viewed within a framework defined primarily by their funding source and, secondarily, by the continuum of services: diversion, foster care, or permanent placement. The decisionmaking process that takes place within this framework ideally is based on an assessment of the families' and children's needs, permanency planning issues, risk and safety issues, and family preservation. Not all kinship care situations need to involve the formal foster care system, and the inception of guardianship subsidies in 1996 created an alternative option for permanent placement.

Prior to 1996, permanency options for children in kinship care were long-term kinship care (with TANF grants or foster care payment), private guardianship (with no payment), or adoption (with or without subsidy). Adoption was the only federally subsidized option for achieving permanency for children who were abused or neglected and unable to return home to their families. With the dramatic increase in kinship foster care placements since the early 1990s (Children's Bureau 2000), and in recognition of the limitations of adoption for kinship placements, subsidized guardianship was proposed as an additional option.

Since 1996, the Department of Health and Human Services has funded seven demonstration projects in the states of Delaware, Illinois,

Maryland, Montana, New Mexico, North Carolina, and Oregon (Administration for Children and Families 2003). All seven states designed their guardianship programs for children whose needs for permanent placement could not be met by reunification or adoption. In addition to the guardianship programs allowed by federal waiver, a majority of states have implemented subsidized guardianship using funds from other sources (U.S. Department of Health and Human Services 2001).

As discussed earlier, research suggests that many kinship caregivers are reluctant to adopt their kin because of family and cultural issues. Guardianship subsidies present an alternative means of changing a temporary care situation into a permanent one. As a permanency option, guardianship subsidies have several advantages: the rights of biological parents need not be terminated, children are removed from the continuing jurisdiction of the court system, kinship caregivers retain their identities (e.g., as grandparents, aunts, uncles), child welfare agencies can end their case management responsibilities, kinship providers are assured some level of financial support, and child welfare agencies and courts save costs. The most important advantage is the underlying assumption that guardianship subsidies provide children with permanent and stable homes that will promote positive developmental outcomes.

In the only published study to date on the effects of guardianship subsidy, Testa (2002) reports that the programs have merit as options to adoption. Illinois, the largest state to receive funding for one of the demonstration projects, provides good evidence of the potential benefits. Children placed in families that were given the option of receiving guardianship subsidies were significantly more likely to achieve permanency than those in families who were not given the option (Testa & Slack 2002). Additionally, withdrawal of administrative oversight and case management from the families did not result in higher rates of child abuse and neglect (Administration for Children and Families 2003).

Final evaluation reports for all seven of the demonstration reports were due by the end of federal FY2003, and the future of guardianship subsidies is unknown. Possibly, subsidized guardianship will become an integral part of the child welfare service system if legislators see the advantages of legal permanency with relatives over temporary foster care for children in need of safe and permanent homes.

Value Conflicts and Ethical Dilemmas
Value Conflicts
The Oxford English Dictionary includes no definition of "value" or "values" that approximates the way the word is used in contemporary U.S. political debate. In our own sense of the meaning, values express preferred norms based on individual or cultural beliefs, rather than on proof or evidence. As might be expected, value issues and conflicts permeate issues surrounding placement of children in state custody. Among them are: How serious should maltreatment, or the risk of it, be before children should be removed from parents? How long should parents have to improve family conditions before losing permanent custody of children? Should relatives be the placement of choice for foster children? These are not questions to which there are verifiable answers, only ranges of perspectives. This section focuses on three value considerations that underpin kinship care policy: the importance of family ties or kinship; the nature of duty to kin; and the role of race, ethnicity, and/or religion in child placement. Each of these complex issues can be considered here only very briefly.

Importance of family ties. At the core of any debate over the use of kinship foster care is the importance of family and blood kinship. American culture, like most others, takes it for granted that children and parents belong together, and a weaker version of this assumption extends to relatives with more distant degrees of kinship. However, we are not as "clan-minded" as some cultures, and it is possible that in many circumstances the societal value we place on individualism tempers our commitment to family ties. Yet it is the intrinsic value of family ties that lawmakers embraced when they legislated preferences for kinship placements in the Indian Child Welfare Act and the Adoption and Safe Families Act. Such legislative preferences are rooted in the "rights paradigm" that bases social policy on legal claims (Rappaport 1981). Some observers who prefer residual, nongovernmental solutions no doubt are also motivated by the hope that the state can be less involved with, and perhaps less financially committed to, kinship placements.

Nature of duty to kin. For many decades, relatives who took care of the children of kin received none of the assistance that society began to make available to non-kin foster parents about 100 years ago (Hegar & Scannapieco 1995). A great many kinship caregivers still receive no such assistance. Why do they continue to engage in kinship foster care?

Testa and Slack (2002) have recently contributed to the literature a thoughtful and scholarly paper that examines kinship foster care as a "gift relationship," in the sense that Titmuss (Titmuss, Oakley, & Ashton 1997) first used the term in 1971 to denote acts of selflessness. They apply the latter's concepts of altruism and reciprocity and incorporate aspects of game and exchange theory to construct hypotheses about what kinship foster parents will do about continuing to provide care in different situations. They also test their hypotheses in a study of a large population of children (983 individuals) in kinship care in Cook County, Illinois. Partway through the study, a change in the state's approach to funding allowed the authors to include the impact of funding levels on participation in kinship foster care. Although funding did have a significant effect on continuing to provide kinship fostering (76.7% of those with full funding continued; 58.7% of

those with reduced funding did so), Testa and Slack (2002:101) conclude that the continued participation of the majority in both groups "suggests that kinship altruism and family duty still play a major role in upholding the willingness of extended families to take responsibility for their dependent kin."

Role of race, ethnicity, and religion. Although the overrepresentation of black children in kinship care has made race an important research variable, the additional dimensions of ethnicity and religion also are relevant in a discussion of value conflicts. It is clear from all available research that both kinship caregiving and kinship foster care are much more prevalent in African American communities and somewhat more prevalent in Hispanic communities than they are in the U.S. population as a whole. Reasons given in the literature are mostly speculative, but they include cultural acceptability of kinship caregiving, historical exclusion from traditional child welfare services, continued belief in family duty and group self-help, economic and employment pressures on parents, and the destructive impact of the drug culture and related criminality on the recent parental generation (Barrio & Hughes 2000; Brown, Cohon, & Wheeler 2002; Hegar 1999b; Hegar & Scannapieco 1995; Minkler & Roe 1993; Scannapieco & Jackson 1996). These speculations suggest that kinship placements are made because specific communities of color are more open to them and, perhaps, in greater need of them.

However, there is also a policy dimension to the issue of the differential use of kinship foster care, one that illustrates a key value conflict. With the passage of the Multiethnic Placement Act of 1994, the Interethnic Adoption Provisions of 1996, and the Adoption and Safe Families Act of 1997, the child placement system was given two directives: First, not to consider race in foster care and adoption decisions, and, second, to give preference to relatives in making placements. It is not possible even to recap here the decades of debate over transracial placements (see Brooks, Barth, Bussiere, & Patterson 1999; McRoy & Hall 1995; McRoy, Oglesby, & Grape 1997; Shireman 1994), but it seems reasonable to say that many social workers in the child welfare field continue to believe that children are best served by placement within their racial or ethnic communities whenever such a placement is possible. There are, of course, other observers who disagree (e.g., Simon & Altstein 1987). Although the Interethnic Adoption Provisions of 1996 declare consideration of race in child placement impermissible, placement of black, Hispanic, or any children in kinship foster care ordinarily allows them to continue life within their specific racial/ethnic/religious communities. Therefore, the use of kinship foster care may allow some child placement staff, members of communities of color, and individual families to pursue values that favor same-race placements in the face of national policy to the contrary.

Ethical Dilemmas

An ethical dilemma arises when two or more ethical precepts conflict and it is impossible to apply them simultaneously. A classic example is the conflict between client confidentiality and child abuse reporting, which the National Association of Social Workers (1999) code of ethics (NASW Code) and state laws address directly, in favor of reporting. However, neither the NASW Code nor laws help social workers resolve all ethical dilemmas. The NASW Code begins with six overarching ethical principles, three of which are highly relevant to policy and practice involving kinship foster care.

One principle is that "social workers recognize the central importance of human relationships" (National Association of Social Workers 1999:113). The NASW Code elaborates that "social workers seek to strengthen relationships among people in a purposeful effort to promote, restore, maintain, and enhance the well-being of individuals, families, social groups, organizations, and communities" (1999:4). The relevance of this ethical mandate for kinship

foster care is immediately evident. When appropriately carried out, kinship placements can indeed strengthen relationships among children, extended families, and their communities. Their capacity to do so has lead many organizations and practitioners to promote the use of kinship foster care (e.g., Child Welfare League of America 1992, 1994; National Black Child Development Institute 1989; National Commission on Family Foster Care 1991).

Two other ethical principles from the NASW Code also have relevance for kinship care policy and practice, and these are the key to the dilemmas that may confront conscientious social workers. They are: "social workers' primary goal is to help people in need and to address social problems," and "social workers challenge social injustice" (National Association of Social Workers 1999:5). It should be clear from the discussion in this chapter that diversion of children from the child welfare system into kinship caregiving is likely to leave many of their economic needs unmet, particularly if the families involved are black, Hispanic, or headed by a single grandmother, because the official poverty rates for these three types of kinship caregiving families range from 46% to 52% (U.S. Census Bureau 2003).

Even for children placed in kinship foster care, the studies cited here (as well as official U.S. policy reports such as the one quoted below) conclude that formal (public) kinship foster parents share many unmet needs for services with informal (private) kinship caregivers: kinship caregivers usually receive little if any advance preparation for assuming their role. Agency-involved and private kinship caregivers are often constrained by limited decisionmaking authority. Public and private kinship caregivers are older, and are more likely to be single and African American. Public kinship caregivers are also more likely never to have married, to be the only adult in the household, and to take care of fewer children. Kinship caregivers' homes are more likely to be in the center of cities, although this appears to be largely because African

Americans are concentrated in urban areas. Both public and private kinship caregivers are likely to have less education and lower incomes and are more likely to receive public benefits than non-kin foster parents. Public kinship caregivers are less likely to report being in good health and appear to be more likely to experience economic hardship (Children's Bureau 2000:39).

Is it ethical for social workers, seeking to recognize and strengthen family relationships, to place children, and to write policies to place children, in conditions rife with human need and social injustice? The differences between traditional foster care and kinship placements, coupled with the racial differences between the children in the two types of placements, have led us and other observers to suggest that a racially segregated, two-tier system of foster care is emerging in the United States (Brown & Bailey-Etta 1997; Hegar & Scannapieco 1995; Scannapeico & Hegar 1999). Kinship foster care poses ethical dilemmas that are not easily resolved!

Case Examples

The following are actual disguised case vignettes from our experience in practice and consultation with social work agencies. They highlight some of the issues raised thus far in this chapter, and each has a bearing on the final section concerning kinship foster care as extended family preservation.

DECIDING WHETHER TO MAKE A PLACEMENT CHANGE

Of the four children of a single mother, none remain with her, and none has had any involvement with their fathers. The oldest girl, now 14, has been raised by her great aunt, a divorced woman of about 58 with several grown children. A boy is in foster care in another state. The two children in agency custody are a girl, 5, and her half-brother, 4, who is HIV-positive and physically frail. These two African American children are placed in a foster home with white parents who specialize in HIV/AIDS children. The other

foster children in the home are all male infants and preschoolers with HIV.

The children's great aunt wishes to offer a permanent home to the 5-year-old girl, who is her godchild and who was placed with her (by another agency) for about a year as an infant. The great aunt is employed full time. She has adult children with their own families, one of whom lives nearby and would offer the child a home if the latter could no longer, for any reason, be cared for by her great aunt. This daughter also would provide after-school care. The great aunt does not have a separate room for the boy, nor does she feel able to cope with his medical needs. The 5-year-old has had many visits in her home, whereas her brother has not. The 5-year-old feels close to her great aunt and to her 14-year-old sister, who has grown up there. Finally, the family attaches cultural and religious significance to the ties between godparent and godchild, which implies that the children's mother gave the great aunt special responsibility for this particular child.

After assessing the children using appropriate doll families and the children's drawings, interviewing all adults, observing in both homes, and reviewing agency records and collateral contacts, an outside evaluator contracted by the public child welfare agency recommended kinship placement for the 5-year-old girl, even though that involved separating the siblings. The major rationale was that the children had different needs for permanence and specialized care.

ASSESSING SERVICES NEEDED IN A KINSHIP PLACEMENT

Sixty-one-year-old Gloria Stewart has been caring for her two grandchildren, Robert, 7, and Marie, 4, for the past 2 years. They live in a small city where Ms. Stewart has a two-bedroom apartment. She has been granted custody of Robert, but not Marie, by the juvenile court. Marie is in the custody of the public child welfare agency. Robert's father is incarcerated; Marie's father lives in the city and has a job at a clothing factory. Once a month, he visits her home and gives Ms. Stewart $30 toward the care of Marie. This is his only contact with his daughter, although he has expressed an interest in seeking custody of her. When asked what prevents his assuming the care of his child, he cites the obstacles of child care, his lack of parenting skills, and his living arrangements. In spite of his failure to address these issues, he has objected to Ms. Stewart having custody of Marie.

The children appear to be attached to their grandmother, who loves them dearly. But she is frustrated because she has had to forfeit several of her favorite activities, including singing in the church choir and her Wednesday Bible class. She also is beginning to show signs of impatience with Robert. Robert has had serious behavioral problems for several years. For a short time, he attended therapy at a local mental health center. Ms. Stewart discontinued the visits because the center was inconvenient to visit and she believes that Robert will outgrow his problems. Meanwhile, Robert continues to become involved in neighborhood fights, steal, and wet the bed nightly.

Marie is also experiencing difficulties. As an infant, she was diagnosed with physical problems as a result of her mother's drug use during pregnancy. She is developmentally delayed in the areas of social and cognitive skills. Lack of custody has prevented Ms. Stewart from adequately addressing Marie's school and medical needs. Ms. Stewart does not seek health check-up visits for either child, only medical treatment for emergencies or symptomatic problems. Robert is on medical assistance and is assigned to a local HMO, and Marie has medical assistance coverage but is not assigned to any participating medical plan.

Ms. Stewart receives TANF payment of $130 a month for Robert and $320 a month in foster care payments for Marie. She does not receive food stamps. Ms. Stewart works at a part-time job for which she earns $500 a month, but she does not receive medical or leave benefits. The child welfare agency provides day care for Marie; however, Robert is ineligible for Title IV-A day care funds, as Ms. Stewart is not a part of his TANF case. Robert might be eligible for Title XX subsidized day care, but, even if he is eligible, there is a long waiting list. At this point, Ms. Stewart is considering allowing the agency to take custody of Robert because the financial al-

lowance for foster care would be much greater. But she is not happy with the requirements of foster care.

Ms. Stewart's situation highlights many common themes in kinship caregiving and kinship foster care. One of these themes is that, although the line between the two roles is somewhat artificial, that artificial line nonetheless determines benefits and services. Another common thread is that the relatives who provide care for children typically require public services themselves, and the additional role of caring for children taxes their emotional and financial resources. Finally, this case, like the previous one, illustrates that children requiring kinship placement frequently have unmet needs for medical, educational, and behavioral intervention.

Kinship Foster Care as Extended Family Preservation

It should be clear from the discussion so far that kinship foster care has become a significant feature of the U.S. child welfare system, just as informal kinship caregiving is an important part of the landscape of American families. Both are more prevalent among families of color, particularly in African American communities, than in the general population. The trend toward kinship placements has been fueled by both the growth of foster care and the shortage of traditional foster homes. Since the 1970s, several federal statutes and court decisions also have worked to promote kinship placement of children, and the most recent, the Adoption and Safe Family Act of 1997, appears likely to shift the emphasis further toward kinship foster care, particularly for children needing placement for longer periods.

Child welfare agencies use kinship placements in three ways: as a means of diverting children from court adjudication and foster care placement, as formal foster homes, and as permanent placements that allow children to grow up within their extended families. Research suggests that many families involved in each of these roles face significant challenges related to low incomes, difficulty accessing services, and lack of support from agencies. Children in kinship care also face academic, emotional, and behavioral challenges, although not necessarily more so than other foster children. Empirical evidence of the outcomes of kinship foster care is still very sparse, but so far, it suggests that children placed with relatives may do as well as other children with similar backgrounds.

Conclusion

Much of the impetus to place children in the homes of kin comes not from evidence that it works but from strong convictions that it is the right thing to do. For many advocates, it is a value-based policy choice that has to do with preserving the extended family when the nuclear family is too stressed to function. As we have discussed, placement within extended families very often also allows children to continue to live in familiar ethnic, religious, and geographical communities. Kinship care is a practice with deep roots in historical and cultural tradition. As a policy direction, it first places

responsibility for children at the family level. It also is a policy that minimizes state involvement in the forms of supervision, provision of services, and financial support.

Although some policy analysts and advocates may accept the ways kinship caregiving and kinship foster care currently operate, as residual services that require less state commitments of staff and funds than traditional foster care, others are more troubled by the value conflicts and ethical dilemmas presented above. We support the role that kinship placements play in extended family preservation but are concerned about the impact on kinship caregivers of federal, state, and local cutbacks in transfer payments and social services. Certainly there have also been some encouraging developments, such as federal waivers to allow subsidized guardianship in several states and other innovative programs to support both permanent and shorter-term kinship placements. Kinship foster care can contribute to family preservation, but few of the families involved are in positions to take on responsibility for children without the support of the larger community and society.

References

Administration for Children and Families. (2003). *Assisted guardianship/kinship permanence.* Retrieved August 1, 2003, from www.acf.dhhs.gov/programs/cb/initiatives/cwwaiver/assisted.

Adoption and Safe Families Act. (1997). P.L. 105-89.

Adoption Assistance and Child Welfare Act. (1980). P.L. 96-272.

American Humane Association. (1996). Family group decision making: A promising new approach for child welfare. *Child Protection Leader,* (July), p. 4.

Axinn, J., & Stern, M. J. (2001). *Social welfare: A history of the American response to need,* fifth ed. Boston: Allyn and Bacon.

Barrio, C., & Hughes, J. M. (2000). Kinship care: A cultural resource of African American and Latino families coping with parental substance abuse. *Journal of Family Social Work, 4*(4), 15–31.

Beeman, S., Kim, H., & Bullerdick, S. (2000). Factors affecting placement of children in kinship and non-kinship foster care. *Children and Youth Services Review, 22,* 37–54.

Benedict, M. I., Zuravin, S., Somerfield, M., & Brandt, D. (1996). The reported health and functioning of chil-

dren maltreated while in foster care. *Child Abuse and Neglect, 20,* 561–571.

Benedict, M., Zuravin, S., and Stallings, R. (1996). Adult functioning of children who lived in kin versus nonrelative family foster homes. *Child Welfare, 75,* 529–549.

Berrick, J. D., Barth, R. P., & Needell, B. (1994). A comparison of kinship foster homes and foster family homes: Implications for kinship foster care as family preservation. *Children and Youth Services Review, 16,* 33–64.

Berrick, J. D., Needell, B., & Barth, R. P. (1995). *Kinship care in California: An empirically-based curriculum.* Berkeley: University of California–Berkeley, Child Welfare Research Center.

Berrick, J. D., Needell, B., & Barth, R. P. (1999). Kin as a family and child welfare resource: The child welfare worker's perspective. In R. L. Hegar & M. Scannapieco (eds.), *Kinship foster care: Practice, policy and research,* pp. 179–192. New York: Oxford University Press.

Bonecutter, F. J. (1999). Defining best practice in kinship care through research and demonstration. In J. P. Gleeson and C. F. Hairston (eds.), *Kinship care:*

Improving practice through research, pp. 37–60. Washington, DC: Child Welfare League of America.

Brooks, D., & Barth, R. P. (1998). Characteristics and outcomes of drug-exposed and non-drug–exposed children in kinship and non-relative foster care. *Children and Youth Services Review, 20*, 475–501.

Brooks, D., Barth, R. P., Bussiere, A., & Patterson, G. (1999). Adoption and race: Implementing the Multiethnic Placement Act and the Interethnic Adoption Provisions. *Social Work, 44*, 167–178.

Brown, A.W., & Bailey-Etta, B. (1997). An out-of-home care system in crisis: Implications for African American children in the child welfare system. *Child Welfare, 76*, 65–83.

Brown, S., Cohon, D., & Wheeler, R. (2002). African American extended families and kinship care: How relevant is the foster care model for kinship care? *Children and Youth Services Review, 24*, 53–77.

Burnette, D. (1999). Custodial grandparents in Latino families: Patterns of service use and predictors of unmet needs. *Social Work, 44*, 22–34.

Burton, L. M. (1992). Black grandparents rearing children of drug-addicted parents: Stressors, outcomes, and social needs. *Gerontologist, 32*, 744–751.

Children's Bureau. (2000). *Report to the Congress on kinship foster care*. Retrieved July 21, 2003, from aspe.hhs.gov/hsp/kinr2o00/full.pdf.

Children's Bureau. (2003). *The AFCARS Report: Preliminary FY 2001 estimates as of March 2003*. Retrieved July 22, 2003, from www.acf.hhs.gov/program/cb.

Child Welfare League of America. (1992). Kinship care: A new look at an old idea. *Children's Voice*, (spring), pp. 6–7, 22.

Child Welfare League of America. (1994). *Kinship care: A natural bridge*. Washington, DC: Child Welfare League of America.

Child Welfare League of America. (2000). *Standards of excellence for kinship care services*. Washington, DC: Child Welfare League of America.

Chipman, R., Wells, S. J., & Johnson, M. A. (2002). The meaning of quality in kinship foster care: Caregiver, child and worker perspectives. *Families in Society, 83*, 508–519.

Courtney, M. E., & Needell, B. (1997). Outcomes of kinship care: Lessons from California. In R. P. Barth, J. D. Berrick, & N. Gilbert (eds.), *Child Welfare Research Review*, vol. 2, pp. 272–293. New York: Columbia University Press.

Dubowitz, H., Feigelman, S., Harrington, D., Starr, R., Zuravin, S., & Sawyer, R. (1994). Children in kinship care: How do they fare? *Children and Youth Services Review, 16*, 85–106.

Dubowitz, H., Feigelman, S., & Zuravin, S. (1993). A profile of kinship care. *Child Welfare, 72*, 153–169.

Dubowitz, H., Feigelman, S., Zuravin, S., Tepper, V., Davidson, N., & Lichenstein, R. (1992). The physical health of children in kinship care. *American Journal of Diseases in Children, 146*, 603–610.

Ehrle, J., & Geen, R. (2002). Kin and non-kin foster care—Findings from a national survey. *Children and Youth Services Review, 24*, 15–35.

Ernst, J. (1999). Whanau knows best: Kinship care in New Zealand. In R. L. Hegar & M. Scannapieco (eds.), *Kinship care: Policy, practice & research*, pp. 112–138. New York: Oxford University Press.

Fields, J. (2003). *Current Population Reports: Children's living arrangements and characteristics: March 2002*. Washington, DC: U.S. Department of Commerce. Retrieved July 21, 2003, from www. census.gov/population/socdemo/nh-fam/cps2002.

Folks, H. (1902, reprinted 1978). *The care of destitute, neglected, & delinquent children*. Washington, DC: National Association of Social Workers.

Gebel, T. J. (1996). Kinship care and non-relative family foster care: A comparison of caregiver attributes and attitudes. *Child Welfare, 75*, 5–18.

Geen, R., & Berrick, J. (2002). Kinship care: An evolving service delivery option. *Children and Youth Services Review, 24*, 1–14.

Gleeson, J. P. (1996). Kinship care as a child welfare service: The policy debate in an era of welfare reform. *Child Welfare, 75*, 419–449.

Gleeson, J. P. (1999a). Kinship care as a child welfare service: Emerging policy issues and trends. In R. L. Hegar & M. Scannapieco (eds.), *Kinship care: Policy, practice & research*, pp. 28–53. New York: Oxford University Press.

Gleeson, J. P. (1999b). Who decides? Predicting caseworkers' adoption and guardianship discussions with kinship caregivers. In J. P. Gleeson & C. F. Hairston (eds.), *Kinship care: Improving practice through research*, pp. 61–84. Washington, DC: Child Welfare League of America.

Gleeson, J. P., & Craig, L. C. (1994). Kinship care in child welfare: An analysis of states' policies. *Children and Youth Services Review, 16*, 7–31.

Gleeson, J. P., O'Donnell, J., & Bonecutter, F. J. (1997). Understanding the complexity of practice in kinship foster care. *Child Welfare, 76*, 801–826.

Glisson, C., Bailey, J. W., & Post, J. A. (2000). Predicting the time children spend in state custody. *Social Service Review, 74*, 253–280.

Gordon, A. L., McKinley, S. E., Satterfield, M. L., & Curtis, P. A. (2003). A first look at the need for enhanced support services for kinship caregivers. *Child Welfare, 82*, 77–96.

Greeff, R. (ed.). (1999). *Fostering kinship: An international perspective on kinship foster care*. Aldershot, England: Ashgate ARENA.

Grogan-Kaylor, A. (2000). Who goes into kinship care: The relationship of child and family characteristics to placement into kinship foster care. *Social Work Research, 24*, 132–141.

Hegar, R. L. (1993). Assessing attachment, permanence, and kinship in choosing permanent homes. *Child Welfare, 72*, 367–378.

Hegar, R. L. (1999a). Kinship foster care: The new child placement paradigm. In R. L. Hegar & M. Scannapieco (eds.), *Kinship care: Policy, practice & research*, pp. 225–240. New York: Oxford University Press.

Hegar, R. L. (1999b). The cultural roots of kinship care. In R. L. Hegar & M. Scannapieco, (eds.), *Kinship care: Policy, practice & research*, pp. 17–27. New York: Oxford University Press.

Hegar, R. L., & Scannapieco, M. (1995). From family duty to family policy: The evolution of kinship care. *Child Welfare, 75*, 200–216.

Hegar, R. L., & Scannapieco, M. (eds.). (1999). *Kinship foster care: Policy, practice, & research*. New York: Oxford University Press.

Hegar, R. L., & Scannapieco, M. (2000). Grandma's babies: The problem of welfare eligibility for children raised by relatives. *Journal of Sociology and Social Welfare, 27*, 153–171.

Iglehart, A. P. (1994). Kinship foster care: Placement, service, and outcome issues. *Children and Youth Services Review, 16*, 107–122.

Indian Child Welfare Act. (1978). P.L. 95-608.

Jackson, S. (1996). The kinship triad: A service delivery model. *Child Welfare, 75*, 583–599.

Jackson, S. (1999). Paradigm shift: Training staff to provide services to the kinship triad. In R. L. Hegar & M. Scannapieco, (eds.), *Kinship care: Policy, practice & research*, pp. 93–111. New York: Oxford University Press.

Jansson, B. (1997). *The reluctant welfare state: American social welfare policies—Past, present, and future*, third edition. Pacific Grove, CA: Brooks/Cole.

Keller, T. E., Wetherbee, K., Le Prohn, N., Payne, V., Sim, K., & Lamont, E. R. (2001). Competencies and problem behaviors of children in family foster care: Variations by kinship placement status and race. *Children and Youth Services Review, 23*, 915–940.

Kelley, S., Whitley, D., Sipe, T., & Crofts Yorker, B. (2000). Psychological distress in grandmother kinship providers: The role of resources, social support, and physical health. *Child Abuse and Neglect, 24*, 311–321.

Kolomer, S. R. (2000). Kinship foster care and its impact on grandmother caregivers. *Journal of Gerontological Social Work, 33*, 85–102.

Leos-Urbel, J., & Geen, R. (2002). The evolution of federal and state policies for assessing and supporting kinship caregivers. *Children and Youth Services Review, 24*, 37–52.

Le Prohn, N., & Pecora, P. (1994). Findings from the Casey Family Program foster parent study. Seattle: Casey Family Program.

Leslie, L. K., Landsverk, J., Horton, M. B., Ganger, W., & Newton, R. R. (2000). The heterogeneity of children and their experiences in kinship care. *Child Welfare, 79*, 315–334.

McRoy, R. G., & Hall, C. (1995). Transracial adoptions: In whose best interest? In M. Root (ed.), *Multiracial people in the new millennium*, pp. 63–78. Newbury Park, CA: Sage.

McRoy, R. G., Oglesby, Z., & Grape, H. (1997). Achieving same-race adoptive placement for African American children: Culturally sensitive practice approaches. *Child Welfare, 76*, 85–104.

Minkler, M., & Roe, K. M. (1993). *Grandmothers as caregivers: Raising children of the crack cocaine epidemic*. Newbury Park, CA: Sage.

Minkler, M., Roe, K. M., & Price, M. (1993). The physical and emotional health of grandmothers raising grandchildren in the crack cocaine epidemic. *Gerontologist, 32*, 752–761.

Multiethnic Placement Act. (1994). P.L. 103-382.

National Association of Social Workers. (1999). *Code of ethics of the National Association of Social Workers*. Washington, DC: National Association of Social Workers. Retrieved August 15, 2003, from www/naswdc.org/Code/ethics.htm.

National Black Child Development Institute. (1989). *Who will care when parents can't? A study of black children in foster care*. Washington, DC: National Black Child Development Institute.

National Commission on Family Foster Care. (1991). *A blueprint for fostering infants, children, and youths in the 1990s*. Washington DC: Child Welfare League of America.

Needell, B., Webster, D., Cuccaro-Alamin, S., Armijo, M., Lee, S., & Brookhart, A. (2001). *Performance indicators for child welfare services in California*. Berkeley, CA: Center for Social Services Research. Retrieved March 20, 2003, from csr.berkeley.edu.

Osby, O. (1999). Child rearing perspectives of grandparent caregivers. In J. P. Gleeson & C. F. Hairston (eds.), *Kinship care: Improving practice through research*, pp. 215–232. Washington, DC: Child Welfare League of America.

Personal Responsibility and Work Opportunity Reconciliation Act. (1996). P.L. 104-193.

Rappaport, J. (1981). In praise of paradox: A social policy of empowerment over prevention. *American Journal of Community Psychology, 9*, 1–25.

Ryburn, M. (1998). A new model of welfare: Reasserting the value of kinship for children in state care. *Social Policy & Administration, 32*, 28–45.

Saluter, A. F. (1989). *Changes in American family life. Current population reports, social studies*. Washington, DC: U.S. Department of Commerce.

Saluter, A. F. (1996). *Current population reports: Marital status and living arrangements. March 1995 (update)*. Washington, DC: U.S. Department of Commerce.

Scannapieco, M. (1999a). Formal kinship care practice models. In R. L. Hegar & M. Scannapieco (eds.), *Kinship care: Policy, practice & research*, pp. 71–83. New York: Oxford University Press.

Scannapieco, M. (1999b). Kinship care in the public child welfare system: A systematic review of the research. In R. L. Hegar & M. Scannapieco (eds.), *Kin-*

ship care: Policy, practice & research, pp. 141–154. New York: Oxford University Press.

Scannapieco, M., & Hegar, R. L. (1995). Kinship care: A comparison of two case management models. Child and Adolescent Social Work, 12, 147–156.

Scannapieco, M., & Hegar, R. L. (1996). A nontraditional assessment framework for kinship foster homes. Child Welfare, 75, 567–582.

Scannapieco, M., & Hegar, R. L. (1999). Kinship foster care in context. In R. L. Hegar & M. Scannapieco (eds.), Kinship care: Policy, practice & research, pp. 1–13. New York: Oxford University Press.

Scannapieco, M., & Hegar, R. L. (2002). Kinship care providers: The array of support and intervention services needs. Child and Adolescent Social Work, 19, 315–327.

Scannapieco, M., Hegar, R. L., & McAlpine, C. (1997). Kinship care and foster care: A comparison of characteristics and outcomes. Families in Society, 78, 480–488.

Scannapieco, M., & Jackson, S. (1996). Kinship care: The African American response to family preservation. Social Work, 41, 190–196.

Shireman, J. (1994). Should interracial adoptions be permitted? In E. Gambrill & T. Stein (eds.), Controversial issues in child welfare, pp. 246–260. Needham Heights, MA: Allyn and Bacon.

Shlonsky, A. R., & Berrick, J. D. (2001). Assessing and promoting quality in kin and nonkin foster care. Social Services Review, 75, 60–83.

Shore, N., Sim, K. E., Le Prohn, N. S., & Keller, T. E. (2002). Foster parents and teacher assessments of youth in kinship and non-kinship foster care placements: Are behaviors perceived differently across settings? Children and Youth Services Review, 24, 109–134.

Simon, R. J., & Alstein, H. (1987). Transracial adoptees and their families: A study of identity and commitment. New York: Praeger.

Testa, M. F. (1997). Kinship foster care in Illinois. In R. P. Barth, J. D. Berrick, & N. Gilbert (eds.), Child Welfare Research Review, vol. 2, pp. 272–293. New York: Columbia University Press.

Testa, M. F. (2002). Subsidized guardianship: Testing an idea whose time has finally come. Social Work Research, 26, 145–157.

Testa, M. F., & Rolock, N. (1999). Professional foster care: A future worth pursuing? Child Welfare, 78, 108–124.

Testa, M. F., & Shook Slack, K. (2002). The gift of kinship foster care. Children and Youth Services Review, 24, 79–108.

Thornton, J. L. (1991). Permanency planning for children in kinship foster homes. Child Welfare, 70, 593–601.

Titmuss, R., Oakley, A., & Ashton, J. (1997). The gift relationship: From human blood to social policy, expanded ed. New York: New Press.

U.S. Census Bureau. (2003). Table C4: Children with grandparents by presence of parents, gender, race and Hispanic origin for selected characteristics: March 2002. Retrieved July 22, 2003, from www.census.gov/population/socdemo/hh-fam/cps2002.

U.S. Department of Heath and Human Services. (2001). On their own terms: Supporting kinship care outside of TANF and foster care. Washington, DC: U.S. Department of Health and Human Services.

U.S. General Accounting Office. (1999). Foster care: Kinship care quality and permanency issues. GAO/HEHS-99-32. Washington, DC: U.S. General Accounting Office.

Usher, C. L., Randolph, K. A., & Gogan, H. C. (1999). Placement patterns in foster care. Social Service Review, 73, 22–36.

Wells, K., & Guo, S. (1999). Reunification and reentry of foster children. Children and Youth Services Review, 21, 273–294.

Welty, C., Geiger, M., & Magruder, J. (1997). Sibling groups in foster care: Placement barriers and proposed solutions. Sacramento: California Department of Social Services.

Wilcox, R., Smith, D., Moore, J., Hewitt, A., Allan, G., et al. (1991). Family decision making, family group conferences: Practitioners' view. Auckland, New Zealand: Practitioners' Publishing.

Wulczyn, F. H., & Goerge, R. M. (1992). Foster care in New York and Illinois: The challenge of rapid change. Social Service Review, 66, 278–294.

Wulczyn, F. H., Kogan, J., & Harden, B. J. (2003). Placement stability and movement trajectories. Social Service Review, 77, 212–236.

Zuravin, S., Benedict, M., & Stallings, R. (1999). The adult functioning of former kinship and nonrelative foster care children. In R. L. Hegar & M. Scannapieco (eds.), Kinship care: Policy, practice & research, pp. 208–222. New York: Oxford University Press.

REBECCA L. HEGAR

Sibling Issues in Child Welfare Practice

urprising controversies arise over the meaning of the word "sibling." Rooted in an archaic word for "kin," sibling most literally means "little kinfolk," and it originally included such relatives as cousins, as well as brothers and sisters. With its first recorded use in 1000 C.E., it is among the oldest of English words (see the Oxford English Dictionary). In contemporary usage, siblings share one or both parents by birth or adoption. However, the operational definition of siblings for research purposes has proved a challenge (Staff & Fein 1993; see also Hipple & Haflich 1993). When should researchers consider half-siblings, stepsiblings, adoptive siblings, birth siblings, or fictive siblings (children who consider themselves brothers and sisters, although not linked by birth, adoption, or marriage, as may occur in foster care or in blended cohabiting households)? Almost invariably, the siblings identified in child welfare research are either full siblings or half-siblings with the same mother. This is because child welfare agencies typically track children based on the mother's identity, unless she is not present in the home. There is a dearth of information concerning paternal siblings, unless they reside in the household of a single father.

In this chapter, I set the context for understanding siblings in child welfare by summarizing demographic trends and patterns involving siblings in the general population. I also provide a brief historical overview and consider how academic research at different times has focused on distinct aspects of sibling relationships. The chapter summarizes the research literature on several topics: aspects of sibling relationships, sibling placements and their outcomes, promising approaches and programs promoting joint placement of or contact among sibs, and tools for those working with siblings to provide assessment and interventions. The chapter concludes with case studies, discussions of value-based issues, and comments on the role of sibling placements in preserving families.

U.S. Demographic Patterns Involving Siblings

Just as research definitions of "sibling" are problematic, startlingly little is known about the population of siblings in the United States. Reports based on census data emphasize that, as a proportion of all families, the number with four or more children has fallen steadily since 1970 (Fields & Casper 2001:6). However, for children, the likelihood of living with siblings has remained constant in recent years. According to census data, 20% of U.S. children under age 18 have no coresident siblings, 39% live with one sibling, 25% live with two sibs, and 15% reside with three or more (Fields 2003:19). These proportions are within 1%, for each category, of those reported almost 10 years previously (Saluter 1996:36). Because of the Census Bureau's focus on households, it is much harder to estimate how many siblings children actually have, as some siblings may live with another parent or relative, reside elsewhere (e.g., in foster care, institutions, prisons), or be adults either at home or in independent households. It can be safely assumed that many children have siblings who are not counted in the census because they are not coresident minors.

Just as 80% or more of U.S. children have siblings, so do children who are served by child welfare agencies. Although conclusive national statistics are lacking because many U.S. government documents (e.g., Children's Bureau 2003) do not report on sibling groups, this may change as the Child and Family Service Reviews being conducted by the U.S. Department of Health and Human Services begin to include sibling placement issues (Christian 2002). For now, the best data come from other sources. The National Adoption Information Clearinghouse estimates that 65% to 85% of foster children come from sibling groups (Corder 1999). Academic research on siblings in the child welfare system suggest that 60% (Welty, Geiger, & Magruder 1997) to 73% (Staff & Fein 1992) of U.S. foster children have siblings who also enter foster care. Many, if not most, of them are separated from some or all of their siblings in care (Drapeau, Simard, Beaudry, & Charbonneau 2000; Kosonen 1996; Maclean 1991; Shlonsky, Webster, & Needell 2003; Staff & Fein 1992; Welty, Geiger, & Magruder 1997).

Societal Context of Siblings: The Role of Research

For many decades, very little professional or academic research was directed to any aspect of siblingship. The effect of birth order on personality development was one of the first issues to attract the attention of researchers (see Toman 1976). When relationships among siblings began to attract professional attention, the issue of rivalry became paramount (e.g., Sewall 1930). By the 1960s, adult researchers were beginning to notice that families had children whose relationships were interesting (e.g., Cummings & Schneider 1961). Irish (1964) explored some of the reasons this realization may have taken so long, such as the dominance of theories of personality rooted in the parent-child relationship. However, Perlman noted crit-

ically in 1967 that the word "sibling" still seldom appeared in the professional literature without being paired with "rivalry" (Perlman 1967).

By the 1970s, theory and research concerning siblings began to mature. Major works about the nature and range of sibling relationships appeared over the course of a decade (e.g., Bank & Kahn 1982; Lamb & Sutton-Smith 1982; Sutton-Smith & Rosenberg 1970). Much of the additional scholarship during and after this period has fallen into the following categories (see Hegar 1988b):

1. Adult sibling relationships (e.g., Campbell, Connidis, & Davies 1999; Cicirelli 1977, 1980; Cicirelli, Coward, & Dwyer 1992; Moser, Paternite, & Dixon 1996; Schulman 1999; White & Reidmann 1992);
2. Rivalry, conflict, and violence (e.g., Garcia, Shaw, Winslow, & Yaggi 2000; McGuire, Manke, Eftikhari, & Dunn 2000; Pfouts 1976; Rinaldi & Howe 1998);
3. Sex between siblings (e.g., Adler & Schutz 1995; Ascherman & Safier 1990; De Giorgio-Miller 1998; Finkelhor 1980; Santiago 1973; Worling 1995);
4. Other relationship issues of juvenile siblings (e.g., Brody, Stoneman, Smith, & Gibson 1999; Epkins & Dedmon 1999; McGuire, McHale, & Updegraff 1996; Updegraff & Obeidallah 1999; Volling, Youngblade, & Belsky 1997);
5. Siblings in therapy (e.g., Gustafsson, Engquist, & Karlsson 1995; Hunter 1993; Lewis 1986, 1991; Ranieri & Pratt 1978);
6. Siblings from stressed and disempowered families, similar in some ways to many of those served by child welfare agencies (e.g., Caya & Liem 1998; Jean-Gilles & Crittenden 1990; Lewis 1991; Minuchin, Montalvo, Guerney, Rosman, & Schumer 1967; Widmer & Weiss 2000); and
7. Sibling loss through death (e.g., Hogan & Balk 1990; Hurd 1999; Robinson & Mahon 1997; Worden, Davies, & Mccown 1999).

Running parallel to professional attention to siblings in general has been increasing attention to siblings in families in which child abuse or neglect occurs. One emphasis has been on siblings as perpetrators of violence or abuse (e.g., Green 1984; Johnston, Grossmen, Connell, & Koepsell 2000; Reid & Donovan 1990; Tooley 1977; Whipple & Finton 1995; Wiehe 1990). Another focus has been on the perceptions of sibling placements by caseworkers (Hegar 1986; Smith 1996), foster mothers (Smith 1996), and foster children (Hindle 2000), as well as on assessing and maintaining the sibling relationships of foster children (Grigsby 1994; Whelan 2003). I consider the issue of assessment of the sibling relationship later in this chapter.

The balance of this review of the research concerns the growing attention given to questions surrounding placement of siblings. There has been a long-standing interest within the child welfare field in siblings who enter foster care (e.g., Berg 1957; Hurvitz 1950; Maas & Engler 1959; Theis & Goodrich 1921). However, most of the early attention to siblings in child welfare was limited to noting the problems associated with finding joint placements and to conveying practice wisdom concerning separation of siblings in foster care.

The first wave of research addressing sibling placement arose in Britain between 1940 and the mid-1960s (Heinicke & Westheimer 1965; Isaacs 1941; Parker 1966; Trasler 1960). These studies concerned populations of children quite different from those in foster care today—for example, children evacuated during the blitz bombings of World War II (Isaacs 1941) and children placed in short-term residential nurseries (Heinicke & Westheimer 1965). It was not until after 1970 that some foster care research in the United States addressed the issue of siblings in child placement (Aldridge & Cautley 1976; Zimmerman 1982). The findings of these and later studies are discussed in the next section.

Outcomes, Risks, and Benefits Related to Sibling Placement

In recent years, there has been a significant increase in the number of studies that have examined sibling placement in parts of the world featuring rather different placement systems and foster care or adoption populations. Sites of recent studies include Canada (Drapeau, Simard, Beaudry, & Charbonneau 2000; Thorpe & Swart 1992); England (Maclean 1991; Rushon, Dance, Quinton, & Mayes 2001; Wedge & Mantle 1991); the Netherlands (Boer & Spierling 1991; Boer, Versluis-den Bierman, & Verhulst 1994; Boer, Westenberg, & van Ooyen-Houben 1995); Scotland (Kosonen 1996), and the United States (Brodzinsky & Brodzinsky 1992; Shlonsky, Webster, & Needell 2003; Smith 1998; Staff & Fein 1992; Welty, Geiger, & Magruder 1997). I have reviewed these and other studies in detail elsewhere (Hegar, in press). As was the case during the earlier period of foster care research discussed above, few recent studies address the ultimate questions of outcome of sibling placements.

Studies that do examine how sibling placements turn out tend to compare placements of siblings with those of other children, using as outcome variables either rates of placement disruption or measures of emotional and behavioral adjustment. Although some studies compare children placed with siblings with those separated from siblings (e.g., Aldridge & Cautley 1976; Drapeau, Simard, Beaudry, & Charbonneau 2000; Thorpe & Swart 1992; Smith 1998), other studies compare sibling placements with those of children placed singly, whether or not the latter come from sibling groups (Barth, Berry, Yoshikami, Goodfield, & Carson 1988; Boer, Versluis-den Bierman, & Verhulst 1994; Boer, Westenberg, & van Ooyen-Houben 1995; Holloway 1997; Rosenthal, Schmidt, & Conner 1988). As discussed earlier, they also define siblings and joint placement in various ways.

Considering all of their differences in settings and research methods, it is interesting that studies consistently have found that disruption rates in sibling placements are either lower than (Drapeau, Simard, Beaudry, & Charbonneau 2000; Rosenthal, Schmidt, & Conner 1988; Staff & Fein 1992; Trasler 1960) or not significantly different from nonsibling placements (Boer, Versluis-den Bierman, & Verhulst 1994; Holloway 1997; Parker 1966; Wedge & Mantle 1991). When disruption does occur, it has been found to be unrelated to sibling issues (Boer & Spiering 1991). One recent study that did not focus specifically on sibling placement does report more placement changes in the case of siblings placed together (Wulcyn, Kogan, & Harden 2003).

Of the studies that assess children's behavior or emotional adjustment, several report better outcomes in sibling placements (Boer, Versluis-den Bierman, & Verhulst 1994; Heinicke & Westheimer 1965; Isaacs 1941; Rushon, Dance, Quinton, & Mayes 2001; Smith 1998), whereas another found no significant differences (Brodzinsky & Brodzinsky 1992). One study has noted more behavior and school problems for siblings placed together (Thorpe & Swart 1992).

Sibling Placement Programs and Promising Approaches

Legal Mandates Concerning Siblings

Among the earlier advocates of sibling rights in child placement situations was a social worker writing in the legal literature. Reddick (1974) argued that siblings have a right of association that should influence judges reviewing child placement decisions. Hegar (1988a) later reasoned that the legal profession and the helping professions approach sibling placement using different paradigms for decisionmaking. Whereas lawyers approach the question from what Rappaport (1981) calls a "rights paradigm," social workers are more inclined to apply a "needs paradigm." Reddick's (1974) argument about a right of association is based on the

former; an example of the latter might be an agency policy mandating that the relationships among members of sibling groups be considered in making placement decisions. These concepts are discussed more fully later, in the context of value conflicts surrounding services to siblings.

State legislatures have been moving steadily to address the issue of siblings in the child welfare system, particularly of those in foster care. A majority of states now gives some statutory attention to placement decisions affecting siblings, although their approaches vary widely (Christian 2002). A number of state laws now express a preference for joint sibling placements whenever possible (Christian 2002). In England, there is also a statutory preference for shared placements.

U.S. courts have also addressed the issue of sibling placement in two contexts: class action suits against state child welfare agencies and cases of individual children separated from siblings. The history of class actions in child welfare and the vulnerability of agencies to such suits are well known (Stein 1987). Several of the prominent class actions of the past 20 years have included claims about unnecessary separation of siblings or poor service to sibling groups (e.g., *Aristotle P. vs. Johnson* [Illinois]; *Del A. vs. Edwin Edwards* [Louisiana]). At least one suit, which like several others was settled by consent, concerned issues of sibling placement exclusively (*Jesse E. vs. New York City Department of Social Services*). Although class actions settled by consent decrees have generally required states to do more to safeguard and promote the ties of siblings in foster care, the most prominent case to date concerning an individual child, *Adoption of Hugo* (Massachusetts), ruled that there is no constitutional basis for sibling rights in child placement cases (Dillard 1999, 2002; Glaberson 1998). This case subsequently was appealed to the U.S. Supreme Court but not accepted for review, so there has been no national resolution of the question of sibling rights.

Social Services Initiatives Concerning Siblings

In 2002, Casey Family Agency convened and sponsored a symposium on siblings in out-of-home care that included presentations about innovative programs designed to serve siblings involved in the child welfare system (Casey Family Programs 2002). An example is the Camp To Belong program founded by Lynn Price in Colorado. Her program allows children separated in foster care or adoption to reunite at a summer camp for sibling groups only (Corder 1999; Price 2002).

There are also foster care programs, many still in the early stages of implementation, designed to keep more siblings in shared placement. In Washington, the Sibling House Foundation offers settings in which siblings can remain together, and in New York City, where the settlement of the *Jesse E. v. New York City Department of Social Services* lawsuit required a new approach to sibling placement, foster parents who accept sibling groups also receive supplemental payments and services (Corder 1999).

Neighbor-to-Neighbor is a specialized foster care program, begun in Chicago by Hull House Association, that provides salaries and extra training to a professionalized cadre of foster parents who accept sibling groups (Corder 1999). This model has been expanded and copied in other communities. One example is Neighbor to Family in Florida, which served 42 sibling groups with 143 children between 1998 and 2002 with very high reported rates of joint sibling placement (100%) and placement stability (82%) (Neighbor to Family 2002). A similar program in Massachusetts, Sib-Links, stands out because case management is provided by the public child welfare agency rather than by a contracted nonprofit group. Sib-Links began placing sibling groups in 2001 (Alvarado 2002).

As with most innovative programs that are relatively new, there is a dearth of published research on the outcomes of most programs described in this section. However, it is clear that the needs of sibling groups in foster care have moved out of obscurity and are attracting the attention of legislators, judges, community advocates, and public and private child welfare agencies.

Assessment Tools

One result of the legal impetus to place siblings together (or facilitate their relationships with one another if they are separated) has been the need for independent evaluations of children and their relationships with siblings. For example, when there is a statutory preference for placing siblings together, courts may require expert testimony to support any recommendation of separate placements. Experts, in turn, require assessment skills and tools to help evaluate sibling relationships.

Many of the standard assessment procedures used in child welfare practice can be used in placement evaluations of siblings. These include observations of interactions among siblings; children's drawings of their families, made with instructions to include whomever they wish; discussions and revelations made by children when they show the evaluator their "life books" or photo albums; nondirective play therapy assessment using doll families and other materials; and direct statements and preferences expressed by the children. Recently, Whelan (2003) has advocated using attachment theory as the basis for assessing whether siblings should be placed together, and he includes case studies illustrating this approach.

There also are standardized assessment instruments designed to gauge the nature of individual sibling relationships, although these are relatively few and recently developed. As is usually the case with new measurement tools, additional research will have to establish their validity, and extensive use may be necessary before they are widely accepted. One is the Sibling Relationship Inventory (SRI) developed by Stocker and McHale (1992), which is designed to measure the dimensions of affection, hostility, and rivalry. Published studies have used the SRI with children between the ages of 5 and 13

(Dunn, Slomkowski, & Beardsall 1994; Stocker & McHale 1992), and one has tested its internal consistency and test-retest reliability, with satisfactory results (Boer, Westenberg, McHale, Updegraff, & Stocker 1997).

Another, newer, instrument is the Social Interactions Between Siblings (SIBS) Interview, first presented by Slomkowski, Wasserman, and Schaffer (1997). Although there are at least three other instruments for use with siblings, Boer, Westenberg, McHale, Updegraff, and Stocker (1997) note that they have been used primarily with adolescents and young adults, and it is not clear that they would be useful in child placement decisions. They are the Sibling Inventory of Differential Experiences (Daniels & Plomin 1985), the Sibling Relationship Questionnaire (Furman & Buhrmester 1985), and the Sibling Inventory of Behavior (Hetherington & Clingempeel 1992).

Value Conflict in Sibling Services: Rights vs. Needs

As with kinship foster care, the issue of how best to serve siblings in child welfare is closely linked to the meaning and value of family ties (see also the chapter by Hegar and Scannapieco). Although parent-child ties have a high degree of legal protection and grandparent-child relationships have come to be recognized in some circumstances, sibling ties are only beginning to be acknowledged in law. Some of that recognition comes in the form of recent state statutes that take various approaches to siblings entering foster care and adoptive placements. As already noted, the majority of states now addresses the issue of siblings in state custody, and a number of these statutes take the form of a general preference for sibling contact and/or placement (e.g., Connecticut, Nevada, Texas) (Christian 2002). When state statutes become more specific, they highlight the distinction that Rappaport (1981) makes between the rights paradigm and the needs paradigm, which forms the basis of the value conflict discussed here.

In the context of social advocacy, the distinction between rights and needs sometimes becomes blurred. Discussion of the needs of some groups can slide into an assertion of rights, almost unnoted. However, many rights are claims that can be legally enforced. Needs, however, may be general human requirements for life or happiness or specific individual necessities, but they are not legally protected or guaranteed. Of course, individual needs do enter into judicial deliberations of what is in a child's best interests. In their recent statutory approaches to sibling placements, states have tended to fall along a continuum from a rights orientation, giving children in foster care enforceable rights with regard to their brothers and sisters, to a needs orientation, mandating that state agencies consider sibling relationships in making placement decisions.

Toward the end of the continuum that emphasizes rights in addition to needs, California allows anyone, including children, to assert the sibling relationship in court as a possible basis for various orders, including as a basis for denying termination of parental rights if that action would interfere with a sibling relationship that outweighs the potential benefits of adoption (Christian 2002). Maryland and Massachusetts also allow children in foster care or adoption to petition for sibling visitation. The Arizona statute uses the language of rights with respect to children in foster care maintaining contact with significant others, including siblings, and with respect to court orders that address visitation in permanent guardianship cases. In both California and Louisiana, there are provisions for courts to order postadoption contact between siblings, which place unusual limitations on parents' rights to make all decisions about contact with their children.

Although states that are beginning to confer sibling rights also incorporate the language of best interests into their statutes as the standard for judicial decisionmaking, other states avoid the language of rights by addressing only how the sibling relationship may serve individual children. For example, Mississippi, Missouri, New Mexico, and South Carolina, among others, list the sibling relationship as one of the factors to be considered in making child welfare placement decisions (Christian 2002). Presumably, an assessment that showed a relatively insignificant sibling relationship would allow a child placement agency and juvenile court to disregard the sibling tie in placement decisions, something that would be more difficult in states that lean heavily toward the rights paradigm.

Sibling Placement Case Examples

THREE SIBLINGS WITH A HISTORY OF SEXUAL ABUSE

Two sisters (aged 13 and 6) and their brother (aged 8) have been in agency custody for 3 years. They were removed for sexual abuse, for which both parents were tried and sentenced. The oldest child disclosed the sexual abuse when it began to affect her younger siblings. The parents remain incarcerated and parental rights have been terminated. For 2 years, the children were placed together in the Ayres foster home with a couple in their 50s who have several adult children no longer living at home. This placement worked well, but the Ayres family felt too old to adopt. Plans were made for all three children to be moved to the Barnes foster/adoption home, with the goal of adoption. The children were moved one at a time, beginning with the youngest, over a period of several months. About 2 months after the placement of the 13-year-old girl, the Barnes family requested her removal. At this point, the child welfare agency arranged for an outside evaluation and requested placement recommendations concerning all three children.

The 13-year-old had been the most seriously abused of the children, and she was in special education as a slow learner. The Barnes family's complaint was that she set a poor example and usurped some of the parental role with her siblings. The family had other adopted children, each younger than 10. The 13-year-old had returned to the Ayres foster family, who then said they wished to adopt her and her siblings. They believed strongly that the children should not be split up. The 13-year-old favored this plan. The Barnes family wanted to adopt the younger sister and brother. Those two expressed a wish to stay with the Barnes family. The two families lived about an hour's drive from one another, had little in common, and were angry with one another about decisions affecting the children. The Barnes family would not allow the 13-year-old to call her siblings or visit in their home. The agency had been arranging and supervising visits, among the children only, in public places like parks and bowling alleys. The children and both families were of the same race and general religious background.

After a placement evaluation involving record reviews and staff interviews, interviews with the three children, observations of their interactions, and the review of such assessment tools as family drawings by each child, the placement consultant recommended placement of the three siblings with the Ayres family. At follow-up 2 years later, the children had been adopted and remained together in the Ayres family. The boy had displayed some sexualized aggression and needed to be supervised closely. The adoptive parents continued to be committed to raising the three children.

THREE SIBLINGS SEPARATED BETWEEN TWO HOMES

In a rural part of the country where few African Americans live, three black children came into care due to parental neglect. Their mother subsequently surrendered custody and the rights of their father were terminated. At the time (before the passage of the Multiethnic Placement Act amendments that prohibit consideration of race in child placement decisions), the agency had only two black foster homes, and both were too full to accept a sibling group of three. Therefore, the two girls (aged 5 and 7) were placed in one of the homes (the Austin family), while their younger brother (aged 2) was placed in a home with white parents (the Booth family) who also had two young adopted children. The Booth family, therefore, included three preschool children. The separated siblings had regular visits, almost always in the home of the Austin family. Meanwhile, the Austins had room in their home and asked to adopt the whole sibling group of three. They had two biological children, one in college and one in middle school. They also provided respite care for a cousin of the three siblings who is in residential care, and their life within the small African American community brought them into regular contact (at church) with the children's biological grandmother.

The placement evaluation included record reviews and staff interviews, interviews with the three children and observations of their interactions, family drawings by the school-aged children, and nondirective play with doll families (both black and white dolls). The placement consultant recommended placement of the three siblings with the Austin family, where they were subsequently adopted.

A third sibling case appears as the first case discussed in the chapter concerning kinship foster care by Hegar and Scannapieco. It illustrates a situation in which separate placements might be recommended for siblings.

Conclusion

Although permanent shared placement of siblings is rarely discussed in the context of family preservation, it should be. Child welfare agencies are ultimately powerless to bring about changes in the behavior and functioning of parents and other adults that might lead to family reunification, guardianship, or adoption within the extended family. Agencies do have legal authority, in the form of temporary or permanent child custody, over the children in their care. Most often, these children belong to sibling groups over which an agency has significant decisionmaking control. Unfortunately, the sibling group is sometimes the only part of a foster child's family that a child welfare agency has a chance of preserving.

One rationale for preserving the sibling subsystem whenever possible is that children have an interest in their future relationships. If siblings are not enabled to have a relationship in childhood, they will have difficulty acting as brothers and sisters in adulthood. There is both evidence from social science research and reasoning in the legal literature to support the significance of sibling relationships that stretch into the future.

Research studies over several decades have documented the significance of siblings in the lives of young adults (e.g., Cicirelli 1980; Moser, Paternite, & Dixon 1996; Shortt & Gottman 1997), those in mid-life (e.g., Bedford 1998; Miner & Uhlenberg 1997; White & Reidmann 1992), and the elderly (e.g., Campbell, Connidis, & Davies 1999; Cicirelli 1977; Cicirelli, Coward, & Dwyer 1992; Connidis & Campbell 1995; Schulman 1999). Recently, legal scholars have repeatedly raised the issue of siblings' rights to associate, including the right to a future that includes sibling relationships (e.g., Elstein 1999; Jones 1993; Markel 1997; Patton 2001; Patton & Latz 1994). Unless child welfare agencies are able to help preserve sibling relationships, foster children and those who are adopted will lose parts of their family and pieces of their future. Efforts are needed at all stages of child welfare intervention to gather information about siblings, obtain and preserve their names and contact information, bring the sibling relationship to the attention of attorneys and judges, recruit and train foster parents so that more placements for siblings will be available, make thoughtful permanent placement decisions that consider the sibling relationships of children, and enable children to have relationships with brothers and sisters from whom they are separated. To do less is to fail in an important aspect of family preservation.

References

Adler, N. A., & Schutz, J. (1995). Sibling incest offenders. *Child Abuse and Neglect, 19,* 811–819.

Aldridge, M. J., & Cautley, P. (1976). Placing siblings in the same foster home. *Child Welfare, 55,* 85–93.

Alvarado, M. (2002). Practice: The Sib-Links program. In *Proceedings of the National Leadership Symposium on Siblings in Out-of-Home Care,* pp. 34–36. Washington, DC: Casey Family Programs National Center for Resource Family Support.

Ascherman, L. I., & Safier, R. J. (1990). Sibling incest: A consequence of individual and family dysfunction. *Bulletin of the Menninger Clinic, 54,* 311–322.

Bank, S. P., & Kahn, M. D. (1982). *The sibling bond.* New York: Basic Books.

Barth, R. P., Berry, M., Yoshikami, R., Goodfield, R. K., & Carson, M. L. (1988). Predicting adoption disruption. *Social Work, 33,* 227–233.

Bedford, V. H. (1998). Sibling relationship troubles and well-being in middle and old age. *Family Relations, 47,* 369–376.

Berg, R. B. (1957). Separating siblings in placement. *Child Welfare, 36,* 14–20.

Boer, F., & Spiering, S. M. (1991). Siblings in foster care: Success and failure. *Child Psychiatry and Human Development, 21*(4), 291–300.

Boer, F., Versluis-den Bierman, H., & Verhulst, F. C. (1994). International adoption of children with siblings: Behavioral outcomes. *American Journal of Orthopsychiatry, 64,* 252–262.

Boer, F., Westenberg, M., McHale, S. M., Updegraff, K. A., & Stocker, C. M. (1997). The factorial structure of the Sibling Relationship Inventory (SRI) in American and Dutch samples. *Journal of Social and Personal Relationships, 14,* 851–859.

Boer, F., Westenberg, P. M., & van Ooyen-Houben, M. (1995). How do sibling placements differ from placements of individual children? *Child and Youth Care Forum, 24,* 261–268.

Brody, G. H., Stoneman, Z., Smith, T., & Gibson, N. M. (1999). Sibling relationships in rural African American families. *Journal of Marriage and the Family, 61,* 1046–1057.

Brodzinsky, D. M., & Brodzinsky, A. B. (1992). The impact of family structure on the adjustment of adopted children. *Child Welfare, 71,* 69–76.

Campbell, L. D., Connidis, I. A., & Davies, L. (1999). Sibling ties in later life: A social network analysis. *Journal of Family Issues, 20,* 114–148.

Casey Family Programs. (2002). *Proceedings of the National Leadership Symposium on Siblings in Out-of-Home Care.* Washington, DC: Casey Family Programs National Center for Resource Family Support.

Caya, M. L., & Liem, J. H. (1998). The role of sibling support in high-conflict families. *American Journal of Orthopsychiatry, 68,* 327–333.

Children's Bureau. (2003). *The AFCARS Report: Preliminary FY 2001 Estimates as of March 2003.* Retrieved July 22, 2003, from www.acf.hhs.gov/program/cb.

Christian, S. (2002). Summary of legislation. In *Proceedings of the National Leadership Symposium on Siblings in Out-of-Home Care,* pp. 63–70. Washington, DC: Casey Family Programs National Center for Resource Family Support.

Cicirelli, V. G. (1977). Relationships of siblings to the elderly person's feelings and concerns. *Journal of Gerontology, 32,* 317–322.

Cicirelli, V. G. (1980). A comparison of college women's feelings toward their siblings and parents. *Journal of Marriage and the Family, 42,* 111–118.

Cicirelli, V. G., Coward, R. T., & Dwyer, J. W. (1992). Siblings as caregivers for impaired elders. *Research on Aging, 14,* 331–352.

Connidis, I. A., & Campbell, L. D. (1995). Closeness, confiding, and contact among siblings in middle and late adulthood. *Journal of Family Issues, 16,* 722–745.

Corder, C. (1999). Sibling bonds. *Children's Voice, 8*(2), 28–29.

Cummings, E., & Schneider, D. M. (1961). Sibling solidarity: A property of American kinship. *American Anthropologist, 63,* 498–507.

Daniels, D., & Plomin, R. (1985). Differential experience of siblings in the same family. *Developmental Psychology, 21,* 747–760.

De Giorgio-Miller, J. (1998). Sibling incest: Treatment of the family and the offender. *Child Welfare, 77,* 335–346.

Dillard, R. S. (1999). *Child in foster care seeks Supreme Court determination that siblings have a right to family integrity when their parents have lost custody.* Retrieved November 30, 1999, from www.adoptioninstitute.org/policy/polsib.html.

Dillard, R. S. (2002). Litigation: Advancing sibling rights? In *Proceedings of the National Leadership Symposium on Siblings in Out-of-Home Care,* pp. 71–74. Washington, DC: Casey Family Programs National Center for Resource Family Support.

Drapeau, S., Simard, M., Beaudry, M., & Charbonneau, C. (2000). Siblings in family transitions. *Family Relations, 49,* 77–85.

Dunn, J., Slomkowski, C., & Beardsall, L. (1994). Sibling relationships from the preschool period through middle childhood and early adolescence. *Developmental Psychology, 30,* 315–324.

Elstein, S. G. (1999). Making decisions about siblings in the child welfare system. *Child Law Practice, 18*(7), 97–98, 102–106.

Epkins, C. C., & Dedmon, A. M. M. (1999). An initial look at sibling reports on children's behavior. *Journal of Abnormal Child Psychology, 27,* 371–381.

Fields, J. (2003). *Current population reports: Children's living arrangements and characteristics: March*

2002. Retrieved July 21, 2003, from www.census.gov/population/socdemo/nh-fam/cps2002.

Fields, J., & Casper, L. M. (2001). America's families and living arrangements: Population characteristics, 2000. In *Current population reports*, pp. 234–252. Washington, DC: U.S. Census Bureau.

Finkelhor, D. (1980). Sex among siblings: A survey on prevalence, variety, and effects. *Archives of Sexual Behavior, 9*, 171–194.

Furman, W., & Buhrmester, D. (1985). Children's perceptions of the qualities of sibling relationships. *Child Development, 56*, 448–461.

Garcia, M. M., Shaw, D. S., Winslow, E. B., & Yaggi, K. E. (2000). Destructive sibling conflict and the development of conduct problems in young boys. *Developmental Psychology, 36*, 44–53.

Glaberson, W. (1998). Case tries to win siblings a right to be together. *New York Times*, (December 29), pp. A1, A12.

Green, A. (1984). Child abuse by siblings. *Child Abuse and Neglect, 8*, 311–317.

Grigsby, R. K. (1994). Maintaining attachment relationships among children in foster care. *Families in Society, 75*, 269–276.

Gustafsson, P. A., Engquist, M. L., & Karlsson, B. (1995). Siblings in family therapy. *Journal of Family Therapy, 17*, 317–327.

Hegar, R. L. (1986). Siblings in foster care: A descriptive and attitudinal study. Doctoral dissertation, Tulane University School of Social Work, New Orleans, LA.

Hegar, R. L. (1988a). Legal and social work approaches to sibling separation in foster care. *Child Welfare, 67*, 131–151.

Hegar, R. L. (1988b). Sibling relationships and separations: Implications for child placement. *Social Service Review, 62*, 446–467.

Hegar, R. L. (In press). Sibling placement in foster care and adoption: An overview of international research. *Children and Youth Services Review*.

Heinicke, C. M., & Westheimer, I. J. (1965). *Brief separations*. New York: International University Press.

Hetherington, E. M., & Clingempeel, W. G. (1992). Coping with marital transitions: A family perspective. Serial number 227. *Monographs of the Society for Research in Child Development, 57*(2–3), 118–131.

Hindle, D. (2000). Assessing children's perspectives on sibling placements in foster and adoptive homes. *Clinical Child Psychology and Psychiatry, 5*, 613–625.

Hipple, L., & Haflich, B. (1993). Adoption's forgotten clients: Birth siblings. *Child and Adolescent Social Work Journal, 10*, 53–65.

Hogan, N. S., & Balk, D. E. (1990). Adolescent reactions to sibling death: Perceptions of mothers, fathers, and teenagers. *Nursing Research, 39*(2), 103–107.

Holloway, J. S. (1997). Outcomes in placements for adoption or long-term fostering. *Archives of Disease in Childhood, 76*(3), 227–230.

Hunter, L. B. (1993). Sibling play therapy with homeless children: An opportunity in the crisis. *Child Welfare, 72*, 65–75.

Hurd, R. C. (1999). Adults view their childhood bereavement experiences. *Death Studies, 23*, 17–41.

Hurvitz, V. (1950). Factors that make for separation of siblings in foster home care. *Jewish Social Service Quarterly, 26*, 503–510.

Irish, D. P. (1964). Sibling interaction: A neglected aspect in family life research. *Social Forces, 42*, 279–288.

Isaacs, S. (ed.). (1941). *The Cambridge evacuation survey: A wartime study in social welfare and education*. London: Methuen.

Jean-Gilles, M., & Crittenden, P. M. (1990). Maltreating families: A look at siblings. *Family Relations, 39*, 323–341.

Johnston, B. D., Grossmen, D. C., Connell, F. A., & Koepsell, T. D. (2000). *Pediatrics, 105*, 562–568.

Jones, B. A. (1993). Do siblings possess constitutional rights? *Cornell Law Review, 78*, 1187–1220.

Kosonen, M. (1996). Maintaining sibling relationships: Neglected dimension in child care practice. *British Journal of Social Work, 26*, 809–822.

Lamb, M. E., & Sutton-Smith, B. (eds.). (1982). *Sibling relationships: Their nature and significance across the life span*. Hillside, NJ: Erlbaum.

Lewis, K. G. (1986). Sibling therapy with multiproblem families. *Journal of Marital and Family Therapy, 12*, 291–300.

Lewis, K. G. (1991). A three-step plan for African-American families involved with foster care: Sibling therapy, mothers' group therapy, family therapy. *Journal of Independent Social Work, 5*(3/4), 135–147.

Maas, H. S., & Engler, R. E. (1959). *Children in need of parents*. New York: Columbia University Press.

Maclean, K. (1991). Meeting the needs of sibling groups in care. *Adoption and Fostering, 15*(1), 33–37.

Markel, C. D. (1997). A quest for sibling visitation: Daniel Weber's story. *Whittier Law Review, 18*, 863–878.

McGuire, S., Manke, B., Eftikhari, A., & Dunn, J. (2000). Children's perceptions of sibling conflict during middle childhood: Issues and sibling (dis)similarity. *Social Development, 9*, 173–190.

McGuire, S., McHale, S. M., & Updegraff, K. (1996). Children's perceptions of the sibling relationship in middle childhood. *Personal Relationships, 3*, 229–239.

Miner, S., & Uhlenberg, P. (1997). Intragenerational proximity and the social role of sibling neighbors after midlife. *Family Relations, 46*, 145–153.

Minuchin, S., Montalvo, B., Guerney, B. G., Rosman, B., & Schumer, F. (1967). *Families of the slums: An exploration of their structures and treatment*. New York: Basic Books.

Moser, M. R., Paternite, C. E., & Dixon, W. E. (1996). Late adolescents' feelings toward parents and siblings.

Merrill-Palmer Quarterly Journal of Developmental Psychology, 42, 537–553.

Multiethnic Placement Act. (1994). P.L. 103-382.

Neighbor to Family. (2002). About Neighbor to Family Florida. In *Proceedings of the National Leadership Symposium on Siblings in Out-of-Home Care,* pp. 88–110. Washington, DC: Casey Family Programs National Center for Resource Family Support.

Parker, R. A. (1966). *Decisions in child care: A study of prediction in fostering.* London: George Allen & Unwin.

Patton, W. W. (2001). The status of siblings' rights: A view into the new millennium. *DePaul Law Review, 51*(1), 1–38.

Patton, W. W., & Latz, S. (1994). Severing Hansel from Gretel: An analysis of siblings' association rights. *University of Miami Law Review, 48,* 745–808.

Perlman, H. H. (1967). Note on siblings. *American Journal of Orthopsychiatry, 37,* 148–149.

Pfouts, J. H. (1976). The sibling relationship: A forgotten dimension. *Social Work, 21,* 200–203.

Price, L. (2002). Camp To Belong. In *Proceedings of the National Leadership Symposium on Siblings in Out-of-Home Care,* pp. 25–27. Washington, DC: Casey Family Programs National Center for Resource Family Support.

Ranieri, R. F., & Pratt, T. C. (1978). Sibling therapy. *Social Work, 23,* 418–419.

Rappaport, J. (1981). In praise of paradox: A social policy of empowerment over prevention. *American Journal of Community Psychology, 9*(1), 1–25.

Reddick, W. H. (1974). Sibling rights in legal decisions affecting siblings. *Juvenile Justice, 25*(4), 31–38.

Reid, W. J., & Donovan, T. (1990). Treating sibling violence. *Family Therapy, 17,* 49–59.

Rinaldi, C., & Howe, N. (1998). Siblings reports of conflict and the quality of their relationships. *Merrill-Palmer Quarterly Journal of Developmental Psychology, 44,* 404–422.

Robinson, L., & Mahon, M. M. (1997). Sibling bereavement: A concept analysis. *Death Studies, 21,* 477–499.

Rosenthal, J. A., Schmidt, D. M., & Conner, J. (1988). Predictors of special needs adoption disruption: An exploratory study. *Children and Youth Services Review, 10,* 101–117.

Rushon, A., Dance, C., Quinton, D., & Mayes, D. (2001). *Siblings in late permanent placements.* London: British Agencies for Adoption and Fostering.

Saluter, A. F. (1996). *Current population reports: Marital status and living arrangements: March 1995 (update).* Washington, DC: U.S. Census Bureau.

Santiago, L. (1973). *The children of Oedipus: Brother-sister incest in psychiatry, literature, history, and mythology.* Roslyn Heights, NY: Libra.

Schulman, G. L. (1999). Siblings revisited: Old conflicts and new opportunities in later life. *Journal of Marital and Family Therapy, 25,* 517–524.

Sewall, M. (1930). Two studies of sibling rivalry: Some causes of jealousy in young children. *Smith College Studies in Social Work, 1,* 6–22.

Shlonsky, A., Webster, D., & Needell, B. (2003). The ties that bind: A cross-sectional analysis of siblings in foster care. *Journal of Social Service Research, 29*(3), 27–52.

Shortt, J. W., & Gottman, J. M. (1997). Closeness in young-adult sibling relationships: Affective and physiological processes. *Social Development, 6*(2), 142–164.

Slomkowski, C., Wasserman, G., & Schaffer, D. (1997). A new instrument of assessing sibling relationships in antisocial youth—The Social Interaction Between Siblings (SIBS) Interview. *Journal of Child Psychology and Psychiatry and Allied Disciplines, 38,* 253–256.

Smith, M. C. (1996). An exploratory survey of foster mother and caseworker attitudes about sibling placement. *Child Welfare, 71,* 257–270.

Smith, M. C. (1998). Sibling placement in foster care: An exploration of associated concurrent preschool-aged child functioning. *Children and Youth Services Review, 20,* 389–412.

Staff, I., & Fein, E. (1992). Together or separate: A study of siblings in foster care. *Child Welfare, 71,* 257–270.

Stein, T. J. (1987). The vulnerability of child welfare agencies to class action suits. *Social Service Review, 61,* 636–654.

Stocker, C. M., & McHale, S. M. (1992). The nature and family correlates of preadolescents' perceptions of their sibling relationships. *Journal of Social and Personal Relationships, 9,* 179–195.

Sutton-Smith, B., & Rosenberg, B. G. (1970). *The Sibling.* New York: Holt, Rinehart & Winston.

Theis, S., & Goodrich, C. (1921). *The child in the foster home.* New York: New York School of Social Work.

Thorpe, M. B., & Swart, G. T. (1992). Risk and protective factors affecting children in foster care: A pilot study of the role of siblings. *Canadian Journal of Psychiatry, 37,* 616–622.

Toman, W. (1976). *Family constellation,* third ed. New York: Springer.

Tooley, K. (1977). The young child as a victim of sibling attack. *Social Casework, 58,* 25–28.

Trasler, G. (1960). *In place of parents: A study of foster care.* London: Routledge & Kegan Paul.

Updegraff, K., & Obeidallah, D. A. (1999). Young adolescents' patterns of involvement with siblings and friends. *Social Development, 8,* 52–69.

Volling, B. L., Youngblade, L. M., & Belsky, J. (1997). Young children's social relationships with siblings and friends. *American Journal of Orthopsychiarty, 67,* 102–111.

Wedge, P., & Mantle, G. (1991). *Sibling groups and social work: A study of children referred for permanent substitute family placement.* Aldershot, England: Avebury.

Welty, C., Geiger, M., & Magruder, J. (1997). *Sibling groups in foster care: Placement barriers and proposed solutions.* Sacramento: California Department of Social Services.

Whelan, D. J. (2003). Using attachment theory when placing siblings in foster care. *Child and Adolescent Social Work Journal, 20,* 21–36.

Whipple, E. E., & Finton, S. E. (1995). Psychological maltreatment by siblings: An unrecognized form of abuse. *Child and Adolescent Social Work Journal, 12,* 135–146.

White, L. K., & Reidmann, A. (1992). Ties among adult siblings. *Social Forces, 71*(1), 85–102.

Widmer, E. D., & Weiss, C. C. (2000). Do older siblings make a difference? The effects of older sibling support and older sibling adjustment on the adjustment of socially disadvantaged adolescents. *Journal of Research on Adolescence, 10,* 1–25.

Wiehe, V. R. (1990). *Sibling abuse: Hidden physical, emotional and sexual trauma.* Lexington, MA: Lexington Books.

Worden, J. W., Davies, B., & Mccown, D. (1999). Comparing parent loss with sibling loss. *Death Studies, 23,* 1–15.

Worling, J. R. (1995). Adolescent sibling-incest offenders: Differences in family and individual functioning when compared to adolescent nonsibling sex offenders. *Child Abuse and Neglect, 19,* 633–643.

Wulcyn, F., Kogan, J., & Harden B. J. (2003). Placement stability and movement trajectories. *Social Service Review, 77,* 212–236.

Zimmerman, R. B. (1982). Foster care in retrospect. *Tulane Studies in Social Welfare, 14,* 1–125.

PEG McCARTT HESS

Visits

Critical to the Well-Being and Permanency of Children and Youth in Care

requent visiting between children and youth in care and their parents consistently has been found to be associated with children's enhanced well-being while in care, the outcomes of placement (particularly family reunification), and decreased length of stay in care. However, despite the wealth of available research and other information concerning the importance of visiting as a component of placement services, many children are not provided frequent visits with their families. A close look at state policies regulating visiting practices reveal that they vary widely, often providing no or limited guidance to those who plan and implement visits. Another measure of the states' attention to family visiting of children in care is the findings from the federal Child and Family Services Reviews. The reviews found that 20 of the 50 states neither achieved substantial conformity nor demonstrated strength in the area of "Facilitating Visitation of Children in Care With Parents and Siblings" (Children's Bureau 2001, 2002, 2003–2004). Although the word "failure" is not used in the review summaries, the finding is equivalent to failure in this area for two out of five of the states.

THE STILLMAN FAMILY

Marty Stillman is a 29-year-old mixed-race mother of two children, Bobby (aged 4) and Javon (aged 2). Marty, who had lost both of her parents as a teenager, longed for a family and very much wanted to have children. After several unsuccessful relationships, Marty met Pete, who was on permanent disability for a physical injury he had sustained as a child.

She and her two children from previous relationships moved into Pete's studio apartment. Unfortunately, Marty began abusing illegal substances with Pete, and this contributed to violence in their newly formed family. At various times over their 3-year relationship, Pete physically abused Marty and both children. Hearing almost constant commotion coming from the small apartment, a neighbor called the state hotline for suspected child abuse. Upon investigation, the police arrested Pete, who acknowledged the physical abuse of the children. Citing imminent risk and safety concerns for the children, the Child Protective Services worker placed Bobby and Javon in a family foster home located within the community. The boys were placed together with Mrs. Jones, a skilled and experienced foster parent. Neither boy had ever been separated from his mother and both were deeply distressed.

The child welfare worker provided Marty with her cell phone number and suggested that she could begin visiting her children within 72 hours. After the mandated 72-hour case conference was held, Marty and the child welfare staff began to develop a plan that would enable her to be reunited with her children. Marty was highly motivated to have her children returned to her care.

During that first week, visits were supervised with a visiting coach present to work with Marty and her children. In the spirit of full and open disclosure, the role of the visiting coach was explained to Marty, who welcomed any intervention that would assist her in reunifying with her children. Marty met weekly with her children and the visiting coach in the foster parent's home. Mrs. Jones, the foster parent, was a seasoned and skilled mentor in her own right and welcomed Marty into her home and kept her abreast of all events in her children's lives. She also welcomed Marty to telephone her any evening before 11 P.M. After 2 months, Marty had moved from the studio apartment she had shared with Pete. With her social worker's help, she moved into a new apartment. She attended a day treatment program to support her decision to abstain from alcohol and substance abuse and made some very positive connections with both staff and fellow program members in that program. Marty was no longer seeing Pete. She was allowed to begin visits with her children in her apartment, with the visiting coach continuing to facilitate the visits.

Bobby and Jovan were thrilled with their new apartment, located in a building with a playground, and seemed to thrive under these new conditions. Marty continued to meet the goals in her plan, spoke by phone with the children daily, and in her words: "I am doing everything I need to do to get my kids back." The visits were increased in length and the visiting coach recommended that visits begin to be unsupervised.

At the 6-month case review, Marty and her caseworker developed a specific plan with steps to reunify her with her children. The steps included moving to overnight visits with both the visiting coach and Mrs. Jones available by phone, and then to visits of several days. Within 3 months, Bobby and Jovan were able to have a visit of 2 weeks, after which they were reunified with Marty. Marty continued to work with the child welfare caseworker in the after-care program. Mrs. Jones, who had developed a strong connection with Marty and her children, chose to continue providing support to Marty and be a part of the Stillman family system.

In this chapter, I review research findings that indicate the importance of frequent visiting and the nature of the states' current visiting policies. Guidelines to visiting practice and the obstacles to achieving optimum visit arrangements for children in care and their families are identified, and several innovative visiting programs are described.

Why Is Visiting Important?

The professional literature has long identified visiting between children in care and their families as essential to maintaining parent-child and other family attachments and to reducing the sense of abandonment that children experience at placement (Beyer 1999; Blumenthal & Weinberg 1983; Elstein 1999; Fahlberg 1979; Fanshel & Shinn 1978; Haight, Black, Workman, & Tata 2001; Haight, Kagle, & Black 2003; Hess 1981, 1982, 1987, 1999, 2003b; Hess & Proch 1988, 1993; Kuehnle & Ellis 2002; Littner 1975; Mapp 2002; McFadden 1980; Weinstein 1960; White 1982; Wright 2000). In 1959, Maas and Engler reported the findings of the first comprehensive study of children in foster care in the United States. They reported that visitation was a variable related to discharge. Since that time, a number of studies have confirmed this finding and identified additional reasons why frequent visiting is important.

First, numerous studies have found a relationship between the frequency of parent-child visiting and children's well-being while in care. Children in care who are visited frequently by their parents are more likely to have high well-being ratings and to adjust well to placement than are children less frequently or never visited (Borgman 1985; Cowan & Stout 1939; Fanshel & Shinn 1978; Weinstein 1960). Fanshel and Shinn (1978) have provided the greatest detail regarding the relationship between visiting and children's personal and social adjustment while in care. Over a 5-year period, they examined the experiences of 624 children who entered foster care in New York City in 1966. They reported that children who were visited more frequently were rated more positively on the indexes of emotional well-being and developmental progress. For example "highly (more frequently) visited children showed significantly greater gains in verbal IQ cores over the full five years of the study" (Fanshel & Shinn 1978:486). During certain periods, frequently visited children showed significantly greater gains in nonverbal IQ scores and in emotional adjustment. In addition, frequent visiting helped predict positive changes in such behaviors as agreeableness, defiance and hostility, and emotionality and tension, and overall positive assessment by the child's classroom teacher (1978:486, 487). Consistent with the findings about frequently visited children's wellbeing while in care, studies (Barth 1986, 1990; Iglehart 1994) conclude that youth who have contact with their birth parents while in foster care have better outcomes following their exit from care than do youth who do not maintain these contacts.

Studies also have found that parental visiting frequency is strongly associated with the outcomes of placement—particularly family reunification—and length of stay in care. Children who are more frequently visited are more likely to be discharged from placement (Davis, Landsverk, Newton, & Ganger 1996; Fanshel 1982; Fanshel & Shinn 1978; Lawder, Poulin, & Andrews 1985; Milner 1987; Sherman, Neuman, & Shyne 1973), to experience shorter placement time in months (Mech 1985), and to experience a successful (i.e., lasting) reunification with their families (Farmer 1996).

The benefits of parental visiting reported by Davis, Landsverk, Newton, and Ganger (1996) are particularly compelling. They report that, in a study subsample of 922 children 12 years old or younger who entered foster care in San Diego and remained in care for more than 72 hours, after up to 18 months in care, 66% of the children were reunified with their families. Just over one-third (34%) had other permanency planning outcomes. In the logistic regression model predicting family reunification, "The .10 odds ratio indicates that when the mother visited as recommended the child was approximately 10 times more likely to be reunified" (Davis, Landsverk, Newton, & Ganger 1996:375). These researchers (1996:381) conclude that "the evidence gathered by the current and other studies of the crucial importance of parental visiting speaks loudly for even stronger alloca-

tions of fiscal and professional resources to foster care practice in order to maximize the benefits inherent in parental visiting."

Thus frequent parental visiting has consistently been found not only to benefit children in care emotionally, but also to affect whether and how quickly they return home. These are significant reasons for policymakers and practitioners to give serious attention to insuring that parents are afforded every opportunity to visit with their children and that, whenever possible, obstacles to parents' visiting are addressed and eliminated. Visiting coaching, an increasingly useful practice that pairs a social worker and parent together in a visiting situation, has also been found to enhance the visiting experience for the child and parent.

Policy Regarding Visiting of Children and Youth in Care

One of the factors contributing to the frequency of scheduled visits is the agency policy for staff regarding planned visit frequency. One study (Hess 1988:315, 323) found that having in place an agency policy that specified minimum parent-child visiting frequency "resulted in the development of visiting plans that complied with the minimum standard required by the agency for visit frequency. . . . Caseworkers with neither agency policy nor norms refer to their own personal guidelines regarding visit frequency." As emphasized in the first published detailed guidelines for visiting practice (Hess & Proch 1988:11):

> Visiting does not occur at the whim of parents and caseworkers, independent of case goals and agency services. Visiting is a planned intervention, and the visiting plan is an essential component of the service plan. The visiting plan is based in part on the permanency goal for the child, and therefore should help achieve the goal and reflect progress toward it.

Two decades ago, a study of the parent-child visiting policies of all state public agencies responsible for placement services examined the extent to which state policies outlined standards and expectations regarding visit frequency and other aspects of visiting, such as visit length, location, participants, and activities. Although almost all states were found to have applicable policies, Hess and Proch (1986:13) reported that "the content of the policies varies widely, indicating there is no consensus on standards concerning any aspect of visiting and raising questions about how well the relationship between children in care and their parents is protected."

In 2002, I completed a study of state policies and procedures regarding visiting to determine the degree to which clear standards were emerging to guide the practice of agency staff responsible for planning visits and implementing family visiting plans. (See Hess 2003 for a description of study methodology and a detailed discussion of findings, including excerpts from the state policies.) Respondents completed a telephone survey and provided materials illustrative of the policies discussed. Analysis of the responses received from 37 states (74%) indicated that all had a policy in place regarding child-family visiting. The majority of these policies addressed not only visiting between children and their parents, but also visiting between siblings separated while in care. The emphasis on visiting between siblings reflected a change in policy since the policy study findings reported by Hess and Proch (1986).

Through content analysis of the policies provided by the respondents, 30 discrete categories of requirements and/or guidance relevant to visiting between children in care, their families, and others were identified. However, only seven of the 30 content areas were addressed by half or more of the responding state policies:

- Development of a written visiting plan, addressed by 78.4% of the responding states;
- Documentation of the visiting plan in the case record, addressed by 78.4%;
- Specification of who may participate in visits, addressed by 73.0%;

- Specification of how frequently visits should occur, addressed by 70.3%;
- Stipulation of agency and/or caseworker responsibilities regarding visits, addressed by 62.2%;
- Specification of the circumstances under which visits should or could be limited or terminated, addressed by 56.8%; and
- Stipulation of where visits should or may occur, addressed by 54.0%.

However, close reading of the content areas that were addressed revealed that in many state policies, the way in which an area was addressed lacked specificity. In addition, when specific guidance concerning visiting was provided, a wide variation was found in state requirements. When states provide guidance in a particular area, such as visit frequency and location, they frequently emphasize different priorities and actions. To illustrate, although 70.3% of the responding states "address" the frequency of visiting in their policies, the ways in which frequency is addressed provide very different messages to those workers responsible for planning the frequency with which visits are scheduled. Nine states recommend or require that children in care be provided with visits with family members at least weekly, yet the minimum recommended visit frequency for children in care and their families in four other states is only monthly. Assuming that caseworkers schedule visits as frequently as required, children in the first nine states would be provided four visits per month, or 48 visits per year, whereas children in the other four states would have only one visit per month, or 12 visits per year. Children in care in an additional seven states are permitted visits "regularly" or "as frequently as possible," phrases that can be and most likely are interpreted very broadly by agency staff. Given the solid research findings documenting the relationship between visit frequency and the outcomes of placement reported above, it is of particular concern that 11 (29.7%) of the responding states' policies do not address visit frequency and thus are fully silent on the critical issue of visiting frequency. These differences in state policies concerning visit frequency almost certainly affect children's well-being, family relationships, and progress toward permanence.

Therefore, although the majority of states have policies that address a core set of content areas with regard to visiting, the message sent through these policies varies radically. It is deeply troubling that the required minimum frequency of children's visits with their parents depends on the jurisdiction in which children enter custody.

In a thoughtful discussion regarding what attorneys need to know about the importance of parent-child relationships and the impact of parent-child separation, Kuehnle and Ellis (2002) highlight the differences regarding minimum frequency of children's visits when they are separated from their parents due to divorce rather than due to "dependency" (child neglect and abuse). They (2002:69) assert "In family court, attorneys and mental health professionals would be outraged if a child were kept from all contact with a parent for weeks, let alone months. In dependency court, why is this tolerated?" This observation is reminiscent of comments often heard from professionals familiar with both the prison and child welfare systems that persons who are incarcerated are typically permitted much more frequent visiting than are children in foster care.

Guidelines for Visiting Practice

Since 1980, when the Adoption Assistance and Child Welfare Act emphasized reunification as a permanency goal for children in care, greater attention has been paid to visiting as an intervention in the practice literature and training curricula for caseworkers and foster parents. As indicated above, most state policies now require that a written visiting plan for children and their families be developed and included in the child's case plan and/or case record. Al-

though state policies vary with regard to the plan's required contents, the practice literature (e.g., Beyer 1999; Hess & Proch 1988, 1993; Maluccio, Fine, & Olmstead 1986; Wright 2000) consistently emphasizes that such plans must address visit frequency, length, location, and participants; whether visits will be supervised; supportive services to facilitate visiting, such as transportation; appropriate visiting activities; and any conditions related to visits, such as the requirement that a parent must call in advance to confirm his or her intention to keep a visit appointment or must refrain from using physical discipline during visits.

Guidelines for practitioners who plan and implement family visits also address the preparation of children and others participating in visits, as well as the provision of opportunities for discussion of the visit experience following the visit. Well-planned visits are individualized. They take into account the developmental age of the child, facilitate natural interaction between parents and their children, and provide opportunities for parents to address those problems that brought the children into care. When the permanent plan is reunification, visiting arrangements should change over time to reflect the family's progress toward that goal. Specifically, as reunification approaches, visits should become more frequent, occur more often in the child's home, and be longer and less frequently supervised. To fully assess the child and family's readiness for reunification, overnight and weekend visits must safely occur. Visits with parents, siblings, and/or others may also be important for children with permanency goals other than family reunification, including emancipation and placement with relatives.

In addition to the sources for practice guidance cited previously, many states and local jurisdictions have developed extensive materials to guide caseworkers, foster parents, family members, and others in visiting planning and activities (e.g., materials developed by Allen and

Hamilton 2001, for Iowa and by Hess 1999, for Pennsylvania).

Standards for visiting practice have also been promulgated. The Child Welfare League of America's standards for family foster care services (1995:48–49, 74–75) stress the importance of children's visits with parents, siblings, kin, and friends. The Supervised Visitation Network (SVN) has also developed extensive standards and guidelines for supervised visiting policy, programs, and practice. Formed in 1992, this organization's individual members and member organizations include those providing supervised visits for children whose parents are divorced, as well as those providing services to children in placement. The SVN's goals are to provide information related to supervised visiting services; develop and maintain standards and guidelines for supervised visiting practice; and advocate for funding, staff training, and the development of new visiting programs to serve families. Practice standards and guidelines are published on the organization's Web site (Supervised Visitation Network 2004).

Obstacles to Planning and Implementing Visiting for Children in Care

As reported elsewhere in this volume (see the chapter by Cohen, Hornsby, and Priester), caseworker contact with parents of children in care is generally infrequent; services to support visits occur even less frequently. For example, a recent study (Hess 2003a) of 251 randomly selected foster children's placement experiences in one state found that, based on information found in the case records of 150 children (where visiting was applicable), only 12.7% of mothers and 5.6% of fathers were visited by their children in care at least once very 2 weeks (i.e., in accordance with agency policy) during one recent 18-month period. For other children, visit frequency ranged from once every 2 to 4 weeks (16.7% of mothers, 4.5% of fathers) to once every 1 to 2 months (13.3% of mothers, 1.1% of fathers) to less frequently than once every 2

months (13.3% of mothers, 13.5% of fathers). Three-quarters (75.3%) of the fathers and 44.0% of the mothers and their children did not visit once during the 18-month period.

Findings concerning the reasons for infrequent visiting have been examined. Fanshel (1982:67–73) reported that the frequency of visiting was lowered by a parent's low motivation (lack of relatedness to child), employment hours, and other child care responsibilities; the distance of parent's home from child's placement address; the lack of funds for transportation or child care; and a parent's physical or mental illness or mental retardation. In addition to these reasons, visits may either occur infrequently or not at all because children refuse visits or foster caregivers do not cooperate with visit arrangements. Unfortunately, visiting also does not occur because visits are not scheduled by agency staff. Caseworkers have reported that the frequency of planned visits is undermined by the lack of agency resources, "especially caseworker time to schedule and coordinate visits, supervise visits needing supervision, transport parents and children, prepare persons for visits, discuss visit reactions with parents, children, and foster parents, and record pertinent information" (Hess 1988:315).

Innovative Programs That Support Visiting

In an attempt to address these obstacles and challenges, public child welfare agencies have begun to purchase visiting services from other agencies and service providers. Consequently, over the past decade, hundreds of visiting programs have been developed throughout the country. Some thrive and grow, whereas others are discontinued, typically due to insufficient funding. (For detailed descriptions of visiting programs and their development, see Hess, Mintun, Moehlman, & Pitts 1992; Hess 2000; Pearson and Thoennes 1997.) To illustrate the diversity of visiting programs that serve children in care and their families, two such programs are described here.

Families Together

Families Together, a program of Providence Children's Museum (PCM), was created in 1992 in collaboration with the Rhode Island Department of Children, Youth, and Families (DCYF). The program provides therapeutic visits for children aged 1 to 11 and their parents throughout Rhode Island who have been separated by court order due to abuse and neglect and who are referred to the program by their DCYF caseworker. Children's museums provide a welcoming, stimulating, and safe environment for family interaction. At PCM, visits occur when the museum is open to the public; therefore, the therapists supervising visits observe parents and children in an active community setting.

Participants—children, their parent or parents, and in some cases extended family members—make a series of visits to the museum, where, under the guidance of the program's family therapists, they play and learn together. The families visit PCM for 1 hour biweekly for 3 to 6 months; some continue visiting for as long as a year. Transportation to and from PCM is provided by Families Together staff. Guided by one of the staff therapists, families engage in healthy play activities and communication necessary for successful reunification. Visiting in this environment gives parents hand-on experience and immediate feedback as they master parenting skills.

Families Together staff members work closely with family caseworkers and other team members to insure the visit strategies are an integral part of the comprehensive case plan. In many situations, PCM is the only provider that sees the entire family together for an extended period. Families Together staff members, all of whom have social service, mental health, and child development training, offer observations and clinical insight into the health of the parent-child relationship to their caseworkers, therapists, and family court judges. In addition, Families Together consultants are available on a weekly basis to caseworkers and supervisors at all regional DCYF offices to assist workers in documenting visits and developing effective visiting plans and strategies for successful visits. Consultants also meet with families and DCYF staff members, observe and participate in visits at the regional offices and in the community, and screen referrals to the Families Together visiting program.

In describing this program, Brinig and O'Donnell (1999) emphasize the collaboration at all levels between the museum and DCYF staff members. Brinig and O'Donnell (1999:2) note that "while it is unusual for museums to be involved to this extent with social service agencies, Families Together does not strike PCM's Board, staff or community as inappropriate to our mission. As most of us in the field know, some of the most important work we do in children's museums has to do with strengthening family relationships."

Family Connections Reunity House
Therapeutic Supervised Visitation Program

Located in Orange, New Jersey, Family Connections (www.familyconnectionsnj.com) offers comprehensive, therapeutic supervised visits at Reunity House. In each phase of this three-phase program, the amount of time a family spends together is increased, along with opportunities to engage in daily family living activities. The program's goal is to achieve safe, successful, and lasting family reunification for children in foster care and their families.

Visiting services are provided in a renovated Victorian house that has two visiting rooms on the first floor, a room for group sessions, and two full apartments in which 2- and 3-hour visits occur. The full apartments give families the opportunity to cook meals together and feel comfortable in a homelike setting.

Each phase of the program includes meetings with children to review feelings about visits; meetings with parents to review visits, discuss relevant parent issues, and plan for subsequent visits; and an ongoing weekly parenting skills training and support group. Phase I includes weekly 1-hour supervised visits and video-taping of an early visit. Phase II includes weekly 2-hour supervised visits, including outings in the community. Phase III includes weekly 2-hour supervised visits, a visiting outing of up to 3 hours, overnight visiting, and a videotaping of a visit during the final stages.

Further Research

Despite the consistent research findings regarding visiting described in this chapter, important questions about visiting policies, programs, and practices remain. Although Haight, Black, Workman, and Tata (2001) report interesting findings regarding parent-child interaction during visits, further systematic study of the nature of the visiting situation is needed. Additional knowledge of the factors that influence the nature of the visiting situation would assist practitioners in planning for successful visits, preparing participants for visits, and assessing parent-child visiting interactions. For example, how does the location of visits (e.g., in the office, foster family home, public community settings, child's home) affect parent-child interaction during visits, achievement of case goals, or the timing of family reunification? How do the auspices of visit services (e.g., public child welfare agency, contractual agency, community mental health agency) affect family members' cooperation with the visiting plan or the information derived from visits available for case decisionmaking?

Visit frequency in combination with other characteristics of visits also requires further study. To date, studies have focused on visit frequency, perhaps because of patterns of agency record keeping. However, a focus solely on visit frequency obscures other dramatic differences in visiting and the contribution of these differences to permanency outcomes. For example, although the planned visit frequency may be once a week, the visit may be limited to 15 minutes or extend over the weekend, may occur in the agency and be closely supervised or be unsupervised in the parent's home, and may

include a range of participants. Although the association of the variable of visit frequency with a range of other variables has produced significant information, other variations in visiting (e.g., visit length, location, supervision) in cases in which visit frequency is the same may also be influencing outcomes and not yet have been identified.

Proch and Howard (1986) detected a relationship between the recorded visiting plan and parental visiting patterns. A number of questions remain unanswered about the process of developing visiting plans and about parents' adherence to the plan. Although the practice literature (e.g., Hess & Proch 1988, 1993) provides guidance on the family- and child-specific factors to be considered in developing individualized visiting plans, questions still remain: what visit arrangements are most effective with whom (e.g., parents with different types of problems, children of different ages) and under what conditions?

Caseworkers often determine the amount of time family members spend together while a child is in care, as well as the nature of the visiting experience. Further examination of multiple agency and placement factors (e.g., foster parents' willingness to assist with visit transportation or to have visits scheduled in their home, availability of community-based visiting services, the location of children's placements in their families' neighborhoods) that support and constrain caseworkers in developing and implementing visiting arrangements would provide information essential to training, program development, and resource development and allocation.

Conclusion

Although ample information is available concerning the critical importance of family visiting to children and youth in care, many states continue to fall short in achieving visiting policies and practices that support both children's well-being in care and achievement of desired permanency outcomes. Resources to support frequent visiting, including caseworker time, are in short supply.

Visiting has been called the "heart" of family reunification (Hess & Proch 1993); yet it appears that the heart will continue to be broken unless specific national standards for minimum visit frequency and other aspects of visiting are developed and promulgated. In addition, sufficient resources for visit planning and implementation must be brought to bear to protect and strengthen the fragile family relationships of children and youth in care.

References

Adoption Assistance and Child Welfare Act. (1980). P.L. 96-272.

Allen, M., & Hamilton, N. (2001). *The visit handbook.* Des Moines: Iowa Department of Human Services.

Barth, R. (1986). Emancipation services for adolescents in foster care. *Social Work, 67,* 165–171.

Barth, R. (1990). On their own. *Child and Adolescent Social Work, 7,* 419–440.

Beyer, M. (1999). *Parent-child visits as an opportunity for change.* Prevention Report 1. Des Moines, IA: National Resource Center for Family Centered Practice.

Blumenthal, K., & Weinberg, A. (1983). Issues concerning parental visiting of children in foster care. In M. Hardin (ed.), *Foster children in the courts,* pp. 372–398. Woburn, MA: Butterworth.

Borgman, B. (1985). The influence of family visiting upon boys' behavior in a juvenile correctional institution. *Child Welfare, 64,* 629–638.

Brinig, H., & O'Donnell, J. (1999). The children's museum: An oasis for troubled families. *Hand to Hand, 13,* 1–2, 7.

Children's Bureau. (2001). *Child and Family Services Reviews: Summary of key findings.* Retrieved December 30, 2004, from www.acf.hhs.gov/programs/cb/cwrp/keyfindings2001.htm.

Children's Bureau. (2002). *Child and Family Services Reviews: Summary of key findings.* Retrieved from www.acf.hhs.gov/programs/cb/cwrp/keyfindings2002.htm.

Children's Bureau. (2003–2004). *Child and Family Services Reviews: Summary of key findings.* Retrieved from www.acf.hhs.gov/programs/cb/cwrp/keyfindings2003.htm.

Child Welfare League of America. (1995). *Child Welfare League of America standards of excellence for family foster care services,* revised ed. Washington, DC: Child Welfare League of America.

Cowan, E., & Stout, E. (1939). A comparative study of the adjustment made by foster children after complete and partial breaks in continuity of home environment. *American Journal of Orthopsychiatry, 9,* 330–338.

Davis, I., Landsverk, J., Newton, R., & Ganger, W. (1996). Parental visiting and foster care reunification. *Children and Youth Services Review, 18,* 363–382.

Elstein, S. (1999). Making decisions about siblings in the child welfare system. *ABA Child Law Practice, 18,* 115.

Fahlberg, V. (1979). *Attachment and separation.* Lansing: Michigan Department of Social Services.

Fanshel, D. (1982) *On the road to permanency.* New York: Child Welfare League of America.

Fanshel, D., & Shinn, E. (1978). *Children in foster care: A longitudinal investigation.* New York: Columbia University Press.

Farmer, E. (1996). Family reunification with high-risk children: Lessons from research. *Children and Youth Services Review, 18,* 287–305.

Haight, W., Black, J., Workman, C., and Tata, L. (2001). Parent-child interaction during foster care visits: Implications for practice. *Social Work, 46,* 325–338.

Haight, W., Kagle, J., & Black, J. (2003). Understanding and supporting parent-child relationships during foster care visits: Attachment theory and research, *Social Work, 48,* 195–207.

Hess, P. (1981). *Working with birth and foster parents.* Knoxville: University of Tennessee, School of Social Work.

Hess, P. (1982). Parent-child attachment concept: Crucial for permanency planning. *Social Casework, 63,* 46–53.

Hess, P. (1987). Parental visiting of children in foster care: Current knowledge and research agenda. *Children and Youth Services Review, 9,* 29–50.

Hess, P. (1988). Case and context: Determinants of planned visit frequency in foster family care. *Child Welfare, 67,* 311–326.

Hess, P. (ed.) (1999). *Enhancing visiting services: Standards, leadership, organization, and collaboration.* Philadelphia: Commonwealth of Pennsylvania Department of Public Welfare.

Hess, P. (2000). The history and evolution of supervised visitation. In A. Reiniger (ed.), *The professionals' handbook on providing supervised visitation,* pp. 11–30. New York: New York Society for the Prevention of Cruelty to Children.

Hess, P. (2003a). *A review of case files of foster children in Fulton and DeKalb counties, Georgia.* New York: Children's Rights.

Hess, P. (2003b). *Visiting between children in care and their families: A look at current policy.* New York: National Resource Center for Foster Care and Permanency Planning, Hunter College School of Social Work.

Hess, P., Mintun, G., Moehlman, A., & Pitts, G. (1992). The Family Connection Center: An innovative visiting program. *Child Welfare, 71,* 77–88.

Hess, P., & Proch, K. (1986). How the states regulate parent-child visiting. *Public Welfare*, (fall), 13–17, 46.

Hess, P., & Proch, K. (1988). *Family visiting of children in out-of-home care: A practical guide.* Washington, DC: Child Welfare League of America.

Hess, P., & Proch, K. (1993). Visiting: The heart of reunification. In B. Pine, R. Warsh, & A. Maluccio (eds.), *Together again: Family reunification in foster care.* pp. 119–139. Washington, DC: Child Welfare League of America.

Iglehart, A. (1994). Adolescents in foster care: Predicting readiness for independent living. *Children and Youth Services Review, 16,* 159–169.

Kuehnle, K., & Ellis, T. (2002). The importance of parent-child relationships. What attorneys need to know about the impact of separation. *Florida Bar Journal, 76,* 67–70.

Lawder, E., Poulin, J., & Andrews, R. (1985). *185 foster children five years after placement.* Philadelphia: Research Center, Children's Aid Society of Pennsylvania.

Littner, N. (1975). The importance of the natural parents to the child in placement. *Child Welfare, 54,* 175–181.

Maas, H., & Engler, H. (1959). *Children in need of parents.* New York: Columbia University Press.

Maluccio, A., Fine, E., & Olmstead, K. (1986). *Permanency planning for children: Concepts and methods.* London: Tagvistock.

Mapp, S. (2002). A framework for family visiting for children in long-term foster care. *Families in Society, 83,* 175–182.

McFadden, E. J. (1980). *Working with natural families, instructors' manual.* Ypsilanti, MI: Foster Parent Education Program.

Mech, E. (1985). Parental visiting and foster placement. *Child Welfare, 64,* 67–72.

Milner, J. (1987). An ecological perspective on duration of foster care. *Child Welfare, 66,* 113–123.

Pearson, J., & Thoennes, N. (1997). *Supervised visitation: A portrait of programs and families.* Denver, CO: Center for Policy Research.

Proch, K., & Howard, J. (1986). Parental visiting of children in foster care: A study of casework practice. *Social Work, 31,* 178–181.

Sherman, E., Neuman, R., & Shyne, A. (1973). *Children adrift in foster care.* New York: Child Welfare League of America.

Supervised Visitation Network. (2004). *Standards and guidelines for supervised visitation practice.* Retrieved August 15, 2004, from www.svnetwork.net/.

Weinstein, E. (1960). *The self-image of the foster child.* New York: Russell Sage Foundation.

White, M. (1982). Promoting parent-child visiting in foster care: Continuing involvement within a permanency planning framework. In P. Sinanoglu & A. Maluccio (eds.), *Parents of children in placement: Perspectives and programs,* pp. 461–475. New York: Child Welfare League of America and the University of Connecticut.

Wright, L. (2000). *Toolbox #1: Using visitation to support permanency.* Washington, DC: Child Welfare League of America.

LLOYD B. BULLARD
KATHERINE JOHNSON

Residential Services for Children and Youth in Out-of-Home Care

A Critical Link in the Continuum of Care

I n this chapter, we provide a comprehensive picture and a historical overview of residential services, as well as a review of the empirical findings regarding the outcomes of residential services. We also profile characteristics of children and youth in residential care, highlight case studies of children that have benefited from residential services, and outline promising practices of some model residential facilities. Finally, we address the challenges that lie ahead as residential services continue to serve increasingly acute populations of children, drawing on limited funds.

Overview of Residential Services

Residential services are an important component in the continuum of child welfare services. The primary purpose of residential care is to address the unique needs of children and youth who require more intensive services than a family setting can provide. Either on-site or through links with community programs, residential facilities provide educational, medical, psychiatric, and clinical/mental health services, as well as case management and recreation (Child Welfare League of America 2004). A variety of types of facilities, ranging from emergency shelter care to secure detention, exist, and the sizes of the facilities range from four-bed group homes to institutions with 250 or more beds. Although residential services are provided in a variety of settings, all facilities are available

and accessible on a 24-hour basis and designed to meet children's basic needs. Residential care is a child welfare service, which can be provided under the auspices of mental health, juvenile justice, education, and/or developmental disabilities.

Scope of Residential Services

Since the 1980s, the number of children entering out-of-home placement has increased dramatically, although no study has been completed to accurately calculate the number of children placed in residential care. There were 532,000 children in out-of-home care in 2002, and it is estimated that approximately 19% (99,936) of those children were in residential care (U.S. Department of Health and Human Services 2004). Most of the children in residential care are older. In 1999, only 8.7% of children placed in group homes were 12 years of age or younger. States that report high percentages of young children in either group homes or institutions attributed the trend to the placement of young children in emergency shelters for brief periods (U.S. Department of Health and Human Services 2002).

Types and Definitions of Residential Services Facilities

The Child Welfare League of America's (2004) *Standards of excellence for residential services* recognizes seven types of facility settings for providing residential services:

1. Supervised/staff apartments (also known as Supervised Independent Living Programs or SILPs);
2. Community-based group homes;
3. Residential treatment centers (RTCs);
4. Intensive residential treatment facilities (RTFs);
5. Emergency shelter care;
6. Short-term/diagnostic reception centers (DRCs); and
7. Detention and secure treatment (secure and nonsecure detention).

Within these settings, many facilities further specialize to provide targeted services to the following groups: pregnant and parenting teens; youth exhibiting sexually offending behaviors, sexually reactive behaviors, fire-setting behaviors, self-injurious behaviors, suicidal ideation, and mental health and/or substance abuse problems; children with fragile medical conditions; and children with serious cognitive limitations. The following definitions describe the residential services available within each setting, the features that are consistent among all residential settings, and the unique characteristics of each setting (Child Welfare League of America 2004):

- Supervised/staffed apartments: Small living units housing no more than four children that may be sited within larger complexes or may be independent. Apartments afford residents opportunities for increasing their independence and for using community resources, such as employment, healthcare, education, and recreation. Apartments can be fully supervised by live-in staff or by shift coverage, or they may be semisupervised, as appropriate for the ages and service plans of the residents.
- Group homes: Detached homes housing 12 or fewer children in a setting that offers the potential for the full use of community resources, including employment, healthcare, education, and recreational opportunities.

- Residential treatment: Treatment that provides a full range of therapeutic, educational, recreational, and support services by a professional, interdisciplinary team. Residential treatment facilities are located so as to afford opportunities for children to be progressively more involved in the community; however, the full range of services is available on site.
- Intensive residential treatment: Treatment that provides more intensive and frequent services and more intensive staffing patterns than offered by residential treatment. Provides staffing, structure, and environment to make possible more intensive child supervision and a higher degree of physical safety. There is a greater capacity to adapt and individualize service delivery.
- Emergency shelter care: Care that provides emergency services to meet basic needs for safety, food, shelter, clothing, education, and recreation on a short-term basis. Allows access and admission on a 24-hour basis. May admit children through self-referral without parental consent for periods as stipulated by state regulation and statute. May have services available on site or may access needed services in the community.
- Short-term/diagnostic care: Care that provides more intensive services than does emergency shelter care. Admission may be planned or emergency. Diagnostic services include a time-limited assessment/diagnostic process that evaluates each child and family's needs.
- Detention: Short-term care that provides supervision to children in the custody of or detained by a juvenile justice authority. Detention facilities may include restrictive features, such as locked doors and barred windows. At a minimum, services provided and available are equivalent to those provided by emergency shelters.
- Secure treatment: Treatment that provides residential or intensive residential treatment

in a secure facility that may include restrictive features, such as locked doors and barred windows. Although some services may be accessed in the community, the full range of services is available on site. Provides staffing, structure, and environment to make possible intensive child supervision and a high degree of physical safety to prevent self-injury, running away, or unplanned entry from outside.

RTC at Girls and Boys Town: A Model Program

The RTC at Girls and Boys Town implements a psychoeducational treatment model. It is a coordinated combination of cognitive-behavioral and educational treatment components designed to supplement and support the more traditional psychiatric and clinical modalities for children and adolescents. The RTC combines psychiatric supervision of psychotropic medication with an integrated treatment plan developed by a multidisciplinary team. The treatment incorporates individual, group, and family psychotherapy and special education.

Minimal treatment components for each youth include weekly meetings with a child psychiatrist, weekly family therapy when feasible, and daily work on academic subjects. Distinctive aspects of the RTC treatment include a contingency-based system of managing behavior and a behaviorally specified social skills curriculum that is used to develop replacement skills for previously problematic behaviors. The youth practice their prescribed social skills and self-control strategies during daily interactions initiated by direct care staff. Staff members are trained in the classroom and on the job to implement treatment and build relationships.

An outcome study of Girls and Boys Town RTC found that children showed improvement on Child Behavior Checklist (CBCL) scores between admission and discharge, and at follow-up on the anxious/depressed, attention problems, delinquent behavior, aggressive behavior, and internalizing, externalizing, and total prob-

lems subscales (Lazelere et al. 2001). Mean scores on the Children's Global Assessment scale found that children moved from "major impairment of functioning in several areas and unable to function in one area" to "variable functioning with sporadic difficulties or symptoms in several, but not all, social areas." Upon discharge, only 9% of the youth moved to a more restrictive setting, 89% were in school, and 7% had graduated from high school and were working. Furthermore, caregivers reported that 76% of youth had a better quality of life postdischarge than they were experiencing prior to their placement in residential treatment. One key to the maintenance of positive treatment gains was utilizing several kinds of outpatient treatment after discharge. Girls and Boys Town serves as a model of what well-administered residential treatment can achieve (Lazelere et al. 2001).

Childhelp USA: Caring for Young Children in the United States

Childhelp USA serves boys and girls aged 4 to 12 (Pugh et al. 1997). At Childhelp, the treatment program emphasizes structure, support, and sensitivity. With a nurturing environment, Childhelp treatment center offers a variety of psychotherapeutic programs for children, including family group, art, play, peer, animal, and individual therapy. Child-staff ratios are kept to a maximum of five children to one adult, allowing each child to receive individual attention. The structured environment consists of a behavior modification system, which emphasizes positive reinforcement through all phases of daily activities, including school behavior, peer relationships, adult interactions, hygiene, and daily chores.

The children live in cottages, which have four bedrooms with three beds in each. Each child has his or her own bed, closet, and toiletries, which gives the children a sense of security and self-worth. The children ride bicycles, skateboards, and play a variety of community sports. The treatment center has its own ranch, with horses, chickens, and cows. The animals are used as "animal therapy" to help teach children the responsibility of caring for and loving the animals. About 75% of the child attend off-grounds elementary schools and have individualized education programs. The remainder of the children stay on grounds and attend classes for the severely emotionally disturbed, with much work devoted to increasing skills to enable these children to transition to off-grounds schools.

Historical Overview of Residential Services

According to McGowan (1983), the first orphanage designed specifically for young people in the United States was the Ursuline Convent, founded in New Orleans in 1727 under the auspices of Louis XV of France. However, prior to 1800, most dependent children and youth were cared for in almshouses and/or by indenture, the most common pattern being that very young children were placed in public almshouses until the age of 8 or 9, and then they were indentured until they reached majority. Bertolino and Thompson (1999) report that during the nineteenth century, the establishment of prisons, juvenile reformatories, asylums, and orphanages proceeded at a rapid pace. The primary purpose of most of these institutions was rehabilitation; however, orphanages were developed solely to care for poor and homeless children. Institutions conducted rehabilitation through isolation, compliance, structure, and punishment, while also providing religious and moral teaching (Bertolino & Thompson 1999).

In the nineteenth century, 104 institutions designed specifically for children and youth were in operation (Tiffin 1982). During the 1820s, institutions for children and youth were developed based on the same model as adult prisons and correctional facilities for juveniles (Levine & Levine 1970). Later in the century, cottage-style care emerged, which consisted of one female houseparent responsible for supervising and caring for up to 50 children and youth at a time (McGowan 1983).

In the early twentieth century, a trend emerged that moved the field from custodial care and rehabilitation toward residential psychotherapeutic treatment programs (Bertolino & Thompson 1999). The regulation of these programs became an area of concern for many states. As a result, states developed and implemented standards for the operation of these programs. Government agencies created programs for visiting and inspecting institutions, and licensing bodies enforced the standards and increased control (Bertolino & Thompson 1999). Unfortunately, standards and thus the quality of care varied greatly from state to state. Some states developed strong standards but fell short on monitoring and enforcement. Others had poor standards but good monitoring and enforcement.

Unsatisfied with state efforts, professionals in the field concluded that higher standards were needed. As a result of their advocacy, the accreditation movement of the twentieth century was born. Returning children and youth to their homes became the overarching goal. Professionals started developing new practices for assuring accurate assessments and categorizing childhood disorders, and facilities began to use standards of psychoanalytic and learning hypotheses to care for children and youth (Stein 1995). In addition, several studies indicated the harmful effects of institutional care on young people and the need to reduce the number of institutional stays experienced by them (Child Welfare League of America 1994).

In the 1930s, many preventive programs were restructured into residential treatment facilities and new treatment facilities were established (Bertolino & Thompson 1999). The concept of a therapeutic environment was introduced. Starting in the 1960s, behavior modification was introduced into residential facilities (Adler 1981). During this time, a considerable amount of information was developed and written on behavioral systems, mainly by professionals in conjunction with their facility treatment modality.

During the 1950s and 1960s, residential care became a widely accepted means of managing and treating emotionally disturbed children and youth. The deinstitutionalization movement in the juvenile justice and mental health fields fueled the expansion of residential services, which forced many facilities to extend their services to address the needs of a more diverse population. Providers expanded their program options by including assistance with family support, foster family support, counseling, individual and group therapy, family therapy, and pre-independent living and life skills. Throughout this period, the residential treatment center and the community-based group home were the two dominant forms of care (Braziel 1996). Community-based programs were less expensive than institutions and kept children and youth connected with their community while still providing them with the supervision and treatment they required (Rosen, Peterson, & Walsh 1980).

Today, residential services are provided by public, private nonprofit, and for-profit child welfare agencies. Residential facilities may be campus-based, community-based, self-contained, or secure. Facilities are located in urban, suburban, or rural areas. In these settings, children, youth, and their families are offered a variety of services, such as therapy, counseling, education, recreation, health, nutrition, daily living skills, pre-independent living skills, reunification services, aftercare, and advocacy (Braziel 1996). It is estimated that there are approximately 10,000 facilities nationwide providing residential services (Bullard & Healy 1998).

The following case story describes an example of reunification through the use of an array of intensive services.

ADAM

Adam was born to a single, 15-year-old mother. As a result, Adam's grandmother became his primary caregiver. Two weeks prior to Adam's tenth birthday, his mother got married and shortly thereafter, Adam's

mother and stepfather decided to move to another state. Both parents thought it would be best for Adam to move with them due to his grandmother's failing health. Before long, Adam's stepfather became physically abusive to both Adam and his mother. Adam had been a better than average student prior to the move, but now his grades and behavior began to deteriorate.

Adam's new teacher noticed several bruises on his arms and legs. The school immediately contacted Child Protective Services (CPS). Through an interview with Adam, the CPS worker learned that Adam's stepfather had spanked him numerous times in recent weeks. Adam's stepfather informed the worker that Adam had received multiple whippings for his poor school performance and that if Adam's poor behavior continued, the beatings would continue. Because CPS could not insure Adam's safety in the home, he was removed and placed in an emergency-diagnostic program.

Adam's caseworker requested a full assessment for Adam and his family. Adam's assessment recommended that he receive Ritalin™ for attention deficit/hyperactivity disorder, weekly individual and family therapy, and be placed in a residential treatment center. Adam's mother and stepfather were ordered to attend weekly family therapy and enroll in parenting classes. Adam's stepfather was also required to attend anger management and domestic violence groups. Because they were invested in Adam's return home, both parents agreed to comply with the recommendations.

Adam's new residential placement invited his parents to participate in the admission process and encouraged them to actively participate in Adam's treatment. Adam's parents were enthusiastic about his placement and were especially pleased that they could visit Adam freely and would be consulted regularly regarding Adam's treatment. The residential facility staff members were not interested in talking about what the parents had done wrong, but instead focused on helping them address their needs and the challenges preventing Adam from returning home.

Adam was able to achieve tremendous success both in the treatment milieu and on-grounds school. Adam found the smaller school class size less threatening and the teachers flexible. Furthermore, Adam and his parents made great strides in individual and family therapy. Adam liked having input in his treatment, service plans, and activities planning. He did well in the structured environment that allowed for some flexibility.

Within 3 months, Adam was spending every weekend at home. Both parents and Adam continued to report good visits. Within 9 months—after Adam's parents had successfully completed their required classes and sessions and Adam had successfully addressed the goals outlined in his treatment plan—he was discharged home from the program.

Prior to Adam's return home, the program arranged for aftercare services, which included scheduling a mentor to meet twice a week with Adam. Adam and his parents were extremely pleased with their accomplishments, the relationship that they established with the facility's staff, and the thoughtful aftercare plan for the family.

In the past 40 years, numerous new approaches and models for altering behavior have emerged within residential facilities; however, no consensus exists regarding which approach or model is best (Bertolino & Thompson 1999). Many models include utilizing behavior modification techniques for the purpose of inducing the desired behavior. Currently, point and level systems are one of the most popular behavior modification approaches employed by residential agencies, despite the widespread belief that point and level systems have many limitations and are not adequate tools for supplying residents with personal interactions (Armstrong 1993; Buckholdt & Gubrium 1980; Durrant 1993; Fox 1994; Goldfried & Castonguay 1993; VanderVen 1993, 1995, 1999).

In the past 20 years, psychotherapeutic milieu models of care have also continued to evolve. This development has spurred a movement away from pathology and problem-centered viewpoints (Bertolino & Thompson 1999) toward expanded competency-centered techniques, such as solution-oriented, solution-focused, narrative, reflexive, workability, and collaborative language methods therapies (Anderson 1997; Berg 1994; de Shazer 1985, 1988; Eron & Lund 1996; Freeman & Combs 1996; Furman & Ahola 1992; Hoffman 1993; Miller, Duncan, & Hubble 1997; O'Hanlon & Weiner-Davis 1989). During the past decade, this shift has encouraged the development of competency-based approaches in residential programs (Booker & Blymer 1994; Freeman, Epson, & Lopovits 1997). Durkin (1990) stated that a competency-based approach is crucial in the healthy development of children and youth, as residential care should promote normal growth and development.

Although residential services and the array of settings have changed greatly over the years, the debate over residential care vs. family foster care remains (Whittaker & Maluccio 2002). Most professionals would agree that the main purpose of residential child welfare facilities should be to address the specific needs of children and adolescents who are unable to live with their families or in family foster care, and for whom a more restrictive setting is not required. It is generally accepted that placements should be based on a full assessment of the child and his or her family's needs; however, research to date implies that optimal placement criteria are equivocal and that no definitive guidelines for placement exist (Segal & Schwarz 1985).

Characteristics of Children and Youth in Residential Group Care

Many children living in residential group care exhibit high incidences of impulsiveness, aggression, truancy, inappropriate sexual behavior, delayed social development, interpersonal and academic problems, conduct disorder, and adjustment disorder (Fitzharris 1985; Whittaker, Fine, & Grasso 1989; Wurtele, Wilson, & Prentice-Dunn 1983; Young, Dore, & Pappenfort 1988). Compared to the general population, children and youth in residential treatment centers are more impoverished, have more behavioral and academic problems, and have more deficits in social competencies (Wells & Whittington 1993).

Perhaps most challenging is the number and severity of mental health problems that youth in residential treatment present. A study using the Behavior Problems index found that children and youth residing in residential group care scored more than two standard deviations above the mean compared to those in the same age range in the general population (Zill & Peterson 1989). A study of children and youth in 15 Illinois residential treatment facilities found that 80% of the sample met the criterion for diagnosis in at least one of the five categories on the Children's Severity of Psychiatric Illness scale, and more than 50% met the criteria for emotional disturbance (Lyons, Libman-Mintzer, Kisiel, & Shallcross 1998). Wells and Whittington (1993) found that 87% of boys and 89% of girls in residential treatment scored in the clinical range on the total problem behavior scale of the CBCL. Studies using the CBCL in Nebraska, California, and the Midwest consistently reveal mean scores in the clinical range on the delinquency, aggression, withdrawn, internalizing, externalizing, and total problems scales (Brady & Caraway 2002; Handwerk, Lazelere, Soper, & Friman 1999; Shennum, Moreno, & Caywood 2002).

The mental health problems that children and youth in residential care face are often acute. A study of young people in 13 residential treatment facilities in New York found that more than one-third had at least one prior psychiatric hospitalization and had exhibited suicidal behaviors or gestures (Dale, Baker, Anastasio, & Purcell, in press). Furthermore, a study of 416 boys who entered the Children's Village RTC in New York between 1995 and 1997 found that 19.5% experienced an acute psychiatric crisis at some point during their stay (Baker & Dale 2002).

Youth in the child welfare system demonstrate greater social, emotional, academic, behavioral, and mental health problems than their peers in the general population, and children and youth in residential care are often the most challenged. Compared to those in treatment foster care, youth living in residential group care tend to be older (Berrick, Courtney, & Barth 1993; English 1993), predominantly male (English 1993), are more likely to have been sexually abused (English 1993; National Survey of Child and Adolescent Well-Being Research Team 2002) and to engage in sexually offending behaviors (A. J. L. Baker & D. Kurland, unpubl. data), and to have a history of running away (English 1993) and contact with the criminal justice system (English 1993; A. J. L. Baker & D. Kurland, unpubl. data).

Although English (1993) found that children and youth living in residential group care and treatment foster care are equally likely to have mental health, anger, and academic problems (English 1993), other professionals have found that those in residential group care have higher levels of mental health disorders (A. J. L. Baker & D. Kurland, unpubl. data). Such studies have shown that children and youth in residential treatment centers were more likely to abuse substances, have a history of suicidal ideation and psychiatric hospitalization, and be taking psychotropic and antipsychotic medications compared to their peers in foster care (A. J. L. Baker & D. Kurland, unpubl. data). These differences remained true even when controlling for demographic and background characteristics.

The evidence regarding the acuity of the behavioral and mental health problems that youth in residential treatment facilities exhibit means facilities face monumental challenges in providing care and treatment. Furthermore, historical evidence suggests that the youths' presenting problems continue to grow more severe. Over the past 10 years, the proportion of youth entering residential treatment with mental health problems and juvenile justice backgrounds has increased dramatically, such that those entering residential treatment centers in New York in 2001 were more likely to have a history of substance abuse, psychiatric hospitalization, association with the juvenile justice system, and psychotropic medication use than their peers who entered care a decade before them (Dale, Baker, Anastasio, & Purcell, in press).

Outcomes of Residential Care

Outcome studies of residential treatment vary widely in scope and suffer from an absence of control conditions, poorly defined service units, limited samples, improper selection of outcome criteria, and improper use by practitioners (Whittaker & Pfeiffer 1994). Those studies that do identify a comparison group often fail to control for the initial level of problems that the children and youth present, making causality especially difficult to determine. Such gaps in research have posed a barrier to identifying best practices in residential services. These gaps are exacerbated by the relative inattention to new models of residential provision by federal agencies and private foundations compared to other types of out-of-home placement (Whittaker & Maluccio 2002). The lack of strong research findings supporting the efficacy of residential care led the U.S. General Accounting Office (1994:4) to observe:

> Not enough is known about residential care programs to provide a clear picture of which kinds of treatment approaches work best or about the effectiveness of the treatment over [the] long term. Further, no consensus exists on which youth are best served in residential care . . . or how residential care should be combined with community-based care to serve at-risk youths over time.

Studies have yielded mixed results. Some have identified positive outcomes associated with residential treatment. Using the Global Assessment scale, a Canadian study of 40 children in a residential treatment center found that for the majority of children, functioning was severely impaired at admission, moderately impaired at discharge, and normal at 1 and 3 years postdischarge (Blackman, Eustace, & Chowdhury 1991). A study of children diagnosed with conduct disorder in residential treatment cen-

ters found that the number of concerns expressed by caregivers decreased between admission, discharge, 6 months, 1 year, and 2 years postdischarge (Day, Pal, & Goldberg 1994). Finally, a retrospective study of 200 children served at group homes in the Midwest found that, as adults, 70% had completed high school, 27% had some college or vocational training, and only 14% were receiving public assistance. Unfortunately, 42% had been arrested since their discharge (Alexander & Huberty 1993).

Family-centered residential treatment centers have shown considerable success. Landsman, Groza, Tyler, and Malone (2001) found that youth in family-centered care had shorter lengths of stay, were more likely to return home at discharge, and had better long-term stability than those in traditional residential treatment centers. Similarly, at 6-, 12-, 18-, and 24-month follow-up, 58% of youth discharged from a family-focused, community-oriented residential treatment program had been involved in no new illegal activity, had continued to participate in educational endeavors, and had not been moved to a more restrictive level of treatment. Ninety percent of the youth accomplished two of the three aforementioned outcomes (Hooper, Murphy, Devaney, & Hultman 2000).

The following case demonstrates the critical importance of family and youth involvement in determining a treatment plan.

ROXANNE

Roxanne was a 16-year-old girl who lived with her mother and her mother's boyfriend. One afternoon, Roxanne shared with her mother that the latter's boyfriend had been sexually molesting her for the past 6 months, including fondling her breasts and genitals, and forcing her to have sexual intercourse. He had threatened to hurt Roxanne if she told anyone. Roxanne's mother confronted her boyfriend and he denied everything. Roxanne's mother immediately chose to believe her boyfriend and punished Roxanne for lying. Roxanne was told not to repeat any of this to anyone.

The following day, Roxanne told a close friend that her mother's boyfriend had been sexually molesting her. Roxanne's friend told her mother, who subsequently called the police. Roxanne was given the choice of going to a foster home or group home. Roxanne decided that a group home would be her best option, because she did not want the pressure of adjusting to the rules of a new family.

Roxanne was placed in a community-based group home near her home. Roxanne's mother attempted to contact Roxanne on several occasions following her placement and tried to influence Roxanne's account of her story. After several failed attempts to coerce Roxanne into altering her story, Roxanne's mother became verbally abusive. After several weeks, Roxanne's mother stopped calling altogether.

Roxanne was given the opportunity to participate in the development of her treatment plan. Roxanne decided that because her mother was not involved in her treatment, she would work toward independent living. She also hoped to reestablish communication with her mother. Roxanne's initial adjustment to the group home was challenging, because she was not accustomed to being held accountable for her actions. Once she learned that completing her responsibilities earned her privileges, her adjustment improved.

Eventually, Roxanne's social worker was able to convince Roxanne's mother to visit her. Shortly after the first visit, Roxanne's mother agreed to participate in weekly family therapy, at which Roxanne was able to express her feelings of abandonment and distrust. Two months later, Roxanne's mother apologized to Roxanne for not believing and supporting her. Roxanne continues to speak with her mother weekly and visits her when the boyfriend is out of town.

Roxanne's relationship with staff and teachers improved after she reestablished contact with her mother. Within 6 months, Roxanne successfully addressed all of her treatment plan goals. Roxanne was discharged to an independent living program, where she was able to find a job and graduate from high school. The following fall, Roxanne left the program to attend college full time.

One of the most promising studies demonstrating the efficacy of group care with young children emerged from a 23-year longitudinal study from Israel. In this study, Weiner and Kupermintz (2001) found that 268 children initially placed as preschoolers in well-designed congregate care settings, some of whom spent long periods in care before being placed in adoptive homes, functioned "adequately or well" as young adults. The finding was contrary to the researchers' initial hypothesis and led them (2001:214) to conclude that "neither preschool institutional care, nor long-term institutional care was found to be harmful for these young people in terms of normative living. . . . In fact, the majority of those who were functioning well have significantly improved since their teenage years."

A study of 246 children at Childhelp found that aggressive behavior, covert conduct problems, attention deficit/hyperactivity disorder, self-destructive behavior, withdrawal/anxiety, toileting problems, and sexual acting out were all reduced in a significant number of children at the time of discharge. Positive attitudes toward staff and responses to discipline also improved (Pugh et al. 1997).

Other studies of residential care have shown less positive outcomes for children and youth. Hoagwood and Cunningham (1992) found that for emotionally disturbed children and youth aged 5 to 18, 63% exhibited minimal or no progress during a 3-year residential treatment program. Furthermore, only 11% demonstrated "good" progress. A study by Asarnow, Aoki, and Elson (1996) examined outcomes and service utilization over a 3-year period following discharge from a residential treatment center in a sample of 51 boys with disruptive behavior disorders. They found that once a pattern of residential treatment was initiated, high rates of continuing placement and dependency continued in the immediate and long-term postdischarge period, such that the risk of replacement was 32%, 53%, and 59% by the end of the first, second, and third postdischarge years, respectively.

It is indisputable that not all residential programs are created equal; thus the outcomes that such facilities achieve vary widely. Characteristics of residential treatment centers that have been correlated with long-term positive outcomes include high levels of family involvement, supervision and support from caring adults, a skills-focused curriculum, service coordination, development of individualized treatment plans, positive peer influences, enforcement of a strict code of discipline, a focus on building self-esteem, a family-like atmosphere, academic support, presence of community networks, a minimally stressful environment, and comprehensive discharge planning (Barth 2002; Curry 1991; Curtis, Alexander, & Lunghofer 2001; Lazelere et al. 2001; Pecora, Whittaker, Maluccio, & Barth 2000; U.S. General Accounting Office 1994; Whittaker 2000). Age, gender, intelligence, length of stay, and presenting problems are all weakly correlated to outcomes (Curry 1991; Pecora, Whittaker, Maluccio, & Barth 2000).

Other studies have found that a positive working alliance between youth and staff after 3 months in care related to positive psychological advances for youth and predicted lower rates of recidivism upon discharge (Florsheim, Shotorbani, Guest-Warnick, Barratt, & Hwang 2000). Substance abuse, difficulty talking with adults, no home visits, teasing others, and prior residential placement have been identified as indicators of unplanned discharge from residential treatment (Sunseri 2001). The same holds true for prior psychiatric hospitalization, juvenile delinquent status at admission, and exhibiting very serious emotional and behavioral problems during the first 2 months of treatment (C. S. Piotrkowski & A. J. L. Baker, unpubl. data). A study of 37 children and youth at Edgewood Children's Center in Missouri found that consistent family counseling resulted in a preponderance of positive outcomes for chil-

dren and youth at discharge, but only discharge destination was significantly related to postdischarge outcomes (Burks 1995).

Outcomes of Residential Treatment Compared to Those of Family and Therapeutic Foster Care

Most of the studies comparing children and youth in foster care to those in residential treatment fail to control for differences in their presenting problems at intake; thus, findings that treatment foster care is a more cost-effective service that produces similar or better outcomes are not altogether surprising, given the characteristics of children and youth in residential care compared to their peers in foster care.

That being said, attempts to compare longterm outcomes for children and youth in residential treatment vs. therapeutic foster care have produced mixed results. Two studies found no difference in the reduction of problem behaviors for children and youth in residential care vs. those in therapeutic foster care (Colton 1988; Rubenstein, Armentrout, Leven, & Herald 1978). A study by Chamberlain and Reed (1998) revealed that 1 year after completing either a residential treatment or a therapeutic foster care program, boys in treatment foster care were less likely to run away, had significantly fewer arrests and a greater probability of no arrests, fewer incarcerations, and were more likely to live at home or with relatives.

Other studies have used personal interviews to determine the long-term outcomes of youth in residential care vs. family foster care. Followup studies with youth who had spent more than 5 continuous years in either family foster or residential care found that those who had lived in family foster care achieved higher levels of education; had fewer arrests or convictions; had fewer substance abuse problems; were more satisfied with their level of contact with their biological siblings; were less likely to move, live alone, be single head-of-household parents, and be divorced; had more close friends and greater informal support; had higher satisfaction with their income level and were more optimistic about their economic future; and generally more positive assessments about their lives (Festinger 1983; Jones & Moses 1984).

The National Survey of Child and Adolescent Well-Being (2002) found that children and youth in group care were four times as likely as those in foster care, and 10 times as likely as those in kinship care to report that they do not like the people with whom they live. They were also more likely to report never seeing their biological mother or father. Barth (2002) found that, compared to children and youth in foster care, reentry rates of individuals in residential treatment were higher and that there were fewer aftercare services available to ease the transition home.

In an extensive review of the literature in support of a research agenda for child welfare, Meadowcroft, Tomlinson, and Chamberlain (1994) concluded that, compared to therapeutic foster care, residential care is more expensive, serves a population with similar problems, places children and youth in more restrictive settings at discharge, and produces fewer behavioral improvements. Such findings led the U.S. surgeon general to report that residential treatment has not shown substantial benefits to children and youth with mental health problems and may have adverse effects because of behavior contagion. The report concludes that for youth who manifest severe emotional or behavioral disorders, the positive evidence for home- and community-based treatments contrasts sharply with the traditional forms of institutional care, which can have deleterious consequences (U.S. Department of Health and Human Services 2000).

Although we have outlined a number of important studies regarding residential care, many questions remain. Pecora, Whittaker, Maluccio, and Barth (2000) suggest several areas that research regarding residential care should address, including subgroups that might be better served in residential settings, community tran-

sitions and maintenance of educational gains, mechanisms for family involvement, and identification of outcome indicators and program components of effective residential settings. Furthermore, it is imperative that residential programs be evaluated, preferably via standardized evaluation procedures that utilize consistent measurements, methodologies, and definitions.

Future Directions

Residential providers must emphasize identifying best practices that lead to successful outcomes. Unfortunately, the identification of best practices is hindered by the historically negative image of group care that stems from the long-established hierarchy of preferred out-of-home care arrangements for children and youth (Whittaker & Maluccio 2002). The hierarchy dictates that family foster care is to be preferred over group care when child dependency is the primary issue. The marginalized position of group care in the continuum of child welfare services has, in many ways, stifled creative interventions in the field. As Wolins (1974:126) eloquently states, "as professionals withdrew their approbation, the [full- and part-time group care] programs deteriorated, innovation ceased and cycles of prediction of bad results, and their fulfillment, spiraled programs downward."

The strict hierarchy of preferred child welfare interventions not only curbs advancement of practices in residential settings, but also forces children and youth who may be in need of intensive residential services to "fail out" of a number of family foster home placements before they are admitted to group care. The history of placement disruption that many children and youth carry into residential treatment increases the challenges that residential providers face. Furthermore, the hierarchy of services is based on the assumption that child dependency is the primary placement issue, when in reality the child welfare system is increasingly caring for children and youth with acute mental health needs that may be best served in residential settings.

Therefore residential providers and researcher also need to work on identifying placement criteria that insure that children and youth who would most benefit from residential services receive them. Current practice wisdom suggests that residential group care is most appropriate for those who need a structured program, who cannot tolerate the emotional intimacy of a therapeutic foster family, whose relationship with biological parents may disrupt foster family efforts, who cannot form age-appropriate relationships, and whose behavioral or emotional problems significantly affect daily functioning (Dore 1994). Barth (2002) suggests that residential services may be most appropriate for children who have previously run away from foster care, youth who are destructive or engage in self-destructive behaviors, and youth who are moving back to the community from more restrictive settings. These findings, however, are only loosely based on empirical evidence; thus it is critical that more research be completed to identify youth that would benefit most from residential services. Indisputably, placements must be based on the needs of the child and his or her family and the level of services required to meet those needs. The placement goal should always be based on the most appropriate and least restrictive environment for meeting the needs of the child.

Along with identifying appropriate placement criteria, funding of residential services is another critical issue facing providers today. Without creating adequate funding streams, facilities cannot provide appropriate services to insure the safety, permanency, and well-being of the youth in their care. Children and youth in residential care have more acute needs than their peers in other sectors of out-of-home care. Unfortunately, most residential care facilities across the country have not been funded at the levels required to provide the intensive services the children, youth, and families in their care require. In most states, there is no formal or consistent methodology used for establishing reimbursement rates for care. Furthermore, it is rarely acknowledged that some group care costs offset expenses that would have been incurred by communities, such as the provision of mental health and educational services. Residential care is an undeniably costly service, but one necessary to provide the best care and intervention to the most vulnerable population in the child welfare system.

A number of other critical issues face residential providers in the future. The federal government, state regulators, and licensing and accreditation bodies are increasingly emphasizing reduction and eventual elimination of the use of restraint and seclusion in facilities serving children and youth, as such interventions have been found to place children, youth, and staff members at risk of physical injury and death, as well as cause emotional and psychological harm. The importance of family involvement to children and youth in residential placements is also becoming more apparent; residential providers must find ways to better engage families in treatment. Residential settings must also begin to embrace new models of care, such as relationship-based and trauma-sensitive treatment milieus, and abandon "management and control" models that have dominated the field in the past. Workforce recruitment and retention issues, which are central to insuring that youth in residential settings are receiving quality and consistent care, continue to be a challenge in all areas of child welfare. Finally, as previously mentioned, program evaluation and empirically based continuous quality improvement need to become institutionalized components of every residential setting.

Conclusions

Residential services are an important component in the continuum of child welfare services. Upon admission, most children and youth in residential treatment exhibit challenging behaviors that require intensive intervention, and providers are often able to meet their needs to help them achieve positive outcomes. Research regarding best practices and appropriate placement criteria will continue to strengthen the field, and adequate funding will insure that youth in care receive the degree of intervention that they require.

References

Adler, J. (ed.). (1981). *Fundamentals of group care: A textbook and instructional guide for child care workers.* Cambridge, MA: Balinger Publishing.

Alexander, G., & Huberty, T. J. (1993). Caring for troubled children: The villages follow-up study. Bloomington, IN: The Villages of Indiana.

Anderson, H. (1997). *Conversation, language, and possibilities: A postmodern approach to therapy.* New York: Basic Books.

Armstrong, L. (1993). *And they called it help.* Reading, MA: Addison-Wesley.

Asarnow, J. R., Aoki, W., & Elson, S. (1996). Children in residential treatment: A follow-up study. *Journal of Clinical Child Psychology, 24,* 209–214.

Baker, A. J. L., & Dale, N. (2002). Psychiatric crises in child welfare residential treatment. *Children's Services: Social Policy, Research, and Practice, 5*(3), 213–229.

Barth, R. P. (2002). Institutions vs. foster homes: The empirical base for a century of action. Chapel Hill: University of North Carolina School of Social Work, Jordan Institute for Families.

Berg, I. K. (1994). *Family based services: A solution-focus approach.* New York: Norton.

Berrick, R., Courtney, M., & Barth, R. P. (1993). Specialized foster care and group home care: Similarities and differences in the characteristics of children in care. *Children and Youth Services Review, 15,* 453–473.

Bertolino, B., & Thompson, K. (eds.). (1999). *The residential youth care worker in action: A collaborative, competency-based approach.* New York: Haworth Mental Health Press.

Blackman, M., Eustace, J., & Chowdhury, M. A. (1991). Adolescent residential treatment: A one- to three-year follow-up. *Canadian Journal of Psychiatry, 36,* 472–479.

Booker, J., & Blymer, D. (1994). Solution-oriented brief residential treatment with "chronic mental patients." *Journal of Systemic Therapies, 13*(4), 53–69.

Brady, K. L., & Caraway, J. S. (2002). Home away from home: Factors associated with current functioning in children living in a residential treatment center. *Child Abuse and Neglect, 26,* 1149–1163.

Braziel, D. J. (ed.). (1996). *Family-focused practice in out-of-home care.* Washington, DC: CWLA Press.

Buckholdt, D. R., & Gubrium, J. F. (1980). The underlife of behavior modification. *American Journal of Orthopsychiatry, 50,* 279–290.

Bullard, L. B., & Healy, J. (1998). *National survey of public and private residential group care facilities and their capacities.* Retrieved June 30, 2004, from www.cwla.org/programs/groupcare/nationalsurvey.htm.

Burks, J. (1995). Edgewood Children's Center outcome study 1991/1992. *Residential Treatment for Children and Youth, 13*(2), 31–40.

Chamberlain, P., & Reid, J. B. (1998). Comparison of two community alternatives to incarceration for chronic juvenile offenders. *Journal of Consulting and Clinical Psychology, 66,* 624–633.

Child Welfare League of America. (1994). *Welfare reform: Facts on orphanages.* Washington, DC: CWLA Press.

Child Welfare League of America. (2004). *Standards of excellence for residential services.* Washington, DC: CWLA Press.

Colton, M. (1988). *Dimensions of substitute care.* Aldershot, England: Avebury.

Curry, J. F. (1991). Outcome research on residential treatment: Implications and suggested directions. *American Journal of Orthopsychiatry, 61,* 348–357.

Curtis, P. A., Alexander, G., & Lunghofer, L. A. (2001). A literature review comparing outcomes of residential group care and therapeutic foster care. *Child and Adolescent Social Work Journal, 18*(5), 377–392.

Dale, N., Baker, A. J. L., Anastasio, E., & Purcell, J. (in press). Characteristics of children in residential treatment in New York State. *Child Welfare.*

Day, D. M., Pal, A., & Goldberg, K. (1994). Assessing the post-residential functioning of latency-aged conduct disordered children. *Residential Treatment for Children and Youth, 11*(3), 45–61.

de Shazer, S. (1985). *Key to solution in brief therapy.* New York: Norton.

de Shazer, S. (1988). *Clues: Investigating solutions in brief therapy.* New York: Norton.

Dicker, S., Gordon, E., & Knitzer, J. (2001). *Improving the odds for the healthy development of young children in foster care.* New York: National Center for Children in Poverty.

Dore, M. M. (1994). Guidelines for placement decision-making. New York: Child Welfare Administration, Human Resources Administration of the City of New York.

Durkin, R. (1990). Competency, relevance, and empowerment: A case for restructuring childrens' programs. In J. Anglin, et al. (eds.), *Perspectives in professional child and youth care,* pp. 231–244. New York: Haworth.

Durrant, M. (1993). *Residential treatment: A cooperative, competency-based approach to therapy and program design.* New York: Norton.

English, D. (1993). *Group care/therapeutic foster care, Part III: A comparison of children currently placed in group care versus those in therapeutic foster care*. Seattle, WA: Office of Children's Administration Research, Children, Youth and Family Services, Department of Social and Health Services.

Eron, J. B., & Lund, T. W. (1996). *Narrative solutions in brief therapy*. New York: Guilford.

Festinger, T. (1983). *No one ever asked us . . . A postscript to foster care*. New York: Columbia University Press.

Fitzharris, T. L. (1985). *The foster children in California: Profiles of 10,000 children in residential care*. Sacramento: California Association of Services for Children.

Florsheim, P., Shotorbani, S., Guest-Warnick, G., Barratt, T., & Hwang, W. (2000). Role of the working alliance in the treatment of delinquent boys in community-based programs. *Journal of Clinical Child Psychology, 29*(1), 94–107.

Fox, L. E. (1994). The catastrophe of compliance. *Journal of Child and Youth Care, 9*, 13–21.

Freeman, J., & Combs, G. (1996). *Narrative therapy: The social construction of preferred realities*. New York: Norton.

Freeman, J., Epson, D., & Lopovits, D. (1997). *Playful approaches to serious problems: Narrative therapy with children and their families*. New York: Norton.

Furman, B., & Ahola, T. (1992). *Solution talk: Hosting therapeutic conversations*. New York: Norton.

Goldfried, M. R., & Castonguay, L. G. (1993). Behavior therapy: Redefining strengths and limitations. *Behavior Therapy, 24*, 505–506.

Handwerk, M., Lazelere, R. E., Soper, S. H., & Friman, P. C. (1999). Parent and child discrepancies in reporting severity of problem behaviors in three out-of-home settings. *Psychological Assessment, 11*, 14–23.

Hoagwood, K., & Cunningham, T. (1992). Outcomes of children with emotional disorders in residential treatment. *Journal of Child and Family Studies, 1*, 129–140.

Hoffman, L. (1993). *Exchanging voices: A collaborative approach to family therapy*. London: Karnac.

Hooper, S. R., Murphy, J., Devaney, A., & Hultman, T. (2000). Ecological outcomes of adolescents in a psychoeducational residential treatment facility. *American Journal of Orthopsychiatry, 70*, 419–500.

Jones, M. A., & Moses, B. (1984). *West Virginia's former foster children: Their experiences in care and their lives as young adults*. New York: CWLA Press.

Krueger, M. A. (1991). Coming from the center, being there. *Journal of Child and Youth Care, 5*(1), 77–88.

Landsman, M. J., Groza, V., Tyler, M., & Malone, K. (2001). Outcomes of family-centered residential treatment. *Child Welfare, 80*, 351–379.

Lazelere, R. E., Dinges, K., Schmidt, M. D., Spellman, D. F., Criste, T. R., & Connell, P. (2001). Outcomes of residential treatment: A study of adolescent clients of Girls and Boys Town. *Child and Youth Care Forum, 30*(3), 175–185.

Levine, M., & Levine, A. (1970). *A social history of helping services: Clinical, court, school, and community*. New York: Appleton-Century-Crofts.

Lyons, J. S., Libman-Mintzer, L. N., Kisiel, C. L., & Shallcross, H. (1998). Understanding the mental health needs of children and adolescents in residential treatment. *Professional Psychology: Research and Practice, 29*, 582–587.

McGowan, B. (1983). Historical evolution of child welfare services. In B. McGowan & W. Meezan (eds.), *Child welfare: Current dilemmas*, pp. 45–90. Itasca, IL: Peacock Publishers.

Meadowcroft, P., Tomlinson, B., & Chamberlain, P. (1994). Treatment foster care services: A research agenda for child welfare. *Child Welfare, 73*, 565–582.

Miller, S. D., Duncan, B. L., & Hubble, M. A. (1997). *Escape from Babel: Toward a unifying language for psychotherapy practice*. New York: Norton.

National Survey of Child and Adolescent Well-Being. (2002). *One year in foster care: Draft report*. Research Triangle Park and Chapel Hill: RTI International and University of North Carolina, School of Social Work.

O'Hanlon, W. H., & Weiner-Davis, M. (1989). *In search of solutions: A new direction in psychotherapy*. New York: Norton.

Pecora, P. J., Whittaker, J. K., Maluccio, A. N., & Barth, R. P. (2000). *Child welfare challenge*, second ed. Hawthorne, NY: Aldine de Gruyter.

Pugh, R. H., Tepper, F. L., Halpern-Felsher, B. L., Howe, T. R., Tomlinson-Keasey, C., & Parke, R. D. (1997). Changes in abused children's social and cognitive skills from intake to discharge in a residential treatment center. *Residential Treatment for Children and Youth, 14*(3), 65–81.

Rosen, P. M., Peterson, L. E., and Walsh, B. W. (1980). A community for severely disturbed adolescents: A cognitive-behavioral approach. *Child Welfare, 59*, 15–25.

Rubenstein, J. S., Armentrout, J. A., Leven, S., & Herald, D. (1978). The Parent-Therapist program: Alternate care for emotionally disturbed children. *American Journal of Orthopsychiatry, 48*, 654–662.

Segal, U. A., & Schwarz, S. (1985). Factors affecting placement decisions of children following short-term emergency care. *Child Abuse and Neglect, 9*, 543–548.

Shennum, W. A., Moreno, D. C., & Caywood, J. C. (2002). Demographic differences in children's residential treatment progress. In N. S. LeProhn (ed.), *Accessing youth behavior: Using the Child Behavior Checklist in family and children's services*. Washington, DC: CWLA Press.

Stein, J. A. (1995). *Residential treatment of adolescents and children: Issues, principles, and techniques*. Chicago: Nelson Hall.

Sunseri, P. A. (2001). The prediction of unplanned discharge from residential treatment. *Child and Youth Care Forum, 30*(5), 283–303.

Tiffin, S. (1982). *In whose best interest: Child welfare reform in the progressive era.* Westport, CT: Greenwood Press.

U.S. Department of Health and Human Services. (2000). *Report of the Surgeon General's Conference on Children's Mental Health: A national action agenda.* Washington, DC: U.S. Government Printing Office.

U.S. Department of Health and Human Services. (2002). *Child welfare outcomes 1999: Annual report.* Washington, DC: U.S. Government Printing Office.

U.S. Department of Health and Human Services. (2004). *Preliminary FY 2002 estimates as of August, 2004. (The AFCARS Report).* Retrieved December 1, 2004, from www.acf.hhs.gov/programs/cb/publications/afcars/report9.htm.

U.S. General Accounting Office. (1994). *Residential care: Some high-risk youth benefit, but more study needed.* Gaithersburg, MD: U.S. General Accounting Office.

VanderVen, K. (1993). Point and level systems: Do they have a place in group care milieu? *R&E: Research and Evaluation in Group Care, 3,* 20–23.

VanderVen, K. (1995). Point and level systems: Another way to fail children and youth. *Child and Youth Care Forum, 24*(6), 345–367.

VanderVen, K. (1999). Point/Counterpoint: Level & point systems. *Residential Group Care Quarterly, 1*(2), 4–6.

Weiner, A., & Kupermintz, H. (2001). Facing adulthood alone: The long-term impact of family break-up and infant institutions: A longitudinal study. *British Journal of Social Work, 31,* 213–234.

Wells, K., & Whittington, D. (1993). Characteristics of youths referred to residential treatment: Implication for program design. *Children and Youth Services Review, 15,* 165–171.

Whittaker, J. K. (2000). Reinventing residential childcare: An agenda for research and practice. *Residential Treatment for Children and Youth, 17*(3), 13–30.

Whittaker, J. K., Fine, D., & Grasso, A. (1989). Characteristics of adolescents and their families in residential treatment at intake: An exploratory study. In E. Balcerzak (ed.), *Group care of children: Transitions toward the year 2000,* pp. 67–87. Washington, DC: Child Welfare League of America.

Whittaker, J. K., & Maluccio, A. N. (2002). Rethinking "child placement": A reflective essay. *Social Service Review, 72,* 108–132.

Whittaker, J. K., & Pfeiffer, S. I. (1994). Research priorities for residential group child care. *Child Welfare, 73,* 583–601.

Wolins, M. (1974). *Successful group care: Explorations in the powerful environment.* Chicago: Aldine.

Wurtele, S., Wilson, D., & Prentice-Dunn, S. (1983). Characteristics of children in residential treatment programs: Findings and clinical implications. *Journal of Clinical Child Psychology, 12,* 137–144.

Young, T. M., Dore, M. M., & Pappenfort, D. M. (1988). Residential group care for children considered emotionally disturbed, 1966–1981. *Social Service Review, 58,* 158–170.

Zill, N., & Peterson, X. (1989). *National longitudinal survey of youth child handbook.* Columbus: Ohio Center for Human Resources Research.

ROBIN NIXON

Promoting Youth Development and Independent Living Services for Youth in Foster Care

Changing the Paradigm of Foster Care Services for Youth

Over the past 20 years, there have been significant efforts to promote a positive youth development approach across many youth services disciplines, including foster care. Efforts in the child welfare and foster care arenas have focused on strengthening services to and improving the outcomes of young people preparing for the transition to adulthood. Despite these efforts, the outcomes experienced by young people leaving the foster care system between the ages of 18 and 21 continue to be challenging and disappointing to child welfare practitioners, policymakers, and communities as a whole (Courtney, Piliavin, Grogan-Kaylor, & Nesmith 1998; McMillen & Tucker 1998; Table 1).

Contributing to these less positive outcomes are current systemic beliefs regarding permanency and family connections for older youth (Nixon, in press). Unfortunately, efforts to increase funding and programmatic support for skill-building and other independent living services in the 1980s have contributed to diminished efforts to help older youth return to their families of origin, to be adopted, or achieve other kinds of permanency, such as permanent or subsidized guardianship. Child welfare workers and/or child welfare policy and funding may push a young person toward a goal of independent living or another planned permanent living arrangement even to the point of abandoning efforts to reunify a youth with his

or her family or to seek permanency for the youth via an adoption—based solely on the child's development as teenager (Ansell & Kessler 2003; Wattenberg 2002). Other factors, such as the number of placements a youth experiences in foster care and the restrictiveness of those placements, also have a significant negative impact on young people's ability to maintain or establish connections to family members and other supportive adults (Freundlich 2003). Young people themselves report that one of the most significant factors in their ability to survive and thrive as a young adult leaving foster care was that one person (e.g., teacher, mentor, foster parent, older sibling) was always there for them (Mallon 1998; Nixon 2000). It is clear that the field of children, youth, and family services is in need of a cognitive and practice-related reorientation toward a positive youth development approach that includes an understanding of a young person's needs for family connections and a social network, supplemented by skills and competencies. In this chapter I discuss and review the confluence of the following themes: positive youth development, independent living services for adolescents, and services to support youth transitioning to independence. The issues of permanency for youth and the issues of the appropriate use of the permanency goal of another planned permanent living arrangement are discussed elsewhere in this volume (see the chapter by Renne and Mallon).

TABLE 1. *Summary of Outcomes for Youth Formerly Served by the Foster Care System*

Study	Homelessness	Education	Employment	Incarceration	Early Parenthood	Cost to Community
Barth (1990) documented the experiences of youth emancipated from foster care	Thirty percent reported having no housing or having to move every week	At follow-up, 45% of 21-year-olds had completed high school	Seventy-five percent were working, with an average annual income of $10,000	Thirty-one percent had been arrested; 26% had served jail time	Forty percent reported a pregnancy since discharge, most were unplanned	Almost 40% received AFDC or general assistance funds
Cook (1991) examined the impact of independent living services on enhancing the ability of foster youth to be self-sufficient, 2.5 to 4 years after discharge	Twenty-five percent reported at least one night of homelessness	Fifty-four percent had completed high school	Thirty-eight percent maintained employment for 1 year	No data reported	Sixty percent of the women had given birth	Forty percent were a cost to the community
Alexander & Huberty (1993) studied a sample of former residents from The Villages in Indiana, with an average age of 22 years	Average number of moves during the past 5 years was 7.4	Twenty-seven percent had some college or vocational training	Forty-nine percent were employed, compared with 67% of 18- to 24-year-olds in the general population	Almost 42% had been arrested, compared to 30.1% of the general population in Indiana	No data reported	Fourteen percent received assistance in the form of food stamps, general assistance, and/or AFDC
Courtney, Piliavin, Grogan-Kaylor, & Nesmith (1998) looked at former youth transitions to adulthood, 12 to 18 months after discharge in Wisconsin	Twelve percent reported living on the street or in a shelter since discharge	At 12 to 18 months after discharge, 55% had completed high school	Fifty percent were employed; average weekly wage ranged from $31 to $450	Eighteen percent experienced post-discharge incarceration	No data reported	Thirty-two percent received public assistance
Reilly (2003) examined outcomes for former foster youth in Clark County, Nevada, 6 months to 3 years after discharge	Thirty-six percent indicated there were times when they had no place to live	Fifty percent left care without a high school degree; 75% wanted to obtain a college degree	Sixty-three percent were employed; average hourly wage was $7.25	Forty-one percent had spent at least 1 night in jail; 7% were incarcerated	Thirty-eight percent had children; 70% of the women had experienced pregnancy	Limited data reported; 25% had Medicaid and 11% received other public assistance

Youth Development, Independent Living, and the Child Welfare System

The federal Adoption and Foster Care Analysis and Reporting System interim estimates for FY2002 indicate that on September 30, 2002, 532,000 children and youths were in foster care (U.S. Department of Health and Human Services 2004). Youth aged 11 and older account for 49% (260,702) of this total number.

Of these children and youth, 61% had been in care more than 12 months, with 29% in care more than 3 years. Despite their reported length of time in care, the largest group of these children and youth had a case goal of reunification, accounting for 45% of the total, with adoption as the second largest group, at 21%. Even though the Adoption and Safe Families Act (ASFA) of 1997 does not recognize long-term foster care as a permanency option, 9% (46,119) of these children and youth had such care as the goal for permanence. Six percent (33,581) of the youths had a goal of emancipation. Although there is no concrete evidence to support this supposition, from a practical perspective, one can hypothesize from these figures that most of these children are teens.

On September 30, 2002, 126,000 children and youths were waiting to be adopted (U.S. Department of Health and Human Services 2004). Waiting children and youth are those who have a goal of adoption or whose parental rights have been terminated. This estimate excludes individuals 16 and older whose parental rights have been terminated and who have a goal of emancipation. Children and youth who were adopted during this period waited an average of 16 months to be adopted after their parents' rights were terminated. Thirty-four percent (42,703) of these young people were between 11 and 18 years old. During FY2002, 53,000 children or youth were adopted from the public foster care system.

These statistics provide some indication of the number and demographic and case characteristics of the thousands of youth in the child welfare system. It is generally agreed that between 20,000 and 25,000 youths age out of the system each year, many unprepared or only marginally prepared to transition to adulthood (Wertheimer 2002). These young people, most of whom leave the system without secure, supportive family connections, steady employment, or stable housing, experience some of the most disturbing outcomes of any client population in human services.

In recent years, a number of studies have examined outcomes for older youth as a result of the Title IV-E Independent Living program. This research has evaluated the effect of services for youth both before and after exiting care. A growing body of knowledge indicates that instruction in life skills has a positive effect on outcomes for older foster youth (Cook 1991, 1994); however, studies have also demonstrated that these youth are still inadequately prepared to make the transition to adulthood (Courtney, Piliavin, & Grogan-Kaylor 1995; Courtney, Piliavin, Grogan-Kaylor, & Nesmith 1998, 2001).

Efforts to Improve Services for Youth

The population of young people aging out of foster care has been of tremendous concern to professionals in the field of children, youth, and family services and to local communities since the mid-1980s. Although many professionals in the field were aware that young people exiting foster care were having difficulty maintaining housing and employment, there was no concerted effort to gather information, evaluate current policy, or create new programming with federal funds until 1985. In 1984, a group of young adults in New York City filed a lawsuit against the city and state child welfare agencies for failing to prepare them adequately for independence (*Palmer vs. Cuomo* [New York]). Six of the named plaintiffs had become homeless after leaving foster care. The court ruled that the state and New York City's child welfare system had not adequately prepared or planned for discharge for these youth (Allen & Nixon 2000). In addition, there was limited research demonstrating the struggles of emancipated, or aged-out foster youth, and in a survey of state agencies carried out by the Child Welfare League of America, agencies reported their own difficulties in funding and delivering services to older teens, as well as the difficulties experienced by teens after leaving care (Allen & Nixon 2000). Although some state-funded services had been available to older youth since the 1970s (Barth 1986), no federal program support or funding was available.

These concerns culminated in the passage of legislation creating the federal Title IV-E Independent Living initiative in 1986. In 1987, funds were allocated and program implementation began in all 50 states and the District of Columbia. In some states, federal funds supplemented state funds that were already being used to provide independent living services to older teens in foster care. From 1987 to 1999, most states provided services to approximately 50% of eligible youth, including life skills training, some educational supports, provision of materials for employment training and education, and provision of household goods (Casey Family Programs 2000).

Despite the new resources available through the Title IV-E Independent Living initiative, research continued to show that young people aging out of care were not achieving very successful outcomes in most areas of life. Of particular concern was the number of former foster youth experiencing homelessness, arrest, early parenthood, failure to complete high school, serious physical and mental health problems, and criminal victimization (Barth 1990; Scannapieco, Schagrin, & Scannapieco 1995; Courtney & Piliavin 1998; Nevada KIDSCOUNT 2001). Research regarding this population has not been limited to independent living services. Some studies of transitioning youth have identified other critical factors impacting successful transitions and healthy adult functioning, particularly length of time in foster care, number of placements, and contact with birth families (Iglehart 1994; Waldinger & Furman 1994). The largest studies of youth in transition out of fos-

ter care (and some small studies) have demonstrated some correlation between participation in independent living programs or other transitional supports and higher levels of achievement and functioning, as well as client perceptions of support and self-confidence (Casey Family Programs 2003; Cook 1991; A. Hailu, pers. comm.). Significant evidence to support the effectiveness of independent living services and other child welfare supports for older youth and young adults, however, has in general been very limited and is challenged by small sample sizes (U.S. General Accounting Office 1999). Research has not addressed the impact of positive youth development-focused programs and opportunities for foster youth.

In the late 1990s, concern regarding the well-being of these vulnerable teens and young adults again gained momentum. Numerous studies and anecdotal evidence presented by a growing number of youth-led advocacy organizations supported the idea that more needed to be done for this population (Boyle 2000). Note that advocacy efforts at that time included the premise that young people making the transition to adulthood require not only services and support, but also opportunities to advocate, participate in decisionmaking, and contribute to their programs, schools, and communities. The passage of ASFA in 1997 highlighted the priority of permanence for children and youth in foster care. Legislators and advocates realized that ASFA did not sufficiently address the challenges for older youth of both attaining permanency and preparation for adulthood. A number of congressional hearings were held, with testimony from advocates and most importantly, with passionate and articulate testimony from young people themselves (Allen & Nixon 2000; Nixon 1999).

This second wave of attention and advocacy culminated in the passage of the Foster Care Independence Act of 1999, Title I of which replaced the existing federal Independent Living Initiative with the John H. Chafee Foster Care Independence program. In addition to a 100%

increase in funds, the act required that states prioritize permanency for older teens, increase youth participation in decisionmaking, provide both participation and services to Native American tribes and tribal youth, and provide services to young people aged 18 to 21 who had already left foster care. States were also given the option to utilize 30% of their Chafee funds for housing, as well as to provide Medicaid to this group of young adults.

Little is known about the effectiveness of the Chafee program after the first 5 years of implementation. The state performance assessment process required by the act has yet to be implemented by the U.S. Department of Health and Human Services, although the information is critical to the analysis of both the effectiveness of the program and the status of the young people served (Nixon 2003). The Chafee program also includes an evaluation component, which will identify and evaluate programs of "potential national significance," as identified by the Office of the Secretary of Health and Human Services (National Foster Care Awareness Project 2000). Four programs are currently undergoing a third-party evaluation, which will result in significant information for the field regarding different types of support and services for youth in transition.

The passage of the Foster Care Independence Act has had a significant impact on the service development and advocacy communities, as well as on the service delivery system. The national dialogue regarding services and supports for older youth in foster care has evolved to focus on how the field addresses the youth development and permanency needs of this population. Various organizations and collaborations have initiated projects, some specific to foster care, others addressing the needs of disadvantaged or vulnerable youth but targeting foster youth as a priority population. Initiatives have included the formation of a Youth Transitions Funders Group (Funders Group & Finance Project 2004) of foundations looking at the need for improved planning and increased funding

of transition initiatives; a White House Task Force on Disadvantaged Youth (2003) that issued a report with recommendations for federal support of youth development programs; and the establishment of a new foundation-funded national youth organization, the Jim Casey Youth Opportunity Initiative (2003), intended to improve outcomes for transitioning foster youth nation wide. The Stuart Foundation (2003) has funded and coordinated a cross-disciplinary group of child welfare experts to frame new approaches to supporting permanency for teens and successful transitions to adulthood in the context of permanency.

Philosophy of Positive Youth Development in Child Welfare

Youth development is the physical, emotional, and cognitive developmental processes in which all youths engage over time. Each child, youth, and young adult moves along this pathway in the context of family, school, and community as they strive to meet their needs and build competencies (Pittman & Fleming 1991). A positive youth development approach by social workers requires personal and professional commitment to building strong positive relationships with young people, sharing program planning and decisionmaking with them, helping them to develop, and supporting them in becoming happy, connected, and contributing citizens (Nixon 1997).

Young people in foster care often do not have access to services designed to promote their positive development or overall well-being. The primary focus of child welfare and other helping systems has been intervening in family dysfunction or addressing other system-defined problems of children, youth, and families. The premise underlying this approach is that fixing the problems will allow the young person to develop in a healthy fashion. However, as Pittman and Fleming (1991) note, being problem-free is not the equivalent of being fully prepared. A problem-focused approach may prevent foster youth from participating in activities designed to nurture leadership, self-efficacy, educational success, holistic physical and emotional health, and the acquisition of skills needed to negotiate communities and society as a whole. To insure that young people are able to make successful transitions to adulthood, caseworkers and out-of-home caregivers must support them in overcoming behavioral, emotional, and family functioning challenges and, in addition, help them envision and achieve a competent and connected adulthood.

Barriers to a more positive, developmental approach have included lack of training for youth services and child welfare staff; continued categorical funding at the state and federal levels; and a focus on clinical diagnosis, treatment, and behavior management for older foster youth. Emphasis should instead be placed on providing opportunities to participate in decisionmaking and on learning and practicing skills, especially those related to leadership, employment, and education (Yu, Day, & Williams 2002).

Standards for Transition, Independent Living, and Self-Sufficiency (TILSS) Services

Various state and national efforts to increase youth participation and leadership in child welfare have developed over the past several years. These include the National Foster Youth Advisory Council at the Child Welfare League of America, Community Youth Councils sponsored by the Jim Casey Youth Opportunity Initiative, and the National Alumni Network (of former foster youth) sponsored by Casey Family Programs. In addition, some state Chafee programs have taken great strides toward youth/adult partnership through advisory councils, including those in Maine and North Carolina.

The Child Welfare League of America (CWLA) is the nation's oldest and largest association of child, youth, and family-serving agencies. Setting standards of excellence and supporting improvements to programs and services have been major goals of CWLA since

its formation in 1920. CWLA standards establish goals for the continual improvement of services for children, youth, and families, and provide the field with a vision to which it can aspire (Child Welfare League of America 2005). CWLA standards have been developed for 13 areas of child welfare and social services practice and have been recognized as an invaluable resource to public and private child welfare agencies, courts, policymakers, community-based organizations, and many other stakeholders.

In 2005, CWLA published new standards for transition, independent living, and self-sufficiency (TILSS) services. These standards represent a road map by which the field can navigate youth development-oriented practice and re-orient itself in ways that promote positive youth development and increase the likelihood of good outcomes for youth after foster care. The principles and assumptions can help to create a new foundation for services to youth in foster care, especially those in transition to adulthood (Child Welfare League of America 2005).

TILSS services should be grounded in the following basic principles and assumptions:

- A family is the best place for the healthy development of children and youth. In the context of family, school, neighborhood, and community, all children and youth need support and opportunities to develop the skills, knowledge, and relationships needed to function as healthy, contributing adults.
- Positive youth development takes place in the larger context of culture, community, and society. TILSS services should build on and respect the strengths of culturally and ethnically diverse individuals, families, and communities.
- All young people have significant gifts and strengths on which they can build their future. Protection and healing are only part of the responsibility of the service community—service providers and other

community members must also strive to nurture individual talents, creativity, leadership, personal efficacy, character, and each youth's ability to contribute to programs and society.

- TILSS services cannot take the place of permanency and family relationships. Youth in out-of-home care, however, may need additional support to learn life skills, achieve educational and career goals, build a network of social support, and develop the confidence and resilience to achieve optimum positive development.

- Healthy, productive adulthood is not "independent." Adults, even those who live alone, live interdependently, within a network of support and connection to family, friends, co-workers, community members, and resources. Self-sufficiency in adulthood is a lifelong process that should be understood in the context of interdependence.

- TILSS services and supports designed to insure safety and well-being, facilitate development, and acquire skills should be available continuously from entry into foster care until such time as a young adult has achieved successful interdependence.

- Services and supports should be provided on the basis of developmental readiness and need rather than arbitrarily by age or placement. The minimum age for discontinuation of support services should be 21 years; the optimal age is 25, the age at which most young people in our communities begin to achieve economic self-sufficiency. No youth should ever be discharged to homelessness or a precarious living arrangement.

- Although they might not require formalized TILSS services, children under the age of 10 will benefit from awareness on the part of caregivers and social workers of their developmental readiness for learning life skills, practicing decisionmaking, and experiencing an appropriate degree of autonomy and participation in planning.

- Children over the age of 10 should experience purposeful learning opportunities related to life skills and preparation for the transition to adulthood, as well as be included in decisionmaking and care/case planning. Children aged 14 and older should participate in structured TILSS services, leadership programs, program planning, individual case planning, and other planned activities that will contribute to their positive development and preparation for the transition to adulthood. All youth in out-of-home care should participate in TILSS services regardless of permanency plan or placement.

- Children and youth enter foster care due to abuse, neglect, emotional distress, and homelessness. The child welfare agency should insure that youth and young adults making the transition to interdependence receive support and services designed to aid them in developing psychosocial coping skills and resolving residual conflicts related to the circumstances that brought them into care. Youth should be informed, involved, and counseled regarding permanency options and processes, including adoption, reunification, termination of parental rights, and permanent guardianship.

- Young people are entitled to participate in the design, implementation, and evaluation of the services and supports intended to assist them. The active participation of youth in decisionmaking, planning, and leadership contributes not only to their own positive development, but also to agency accountability and the quality of service delivery.

- Planning for the transition from foster care to adulthood requires a clearly stated, written transition plan developed in partnership with the youth. An effective plan requires an accurate assessment of the young person's strengths and needs, clearly stated objectives, and identification of what supports will be necessary to accomplish the objectives, including linkages with the adult serving system, if necessary. The transition plan should establish realistic timelines for accomplishment of objectives and be reviewed and updated periodically with the youth.

- Young people—in fact, all people—learn by doing. TILSS services should emphasize the acquisition of life skills through learning, practicing, and doing in preference to classroom style learning. Many opportunities to learn by doing can take place in the youth's placement setting, supported by caseworkers or foster/kinship parents. Independent living programs, whether residential or nonresidential, should emphasize learning through supported experience in real-life settings.
- The child welfare agency and other service providers must strive to collect, analyze, and disseminate data that demonstrate the effectiveness of program strategies and funding, facilitate accountability, and provide a solid foundation for ongoing program development. Longitudinal data regarding the community functioning and well-being of young adults who have left out-of-home care are critical to this process.

Conclusion

The dialog regarding youth development, permanency, and independent living/transition services has significant implications for how child welfare theory and practice will develop over the next several years. Practitioners and community members will have to broaden their perspectives regarding youth permanency. They must not only understand, but also actively pursue goals that include supporting a young person in finding lifelong family relationships and helping them prepare for adult life, parenting, employment, and citizenship. Practitioners must overcome such barriers to permanency as long-held beliefs regarding the unadoptability of teens or teens' unwillingness to be adopted. They will have to be creative in finding alterna-

tive permanency strategies, such as guardianship, for those youth who choose not to sever ties with their families of origin. The child welfare system must strive concurrently to help youth in foster care achieve permanency while insuring that they are learning the skills they need to function as adults. There is no inherent conflict in the idea of concurrent permanency and independent living services; however, the system tends to focus on barriers to permanency for older youth and thus prioritize preparation for independence. Services should promote successful interdependence. Older youth, who may have spent several years in foster care and experienced more disruptions in placement, must be included in decisionmaking about their lives. In addition, extra effort should be made on their behalf to fully address both competency development and the establishment of family connections.

Most importantly, practitioners, policymakers, and community members need to view young people in foster care through a different lens, one that magnifies their strengths, their potential, and their right to participate in decisions about their lives, rather than one that emphasizes their challenges and problems. The experience of foster care can contribute to feelings of dependence and disempowerment for youth, who are often excluded from decisionmaking in case management and court processes. Young people must be included extensively in both individual case planning and program planning for foster care and independent living services. By engaging foster youth in decisionmaking, an environment is created in which they are more likely to be motivated to develop needed competencies and to succeed in developing or strengthening critical family ties. The growth of youth advocacy and leadership organizations, led by the exemplary and effective California Youth Connection, has insured that more youth and young adults are able to participate in discussions and planning around services designed to help foster teens and those who have aged out of care.

Consistent with a youth development approach, many child welfare professionals and advocates now see youth participation as a critical component of successful program planning, implementation, and evaluation, rather than as something that only helps youth develop their skills and character.

References

Adoption and Safe Families Act. (1997). P.L. 105-89.

Alexander, G., & Huberty, T. (1993). *Abused and neglected children as adults: Does the past predict the future?* Abstract presented at the University of Illinois Invitational Research Conference on Preparing Foster Youths for Adult Living, Indianapolis, IN, September 1993.

Allen, M., & Nixon, R. (2000). The Foster Care Independence Act and John H. Chafee Foster Care Independence Program: New catalysts for reform for young people aging out of foster care. *Journal of Poverty Law and Policy, 23,* 197–216.

Ansell, D. I., & Kessler, M. L. (2003). Rethinking the role of independent living in permanency planning. *Child Law Practice, 22*(4), 66–68.

Barth, R. P. (1986). Emancipation services for youth in foster care. *Social Work, 31,* 165–171.

Barth, R. P. (1990). On their own: the experiences of youth after foster care. *Child and Adolescent Social Work Journal, 7*(5), 419–440.

Boyle, P. (2000). Young advocates sway Washington: Odd fellows team scores $70 million hike for independent living. *Youth Today, 9*(2), 1, 52–57.

Casey Family Programs. (2000). *Transition from foster care: A state-by-state data base overview. Executive summary.* Seattle, WA: Casey Family Programs.

Casey Family Programs. (2003). *The foster care alumni studies: Stories from the past to shape the future.* Seattle, WA: Casey Family Programs.

Child Welfare League of America. (2005). Foreword. In *Standards of excellence for transition, independent living, and self sufficiency services,* pp. 1–4. Washington, DC: CWLA Press.

Cook, R. (1991). *A national evaluation of Title IV-E foster care independent living programs for foster youth: Phase 2 final report.* Rockville, MD: Westat.

Cook, R. (1994). Are we helping foster youth prepare for their future? *Children and Youth Services Review, 16,* 213–229.

Courtney, M., Piliavin, I., & A. Grogan-Taylor. (1995). *The Wisconsin study of youth aging out of out-of-home care: A portrait of children about to leave care.* Madison, WI: Institute for Research on Poverty.

Courtney, M., Piliavin, I., Grogan-Kaylor, A., & Nesmith, A. (1998). *Foster youth transitions to adulthood: Outcomes 12–18 months after leaving out-of-home care.* Madison: University of Wisconsin–Madison.

Courtney, M., Piliavin, I., Grogan-Kaylor, A., & Nesmith, A. (2001). Foster youth transitions to adulthood: A longitudinal view of youth leaving care. *Child Welfare, 80,* 685–717.

Foster Care Independence Act. (1999). P.L. 106-169.

Freundlich, M. (2003). *Time running out: teens in foster care.* New York: Children's Rights.

Funders Group & Finance Project. (2004). *Connected by 25: A plan for investing in successful futures for foster youth.* Washington, DC: Foster Care Work Group, Youth Transitions Funders Group, and Finance Project.

Iglehart, A. P. (1994). Adolescents in foster care: Predicting readiness for independent living. *Children and Youth Services Review, 16,* 159–169.

Jim Casey Youth Opportunities Initiative. (2003). *Public opinion about youth transitioning from foster care to adulthood.* St. Louis, MO: Jim Casey Youth Opportunities Initiative.

Mallon, G. P. (1998). After care, then where? Evaluating outcomes of an independent living program. *Child Welfare, 77,* 61–78.

McMillen, J., & Tucker, J. (1998). The status of older adolescents at exit from out-of-home care. *Child Welfare, 78,* 339–360.

National Foster Care Awareness Project. (2000). *Frequently asked questions about the Foster Care Independence Act and the John H. Chafee Foster Care Independence program.* Seattle, WA: Casey Family Programs.

Nevada KIDSCOUNT. (2001). *Transition from care: The status and outcomes of youth who aged out of the foster care system in Clark County, Nevada: Issue Brief II.* Las Vegas: University of Nevada.

Nixon, R. (ed.). (1997). Positive Youth Development. Special issue. *Child Welfare, 76*(5).

Nixon, R. (1999). *Improving independent living services for foster youth.* Hearing before the Subcommittee on Human Resources of the Committee on Ways and Means, U.S. House of Representatives, 106th Congress, Washington, DC, March 9, 1999.

Nixon, R. (2000). *Improving transitions to adulthood.* Washington, DC: Child Welfare League of America.

Nixon, R. (2003). The National Youth in Transition database. *Voice, 4*(2), 32–33.

Pittman, K., & Fleming, W. (1991). *A new vision: Promoting youth development.* Washington, DC: Academy for Educational Development.

Reilly, T. (2003). Transition from care: Status and outcomes of youth who age out of foster care. *Child Welfare, 82,* 727–746.

Scannapieco, M., Schagrin, J., & Scannapieco, T. (1995). Independent living programs: Do they make a difference? *Child and Adolescent Social Work Journal, 12,* 381–389.

Stuart Foundation. (2003). *Stuart Foundation convening on permanency for older youth in foster care.* San Francisco: Stuart Foundation.

U.S. Department of Health and Human Services. (2004). *Preliminary FY 2002 estimates as of August, 2004. (The AFCARS Report).* Retrieved December 1, 2004, from www.acf.hhs.gov/programs/cb/publications/afcars/report9.htm.

U.S. General Accounting Office. (1999). *Foster care: Effectiveness of independent living services unknown.* HEHS 00-13. Washington, DC: U.S. General Accounting Office.

Waldinger, G., & Furman, W. M. (1994). Two models of preparing foster youths for emancipation. *Children and Youth Services Review, 16,* 362–381.

Wattenberg, E. (2002). *Debating the options for adolescents at risk: Can we safeguard the interests of endangered adolescents?* St. Paul: University of Minnesota.

Wertheimer, R. (2002). *Youth who "age out" of foster care: Troubled lives, troubling prospects.* Vol. no. 2002-59. Washington, DC: ChildTrends.

White House Task Force on Disadvantaged Youth. (2003). *Final report.* Washington, DC: The White House.

Yu, E., Day, P., & Williams, W. (2002). *Improving educational outcomes for youth in care.* Washington, DC: Child Welfare League of America.

LOIS WRIGHT
MADELYN FREUNDLICH

Post-Permanency Services

Although permanency planning and achieving permanency have been the focus of child welfare since the early 1980s, post-permanency planning—sustaining permanency—has received less attention. The Adoption and Safe Families Act (ASFA) heightened focus on permanency. Although it places emphasis on speedier discharges of children and youth from foster care and accelerated planning related to termination of parental rights and adoption, it does not address sustaining permanency. Yet there is evidence that permanency is not simply a placement event but rather a process that implicates a range of issues related to child and family well-being. Of critical importance in this process are the post-permanency service needs of children, youth, and families (birth, kinship, and adoptive) as they confront these issues. This aspect of permanency—sustaining permanency through post-permanency services that address ongoing child and family well-being—is the subject of this chapter.

In this chapter, we present an overview of the research, theory, and values related to post-permanency, offer guiding principles for post-permanency services, and suggest how those principles translate into a coherent system of post-permanency services.

Research

The knowledge base related to post-permanency needs and services is better described as a patchwork of information than a coherent set of principles, policies, programs, and practices. With the implementation of federal data collection and reporting system requirements (Adoption Foster Care and Analysis Reporting System [AFCARS]), a wider range of data has become available regarding outcomes for children and youth who exit foster care. These data, however, are generally limited to demographic information and permanency destinations; the data are far more complete on children and youth who achieve permanency through adoption. Data on children and youth who leave care through reunification or through arrangements with kin and the post-permanency needs of these families remain extremely limited (U.S. Department of Health and Human Services 2004).

Research on post-permanency status and needs also is more extensive with regard to adoption. Much of the research on the needs of adopted children and youth and their new families has focused on their histories of abuse and neglect prior to entering foster care, foster care experiences, ages at the time of adoption, and the impact of these factors on later service needs in the areas of physical health, mental health, and education (Avery & Mont 1994; Barth & Berry 1988; Lakin 1992; Simms, Dubowitz, & Szilagyi 2000; Smith & Howard 1994). Research also has attempted to assess adoption stability by determining the rates of adoption disruption and dissolution (see the chapter by Festinger). Disruption rates for children and youth with physical, mental health, and developmental problems have been found to range from 10% to 25% (Berry 1997; Festinger 1990; Goerge, Howard, Yu, & Radomsky 1997). The few studies that have calculated dissolution rates found rates of 6.6% (Goerge, Howard, Yu, & Radomsky 1997) and 5.4% (Festinger 2001).

Studies by Barth and Berry (1988), Festinger (1990), Holloway (1997), and Smith and Howard (1999) suggest that disruption is the result of child factors (age at time of placement, number of prior placements, and emotional and/or behavioral problems), adoptive parent factors (educational level and parental expectations), and system factors (provision of inadequate or overly optimistic information at time of placement and inadequate preparation of adoptive parents regarding children and youth's special needs). A growing body of research has addressed the service needs of adoptive families. Barth, Gibbs, and Siebenaler (2001) have summed up these findings as indicating needs for services in four areas: educational and informational services, clinical services, material services, and support networks.

Permanency through placement with relatives is an arrangement about which little has been written and on which research has focused to a very limited degree (Terling-Watt 2001; see the chapter by Hegar and Scannapieco). Nonetheless, a number of permanency arrangements currently are being made that provide children and youth in foster care with permanency through placement with relatives: custody transferred from child welfare agencies to kin; placement with kin through guardianship arrangements that carry no financial support for the family; subsidized guardianships that provide kin with legal authority and financial support; and adoption by kin (U.S. Department of Health and Human Services 2004).

Very little data are available regarding the stability of placements with relatives. Barth, Gibbs, and Siebenaler (2001) reported that guardianships disrupt at a rate of 10% to 16%. Terling-Watt (2001) found that 29% of relative placements disrupt in the first 6 months following placements and that almost half (49%) disrupt in the second and third year following placement. Research suggests that disruption of permanent kinship placements is not associated

with the level of relatives' commitment to the children and youth in their care or to child maltreatment issues, but, instead, to the continued influence of biological parents; adolescents' difficulties in adapting to life with their relatives; children and youth's psychological and behavioral problems; relatives' age and health limitations; and the limited information, training, and support that are made available to relatives (Terling-Watt 2001). The literature on kinship care generally has mentioned post-permanency services only in passing (see Cornerstone Consulting Group 2001; Kruegman 1992; Neal 1992). One study, however, found that kin who become guardians need services in the areas of respite care, child care, financial support for caregivers, and mental health services for children and youth (Cornerstone Consulting Group 2001).

Although reunification is the preferred permanency option for children and youth in foster care, data and research are limited regarding the post-reunification needs of children, youth, and families. There continues to be no definitive determination of the actual reentry rate to foster care following reunification, nor is there a standard against which to determine whether a particular reentry rate is high or low. Several studies have found reentry rates following reunification to range from a low of 3% to a high of 37% (Block 1981; Fanshel & Shinn 1983; Fein, Maluccio, Hamilton, & Ward 1983; Fein & Staff 1993; Mech 1983; Terling 1999).

Research has identified six groups of factors associated with reentry to foster care following reunification: placement-related factors (length of stay, number of placements, and type of placements); children's older age at time of reunification; children's behavioral and psychological problems; families' circumstances (particularly housing problems and low income); parents' problems (particularly substance abuse); and service availability and accessibility (Courtney, Pilavin, & Wright 1997; Festinger 1996; Frame, Berrick, & Brodowski 2000; Goerge & Wulczyn 1990). Relatively little is known about the types of services that families need or actually receive post-reunification. Studies, however, have suggested that families need basic resources, such as housing, employment, and income, as well as counseling, health services, educational services, and respite care (Fein & Maluccio 1984). In addition, research has highlighted the importance of services that address children and youth's emotional and behavioral problems and learning disabilities after they return home (Biehal & Wade 1996; Farmer 1996; Landsverk, Davis, Granger, Newton, & Johnson 1996).

Theoretical Considerations

In addition to research, theory suggests the need for post-permanency services. Although there are no generally agreed-upon best approaches, attachment theory, role theory, family systems theory, and ecological theory are particularly useful in explaining why permanency arrangements can be difficult to sustain and why families, children, and youth may need a variety of post-permanency services. Developmental theory will not be discussed here separately, but it is important to note the ongoing influence of the developmental stage throughout the child and family's time together, as described later.

Attachment theory has been most influential in the field of child welfare (e.g., Bowlby 1969, 1973; Goldstein, Freud, & Solnit 1979; Jewett 1982; O'Connor, Rutter, English, & Romanian Adoptees Study Team 2000). Given that disrupted early relationships and subsequent separations (presumed contributors to attachment difficulties) are ubiquitous in child welfare, it is understandable that attachment theory has been dominant. Parents who adopt with incomplete knowledge of the child's attachment history may be disappointed and frustrated with the latter's limited ability to relate and to own the family. Often, attachment difficulties surface during adolescence, particularly when a child was adopted as an adolescent, as the parents are trying simultaneously to

attach to the child and to support independence (Barth & Berry 1988). In terms of kinship care, Reitz and Watson (1992) note the child and family's difficulty in sorting out the child's dual parentage and the possible discrepancies between attachments and legal authority. In reunification, professionals must consider how existing attachment issues were addressed during the period of separation. The mother and infant in the following scenario were fortunate in having frequent and productive visits together during the child's time in foster care:

> I was really messed up. Drugs and alcohol. Mostly alcohol. Jeremy was just a baby. I knew I couldn't take care of him until I got straightened out, but that didn't make it any easier. I was out of it more than I was sober during his first 3 months of life, so we never really got to know each other. But I was lucky, because the caseworker and the foster mom said I could visit every day as long as I was sober. At first, I didn't even know how to relate to him. They helped me learn to take care of him, and that really motivated me to stay sober. After 6 months, they let me have him back. He likes me to hold him, and he looks at me and giggles.

Role theory is also well suited to explaining post-permanency familial difficulties, as every coming and going leaves some family role unfulfilled, presents unfamiliar and unscripted roles, challenges an existing role structure, and requires negotiation for defining the new role structure. Bullock, Little, and Millham (1993) provide an extensive discussion of roles in relation to reunification, including the complexities and difficulties in resuming roles and the need for renegotiations of roles when a child returns. Differences between how parents and the agency see the adoptive parents' role can result in role conflict and ambiguity; rigid expectations regarding the role the child is to fill in the family may increase the anxiety in the parent-child relationship, particularly when the child reaches adolescence (Reitz & Watson 1992). The recent practice of concurrent planning, in which reunification and another permanency goal (e.g., adoption) are pursued simultaneously, further complicates the role of the foster parent wishing to adopt, increasing the potential for role confusion that could strain both child and foster family loyalties (Barth & Berry 1988). Examining kinship care in terms of role theory reveals more of the complexity of that arrangement (Le Prohn 1994). As kinship adoptions are most likely open, the issue of dual parentage must be addressed, expectations expressed, and ground rules determined (Hochman 1997; Reitz & Watson 1992), as demonstrated in the following scenario:

> My daughter Jill tried to pull her life together, but she was not prepared to care for a baby and couldn't keep off drugs. I hadn't known how bad it was, or I would have done something earlier. Her caseworker contacted me about it, because they were going to terminate her rights. Jill seemed relieved when I said I would adopt Jamie, keeping it all in the family. But she doesn't understand that I am his mother now. She still wants to make all the decisions for him and is upset when I disagree and make my own decisions. I want her to continue to come see him whenever she wants, but we really have to talk about some limits, and the final decisions are mine now.

Fundamental to all family systems thinking is the idea that individuals cannot be adequately understood outside the context of the family (immediate, extended, and historical) of which they are a part and that a problem in any part of the family reverberates throughout the system (Bowen 1978; Minuchin 1974; Watzlawick, Beavin, & Jackson 1967). Particularly important is the understanding that a child's presenting problem may be symptomatic of a family interactional issue and thus the child is only the symptom-bearer. In reunification, boundary issues influence how readily the family accepts the child back into the home. Family subsystems may be rigid, and the new coalitions that formed in the child's absence may freeze him or her out of important relationships:

> I was really close to my sister, Kisha. We are just 1 year apart, and we did everything together. At home we did dishes together and played computer games together. Everybody at school knew if you saw one of us, you saw the other. After Mom beat me so bad, I was in foster care for 3 months. You wouldn't think in only 3 months that things could have changed so much. But they did. When I came home, Kisha was stuck like glue to our half-sister, Theresa; she had moved in while I was gone. I felt like nobody even wanted me back home. I was lonely and depressed and ran away once.

Reitz and Watson (1992) describe family system scenarios in which parents adopt to distract from their marital difficulties, and the child, caught in the middle of marital tensions, becomes anxious and symptomatic. Kinship care presents more complicated family system issues, with boundary issues intensified and children often reflecting confusion in the family (Reitz & Watson 1992).

Much of modern ecological theory derives from the work of Brofenbrenner (1979), who showed how the socialization that occurs between parent and child is embedded in complex systems of social networks and societal, cultural, and historical influences. Garbarino (1982) introduced the concept of sociocultural risk and opportunity, which challenges notions of family responsibility and independence and suggests instead that shared responsibility and interdependence are more facilitative of healthy development. In terms of adoption, critical ecological issues include the sensitivity of friends and relatives to the arrangement, the extended family's acceptance of the child as part of the family, availability of supports to ease family burdens, and the competence of community institutions and service providers regarding adoption issues:

> We thought the whole family was behind us when we decided to adopt. But when they found out that Michael was a biracial adolescent, they just kind of raised their eyebrows. My family won't even talk

about it, and I don't think they'll ever accept him as part of the family. Jim's family has come around some. They are really nice to him and have stopped looking shocked when he brings his black friends to the house. The community? That's another story. I never felt any support coming from the community. I feel like people are always looking at us and wondering. I know Michael can feel this, and some day we'll have to deal with it.

Poverty is an important ecological consideration, and kinship care providers are more apt than nonrelative adopters to live in poverty (McDonald, Propp, & Murphy 2001). Likewise, research on reentry into care (cited above) suggests that many of the difficulties of reunified families are ecological in nature (e.g., poverty, housing problems, low positive social support, dangerous environments), difficulties often not addressed during the child's stay in care.

Values and Post-Permanency Services

Societal and personal values lie at the heart of any consideration of post-permanency services. Answers to a range of questions—What is society's responsibility to invest in families through offering post-permanency services? To whom should they be offered, to what extent, with what conditions, for how long, and at whose expense? —are based on strongly held beliefs about child and family rights and responsibilities.

Certainly the entire field of child welfare is undergirded by values and riddled with values tensions (see Barth, Goodhand, & Dickinson 1999). As a society, we value our children and youth and accept an obligation to protect them. We also value families' privacy, freedom from state intrusion, and responsibility to care for their own. Child protection reflects a resolution of the tension between these values—parents' rights and responsibilities are honored until a child's safety is brought into question, at which point the child's rights take precedence. More recently, a child's right to permanency has been recognized by society, carrying state responsi-

bility beyond insuring safety to also include protecting ongoing nurturing relationships, as reflected in the Adoption Assistance and Child Welfare Act of 1980 and ASFA. Still, the strong societal belief that individual families are responsible for the welfare of their children has always made efforts to address children and youth's concerns problematic for U.S. political institutions, and individualism and social justice have been difficult to reconcile (Hutchinson & Charlesworth 2000).

The relatively recent recognition of the need for post-permanency services, along with the extension of child welfare goals beyond child safety and permanency to include the more illusive goal of well-being, signals the beginning of an important shift in resolving the ongoing puzzle of reconciling family responsibility and the public assumption of responsibility for the welfare of children and youth. In the context of societal changes (e.g., greater interdependence, multiculturalism, economic disparity), changes in the child welfare population (i.e., more children and youth with a variety of special needs), and the current policy pressure toward permanency (ASFA), a compelling case is made for supporting families in claiming their rights and carrying out their responsibilities toward their children.

Post-permanency services have received the greatest support in relation to adoption, and families who adopt are seen as providing a service to children, youth, and society. However, in relation to other permanency arrangements—kinship care and reunification—inequity becomes apparent, as notions of parental responsibility and deservedness come into play. Thoughtful observers must ask themselves whether society is less willing to help some families than others, to the detriment of the safety, permanency, and well-being of some children and youth.

Our position is that, although we value family privacy, sanctity, and responsibility, serving the needs of children and youth is a higher obligation. The debate must move beyond privacy vs. intrusion or family vs. public responsibility and must put children and youth in the forefront. Services should be connected to the individual child rather than to the post-permanency arrangement, and should be extended to children and youth in need, regardless of the arrangement.

Convergence of Research, Theory, and Values

In the relatively new area of post-permanency services, it is important to articulate an underlying philosophy—based on research, theory, and values as previously discussed—to guide policymakers and child welfare agency staff at all levels through subsequent decisionmaking. This umbrella philosophy can keep the process focused and consistent as they begin to design a coherent post-permanency approach and consider various aspects of post-permanency law, policy, and practice. We have identified seven principles that may be considered elements of an umbrella philosophy: social obligation, the ideal of services following the child, permanency as an ongoing process, a developmental view of permanency, service accessibility and acceptability, service integrity, and public agency leadership.

Social Obligation

It would be difficult to move toward designing a coherent system of post-permanency services absent an underlying conviction that there is a social obligation to families post-permanency, whether these are reunified birth families, extended families, or adoptive families. Practitioners must promote efforts to support and strengthen these families in ways that meet their needs, thereby maximizing positive outcomes for children and youth in terms of their safety and well-being. An acceptance of social obligation also takes a longer view of outcomes for children, youth, families, and society as a whole. It recognizes the long-range consequences (e.g., mental health problems, substance abuse, home-

lessness, incarceration) of failing to follow through on societal obligations in the present that are likely to impact the overall health and well-being of U.S. society. Moving into post-permanency services signals a shift for child welfare, suggesting that the social obligation is far broader than insuring safety and that having intervened, society continues to carry some responsibility for the outcomes for children and youth.

Services Follow the Child

Currently there is inconsistent availability of post-permanency services according to the particular arrangement, with more services available for families who have adopted and less for kinship care and reunification arrangements. Through an examination of values, we suggest that those who develop policies and programs—as well as practitioners who serve families—recognize the legitimacy of post-permanency services across arrangements and focus on the child. Thus, dollars and services should follow the child rather than the arrangement. An approach avowing that a child who is adopted "deserves" assistance more than a child who is returned home or whose grandmother makes the decision to raise him or her would be very difficult to justify. Indeed, assuming that the intent of child welfare programs is to achieve good outcomes for children and youth, it would be counterproductive to exclude a whole class of children and youth from services based on their living arrangements. Optimally, programs need to incorporate approaches in which services both follow the child and provide families the tools they need to become stronger and more competent at handling their responsibilities.

Permanency as an Ongoing Process

Permanency planning must recognize that placing a child with the intent of permanency is only one step in a process that begins with the agency's first intervention and continues far beyond the child's return home, placement with kin, or placement with an adoptive family. Post-permanency support and services are a natural extension of earlier phases of the permanency planning process. Indeed, agency choices and actions in earlier phases (e.g., the quality of investigations, application of reasonable efforts, initial placement, availability and quality of services, use of visiting, ability to work with the courts, interpretation of ASFA) influence what the permanency destination will be and how the plan is implemented. Child welfare agencies are co-creators of children and youth's pre-permanency experiences and outcomes and thus have a continuing responsibility.

Developmental View
Ongoing normal developmental processes present important challenges to sustaining permanency, as every life stage presents new demands on the child, the family, and the environment. As the child and his or her relationship with the family develop, the post-permanency services and supports that are needed may change, both in terms of the nature and intensity of services and in terms of supports. The adoption literature focuses on the normal developmental trajectory of adoptive families, with certain anticipated crises triggering the need for service (Modell 1994; Pavao 1998). However, there is little discussion of these issues with regard to reunited families and kinship arrangements. All families, irrespective of permanency arrangement, require the caseworker's understanding of the developmental nature of child and family issues and the episodic family challenges these issues present. Furthermore, families should be encouraged to seek services in an environment that recognizes episodic need as normal and supported in doing so.

Service Accessibility/Acceptability
Both pre- and post-permanency services are meaningful and supportive of positive outcomes for children, youth, and families only if they are both accessible and acceptable. Accessibility is a broad concept, covering a range of factors re-lated to the ease of using services. It includes accessibility in many forms: financial, temporal, geographic, cultural, and psychological. Acceptability, which is closely related to psychological accessibility, refers to the users' view of services, their comfort level with the services, and how services are provided. Taken together, accessibility and acceptability suggest the need for a range of services with options and choices (e.g., formal and informal, private and public).

Without full acceptance of social responsibility for children and youth in post-permanency arrangements, implementation of accessibility and acceptability may be hampered by lingering views of services as a privilege rather than a right, implying that social obligation ends with providing services, leaving families with the challenges of accessing them. This viewpoint runs counter to the goals of child safety, permanency, and well-being and is inconsistent with a value of shared social responsibility for children and youth. The most important assurance of acceptability is that the voices of all families are heard fully and equally and that social services are responsive to these voices.

Service Integrity
Service integrity refers to societal confidence that services do what they are designed to do—that they are producing or contributing toward intended outcomes. In the arena of post-permanency services, it is essential that a system be in place to evaluate the impact of services and insure service quality and effectiveness. Even when formal evaluation of services is not possible, they can still be assessed—based on theory, informal feedback, or practice wisdom—to determine whether services are effective and thus have integrity. Practitioners may need to reexamine the current processes of planning services to insure that they include ongoing conversations with families and children about not only their needs but also service effectiveness. Examining outcomes is challenged by the inclusion of child well-being (Children's Bureau 2001) as a child welfare goal, as the concept

has yet to be specifically and fully defined. Still, there is a need for some combination of informal and formal processes, including standard measures of effectiveness and ways of incorporating the feedback of families and their children regarding their service experiences.

Public Agency Leadership

To meet the variety of child and family needs and insure service acceptability, a system of mixed public and private, formal and informal services is needed. Although a public role in post-permanency services is already accepted on some level, particularly in terms of post-adoption services, the issue of the extent of public involvement remains unresolved. Only with strong public leadership and resource commitment will the principles that we have delineated be integrated into the development and delivery of post-permanency services and support.

The public agency must assume a role that includes leadership, support, and integration of services. However, the public sector cannot be the sole, nor perhaps even the major, provider of post-permanency services. Rather, the public sector's role is to determine need and, while directly offering some services, to support and encourage private and informal services. We suggest that the public agency should be viewed not so much as "leader" as "convener," with coordinating responsibility that extends to private agencies, community-based resources, and neighborhood supports for families. Under this approach, the public agency would create the framework and support it and then, essentially, get out of the way.

A System of Post-Permanency Services

The translation of these seven principles into improved practice requires a coherent post-permanency service system. Two initial steps in the creation of such a system are a delineation of the components of such a system and an exploration of how these components might be implemented in light of the principles.

Components of a Coherent System of Post-Permanency Services

Six components characterize a coherent system of post-permanency services: law, policy, programs, services, system of care, and the environmental context.

Law. As is the case with child welfare services in general, federal and state laws play a key role in shaping the nature and scope of post-permanency services. Of perhaps greatest impact is the extent to which the law recognizes the value of certain services through the allocation of public funds to support the development and provision of those services. Financial support for post-permanency services may take a variety of forms—the earmarking of funds specifically for this purpose; statutory provisions that allow state or local authorities the flexibility to use funds for services most needed by families; legal frameworks that endorse "blended" funding to meet families' needs for cross-system services; fiscal incentives when states develop and invest in post-permanency services; inclusion of post-permanency outcomes in evaluative reviews required by law; and funding structures that recognize the strengths of both the formal and informal service systems. The law also defines the extent to which financial benefits may be available to families—for example, the extent to which tax benefits are extended to all or only certain groups of families and whether ongoing financial support is available to reunified, kin, and adoptive families. Finally, and importantly, the law establishes benefits to which certain individuals are entitled and mechanisms to insure that the rights of individuals to these benefits are protected.

Policy. Broader than the law, policy articulates general program parameters based on publicly stated values. Policy sets the overall course of program development and implementation at the federal and state levels, grounded on broad principles that guide planning and decision-making. In the context of child welfare policy, these principles historically have focused on child safety and permanence, with recognition of, but less emphasis on, child and family well-being. Support for post-permanency services is dependent on the extent to which policy articulates a broad commitment to child safety, permanency, and child and family well-being and the extent to which policy places priority on the development and implementation of services that extend beyond the initial achievement of permanency.

Programs. Programs are organized systems of service delivery that provide a set of related services to a specific population of clients or provide a single service to a broad or diverse population of clients. Post-permanency programs may take a variety of forms—ongoing programs of services provided by public and/or private child welfare agencies, special initiatives funded by federal or state governments (e.g., programs developed through the federal Adoption Opportunities Program or through state-funded programs to expand post-adoption or post-guardianship services), advocacy initiatives linking families with formal and informal resources in their communities, and foundation-supported initiatives to support needed program development and implementation. To date, post-permanency programs have tended to provide a range of services (of varying scope) to a defined group of post-permanency families—most often, adoptive families.

Services. Although a somewhat elusive concept to define, services may be viewed as the specific types of assistance that individuals and/or families receive in relation to identified needs. Services are extremely variable, ranging from highly formal (e.g., therapy for a child's emotional problems) to highly informal (e.g., a parent support service that begins when families meet one another at an agency orientation and then evolves into regular get-togethers over coffee to discuss common parenting challenges). A number of service considerations arise in connection with the development of a post-

permanency system: families' eligibility for services (which is tied to a host of other factors, including the nature of the post-permanency arrangement), accessibility to services (which involves the cost of the services and where the services are provided), the acceptability of services (which implicates personal, social, and cultural factors), and the extent to which services actually make a difference in outcomes for families (an issue that reflects the need for evidence-based practice). Services depend on law and policy to provide the necessary financial resources, but even when funding is available, there is no guarantee that services will be appropriately offered and provided to all families who need them.

System of care. The concept of system of care, perhaps most fully developed in the field of mental health (Lourie, Katz-Leavy, & Stroul 1996), encompasses a range of interconnections in the context of post-permanency services and supports. These interconnections exist

1. Among the various child welfare services provided by public agencies—child protective services, family preservation, foster care, and adoption—all of which must work together to maximize positive post-permanency outcomes;
2. Between public child welfare agencies and the private child welfare agencies that share responsibility for permanency planning with families and achieving positive outcomes in relation to child safety, permanency, and child and family well-being;
3. Between child welfare services (whether provided by public or private agencies) and other service systems that play vital roles in promoting the well-being of children, youth, and families, including the mental health, healthcare, and educational systems; and
4. Between the formal, professionalized service systems and informal (or "nontraditional") service systems—extended family, friends, neighborhoods, churches, and other

neighborhood supports—which families often identify as the most important and helpful resources for them. This multitiered framework for a post-permanency system of care highlights the importance of identifying all the essential partners in the development and implementation of quality post-permanency services. It also points to the need to develop effective channels of communication and other mechanisms that support strong collaboration among the key participants.

Environmental context. However post-permanency services may be defined, developed, and implemented, they interact with other social and service environments. The larger social environment affects how the post-permanency needs of families are viewed. Social attitudes about children's birth, kin, and adoptive families affect whether services are supported by the public for all families, irrespective of the nature of the permanency arrangement. Social and cultural values and perceptions also affect the extent to which policy (as articulated in law and in federal and state initiatives) endorses post-permanency services, programs are developed to address these needs, and resources are mobilized. A normative, developmental conceptualization of the post-permanency needs of families would impact societal understanding of the role of ongoing supports and services. In this connection, public agency leadership—with the goal of drawing together partners from many different systems and perspectives—becomes particularly critical.

There also are key considerations in relation to post-permanency services in the context of specific program and service system environments. These issues include the policies of child welfare agencies (whether public or private) and other service systems that guide the provision of such services; the training of professional and paraprofessional staff who provide services; staff attitudes and expectations regarding families' needs for and responses to services, particularly as staff relate directly to families; and the physical environments in which services are provided (i.e., whether services are provided at home or at an office and the physical surroundings when services are provided outside the home).

Analysis of the Principles and Components of a Coherent System of Post-Permanency Services

A second step in creating a coherent post-permanency service system is an exploration of each component in light of the principles of social obligation, services following the child, permanency as an ongoing process, developmental view of families' needs, service accessibility and acceptability, service integrity, and public agency leadership. This process requires that attention be given to each individual component but also that focus be maintained on the interaction of the various components with one another as an analysis is undertaken of (1) the current status of each component of post-permanency services; (2) where improvement is needed; and (3) the effect of changes in one component on other components.

This process is likely to be most meaningful and hold the promise of greatest benefit if there is active participation of public and private child welfare agencies staff, community representatives, and, perhaps most importantly, families themselves. An inclusive approach also can be expected to generate more comprehensive information than would be possible if participants are limited to professionals in the field of child welfare. A broadly inclusive process is likely to serve an educational function of its own, providing participants with opportunities to enrich their own understanding of families' post-permanency needs and achieve greater clarification of all parties' roles, responsibilities, and potential contributions.

Many approaches may be taken in the analysis of the issues that have been raised in this chapter. One approach is to use a matrix structure that guides the consideration of each component in terms of each guiding principle. The following matrix offers a guide and stimulus for the consideration of these issues.

	Principles						
	Social Obligation	Services Follow the Child	Permanency as an Ongoing Process	Families' Needs as Developmental	Accessibility and Acceptability	Integrity	Public Leadership
Components							
Law							
Policy							
Program							
Services							
System							
Environment							

As one example of what the matrix approach might yield, policy could be considered through the lens of the principle of "services follow the child." This consideration might lead to a comparison of policy initiatives that promote ongoing services for children and youth who are adopted, who are placed permanently with relatives, and who are reunited with their parents. The dearth of policies that support services for children who leave foster care to live with their birth parents and relatives may lead to an examination of the factors that have supported policies that favor one group of children and youth (or type of parent) over others. What factors explain the policy emphasis on adoption-related services as opposed to reunification- or kinship-related services? What changes would be needed to shape a more inclusive child-focused policy? What are the barriers to policies that promote post-permanency services for all children and youth, irrespective of the nature of the family arrangement? This example suggests how the matrix approach can stimulate consideration of the key issues in light of both the principles and components that have been identified.

Conclusion

In this chapter, we document what is known about outcomes for children and youth after they have exited foster care to return to their birth parents, live permanently with relatives, or be adopted. We outline the theoretical considerations that can provide a basis for post-permanency services and systems, and describe the importance of delineating the values on which work in this area must proceed. The chapter sets forth a philosophical and conceptual framework for the development of a coherent post-permanency service system, outlining seven key principles and six components of such a system. Finally, we suggest a method for applying the presented information in a way that can lead to the development of effective post-permanency services and service systems. Work on post-permanency is still in an early, formative stage, and much more needs to be understood and documented. This chapter provides a framework for those involved in planning, delivering, and advocating for post-permanency services as they undertake this critical work.

References

Adoption and Safe Families Act (1997). P.L. 105-89.

Adoption Assistance and Child Welfare Act. (1980). P.L. 99-272.

Avery, R. J., & Mont, D. M. (1994). *Special needs adoption in New York State: Final report on adoptive parent study. Final Report to the U.S. Department of Health and Human Services.* Washington, DC: U.S. Department of Health and Human Services.

Barth, R. P., & Berry, M. (1988). *Adoption and disruption: Rates, risks, and responses.* Hawthorne, NY: Aldine de Gruyter.

Barth, R. P., Gibbs, D. A., & Siebenaler, K. (2001). *Assessing the field of post-adoption services: Family needs, program models, and evaluation issues.* Washington, DC: U.S. Department of Health and Human Services.

Barth, R., Goodhand, J., & Dickinson, N. (1999). Reconciling competing values in the delivery of child welfare services under ASFA, MEPA, and community-based child protection. In U.S. Department of Health and Human Services (ed.), *Changing paradigms of child welfare practice: Responding to opportunities and challenges,* pp. 7–23. Washington, DC: U.S. Department of Health and Human Services.

Berry, M. (1997). Adoption disruption. In R. J. Avery (ed.), *Adoption policy and special needs children,* pp. 77–106. Westport, CT: Auburn House Press.

Biehal, N., & Wade, J. (1996). Looking back, looking forward: Care leavers, families and change. *Children and Youth Services Review, 18,* 425–446.

Block, N. M. (1981). Toward reducing recidivism in foster care. *Child Welfare, 60,* 597–610.

Bowen, M. (1978). *Family therapy in clinical practice.* New York: Jason Aronson.

Bowlby, J. (1969). *Attachment and loss.* Vol. 1: *Attachment.* London: Hogarth Press.

Bowlby, J. (1973). *Attachment and loss.* Vol. 2: *Separation, anxiety and anger.* London: Hogarth Press.

Bronfenbrenner, U. (1979). *The ecology of human development: Experiments by nature and design.* Cambridge, MA: Harvard University.

Bullock, R., Little, M., & Millham, S. (1993). *Going home: The return of children separated from their parents.* Brookfield, VT: Dartmouth Publishing.

Children's Bureau. (2001). *Assessing the context of permanency and reunification in the child welfare system.* Washington, DC: Children's Bureau.

Cornerstone Consulting Group. (2001). *Guardianship: Another place called home.* Houston: Cornerstone Consulting Group.

Courtney, M. E., Pilavin, I., & Wright, R. (1997). Transitions from and returns to out-of-home care. *Social Service Review, 71,* 652–667.

Fanshel, D., & Shinn, E. B. (1983). *Children in foster care: A longitudinal investigation.* New York: Columbia University Press.

Farmer, E. (1996). Family reunification with high-risk children: Lessons from research. *Children and Youth Services Review, 18,* 403–424.

Fein, E., & Maluccio, A. N. (1984). Children leaving foster care: Outcomes of permanency planning. *Child Abuse and Neglect, 8,* 425–431.

Fein, E., Maluccio, A. N., Hamilton, V. J., & Ward, D. E. (1983). After foster care: Outcomes of permanency planning. *Child Welfare, 62,* 483–558.

Fein, E., & Staff, I. (1993). Last best chance: Findings from a reunification services program. *Child Welfare, 72,* 25–41.

Festinger, T. (1990). Adoption disruption. In D. M. Brodzinsky & M. D. Schechter (eds.), *The psychology of adoption,* pp. 254–273. New York: Oxford University Press.

Festinger, T. (1996). Going home and returning to foster care. *Children and Youth Services Review, 18,* 383–402.

Festinger, T. (2001). *After adoption: A study of placement stability and parents' service needs.* New York: Shirley M. Ehrenkranz School of Social Work, New York University.

Frame, L., Berrick, J., & Brodowski, M. (2000). Understanding reentry to out-of-home care for reunified infants. *Child Welfare, 79,* 339–370.

Garbarino, J. (1982). *Children and families in the social environment.* New York: Aldine.

Goerge, R. M., Howard, E. C., Yu, D., & Radomsky, S. (1997). *Adoption, disruption, and displacement in the child welfare system, 1976–94.* Chicago: Chapin Hall Center for Children, University of Chicago.

Goerge, R. M., & Wulczyn, F. H. (1990). *Placement disruption and foster care reentry in New York and Illinois.* Vol. II: *Supplementary statistical tables.* Chicago: Chapin Hall Center for Children, University of Chicago.

Goldstein, J., Freud, A., & Solnit, A. (1979). *Beyond the best interests of the child.* New York: Free Press.

Hochman, G. (1997). *Keeping the family tree intact through kinship care.* Retrieved June 26, 2001, from www.calib.com/naic/pubs/f_kinshi.htm.

Holloway, J. S. (1997). Outcome in placements for adoption or long-term fostering. *Archives of Disease in Childhood, 76*(3), 227–230.

Hutchinson, E., & Charlesworth, L. (2000). Securing the welfare of children: Policies past, present, and future. *Families in Society: The Journal of Contemporary Human Services, 81,* 575.

Jewett, C. (1982). *Helping children cope with separation and loss.* Harvard, MA: Harvard Common Press.

Kruegman, D. C. (1992). *Services for kinship foster families.* Paper presented at Kinship Foster Care: The Issues, Needs and Possibilities. Association for the Bar of the City of New York, New York, January 29, 1992.

Lakin, D. (1992). Making the commitment to adoption. In Spaudling for Children (ed.), *Trainers guide: Special needs adoption training curriculum.* Southfield,

MI: National Resource Center for Special Needs Adoption.

Landsverk, J., Davis, I., Granger, W., Newton, R., & Johnson, I. (1996). Impact of child psychosocial functioning in reunification from out-of-home placement. *Children and Youth Services Review, 18,* 447–462.

Le Prohn, N. (1994). The role of the kinship foster parent: A comparison of the role conceptions of relative and non-relative foster parents. *Children and Youth Services Review, 16,* 65–84.

Lourie, I. S., Katz-Leavy, J., & Stroul, B. A. (1996). Individualized services in a system of care. In B. A. Stroul (ed.), *Children's mental health: Creating systems of care in a changing society,* pp. 429–452. Baltimore: Paul H. Brookes Publishing.

McDonald, T. P., Propp, J. R., & Murphy, K. C. (2001). The post-adoption experience: Child, parent, and family predictors of family adjustment to adoption. *Child Welfare, 80,* 71–94.

Mech, E. V. (1983). Out-of-home placement rates. *Social Service Review, 57,* 659–667.

Minuchin, S. (1974). *Families and family therapy.* Cambridge, MA: Harvard University Press.

Modell, J. S. (1994). *Kinship with stranger: Adoption and interpretation of kinship in American culture.* Berkeley: University of California Press.

Neal, L. (1992). *An African American perspective on kinship foster care.* Paper presented at Kinship Foster Care: The Issues, Needs and Possibilities. Association for the Bar of the City of New York, New York, January 29, 1992.

O'Connor, C., Rutter, M., English, D., & Romanian Adoptees Study Team. (2000). Attachment disorder behavior following early severe deprivation: Extension and longitudinal follow-up. *Journal of the American Academy of Child and Adolescent Psychiatry, 39,* 703–712.

Pavao, J. M. (1998). *The family of adoption.* Boston: Beacon Press.

Reitz, M., & Watson, K. (1992). *Adoption and the family system.* New York: Guilford Press.

Simms, M., Dubowitz, H., & Szilagyi, M. A. (2000). Health care needs of children in the foster care system. *Pediatrics, 106,* 909–918.

Smith, S. L., & Howard, J. A. (1994). *The adoption preservation project.* Normal: Illinois State University, Department of Social Work.

Smith, S. L., & Howard, J. A. (1999). *Promoting successful adoptions: Practice with troubled families.* Thousand Oaks, CA: Sage.

Terling, T. (1999). The efficacy of family reunification practice: Reentry rates and correlates of reentry for abused and neglected children reunited with their families. *Child Abuse and Neglect, 23,* 1359–1370.

Terling-Watt, T. (2001). Permanency in kinship care: An exploration of disruption rates and factors associated with placement disruption. *Children and Youth Services Review, 23,* 111–126.

U.S. Department of Health and Human Services. (2004). *Preliminary FY 2002 estimates as of August, 2004. (The AFCARS Report).* Retrieved December 1, 2004, from www.acf.hhs.gov/programs/cb/publications/afcars/report9.htm.

Watzlawick, P., Beavin, J., & Jackson, D. (1967). *Pragmatics of human communication.* New York: Norton.

SECTION IV
Systemic Issues in Child Welfare

❖   ❖   ❖   ❖   ❖   ❖   ❖

Overview

Facilitating an agenda of well-being, safety, and permanency requires that child welfare systems and the professionals who work in them institutionalize safety-focused, family-centered, and community-based approaches as the foundation of service delivery. Timely, quality services require policy, fiscal, and organizational cultures that promote and encourage effective practice with and on behalf of children, youth, and families.

To support the institutionalization of quality services, several components of an agency's infrastructure, such as its mission, goals, policies, and procedures, will need to be aligned with current practice standards as well as federal and state policy. Consideration must also be given to appropriate caseloads, accountability at all levels, agency staff and caregiver qualifications and ongoing training, and partnerships with legal entities and others from the court system, with other service delivery systems serving families, children, and youth, and with the community and its formal and informal provider networks.

Identifying the criteria and developing a process for determining how to make organizational-level decisions are complex tasks. To facilitate this process, managers are urged to familiarize themselves with child welfare practice standards, federal and state policies, and child welfare data for the state, and, where applicable, the local jurisdiction. The analysis of the data assists in identifying the needs of children and youth who most often are placed in foster care and may support further evaluation of outcomes of services provided to them, as well as the strengths and weaknesses of the service system. Such data are useful in identifying the most frequently needed services, issues regarding caseload size, the nature of practice decisions by supervisors and frontline staff, and the need for resources to be allocated for program development, training, and accountability at all levels.

In addition to the systemic challenges related to increased emphasis on data collection and analysis for service planning and accountability, child welfare in the twenty-first century requires achieving case goals within briefer specified time frames.

Time Frames for Decisionmaking

The Adoption and Safe Families Act (ASFA) requires that states hold the child's first permanency hearing within 12 months, rather than 18 months, as previously required. Furthermore, it requires that states initiate or join proceedings to terminate parental rights for parents of children who have been in care for 15 of the past 22 months, except in situations in which the child is placed safely with relatives, there is a compelling reason why termination of parental rights is not in the child's best interest, or the family has not received the services that were part of the case plan.

These time frames have required supervisors and frontline workers to approach their work differently, as they must move quickly to complete comprehensive child and family assessments, provide services, assist the family in connecting with other supports in the community, and evaluate progress. Achieving case goals within specified time frames requires that resources are provided for sufficient casework and other positions within the child welfare agency. In addition, it requires individualized service plans, high-quality, comprehensive, and coordinated services and supports, and, to support such services and support, effective collaboration with other service providers.

Collaboration with Other Service Providers: The Service Array

No one agency or program has the resources or expertise to develop a comprehensive response to the needs of all families that come in contact with the child welfare system. Families served by this system typically experience complex and interrelated problems, such as child maltreatment, poverty, unemployment, poor housing, substance abuse, domestic violence, and mental illness. The degree to which community-based social service agencies and courts can be effective in helping children and families depends in a large part on their ability to connect families with the resources available from various agencies, community-based organizations, and other formal and informal supports in the community.

To achieve positive outcomes for children and families, it is essential that all components of the community work together to provide the child and family an individualized array of comprehensive, coordinated, family-centered, and community-based services and supports. A lack of collaboration and coordination of services among these agencies can undermine the efforts to create safe, stable family environments; it can also result in unnecessary and duplicated requirements and services that complicate rather than simplify and support family life.

Collaboration of multiple services, particularly when various interdisciplinary styles are involved, is not a simple task. With resources stretched throughout the human services system and with differences in philosophy and practice approaches in various systems, collaboration can be perceived as a real challenge. However, many child welfare systems are beginning to effectively forge collaborative partnerships that acknowledge the limitations of each agency and yet find ways to work effectively together to provide the individualized services that families need.

For collaboration to be successful, partnering agencies must be guided by a common vision and commitment. Therefore, the child welfare system, together with other service systems and community providers, must form partnerships that select and focus on the same goals (e.g., creating more substance-abuse resources or programs to prevent family violence), even if the mandates for and means of attaining that goal differ for each agency. Responsible parties must outline the concrete tasks and functions to be performed by each agency. This means that interagency agreements must be specific about the purpose of collaborative efforts (e.g., providing cross-training to the courts, mental health, substance abuse, and other service providers regarding ASFA time limits and other mandates; developing interagency referral protocols and/or contracts to provide services to families). Community partnerships must subsequently evaluate their effectiveness and identify policies and practices that would benefit from modification. Thus these partnerships will be continually evaluating and advancing efforts to insure that families receive the most comprehensive, coordinated, individualized supports and services possible to promote safe, stable family environments.

Beyond collaboration, child welfare agencies must take a leadership role to expand the network of services available at the neighborhood level, including those provided by schools, churches, health and child care centers, and other family support agencies. This requires a clear understanding of trends, of the services families need but are not provided, and of strategies to elevate critical issues and obtain responses from agency administrators and policymakers. Agencies may also find it useful to enlist the court's help in working with these and other providers.

Use of the Agency's Legal Authority

In all child welfare agencies, the principles of good practice must be addressed in the context of the agency's authority and responsibilities. All agency staff—from administrators to frontline practitioners—must recognize that they function as agents of the state's authority and responsibility to insure the safety, permanency, and well-being of children. They also need to educate other systems (e.g., employment, housing, health, mental health, substance abuse treatment, schools) involved with the child and family regarding the unique authority role of the child welfare agency and on the requirements of federal and state legislation.

The decisionmaking process in child welfare takes place in the context of deeply held, but often competing, societal values. Society recognizes that parents have the fundamental right and responsibility to protect and nurture their children. However, when parents are unable or unwilling to do so, the public child welfare agency has the societal and legal mandate to intervene promptly to insure the child's safety. Most families become involved with the child welfare system involuntarily due to abuse and neglect. This nonvoluntary nature of child protective services creates special challenges for child welfare agencies. Frontline practitioners must take into account the possible existence of competing goals among different members of the system—the child, the family, out-of-home caregivers, the agency, and the courts.

Placement Stability as a Systemic Factor

The first chapter in this section, by D'Andrade, focuses on placement stability. This chapter explores a phenomenon in child welfare that might be considered the antithesis of permanence: placement instability, which occurs when children experience a series of homes or facili-

ties while in care. Placement instability was first identified in studies examining the child welfare system in the 1950s, 1960s, and 1970s, with findings that many children and youth were "drifting" in care, often enduring multiple placements, with no actions being undertaken on their behalf to find them permanent homes. The consequences for children that are associated with placement stability, we believe, should cause readers to consider this subject, not only as a practice issue, but also as a broader systemic matter to be considered in the context of necessary child welfare reform. The problem of children and youth "drifting" in foster care is still unresolved in the twenty-first century. According to D'Andrade, approximately 20–25% of children and youth who enter out-of-home care are neither reunified with their families nor placed in other permanent homes through adoption or guardianship; for these young people, placement instability remains an ongoing concern. D'Andrade's chapter describes the challenges involved with defining instability and details the evidence regarding its effects on children and youth. Promising approaches are considered, along with evidence regarding their effectiveness.

Placement instability potentially affects any child or youth entering out-of-home care. The next three chapters in this section address systemic issues that have been found to negatively affect specific groups of children and youth in the child welfare system and their families: children and youth of color; African American fathers; and immigrant children and youth.

Overrepresentation of Children and Youth of Color in Foster Care

Children of color, belonging to various cultural, ethnic, and racial communities (primarily African American, Hispanic, and Native American), are disproportionately represented in the child welfare system and frequently experience disparate and inequitable service provision. The overrepresentation of children of color in child welfare and other social service systems (e.g., juvenile justice) is linked to social class, economic, and other factors that must be addressed to insure that the needs of all children are fairly and appropriately served. In her chapter on overrepresentation of children and youth of color in foster care, McRoy takes a close look at the latest statistics available from the Adoption and Foster Care Data Analysis System (U.S. Department of Health and Human Services 2004). These reveal that in 2002, 59% of the 532,000 children in the U.S. foster care system were children of color, yet only 38% of all U.S. youngsters are children of color. The inverse is true for white children, who represent 61% of the U.S. child population, and only 37% of the children in out-of-home care. McRoy's chapter reviews the literature on the causes and correlates of overrepresentation and presents systemic strategies for addressing this growing problem.

Fathers and Their Involvement in the Child Welfare System

There is a dearth of information on the involvement of fathers in the child welfare system; yet every child who has a mother, also not only has a father, but an entire set of paternal resources as well. The majority of state child welfare systems have failed in their attempts to locate and involve fathers and paternal resources in meaningful ways in the lives of children and youth. The chapter by Pate focuses on African American children who are disproportionately represented in the child welfare system and highlights narratives from in-depth interviews with five fathers. Pate gives a "voice" to this underrepresented group in the child welfare system by discussing the importance of involving fathers in the lives of children and youth.

Immigrant Children and Youth in the Child Welfare System: Immigration Status and Special Needs in Permanency Planning

Child welfare workers do not routinely identify their clients' immigration-related needs; nor do they make referrals for immigration legal services. Although a great deal of attention is given to laws and systems governing the entrance of new immigrants into the United States, there is little coordination between federal and state policies for addressing the human service needs of these newcomers once they are here. The result is an ad hoc, patchwork approach to federal, state, and local services that can permit new immigrants, especially children and youth, to fall between the cracks. In her chapter on immigrant needs, Earner focuses specifically on how immigration status affects permanency planning for youth in out-of-home care. The different types of immigration status of children and youth in care and the importance of early identification and assessment of immigration status and guidelines for effective intervention are highlighted. Earner also provides examples of collaborative programs between public child welfare systems and community-based immigration services providers that enhance capacity to meet the permanency planning needs of this population.

Foster Parent Recruitment, Development, Support, and Retention

The increased emphasis on achieving permanency for children in a timely manner has prompted professionals and policymakers to focus on finding more effective ways to recruit and retain resource families for children in need of permanent homes. Increasingly, the child welfare system is relying on foster parents to fill the gap. Foster parents, rather than newly recruited adoptive parents, are serving as the most consistent and viable option for permanence for large numbers of children and youth in care. Most children separated from their families reside with licensed foster parents in family-like, community-based settings.

According to the *Children's Bureau Express* (Children's Bureau 2000), 64% of children adopted from the child welfare system are adopted by their foster parents (although not necessarily the families with whom they were first placed). In some states (e.g., Virginia), almost 81% of all adoptions are finalized with foster parents. Not only are foster parents adopting children in their care, but also, according to the National Adoption Information Clearinghouse, these adoptive placements are very successful, with 94% remaining intact for the life of the child (U.S. Department of Health and Human Services 2004). Thus the promise of permanency for children and youth in the child welfare system who are unable to return to their birth parents lies in many instances with their foster parents. This reality has far-reaching practice and policy implications. One of the critical practice implications is the need to keep the pool of foster parents growing, because as foster families take on the role of adoptive parents to children in their care, the pool of foster parents naturally diminishes.

Foster parents have historically been viewed as temporary caregivers or in some cases, as "babysitters" for children in foster care (Barbell & Freundlich 2002). Traditionally, foster parents have not been considered as potential adoptive parents for the children cared for in their homes, even when the children had deeply bonded with them (Dougherty 2001).

Mallon (2004:58) in his research on gay dads provided this observation about foster parents from Terry Boggis, the director of CenterKids in New York City:

> I think it takes a very different, almost enlightened being to be a good foster parent. You have to be willing to love them [the children] on a spiritual level, totally embracing them and accepting that you must ultimately be willing to say good-bye. In this one way, it's a dramatically different approach to the kind of parenting most of us imagine; it's not about claiming and owning. It's not about saying "This child is mine." But you have to say, "This child is a gift in my life, someone I am allowed to love and nurture and then, perhaps, let go." All parenting is about that, really, but it's a greater likelihood—a bigger risk looms larger with foster children.

A foster parent maybe able to adopt the child, but that is not the deal when you go into the relationship. You absolutely have to be willing to share in the role of parent, but understand that you are not, in the end, their parent. Just because you set the meals on the table and cuddle with them and read them bedtime stories does not erase the fact that they already have a mother and/or father somewhere.

I have the greatest respect for foster parents. They have to be really centered and mature to approach parenthood through that channel because they have to want the child to be reunited with his or her biological family. They have to want the parent to get to the place where he or she is able to take care of the child they are raising. People tend to enter into parenting assuming there it will be a permanent relationship. But foster parents have to say, "Until your parents are able to take care of you, I will love you like my own." It requires a lot of maturity to tolerate that reality.

You also have to be willing to see your home as a revolving door, but at the same time consider permanency planning as a possible outcome. The reconciliation with birth parents might not work out, and then the child might be freed for adoption. It is hard to sign on to both of these realities at the same time. Again, you have to be able to say, "However this goes, I am willing to attach my fate to this child's life and do whatever is best for this child."

In their chapter, Pazstor, McNitt, and McFadden provide a framework for an approach to finding and maintaining foster parents, a critical area of systemic reform.

Families, Children, and the Law

Court systems and child welfare legislation are indispensable components of child welfare practice. Social workers, attorneys, judges, guardians ad litem, court-ordered special advocate volunteers, and others involved in the legal and judicial system are key actors in promoting systemic child welfare reform. But without laws authorizing the agency, police, and courts to intervene on behalf of abused and neglected children, society would be powerless to become involved in child protection.

Juvenile and family courts, as well as tribal and many general trial courts, have jurisdiction over cases involving child abuse and neglect. Only children who are identified in a state's law as needing the court's protection may become the subject of a child protection petition. Each state has its own terms and definitions related to the jurisdiction of these cases and each has its own court structure for handling such cases.

The passage of ASFA expanded the role of juvenile and family courts in several ways, as elaborated throughout this volume. Although these changes have been important for improving outcomes for children, ASFA did not address the systemic challenges faced by courts in meeting these new requirements, nor did it provide additional resources to assist courts in overcoming these challenges. In his chapter on families, children, and the law, Harden provides a comprehensive review of the salient issues involved in family, child welfare agency, community, and legal collaboration.

Child and Family Services Reviews

The collection and analysis of child welfare data has formed the foundation for the Child and Family Services Reviews (CFSRs) that have occurred in all 50 states, the District of Columbia, and Puerto Rico. In 1994, prior to the enactment of ASFA, Congress directed the U.S. Department of Health and Human Services to develop regulations for reviewing state child and family service programs administered under Titles IV-B and IV-E of the Social Security Act. Dissatisfaction among states and the federal government with prior federal reviews led, at least in part, to the passage of ASFA legislation. Although prior review processes had been effective in holding states accountable for meeting procedural requirements associated with the foster care program, they were less successful in insuring positive outcomes for the children, youth, and families served by state child welfare

agencies, especially those outside the foster care program—those children, youth, and families served by in-home family support programs.

Following the 1997 ASFA legislation, the Administration for Children and Families (ACF) within the U.S. Department of Health and Human Services, in consultation with the child welfare field, developed and field-tested the new CFSRs in 14 states, prior to implementing the reviews officially in federal FY2000. As noted by Milner, Mitchell, and Hornsby in their chapter, the CFSRs examine child welfare practices at the ground level, capturing the interactions among caseworkers, children, families, and service providers and determining the effects of those interactions on the children and families involved. The reviews stress practice and are based on the belief that, although certain policies and procedures are essential to an agency's capacity to support positive outcomes, it is the day-to-day casework practices and the underlying values that most influence such outcomes. In addition, the CFSRs are the federal system's primary mechanism for promoting an agenda of change and improvement in services to children and families nationally. With a focus on program improvement planning, the reviews are intended to stress thoughtful planning and the development of lasting solutions.

In addition to the limitations of the CFSR process identified by Milner, Mitchell, and Hornsby, conceptual limitations of the current national standards have been described by Courtney, Needell, and Wulczyn (2003:15), who have called for the federal government to "replace the current measures" used in the CFSRs. It can be anticipated that ongoing examination and refinement of the CFSR process will further enhance the prospects for systemic reforms that realize improved outcomes for children and families.

Supervisory and Quality Assurance Practices

Supervisors and administrative staff play a critical role in insuring that state and federal policies as well as local, regional, and federal initiatives are fully supported and that outcomes focused on safety, permanency, and well-being of children and families are achieved through the delivery of competent, individualized, and timely services.

Supervisors and other administrative level staff convey the mission, policies, procedures, and resources of the organization and direct the frontline action—the point of contact with children, youth, and families. Simultaneously, these professionals communicate information from the direct practice level to upper management to help agency administrators plan and allocate resources. As such, effective supervision is essential to achieving quality child welfare services.

Therefore, supervisory skills and ongoing training are critical to enhance supervisory capabilities in managing the practice-level staff and caseloads. Supervisors are increasingly more computer savvy and use their computer skills to access state child welfare data systems to monitor the practice-level work and individual worker performance. Understanding the data reports enables supervisors to identify outcome trends, more effectively manage frontline staff, and influence necessary changes in policies and procedures within agencies to yield better outcomes for children and their families.

To achieve positive outcomes, child welfare organizations must have a vision of what they hope to achieve and a strategy to guide their practice. With competing and often changing demands, organizing this work to achieve selected outcomes can be an arduous task. There is frequently a lack of direction, agreement, or understanding as to the outcomes that the organization is working to achieve. Unfortunately there is often a contradiction between what is targeted in practice and what is targeted by administration and supervision. Similarly the systems that have been implemented to support the staff, such as information systems and training, sometimes might appear to be focused in different directions.

In their chapter, Sahonchik, Frizsell, and O'Brien discuss the need for organizations to develop a quality assurance plan to guide and provide focus for their work with children, youth, and families. This chapter is intended to help students and practitioners understand how a strategic planning process can help child welfare agencies achieve desired results and how the rationalizing and all-encompassing features of strategic planning offer what may be the best prospect currently available to overcome obstacles to change. Toward this end, the chapter authors address three key questions: What is strategic planning? Why should a child welfare organization engage in it? How do professionals in a child welfare organization develop, implement, and monitor a strategic plan?

Accreditation of Organizations

Accreditation of child welfare organizations is yet another venue for systemic evaluation of and ultimate improvement in services to children, youth, and families. Accreditation, as noted in the chapter by Morison, is a well-established process for public and private social service and behavioral healthcare providers. The accreditation activities of self-study, review, and recognition can pinpoint strengths and areas of needed improvement in an organization's governance, operations, and services. Agencies that pursue accreditation are prompted to rigorously plan for optimal use of resources, upgrade core conditions, enhance services, reduce preventable untoward events, and improve organizational performance and outcomes.

The chapter by Morison sets forth the current context for accreditation in child welfare organizations, including broadened advocacy for the implementation of research-based practice and achievement of positive outcomes during a time of severely reduced budgets. It examines the role that accreditation can play to help agencies meet demands for accountability, and provides readers with insight into how accreditation is facilitated and implemented. Accreditation standards, like continuous quality improvement strategies and the federal CFSR process, offer practice guidelines that support positive outcomes. Accreditation can be valuable when viewed as a means to facilitate continuous long-term planning, achieve ever-stronger operations, and promote better outcomes for those served by organizational professionals.

Seven Systemic Factors Measured by CFSR

In the CFSR process, there are seven systemic factors that are evaluated. These factors, along with the safety, permanency, and well-being outcomes, provide those charged with evaluating the state's performance with a comprehensive overview of the state's capacity to work with children, youth, and families. As part of the review of systemic factors, each state must have a well-developed child welfare program to produce consistently positive outcomes for children and families. One of the goals of the federal reviews is to identify areas in each state's system that can be improved. The following identifies and elaborates on these seven systemic factors and related indicators that are measured in the CFSR process for each state:

1. Statewide information system. The state can readily identify the status, demographic characteristics, location, and goals for the placement of every child who is—or has been in the preceding 12 months—in foster care.
2. Case review system. The state provides a written case plan for each child to be developed jointly with the child's parent(s); provides a periodic review of the status of each child no less than once every 6 months; insures that each child in foster care has a permanency hearing no later than 12 months from the date the child entered foster care and not less than every 12 months thereafter; provides a process for termination of parental rights proceedings; and provides foster parents, pre-adoptive parents, and relative caregivers of children in foster care with

notice of and an opportunity to be heard in any review or hearing.
3. Quality assurance system. The state insures that children in foster care placements receive quality services that protect their safety and health and evaluates and reports on these services.
4. Staff training. Development and training programs support the goals and objectives in the state's Child and Family Services Plan; address services provided under both subparts of Title IV-B and the training plan under Title IV-E of the Social Security Act; and provide training for staff members who work in family preservation and support services, as well as child protective, foster care, adoption, and independent living services. Ongoing training that addresses the skills and knowledge necessary to carry out their duties in the state's Child and Family Services Plan is also provided for staff. Short-term training is offered for current or prospective foster parents, adoptive parents, and the staff of state-licensed/approved child care institutions that care for foster and adopted children.
5. Service array. The state has an array of services that assesses the strengths and needs of children and families; addresses the needs of the family, as well as the individual child, to create a safe home environment; and enables children at risk of foster care placement to remain with their families when their safety and well-being can be reasonably assured. Services are designed to help children achieve permanency; to be accessible to families and children in all political subdivisions covered in the state's Child and Family Services Plan; and to be individualized to meet the unique needs of each child and family.
6. Agency responsiveness to the community. The state engages in ongoing consultation, coordination, and annual progress reviews with a variety of individuals and organizations representing the state and county

agencies responsible for implementing the Child and Family Services Plan and other major stakeholders in the services delivery system. The stakeholders include, at a minimum, tribal representatives, consumers, service providers, foster care providers, the juvenile court, and public and private child and family serving agencies.

7. Foster and adoptive parent licensing, recruitment, and retention. The state establishes and maintains standards for foster family homes and child care institutions, applies standards to every licensed/approved foster family home or child care institution that receives Title IV-E or IV-B funds, and complies with the safety requirements for foster care and adoption placements. In addition, each state has a process that recruits foster and adoptive families who reflect the racial diversity of the children in the state, and develops and implements plans for the effective use of cross-jurisdictional resources to facilitate timely adoption or permanent placement.

Strategic planning strategies, accreditation, and the CFSR represent an unprecedented opportunity and an enormous responsibility for child welfare systems to address issues affecting the system's overall functioning. The opportunity to work collaboratively with the courts and legal entities, to address broader issues of practice involving fathers, insuring placement stability, reducing the overrepresentation of children and youth of color in foster care, enhancing responsiveness to immigrant communities, and effecting lasting changes in the ways that public child welfare systems develop resources and respond to the needs of children and families carries with it the responsibility to diligently strive to implement changes that will reform systems. By focusing on both frontline child welfare practice and the systemic supports for practice at the local level, there are opportunities for those at every level to make changes where the effects can be felt the most: in the lives of children, youth, and families.

References

Adoption and Safe Families Act. (1997). P.L. 105-89.

Barbell, K., & Freundlich, M. (2002). *Foster care today.* Washington, DC: Casey Family Programs.

Children's Bureau. (2000). Promising practices: States streamline foster and adoptive home approval process. *Children's Bureau Express, 1*(7), 1–4.

Courtney, M., Needell, B., & Wulczyn, F. (2003). National standards in the Child and Family Services Reviews: Time to improve on a good idea. Paper prepared for the Joint Center for Poverty Research. Child Welfare Services Research and its Policy Implications. Washington, DC. Retrieved May 18, 2005, from www.jcpr.org/wpfiles/needell.pdf?CFID=6095693&CFTOKEN=71821970.

Dougherty, S. (2001). *Engaging foster families. Toolbox 1.* Washington, DC: Child Welfare League of America.

Mallon, G. P. (2004). *Gay men choosing parenthood.* New York: Columbia University Press.

U.S. Department of Health and Human Services. (2004). *Preliminary FY 2002 estimates as of August, 2004. (The AFCARS Report).* Retrieved December 1, 2004, from www.acf.hhs.gov/programs/cb/publications/afcars/report9.htm.

AMY C. D'ANDRADE

Placement Stability in Foster Care

Permanency is a central aim of the child welfare system. The Adoption Assistance and Child Welfare Act of 1980 and more recently, the Adoption and Safe Families Act (ASFA) of 1997, emphasize the idea that every child should have a permanent home. In this chapter, I explore a phenomenon in child welfare that might be considered the antithesis of permanence: placement instability, which occurs when children and youth experience a series of homes or facilities during their time in foster care.

Placement instability was first identified in studies examining the child welfare system in the 1950s, 1960s, and 1970s (Fanshel 1971; Maas & Engler 1959; Malone 1960). These studies showed that for many children and youth, the agency responsible for their care had no articulated plan either for reunifying them with their parents or for making other arrangements for a permanent placement. As a result, children and youth were "drifting" in care, often enduring multiple placements, with no actions being undertaken on their behalf to find them permanent homes. The Adoption Assistance and Child Welfare Act was enacted to combat what was labeled "foster care drift." The law created financial incentives for the development of preventive and reunification services, required states to make reasonable efforts to provide these services as a condition of funding, and also required the development of a permanent plan—adoption, guardianship, or another permanent living arrangement—for every child not reunified within 18 months of being taken into care. The hope was that these reforms would insure that every child found a legally permanent home or at least a stable one.

Although changes brought about by the Adoption Assistance and Child Welfare Act have been instrumental in facilitating permanence for some children and youth, the problem of children and youth drifting in foster care has not been solved. Approximately 20–25% of children and youth who enter out-of-home care are neither reunified nor find other permanent homes through adoption or guardianship; for these youngsters, placement instability remains an ongoing concern. This chapter begins by describing some of the challenges involved with defining instability and details the evidence regarding its effects on children and youth. The magnitude of the problem is reviewed and various risk factors explored. Promising approaches are considered, along with the available evidence regarding their effectiveness. The chapter concludes by calling for expanded efforts on the part of researchers, program developers, practitioners, and policymakers to improve the situation for children and youth in foster care.

Defining Placement Instability

A number of challenges exist in defining placement instability (James, Landsverk, & Slymen 2003; Newton, Litrownik, & Landsverk 2000). The simplest approach is to merely count the number of placements or placement changes a child has had. Many of the studies exploring the phenomenon have framed the issue in this manner. However, placement instability is considerably more complex than this conceptualization suggests.

Placement changes in foster care can occur for a number of reasons: the current situation may not be beneficial to the child; the foster parent may find the child's behavior too difficult; or the foster parent's circumstances may change unexpectedly, resulting in an inability to care for the child (James 2004; Kadushin & Martin 1988). Although some researchers assert that even the most carefully planned moves are a disruption in the continuity of care and a cause for concern (Webster, Barth, & Needell 2000), others argue that placement changes should not necessarily be considered a negative experience; a change could result in an environment better suited to the child's needs (Festinger 1983; Usher, Randolph, & Gogan 1999). Some researchers (Proch & Taber 1985:309) then define the problem as "placement disruption": "an unplanned change in foster placement made in response to a demand for replacement by a child's caregiver."

Other aspects of the child welfare placement process complicate the task of defining placement instability. Children with the same number of placements may have different patterns of placement: some children with multiple placements may be tending toward increased stability and permanence, whereas others may be moving toward continuing instability and more restrictive settings (Berrick, Needell, Barth, & Jonson-Reid 1998; James, Landsverk, & Slymen 2003; Usher, Randolph, & Gogan 1999). Emergency shelter care—a brief placement in group care or a specialized short-term foster family home for assessment purposes—is sometimes considered to add to the overall total placement count (Newton, Litrownik, & Landsverk 2000), and sometimes not (Webster, Barth, & Needell 2000). Although placement stability is generally considered with respect to a single period in care, one could also expand the concept to account for reentry into foster care, with subsequent entries considered additional placements. Interrupted placements can also be problematic. If a child is placed for 2 weeks in a psychiatric hospital from a foster home, and

then returns to the same home, it is not clear whether that experience should be counted as one, two, or three placements (Newton, Litrownik, & Landsverk 2000).

Clearly, there is no single agreed-on definition of placement instability or strategy for handling the myriad situations that complicate the placement process. However, there is somewhat more consensus regarding the deleterious effects of placement instability.

Effects of Placement Instability

Most professionals agree that placement instability is harmful to children and youth in foster care. When children change placements, they are likely to experience rejection by a caregiver as well as loss of a familiar social environment and its associated relationships, and must adapt to a new environment and new caregivers. However, there is surprisingly little evidence that multiple placements are detrimental (Barber & Delfabbro 2003; Proch & Taber 1985). Empirical research is limited; there are relatively few studies examining the issue, and most of those conducted rely on bivariate tests of association, which cannot rule out alternate explanations for the outcomes found. Here I present empirical evidence regarding the effects of placement instability on children and youth, as well as concerns generated from related theory. Those studies in which authors have attempted to control for extraneous factors through the study design or statistical analysis are noted in the text.

Attachment

Many researchers and theorists have expressed concerns about the effects of multiple placements on a child's ability to form healthy attachments with people (Cox & Cox 1985; Littner 1956; Maas & Engler 1959; Meezan 1983; Shireman 1983). Several decades of research on attachment provide a basis for this concern. Attachment theorists stress the importance of the infant-parent attachment and note that mothers who are neglectful, abusive, or inconsistent have infants who show insecure patterns of attachment. These patterns of attachment tend to self-perpetuate, as the child's attachment behavior tends to elicit responses from the caregiver that strengthen the behavior pattern (Bowlby 1988; Goldberg 2000). Although early patterns established between the mother and infant continue to influence the child's behavior, there is also an ongoing interaction between the child's personality and his environment. This can bode well for a child or youth moved from a damaging environment to a supportive, healthy foster home, but has less hopeful implications for those who experience a series of rejections as they change placements, with each rejection potentially affecting their attachment behavior and ability to form positive connections with people.

Education

It is well established that foster children and youth lag behind their peers in educational achievement (Ayasse 1995; Slater & Smith 1993). Few studies, however, have examined the degree to which placement stability may be contributing to these poor outcomes. Available studies do suggest that movement in foster care has negative consequences for educational achievement. A study of the effects of residential and school mobility on academic outcomes for a stratified sample of 726 maltreated and matched nonmaltreated children in New York found that mobility was negatively associated with such academic outcomes as test scores, English grades, and grade repetition (controlling for gender, age, and public assistance status) (Eckenrode, Rowe, Laird, & Braithwaite 1995). In addition to affecting current academic functioning, placement instability appears to hinder overall educational outcomes. Higher numbers of placements have been found to be associated with lower levels of overall educational achievement (Zimmerman 1982) and with a depressed likelihood of earning credits at a community college in early adulthood (controlling for age, ethnicity, placement type, gender, and county

size) (Needell, Brookhart, Jackman, Cuccaro-Alamin, & Shlonsky 2002).

Mental Health and Behavioral Problems

Many studies have found that placement instability is associated with behavioral and emotional problems for children in care. More than four decades ago, Maas and Engler (1959) reported that problem behaviors in children and youth appeared to be associated with the number of moves they had made in foster care. Similarly, a study of the population of children ($n = 585$) who exited the Casey Family Programs from 1966 through 1984 found that children with more placements prior to entering the program were more likely to be considered hostile and negative when assessed upon entry. Additionally, children and youth who experienced more placements while in Casey care were in poorer condition at departure from the program (Fanshel, Finch, & Grundy 1990). Those with more placements have also been found to be more likely to receive mental health services while in care (Needell, Brookhart, Jackman, Cucarro-Alamin, & Shlonsky 2002), suggesting they may have greater mental health needs than children and youth with fewer placements.

The association of more problematic behaviors with the number of placements could be simply because children and youth with more difficult behaviors are harder to care for and hence move more frequently. One study (Newton, Litrownik, & Landsverk 2000) attempts to disentangle this relationship and test the hypothesis that placement instability negatively affects behavior. A sample of 415 children who had been in care at least 5 months were assessed approximately 5 months after entry to care (Time 1), and again a year later (Time 2). A version of Achenbach's Child Behavior Checklist (CBCL) was used to assess problem behaviors on three domains. The sample was divided into two groups: children whose scores on all domains were below all borderline cut points, and a more disturbed group of children, who scored above the cut point on at least one of the domains. The more disturbed group had a higher average number of placements (4.6) than those without problems (3.9). For the whole sample, more problems were associated with more placement changes at both measurement points. This association between number of placements and problem behaviors is well known. However, if multiple placements in turn *cause* emotional and behavioral problems, CBCL scores at Time 2 should worsen for children with more placements. The researchers assessed this with a linear regression using Time 2 CBCL scores as the outcome, and controlling for Time 1 CBCL scores as well as race, age, and gender. When subjects had five or more placements, the number of placements did have a significant negative effect on Time 2 CBCL scores, supporting the hypothesis that placement movement itself negatively affects behavior.

Not all studies have found an association between behavioral and emotional problems and placement instability, however. A recent examination (Barber & Delfabbro 2003) of the association of child well-being with placement instability found that children and youth with unstable placement patterns were just as likely to have improved well-being scores across an 8-month period as were those with stable placement patterns. Similarly, a study of a random sample of 492 foster children in Oregon under 12 who had been in care for more than 1 year found that multiple placements were not associated with lower levels of child well-being (Lahti 1982).

Preparation for Independent Living

There are an estimated 20,000 youths who emancipate from the foster care system each year at age 18 or 19 (Courtney, Piliavin, Grogan-Kaylor, & Nesmith 2001). Taber and Proch (1987:433) assert adolescents with multiple placements:

Cannot master developmental tasks or achieve permanency goals because they are not in one place long enough to benefit from services. With each move, they fall farther behind in school and become more alienated from adults. They ultimately "age out" of foster care lacking urban survival skills and without adults upon whom they can rely.

Indeed, youth with more placements appear to be less equipped for independence. Those with more placements were found to be more likely to have psychological problems at emancipation (Festinger 1983). Another study (Iglehart 1994) found that for a random sample of 152 adolescent foster youth in Los Angeles aged 16 or older, those with fewer placements were more likely to be perceived by their caregivers as having the ability to create a supportive environment for themselves: to choose friends, take care of their homes, and know where to turn for help (controlling for the presence of a mental health problem and school performance).

Adult Outcomes

The relationship of placement instability to a number of adult outcomes has been assessed, with contradictory findings. Although Festinger (1983) found no association between the number of placements and the frequency with which young adults had moved since leaving care, or with their overall sense of well-being as an adult, adults who had more placements during their childhoods in care were found to be more likely to be functioning poorly (Zimmerman 1982), less likely to have remained in contact with foster parents (Festinger 1983), and more likely to be emotionally disturbed (Fanshel, Finch, & Grundy 1990). Young women who emancipated from care with over five placements have been found to be more likely to be receiving Aid to Families with Dependent Children (AFDC)/Temporary Assistance to Needy Families (TANF) than those with only one placement (controlling for age, ethnicity, placement type, gender, and county size). Although the number of placements was not significantly associated with whether a youth earned any money after emancipation, youth who experienced five or more placements were less likely to earn at least $1,250 or more quarterly than those with only one placement (Needell, Brookhart, Jackman, Cucarro-Alamin, & Shlonsky 2002).

Fanshel (1992) expresses a concern that multiple placements will contribute to the likelihood of a child engaging in criminal activity as an adult. Research in this area is inconclusive: some bivariate studies have found such an association (Zimmerman 1982), whereas others have not (Festinger 1983). In a multivariate analysis controlling for age, ethnicity, placement type, gender, and county, the more placements a boy had while in care, the more likely he was to have a felony conviction (Needell, Brookhart, Jackman, Cucarro-Alamin, & Shlonsky 2002).

Overall, multiple placements appear to be damaging to children and youth. Although results are equivocal, many researchers have found higher numbers of placements to be associated with problems in education, behavior, mental health, preparation for independent living, and adult functioning. In the next section, I consider how many children and youth are being affected by the problem of placement instability.

Demographics and the Extent of the Problem

Comparing findings of studies that examine placement stability is difficult because researchers study different subpopulations of children and youth in care, examine different periods of time, use different study methodologies, and apply different definitions of "instability." However, the literature does provide a general sense of the issue, and indications as to which groups might be most greatly affected.

Findings from several studies of placement stability that use samples drawn from the overall child welfare population suggest that approximately half of all foster children and youth experience only one or two placements. In a longitudinal study of all 1993 first entries to care in one Ohio county ($n = 1456$), 56% of all children had only one placement over 3 to 4 years (Usher, Randolph, & Gogan 1999). Similarly, a study examining all children and youth emancipating from care in California from 1992 to 1997 from the child welfare system ($n = 11,060$) found that 42.5% had experienced only one or two placements during their stay in care (Needell, Brookhart, Jackman, Cuccaro-Alamin, & Shlonsky 2002).

However, sampling child welfare populations entering or exiting care ignores an important element necessary in understanding placement instability. When time in care is taken into account, it can be seen that placement instability is more of a problem for children in long-term care than for those who reunify or are adopted or placed in guardianship within a year or two. Approximately 20–25% of all children who enter care do not reunify or enter into other permanent arrangements, such as adoption or guardianship, but remain in long-term foster care (Berrick, Needell, Barth, & Jonson-Reid 1998). In comparison to the overall population of youngsters in care, for which one or two placements is the norm, longitudinal studies examining the placement stability of those in long-term care commonly find that more than half had three or more placements.

In Usher, Randolph, and Gogan's (1999) study, almost 60% of the children still in care after 3 or 4 years had three or more placements: 21% had three, 16% had four, and just under 15% had five or more placements. Less than one-fourth remained in their first placement (1999). Data from the national Foster Care Information System (FCIS) on children and youth who had been in care more than 6 years show that only 18% of children who entered care before the age of 5 and whose predominant placement was with non-kin had one placement during that time; 58% had three or more placements, and 28% had five or more. Children and youth in kin placements fared somewhat better; 38% remained in their first placement after 6 years, 33% had three or more placements, and 10% had five or more (Berrick, Needell, Barth, & Jonson-Reid 1998). Webster, Barth, and Needell (2000) examined the experiences of all children under the age of 6 who entered care in California between January 1988 and December 1989, and who were still in care 8 years later. Only 21.5% of these children in non-kin care had one placement after 8 years; 52% had three or more placements, and 21% had five or more. Placements with kin were more stable, with 37% still in their first placement, 29% experiencing three or more, and 8.5% five or more placements.

Other studies of long-term care show similar findings. Less than half of a sample of Connecticut youth who had been in foster family care at least 2 years had only one placement; one-third had had three or more (Fein, Maluccio, & Kluger 1990). Just over 30% of a sample of 2,653 emancipating California adolescents who had been in care for at least 18 months experienced a single placement while in care; 19% had two placements; and 25% had five or more placements (Courtney & Barth 1996).

Two other subgroups of the foster care population also appear to be at higher risk for experiencing multiple placements: children and youth who have already begun to experience placement instability, and those in treatment placements. As part of an evaluation of an intervention to reduce placement instability, Taber and Proch (1987) studied 51 youths who had at least two placement disruptions within the past 2 years, and had been in care for a median of 3 years and 5 months. Over 80% of this group had experienced more than five placements so far during their sojourn in care, with a median of nine placement moves. In Needell, Brookhart, Jackman, Cuccaro-Alamin, and Shlonsky's study of emancipating foster youth, for the 15% of those whose last placement was a group home, more than half experienced five or more placements during care. For those emancipating from treatment foster care, 47% had five or more placements (2002).

One promising approach to understanding placement instability is to examine the patterns of placements. This approach allows the timing of placement changes and the type of placement setting to be considered in addition to the number of placements. Festinger (1983) noted that for certain outcomes, the pattern of placements was more important than the number. For example, a current sense of well-being was less likely for those who moved from foster home to group home than for those who moved from group home to group home. Zimmerman (1982) went a step further by identifying four placement patterns: (1) reunification within 6 years and one or two placements (49% of the sample); (2) long-term foster care with one or two placements (31%); (3) long-term foster care with one or two placements, one of which was a treatment facility (5%); and (4) what she calls an "abnormal" pattern, long-term foster care with three or more placements of a "seemingly unplanned nature" (16%). Zimmerman found that children and youth with "abnormal" patterns were more likely to respond to the question "by whom were you really loved when you were growing up?" with the answer, "no one."

More recently, researchers have begun to expand upon this approach. Five general patterns of movement were identified in a cohort of 430 children aged 1–16 who entered care in one California city between May 1990 and October 1991 and were still in care 18 months later. "Early stability" children (35.6% of the sample) may have had several placements early in their stay in the system, but were placed within 45 days in a home in which they stayed the remainder of the 18-month period; "later stability" children (28.6%) experienced multiple placements during the first half of the study period, but attained stability between the forty-sixth day and the ninth month; "variable pattern" children (16.0%) spent at least half the study period in one placement, but disrupted before the study period was over; and, of greatest concern, "unstable pattern" children (19.8%)

experienced multiple placements, with none lasting longer than 9 months. Children and youth with higher levels of externalizing problems were more likely to experience increasingly unstable placement patterns (James, Landsverk, & Slymen 2003).

Wulczyn, Kogan, and Harden (2003) continue this line of inquiry by considering placement trajectories of children and youth. Using statistical techniques, common trajectories were extracted from a large sample of 16,170 children in care over a period of 3 years. This classification strategy revealed that children with the same number of placements differed in important ways. Older youth, for example, were more likely to experience changes later in their placement histories, whereas younger children tended to experience changes earlier, and then settle into a stable home. This avenue of research seems a fruitful one to pursue. It facilitates a more nuanced understanding of the phenomenon of placement instability—one that encompasses placement restrictiveness and placement timing, in addition to the number of placements. Such a measure is able to identify the important differences between those children who, after an initial series of placements, quickly settle in to a stable home, and those who may experience perhaps the same number of placements, but are tending toward greater instability over time. If characteristics can be identified that predict which children are most likely to experience variable or unstable patterns, then appropriate interventions can be targeted.

However defined and examined, placement stability remains a problem for many youngsters in out-of-home care. Those who remain in foster care long-term, who have begun to exhibit a pattern of placement disruption, older youth, and children in treatment placements appear to be at greatest risk for continued instability.

Risk (or Contributing) Factors

The cause of placement instability has not been widely studied. Here I consider three broad categories of contributing or causative factors: limited agency resources, the nature of foster care itself, and aspects of the individual child.

Agency Resource Issues

Due to resource constraints, social workers in child welfare agencies tend to have very large caseloads, making it "unlikely that sustained attention can be given to any one family" (Cox & Cox 1985:12). Caseload demands can also result in social workers having insufficient time to make complete assessments of children necessary for appropriate matches between the child's needs and foster home characteristics. Placements that have a higher likelihood of disrupting might result (Berrick, Needell, Barth, & Jonson-Reid 1998; Cox & Cox 1985).

The low reimbursement rate for foster care providers, coupled with the movement of women to the workforce, has resulted in a continual decrease in the availability of foster homes (Fanshel 1992; Testa & Rolock 1999). As a result, children are often placed in homes based on what is available rather than what might best meet the children's needs (Lutz 2003; McGowan 1983). Additionally, support services provided to foster parents tend to be minimal (Berrick, Needell, Barth, & Jonson-Reid 1998; Cox & Cox 1985; Knitzer & Allen 1978). It may be that if more training and support were provided to caregivers, fewer foster home placements would fail (Lutz 2003).

Nature of Foster Care

Historically, foster parents were discouraged from forming strong connections with the children placed with them (Bartholet 1999); in fact, social workers sometimes moved children and youth whom they felt were becoming "too attached" to their foster parents (Knitzer & Allen 1978). Although child welfare agencies no longer explicitly discourage strong attachments between foster parents and their charges, some professionals have argued that foster care by its very nature cannot provide a critical sense of permanence and security to children (Bryce &

Ehlert 1971; Goldstein, Freud, & Solnit 1973). "Even the most well-intentioned foster parent must view themselves as temporary providers, and this perception is bound to place barriers in the path of their forming intimate, loving relationships with the foster children and youth they care for" (Berrick, Needell, Barth, & Jonson-Reid 1998:107).

However, some researchers have found that foster care can provide adequate security and permanence for children. Lahti (1982) found that foster parents often considered a child a permanent member of the family. Caregivers' assessments of children's well-being was unrelated to their legal status, but positively associated with the caregiver's sense of the child's entrenchment in the family.

Although foster care by its essence may not necessarily preclude a sense of permanence for a child, certain aspects inherent to the placement process may threaten the likelihood of stability. First, most of the children in foster care have suffered some form of significant abuse or neglect. Attachment theorists posit that abused or neglected children develop attachment patterns that can be challenging for caregivers to deal with, such as whining, clingy, or distant behavior (Bowlby 1988). Studies of children who have been abused in infancy suggest that as toddlers and preschoolers, they have difficulty relating to adults and peers, reacting with overt hostility or withdrawal and avoidance (Dore & Eisner 1993).

Compounding the problem is that the behavioral patterns tend to be self-perpetuating. The behavioral pattern developed by a child in response to a dysfunctional parent is likely to elicit responses from any new caregivers that reinforce the pattern (Bowlby 1988; Penzarro & Lein 1995). According to the theory, children's environments influence their behavior, so one could hope that the pattern could be altered upon their placement in foster care; however, it is also argued (Bowlby 1988:170) that as children get older, the behavior patterns become "increasingly a property of the child himself,

and also increasingly resistant to change. This means he tends to impose it . . . upon new relationships" such as a foster parent. These difficult behaviors are often interpreted by caregivers as a rejection of their well-intentioned efforts (Dore & Eisner 1993), and could result in sufficient foster parent frustration to cause a disruption.

Characteristics of the Child
A number of studies have examined characteristics of children and youth associated with placement instability. Boys (Palmer 1996; Webster, Barth, & Needell 2000), white children and youth, and those with more placements in the first year of care (Webster, Barth, & Needell 2000), older children and those not living with kin (Webster, Barth, & Needell 2000; Wulczyn, Kogan, & Harden 2003), and children and youth with emotional or behavior problems (Palmer 1996; Pardeck 1983) have been found to be more likely to experience placement instability.

Although the troublesome behavior of foster children is often assumed to be behind a placement move, a recent study examining reasons for placement changes in foster care suggests that child behaviors are in fact not the most common cause of placement changes. One study (James 2004) sampled 454 children and youth entering care between May 1990 and October 1991, who together experienced 1,358 placement changes over 18 months. Only 21% of the placement changes that occurred were prompted by the behavior of the child; the rest were due to such reasons as moving to a placement with siblings, to long-term placement, to or within a short-term placement (31%), to placement with a relative (36%); or foster family personal issues or complaints against the foster parents (8%).

Unfortunately, as this brief review suggests, little is known about the causes of placement instability. What additional factors may be involved and the degree to which factors considered here might interact with one another is unknown. Clearly, much work remains to be done in this area.

Promising Approaches

Most of the legislative efforts to improve the child welfare system have consisted of policies that attempt to keep children and youth out of foster care, shorten their time in care, or move them out of foster care as quickly as possible. In the context of the problem of placement instability, these efforts could be considered preventive, in the sense that they attempt to prevent children from entering the environment in which they are at risk for experiencing the problem, or reduce the time they spend in that risk environment. For example, the Adoption Assistance and Child Welfare Act attempted to decrease the number of children and youth entering long-term foster care by minimizing federal incentives within AFDC for custodial use of foster care and increasing funding for placement prevention and reunification services. Family preservation programs further prompted by the 1993 Family Preservation and Support Act also attempted to decrease the number of children entering foster care by providing intensive services to parents in an attempt to keep children in the home. To limit the amount of time spent in foster care, time frames were mandated by which a permanent plan had to be in place for each child in care. ASFA shortened those time frames in many states and emphasized efforts to find adoptive homes for children and youth.

Other reform efforts could be seen as ameliorative, as they attempt to address some of the possible effects of placement instability. For example, the federally funded Independent Living Skills program provides services to prepare adolescents in foster care for independent living in the community when they age out of the system. Programs like Foster Youth Services (for education) or the California Health Passport Program (for healthcare) attempt to track children and youth's records as they "bounce" from placement to placement.

Although valuable, these programs and policies do not target the underlying problem of placement instability. Few programs have developed specifically to address the issue. However, other innovations in child welfare services have shown some promise in decreasing placement instability; these programs are described here, along with one program, developed and evaluated in the late 1980s, which specifically targeted placement instability.

Placements with Kin

About 25% of children placed in foster care are placed with members of their extended families (Geen 2003). These kin placements have been shown to offer considerably more stability for the increasing numbers of children placed in them than do other kinds of foster care placements (Berrick, Needell, Barth, & Jonson-Reid 1998). One study of kin care in California examined placement stability rates over 4 years for the population who entered care in the first 4 months of 1988 ($n = 11,189$). For those cases that remained open after 4 years, 62.9% of children initially placed with kin (compared to 21.3% of children in non-kin placements) remained in the same home; 17.2% of children in kinship care had two placements (compared to 30% of those in non-kin care). Almost 16% of those in non-kin care had five or more placements, over twice the rate for the group in kinship care. Similar disparities in placement stability rates existed for children and youth who had been reunified or adopted within 4 years. Although some children placed with kin did change placements, 85% of these new placements were with other kin members (Courtney & Needell 1997).

Casey Family Services

Casey Family Services is a privately endowed agency with the distinct purpose of providing quality long-term foster care to children (Fanshel, Finch, & Grundy 1990). The program provides higher payments and services to caregivers, as well as more services and supports to children, including such services for emancipated youth as financed apprenticeships and advanced education. The average number of placements per child decreases once the child is in the Casey program; from over six at the time of entry to the program to 3.3 placements while in Casey care (Casey Family Programs 1997). The program claims that although children and youth may have multiple placements while with Casey, they still benefit from having their cases managed by the agency. "Sometimes a child who has been unable to establish a permanent relationship with any family comes to regard the agency and the division social worker as the stable center of his or her life" (Fanshel, Finch, & Grundy 1990:8).

Professional Foster Parents
A related approach to the Casey program is the professionalization of foster parents, based on the notion that higher compensation and professional treatment will act as an incentive to foster parents to encourage them to keep children and youth (Testa & Rolock 1999). Although the concept of professional foster parenting is only vaguely defined, there is general agreement that it includes adequate compensation; benefits based on training, experience, and merit; and participation of the caregivers as a member of the agency service team (Pecora, Whittaker, Maluccio, & Barth 2000; Testa & Rolock 1999). Testa and Rolock (1999) state that salaries legitimize the increasingly complex demands placed on foster parents, such as caring for difficult children and dealing with the bureaucracy of a child welfare agency, and provide acknowledgment for the work of foster parents in universally understood terms.

There is some evidence that professional foster homes provide more stability for children and youth. One study (Testa & Rolock 1999) compared kinship caregivers, non-kin foster parents, and two types of professional foster parents (a group compensated with a salary and a group compensated with a housing voucher). Homes that received children between December 1994 and September 1996 ($n = 2,062$) were tracked through September 1997. Almost 60% of the professional foster parents who received a salary were caring for the same children at the assessment date as they were at the start of the study. Kinship care provided the next highest degree of stability, with 46.8% caring for the same children. Professional foster parents who received housing vouchers had the next highest degree of stability, with 36–40% of them continuing to care for the same children. Least stable was regular foster care, with only 20.2% of the homes caring for the same children at the assessment point.

Court-Ordered Special Advocates
The Child Abuse Prevention and Treatment Act of 1976 mandated that all children and youth in the system due to abuse or neglect must have a guardian ad litem representing them in court. Although many states use attorneys for this role, others use court-ordered special advocates (CASAs) or assign CASAs to certain children and youth in addition to an attorney. CASA volunteers speak for children in dependency proceedings, investigate the facts of a case, advocate for the children's best interests, insure services are provided, and monitor court orders to insure compliance. In 1998, there were 843 CASA programs in the United States, with 47,000 volunteers serving 183,339 children (Calkins & Millar 1999; Litzenfelner 2000).

A study of two CASA sites in Kansas compares children and youth entering care who were assigned CASAs to a matched group who did not receive CASAs ($n = 81$). After 2 years, the CASA group had fewer placements, averaging 3.9 to the comparison group's 6.6 (Litzenfelner 2000). Another study examined all children who entered care in one county in 1994. Those who were assigned CASAs had fewer placements than those not assigned CASAs; groups did not differ by gender, ethnicity, or "case severity" (Calkins & Millar 1999). However, neither study makes use of random assignment or statistical controls; differences between children assigned and those not assigned CASAs could be due to other factors than the CASA program.

Group Care

It has long been the consensus in child welfare that a family environment is preferable to an institutional one in facilitating healthy child development (Whittaker 2000). Group care has been generally distrusted due to its potential for abuse and institutional neglect, its history of poor living conditions, minimal evidence regarding its effectiveness, and its high cost (Whittaker 2000). Most often, group care is considered an unpleasant but regrettably necessary component of the continuum of placement services available for children in out-of-home care, reserved for those so disturbed that they require extraordinary structure and supervision (Allen & Knitzer 1983; Bartholet 1999). However, it has been argued that there are other populations for whom group care may be an appropriate placement. Some researchers have theorized that the task of relating to new parent figures may be too difficult for children and youth with very troubled relations with their own parents. Relating to professional staff can be less emotionally taxing, and provide "diluted" emotional relationships that allow a child to maintain a "safe" psychological distance from caregivers and "moderate contact in accordance with emotional needs" (Kadushin & Martin 1988:676). As a result, the child experiences less distress and engages in less acting out, obviating the need for a replacement (Rosenberg 1983).

There is some evidence to support the idea that group care may reduce placement instability for some young people. Wulczyn, Kogan, and Harden (2003:232) found a subgroup of children in group care who had fewer placements than those in foster home care and conclude that "group care may be preferable if it averts the multiple placements that some children and youth may experience (e.g., adolescents)." Penzarro and Lein (1995) and Benoit (1994) also argue that stability in residential care would be less damaging for children than multiple placements in foster care. Although group care is likely to remain a controversial approach to reducing placement instability, for some troubled adolescents, it may be worth further consideration.

Intensive Case Management

One program specifically designed to address placement instability has been found to be effective. In 1987, Taber and Proch reported on a program for youth at high risk of placement instability: those aged 12 to 18 who suffered at least two disruptions in the past 24 months and who had significant problem behaviors ($n = 51$). These youth received support services, careful assessment, and were actively involved in case planning with the agency. To assess the success of the program, the authors compared the number of moves each child experienced from the time of program completion to the time of assessment ("after" scores) to the number of moves experienced over the same length of time just prior to the service (this time frame varied for each child). The median number of moves was significantly reduced from 4.8 to 1.8. Overall, placement moves were reduced 60%; additionally, those moves experienced after the child's participation in the program tended to be to less restrictive placements.

More recently, some states have developed innovative programs targeted specifically at reducing placement instability. Connecticut initiated a shelter/assessment strategy, in which children are first placed in an assessment center for up to 45 days. This allows time for them to have a thorough assessment, so that they may be placed in homes most suited for them, and thus be less likely to disrupt. In the same state, an emergency mobile crisis unit can be called on to assist in a crisis situation at a foster home, in the hopes of salvaging the placement. Mississippi requires some placement providers to agree to a "no decline, no dismiss" policy, in which children are to remain with that provider unless another level of care is appropriate. Vermont enhanced its management information data system to include reasons for placement changes. This enhanced understanding enabled professionals to target interventions appropriately. Arizona has been focusing on expanding respite care for foster parents (Lutz 2003). Evaluations of these efforts are not yet available, but program descriptions sound promising.

Discussion and Conclusion

Family preservation programs, reunification services, concurrent planning, and adoption services are commendable child welfare programs and should continue. But equally important—and currently neglected—are efforts to reduce placement instability for children and youth in care. Research reviewed here suggests that placement instability negatively affects school performance and educational attainment, condition at exit from care, and behavioral and emotional health while in care. Youth with multiple placements are less equipped for independent living and function less well as adults.

In spite of the substantial number of children and youth affected and the potential negative consequences of placement instability, the issue has received surprisingly little attention from the child welfare field. In the research arena, although information on number of placements is sometimes gathered as a variable in studies assessing the effects of foster care, it too seldom has been the subject of study in its own right. More sophisticated measurement strategies than simply counting the number of homes a child has experienced should be used; for example, strategies that incorporate the timing and restrictiveness of placements. Existing literature suffers from too much variability in time frames, populations studied, and definitions. Few studies consider the reason behind a placement change or even track such changes; thus little is known about the proportion of moves due to the child's behavior, the proportion thoughtfully planned, and that due to such

reasons as the death of illness of a foster parent. Without this kind of basic information, developing effective interventions will be very difficult.

Other neglected subjects of study regarding placement instability include the effects on caregivers, on siblings and foster siblings, and on the agency in terms of time and resources. Additionally, other aspects of foster care that may affect a child's experience of stability should be studied, such as the number of caregivers, placement with and movement of siblings (Fanshel 1992) or foster siblings, and number of caseworkers. The number of episodes should also be considered. Reentry to care is not infrequent: one study of youth emancipating from care in California found that 40% had at least two separate episodes in foster care (Needell, Brookhart, Jackman, Cuccaro-Alamin, & Shlonsky 2002). Studies that do not take reentry into account may be underestimating the problem of placement instability for a substantial number of children and youth.

The problem of placement instability has been neglected in the policy arena as well. National policy has focused on preventing entrance into care, shortening foster care stays, and moving children into adoptive homes. Studies reviewed here suggest that targeted attention in the form of advocates, intensive services and case planning involving the child or youth, and increased foster parent supports may make a meaningful difference in placement stability. However, little has been done to require or facilitate such efforts by agencies, or to encourage exploration of these or other alternatives for some older children, such as group home care (Goldsmith 1999). Although such ameliorative programs as Independent Living Services are a tacit acknowledgment of both the existence of the problem of placement instability and the government's responsibility to address it, they are inadequate as the primary policy intervention.

Some progress has been made, in that states are required to report placement change information to the federal government. Additionally, a national standard for placement stability has been set. In each state, 86.7% of all children in foster care for less than 12 months should have two or fewer placements. States are required to meet this standard, or present a plan to achieve it, to maintain federal funding (U.S. Department of Health and Human Services 2001). Although this standard uses a very simple measure of placement instability and considers only a portion of foster care stays, it is a first step toward directing more attention to this important issue. It should be accompanied by funding specifically targeted at reducing placement instability, particularly for children and youth in long-term care. Productive efforts might include research investigating causes of placement breakdown, development of model programs and their evaluation, and exploration of alternative living arrangements that may better meet the critical need of this population for a stable home.

Improving placement stability for children and youth in foster care is essential. There is still much to do: the most recent data from the Child and Family Services Reviews show that 36 of the 50 states that have undergone a review did not achieve substantial conformity in meeting the placement stability national standard (U.S. Department of Health and Human Services 2004). Researchers, policymakers, and practitioners share the responsibility of understanding the extent of the problem and developing and evaluating innovative solutions. Research efforts should explore causes and associated characteristics of instability, using expanded and more sophisticated definitions of the problem. In the practice arena, programs that have some empirical support, such as intensive case management services and improved supports and services to foster parents, should be pursued. Federal and state policy could do more to facilitate these efforts. Child welfare professionals should not continue to allow a substantial portion of foster children and youth to experience placement instability, and trust ameliorative programs to address the consequences.

References

Adoption and Safe Families Act. (1997). P.L. 105-89.

Adoption Assistance and Child Welfare Act. (1980). P.L. 96-272.

Allen, M., & Knitzer, J. (1983). Child welfare: Examining the policy framework. In B. McGowan & W. Meezan (eds.), *Child welfare: Current dilemmas, future directions*, pp. 93–142. Itasca, IL: Peacock Publishers.

Ayasse, R. (1995). Addressing the needs of foster children: The Foster Youth Services program. *Social Work in Education, 17*(4), 207–216.

Barber, J. G., & Delfabbro, P. H. (2003). Placement stability and the psychosocial well-being of children in foster care. *Research on Social Work Practice, 13,* 415–431.

Bartholet, E. (1999). *Nobody's children: Abuse and neglect, foster drift, and the adoption alternative.* Boston: Beacon Press.

Benoit, M. (1994). The quality—not the category—of care. In D. Besharov (ed.), *When drug addicts have children,* pp. 239–248. Washington, DC: Child Welfare League of America.

Berrick, J., Needell, B., Barth, R., & Jonson-Reid, M. (1998). *The tender years: Toward developmentally sensitive child welfare services for very young children.* New York: Oxford University Press.

Bowlby, J. (1988). *A secure base: Parent-child attachment and healthy human behavior.* London: Basic Books.

Bryce, M., & Ehlert, R. (1971). 144 foster children. *Child Welfare, 50,* 499–503.

Calkins, C., & Millar, M. (1999). The effectiveness of court appointed special advocates to assist in permanency planning. *Child and Adolescent Social Work, 16,* 37–45.

Casey Family Programs. (1997). *The first thirty years: What we have learned.* Seattle: Casey Family Programs.

Child Abuse Prevention and Treatment Act. (1976). P.L. 93-274.

Courtney, M., & Barth, R. (1996). Pathways of older adolescents out of foster care: Implications for independent living. *Social Work, 41,* 75–83.

Courtney, M., & Needell, B. (1997). Outcomes of kinship care: Lessons from California. In J. Berrick, R. Barth, & N. Gilbert (eds.), *Child welfare research review*, vol. 2, pp. 130–149. New York: Columbia University Press.

Courtney, M., Piliavin, I., Grogan-Kaylor, A., & Nesmith, A. (2001). Foster youth transitions to adulthood: A longitudinal view of youth leaving care. *Child Welfare, 80,* 685–717.

Cox, M., & Cox, R. (1985). A history of policy for dependent and neglected children. In M. Cox & R. Cox (eds.), *Foster care: Current issues, policies and practices*, pp. 1–25. Norwood, NJ: Ablex Publishing.

Dore, M., & Eisner, E. (1993). Child-related dimensions of placement stability in treatment foster care. *Child and Adolescent Social Work, 10*, 301–317.

Eckenrode, J., Rowe, E., Laird, M., & Brathwaite, J. (1995). Mobility as a mediator of the effects of child maltreatment on academic performance. *Child Development, 66*, 1130–1142.

Family Preservation and Support Act. (1993). P.L. 103-66.

Fanshel, D. (1971). The exit of children from foster care. *Child Welfare, 50*, 65–81.

Fanshel, D. (1992). Foster care as a two-tiered system. *Children and Youth Services Review, 14*, 49–60.

Fanshel, D., Finch, S., & Grundy, J. (1990). *Foster care in a life course perspective.* New York: Columbia University Press.

Fein, E., Maluccio, A., & Kluger, M. (1990). *No more partings: An examination of long-term foster care.* Washington, DC: Child Welfare League of America.

Festinger, T. (1983). *No one ever asked us: A postscript to foster care.* New York: Columbia University Press.

Geen, R. (2003). Kinship foster care: An ongoing, yet largely uninformed debate. In R. Geen (ed.), *Kinship care: Making the most of a valuable resource.* Retrieved June 30, 2004, from www.urbaninstitue.org/pubs/kinshipcare/chapter1.html.

Goldberg, S. (2000). *Attachment and development.* New York: Oxford University Press.

Goldsmith, H. (1999). Foreword. In R. McKenzie (ed.), *Rethinking orphanages for the 21st century*, pp. ix–xiii. Thousand Oaks, CA: Sage.

Goldstein, J., Freud, A., & Solnit, A. (1973). *Beyond the best interests of the child.* New York: Free Press.

Iglehart, A. (1994). Adolescents in foster care: Predicting readiness for independent living. *Children and Youth Services Review, 14*, 159–169.

James, S. (2004). Why do foster care placements disrupt? An investigation of reasons for placement change in foster care. *Social Services Review, 78*, 601–627.

James, S., Landsverk, J., & Slymen, D. J. (2003). Placement movement in out-of-home care: Patterns and predictors. *Children and Youth Services Review, 26*, 185–206.

Kadushin, A., & Martin, J. (1988). *Child welfare services.* New York: Macmillan Publishing.

Knitzer, J., & Allen, M. (1978). *Children without homes: An examination of public responsibility to children in out-of-home care.* Washington, DC: Children's Defense Fund.

Lahti, J. (1982). A follow-up study of foster children in permanent placement. *Social Service Review*, 556–571.

Littner, N. (1956). Traumatic effects of separation and placement. New York: Child Welfare League of America.

Litzelfelner, P. (2000). The effectiveness of CASAs in achieving positive outcomes for children. *Child Welfare, 79*, 179–193.

Lutz, L. L. (2003). *Achieving permanence for children in the child welfare system: Pioneering possibilities amidst daunting challenges.* Retrieved June 30, 2004, from www.hunter.cuny.edu/socwork/nrcfcpp/.

Maas, H., & Engler, R. (1959). *Children in need of parents.* New York: Columbia University Press.

Malone, B. (1960). Help for the child in an in-between world. *Child Welfare, 39*, 17–22.

McGowan, B. (1983). Historical evolution of child welfare services. In B. McGowan & W. Meezan (eds.), *Child welfare: Current dilemmas, future directions*, pp. 45–90. Itasca, IL: Peacock Publishers.

Meezan, W. (1983). Child welfare: An overview of the issues. In B. McGowan & W. Meezan (eds.), *Child welfare: Current dilemmas, future directions*, pp. 5–44. Itasca, IL: Peacock Publishers.

Needell, B., Brookhart, A., Jackman, W., Cucarro-Alamin, S., & Shlonsky, A. (2002). *Youth emancipated from foster care: Findings using linked administrative data.* Berkeley, CA: Center for Social Services Research.

Newton, R., Litrownik, A., & Landsverk, J. (2000). Children and youth in foster care: Disentangling the relationship between problem behavior and number of placements. *Child Abuse and Neglect, 24*, 1363–1374.

Palmer, S. E. (1996). Placement stability and inclusive practice in foster care: An empirical study. *Children and Youth Services Review, 18*, 589–601.

Pardeck, J. (1983). An empirical analysis of the behavioral and emotional problems of foster children as related to re-placement in care. *Child Abuse and Neglect, 7*, 75–78.

Pecora, P., Whittaker, J., Maluccio, A., & Barth, R. (2000). *The child welfare challenge: Policy, practice and research.* Hawthorne, NY: Walter de Gruyter.

Penzarro, R., & Lein, L. (1995). Burning their bridges: Disordered attachment and foster care discharge. *Child Welfare, 74*, 351–366.

Proch, K., & Taber, M. (1985). Placement disruption: A review of research. *Children and Youth Services Review, 7*, 309–320.

Rosenberg, L. (1983). The techniques of psychological assessment as applied to children in foster care and their families. In M. Hardin (ed.), *Foster children in the courts*, pp. 550–574. Boston: Butterworth Legal Publishers.

Shireman, J. (1983). Achieving permanence after placement. In B. McGowan & W. Meezan (eds.), *Child welfare: Current dilemmas, future directions*, pp. 377–424. Itasca, IL: Peacock Publishers.

Slater, J., & Smith, C. (1993). *Meeting the education needs of foster children in California: Strategies for improving academic success*, vol. 1. Sacramento: California Department of Education.

Taber, M., & Proch, K. (1987). Placement stability for adolescents in foster care: Findings from a program experiment. *Child Welfare, 66*, 433–445.

Testa, M., & Rolock, N. (1999). Professional foster care: A future worth pursuing? *Child Welfare, 78,* 108–124.

U.S. Department of Health and Human Services. (2001). *Background paper: Child and Family Services Reviews national standards.* Retrieved June 30, 2004, from www. acf.hhs.gov/programs/cb/hotissues/background.htm.

U.S. Department of Health and Human Services. (2004). *Findings from the initial Child and Family Services Reviews 2001–2004.* Retrieved October 1, 2004, from www.acf.hhs.gov/programs/cb/cwrp/2004cfsrresults. htm.

Usher, C., Randolph, K., & Gogan, H. (1999). Placement patterns in foster care. *Social Services Review, 73,* 22–36.

Webster, D., Barth, R., & Needell, B. (2000). Placement stability for children in out-of-home care: A longitudinal analysis. *Child Welfare, 79,* 614–632.

Whittaker, J. (2000). The future of residential group care. *Child Welfare, 79,* 59–74.

Wulczyn, F., Kogan, J., & Harden, B. J. (2003). Placement stability and movement trajectories. *Social Service Review, 77,* 212–236.

Zimmerman, R. (1982). *Foster care in retrospect.* New Orleans: Tulane University.

RUTH G. McROY

Overrepresentation of Children and Youth of Color in Foster Care

Overrepresentation (also termed "disproportionality") refers to the current situation in which particular racial/ethnic groups of children are represented in foster care at a higher or lower percentage than their representation in the general population. Disproportionality refers both to the overrepresentation of children of color in foster care and to the disparate outcomes they experience while in foster care.

Children of color, belonging to various cultural, ethnic, and racial communities (primarily African American, Hispanic, and Native American) are disproportionately represented in the child welfare system and frequently experience disparate and inequitable service provision. The overrepresentation of children of color in child welfare and other social service systems (e.g., juvenile justice) is linked to social class, economic, and other factors that must be addressed to insure that the needs of all children are fairly and appropriately served.

A closer look at the latest statistics available from the Adoption and Foster Care Data Analysis System (U.S. Department of Health and Human Services 2004) reveals that in 2002, 59% of the 532,000 children in the U.S. foster care system were children of color, yet only 38% of all U.S. children are children of color. The inverse is true for white children, who represent 61% of the U.S. child population, and only 37% of the children in out-of-home care.

Sections of the literature review in this chapter appear also in R. McRoy (2004), The color of child welfare. In K. Davis & T. Bent-Godley (eds.), *The color of social policy.* Washington, DC: Council on Social Work Education.

Further examination of ethnic differences among the populations of color reveals that African Americans have the highest overrepresentation of all ethnic groups in foster care. They make up 37% (195,040) of those in out-of-home care, yet consititute only 15% of the U.S. child population. Native Americans are also overrepresented in foster care, as they make up 2% of the foster care population and only 1% of the U.S. child population.

Asian American and Hispanic children tend to be underrepresented in foster care. In 2002, Asian/Pacific Islanders represented less than 1% of the foster care population, but 4% of the U.S. child population. Hispanic children represented 17% of the U.S. child population, and equally 17% of the foster care population. Even in states like California with large Hispanic populations, Hispanics are underrepresented in foster care (Roberts 2002).

The majority of the research literature on disparities in foster care has focused on the African American population (Billingsley 1992; Billingsley & Giovannoni 1972; Chestang 1972; McRoy 1994), due to their very significant overrepresentation. In this chapter, I review the literature on the causes and correlates of overrepresentation and present strategies for addressing this growing problem. I conclude with a discussion of the implications for child welfare practice with children, youth, and families of color.

Key Facts

To gain a more complete understanding of the issues of disporportionality of children of color in foster care, readers should consider some key factors about overrepresentation (see Dougherty 2003). Research indicates that children of color are not at greater risk for abuse and neglect than are white children and that there are no differences in the incidence of maltreatment (Ards, Chung, & Myers 1999; Sedlak & Schultz 2001).

Yet children and youth of color experience disproportionately higher rates of maltreatment investigation and of abuse and neglect substantiation (Fluke, Yuan, & Edwards 1999). Children of color are more likely to be removed from their parents and placed in foster care, they stay in foster care for longer periods of time, and they are less likely to be either returned home or adopted.

African American children in New York State were ten times as likely as white children to be in state protective custody. The phenomenon is even more pronounced, however, in cities where children of color constitute a smaller percentage of the population. In areas where they comprise less than 2% of the population, their foster care placement rate was 15 times their proportion of the population (Fluke, Yuan, & Edwards 1999).

According to the Adoption and Foster Care Data Analysis System 8 datasets, as analyzed by the Child Welfare League of America (2003), for every 1,000 white children in the U.S. population, five were in foster care on September 30, 2000. Although white children represented 61% of the total population under the age of 18, they constituted 38% of the foster care population. For every 1,000 African American children in the U.S. population, 21 were in foster care on September 30, 2000. Although African American children represented 15% of the total population under the age of 18, they made up 40% of the foster care population. In addition, African American children experience longer stays in care.

For every 1,000 Hispanic children in the U.S. population, seven were in foster care on September 30, 2000. Although Hispanic children represented 17% of the total U.S. population under the age of 18, they constituted 15% of the foster care population (Child Welfare League of America 2003). For every 1,000 Native American children in the U.S. population, 16 were in foster care on September 30, 2000. Native American children represented 1% of the total population under the age of 18 and 2% of the foster care population. For every 1,000 Asian/Pacific Islander children in the U.S. population, two were in foster care: these children represented 3% of the total U.S. population under the age of 18, and accounted for 1% of the foster care population.

Why does it matter that there are more children and youth of color in the foster care system? As discussed in the following sections, it matters that more children of color are removed from their families and placed in foster care, because they fare less well while in care than do white children. These children:

- Remain in care longer;
- Are less likely to return home to their families of origin;
- Are less likely to be adopted; and
- Are more likely to emancipated from the child welfare system without permanent connections with at least one adult.

In addition, the instability in foster children's lives makes it difficult for them to become productive citizens as they mature. Educational delays and emotional stress are associated with both maltreatment and multiple placements. Finally, youth of color aging out of care are at high risk for depression, homelessness, and economic dependency.

Review of the Literature

A number of factors have been identified as potentially contributing to the disproportionate representation of African American children in the foster care system, including disproportionate poverty among African Americans, vulnerable single parent households, greater visibility to authorities responsible for child maltreatment reporting, racism and bias in reporting, welfare policies, lack of resources, community of residence, and increasing substance abuse and lack of community-based treatment (Bass, Shields, & Behrman 2004; Chipungu & Bent-Goodley 2004; Green 2002; Hill 1997).

Some observers suggest that the interaction of race and class may be causing disproportionate representation in the out-of-home care system. Although African Americans represent only about 12.9% of the population, they continue to be disproportionately poor. In 1999, 23.6% (8.4 million) of African Americans were poor and nearly half of all poor blacks were less than 18 years old. Although the poverty rate for African Americans is the lowest ever measured by the U.S. Census Bureau, it is still much higher than for whites—7.7%, or 14.9 million people (U.S. Census Bureau 2000).

According to Pelton (1989), there is a strong relationship between child abuse and neglect and poverty. It is a well-established fact that most of the children in foster care come from single parent households (Lindsey 1991). As the poverty rate for children is 46.1% in female headed families compared to 9.7% in all other family types (Children's Defense Fund 2000), it is no surprise that these families would be more vulnerable. Single mothers rarely receive child support and low wages make it very difficult to afford good child care.

Courtney (1998:95) reports that "the incidence of abuse and neglect is approximately 22 times higher among families with incomes less than $15,000 per year than among families with incomes of more than $30,000 per year." Note also that physicians and other service providers may be more likely to attribute an injury to abuse in cases of children in low-income homes and attribute the same injury to an accident in families of higher income (Newberger, Reed, Daniel, Hyde, & Kotelchuck 1977; O'Toole, Turbett, & Nalpeka 1983). These differential

attributions and labeling biases against low-income families may account for some of the relationships that have been found between poverty and abuse.

Stehno (1990), acknowledging that African American children are much more likely to be poor than are white children, suggests that growing depression and substance abuse of impoverished parents can also lead to neglect. In fact, according to the Child Welfare League of America (1997), in 1995, about one million children were found to be substantiated victims of child abuse and neglect and at least 50% had chemically involved caregivers. Parental substance abuse is one of the leading contributors to children being removed from home and placed in care.

Parental incarceration is another factor leading more children into the child welfare system. Drug and alcohol abuse are clear factors contributing to the incarceration of 80% of the 1.7 million men and women in prison today. In 2000, 1.5 million children had at least one parent in prison and disproportionately high numbers of these parents were African American (U.S. Department of Justice 2000).

Cumulative Effect: The Path to Overrepresentation in the Child Welfare System

Poverty, child abuse and neglect, parental substance abuse, and parental incarceration all combine to impact the potential vulnerability of African American children. However, these factors alone do not fully explain their overrepresentation in the child welfare system. Barth (2001); Kapp, McDonald, and Diamond (2001); and others have suggested that it is important to understand disproportionality by examining a child's path into the system, beginning with research findings of the likelihood of maltreatment of African American and white children. For example, although Fluke, Yuan, Hedderson, and Curtis (2002) found that African American, Hispanic, and Asian/Pacific Islander children have a disproportionately higher rate of maltreatment investigations than whites, several researchers (Ards, Chung, & Myers 1999; Sedlak & Schultz 2001) have found that African American children are not at greater risk for abuse and neglect. Also, the National Incidence Study-3 data (U.S. Department of Health and Human Services 1996) also found no significant race differences in the incidence of maltreatment.

Despite the lack of differences in incidence between groups, differences have been found in the substantiation of abuse/neglect in cases of African American children. Eckenrode, Powers, Doris, Munsch, and Bolger (1988) reported study findings that suggested that child maltreatment reports are much more likely to be substantiated for African American and Hispanic children than are those for white children. Using hypothetical vignettes of cases of sexual abuse, Zellman (1992) found that survey participants were more likely to believe that the law required a report to be made when children of color were described in the vignettes than when white children were described.

Although some studies have found no racial differences in allegations of sexual abuse by race or ethnicity (National Center on Child Abuse and Neglect 1981, 1988), some have found differences in type of abuse by race. For example, Cappelleri, Eckenrode, and Powers (1993) and Jones and McCurdy (1992) found that white children were more likely to experience sexual abuse (as compared to neglect) than were African American children.

Outcome Disparities: Contemporary and Historical Analysis

Not only are African American children and youth overrepresented in the child welfare system, researchers have found numerous racial inequities in service delivery. Courtney and colleagues (1996) reviewed much of the literature on disparities in service provision and found research accounts of inequities in child maltreatment reporting, child welfare service provision, kinship care, family preservation ser-

vices, exit rates and length of care, placement stability, and adoption. Although a few studies they reported did not find an association with race, the majority did. They also found that most of the racial differences reported were found between African Americans and whites rather than among other racial groups.

Overrepresentation and differential service delivery are not new issues in foster care. According to Lawrence-Webb (1997), under the Aid to Dependent Children program, established in 1935, states could determine eligibility for receiving public assistance. Therefore, to rule out "immoral families" from receiving public welfare benefits, many states established "home suitability" and "illegitimate child" clauses. During this period, Florida removed 14,000 children (more than 90% of them African American) from public assistance, and in 1960 23,000 children were removed from the welfare roles in Louisiana (McRoy 2004). Once children and their families were declared ineligible for public assistance, their children were often labeled as "neglected" due to lack of financial resources and were subsequently brought before the court for child protection issues.

In response, the Flemming rule, named after U.S. Department of Health, Education and Welfare Secretary Arthur Flemming, was passed in 1961, which required the provision of service interventions to families identified as being "unsuitable" (see Murray & Gesiriech 2004:2). Although services were to be provided, many caseworkers began to emphasize removal of the child from the home as opposed to working with the family to correct the conditions. At the time, most eligibility workers were not trained social workers and lacked the skills needed for understanding family dynamics and clinical intervention techniques (Lawrence-Webb 1997: 13). Moreover, according to Lawrence-Webb (1997:14), these workers serving African American families were untrained in cultural sensitivity and held racial stereotypes of African American clients. Therefore, they were more likely to push for child removal.

Once removed from their birth homes and placed in foster care, these children were not given equal access to services. For example, in 1959, Maas and Engler reported that many African American children in foster care were in need of adoption, but were less likely to be adopted than were white children.

Beginning with the 1962 amendments to the Social Security Act, which made open-ended funds available for out-of-home placements, children began to be removed from "undesirable family situations." Jeter (1963:32) reported that 81% of children entered care because their parents were either unmarried or the children came from "broken homes, and in public agencies, the largest groups of children placed in foster care consisted of both Negro and American Indian children, 49% of the Negro children, and 53% of the American Indian children. In voluntary agencies the proportions were even higher, 57% and 59% [respectively] in foster care." Jeter (1963) also found ongoing discrimination in service provision, noting that African American children were primarily being served by public agencies and private voluntary agencies were primarily serving white children. Black children were remaining in foster care for longer periods of time than were white children, and adoption was not being offered on an equitable basis.

Over the years, additional studies have been published that documented differential service provision. In 1982, Olsen found that white and Asian American families had the greatest chance for receiving recommendations for services and Native American families had the least chance. African American and Hispanic children were least likely to have plans for contact with their families. Barth and colleagues (1986) reported that in their study of 101 physically abused children in California, African American children were more likely than other children to experience permanent out-of-home placement. Close (1983) and Stehno (1990) found African American children in care are more likely to remain in care longer, be less likely to have visits

with their families, and have fewer contacts with workers. Similarly, Fein, Maluccio, and Kluger (1990) found in their study of 779 children who had been in out-of-home care in Connecticut for at least 2 years in 1985 that white children and foster families received more services and support than did children and foster families of color.

Goerge (1990) found that over an 8-year period, African American children in Cook County remained in care for a median of 54 months, whereas the median length of stay for all other children was 18 months. Goerge, Wulczyn, and Harden (1994) reported significant differences in the median duration in care for African Americans and whites. In California, the time in care was 30.8 months for African American children compared to 13.6 months for white children. In Illinois, African Americans had a median duration of 36.5 months compared to 6.6 months for whites. In Michigan, African Americans remained in care 17.5 months, whereas whites had a median duration of 11.2 months. In Texas, although the duration of care was not as great, there was a difference of 7.3 months for whites and 9 months for African Americans.

McMurtry and Gwat-Yong (1992) reported in their study of 775 foster children in Arizona that African American children were half as likely to be returned home as white children. These authors also found that African American children were three times as likely to be in the foster care system and that they had been in care for longer periods than the other three ethnic groups studied. Black children spent an average of 3 or more years in out-of-home care; in contrast, white and Hispanic children spent an average of 2.5 years, and other children of color, 2 years. The third group consisted of children from mixed race backgrounds.

Berrick, Barth, and Needell (1994), studying 600 kinship foster parents and nonrelative foster parents in California, noted that white foster parents were receiving more services than were other foster parents and that kinship foster parents (mostly African American) were less likely to have been offered such services as training, respite care, and support groups than were nonrelative foster parents.

Courtney (1994) found that in California, African American children placed in kinship care went home at about half the rate of similarly placed white children. According to Courtney (1995), African American children have significantly higher reentry rates into foster care than all other children, even after controlling for the child's age, health problems, placement history, and Aid for Families with Dependent Children program eligibility. Finally, Courtney and colleagues (1996) reported that African American children are also less likely to be adopted than white or Hispanic children.

Some of the most compelling findings of service disparities were reported by Barth in 1997. In his longitudinal study of 3,873 children in California who were younger than 6 upon entry into care, age and race had substantial independent effects on outcomes. "Controlling for age, African American children were considerably less likely to be adopted than Anglo or Latino children. The estimated adopted/remained in care odds ratio was more than five times as great for Caucasian children as for African American children" (Barth 1997:296). An African American infant had nearly the same likelihood of being adopted as a white 3- to 5-year-old. Also, the odds of African American children being reunified from non-kinship foster care were one-fourth those of white children in care. Barth (1997:296) concluded that "current practices clearly appear to inadvertently discriminate the most against African American children who do not have the same opportunity as other children—all other things being equal—to be adopted."

Other states have reported disparities as well. For example, a study by the Minnesota Department of Human Services (2002) to the state legislature on outcomes for African American children in Minnesota's child protection system noted significant disparities:

> Black children are more likely to be reported as suspected victims of maltreatment by teachers, police, nurses, family members or neighbors. And after an initial screening, black children are six times as likely as white children to be referred for a more formal investigation. Black children are nearly eight times as likely as white children to be determined victims of maltreatment. Only two in five African American families receive counseling, compared to three in five white families. If a child becomes legally free for adoption, black children stay in care two years and three months, which is about six months longer than white children. One of the largest areas of disproportionality in Minnesota occurs in Hennepin County in which African American children represent 10% of the child population, yet 60% of the placement population.

Disparate outcomes are not only reported for African American children in the foster care system: similar patterns are found in the juvenile justice system. African American youth in 1997 accounted for 26% of those arrested, 31% of referrals to juvenile court, 44% of youth detained, 56% of those waived to criminal court, 40% sent to residential placement, and 58% of those admitted to state prison. Although white youth were reported as committing higher levels of weapons-possession crimes, African American youth were arrested at 2.5 times the rate of whites for weapons offenses (Green 2002; Building Blocks for Youth 2000).

Moreover, according to the Child Welfare League of America, there is a link between child abuse and later juvenile delinquency arrests. A study in Sacramento, California, indicated that children reported abused and neglected were 67 times more likely to be arrested between the ages of 9 and 12 than were other children (Johnson 1997). This link suggests even more dire long-term consequences for minority children, because they are disproportionately represented in abused and neglected populations.

Addressing Foster Care Inequities

Court-Mandated Systems Improvement

Over the years, there has been growing concern about state systems failing to correct the problematic outcomes for children in out-of-home care. Since 1995, Children's Rights of New York, a legal advocacy organization whose mission is to promote and protect the rights of abused and neglected children in foster care systems, has filed suits or begun investigations against many states, including Connecticut, the District of Columbia, Florida, Georgia, Missouri, New Jersey, New Mexico, New York, Tennessee, and Wisconsin. For example, Children's Rights filed a class action law suit against Governor Donald Sundquist and George Hattaway, then commissioner of the Tennessee Department of Children's Services (DCS), for failure to protect the approximately 10,000 children dependent on DCS for care and protection. The complaint was filed specifically on behalf of BRIAN A., and eight other named plaintiffs who were in the Tennessee foster care system. According to the complaint:

> The Plaintiff Class includes approximately 9,000 children reported by the state to be in DCS custody who are dependent and neglected, "unruly" or were placed into custody voluntarily by their parent(s) or guardian(s). There are approximately 4,400 African-American children in DCS custody. The questions of law and fact raised by the claims of the named Plaintiffs are common to and typical of those raised by the claims of the putative Class members. Each named Plaintiff and each putative Class and Subclass member is in need of child welfare services, must rely on Defendants for those services, and is harmed by DCS's systemic deficiencies.

The Tennessee Department of Children's Services was charged with (Children's Rights 2004:12):

Lack of appropriate foster care placements, lack of adequate assessments, investigations and services to insure safety of children returned to home of parents or relatives. Also DCS routinely fails to provide appropriate caseworker, monitoring and supervision. Children often face abuse and neglect while in care, do not receive necessary services and treatment, and frequently spend many years moving from one inappropriate placement to another. The comptroller's report stated, "upon entering custody, African American children are not as likely to receive adequate services crucial to achieving permanency and improving family participation." Defendants' criteria or methods of administering adoption and permanency services also have a discriminatory effect on African-American foster children. Children spend years of time in care, lose much of their childhoods, move from one inadequate placement to another, lack appropriate services, are discharged at 18 without life skills, and the turnover rates for caseworkers are unmanageably high.

On July 30, 2001, a federal district judge approved the settlement reached by these parties. The settlement called for a technical assistance committee of five national experts in the child welfare field to assist in implementation of the agreement; an independent monitor to determine whether the state is making reforms; a quality assurance program for statewide implementation; a system for receiving screening and investigating reports of child abuse and neglect; regional services to support and preserve foster children in the state's custody; maximum limits on caseloads and number of caseworkers overseen by a single supervisor; and time periods within which children must be moved through the adoption process. The agreement also called for the state to hire an independent consultant to conduct a statewide evaluation of the Tennessee foster care program to determine whether African American children in the plaintiff class receive disparate treatment or suffer disparate impact, to assess the causes for such disparities, and recommend solutions.

This is perhaps one of the most comprehensive settlement agreements rendered in this type of case. Through monitoring the state's delivery system and mandating caseload size and service outcomes, the state will be held accountable for its actions on behalf of children, youth, and families of color.

State-Initiated Reforms

Other states, such as California and Minnesota, have also begun to evaluate their service delivery. In 2000, the California Department of Social Services and then-Governor Gray Davis launched a Child Welfare Redesign initiative to overhaul the state's child welfare system to improve outcomes. Included in this effort is a focus on achieving fairness and equity for all children; although only 7% of the California child population is African American, more than 33% of children in supervised care are African Americans.

The Minnesota Department of Human Services (2002) completed a study for the state legislature on outcomes for African American children and has established a goal of reducing disparities at each decision point in the child welfare system. Other states are also beginning to examine these issues.

Conclusions and Implications for Practice

Child welfare systems have a history of cultural preference and focus on the Americanization of immigrant children. The system was not designed to serve culturally and racially diverse populations.

Until the 1960s, public child welfare services —and specifically, adoption services—systematically excluded African American children. Over the past four decades, the public child welfare system has become increasingly diverse, and for some populations, a system that is overly inclusive. Currently child welfare systems attempt to protect children by relying on placement with less attention to the family and

community issues that make families and children of color more vulnerable.

Overrepresentation and racial disparities in child welfare service provision must be recognized and addressed in state systems. If not, it is likely that there will be more class action suits on behalf of African American children in care. More effective service provision can be achieved by addressing the problems of high caseloads; a shortage of experienced professional social workers, especially minority professionals (Stehno 1990); inadequate and minimally funded family preservation services; limited data and reporting capability; and insufficient alternatives to out-of-home placements.

Biased assessments may occur due to the lack of culturally competent child protective service workers who are aware of cultural differences and variations in child rearing (Cross, Bazron, Dennis, & Isaacs 1989; Leashore, Chipungu, & Everett 1991; Stehno 1982) and therefore be more likely to remove African American children from their birth families. McMurtry and Gwat-Yong (1992:47) suggested that the nonminority staff lacking familiarity with black family norms may have been more likely to find these families dysfunctional and to view reunification as not feasible. Almost 20 years ago, Vinokur-Kaplan & Hartman (1986) reported that 78% of workers and 87% of supervisors are white and that the majority of them have not received cultural competency training. In 2004, Bozanich, Molinar, Lefler, Cole, and Crumpton (2004) called for developing cultural competence through training, assessment, analysis, and implementation.

Exacerbating the situation of lack of culturally competent staff, is the lack of tenured staff in general in the child welfare system. According to the U.S. General Accounting Office (1995), the average tenure of a child welfare worker is less than 2 years. Thus inexperienced workers are responsible for large caseloads, including complex cases that may have issues pertaining to substance abuse, mental illness, domestic violence, HIV/AIDS, and other poverty-related problems. Schools of social work must partner with state child welfare systems to develop specialized training for staff on such topics as social justice, cultural competence, and assessing family strengths, in addition to substance abuse and family violence.

Growing attention is now being focused on the link between child maltreatment and juvenile justice. In 1997, the Child Welfare League of America cited a Sacramento, California, study that found that children reported abused and neglected are 67 times more likely to be arrested as pre-teens (Johnson 1997). These dire predictions make it even more critical to find ways to integrate service delivery systems and design child abuse prevention programs.

Acknowledging the problem of disproportionality, the Child Welfare League of America has committed to a number of activities to address the issue, including: "engage member agencies to establish an action agenda to address this issue; present data and research; engage task forces to develop culturally competent policies, services and practices; address workforce recruitment and retention issues to enhance diversity and cultural competence of staff; and address these issues at the national conference" (Child Welfare League of America 2003:29).

The Pew Commission on Children in Foster Care was launched on May 7, 2003, as part of a grant from the Pew Charitable Trusts to the Georgetown University Public Policy Institute to find ways to improve outcomes for children in care. One of their first initiatives is to find ways to improve the federal financing structure for foster care, which far overshadows the minimal funding of other approaches to providing safety for children and assistance to their families. Finding ways to structure funding so that states will have an incentive to preserve and maintain families rather than one to place children in out-of-home care should begin to impact the growing number of children in care.

The Children's Bureau–sponsored Child and Family Service Reviews offer an excellent opportunity to mandate accountability for service delivery (Chibnall et al. 2003). During these state reviews, case records should be assessed for service delivery inequities, so that states can self-correct and develop aggressive program improvement plans without the need for lawsuits to force them to address disparate outcomes.

Most importantly, ways must be found to help families so they are not at risk for having their children removed. Pelton (1989:52–53) suggests that the reason for placement is that the family, frequently due to poverty, "does not have the resources to offset the impact of situational or personal problems which themselves are often caused by poverty, and the agencies have failed to provide the needed supports, such as baby sitting, homemaking, day care, financial assistance, and housing assistance." Community-based organizations that provide comprehensive wraparound services, including employment assistance, substance abuse prevention, and treatment, are essential.

Community-based, family-centered prevention programs, particularly those with a built-in differential response (in which more than one response to a report is possible) must be explored by child welfare systems. Responses to cases in which a family is at risk should include support and preservation services. Promising practices include family group conferencing, family group decisionmaking, and other strategies that involve families and/or youth in case planning and deciding what is right for the family.

Further exploration of the permanency option of legal guardianship, which permits an alternative to termination of parental rights and permits families to stay connected, is essential. Kinship care has the potential to become prevalent, with ongoing support from states and local districts. These permanency goals are in many ways more concordant with many cultural and racial traditions that support the maintenance of strong ties with extended family.

The Black Association of Social Workers and its partners believe that African American children who require foster care should be placed with African American families (National Association of Black Social Workers 1972). This organization recognizes that in rare instances, the special needs of a particular child may indicate placement with a non–African American family. Such a placement should be made only when an African American family cannot be found for the child. Lack of appropriate resource families can increase the chances of disparity in outcomes.

Several years ago, President Clinton appointed a national commission to study racial disparities in mental health service provision. It is my belief that a similar commission should be appointed to study the child welfare system. Federally mandated initiatives are needed to rectify the disproportionate impact of child welfare policy and practice decisions on children and youth of color.

References

Ards, S., Chung, C., & Myers, S. (1999). Letter to the editor. *Child Abuse and Neglect, 23,* 244.

Barth, R. (1997). Effects of age and race on the odds of adoption versus remaining in long-term out-of-home care. *Child Welfare, 76,* 285–308.

Barth, R. (2001). Child welfare and race: Reviewing previous research on disproportionality in child welfare. Paper presented at the Race Matters Forum, Chevy Chase, MD, January 8–9, 2001.

Barth, R. P., Berry, M., Carson, M., Goodfield, R., & Feinberg, B. (1986). Contributors to disruption and dissolution of older child adoption. *Child Welfare, 65,* 359–371.

Bass, S., Shields, M., & Behrman, R. (2004). Children, families, and foster care: Analysis and recommendations. *Future of Children, 14,* 5–29.

Beckstrom, M. (2002). Minnesota child welfare: Black kids more likely to be taken from homes. Pioneer Press. Retrieved April 4, 2002, from www.twincities.com/mld/pioneerpress/news/local/2993303.htm.

Berrick, J., Barth, R., & Needell, B. (1994). A comparison of kinship foster homes and foster family homes: Implications for kinship foster care as family preservation. *Children and Youth Services Review, 16,* 33–63.

Billingsley, A. (1992). *Climbing Jacob's ladder: The enduring legacy of African American families.* New York: Simon and Schuster.

Billingsley, A., & Giovannoni, J. M. (1972). *Children of the storm.* New York: Harcourt Brace Jovanovich.

Bozanich, D., Molinar, L., Lefler, J., Cole, C., & Crumpton, J. M. (2004). *Developing cultural competence through training, assessment, analysis, and implementation.* Paper presented at the second annual Symposium on Fairness and Equity Issues in Child Welfare Training, University of California, Berkeley, April 27–28, 2004.

Building Blocks for Youth. (2000). *And justice for some: Differential treatment of minority youth in the justice system.* Retrieved April 18, 2004, from www.building blocksforyouth.org.

Cappelleri, J. C., Eckenrode, J., & Powers, J. L. (1993). The epidemiology of child abuse: Findings from the second National Incidence and Prevalence Study of Child Abuse and Neglect. *American Journal of Public Health, 83,* 1622–1624.

Chestang, L. (1972). *Character development in a hostile environment.* Occasional paper no. 3. Chicago: University of Chicago.

Chibnall, S., Dutch, N. M., Jones-Harden, E., Brown, B., Gourdine, R., et al. (2003). *Children of color in the child welfare system: Perspectives from the child welfare community.* Washington, DC: Children's Bureau.

Children's Rights. (2004). *Annual DCS case file review report for the State of Tennessee.* Retrieved June 30, 2004, from www.childrensrights.org/PDF/TAC_Report_Oct.pdf.

Child Welfare League of America. (1997). *Child abuse and neglect: A look at the states.* Washington, DC: CWLA Press.

Child Welfare League of America. (2003). Children of color in the child welfare system statement. Washington, DC: Child Welfare League of America.

Chipungu, S., & Bent-Goodley, T. (2004). Meeting the challenges of contemporary foster care. *Future of Children, 14,* 75–93.

Close, M. (1983). Child welfare and people of color: Denial of equal access. *Social Work, 28,* 13–20.

Courtney, M. E. (1994). Factors associated with the reunification of foster children with their families. *Social Service Review, 68,* 82–108.

Courtney, M. E. (1995). Reentry to foster care of children returned to their families. *Social Service Review, 69,* 226–241.

Courtney, M. E. (1998). The costs of child protection in the context of welfare reform. *Future of Children, 8,* 88–103.

Courtney, M. E., Barth, R. P., Berrick, J. D., Brooks, D., Needell, B., & Park, L. (1996). Race and child welfare services: Past research and future directions. *Child Welfare, 75,* 99–137.

Cross, T., Bazron, B., Dennis, K., & Isaacs, M. (1989). *Toward a culturally competent system of care.* Washington, DC: Child and Adolescent Service System Program Technical Assistance Center.

Dougherty, S. (2003). Practices that mitigate the effects of racial/ethnic disproportionality. Washington, DC: Casey Family Programs.

Eckenrode, J., Powers, J., Doris, J., Munsch, J., & Bolger, N. (1988). Substantiation of child abuse and neglect reports. *Journal of Consulting and Clinical Psychology, 56,* 9–16.

Fein, E., Maluccio, A., & Kluger, M. (1990). *No more partings. An examination of long-term foster care.* Washington, DC: Child Welfare League of America.

Fluke, J. D., Yuan, Y. Y. T., & Edwards, M. (1999). Recurrance of maltreatment: An application of the National Child Abuse and Neglect Data System (NCANDS). *Child Abuse and Neglect, 23,* 633–650.

Fluke, J. D., Yuan, Y., Hedderson, J., & Curtis, P. (2002). Disproportionate representation in child maltreatment. Paper presented at the Research Roundtable on Children of Color in Child Welfare, Washington, DC, June 30, 2004.

Goerge, R. M. (1990). The reunification process in substitute care. *Social Service Review, 64,* 422–457.

Goerge, R. M., Wulczyn, F. H., & Harden, A. W. (1994). *Foster care dynamics 1983–1992, California, Illinois, Michigan, New York and Texas: A report from the Multistate Foster Care Data Archive.* Chicago: Chapin Hall Center for Children, University of Chicago.

Green, M. (2002) Minorities as majority: Disproportionality in child welfare & juvenile justice. *Children's Voice, 6,* 9–13.

Hill, R. B. (1997). *The strengths of African American families: Twenty-five years later.* Washington, DC: R & B Publishers.

Jeter, H. R. (1963). *Children, problems and services in child welfare programs.* Children's Bureau publication no. 403-1963. Washington, DC: U.S. Department of Health, Education, and Welfare.

Johnson, J. (1997). Study shows children reported abused and neglected are 67 times more likely to be arrested as pre-teens. Washington, DC: Child Welfare League of America.

Jones, E. D., & McCurdy, K. (1992). The links between types of maltreatment and demographic characteristics of children. *Child Abuse and Neglect, 16,* 201–214.

Kapp, S., McDonald, T., & Diamond, K. (2001). The path to adoption for children of color. *Child Abuse and Neglect, 25,* 215–229.

Lawrence-Webb, C. (1997). African American children in the modern child welfare system: A legacy of the Flemming Rule. *Child Welfare, 76,* 9–30.

Leashore, B. R., Chipungu, S. S., & Everett, J. E. (1991). *Child welfare: An Africentric perspective.* New Brunswick, NJ: Rutgers University Press.

Lindsey, D. (1991). Adequacy of income and the foster care placement decision: Using an odds ratio approach to examine client variables. *Social Work Research and Abstracts, 28,* 29–36.

Maas, H. S., & Engler, R. E., Jr. (1959). *Children in need of parents.* New York: Columbia University Press.

McMurtry, S. L., & Gwat-Yong, L. (1992). Differential exit rates of minority children in foster care. *Social Work Research and Abstracts, 28,* 41–48.

McRoy, R. G. (1994). Attachment and racial identity issues: Implications for child placement decision making. *Journal of Multicultural Social Work, 3*(3), 59–74.

McRoy, R. G. (2004). The color of child welfare. In K. Davis & T. Bent-Goodley (eds.), *The color of social policy,* pp. 112–123. Washington, DC: Council on Social Work Education.

McRoy, R. G., Oglesby, Z., & Grape, H. (1997). Achieving same-race adoptive placements for African American children: Culturally sensitive practice approaches. *Child Welfare, 76,* 85–104.

Minnesota Department of Human Services. (2002). Children's services study of outcomes for African American children in Minnesota's child protection system. St. Paul: Minnesota Department of Human Services.

Murray, K. O., & Gesiriech, S. (2004). A brief legislative history of the child welfare system. In Pew Charitable Trust (ed.), *The Pew Commission on children in foster care,* pp. 1–6. Washington, DC: Pew Charitable Trust.

National Association of Black Social Workers. (1972). *Resolution opposing the practice of placing African-American children in need of adoptive homes with Caucasian parents.* Washington, DC: National Association of Black Social Workers.

National Center on Child Abuse and Neglect. (1988). *Study findings: Study of national incidence and prevalence of child abuse and neglect.* Washington, DC: U.S. Government Printing Office.

National Center on Child Abuse and Neglect. (1996). *Child abuse and neglect state statute series.* Vol. 1: *Reporting laws.* Washington, DC: U.S. Department of Health and Human Services.

Newberger, E., Reed, R., Daniel, J. H., Hyde, J., & Kotelchuck, M. (1977). Pediatric social illness: Toward an etiologic classification. *Pediatrics, 60,* 178–185.

Olsen, L. (1982). Predicting the permanency status of children in family foster care. *Social Work Research and Abstracts, 18*(1), 9–19.

O'Toole, R., Turbett, P., & Nalpeka, C. (1983). Theories, professional knowledge, and diagnosis of child abuse. In D. Finkelhor, R. J. Gelles, G. T. Hotaling, & M. A. Straus (eds.), *The dark side of families: Current family violence research,* pp. 349–362. Beverly Hills, CA: Sage.

Pelton, L. H. (1989). *For reasons of poverty.* New York: Praeger.

Personal Responsibility and Work Opportunity Reconciliation Act. (1996). P.L. 104-193.

Roberts, D. (2002). *Shattered bonds: The color of child welfare.* New York: Basic Books.

Sedlak, A., & Broadhurst, D. (1996). *Executive summary of the Third National Incidence Study of Child Abuse and Neglect*. Washington, DC: U.S. Department of Health and Human Services.

Sedlak, A., & Schultz, D. (2001). Race differences in risk of maltreatment in the general population. Paper presented at the Race Matters Forum, Chevy Chase, MD, January 8–9, 2001.

Stehno, S. (1982). Differential treatment of minority children in service systems. *Social Work, 27,* 39–45.

Stehno, S. (1990). The elusive continuum of child welfare services: Implications for minority children and youth. *Child Welfare, 69,* 551–562.

Vinokur-Kaplan, D., & Hartman, D. (1986). A national profile of child welfare workers and supervisors. *Child Welfare, 65,* 323–325.

U.S. Census Bureau. (2000). *Poverty rate lowest in 20 years, household income at record high, Census Bureau reports.* Retrieved June 30, 2004, from www.census. gov/Press-Release/www.2000/cb00-158.html.

U.S. Department of Health and Human Services. (1996). *The third National Incidence Study of Child Abuse and Neglect.* Washington, DC: U.S. Government Printing Office.

U.S. Department of Health and Human Services. (2004). *Preliminary FY 2002 estimates as of August, 2004. (The AFCARS Report).* Retrieved December 1, 2004, from www.acf.hhs.gov/programs/cb/publications/ afcars/report9.htm.

U.S. Department of Justice. (2000). *Sourcebook of criminal justice statistics 2000.* Washington, DC: U.S. Department of Justice, Bureau of Justice Statistics.

U.S. General Accounting Office. (1995). Child welfare: Complex needs strain capacity to provide services. GAO/HEHS-95-208. Washington, DC: U.S. General Accounting Office.

Zellman, G. L. (1992). The impact of case characteristics on child abuse reporting decisions. *Child Abuse and Neglect, 16,* 57–74.

DAVID PATE, Jr.

African American Fathers and Their Involvement in the Child Welfare System

here is a dearth of information on the involvement of fathers in the child welfare system (O'Donnell 1999). Slight attention has been paid to the issue in the academic and general literatures (National Child Welfare Resource Center for Family-Centered Practice 2002; Pate 2002).

A recent report from the U.S. Department of Health and Human Services noted that states have done poorly in their child welfare programs. The majority of states has failed in attempts to locate and involve fathers (Pate 2003). A study at the Urban Institute examined the intersection of father involvement and child welfare in the states. One of its reports recommends that locating the fathers of foster children should be a priority among child welfare agencies. Not only do many of the mandates of the Adoption and Safe Families Act (ASFA) require this, but anecdotal evidence also suggests quicker, more informed permanency outcomes are likely for children and youth in the foster care system if fathers are more consistently identified and located (Sonenstein, Malm, & Billing 2002; U.S. Department of Health and Human Services 2002). Although there is no easy answer to this problem, the examples below provide insight into the rationale for locating fathers and involving them in the lives of their children. The goal of ASFA is to make reasonable efforts to preserve and reunify families. In this chapter, I discuss four fathers—Mansour,

An earlier version of this chapter appeared in Paternal resources. *Focus*, 2002 (spring), 11–22.

Ivy, P-nut, and John—who have had experiences with the child welfare system. These fathers are described not because they are representative of all fathers who interface with the system, but rather because their situations may provide the reader with important knowledge about the role of the father in the child welfare system.

The purpose of this chapter is to discuss the involvement of fathers with children in the child welfare system. The chapter focuses on African American children who are disproportionately represented in the child welfare system. Race continues to be a very important factor in child welfare policy and·practice. "Racial disproportionality" refers to the disproportional representation of some racial or ethnic groups of families and children in child welfare populations compared to their numbers in the general population (Courtney & Sykes 2003; Harris & Courtney 2003; see also the chapter by McRoy). The information presented here helps fill a significant gap in our understanding of African American noncustodial fathers. Using a study of noncustodial fathers conducted in Wisconsin during the period 1999 through 2001 and highlighting salient findings from the Urban Institute's study on permanency for fathers, I address the question: what is the experience of fathers in the child welfare system? Highlights from in-depth interviews with five noncustodial fathers (Pate 2003) give "voice" to this underrepresented group in the child welfare system. I conclude with recommendations for future research and practice.

Background

Since passage of the Personal Responsibility and Work Opportunity Reconciliation Act of 1996, policymakers, academics, and philanthropic foundations have actively engaged in discussion of the role of divorced or unmarried low-income fathers in the lives of their children. Bills have recently been introduced in the U.S. House of Representatives and the Senate. Between May and December 2002, both chambers introduced fatherhood legislation. The House of Representatives bill passed on May 16, 2002. The Personal Responsibility, Work, and Family Promotion Act of 2002, H.R. 4737, contains fatherhood legislation titled "Promotion and Support of Responsible Fatherhood and Healthy Marriage Act of 2002." It is proposed as Title IV-C of the Social Security Act, sponsored by Representative Wally Herger (R-CA), Buck McKeon (R-CA), and Benjamin Cardin (D-MD). The Senate bill, Work, Opportunity, and Responsibility for KIDS (Work) Act of 2002, was approved by the Senate Finance Committee on June 26, 2002. The bill contains fatherhood legislation titled "Noncustodial Parent Employment Grant Program." It is proposed as Title IV-D, section 469C. The most recent support of fatherhood legislation was submitted by Senator Evan Bayh (D-IN) on March 11, 2004, in support of the Responsible Fatherhood Act of 2003, which is included in the welfare reform bill. Discussions have focused particularly on the emotional and financial role of the fathers in their children's lives, and much attention has focused on the desirability of increased involvement of unmarried low-income fathers by marrying the mothers of their children. This concern has been based on the assumption that noncustodial fathers have not been involved in their children's lives.

Yet child support and welfare research on low-income noncustodial fathers over the past 7 years has challenged this assumption, documenting that fathers are indeed involved with their children and that basing policy on the presumption that they are not is misguided. A report from the Fragile Families and Child Well-Being study (McLanahan et al. 2001) was based on research conducted in Milwaukee, Wisconsin. One of the findings concerned the proportion of fathers living with their children. The analysis suggested that 43% of the unmarried parents are cohabiting. Qualitative research into the complex lives of noncustodial fathers (Edin, Lein, Nelson, & Clampet-Lundquist 2001; Johnson, Levine, & Doolittle 1999; Sorensen & Zibman 2000; Waller & Plotnick 2001) has demonstrated that many of them are involved with their children and make informal child support payments even while paying into the formal child support system. Many live with the mothers of their children, provide financial support in excess of the monthly child support order, and have physical and legal custody of their children. They also face limited employment opportunities.

In November 1997, ASFA was approved by Congress and signed by the president. Its intent was to improve the safety for children, to promote adoption and other permanent homes for children, and to support their families. ASFA requires that the courts begin the process of terminating the parental rights of men and women who have had children in foster care for 15 out of the past 22 months. Available data show that more than 50% of children in foster care come from single-parent, female-headed families (Sonenstein, Maim, & Billing 2002). ASFA authorized the use of the Federal Parent Locator Service (FPLS), the system for locating parents delinquent in child support payments. Another technique to increase the involvement of fathers and to build family responsibility and community accountability for protecting children is family group decisionmaking (FGDM), which invites concerned individuals, including noncustodial fathers and their family members, to participate in creating permanency plans for children. Early findings are showing favorable results in increased involvement of paternal relatives. However, more research on noncustodial parents' involvement in the child welfare permanency planning process is needed. (An article in the *Milwaukee Journal Sentinel* 2004 discussed the increased number of women who are noncustodial parents. The number has increased from 4% to 15% in the past 5 years.)

Since the early 1990s, many public and private child welfare agencies have been organizing FGDM meetings to capitalize on the family's strengths and wisdom in developing service plans for children who had been maltreated to insure their well-being and safety. "FGDM" is an umbrella term that encompasses a number of models for organizing family meetings. The most common model used in the United States is family group conferencing, which originated in New Zealand in the late 1980s. FGDM involves families, including extended relatives (e.g., grandparents, cousins), perpetrators, victims, and others considered by the family as important to their lives (e.g., tribal elders, clergy, neighbors, fictive kin) in making care and protection decisions. In 1998, it was estimated that more than 50 U.S. communities (cities or counties) had FGDM initiatives, a significant increase from the five communities identified in a 1995 American Humane Association (AHA) survey on innovative practices and system reform. A 2003 AHA study has shown a 200% increase in U.S. communities implementing FGDM in their communities (Children's Bureau Express 2003; Merkel-Holguin 2003).

At present, analysts and practitioners no longer believe that fathers fill a unidimensional role in their families and in their children's eyes; they find instead a number of significant roles and a variety of reasons for paternal involvement. Most researchers have implicitly assumed that variations in the definition of fatherhood are primarily the product of subcultural and cultural factors rather than of individual characteristics. As discussed below, most men set goals that reflect their own childhood experiences, choosing either to compensate for their fathers' deficiencies or to emulate them. Parental involvement can be determined by personal motivation (Lamb 1987), skills self-confidence in the role of parent, and support, especially support in the family from the mother (Pleck 1982).

Early Identification of Paternal Resources

Early identification of paternal family members as permanency resources for children in foster care is frequently overlooked by social workers who work with families. The field of children, youth, and family services has had a long history of not including fathers in planning for children and youth. For decades, social workers in the child welfare field have listed "father unknown" on forms; or have not thought about inquiring as to a father's whereabouts in the case assessment because the assumption was that most fathers were uninvolved in the lives of their children. If a child's father was uninvolved, the social worker surmised, then that father's family was most likely uninvolved as well. In many cases, nothing could be further from the truth, as many mothers not only know about their child's father, but also know about and rely on his family for support as well. Not asking about, or assuming uninvolvement, or accepting "I don't know where my child's father's family lives" are all examples of inadequate approaches to seeking out fathers in the lives of children in foster care—and not just fathers, but their families as well. Paternal aunts, uncles, grandparents, great-grandparents, and cousins are all part of the paternal web of resources that may exist for a child in need of permanency and may also remain untapped as resources because of our acceptance of the "I don't know" answer.

Children in the child welfare system are clearly affected by their fathers' absence. There is evidence that the majority of children in the system have noncustodial fathers, although the exact proportion is unclear. Furthermore, some of the recent shifts in child welfare policy have had ramifications for how noncustodial fathers are involved in case planning. According to a report issued by the Urban Institute (Sonenstein, Malm, & Billing 2002), there is evidence that some child welfare agencies, in conjunction with child support enforcement programs, are working diligently to identify and locate noncustodial fathers. Here I summarize the policies and practices identified in the report that affect the involvement of noncustodial fathers.

There are a number of shifts in child welfare policies and practices that could make the involvement of noncustodial fathers in child welfare case planning more likely. These include the provisions of ASFA, the nationwide movement of the field toward concurrent case planning, the increasing use of kinship placements, and the growing popularity of FGDM in case planning. These trends and their potential for increasing the role of noncustodial fathers in case planning are described below. To date, however, no research has been identified that examines whether these practices actually increase the involvement of noncustodial fathers.

ASFA requires the reduction of the time in which child welfare agencies must make permanency decisions for children in custody from 18 months to 12 months, making the early identification and location of noncustodial fathers more important. In addition, ASFA both allows and encourages states to use the FPLS employed by child support enforcement programs to locate fathers and other relatives.

Child welfare agencies routinely identify and assess noncustodial parents as potential placement resources, and some states' policies explicitly give preference to them. Malm (2004: 22) notes that California's policy, for example, is that "the first placement priority is for placement in the home of the non-custodial parent, or in the home of a suitable relative (if a noncustodial parent is unavailable)." Other states' policies are more general, such as the policy in Texas that requires the agency to verify that parents are unable or unwilling to provide care prior to placing a child in out-of-home care. Michigan's policy manual states that although return home is usually the most appropriate goal when a child is first placed in foster care, where indicated, the focus may shift to the noncustodial parent's home.

Agencies must identify noncustodial parents as early as possible so that termination of their rights, when needed, can occur swiftly. The *Adoption and permanency guidelines* from the National Council of Juvenile and Family Court Judges (2000:22) state that "at the very first hearing on a petition alleging abuse or neglect, efforts should begin to include all parents involved in the life of the child and to locate absent parents." The guidelines further discuss the importance of locating putative fathers and bringing them into court early in the process, both to resolve paternity issues and avoid court delays later in the process (Grossmann, Funk, Mentaberry, & Seibel 2000). Judicial guidelines have long sought this early identification, and the implementation of ASFA has increased the likelihood that identification will be pursued. In addition to identifying and locating noncustodial fathers for the express purpose of accelerating the termination of parental rights, finding these fathers is important to the adoption proceedings so that the paternal side of the child's background and medical history can be obtained prior to adoption. Finally, the resolution of such paternity issues may also be instrumental in locating and securing other paternal relatives who may be utilized in permanency planning.

Another increasingly common practice in child welfare agencies is the use of concurrent planning (National Resource Center for Foster Care and Permanency Planning 1999). This practice encourages caseworkers to pursue more than one goal for the child. From the beginning of the case process, caseworkers can simultaneously attempt to locate a permanent or adoptive home for a child while they seek to preserve or reunite the child with his or her family. Efforts to locate noncustodial fathers may occur much earlier when child welfare agencies support concurrent planning because fathers or their relatives may be a placement resource. Moreover, fathers need to be identified and located to obtain termination of parental rights if adoption is pursued as an option.

Two other trends in child welfare practice, the increasing use of kinship placements and the use of family decisionmaking models, may affect the ways in which caseworkers identify, locate, and involve noncustodial fathers. The use of relatives or kin as foster parents increased significantly in the 1980s and early 1990s. One of the main factors contributing to the use of kinship care is that child welfare agencies have developed a more positive attitude toward the use of kin as foster parents. In addition, the number of non-kin foster parents has not kept pace with the number of children requiring out-of-home care. The increased use of kinship care may also reflect recent court decisions upholding the rights of relatives to act as foster parents and to be financially compensated for doing so. Policies and practices geared toward identifying and locating relatives as potential placements may lead workers to identify and locate noncustodial parents. Not only have agency policies shifted in favor of placement with relatives, but the focus is also on finding these relatives early in the process, prior to having to place the child in a non-kin foster home.

The increased use of kinship care in child welfare can also hasten the involvement of the noncustodial father to the extent that financial support is sought. Relatives who receive a Temporary Aid to Needy Families (TANF) payment or foster care payment on behalf of a related child are required to cooperate with child support enforcement. States are increasingly seeking reimbursement for the cost of care of foster children through child support enforcement efforts. A significant proportion of children in foster care are eligible for federal Title IV-E reimbursement funds to the state. Also, child welfare agencies increasingly require parents to repay the cost of out-of-home placement for children ineligible for Title IV-E reimbursement.

In addition, as discussed above, child welfare agencies are also increasingly utilizing family group conferencing or family meetings. These techniques seek to include a range of individuals for all immediate and extended family members, child welfare staff, and community provider staff members in the case process. Through the family meetings, agency staff members are able to inform family members of the case particulars, the case process, agency and court procedures, as well as to solicit their input on case planning, identification of potential placement options, and permanency outcomes. During the organization and facilitation of these family meetings, agency workers are likely to obtain extensive information about the noncustodial father from other family members. Thus, agencies using this form of casework practice are probably in a better position to identify, locate, and involve noncustodial fathers in case planning.

Promising Practices for Locating and Involving Noncustodial Fathers in Child Welfare

ASFA both allows and encourages states to begin to use the FPLS to locate fathers and other relatives. ASFA authorizes child welfare and child support enforcement agencies to request information from the FPLS to locate individuals who have or may have parental rights to a child. Interagency agreements between the agencies were also encouraged. An informational memorandum sent January 1, 1999, to state agencies administering Title IV-D and Title IV-E funds provided information on using the FPLS for child welfare services. In addition, the 1993 federally mandated Statewide Automated Child Welfare Information Systems being implemented by state child welfare agencies required a link to child support data.

Efforts to coordinate child welfare and child support services, notes the Urban Institute (Sonenstein, Malm, & Billing 2002), may offer promise. Results from an evaluation of South

Carolina's Department of Social Services' diligent search project (Sonenstein, Malm, & Billing 2002) showed that missing parents were located in more than 75% of the cases referred by child welfare staff, and more than half of these cases were located in less than a month. Fathers were far more likely to be the subject of the search than mothers, representing 72% of the total referrals. The results also showed that in 15% of families, referrals were made to locate more than one father. This occurred both in cases involving undetermined paternity and for families in which multiple children had different fathers. It is important to note that 10% of fathers were found through the prison, probation, or parole systems. There is also some evidence, the report notes, of increased state-level coordination between child welfare and child support agencies in a handful of states. Interviews being conducted with child welfare administrators in all 50 states by the Urban Institute have identified a few states with increased coordination. In Kansas, for example, the child support enforcement and child welfare agencies both emphasize the involvement of fathers, although no joint activities are currently being undertaken. In addition, Wisconsin's child support agency has hired paternity specialists who are available to child welfare workers to assist in identifying and locating noncustodial fathers (Bess, Andrews, Jantz, & Russell 2003). During the Urban Institute's study of kinship care, some agencies reported that, with the increased focus on kinship care placements, specialized units have been created specifically to search for relatives, including noncustodial fathers. In other agencies, no special unit was created, yet individual caseworkers had access to the welfare agency's data system to help locate noncustodial fathers and other relatives. Note, however, that very few of the local child welfare administrators interviewed had implemented the FPLS to locate noncustodial fathers. In fact, some administrators were unaware that this resource could be utilized by the child welfare system.

Other examples of promising new approaches are communities receiving Model Court project grants from the Office of Juvenile Justice and Delinquency Prevention (Mentaberry 1999). Some of these communities are implementing innovative approaches to expediting permanency for children, including projects that focus on paternity establishment and locating absent parents as primary goals. Responsible fatherhood programs and programs for incarcerated parents also provide examples of promising practices. Programs focused on prisoners, such as Long Distance Dads, implemented by the Pennsylvania Department of Corrections, address the needs of incarcerated fathers. This is a 12-week program designed to promote fatherhood and empower fathers to assume responsibility for their children both during and after incarceration.

Other promising models include the F.A.C.T. Program in Kentucky, a collaborative effort between Prevent Child Abuse Kentucky and the Blackburn Correctional Complex. This program teaches fathers who are incarcerated responsible parenthood and abuse prevention, with graduates of the program entitled to special visits with their children in less restrictive environments. Another program, Papas and Their Children, has been developed in San Antonio, Texas. This weekly program facilitates participatory activities between children and their incarcerated fathers at several state jails. The Urban Institute's (Sonenstein, Malm, & Billing 2002) review of responsible fatherhood programs found two programs with components that may address child abuse and neglect. A fatherhood program in Hawaii is providing parenting skills for fathers in families identified as at risk for child abuse and neglect. The participating fathers are being served by a Healthy Start child abuse prevention program. In Chicago, the Paternal Involvement project has been a strong advocate for fathers since 1992 and was instrumental in drafting legislation that created the state's first noncustodial parent services unit. The group is currently participating in a pilot project with the Illinois Department of Children and Family Services in an effort to promote noncustodial fathers as custodial alternatives to mothers who are unable to care for children (Jeffries, Menghraj, & Hairston 2001).

The Urban Institute's review uncovered a few examples of promising new efforts to involve noncustodial fathers in child welfare case planning. However, as indicated, these efforts are fairly limited, and no rigorous evaluations have been conducted to assess whether the efforts lead to positive outcomes.

Ethnographic Study

Low-income noncustodial fathers are often stereotyped as irresponsible absentee parents who must be legally compelled to fulfill their obligations (for a summary and review, see Johnson, Levine, & Doolittle 1999). Some fathers do indeed fit the stereotype. However, the findings discussed here document that many noncustodial fathers are closely connected with their children; they make informal payments in excess of their support obligations and have physical custody of children. Often they do so while confronting a daunting array of economic and personal disadvantages.

The ethnographic research discussed in this chapter forms part of the Child Support Demonstration Evaluation (CSDE), a federally mandated evaluation of Wisconsin's innovative child support policies implemented in 1997, under the rubric of the Wisconsin Works (W-2) welfare reforms. These policies allowed all child support paid by noncustodial parents to be passed through to the child, regardless of the mother's welfare status, and to be ignored in the calculation of the family's benefit amounts (for details, see Meyer & Cancian 2001). The purpose of this qualitative, 2-year study was to provide a deeper understanding of the life experiences of noncustodial fathers in light of the changes to welfare and child support programs (Pate 2002).

There were 36 fathers in the ethnographic study, all African American and all from the city of Milwaukee (Meyer & Cancian 2001). All were fathers of children receiving public assistance. In extended interviews, the author explored the nature and extent of fathers' responsibilities, their concepts of their parental role, their experiences finding and holding work, the ways in which these experiences affected their family roles, and their understanding of the child support system and of welfare reform. Sixteen of the fathers were interviewed again a year later.

Because the CSDE project was particularly concerned about fathers who had participated in job search and job training programs, 11 of these fathers were specifically drawn from among participants in the Children First program administered through two W-2 agencies in Milwaukee, United Migrant Opportunity Service, and Employment Solutions. Children First provides work experience and training to unemployed and underemployed noncustodial parents who are unable to meet child support obligations; participation is generally court-ordered.

A distinctive and challenging feature of this project was that the majority of the participants was randomly selected from an administrative dataset, Wisconsin's automated child support data system, Kids Information Data System. It was, as a consequence, hard to gain access to prospective informants and to persuade them that there would be no negative repercussions from participating. Many of the men had had consistently difficult interactions with police and government officials, and the ability to assure them of a high standard of confidentiality was extremely important.

Paternal Characteristics

The men who were interviewed ranged in age from 21 to 57. Ten had only one child and two had more than 10 apiece; 22 of the fathers had children by more than one woman. Thirty-one fathers had lived with their biological children, and 21 had lived with children they did not father (primarily children of their partner at the time). Most fathers were currently not living alone; about half lived with a female friend or partner, and some lived with their mothers. The majority of the men were neither home owners nor listed on the lease at their current address; some, indeed, had no stable address and were in transit among the homes of family members and friends. Eight of the 16 fathers who had ever been married were currently married, but not necessarily living with their wives.

Because these fathers were part of the larger CSDE, the author was able to access the state's administrative records of their formal earnings and child support payments. All fathers had very low formal earnings, averaging $9,600 in 1999 and $8,000 in 2000. Those in the Children First sample reported even less: $5,000 in 1999 and $7,500 in 2000. All had a child support order at the time of the interview. In 1999, they paid an average of $1,400 in child support; in 2000, they paid $1,200. Those in the Children First sample paid $800 in 1999 and $1,200 in 2000. Men in both groups averaged support arrearages of $6,200 when their children entered W-2, although these amounts diminished over the 2 years of the interviews. Both groups owed substantial amounts to the state for hospital costs associated with a child's birth, interest on support arrears, and public assistance reimbursements. (Aid to Families with Dependent Children and TANF recipients must give to the state their right to prior child support arrears and amounts due during benefit periods.) In addition to the child support they did (or did not) pay, many of the fathers provided other support, not directly monetary: outings, supplies, such as diapers and clothes, and child care.

Many of these men faced formidable barriers to involvement in their children's lives. For some, family was often the only significant source of support. Their most serious problems revolved around employment, housing, and interactions with the criminal justice system.

Employment
Just about 70% of the men were employed at the first interview. Their educational backgrounds ranged from less than a high school education to some college. In fact, nine fathers had attended college. (Wisconsin is ranked near the top in the overall rate of high school graduation, but has the worst graduation rate in the nation for African Americans: 40%; see Manhattan Institute 2004). Among those working, the average wage was $7 an hour; full- and part-time jobs included temporary services, painters, maintenance workers, fast food workers, child care workers, and meatpackers. Of those not employed, three were recipients of Social Security Disability Income.

Many of the men discussed employment opportunities in the suburbs, as opposed to the central city. Obstacles they reported in accessing suburban jobs included lack of reliable transportation, long bus rides, unwarranted police harassment, and discomfort in communities where they did not feel welcome. Temporary employment agency jobs paid slightly above minimum wage, but appeared to offer little stability (Pate 2002:58):

> They promise you that, you know, this job might be long-term. After 90 days, you are supposed to be hired. But then the company can work you 89 days, and say "we don't need you." So then you into a job, get settled into it, think this is going to be it. Then boom. You back on the unemployment list waiting on another job.

A few of the men had social networks that could provide them with access to a stable job, generally a family member or a very close friend; about 20% of fathers had secured work in this way. But even these jobs offered limited opportunities. Only one man had been employed 25 years at a company where his father had worked; he was currently earning $8 an hour.

Some men "hustled" in the informal economy, doing auto repair, yard work, or trafficking in drugs. Drug dealing, to some of these men, appeared to be the only realistic way to make enough money to support themselves and meet their other responsibilities. One trafficker, a father of five children who lived with one of the children's mother, had no high school diploma. He had dreamed of being married and working as a truck driver, but those dreams, he said, were destroyed when he came to police attention as a result of an accident in which he was found to be driving with only a permit. Over the years, he was not able to attend to the traffic violation and accumulated substantial financial penalties that he could not pay. He had recently put out 10 job applications, for "any kind of job," but had received no calls. "Mostly, I'm selling marijuana. I ain't never heard it killing no one at work" (Pate 2002:62).

Housing
Many fathers did not make enough money to pay for an apartment. Many fathers, both younger and older, lived with their mothers, who constituted almost their only—and sometimes reluctant—social safety net. Some men had lived with a female partner but were not on the lease and as a consequence, had lost shelter when the relationship ran aground.

Interactions with the Justice System
Of all the issues that confronted fathers, encounters with the justice system seemed to be the most compelling. In the first year of this research, 24 of the 36 fathers had had a criminal charge or a civil action against them. By the end of the second year, 33 were in this position —92% of the sample. There were 11 felonies and 14 misdemeanors, the majority for traffic violations, but also others, including assault and battery. Eleven fathers had experienced a period of incarceration for nonpayment of child support, although only three had been charged with a felony for failing to pay. Jail stays ranged from 1 day to 6 months. In Milwaukee County from April 1999 to April 2001, over 6,200 people were booked into Milwaukee County jail with "nonpayment of child support" listed as one of their offences. These were all criminal offenses; about 75% were misdemeanors and the rest felonies. Child support was not the primary reason for the arrest. The overwhelming

point of initial police contact was a traffic stop, the second most common reason being a public peace disturbance (Milwaukee County Sheriff's Department, unpubl. data).

Fathers and Child Support Policy
Many of the fathers had neither the education nor the knowledge to grasp the basics of the child support system. They did not understand that an order establishing legal fatherhood led to a child support order. They did not understand that mothers receiving welfare were required to cooperate with the child support agency in collecting support due and to assign it to the agency as partial reimbursement for the cost of the welfare. Nor did they understand the procedures for modifying a support order if circumstances changed, or their right to initiate legal actions. They did have a better grasp of the state's enforcement tools—criminal charges, liens, credit bureau reporting, and suspension of the driver's license for nonpayment. Partly as a consequence, the child support system itself was rather widely viewed as an intruder in people's private affairs.

The majority of fathers had been proud to acknowledge the birth of their children, and all had been present at the birth of one or more of the children. But questions of legal paternity brought to the fore a mass of misunderstandings. Many of the interviewees believed that their acceptance of the role of father was sufficient. They did not understand the rationale for legal paternity when they felt they had taken on the social, financial, and moral roles of fatherhood. One father could not understand why legal paternity did not mean that the child automatically received his last name, since he had to pay support for 18 years.

As for the support payments themselves, the views were fairly predictable. Many subjects said that they had no problem with paying support so long as it helped their children. Others complained that the system in Milwaukee viewed them as "deadbeat dads" as a matter of course. Fathers who lived with their children but did not have court-ordered custody did not understand why they continued to owe child support. Fathers who made substantial contributions to other expenses (e.g., paying for child care) did not understand why no adjustment was made for these contributions. Most had not heard about the W-2 pass-through policy that was the primary subject of the CSDE research.

In April 2002, 27 states had opted not to finance a pass-through of child support collected to welfare-reliant families, five states had complicated pass-through and disregard policies, and 17 states provided a $50 pass-through to welfare-reliant families. Wisconsin provided a full pass-through and disregard of current child support collected (Turetsky 2004).

Note, however, that even in Wisconsin, families in the control group of the CSDE did not receive all support paid on their behalf. Moreover, even in the full pass-through group, amounts paid in excess of the current amount due could accrue to the state rather than to the family. As of July 1, 2002, all Wisconsin families were eligible for the full pass-through and disregard of current child support.

Some fathers owed quite enormous bills, considering their low incomes. Debts could include childbirth costs, court costs, child support interest, and partial reimbursement of past welfare costs. When men with child support orders are employed, child support payments are generally made through income withholding by their employer; 90% of those paying child support in this sample of fathers did so through wage garnishment. (Garnishment is not a choice of the employee. By federal law, all employers are required to submit information about newly hired employees to the state Directory of New Hires. Under that law, the employer must be informed about the employee's child support obligation as soon as possible and wage garnishment instituted.) Tax interception is another enforcement tool, and a profoundly resented one. State administrative data show 58% of the fathers in this study had had taxes intercepted since 1997.

Fathers' Relationships with Children and Mothers

All but two fathers in the study reported telephone or in-person contact with at least one of their children in the 3 months before the first interview. All made efforts to be involved —indeed, took it for granted that they ought to be involved—with their children. Particularly for the younger men, being a good father was equated with a quality of manhood, sometimes in emulation of their own fathers, sometimes in a conscious choice to be a different kind of father. A 32-year-old father of six children by five different women said: "You know, I don't even know who my dad is. And I wish that I wouldn't be like my dad. And that is the main reason why I am a man now and I take care of my kids" (Pate 2002:43). This sentiment was on occasion echoed by mothers who encouraged the father to be involved with his child. One father commented that his former partner had been upset when they split, but would not let that interfere with his relationship with their daughter "because when she [the mother] was growing up, her father wasn't around. . . . She won't take that away from me because she never had it" (Pate 2002:47). Fathers who have been involved with multiple women may experience particular difficulty in negotiating those relationships and keeping in touch with their children.

It is difficult to categorize the extent of fathers' involvement with their children because it varies, especially for fathers with more than one child. Frequently it depends on the relationship with the mother. If the child with whom the father has had the most contact is considered, we can identify four main categories of involvement: custody, frequent visiting, regular visiting, and contact (fig. 1).

"Custody" is defined in this study as meaning that the father had one or more of his children living in his principal residence. Generally, this was the only residence for the child. Thirteen fathers had informal custody or formal custody (that is, a legal determination by the court).

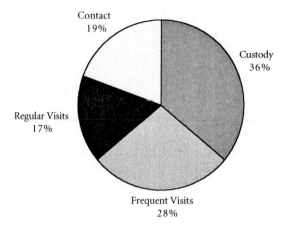

FIGURE 1. Fathers' involvement with their children.

Five fathers had sole formal custody, four of them because the mother had been declared unfit on grounds of drug use; all of these men had fathered children in other relationships and maintained contact with them. In one case, formal custody was held by the child's paternal grandfather. Seven fathers had informal custody. All seven had active child support orders and were accruing arrears, and in a formal determination in a court of law, might well have been awarded joint or sole custody. All of these seven fathers were cohabiting with the mother of one of their children.

"Frequent visiting" may include extended overnight visits of 4 or more days; it is an arrangement very similar to legally established joint custody, although it is usually informal. Six of the fathers, all with active child support orders, visited with at least one of their children three or four times a month, mostly through informal arrangements with the mother ("regular visiting"). "Contact" basically consists of infrequent visits and telephone contact. Seven fathers were in this category; some had children over 18 who no longer lived with them; others had poor and hostile relations with the mothers of their children.

The remainder of this section focuses on fathers with legal custody of their children. Thirteen fathers had custody, and five had been

awarded sole custody. Four of them were awarded sole custody (physical placement) because the mother was declared unfit based on drug-related problems. (Edin and Lein [1997] discuss the number of welfare-reliant mothers who have resorted to prostitution and drug trafficking because the welfare check was not enough for the family to survive. Men in this study also told the same story about some of the mothers of their children. These were the two primary reasons for which fathers would gain custody of the children.) One of these fathers had children who were placed with his mother in a kinship care placement. In addition, one father, a Social Security Disability Insurance recipient, had been designated the legal guardian of his three grandchildren, who lived with him, because his daughter was in prison for a drug-related offense. Four of these fathers are discussed in the next section, which describes their experience with the child welfare system.

Case Examples

Mansour is a 39-year-old father of 11 children by seven mothers. He had his first child at the age of 18. He graduated from high school, and then served in the Marine Corps for 6 years. He married, and during the first year of marriage, his wife was killed in a car accident. His oldest child was 22, and his youngest was 6. He works as a chef at $9 an hour. His housing is a rented home on the northwest side of Milwaukee, Wisconsin. He was awarded sole custody of his five youngest children, ranging in age from 6 to 9.

The second father is P-nut, a 23-year-old father of four. He is living with his current girlfriend. He is unemployed, although he had worked at a home health center for a limited time. One of his children lived with the biological grandmother. She was awarded legal guardianship of her biological grandson and his brother. His mother has had legal guardianship for his biological son since the latter was 3.

The third father is John, a 43-year-old father of three daughters. He had maintained a relationship with all three of the mothers of his children. At the time, he was employed as a quality control manager in a welding company that paid him in excess of $40,000. John joined the Marines at the age of 18 and remained in the service for years. He was a home owner and the main caregiver of his own father. He was one of six siblings. He was formerly married to the mother of the daughter for whom he was awarded sole custody, when she was 7 years old.

The fourth father, Ivy, is the 31-year-old father of eight children, five girls and three boys, ranging in age from 12 to 2. He matriculated from a local community college with an associate degree in microcomputers. Four years ago, he was incarcerated for possession with intent and charged with a felony. He is currently unemployed from his last job as a manager of a local fast food restaurant. His situation at the time of the interview, 3 days before Thanksgiving, was not good. His unemployment payments had just ceased. At the time of the interview, he was behind in his rent and facing eviction in 2 days. Both the electric and gas bills were in arrears. In addition, his youngest brother was living with him. He had physical custody of his two oldest children by the first mother. At the time of the first interview, Ivy stated that he was the custodial parent of two children. Throughout the interview, he made

it clear that he had sole responsibility for the well-being of these children. He handled all of their needs. In later discussions, he stated that he had to go back to court to finalize his custody in Wisconsin.

It is important to note that these men often do not know the legal status of their relationship with their children regarding paternity or custody and access. Therefore, research findings that rely on the informants' report may be at variance with actual legal status of the parent-child relationship. The complexities of legal processes are difficult for most laypersons to understand, and without the financial resources to secure legal representation, these parents may not be in a position to report accurately the legal status of the parent-child relationship.

All of these fathers had paternity established because they had a child support order stating they were the legal father; however, they had no legal visiting or custody order until the custody hearing took place. (Paternity establishment is the first step of a multistep process in the child support enforcement process for children of unmarried parents. If a child is born to parents who were married when the child was born or conceived, the law presumes that the husband is the father; no additional action is required to establish the child's paternity; Pate 2003). In addition, all four fathers had child support arrearages and had children who had been or were currently using services provided by the welfare system.

Contact with the Child Welfare System
Mansour discussed how he was notified by his ex-girlfriend's mother that the child welfare system had received information that his children were living in an unsafe environment and were about to be placed:

The system was fittin [getting ready] to get my kids. Because she's [the mother] on drugs and you know how people calling in on you.... The state take[s] over your kids.... Her mother called me in Chicago

... told me ... "Mansour, you got to come up here because your kids are about to go into the system." ... What, mamma? I left my job in Chicago, moved to Milwaukee, went to court. . . . Brother, let me tell you, honest to God truth, they could not have took my kids from me. . . . I came . . . now they did grant them to me. . . . But they could [not] have took my kids, because I would have went to jail, cause they could not have took mine. . . . Because I didn't do anything wrong, it was their momma. And I took my three kids, plus she already had three kids when I met her, and I raised two of those out of the three. So I raised five by myself for at least five years. I was working and hustling at the same time. And I'm [a]shamed to say this. But I took care of my kids. I could cook, I could clean, I could French braid. I could French roll. Whatever it took to do. You see, I had two girls and four boys. See what I'm saying, I had to do all them things. So, I'm saying, I became the mommy and the daddy. And I . . . didn't . . . I . . . this stuff didn't bore me because my momma is the same way. . . . That's why I stepped in and took my shorties. To make my daddy feel good in his grave. I did it out of my heart because it was born in me.

Mansour explains the daily fear of not getting his "babies" because he felt that he was under the watchful eye of the courts for 6 years to prove his fitness as a parent: "okay, so for the next 6–7 years I had to be in court every year, every year, every year."

Were they checking up on you?

No, because she [the mother of the children] would bring in a suit. You know, I want visitation, I want custody. Every year it would change. So for like 6 years I did this. And then every time I was on pins and needles. At any moment I might get a crazy judge and [have to] give them back because they feel kids should be with their mother, even though I had them in the best school in the city of Milwaukee. . . . I'm doing a good job. . . . The school, everybody's sending letter[s] and they were still crazy and indifferent and then I finally got a black guardian ad litem who's now a commissioner, a judge. And he looked at everything and

he said, "I'm going to tell you something. I've seen how you interact with them and . . . I could not do what you're doing. I'll be very honest with you, if it was . . . I could not do what you're doing and I don't know how you do it." My God. When a lot of people say they would die for their kids they don't really mean it. Other than that, I would lay down my life with no reservation and be happy, totally happy, for my children. Totally. No question, no doubt. . . . I really have to focus and get them through college.

John was formerly married to the mother of his child and maintained relations with his daughter's family members. He was living in Milwaukee when he received notification that his daughter would be placed in foster care. He discusses the phone call he received from his ex-sister-in-law in California:

It was approaching the next school year, I mean it was October, something like that. My ex-sister-in-law called me. . . . [She said] "What I want to tell you is I think you better get your baby." I said, "What do you mean?" She said, "Well ah, just, just get your baby." I said, "Talk to me! Tell me what are you speaking of?" Well, you know, the child services and all that had gotten involved, [I] guess my daughter was living in motels. She [his wife] had lost the house, had lost everything. My daughter was living in a motel where guys were coming in and out of this motel. My baby's seven years old. Ah, I said, "Well who do I talk to? Give me a name and give me a number. That's all I want." She gave me a name; she gave me a number, and I took over from there. That person was a child [welfare] services . . . agent from northern California, and from the time I talked to her I let her know, she told me the first thing, "We're about to place your daughter in a foster home." I said, "No, the hell you ain't. No, the hell you ain't. I am her father. Why am I not there involved with this? Why have I not been contacted in this matter?"

What did they [child welfare staff person] say to you?

They did not have an answer for me. . . . I could not get a full explanation of why I was not considered from the start. And when my sister-in-law told me they were about to do it in two weeks. I said, "I tell you what. If you attempt to, to complete this action, I will sue you, the [state] of California, [for] everything that you got. *My daughter [is]coming to me.* You make sure of this." "Well, ah, it's not that simple." "Well you tell me what I got to do." And, ah, she said, "Well first of all, you know, you fill out this . . . blah blah blah. . . . Put in for the petition, you know, for the custody and all this . . . you know, we [will] send people out.

John explained that his child's case was eventually transferred to the Wisconsin child welfare services bureau. The child welfare workers began to investigate for his suitability as an adoptive parent.

[The state of California] child welfare services [staff person] said, "Well, we got you in contact with the Wisconsin people now. They're going to take over, and they're going to follow up with what, what we tell them to follow up on." I guess they have the same system procedures that they go through. They came to my house for an entire year to check up on me. [He said that the child welfare worker would say] "Well where's your daughter going to stay?" You know, "Well this is her bedroom." I had to show them that I had adequate space . . . a bedroom, this and that. My daughter was in here. [I had to show them:] this is her bedroom, this is her dresser. You know, girls' color [in her] bedroom, you know, bicycle, all this was hers when she comes. Refrigerator's full, house is clean, you know, keep coming. This is no act! I'm not doing this just for you, you know. . . . They kept coming, unannounced. They'd [even] come at eight o'clock at night. . . . This is '91 to '92. . . . They came to my house for a whole year. They [generally] came unannounced. . . . Saturday morning, it could be seven o'clock; Saturday evening, it could be five. They came. And every time they came I was ready. Not [one] time they didn't come that I didn't have food in my refrigerator, that her room wasn't like it was the last time

[they] came. I'm just waiting for her to come and occupy it [her room].

Was she in foster care [during this period of investigation]?

She was with the ex-sister-in-law who was taking care of her.

Okay, all right.

Ah, got a call April 1st, 1992. It was a caseworker. Said, "Ah, what you doing right now?" I said, "Um, nothing. . . . I'm doing a little work in the garage," something I was doing. Said, "Well, [I] want you to take a seat." I said, "For what?" cause I don't even know who I'm talking to, I'm thinking he [is] going to tell me something: "Well, won't you take a seat?" [Brief silence, sighs]. He said, "Ah, got some news for you." He said, "Your baby's coming." My baby came to me on Easter Sunday.

He discusses his first reaction to being the primary parent of his child:

When she [arrived at the airport], she had a long old dress on . . . wearing sandals. She had braids in her hair and—. . . I got my baby in my arms. I took them braids out of her hair, man, the dirt was thick and I cried. I took her hair out. I washed it. —. . . that was the beginning of my knowing what I had to do, was taking her hair out, looking at that dirt. Somebody gotta wash this. That's when I started doing my baby's hair. I was the braider, man. I did it. Combed it, washed it, greased it, braided it. She can tell you right now, she got tired of looking like Pippi Longstocking. [Laughter] That's right. Straight off the sides, cause I couldn't do it right.

Ivy was 18, and the mother of his first child was 15 when the child was born. They were high school sweethearts. In the following passage, he discusses his willingness to take care of his ex-girlfriend, her desire to place the children with an adoption agency, and his determination to adopt his children:

I did not want my baby's momma to be in the streets. That's one thing that I knew in my mind.

... So I told my grandmother at the time "—, Granny, my girl friend pregnant." And her mom put out. ... And so we moved into the projects [with my grandma] and I been taking care of her, and then she got a little bit promiscuous on the street. ... And so she wanted to move out with one of the dudes she sleeping around with, which was right down the porch from where we lived. ... She moved out, [however], she was pregnant again by me. ... Later on down the line ... she didn't want the kids. She was going to put them up for adoption. ... I said, "don't put my kids up for adoption. Give my kids to me—." ... We went to the court down in Illinois.

You had to do this in Chicago?

Yea. My first two [children] were in Chicago. All the rest was up here in Milwaukee—. ... First I had trouble [with the courts]. ... They gave me my son easy. But giving me my daughters, [which] the childs' maternal grandmother didn't want to do ... she wanted to separate my kids, but I said "—, no, my kids stay together."

Another issue shared by these men was their continued interaction or desire for continued interaction with the mothers of their children. Ivy discussed his attempts to sustain a relationship with the mother of their children:

[The mother is] still in Decatur. I was going to call 1-800-USA-SEARCH, you know, but she know her kids, she know they up here in Milwaukee. We been living up here going on ten years now. So she know where they are. And I never even tried to get child support from her. I don't want child support from her. You know what I mean? Personally, I been doing good, this much good, without it. ... Only thing I want her [the mother of the children] to do is say "hi" to her kids. Send a picture. Write a letter. ... You don't even have to come around. Just send a card. I don't want no child support from her. I don't want the state to find me to give me child support. You should not have to make a grown person take care of their kid.

Did you hire a lawyer or did you by yourself?

No. Pro se.

Many of these fathers do not understand their child support order for their biological children, particularly if they care for the child everyday. P-nut discusses his child support order for his son living with his biological mother. His mother was awarded legal guardianship of his son and his son's brother. His son's brother is the result of a previous relationship:

[Please explain:] you [stated] you had a child support order for your biological son, too?

Yea. ... I had told the judge ... my son had been with my mother ... ever since he was 3 [days old]. So, I [had] been with him like all his life— he been with me. So the judge, like, "well, you don't have to pay no child support, just drop it." I had took a bill down there [court]. He was like, "you no longer [have to] pay child support." I had it signed by the judge. I took it to Room 707 in the building. ... And I thought they put it in the computer from there. So, for a long time I stopped getting child support orders ... child support forms. Then all of a sudden the child support forms pops up. They saying I owe them a thousand and some dollars. But it is for foster care. And I'm like ... I don't know how that is possible. Know what I'm saying? And the judge, now they saying, "it's not for the judge." They want me to pay foster care.

She [your mother] had both your kids?

Yea. I say, we have, my mother has both my son and his brother. The mother's ... well, only one of them is mine. Know what I'm saying? But both of them call me "daddy."

Why did your mom [take legal guardianship] for both boys?

She [the mother of the children] was in the system ... know what I'm saying? ... We different. ... We from down South, I guess, so, like, we look at it like, okay, it's his brother. He's been here since he was 3 days old. He [his brother] was like 1 or 2. We like, the only thing he know. We [his biological mother and him] have tried ... to let them see [their] mother [and her family]. ... And, [they would say], ... "Daddy, who [are] these people?"

Although the children have had a negative reaction to their biological mother's family, P-nut has attempted to maintain a relationship with the mother of the children under his biological mother's legal guardianship even though there is a court order for her to not be around the children:

> I see [their] mother on the street.... I told her she could go home and put on some clothes. We went out to eat and I let her visit the boys [even though] there [is] an order [that] she is not supposed to be around them. But she chose not to clean herself up. So, I'm like, I take you out to eat, you can visit the boys spend a little time with them. She didn't want that.

He continues to work on getting sole custody of his biological son and his brother, but has had a difficult time maintaining a stable job, and his efforts are being met without much success.

Responsible Fatherhood

John discusses the daily challenges of balancing responsible parenthood and work. His thoughts were similar to those of all four of these parents:

> There was the initial impact for me of what, the work I had to do. Whether it be wash [her] hair, take it down. Whether it be make sure you go to bed; whether it be make sure you get in the bathtub, um, things like that. Ah, so 7 years old, put her in school. They put my daughter back a grade because of that 43-day stint the previous year. [One of the reasons child welfare became involved in this child's life was because she had only attended 43 days of school in the previous year.] She had to start that year all over again. Uh, she should be in tenth grade now, but she's in ninth. But again, doing the wash gave me the drive of what I had to do to keep her ready every day. Going to work, my employers understood, uh, what I was going through, which is good that they did understand. Ah, that I was going to take this role on, that I had nobody else. So they were cooperative, you know, eight o'clock, fine, take my daughter to school,

> then I go to work. And it's been like that for the last 8 years. . . . We went to a Catholic school for 8 years. I know what it felt like to have my mother there for teacher conferences, programs, 4 o'clock meetings. So I knew right away what I had to do. My parents did it, so I knew I could do it. So I didn't miss no programs; I didn't miss no conferences. My daughter there has been a straight-A student for 3 years straight.

John provides us some reflection on the role of parenting and the mothers of his children:

> And I don't want mine to be like me. You know, I want them to have better than me. And even though I know what I got out of this system . . . the opportunities it gave me to go to the service, go to college, you know, get a good job, this and that, I took advantage of it. And for the opportunities that I missed taking advantage of, I can't lose sleep over it. Um, again, Milwaukee is not conducive to a black man surviving. Not at all. If it was, I wouldn't have left 10 years ago, probably. Or let's say, ah, 20 years ago, or 25 when I left. I left in '75, so I didn't come back until '89. Twenty-four years. And ah, you know, my kids are my life. I would love to work a second job, so that I could offset some of this [financial] burden. But ah, like I said, that one in there just got her hair done yesterday. Fifty bucks . . . went to Afrofest last night. Another twenty bucks in the park. [Laughter] But, you know for a parent, a man to be involved with his kids is one of the greatest things a kid can experience other than the mom. She knows it, cause her mom still calls. Oh yeah, every now and then, Mom still [shows her] loves [for her daughter]. I'm a fearful dad, I don't want them out of my sight. I'm like that lion with the puppies, don't go too far, get back here. You know. Ah, make sure they're safe. They don't call home on time, I'm on pins and needles, stuff like that; I'm like that. Ah. So if I can train 'em right, put 'em out in the world, I'll have less of a fear when they're gone.

Ivy discusses his views on the responsibility of fathers to their children and the lack of social services for fathers:

You got men out here who do take care of their responsibilities. You do got men out here like myself who is trying to do the best I can for his family. They ain't seen their mom in 12 years, 11 years. They have not. I am the one who was there all those nights, I'm the one. You don't see no special in TV, My Favorite Dad, or Father's Day, don't get blown out of proportion like Mother's Day do. And, God knows, I'm not trying to say give me some kind of special award. No —. That's not what I want —. I just want someone to acknowledge that it be an equal thing. We [are] not equal because if there was a woman in my situation, I would be able to go somewhere and get a grant, somebody could help me pay my rent. When I try to go to Salvation Army, when I try to go certain places, they tell me, "why, we can't help you, [because] we only have grants for battered women or homeless women . . . You can't be a man with kids. You can't do that—," . . . You can be a woman with kids. At the Salvation Army, you can be a woman with kids. Kids on this side with a woman. But if you a man with kids, then the man got to go over there and the kids go over here. That's crazy. I'm not going to be separated from my kids. I [am] not saying that I will resort to selling dope [to survive], I'm not saying that. I would not say that ever. But, however, I am saying I will shovel snow, rake leaves, fill beer cans, collect cans, or something to survive for me and my kids. You know?

Social Services for Custodial Fathers

It is often assumed that single men with custodial children will have easier access to social services for their children. The majority of the fathers in this study who had children in their care complained about the bias in human services for providing assistance to men with children. Ivy discusses his experience with accessing services for himself and his children:

My reality is that [the provision of social services is] prejudiced, it's biased. I mean, it's not biased, it's prejudiced. It's one-sided.—Because W-2 women's works, not for men. I'm a man, I'm a parent. I do the same thing that a woman do. . . . More is expected of me. I can raise my daughter the best I

can. Wisconsin Works . . . say they provide child care. When it's time for me to try to get child care, they send me through the red tape. Yeah! . . . Cause I'm a man. Like I said it before, I tried to get a low-income house. But because I was a man who had a felony back in '93, they gave me red tape so they can't give me a place to stay. I said, "well, what are me and my kids supposed to do? Do I not supposed to take care of my kids?" They say, "well, we can't help you there. We can't accept men with families here." I said, "well, women with families, y'all accept them." "Well, we specialize in helping women . . . [to] become independent under W-2—." I said, "what about me? Do I . . . need to get a wig and change my name?" You know, tell me something. What am I supposed to do to get some help [for me and my children]? This is not right. This is not right at all.

It is generally the fathers' assessment that the lack of provision of services to them is based on bias. Several subjects complained about the receptivity of the caseworkers when they requested services.

Promoting Responsible Fatherhood

Studies show that children who grow up without responsible fathers are significantly more likely to experience poverty, perform poorly in school, engage in criminal activity, and abuse drugs and alcohol. The U.S. Department of Health and Human Services supports programs and policies that reflect the critical role that both fathers and mothers play in building strong and successful families and in the well-being of children. (For a variety of information on fatherhood, see www.hunter.cuny.edu/socwork/nrcfcpp/info_services/fatherhood.html.)

The U.S. Department of Health and Human Services (2004) has developed a special initiative to support and strengthen the roles of fathers in families. This initiative is guided by the following principles:

- All fathers can be important contributors to the well-being of their children;

- Parents are partners in raising their children, even when they do not live in the same household;
- The roles fathers play in families are diverse and related to cultural and community norms;
- Men should receive the education and support necessary to prepare them for the responsibility of parenthood; and
- Government can encourage and promote father involvement through its programs and through its own workforce policies.

Conclusions

It seems clear that recent trends that emphasize the involvement of noncustodial fathers in their children's lives are likely to affect the families served by child welfare agencies. Although the nature of recent policy reforms and program initiatives, such as expedited permanency planning, concurrent planning, and family group meetings, may lead observers to believe that child welfare agencies will increasingly identify, locate, and involve noncustodial fathers in casework and permanency planning, there is no empirical evidence to predict the likely effects of these shifts in case practice.

The low-income fathers described in this chapter faced formidable hurdles to secure and maintain that contact with their children. Most were not notified by a child welfare worker that the child was being considered for placement with the state; they instead received notification from an ex-kin member or the biological mother. Economically, the fathers appear to be caught in poverty traps as deeply as any single mother. Poor education, criminal records, and perceived race and class prejudice limit their employment opportunities. Yet under these difficult circumstances, more than half of the fathers considered themselves emotionally and financially responsible for their children. In sum, this group of low-income African American fathers had high levels of involvement with at least some of their children, long-term rela-

tionships with at least one of the mothers, and sporadic to long-term employment.

It is important for child welfare staff members to consider all of the relationships that a child may have, including the one with the "other" biological parent. In research conducted by me (Pate 2003), it was found that the fathers maintained a relationship with their former kin because of their relationship with their child. To conduct more diligent searches, it is important for the worker to broaden their definition of family and look at the kinship relationship that will include the father's family as a resource for locating the father, as well as a possible option for placement of the child.

From a broader perspective, there are some limited efforts to promote collaborations between child welfare and child support enforcement agencies. The results of the South Carolina Diligent Search Project appear promising. The focus of this effort thus far appears to be on identifying and locating fathers primarily for the purposes of expediting the termination of parental rights, thereby hastening adoption proceedings. Other collaborative efforts are focused on increasing child support collections. Few programs, with the exception of the parental involvement project in Illinois, focus attention on finding noncustodial fathers as placement resources. The lack of basic research about how noncustodial fathers are involved in the child welfare permanency planning process provides a strong rationale for the current study conducted by the Urban Institute, which examines casework practices in five states. For these five states, the study will provide information that is currently not available:

- How many children in foster care have noncustodial fathers?
- How do child welfare policies and caseworker practices currently involve noncustodial fathers in case planning?
- What are the perceived barriers to involving noncustodial fathers in case planning?

- What are the perceived likely effects of noncustodial father involvement?
- How many children in foster care are known to the child support program and can child support locator services assist child welfare agencies in identifying and locating noncustodial fathers?

- What promising practices are currently being implemented to identify, locate, and involve noncustodial fathers in child welfare cases?

References

Adoption and Safe Families Act. (1997). P.L. 105-89.

Bess, R., Andrews, C., Jantz, A., and V. Russell. (2003). The cost of protecting vulnerable children III: What has happened since welfare reform and ASFA? Washington, DC: Urban Institute.

Courtney, M., & Sykes, A. (2003). Racial disproportionality in the child welfare system. *Children and Youth Services Review, 25,* 355–358.

Edin, K., & Lein, L. (1997). *Making ends meet: How single mothers survive welfare and low-wage work.* New York: Russell Sage Foundation.

Edin, K., Lein, L., Nelson, T., & Clampet-Lundquist, S. (2001). Talking with low-income fathers. *Poverty Research News, 4*(2), 10–12.

Grossmann, D. E., Funk, D. A., Mentaberry, M. V., & Seibel, B. (2000). *Adoption and permanency guidelines: Improving court practice in child abuse and neglect cases.* Reno, NV: National Council of Juvenile and Family Court Judges.

Harris, M., & Courtney, M. (2003). The interaction of race, ethnicity, and family structure with respect to the timing of family reunification. *Children and Youth Services Review, 25,* 409–429.

Jeffries, J. M., Menghraj, S., & Hairston, C. F. (2001). *Serving incarcerated and ex-offender fathers and their families.* Washington, DC: U.S. Department of Justice and the Charles Stuart Mott Foundation.

Johnson, E., Levine, A., & Doolittle, F. (1999). *Fathers' fair share: Helping poor men manage child support and fatherhood.* New York: Russell Sage Foundation.

Lamb, M. E. (ed.). (1987). *The father's role: Cross cultural perspectives.* Hillsdale, NJ: Erlbaum.

Malm, K. E. (2004). *Getting noncustodial dads involved in the lives of foster children.* Caring for Children: Facts and Perspectives brief no. 3. Washington, DC: Urban Institute.

Manhattan Institute. (2004). *High school graduation rates in the United States.* Retrieved June 30, 2004, from www.manhattaninstitute.org/html/cr_baeo.htm.

McLanahan, S., Garfinkel, I., Reichman, N. E., Teiber, J., Carlson, M., & Audgier, C. N. (2001). *The Fragile Families and Child Wellbeing Study—National baseline report.* Princeton, NJ: Center for Research on Child Well-Being.

Mentaberry, M. (1999). *Model courts serve abused and neglected children.* Fact sheet no. 90. Washington, DC: U.S. Department of Justice.

Merkel-Holguin, L. (2003). Fathers and their families: The untapped resource for children involved in the child welfare system. *American Humane Association, 4*(8), 121–127.

Meyer, D. R., & Cancian, M. (2001). *The W-2 child support demonstration evaluation phase I: Final report.* Vol. I: *Effects of the experiment.* Madison: The W-2 Child Support Demonstration Evaluation, Institute for Research on Poverty, University of Wisconsin–Madison.

Milwaukee Journal Sentinel. (2004). More moms made to pay child support. *Milwaukee Journal Sentinel,* (May 3), p. 15.

National Child Welfare Resource Center for Family-Centered Practice. (2002). *Father involvement.* Washington, DC: National Child Welfare Resource Center for Family-Centered Practice.

National Council of Juvenile and Family Court Judges. (2000). *Adoption and permanency guidelines.* Washington, DC: National Council of Juvenile and Family Court Judges.

National Resource Center for Foster Care and Permanency Planning. (1999). *Concurrent planning curriculum.* New York: National Resource Center for Foster Care and Permanency Planning.

O'Donnell, J. M. (1999). Involvement of African American fathers in kinship foster care services. *Social Work, 44,* 428–441.

Pate, D., Jr. (2002). An ethnographic inquiry into the life experiences of African American fathers with children on W-2. In D. Meyer & M. Cancian (eds.), *The W-2 child support demonstration evaluation report on nonexperimental analyses.* Vol. II: *Fathers of children in W-2 families,* pp. 223–251. Madison: Institute for Research on Poverty, University of Wisconsin–Madison.

Pate, D., Jr. (2003). *Documenting the perspectives of fathers with children on welfare in the post entitlement era: The life experiences of thirty-six African American fathers in Milwaukee, Wisconsin.* Doctoral dissertation, University of Wisconsin, Milwaukee.

Personal Responsibility and Work Opportunity Reconciliation Act. (1996). P.L. 104-193.

Pleck, J. H. (1982). *Husbands and wives paid work, family work, and adjustment.* Wellesley, MA: Wellesley College Center for Research on Women.

Responsible Fatherhood Act. (2003). P.L. 104-193.

Sonenstein, F., Malm, K., & Billing, A. (2002). *Study of fathers' involvement in permanency planning and child welfare casework.* Washington, DC: Urban Institute.

Sorensen, E., & Zibman, C. (2000). *To what extent do children benefit from child support?* Washington, DC: Urban Institute.

Turetsky, V. (2004). *Child support, fatherhood, and marriage provisions in TANF reauthorization bills.* Washington, DC: Center for Law and Social Policy.

U.S. Department of Health and Human Services. (2002). *Study of fathers' involvement in permanency planning and child welfare casework.* Retrieved June 30, 2004, from aspe.hhs.gov/hsp/CW-dads02/.

U.S. Department of Health and Human Services. (2004). *Fatherhood initiative.* Retrieved June 30, 2004, from http://www.fatherhood.hhs.gov/index.shtml.

Waller, M. R., & Plotnick, R. (2001). Effective child support policy for low-income families: Evidence from street-level research. *Journal of Policy Analysis and Management 20,* 89–110.

ILZE EARNER

Immigrant Children and Youth in the Child Welfare System

Immigration Status and Special Needs in Permanency Planning

REBECCA

Rebecca was 14 years old when she was sent from Jamaica to live in New York with her mother's sister in Brooklyn. Within 3 months of her arrival, her aunt's live-in boyfriend began to sexually abuse her. When her aunt discovered what was going on, the fight between her and her boyfriend brought the police and child welfare authorities. Rebecca was placed in a group home where she stayed until she was discharged at the age of 18 years. During her 4 years in the care of the state, she received an array of services, including independent living skills training. It was only after she left care that Rebecca discovered she was an undocumented immigrant and could not legally study, live, or work in the United States. Rebecca lost the only opportunity she had to legally change her immigration status because the foster care agency failed to make an application on her behalf while she was in their care.

Cases like Rebecca's are not uncommon as new immigrants, especially children and youth, continue to change the demographic face of the country. As illustrated by Rebecca's case, the problem is that mainstream institutions, like child welfare systems, have been slow to recognize, respond to, and appropriately address the special needs of immigrant children and youth who come into their care. Child welfare workers do not routinely assess clients for immigration-related needs; nor do they make referrals for immigration legal services. The primary reason for this oversight is that although a great deal of attention is often given to laws and systems governing the entrance of new immigrants into the United States, there is little coordination between federal and state policies for addressing the human service needs of these newcomers once they are here. The result is an ad hoc, patchwork approach to federal, state, and local services that can leave new immigrants, especially children and youth, falling between the cracks. In this chapter, I focus specifically on how immigration status affects permanency planning for adolescent youth in out-of-home care. The different types of immigration status of immigrant children and youth in care, early identification and assessment of immigration status, and guidelines for effective intervention are highlighted. I also describe examples of collaborative programs between public child welfare systems and community-based immigration services providers that enhance capacity to meet the permanency planning needs of this population.

The range of special needs presented by immigrant children and youth who come to the attention of the public child welfare system is broad and can include issues related to language and culture (Suleiman 2003), special health problems (Guendelman, Schauffler, & Pearl 2001), and educational needs (Qin-Hilliard 2002), as well as psychosocial and mental health problems that result from migration and subsequent adjustments (James 1997). Immigration status affects the ability of all immigrants to access certain public services and benefits; however, immigrant children and youth are often eligible for certain types of services apart from their parents or other adult members of a household. Ignorance on the part of both service providers and consumers often results in many immigrant children and youth not getting services to meet their special needs.

New immigrants and their children are a fact of American life. From 1990 to 2000, more immigrants came to live in the United States than in any other historical time frame (Fix & Passel 2001). In 1970, the foreign-born population represented less than 5% of the total population. Current data indicate that 31 million residents presently in the United States are foreign-born, representing roughly 11% of the total population. Of these, 60% are either legal permanent residents or naturalized citizens; refugees and asylum seekers make up another 7%. However, an estimated 28% are undocumented aliens (U.S. Census Bureau 2001). Further complicating this demographic picture is that noncitizen households are far more likely to contain children (55% vs. 35%) and that 85% of immigrant families with children are so-called "mixed-status" families—a situation in which members of the same family may include various combinations of citizens and noncitizens (e.g., undocumented parents, citizen children, undocumented siblings) (Fix & Zimmerman 1999). These families present distinct challenges for child welfare services providers in the face of recent federal legislation that has sought to substantially restrict the legal and social rights of immigrants (Baum & Goldstein 2002).

Immigrant policy, as distinct from immigration policy, is generally construed as the laws, regulations, and programs that affect immigrants' access to health and human services, including preventive and primary health care, housing, job placement, counseling, and other social services programs (Siegel & Kappaz 2002). Since 1996, only a categorical group of "qualified" immigrants is entitled to receive assistance from federal benefits programs. With the passage of the Personal Responsibility and Work

Opportunity Reconciliation Act, all new legal immigrants were barred for a period of 5 years from accessing federal means-tested benefits, including Temporary Assistance to Needy Families, Medicaid, and the Child Health Insurance program, while states were given the option to define to what extent they wished to pursue these categorical distinctions for immigrants to access state aid programs. Immigrants generally not qualified for benefits include the undocumented, but also many others legally present in the United States, such as applicants for family unity or other adjustment of status categories, asylum seekers, students, visitors, and temporary workers (Siegel & Kappaz 2002). The unintended consequence of this policy has been an overall "chilling" effect that has kept many immigrant families from accessing services to which they are legally entitled, including healthcare for their children and food stamp programs (Fix & Zimmerman 1999). According to some studies, as a result immigrant families and their children are disproportionately poor and lack adequate healthcare, food, and shelter (Capps et al. 2002).

Little is known about how or why immigrant children and youth come to the attention of the child welfare system, or for that matter even of the numbers of children and youth involved. Anecdotal evidence, limited studies, and reports from observers suggest, however, that their numbers are increasing, especially in the long-term foster care population (Earner, in press; Lutheran Immigration and Refugee Services & U.S. Conference of Catholic Bishops 2003).

In the absence of specific data, it can be assumed that the issues that bring immigrant children and youth into contact with the child welfare system are often the same as those for their American counterparts: a combination of the normative changes that occur during childhood and adolescence and of exceptional family and environmental stressors (Loppnow 1985). However, in the case of immigrant children and youth, the stressors may be exacerbated by experiences unique to this population that may also place them in situations where the risk for abuse and neglect is high. For example, some immigrant children and youth residing in the United States have been sent by their families and are living with extended family members (Baum & Goldstein 2002; Haines 2001). In other cases, immigrant children and youth may experience being left behind in their native country with grandparents or other relatives while their parents travel to the United States to find employment. They may then be reunified many years later with parents they hardly know and find themselves in a situation of having to adjust not only to their parents and a new country, but perhaps a new family as well, with siblings or step-siblings that are U.S. born (Kandel & Kao 2001). For immigrant children and youth who migrated with their parents, the migration experience itself, especially if it included illegal border crossings, may have been traumatic. Psychological suffering can continue and profoundly affect adjustment to the reality of life in a new country; in addition, undocumented immigrants must cope with the constant fear of being found out (James 1997).

Other unique issues that place immigrant children and youth at risk may be cultural dissonance between immigrant parents and their American-raised children (Ojito 1997); disciplinary practices on the part of parents that differ from accepted standards in this country (Gopaul-McNichol 1999); language barriers (Carliner 2000); untreated mental health problems in families, including substance or alcohol abuse (Vega, Kolody, & Aguilar-Gaxiola 2001); and individual difficulties with assimilation and acculturation (Beiser, Hou, Hyman, & Tousignant 2002; Rumbaut 1996). Much less is known about a growing number of disturbing cases involving immigrant children and youth who may be victims of trafficking, either with or without their families' knowledge and complicity, for the purposes of employment or pros-

titution (Franken 2002). Another small but growing phenomenon is that of unaccompanied minors, some of whom may be refugees, although others are often picked up by immigration officials at ports of entry with no official status (Solomon 2002).

Once immigrant children and youth are involved with the child welfare system, they and their families face a unique set of obstacles that may keep them in care longer and affect permanency planning outcomes. In some cases, immigrant parents are unable to meet the service plan requirements for family reunification because they are ineligible, based on their immigration status, for certain federal or state-funded services (e.g., alcohol or substance abuse counseling, mental health services) (Baum & Goldstein 2002). In other cases, parents may be unfamiliar with or afraid to engage with child welfare authorities and do not understand, either because of language or cultural barriers, the consequences of their failure to comply with service plan requirements (Earner 2004). Child welfare workers may also be hesitant to place immigrant children and youth in kinship care with undocumented relatives even though the mandates of the Adoption and Safe Families Act of 1997 can result in permanent separation from family and kin for these children and youth in care (Wexler 2002).

Finally, because of widespread unfamiliarity with immigration laws and a lack of legal resources, foster care services providers may altogether fail to address immigration status irregularities of children and youth in their care. In the case of Rebecca, adjustment of immigration status could have been facilitated through a Special Immigrant Juvenile Status application to the U.S. Citizenship and Immigration Services. Under the Immigration Act of 1990, immigrant children and youth in long-term foster care can become permanent residents and obtain legal resident status (a "green card") that allows them to fully participate in society once they leave out-of-home care.

Definitions and Implications of Immigration Status on Service Needs and Permanency Planning

A critical first step for child welfare workers in beginning to address the special needs of immigrant children and youth is learning to recognize the impact that immigration status has on an individual's ability to function in society and to address this issue appropriately in developing service plan needs. Although most immigrant children and youth in care will receive all necessary services regardless of their status, it is important to stress that once a child leaves care, the ability to achieve independent living can be severely curtailed by immigration status problems. Undocumented persons cannot obtain a social security card, live permanently in the United States, obtain legal employment, travel freely, receive financial aid for college, or access most forms of public benefits. Permanency planning for immigrant children and youth in foster care must therefore address their specialized need for immigration-related legal services.

Immigration law is both complex and subject to change. Therefore, it is unreasonable to expect that child welfare workers will become sufficiently proficient to be able to give expert advice to children and youth in their care. However, through regular training, workers can achieve a general knowledge and familiarity with common immigration statuses and the ability both to assess immigration status, especially for youth in foster care, and to refer children to specialized immigration and legal resources when appropriate. Important to the issue of assessing immigration status are agency guidelines for workers to insure that this information is protected by confidentiality protocols; many immigrants are reluctant to interact with government officials or employees for fear that they will be reported. Providing both verbal and written assurances that information about immigration status is sought strictly for the purposes of identifying programs for which a family or child may be eligible would help alleviate this fear. Unfortunately, few state or local child welfare agencies have developed such handbooks or implemented guidelines for child welfare workers on these issues.

Identifying the immigration status of children, especially adolescents, in foster care is necessary and should be a routine part of concurrent planning protocols. Even if children or youth are reunified with their families, those with immigration status irregularities can and should be referred to immigration-related legal services or community-based immigration advocacy organizations that are qualified to provide expert advice. Furthermore, even if a child is a U.S. citizen but the worker recognizes that the family includes new immigrants, the family may benefit from such a referral. For adolescents in care, there is a limited window of opportunity to file for immigration status adjustments. The sooner the process is initiated, the more likely it will be successful. Assumptions about immigration status should not be made based on a family or child's ability or lack of ability to speak English or on the family's ethnic background or country of origin.

Documents that identify immigration status may become lost over the years, but the statuses do not expire. So, for example, although a green card, officially known as an "Alien Registration Card," may be lost or the card itself may have expired, the individual continues to be a lawful permanent resident. Child welfare caseworkers can assist individuals with the replacement of documents through the U.S. Citizenship and Immigration Services (USCIS) or refer individuals to qualified immigration advocacy organizations for assistance (New York City Administration for Children's Services 2004).

The following is a brief overview of common immigration statuses that child welfare workers may encounter with children and youth in care as well as a description of how these statuses impact services.

"Legal permanent residents" are immigrants who have been granted permission to live and work in the United States permanently; they possess a green card and have a social security number. They are still citizens of their country of origin but can exercise most of the rights of American citizenship. One difference is that they can be deported or denied permission to reenter the country if they are convicted of certain felony crimes or other special circumstances. Under current legislation, they may be considered "qualified aliens" and be eligible for federally funded government benefits after they have had a green card for 5 years. This status has no implications for permanency planning.

"Refugees/Asylees" are individuals who must flee their country to avoid persecution and may be granted refugee or asylee status. The difference between a refugee and an asylee is that refugee status is conferred upon individuals while they are still outside of the United States; an asylee is an individual who is granted status after he or she has arrived. The Office of Refugee Resettlement, a division of the U.S. Department of Health and Human Services, is responsible for resettlement of refugees, including unaccompanied refugee minors who receive foster care and other services and benefits. Presently the Office of Refugee Resettlement contracts with voluntary agencies, primarily Lutheran Immigration and Refugee Services and the U.S. Conference of Catholic Bishops, to assist in locating foster care placements for refugee and asylee minors (Office of Refugee Resettlement 2002). Because of their status and the special circumstances surrounding their entrance to the United States, these individuals are entitled to certain services not otherwise available to other immigrants in foster care. They can be identified by a green card, a stamp in their passport, or a letter from the USCIS. The Office of Refugee Resettlement should be notified if individuals with this type of status are identified (New York City Administration for Children's Services 2004).

Under a collection of federal laws known generally as the "Violence Against Women Act" (VAWA) of 1994, battered immigrant spouses and/or their children can obtain legal immigrant status without the abuser's knowledge or permission. To be eligible, the batterer must either be a legal permanent resident or a U.S. citizen. If professionals believe that a child or parent might qualify, a referral should be made for domestic violence-related legal services immediately. Each state has an Office on Violence Against Women and further information can be accessed from the National Domestic Violence Hotline (1-800-799-SAFE) (U.S. Department of Justice 2003).

Currently U.S. law recognizes as "trafficked persons" those individuals who can prove that they were brought across international borders for the purpose of forced labor or prostitution. The Victims of Trafficking and Violence Prevention Act of 2000 grants these individuals the possibility of obtaining legal permanent status if they met these criteria and agree to cooperate in criminal investigations of their traffickers. Advocates estimate that approximately 50,000 women and children are brought each year to the United States under these circumstances (Franken 2002). Presently there are only ad hoc procedures in place to address the needs of minor children who are identified as victims of trafficking, including placing them in state foster care services rather than federal immigration detention facilities. The Office of Refugee Resettlement has been designated as the lead organization to address this situation and should be contacted if someone suspects that an individual meets the criteria of a trafficked person (Office Refugee Resettlement 2003).

"Undocumented Aliens" are individuals who either entered the United States unlawfully or overstayed a visa. Undocumented minors often may not know their status because they were not informed of their status by parents or relatives. Undocumented immigrants are eligible for limited services and benefits, such as Child Health Plus, emergency Medicaid, and some state-funded programs. Undocumented immigrants, especially children, may be eligible to apply for lawful immigration status and should be referred to appropriate immigration legal services as soon as possible. Undocumented immigration status has significant implications for permanency planning because of the limits it places on an individual's ability to live independently once he or she leaves out-of-home care. The next section discusses immigration law relief available to undocumented minors in long term foster care placement.

Special Immigrant Juvenile Status

In 1990, the Special Immigrant Juvenile Status Law (SIJS) was created and incorporated into the Immigration and Nationality Act. It allows unmarried minors under the jurisdiction of a juvenile court who are under the age of 21 and deemed eligible for long-term foster care to apply to USCIS for special immigrant status and subsequently for lawful permanent residency. Certain criteria must be met: (1) the minor must qualify for long-term foster care; (2) the court must rule that family reunification is not an option; (3) the minor must remain in foster care or go on to adoption or guardianship; (4) the court must find that it is not in the best interests of the minor to be returned to their country of origin; and (5) the minor must be in care because of neglect, abuse, or abandonment (Catholic Legal Immigration Network and Immigrant Legal Resource Center 2002).

SIJS proceedings are initiated by child welfare workers and consist of a two-part application, one with the juvenile court and the other with the USCIS. It is imperative that potential applicants are identified early because current USCIS regulations stipulate that the minor remain under jurisdiction of the court until the immigration application is decided. This can take anywhere from 6 to 36 months or longer. Some states end dependency at the age of 18, whereas others extend it to age 19, especially if the minor must complete high school. Other states extend dependency to the age of 21. Therefore it is critical that workers make judges aware of and advocate for the need to extend dependency as long as the SIJS application is in

process. If the minor leaves care, ages out of the system, or turns 21 years old, the immigration application becomes moot and regardless of the circumstances the minor will lose this opportunity to change his or her immigration status.

Once the SIJS application is approved, the minor can apply for lawful permanent residency. However, he or she will be required to meet all of the requirements that apply to this status. Applicants might be denied permanent residency if they have a record of involvement with drugs or have committed certain felony crimes, are HIV positive, have committed visa fraud, or had previously been deported. Minors with these potential problems should be advised to consult an immigration attorney who may be able to resolve their case with special waivers (Catholic Legal Immigration Network and Immigrant Legal Resource Center 2002).

Child welfare workers should explain to youth in care the benefits and risks involved prior to making an SIJS application. For some undocumented children and youth, an SIJS application might be the only route to gain lawful permanent resident status in the United States. Not only does this insure the long-term benefit of guaranteeing an individual's ability to live and work permanently in the United States, a more immediate benefit is that once an SIJS application is made, the minor can also be granted work authorization until his or her case is decided. These minor children are also then protected from deportation proceedings. The greatest risk in making the SIJS application is that it alerts the USCIS to the existence of the undocumented minor in the United States. The SIJS application process is not confidential; the USCIS can use this information at a later date to initiate removal proceedings if the application is unsuccessful. Therefore it is crucial that all potential applicants are referred to appropriate and qualified legal advice prior to initiating the application process. It should be noted that even if a child is not likely to win SIJS status, a qualified legal expert may still be able to get them legal status in some other way (Catholic Legal Immigration Network and Immigrant Legal Resource Center 2002).

Finally, immigrant children and youth who apply for change of status through SIJS should also be made aware that they will not be able to use their new lawful immigration status to petition for either their original parents or siblings. A legal permanent resident can usually help their family members to change their immigration status. This rule was enacted to insure that parents who abused, neglected, or abandoned their children would not benefit from their children's new legal status (Catholic Legal Immigration Network Immigrant Legal Resource Center 2002).

Collaborative Endeavors between Public Child Welfare and Immigrant Services Providers

Beginning in the mid-1990s, immigrants' rights advocates and community-based organizations that serve immigrant communities began to draw attention to the systemic barriers immigrant families, children, and youth face in negotiating mainstream social service institutions. A number of national, state, and local studies identified problems immigrants encounter accessing health care (Hagen, Rodriguez, Capps, & Kabiri 2003), education (Yeh & Inose 2002), legal services (Lee 2000), mental health and social services (Vergara, Miller, Martin, & Cookson 2003). Recommendations for change have included a public health model approach with an emphasis on prevention and well-being (i.e., better coordination of services and collaboration between providers, expanding cultural and linguistic competence, and improving outreach to immigrant communities) (Cress 2003; Kullgren 2003; Taylor 2004). Advocates for social change have focused on the need for developing an agenda for action in the arena of immigrant policies, such as promoting social justice through legislative change, community-building, and enhancing the capacity of ethnic

and community-based organizations to help integrate immigrants into full participation in society (Siegel & Kappaz 2002).

Scant attention has been paid to the issues and problems faced by immigrant families, children, and youth who come into contact with this system. This situation has slowly begun to change through local efforts by both immigrant and child welfare advocates (Baum & Goldstein 2002). There are two promising approaches for change. One involves cross-service training between public child welfare agencies, refugee-serving agencies, and refugee community representatives. The other illustrates the role that an advisory committee composed of consumer groups can play in shaping services to immigrants in the child welfare system.

Bridging Refugee Youth and Children's Services (BRYCS; Bridging Refugee Youth and Children's Services 2003) is a joint project of the Lutheran Immigration and Refugee Services and the U.S. Conference of Catholic Bishops/ Migration and Refugee Services. Through funding received from the U.S. Department of Health and Human Services, Administration for Children and Families, and the Office of Refugee Resettlement, BRYCS has sought to develop a model mechanism for how public child welfare agencies, refugee services providers, and representatives of refugee community-based organizations can inform one another about their operating structures, objectives, needs, and resources. The goal is to enhance communication and understanding between these groups and increase the effectiveness of service provision to refugee families and children.

In 2000, BRYCS began with an initial short-term project, Community Conversations, which consisted of focus group meetings with public child welfare officials and representatives of African refugee groups living in Seattle, Washington; Omaha, Nebraska; and Baltimore, Maryland. These meetings explored such issues as child-rearing practices, knowledge about relevant U.S. laws and the child welfare system among refugee families, as well as public child welfare officials' concerns and questions about refugee communities and family practices. It became apparent from these conversations that there were issues and recommendations frequently raised by these groups that could be applied to all immigrant refugee communities and the child welfare system (Bridging Refugee Youth and Children's Services 2003).

The pilot programs in Atlanta, Georgia; Cleveland, Ohio; and St. Louis, Missouri resulted in the development of a model of cross-training whereby an array of service providers who work with immigrant families in any given community are brought together by a lead organization to discuss how to coordinate, collaborate, and share resources to strengthen services to immigrants. The lead organization may either be a public child welfare agency or a community-based organization; in either case, it should be an organization with recognition in the community. Because this training is focused on refugees, participants include resettlement organizations, ethnic mutual assistance associations, community-based organizations, mainstream organizations (e.g., schools, healthcare providers, domestic violence programs, mental health services, substance and alcohol abuse services, adult education), and public child welfare agencies. Ideally the final outcomes of this task force are the development of a resource manual that describes available services and identifies liaison personnel, as well as the creation of a natural network of services providers who have an incentive to collaborate in meeting the needs of the refugee population (Bridging Refugee Youth and Children's Services 2003). This model can be adjusted to accommodate immigrant populations other than refugees.

In New York City between 1999 and 2002, several media stories documented the experiences of immigrant parents and children who were involved with the city child welfare system (Gonzalez 1999a,b; Hurley 2002). At the same time, several immigrant rights and child welfare advocates released reports attesting to the systemic barriers immigrants faced that amounted to de facto discrimination (Coalition for Asian American Children and Families 2001; Coalition for Hispanic Children and Families 2001). Pressure from immigrants' right and child welfare advocates prompted the New York City Administration for Children's Service to create a special advisory group composed of consumer groups whose task was to address immigrant issues in the child welfare system.

In 2003, the Commissioner's Advisory Board Subcommittee on Immigrant Issues initiated work on developing a collaborative agenda for improving services to immigrant families, children, and youth. The group, composed of representatives of parents' rights organizations, immigrant's right groups, child welfare advocates, legal experts, members of faith-based and ethnic-community–based organizations, and members of the public child welfare agency worked together to develop a handbook and training curriculum. The handbook, one of the few that exist in any local or state public child welfare system, identifies different types of immigration statuses child welfare workers may encounter, provides assessment guidelines, and details regulations regarding confidentiality. It also covers issues related to language access, the use of interpreters, and translation services.

Training curriculum on immigrant issues specifically in relationship to child welfare services was developed by the Immigrants and Child Welfare project in collaboration with other community-based groups and is now offered regularly to all child welfare workers in New York City (Earner 2004). This training, aside from providing basic information about immigration status and immigrants' access to public benefits, also addresses the migration experience and how that affects immigrant families and their children. Both the handbook and the training guide include a community resource manual specific to immigrant family needs.

Conclusion

The child welfare system must become more sensitive to the special needs of immigrant families, children, and youth who become involved in services. Immigrant children and youth may be able to legalize their immigration status while in care and should be referred to specialized legal services in a timely manner. Child welfare workers should become knowledgeable of the ways in which immigration status affects individuals' ability to function, especially once they leave care. In addition, workers should have knowledge of the common immigration statuses and the impact of these on permanency planning. Agencies can insure that workers are trained to engage in early identification of immigration status–related needs of children and youth and, when appropriate, are prepared to routinely refer all immigrant families, children, and youth to immigration law legal services and assistance. Handbooks should also be developed that provide policy and protocol guidelines and information about resources, so that caseworkers provide up-to-date and current information and referrals to immigrant families. Confidentiality protocols regarding information about immigration status can alleviate immigrants' fears about interacting with government officials and employees.

Immigrants present numerous challenges to the public child welfare system; however, in partnership with community-based organizations and other services providers who work with this population, it is possible to create a comprehensive continuum of care for these newcomers that addresses immigration-related issues. For immigrant children and youth in care, this is critical to ensure their future ability to live and work as independent adults in American society.

References

Adoption and Safe Families Act. (1997). P.L. 105-89.

Baum, J., & Goldstein, B. (2002) *Problems facing immigrant families in the child welfare system*. Testimony to the New York State Assembly Standing Committee on Children and Families and New York State Assembly Legislative Task Force on New Americans, July 11, 2002.

Beiser, M., Hou, F., Hyman, I., & Tousignant, M. (2002). Poverty, family process and the mental health of immigrant children in Canada. *American Journal of Public Health, 92*(2), 220–228.

Bridging Refugee Youth and Children's Services. (2003). *Immigrant issues in child welfare*. Retrieved June 30, 2004, from www.brycs.org.

Capps, R., Ku, L., Fix, M. E., Furgiuele, C., Passel, J. S., et al. (2002). *How are immigrants faring after welfare reform? Preliminary evidence from Los Angeles and New York City. Final report*. Washington, DC: Urban Institute.

Carliner, G. (2000). The language ability of U.S. immigrants: Assimilation and cohort effects. *International Migration Review, 34*(1), 158–182.

Catholic Legal Immigration Network & Immigrant Legal Resource Center. (2002). *Special immigrant juvenile status for children under juvenile court jurisdiction*. Retrieved June 30, 2004, from athena.ilrc.org.

Coalition for Asian American Children and Families. (2001). *Crossing the divide: Asian American families and the child welfare system*. New York: Coalition for Asian American Children and Families.

Coalition for Hispanic Children and Families. (2001). *Building a better future for Latino families*. New York: Coalition for Hispanic Children and Families.

Cress, C. (2003). Making community-based learning meaningful: Faculty efforts to increase student civic engagement skills. *Transformations, 19*(2), 87–94.

Earner, I. (in press). Immigrant families and public child welfare: Barriers to services and approaches to change. *Child Welfare*.

Fix, M. E., & Passel, J. (2001). *U.S. Immigration at the beginning of the 21st century*. Testimony to the Subcommittee on Immigration, Committee on the Judiciary, U.S. House of Representatives, August 2, 2001.

Fix, M. E., & Zimmerman, W. (1999). All under one roof: Mixed-status families in an era of reform. Washington, DC: Urban Institute.

Franken, M. (2002). Rescue and protection of trafficked victims: The experience of the Catholic Church in the United States. Address presented at Conference on 21st Century Slavery, United States Conference of Catholic Bishops, Rome, Italy, May 25–28, 2002.

Gonzalez, D. (1999a). Empty crib, full schedule in court. *New York Times*, (April 10), p. 23.

Gonzalez, D. (1999b). Still unable to proclaim: "This is mine." *New York Times*, (May 15), p. 25.

Gopaul-McNichol, S. A. (1999). Ethnocultural perspectives on childrearing practices in the Caribbean. *International Social Work, 42*(1), 79–86.

Guendelman, S., Schauffler, H. H., & Pearl, M. (2001). Unfriendly shores: How immigrant children fare in the U.S. health system. *Health Affairs, 20*(1), 257–266.

Hagen, J., Rodriguez, N., Capps, R., & Kabiri, N. (2003). The effects of recent welfare and immigration reforms on immigrants' access to health care. *International Migration Review, 37*(2), 444–452.

Haines, D. W. (2001). Helping out: Children's labor in ethnic businesses. *International Migration Review, 35*(1), 340–341.

Hurley, K. (2002). *Card me: Immigrants in foster care may finally get help getting legal. City Limits.* Retrieved June 30, 2004, from www.citylimits.org.

Immigration Act. (1990). P.L. 101-649.

Immigration and Nationality Act. (1996). P.L. 104-208.

James, D. C. S. (1997). Coping with a new society: The unique psychosocial problems of immigrant youth. *Journal of School Health, 67*(3), 98–113.

Kandel, W., & Kao, G. (2001). The impact of temporary labor migration on Mexican children's educational aspirations and performance, *International Migration Review, 35*(4), 1205–1231.

Kullgren, J. T. (2003). Restrictions on undocumented immigrants' access to health services: The public health implications of welfare reform. *American Journal of Public Health, 93*(10), 1630–1633.

Lee, R. (2000). Are religiously affiliated law schools obsolete in America? The view of an outsider looking in. *St. John's Law Review, 74*(3), 655–666.

Loppnow, D. M. (1985). Adolescents on their own. In J. Laird & A. Hartman (eds.), *A handbook of child welfare.* New York: Free Press.

Lutheran Immigration and Refugee Services & U.S. Conference of Catholic Bishops. (2003). Serving foreign-born foster children: A working paper and resource guide for meeting the special needs of refugee youth and children. Paper presented at the Bridging Refugee Youth and Children's Services Roundtable, Washington, DC, July 16–19, 2003.

New York City Administration for Children's Services. (2004). *Immigration and language guidelines for child welfare staff.* New York: New York City Administration for Children's Services.

Office of Refugee Resettlement. (2002). *The unaccompanied refugee minors program.* Retrieved June 30, 2004, from www.acf.dhhs.goc/program/orr/.

Ojito, M. (1997). Culture clash: Foreign parents, American child rearing. *New York Times*, (June 29), p. 3.

Personal Responsibility and Work Opportunity Reconciliation Act. (1997). P.L. 104-193.

Qin-Hilliard, D. B. (2002). Overlooked and underserved: Immigrant students in U.S. secondary schools. *Harvard Educational Review, 72*(3), 402-406.

Rumbaut, R. G. (1996). The crucible within: Ethnic identity, self-esteem, and segmented assimilation among children of immigrants. *International Migration Review, 28*(4), 749–794.

Siegel, W. L., & Kappaz, C. M. (2002). *Strengthening Illinois' immigrant policy: Improving health and human services for immigrants and refugees.* Chicago, IL: Illinois Immigrant Policy.

Solomon, A. (2002). Kids in captivity. *Village Voice.* Retrieved June 30, 2004, from www.villagevoice.org.

Suleiman, L. P. (2003). Beyond cultural competence: Language access and Latino civil rights. *Child Welfare, 82*, 185–200.

Taylor, J. A. (2004). Teaching children who have immigrated: The new legislation, research and trends in immigration which affect teachers of diverse student populations. *Multicultural Education, 11*(3), 43–44.

U.S. Census Bureau. (2001). *Profiles of the foreign-born population in the United States: 2000.* Current Population Reports P23-206. Washington, DC: U.S. Census Bureau.

U.S. Department of Justice. (2003). *Protections for battered immigrant women and children.* Retrieved June 30, 2004, from www.ojp.usdoj.gov/vawo/laws/vawa/vawa/htm.

Vega, W. A., Kolody, B., & Aguilar-Gaxiola, S. (2001). Help seeking for mental health problems among Mexican-Americans. *Journal of Immigrant Health, 3*(3), 133–143.

Vergara, A. E., Miller, J. M., Martin, D. R., & Cookson, S. T. (2003). A survey of refugee health assessments in the United States. *Journal of Immigrant Health, 5*(2), 67–78.

Victims of Trafficking and Violence Prevention Act. (2000). P.L. 106-386.

Wexler, R. (2002). Take the child and run: Tales from the age of ASFA. *New England Law Review, 36*(1), 129–152.

Yeh, C., & Inose, M. (2002). Difficulties and coping strategies of Chinese, Japanese and Korean immigrant students. *Adolescence, 37*, 69–82.

EILEEN MAYERS PASZTOR
MYRNA L. McNITT
EMILY JEAN McFADDEN

Foster Parent Recruitment, Development, Support, and Retention

Strategies for the Twenty-First Century

---

hild welfare literature dating back for more than 150 years documents the need and search for foster parents (McGowan 1983). Originally sought for dependent, neglected, and orphaned children, in more recent times, foster parents have been needed to provide care for children separated from their parents because of the tragedies of physical abuse, sexual abuse, neglect, and emotional maltreatment (National Commission on Family Foster Care 1991). Even though the literature has consistently focused more on recruitment than on retention, an adequate supply of foster parents —so that children could be placed by choice and not chance—has never been documented. Research does indicate that many foster parents discontinue fostering during their first year of service, and a major reason is the lack of dignity and respect afforded them by the agencies with which they affiliate (Baring-Gould, Essick, Kleinkauf, & Miller 1983; Behana 1987; Casey Family Programs 2000: Chamberlain, Moreland, & Reid 1992; Pasztor 1985; Pasztor & Wynne 1995; Ryan 1985; U.S. General Accounting Office 1989). This dynamic may indicate that there is a fundamental flaw with the way foster parents are viewed and treated in the delivery of child welfare services. In this chapter, we provide a framework for an approach to finding and keeping foster parents because, as noted more than 20 years ago, we would not have to work so hard to *find* them if only we could *keep* them (Pasztor & Burgess 1982).

This chapter begins with a historical perspective on foster parent recruitment and retention. Then we address the challenge of both keeping and finding foster parents by:

- Affirming the role of foster parents as resource families who are essential to provide a therapeutic family setting for abused and neglected children; and
- Investing in a comprehensive action plan that uses community problem solving, appreciates diversity, and builds collaborative relationships.

Back to the Future

Orphan's Prayer
People waited at the stations
For the child they know would be
Coming to join their home fires
Orphans now with family.
(Christiansen 1985:1)

Endeavors to recruit and retain foster parents began before there was any formal child welfare system. From the mid-nineteenth century until 1929, the Orphan Train movement relocated more than 100,000 destitute immigrant children from the streets of New York City to families in America's heartland (see O'Connor 2001).

Handbills announcing the arrival of yesterday's orphan trains have been transformed into contemporary mass marketing messages on billboards, city buses, the Internet, and "Wednesday's Child" television segments. Simple contracts of indenture for families selecting a child from an orphan train have given way to a complicated maze of modern child welfare law, ranging from practices established in the 1970s, when foster parents had to sign documents indicating that they would not attempt to adopt children placed with them, to current trends of pressuring a foster parent to adopt at time of initial placement with the foster family. Some dynamics remain the same. Caseworkers, along with the media, still refer to children being "up for adoption." (We believe that only professionals with degrees in social work (BSW, MSW, Ph.D., or DSW) should be titled "social workers." As most children in family foster care are served by individuals without those degrees, we use the generic term "caseworker" in this chapter). This reference comes from the 150-year-old practice of placing children up on train station platforms and theater stages so they could be viewed for selection. The notion that foster parents take children for the money derives from the orphan train days, when older children were selected first, because they could help work on farms. The challenges of placing nineteenth-century immigrant children having Italian, Irish, and German accents and Catholic religious affiliation with well-established Protestant families in rural America have given way to new cross-cultural placements of ethnic minority children from African American, Latino, and other cultures.

In a global context, societies are being transformed and families are buffeted by economic dislocation. Once again, patterns of immigration bring families into new and difficult circumstances. Although immigrants offer a cheap labor force to industrialized nations, they also bring their cultural traditions and familial attitudes that often run counter to the dominant culture they enter. Therefore child welfare issues must be considered in a global context. The U.N. Convention on the Rights of the Child mandates (Articles 19 and 20) that alternative care must be available for abused, neglected, and abandoned children. "Increasingly, countries around the world have recognized the benefits to child well-being of family-based care as an alternative to institutional care" (Herczog, van Pagee, & Pasztor 2001:632).

In the United States, the convergence of many systemic issues has impacted foster parent recruitment, selection, development, and retention. Immigration, demographic shifts found in an aging society, globalization of the economy (destroying jobs in manufacturing), and a shift to a service economy have resulted in an ongoing increase of households with two working parents. Consequently, the traditional stereotype of the stay-at-home mother and wage-earning father has been transformed into the present-day reality of stressed families lacking the time to support and plan for the needs of dependent family members. In fact, the definition of family in the United States is changing to include not only the traditional heterosexual two-parent family (either married or living together without marriage) but also single parents, stepfamilies, and same-gender partner families (Downs, Moore, McFadden, Michaud, & Costin 2004). Rigid gender roles and agency efforts to recruit the "perfect family" may overlook many families both willing and able to foster. One of the issues, then, facing foster parent recruitment is how the state or community defines "family." The need for social justice impels society to serve the children, but also to recognize the value of historically underutilized groups—such as single parents, people with limited incomes, kinfolk, gays, and lesbians—to provide permanency for children (Mallon 2004).

The disconnect between resources and the needs of a changing and aging population surely affects foster parent availability. Historically, a shortage of affordable, accessible child day care has meant that prospective foster parents could not find care for their own children, much less someone else's. Now families struggle to find adult day care for dependent parents. Current foster parents themselves may be aging to the extent that they are unable to care for children. Some single foster parents have never been covered by social security and find in senescence a struggle to maintain a subsistence standard of living. The healthcare insurance crisis leaves many families underinsured or uninsured. Mental health and family support services are financially diminished and struggle for public support.

As the national debt has grown by billions of dollars and personal debt in the United States is at an all-time high, families wonder about their future economic situation. The impact of terrorism and war has not only absorbed an ever-increasing amount of federal funds but has also caused many U.S. citizens to be fearful about their safety. How may the war on terrorism after September 11, 2001, impact child welfare in general and foster parent recruitment specifically? Children orphaned by the events of September 11 were absorbed into their kinship networks outside the formal child welfare system. However, in a time when there is an increase in military spending and continuing high unemployment rate, states consistently report underfunding by the federal government for state-operated child welfare programs. Once the American dream was to achieve a comfortable middle-class living. Now families struggle to meet day-to-day financial obligations and maintain hope for the future.

Social and economic stress, family violence, and the continuing failure to win the war on drugs take a toll on children. With an increase in abused and neglected children coming into the foster care system in the 1970s, the term "special needs" was coined to differentiate between the dependent/neglected children of the orphan train era and a new population of children with diagnosed emotional and behavior challenges. By 1991, the National Commission on Family Foster Care—convened by the Child Welfare League of America and the National Foster Parent Association—proposed that one problem in foster care was not only the increasing number of children, but also the severity of the children's needs. Special needs children were the least challenging; a new category, "extraordinary needs," also has to be served. More recently, the David and Lucile Packard Foundation (2004:2) reported that by the time children enter the foster care system, "much emotional—if not physical—damage has already occurred. Many children in foster care come from families struggling with complex and interrelated problems including mental illness, substance abuse, homelessness, domestic violence, incarceration, and HIV/AIDS."

The Oregon project in the 1970s provided the conceptual framework for the Adoption Assistance and Child Welfare Act of 1980 by documenting children's needs for continuity, commitment, and legal and social status (Pike, Downs, Emlen, Downs, & Case 1977). More recently, the Adoption and Safe Families Act (ASFA) of 1997 expanded the goal, requiring states to meet measurable indicators of child safety, well-being, and permanency. According to Moye and Rinker (2002:375), "the child welfare system is larger, more expensive, and in a greater crisis than most Americans probably realize." An indicator of the extent of the problem is the discrepancy between the number of children needing family foster care, which has doubled in the past two decades and now amounts to two-thirds of the out-of-home care population (U.S. Department of Health and Human Services 2003, 2004), and the decreasing number of qualified foster families.

Rather than experiencing foster care as a healing opportunity, children continue to suffer because "too often the system lets those children down" (David and Lucile Packard Foundation 2004:2). The David and Lucile Packard Foundation (2004:2) attributed this failure in part to overburdened caseworkers and foster parents who do not get the help that they need. Kortenkamp and Ehrle (2002:4) documented that the caregivers of many children in foster care are themselves "aggravated" by the demands of caregiving. According to the National Commission on Family Foster Care (1991), children with special if not extraordinary needs must be cared for in a therapeutic environment by foster parents who have special if not extraordinary skills. Pasztor and Wynne (1995) suggest that foster parents must have strengths and supports, in addition to skills. This outcome can only be achieved when the public is concerned about the discrepancy between the number of children needing care and the number of quality foster families. Furthermore, it must be recognized that "crisis" is a misleading word, implying a temporary condition. Actually, the foster care system has been "in crisis" for more than two decades, indicating that the ongoing state of dysfunction has become a de facto way of doing business. According to Pasztor, Hollinger, Inkelas, and Halfon (2004), given the ASFA mandates, bold steps must be taken to insure that foster parents can access the resources needed for the children in their care, and that they are essential members of the caregiving team. This desired goal requires recruitment, development, and support that leads to the retention of a sufficient quantity of quality foster parents.

Affirming the Role of Foster Parents as Resource Families

The Family and Children's Services Division of the Hamilton County Welfare Department receives about 60 calls per month concerning the foster care program. About 40 applicants are rejected immediately because they cannot meet the basic requirements. As badly as we need *homes,* usually only one *client* per month becomes a foster parent.
(*Cincinnati Enquirer* 1975:21)

This statement (emphasis ours) exemplifies that, as recently as 30 years ago, foster parents were considered clients. Foster parent training programs, such those developed by Eastern Michigan University and Nova University in the late 1970s and Child Welfare Institute's Model Approach to Partnerships in Parenting (MAPP) in the 1980s, emphasized a shift in the role of foster parent from a client receiving services to a service provider needing supports. These programs recognized that there had to be congruence between role definition and the training to fulfill that role. This new focus also, by necessity, had to address how casework staff should interact with foster parents as their team members, partners, or collaborators.

In 1991, the National Commission on Family Foster Care outlined a strategic plan to reframe family foster care with a clear and valued role for foster parents. Infants, children, and youth placed in family foster care should only be placed with foster parents who have the competencies and supports to meet their unique needs. Foster parents must have a collaborative role in the delivery of services, including participation in case planning, administrative reviews, and court proceedings. It was also noted that foster parents could have specialized roles, such as caring for children with HIV/AIDS, managing youth with behavior challenges, or serving as role models for parents of children in care. In addition, some foster parents were being selected, trained, and supported to provide treatment foster care (National Commission on Family Foster Care 1991:40). However, given the trauma that children have endured prior to being placed in family foster care, we think that all foster care should take place in a therapeutic or treatment setting.

By the mid 1990s, the role of foster parents was clarified again through the Parent's Resource for Information, Development & Education (PRIDE) model of foster parent recruitment, assessment, selection, and training, which advanced the child welfare field by referring to both foster and adoptive parents as "resource families" (Pasztor & Wynne 1995:33). The PRIDE training identified five competencies for resource parents based on the recommendations by the National Commission on Family Foster Care: (1) protecting and nurturing; (2) meeting developmental needs and addressing developmental delays; (3) supporting children's relationships with their parents; (4) connecting children to safe and nurturing lifetime relationships; and (5) working as a member of a professional team (Leighton et al. 2003). This training approach, now used across the United States and in more than a dozen other countries, reconceptualized recruitment and retention as development and support. The premise is that most new resource parents do not initially possess the competencies needed to work with challenging children; these competencies must be developed through preservice training, on-the-job experience, collaboration with skilled casework staff, and interactions with the agency, other resource parents, and the community. No fewer than 25 supports have been documented in the literature, including in-service training, mentoring, respite care, reimbursement for the full cost of fostering, access to community resources, insurance, and a grievance and appeals process (Pasztor & Wynne 1995). The role of staff in providing support is essential, such as the creation of resource family developers, who have expertise in community organization, cultural sensitivity, and the child welfare system (Lutz 2002). Thus recruitment (an activity) and retention (an outcome) become, according to PRIDE, integrated processes of development and support.

With new language of "development and support" and "resource families," additional language can be included to affirm the role of persons providing out-of-home care for children. This would, for example, eliminate the use of the phrase "foster home" (as indicated in *Cincinnati Enquirer* 1975) when referring to foster families. Typically, caseworkers, educators, administrators, and researchers refer to foster "homes" rather than to foster families. This usage discounts resource families by forgetting that real people with real feelings are involved in the therapeutic care of children. It is not the *home* that hurts or heals a child, but the individuals living there. Families are further

marginalized when expressions like "screening out" and "weeding out" are used to refer to the selection process, as opposed to the less pejorative concept of "selecting in," as advanced by MAPP.

Youth transitioning from foster care can be an effective resource for recruitment and public awareness; such youth may also have strong feelings concerning child welfare language. Youth representatives on the National Commission on Family Foster Care explained that "being removed" refers to snow or garbage, whereas they experienced the trauma of "separation" from all that was familiar. They did not like to be referred to as a "damaged child" when discussing their needs. Efforts to change perceptions rooted in the language of child welfare will involve a shift to strength-based practice. In an admonition to practitioners, Saleebey (2002:81–82) states, "it will take genuine diligence on your part to begin to appreciate and utilize strengths in practice. . . . The system is against you, the language and metaphors of the system are against you." Youth desire this change, harboring strong feelings about labels attached to foster care. "I am not a label. I am a person who has been labeled all my life and I've always fought it" (Desetta 1996:155). Box 1 provides examples of strengths-based language, as opposed to stigmatizing language (Silverstein, Roszia, Pasztor, & Clark 2004).

The causes of the problems in recruiting and retaining, or developing and supporting, resource families, are well documented throughout the literature, along with research regarding effective solutions (Pasztor & Wynne 1995). Adopting the multifaceted approaches outlined in the knowledge base is essential, and begins with a clear definition of the *role* of resource families in the delivery of family foster care services. The field has been struggling to define this role as client, colleague, or something in-between for more than 50 years (Anderson 1988; Hanford 1941; Maas & Engler 1959; McFadden 1996; Pasztor & Burgess 1982; Pasztor & Wynne 1995). It is not effective, efficient, or ethical to

BOX 1. *Strength-Based Language for Family Foster Care*

From	To
Hard-to-place child	Hard-to-find family
Damaged child	Fragile or challenging child
Biological/natural/real parent	Birth parent
Pulled/removed from parents	Separated from parents or family
Up for adoption	Needing an adoptive family
Foster homes	Resource families
Slots/homes/beds	Families
Weeding out/screening out	Mutual selection/selecting in
Home study	Family assessment

recruit individuals for a position that is not established and supported in an organization. Once the role is clearly stated and valued, then the community can be engaged to find and keep resource parents who are willing and able to fulfill that role.

Investing in a Multifaceted Community Approach

Recommendation: Develop and implement a sustained plan for foster parent and staff recruitment and retention so that each infant, child, and youth placed in family foster care has a foster parent and social worker prepared and supervised to support fully the child's cultural, developmental, and permanency needs.

Action: Convene local, regional, and state task forces (comprising, for example, foster parents, agency staff, elected officials, leaders from civil and religious groups) to formulate strategic plans for retention and recruitment.

(National Commission on Family Foster Care 1991:63)

If communities value families as the best places for children to grow up, then communities must take responsibility to develop and implement "a comprehensive, culturally responsive, community-based strategic plan" (Pasztor & Wynne 1995:65) for the recruitment, development, support, and retention of resource parents. The support plan for retention must be in place before recruitment and development begins, to avoid a revolving-door effect. Scattershot approaches fail to achieve adequate numbers of quality resource families to meet the needs of children separated from their parents or kin. The field of child welfare must approach the recruitment and retention of resource families from a different perspective, one that entails a specific plan for change.

A framework for child welfare systems reform has been developed by the W. K. Kellogg Foundation (2003):

- We know better than we do;
- Change takes community problem solving;
- Change requires collaboration;
- Diversity must be respected; and
- A comprehensive action plan is essential.

The foundation also presented a set of core values:

- Expect that a new start is possible and shape new systems of care;
- Practice diversity and community engagement;
- Invest in people and build collaborative relationships;

- Pursue a multitude of approaches simultaneously; and
- Expand the reach of known best practices.

"We Know Better than We Do"

Recently, Casey Family Programs (2003), in its Breakthrough Series, posed the question "what would a successful system of recruitment and retention look like?" Eight challenges were addressed:

- Getting the message out: How can public awareness be raised about the needs of children in the public child welfare system?
- Turning interest into commitment: How can the number of interested families who decide to become resource families be increased?
- Preparing families and children for placement: How can they be better supported through the recruitment process and before placement?
- Streamlining licensing: How can qualified families be licensed in a timely and supportive way?
- Providing services and supports: What do resource families need to provide appropriate care?
- Developing a partnership: How can resource families, youth, and birth families be made true partners with the agency?
- Involving the community: How can communities be active partners in recruiting and supporting resource families, youth in care, and birth families?
- Training staff: How can well-trained staff be recruited and retained throughout the agency who can recruit, support, and engage resource families, children in care, and the children's families?

Successful strategies and tools included (Casey Family Programs 2003):

- Using experienced resource families as mentors to prospective and newly enlisted families;

- Making information about resource families (e.g., pictures, videos, information forms) available to the child or youth and the birth family before placement;
- Assigning new agency workers to shadow a foster parent for a day;
- Holding family team meetings that include birth families, resource families, youth, and agency staff;
- Improving relationships with schools; and
- Setting up an Internet listserve for resource families.

The implementation of these eight elements along with the six applied strategies resulted in improved outcomes, including an increase in the number of prospective families, greater inclusion of resource families in case planning, and a reduction of days of foster care before placement with kinship caregivers (Casey Family Programs 2003).

Burdened state agencies and the private agencies with which they contract must stay the course if these promising practices are to be realized in bringing about long-term change. Development and support is time consuming and costly. At times of economic crisis, legislatures and agency administrators cut budgetary line items designated for recruitment. Economics definitely impact resource family development and support. A 1999 Child Welfare League of America report (Barbell 1999) noted that 80% of American households have not recovered from the recession of 1990 and their median income was actually below what they were earning in 1989. Most resource families have less income in 2005 than in 1989 and, in addition, fostering usually creates a financial hardship. Lower-income households typically represent the potential pool of foster families. These families need an array of supports, from per diem foster care reimbursements aligned with what it actually costs to raise a child to having quality child care options that may be available to households with two working parents. It is likely that without relief from the financial

stress of raising a child, families with the motivation and skills to foster may be increasingly
hard to engage. According to Rhodes, Orme,
Cox, and Buehler (2003), family resources have
been associated positively with willingness to
care for special needs children. For many American families, these resources are depleted. Along
with the pressures of family finances, it should
be anticipated that resource families, like other
American families, will have their share of problems with physical and mental health, parenting, and marital issues. When such problems
occur, it may be difficult for families to continue fostering.

State legislatures can set the tone for the importance of family foster care by creating a
favorable environment for the development of
resources. Positive attention by legislatures
may improve the often-tarnished image of foster care. The National Foster Parent Association
(2003), through the Council of State Presi-
dents, has endeavored to seek universal passage
of a Foster Parent Bill of Rights. According to
the National Foster Parent Association, thus
far only Illinois, Maryland, Mississippi, Oklahoma, Tennessee, and Washington have passed
such legislation. Such bills address the essential
role of resource families by serving vulnerable
children and participating with state child welfare agencies in the creation and implementation of relevant policies and procedures. A mass
marketing message about the value of resource
families is achieved when legislatures partner
with foster parent associations and agencies in
the passage of a Foster Parent Bill of Rights.

Prospective resource families often consider
fostering for more than a year before making
the first inquiry call (Coyne 1986; Pasztor &
Burgess 1982; Pasztor &Wynne 1995). Many
times, the first contact with the agency is the
voice mail message of the recruiter. This impersonal response to the tension of finally making
this call can be disconcerting. The information
packet typically mailed to the resource parent
contains a description of the types of children
in need of care and the statutory requirement
to become a foster parent. This information
can be daunting without a guide to interpret
the process. Literature from the Child Welfare
League of America (Dougherty 2001) explains
that current resource parents can be recruiters,
trainers, and mentors to new resource parents.
Similarly, North Carolina has suggested a mentoring program (Jordan Institute for Families
1999). Satisfied, competent resource parents can
influence those who are considering foster care.

During the past two decades, the role of experienced resource parents as one of the most
effective tools for new resource parent development has continued to be reinforced (Friedman,
Lardieri, Murphy, Quick, & Wolfe 1980; Pasztor
& Burgess 1982; Pasztor & Wynne 1995; Wasson & Hess 1989). All too often, the role that
an experienced resource parent can have is not
formalized by agencies. The use of the social
network of experienced resource parents opens
the door for targeted marketing. The Iowa Foster and Adoptive Parent Association created a
mentoring program that is an integral part of
the recruitment, development, and support process (L. Stout, pers. comm.). Twelve independent contractors who are resource parents have
a toll-free telephone line at home. They welcome newly licensed resource families, contact
families who are leaving fostering, and assist
with support groups and training. They also
are available to assist other resource parents on
a one-to-one basis with concerns, questions, and
problems. Other states, including Connecticut,
Iowa, Nebraska, and Washington, also have
mentoring programs.

Research has shown that there is a significant
attrition problem reflected in the number of
prospective resource parents recruited and those
who get "lost" in the licensing or approval process (Friedman, Lardieri, Murphy, Quick, &
Wolfe 1980; Rodwell & Biggerstaff 1995; Siegel
& Roberts 1989). Prospective families are selected out or select themselves out due to a myriad of reasons. Although some of these families
might not have been a good match for fostering,
the vast majority that do not become licensed

BOX 2. *Should I Become a Foster Parent?*

YES:

1. I enjoy being around children.
2. I have the time and energy to devote to working through behavior problems of children.
3. I want to contribute to the life of a special needs child/youth.
4. I enjoy teamwork and working with other people.
5. I am naturally optimistic and embrace the many challenges of life.

NO:

1. I have a full-time job and other time-consuming commitments.
2. I have a job that will not allow me to occasionally miss work or phone calls because of the foster child's/youth's needs (e.g., school meetings, emergencies, medical appointments).
3. I am going through a major life change (e.g., divorce, marriage).
4. I prefer to work through problems alone and do not like others to suggest or ask too many questions.
5. I have difficulty coping with stress and excessive demands.
6. I am not ready or willing to experience the huge change in lifestyle or decrease in personal time that working with an abused or neglected child entails.

Source: National Center for Children and Families (2003).

---

or approved drop out of their own volition (Kadushin & Martin 1988; Pasztor 1985; Smith & Gutheil 1988).

Recruited resource families can be encouraged to engage in a self-assessment process regarding fostering. The National Center for Children and Families posts a series of questions for self-assessment on its Web site to assist in this process (box 2). This type of query is not research-based, but does raise pertinent questions for the recruited family regarding the basic dynamics of fostering. By contrast, the Casey Family Project (Casey Family Programs 2003) is working with the University of Tennessee to standardize two tools, the Casey Foster Applicant Inventory and the Casey Home Assessment Protocol. The goal is to improve techniques for the development and support of resource parents. Ethical issues concerning cultural sensitivity and the use of assessment tools with prospective resource parents must be considered.

Development and support activities are often grouped together, but they involve different strategies. Groze, McMillen, and Haines-Simeon (1993) noted that contact with someone who has received foster care or who has fostered is related to the motivation to foster. Using this information, Scotland has employed young people transitioning from foster care to recruit resource parents. This strategy has created a "hold-even" process in that country by recruiting as many foster parents each year as leave the child welfare system (International Child and Youth Care Network 2003).

There is much conventional wisdom about how best to retain and recruit, or support and develop resource families. Qualitative and quantitative research typically has not guided that wisdom. Evaluation of practice to determine what works under what circumstances is necessary. However, the value of systematic training for foster parents is well established: "Foster parent training has been shown to reduce the incidence of failed placements, increase the number of desirable foster parents, and to encourage foster parents to remain licensed" (Downs, Moore, McFadden, Michaud, & Costin 2004:351).

Change Requires Community Problem Solving
Abused and neglected children requiring family foster care belong to and in their communities. A community cannot be a place where children are harmed and then cast aside to a different community to be healed. A real community takes care of its own. Resource families are community members who merit their neighborhood's support. Child welfare agencies, both public and private, must work together to identify resources and challenges in communities that promote or hinder effective fostering. Perceptions of the agencies, their staff, and their current resource families are key to the effort of engaging the community. One comprehensive approach to community support of its foster families was the federally funded Project CARR (Community Approach to Foster Family Recruitment and Retention), implemented in the greater Houston, Texas, area to integrate recruitment with retention (Pasztor et al. 1989).

Child-placing agencies must be aware of their reputation within their communities. Distrust of the dominant culture is found in communities of color, whose children are overrepresented in out-of-home care. This has not always been the case as, in the early twentieth century, African American children were excluded from the child welfare system (Roberts 2001). Yet currently, "although only 17% of the nation's children are African Americans, they represent 42% of the children in foster care" (Roberts 2001:7). This overrepresentation is also true of Native American and Hispanic children. Ethnicity has been a barrier to licensing as resource parents, with African Americans being less likely to be approved to foster than their white counterparts and, once licensed or approved, having more difficulty with the placement agency (Downs 1986; Ougheltree 1957). Denby

and Rindfleisch (1996) reported that African American foster families are three times more likely to be closed involuntarily than white foster families. Leaders from all sectors of the community must be involved in resource parent development and support activities, if the historical distrust of the formal system is to be overcome.

Places of worship are often linked with a potential resource family's willingness to foster children who have been neglected or abused (Cox, Buehler, & Orme 2002). Programs such as One Church One Child make use of trusted leadership in the faith community to locate resource families. It has been suggested that formal arrangements should be negotiated with such denominations as the Church of the Latter Day Saints (Mormons), Seventh Day Adventists, members of the Islamic community, and Christian Scientists to foster children from their faith communities. The Reverend C. W. Martin from Possum Corner, Texas, has made child welfare a church mission, with his rural congregation adopting more than 70 children with special needs.

Literature dating back over 20 years describes the health and mental health needs of abused and neglected children requiring family foster care, and the challenges of serving them from the perspectives of physicians, agencies, and resource parents themselves (Pasztor, Hollinger, Inkelas, & Halfon 2004). Professionals who served or are serving at-risk populations represent a possible source of resource parents with the knowledge and skills to care for special children with extraordinary needs. This group of professionals may not only provide children with specialized care but may also engender a community dialog on multidisciplinary delivery of services, as they have learned to work across disciplines in advocating for the needs of their clients. Multidisciplinary community teams working with resource families on behalf of young children in foster care at risk for special educational services have been successful in early identification of needs. Wraparound services for children and youth have been successful in keeping children and youth in the least-restrictive community placement possible (Walker & Bruns 2003).

Prospective resource parents need to have a clear role definition of how to work with other professionals in the community. The children placed in their care must have accessible, culturally competent services, and the resource families themselves must have similar supports. Ongoing support of foster parents is associated with a sense of satisfaction that the needs of the children placed with them are being met. Support and satisfaction are key elements of retention. Love is not enough to care for today's foster children.

Given the situations of children entering foster care today, supports to resource parents must connect with the specific conditions and needs of the children, so that foster parents can meet the demands of their role. "Children who are more aggressive and poorly socialized are more likely to experience unsuccessful placements" (Baum, Crase, & Crase 2001:203). When a system is burdened, it is essential that resource parents are not asked to work beyond their skills and abilities by pressuring them to take increasing numbers of children until their capacity to function is compromised and children are further maltreated (McFadden & Ryan 1991). Ethically, child welfare workers at all levels of practice must guard against the exploitation of resource parents and understand the imperative of protecting children while they are in the public's care.

Allegations of maltreatment made against resource families affect retention. Reducing the fear of how complaints will be handled and providing training that inoculates foster parents against the likelihood of allegations are helpful practices for retaining foster parents. The Outcome Pioneers Project in Los Angeles is investigating the impact of abuse allegations on both child attachment and resource family retention, because not only is the impact on foster parents of concern, but the impact of unfounded or inconclusive investigations can traumatize the children involved as well (Pasztor 2004). Best practice is further complicated because individual jurisdictions have varying responses to the challenge of allegations against resource families (Child Welfare League of America, Casey Family Programs, & National Center for Resource Family Support 2002).

Change Requires Collaboration

As resource families are service providers (not service recipients), development and support initiatives must insure that they are included in all aspects of service delivery. Resource parents have variously been termed "team members" and "partners." They must work with a wide range of professionals in their communities, such as schools, healthcare providers, and mental health practitioners. They have connections to civic organizations, unions, and places of worship. Those groups could be engaged strategically in the development and support of resource families, or might even become resources themselves. Community members are essential to the support of resource families, and everyone in the community is a potential resource family developer and champion.

As part of ASFA, incentives were given to states to develop post-legal services for adoptive families. Many of the completed adoptions were foster parent adoptions of children in their care. Across the nation, states made decisions about the use of the incentive funds. "No state indicated that they had a process that included foster families or the general public in decision making about how incentive funds would be used" (Cornerstone Consulting Group 2001:5). Public welfare administrators, in making such decisions, were aware that there would be a loss of temporary foster care resources through the adoption of children with special needs. Opportunity to collaborate was lost by not asking foster and adoptive families, or the families of the children, what their needs were. That knowledge could have enriched concurrent planning processes on behalf of children and families through joint recruitment, retention, and post-legal services.

Pasztor and Wynne (1995) emphasized community collaboration with a focus on the important role that local and state foster parent groups and associations must have in the process of developing and supporting resource families. Collaboration can be a statewide strategy, with application of practice expressed at the local level. Collaboration and processes of systemic change involve a long-term commitment if positive outcomes are to be realized, as demonstrated by the Annie E. Casey's Family to Family foster care systemic change process. This program requires a commitment to community and the inclusion of birth, kinship, and resource parents in the delivery of services. Family to Family began in 1993 with six jurisdictions in Georgia, Alabama, Maryland, New Mexico, Ohio, and Pennsylvania. Other states and jurisdictions have since joined (Omang & Bonk 1999). Family to Family is a values-driven process that is grounded in neighborhood child welfare work. Using nontraditional community organizations that can work with child welfare agencies, family resources are identified for children within their neighborhoods. For example, the Franklin Wright Settlement House in Detroit develops resource families that are then referred for licensing. This is a good fit, as the agency has the trust of the local citizens in a neighborhood that had a high foster care disruption rate.

Other states and jurisdictions involved in Family to Family report fewer disruptions for children(Omang & Bonk 1999:17):

Hardly anyone disagrees in theory with the most basic Family to Family principle, which is that of child welfare partnerships with foster and adoptive families and relatives, with neighborhoods and communities, and with other public and private agencies. But in practice, child welfare workers have always run the procedure and made the critical decisions, too often regarding birth parents

as adversaries and foster parents as employees in the day-to-day work of caring for children at risk.

Collaboration requires a sharing of power and resources. When done well, options for children and families are expanded. It is labor intensive and requires that child welfare staff members go beyond their traditional role in the development and support of resource families.

Community collaborative relationships with law enforcement and child welfare agencies concerning the fingerprinting and timely records checks of prospective resource parents assist in the licensing process. If the family is unable to meet standards of safety set by state licensing standards, further training and development activities are not expended.

Collaboration occurs when tasks are divided among the child welfare agencies responsible for licensing and community organizations that partner to develop and support foster families. The Utah Foster Care Foundation, a private organization, develops foster parents and provides training. Sisco (2001) reported an improvement in quality with this public/private partnership. Similarly, Iowa's Foster Parent Association holds contracts with its state child welfare agency to participate in an array of resource family development and support initiatives. It has established the KidSake Recruitment and Retention project, which includes contracts with 22 child-placing agencies. The project handles calls of inquiry, operates a recruitment information Web site, refers inquirers to an agency in their county, and sends a confirmation letter to the county. The project also holds a "Meet the Worker Night," hosts a statewide foster care/adoption event at an amusement park, and sponsors a statewide training for resource families (L. Stout, pers. comm.).

Although there is a considerable literature on agency collaboration and interdisciplinary collaboration, the child welfare field is less informed about collaboration between individuals who are involved in the unique dynamics of family foster care. There are two dynamics that must be considered: the challenge of demographic diversity, and the challenge of authority vs. attachment (Pasztor, Goodman, Potts, Santana, & Runnels 2003). Resource parents tend to be demographically different from caseworkers, their role reciprocals. Compared to a new child welfare caseworker, resource parents tend to be older and more likely to be married. They also are more likely to have children by birth and be of color. They are less likely to have a college degree. Most Americans tend not to associate with individuals who are demographically different from themselves; yet these diverse groups of resource parents and caseworkers must learn to collaborate on emotionally charged issues in spite of their differences.

Other conflicts arise because resource families often have attachments to children but no real authority over them. Caseworkers have authority but no deep attachment—otherwise, there could be a "boundary issue." Although conflict is inherent, if not inevitable, in these relationships, conflict resolution training typically is not on the list of preservice and inservice training topics (Pasztor, Goodman, Potts, Santana, & Runnels 2003). As the role of the resource parent as a collaborative partner is further defined, child welfare agencies must also be respectful of the potential for conflict inherent in the agency/resource family relationship. In the traditional sense, the resource parent is neither a full colleague nor a client. Agency administrators, along with caseworkers and their supervisors, must be cognizant and respectful of these role conflicts.

Respect for Diversity

A community strengths and needs assessment, such as community mapping, can identify resources for children in care. The PRIDE program defines a specific competency that staff must have to target the recruitment of families with the willingness, ability, and resources to foster children who are demographically diverse

(Leighton et al. 2003; Pasztor & Wynne 1995). Children in family foster care are overrepresented from African American and Hispanic communities (Needell et al. 2002). According to the Child Welfare League of America (2003), in 1980, 47% of the children in foster care were of color. By 2000, that number had climbed to 66%. This change is largely attributed to the relationships between poverty, abuse, and neglect, and institutional racism (Cahn 2002).

Historically, foster care was seen as a service for white children. Dating back to the orphan trains, children going into foster care were predominantly white. Prior to World War II, black children were virtually excluded from child welfare services (Roberts 2001:7). African American children were typically cared for by kin. Children not taken in by relatives might be labeled delinquent and thus imprisoned (Roberts 2001). The Civil Rights movement prompted attention to the needs of all children in the child welfare system. As social and economic conditions of the 1980s worsened (e.g., epidemics of crack-cocaine use and HIV/AIDS, the shredding of the social safety net during the Reagan administration), more children—especially poor children of color—came into the foster care system (National Commission on Family Foster Care 1991). With an increasing and troubling number of children of color needing foster and adoptive families, the child welfare workers began to look at transracial or cross-cultural placements, and social work and political battles thus began.

In 1972, the National Association of Black Social Workers (1972:22) stated that black children should be placed only with black families, whether in foster care or for adoption:

> Black children belong, physically, psychologically and culturally in black families in order to receive the total sense of themselves and develop a sound projection of their future.... The socialization process in the child's cultural heritage is an important segment of the total process. This must begin at

the earliest moment; otherwise our children will not have the background and knowledge which is necessary to survive in a racist society. This is impossible if the child is placed with white parents in a Caucasian environment.

Today, other groups of children living in ethnic enclaves, such as the Hmong in central California and children of Middle Eastern descent in southeastern Michigan, are appearing in foster care populations. Native American children were afforded some protection through the Indian Child Welfare Act of 1978, which strengthens the role of tribal governments in determining custody and requires keeping Native American children within their tribe, or at least their cultural group.

Contrary in many ways to the Indian Child Welfare Act, the Multiethnic Placement Act was passed into law in 1994. Provisions of the Multiethnic Placement Act prohibit foster care, adoption agencies, and other entities that are involved in the placement of children and that receive federal funds from delaying and denying, or otherwise discriminating, in making a placement decision solely on the basis of race, color, or national origin. The act requires states to develop plans for the diligent recruitment of potential resource families that reflect the ethnic and racial diversity of the children in the state who need them (Bussiere 1995).

The 1972 position of the National Association of Black Social Workers can serve as a value framework in considering how to enhance collaboration between agencies associated with the dominant culture and communities of color. Social work skills, using strength-based practice that identifies trusted leaders—both formal and informal—in communities of color should provide a foundation of practice. We cannot expect that the urgency of the need for more resource families of color will immediately engender a spirit of trust after centuries of mistrust.

Development and support activities must be neighborhood based and easily accessible, using places of worship and community centers where families of color may be comfortable. The Multiethnic Placement Act allows and encourages targeted recruitment. Bausch and Serpe (1999) developed strategies for the recruitment of Mexican American adoptive parents, which may serve as a template for the development of resource families from other ethnic groups:

- Disseminate more information about the need for families and the child in need of placement within the Mexican American community;
- Offer support groups for parents led by Latinos;
- Adjust assessment criteria, particularly as they relate to income and marital status;
- Recruit from the child's extended family network; and
- Prepare families parenting cross-culturally with skills in understanding racism, discrimination, possible identity conflicts, and cultural continuity.

Agencies should apply licensing standards consistently, and not raise the bar for families of color. The law does not allow discrimination against white families in the placement of a child of color. So, too, families of color cannot be discriminated against in setting standards for licensing that can become a barrier to resource development. How families are treated in the process may set the stage not only for the successful completion of the licensing process, but also determine how long the family remains a resource for children. Responsiveness of the agency to the recruited family and a positive approach to the families in the development process is essential (Bussiere 1995).

Agencies need to insure that staff members are culturally competent in all endeavors to develop and support resource families. Child welfare practitioners should engage with their potential partners so that issues of historical racism, cultural norms, and practices are heard and seen as a strength in the prospective family.

Minimally, this will require a redefinition of power sharing, as the agency brings new partners to the table. Guidelines for culturally competent foster care services can be obtained from the Child Welfare League of America's foster care programs Web site.

Child welfare professionals must be committed to the value and ethic of self-determination. The Multiethnic Placement Act was intended to insure that children are placed in families willing to nurture their development. This is not mutually exclusive to actively working with diverse communities to identify potential resource families and to support them. Activities that specifically target development and support of resource parents should be representative of the children needing placement. Often this goal is framed as giving voice to communities of color, silenced too long by forces of the dominant culture.

Consideration of the unique needs of sexual minority children is also part of resource parent development and support. The needs of gay, lesbian, bisexual, transgender, and questioning (GLBTQ) youth have only started to be addressed in the past decade (DeCrescenzo & Mallon 2002; Mallon 1997). Similarly, policies and practices for the development and support of gay and lesbian resource parents should be implemented. Just as there is concern regarding cross-cultural or transracial placements, attention must be given to the diverse ways that gay and straight resource parents may work differently with GLBTQ youth in their care. There are dynamics that must be considered when sexual minority youth are or are not placed with resource parents of the same sexual orientation (Ramos & Pasztor 2003). Gay and lesbian communities should be approached for leadership and assistance in finding and keeping resource parents who can meet the special if not extraordinary needs of sexual minority youth, especially those who are at risk of transitioning from foster care without connections to at least one safe, nurturing adult. Both the North American Council on Adoptable Children and the Child Welfare League of America support policies and practices that entitle potential gay and lesbian resource families to fair and equal consideration (Mallon 2004).

Comprehensive Action Plan

Once the role of resource families is clearly defined and accepted by agencies and communities, a comprehensive action plan for initial support and then recruitment and development can be created. Part of that plan must include how resource parents are developed through competency-based preservice training programs that are integrated with the mutual assessment (formerly known as the "home study" process). There must be competency-based in-service training as well. Most agencies provide training that is either money-driven, based on available funding, or time-driven, based on how many hours they believe resource parents will devote to participating. However, training is only as effective as the policy that directs it and the supervision that reinforces it. Training, no matter how excellent, cannot compensate for deficits in the system. Nonetheless, foster parent associations can and do provide realistic training and support for both new and experienced resource parents. In acknowledgment of professionalism, foster parent associations should have paid contracts to do the essential work of training and support.

With a comprehensive retention plan in place (e.g., the 25 research-based components outlined in Pasztor & Wynne 1995), a multifaceted recruitment plan can be established. One-shot recruitment activities are rarely effective; recruitment efforts need to be ongoing, consistent, and persistent (Coyne 1986; Moore, Grandpre, & Scoll 1988; Pasztor et al. 1989; Rodwell & Biggerstaff 1995). The method of communicating the need may vary from community to community, but keeping the message in the public eye on a regular basis is essential. Brochures, posters, fliers, billboards, outreach at community events, inserts in utility bills, awards banquets, and public service announcements on

---

BOX 3. *Opening Doors for Resource Families with Technology*

Adopt US Kids, a service of the U.S. Children's Bureau:
www.adoptuskids.org

National Foster Parent Association:
www.fosterparentnet.org/nfpa.aspx

National Resource Center on Family-Centered Practice and Permanency Planning,
Hunter College School of Social Work, City University of New York:
www.hunter.cuny.edu/socwork/nrcfcpp/

North American Council on Adoptable Children:
www.nacac.org/

Northwest Resource Associates:
home.gci.net/~afptc/

---

the radio and television are but a few of the possible approaches. Having a slogan or logo helps institutionalize the message. The message should be positive and focus on the strengths of fostering rather than the rescue of children.

Mass marketing is needed to address the negative image held by the public at large of foster care. For every article that is written about a foster care tragedy, letters to the editor should flood the newspaper regarding positive interventions. It may be helpful to build community support for fostering by offering opportunities for volunteers—tutoring, for example —with the message: "you don't have to be a foster parent to help a foster child." The Internet is a new medium in foster parent development and support (box 3).

There can be agency-hosted Web sites, and e-mail is a means for resource parents to communicate with staff and one another. However, the digital divide must be taken into consideration for resource families who tend to be less resourced. Knowledge of demographic and census data concerning resource parents may identify community places where other families might be found. Knowing where resource parents shop and what radio stations they listen to may provide effective outreach,

and ethnic media offer new opportunities for recruitment.

For example, Alaska relies on a contract with a nonprofit organization in Oregon to provide the in-service training for resource families. This contract provides on-site, self-study, computer tracking, and telephone support to resource families. Support groups for resource families have organized through chat rooms over the Internet. The Iowa Foster and Adoptive Parent Association established the KidSake Web site as part of a recruitment initiative. The Web site provides information on fostering, the process of becoming a resource parent, and lists publications available on topics related to fostering and adoption.

A national recruitment strategy is in place to identify potential resource families. Federal sponsorship enables dignitaries such as the U.S. president and state governors to involve all 50 states. Every state has a recruitment campaign and a recruitment and response strategy to respond in a timely fashion to families inquiring about providing temporary or permanent care for children and youth. "Welcome to Adopt US Kids—together, we will find families for our children" is the on-line greeting for this Web site sponsored by the Children's Bureau Administration for Children and Families, U.S. Department of Health and Human Services. The Adopt US Kids Web site provides an extensive on-line photo listing of children in foster care nationwide who need adoptive families. Adopt US Kids also provides an array of training and technical assistance services to states to enhance their capacity in the area of recruitment and retention of resource families. In 2004, along with the Ad Council, Adopt US Kids launched a national recruitment campaign.

Over the past decade, foster parent adoption of their foster children represents more than 50% of all adoptive placements; literature dates back 20 years in documenting the benefits of this practice (Meezan & Shireman 1985). However, it is necessary to recruit other families not already known to waiting children, and the Adopt US Kids Web site offers one such option. Interested families at all stages of the adoption process can register on-line to indicate the child they are interested in adopting. The inquiries are linked to the identified state agency having knowledge of the need for the child to have a family. Within hours of their inquiry, families have knowledge of their role in process and placement. For the families filling out the inquiry form, their hopes of becoming a resource to children can be uncertain. The excitement of seeing a photo listing of a child only to find that the child has already been placed can be frustrating to a family not experienced with the child welfare system. Ongoing communication with families interested in working with special needs children in foster care and adoption must be nurtured, even with this state-of-the-art recruitment process, so as not to lose contact with prospective resource families. It is also important to acknowledge practices found in communities of color, where narrative traditions concerning matters of family are essential to culturally sound practice. Technology should be used as an aid and not as a substitute for the teamwork relationship.

As communities define their needs for family foster care, the range of fostering options should be addressed. What has been termed "general foster care" may serve some children. Given the trauma that most children entering care are reported to have experienced because of physical abuse, sexual abuse, and neglect, it appears that most should have access to treatment foster care, requiring resource parents with special training and skills. Research documents the effectiveness of therapeutic foster care with salaried foster parents who can file treatment plans, work with the parents of children in care, and produce measurable outcomes. This form of professional foster care is promising for the seriously disturbed children who increasingly make up the foster care population. The Foster Family-Based Treatment Association headquartered in New Jersey provides models. Pilots for this type of care are taking place in parts of Illinois, Florida, and Massachusetts (Christian 2002).

A comprehensive plan for the support and development of resource parents ultimately hinges on their value to their communities in general, and their agencies specifically. At the core is the relationship between resource parents and caseworkers. There is considerable literature on why foster parents discontinue their critical work. A key variable that has been consistently reported for at least 20 years is the lack of agency support and communication, whether it is addressing a child management issue, a resource challenge, a birth parent conflict, or the trauma of abuse allegations (Anderson 1988; Behana 1987; Carbino 1991; McFadden 1985; Pasztor & Burgess 1982). Foster parents' role reciprocals—caseworkers and the supervisors for both caseworkers and foster parents—must be developed and supported to work collaboratively with foster parents.

Culturally competent, proactive staff members are essential to all components of resource family development and support. For example, they must understand the salient issues of working with potential resource families who are gay and lesbian. Training can incorporate the findings of research studies indicating that children of gay and lesbian parents show no differences from children of heterosexual couples in intellectual and behavioral functioning, friendships, peer relationships, and social adjustment. Furthermore, methods of handling the mutual assessment process should be included in staff training, including when to write down sensitive information and when to omit it. Most important, resource families who are gay and lesbian should address their orientation with the children in their care as a parenting issue, at the right time and place (Mallon 2004).

At the same time, finding and keeping casework staff is an enormous struggle. At least two decades of research identifies strategies to retain casework staff and recruit others (Alliance for Children and Families, American Public Human Services Association, & Child Welfare League of America 2001; Annie E. Casey Foundation 2003; Helfgott 1991; Jayaratne & Chess 1985; Malm, Bess, Leos-Urbel, Geen, & Markowitz 2001; National Association of Social Workers 2003; Pecora, Briar, & Zlotnik 1989; Rycraft 1994; U.S. General Accounting Office 2003). Social work educators and agency administrators have begun meeting nationally to address the imperative need to professionalize and credential the child welfare workforce. The National Association of Social Workers is involved at state and national levels, and the Child Welfare League of America has a national task force addressing the issue.

Resource families cannot be fully supported and developed by staff who lack a comprehensive social work education, or who fail to have a mandated code of ethics, which includes competence, dignity, the importance of human relationships, integrity, service, and social justice (National Association of Social Workers 1996:1). A comprehensive strategic plan to develop and support child welfare social workers is essential to meet the safety, well-being, and permanency needs required by ASFA. However, agencies suffering high administrative turnover lack leadership with the institutional memory of viable policy and practice. Administrators

without social work backgrounds in general, or child welfare expertise in particular, also lack knowledge of salient research findings. Politicians and administrators who do not know what to do—or do not want to invest in what is known to work—tend to commission new studies or implement reorganizations. This practice gives the illusion of affecting change, whereas the reality is "running to keep in place," as the Urban Institute's recent report on the child welfare system was titled (Malm, Bess, Leos-Urbel, Geen, & Markowitz 2001).

As indicated in a recent study for the California legislature (Pasztor, Saint Germain, & DeCrescenzo 2003:38), without a comprehensive, strategic plan to find and keep casework staff (or resource families), "a new generation of politicians, lawmakers, agency administrators, and educators will struggle with the same problems. Another shortage study will be commissioned, and the cycle will begin again."

In collaboration with foster parent associations, child welfare agency administrators and staff must continue to be diligent in seeking solutions to the complex and perplexing problems of foster care and, in a larger sense, child welfare. Social justice is the ethical imperative at the core of finding and keeping resource families for children with special and extraordinary needs. As more and more children and youth are being adopted by their resource parents, issues of "dual licensure" (Greenblatt & Lutz 2000), with commensurate post-adoption supports, must be addressed.

Conclusion

Collectively, we have been resource families over the past 30 years through kinship care, family foster care, and adoption. Our perspective is shared as an expression of the need for sustained collective knowledge and experience, with the passion to support and develop resource families. Inevitably, the efficacy of family foster care as a service to children and their birth families will continue to be questioned. If not family foster care, then what? Our experiences have included giving children and adolescents life in a family; finding appropriate health, mental health, and educational services; meeting the challenges of maintaining birth family bonds; and connecting children to safe, nurturing relationships intended to last a lifetime. Foremost, each of us has come to realize that by being a resource family, our children (the oldest now 42) have achieved—albeit to varying degrees—a sense of safety, well-being, and permanency because of the community resource of family-based care.

In addressing the recruitment, development, support, and retention of resource families, it may be helpful to consider what has been stated in the National Association of Social Worker's *Child welfare section connection* (King 2003:4). Offered is a six-step process, adapted from Maxwell (1996):

- When we change our thinking, we change our beliefs.
- When we change our beliefs, we change our expectations.
- When we change our expectations, we change our attitudes.
- When we change our attitudes, we change our behaviors.
- When we change our behaviors, we change our performance.
- When we change our performance, we change our practice.

References
Adoption and Safe Families Act. (1997). P.L. 105-89.
Adoption Assistance and Child Welfare Act. (1980). P.L. 96-272.
Alliance for Children and Families, American Public Human Services Association, and Child Welfare League of America. (2001). *The child welfare workforce challenge: Results from a preliminary study.* Washington, DC: Child Welfare League of America.
Anderson, S. (1988). *Foster home retention survey: Findings from former foster parents in 10 Bay Area counties.* San Francisco: Bay Area Community Task Force on Homes for Children.
Annie E. Casey Foundation. (2003). *The unsolved challenge of system reform: The condition of the frontline human services workforce.* Baltimore: Annie E. Casey Foundation.
Barbell, K. (1999). *The impact on financial compensation, benefits, and supports in foster parent retention and recruitment.* Washington, DC: Child Welfare League of America.
Baring-Gould, M., Essick, D., Kleinkauf, C., & Miller, M. (1983). Why do foster homes close? *Arete, 8*(2), 49–63.
Baum, A. C., Crase, S. J., & Crase, K. L. (2001). Influences on the decision to become or not become a foster parent. *Families in Society, 82,* 202–213.
Bausch, R. S., & Serpe, R. T. (1999). Recruiting Mexican American adoptive parents. *Child Welfare, 78,* 693–727.
Behana, N. (1987). *Foster parents' perceptions of agency support.* Master's thesis, San Diego State University, School of Family Studies and Consumer Science, San Diego, CA.
Bussiere, A. (1995). *A guide to the Multiethnic Placement Act of 1994.* Washington DC: American Bar Association.
Cahn, N. (2002). Race, poverty, history, adoption, and child abuse: Connections. *Law & Society Review, 36*(2), 461–490.
Carbino, R. (1991). Child abuse and neglect reports in foster care: The issue of foster families and "false" allegations. *Children and Youth Services Review, 15,* 233–247.
Casey Family Programs. (2000). *Lighting the way: Attracting and supporting foster families.* Seattle: Casey Family Programs.
Casey Family Programs. (2003). *The Foster Family Assessment Project.* Retrieved October 25, 2003, from www.casey.org.
Chamberlain, P., Moreland, S., & Reid, K. (1992). Enhanced services and stipends for foster parents: Effects on retention rates and outcomes for children. *Child Welfare, 71,* 387–401.
Child Welfare League of America. (2003). *National data analysis system.* Retrieved June 30, 2004, from www.cwla.org/ndas.htm.
Child Welfare League of America, Casey Family Programs, & National Center for Resource Family Support. (2002). *State response to allegations of maltreatment in out-of-home care.* Washington, DC: Child Welfare League of America, Casey Family Programs, & National Center for Resource Family Support.
Christian, S. (2002). Supporting and retaining foster parents. *State Legislative Report, 27*(11). Retrieved June 17, 2003, from www.ncsl.org/programs/cyf/slr2711.htm.
Christiansen, M. A. (1985). *An orphan's prayer.* Lake Mills, IA: Graphic Publishing.
Cincinnati Enquirer. (1975). Want to be a foster parent? *Cincinnati Enquirer,* (May 22), p. 21.

Cornerstone Consulting Group. (2001). *A carrot among the sticks: The adoption incentive bonus.* Houston: Cornerstone Consulting Group.

Coyne, A. (1986). Recruiting foster and adoptive families: A marketing strategy. *Children Today, 25,* 30–33.

Cox, M. E., Buehler, C., & Orme, J. G. (2002). Recruitment and foster family service. *Journal of Sociology and Social Welfare, 29*(3), 151–177.

David and Lucile Packard Foundation. (2004). *Children, families, and foster care: Issues and ideas.* Los Altos, CA: David and Lucile Packard Foundation.

DeCrescenzo, T., & Mallon, G. P. (2002). *Serving transgender youth—The role of child welfare systems.* Washington, DC: Child Welfare League of America.

Denby, R., & Rindfleisch, N. (1996). African American's foster parenting experiences: Research findings and implications for policy and practice. *Children and Youth Services Review, 18,* 523–551.

Desetta, A. (ed.). (1996). *The heart knows something different: Teenage voices from the foster care system.* New York: Persea Books.

Dougherty, S. (2001). *Toolbox No. 2: Expanding the role of foster parents in achieving permanency.* Washington, DC: Child Welfare League of America.

Downs, S. W. (1986). Black foster parents and agencies: Results of an eight state survey. *Children and Youth Services Review, 8,* 201–218.

Downs, S. W., Moore, E., McFadden, E. J., Michaud, S., & Costin, L. (2004). *Child welfare and family services: Policies and practice.* New York: Pearson.

Friedman, R. M., Lardieri, S., Murphy, R. E., Quick, J., & Wolfe, D. (1980). The difficult job of recruiting foster parents. *Public Welfare, 38,* 10–17.

Greenblatt, S., & Lutz, L. (2000) *Dual licensure of foster and adoptive families—Evolving best practices.* Seattle: Casey Family Programs.

Groze, V., McMillen, C., & Haines-Simeon, M. (1993). Families who foster children with HIV: A pilot study. *Child and Adolescent Social Work Journal, 10,* 67–87.

Hanford, J. (1941). Child placement and the family agency. *Social Service Review, 15,* 706–711.

Helfgott, K. (1991). *Staffing the child welfare agency: Recruitment and retention.* Washington, DC: Child Welfare League of America.

Herczog, M., van Pagee, R., & Pasztor, E. M. (2001). The multinational transfer of competency-based foster parent assessment, selection, and training: A nine-country case study. *Child Welfare, 80,* 631–644.

Indian Child Welfare Act. (1978). P.L. 95-608.

International Child and Youth Care Network. (2003). *Foster parent recruitment and retention.* Retrieved June 10, 2003, from www.cyc-net.org.

Jayaratne, S., and Chess, W. (1985). Factors associated with job satisfaction and turnover among child welfare workers. In J. Laird & A. Hartman (eds.), *A handbook of child welfare,* pp. 760–766. New York: Free Press.

Jordan Institute for Families. (1999). Assessing your agency's foster parent recruitment needs. *Children's services practice notes, 4*(3). Retrieved October 24, 2003, from ssw.unc.edu frcp/Cspnvol14_no3.htm.

Jordan Institute for Families. (1999). Foster parent associations: A valuable recruitment resource. *Children's services practice notes, 4*(3). Retrieved June 17, 2003, from ssw.unc.edu/fcrp/Cspan/vol14_no3/foster_parent_associations.htm.

Kadushin, A., & Martin, J. A. (1988). *Child welfare services,* fourth ed. Upper Saddle River, NJ: Prentice Hall.

King, G. (2003). The face of adoption and foster care has changed: What about our beliefs? *NASW Child Welfare Section Connection,* (July), p. 3.

Kortenkamp, K. & Ehrle, J. (2002). *The well-being of children involved with the child welfare system: A national overview.* Washington, DC: Urban Institute.

Leighton, M., Mathews, J., Pasztor, E., Polowy, M., Watson, J., et al. (2003). *Foster PRIDE/Adopt PRIDE—Trainer's guide revised.* Washington, DC: Child Welfare League of America.

Lutz, L. (2002). *Recruitment and retention of resource families—The promise and the paradox.* Seattle: Casey Family Programs.

Maas, H. S., & Engler, R. E. (1959). *Children in need of parents.* New York: Columbia University.

Mallon, G. P. (1997). Basic premises, guiding principles and competent practices for a positive youth development approach to working with gay, lesbian and bisexual youth in out-of-home care. *Child Welfare, 76,* 591–610.

Mallon, G. P. (2004). *Recruiting and retaining lesbian and gay foster and adoptive parents.* Washington, DC: Child Welfare League of America.

Malm, K., Bess, R., Leos-Urbel, J., Geen, R., & Markowitz, T. (2001). *Running to keep in place: The continuing evolution of our nation's child welfare system. Assessing the new federalism,* occasional paper no. 54. Washington, DC: Urban Institute.

Maxwell, J. C. (1996). *Thinking for a change.* New York: Warner Books.

McFadden, E. J. (1985). *Preventing abuse in family foster care.* Ypsilanti: Eastern Michigan University.

McFadden, E. J. (1996) Family-centered practice with foster parent families. *Families in Society, 77,* 545–557.

McFadden, E., & Ryan, P. (1991). Maltreatment in family foster homes: Dynamics & dimensions. *Children and Youth Services, 15*(2), 209–231.

McGowan, B. (1983). Historical evolution of child welfare services. In B. McGowan & W. Meezan (eds.), *Child welfare: Current dilemmas, future promises,* pp. 45–90. Itasca, IL: Peacock Publishers.

Meezan, W., & Shireman, J. (1985). Antecedents to foster parent adoption decisions. *Children and Youth Services Review, 7,* 207–224.

Moore, B., Grandpre, M., & Scoll, B. (1988). Foster home recruitment: A marketing approach to attracting and licensing applicants. *Child Welfare, 67,* 147–160.

Moye, J., & Rinker, R. (2002). It's a hard knock life: Does the Adoption and Safe Families Act of 1997 adequately address problems in the child welfare system? *Harvard Journal on Legislation, 39*(2), 375–394.

Multiethnic Placement Act. (1994). P.L. 103-382.

National Association of Black Social Workers. (1972). *Position statement on transracial placement.* Washington, DC: National Association of Black Social Workers.

National Association of Social Workers. (1996). *NASW code of ethics.* Washington, DC: National Association of Social Workers.

National Association of Social Workers. (2003). Deprofessionalization and declassification. In *Social work speaks: National Association of Social Workers policy statements,* sixth ed., pp. 22–34. Washington, DC: National Association of Social Workers.

National Center for Children and Families. (2003). *Should I become a foster parent?* Retrieved October 23, 2003, from www.nccf-cares.org/foster.htm.

National Commission on Family Foster Care. (1991). *A blueprint for fostering infants, children, and youths in the 1990's.* Washington, DC: Child Welfare League of America.

Needell, B., Webster, D., Cuccaro-Alamin, S., Armijo, M., Lee, S., et al. (2002). *Child Welfare Services Reports for California.* Retrieved November 30, 2003, from cssr.berkeley.edu/CWSCMSreports.

O'Connor, S. (2001). *Orphan trains: The story of Charles Loring Brace and the children he saved and failed.* Boston: Houghton Mifflin.

Omang, J., & Bonk, K. (1999). Family to family: Building bridges for child welfare with families, neighborhoods, and communities. *Policy and Practice of Public Human Services, 57*(4), 15–21.

Ougheltree, C. (1957). *Finding foster homes.* New York: Child Welfare League of America.

Pasztor, E. M. (1985). Permanency planning and foster parenting: Implications for recruitment, selection, training, and retention. *Children and Youth Services Review, 7,* 191–206.

Pasztor, E. M. (2004). *The impact of abuse allegations on children and foster parents—Scholarly and creative activities grant.* Long Beach: Department of Social Work, California State University, Long Beach.

Pasztor, E. M., & Burgess, E. (1982). Finding and keeping more foster parents. *Children Today, 36,* 2–5.

Pasztor, E. M., Goodman, C., Potts, M., Santana, M., & Runnels, R. (2003). *Kinship caregivers and social workers: The challenges of collaboration (An evidence based curriculum).* Berkeley: California Social Work Education Center.

Pasztor, E. M., Hollinger, D., Inkelas, M., & Halfon, N. (2004). Health and mental health services for children in family foster care: Foster parents' perspectives. *Child Welfare, 83,* 220–233.

Pasztor, E. M., Saint-Germain, M., & DeCrescenzo, T. (2003). *Demand for social workers in California.* Retrieved from June 30, 2004, from www.csus/edu/calst/Government_Affairs/faculty_program.html.

Pasztor, E. M., Shannon, D., Buck, P., Roberts, A., Green, R., & Morton, T. (1989). *Community approach to foster parent recruitment and retention: A strategies guidebook.* Atlanta: Child Welfare Institute.

Pasztor, E. M., & Wynne, S. (1995). *Foster parent retention and recruitment: State of the art in practice and policy.* Washington, DC: Child Welfare League of America.

Pecora, P., Briar, K., and Zlotnik, J. (1989). *Addressing the program and personnel crisis in child welfare.* Silver Spring, MD: NASW Press.

Pike, V., Downs, S. W., Emlen, A., Downs, G., & Case, D. (1977). *Permanent planning for children in foster care.* No. OHDS 77-30124. Washington, DC: U.S. Department of Health, Education, and Welfare.

Ramos, D., & Pasztor, E. M. (2003). Preparing heterosexual and sexual minority youth in foster care for independent living. Poster presentation at the CWLA National Conference on Research in Child Welfare, Miami, November 13, 2003.

Rhodes, K. W., Orme, J. G., Cox, M., & Buehler, C. (2003). Foster family resources, psychosocial functioning, and retention. *Social Work Research, 27,* 243–255.

Roberts, D. (2001). *Shattered bonds: The color of child welfare.* New York: Basic Books.

Rodwell, M. K., & Biggerstaff, M. A. (1995). Strategies for recruitment and retention of foster families. *Children and Youth Services Review, 15,* 403–419.

Ryan, P. (1985). Analysis of foster parents who leave fostering. *Impact, 1,* 3–13.

Rycraft, J. R. (1994). The party isn't over: The agency role in the retention of public child welfare caseworkers. *Social Work, 39,* 75–80.

Saleebey, D. (2002). *The strength perspective in social work practice,* third ed. Boston: Allyn and Bacon.

Siegel, M. M., & Roberts, M. (1989). Recruiting foster families for disabled children. *Social Work, 34,* 551–553.

Silverstein, D., Roszia, S., Pasztor, E., & Clark, H. (2004). *Adoption Clinical Training (ACT).* Monterey, CA: Kinship Center.

Sisco, C. (2001). Utah: Private foundation helps Utah recruit, train, retain foster parents. *Policy and Practice of Public Human Services, 59*(2), 12–14.

Smith, E. P., & Gutheil, R. H. (1988). Successful foster parenting recruiting: A voluntary agency effort. *Child Welfare, 67,* 137–146.

U.S. Department of Health and Human Services. (2003). *Necessary components of effective foster care and adoption recruitment.* Retrieved June 10, 2003, from www.acf.dhhs.gov/programs/.

U.S. Department of Health and Human Services. (2004). *Preliminary FY 2002 estimates as of August, 2004.*

(The AFCARS Report). Retrieved December 1, 2004, from www.acf.hhs.gov/programs/cb/publications/afcars/report9.htm.

U.S. General Accounting Office. (1989). *Foster parents: Recruiting and pre-service training practices need evaluation.* Washington DC: U.S. General Accounting Office.

U.S. General Accounting Office. (2003). *Child welfare: HHS could play a greater role in helping child welfare agencies recruit and retain staff.* Washington, DC: U.S. General Accounting Office.

Walker, J. S., & Bruns, B. (2003). Quality and fidelity in wraparound. *Focal Point: A National Bulletin on Family Support and Children's Mental Health, 15,* 21–26.

W. K. Kellogg Foundation. (2003). *Families for kids: A powerful approach to system reform.* Retrieved November 5, 2003, from www.wkkf.org.

Wasson, D., & Hess, P. (1989). Foster parents as child welfare educators. *Public Welfare, 47,* 16–22.

MARK HARDIN

Role of the Legal and Judicial System for Children, Youth, and Families in Foster Care

ourt systems and child welfare legislation are indispensable components of child welfare practice (Hardin 1985, 1998). Without a doubt, social workers, attorneys, judges, guardians ad litem, court-ordered special advocate (CASA) volunteers, and others involved in the legal and judicial system are key actors in promoting systemic child welfare reform. Without laws authorizing the agency, police, and courts to intervene on behalf of abused and neglected children, society would be powerless to become involved in child protection.

Juvenile and family courts, as well as tribal and many general trial courts, have jurisdiction over cases involving child abuse and neglect. Only children who are identified in a state's law as needing the court's protection may become the subject of a child protection petition. Each state has its own terms and definitions related to jurisdiction of these cases, and each state has its own court structure for handling these cases.

As noted by Badeau (2004) in her comprehensive review of child welfare and the courts, state courts are key decisionmakers in the lives of children involved in the child welfare system (Feller, Davidson, Hardin, & Horowitz 1992). The responsibilities of juvenile and family court judges include decisions and determinations of whether child abuse or neglect actually occurred, whether the parent(s)' rights should be terminated, and whether a child should be adopted or placed in another permanent setting.

Passage of the 1997 Adoption and Safe Families Act (ASFA) clearly expanded the role of juvenile and family courts in several ways (Harden 1998):

- Establishing a judicial role in decisions about whether and what reunification services are required;
- Requiring earlier and more comprehensive permanency hearings than previously mandated (these hearings must be held within 12 months of initial placement, instead of the prior 18-month requirement);
- Setting deadlines for filing termination of parental rights petitions; and
- Establishing the rights of foster and adoptive parents to receive notice of and appear in juvenile and family court proceedings.

Although these changes were important for improving outcomes for children, ASFA did not address the systemic challenges faced by courts in meeting these new requirements, nor did it provide additional resources to assist courts in overcoming these challenges. As the number of children in state custody has grown and as the court's legal responsibilities for these children have increased, many courts have struggled to handle expanded caseloads, often with limited resources. Indeed, in earlier times, the authority of the state to protect abused children was extremely limited. State laws did not require child abuse and neglect reporting. They did not establish child protection agencies and empower them to investigate child abuse and neglect or to provide safe placements for maltreated children. Modern child protection laws establish guidelines and procedures for state actions to protect children and help to insure greater consistency, fairness, and impartiality in decisions about when and how states intervene to protect children.

Although most child welfare officials and workers would no doubt continue to operate with professional care, good faith, and minimal bias, one can imagine the disempowering effects that state agencies would have if they were empowered to intervene and remove children without a legal hearing or trial. When courts operate properly, they provide an orderly and meticulous decisionmaking process, which is not duplicated by the child welfare agency, but is intrinsically linked to it. Court rules, procedures, and standards of evidence mandate a highly exacting sifting and evaluation of information before decisions critical to the family are made. Although juvenile courts do approve agency recommendations and sustain agency petitions in the vast majority of juvenile cases, the legal process also shapes and disciplines agency fact gathering and decisionmaking.

Of course, courts do not always operate as well as they should. Sometimes judges or referees may rush too quickly through child protection hearings, especially if the facts are not in dispute. Sometimes attorneys appear in court ill prepared and uninformed about their cases; like their casework counterparts, they may have too many children and families on their caseloads. At times the court process itself is cumbersome. Nevertheless, even considering such imperfections, courts are essential in child welfare. Therefore child welfare workers, the agencies they work with, and the legal system and its personnel should work to improve the quality and integrity of the court process. In this chapter, I review the role of the court system and focus on the various roles of those professionals, both social work and legal, that interface with the legal and judicial systems for children, youth,

and families in foster care. I offer practical guidance on how best to understand the court system, as these key players in the child welfare system and the legal system interact. Each type of possible court hearing is identified and reviewed for the reader, providing a comprehensive review of the various hearings that are related to child welfare. The chapter concludes by reviewing reform efforts for enhancing practice and promoting collaboration between professionals in both fields.

Unique Characteristics of Juvenile and Family Courts

As noted by Badeau (2004), state and local juvenile and family courts have the ability to hasten or delay children's movement in and out of foster care. Most courts that oversee the cases of children in foster care struggle to balance the competing needs of (1) protecting children from further harm, (2) making timely decisions about their futures, and (3) respecting their parents' due process rights. In meeting these needs, the courts, judges, and attorneys rely on more nonlegal professionals than do their counterparts in other court systems. These professionals include child welfare agency caseworkers, private agency social workers, volunteer CASAs, mental health and healthcare professionals, educators, and citizen review panels.

In essence, the juvenile and family courts are both the "gate-keepers" and the monitors of the nation's child welfare system. To a large extent, judges control which children and families are served by the child welfare system, as well as the nature of the services they are provided. More so than other members of the judiciary, juvenile and family court judges are expected to understand child and adolescent development, family dynamics, and the impact of substance abuse, mental health problems, and the concepts and desired outcomes of concurrent and permanency planning. They are further expected to determine which services and resources would be most appropriate for each individual child and family. These unique expectations have led to the creation of a complex and often cumbersome court structure and process for managing child welfare cases.

Overview of the Juvenile and Family Court Structure

Badeau (2004) makes clear that although some states have a juvenile and family court system that is separate from the courts that handle adult matters, in other states, the juvenile and family courts fall within the larger court structure. Some state court systems have dedicated career tracks for juvenile and family court judges; in other states, the juvenile and family courts are one of several rotations. In the latter states, child abuse and neglect cases are typically heard in juvenile sessions of the general courts.

The court structure used for hearing child abuse and neglect cases is likely to affect some aspects of how the case is handled. For example, a court responsible for general civil and criminal matters may find that children's cases constitute only a small fraction of its overall areas of responsibility. As a result, these cases may not receive the time, attention, or other unique resources warranted. Additionally, the judges hearing these cases may be less familiar with child welfare issues than are juvenile and family court judges, who have the opportunity to develop special expertise in child welfare and dependency issues. In recent years, states have addressed these issues by experimenting with a number of variations on traditional court structures.

Collaboration between Social Workers and Attorneys

Social workers and attorneys are trained in very different practice styles. Social workers believe in the self-determination of the client. Attorneys are guided by the written law and legal precedents. There are at times philosophical differences that can appear to make collaboration a challenge when social workers and attorneys attempt to work together with the same

clients. Courts are the legal entity for making many key decisions in collaboration with child system personnel and families that determine the direction of practice in individual cases, all of which are influenced by social workers. Although the focus here is on collaboration between these systems, it is the courts that ultimately decide whether a child will be removed from the home, placed in foster care, freed for adoption, and many other matters. The input of social workers affects all of these decisions.

Although individual differences among lawyers and judges do affect legal decisions, the social worker or case manager who represents the child welfare agency also has an enormous influence on juvenile court proceedings. The quality of day-to-day practice, the thoroughness and precision of fact gathering by the worker, and the communication of this information to the attorney greatly influence the ultimate outcome of cases. Social workers must share with the attorney responsibility for preparation in juvenile court cases. In fact, the social worker is responsible for the majority of information available to attorneys about their clients and in many ways determines what is presented to the court. This is one of the principal reasons why social work practice skills have such an important bearing on courtroom success.

At the same time, social workers should be familiar with the working of the legal system as they proceed in their daily practice. Many specific laws and government regulations govern work with children, youth, and families in the foster care system. The daily actions and decisions of social workers affect their success in later court proceedings; thus even though many courts place broad responsibility over the care of abused and neglected children on child welfare agency personnel, social workers must constantly be mindful of legal expectations and requirements.

One area of expertise that is essential to the role of the child welfare practitioner is that of gathering reliable and objective case information. Whether this is labeled as "investigation" or "assessment," workers must be capable of carefully observing, analyzing, and reporting the conditions and circumstances surrounding abuse or neglect and of obtaining social, medical, and other information important to a full understanding of the situation. In some cases, workers need to collect physical evidence, and carefully interview individuals known to the client who may have important information regarding the abuse or neglect. Social workers may be asked to take photographs, help prepare written statements, and gather and analyze data from multiple sources. Child welfare practitioners must become skillful at recognizing and following leads to draw down further information about the case. They must know when and how to involve the police if needed for protective purposes or to proceed in cases for which there is clear malfeasance. A social worker who is prevented from gathering necessary information should know how to draw on the authority of the court to gain access.

Documentation of case information is another critical role of the social worker. Documentation involves the recording of case activities as a matter of routine, including what the client does and says, what services are provided, the directions given by the agency to the parent, and other critical information. Important documentation skills include the ability to focus on concrete sights, sounds, and facts that can be substantiated by evidence, rather than personal impressions or broad generalizations.

Proper documentation also requires that child welfare practitioners know which records need to be gathered and when and how it should be done. At times this requires knowledge of how to use the court process for collection of information from out of state. Documentation is not only crucial in obtaining fair court decisions, but critical for good child welfare practice. Specific, concrete information enhances work with families. Overreliance on impressions and unverified facts can limit the practice effectiveness.

Another important skill for the social worker involves the preparation and presentation of written information for the attorney. Social workers should be familiar with the facts that are essential to the legal proceeding. They then become skillful at organizing information in a manner useful to the key actors in the legal process—namely, the attorney, the guardian ad litem, and the judge or referee. Because the attorney is generally the conduit through which case information reaches the attention of the court, incomplete documentation may lead to ill-informed decisions by the judge. Social workers bear the ethical responsibility for presenting documentation in an organized, tactful, and assertive fashion with the client's legal counsel.

The courtroom might be a familiar place for attorneys and judges, but its formality and its rules can make it a formidable setting for a novice social worker. Therefore, performance in the courtroom may take some practice for social workers. Nonetheless, social workers must learn courtroom norms and demeanor. They must acquire the requisite skills for presenting facts and responding competently to cross-examination. Social workers must learn how to become familiar with the courtroom and develop a level of competence in preparing and presenting opinions, when necessary.

Finally, social workers must understand how their work with the family affects the legal case. For example, over time, effective child welfare pracitioners develop an understanding of what specific facts must be documented for the court. They should recognize the legal importance of giving early notice to noncustodial parents, including unmarried fathers. (Failure to give early notice can lead to serious delays later in the case and is counterproductive to good child welfare practice.) In general, child welfare practitioners should be able to provide complete, competent, and comprehensive case plans and focus on those agency efforts most likely to illustrate for the court the merits of their work on behalf of the child and his or her family.

Role of the Parents' Attorney in Child Welfare Cases

The parents' attorney should not be passive and uncritical of child welfare agency practice. The diligent parents' attorney will perform an independent investigation and consult with independent experts. The job of the parents' attorney is to advocate the will of the parents, not what the attorney believes is best for the child. Parents' attorneys often perform a constructive role that ultimately benefits the child. Because the juvenile court focuses on the interests and welfare of the child, parents' attorneys advise their clients to make specific improvements or to cooperate. They advise their clients to do these things to create a favorable impression with the court.

Competent parents' attorneys can help sharpen child welfare decisionmaking. By criticizing and attacking information adverse to the client, often using adversarial tactics unfamiliar to social workers, the attorney imposes a different type of structure on the court proceeding. This argument presupposes, however, that the court holds a reasonable balance in the quality of advocates on both sides and has an attentive judge. Just as a skilled parents' attorney sometimes can exclude important information concerning mistreatment of the child, a more skillful and seasoned agency attorney can at times successfully win a case against a parent, even when the case may be based on a haphazard investigation and erroneous conclusions.

Often parents' attorneys cause delays in the court process, particularly if they are appointed late in the proceedings and are unprepared at the time of the trial. For example, when the child is already in the parents' custody or when the attorney feels that parents need more time to improve and make a favorable impression on the court, the attorney is likely to seek delays. However, parents' attorneys are sometimes strong advocates of speedy court proceedings, particularly when the child has been taken from the parents and the attorney sees a good chance to regain custody at the next court hearing. A good attorney realizes that the longer the child remains in the custody of the agency, the more difficult it can be for parents to have the child returned to their care and custody.

Another important way in which parents' attorneys seek to influence court proceedings is by creating a favorable record of the facts in the case. For example, an attorney may want to prevent the judge from deciding that the parents committed serious acts of abuse or neglect because that might make it more difficult to return the child home later. For this reason, a parents' attorney who views the chances of a favorable finding as poor may offer not to oppose a finding of abuse or neglect and to agree to placing the child into foster care, in exchange for the judge not finding that the parent has committed specific serious acts of abuse or neglect. Although this practice is sometimes justified as a means to maintain a "positive relationship" between client and agency, it can also make it more difficult to prevent the child's premature return home or to terminate parental rights after a parent has failed to improve.

Role of the Guardian ad Litem or Attorney for the Child

There is considerable variation among state and local courts concerning who, if any one, represents the child. For example, depending on the location, attorneys, laypersons, or some combination may always represent children in every case, or different children may be represented differently in the same court.

Not only are there differences in who represents the child, but also in the mission of the person doing the representation. Some children's representatives are supposed to strictly represent the wishes of the child (if capable of forming and articulating wishes), others are supposed to represent their own independent opinion of what is in the child's best interests, and still others are supposed to represent their independent opinion of the child's best interests while also informing the court of the child's wishes. A common practice in many states is for the child's attorney or guardian ad litem to advocate for what he or she believes is the child's best interest, while informing the court of the views and preferences of the child. In practice, the older the child, the more likely is it that the child's views will be reported in court.

Clearly, to investigate and represent the best interests of the child, the attorney or guardian ad litem needs expertise and training, as well as access to independent consultants. The attorney or guardian ad litem who passively and uncritically accepts the facts of the case as presented by the agency is not performing professionally. Instead, the child's representative should conduct a thorough review of records, interview the parties, carry out a follow-up investigation when called for, and arrange for independent experts when needed. The thoroughness of such an investigation and consultation will depend in part on the apparent thoroughness of the work already done by the agency.

Many social workers ask why it is necessary to have a special representative for the child, when the agency itself is charged with the child's protection and supervision. This question is reasonable. If an independent advocate is really needed, some interest of the child must not be already fully represented or protected; some gap in agency representation or flaw in agency social work may exist. The primary argument for independent legal advocates for children is that the agency itself is an interested party in the case and the agency's practices require court scrutiny. The independent child representative is, according to this argument, substantially free of constraints in expressing any concerns for the child. By contrast, the agency's attorney may not be free to point out flaws in agency policies and services, deficiencies in resources, or needed improvements in practice. However,

the child's representative is often an important ally of the worker. The representative may push the case forward when the agency attorney is less responsive. The judge may place special trust in the child's representative.

Role of the Government Attorney

There is perhaps an even greater variation in who presents the case on behalf of the government than in who performs the role of the child's representative. Among the types of attorneys who may represent the government are district attorneys, state's attorneys, county counsel, corporation counsel, city solicitors, city attorneys, attorneys general, attorneys employed by the public child welfare agency, or even private attorneys. More significant than the title or type of attorney is whether individual government attorneys are assigned to child welfare cases on a long-term basis. Long-term work assignments help attorneys develop expertise. Such assignments also make it easier to recruit attorneys with a strong interest in handling child welfare cases.

Specialized units of attorneys represent many urban child welfare agencies, but relatively few rural agencies. Such units may, for example, work for the state attorney general or the agency itself. If the specialized attorneys are recruited and hired based on their skills and experience and they are permanently assigned to child welfare cases, they can be a real advantage for the agency.

Finally, hybrid arrangements exist in a number of states, in which agencies are represented by local attorneys in some matters and by state attorneys in others. For example, in one agency, local attorneys handle juvenile court cases, whereas an attorney working for the state provides advice on policy. Unfortunately, the state attorney in question lacks experiences in abuse and neglect cases and has no special expertise to contribute to policy development. In another state, however, the attorney general has hired several full-time attorneys to provide back-up to local prosecutors. These attorneys, in addition to assisting local prosecutors where there is a backlog or a complicated case, provide training to workers and help the state agency formulate policy.

An important issue in the representation of child welfare agencies concerns who makes the decision when an attorney and social worker disagree on how to handle a case. A common view is that the attorney should decide clearly "legal" issues, whereas the social worker should have a say in "social work" concerns. Unfortunately, issues in juvenile court cases do not neatly divide into purely legal and purely social work concerns. This is especially true when workers and attorneys cannot agree on whether to take a case to court. Agency workers may feel that a case is so urgent that it is worth initiating legal proceedings, even though the attorney advises that the documentation of abuse or neglect is inadequate. The attorney may feel that bringing the case to court will undermine agency credibility with the court.

In some agencies, the final decision on whether to file a case in court is clearly made by the attorney and not the agency, as, for example, when an attorney employed by an elected district attorney represents the agency. Many publicly elected district attorneys regard their job as representing the "public interest" as they see it in child welfare cases. According to this view, which may or may not be supported by state law, they are not bound to represent the views of the agency. However, in some states, government attorneys believe that agency staff must decide whether to file a petition—assuming there is a legal basis for a petition. In a few states, independent "intake officers" make the decision on whether to file petitions.

Perhaps the most appropriate solution concerning who should make decisions is that the agency should have the prerogative to decide whether a case should be filed as long as the case is not legally frivolous. The attorney, however, should have some control over the timing of the case and perform a supervisory role concerning case preparation. In many agencies, the agency attorneys are insufficiently utilized. This sometimes occurs in jurisdictions in which parents are denied or receive insufficient representation themselves.

Besides determining who decides what, some agencies and government attorneys have developed procedures to resolve disagreements about cases. Such procedures allow workers or attorneys to take disputes to supervisors or to convene a committee to resolve the issue. There are three key differences in the duties of agency attorneys in child welfare cases: lawyers' presence in court, attorney preparation, and lawyers' involvement in case planning while litigation is inactive. With regard to the attorneys' presence in court, although child welfare workers are generally not expected to appear unrepresented in contested abuse or neglect proceedings and termination of parental rights hearings, there are still courts in which workers have to represent the agency in court alone, even when the parents have their own attorneys. There are even more courts in which government attorneys are typically not present at emergency shelter care and foster care review hearings.

In the best possible circumstances, cases should be reviewed with ample time for all involved parties. In some courts, government attorneys often first discuss their cases on the day of the court hearing, shortly before the hearing begins. To avoid such poor practice, agencies and government attorneys need to work out specific procedures to prepare for hearings. For example, social workers should understand why it is important to call attorneys before every hearing to arrange for a conference about the case—either by telephone or in person. The conference should be scheduled to occur well before the date of the hearing. Of course, agencies also must see to it that they have enough attorneys to make such conferences practical.

Complicated procedures may be required to initiate a case. For example, agencies may require a detailed checklist that its social workers must follow in preparing written information for the attorneys. The written information is submitted before a petition is filed. The attorney then must review the information and contact the worker before drafting a child abuse, termination, or parental rights petition. Later, if the case is contested, the worker and attorney must arrange a conference at least a week before the trial. At the conference, they determine which witnesses must be subpoenaed. The attorney meets with and prepares the witnesses at least a day before trial.

This kind of process represents minimal trial preparation in other types of legal practice, but many child welfare agencies practice relatively lax case preparation. In some agencies, child welfare workers draft petitions, typically filling in preprinted forms. In other agencies, workers can obtain the help of court liaison workers or intake officers in planning the case or drafting the petition. However, such court liaisons generally have not received legal training and usually work independently from the attorneys representing the agency.

Periodic Consultation to Promote Collaboration

As for periodic case consultation between hearings, many agencies require a strategy session with their attorney whenever social workers and supervisors tentatively decide to change their case goal, such as from reunification to adoption or some other permanency option (see Fiermonte & Renne 2002). Some agencies require an attorney to be present during internal periodic agency case review meetings. A few agencies expect social workers to periodically consult with their attorneys on each case. Periodic legal consultation helps child welfare workers identify legal problems that can cause substantial delays later, such as failure to prepare documentation on issues that may come up in court later or failure to locate missing parents and relatives. Periodic legal consultation also can help insure that the agency is pursuing a legally sound long-term case strategy, without waiting for the worker to single-handedly

take the initiative to raise the issue. Case consultation also assists in building professional relationships between social workers and legal personnel.

Some social workers may be free to telephone or make appointments with attorneys to obtain ad hoc advice on case strategy, whereas others may not be permitted to do this. In practice, the average social worker seldom calls the attorney, except regarding imminent litigation. This situation may be due to the difficulties in obtaining access to the attorney, tension between the two professional groups, a lack of confidence in the attorney, or simply insufficient knowledge as to what information might be obtained from the attorney. Whatever the reason, however, it is important for child welfare agencies and legal personnel to improve their communications with one another. One way to do this is to involve attorneys and social workers in joint training on issues specific to child welfare.

Because the quality of legal counsel is so critical to the success of child welfare practice, agencies need to concentrate both on working more effectively with their attorneys and on getting better services from them. Of course, getting better services from attorneys can be more difficult when attorneys are ultimately accountable to someone other than child welfare agency executives, but the Child and Family Services Review process is making it clear that collaboration between stakeholders in the child welfare profession and in the legal arena is essential to promoting positive outcomes for children, youth, and families.

Juvenile Court Process: Neglected and Abused Children

Here I describe the key stages of the juvenile court process in proceedings brought for the protection of abused and neglected children and propose practices for social workers at each of these stages. Before proceeding to the specific stages of the legal process, it is helpful to consider two basic principles that should guide the agency at every stage. First, the juvenile court process is best understood as a series of decisions concerning the future of the child, and each hearing should logically flow from the previous hearing and set the stage for the future hearings. That is, each hearing and decision must be handled both in light of its immediate and long-term consequences. Second, child welfare agencies need to be conscious of how they affect the speed of the court proceedings. Unwarranted delays in court proceedings interfere with case planning and ultimately delay legal permanency for children.

Emergency Removal Hearings

In certain emergency situations involving suspected child abuse or neglect, the law permits police officers and (in some states) child welfare workers to remove children from their parents without first getting permission from a judge or judicial officer. In emergency situations for which it is safe to delay removal so that a judge or judicial officer can first be contacted, however, many states require police or social workers to apply for a court order before removal.

When a child is removed from home in an emergency, there must be an emergency removal hearing. This hearing (which, depending on the state, may also be called a "shelter care hearing," "detention hearing," "preliminary hearing," or "preliminary protective hearing") is required whenever a child is removed without first giving the child's parents or custodian the opportunity to challenge the decision in court. An emergency removal hearing must also be held within a short time after removal of the child, most typically between 1 and 3 days. Such hearings tend to be very brief and informal. In some courts, emergency hearings are conducted without attorneys.

The central issue at the emergency hearing is whether the child should be held in foster care, returned home, or temporarily placed with a relative or familiar caregiver until the time of the trial of the case. In deciding whether the child can safely remain at home, the court may take into account the availability of services and supervision in the home that might be provided to the family. Other issues that may come up in the hearing include the expulsion of an alleged abuser from the home rather than removing the child, ordering evaluations of children and parents, and ordering temporary services.

Agencies should notify and involve parents in the legal proceedings as rapidly as possible after the child's removal. This involvement speeds the legal proceedings and in some cases can speed family reunification, which limits the traumatic effect of parent-child separation. To notify and involve parents, social workers must make diligent and immediate efforts to locate the parents, notify them that the child is in custody, and advise them of the time and place of the next court proceeding.

Prompt appointment of advocates for the parents and for the child also helps to speed the neglect or abuse case. Parents should be given the opportunity to meet with their attorneys before the emergency removal hearing. However, it is permissible and reasonable for child welfare workers to interview parents before they have attorneys so long as the parents are not in police custody.

It is essential that child welfare workers document the circumstances surrounding the emergency removal, not only to prepare for the neglect or abuse trial, but also to be prepared for subsequent court proceedings. A vivid and accurate account of the circumstances compelling removal of the child can set the tone for the case throughout the court process. Accordingly, workers should consistently prepare factual and precise descriptions of what they saw and heard to convince them to remove the child; take written or recorded statements from important witnesses at the time of the removal; preserve not only the names and addresses of witnesses, but also means of contacting the witnesses should they change address; and take photographs and preserve physical objects that are important evidence in the case.

Adjudication

The adjudication, which is also sometimes referred to as the "fact-finding hearing," or "jurisdictional hearing," is the trial at which it is decided whether the child has in fact been abused or neglected. The adjudication is based on facts or circumstances stated ("alleged") in the petition, the legal document outlining the state's case against the parents. Testimony and documents submitted at the adjudication generally must conform to relatively strict rules of evidence. If the court finds that the facts alleged in the petition are accurate, the court can assume "jurisdiction" over the case. This term means that the juvenile court has the power to make certain critical decisions concerning the child's future, including who will have the responsibility for the child's placement and care.

Child welfare agencies and their attorneys should exercise extreme caution when entering into compromises concerning the allegations of mistreatment of the child. That is, the petition and findings of the court should accurately reflect how the child was mistreated, the dangers confronting the child, and why it is necessary for the court to intervene. This is critically important, because subsequent agency work with and planning for the family will be evaluated partly in terms of how well they address those family problems that were proved during the adjudication. The following example illustrates the pitfalls of negotiating about the court record.

JENNIFER

Jennifer, 5, came into care as the result of severe burns on her left hand and upper arm. Jennifer's aunt reported that the burns were a result of the mother holding the child's hand against a hot clothes iron, as a punishment. At the urging of the defense attorney and to avoid a contested trial, the agency filed a petition alleging the child to be "in need of care and services that the mother is unable to provide." No written statement was ever taken from the aunt, who later recanted the story under pressure from the mother.

After Jennifer was placed in care, her mother secured a steady job and found suitable housing, but consistently refused to cooperate in any training or therapy to examine her relationship with Jennifer and to enhance her parenting skills. The mother visited Jennifer as permitted by the agency, but Jennifer remained distant and withdrawn from her mother.

Eighteen months after Jennifer was removed, the agency remained reluctant to return her to her mother, but did not know how to prove that the mother caused Jennifer's burns. Because of the agency's failure to make an accurate record of the abuse in the original court proceedings, not only did case planning go awry, but it became difficult to free the child for adoption, condemning Jennifer to long-term "temporary" care.

To create a strong record, the agency attorney should draft petitions, stating the nature of the abuse and neglect as accurately and completely as possible. If the initial petition proves to be inaccurate and incomplete, generally it can be amended before or even during the trial. At the close of the trial, the attorney should prepare and try to convince the judge to adopt helpful "findings of fact" (a detailed statement of the facts of the case). If the attorney has prepared a detailed petition, it is easier to persuade the court to determine the specific nature of the abuse or neglect. With a detailed petition, the attorney may simply ask the judge to determine that the government proved each allegation in the petition. Another important way to be prepared for later stages of the case is to retain significant photographs and other evidence that are not part of the court's file.

In addition to setting forth the nature of the child abuse or neglect, the petition might also describe the efforts and services of the agency to prevent removal of the child or to reunify the family. If the agency is to claim federal matching funds for a child in foster care, the court must find the government made reasonable efforts to try to prevent the need to remove the child from home—and the court should describe these efforts in writing. The agency makes it easier for the judge to say what the agency has done to try to prevent removal when the agency puts this information in the petition.

Note, however, that in some courts, judges makes reasonable efforts findings during the emergency removal hearing, not during adjudication. Reasonable efforts are not easily defined. To provide a definition, notes the *Child welfare policy manual* (U.S. Department of Health and Human Services 2005) would be a direct contradiction of the intent of ASFA. The statute requires that reasonable efforts determinations be made on a case-by-case basis. It is believed that a definition would either limit the courts' ability to make determinations on a case-by-case basis or be so broad as to be ineffective. In the absence of a definition, courts may entertain actions that would determine whether reasonable efforts were made. If so, the agency needs to submit a brief report describing its reasonable efforts before the emergency removal hearing. In such courts, it is too late to first report on reasonable efforts in the predisposition report.

It is very important to give both parents formal notice when the agency's case is opened. This not only includes parents who have lost legal custody after a divorce proceeding, but also includes unmarried, absent fathers. Involving noncustodial parents and unmarried fathers not only protects both parents' rights but also helps avoid long-term case delays. For example, when a parent is first brought into a case long after the child has been placed in foster care—and after the agency has finally given up work with the custodial parent—work with the newly identified parent must begin from scratch. But when both parents are involved from the beginning, agencies can reach a final decision concerning the child more rapidly. Furthermore, noncustodial parents or their close relatives sometimes may either be able to help the child while the latter is in foster care (e.g., through providing child support or visiting the child) or may even become caregivers.

Cases may be delayed when a noncustodial parent or unwed father is missing, when a parent lives out of state, or when paternity has not been legally determined. In any of these situations, it may make sense to go ahead with adjudication before providing notice or determining paternity. If the court proceeds with the adjudication, then, as soon as possible after adjudication, the agency should give proper legal notification ("notice") about the case to the missing or out-of-state parent—or should take immediate steps to resolve the question of paternity. Whether the court should go ahead with the adjudication before notifying both parents or before resolving paternity may depend on state law, or may be a judgment call for the court.

Legal notice should be given to a noncustodial parent or unwed father as soon as possible, because the noncustodial parent should have the opportunity to come to court and to seek custody of the child and because delays in notice can delay permanency for the child. Likewise, when there is a possible ("putative") unmarried father, it is critical to establish quickly whether he has legal rights as a parent. In many cases, this requires early paternity testing to determine if he is in fact the child's biological father. If a putative father does turn out to have parental rights, he should be able to participate in the court proceedings.

Disposition

Disposition is that stage of the juvenile court process in which, after adjudication, the court determines whether the child may be placed in foster care, determines who will be awarded the authority to care for and supervise the child, and, in some cases, sets the conditions under which the child is placed. State law distinguishes between the adjudication and disposition in all but a few states, although not all states use the terms "disposition hearing" or "dispositional hearing." The exact timing of the disposition hearing depends on both state law and the practice of the particular court. Disposition may occur at a separate hearing some time after adjudication or may take place immediately following adjudication. Although disposition typically occurs within several weeks of removal in some courts, it can occur many months after removal in other courts.

In most states, many rules of evidence that must be followed at the adjudication do not apply at the disposition hearing. For example, the court may receive and consider second-hand ("hearsay") evidence during the disposition hearing. But even in states where hearsay evidence is allowed during the disposition hearing, opposing attorneys generally have the right to subpoena and cross-examine the authors of any agency disposition reports submitted to the court. In addition, because the court decides different issues at disposition than at adjudication, the parties have the right to present additional evidence about disposition after the adjudication has been completed.

The predisposition report needs to be made available to the parties at least several days in advance of the disposition hearing to give them the opportunity to analyze and critique the agency's recommendations. Agency policy should rigorously require such a practice, so that the report can meaningfully contribute to an intelligent disposition decision.

In most courts, agency workers and their attorneys should plan and conduct disposition proceedings with great care and attention. The court not only makes important decisions at the disposition hearing and also decides whether to place the child in foster care, but also may create an important record. That is, besides deciding whether the child will remain in foster care for an extended period of time, the court may specify what the agency and parents are expected to accomplish over the next several months.

Most states require the agency to submit a written predisposition report to the court for the purpose of explaining and justifying its recommendations and proposed plan. This report can be very influential in court. Therefore it is important that the report not only inform the judge about the case, but also help the judge decide what to include in the court order following the hearing. To inform and help the judge, the report should both explain the family problems that contributed to the abuse or neglect and should suggest exactly what the agency and parents should do to resolve these problems and meet the child's immediate needs.

A disposition report should include recommendations for disposition and explain the reasons for the recommendations. For example, if removal is recommended, the report should outline how the child is likely to be harmed if left in the home, what services were provided to keep the child at home, and what should be done after removal to minimize the adverse affects of the family's separation. Among other things, this report should include recommendations on visiting and contacts between parents and child. The disposition report should not include details that the judge will view as extraneous. It is not necessary to describe every bit of information the agency has concerning the child or family. If the report seems unfocused or needlessly long, the judge is less likely to read it or follow its recommendations.

If a case plan is completed prior to disposition, it might be attached to or incorporated into the predisposition report. The court's disposition order then may approve or modify the plan that the worker proposes in the predisposition report. Because of this possibility, the plan should be clear, specific, and fair to both the agency and the parents.

At a minimum, the predisposition report should outline what the parents and agency should do before the court next hears the case. Depending on how much the agency knows about the parent and child, the report may propose detailed goals and tasks for the agency and parents or may set forth only the broadest outline of subsequent steps. Agencies should be aware of both the benefits and risks of submitting a detailed plan to the court to consider at the disposition hearing. On the positive side, when a court order specifies in detail what the parent and agency are expected to do, it will be more clear in future hearings whether the parents and the agency have met their legal obligations.

When a specific, court-ordered case plan has been in effect, it often is easier for a judge to resolve a case decisively. For example, after a parent has fully complied with a court-ordered case plan and met all conditions for the child's return, the judge is more likely to return the child home without further delay. However, if a parent has failed to comply with the plan and has failed to make progress, the judge is more likely to be willing to approve a new permanent plan for the child, such as adoption. Overall, a judge is more likely to rely on a case plan that was approved by the court as opposed to one unilaterally prepared by a caseworker. This is especially true when all parties had the opportunity to present evidence before the court approved the plan.

Another possible reason to propose a detailed disposition order is to try to get the court to resolve disagreements. For example, the agency may ask the court to settle disagreements concerning services, visiting, or medical or mental health evaluations. When the court resolves such disagreements, parents and their attorneys may be encouraged to cooperate with the agency. By resolving disagreements, the court may also make it harder for parents' attorneys to argue in later hearings that the agency was unreasonable or that parents had good reasons for refusing to cooperate.

Of course, there are also risks in seeking detailed disposition orders. The court may order an ill-advised plan. There also is the risk that the agency will become "locked into" the plan after circumstances change or new information comes to light. In other words, except in emergency situations, workers may be forced to follow a case plan that has become obsolete, until there is a court hearing in which the judge approves changes in the plan. How much should child welfare workers worry about locking in

an obsolete case plan? The answer depends, in part, on how long it takes the court to schedule hearings. Another consideration is how many hours a worker will typically have to spend to prepare the paperwork, meet with the attorney, and go to court to modify the court order.

Once the agency submits the predisposition report, it is the job of the attorneys and judge to critique, refine, and (hopefully) improve on the original product. Workers should view their report as a success when the attorneys and judge help to refine and improve their recommendations. They should be encouraged when, after the parents' attorneys have successfully proposed reasonable changes in the plan, the parents feel more involved in the case plan. The report is not a success if it is disregarded or misunderstood. To reduce this risk, the caseworker and attorney should meet well before the hearing to make sure that the plan will be explained convincingly to the judge.

Fashioning a good disposition report and order is a high art. Disposition reports and orders should balance the needs for flexibility, a clear court record, and anticipating and resolving disputes that may later hamper case progress.

Court Review Hearings

Court review hearings, which take place after disposition, examine case progress and the current well-being of the child. During review hearings, the judge decides whether and how to modify court orders concerning the child's placement and care and the agency's efforts to secure long-term safety and permanency for the child.

A review hearing may take place at predetermined intervals, such as once every 6 months, but many judges set the times of review hearings based on the particular circumstances of the case. For example, a judge may schedule the next review hearing at a date soon after the result from an anticipated psychiatric evaluation is expected, enabling the court and the parties to readjust the case plan based on the new information. Judges may set especially frequent review hearings in cases that, for a variety of possible reasons, seem to require more intense judicial monitoring.

Not every state's laws require courts to conduct review hearings following disposition. In some states, periodic reviews may be conducted entirely by the agency itself or by volunteer citizen review boards. In states that do require periodic judicial review hearings, there are substantial differences in their requirements. State law varies, for example, regarding how often the review must take place, the issues the court is to examine during the review, and the exact procedure followed during the hearing.

In some states, court review proceedings often build on earlier reviews conducted by the child welfare agency or citizen review boards. Federal law requires a review at least once every 6 months and may be conducted by a court, an agency, or a citizen review board. Some states use a combination of judicial and nonjudicial periodic reviews. An agency's prereview hearing report serves the same basic purposes as a predisposition report. Accordingly, like the predisposition report, it is important to send the prereview hearing report to the parties well in advance of the hearing. This practice allows better, more informed testimony at the review hearing. Generally, a prereview hearing report should describe the efforts the agency and parents have made to achieve safety and permanency for the child, explain what progress has occurred in the case, describe the current circumstances and condition of the child, and recommend changes in case goals and activities.

Review proceedings provide a special opportunity to record how the case has progressed since the last court hearing. Because both parties may still be working toward a common goal of family reunification, a full and frank disclosure of how the case is progressing may be much more likely than in a later and more adversarial proceeding, such as in a hearing for termination of parental rights. The agency may wish to place in the record what services it has offered to the family since the last court hearing, what efforts and progress the parents have made to respond to such services, what strengths the family has demonstrated, and what problems remain in the family.

Because the case may have gone on for a long time by the time of review, fewer risks are taken when asking the court to approve a case plan. After the agency has exercised responsibility for the child for an extended period, it should be possible to specify detailed tasks and goals to be met by the parties and to specify the consequences of failing to do so. In many cases, the judge will not only endorse the case plan, but also state that termination of parental rights should be initiated should the plan be unsuccessful.

Not all courts are willing to specify goals, tasks, and services for the parties as part of the court order. In some cases, state law may limit what the judge can order. If the judge is unwilling or unable to order the parties to follow a case plan, agency attorneys may request that the judge urge the parties to comply. Such a recommendation can be reduced to writing and included in court documents. When parents are working toward reunification, such recommendations may carry considerable weight with them and their attorneys.

Permanency Hearings

Permanency hearings are supposed to be different from review hearings. Whereas the purpose of a review hearing is to oversee and refine the case plan, that of a permanency hearing is to concretely determine a permanent goal ("permanency plan") for the child. Although either a court or a court-appointed or approved administrative body may hold a permanency hearing, in practice, courts nearly always conduct permanency hearings. The parties, including age appropriate children, must be able to participate in the permanency hearing. As in review hearings, foster parents must receive notice and have the opportunity to be heard.

When deciding on a permanency plan, the court is to place highest priority on return home, adoption, legal guardianship, or other permanent placements with relatives. Before approving the placement of a child in some other "planned, permanent living arrangement," the agency must document and the court must find that there is a compelling reason why the higher priority options are not in the child's best interests.

The court must conduct permanency hearings within 12 months after a child is considered to have entered foster care and then at least once every 12 months thereafter, for as long as the child remains in foster care. There is a shorter deadline for permanency hearings after a court decides that the agency is not required to try to help a child safely return home. After the court has made such a determination, the court must conduct a permanency hearing within 30 days.

Although there are similarities in some of the issues that come up in review and permanency hearings, there also are important differences. In both types of hearings, the agency presents what it has done to try to achieve a safe and permanent placement for the child. In the permanency hearing, however, the agency must also convince the court to make a finding that the agency has made reasonable efforts to achieve this goal. If the case goal is family reunification, in both types of hearings, the agency presents evidence concerning the parents' efforts to make it possible for the child to safely return home and concerning what progress parents have made in achieving those goals.

Whereas the review focuses on possible adjustments and refinements in the current case plan, the permanency hearing selects the most appropriate permanency plan for the child. Accordingly, the agency's preparation for the two types of hearings can vary. For the review hearing, the agency must prepare to explain and defend needed adjustments in the case plan. For the permanency hearing, the agency must show why it proposes return home, adoption, legal guardianship, permanent placement with a relative, or another planned permanent living arrangement. The agency must show why all other choices are not practical or not in the child's best interests. The agency's permanency hearing report should describe the agency's recommended permanency plan, explain why other alternatives are not recommended, and should propose specific steps and timetables to finalize the permanency plan. As with other court reports, it is important that the agency submit it well before the hearing takes place.

In practice, the distinction between review hearings and permanency hearings can be blurred. As time passes and it becomes increasingly apparent whether the child will eventually be returned home, review hearings often become more like permanency hearings. Although a hearing is initially scheduled as a review hearing, the court need not wait until the permanency hearing to decide to return a child home, approve proceedings for legal guardianship, or permanently place a child with a relative. Similarly, agencies need not wait until the permanency hearing to initiate court proceedings to legally free a child for adoption (terminate parental rights).

Termination of Parental Rights

Termination of parental rights is a decision with extremely important implications for the child and the family. Termination involves complete and final severance of a parent's legal rights and responsibilities to the child. In some states, termination is referred to as "permanent commitment" or "permanent guardianship" with the right to consent to adoption. Whatever term is used, this legal action permanently ends the parents' rights to visit or communicate with the child and removes the parent's right to make any decisions concerning the child. It also eliminates the need for parental consent as a precondition for the child's adoption.

In most states, termination of parental rights requires a new set of legal proceedings, including a new written set of allegations against the parent (the petition), new formal notice to the parents (summons), and a separate hearing or set of hearings. In many states, termination is the most formal of legal proceedings in child protection cases, even more so than the adjudication. It is the most likely to be appealed to a higher court. In some states, termination is heard in a different court than the one that heard the earlier stages of the child protection proceedings.

Preparation for a contested termination case usually requires the agency to put together a detailed and focused case history. In the course of a typical termination proceeding, the agency must demonstrate the original parental problems or maltreatment causing the child to be placed in foster care, show the efforts by the child welfare agency and others to resolve the problem and unify the family, show the inadequacy of the response by the parents to agency efforts to help, and demonstrate that termination is needed to meet the current needs of the child. In addition to these requirements, the agency may need to present a plausible plan to secure a new permanent home for the child.

The success of a termination case depends in part on the facts of the case and on how well the child welfare worker has recorded and documented those facts, prepared a case summary, identified strong potential witnesses, and testified during the trial. The most basic issue in a termination of parental rights proceeding is whether a reasonable likelihood exists for the child to be safely returned to the parent. Although the grounds for termination of parental rights set forth in state law do vary and must be carefully adhered to, the chief focus of termination cases concerns whether the child cannot or should not be reunited with the parents.

Five basic types of indicators can show that a child should not return home. When the facts are strong enough one indicator alone may be sufficient to demonstrate that a return is unlikely, but more often, a combination of indicators will apply in a particular case. First, the child may be unable to return because the parent has demonstrated an extreme lack of interest or commitment toward the child. Key examples of extreme lack of motivation and concern are a parent's failure to visit or communicate with the child while the child was in foster care and a pattern of needlessly leaving the child with others for prolonged periods of time and then failing to pick up the child as agreed. When such behavior has extended over time and the agency has been liberal in assisting the parent to maintain contacts and a relationship with the child, parental disinterest can be a strong basis for termination. In many states, parental disinterest comes under the legal heading of "abandonment," although abandonment grounds can be more-or-less strict, depending on the particular state.

Second, the child may be unable to return because the parent has failed to make necessary adjustments to prepare for the child's return, in spite of help from the child welfare agency. This is the most common and basic ground for termination of parental rights. In short, the agency must prove that a child is unable to return by demonstrating that it has tried everything reasonable and possible to reunify the family, but the parent is still not ready to care for the child. To present proof of this type, the agency should be prepared to demonstrate that the court and the child welfare agency formulated a program for the parent designed to alleviate the problems that caused the continued parent-child separation. The agency also needs to prove that it diligently attempted to follow through with its program of assistance, and prove that the parent persists in conduct that prevents the return of the child. Proving this particular basis for the termination of parental rights is specifically centered on the history of the parent's problems and behavior toward the child, as well as on the agency's involvement with the family.

Third, return may be inappropriate because of the unusual severity or repetition of abuse or neglect. Parental mistreatment of a child may be so chronic or severe that returning the child home presents an unacceptable risk. Consider the following case.

ESCALATING ABUSE

A father constantly abused his young son, causing an escalating series of injuries. Eventually, the child was hospitalized and placed in foster care after suffering from serious burns and broken ribs. The agency first learned of the case as the result of the hospitalization. While the child was in foster care, a younger sibling died as a result of the father's abuse. In this case, no further efforts to work with the father were appropriate as a precondition to a termination of parental rights, as unacceptable danger was involved in returning the child.

Even in less extreme cases, where it is necessary to show efforts to work with the family, the severity and persistence of mistreatment is important in determining whether termination is supportable.

Fourth, return may be impractical because a diagnosable condition may make the parent unable to assume care of the child. Parental "condition" refers to incapacities so severe that the parent cannot care for the child, such as intractable mental illness, mental deficiency, or in rare cases, extreme physical disability. Cases of this type should be provable without reference to parental fault. A diagnosis made by an expert is usually critical proof in condition cases. If a parent suffers from a condition that renders him or her totally unable to care for the child, it should not be necessary to show that the agency has attempted to work with the parent. However, where the agency has made futile efforts to help the parent, such efforts can help demonstrate the intractability of the condition and reinforce the prognosis of the expert witness. Furthermore, in the many cases in which the parent is partially incapacitated, a combination of evidence of incapacity and unsuccessful agency efforts to work with the parent may be required.

Fifth, return may be inappropriate because, as a result of the parent's past behavior, the child is unalterably averse to return. Return home may trigger a severe emotional reaction in a child due to past experiences in the home.

Even though the parent may now be capable of providing appropriate care for the child, traumatic memories or new relationships may make return profoundly painful or frightening. This basis for termination, ironically, is perhaps the least used, in part because it is difficult to prove precisely why and how return home will harm the child and in part because state law may not authorize termination solely on this basis.

In some cases, however, proof of potential emotional harm to the child may be compelling. A dramatic example might be a child who, upon being visited by a birth parent, retreats into a corner of a room, coils into a fetal position, and rhythmically knocks his head against the wall. In such a case, mental health experts may testify that such behavior shows that return home will trigger an extreme and possibly irreversible emotional reaction by the child. In such a case, it may be possible to prove that returning the child to the parent will be inappropriate, no matter how well rehabilitated the parent. Unfortunately, however, state law may not allow termination of parental right based only on the clear emotional needs of the child.

Less dramatic examples can also be helpful in a termination case. Even if the evidence that return home will harm the child cannot be the sole basis for a termination of parental rights decision, it may be combined with other types of proof. If fact, in every termination case there should be evidence focusing precisely on how return home will affect the individual child in the proceeding. This issue needs to be given considerable thought by the worker and should be reflected not only in testimony, but also in the arguments of the agency attorney.

Besides demonstrating that a child is unable to return home and to satisfying the specific statutory grounds for termination, it is important to be prepared to demonstrate that termination will actually result in an appropriate permanent placement for the child. Usually this demonstration entails offering evidence that the child actually will be adopted within a reasonable time. Although most judges do not require that a specific adoptive home be selected before granting termination, many do expect testimony from adoption specialists indicating that the particular child can be adopted. Other judges deal with the issue by terminating parental rights but retaining jurisdiction and periodically reviewing the case to be sure that the agency is conducting an adequate adoptive search and is *not* excluding suitable adoptive parents.

Adoption or Guardianship Hearing

To make the child legally part of another family, either through adoption or by establishing legal guardianship, is the final type of hearing. These areas are reviewed extensively elsewhere in this volume (see the chapter by Groza, Houlihan, and Wood on adoption and that by Testa and Miller on guardianship).

Current Reform Efforts

Clearly there are changes that should be made to improve the collaboration between the court and child welfare systems (Grossman 1995). The Pew Commission on Children in Foster Care (Pew Charitable Trust 2004) specifically highlights several critical themes that point practitioners and policymakers toward better collaboration between the courts and the child welfare system. In addition, the U.S. General Accounting Office (1999) report identified significant problems facing juvenile and family courts. The identified problems fell into two broad categories: (1) lack of cooperative working relationships between the courts, tribes, and child welfare agencies; and (2) difficult personnel and data management issues. A subsequent report (U.S. General Accounting Office 2002) noted that most states indicate some significant court challenges that hinder efforts to achieve permanency for children in foster care. For example, caseloads for both the judges and the attorneys involved in child welfare cases are often very large, at times exceeding 1,000 cases per year. With such high caseloads, judges often have as little as 4 minutes to devote to a protective

hearing, and rarely do they have enough time to adequately consider all of the information presented at subsequent hearings. Yet without current data at their fingertips, most judges and court administrators are not able to track the amount of time spent on each case or the number of continuances. According to Badeau (2004), several court reform efforts are currently underway, including the following.

Model Courts

In 1980, the National Council of Juvenile and Family Court Judges created the Model Courts program with funding from the Edna McConnell Clark Foundation. The purpose was to create model approaches to assist courts with the implementation of the "reasonable efforts" requirements related to family preservation and reunification. Since then, the focus of the Model Courts program has expanded, and the number of jurisdictions with model courts has grown from the original 14 to 25. These courts have engaged in a number of innovative strategies to improve both court performance and outcomes for children. Model Court judges have taken a leadership role in improving court and agency collaboration, increasing the role of community leaders in court activities, enhancing availability of and access to services (e.g., providing on-site mental health or substance abuse assessments). Other reforms have involved redesigning courtrooms and reorganizing court calendars to be more child- and family friendly, and improving court access to and utilization of data.

Court Improvement Program

The Court Improvement Program (CIP), established in 1993, was recently reauthorized through 2006. Under this program, the highest court in each state is eligible to apply for grants to make specific improvements to their juvenile and family court systems. The U.S. Department of Health and Human Services has funded the American Bar Association (ABA) Center on Children and the Law to provide technical assistance to states with CIP grants. According to the ABA, states have targeted their improvement efforts in the following areas:

- Improving the quality and depth of court hearings in child welfare cases;
- Improving legal representation of all parties;
- Improving timelines of decisionmaking through improved usage of technology and data management and other management tools;
- Addressing issues of court staffing and the quality of the judiciary; and
- Increasing community collaboration between agencies, tribes, and courts.

Development of Juvenile and Family Court Performance Standards

In 2001, three of the largest national organizations with interest in juvenile and family courts —the National Council of Juvenile and Family Court Judges, the National Center for State Courts, and the ABA—with funding from the Packard Foundation, came together to develop juvenile and family court performance standards and to pilot these standards in several jurisdictions around the country. Building on the outcome measures included in the Child and Family Services Reviews, this project developed measures to help courts identify problems, set priorities, develop solutions, and evaluate their impact. A few states and individual courts have approved policies (through administrative directives or legislation) requiring case tracking and performance measures.

Conclusion

Passage of ASFA in 1997 expanded the role of juvenile and family courts in several ways. Although the courts ultimately decide whether a child will be removed from the home, placed in foster care, or freed for adoption, and determine the nature and extent of services provided to children, youth, and their families, the input of child welfare workers affects all of these deci-

sions. Therefore, it is essential that social workers involved in the child welfare system understand the role of the court as it relates to critical case decisions, permanency planning, and permanency outcomes, and are fully prepared to interface with the legal and judicial systems on behalf of the children, youth, and families that workers serve. Further, in their day-to-day practice, child welfare workers must constantly be mindful of legal expectations and requirements.

In this chapter, I have reviewed the types of court hearings that child welfare workers will encounter and provided a comprehensive overview of the various legal proceedings that affect those served by the child welfare system. In addition, I have offered practical guidance on how social workers can function most effectively as they collaborate with attorneys and others in the legal and judicial system. Child welfare workers are responsible for the majority of information available to attorneys about their clients and in many ways workers determine what is presented to the court. For example, the success of a termination case depends in part on the facts of the case and on how well the child welfare worker has recorded and documented those facts, prepared a case summary, identified strong potential witnesses, and testified during the trial. Therefore, thorough fact gathering by the worker and the communication of this information to the attorney is essential.

Finally, I have reviewed current reform efforts for enhancing practice and promoting collaboration between professionals in both fields. Most states indicate some significant court challenges that hinder efforts to achieve children's safety, permanency, and well-being. At times the court process itself is cumbersome. In other instances, judges and attorneys, like their caseworker counterparts, may have too many children and families on their caseloads. Therefore, child welfare workers, the agencies they work with, and the legal system and its personnel should work to improve the quality and integrity of the court process.

References

Adoption and Safe Families Act. (1997). P.L. 105-89.

Badeau, S. (2004). *Child welfare and the courts.* Washington, DC: Pew Charitable Trust.

Feller, J. N., Davidson, H., Hardin, M., & Horowitz, R. (1992). *Working with the courts in child protection.* Washington, DC: U.S. Department of Health and Human Services.

Fiermonte, C., & Renne, J. L. (2002). *Making it permanent: Reasonable efforts to finalize permanency plans for foster children.* Washington, DC: American Bar Association, Center on Children and the Law/NRC on Legal and Judicial Issues.

Grossman, D. E. (1995). *Resource guidelines: Improving court practice in child abuse & neglect cases.* Reno, NV: National Council of Juvenile and Family Court Judges.

Hardin, M. (1985). Families, children, and the law. In A. Hartman & J. Laird (eds.), *The child welfare handbook,* pp. 213–236. New York: Free Press.

Hardin, M. (1998). *Impact of the Adoption and Safe Families Act on judicial resources and procedures.* Washington, DC: American Bar Association.

Laver, M. (1998). Advice for agency attorneys: Implementing ASFA: A challenge for agency attorneys. *Child Law Practice, 12,* 12–17.

Pew Charitable Trust. (2004). *Pew commission on children in foster care.* Washington, DC: Pew Charitable Trust.

U.S. Department of Health and Human Services. (2005). *Child welfare policy manual.* Washington, DC: U.S. Department of Health and Human Services.

U.S. General Accounting Office. (1999). *Juvenile courts: Reforms aim to better serve maltreated children.* HE-HS-99-13. Washington, DC: General Accounting Office.

U.S. General Accounting Office. (2002). *Foster care: Recent legislation helps states focus on finding permanent homes for children, but long-standing barriers remain.* GAO-02-585, 12 GAO HE-HS-99-13. Washington, DC: U.S. General Accounting Office.

JERRY MILNER
LINDA MITCHELL
WILL HORNSBY

Child and Family Services Reviews

An Agenda for Changing Practice

In 1994, Congress directed the U.S. Department of Health and Human Services to develop regulations for reviewing state child and family service programs administered under Titles IV-B and IV-E of the Social Security Act. Dissatisfaction among states and the federal government with prior federal reviews led, at least in part, to the passage of the legislation. Although prior review processes had been effective in holding states accountable for meeting procedural requirements associated with the foster care program, they were less successful in insuring positive outcomes for the children and families served by state child welfare agencies, especially those outside the foster care program.

Following the 1994 legislation, the Administration for Children and Families (ACF) in the U.S. Department of Health and Human Services, in consultation with the child welfare field, developed and field-tested the new Child and Family Service Reviews (CFSRs) in 14 states, prior to implementing the reviews officially in federal FY2000. ACF shaped the CFSRs around the goals of capturing the actual experiences of children and families served through state child

welfare programs and evaluating programs on the basis of outcomes, rather than focusing exclusively on federal requirements pertaining to procedures and documentation. Using the statutory and regulatory underpinnings of the Title IV-B Child and Family Services Plan (the state plan), including the principles that guide the development of the state plan, ACF developed measures that reflect the substance and intent of those requirements through actual casework with children and families (Child and Family Services 2000).

The CFSRs examine child welfare practices at the ground level, capturing the interactions among caseworkers, children and families, and service providers, and determining the effects of those interactions on the children and families involved. The emphasis on practice is based on a belief that, although certain policies and procedures are essential to an agency's capacity to support positive outcomes, it is the day-to-day casework practices and their underlying values that most influence such outcomes.

The CFSRs also serve a much broader purpose than simply evaluating state performance relative to state plan requirements. The reviews are ACF's primary mechanism for promoting an agenda of change and improvement in services to children and families nationally. With a solid focus on program improvement planning, they provide an opportunity for states and the federal government jointly to implement reforms at a systemic level that will realize and sustain improved outcomes for children and families. Rather than seeking quick, and possibly ineffective, answers to the complex problems that weaken the responsiveness of state child welfare programs, the CFSRs promote thoughtful planning and the development of lasting solutions. Furthermore, the reviews offer opportunities to frame solutions clearly in the context of practice principles that reflect the mission and intent of federally funded child and family service programs and state-of-the-art thinking on the most effective approaches to serving children and families.

Four broad practice themes form the conceptual framework for evaluating state child and family service programs through the CFSRs and for crafting the program improvement plans that result from the reviews. Those themes are family centered practice, strengthening parents' capacity to provide for their children's needs, individualizing services to children and families, and community-based services. Family-centered practice is a conceptual framework that incorporates a set of principles for working with families "based on the belief that the best way to protect children in the long run is to strengthen and support their families, whether it be nuclear, extended, foster care, or adoptive," and that strengthening parental capacity to provide for their children is a core essential (National Child Welfare Resource Center for Family-Centered Practice 2000:12). Family-centered practice is also an approach to service delivery, but must be distinguished from family preservation programs, which are specific types of services (Zlotnik & John-Langba 2002). Literature on family-centered practice (Hartman & Laird 1985) points to its inception in the mental health field, through the creation of the Child and Adolescent Service System program (CASSP) (Johnson et al. 2003) and notes current use in many disciplines and with various populations, including physical and mental health programs, gerontology, child welfare, juvenile justice, and education (Zlotnik & John-Langba 2002). The origins of the themes

of individualizing services to children and families and the need for community-based services can also be traced to the federal CASSP and are important components of the systems of care values and principles (Stroul & Friedman 1986). In efforts to meet the needs of children and families in various populations, the systems of care values and principles "are being applied in all systems of care building, that is, regardless of whether the focus is on only children with serious disorders" (Pires 2002:25). By evaluating state programs in the context of these themes, ACF strives not only to help child welfare systems nationwide conform to relevant laws and regulations but also to increase their capacity to respond to the needs of children and families and afford them meaningful opportunities to achieve their goals.

Approach

CFSRs examine state child and family service programs from two perspectives, (1) the outcomes of services provided to children and families and (2) systemic factors that affect the state's ability to help children and families achieve positive outcomes. Seven outcomes within the reviews are grouped into the three domains of safety, permanency, and child and family well being, as shown in fig. 1.

Each outcome is evaluated, first in the individual cases reviewed and then for the state as a whole, on the basis of a series of performance indicators. For example, reviewers rate individual cases on the outcome, "children have permanency and stability in their living situations," by considering the incidence and reasons behind foster care reentries, the stability of foster care placements, the timely and appropriate establishment of permanency goals, and the achievement of the specific permanency goal for the child. ACF then uses information from individual cases, supplemented by statewide data indicators (i.e., incidence of foster care reentries, number of placement changes for children in foster care, and length of time to achieve adoption and reunification for children with

Safety	Permanency	Child and Family Well-Being
• Children are, first and foremost, protected from abuse and neglect • Children are safely maintained in their homes whenever possible and appropriate	• Children have permanency and stability in their living situations • The continuity of family relationships and connections is preserved for children	• Families have enhanced capacity to provide for their children's needs • Children receive appropriate services to meet their educational needs • Children receive adequate services to meet their physical and mental health needs

FIGURE 1. Outcomes evaluated in the Child and Family Services Reviews.

those goals) to determine the state's conformity with the outcome.

The primary sources of information in individual case reviews are interviews with the children, parents, foster parents, caseworkers, and service providers involved in each case. Although the actual case files are a source of information, reviewers obtain a more complete picture of what has occurred by interviewing the actual parties to any individual case.

In addition to the outcomes, the reviews evaluate the level of functioning for the following seven systemic factors (Child and Family Services 2000):

- Statewide information system;
- Service array;
- Case review system;
- Staff training;
- Quality assurance system;
- Agency responsiveness to the community; and
- Foster and adoptive parent licensing, recruitment, and retention.

The review team evaluates the seven systemic factors on the basis of state plan requirements related to each factor. For example, the review team rates the systemic factor, "case review system," based on the effectiveness of procedures for the timely termination of parental rights when appropriate, periodic case reviews and permanency hearings for children in foster care, joint development of written case plans with the

child's parents, and notification of foster and preadoptive parents of hearings and reviews.

The primary sources of information used to evaluate the systemic factors are a statewide assessment, completed prior to the on-site review, and stakeholder interviews with key state and community representatives. In both the statewide assessment and the stakeholder interviews, representatives from within and outside the state's child welfare agency are asked to provide information and perspective on the issues under review. This practice has the added benefits of increasing community understanding of the issues in child welfare and building support for the agency's efforts to make needed improvements.

By using a mix of quantitative and qualitative measures whenever possible, the reviews present a broad view of statewide performance in certain critical areas while providing much needed insight into the policies, practices, and circumstances that affect the numbers. The use of multiple sources of information also helps clarify how data reflect practice and how qualitative information can, in turn, be used to explain the data. There are limits to this approach, however, particularly in those areas of the review in which quantitative measures at a national or statewide level are missing. This shortcoming is particularly evident in the three well-being outcomes.

The lack of national data on well-being for use in the reviews is a major limitation to reviewing for the well-being outcomes. Unlike the safety and permanency outcomes, for which there are national sources from which data indicators for individual states can be extracted, there is no source of national data that fits the parameters of the CFSRs. (The Adoption and Foster Care Reporting and Analysis System is the data source for the permanency measures and the National Child Abuse and Neglect Data System is the data source for the safety measures.) Another limitation pertains to the scope of ACF's authority to review for, and hold states accountable for, well-being indicators and outcomes. The CFSR process, by definition, examines those indicators that fall within the scope of state plan requirements under Titles IV-B and IV-E. Although there are national sources of information that offer valuable information on the well-being of children and families on a broader scale (e.g., Annie E. Casey Foundation 2004), ACF reviews only for indicators that fall within its authority, such as certain requirements associated with education, physical health, and mental health. Beyond these measures, the well-being indicators used in the reviews primarily evaluate child welfare practices that support the well-being of children and families.

Here we describe the content in the CFSRs that addresses and promotes each of the four underlying themes of the reviews.

Family-Centered Practice

Various elements in the CFSR process direct the attention of child welfare agencies toward interventions that address the needs of entire families. Although few observers would argue the merits of approaching child welfare practice from a family-centered perspective, it is difficult to operationalize the concept in actual practice and to measure it in the review process. CFSRs are based on an assumption that the most fundamental needs of children, such as needs for nurturing, belonging, and safety, cannot be addressed effectively without attending to the entire family's needs. Furthermore,

efforts to make systemic improvements in critical indicators pertaining to safety, permanency, and well-being rely on agency interventions designed to address the effects of the family's behaviors and conditions on the recurrence of negative indicators.

The two safety outcomes having the highest priority for program improvement efforts generated by the CFSRs include examples of indicators that focus on the entire family rather than on identified children. For such indicators as the timeliness of initiating investigations of reports of maltreatment and the recurrence of maltreatment, reviewers must address all children in the family and gather information that sheds light on the causes and nature of the maltreatment, such as recurring risks in the family or the involvement of similar offenders in multiple incidents. As reviewers rate the services provided by the agency to protect children in their homes and mitigate the risk of harm, they are able to evaluate the extent to which the agency appropriately directed its interventions toward issues in the family that affect the safety of children.

For the permanency outcomes, reviewers use the same approach to evaluate such indicators as multiple entries into foster care by comparing the family-related factors that affected initial and subsequent entries into care with efforts to resolve those issues. Other indicators used in the permanency outcomes also emphasize family-centered practice by focusing attention on the needs of children in foster care relative to their families. Examples of those indicators include the child's relationship with his or her parents during an episode of foster care, the frequency and quality of visiting that occurs between children in foster care and their parents and siblings, and the use of relatives as placement resources. In training for the reviews, reviewers receive information on the importance of family relationships to children in foster care and family involvement in case planning activities. Trainers caution reviewers not to assume that indicators pertaining to children's relationships with their families be rated "not applicable" solely because parental rights have been terminated or because reunification is not the case goal. In this manner, the reviews not only evaluate the effectiveness of specific family-centered activities, but also highlight the importance and priority associated with such activities.

Finally, the well-being outcomes contain indicators that focus on the assessment of needs and subsequent delivery of services, which not only promote well-being within the family, but also have a cross-cutting effect on the safety and permanency outcomes. In reviewing for the quality of needs assessments for general case planning purposes, as well as for more specific areas, such as health and education, reviewers must determine whether the needs of all relevant family members have been addressed. Not surprisingly, reviewers often find that needs assessments focus on a targeted individual in the family rather than on all family members. This focus, in turn, often leads to service delivery that is fragmented and ineffective in making improvements in the family that are essential to the family's long-term ability to sustain and protect its members.

At times, this view of family-centered practice challenges the agencies' internal perception of their roles. For example, they may be reluctant to assume responsibility for assessing or serving family members who do not present obvious needs, who are not the subject of an allegation of maltreatment, or who are not considered to be the focus of casework activity. Similarly, agencies may direct efforts exclusively toward one dimension of need in the family, such as alleged maltreatment, when a comprehensive assessment might reveal needs for service in other areas, such as education, domestic violence, or mental health. In such situations, the CFSRs are effective in underscoring both the need and the challenge of using a family-centered approach to serving children and families.

Strengthening Parental Capacity to Provide for Their Children

In promoting the theme of strengthening parental capacity to provide for their children, the CFSR process takes the family-centered practice concept to the next level. The underlying value here is that when they can care for their children in ways that protect their safety and well-being, parents are a better choice to provide that care than are state agencies. This theme also carries the implicit message that the correct role of agencies is working with families to help prepare them to sustain their children over time when that is possible and appropriate, rather than assuming the role of long-term caregiver.

Central to this message is the premise that engaging parents in decisions and assessments related to their strengths and needs, establishing case plan goals, and providing services are more likely to support the timely and effective achievement of positive outcomes for children. It follows that parents are more likely to engage and commit to those services and plans in which they have had a voice in identifying and developing. Having systems in place that support such parental involvement requires policies, established practices, and clear expectations in the agency that promote this philosophy. From a systemic perspective, the reviews examine the capacity of agencies in this area primarily through evaluation of the case review system. In this evaluation, indicators address parental involvement in case planning activities and participation in hearings and reviews pertaining to their children, as well as through other systemic factors, such as staff training, quality assurance, and service array. By reviewing systemic factors with this theme in mind, the reviews provide information to states on how the functions of different aspects of the agency come together to either support or inhibit the agency's ability to strengthen parental capacity.

At the practice level, all three outcome domains address parental capacity to one extent or another. In the area of safety, reviewers explore services that are provided to families to protect children in their own homes and to prevent removal, such as family preservation, family support, and other types of placement prevention services. Reviewers address not only the types of services provided, but review the match of those services to needs associated with the parents' capacity to keep their children safe and to improve their abilities to care for their children. When rating cases on how well the risk of harm has been managed, reviewers also consider the effectiveness of services in reducing the risk of harm to children. They also take into account other interventions used by the agency to ameliorate the risk, such as developing safety plans, arranging respite care to assist parents, making temporary informal placements, or placing the child in foster care.

For the permanency outcomes, reviewers explore the steps taken by the agency to strengthen parents' relationships with their children who are in foster care. An example of this is the agency's efforts to support regular visiting and other forms of contact. Such efforts include coordinating or providing transportation, developing clear visiting plans, using flexible meeting locations for visits, and communicating to families the reasons for restrictions or prohibitions on visits. Recognizing the effects of placement proximity on visiting frequency, the reviews also address the proximity of the child's foster care placement to the parents. Here reviewers examine how the location of the child's placement supports the achievement of the case plan goal and affects the ability of parents to maintain a meaningful role in the lives of their child in foster care, including decisionmaking on important issues, participating in activities with the child, attending school functions, and sharing special occasions with the child. In rating cases, distinctions are made with regard to placements outside the child's community, county, or state for reasons of convenience or the lack of closer placement resources, as opposed to making such placements to meet specialized needs of a child that cannot be met otherwise.

The well-being outcomes also address parental capacity to care for their children in several ways, most notably in that one of the three well-being outcomes is "families have enhanced capacity to provide for their children's needs." One indicator of this outcome captures how the needs of family members are assessed and matched to services, thus emphasizing the importance of identifying and responding to underlying needs of parents that may be far more significant than the presenting problems that parents bring to the agency. This indicator acknowledges that when agencies only address presenting symptoms and not the underlying needs behind those symptoms, the likelihood is greatly diminished that parents can achieve a level of change sufficient to adequately care for their children. Identifying and addressing underlying needs requires a more comprehensive case planning and assessment process than many state agencies now use. By including such measures as described above, the review process itself serves as an advocate for the use of meaningful case planning approaches.

In another well-being example, an indicator addresses the level of contact between caseworkers and parents, including the frequency, quality, and substance of contacts. This indicator is based on the assumption that caseworkers must have consistent and meaningful contact with parents if they are to help parents improve their ability to meet their children's needs and to actively engage parents in activities that support this goal.

Finally, it is worth noting that the actual process of gathering information in the CFSRs, apart from the indicators and outcomes subject to review, serves to promote the theme of strengthening parental capacity by requiring reviewers to actually interview parents and ask them about issues that are critical to their functioning. Although it would be easier, and certainly more expedient, to rely on written documentation to gather information and assess outcomes, the reviews require the input of parents and others in coming to conclusions about states' performance. Through such heavy reliance on parental input, the reviews model the concept that similar levels of input are essential to the day-to-day case practices that occur between state child welfare agencies and the families they serve.

Individualizing Services to Children and Families

The ability of state agencies to individualize services to children and families is linked programmatically to the theme of strengthening parental capacity, in that parental capacity is not likely to be strengthened if the unique strengths and needs of the parents are not addressed through case planning and service delivery. Both themes are played out in the reviews in a systemic perspective through the service array available to children and families and, from a practice perspective, through the indicator that addresses assessment and service provision.

Systemically, the reviews cover the capacity of states to provide services that can be designed and tailored to the unique needs of children and families, as opposed to offering predetermined categories of services, regardless of their fit to individual needs. The tasks confronting states here include providing funds for services that are flexible enough to permit developing individualized services as needed, training staff to identify and assess for individual needs, and developing the capacity of service providers to respond to the individual, and sometimes highly unusual, needs of children and families with appropriate services.

Arguably, among the most difficult tasks of states in this area are coming to consensus over what it means to individualize services and orienting staff at the front line to think in terms of assessing for individual needs as they approach their work with children and families. In training reviewers to evaluate this area, distinctions are made between needs, such as a parent's need to control substance abuse or a child's need to

control behavior in school, and services, such as parenting classes or respite care. The reviews model the approach of first assessing what is needed by the individuals in a case before deciding which services are most appropriately matched for the identified needs. This approach is also designed to point out the pitfalls of approaches to case planning that might conclude, for example, that an individual needs parenting classes (a service), when the real need might be to control substance abuse, a need for which parenting classes would likely be ineffective.

Although this distinction may seem fairly simplistic, it carries major implications for a state agency's capacity to serve children and families in an individualized manner, because identifying individualized needs serves no useful purpose if the agency is not equipped to respond to those needs with appropriate services. Thus in evaluating the service array from a systemic perspective, the reviews address the states' flexibility to create new services when needed and to adapt existing services to respond to individual needs. The issue of accessibility, as with community-based services, is also a systemic consideration. Frontline staff must be able to access the funds and service providers required to put the correct services in place when necessary. Through the statewide assessment, the state evaluates its own system in this light, considering its capacity to individualize across the array of services, the effectiveness of the services it has in place, and gaps in the service array. In the on-site review, stakeholders are asked to consider the capacity of the system to individualize services and the adequacy of existing services to meet identified needs. This information can then be used by the state to shape plans to strengthen its capacity to support practice that individualizes services.

In reviewing at the practice level, reviewers examine how the individual needs of children and families are met in specific cases. With regard to permanency outcomes, for example, reviewers explore the fit of services in relation to the child's established permanency goal. In the well-being outcomes, reviewers evaluate specific services provided to meet the educational, physical, and mental health needs of children. In the safety outcomes, they evaluate services provided to protect children in their homes and prevent removal, when remaining at home is the appropriate plan for a child. It has not been uncommon for reviewers to identify concerns with the quality and thoroughness of assessments in identifying the needs of family members, particularly those needs that contribute to abuse and neglect of children or unresolved permanency issues. Furthermore, the reviews have the ability to note those situations in which needs have been correctly identified, but not responded to through the provision of individualized services, such as responding to a child's trauma from sexual abuse or witnessing domestic violence.

The theme of individualizing services to children and families is one that affects state performance across all the outcomes, as the safety, permanency, and well-being of children can be easily compromised if the root problems affecting the outcomes are not identified and treated. At best, in the absence of adequate capacity in this area both systemically and in daily practice, agencies risk making faulty decisions about permanency goals or extend the time needed to achieve permanency for children.

Community-Based Services

Finally, following the theme of community-based services, the CFSRs build on the principles outlined in federal regulations designed to guide states in developing the state plans. These principles frame the concept of community-based services in such terms as timeliness, flexibility, coordination, and accessibility of services; provision of services in the families' home or community; parental involvement in service design and delivery; and respect for the culture and strengths of families and their communities.

Similarly, one way in which the reviews evaluate community-based service delivery from a systemic perspective is by examining the array of services offered to meet the needs of children and families, first through the types of services available and second through the accessibility of those services. The reviews evaluate the range of services on the basis of available services to support families and prevent the removal of children, to protect children in their homes, and to support reunification or achievement of other permanency goals. In locations where there is a prominent incidence of specialized service needs, such as needs to control substance abuse or domestic violence or to help children deal with the effects of sexual abuse, the reviews also address the availability of services to address those particular needs.

In evaluating the accessibility of services, reviewers look not only at where the services are actually located, but also at such issues as waiting lists and the costs of services, the extent to which available providers are able to work in the social context of the families they serve, and the flexibility of the agency and providers in bringing services to children and families. It has not been uncommon for the reviews to identify a broad array of services in place in a state, albeit with significant barriers to children and families accessing the services to the degree necessary to achieve their goals. In particular, and not surprisingly, the reviews have identified major challenges for states in providing the range of services needed in rural environments, where providers are sparse. However, the reviews have identified a number of effective approaches that support the availability and accessibility of services, such as states arranging for providers from more heavily populated areas to make periodic visits to less populated areas, the use of paraprofessionals as service providers, arranging for service provision on a regional level, and providing supports (e.g., transportation) to children and families that enable them to access services.

The focus on community-based services in the CFSRs also carries through to the systemic factor of agency responsiveness to the community. Clearly, many needs of children and families for services related to their safety, permanency, and well-being cross the boundaries of agencies other than the state or local child welfare agency. Furthermore, the ability of families to meet the long-term needs of their members is tied to the nurture and ongoing support they obtain from their communities. Therefore, the reviews evaluate the extent to which the states engage in collaboration and coordination of services with a range of stakeholders, such as other public and private child and family services agencies, tribes, faith-based organizations, and leaders and providers, to create a strong community-based array of services.

Beyond the systemic perspective, the reviews evaluate how well actual case practice reflects community-based service delivery. The permanency outcome, "the continuity of family relationships and connections is preserved for children," is an example of how some outcomes and indicators evaluate and underscore the importance of community-based services. Reviewers evaluate this outcome on the basis of such indicators as the proximity of a child's foster care placement to his or her parents, recognizing that close proximity supports increased visiting, more opportunity for parents to participate in planning and caring for their children in foster care, and the timely achievement of permanency goals. The outcome also includes indicators that evaluate the use of relatives as placement resources for children and the agency's efforts to preserve the primary connections and characteristics of children in foster care. This inclusion recognizes the inherent tie between these indicators, the child's community or cultural context, and the services needed.

Similarly, reviewers rate the two well-being outcomes, "children receive appropriate services to meet their educational needs" and "children receive adequate services to meet their physical and mental health needs," on the basis of indicators tied closely to the community-based services theme. The education outcome includes, among other items, an evaluation of

whether children must change schools as a result of being placed in foster care and of agency efforts to maintain some measure of continuity in the child's school placement. The physical and mental health outcome presents an opportunity to determine how effectively the agency is providing for health screening, preventive care, and treatment of identified needs for children, as well as the accessibility of services to meet these specialized needs. The reviews focus attention on both the agency's ability to meet these needs and the strengths and gaps in the service array. Common examples of such gaps identified by the reviews include the lack of dental providers in some communities to provide services to children served by the child welfare agency and a lack of flexible, community-based mental health providers to serve emotionally disturbed children.

Implications for Program Improvements

The goal of the CFSRs is to help states realize improved outcomes for the children and families they serve. Although the information-gathering portion of the CFSR process is critical, the most important aspect of the review is how states use the information to make needed program improvements. In identifying both strengths and needs in state programs, the reviews provide the basis for meaningful program improvement plans (PIPs) that have the potential to create lasting systemic change in state child welfare programs.

The implications for states as they develop and implement PIPs following the CFSRs are substantial. To achieve true systemic reforms that reflect the themes of family-centered practice, strengthening parents' capacity to provide for their children's needs, individualizing services to children and families, and community-based services, state child welfare agencies must engage other systems that serve the same populations. For example, the courts, education system, mental health system, juvenile justice, tribes, and others in the child welfare field must have meaningful roles in developing and implementing PIPs if states are to see major improvements in outcomes. As evidence, in examining the findings across the states that ACF reviewed in the first 2 years of the initial CFSR, ACF found that states with strong case review systems were more likely to have positive findings on certain other performance measures, including timely adoptions, performing adequate needs assessments of family members and providing appropriate services, engaging parents in case planning decisions, and frequent caseworker visits with parents (Administration for Children and Families 2004). Because the case review system evaluates the interface between the courts and child welfare agencies in certain activities, the implication is that collaboration between child welfare agencies and the courts is an important component of seeking improved practices and outcomes.

States will also need to examine how and if frontline practices reflect the principles that underlie the agency's goals and mission. For example, although strengthening parents' capacity to provide for their children's needs is an underlying principle of the CFSR, and probably one that most child welfare agencies would ascribe to, among the 15 states that ACF reviewed in federal FY2002, ACF found significantly higher ratings on certain items in foster care cases than in cases involving intact families receiving services in their own homes. The differences included such important indicators as controlling the risk of harm to children; the frequency of caseworker visits with children; and addressing children's educational, physical health, and mental health needs. Similarly, although most child welfare agencies would probably see family-centered practice as a part of their mission and goals, among this same group of states, ACF found significantly more positive performance in how the agencies addressed the mothers' needs in families in comparison to the fathers' needs (Administration for Children and Families 2004). Both examples signal the need to examine practice in light

of mission and goals as agencies seek to improve outcomes.

In the future, the states will need to approach program improvement planning in very thoughtful ways to address the scope of changes needed. For example, given the time frames associated with PIPs, states need to approach planned changes incrementally and identify realistic goals. The PIP should include goals that clearly prioritize improvements in those areas having the direst consequences for children and families, particularly areas of practice that affect child safety, while giving due attention to all areas identified as needing improvement. States also need to address those areas needing improvement that cross the lines of outcomes and systemic factors covered in the CFSRs. For example, improvements in comprehensive assessments and improving case planning will not only affect the well-being outcomes subject to review, but can be expected to affect the safety and permanency of children served by the agency. Again, the findings of the reviews conducted over the first 2 years of the CFSR support this concept. Among the 15 states that ACF reviewed in federal FY2002, for example, there was a correlation between frequent caseworker visits with children and positive performance on five of the seven CFSR outcomes, including one safety outcome, both permanency outcomes, and two of the well-being outcomes. There was also a correlation between frequent caseworker visits and 14 of the 23 individual performance indicators in the CFSR, crossing the lines of the safety, permanency, and well-being outcomes (Administration for Children and Families 2004). This finding suggests that improvements in certain day-to-day practices, such as the frequency of caseworker contact with children, can have far-reaching effects in multiple outcomes for children and families.

Finally, the states are faced not only with developing and implementing strategies for change, but with determining how to measure and evaluate the effectiveness of those changes on the lives of children and families and on the agency's ability to serve them. Implementing measurable improvements is central to the PIP process. Requirements include that the PIP establish benchmarks of progress toward final goals, identify specific percentages of improvement to be made in data indicators, and prescribe methods to be used in evaluating the success of the plan. This focus extends to developing the agency's capacity to monitor itself over time, especially from an outcome-based perspective. In this sense, quality assurance is both a systemic factor subject to the CFSRs and an effective way for states to monitor and measure their progress as they implement PIPs. Where states either develop or adapt their internal quality assurance systems to track and measure program improvements, they should expect to greatly increase their ability to gauge their progress over time, make corrections as needed, and gain the information needed to maintain progress.

Conclusion

CFSRs represent an unprecedented opportunity and an enormous responsibility for both the states and the federal government. The opportunity to work collaboratively to effect lasting changes in the ways that public child welfare systems respond to the needs of children and families carries with it the responsibility to make the most of the opportunity by implementing changes that will stand the test of time. By focusing on both frontline child welfare practice and the systemic supports for practice at the local level, the reviews present an opportunity for states to make changes where

their effects can be felt the most, in the lives of children and families. Furthermore, by framing the review process and program improvement planning within well-established, practice-oriented themes, the reviews provide context and standards against which states can evaluate their current functioning and the goals they are working to achieve.

The CFSRs also provide an agenda for change in the nation's child welfare system that will be judged according to what happens to children and families as a result of their involvement with child welfare. However, along with the expectations for change brought forward by this process comes the reality that significant and lasting change will not be achieved easily or quickly. The needs for improvement identified by the reviews thus far are significant. They require substantial resources and thoughtful planning to correct. States that failed to achieve substantial conformity on all or most of the seven outcomes examined in the first round of reviews cannot be expected to suddenly bring all of those outcomes into substantial conformity over the course of one or two program improvement plans. Instead, the CFSRs represent a long-term approach to dealing with the very complex problems in public child welfare services. Although everything cannot be repaired at once, the careful use of information from the reviews, coupled with reasoned planning through the PIP process, offers the hope of immediate changes in some of the most critical areas of practice, followed by measurable and lasting improvements across the spectrum of child and family services.

References

Administration for Children and Families. (2004). *Key findings from the initial Child and Family Service Reviews 2001 to 2004.* Retrieved October 30, 2004, from www.acf.hhs.gov/programs/cb/cwrp/results/index.htm.

Annie E. Casey Foundation. (2004). *Kids count data book: State profiles of child well-being.* Baltimore: Annie E. Casey Foundation.

Child and Family Services. (2000). *Procedures manual.* Washington, DC: U.S. Department of Health and Human Services.

Hartman, A., & Laird, J. (eds.). (1985). *The child welfare handbook.* New York: Free Press.

Johnson, H., Cournoyer, D., Fliri, J., Flynn, M., Grant, A., et al. (2003). Are we parent-friendly? Views of parents of children with emotional and behavioral disabilities. *Families in Society, 84,* 231–244.

Milner, J., Mitchell, L., & Hornsby, W. (2001). The Child and Family Service Review: A framework for changing practice. *Journal of Family Social Work, 6*(4), 5–18.

National Child Welfare Resource Center for Family-Centered Practice. (2000). *Best practice, next practice.* Washington, DC: National Child Welfare Resource Center for Family-Centered Practice.

Pires, S. (2002). *Building systems of care, a primer.* Washington, DC: Georgetown University Child Development Center, National Technical Assistance Center for Children's Mental Health.

Stroul, B., & Friedman, R. (1986). *A system of care for children and youth with severe emotional disturbances,* revised ed. Washington, DC: Georgetown University Child Development Center, National Technical Assistance Center for Children's Mental Health.

Zlotnik, J., & John-Langba, J. (2002). *Research on family-centered practice: An annotated bibliography with commentary.* Washington, DC: Institute for the Advancement of Social Work Research.

KRIS SAHONCHIK
BETH FRIZSELL
MARY O'BRIEN

Strategic Planning for Child Welfare Agencies

"Would you tell me, please, which way I ought to go from here?"

"That depends a good deal on where you want to get to," said the cat.

"I don't know where . . . ," said Alice.

"Then it doesn't matter which way you go," said the cat.

Lewis Carroll's *Alice in Wonderland*

To achieve outcomes for children and families professionals in the field of child welfare must have a vision of what they hope to achieve and a strategy to guide the way. But organizing work to achieve selected outcomes is difficult with competing, and often changing, demands. Frequently there is a lack of direction —a lack of agreement or understanding—as to the desired outcomes. Contradictions exist between what is targeted in practice and what is targeted by management and supervision. Similarly, the systems that support the work— information, training, and services—appear to be focused in different directions (Edwards, Yankey, & Altpeter 1998; Herman & Associates 1994).

In this chapter, we explain how a strategic planning process can help agencies serving children and families achieve desired results and how the rational and all-encompassing features of strategic planning can overcome barriers to change. We address three key questions: What is strategic planning? Why do it? How does one develop, implement, and monitor a strategic plan?

What Is Strategic Planning?

Strategic planning is a continual process for improving organizational performance by developing strategies to produce results. It involves looking at where the agency wants to go, assessing the agency's current situation, and developing and implementing approaches for moving forward (Blackerby 1994; Boyle 2001; Bryant 1997; Bryson 1995). Planning is strategic when it focuses on what the agency wants to accomplish and on moving the agency toward these larger goals. By constantly focusing attention on a shared vision and on specific goals and objectives, strategic planning has the potential to permeate the culture of the agency, becoming a tool for creating systemic change. Leaders at all levels—directors, managers, supervisors, and caseworkers, as well as external partners—are engaged in developing a sense of direction and identifying priorities (Barry 1986).

Strategic planning is not a one-time event, but an ongoing process for systemic change. Agencies need to prepare to plan by developing a vision, conducting assessments, and implementing a planning process (Harper 2001; Pearlmutter 1998). They can then develop, write, and finalize the plan. Implementation includes managing, supervising, and monitoring progress on the plan. Finally, the plan is revised as needed to keep it current and active. Ongoing communication is critical throughout the process.

This continuous cycle is similar to the child and family assessment and case planning process (Cassafer 1996; Romney 1996). The strength of the family case plan or service plan is dependent on the quality of the assessment of the family's needs and the strategies developed in the plan to use appropriate services and resources to build on the family's strengths. Routine case reviews help to monitor the implementation, progress, and effectiveness of the plan. If the plan is not helping the families reach their goals or outcomes, it is time to reassess and revise the strategies (Hodge-Williams, Spratley, & Wynn 1998). Just as a strong case planning process is critical to achieving individual child and family goals, a strong strategic planning process is critical to achieving agency goals.

Why Conduct Strategic Planning?

Outcomes: The strategic planning process is a powerful tool that agencies can use to improve outcomes for children and families (Kaufman 1992; Lorange & Vancil 1977). Such improvement is especially important as federal and state funding sources require defined and measurable outcomes and monitor agency performance on these outcomes.

Best practice: Organizations that have developed national standards for the management of child welfare agencies—the Child Welfare League of America, the Council on Accreditation of Services for Children and Families, and the National Association of Public Child Welfare Administrators—all specify that agencies develop a strategic plan (Cassafer 1996).

Accountability: There is a national movement to increase accountability for child welfare services in light of media coverage regarding tragic child abuse and neglect cases, child fatalities, children "lost" in child welfare systems, and the lack of data on child welfare. Strategic planning can produce data on agency performance and show the agency's commitment to quality services for children and families.

Focus: Joint development, distribution, and implementation of the strategic plan make all staff members and stakeholders more aware of the agency's purpose and overall direction. It helps insure that everyone is working together in a concerted effort for the same purpose.

Strategic allocation: A strategic planning process provides a framework within which agencies can make decisions about priorities and allocation of resources. Administrators and supervisors can determine how resources, time, and effort will be deployed.

Direction and meaning: When strategic plans are fully implemented, they help caseworkers see how their day-to-day work with children and families connects to agency goals. A strategic plan can also help managers at all levels see how the work they supervise helps the agency move in desired directions.

Change: The continual cycle of strategic planning allows state agencies to look at needs, evaluate progress, and adapt as needs change.

Strengths: Strategic planning processes identify areas needing improvement and areas of strength in the agency and in the environment. When the planning group is selecting and prioritizing outcomes and strategies, they can build on strengths to address areas of need.

Multiple plans: Federal requirements for the 5-year Child and Family Service Plan (CFSP) include integration of multiple plans, such as elements of the Program Improvement Plan (PIP), the Title IV-E training plan, the Child Abuse Prevention and Treatment Act (CAPTA) annual plan, statewide foster and adoption recruitment plan, and the Chafee Independent Living Five-Year plan. Although many states have just appended each plan as separate sections or appendixes, strategic planning can provide a forum to examine and integrate multiple plans. At any opportunity, such as when a new 5-year CFSP is due, the state should work toward integrating other state plans that may have been developed since the previous CFSPs were completed.

Coordinate efforts: A strategic planning process helps agencies coordinate work across units and divisions to avoid duplication. For example, human service agencies that have a common vision to support families can coordinate Title IV-B family support programs with prevention efforts funded under the economic assistance/ Temporary Aid to Needy Families program and maximize the effectiveness of both programs.

Federal and State Requirements

CFSP. State child welfare agencies are required to develop comprehensive 5-year CFSPs under Title IV-B. The Child and Family Services Review process was developed in response to a 1994 Congressional mandate to insure compliance with state plan requirements. The review builds directly on requirements for the CFSP; elements of the PIPs developed in response to the Child and Family Services Review process must be integrated into the CFSP.

PIP. The Child and Family Services Review process is a comprehensive assessment of agency strengths and needs, focused on seven specific outcomes and seven systemic factors. The final report specifies the areas needing improvement to reach substantial conformity with federal standards. States must then develop PIPs that specify how they will make systemic improvements.

Federal and state requirements for planning have often been established in response to calls for greater efficiency and/or increased accountability. Federal and state legislators have increasingly required child welfare agencies to define agency goals and priorities, and/or to report regularly on outcomes. In some states (e.g., California), legislation has launched planning initiatives to move the government forward, requiring agencies to participate in a process of setting goals, developing work plans to achieve them, and regularly assessing progress (Osborne & Gaebler 1992; Osborne & Pastrik 1997). To the extent possible, these state planning processes

should be coordinated with federally required planning processes.

How to Develop a Strategic Plan
Define the Terms, Develop a Process, and Select a Format

All planners have experienced the confusion that results when a planning process uses undefined or inaccurate terms. Sometimes what one person says in no way resembles what another person hears. When this happens in an organization, the confusion can lead to frustration, misunderstanding, and mistakes. When it happens in the strategic planning process, it can lead to wasted effort and even failure of the plan.

Child welfare agencies use a wide variety of terms to describe the content of strategic plans. For example, some use "goals" and others use "outcomes" to describe the aim or result of the agency's work. In its annual report to Congress, the federal government calls "reduce recurrence of abuse and neglect" an outcome, whereas in the Child and Family Service Review process, it is referred to as a "performance indicator" of progress toward a broader outcome of children being protected from abuse and neglect (U.S. Department of Health and Human Services 2002:1212). The use of terms is guided by the context in the agency—the federal requirements for the planning process, the terms required by state processes or laws, or the terms that are familiar to those involved in the planning process (Bryson & Alston 1996; California State Department of Finance 1998). To avoid misunderstanding and confusion, planners should choose terms early on, define them, and insure that everyone understands, agrees with, and uses the same terms throughout the planning process (Admininstration for Children and Families 1997).

Planners should examine the principles, values, and beliefs that guide the agency and the vision that defines the ultimate goal and purpose of the agency. The vision provides a framework for the strategic planning process by defining the direction and results the agency hopes to achieve.

The planning process should include input from agency administrators and staff and community stakeholders. Federal requirements, national standards, and strategic planning literature consistently point to the need to involve a broad range of stakeholders in planning. A planning group, with clearly defined roles and responsibilities, facilitates an effective planning process.

Those involved in planning need to choose a format for the type of plan they want to produce. A matrix that creates a visual picture of the agency's plan is an effective way to organize a large amount of information in a format that is easy to communicate and share with staff, stakeholders, and external partners. An accompanying narrative can provide information necessary to understand the matrix and to further explain the content of the plan. The format should enable planners to test the feasibility of the strategy with regard to the outcomes desired.

A standard format for any strategic plan should include:

- Outcomes (the desired results or expected consequences of the plan) and/or goals (the aim, purpose, directions, or priorities of the plan that can be measured);
- Strategies (the broader efforts undertaken to achieve agency goals or outcomes);
- Objectives (the measurable steps taken to accomplish the goal or outcome within the established time frames);
- Action steps (more specific actions undertaken to accomplish the strategies or objectives and demonstrate progress toward the goals or outcomes);
- Quantitative measures (indicators of progress that can be expressed in numerical terms, counted, or compared on a scale);
- Qualitative measures (indicators of progress that are process-oriented and difficult to capture in numerical terms);

- Benchmarks (defined in federal PIP instructions as "interim and measurable indicators that will be assessed to determine if progress is being made towards achieving the established goal"; Administration for Children and Families 1997:122);
- Responsible parties (individuals or units assigned responsibility for carrying out the strategies, objectives, or action steps); and
- Time frames (expectations about when plan activities and goals will be initiated and accomplished).

Define Priorities and Conduct an Assessment

To identify priority areas, planners should consider both the needs of the agency and how they can build on agency strengths. Questions to consider include:

- What are the most significant issues the agency faces?
- Where can improvements be made?
- What strengths can be built on?
- Which target areas will have the greatest impact on outcomes?
- What resources (e.g., staff, funds) are available or could be made available?

An analysis of performance and infrastructure provides a basic understanding of organizational capacity. A strong assessment can help agencies identify strengths that can be used to address weak areas and become familiar with the capabilities of existing data sources. Planners can draw on this knowledge to establish agency goals and the measures and indicators that will be used to track progress.

Write the Plan

After reviewing the assessment and prioritizing target areas, planners need to develop the content of the plan. They need to answer three key questions and insure that leads and time frames are identified.

What Does the Agency Need to Accomplish?

Planners must define clearly what the agency needs to accomplish, often expressed as the agency goals or outcomes. Outcomes are often broader statements about the desired results of agency work, whereas goals are more specific priorities that can be measured. Often several goals relate to an outcome. These statements should build directly on the analysis done during the assessment. Some guidelines for developing specific statements that express what the agency should accomplish are:

- Use the agency vision to guide the selection of goals and outcomes. This is critical to institutionalizing the vision within the agency.
- Develop clear statements of goals and outcomes.
- Consider any mandated goals or outcomes for the type of plan being developed.
- Look for opportunities to build on strengths. Although agencies may be failing to meet certain standards, virtually all agencies do some things well and such strengths should not be ignored.
- Consider how to track progress, including identifying indicators/measures that will be used and considering the state of the available data and data systems. Planners can build on available data or consider strategies for obtaining additional information.
- Consider whether the goals, outcomes, and related activities of the plan could be integrated with other plans that guide the agency's work.

What Can Be Done to Accomplish the Goals?

After determining what the agency wants to accomplish, the planning focus becomes what will be done to reach those goals and/or outcomes. Drawing on the assessment, the planning group needs to brainstorm and choose strategies, objectives, and/or action steps that address these areas. The agency can consider:

- Strategies most likely to produce the desired results, from model programs, benchmarking, or improvements made by similar agencies;

- Strategies and action steps that make the most sense to stakeholders and staff;
- Activities that can be undertaken with available resources;
- Strategies and activities that can be sustained over time;
- Approaches that address significant barriers to change;
- Strategies that take advantage of agency strengths;
- Pilots, demonstration projects, or practice strategies implemented in targeted sites; and
- Evidence-based practice initiatives—national review of evaluation and research results from various state initiatives or models.

Many problems that child welfare agencies face, such as low permanency rates or high levels of reabuse, are multifaceted and complex. Agencies are often tempted to implement a simple improvement to attempt to fix the problem in the short-term. However, systemic change that will be sustained over time often requires broader strategies that impact a number of different systems.

How Will Progress Be Defined and Measured?

A common mistake made by planners is to develop a plan that clearly defines what the agency wants to accomplish and what the agency will do to get there, but does not include a strategy for measuring progress. For example, some plans do not include measures or indicators to track progress, whereas others include these in the plan but never implement monitoring and reporting systems. Without knowing if implementation of the plan has made any difference, the planning process risks being judged an unproductive drain on agency resources. To know if a plan is effective, it is essential to routinely measure, review, and evaluate all components of the plan (Mercer 1991; Monahan 2001; Rossi & Freeman 1985).

There are two ways to monitor progress. The first is to track the progress made toward the goals and outcomes, or toward what the agency wants to accomplish. This method tracks the impact of what the agency is doing. The second is to track implementation of the specific strategies and action steps in the plan or the activities the agency is implementing to accomplish the goals or outcomes. There are different types of indicators or measures that agencies can use to monitor progress in these two areas: quantitative and qualitative.

Quantitative measures reflect information that can be expressed in numerical terms, counted, or compared on a scale. These are the numbers, rates, percentages, or statistics that are used to measure progress, such as the number of available foster families or the number of children adopted. Sources for these measures can be either agency data systems or program reports.

Qualitative measures reflect information that is difficult to measure, count, or express in numerical terms (Administration for Children and Families 1997). These measures include processes that assess participants' impressions, judgments, or experiences with services, often through observation, intensive case reviews, interviews, or focus groups. Examples include families' impressions about their involvement in the case planning process.

For any measure or indicator that uses numbers, the agency must gather baseline information on performance on that indicator. Having the baseline allows agencies to track trends over time and judge the significance of changes in the numbers. This tracking will help the agency establish performance targets over specified periods. For example, the agency might aim to increase the percentage of foster and/or adoptive homes that reflect the racial or ethnic makeup of children in foster care. If 54% of the children in out-of-home care are children of color and 36% of foster home placements are with families of color, the agency might aim to increase from the baseline of 36% to 40% over a 12-month period.

In monitoring progress toward goals and outcomes, agencies need to choose indicators that measure the result of the activities and processes with respect to the established goals. The ultimate result or outcome that the agency is aiming for must be measured and tracked over time. In choosing indicators or measures, agencies also need to consider the data they have available and how they can obtain additional data.

To monitor progress on strategies and action steps, agencies often use qualitative measures. For example, an action step might be: establish an adoptive parent advisory board to help the agency develop innovative strategies for adoptive parent recruitment. The measure would then be: the adoptive parent advisory board is established within 3 months. An adoptive parent recruitment plan, including innovative strategies, is then developed in 6 months.

To the extent possible, these measures should also reflect the impact of the activities. For example, a measure that reflects the impact would be: increase in the number of adoptive parent inquiries resulting from the implementation of the new recruitment strategies.

For most plans, there will be both long-term and short-term indicators of progress. For example, if a long-term goal is to increase the number of foster families from 1,700 to 2,000 over the next 2 years, a short-term indicator might be increasing the number of African American foster families from 500 to 600 in 1 year.

Determine Oversight Responsibility and Time Frames

In developing the plan, two additional components need to be addressed: Who will be responsible for the activities within the plan? When will the activities and goals be completed?

Assigning responsible parties is critical to insuring that the plan is fully implemented; such assignments are typically made by senior management or the core planning group. The person who is responsible should have in his or her purview of authority the ability to accomplish the task. These staff will also play an important role in the management and supervision of the plan and will routinely report progress to the plan manager and/or planning group. Staff responsible for various activities must be clearly identified and must understand their responsibilities (Edwards, Yankey, & Altpeter 1998; Herman & Associates 1994; *Notes from the Field* 1998).

The agency senior management or core planning group needs to review the overall plan and determine appropriate time frames for initiating and completing the activities. Activities need to be sequenced, based on realistic increments of time and the availability of resources necessary to carry out the required work. The priority assigned to these activities needs to be reflected in the time frames for initiation and completion in the plan. For example, safety is paramount, so if response times on child protection investigations need to be improved, the timeframe for the activities to improve response time should be immediate.

Once those involved in planning have developed a draft plan, the draft should be circulated for additional input, and revised as necessary. Finalizing the plan involves two steps. The first is sharing the final plan with the stakeholders and staff who provided input throughout the process. This review gives the planning group an opportunity to explain how and why input was or was not incorporated. It also gives staff and stakeholders an opportunity to review the plan in its final form and builds consensus on the plan.

After the plan is finalized and approved, the second step is to publish the plan and share it with everyone who will implement the plan, including the planning group, agency staff, and other external partners or stakeholders (Fogg 1999). Approaches to distributing the plan include:

- Publish hard copies and distribute them to the press, legislators, agency heads, community leaders, tribes, and other stakeholders;
- Post the plan on a state or department Web site;
- Hold a press conference to announce the plan;
- Convene stakeholder forums to disseminate the plan;
- Distribute copies to all staff;
- Train managers, supervisors, and staff on the contents of the plan; and
- Reconvene the planning group to share and review the final plan.

As the plan is implemented and revised, it needs to be continually communicated. Just like the agency vision, the components of the plan must be communicated and reinforced throughout the agency and the community. Approaches include:

- Insuring that any decisionmaking processes in the organization (e.g., policy, budget) consider the elements of the strategic plan;
- Presenting updates on progress in meetings with agency managers; and
- Incorporating components of the plan into both initial and ongoing in-service training for managers, supervisors, and staff.

Implement the Plan

Too often, strategic plans are written but never implemented, sitting unused on office shelves. In an effective strategic planning process, a plan is written that is then widely shared and used both in the agency and the broader community. The implementation stage involves communicating the plan, managing its implementation, supervising the actual work, and monitoring and reporting progress (Barry 1986).

Agency leaders are responsible for implementing and managing the plan. Usually, they assign managers with the authority to delegate responsibilities. As the plan often requires changes or actions by stakeholders outside the child welfare agency, plan managers, in conjunction with other agency managers, need to communicate and coordinate with other agencies and community-based groups.

As the planning groups were instrumental in developing the plan, they also have a key role in ongoing management of the plan. Planning groups should convene on a regular basis to maintain a focus on the activities and outcomes in the plan (Edwards, Yankey, & Altpeter 1998; Herman & Associates 1994; *Notes from the Field* 1998). Their roles can include:

- Reviewing the implementation of activities;
- Monitoring progress on the outcomes and measures;
- Assisting agency management and the plan manager in carrying out the plan (e.g., by identifying additional resources, brainstorming on approaches to overcoming barriers);
- Assisting in the development of quarterly and annual reports on progress; and
- Using data or information from assessments to guide revisions to the plan.

Plan managers and planning groups should consider how to integrate the goals and outcomes of different plans developed by the agency. Coordinating agency plans can reduce the workload of implementing and reporting on separate plans and can increase the effectiveness of the efforts to move toward goals.

Managers at all levels—state, regional, or county, district, and unit—must supervise the work being done on the plan. Supervision must take place as the plan is being implemented and communicated to staff, as specific work plans are developed at various levels, and as data on progress are being reviewed.

Developing local plans engages managers and staff in implementing the strategic plan, as they take ownership of local goals, strategies, and action steps. These local plans translate the state plans into guides for the day-to-day work of local managers, supervisors, and caseworkers. Such local plans help insure that statewide strategic plans impact practice. For statewide PIPs, some states are asking counties or regions to develop their own plans for how they will implement the statewide plan in their

areas (U.S. Department of Health and Human Services 2001).

Local planning groups and staff can also be involved in the ongoing process of reviewing progress and revising the state and local plans as necessary. To support local planning, states must:

- Structure the planning process on the local level, clearly defining roles, responsibilities, and timeframes;
- Provide guidance on the state-level vision, outcomes, strategies, and objectives;
- Provide a format for local plans; and
- Provide a structure for reporting and monitoring local performance on outcomes, possibly linked to state quality assurance and information systems.

Monitoring the Plan

In the implementation stage, agencies need to develop reports and use them on a regular basis —daily, weekly, or monthly—to monitor progress on the plan. In addition to such routine monitoring, a comprehensive review of progress should take place on an ongoing basis quarterly, biannually, or annually, depending on the reporting requirements of the plan. For example, PIPs require quarterly and CFSPs require annual reports on progress. As progress is reviewed, those involved in planning should coordinate with quality assurance and information systems staff to build on and integrate plan reports with existing and new agency systems. The ongoing monitoring and comprehensive reviews of progress should assess both progress toward the goals and outcomes and that being made on implementing the plan.

In the process of reviewing progress on the plan, agency managers continually repeat the strategic planning process. The agency conducts ongoing assessments of its performance by gathering and analyzing information on agency performance. The planning structure is reconvened so that planning groups review performance and reassess the goals, outcomes, strategies, and action steps in the plan (Rainey 1997). The staff and stakeholders involved in the planning process consider changes to the plan, and the draft revised plan is circulated for comment and finalized. The revised plan is communicated widely, and responsibilities and work plans are revised. The revised plan is monitored and then revised again in this on-going process. To the extent that the plan is updated, it can stay current and meaningful to the organization.

Conclusion

As agencies serving children and families, guided by a vision, develop and communicate clear goals, outcomes, strategies, and measures, the resultant strategic planning can in turn be used to build consensus on a clear mission for the agency that provides direction and guides choices. The continual cycle of planning—including regular reassessment of needs and strategies—helps agencies adapt to change, correct mistakes, and allocate resources to areas of greatest need.

References

Administration for Children and Families. (1997). *The program managers' guide to evaluation.* Washington, DC: U.S. Department of Health and Human Services.

Barry, B. W. (1986). *Strategic planning work for nonprofit organizations.* Indianapolis, IN: Wilder Foundation.

Blackerby, P. (1994). History of strategic planning. *Armed Forces Comptroller, 39*(1), 23.

Boyle, P. (2001). From strategic planning to visioning: Tools for navigating the future. *Public Management, 83*(4), 23–27.

Bryant, S. (1997). Strategic management: Developing and realizing a strategic vision. *Public Management, 79*(1), 28–32.

Bryson, J. M. (1995) *Strategic planning for public and nonprofit organizations: A guide to strengthening and sustaining organizational achievement,* revised ed. San Fransisco: Jossey-Bass.

Bryson, J. M., & Alston, F. (1996). *Creating and implementing your strategic plan: A workbook for public and non-profit organizations.* San Francisco: Jossey-Bass.

California State Department of Finance. (1998). *Strategic planning guidelines.* Sacramento: California State Department of Finance.

Cassafer, D. J. (1996). How can planning make it happen? In P. Pecora, W. Seeling, F. Zirps, & S. Davis (eds.), *Quality improvement and evaluation in child and family services: Managing into the next century.* Washington, DC: Child Welfare League of America.

Edwards, R. L., Yankey, J. A., & Altpeter, M. A. (1998). *Skills for effective management of nonprofit organizations.* Washington, DC: NASW Press.

Fogg, C. D. (1999). *Implementing your strategic plan: How to turn intent into effective action for sustainable change.* New York: American Management Association.

Harper, S. C. (2001). *The forward thinking organization: Visionary thinking and breakthrough leadership to create your company's future.* New York: American Management Association.

Herman, R. D., & Associates. (1994). *The Jossey-Bass handbook on nonprofit leadership and management.* San Francisco: Jossey-Bass.

Hodge-Williams, J., Spratley, J. F., & Wynn, C. M. G. (1998). *Quality-centered, team-focused management.* Washington, DC: CWLA Press.

Kaufman, R. (1992). *Strategic planning plus—An organizational guide.* Newbury Park, CA: Sage.

Lorange, P., & Vancil, R. F. (1977). *Strategic planning systems.* Englewood Cliffs, NY: Prentice-Hall.

Mercer, J. L. (1991). *Strategic planning for public managers.* Westport, CT: Quorum Books.

Monahan, K. (2001). *Balanced measures for strategic planning: A public sector handbook.* Vienna, VA: Management Concepts.

Notes from the Field. (1998). Total quality management and the not for profit. *Administration in Social Work, 8*(1), 75–86.

Osborne, D., & Gaebler, T. (1992). *Reinventing government: How the entrepreneurial spirit is transforming the public sector.* Reading, MA: Addison-Wesley.

Osborne, D., & Pastrik, P. (1997). *Banishing bureaucracy: The five strategies for reinventing government.* New York: Penguin.

Pearlmutter, S. (1998). Self-efficacy and organizational leadership. *Administration in Social Work, 22*(3), 23–38.

Rainey, H. G. (1997). *Understanding and managing public organizations.* San Francisco: Jossey-Bass.

Romney, V. A. (1996). *Strategic planning and needs assessment.* Fairfax, VA: National Community Education Association.

Rossi, P., & Freeman, H. (1985*) Evaluation: A systemic approach.* Beverly Hills, CA: Sage.

U.S. Department of Heath and Human Services. (2001). *Child and Family Service Reviews procedure manual 2000:* Washington, DC: U.S. Department of Heath and Human Services.

U.S. Department of Heath and Human Services. (2002). *Child welfare outcomes 2001: Annual report.* Washington, DC: U.S. Department of Heath and Human Services.

ANN MORISON

Accreditation of Child Welfare Organizations

Accreditation is a well-established self-study and review process that can pinpoint strengths and areas of needed improvement in an organization's governance, operations, and services for public and private social service and behavioral healthcare providers. Agencies that pursue accreditation are prompted to rigorously plan for optimal use of resources, upgrade core conditions, enhance services, reduce preventable untoward events, and improve organizational performance and outcomes.

There are different approaches to accreditation, including variations in the elements of practice that are reviewed, how a self-assessment is developed, and how site visits are conducted. In this chapter, I do not compare and contrast accreditation methods. Instead, I describe in general terms the purpose and process of accreditation, using as my primary example the Council on Accreditation (COA). Founded in 1977 by Family Service of America and the Child Welfare League of America, COA is the principal accreditor of public and private child welfare agencies/providers. COA is one of three leading accreditors of child and family service organizations and behavioral healthcare services in the United States and Canada. Other prominent accreditors of health and human services in the United States include the Joint Commission on Accreditation of Healthcare Organizations, the Commission on Accreditation of Rehabilitation Facilities, and the National Association for the Education of Young Children.

In this chapter I also set forth the current context for accreditation, including broadened advocacy for implementation of research-based practice and achievement of positive outcomes during a time of severely reduced budgets, and examine the role that accreditation can play to help agencies meet demands for accountability.

The following section suggests that the methods used to manage and implement accreditation are of considerable importance. Accreditation standards offer practice guidelines that support positive outcomes; therefore, it becomes important for an organization to not "put on the shelf" what is learned about its practice. The accreditation process generates much information of potential use for planning and growth but, as is true of all data collection efforts, it should not be embarked on without a clear understanding of how the information will be used. Use is also a key topic because agency-based service providers are becoming more visibly attuned to concerns that emanate primarily from researchers in social services and healthcare about how frequently best practice guidelines are put into practice (Gambrill 1999; Rosen 2002; Zlotnik 2002). There now is a strong interest in human services fields in identifying methods that can increase the use of research in practice (Gira, Kessler, & Poertner 2001). Two perspectives are offered on the utility of accreditation. One perspective views accreditation as an end in itself; the second views accreditation is a means to an end. The former is of limited value: it does little to advance either ongoing learning or the flexibility that changing conditions and partnerships require. The chapter proposes that, alternatively, accreditation can be of unlimited value when viewed as a means to facilitate continuous long-term planning, achieving ever-stronger operations and better outcomes. The second perspective is advantageous, and necessary, for agencies receptive to new and fluid conditions and opportunities. A means-to-an-end view would be responsive, in particular, to child and family services providers that are committed to functioning as part of a system of care.

The decision for an agency to become accredited is usually voluntary and requires a significant commitment of resources. Thus it is advisable for child, youth, and family services professionals to have an understanding of how and why agencies choose to pursue accreditation.

Background

Although this chapter is concerned with accreditation of child welfare organizations, there are familiar examples from everyday life of how standards are set to encourage high quality. Standards to promote quality and protect health and safety are developed in many fields for various purposes.

Standard Setting in Everyday Life

Standards are developed for many different aspects of life, including stress testing limits for metals, hotel service and comfort ratings, sanitary ratings for restaurant kitchens, and energy efficiency ratings for appliances. Some standards, such as permissible auto emissions levels, are crafted in accordance with government mandates and can be developed in response to national public health and safety concerns. In this example, the cost of implementing the standard is shared among auto manufacturers, state inspection programs, and drivers. Other standards sort products into categories of quality or efficiency. All involve the application of standards developed through research and consultation with experts in a particular industry or field and are directed at making more open to public scrutiny practices that otherwise would be strictly internal (Hamm 1997). In the aforementioned examples, the process is not educa-

tional or participatory per se. The item to be approved or recognized is tested or reviewed on the basis of data and documentation, does or does not "measure up," and can be retested after corrective action is taken.

Standard Setting and Self-Examination for Providers of Child and Family Services

The field of child and family services, inclusive of child welfare and behavioral healthcare, has instituted accreditation for another purpose. In the field of child and family services, accreditation is a self-regulatory mechanism that promotes professionalism and provides a means for the field to continually search for the strongest evidence available to support best practice. An organization that pursues accreditation is saying, in effect: "let us examine our policies, procedures, and operations and compare them with nationally accepted standards of practice, so we can endorse or strengthen them as necessary to promote increased health, safety, and other positive outcomes for children and families." Such self-examination requires openness to learning and change. Those who complete the process attest that such a review is a catalyst for change and that change, especially deep, transformational change, is best accomplished by adopting a system-wide approach to accreditation. In this way, departments and staff normally separated by discipline and geography can appreciate how strategic planning guides resource allocation, how policies and procedures provide guidance, how services mesh across and beyond the organization, and how the components of multiservice efforts can combine to support positive change for children and families.

Depending on the philosophy and mission of the accreditation body, in addition to specific services, such as child protection and foster care, standards may cover leadership and management practices. The belief that governance, management, programs, and services are vital components of a well-functioning human services organization is consistent with recent efforts to identify key elements for a nonprofit capacity-building framework (DeVita & Fleming 2001). It is also in accordance with recent research on pathways to nonprofit excellence (Light 2002), described in greater detail later in the chapter. Although most accreditors concentrate on specific services, some focus on an entire organization. In either case, standards are typically written at the level of critical service components and generally do not prescribe at the microlevel of practice; that is, the standards do not get between the practitioner and service recipient. (However, some accreditation entities, such as National Association for Education of Young Children, do write standards at a practitioner level; e.g., the qualities of a positive teacher-parent relationship might be defined and reviewers would look for such qualities in teacher-parent interactions.)

Accreditation standards are based on research, expert opinion, and field comment; standards are reviewed and updated periodically in response to trends in the field and new practice knowledge. Some accreditation bodies revise select standards annually; others, such as COA, publish updates on an ongoing basis in response to requests from the field for a reassessment of practical application, in between publishing a complete new edition and support material every 4 or 5 years. Entities that develop policy advocacy oriented standards, such as the Child Welfare League of America, may operate on a timetable with a long horizon.

Accreditation standards are national standards that cite the need for professionals and organizations to hold proper credentials and licenses; thus accreditation endorses and is different from state licensing. Accreditation regards state and local licensure as a necessary but not always sufficient condition for insuring quality services.

Value Base and Value of Accreditation

Standards are not value free. For example, the values reflected in COA standards are: inclusion and respect for persons served; recognition of, connections with, and service in the child's and family's community; a strengths orientation; and cultural diversity and competence. Accountability is achieved through an organization's demonstrated effort to measure whether services provided in accordance with standards make a positive difference.

A core belief that undergirds accreditation is that productivity and accountability are necessary for achieving mission. More specifically, COA believes the value of accreditation for an organization rests with a guided self-examination of mission, governance, and resources (leadership and assets) directed at promoting high-quality performance (efficiency, sustainability, and outcomes measurement capacity), and of resource allocation through effective relationships and service delivery (services), aimed at achieving positive results.

This expectation is compatible with managed care, but accreditation should not be confused with managed care. A fundamental difference between accreditation and managed care is the emphasis managed care places on cost containment vs. an emphasis on service quality that leads to positive outcomes. Although accreditation standards promote skilled stewardship of limited resources, accreditation goes beyond an interest in measures of agency performance and amount of service delivered, sometimes referred to as "output," to support positive outcomes.

Human services organizations seek accreditation because accreditation is considered to be of direct benefit to agency staff members dedicated to a high standard of service delivery. Two recent surveys (M. Christopher, pers. comm.) of accredited private agencies conducted by a national and state association on behalf of members identified benefits at the level of improved agency performance. The surveys were designed to identify areas of satisfaction with and needed improvement in the COA accreditation process. Perceived benefits included:

- Clarification of policy;
- Improvement and standardization of procedures;
- Facilitation of internal administrative and service consistency;
- Adoption of best practices;
- Eligibility to apply for and receive contracts;
- Support for credibility, marketability, professionalism; and
- Support for program funding.

At a recent national forum of large, multiservice agencies, inclusive of ancillary personnel and consultants, an organization's increased ability to negotiate lower insurance rates based on reduced risk was identified as a further benefit. Other benefits of accreditation, noted by public agency directors, have included the ability to answer concerns identified in a consent decree, reduce staff turnover, and attract higher qualified professional staff (U.S. General Accounting Office 2003).

Accreditation Process

Several factors logically impact on whether accreditation achieves maximum benefit to an organization. Years of accreditation experience suggest that several variables make a difference in both public and private agency satisfaction, including:

1. The reasons an organization's leaders seek accreditation;
2. The productivity of the accreditation facilitation process;
3. The clarity and strength of the guidelines offered to support positive outcomes;
4. The degree of commitment to comparing agency practices to national standards; and
5. The use of the accreditation once attained.

Each of these variables merits discussion and investigation. The primary focus of this chapter, however, is where the process begins and ends: with leadership and anticipated use of accreditation.

Accreditation Basics

There are steps that move an agency—private or public—forward in the process from point of application through notification of accreditation. These steps are straightforward and agencies that keep them in mind can, with the help of an accreditation staff facilitator, complete the process in 12 to 18 months or less. An organization initiates the accreditation process by contacting an accrediting body whose fields of interest matches the organization's fields of practice and completing an application. Agencies eligible to apply for COA accreditation hold necessary licenses, have been in operation for at least 1 year, and deliver programs in one or more of the service areas for which standards have been developed. An agreement is reached about the scope of accreditation based on the breadth and structure of the full organization as a distinct governable entity, and on applicability of standards for the services an agency provides. The organization then receives and applies standards set forth by the accrediting body to develop a comprehensive self-assessment, or self-study.

A site visit conducted by a team of peer volunteers, either at the agency or the agency's central or regional offices, provides an independent appraisal of how fully the agency has implemented standards of practice, as described in the organization's self-study. Site-visit results are reported to the agency on a preliminary basis and the agency is encouraged to respond prior to the decision of a commission whose members are senior agency executives and experienced team leaders with no connection to the agency under review. These commissioners can decide to accredit, defer accreditation pending completion of additional activities, or deny accreditation. Once accredited, an agency receives a final report to assist leadership with continuous goal setting and program development.

Just as licenses are granted for a specific period, agencies are accredited for a period of 3 to 4 years, at which time reaccreditation can be pursued. During this time the agency continues to be responsible for implementation of standards, just as the responsibility to maintain conditions that warrant continued licensure remain in force and effect. Should significant, uncorrected lapses occur in how an organization protects and serves clients, accreditation can be suspended or revoked. The next frontier for accreditation is to partner with agencies to build into their operations productivity and outcomes assessment with the maintenance of accreditation feedback loop to the accreditor.

Accreditation of Public Child Welfare Agencies

Public agencies and private service providers follow essentially the same steps in the process of accreditation; however, governmental entities bring some special considerations to the process. At the outset, decisions regarding public agencies are made about accrediting either cohorts of regions or counties over several years, or throughout the state simultaneously. Preliminary discussions to establish parameters can address how implementation of the standards in a state office or department is likely to involve, or stand apart from, related offices and departments. Guidance is often sought and provided at some level of detail on the practicality and sensibility of implementing administration and management standards, in particular.

These discussions and the decisions that follow are influenced by many factors, including legislation, initiatives planned or underway, consent decrees, and the structure of state services. A key factor in determining scope and time frames is state leadership, as expressed through the state's and state department's vision, strategic plan, and goals. Experience indicates that when significant organizational change is anticipated, there will be several basic factors: (1) a clearly articulated and shared vision, (2) total leadership buy-in, (3) a commitment to bringing change to all levels of the organization, (4) a commitment to being a learning organization, and (5) a willingness to take risks and an environment that allows for mistakes.

As with private organizations, state and county systems have an opportunity to assess and improve their organization and management practices through accreditation. Some standards, such as those regarding governance, are adapted to fit the particular administrative code and language of the state. Standards in burgeoning areas, such as contracting for services, invite almost continual refinement and enhancement. In addition, critical areas have recently been identified that logically have an impact on outcomes achieved at a local level. Some state systems, fully recognizing local authority and partnerships, increasingly want to include in their agency review standards that cover such areas as policy development, implementation, and monitoring; technical assistance; and alliances with other state departments and local providers.

The latest report on accreditation of public child welfare agencies available at the federal level (U.S. Department of Health and Human Services 1994) equivocates on the feasibility, benefits, and costs of looking toward accreditation of state agencies. The report's conclusions were based on little data and limited actual public sector accreditation experience: in 1994, COA accredited 604 agencies, and 25 (4%) were public sector. Today, approximately 1,400 agencies are accredited or are pursuing accreditation. Of these, three state systems (Kentucky, Illinois, and Louisiana) and 74 counties from 13 states have been COA accredited; nine states are pursuing accreditation at the state (six) or county level (two), or at both levels (one). In addition, COA accreditation has gained official recognition by numerous state departments as an indication of service delivery that merits approval of funding. An updated report would bring timely, warranted attention to developments related to public sector accreditation that have occurred since this report was issued, including accountability in service delivery that has changed dramatically in the interim.

Significance of Accreditation for Professionals in a Service System

For an individual in a system, the meaning of accreditation will vary, depending on professional practice and policy interests. On a practice level, accreditation has a direct bearing on how a service environment operates and how an agency organizes personnel and processes to continually improve agency performance and service delivery outcomes. The work environment—including supervision, peer support (Cicero-Reese & Black 1998), and organizational climate (Glisson & Hemmelgarn 1998)—has been found to impact on worker retention and positive child outcomes. Through its self-study, an agency creates and fortifies such structures and supports. Those same supports are needed to help the agency at large and individuals in it work toward measuring the difference in outcomes for children and families over the 3- to 4-year accreditation period.

Accredited organizations report that completing the self-examination process often also prompts individuals in different parts of the organization to think of the organization as a system of interrelated efforts. A central question becomes: how does the work or productivity of one unit impact on the work or ability of another unit to provide direct services? Support and clinical staff can become more attuned to, for example, the role of governance, the value of data to inform decisionmaking, and the necessity of well-trained staff members for service recipients to remain safe and healthy and achieve positive results.

There are also implications at the policy level associated with approval of measures that support safety and quality. The public at large cannot overlook, for example, national news accounts of the devastating consequences of "a complacent, sleepy culture" and management practices at the National Aeronautics and Space Agency that may discourage questioning at certain levels (Sanger 2003), and is then left to debate how well spent are the millions of dollars for the nation's space exploration program. Similarly, when reports are issued on violations of rules that limit to 12 the number of hours nurses can work, based on findings that patient errors climb after so many hours (Pear 2003b), a debate will ensue about how much funding a service sector already receives and the cost of additional mandates. Headlines also call attention to the cost in human life of failures to closely monitor cases in a social services system (Grimm 2004), to keep caseloads at a manageable level (Jones 2004; Jones & Kaufman 2003), and to provide treatment to children who receive mental healthcare under healthy, humane, and lawful conditions (Pear 2003a).

For such reasons, and to reduce "revolving door" overuse of services, proponents of quality services believe funds spent for quality services are funds well spent. Quality at a reasonable cost is good human service and economic policy. Direct service providers know, however, that although the average citizen may endorse quality, gaps frequently exist between policy and resources allocated at national, state, and local levels. Professionals who stand nearest in relationship to children and families seeking services have a special responsibility, then, to decide how good is "good enough" and to understand the choices available to an agency to verify and maintain quality services.

Context for Accreditation

Demands for improved service quality and results present a significant challenge for agency leaders and for state and local governments in today's harsh funding environment. Governmental and nonprofit organizations that remain mission driven, adopt a continual learning stance (Heuer 1999), and appreciate the importance of maintaining both organization and service integrity, can, however, identify and make needed reforms. Accreditation, with due consideration of the relevance of standards and processes and the pressure agencies feel to demonstrate results, can play a role in helping agencies build sustainable capacity to implement procedures that produce positive outcomes.

Three Interests: Reasonable Cost, Provider Accountability, and Service Recipient Outcomes

Accreditation represents quality, continual improvement, and other benefits associated with insuring safety and good outcomes, albeit at a cost. An accreditation fee calculated on a sliding scale to accommodate a range of budgets, and spread over 4 years, hundreds of staff members, and hundreds or thousands of service recipients, is reasonable. To this fee is added the cost of bringing service delivery to a level that research and experience indicate is safe and effective. Depending on many factors—number and kind of funding sources, alliances and partnerships, creativity, and current mode of operations—improvements can incur additional costs, ranging from minor to moderate.

The costs and benefits of services have always been a matter for the public and policymakers to debate, but analyzing costs and benefits has dominated discussions during the past several years of fiscal unrest. Along with a dour funding outlook in the states (Finegold et al. 2003) it has been noted that some organizations "struggle not only to remain vital and effective but just to survive" (Perlmutter & Gummer 1994:227). Since September 2001, funds in federal and state budgets have shifted to cover new and unanticipated expenses, principally homeland security and a war effort. Simultaneously, businesses have downsized, jobs have been lost, individual and corporate investments have diminished, and philanthropic giving has been reduced dramatically. A critical question is then: how do organizations make the most of available resources to maintain service quality and achieve positive outcomes?

Meanwhile, for more than a decade, an interest in accountability and results-based accountability at a federal, state, and local level has grown and prompted states to put in place ac-

countability systems (Hatry 1999; Schorr, Farrow, Hornbeck, & Watson 1994). The Government Performance and Results Act of 1993 provided the impetus for more and better accountability by requiring all programs receiving federal funds to provide plans and annual reports on results. More recently, tightened foster care and adoption timeframes, to address concerns about the time children spent in care, were attached to the Adoption and Safe Families Act of 1997. These measures were followed by calls for better government oversight for achievement by states of more specific indicators of child safety, permanency, and well-being, which gave rise, in 2001, to establishment of Child and Family Service Reviews (CFSRs). These reviews—and accreditation—also support improvement of systemic factors known to influence outcomes, including implementation of a quality assurance system and basic information system; a participatory case review system; training; an adequate array of services; responsiveness to the community; and standards for foster and adoptive parent licensing, recruitment, and retention. Along with federal efforts, many states have engineered systems intended to measure and report results for the state as a whole and to determine achievement of substantial conformity by parts of the service system—education, human services, mental health, and juvenile justice (*Georgia Academy Journal* 1997; Weiss 1997).

Movement toward Evidence-Based Practice

In light of these realities, professionals in the child welfare field and related fields, court judges, and mental health service providers are more aggressively considering the merits and feasibility of using evidence-based practice to guide decisions (Gambrill 1999; Rosen 2002; Zlotnik 2002). There now is a strong interest in both defining evidence-based practice and identifying methods that can increase the use of research in practice (Gira, Kessler, & Poertner

2001). Although concerns have been raised about the use of practice models that have not been demonstrated to be effective with various client groups, or under particular conditions, the trend is leading to an explication of practices that support positive outcomes on topics ranging from maltreatment interventions (Thomlison 2003) to community-based child welfare systems (Usher & Wildfire 2003).

Because good practices—making difficult decisions, conducting comprehensive assessments —need to be carried out by competent professionals, the child welfare field is now contemplating how to meet the need for well-prepared social workers (Child Welfare League of America 2003). Research indicates that downgrading education or job requirements has a negative effect on retention and positive outcomes. Yet a recent study of the human services workforce (Light 2003) and a foundation report (Annie E. Casey Foundation 2003) paint a grim picture: a sufficient, adequately educated and trained human services workforce is unlikely to be in place in the near future unless a concerted effort is made on several fronts to meet numerous identified challenges.

Role of Accreditation

The two movements—results-based accountability for providers and good results at a reasonable cost—are merging in a way and at a point in time that could promote genuine reform. Should it become clear that our society has a moral imperative to fund what works (Bruner et al. n.d.), and that mechanisms are needed to build sustainable capacity to implement what works, accreditation has a role to play. The mission and goals of an organization guide the choices it makes. Although an organization can change its mission, most agencies reexamine mission and sharpen goals through the accreditation process. Accreditation supports an organization in increasing its performance— being more efficient, more targeted in service delivery, and more vigilant in case management

and supervision—to achieve better outcomes. Doing so requires clarity of mission, long- and short-term planning, and data collection and use. These factors are key for a successful non-profit organization.

Recent efforts to determine the elements of a nonprofit capacity-building framework that could be applied not just at an organizational level but at a community level (DeVita & Fleming 2001) allow for tremendous variation in the methods used and capacity developed. This effort to better describe key factors for the nonprofit sector has added credence to the inclusion of vision and mission, leadership, resources, an outreach component, and services and products (performance, outputs, and outcomes). A recent survey seeking to determine the set of factors that stand for nonprofit "excellence" in the minds of 250 opinion leaders and 250 executives who lead private, nonprofit organizations (Light 2002) can shed more light in this regard. The blend of managerial integrity and programmatic impact emerged as a common trait among the high-performer nonprofit organizations included in the study (Light 2002: 72). Most executives did not believe that an organization could be effective, that is, achieve its missions and goals, and not be well managed. The same study, seeking to learn about motivation to improve, identified as strongly felt the pressure to be more effective and to improve. The comments of most executives reflected that the pressure to improve was at some point largely internal. As a result, these leaders say they are applying pressure to themselves: "it's just an ongoing process of looking at what we're doing and how we're doing it; what are the needs that we haven't met?" (Light 2002:77).

Facilitating documentation of "what works" at an agency level in both realms—management and services—is not a role all accreditation entities may intend or be able to assume. From COA's perspective, for example, the challenge will include instituting a multiyear individual accreditation plan that will help agencies assess their starting point, along a road leading to an increased ability to measure the difference that service delivery makes for children, youth, and families. An accreditor will also need to clarify the evidence base for the standards it promulgates, as COA is doing in its forthcoming standards. This clarification involves highlighting how standards for both public and private agencies promote sound assessment and case planning; effective service delivery; and desired safety, permanency, and well-being outcomes. Both measures are expected to increase the likelihood that accreditation will be perpetually useful.

Another challenge is for accreditation entities to answer effectively, through their philosophy, values, standards, and process, questions about the utility of accreditation for agencies seeking to work in partnerships and participate in reform efforts across systems. The final section of the chapter addresses this challenge.

Accreditation Implementation

In the hands of visionary leaders, accreditation can promote flexibility and inclusive practice when viewed as a means to promote professionalism and positive outcomes.

Promoting Structure and Change: A Tool for Leaders

Accreditation can support independent activity of an organization's members when used as a strong frame of reference (Wheatley 1994) by strong leadership. In agencies of every description—small and large, rural and urban, public and private—the use of accreditation depends largely on how the agency head portrays accreditation, and on the support from a board (Heuer 1999) or cabinet for increasing organizational performance. Does leadership see it as a means for maintaining existing operations, whereby information is made to fit a structure so minimal change is required, or is it framed as a means to making the organization open to new possibilities? To helping the organization mature? To solidifying basic infra-

structure, so no matter the age, size, or institutional maturity, an organization can better function in a complex, competitive environment?

Like any instrument, when used as intended, accreditation can take care of the basics, leaving an organization the time and energy to manage complex financial arrangements and balance competition and collaboration. According to Wheatly (1994:91), structure does not necessarily discourage change; instead, it can serve as a kind of "insulation from the environment that protects the system from constant, reactive changes." Accreditation invites a look at the structures an organization already has in place: for monitoring untoward events, to discover patterns, to look at tolerances and steps taken within the culture for insuring sufficient and timely oversight, and to make sure case reviews take place routinely so that cases are not lost in the system. Accreditation can also promote added structure where it is needed, introducing consistency to assessment and case planning, or greater involvement of an oversight committee. Altogether, looking at structure can help an agency shift away from perpetual reactive, crisis-driven, "too little, too late" activities.

Agencies completing the accreditation process comment that it sets in motion a change process through which it is possible to insure steps have been taken to provide a sound management and appropriate service delivery environment. Change that occurs as an organization pursues accreditation can have a profound effect on both its internal operating systems and on how the organization interacts as part of the community of service providers. In sum, the very culture of an organization can, and often does, shift in some positive, fundamental ways as a result of the decision to pursue accreditation (McDonald & McCarthy 2000; Miller 2003).

Qualities That Promote Change

Against this backdrop, an accreditor needs to carefully consider how to facilitate growth. An accreditation body must itself operate as a system taking responsibility for facilitating a smooth process of systemic assessment and effectiveness. An accreditor must recognize that to be truly useful, the entire accreditation process—standards, self-study, peer review, training/technical assistance, and decisionmaking—must be rigorous but flexible and offer consistency while being individualized. One way for an accreditor to understand the impact of its process is to undergo, itself, an in-depth self-study. In doing so, it can discover myriad ways to engage in internal study and, in so doing, become better prepared to guide others in a productive self-study process. Through undergoing a self-study and putting in place a strong continuous improvement process, COA has noted, for example, that standards written to be flexible can fail to provide promised relief if those standards are interpreted as rigid during a self-study. With standards development, then, comes a need to reach into other divisions to make sure interpretations are accurate, sufficient information is available for training purposes, and peer reviewers and organizations can easily access updates.

Means to An End

An accreditor that is committed to insuring that accreditation is useful, that it does not get in the way of the very thing it promotes—quality programs and good results—must ask hard questions of the process. A compendium like that of Schorr (1997) promotes consideration of exactly that: what encourages, and what gets in the way of, quality programs and good results. By looking at impediments to a good process, the accreditor seeks to clarify, first within the accreditation process, and then in the child and family services community at large, how facilitative the accreditation process actually can be. In doing so, it is possible to better specify how a utilitarian, means-to-an-end approach to human services accreditation differs from what could be considered a limited utility, end-in-itself perspective (table 1).

Both perspectives accommodate the possibility that accreditation for some organizations is a validation of already strong management and service delivery practice. That said, the two perspectives contrast sharply and challenge the reader to think critically about how accreditation can be useful for not only promoting, but sustaining, excellence.

The material in the left column of the table highlights the major barriers to service integration that Schorr (1997) identifies. Accreditation

TABLE 1. *Human Services Accreditation: Two Perspectives*

"End-in-Itself" Perspective	"Means-to-an-End" Perspective
Is inflexible, rule-bound	Recognizes that there is no one best way
Focuses on control and compliance—strives to eliminate frontline discretion	Promotes well-trained, adequate supervisory staffing to guide frontline decisionmaking
Cements the status quo	Promotes continuous examination of the status quo through CQI on behalf of and inclusive of stakeholders
Is categorical, inhospitable to family and community development	Recognizes that organizational growth and improvement involves changing over time and making connections, and that effective service delivery is well managed and occurs in collaboration with others
Uses macroeconomic, one-size-fits-all thinking	
Focuses on structure and process	
Denigrates strategy and outcomes	Emphasizes that each organization has a mission, long-term strategic plan, short-term plans, and desired outcomes that are linked and appropriate for that particular organization
Advocates for policies and mandates that work in a traditional office setting but creates obstacles for services delivered in home and community settings or in scarce resource settings	Promotes strategic planning and outcomes measurement as critical for unifying organization and management functions
Monitors productivity	Promotes implementation of core health and safety policies and procedures that can help management reduce the incidence of preventable, untoward events
	Advocates for development of a productivity self-assessment system

could be, and is sometimes, similarly characterized by those who equate accreditation with regulations and directives. The constraints listed in the table are familiar to service providers that encounter intractable guidelines and unbending officials committed to a "this is the way it is" approach. COA's experience, however, is one of working with agencies that are determining, every day, "how it is going to be." These agencies are providing "blended" services, services through community-based organizations that are merging, services as "lead agencies" and through other contemporary partnership configurations. The challenges listed on the left would be antithetical to making small, necessary reforms—through creative alliances, waivers, and other innovative practices—at the local level. As such, it is essential that an accreditation process invite best practice of a boundary-crossing kind that recognizes that families and children are cared for by many, using the resources of many, and with results that are desired and the province of many.

The accreditor that advocates for a framework with the capacity to flex and adjust, and one that promotes the concepts listed on the right side of the table, need not lower standards. Instead, accreditors can help organizations see the merits of moving from an approach that emphasizes a rigid adherence to standards to a stance that encourages exploration of appropriate and innovative ways in which standards can be met. Such an approach is established by the accrediting body not only through the content of standards but also through the language of technical assistance that is used by accreditation coordinators and by peer reviewers throughout the process.

Conclusion

Accreditation helps organizations apply national standards, at the same time recognizing differences in individual initiatives and in resource allocation among states, counties, and communities. In a nation that offers a patchwork of state service provider arrangements for the delivery of child welfare services, along with overall guidance about safety, continuity, well-being, and system indicators, accreditation is a kind of leveler. As an educational opportunity, accreditation has shown that it can both inform an organization's staff members and the community about mission, purpose, implementation of best practice, and measurement of positive change for service recipients. Accreditation, by identifying assets and constraints, also can serve to inform consumers who want to distinguish among service providers.

Setting standards to protect health and safety is a time-honored endeavor in many fields, including child welfare. However, in a society perceived by some observers to be excessively regulated, accreditation can be seen as an added layer of mandates and, therefore, is not without its detractors. However, members of organizations that have experienced an accreditation process that facilitates learning, growth, and measurement of results over time describe positive change that is profound.

Accreditation and reaccreditation processes provide the means to support ongoing self-study and improvement and can facilitate a shift in an agency's culture from being reactive and crisis driven to being proactive and plan driven. Organizations that have been accredited are encouraged to keep asking and answering: Who are we? Who do we serve? What do we do? How do we know that what we do contributes to better outcomes for children and families? The goal of accreditation, as described in this chapter, is not to enforce compliance with standards but to improve services provided to children and families. The mission is to see those who receive services living safe, healthy, and productive lives.

References

Adoption and Safe Families Act. (1997). P.L. 105-89.

Annie E. Casey Foundation. (2003). *The unsolved challenge of system reform: The condition of the frontline human services workforce.* Baltimore: Annie E. Casey Foundation.

Bruner, C., Greenberg, M., Guy, C., Little, M., Schorr, L., & Weiss, H. (n.d.). *Funding what works: Exploring the role of research on effective programs and practices in government decision-making.* Des Moines, IA: Child and Family Policy Center, National Center for Service Integration.

Child Welfare League of America. (2003). *Annotated bibliography: Child welfare workforce.* Retrieved June 30, 2004, from www.cwla.org/programs/r2p/bibliowf. pdf.

Cicero-Reese, B., & Black, P. (1998). Research suggests why child welfare workers stay on the job. *Partnerships for Child Welfare,* 5(5), 5, 8–9.

DeVita, C. J., & Fleming, C. (2001). Building nonprofit capacity: A framework for addressing the problem. In C. J. DeVita and C. Fleming (eds.), *Building capacity in nonprofit organizations,* pp. 5–32. Washington, DC: Urban Institute.

Finegold, K., Schardin, S., Maag, E., Steinbach, R., Merriman, D., & Weil, A. (2003). *Social program spending and state fiscal crises.* Washington, DC: Urban Institute.

Gambrill, E. (1999). Evidence-based practice: An alternative to authority-based practice. *Families in Society: The Journal of Contemporary Human Services,* 80(4), 341–350.

Georgia Academy Journal. (1997) Managing by outcomes changes everything. *Georgia Academy Journal,* 5(2). Retrieved June 30, 2004, from ahs.state.vt.us/981chgaj.htm.

Gira, E. C., Kessler, M. L., & Poertner, J. (2001). *Evidence-based practice in child welfare: Challenges and opportunities.* Urbana-Champaign: Children and Family Research Center, School of Social Work, University of Illinois at Urbana-Champaign.

Glisson, C., & Hemmelgarn, A. (1998). The effects of organizational climate and interorganizational coordination on the quality and outcomes of children's service systems. *Child Abuse and Neglect,* 22, 401–421.

Government Performance and Results Act. (1993). P.L. 103-62.

Grimm, F. (2004). Fixing child welfare: Words are not enough. *Miami Herald,* (May 2), p. 1BR.

Hamm, M. S. (1997). *The fundamentals of accreditation.* Washington, DC: American Society of Association Executives.

Hatry, H. P. (1999). *Performance measurement: Getting results.* Washington, DC: Urban Institute.

Heuer, M. (1999). *Nonprofit organizational effectiveness: A literature review.* Washington, DC: Innovation Network.

Jones, R. L. (2004). New Jersey plans to lessen the load for child welfare workers. Retrieved June 30, 2004, from www.nytimes.com/2004/06/09/nyregion/09child. html#.

Jones, R. L., & Kaufman, L. (2003). Worker in abuse case in Newark juggled 107 child care inquiries. *New York Times,* (January 8), pp. A1, B6.

Light, P. C. (2002). *Pathways to nonprofit excellence.* Washington, DC: Brookings Institution Press.

Light, P. C. (2003). *The health of the human services workforce.* Washington, DC: Brookings Institution.

McDonald, J., & McCarthy, B. (2000). Effective partnership models between the state agencies, community, the university, and community service providers. In *Child welfare training symposium: Changing paradigms of child welfare practice: Responding to opportunities and challenges, Washington, DC, June 28–29, 1999,* pp. 43–72. Washington, DC: Children's Bureau.

Miller, V. (2003). Real change: Transforming the culture of an entire child welfare system. Presentation given at the National Public Agency Roundtable on Quality Service Delivery, Lexington, KY, May 28, 2003.

Pear, R. (2003a). Mental care poor for some children in state custody. *New York Times,* (August 31), pp, A1, A13.

Pear, R. (2003b). Report cites danger in overtime for nurses. *New York Times,* (November 5), p. A22.

Perlmutter, F. D., & Gummer, B. (1994). Managing organizational transformations. In R. D. Herman (ed.), *The Jossey-Bass handbook of nonprofit leadership and management,* pp. 227–246. San Francisco: Jossey-Bass.

Rosen, A. (2002). Evidence-based social work practice: Challenges and promise. Presentation given at the Society for Social Work and Research, San Diego, CA, January 24–27, 2002.

Sanger, D. E. (2003). Report on loss of shuttle focuses on NASA blunders and issues somber warning. *New York Times,* (August 27), pp. A1, A16.

Schorr, L. B. (1997). *Common purpose: Strengthening families and neighborhoods to rebuild America.* New York: Anchor Books.

Schorr, L. B., Farrow, F., Hornbeck, D., & Watson, S. (1994). *The case for shifting to results-based accountability.* Washington, DC: Center for the Study of Social Policy.

Thomlison, B. (2003). Characteristics of evidence-based child maltreatment interventions. *Child Welfare,* 82, 541–570.

U.S. Department of Health and Human Services. (1994). *Accreditation of public child welfare agencies.* OEI publication no. 04-00010. Rockville, MD: U.S. Department of Health and Human Services.

U.S. General Accounting Office. (2003). HHS could play a greater role in helping child welfare agencies recruit and retain staff. GAO-03-357. Washington, DC: U.S. General Accounting Office.

Usher, C. L., & Wildfire, J. B. (2003). Evidence-based practice in community-based child welfare systems. *Child Welfare,* 82, 597–614.

Weiss, H. B. (1997). Results-based accountability for child and family services. In E. J. Mullen & J. Magnabosco (eds.), *Outcomes measurement in the human services*, pp. 173–180. Washington, DC: National Association of Social Workers Press.

Wheatley, M. J. (1994). *Leadership and the new science: Learning about organizations from an orderly universe*. San Francisco: Berret-Koehler Publishers.

Zlotnik, J. L. (2002). *Evidence-based practice: Perspectives and possibilities.* Presentation given to the Institute for the Advancement of Social Work Research Board of Directors, Washington, DC, April 28, 2002.

Gerald P. Mallon

Gerald P. Mallon, DSW, is professor and executive director of the National Resource Center for Family-Centered Practice and Permanency Planning at the Hunter College School of Social Work, New York City. For more than 29 years, Dr. Mallon has been a child welfare practitioner, educator, advocate, and researcher. He is the author or editor of 17 books and numerous peer-reviewed publications in professional journals. His most recent publications from Columbia University Press are *Gay men choosing parenthood; We don't exactly get the Welcome Wagon: The experiences of gay and lesbian adolescents in child welfare systems;* and *Let's get this straight: A gay and lesbian affirming approach to child welfare.* Dr. Mallon earned his doctorate in Social Welfare from the City University of New York at Hunter College and holds an MSW from Fordham University, New York, and a BSW from Dominican College, Blauvelt, NY. Dr. Mallon has lectured extensively in the United States, Ireland, Australia, Canada, and the United Kingdom. He can be reached via e-mail at gmallon@hunter.cuny.edu.

Peg McCartt Hess

Peg McCartt Hess, PhD, is consultant expert on child welfare practice for Children's Rights, Inc., and consultant, National Resource Center for Family-Centered Practice and Permanency Planning at the Hunter College of Social Work, New York. Dr. Hess has been professor at the University of South Carolina College of Social Work, Columbia, and Columbia University School of Social Work, New York City. For 35 years, Dr. Hess has been a child welfare practitioner, educator, advocate, and researcher. She has participated in the evaluation of child welfare practice in numerous states. Dr. Hess is the author or editor of seven books and numerous peer-reviewed publications in professional journals. Her most recent publications from Columbia University Press are *Nurturing the one, supporting the many: The Center for Family Life in Sunset Park, Brooklyn,* with Brenda McGowan and Michael Botsko, and *Empowering community organizations: The mediating role of consultation and technical assistance,* with Patricia Stone Motes, currently in press. Dr. Hess earned her doctorate at the University of Illinois at Urbana-Champaign, School of Social Work, Urbana, and her masters at the University of Chicago, School of Social Service Administration, Chicago. She can be reached via e-mail at peghess@charter.net.

❖ CONTRIBUTORS

Amy Ackroyd, LMSW, is clinical manager at Sweetser, in Saco, ME. She can be reached via e-mail at amy@dbsinyc.com.

Frank Ainsworth, PhD, is lecturer at Edith Cowan University, School of International, Cultural, and Community Studies, Joondalup Campus, Perth, Australia. He can be reached via e-mail at frankainsworth@hotmail.com.

Kara Allen-Eckard, MSW, is the family-centered meetings project trainer at North Carolina State University, Raleigh. She can be reached via e-mail at krallene@chass.ncsu.edu.

Julie C. Altman, PhD, is assistant professor at Adelphi University School of Social Work, Garden City, New York. She can be reached via e-mail at altman@adelphi.edu.

Wendy F. Auslander, PhD, is professor at the George Warren Brown School of Social Work, Washington University, St. Louis, MO. She can be reached via e-mail at wauslander@wustl.edu.

Kathy Barbell, MSW, is associate vice president for program operations at the Child Welfare League of America, Washington, DC. She can be reached via e-mail at kbarbell@cwla.org.

Melissa F. Becker is research associate at the University of Washington School of Social Work, Seattle. She can be reached via e-mail at socialwork@fullerbecker.com.

Marianne Berry, PhD, is professor at the University of Kansas School of Social Welfare, Lawrence. She can be reached via e-mail at andysmom@ku.edu.

Lloyd B. Bullard, M.Ed., is director of residential care and behavior support specialist at the Child Welfare League of America, Washington, DC. He can be reached via e-mail at lbullard@cwla.org.

Tracey K. Burke, PhD, is assistant professor at the University of Alaska at Anchorage School of Social Work. She can be reached via e-mail at tkburke@uaa.alaska.edu.

Zeinab Chahine, MSW, is executive deputy commissioner for child welfare programs at the Administration for Children's Services, New York. She can be reached via e-mail at zchahine@acs.gov.

Elena Cohen, MSW, is senior associate at Center for the Study of Social Policy, Washington, DC. She can be reached via e-mail at ecohen@cssp.org.

Antonia Cordero, DSW, is assistant professor at the University of Connecticut School of Social Work, West Hartford. She can be reached via e-mail at antonia.cordero@uconn.edu.

Terry L. Cross, MSW, is executive director of the National Indian Child Welfare Association, Portland, OR. He can be reached via e-mail at tlcross@nicwa.org.

Amy C. D'Andrade, MSW, is doctoral student researcher at the Child Welfare Research Center, University of California at Berkeley. She can be reached via e-mail at amycd@berkeley.edu.

Diane DePanfilis, PhD, MSW, is associate professor at the University of Maryland School of Social Work, Baltimore. She can be reached via e-mail at ddepanfi@ssw.umaryland.edu.

Martha M. Dore, PhD, is visiting professor at Adelphi University School of Social Work, Garden City, NY. She can be reached via e-mail at dore@adelphi.edu.

Ilze Earner, PhD, is assistant professor at the Hunter College School of Social Work, New York. She can be reached via e-mail at iearner@hunter.cuny.edu.

Diane E. Elze, PhD, is assistant professor at the George Warren Brown School of Social Work, Washington University, St. Louis, MO. She can be reached via e-mail at delze@wustl.edu.

Irwin Epstein, PhD, is the Helen Rehr Professor of Applied Social Work Research at the Hunter College School of Social Work, New York. He can be reached via e-mail at iepstein@hunter.cuny.edu.

Judy Fenster, PhD, is assistant professor at Adelphi University School of Social Work, Garden City, NY. She can be reached via e-mail at fenster@adelphi.edu.

Trudy Festinger, DSW, is professor at the New York University School of Social Work, New York. She can be reached via e-mail at trudy.festinger@nyu.edu.

Kathleen Fox, PhD, is director of research at the National Indian Child Welfare Association, Portland, OR. She can be reached via e-mail at kathleen@nicwa.org.

Mark W. Fraser, PhD, is John A. Tate Distinguished Professor for Children in Need at the School of Social Work, University of North Carolina, Chapel Hill. He can be reached via e-mail at mfraser@email.unc.edu.

Madelyn Freundlich, MSW, JD, is director of policy at Children's Rights, Inc., New York. She can be reached via e-mail at mfreundlich@childrensrights.org.

Beth Frizsell, LCSW, is at the Mississippi Department of Human Services, Division of Family and Children's Services, Jackson, MS, Ciber contractor–PIP consultant. She can be reached via e-mail at efrizsel@ciber.com.

Eileen D. Gambrill, PhD, is Hutto Patterson Professor at the University of California at Berkeley School of Social Welfare, Berkeley. She can be reached via e-mail at gambrill@berkeley.edu.

Stephanie Gosteli, MSW, LCSW, is senior program associate for field operations at Casey Family Services, New Haven, CT. She can be reached via e-mail at sgosteli@caseyfamilyservices.org.

Victor Groza, PhD, is professor at the Mandel School of Applied Social Sciences, Case Western Reserve University, Cleveland, OH. He can be reached via e-mail at victor.groza@case.edu.

Neil B. Guterman, PhD, is associate professor at Columbia University School of Social Work, New York. He can be reached via e-mail at nbg2@columbia.edu.

Mark Hardin, JD, is director of the National Child Welfare Resource Center on Legal and Judicial Issues, American Bar Association Center on Children and the Law, Washington, DC. He can be reached via e-mail at markhardin@staff.abanet.org.

Catherine A. Hawkins, PhD, is professor at the School of Social Work, Texas State University, San Marcos. She can be reached via e-mail at ch11@txstate.edu.

Rebecca L. Hegar, PhD, is professor at the University of Texas at Arlington, School of Social Work. She can be reached via e-mail at rhegar@uta.edu.

Judith Cooper Heitzman, MSSW, LCSW, is doctoral candidate at the Kent School of Social Work at the University of Louisville, KY. She can be reached via e-mail at judy.heitzman@louisville.edu.

Selina Higgins, MSW, LCSW, is director of field operations and coordinator for the Family Team Conferences, Child Evaluation Specialist, and Family Assessment Programs, New York City Administration for Children's Services, New York. She can be reached via e-mail at Selina.Higgins@Dfa.state.ny.us.

Leslie Doty Hollingsworth, PhD, is associate professor at the University of Michigan School of Social Work, Ann Arbor. She can be reached via e-mail at lholling@umich.edu.

Donna T. Hornsby, MSW, is director of the Office of Children and Family Services at the Maryland Department of Human Resources, Social Services Administration, Baltimore. She can be reached via e-mail at DHornsby@dhr.state.md.us.

Will Hornsby, MSW, is child welfare program specialist at the Children's Bureau, Administration for Children and Families, U.S. Department of Health and Human Services, Washington, DC. He can be reached via e-mail at whornsby@acf.hhs.gov.

Lindsey Houlihan, MSSA, is project coordinator of PARTners, Center for Interventions for Families and Children at the Mandel School of Applied Social Sciences, Case Western Reserve University, Cleveland, OH. She can be reached via e-mail at lgm4@case.edu.

Katherine Johnson, MSW, is research associate at the Child Welfare League of America, Washington, DC. She can be reached via e-mail at kjohnson@cwla.org.

Diane W. Keller, PhD, is associate professor at the Marywood University School of Social Work, Scranton, PA. She can be reached via e-mail at keller@es.marywood.edu.

Susan P. Kemp, PhD, is associate professor at the University of Washington School of Social Work, Seattle. She can be reached via e-mail at spk@u.washington.edu.

Ann H. Loyek is graduate assistant at the Marywood University School of Social Work, Scranton, PA. She can be reached via e-mail at loyek@ac.marywood.edu.

Anthony N. Maluccio, DSW, is professor at Boston College Graduate School of Social Work, Boston. He can be reached via e-mail at maluccio@bc.edu.

Jan McCarthy, MSW, is director of child welfare policy at the National Technical Assistance Center for Children's Mental Health at Georgetown University, Washington, DC. She can be reached via e-mail at jrm33@georgetown.edu.

Emily Jean McFadden, MSW, is professor at the School of Social Work, Grand Valley State University, Grand Rapids, MI. She can be reached via e-mail at mcfaddej@gvsu.edu.

Brenda G. McGowan, DSW, is Ruth Harris Ottman Professor of Family and Child Welfare at Columbia University School of Social Work, New York. She can be reached via e-mail at bgm1@columbia.edu.

Curtis McMillen, PhD, is associate professor at the George Warren Brown School of Social Work, Wash-

ington University, St. Louis, MO. He can be reached via e-mail at cmcmille@wustl.edu.

Myrna L. McNitt, MSW, is child welfare consultant at Holland, MI. She can be reached via e-mail at foster@macatawa.org.

Ruth G. McRoy, PhD, is Ruby Lee Piester Centennial Professor in Services to Children and Families at the University of Texas at Austin School of Social Work. She can be reached via e-mail at r.mcroy@mail.utexas.edu.

Jennifer L. Miller, MSW, is senior associate at Cornerstone Consulting Group, Houston, TX. She can be reached via e-mail at jmiller@cornerstone.to.

Jerry Milner, DSW, is senior child welfare specialist at the Children's Bureau, Administration for Children and Families, U.S. Department of Health and Human Services, Washington, DC. He can be reached via e-mail at jmilner@acf.hhs.gov.

Linda Mitchell, MS, is senior child welfare specialist, the Children's Bureau, Administration for Children and Families, U.S. Department of Health and Human Services, Washington, DC. She can be reached via e-mail at lmitchell@acf.hhs.gov.

Ann Morison, PhD, is director of standards at the Council on Accreditation, New York. She can be reached via e-mail at amorison@coa.org.

Robin Nixon is executive director of the National Foster Care Coalition, Washington, DC. She can be reached via e-mail at robinnixon@msn.com.

Mary O'Brien is staff at the Institute for Child and Family Policy at the Muskie School of Public Service and the University of Southern Maine, Portland. She can be reached via e-mail at mobrien2@bowdoin.edu.

Eileen Mayers Pasztor, DSW, is assistant professor at the Department of Social Work, California State University, Long Beach. She can be reached via e-mail at epasztor@csulb.edu.

David Pate, Jr., PhD, is executive director at the Center for Family Policy and Practice, Madison, WI. He can be reached via e-mail at dpate@cffpp.org.

Barbara A. Pine, PhD, is professor at the University of Connecticut School of Social Work, West Hartford. She can be reached via e-mail at barbara.pine@uconn.edu.

Judy L. Postmus, PhD, is assistant professor at the University of Kansas School of Social Welfare, Lawrence. She can be reached via e-mail at postmus@kansas.edu.

Steven Priester, DSW, is staff at Institute for Child and Family Policy at the Muskie School of Public Service and the University of Southern Maine, Portland. He can be reached via e-mail at spreister@usm.maine.edu.

Jennifer Renne, JD, is assistant director of the National Child Welfare Resource Center on Legal and Judicial Issues, American Bar Association Center on Children and the Law, Washington, DC. She can be reached via e-mail at rennej@staff.abanet.org.

Kris Sahonchik, JD, is director of the Institute for Child and Family Policy at the Muskie School of Public Service and the University of Southern Maine, Portland. She can be reached via e-mail at Kriss@usm.maine.edu.

Susan Saltzburg, PhD, is assistant professor at the College of Social Work at Ohio State University, Columbus. She can be reached via e-mail at salzburg.1@osu.edu.

Maria Scannapieco, PhD, is professor at the University of Texas at Arlington School of Social Work. She can be reached via e-mail at mscannapieco@uta.edu.

Aron Shlonsky, PhD, is assistant professor at Columbia University School of Social Work, New York. He can be reached via e-mail at as2156@columbia.edu.

Robin Spath, PhD, is assistant professor at the University of Connecticut School of Social Work, West Hartford. She can be reached via e-mail at robin.spath@uconn.edu.

Karen M. Staller, PhD, JD, is assistant professor at the University of Michigan School of Social Work, Ann Arbor. She can be reached via e-mail at kstaller@umich.edu.

Arlene Stiffman, PhD, is Barbara A. Bailey Professor of Social Work at the George Warren Brown School of Social Work, Washington University, St. Louis, MO. She can be reached via e-mail at arstiff@wustl.edu.

Catherine A. Taylor, PhD, is post-doctoral research scholar at Columbia University School of Social Work, New York. She can be reached via e-mail at ct2125@columbia.edu.

Mary A. Terzian, PhD, is a doctoral student at the School of Social Work University of North Carolina, Chapel Hill. She can be reached via e-mail at mterzian@email.unc.edu.

Mark F. Testa, PhD, is associate professor at the University of Illinois at Urbana-Champaign School of Social Work, Urbana. He can be reached via e-mail at mtesta@uiuc.edu.

Elaine M. Walsh, PhD, is associate professor in the Department of Urban Affairs and Planning at Hunter College, New York. She can be reached via e-mail at ewalsh@hunter.cuny.edu.

Cynthia J. Weaver, D. Min., MSW, is assistant professor at the Marywood University School of Social Work, Scranton, PA. She can be reached via e-mail at cw@jbs1.com.

Zoe Breen Wood, MSW, is the director of the Ability-Based Learning Environment Program at the Mandel School of Applied Social Sciences, Case Western Reserve University, Cleveland, OH. She can be reached via e-mail at zbw@case.edu.

Maria Woolverton, MSW, is senior research associate at the Georgetown University Center for Child and Human Development, Washington, DC. She can be reached via e-mail at woolverm@georgetown.edu.

Lois Wright, MSSW, EdD, is director of evaluation and education, School of Social Work/VISSTA at the Virginia Commonwealth University, Richmond. She can be reached via e-mail at lewright@vcu.edu.

❖ INDEX